D0160748

The Dictionary of the Bible and Ancient Media

The Dictionary of the Bible and Ancient Media

Edited by Tom Thatcher (Lead Editor), Chris Keith,
Raymond F. Person, Jr. and Elsie R. Stern

Judith Odor, Managing Editor

BLOOMSBURY
LONDON • OXFORD • NEW YORK • NEW DELHI • SYDNEY

Bloomsbury T&T Clark
An imprint of Bloomsbury Publishing Plc
Imprint previously known as T&T Clark

50 Bedford Square
London
WC1B 3DP
UK

175 Fifth Avenue
New York
NY 10010
USA

www.bloomsbury.com

BLOOMSBURY, T&T CLARK and the Diana logo are trademarks of Bloomsbury Publishing Plc

First published 2017

© Tom Thatcher (Lead Editor), Chris Keith, Raymond F. Person, Jr., Elsie R. Stern and Judith Odor 2017

Tom Thatcher (Lead Editor), Chris Keith, Raymond F. Person, Jr., Elsie R. Stern and Judith Odor have asserted their right under the Copyright, Designs and Patents Act, 1988, to be identified as Authors of this work.

All rights reserved. No part of this publication may be reproduced or transmitted in any form or by any means, electronic or mechanical, including photocopying, recording, or any information storage or retrieval system, without prior permission in writing from the publishers.

No responsibility for loss caused to any individual or organization acting on or refraining from action as a result of the material in this publication can be accepted by Bloomsbury Academic or the author.

British Library Cataloguing-in-Publication Data
A catalogue record for this book is available from the British Library.

ISBN: HB: 978-0-5672-2249-7
ePDF: 978-0-5676-7838-6
ePUB: 978-0-5676-7837-9

Library of Congress Cataloging-in-Publication Data
Names: Thatcher, Tom, 1967- editor.
Title: Dictionary of the Bible and ancient media / edited by Tom Thatcher (lead editor), Chris Keith, Raymond F. Person, Elsie R. Stern; Judith Odor, production manager.
Description: 1 [edition]. | New York : Bloomsbury Academic, 2017. | Includes bibliographical references. |
Identifiers: LCCN 2017024236 (print) | LCCN 2017033169 (ebook) | ISBN 9780567678379 (epub) | ISBN 9780567678386 (ebook) | ISBN 9780567222497 (hb)
Subjects: LCSH: Bible–Dictionaries. | Bible and literature–Dictionaries. | Literature, Ancient–History and criticism–Dictionaries.
Classification: LCC BS440 (ebook) | LCC BS440 .D535 2017 (print) | DDC 220.8/30223–dc23
LC record available at https://lccn.loc.gov/2017024236

Typeset by Deanta Global Publishing Services, Chennai, India
Printed and bound in Great Britain

Contents

List of Contributors

Ellen Bradshaw Aitken (McGill University, Canada)
David M. Allen (Queen's Foundation for Ecumenical Theological Education, UK)
Coleman A. Baker (Texas Christian University, USA)
Leslie Baynes (Missouri State University, USA)
Deborah Beck (University of Texas at Austin, USA)
Drew W. Billings (Hobart and William Smith Colleges, USA)
Fiona C. Black (Mount Allison University, Canada)
Tomas Bokedal (University of Aberdeen, UK)
Ryan Bonfiglio (Columbia Theological Seminary, USA)
Thomas E. Boomershine (United Theological Seminary, USA)
Jo-Ann A. Brant (Goshen College, USA)
Marc Bregman (University of North Carolina, Greensboro, USA)
Jeff Brickle (Urshan Graduate School of Theology, USA)
Joshua Ezra Burns (Marquette University, USA)
Aubrey E. Buster (Emory University, USA)
Samuel Byrskog (Centre for Theology and Religious Studies, Lund University, Sweden)
Stephen Carlson (Australian Catholic University, Australia)
Warren Carter (Brite Divinity School, USA)
Tony Cartledge (Campbell University, USA)
Sidnie White Crawford (University of Nebraska-Lincoln, USA)
Katharine J. Dell (University of Cambridge, USA)
Natalie Dohrmann (University of Pennsylvania, USA)
Nicholas A. Elder (Marquette University, USA)
Philip Esler (University of Gloucestershire, UK)
Craig A. Evans (Houston Baptist University, USA)
Eric Eve (Oxford University, UK)
Everett Ferguson (Abilene Christian University, USA)
Rob Fleenor (Johnson University, USA)
Carol Fontaine (Andover Newton Theological School, USA)
Ida Fröhlich (Pázmány Péter Catholic University, Hungary)
Edmon L. Gallagher (Heritage Christian University, USA)
Lori Ann Garner (Rhodes College, USA)
R. Scott Garner (Rhodes College, USA)
Kathleen Gibbons (Washington University, USA)
Susan Gillingham (University of Oxford, UK)
Heather Gorman (Johnson University, USA)
Barbara Green (Dominican School of Philosophy and Theology, USA)
Hannah K. Harrington (Patten University, USA)

Barry Hartog (Kathlolieke Universiteit Leuven, Belgium)
Katherine M. Hayes (St. Joseph's Seminary, USA)
Catherine Hezser (SOAS University of London, UK)
Sandra Hubenthal (Universität Passau, Germany)
Michael Hundley (Syracuse University, USA)
Sandra Jacobs (King's College London, UK)
Brice Jones (University of Louisiana at Monroe, USA)
Joel Kalvesmaki (Dumbarton Oaks, USA)
John Kampen (Methodist Theological School in Ohio, USA)
Craig Keener (Asbury Theological Seminary, USA)
Chris Keith (St. Mary's University, UK)
Werner H. Kelber (Rice University, USA)
Allen Kerkeslager (Saint Joseph's University, USA)
Alan Kirk (James Madison University, USA)
Michael Labahn (Martin Luther Universitäte Halle-Wittenberg, Germany)
Tim Langille (Arizona State University, USA)
Matthew D. Larsen, (Yale University, USA)
Anthony Le Donne (United Theological Seminary, USA)
Margaret E. Lee (Tulsa Community College, USA)
Sang-Il Lee (Chongshin University, South Korea)
Marcie Lenk (Shalom Hartman Institute, Israel)
Verena Lepper (Ägyptisches Museum und Papyrussammlung, Staatliche Museen zu Berlin & Humboldt University of Berlin, Germany)
Britt Leslie (United Theological Seminary, USA)
Andrea Lieber (Dickinson College, USA)
Laura S. Lieber (Duke University, USA)
Bruce Longenecker (Baylor University, USA)
Ingeborg Löwisch (Universiteit Utrecht, Netherlands)
Randy Lumpp (Regis University, USA)
James Maxey (Nida Institute for Biblical Scholarship, USA)
Robert K. McIver (Avondale College, Australia)
John Meade (Phoenix Seminary, USA)
Carol Meyers (Duke University, USA)
Eric M. Meyers (Duke University, USA)
Wolfgang Mieder (University of Vermont, USA)
Shem Miller (University of Mississippi, USA)
Christine Mitchell (St. Andrew's College, University of Saskatchewan, Canada)
Terrence Mournet (Ashland Theological Seminary, USA)
Eva Mroczek (University of California Davis, USA)
Dan Nässelqvist (University of Gothenburg, Sweden)
Tobias Nicklas (Universität Regensburg, Germany)
Herbert Niehr (Universität Tübingen, Germany)
Peter Oakes (University of Manchester, UK)
Judith Odor (Asbury Theological Seminary, USA)

Suzie Park (Austin Presbyterian Theological Seminary, USA)
Andrew B. Perrin (Trinity Western University, USA)
Raymond F. Person, Jr. (Ohio Northern University, USA)
John C. Poirier (Kingswell Theological Seminary, USA)
Mladen Popović (Groningen, Netherlands)
Stanley E. Porter (McMaster Divinity College, Canada)
Melissa D. Ramos (University of California, Los Angeles, USA)
Bennie H. Reynolds, III (Medical University of South Carolina, USA)
David Rhoads (Lutheran School of Theology at Chicago, USA)
Jason A. Riley (Fuller Theological Seminary, USA)
Rafael Rodríguez (Johnson University, USA)
Christopher Rollston (George Washington University, USA)
Dieter T. Roth (Johannes Gutenberg Universität Mainz, Germany)
Jens Schröeter (Humboldt University of Berlin)
Barry Schwartz (The University of Georgia, USA)
Beth M. Sheppard (Duke University, USA)
Minna Shkul (University of Sheffield, UK)
John Arthur Smith (Church of Norway)
H. Gregory Snyder (Davidson College, USA)
Julia Snyder (Universität Regensburg, Germany)
Elsie R. Stern (Reconstructionist Rabbinical College, USA)
Marti Steussy (Christian Theological Seminary, USA)
Tyler Stewart (Marquette University, USA)
Aaron P. Tate (University of Wisconsin, USA)
Tom Thatcher (Cincinnati Christian University, USA)
Emanuel Tov (Hebrew University of Jerusalem, Israel)
Erin K. Vearncombe (Princeton University, USA)
Tommy Wasserman (Örebro School of Theology, Sweden)
David Wenkel (Moody Bible Institute, USA)
Rodney A. Werline (Barton College, USA)
Angela Yarber (Wake Forest University, USA)
Mark Ziese (Johnson University, USA)

Table of Abbreviations

Explanation of Talmudic Abbreviations

The distinct versions of Talmudic tractates are indicated by the single-letter abbreviation preceding the named tractate, where *y*. indicates Jerusalem and *b*. indicates Babylonian. A preceding *t*. denotes a tractate of the Tosefta, while an *m*. indicates the Mishnah and *b*. a baraita (a Tannaitic rule bearing an authoritative voice yet outside the Mishnah).

List of Journal Abbreviations

AB	Anchor Bible
ANRW	Aufstieg und Niedergang der römischen Welt: Geschichte und Kultur Roms im Spiegel der neueren Forschung
AOAT	Alter Orient und Altes Testament
AOS	American Oriental Series
AYBRL	Anchor Yale Bible Reference Library
BASOR	*Bulletin of the American Schools of Oriental Research*
BBR	*Bulletin for Biblical Research*
BEvT	Beiträge zur evangelischen Theologie
BRev	*Bible Review*
BZAW	Beihefte zur Zeitschrift für die alttestamentliche Wissenschaft
BZNW	Beihefte zur Zeitschrift für die neutestamentliche Wissenschaft
CBR	*Currents in Biblical Research*
CJ	*Classical Journal*
ConBNT	Coniectanea neotestamentica or Coniectanea biblica: New Testament Series
CRINT	Compendia rerum iudaicarum ad Novum Testamentum
DJD	*Discoveries in the Judaean Desert*
DSD	*Dead Sea Discoveries*
EDSS	*Encyclopedia of the Dead Sea Scrolls*. 2000. Edited by L. Schiffman and J.C. VanderKam. 2 vols. Oxford: Oxford University Press.
ESCO	European Studies of Christian Origins
FRLANT	Forschungen zur Religion und Literatur des Alten und Neuen Testaments
HBS	Herders Biblische Studen
HSM	Harvard Semitic Monographs
HSS	Harvard Semitic Studies
HUCA	*Hebrew Union College Annual*
JAAR	*Journal of the American Academy of Religion*
JAOS	*Journal of the American Oriental Society*
JBL	*Journal of Biblical Literature*
JJTP	*Journal of Jewish Thought and Philosophy*
JPTSup	*Journal of Pentacostal Theology Supplement Series*

JQR	*Jewish Quarterly Review*
JSJ	*Journal for the Study of Judaism in the Persian, Hellenistic, and Roman Periods*
JSJS	Supplements to the Journal for the Study of Judaism
JSNT	*Journal for the Study of the New Testament*
JSNTSup	Journal for the Study of the New Testament: Supplement Series
JSOT	*Journal for the Study of the Old Testament*
JSOTSup	Journal for the Study of the Old Testament Supplement Series
JTS	*Journal of Theological Studies*
LCL	Loeb Classical Library
LHBOTS	Library of the Hebrew Bible/Old Testament Studies
LNTS	Library of New Testament Studies
NovT	*Novum Testamentum*
NTS	*New Testament Studies*
OIS	Oriental Institute Seminars
PMLA	Publications of the Modern Language Association
RBL	*Review of Biblical Literature*
ResQ	*Restoration Quarterly*
RevExp	*Review and Expositor*
RGG	*Religion en Geschichte und Gegenwart*
SBLDS	Society of Biblical Literature Dissertation Series
SBLRBS	Society of Biblical Literature Resources for Biblical Study
SBLSCS	Society of Biblical Literature Septuagint and Cognate Studies
SBTS	Sources for Biblical and Theological Study
SemeiaSt	Semeia Studies
SFMA	Studien zu Fundmunzen der Antike
SJLA	Studies in Judaism in Late Antiquity
SNT	Supplements to Novum Testamentum
SNTSMS	Society for New Testament Studies Monograph Series
STAC	Studien und Texte zu Antike und Christentum
STDJ	*Studies on the Texts of the Desert of Judah*
TANZ	Texte und Arbeiten zum neutestamentlichen Zeitalter
TSAJ	Texte und Studien zum antiken Judentum
UTB	Uni-Taschenbücher
VT	*Vetus Testamentum*
VTSup	Vetus Testamentum Supplements
VWGT	Veröffentlichungen der Wissenschaftlichen Gesellschaft für Theologie
WMANT	Wissenschaftliche Monographien zum Alten und Neuen Testament
WUNT	Wissenschaftliche Untersuchungen zum Neuen Testament
ZAW	*Zeitschrift für die alttestamentliche Wissenschaft*
ZNW	*Zeitschrift für die neutestamentliche Wissenschaft und die Kunde der älteren Kirche*
ZPE	*Zeitschrift für Papyrologie und Epigraphik*

Editor Biographies

Tom Thatcher is professor of biblical studies at Cincinnati Christian University. He is the author/editor of numerous books and articles on the Gospels, the Johannine literature, and early Christian media culture, including *The Riddles of Jesus in John*; *Jesus in Johannine Tradition* (with Robert Fortna); *Memory, Tradition, and Text: Uses of the Past in Early Christianity* (with Alan Kirk); *Why John Wrote a Gospel: Jesus-Memory-History*; *Jesus, the Voice, and the Text*; *The Fourth Gospel in First-Century Media Culture* (with Anthony LeDonne); and *Memory and Identity in Ancient Judaism and Early Christianity*. Tom was a founder of the John, Jesus, and History Group and the Mapping Memory Group in the Society of Biblical Literature, and serves as co-chair of SBL's Bible in Ancient and Modern Media Section, as well as series editor for SBL's Resources for Biblical Studies line.

Chris Keith is professor of New Testament and Early Christianity and director of the Centre for the Social-Scientific Study of the Bible at St Mary's University, Twickenham. He currently serves as series editor for T&T Clark's Library of New Testament Studies series.

Raymond F. Person, Jr. is professor of religion at Ohio Northern University. A primary focus of his research concerns refining methodological approaches based on interdisciplinary work, as evident in his most recent books: *The Deuteronomic History and the Book of Chronicles: Scribal Works in an Oral World*, *Deuteronomy and Environmental Amnesia*, *From Conversation to Oral Tradition: A Simplest Systematics for Oral Traditions* and *Empirical Models Challenging Biblical Criticism* (with Robert Rezetko).

Elsie R. Stern is associate professor of Bible and vice-president for academic affairs at the Reconstructionist Rabbinical College. She is the author of *From Rebuke to Consolation: Exegesis and Theology in the Liturgical Anthology of the Ninth of Av Season* and of several articles on the ideological construction and public reception of scripture in early Judaism. She is also a contributor to the *Jewish Study Bible* and the *Women's Torah Commentary*.

How to Use this Book

Media studies, as a broad and multifaceted academic discipline, is concerned with the history of the affects of communications media on human culture. Within this larger universe of research, the *Dictionary of the Bible and Ancient Media* (*DBAM*) focuses specifically on the Bible and related literatures as understood within, and as products of, their original communication contexts. Media scholars view this emphasis on ancient communications culture as a corrective to presuppositions about the Bible that are informed exclusively by the dynamics and aesthetics of modern media, most particularly the print medium. *DBAM* seeks to introduce researchers at all levels to this growing field by providing a convenient handbook of key terms, concepts, methods, and voices that are frequently encountered in media-critical studies of the Bible.

The Hebrew Bible and the New Testament – the Jewish Scriptures and the Christian Scriptures – are the primary focus of this book. However, the study of other ancient Near Eastern and Hellenistic literatures can provide tremendous insight into the ancient media culture in which the Bible was composed, published and transmitted, and references to such texts are common in media-critical studies of the Bible. *DBAM* therefore includes entries on a number of non-canonical texts and issues surrounding their study, including, for example, Jewish and Christian Apocalypses, the Cave of Letters (Naḥal Ḥever), the Dead Sea Scrolls and other Judean Desert Texts, the Elephantine Papyri, the Enochic literature, Jubilees, letters, pesharim, Ras Shamra, rabbinic literature, testaments, and testimonia. Since *DBAM* is concerned with the period in which the biblical books were composed, the historical and geographical scope of the book is limited to the time periods of the Assyrian, Babylonian, Persian, Greek, and Roman empires and the lands included within these empires, with an emphasis on Israel/Palestine and other areas in which ancient Israelites, Jews, and Christians lived during these times.

Beyond these historical and geographical considerations, the scope and content of *DBAM* reflect the current contours of the field of biblical media studies. Most Bible dictionaries (e.g. the *Anchor Bible Dictionary* and the *HarperCollins Bible Dictionary*) strive to be comprehensive in scope, covering a very broad range of historical, interpretive, and critical concerns related to the biblical texts. *DBAM* strives to comprehend only the scope and distinct concerns of media criticism of the Bible, with emphasis on terms, themes and theories that might be encountered while reading a media-critical study. Reflecting this unique focus, *DBAM* omits many entries that might appear in other reference tools (e.g. on specific biblical characters or books of the Bible and their histories of research) and includes entries not found in most other Bible dictionaries (e.g. on terms and concepts such as cultural memory and pluriformity) that are specific to media studies. Further, those entries that *DBAM* may share with other Bible dictionaries reflect the distinctive concerns of media studies, and may therefore introduce issues that others do not or may exclude the more familiar themes upon which they focus. For example, many Bible reference works will include an entry on Poetry in the Hebrew Bible, but in *DBAM* this entry explores how the comparative study of oral traditions, as founded by Milman Parry and Albert Lord, can inform the study of biblical poetic texts. In this respect, *DBAM* seeks to supplement, rather than replace, the existing library of biblical reference tools, specifically by providing both students and scholars with a comprehensive and accessible handbook for understanding the significant contribution that media studies is providing to the study of the Bible.

DBAM begins with an introduction to media studies and biblical studies by Raymond Person and Chris Keith. The introduction not only summarizes the history of the field, but will also provide readers a framework for understanding the remaining entries, which are listed in alphabetical order. In the introduction and throughout *DBAM*, cross references to other entries within the book are indicated by SMALL CAPS, and most entries conclude with a suggested bibliography for further reading. Longer and more substantial entries seek to provide a conceptual framework for shorter ones, which define individual concepts and illustrate their significance to research on the Bible. While complete neutrality is impossible, the editors have attempted to ensure that all entries accurately reflect how the term or concept in question is broadly defined and understood within the field, rather than representing the nuanced perspectives of the individual contributors.

Finally, please note that the list of entries in *DBAM* is not comprehensive, and cannot be. In recent decades, interest in media-critical study of the Bible has grown exponentially, with new monographs and collections appearing every month. *DBAM* attempts to help interested readers navigate this growing field, in hopes that the exploration will open new insights. The editors have found that the process of developing this work, and of engaging with its contributors, has significantly expanded their own understanding, and we trust that the same will be true for our readers as well.

Tom Thatcher, Lead Editor

Media Studies and Biblical Studies: An Introduction

RAYMOND F. PERSON, JR. AND CHRIS KEITH

The *Dictionary of the Bible and Ancient Media* (hereafter *DBAM*) is the first reference work designed for scholars and students that introduces terms and concepts relating to the study of the Bible and related literature in ancient communications culture. Although media studies as a discipline is primarily concerned with modern culture, discussions of the influence of various media in ancient societies, such as the difference between oral and written traditions, have a long history. Biblical scholars have discussed issues relating to ancient media for some time (even when not using the term *media*). Particularly since the early 1980s, scholars have explored the potentials of interdisciplinary theories of ORAL TRADITION, oral performance, ancient LITERACY and scribality, ritual, PERSONAL and COLLECTIVE MEMORY, VISUAL CULTURE, and MUSIC for considerations of critical and exegetical problems in the study of the Hebrew Bible, the NT, the DEAD SEA SCROLLS, RABBINIC LITERATURE, and related literatures.

As with any form of interdisciplinary research, the study of these ancient works in their native media contexts has challenged researchers to become acquainted with the technical jargon of a variety of disciplines and approaches. Heretofore, students and scholars had to become familiar with this jargon primarily through reading monographs and articles outside their field, as a reference work specifically dedicated to this sub-discipline was lacking. *DBAM* fills this lacuna by providing introductory entries of 300–5,000 words on terms and topics commonly encountered in studies of the Bible in ancient media culture. For the reader's convenience, entries are listed in alphabetical order by title with cross references (denoted in SMALL CAPS), for those who are interested, to other sections of the book. The remainder of this introduction will offer a high-level orientation to media studies of the Bible and related literature, with a view to providing a framework for the individual entries.

Important Factors in Understanding Ancient Media

In modern times, we often perceive strict dividing lines between different media, so that, for example, there are separate academic disciplines for the study of literature, speech, drama, music, and DANCE. Even if there is some justification to our cultural division of some forms of media in modern times, such divisions can obscure even modern artistic expressions. For example, some modern poetry is written to be read in silence, whereas poetry performed at a poetry slam often has a more musical, rap-like cadence combined with body movements for visual effects. This reality is even more so the case for ancient performances, which often combined what we might identify as poetry, music, and even dance. For example, Homer's Demodokus sings his epic poetry while playing the harp (*Odyssey* 8.44–559; Beck 2012), and Moses' sister Miriam leads the women of Israel in singing an epic celebrating the victory over the Egyptians complete with hand drums and dancing (Exod. 15.20-21; Meyers 1999). Both texts were composed and performed orally, probably for many generations, before being committed to WRITING, and many of these original performances doubtless involved actual singing. The composite character of such ancient performances finds a contemporary analogy in some more recent performance traditions – for example, the South Slavic bards (see GUSLAR) sing their oral epics while bowing the traditional one-stringed musical instrument called a *gusle* (Lord 1960). Modern students and scholars, however, encounter these SONGS as written texts on a printed page, and it is this very difference between their function in ancient media contexts and modern media contexts that reveals the need for media criticism in the study of the Bible. Further, even though *DBAM* divides entries into various forms of media (e.g. DRAMA, MUSIC, DANCE, NONVERBAL COMMUNICATION, POETRY IN THE HEBREW BIBLE, VISUAL CULTURE, and EXEGESIS), readers of *DBAM* should keep in mind that it is important not to overemphasize such divisions to the detriment of our analyses.

The differences between the communications contexts in which the biblical texts were produced and the print-based cultures in which they are now studied were a primary focus of the first generation of biblical media critics. Much seminal research in the field was characterized by an understanding of the interfaces between media, specifically between ORALITY and writing, that is now known as the GREAT DIVIDE thesis. Following this approach, and building on the pioneering research of scholars such as ALBERT LORD, ERIC HAVELOCK, and WALTER ONG, biblical media scholars often posited dramatic differences between speech and writing, differences that extended even to the cognitive potentials of individuals living in cultures dominated by one medium or another. A tensive relationship was often posited between oral traditions and the community lifeways and rituals that supported them and written texts, with the latter and their producers sometimes portrayed as opposed to, or even the death of, the former.

Again, even though there is some justification for this division in some settings, even some modern artistic expressions complicate this dichotomy. To return to the example of poetry, the poetry performed at poetry slams is sometimes written and then memorized to be delivered orally. Likewise, some forms of electronic written communication (such as chatting and texting) have what might be called a more *oral* feel, and for this reason Walter Ong refers to such modern expressions as a form of SECONDARY ORALITY (2002: 3, 11, 133–5). The limitations of the Great Divide thesis are even more pronounced when discussing ancient societies, in which only a minimal proportion of the population could read or write. Even within those ancient societies in which reading and writing (two distinct and separate skills) existed, written texts must be understood in relationship to the orality of the masses. In such a context, even though the masses may have been aware of cultural texts, most people experienced their contents by hearing them read aloud, recited from memory, or memorialized in visual arts such as paintings and statues. Readers of *DBAM* should keep in mind the intricate interplay of orality and literacy as two sometimes competing and sometimes complementary modes of expression, both of which served as tools to facilitate personal and COLLECTIVE MEMORY. Again, this point is reinforced below and in separate entries throughout the book.

While most scholars today view ancient communications culture as a continuum that includes all channels for the production and exchange of messages, media study of the Bible tends to focus on three broad categories of research and the interfaces between them: orality/speech, writing/literacy, and memory. Of course, personal and CULTURAL MEMORY provides much of the content for communication through speech, writing, and other forms of media as well. It will also be helpful here to review the roles of orality, literacy, and memory in antiquity and the ways in which these issues have impacted the study of the Bible.

Orality as Medium

Both in terms of individuals and entire cultures, the earliest forms of human communication – whether the cry of a newborn baby or the first vocal sounds by our mammalian ancestors – are sounds made by the mouth and received by the ear. While some modes of expression do not include oral elements (e.g. sculpture), orality is a critical component of human communication, often occurring alongside other modes of expression (such as body movement). In fact, even those modes that do not include oral elements may nevertheless require some type of oral interpretation for their communicative function to have social implications – for example, a docent in a museum who helps the public interpret a sculpture. Orality is also foundational to, and implicit in, many modern alphabetic writing systems, which convert sounds to visual symbols by utilizing alphabetic letters that represent sounds. When we consider the pervasiveness of orality in human cultures and how it combines with other modes of expression (including written texts), we must recognize that orality is a term that covers many different forms of communication.

The most basic form of orality is everyday conversation, which we begin learning from our families even in the womb. As we mature, our language skills become more sophisticated, so that we can change linguistic REGISTERS from one social setting to another – for example, 'talking trash' with close friends in a pub but using 'the Queen's English' in formal settings. These forms of orality are the domain of disciplines such as CONVERSATION ANALYSIS and DISCOURSE ANALYSIS that study human communication that can be recorded with modern video/audio cameras, but are beyond the reach of those with interests in ancient societies. Because of this difficulty, biblical scholars have primarily been interested in the comparative study of the oral tradition and FOLKLORE that purportedly lie behind the biblical texts. Since reconstruction of the oral traditions behind the Bible depends on our reading of the text – that is, we only can know of the possible existence of such traditions from the written Bible itself – scholars have often sought analogies to the biblical material in the study of contemporary oral cultures, so that they can know more about how, for example, PROVERBS, PARABLES, and RIDDLES work in various cultures. Such a comparative method provides some guidelines for understanding the orality behind, and sometimes embedded within, the biblical texts.

Writing as Medium

Since the books of the Bible are obviously written, and since they were written in cultural contexts where writing was available and used as a communications technology, the study of the development and use of writing in the ancient world is significant for understanding the composition and early reception of the biblical texts. Some media critics have given particular attention to the nature of writing and reading in antiquity and to the interfaces between writing and orality. This topic is of considerable interest simply because biblical scholarship, especially in the West, has traditionally assumed that ancient writings were produced, published, and used in ways similar to modern print books. Recent research, however, has produced a much more nuanced understanding of the place of writing, the levels and social implications of literacy, and the role of scribes in antiquity.

In general, 'literacy' refers to the (separate) skills of reading and writing. Today literacy is rarely an important topic because publicly funded elementary schools ensure that most individuals in the industrialized world, even those living in poverty, are taught to read and write. Under such conditions, literacy is typically notable only when absent. In the ancient world, however, there was nothing like the public education that we know today in modernized cultures. Only a slim minority of people (probably 10% or less of the population) in the cultures that transmitted the Bible and related literature attained literate skills to a degree of proficiency. Even among these few, compositional writing ability (i.e. advanced writing beyond signature literacy) was less common than reading because it was acquired in the later stages of education and very few progressed to those stages. Most of these literate individuals were either members of the wealthy classes or slaves in their employ.

At the same time, these predominantly illiterate cultures were characterized by a high degree of textuality. That is, although most individuals could not read or write themselves, they were nevertheless thoroughly aware of writing, MANUSCRIPTS, and the power these texts could wield over their lives. This was true especially in the case of sacred texts but also of more mundane documents, such as land deeds, tax receipts, or marriage contracts. If nothing else, imperial signage, coinage, and public inscriptions often brought the written word before the illiterate populace.

These realities – especially the fact that the books of the Bible were produced in a world where the large majority of people could not read them – have a number of implications for how one understands various forms of media in the ancient world. As a matter of first importance, and in contrast to some previous scholarship, no matter how much significance one attributes to orality and illiteracy for understanding biblical and related traditions, one should not conceptualize such phenomena as entirely detached from literacy and its cultural influence. None of the cultures under discussion in *DBAM* could be characterized by what Ong referred to as *primary orality* – lacking knowledge of writing and its effects altogether (Ong 2002: 11). In other words, the cultures that produced the Bible were not oral or textual but oral *and* textual. We must therefore expect a complex interplay between orality and textuality, and likewise between literacy and illiteracy. The usage and social values of manuscripts in these cultures emerged from and reflected a context where most individuals could not access those texts themselves.

A related further impact of restricted literacy on the ancient media environment is that the production and copying of manuscripts, as well as the reading of manuscripts, were specialized trade skills. We often think of reading and writing as simple acts that are quickly performed, but this is a projection of our own reading and writing practices upon the ancient world (see EDUCATION IN ANCIENT ISRAEL; EDUCATION, HELLENISTIC; SCRIBES). In the ancient context, proficient reading and writing required training and practice. Reading eloquently, and especially publicly, necessitated familiarity with the script and spacing of the individual manuscript being read, and no one manuscript was exactly the same as another since each was handwritten. Similarly, writing often required not only the ability to form letters, syllables, and words correctly, but also the abilities to prepare the WRITING MATERIALS being used, including animal skin or PAPYRUS and the ink and writing instrument being used. Of course, less skill was required to write a household list on a wax tablet, or to carve GRAFFITI on the wall of a building. But one should generally consider proficient readers and writers in antiquity as artisans of literacy (see SCRIBES/SCRIBALITY).

The biblical world – at least, the world of the late Second Temple period – attributed high social value to the sacred and legal written texts that the large majority of people could not read. In such a context, the possession and usage of literate skills enabled some groups to function as part of the intellectual and political elite, as was the case for priests and Torah scribes or many of the great rabbis of the MISHNAH and Talmudim. In other cases, the possession and usage of these skills reflected a group's servile status or role as workaday members of the imperial bureaucracy. This was the case for slaves who were LECTORS in wealthy Roman households, reading aloud at dinner for the owner's guests, or village scribes who copied formulas mechanically on contracts for customers in the *agora*. Thus, although the possession of specialized literate skills could and often did coincide with high social status, it did not always. A host of other factors – including the specific texts read or written, the language in which they were read or written, and the social contexts for the reading and writing – affected the significance of any given instance of the employment of literate skills.

Nevertheless, in text-centred communities such as ancient Judaism and early Christianity, those literate individuals who used their abilities for the reading, copying, and interpretation of authoritative documents often attained a high degree of power as interpretive authorities (see TEXTUAL COMMUNITIES). Thus, the complexities of the ancient media culture meant that literacy was sometimes a primary and demonstrative means by which authorities exercised power over the illiterate masses or, alternatively, the means by which other groups resisted those powers (e.g. Jer. 8.8; 1 Enoch 69.8-9). The same dynamic often prevails in modern religious communities, as when a rabbi reads Hebrew in synagogue, a preacher explains the meaning of Greek words to a congregation, or someone challenges such individuals by appealing to the original languages.

Memory and Media Studies

Alongside literacy, one of the most important recent interdisciplinary developments in the study of ancient media culture has been its convergence with the study of memory. Most of us think of memory as an individual recall facility that allows us to access the past in our brains, similar to opening a filing cabinet and taking out a document that we filed some while ago. In both the sciences and the humanities, however, researchers have demonstrated that memory is a much more complex phenomenon of human activity and is intricately tied to the present social realities of the remembering person or group. Except in the cases of injury or brain damage, the reason that we forget the majority of the past is that it ceases to be relevant to us in the present.

There are a number of scholarly approaches to memory, each with its own focus and application to scholarship surrounding the Bible and the cultures that produced it. Cognitive and autobiographical approaches to memory concern the working of the brain and its neural activity (see COGNITIVE/PERSONAL MEMORY), focusing on ways that individuals store, access, and use the past. Such studies often involve lab tests and scientific reports, which biblical scholars must then apply to the ancient context while attempting to account for the sometimes significant cultural differences. Applications of this approach in biblical studies have included studies of eyewitnesses of Jesus, for example, and the historical reliability of the written Gospels vis-à-vis the past they purport to reflect. Other applications of this approach have overlapped with orality studies, with their shared interest in how individual storytellers are capable of remembering very lengthy epic poems, passed down over generations, often without being written, or with how scribes draw from the larger oral-literate tradition even in the process of copying individual manuscripts (see SCRIBAL MEMORY).

Another major influence on biblical studies has been social or cultural memory theory (see COLLECTIVE/SOCIAL MEMORY and CULTURAL MEMORY). In general terms, both social memory theory and cultural memory theory study ways in which groups employ the remembered past on a culture-wide level for the purposes of creating, affirming, or challenging group identity. Particular emphasis is placed upon the political usages of the past – how those in power, and those who wish to challenge power, shape the past for their own purposes, whether that means highlighting it, fabricating it, or attempting to silence it, among other things. Social memory theory stems from the work of MAURICE HALBWACHS, a French sociologist, while cultural memory theory refers to the adaptation of Halbwachs's work by the German Egyptologist JAN ASSMANN, as well as his wife Aleida Assmann, a cultural theorist. Jan Assmann frequently utilizes ancient Israel's Scriptures and history as case studies to illustrate his conclusions, and Hebrew Bible scholars have often interacted with his work. NT scholars have interacted broadly with social and cultural models of memory as a framework for understanding the development and preservation of tradition in early Christianity.

The Social Contexts of Ancient Media

As noted earlier, speech and writing, along with other media of communication, functioned in antiquity (as they do today) alongside one another on a continuum. By definition, all communication occurs in a social context, and these contexts are significant to the chosen medium, as well as the content and shape of exchanges that occur within them. Three such social contexts are particularly significant to media study of the Bible and all are represented and discussed, in various ways, in entries in this book: daily life, WORSHIP, and EDUCATION. Of course, these three contexts are not mutually exclusive, and they also should be viewed as a continuum of experience, but each was characterized by its own emphases in the use of communications technologies.

Obviously, the structure and rhythm of daily life is a significant context for communication in any society. We learn our language and culture in the family household as infants by observing the daily activities of our elders, siblings, and other household members. Even before we obtain the verbal linguistic skills to say what we want, we learn the meaning of objects related to their functions and learn to ask for what we want by looking at and pointing to an object. Thus, looking at and pointing to a stew pot, even if it is empty, communicates to others that we are hungry, because we have learnt what cooking pots are for. In this way our built environments can communicate a lot to us nonverbally. The physical structure of the home and the HOUSEHOLD ITEMS found within it often communicate the security and care provided by the family that lives in the structure or, in contrast, in times of famine the emptiness of the household's storage facilities communicates how severe the threat to life really is. Furthermore, at an early age we also begin to learn our place in certain daily rituals that are a part of household WORSHIP – for example, in prayers of thanksgiving before or after MEALS. Of course, such rituals would consist not only of spoken words but also of body movements (see NONVERBAL COMMUNICATION IN PERFORMANCE).

As individuals gain linguistic abilities, STORYTELLING within the family household adds depth to our knowledge of our culture. We hear stories about our ancestors – those who live with us, those who live some distance from us, and those who have already died – as told by our elders, so that the memories of them continue to the next generation. Although the Bible is clearly the product of literate elites recording selective cultural traditions in writing, some of what is recorded may have roots in the daily life of the common people. For example, many biblical PROVERBS likely arose in the oral environment of ancient agrarian households and were effective means of transmitting cultural knowledge within the daily lives of the people. The Bible may point to some limited examples of such linguistic artefacts from the daily life of the masses in addition to the archaeological remains of ancient material culture.

Much like current liturgy, various forms of media played prominent roles in ancient worship (see WORSHIP, ANCIENT ISRAELITE; WORSHIP, ANCIENT JEWISH; and WORSHIP, EARLY CHRISTIAN). The reading of manuscripts containing authoritative texts was a core element in Jewish SYNAGOGUES and Christian churches alike (see GOSPELS, PERFORMANCE OF; TORAH READING). When conceptualizing such practices, however, one must keep in mind the effects of restricted literacy and the dynamic interaction of oral and written tradition. In contrast to the reading of texts in modern liturgical settings where individuals might hold a personal copy of a text and follow along with the liturgist's reading, in the ancient context many synagogues (especially those geographically distant from Jerusalem) and churches likely had only a few, or perhaps one, copy of a text. Almost all public readings consisted of reading a single manuscript aloud for the sake of an illiterate listening audience. Thus, most ancient worshippers experienced their holy texts aurally by listening to the designated reader or readers vocalize the text. This reality also means there was an inevitable performative element to the reading of manuscripts in worship, with the reader choosing which passages to highlight and how to highlight them vocally. These visual, oral, and aural factors in the reading of texts thus created a context of audience participation in the reading, as one may easily assume that the reader of the text could have responded to audience requests or prompts. Some manuscripts even seem to prompt or assume such audience participation, as is the case when Paul asks the readership of his letter to the Galatians to inspect the large letters with which he signed the letter (Gal. 6.11) or chastises the Corinthians for their abuse of ritual meals (1 Cor. 11). Some biblical authors give instructions to the lector (Mk 13.14; Mt. 24.15).

Furthermore, worship certainly includes much more than verbal communication. Liturgical rituals certainly include body movement as is most obvious in INITIATION RITUALS, such as CIRCUMCISION and BAPTISM, or festivals that require PILGRIMAGE. The very space in which worship occurs may communicate much to the worshippers, such as the table for the reading of the Torah in SYNAGOGUES (see TORAH READING). In fact, even the absence of the physical Temple after its destruction in 70 CE continued to influence Jewish and Christian worship in the collective memory of these communities (see SECOND TEMPLE; TEMPLES).

A third significant context for considerations of the media culture of antiquity relates to practices and institutions of education (see EDUCATION IN ANCIENT ISRAEL; EDUCATION, HELLENISTIC). Modern studies confirm that children who are read to at early ages, and therefore become comfortable with books, are much more likely to succeed in their later formal education. The same principle applies to the ancient world (Rollston 2010: 122–6). As noted above, education begins in the home and, since the vast majority of family households in ancient and Hellenistic Israel had no need for writing as a technology to support the family business (most often farming, but this is even the case with most of the urban specializations like metallurgy), the education that most ancients received did not include literacy. In fact, when we think of education today, we tend to think of formal contexts in which a professional teacher is paid by the family or community to provide formal instruction that includes reading, writing, and arithmetic. However, for most of the peoples of the ancient world, education occurred in the informal setting of daily family life. For some families (especially in urban areas), their daily lives may have involved the family business possibly within a family-oriented guild, such as pottery, metallurgy, and carpentry. Formal education provided by the state was extremely rare, and even the training of scribes likely occurred within families in the scribal guilds (Hezser 2001; Rollston 2010), which means that the teaching of reading, writing, and basic mathematics that we today associate with formal education most likely still occurred within the confines of scribal families connected to the central bureaucracy. Later in the Greco-Roman world, wealthy individuals might secure instruction for their children through a private tutor or, in more urban areas, a school, where students could study reading, writing, mathematics, and RHETORIC.

The Study of the Bible as/in Ancient Media

Obviously, no dictionary, not least this one, emerges from a vacuum. This book in many respects seeks to summarize and document the emergence of a broad movement within biblical scholarship towards consideration of the media dynamics of the Bible as key to its interpretation. As noted earlier, this movement has been driven, from the outset, by interdisciplinary research in a wide range of disciplines. Any discussion of the history of media criticism of the Bible therefore requires consideration of scholarship outside the field, particularly with reference to developments in the study of orality and oral cultures, writing and the implications of literary, and personal and collective/cultural memory over the past century.

Studies in Orality and Literacy

Probably due in part to PLATO's denigration of oral discourse in comparison with written discourse, Western scholars have long been interested in the relationship between orality and literacy (see ORAL TRADITION, THE COMPARATIVE STUDY OF). These past discussions were primarily based on the assumption noted earlier, and now referred to as the GREAT DIVIDE thesis, that speech and writing should be sharply differentiated as forms of communication. Because of this assumption, earlier scholarship was primarily interested in written literature, even when scholars allowed that there might be forms of oral tradition behind the literary texts. That is, they assumed that even though oral traditions may lie behind the texts, the process of writing down these oral traditions dramatically changed them, so much so that there was little oral residue remaining. Thus, scholars of ancient Near Eastern literature, classical Greek and Roman literature, and medieval literature often approached the literary texts produced in these periods from the perspective of having been produced by authors in literate societies. Often these same scholars viewed these ancient and medieval societies as having high levels of literacy, a conclusion that was deemed largely self-evident by the simple fact of the high literary production of these societies.

In many ways, the modern study of orality, oral cultures, and oral-based texts originates in the seminal work of MILMAN PARRY and ALBERT LORD on the HOMERIC QUESTION in the early twentieth century. Advances in Greek philology had suggested that the *Iliad* and the *Odyssey* each must have been composed by more than one author, because these literary texts include Greek from different historical periods and different regional dialects. The Homeric Question asked whether a single genius, 'Homer', was responsible for these variegated texts, or whether the name 'Homer' should be understood as a collective reference to a larger group of anonymous authors. Rather than attributing individual passages to different authors and scribes, Parry attempted to solve the problem by drawing upon MARCEL JOUSSE'S theory of oral style and Matija Murko's work on the living oral traditions of South Slavic epic. To test these models, Parry and his student Albert Lord collected a large corpus of South Slavic epics performed by living performers and used this material to demonstrate how even illiterate bards (such as the GUSLAR Avdo Međedović) can compose long poetic epics using conventional formulas and themes. Because this oral-traditional style emerges over time and is transmitted across generations of storytellers, epics composed in performance often have what appears to be a linguistic mixture from different historical periods and regional dialects of the same language (see REGISTER; SPECIAL GRAMMAR). With this comparative evidence, Parry and Lord could insist that the Homeric epics were the product of one Homer, a single oral performer, who drew upon a long-standing tradition of composition in performance.

Although their work was not widely accepted in Greek philology, Parry and Lord's thesis contributed significantly to discussions of orality and literacy. Probably because their strong thesis contradicted so much earlier work in ancient and medieval studies, many of the early scholars influenced by their work continued their own work within the tradition of the GREAT DIVIDE or were at least interpreted by others as doing so (e.g. WALTER ONG, ERIC HAVELOCK, and JACK GOODY). However, some other early scholars saw how the Parry-Lord approach undercut significantly the Great Divide thesis. For example, RUTH FINNEGAN drew from her extensive fieldwork in African oral traditions to provide additional support to the comparative study of oral tradition, William Harris used a variety of social science models to estimate the level of literacy in ancient Greece to be low (about 10%), and ROSALIND THOMAS described the interplay between orality and literacy in classical Athens as well as provided important nuances concerning the many varieties of both orality and literacy.

Probably the scholar who had the greatest affect upon broadening the Parry-Lord approach to other literatures and oral traditions was JOHN MILES FOLEY. Although his own primary expertise was Homeric epic, Old English epic, and South Slavic epic, Foley's many research projects, especially his founding and editing of the journal *Oral Tradition*, encouraged scholars throughout the world to apply insights from the comparative study of oral traditions to folklore and literature from every continent and spanning the ancient and modern periods. Foley also encouraged discussions with other relevant approaches to oral traditions – for example, the work of RICHARD BAUMAN, DENNIS TEDLOCK, and DELL HYMES (see also ETHNOGRAPHY OF SPEAKING; ETHNOPOETICS).

Studies in Personal and Collective Memory

As noted earlier, scholarly discussion of memory has taken a variety of forms that span the hard sciences and the humanities. Within that broad discussion, the model most relevant for media studies is associated with Jan Assmann (2006 [2000]; 2011 [1992]), who built upon the earlier work of Maurice Halbwachs (1980 [1950]; 1992 [1941, 1952]). Halbwachs is widely viewed as the first scholar to develop a systematic approach to memory as a collective, or social, phenomenon, rather than an individual capacity (see SOCIAL/COLLECTIVE MEMORY). Rather than viewing memory as a store-and-retrieve function, wherein individuals package the past in some recess of the brain to retrieve it when needed, Halbwachs viewed memory as the product of a dynamic process of construction carried out dually by the individual remembering and the society in which he or she remembers.

Halbwachs' definition of memory differed from common understandings of that term in at least two important ways. First, for him, memory was not primarily about the individual. Although his sometimes less-than-careful language left him open to the accusation that he removed the role of the individual from the formation of memory, this strictly is not accurate. Halbwachs preserved the role of the individual in memory formation, but emphasized strongly the influence of society at large and of discrete social groups (e.g. the family, religion) on the individual's ability to articulate the past and form judgements about it. For Halbwachs, society provides the impetus for what the individual remembers and how the individual remembers it, which gives present social realities a significant, and at times determinative, role in what is remembered and how it is commemorated. He thus stressed that, while individuals remember and communicate about the past, they do so always as members of larger groups.

Second, and as should already be clear, for Halbwachs, memory was not primarily about the ACTUAL PAST – 'what happened' in time and space. If current social realities are what enable, and sometimes even dictate, how the individual recalls the past, then the act of remembering is more about the present and the forces at work in it than about what happened (see PRESENTISM). Indeed, for Halbwachs, memory was so thoroughly related to society and so thoroughly reflective of the present that he located scholarly interest in an individuals' retention of the past outside the concerns of his collective memory theory altogether (Halbwachs 1992: 40 n.3).

Although Halbwachs was not particularly interested in issues surrounding media studies, it was perhaps inevitable that his work would be appropriated in this manner because it highlighted the role of language (Halbwachs 1980: 51), ritual, organizations of space (geography) and time (calendar), and identity formation in all discourse about the past – factors that similarly lie at the foundation of media studies. Jan Assmann, building upon Halbwachs' arguments, took memory studies more purposefully in the direction of ancient media culture. Whereas Halbwachs was primarily concerned with the social formation of the past in the living generation (what he termed collective memory), Assmann was concerned with how socially formed images of the past are passed onto subsequent generations and persist for long durations. Assmann termed this multigenerational form of tradition as cultural memory and renamed Halbwachs' collective memory as COMMUNICATIVE MEMORY, capturing the distinction in chronological focus by saying, 'With cultural memory the depths of time open up' (Assmann 2006: 24). Stated otherwise, Assmann focused on how some versions of the past eventually become canonical versions of the past, and here he discussed ancient Israel repetitively. Assmann asserted a key role for manuscripts in enabling this transition, as they permitted the tradition to cross space and time rather than require the immediacy of oral transmission. Manuscripts furthermore enabled a culture of interpretation to arise around the cultural memory, wherein the authoritative interpreters functioned as points of access to the tradition. Clearly, one can think here of the priests, scribes, rabbis, and philosophers of antiquity who served as TEXT BROKERS between highly regarded forms of cultural memory and the largely illiterate groups that esteemed them (Snyder 2000).

Media and the Study of the Hebrew Bible

Early applications of media studies to the Hebrew Bible were primarily interested in the oral traditions behind the biblical text and how these traditions influenced (or did not) the written text (see also ORAL TRADITION AND the Hebrew Bible). This early interest in oral traditions is most evident in the form-critical approach to the Hebrew Bible developed by Hermann Gunkel and the work of the Scandinavian school of oral traditions represented by Ivan Engnell and Eduard Nielsen (Culley 1986; see also form criticism; folkloristics).

The Parry-Lord approach to oral traditions initiated a renewed interest in the study of oral traditions from a comparative perspective, including early references to their work by their Harvard colleagues, William F. Albright and Frank Moore Cross (Culley 1986). One of the earliest scholars of the Hebrew Bible to utilize the Parry-Lord oral-formulaic theory was Robert Culley, who applied the model to the book of Psalms, arguing that one can discern traces of oral-formulaic composition in the biblical psalms. In his later work, Culley applied these insights to other poetic and narrative texts in the Hebrew Bible. Following the strong arguments of Parry and Lord and their early development by other scholars, Culley's early works tended to sharply distinguish between oral and literate features of the biblical texts, while his later research moved away from the Great Divide thesis to reflect a more nuanced perspective.

The scholar most closely identified with the comparative approach to oral traditions and folklore as applied to the Hebrew Bible is Susan Niditch. During her doctoral programme at Harvard, she studied under both Frank Moore Cross and Albert Lord, so that her continuing research in folklore and epic demonstrates their significant influence. Her 1996 monograph *Oral World and Written Word* remains the most thorough application of the Parry-Lord approach to the Hebrew Bible to date. In this work, she directly challenged the methodological assumptions of source criticism and concluded that the traditional higher-critical approach required significant modification in light of the oral register found in the Hebrew Bible.

Another scholar whose work has drawn significantly from the comparative study of oral tradition is Raymond F. Person, Jr., who studied briefly under John Miles Foley. Influenced by analogous arguments by A. N. Doane and Kathleen O'Brien O'Keeffe for Anglo-Saxon scribes, Person has argued that the ancient Israelite scribes should be understood as performers of the biblical texts, even in their acts of copying manuscripts (1998; 2010; 2015). An important theme in his work is how the current aversion in textual criticism to the reconstruction of the original text of a biblical book aligns especially well with the discounting of the original text in the work of Lord and Foley, so that what are often understood by scholars of literature as variants that have corrupted the original text should better be understood within the context of multiformity, a characteristic of oral traditions, as well as the textual plurality so evident in late Second Temple literature (2015). Thus, like Niditch, Person has provided a strong critique of the assumptions behind current source-critical and redaction-critical approaches (see especially 2016). He has also drawn significantly from the discipline of conversation analysis, demonstrating how this method combines with the comparative study of oral traditions to illuminate our understanding of storytelling and what Lord called the special grammar of oral traditions.

Possibly the most influential discussion of orality and literacy in relationship to literature of the Hebrew Bible has been the recent advances in the understanding of the oral origins of the prophetic literature, especially in the work of Martti Nissinen and his colleagues (see prophecy). The publication of ancient Mesopotamian literature, especially from Mari and Nineveh, has opened up a wealth of comparative material concerning prophecy in the ancient Near East. This has led to more precise definitions of prophecy as a form of intermediation and much better understandings of the role of orality and literacy as they relate to prophecy and prophetic literature. Although he does not draw directly from the comparative study of oral traditions, Nissinen has acknowledged how well his conclusions coincide with the conclusions of Niditch, Person, David Carr, and others concerning orality and literacy in the ancient world. Thus, the comparative approach to oral traditions has more to contribute to the study of prophetic literature.

Although discussions of orality and literacy have a long history in the study of the Hebrew Bible, memory studies are a more recent phenomenon. Here the work of Egyptologist Jan Assmann, which includes significant discussion of ancient Israelite tradition, has been especially influential. Perhaps the most significant application of memory research to critical problems relating to the Hebrew Bible is David Carr's *Writing on the Tablet of the Heart* (2005). Carr's approach is decisively comparative, drawing from discussions of orality and literacy from the ancient Near East and the ancient Mediterranean world. After discussing how the visual presentation of texts required that the reader be already familiar with the text (especially in those writing systems before the development of the Greek vowel-consonant alphabet), Carr concluded that the 'written copies of long-duration texts like the Bible, Gilgamesh, or Homer's works' (2005: 5) primarily served the purpose of aiding in the memorization and enculturalization of the texts in educational contexts. 'Orality and writing technology are joint means for accomplishing a common goal: accurate recall of the treasured tradition' (2005: 7).

In his later *The Formation of the Hebrew Bible*, Carr developed the idea of 'memory variants', such as the 'exchange of synonymous words, word-order variation, [and] presence and absence of conjunctions and minor modifiers' (2011: 33). He concluded that scribal copies of texts that include memory variants, cases of harmonization with other texts, and/or expansions based upon traditional material nevertheless could be understood by the ancients as 'reproductions of what was essentially the "same" tradition' (2011: 100; see SCRIBAL MEMORY). Carr's work thus significantly challenges the key premises of source and redaction criticism.

Ehud Ben Zvi is another scholar who has applied memory theory to a range of issues in the study of the Hebrew Bible, and who has engaged other biblical scholars in the conversation by editing collections of essays on the subject (see Ben Zvi and Levin 2012; Edelman and Ben Zvi 2014). His works are primarily interested in how the Persian period literati remembered Israel and Judah's past, especially focusing on the Deuteronomistic History and the book of Chronicles. Ben Zvi emphasizes how the literati's cultural memory of past events influenced their literary production and, in turn, the identity formation and acculturation of the early Second Temple community.

One of the most promising applications of memory studies to the Hebrew Bible is the recent work of Daniel Pioske. Combining discussion of archaeological evidence of the history of Jerusalem with biblical texts and memory studies, Pioske has advanced an innovative argument on the history of Jerusalem that includes the history of the memory of David's Jerusalem through time. He asks how tenth-century Jerusalem, relatively less important than some other sites (e.g. the forgotten city of Khirbet Qeiyafa), became remembered in even grander terms in the later memory of the biblical authors, and concludes that the biblical authors' memory of Jerusalem was significantly influenced by their experience of the later Iron Age capital with its grander buildings and established kingdom (2015a,b), in contrast to other sites that had fallen into obscurity by the time the biblical texts were composed. Illustrating the interfaces between collective memory and current social realities, the biblical authors' memories of Jerusalem can be seen to be a product of their own environments. In an excellent review article (2015c), Pioske critiques most studies applying memory theory to the Hebrew Bible as being too ahistorical – that is, they do not engage adequately in the possible interactions of the actual past of the narrated events and the historical time contemporary to the biblical authors as a useful tool for diachronic historical reconstruction.

Media and the Study of the New Testament

Historically speaking, the majority of applications of media studies in NT criticism have involved attempts to understand the oral Jesus tradition's relationship with the written Gospels. One can trace this scholarly interest in the oral JESUS TRADITION at least back to Herman Gunkel in the late nineteenth century (see Lee 2012: 1–73). Gunkel's work was influential on the leading NT form critics of the early twentieth century,

Martin Dibelius and Rudolf Bultmann. In many respects, their work, and related research developing and utilizing form-critical models, paved the way for the later introduction of media studies into research on the Gospels and NT criticism.

Early Form Criticism viewed the media transition from the oral Jesus tradition to the written Gospels as both significant and insignificant. This transition was significant insofar as it represented, in material form, a key threshold between the two great epochs of the early church – earliest Palestinian, Aramaic-speaking Christianity and later Hellenistic, Greek-speaking Christianity. Dibelius and Bultmann both assumed that the Palestinian Christians were too illiterate to be capable of writing Greek Gospels, which, although not in their view formal literature, were still pretensions to literature requiring some degree of literate abilities. They thus viewed the Palestinian Christians as the crafters of the oral tradition and the Hellenistic Christians as the educated later group that reorganized the oral tradition into the written Gospels, imbuing it with their own theology in the process, a theology that differed from the Palestinians' theology. Both Dibelius and Bultmann sought to reconstruct this earlier, more primitive oral tradition from its traces in the written Gospels, thereby discovering what the earliest Christians thought about Jesus. This transition from oral to written gospel tradition was, at the same time, insignificant for the form critics from a media perspective, inasmuch as they viewed the move from speech to text as essentially seamless and inevitable. Thus, while the production of written Gospels was a watershed in early Christian history, it was not particularly significant in media terms.

To a large extent, media studies emerged within biblical studies as NT scholars began to challenge the assumptions of Form Criticism, specifically the notion that the medium of a communication (e.g. oral vs. written) is not significant for understanding its structure and content. With regard to the malleability of the oral Jesus tradition, Birger Gerhardsson argued, contrary to the form critics, that the driving force behind the shaping of the oral Jesus tradition was not anonymous communities or later Christians but rather the first disciples of Jesus, who formed a collegia of authoritative interpreters (1998 [1961]: 331). Gerhardsson arrived at this conclusion through study of the role of the memory of texts and traditions in ancient Jewish education, and by casting Jesus as a formal rabbi (in contrast to, e.g. an itinerant preacher) and the disciples as his students, an approach that allowed him to apply the pedagogical model evident in the later rabbinic documents to the practices of Jesus and his first followers. Though controversial at the time (see Kelber and Byrskog 2009), Gerhardsson's model prefigured many subsequent appeals to memory and orality as important analytical categories.

Equally unimpressed with the form-critical model for the transmission of Jesus tradition was Werner Kelber, who published his groundbreaking *The Oral and the Written Gospel* in 1983. Kelber agreed with the form critics that the Christologies of Mark, Q, and Paul differed from those of their oral predecessors, but argued that the decision to shift the Jesus tradition from an oral to a written form was in fact a tactical response to these differences, not an inevitable or incidental move. To support his thesis, Kelber highlighted the differences between the oral medium and written medium in service of ultimately arguing that the author of Mark's Gospel textualized the Jesus tradition precisely in order to supplant the Christology of the oral tradition and diminish the authority of its key bearers (e.g. the disciples, Jesus' family members, early Christian prophets). Although one could still detect traces of orality in Mark's Gospel, by textualizing the tradition the author had frozen a once fluid and living oral stream of tradition into a fixed text. He also argued that Paul worked to overcome the power of the written Torah by employing oral hermeneutical techniques, thus seeing an analogous contentious relationship between orality and textuality in the Pauline corpus. Particularly significant to subsequent study, Kelber's enormously influential work introduced biblical scholars to a wide range of research in the comparative study of oral tradition, including the works of Walter Ong, Milman Parry and Albert Lord, Ruth Finnegan, and John Miles Foley.

Since its release, the method and conclusions of *The Oral and the Written Gospel* have been significantly debated, and no NT media scholar today (including Kelber himself) would accept its arguments in toto. The book's lasting influence, however, has been tremendous in terms of awakening biblical scholars to the significance of the oral milieu of early Christianity and the interdisciplinary field of media studies. Almost all subsequent applications of media studies to the Gospels implicitly or explicitly take their bearings from *The Oral and the Written Gospel* (see Hearon 2006).

Heavily influenced by Kelber's early work, and in dialogue with the contemporary emphasis on narrative-critical study of the Bible in the 1980s, a group of scholars led by David Rhoads and Tom Boomershine developed PERFORMANCE CRITICISM (see Rhoads 2010). Highlighting the illiterate nature of early Christianity and the prominent role of oral speech in antiquity, performance critics argue that the NT documents were *performative* in the sense that they were orally composed and normally published through oral recitation. Building on this premise, performance critics seek to gain new understandings of the biblical texts by performing them orally, or viewing them performed orally, in modern contexts, often through verbatim memorization and repetition of passages or entire biblical books. Performance criticism now has its own monograph series, *Biblical Performance Criticism* (Cascade Books), and largely informs the work of the international Network of Biblical Storytellers. It has also attracted criticism from scholars of ancient book culture for its perceived misunderstanding of the roles of manuscripts in an oral environment (Hurtado 2014), a debate that serves as witness to the continuing relevance of media-critical enquiry.

As noted earlier, NT scholarship in general has moved away from the Great Divide thesis to emphasize the many interfaces of memory, orality, writing, and other media in antiquity. Two recent textbooks, one of which focuses upon scholarly conceptions of the oral Jesus tradition (Eve 2013) and the other of which focuses upon orality in NT studies more broadly (Rodríguez 2014), impress upon introductory readers the need to not overemphasize the differences between oral and written communication in antiquity. Rodríguez's study reconceives media criticism of the NT as less concerned with discovering traces of orality that linger in manuscripts and more concerned with understanding the ancient media context in which early Christians actualized their traditions, contexts in which orality and textuality could intertwine seamlessly.

Contributing to the breakdown of the notion of the Great Divide among NT media critics has been a developing stream of scholarship on ancient book culture from a memory perspective. Kelber's more recent work, sometimes overshadowed by the influence of *The Oral and the Written Gospel*, has been important here. As a recent collection of his essays (Kelber 2013) indicates, Kelber has more recently moved to a position of seeing manuscripts themselves as exhibiting the earmarks that his earlier work attributed to oral tradition alone, such as flexibility and fluidity. Kelber's more recent research frequently appeals to the cultural memory theory of Jan Assmann, as do Alan Kirk (2008) and Chris Keith (2011) in making similar arguments, thus demonstrating once more the interrelated nature of memory theory and media studies. Along with Tom Thatcher, Kirk formally introduced social and cultural memory theories to NT scholarship in an edited Semeia Studies volume (Kirk and Thatcher 2005). The contributors to this book consistently recognize the overlapping nature of some aspects of memory studies and media criticism.

As Eve's and Rodríguez's textbooks make clear, another development among NT media critics reflects advances in studies of ancient literacy. This line of research proceeds from the recognition that the majority of individuals in the Greco-Roman world, including the late Second Temple period, were illiterate (see Harris 1989; Hezser 2001). The implications drawn from this observation vary. In a 1998 article, for example, Tom Thatcher highlights the significance of this cultural environment for understanding the portrayal of textual communities in Josephus. In numerous publications in the aforementioned field of performance criticism, Richard Horsley and David Rhoads preface their arguments for the oral performance of ancient texts by noting widespread illiteracy and asserting that written documents played little role in early Christian culture (e.g. Horsley 2007: 91–3; Rhoads 2010: 167). Alternatively, Gamble appeals to widespread illiteracy as a factor in explaining why books did play such an important role in early Christianity, arguing that literacy was an important factor in the process of the development of the canon (Gamble 2004). Citing the various forms of literacy in the ancient world and the important role of perception in the attribution of literate authority, Chris Keith has argued that Jesus was likely not a scribal-literate teacher, but likely was confused as one on certain occasions (Keith 2011).

As this brief and incomplete survey makes clear, NT scholars have applied media studies to their discipline in a variety of manners. This line of enquiry shows no sign of easing in the near future, as media studies – and especially those associated with memory studies and ancient scribal culture – continue to force scholars to reassess many assumptions about the creation, transmission, and circulation of traditions in early Christianity. There remains, furthermore, a strong need to apply media studies in areas outside Gospels scholarship as vigorously as it has been applied inside Gospels scholarship. In this sense, one can rightly observe that applications of media studies in NT scholarship, like their counterparts in Hebrew Bible scholarship, have a bright future to match their past.

Bibliography

Assmann, Jan. 2006. *Religion and Cultural Memory*. Translated by Rodney Livingstone. Cultural Memory in the Present. Stanford: Stanford University Press. [German original 2000].

Assmann, Jan. 2011. *Cultural Memory and Early Civilization: Writing, Remembrance, and Political Imagination*. Translated by David Henry Wilson. Cambridge: Cambridge University Press. [German original 1992].

Beck, Deborah. 2012. 'The Presentation of Song in Homer's Odyssey'. In *Orality, Literacy and Performance in the Ancient World: Orality and Literacy in the Ancient World, vol. 9*. Edited by Elizabeth Minchin. Mnemosyne Supplements 335. Leiden: Brill, pp. 25–53.

Ben Zvi, Ehud, and Christoph Levin, eds. 2012. *Remembering and Forgetting in Early Second Temple Judah*. Tübingen: Mohr Siebeck.

Carr, David M. 2005. *Writing on the Tablet of the Heart: Origins of Scripture and Literature*. Oxford: Oxford University Press.

Carr, David M. 2011. *The Formation of the Hebrew Bible: A New Reconstruction*. Oxford: Oxford University Press.

Culley, Robert C. 1986. 'Oral Tradition and Biblical Studies'. *Oral Tradition* 1(1): 30–65.

Edelman, Diana and Ehud Ben Zvi, eds. 2014. *Memory and the City in Ancient Israel*. Winona Lake: Eisenbrauns.

Hezser, Catherine. 2001. *Jewish Literacy in Roman Palestine*. Texts and Studies in Ancient Judaism 81. Tübingen: Mohr Siebeck.

Gamble, Harry Y. 2004. 'Literacy, Liturgy, and the Shaping of the New Testament Canon'. In *The Earliest Gospels: The Origins and Transmission of the Earliest Christian Gospels – The Contribution of Chester Beatty Gospel Codex P45*. Edited by Charles Horton. London: T&T Clark, pp. 27–39.

Gerhardsson, Birger. 1998. *Memory and Manuscript: Oral Tradition and Written Transmission in Rabbinic Judaism and Early Christianity with Tradition and Transmission in Early Christianity*. Translated by Eric J. Sharpe. Combined ed. The Biblical Resources Series. Grand Rapids: Eerdmans. [Swedish originals 1961 and 1964, respectively].

Halbwachs, Maurice. 1980. *The Collective Memory*. Translated by Francis J. Ditter, Jr. and Vida Yazdi Ditter. New York: Harper Colophon. [French original 1950].

Halbwachs, Maurice. 1992. *On Collective Memory*. Edited and translated by Lewis A. Coser. Chicago: University of Chicago Press. [French originals 1941, 1952].

Hearon, Holly E. 2006. 'The Implications of Orality for Studies of the Biblical Text'. In *Performing the Gospel: Orality, Memory, and Mark*. Edited by Richard A. Horsley, Jonathan A. Draper, and John Miles Foley. Minneapolis: Fortress, pp. 3–20.

Horsley, Richard A. 2007. *Scribes, Visionaries, and the Politics of Second Temple Judea*. Louisville: Westminster John Knox.

Hurtado, Larry W. 2014. 'Oral Fixation in New Testament Studies? "Orality," "Performance," and Reading Texts in Early Christianity'. *New Testament Studies* 60(3): 321–40.

Keith, Chris. 2011. 'A Performance of the Text: The Adulteress's Entrance into John's Gospel'. In *The Fourth Gospel in First-Century Media Culture*. Edited by Anthony Le Donne and Tom Thatcher. European Studies on Christian Origins/Library of New Testament Studies 426. London: T&T Clark, pp. 49–69.

Keith, Chris. 2011. *Jesus' Literacy: Scribal Culture and the Teacher from Galilee*. Library of Historical Jesus Studies 8/ Library of New Testament Studies 413. London: T&T Clark.

Kelber, Werner. 1983. *The Oral and the Written Gospel: The Hermeneutics of Speaking and Writing in the Synoptic Tradition, Mark, Paul, and Q*. Voices in Performance and Text. Bloomington: Indiana University Press.

Kelber, Werner. 2013. *Imprints, Voiceprints, and Footprints of Memory: Collected Essays of Werner H. Kelber*. Resources for Biblical Study. Atlanta: Society of Biblical Literature.

Kelber, Werner, and Samuel Byrskog, eds. 2009. *Jesus in Memory: Traditions in Oral and Scribal Perspectives*. Waco: Baylor University Press.

Kirk, Alan. 2008. 'Manuscript Tradition as a *Tertium Quid*: Orality and Memory in Scribal Practices'. In *Jesus, the Voice, and the Text: Beyond The Oral and the Written Gospel*. Edited by Tom Thatcher. Waco: Baylor University Press, pp. 215–34.

Kirk, Alan, and Tom Thatcher, eds. 2005. *Memory, Tradition, and Text: Uses of the Past in Early Christianity*. Semeia Studies 52. Atlanta: Society of Biblical Literature.

Lee, Sang-Il. 2012. *Jesus and Gospel Traditions in Bilingual Context: A Study in the Interdirectionality of Language*. BZNW, 186. Berlin: Walter Mouton de Gruyter.

Lord, Albert B. 1960. *The Singer of Tales*. Cambridge, MA: Harvard University Press.

Meyers, Carol. 1999. 'Mother to Muse: An Archaeomusicological Study of Women's Performance in Ancient Israel'. In *Recycling Biblical Figures: Papers Read at a Noster Colloquim in Amsterdam 12–13 May 1997*. Edited by Athalya Brenner and Jan Willem Van Henten. Studies in Theology and Religion 1. Leiden: Deo, pp. 50–77.

Niditch, Susan. 1996. *Oral World and Written Word: Ancient Israelite Literature*. Louisville: Westminster.

Ong, Walter J. 2002 [1982]. *Orality and Literacy: The Technologizing of the Word*. New Accents. New York: Routledge.

Person, Raymond F., Jr. 1998. 'The Ancient Israelite Scribe as Performer'. *JBL* 117: 601–9.

Person, Raymond F., Jr. 2010. *The Deuteronomic History and the Book of Chronicles: Scribal Works in an Oral World*. Atlanta: SBL Press.

Person, Raymond F., Jr. 2015. 'Text Criticism as a Lens for Understanding the Transmission of Ancient Texts in Their Oral Environments'. In *Contextualizing Israel's Sacred Writing: Ancient Literacy, Orality, and Literature Production*. Edited by Brian Schmidt. Atlanta: SBL Press, pp. 197–215.

Person, Raymond F., Jr. 2016. 'The Problem of "Literary Unity" from the Perspective of the Study of Oral Traditions'. In *Empirical Models Challenging Biblical Criticism*. Edited by Raymond F. Person, Jr. and Robert Rezetko. Atlanta: SBL Press, pp. 217–37.

Pioske, Daniel D. 2015a. *David's Jerusalem: Between Memory and History*. London: Routledge.

Pioske, Daniel D. 2015b. 'Memory and Materiality: The Case of Early Iron Age Khirbet Qeiyafa and Jerusalem'. *ZAW* 127: 78–95.

Pioske, Daniel D. 2015c. 'Retracing a Remembered Past: Methodological Remarks on Memory, History, and the Hebrew Bible'. *Biblical Interpretation* 23: 291–315.

Rhoads, David. 2010. 'Performance Events in Early Christianity: New Testament Writings in an Oral Context'. In *The Interface of Orality and Writing*. Edited by Annette Weissenrieder and Robert B. Coote. WUNT 260. Tübingen: Mohr Siebeck, pp. 166–93.

Rollston, Christopher A. 2010. *Writing and Literacy in the World of Ancient Israel: Epigraphic Evidence from the Iron Age*. SBL Archaeology and Biblical Studies. Atlanta: Society of Biblical Literature.

A

Abecedaries An *abecedary* is a text that consists of, or contains, the letters of an alphabet (cf. English 'A-B-Cs') written in a conventional order. An *alphabetic* WRITING system is one in which the written characters are understood to represent sounds, so that written texts essentially reproduce their spoken counterparts. The number of letters in an alphabetic writing system normally ranges from twenty to forty (sometimes with additional diacritics). The primary biblical languages are consistent with this pattern: Hebrew has twenty-two letters in its alphabet, while Greek has twenty-four letters. By contrast, in *a logographic* writing system, written characters represent words, phrases, or concepts themselves, not the sounds of spoken words that would orally communicate these concepts. An abecedary is, then, a listing of those written characters that represent the sounds of the spoken language(s) with which it is associated.

Not all writing systems in antiquity were alphabetic – this was true, for example, of the world's earliest writing systems, developed in Mesopotamia and Egypt during the late fourth millennium BCE. Alphabetic writing was not invented until sometime in the early second millennium BCE. The linear alphabetic inscriptions from Serabit el-Khadm and Wadi el-Hol are among the earliest attested examples of such alphabetic writing. The preferable term for the earliest alphabetic writing system is *Early Alphabetic* (rather than Proto-Sinaitic or Proto-Canaanite), which was invented by Semitic peoples who were familiar with the Egyptian writing system. All alphabetic writing systems (e.g. Phoenician, Aramaic, Hebrew, Greek, Latin, Armenian, etc.) derive from the linear Early Alphabetic writing system.

Among the most famous of the attested ancient abecedaries in a linear alphabetic script is the abecedary in the fifth line of the 'Izbet Ṣarṭah Inscription, written in the Early Alphabetic script of the twelfth or eleventh century BCE (Cross 1980). Similar in prominence is the Tel Zayit abecedary, which dates to the late tenth or very early ninth century BCE. The Tel Zayit abecedary was written in the Phoenician script because this was the script used in Israel during this early period (Rollston 2008; cf. Tappy, McCarter, Lundberg, and Zuckerman 2006). The abecedaries from 'Izbet Ṣarṭah and Tel Zayit were both inscribed in stone. Several abecedaries from the late ninth and early eighth centuries were found at Kuntillet Ajrud (modern Hebrew: *Horvat Teiman*) in the Sinai. These abecedaries were written in the Old Hebrew script with ink on pottery (Ahituv, Meshel, and Eshel 2012) (see OSTRACA).

The abecedaries from 'Izbet Ṣarṭah, Tel Zayit, and Kuntillet Ajrud are written in the 'Abgad Order' (i.e. with the first four letters of the alphabet being *alep*, *bet*, *gimel*, *dalet*). This order became the standard sequence in the Iron Age for Northwest Semitic. Minor variations in this sequence are, however, sometimes evident in antiquity: for example, the letter *'ayin* sometimes precedes *peh*, while *peh* sometimes precedes *'ayin* (note this same variation in the alphabetic acrostics of Psalm 119 and Lamentations 2–4). Within South Semitic, the order of the alphabet was normally the 'Halḥam Order' (i.e. with the first four letters of the alphabet being *he*, *lamed*, *ḥet*, and *mem*). This order is represented, for example, in Ge'ez Ethiopic. At Late Bronze Age Ugarit (1550–1200 BCE), both the Abgad Order and the Halḥam Order are attested in abecedaries. The Halḥam Order is also attested in an Ugaritic abecedary from Beth-Shemesh (Bordreuil and Pardee 1995).

The totality of this evidence demonstrates that there were (at least) two major rivalling orders for the writing of the alphabet in antiquity: the Abgad Order and the Halḥam Order, with minor variations attested within each of these orders.

Significantly, Greek abecedaries have been found at a number of archaeological sites of the Late Second Temple period, including Masada (Carr 2005: 242) and elsewhere in Greco-Roman Palestine (Hezser 2001). One of the more interesting examples is a putative potter's abecedary from Khirbet Qana (Eshel and Edwards 2004: 49–55). Another notable example is an ostracon, apparently the product of a school exercise, that includes the name of the student and the first four letters of the Greek alphabet – perhaps reflecting the fact that among the first things that a student learnt was to write the alphabet and their own name.

It has often been argued that the extant abecedaries are products of educational contexts. For example, Puech has asserted that there can be little 'doubt that the majority of the abecedaries are related to education in the art of writing' (1988: 189). However, Haran (1988: 85–91) has argued that there is no necessary connection between many of the abecedaries and schools, and some scholars have suggested that abecedaries served a mantic, rather than educational, function (see Weeks 1994: 150–1). While the writing of the alphabet, or objects bearing such writing, may sometimes have served a religious or magical purpose, it seems most likely abecedaries functioned primarily as the starting point for teaching students to write. Once pupils had mastered the alphabet (including the size, shape, and proper stance of the letters), the teacher could introduce them to the copying of longer texts, from the most basic to the most difficult of literary texts. The critical role of reproducing the alphabet as a fundamental aspect of scribal training doubtless explains the prominence of abecedaries in antiquity and their representation in the extant archaeological record.

Christopher A. Rollston (George Washington University, USA)

Further Reading

Ahituv, S., E. Eshel and Z. Meshel. 2012. 'The Inscriptions'. *Kuntillet Ajrud (Horvat Teiman)*, 73–142. Jerusalem: Israel Exploration Society.

Bordreuil, P., and D. Pardee. 1995. 'Un abécédaire du type sud-sémitique découverte en 1988 dans les fouilles archéologiques françaises de Ras Shamra-Ougarit'. *Comptes rendus de l'Académie des Inscriptions et Belles-lettres* 139: 855–60.

Carr, D. M. 2005. *Writing on the Tablet of the Heart: Origins of Scripture and Literature*. Oxford: Oxford University Press.

Cribiore, R. 2001. *Gymnastics of the Mind*. Princeton: Princeton University Press.

Cross, F. M. 1980. 'Newly Found Inscriptions in Old Canaanite and Early Phoenician Scripts'. *BASOR* 238: 1–20.

Eshel, E., and D. R. Edwards. 2004. 'Language and Writing in Early Roman Galilee: Social Location of Potter's Abecedary from Khirbet Qana'. In *Religion and Society in Roman Palestine: Old Questions, New Approaches*. Edited by D. Edwards. New York: Routledge, pp. 49–55.

Haran, M. 1988. 'On the Diffusion of Literacy and Schools in Ancient Israel'. In *Congress Volume, Jerusalem 1986*. Edited by J. A. Emerton. VTSup 40. Leiden: Brill, 81–95.

Hezser, C. 2001. *Jewish Literature in Roman Palestine*. Tübingen: Mohr.

Puech, E. 1988. 'Les écoles dans l'Israël préexilique: Données épigraphiques'. In *Congress Volume: Jerusalem 1986*. Edited by J. A. Emerton. VTSup 40. Leiden: Brill, 189–203.

Rollston, C. A. 2008. 'The Phoenician Script of the Tel Zayit Abecedary and Putative Evidence for Israelite Literacy'. In *Literate Culture and Tenth-Century Canaan: The Tel Zayit Abecedary in Context*. Edited by R. E. Tappy and P. K. McCarter. Winona Lake: Eisenbrauns, pp. 61–96.

Tappy, R. E., P. K. McCarter, Jr., M. Lundberg, and B. Zuckerman. 2007. 'An Abecedary of the Mid-Tenth Century B.C.E. from the Judaean Shephelah'. *BASOR* 344: 5–46.

Weeks, S. 1994. *Early Israelite Wisdom*. Oxford: Clarendon.

Actual Past The term *actual past* is used in discussions of COLLECTIVE/SOCIAL MEMORY to differentiate 'what happened' from its subsequent recollection and commemoration. The actual past consists of events, situations, individuals, and places that existed in time and space outside of any individual's recollection of them or any group's commemorative activities. Put another way, the actual past is the raw past, 'reality' outside the imposition of frames, SCHEMAS, or even language to recall and discuss it. For example, the sayings and actions of the historical Jesus would constitute the actual past of his life, as distinct from subsequent Christian recollections of him or traditions about him, such as the written Gospels. Studies of personal and collective memory frequently discuss the relationship between the actual past and personal and group recollections of it, particularly with reference to the possibility of recovering the past from memory and to the impact of the actual past (if any) on its subsequent representations. Theories that emphasize the determinative influence of the actual past on memory are broadly labelled *traditionalist* or *realist* (see REALISM), while theories that emphasize the politics of memory (ways that the actual past is suppressed or manipulated in service of ideological interests) are broadly labelled CONSTRUCTIONIST or PRESENTIST.

Tom Thatcher (Cincinnati Christian University, USA)

Alexandria, Library of The great Library of Alexandria was founded in the early third century BCE by scholar and autocrat Demetrios of Phaleron under the patronage of Ptolemy I Soter. Celebrated as the world's first attempt at a global collection of human knowledge, the library's holdings were reckoned in antiquity at more than 400,000 volumes, an exaggeration, probably by an order of magnitude, that illustrates how large the library and the aspirations behind it have loomed in the collective imagination in the West.

The Ptolemies avidly acquired new books. They are said to have confiscated MANUSCRIPTS found in docked ships, returning copies in lieu of the originals. Ptolemy III (Euegertes I, 246–221 BCE) refused to send grain to Athens until the city loaned him master copies of plays by Aeschylus, Sophocles, and Euripides; he returned only copies and forfeited his deposit of fifteen talents. The Ptolemies commissioned translations into Greek from non-Greek literature as far away as India, thereby creating what was at the time the world's largest translation movement. The most famous of these translations was that of the Hebrew Torah, commissioned by Ptolemy II (Philadelphos, 283–246 BCE). Named after its alleged seventy translators, the SEPTUAGINT came to include other Greek translations of Hebrew Scriptures that emerged in the following decades.

Although material evidence for the library is wholly lacking, textual sources attest to its having been built near the eastern harbour of the city. It was but part of a fully fledged religious and intellectual centre, the *mouseion*, which included a lecture and study hall, a colonnaded walk, dormitories, artwork, and most importantly a temple dedicated to the Muses, after whom the institution had been named. The library proper was integrated into the temple, a synthesis of scholarship and cult that imitated not only the Athenian Lyceum but the Houses of Life that were typically part of Egyptian temples. SCROLLS in the main temple were kept not in a separate room but in bookshelves or niches carved into the temple's hallways. A SCRIPTORIUM is reasonably presumed to have been located on site, or nearby since books would have deteriorated in the humid conditions of the city. As the holdings grew through acquisition, commission, and copying, annexes storing excess books were placed in temples throughout Alexandria.

A private royal institution, the *mouseion* brought together selected scholars to live and work within the precincts. These scholars were given room, board, and stipends, and were exempt from taxation. It was primarily a research institution. Although no teaching is known to have taken place in the *mouseion* until Roman times, young research assistants served apprenticeships that many times resulted in their becoming senior scholars. Residents capitalized on the benefits and unprecedented holdings of the library to pursue new forms of philological inquiry. The holdings drew from a broad range of Greek literature, allowing for the invention of comparative studies in lexicography and grammar. The first treatises on dialects, prosody, and punctuation were created here. The scholarship of critical editing was invented, with the *Iliad* and the *Odyssey* as the primary texts of interest. Critical editing began with Zenodotos of Ephesus and continued with many others, most famously and influentially Aristarchus (second century BCE), whose edition came to dominate the textual tradition. Scholar-editors such as Callimachus used their studies to compose their own literature, advancing horizons in prose and poetry. Scientific writers developed new research into medicine, philosophy, astronomy, and other sciences.

Under Roman rule, the *mouseion* began to take on a pedagogical role, and many Alexandrian scholars migrated to Rome. The library continued to be the centre of a vibrant intellectual culture in Alexandria that lasted well into late antiquity. The destruction of the library has been blamed variously upon a Muslim army led by Caliph 'Umar in 642 CE, a Christian mob led by Bishop Theophilus in 391 CE, and a conflagration ignited by Julius Caesar in 48 BCE. The account supporting the first proposal is a fabrication; the account supporting the second is genuine, but the riot described affected only the smaller 'daughter' library; the third account is also genuine, but of disputed impact. Ultimately, the most important factor leading to the demise of the library was the gradual erosion of its required funding.

Joel Kalvesmaki (Dumbarton Oaks, USA)

Further Reading

Bagnall, Roger S. 2002. 'Alexandria: Library of Dreams'. *Proceedings of the American Philosophical Society* 146(4): 348–62.

Delia, Diana. 1992. 'From Romance to Rhetoric: The Alexandrian Library in Classical and Islamic Traditions'. *American Historical Review* 97: 1449–67.

El-Abbadi, Mostafa. (1992), *The Life and Fate of the Ancient Library of Alexandria*. 2d rev. ed. Paris: UNESCO/UNDP.

El-Abbadi, Mostafa, and Omnia Mounir Fathallah. 2008. *What Happened to the Ancient Library of Alexandria?* Library of the Written Word 3. Leiden: Brill.

Hatzimichali, Myrto. 2013. 'Ashes to Ashes? The Library of Alexandria after 48 BC'. In *Ancient Libraries*. Edited by Jason König, Aikaterini Oikonomopoulou, and Greg Woolf. Cambridge: Cambridge University Press, pp. 167–82.

Amarna Letters Since 1887, approximately 400 cuneiform tablets from an ancient archive have been found in the city of Amarna. Tell el-Amarna was the newly founded capital of Egypt during the reign of Amenhotep IV/Akhenaten (fourteenth century CE) and his successors. The tablets are copies of official letters drafted in the Babylonian language (Akkadian) and in cuneiform script (the diplomatic language of that era) and were kept at the Bureau of the Correspondence of the Pharaoh in Amarna. The archive includes both letters dispatched from officials in Egypt and communications sent back from distant locations, including Babylonia, Assyria, and Mittani. The Amarna Letters span a period that starts with the 30th regnal year of Amenhotep III and ends with the first regnal year of Tutankhamun. Today, more than 200 of the Amarna tablets are preserved at the Vorderasiastisches Museum in Berlin.

The Amarna archive provides unique glimpses into the day-to-day political dynamics of the Egyptian empire. For example, a cuneiform letter (VAT 347: EA 162) from Pharaoh Amenhotep IV accuses Aziru, a vassal ruler of the province of Amurru in Syria, of conspiring with Egypt's enemies, the local chieftains of Byblos and Kadesh. The Pharaoh does not mince words, threatening Aziru and his family with death for betrayal and promising rewards if Aziru remains loyal. The letter concludes with a list of those whom the ruler of Amurru is to turn over. As an example of communications from the provinces back to Egypt, another tablet (VAT 1645 + 2709: EA289) expresses the fears of Abdi Heba, the ruler of Jerusalem, regarding an impending attack by the chieftains of the surrounding cities of Gazru (Gaza) and Shakmu.

As a safeguard, he asks Pharaoh to send fifty men for the city's protection and a representative to observe the Egyptian provinces.

Some of the Amarna Letters also provide clues on the ancient management of government ARCHIVES. For example, the famous gold scandal of Amarna is described in another cuneiform script text (VAT 233 + 2197: EA 27). This document offers evidence of a dispute between Tushratta, king of Mittani, and Pharaoh Amenhotep IV. According to Tushratta, two gold statues were missing from the bridal gifts of the Mittani princess Tadu-Hebaare. Tushratta claims that the statues that had made their way to him were merely gilded wood, even though Egypt possessed 'gold like dirt'. The foreign ruler urges Pharaoh to honour the agreement regarding the bride price that had been reached with his father, Amenhotep III. Added to this letter is a hieratic (Egyptian) inscription that reads 'copy of a letter from Naharin (the Egyptian name for Mittani)', obviously an archival note for later reference. Mineralogical analysis of the clay tablet has revealed that this object, along with the other letters of this set, came from Mittani rather than having been copied in Egypt. It must be assumed therefore that an Egyptian SCRIBE added the hieratic inscription after the letter arrived in Egypt before the letter was stored.

Knowledge of the cuneiform script in Egypt itself must have been very limited. Also, the Akkadian language used in these tablets reflects the writing culture of the time. The texts also include several traces of an early form of Canaanite, suggesting that the authors from the various regions of the ancient Near East used their own style of language. Therefore these texts are linguistically of highest interest and importance and reflect the media environment of the time.

Verena Lepper (Ägyptisches Museum und Papyrussammlung, Staatliche Museen zu Berlin & Humboldt University of Berlin)

Further Reading

Moran, William L. 1992. *The Amarna Letters*. Baltimore: Johns Hopkins University Press.

Answerability *Answerability* (sometimes translated 'responsibility') is an element of Russian literary theorist M. M. BAKHTIN's theoretical model that builds on the same dialogic sense of reality that permeates all of his thought and writing. Most succinctly, answerability is the integrative lifework of becoming a self. Since each individual (whether author/artist, character, or reader) occupies a unique time and place in life while also intersecting the lives of others, Bakhtin conceives existence as the product of many complex choices that calibrate the circumstances of our ever-shifting position in relation to the existence of diverse others. Answerability is not simply the performance of abstract principles but the pattern of actual deeds performed in the event that is a life (or a text). Thus the answerable self emerges as we (author, character, reader) negotiate our own set of acts in the world, acts particular to ourselves but also vastly interrelated with those of others. Bakhtin uses the image of 'signing' for answerability: to sign an utterance, an action, or a life is to take responsibility for making it one's own, performing it with integrity.

Barbara Green (Dominican School of Philosophy and Theology, USA)

Apocalypses, early Christian Early Christian apocalypses are those documents written in the apocalyptic GENRE by Christian authors in the first four centuries CE. Understood as a literary genre, *apocalypse* – broadly speaking – refers to works containing a revelation (which is what the Greek *apocalypsis* means) in narrative form by a heavenly figure to a human being concerning the secrets of the cosmos and the secrets of God's divine purpose for humanity and for creation. Apocalypse is therefore tied to the communication of a significant message and reveals its natural home among ancient media. At the same time, the liveliness of the apocalyptic tradition, with a succession of texts appearing over some six or seven centuries from the third century BCE, attests to the importance of these works in the COLLECTIVE MEMORY of Jews and early Christ-followers and their interest in modifying the tradition to accord with evolving needs and situations.

There are many apocalyptic works extant from antiquity of both Jewish and Christ-movement origin; the latter are generally much indebted to the former, the oldest of which are 1 En. 1-36 (the Book of the Watchers) and 1 En. 72-82 (the Book of Heavenly Luminaries), both probably from the third century BCE (see 1 ENOCH/ENOCHIC TRADITIONS). These earliest apocalypses are remarkably embedded in the communications culture of ancient Israel in that they expressly describe the human being to whom the revelations are delivered, Enoch (the seventh patriarch after Adam), as a SCRIBE, or at least portray him as acting as one. Thus the Book of the Watchers states that Enoch is a scribe (1 En. 12.3, 4; 15.1) and also has him engaging in scribal practice: first, he writes down a memorandum from the Watchers who have seceded from heaven seeking divine forgiveness and reads it out to God (1 En. 13-14) and, secondly, he records heavenly phenomena in WRITING (1 En. 33.4). In the Book of Heavenly Luminaries, where the revelation is described as a book (Ethiopic: *mashaf*; 1 En. 72.1), Enoch says he 'wrote down' the fixed positions of heavenly bodies as Uriel showed them to him (1 En. 74.2); thus he is a scribe by implication.

The diverse nature of the secrets revealed in the apocalyptic texts renders unwise attempts to tie them too closely to any particular subject matter, such as end-time phenomena. On the other hand, most of the extra-canonical Christ-movement apocalypses do focus on the last judgement and the fate of the dead. Most of these apocalypses, like their Jewish precedents, were pseudonymous, but the Apocalypse of John and the Shepherd of Hermas (a revelation granted to Hermas but with contents unlike those of other apocalypses) broke with this tradition by naming their authors. This makes good sense in works where the person receiving the revelation is asked to write it down.

The Synoptic Apocalypse, Mk 13.3-37 (paralleled in Matthew 24 and Luke 21), is often called the *Little Apocalypse*. Although it does contain a description of end-time phenomena similar to those in apocalyptic texts, its form consists of a direct address by Jesus to his followers, not a message conveyed by a heavenly figure to a human being for onward transmission by him. Thus its dramatic mode is one of oral proclamation. The NT Apocalypse of John, while also drawing upon the genres of LETTER and PROPHECY, takes the form of an apocalypse that God made known by sending his angel to John (Rev. 1.1) and culminates in John's vision of the New Jerusalem in Revelation 21–22. It is by far the longest and most elaborate of all the early Christian apocalypses and covers a wide range of subject matter. Throughout the text reminders are given of the revealed nature of what is described by statements such as 'And I saw', 'Then I looked', and 'I heard a voice'. At the same time, this is a text with a remarkable amount of visual imagery. Perhaps its overall aim is to reveal (a) the necessity of worship of God and of the Lamb in preference to idolatry in all its forms and (b) the ultimate triumph of God over evil. At the same time, it is a text pervasively and self-consciously focused on communication.

Many extra-canonical Christian apocalypses are extant. They often draw more upon extra-canonical Jewish ones than on the canonical texts like Daniel and Revelation. A frequently recurring topic in these early Christian apocalypses is a tour of the underworld. This motif originates in the cosmic tour in Jewish apocalypses, beginning with the mountain of the dead in 1 Enoch 22, which is itself part of a larger tour of the cosmos in 1 Enoch 17–36. Such an astronomical interest is also at the centre of the Book of Heavenly Luminaries (1 En. 72.82). In the first and second centuries CE the tradition of the cosmic tour was modified in the light of a developing cosmology to the effect that above the earth's atmosphere were arrayed seven heavens, the seventh and highest of which was God's throne-room (a feature adopted from 1 En. 14). In addition, while earlier examples of the cosmic tour (such as 1 En. 22) presented the dead as held in underworld places until the last judgement, later texts reflected a belief that arose in the first and second centuries CE that the souls of the wicked dead would be tormented in the underworld as soon as they were admitted to it. The Apocalypse of Zephaniah (probably originating among Jews rather than Christ-followers), written in the first century BCE or first century CE, is among the oldest representatives of this understanding. The (Christian) Apocalypse of Paul combines an ascent to the throne of God followed by a visit to the places of the dead. Its descriptions of what happened to the dead, more detailed than in any other source, had a profound impact on the Christian West – especially on the popular imagination, as seen in literary works (like Dante's *Inferno*) and on art (including the works of Hieronymus Bosch).

The Ascension of Isaiah (late first or early second century CE) is a largely if not wholly Christian work of eleven chapters that falls into two parts with scholars divided on whether they are the work of one or more authors. The first part (Chapters 1–5) comprises a narrative about Isaiah and his interactions with Hezekiah and Manasseh, which includes a report of his vision (Ascension of Isaiah 3.13–4.22) and culminates in a description of his death by being sawn in half. The second part (Chapters 6–11) consists of a first-person account of Isaiah's vision (Ascension of Isaiah 7.2–11.35) with the remaining material constituting a third-person narrative framework. The first vision focuses on the origins and crisis of the church on earth and the Parousia, while the second describes Isaiah's ascent through the seven heavens and the descent and subsequent ascent of the Beloved. The Apocalypse of Peter (pre-150 CE, possibly c. 135 CE) presupposes Peter as the decisive witness of the resurrection event to whom further revelations are appropriate. The bulk of the text, much of it an elaboration of certain parts of Matthew 24, concerns the final judgement and the fate of human beings after death, especially the graphically described punishments that will be inflicted on the wicked, with the punishment apt for the sin, and the rewards for the righteous. In time, the Apocalypse of Peter appears to have fallen out of favour and its role in describing the fate of the dead was taken over by Apocalypse of Paul and the Apocalypse of Mary.

Other examples of Christ-movement apocalypses include the Coptic Gospel Apocalypse of Paul, the Coptic Gospel Apocalypse of Peter, the Apocalypse of Thomas, and certain sections of the Sibylline Oracles.

Lastly, several Christ-movement apocalypses follow 1 Enoch in presenting the person receiving the revelation as scribal or as having scribal skills or activity, or as exhibiting an interest in books. This is the case with the Apocalypse of John (Rev. 1.1-3, 11) and the Ascension of Isaiah (1.5). In addition, John is also asked to write letters to the seven churches of Asia (Revelation 2-3). In the Shepherd of Hermas the narrator is asked to write two books (8.2-3). The Apocalypse of Peter concludes with a reference to the 'book of life' (17). Thus the whole genre of apocalypse reveals its origin in ancient Jewish and Christ-movement communication cultures and the way in which they allowed traditions rooted in the collective memories of communities to be preserved and adapted to contemporary requirements.

Philip Esler (University of Gloucestershire, UK)

Further Reading

Bauckham, Richard. 1998. *The Fate of the Dead: Studies on the Jewish and Christian Apocalypses*. SNT 93. Leiden: Brill.

Carey, Greg. 2005. *Ultimate Things: Introduction to Jewish and Christian Apocalyptic Literature*. St. Louis, MO: Chalice Press.

Collins, John J., ed. 1979. *Apocalypse: The Morphology of a Genre*. Semeia 14. Atlanta: SBL Press.

Collins, John J., ed. 2014. *The Oxford Handbook of Apocalyptic Literature*. Oxford: Oxford University Press.

Himmelfarb, Martha. 1983. *Tours of Hell: An Apocalyptic Form in Jewish and Christian Literature*. Philadelphia: University of Pennsylvania Press.

Lewis, Scott M. S.J. 2004. *What Are They Saying about New Testament Apocalyptic?* New York: Paulist Press.

Schneemelcher, Wilhelm, ed. 1992. *New Testament Apocrypha*. Vol. II of *Writings Related to the Apostles, Apocalypses and Related Subjects*. Revised edition of the collection initiated by Edgar Hennecke. Translated and edited by R. McL. Wilson. Cambridge: James Clark & Westminster/John Knox Press.

Apocalypses, Early Jewish An *apocalypse*, from the Greek *apocalypsis*, 'unveiling', is a revelation or uncovering of secrets. As a literary genre, apocalyptic texts purport to reveal or disclose divine secrets, including information regarding forces of nature and other more esoteric realities that would not be so readily apparent. From the beginning, the production of apocalypses seems to have been associated with SCRIBES and scribal culture more explicitly than were other literary genres in early Judaism, not only in terms of the composition and origin of these works, but also in their utilization of metaphors and motifs that emphasize communications media, particularly speech and WRITING.

This thematic emphasis on the technology of writing is illustrated by the first Jewish literary apocalypse, a collection of discrete but interrelated works now known as 1 ENOCH. Its earliest sections, the Book of the Watchers and the Astronomical Book, may date to the third century BCE, while the latest major section, the parables (or Similitudes) of Enoch, was probably composed around the turn of the first millennium CE. All are pseudepigraphal, falsely attributed to Enoch, the enigmatic figure of Gen. 5.21-24 who walked with God, 'then was no more, for God took him'. This laconic tale naturally raised questions. Where did Enoch go? What did he see and hear, and what did he do? In addressing them, the Book of the Watchers expands upon another puzzling text, Gen. 6.1-4. The titular 'Watchers' are 'the sons of God' who leave heaven to claim human wives and beget children. 1 Enoch also builds upon the biblical storyline that follows Gen. 6.1-4, in that the wickedness that engulfs the earth in Gen. 6.5 is a direct result of the Watchers' acts: they revealed forbidden heavenly secrets to humanity, and their children turn out violent and bloodthirsty. Thus the flood is an attempt to wipe the earthly slate clean, as the Watchers' children will die and the Watchers themselves will be bound in a fiery abyss until the day of judgement. It is the job of Enoch, now called 'the righteous scribe', to deliver the bad news to these fallen beings. They in turn ask Enoch to write a petition to God begging forgiveness for their actions.

From this point forward, Enoch is associated with books and writing in almost every ancient work in which he appears. These media, indispensable to all apocalyptic authors to promulgate their message, also play an important role within the narrative of almost every early Jewish apocalypse. Two types of books, fictional and actual, often intersect with one another, as in the Astronomical Book when the angel Uriel bids Enoch to read and understand all that is written on heavenly tablets. When he returns from his celestial journey, Enoch tells his son that he has written down everything that he has seen, so that his descendants will have wisdom and pass it down through the generations – via the actual book that the reader now holds.

As the character of Enoch develops in later apocalyptic literature, his scribal role becomes more pronounced, and he is a composer, not just a reader or copier, of heavenly books. In JUBILEES (ca. 160 BCE), which some have argued is an apocalypse, Enoch dwells in the Garden of Eden and writes the condemnation and judgement of the world. In the misleadingly named Testament of Abraham (first to second century CE), which is in fact an apocalypse, Enoch is once again the 'scribe of righteousness', but now transformed into an imposing figure who wears three crowns and writes judgement with a golden pen. In 2 Enoch (first to second century CE) he is even more exalted, receiving a pen specifically for speedwriting, which he will need to record everything in heaven and on earth, including the fate of all humanity from creation until the end of the age.

In early Jewish apocalyptic literature Enoch is always privy to the revelation of heavenly secrets as their reader, purveyor, recorder, or composer, but he is not the only figure associated with such books. Throughout most of the Hebrew Scriptures, heavenly books are in the hands of God, but in apocalypses, they move into the care of angels who mediate them to human beings. For example, in Daniel, the only full-fledged apocalypse in the Hebrew Scriptures, 'books are opened' during the judgement of the fearsome fourth beast (Dan. 7.10). Whether these books belong to God or to the myriads of heavenly beings around the throne is unclear, but the content of 'the book of truth' (10.21) is given to Daniel by the angel Gabriel in chapter 11. At the beginning of chapter 12, Daniel learns that those whose names are written in yet another book will survive the time of trial inflicted by the fourth beast. Finally, like the writings attributed to Enoch, Daniel's record of what he has seen and heard becomes the actual book of Daniel, which only the wise will understand.

Similarly, the late-first-century CE apocalypse 4 Ezra (2 Esdras) introduces another figure from Israel's past who produces earthly books ostensibly from the revelation of heavenly secrets. While the pseudonymous author of 4 Ezra writes after the fall of the Second Temple (70 CE), he sets his protagonist in the aftermath of the fall of the First Temple (sixth century BCE). At the end of the apocalypse, God calls Ezra to become a new Moses by reproducing the Hebrew Scriptures that Ezra says were burnt in the Babylonian destruction. Ezra must employ five scribes who can write quickly. Then God inspires him with a fiery drink so that he can dictate to them for forty days and nights, producing ninety-four books in all. Twenty-four of these, the reconstituted Scriptures, may be read by a general audience, but seventy are esoteric, only for the consumption of the wise. Presumably among these books is 4 Ezra itself (cf. 12.37-38).

This small sample of material from early Jewish apocalypses demonstrates in nuce the importance of scribes and the media of books and writing within the genre. The written word's power to preserve a record of what has been seen, heard, done, and thought enables real ancient authors and fictional apocalyptic seers alike to transmit their experiences to the wise of their own generation and beyond.

Leslie Baynes (Missouri State University, USA)

Further Reading

Baynes, Leslie. 2012. *The Heavenly Book Motif in Judeo-Christian Apocalypses 200 BCE-200 CE.* JSJS 152. Leiden: Brill.

Collins, John J. 2016. *The Apocalyptic Imagination: An Introduction to Jewish Apocalyptic Literature*. 3rd ed. Grand Rapids: Eerdmans.

Harkins, Angela Kim, Kelley Coblentz Bautch, and John Endres, S.J., eds. 2014. *The Watchers in Jewish and Christian Tradition.* Philadelphia: Fortress Press.

Nickelsburg, George W. E., and James C. VanderKam. 2001 and 2012. *1 Enoch 1* and *1 Enoch 2*. Minneapolis: Fortress Press.

Orton, David E. 1989. *The Understanding Scribe: Matthew and the Apocalyptic Ideal*. JSNTSup 25. Sheffield: Sheffield Academic Press.

Rowland, Christopher. 1982. *The Open Heaven: A Study of Apocalyptic in Judaism and Early Christianity*. New York: Crossroad.

Archives and Libraries Broadly speaking, in the ancient world libraries and archives were places where people collected written texts. In general, a library housed literary texts, while an archive preserved records, technical, documentary, legal, or other less literary texts. Libraries and archives, however, had overlapping constellations of meanings and uses. While each historical example must be considered in its own context, a general understanding of ancient libraries and archives enhances our understanding of ancient media by illustrating communities' reading practices and physical experiences of texts.

Important differences between modern and ancient libraries must be kept in mind to avoid anachronism. First, most ancient libraries or archives were not borrowing libraries. In some instances, borrowing was explicitly forbidden, as an inscription in the Athenian *agora* demonstrates (*Supplementum Epigraphicum*

Graecum 21:500). Further, unlike modern libraries, many ancient libraries or archives were not architecturally designed as social spaces for education and study. Frequently they were simply rooms where texts were kept on shelves, often with no space where someone could work, such as a reading room. Whereas modern Western libraries tend to have mostly printed and published books, an ancient archive or library could contain a wide variety of textual objects. A government archive would hold notes, records, rulings, or LETTERS pertinent to later political figures or history writers – for example, the royal Persian book of records in the book of Esther, the court trial records in Ciceronian Rome (Gurd 2010: 80–101), and the *acta* of later church councils. Other libraries would contain more recognized and public books. Personal libraries would contain texts of subjects curated by and directly pertinent to the owners.

Libraries or archives could be assembled in a variety of ways and for different purposes. Galen relates a tale about the Ptolemaic king of Egypt having all the boats docked in Alexandria searched for books. If any were found, he would have them copied, returning the new copy to the owner and keeping the original in the famous library in Alexandria (*On Hippocrates' 'Epidemics III'*). Houston mentions several ways to assemble a collection of texts: copying, buying, gifting, borrowing, confiscating, plundering, or writing your own (2015: 13–37). As a second example, the SCROLLS from Qumran, which represent something between a library and archive, preserve texts relevant to and written by a particular community. Third, and on a more individual scale, the Cave of Letters at NAḤAL ḤEVER includes personal archives with letters and legal documents connected to the Bar Kokhba revolt and reflecting make-shift archival practices as a result of duress (see Wise 2015).

Libraries or archives served a variety of different social functions. Public book collections were performative and represented cultural capital. The Ulpian Library in Trajan's forum and Hadrian's Library in Athens, for example, served a goal that was greater than preserving books: they memorialized the creator of the library and made a cultural and political statement. Trajan and Celsus are both buried near libraries. Roman libraries would often have had Greek and Latin sections that mirrored each other both physically and culturally. While many people in the urban ancient world would have seen public libraries, few would have actually entered the libraries and used them. Political archives often would have been less visible to the masses. These functioned to preserve practical records rather than high literature, and may have been little more than storerooms with shelves for scrolls. Political archives saved records potentially important to later rulers or history writers. Libraries or archives in TEMPLES, baths, and other places would likewise have had their own unique social functions.

Many libraries were personal. Cicero's comment to Varro in *Ad familiares* 9.4 is illustrative: 'If you have a garden in your library, you will have everything you need.' Cicero clearly envisions that a person of leisure might sit in a garden reading and conversing. The advantage of a personal library over a more public library was that owners could curate the collection and arrange the texts in a way most amenable to their literary purposes and desired self-representation. While borrowing from public libraries was rare, it was common for individuals to share books within their social circle. Living in a large, famous city, one known for its book-friendliness, was an advantage to those engaged in literary pursuits (Plutarch, *Demosthenes* 2). Book collections brought together like-minded literary people.

While modern libraries are often thought of as places of education and schools are expected to have libraries, it was not necessary for ancient schools to be connected to a library or archive, although it is possible that the collections at Herculaneum and Qumran played a pedagogical role. Herculaneum's VILLA OF THE PAPYRI, which includes a significant number of literary and philosophical works, is a clear example of a personal library. Other archives, like the trash heaps of Oxyrhynchus or the VINDOLANDA tablets, do not show archival practices; they become archives to modern users only after their excavation.

The more archive-like a collection, the more it tended to collect less published and more functional texts, like records, technical works, or unpublished letters. The more library-like a collection, the more it tended to collect published literature by known authors. The scrolls in a library, both public and private, often had marginal notes and corrections by users (Galen, *Avoidance of Grief*; Galen, *On Hippocrates' 'Epidemics III'* 2). In Herculaneum and in the caves of Qumran, scholars have found multiple versions of the same text, often in different stages of textual development.

An archive or library could be destroyed in a variety of ways. Plundering of books in war was common. Libraries could also burn, resulting in great loss of texts and cultural capital. Patrons would house texts in places less susceptible to fire, though fires could occur nonetheless (see Galen, *Avoidance of Grief*). The lifespan of a text depended upon the quality of its materials and craftsmanship (see Writing and Writing Materials). A cheaply made book would not last nearly as long as an expensive one. Ancient readers would likely have been more aware than modern readers that every time a text was used, its lifespan was partially consumed.

Long before the Hebrew Bible or NT canon took shape, Jews and Christians began to collect certain types of documents into groups. For instance, Eva Mrocrek has shown that while there was no 'book of the Psalms' in the Second Temple period, there was a collection of Psalms at Qumran, although it was unbounded in number and content (2016: 19–50, 156–83). Similarly, early Christians began to collect some of Paul's letters together into a dossier in the second century CE, and the four canonical Gospels by the end of the second century CE. Origen is reported to have had a library in Alexandria in the first half of the third century CE, which would have contained many Jewish and Christian Scriptures. The earliest explicit evidence of a Christian congregational library comes from Cirta in Numidia in the early fourth century CE (Gamble 1995: 144–54).

Matthew D. Larsen (Yale University, USA)

Further Reading

Crawford, Sidnie White, and Cecilia Wassen, eds. 2016. *The Dead Sea Scrolls at Qumran and the Concept of a Library*. STDJ 116. Leiden: Brill.

Gamble, Harry Y. 1995. *Books and Readers in the Early Church: A History of Early Christian Texts*. New Haven: Yale University Press.

Gurd, Sean A. 2010. 'Verres and the Scenes of Rewriting'. *Phoenix* 64: 80–101.

Houston, George W. 2014. *Inside Roman Libraries: Book Collections and their Management in Antiquity*. Chapel Hill: University of North Carolina Press.

König, Jason, Katerina Oikonomopoulou and Greg Woolf, eds. 2013. *Ancient Libraries*. New York: Cambridge University Press.

Mroczek, Eva. 2016. *The Literary Imagination in Jewish Antiquity*. New York: Oxford University Press.

Wise, Michael O. 2015. *Language and Literacy in Roman Judaea: A Study of the Bar Kokhba Documents*. New Haven: Yale University Press.

Assmann, Jan Jan Assmann (b. 1938) is professor emeritus of Egyptology at the University of Heidelberg and an honorary professor at the University of Konstanz. Primarily an Egyptologist, Assmann's publications have broadly addressed the cultures of the ancient Near East, including and especially ancient Israel. For scholars of the Hebrew Bible and NT, Assmann's most substantial contribution has been his theory of cultural memory. He articulated this theory most fully in his groundbreaking *Das kulturelle Gedächtnis: Schrift, Erinnerung und politische Identität in frühen Hochkulturen*, which, as of 2013, had been published in seven editions (Assmann 2013). In 2011, an English translation was published as *Cultural Memory and Early Civilization: Writing, Remembrance, and Political Imagination* (2011), largely at the insistence of NT media critic Werner Kelber (Assmann 2011: xii). Assmann also interacted with biblical studies in his study of the cultural portrayals of Moses, *Moses the Egyptian* (1997).

Assmann built his theory of cultural memory upon the prior work of French sociologist MAURICE HALBWACHS. The first scholar to propose a robust sociological approach to memory (as opposed to cognitive or psychological approaches), Halbwachs was most interested in the social formation of the past in the current generation, which he termed the COLLECTIVE MEMORY. Assmann, however, was concerned with how socially formed images of the past are passed on to subsequent generations and persist for long durations. Assmann termed this multigenerational form of memory *cultural memory* (*kulturelle Gedächtnis*) and renamed Halbwachs' collective memory as COMMUNICATIVE MEMORY (*kommunikatives Gedächtnis*), capturing the distinction in chronological focus by saying, 'With cultural memory the depths of time open up' (Assmann 2006: 24). Cultural memory studies investigate how some versions of the past (such as the formative stories of Israel's history) become canonical and remain durable for generations as the group's perception of its founding events. Assmann appealed often to the texts and traditions of the Bible and related literature as prime examples of cultural memory.

Assmann articulated his answer to the question of how some versions of the past become so widely accepted for so long as to become canonical in media terms, noting the relationship between oral and written traditions. Assmann believed that oral tradition could sustain communicative memory for only around eighty to one hundred years (Assmann 2006: 24) – essentially, the lifespan of a single generation. Oral tradition is dependent upon the speaker and hearer being co-present; for a culture to transmit its memory across multiple generations, where speakers and hearers are not co-present and perhaps separated by centuries, a more durable medium is necessary that simultaneously provides preservation and access. For Assmann, writing rose to meet this need in antiquity in a special way. In written form, a version of the past – whether the Epic of Gilgamesh, the *Iliad*, the Pentateuch, or stories about Jesus – could detach from its original context of oral storytelling and reach a later context. He referred to the hermeneutical phenomenon created by written tradition's capacity to span two or more places in time and space as the *extended situation* (*zerdehnte Situation*; Assmann 2006: 103). In this sense, writing's preservative function made it possible for multiple generations to accept and revere a particular version of the past, which helped lead to its status as canonical.

Like many media theorists, then, Jan Assmann viewed the transition between oral word and written word as a 'watershed' (2006: 39). The physical nature of the written tradition as material artefact opened up further hermeneutical activities for the group that reinforced its status, such as the material decoration OF MANUSCRIPTS and the rise of a class of authoritative interpreters, whose maintenance of the group's social memory now depended on their expertise in the maintenance of the sacred texts. The latter served as mediators between the present group and the written form of the cultural memory.

As sociological theories of memory have increasingly been applied to biblical studies, Assmann's theory of cultural memory has had an important impact on scholars of the Hebrew Bible such as David Carr and Philip Davies, as well as NT scholars such as Werner Kelber and Alan Kirk.

Chris Keith (St. Mary's University, UK)

Further Reading

Assmann, Jan. 1997. *Moses the Egyptian: The Memory of Egypt in Western Monotheism*. Cambridge, MA: Harvard University Press.

Assmann, Jan. 2006. *Religion and Cultural Memory: Ten Studies*. Translated by Rodney Livingstone. Cultural Memory in the Present. Stanford: Stanford University Press.

Assmann, Jan. 2011. *Cultural Memory and Early Civilization: Writing, Remembrance, and Political Imagination.* Translated by David Henry Wilson. Cambridge: Cambridge University Press.

Assmann, Jan. 2013. *Das kulturelle Gedächtnis: Schrift, Erinnerung und politische Identität in frühen Hochkulturen.* 7th edn. München: C. H. Beck.

Audience Address *Audience address* is a central dynamic of STORYTELLING performance in which both the storyteller and the audience enter into the roles of characters in the story. For example, in oral performances of episodes or speeches from the Gospels, the storyteller speaks at once both to the audience as her/himself and to characters in the story (e.g. the scribes or the disciples) as Jesus. The term *audience address* can also be used in a way roughly parallel to *asides* in literary studies, in reference to side comments a storyteller might make to the audience to explain a setting or define a character's motives. The concept, as used by biblical scholars, is largely based on the conclusions of narrative criticism on the relationships between authors/narrators and their implied (within the text) and real-world audiences. Audience address is a significant dimension of the reconception of the receivers of the Bible as audiences addressed by performers rather than as private readers of texts (see PERFORMANCE CRITICISM).

By nature, storytelling (whether oral or in the form of recitations of written manuscripts) involves two parties: the storyteller and her/his audience, who are physically present during the performance and can react immediately and directly to, and thus influence the flow and contours of, the storyteller's presentation (see BIOSPHERE). In such contexts, the storyteller acts, first and foremost, as performer, speaking as her/himself directly to the audience to describe the settings and actions of the story; at the same time, when recounting the words of individual characters, the storyteller speaks as those characters to other characters in the story world. This dynamic can provide storytellers with many opportunities to enliven the presentation by presenting different characters with distinctive voices, gestures, and attitudes.

In the case of ancient Israel and early Christianity, the more informal settings of traditional storytelling (e.g. homes, festivals, intergenerational transmission of religious ideals) meant that audience address was an aspect of face-to-face encounters in which the audience could interact directly with the storyteller and the characters he or she presented. A particular dimension of that interaction related to oral accounts of direct discourse. During long speeches by a character such as Moses or Jesus, the audience was addressed as the character(s) in the story being addressed by that speaker. For example, in the stories of Exodus, traditional Israelite storytellers may have presented Moses addressing the audience as the people of Israel (e.g. Exod. 13.3-16; 35.1-19, 30-35). Virtually the entire book of Deuteronomy is structured as an interaction between Moses as the speaker and the Israelites just before their entry into the Holy Land. The audiences who heard a subsequent performance of Deuteronomy or passages from it might identify with the Israelites and would have experienced, in the performance moment, the storyteller as Moses addressing them as Israelites. Similarly, the audiences at the various performances of material from the other books of the Pentateuch in later periods of Israel's history could have imaginatively entered into the stories and been addressed as the Israelites during and after the exodus from Egypt.

In the Gospels, the dynamics of audience address are complex, since these stories and their subunits portray Jesus variously addressing a wide range of characters from different backgrounds and perspectives, including, for example 'the twelve' or 'the disciples' (e.g. Mt. 10.5-42; 18.1-21; 24.4-25.46; Mk 4.11-30; 7.15-21; Lk 17.22-18.8; Jn 13.31-16.33) as well as Jesus' various conversation partners (e.g. Nicodemus or the Samaritan Woman; John 3–4) and opponents (e.g. the Pharisees). While Jesus is the main speaker presented by the gospel storyteller, the persons and groups whom he addresses would change frequently in the course of performances of larger blocks of gospel material. At the same time, and reflecting the historical setting envisioned within those stories, the audiences of the Gospels are almost always addressed as various groups of Judeans. In the long speeches of Jesus in Mark, for example, the Marcan audiences are variously addressed as the scribes from Jerusalem (3.23-30); the crowd (4.1-11); those around him with the Twelve (4.11-32); the Pharisees and scribes (7.6-13); the disciples (7.18-22); the crowd with the disciples (8.34-9.1); and Peter, James, John, and Andrew (13.3-37).

From this perspective, the most structured development of the storyteller as Jesus addressing the audience as various groups of Judeans appears in the Gospel of John, reflecting the fact that the Fourth Gospel includes a large amount of direct discourse uttered by Jesus, sometimes apparently directed to later audiences more than to characters in the story. The first element in the structure of audience address begins with the audience being addressed by Jesus and John the Baptist as Galileans – followers of John the Baptist, common folk, Pharisees, and Samaritans – who are drawn to Jesus and many of whom believe in him (Jn 1–4). The middle section of the narrative includes a series of long speeches by Jesus that are addressed to the audience as groups of Judeans who want to kill him and who believe in him (5.17-47; 6.25-59; 8.12-58; 9.41-10.38). Finally, in the longest address to the audience at the Last Supper and footwashing (13.31-16.33), Jesus addresses the audience as the disciples.

It is probable that the historical audiences of the Gospels in the late first century included Greco-Roman Gentiles who identified with Israelite traditions. Reflecting the conclusions of narrative criticism, the data of audience address suggest that the implied audiences of the Gospels (the audiences envisioned within the texts themselves, regardless of the identities of actual readers) were predominantly Judeans but also included Gentiles, both of whom were part of the often heterogeneous groups of Hellenistic Judeans and Greco-Romans in the cities and towns of the late first-century Roman empire.

While initial research into the dynamics of audience address in biblical compositions has focused on the Gospels, audience address is a literary feature of all narratives and would have been an aspect of all ancient performances of the books of the Bible, including the Hexateuch, the prophets, and wisdom teachers of Israel, Acts, and the LETTERS of Paul. Recognition of the unique dynamics of audience address in oral storytelling can lead to new perspectives on the impact and meaning of biblical compositions in their original historical contexts.

Thomas E. Boomershine (United Theological Seminary, USA)

Further Reading

Kelly, R. Iverson, ed. 2014. *From Text to Performance: Narrative and Performance Criticisms in Dialogue and Debate*. Biblical Performance Criticism Series 10. Eugene: Wipf & Stock.

Boomershine, Thomas E. 2011. 'Audience Address and Purpose in the Performance of Mark'. In *Mark as Story: Retrospect and Prospect.* Edited by Kelly R. Iverson and Christopher W. Skinner. SBLRBS 65. Atlanta: SBL, pp. 115–44.

Boomershine, Thomas E. 2011. 'The Medium and Message of John: Audience Address and Audience Identity in the Fourth Gospel'. In *The Fourth Gospel in First-Century Media Culture.* Edited by Tom Thatcher and Anthony LeDonne. LNTS 426. London: T&T Clark, pp. 92–110.

Boomershine, Thomas E. 2014. 'Audience Asides and the Audiences of Mark'. In *From Text to Performance: Narrative and Performance Criticisms in Dialogue and Debate*. Biblical Performance Criticism Series 10. Eugene: Wipf & Stock, pp. 80–96.

Boomershine, Thomas E. 2014. *The Messiah of Peace: A Performance Criticism Commentary on Mark's Passion Resurrection Narrative*. Biblical Performance Criticism Series 12. Eugene: Wipf & Stock.

Maxwell, Kathy Reiko. 2010. *Hearing Between the Lines: The Audience as Fellow-Worker in Luke-Acts and Its Literary Milieu.* LNTS 425. London: T&T Clark.

Authorship See PUBLICATION (IN ANTIQUITY).

B

Bakhtin, Mikhail (M. M.) Mikhail Mihailovich Bakhtin (1895–1975) was a Russian Orthodox thinker, philosopher, anthropologist, historian of Hellenistic literature, literary theorist, and specialist in the works of Rabelais and Dostoevsky. Though his historical circumstances dictated that he worked in substantial isolation from contemporary European language philosophers, those familiar with Heidegger, Gadamer, Ricoeur, and Levinas will recognize much in Bakhtin, granted his idiosyncratic terminology and tangled concepts. His writings – accumulated in notebooks over a lifetime rather than prepared for publication – resist consultation in an orderly or convenient way.

Bakhtin was consumed by two major interests that he continuously developed and re-positioned: 1) the unity comprising an artist's creation of a work or of a human being's living a life and 2) the umbrella concept of DIALOGISM comprising the vast set of ways in which humans intersect in being, in ethical acts, and in language while also remaining distinct and non-coinciding. He early argued for – and demonstrated the unity of – matters sometimes thought discrete: historical-social circumstances, linguistic or literary features of art, and the situated position of a participant in a life situation (whether as author, character, or reader). His understanding of these reverberating processes has been shown to rise from the basic movement of the biblical narrative from creation to breach between Creator and creatures to processes of grace and reconciliation. Thus, without claiming or perhaps even appearing to be a Christian theorist, Bakhtin makes profound and pervasive use of the SCHEMA underlying Christian texts, liturgy, theology, and ethics.

Though Bakhtin himself did not comment on biblical texts, his ideas have been employed fruitfully to issues in biblical interpretation. For the most part eschewing issues in the history of philosophy (which comprises a substantial portion of Bakhtin studies), biblical scholars have been drawn to his more literary concepts, with particular attention to three major premises of his work.

First, Bakhtin's insights into how language is often shared ambiguously among authors, narrators, and various characters provide opportunity to examine and exploit passages where a character may participate in discourse without actually taking responsibility for what is said, may be quoting another with or without accuracy or approval, or may be assigned language by the author or narrator that links to another character or situation. For example, the utterance of 1 Sam. 24.4 (The men of David said to him, 'Here is the day of which the Lord said to you, "I will give your enemy into your hand, and you shall do to him as it seems good to you."' NRSV) reverberates in the speech of various characters and exerts a powerful influence without ever being substantiated. Has God thus promised? Do David's men believe what they say? Does David accept it and act on it, or does he refuse it – or some of each? When a character claims divine approval or permission for a dubious deed, makes assertions that are contested elsewhere in a work, or borrows language from another site, space is opened for interpretation and motive becomes more complex than if the language is attributed in a more uncomplicated manner.

Second, biblical scholars have built upon Bakhtin's approach to GENRE. For Bakhtin, genre is most fundamentally a way of thinking, the shape that thinking tends to take, and hence a strategy for crafting an utterance, a way of envisioning – not simply a form or template to be diagnosed. Bakhtin's insights into the abundance of genres and the multiple and even uncountable ways in which their elements nest and collaborate has provided a fresh and freeing path beyond the more classical and morphologically tight FORM CRITICISM, which is hampered by its obsession to classify constitutive elements and determine precise life setting. As genre moves from more prescriptive to more descriptive, from a few carefully tended forms to a near-infinite set, anomalies can be exploited rather than smoothed away and the rich diversity of genre possibilities can be exploited rather than shrunk. The more plentiful and diverse the genres, the richer the likely interpretation.

Third, Bakhtin's researches into the carnivalesque features of culture and literature have provided a popular way to investigate biblical texts like Esther and Daniel, rendering their otherwise unrealistic and even grotesque features more understandable by suggesting how they share a heritage with other great works of literature and culture. To consider how biblical books once presumed to be primarily historical in reference might be responding to deeper cultural prompts exposes an alternative hermeneutic more political than historical. Here the interest moves from when or how Esther, a Jewish woman, became queen of Persia or how a doltish king could possibly govern an empire to how power structures are subverted and even overturned completely, if briefly and temporarily, in the biblical narrative, and to the complex question of how we imitate our rivals.

In each case, Bakhtin's refusal to separate the artistic features of a text from its socio-historical and ethical dimensions has prompted biblical scholars to engage more deeply in the questions of how biblical characters can be shown responsive to the situations they face and has provided categories for examining whether such characters are evading the challenges with which they are presented, rendering more subtle the ways in which biblical texts continue to offer vast insight into the human condition. The complexity of Bakhtin's thought is challenging, not least because the individual elements of his approach cannot be isolated: each is part of a tightly woven skein of insights with linked and mutually intensifying implications. The best Bakhtinian readings are those that engage multiple issues and levels to investigate socio-historical context, literary features, anthropology, and ethics.

Barbara Green (Dominican School of Philosophy and Theology, USA)

Further Reading

Bakhtin, M. M. 1984. *Problems of Dostoevsky's Poetics*. Edited and translated by Caryl Emerson, with an introduction by Wayne C. Booth. Minneapolis: University of Minnesota Press.

Bakhtin, M. M. 1984. *Rabelais and His World*. Translated by Helene Iswolsky. Bloomington: Indiana University Press.

Bakhtin, M. M. 1986. *Speech Genres and Other Late Essays*. Edited by Caryl Emerson and Michael Holquist. Translated by Vern W. McGee. Austin: University of Texas Press.

Boer, Roland, ed. 2007. *Bakhtin and Genre Theory in Biblical Studies*. Semeia Studies. Atlanta: SBL Press.

Craig, Kenneth. 1995. *Reading Esther: A Case for the Literary Carnivalesque*. Louisville: Westminster John Knox Press.

Green, Barbara. 2000. *Mikhail Bakhtin and Biblical Scholarship: An Introduction*. Semeia Studies. Atlanta: SBL Press.

Green, Barbara. 2003. *How Are the Mighty Fallen? A Dialogical Study of King Saul in 1 Samuel*. Sheffield: Sheffield Academic Press.

Newsom, Carol A. 1996. 'Bakhtin, the Bible, and Dialogic Truth'. *Journal of Religion* 76(2): 290–306.

Newsom, Carol A. 2003. *The Book of Job: A Contest of Moral Imaginations*. Oxford: Oxford University Press.

Banquet/Meals A banquet is a formal gathering centred around a festive, communal meal. Modern banquets typically involve special invitations, appetizers, and cocktails prior to the main course, and in some cases assigned seating – features that distinguish them from more ordinary dining events. In antiquity, banquets also had unique features that set them apart from ordinary meals. In the Greco-Roman period, such celebratory feasts would include a meal with several courses, wine or other libations, formal speeches, and ceremonial practices like reclining, handwashing, and seating that reflected a social hierarchy. Frequent references to banquets throughout Jewish literature of the Second Temple and Early Rabbinic periods indicate that ritual meals were an important social form that held symbolic power for ancient authors and their audiences, much the way they still do today. It is thus not surprising that banquets are frequently presented as the setting for PARABLES and midrashic narratives that wrestle with questions about social status.

Feasting, both as a literary metaphor and a lived social phenomenon, offered ancient Jews a rich site for thinking through complicated issues of identity and belonging in the wake of the destruction of the Jerusalem TEMPLE. Who has the means to prepare an elaborate banquet? Who is invited and who is excluded? What customs must be upheld at the table? What foods will be served? Does it matter if the meat was sacrificed to idols? Can one share a meal with people from outside the community? In opening up key questions such as these, banquets provided an important framework for social formation among both Jews and early Christians.

Sacrificial Meals

While references to formal banquets are rare in the Hebrew Bible, later meal traditions do draw on imagery rooted in the Israelite tradition of cultic sacrifice. Sacrifice was a ritual practice that, in the minds of the Israelites, established communication between themselves and their deity. As a mechanism for atonement and thanksgiving, it also affirmed God's presence in the ancient temple. The priests would draw near to the divine presence to present an offering of livestock or grain, which would then be consumed by fire on the altar, and sometimes shared in part by the priests. While not a banquet in the formal sense of the term, the metaphor of feasting is key to understanding the logic of sacrifice. God 'consumed' the sacrifices offered by the priests, making the temple altar analogous to the dining table, an idea that became further developed in early rabbinic traditions. That the Jerusalem temple was a site of PILGRIMAGE during the seasonal Jewish festivals also reinforced the temple's role as a social centre.

Hellenistic Judaism

In the post-exilic period, with the loss of a single centre for cultic practice, there is ample evidence to suggest that the banqueting cultures of Greece and Rome had a profound impact on Hellenistic Jewish society. Ritual meals held in celebration of the biblical festivals marked the sacred calendar, and the dietary laws prescribed in the Torah became increasingly important as a means of differentiating Jews from their non-Jewish neighbours. The book of Esther, which takes place during the Persian period, culminates in the creation of an annual celebratory feast to mark the new festival of Purim (9.16-22).

Textual and archaeological remains concerning sectarian groups indicate that meals played a pivotal role in forging group IDENTITY. Wisdom of Ben Sira, for example, includes detailed discussion of etiquette and social expectations for participating in a ritual meal (31–32). Analysis of the archaeological remains from Qumran suggests that a communal dining area was a prominent architectural feature of their settlement, and the Community Rule states specifically that the group is expected to hold a regular communal meal (1QS 6.2-3). Philo's extensive discussion of the THERAPUTAE in *The Contemplative Life* provides great detail about the feasting practices of this monastic group, revealing many motifs in common with Greco-Roman traditions.

The notion that the Jewish dietary practices are intended to set Jews apart from their Gentile neighbours is reflected in a motif that appears in the Letter of Aristeas (142). In the Hellenistic romance *Joseph and Aseneth*, Joseph makes a point of rejecting Aseneth specifically because her mouth is defiled by idol worship – 'eating the bread of anguish' from their table (8.4-5).

Early Christianity

Given the significance of banqueting in ancient Mediterranean societies, it is no surprise that communal feasting also became an important, defining practice among early Christians. Ritual meals, modelled in part on Greco-Roman banquets, were a forum to develop and share a collective vision for the community. Paul's epistles to the early Christian communities frequently reference conflicts related to food, such as whether it is permissible to eat meat that had been sacrificed to idols (1 Cor. 8; 10), or whether the EUCHARIST is being consumed with appropriate intention (1 Cor. 11). Perhaps these LETTERS were first shared aloud at communal meals among early Christians?

In other NT sources, the dining table appears as an instructive metaphor, most specifically in the Gospels and as a setting for many of the parables of Jesus. Jesus is described as dining with 'tax collectors and sinners', an indication of low social status (Mt. 9.10-11; Mk 2.15-16; Lk. 5.30). In other narratives, Jesus challenges conventional ideas about social hierarchy symbolized by one's place at the table (Lk. 14.7-10), or uses a banquet as a metaphor for the kingdom of heaven (Lk. 14.15-23). The iconic Last Supper (Lk. 22.7-23; Mt. 26.17-30) is perhaps the most noted example of a sacred feast in the NT, especially important in that it is the basis for the ritual practice of the Eucharist in the early church.

Rabbinic Judaism

Rabbinic texts frequently turn to the dining table to explore issues of identity. In particular, they are interested in the boundaries that one must maintain in establishing relationships between Jews and non-Jews. For the rabbis, consumption of food was a sacred activity. Since their Roman neighbours could potentially be consuming meat or wine that had been dedicated or sacrificed to pagan gods, early rabbinic traditions are very anxious about commensality.

The motif of an eschatological banquet, a feast that takes place among the righteous in the messianic era, is one that reappears with some regularity throughout the corpus of rabbinic literature, even in early Tannaitic sources. For example, 'Rabbi Yaakov said: This world is like an ante-chamber (*prozdor*) before the world to come; prepare yourself in the antechamber so that you may enter the banquet hall (*m. Avot* 4:6).'

Perhaps the most vivid picture of the eschatological meal is preserved in those traditions dealing with the Leviathan and Behemoth, the two mythic beasts engaged in primordial struggle whose corpses are consumed by the righteous in the world to come. After the resurrection, judgement, and cosmic wars have taken place, the righteous are entertained at God's table, where God joins them in this festive meal (*b. Baba Bathra* 74b-75a). That the world to come is envisioned as a banquet conveys a powerful sense of both inclusion and exclusion. To envision the messianic age as one great feast is to celebrate the future unity of the exiled Jewish people. Nevertheless, this inclusive meal simultaneously distinguishes the Jewish people as a holy nation, a nation set apart from other nations.

The Passover seder is most certainly the ancient banquet that has received the most scholarly attention, particularly among scholars exploring the relationship between the Seder and the Gospels' description of Jesus' Last Supper (Lk. 22.7-23; Mt. 26.17-30; see EUCHARIST). The seder is a clear example of a ritual meal that blends elements of the Greco-Roman culture, specifically the symposium tradition, with Jewish sacrificial symbolism.

Andrea Lieber (Dickinson College, USA)

Further Reading

Bokser, Baruch M. 1984. *The Origins of the Seder: The Passover Rite and Early Rabbinic Judaism*. Berkeley: University of California Press.

Marks, Susan, and Hal Taussig, eds. 2014. *Meals in Early Judaism: Social Formation at the Table*. London: Palgrave Macmillan.
Rosenblum, Jordan. 2010. *Food and Identity in Early Rabbinic Judaism*. Cambridge: Cambridge University Press.
Smith, Dennis E. 2003. *From Symposium to Eucharist: The Banquet in the Early Christian World*. Minneapolis: Fortress Press, 2003.
Smith, Dennis E., and Hal Taussig, eds. 2012. *Meals in the Early Christian World: Social Formation, Experimentation, and Conflict at the Table*. London: Palgrave Macmillan, 2012.
Taussig, Hal. 2009. *In the Beginning was the Meal: Social Experimentation and Early Christianity*. Minneapolis: Fortress Press.

Baptism (Christian) Baptism was the ceremony of admission into the early Christian community. In the first four centuries it was normally administered by immersion in water (Mt. 3.6, 16; Acts 8.38-39) and accompanied by a confession of faith.

The usual order in religious history is that ritual action comes first and interpretation comes later. Sometimes, however, the significance of a ceremony is enacted in order to exemplify its implied meaning. Baptism offers examples of movements in both directions.

Paul drew from the physical act of dipping into water and then lifting out the meaning of baptism as a participation in the death and burial of Jesus, so that baptism pictured death to sin and resurrection to new life (Rom. 6.2-5; cf. Col. 2.12). Since Paul expected the Christians at Rome, where he had not visited, to know this significance of baptism, the association of baptism with the atoning death of Jesus must have been present from quite early in apostolic teaching. This theology of baptism was perhaps suggested by Jesus' own use of baptism in a metaphorical sense for his being overwhelmed in suffering (Mk 10.38; Lk. 12.50). Such association agrees with the common use of the verb 'baptize' for death by drowning (Lucian, *The Misanthrope* 44; Josephus, *The Jewish War* 1.437). The meaning of baptism as being united with the death and resurrection of Christ became common in the catechetical instruction of the fourth century (Cyril of Jerusalem, *Mystagogic Catecheses* 2.4-8; John Chrysostom, *Baptismal Instructions* 2.11; Ambrose, *On the Sacraments* 2.7.23).

The promise of the Holy Spirit connected with baptism (Acts 2.38) came to be represented by a laying on of hands and an anointing with olive oil (Tertullian, *On Baptism* 7.1; 8.1; Hippolytus, *The Apostolic Tradition* 21.21-22). Tertullian's placing of the bestowal of the Holy Spirit at these post-baptismal ceremonies was facilitated by the earlier example of conferral of the Spirit by the imposition of hands (Acts 8.17) and the metaphorical association of anointing with the Holy Spirit (Acts 10.38; 1 Jn 2.20, 27). This identification prepared for the later development of confirmation as a separate sacrament.

A classic example of a ritual practice preceding theology is infant baptism, which arose in the second century CE in emergency cases to assure that a dying child would enter the kingdom of heaven. The understanding of the church was that baptism granted 'forgiveness of sins' (Acts 2.38); the question then arose, 'Why baptize infants who have no sins?' (cf. Origen, *Homily on Luke* 14.5). Augustine used the established practice of infant baptism as the decisive argument for original sin against the Pelagians, who denied original sin but allowed the baptism of babies – since babies had not sinned but were baptized for the forgiveness of sins, they must carry the guilt of Adam's transgression (*Guilt and Remission of Sins* 1.26.39). Subsequent history illustrates the opposite relationship, as original sin eventually became the rationale for baptizing the newborns.

Baptism was associated with forgiveness of sins (Mk 1.4; Acts 22.16). The use of water for ceremonial PURIFICATION was common in paganism and Judaism, so the relating of 'washing with water' (Eph. 5.26) to moral cleansing came naturally. Early Christian authors stress, however, that the benefits were attributed to deity at the time of the water rite, not to the water itself (Gregory of Nyssa, *Catechetical Oration* 40; Theodore of Mopsuestia, *Catechetical Homily* 14).

Baptism also offers examples of a doctrinal meaning illustrated by liturgical actions. Triple immersion is first attested with certainty about 200 CE (Tertullian, *The Crown* 3). A plausible explanation for the practice is the administration of baptism 'in the name of the Father and of the Son and of the Holy Spirit' (Mt 28.19), and the *Apostolic Tradition* instructs the administrator to dip the candidate's head after a confession in each of the triune names (21.14-18). A common image for baptism in the second century was new birth. This meaning for baptism (cf. Jn 3.5) was symbolized by the giving of a cup of milk and honey, the food of infants, in the first EUCHARIST of the newly baptized (*Apostolic Tradition* 21.28, 33). The milk and honey also represented entrance into the promised land (based on Lev. 20.24) of eschatological paradise, with the two associations combined in *Barnabas* 6.8-17. The new birth motif probably is a factor in the depiction of Jesus, at his baptism in early Christian art, as small of stature and nude. The significance of baptism as being clothed with Christ (Gal. 3.27) prompted the clothing of those who emerged from the baptismal font with a white robe, first attested in the fourth century (John Chrysostom, *Catechetical Lectures* 7.24; Asterius, *Homily* 12). The interpretation of putting on a garment may be seen also as the giving of a symbolic meaning to the functional act of reclothing after baptism.

The motif of 'enlightenment' (Heb. 6:4) was an early and popular description of baptism (Justin, *1 Apology* 61.12), and those undergoing instruction for baptism were called 'those being enlightened' (Cyril of Jerusalem, *Catechetical Homilies* 18.32). The annual commemoration of the baptism of Jesus in the Greek church was known as the Festival of Lights, and sermons on baptism for this occasion are extant (Gregory of Nazianzus, *Oration* 39; Gregory of Nyssa, *Lights*). A liturgical expression of this theme was the carrying of lamps by the newly baptized into the assembly of the church (Proclus, *Homily* 27.8.50).

Ritually, baptism marked the transition from the non-Christian world to incorporation into the church (1 Cor. 12.13). This entrance into the Christian community was illustrated by the person being led into the assembly, receiving the kiss of peace, and partaking of the Eucharist (Justin, *1 Apology* 65).

Everett Ferguson (Abilene Christian University, USA)

Further Reading

Ferguson, Everett. 2009. *Baptism in the Early Church: History, Theology, and Liturgy in the First Five Centuries*. Grand Rapids: Eerdmans.

Hellholm, David, Tor Vegge, Øyvind Norderval and Christer Hellholm, eds. 2011. *Ablution, Initiation, and Baptism: Late Antiquity, Early Judaism, and Early Christianity*. 3 vols. BENW 176. Berlin: Walter Mouton de Gruyter.

Jensen, Robin M. 2012. *Baptismal Imagery in Early Christianity: Ritual, Visual, and Theological Dimensions*. Grand Rapids: Baker Academic.

Bauman, Richard Richard Bauman has had a long, distinguished, and varied academic career at the interstices between FOLKLORE, anthropology, history, linguistics, semiotics, and speech communication, contributing to the development of both theory and method in the ETHNOGRAPHY of language, performance studies, and the ideology of language. In this last area, especially in collaboration with Charles L. Briggs, Bauman charted the role of modern language ideologies in sociopolitical inequality. Bauman's approach to performativity is in some ways more saliently postmodern than that of many scholars interested in these questions. In the course of his career, Bauman has served as director of the Center of Intercultural Studies in Folklore and Ethnomusicology at the University of Texas and chair of the Department of Folklore and Ethnomusicology at Indiana University. He was president of the Semiotic Society of America, the Society for Linguistic Anthropology, and the Society of Fellows of the American Folklore Society, chair of the Folklore Advisory Council of the Smithsonian Institution, and editor of the *Journal of American Folklore*.

As wide ranging as Bauman's scholarship is, it centres nonetheless on his appreciation of the essential role that verbal art plays in human reality, something he acknowledged in his early and influential monograph *Verbal Art as Performance* (1977). This work put him in the company of the major explorers of verbal art forms who, beginning notably in the mid-twentieth century, blazed many trails across academic disciplinary boundaries. In this rich scholarly environment, regard for traditional verbal art moved from treatment of speech as static material record or inert artefact to dynamic communicative performance, an act and event that expresses and shapes communities and cultures.

Bauman resisted a perceived effort by certain schools of analysis to maintain a clear theoretical dichotomy between ORALITY and LITERACY, (see GREAT DIVIDE) arguing that an understanding of speaking and WRITING in human life can be achieved only by empirically sound, cross-cultural studies. Bauman's own fieldwork includes research on STORYTELLING in Scotland, Nova Scotia, Mexico, and rural West Texas.

The postmodern qualities of Bauman's work perhaps appear mostly obviously in his attention not only to the necessity of interdisciplinary approaches to the study of verbal art but to various challenges posed by the concatenation of the disciplines themselves. Taken together, these disciplines reveal the social constitution of communicative forms, but they also show that society itself is constituted by communicative acts. These forms offer insight into the societies they produce and express. They serve as cultural resources for their societies, and they establish and express a society's values even as they vary historically and culturally. In his capstone work with Charles Briggs, *Voices of Modernity*, Bauman investigated how thinking about language by modernity's framers contributed to forms of political and social inequality in the modern era.

Randy Lumpp (Regis University, USA)

Further Reading

Bauman, Richard. 1977. *Verbal Art as Performance*. Prospect Heights, IL: Waveland Press.

Bauman, Richard. 1986. *Story, Performance and Event: Contextual Studies of Oral Narrative*. New York: Cambridge University Press.

Bauman, Richard. ed. 1992. *Folklore, Cultural Performances, and Popular Entertainments: A Communications-Centered Handbook.* New York: Oxford University Press.

Bauman, Richard., and Charles L. Briggs. 1990. 'Poetics and Performance as Critical Perspectives on Language and Social Life'. *American Review of Anthropology* 19: 59–88.

Bauman, Richard, and Charles L. Briggs. 2003. *Voices of Modernity: Language Ideologies and the Politics of Inequality*. New York: Cambridge University Press.

Bible in Ancient and Modern Media Research Unit (Society of Biblical Literature) The Bible in Ancient and Modern Media Section (BAMM) is a collaborative research unit founded in the Society of Biblical Literature in 1983 to promote media-critical study of the Bible. Since its formation, BAMM has sought to initiate research into the interrelationship of the Bible and communications technology, from the oral traditions and early writings of ancient Israel in the mid- to late second millennium BCE to the present technological revolution of electronic and now digital media. The initial conception of the group emerged in the context of two areas of inquiry: studies of the media culture of the Bible in the ancient world, and research exploring the interpretation of the Bible in and for the electronic culture of the late twentieth century.

Biblical Scholarship and the Rise of Media Criticism

The field of media studies emerged in the twentieth century from a broad academic interest in understanding the impact of the rise of modern communications technologies, such as the telephone, motion pictures, television, and computers. Seen in the context of the history of civilization, the development of electronic media represents a comprehensive shift in communications technologies on a scale comparable to the invention of the printing press in the fifteenth century and of the technology of WRITING in the ancient world. Major figures in this initial wave of research into the impact of communications technology included Harold Lazenfeld, Harold Innis, ERIC HAVELOCK, MARSHALL MCLUHAN, and WALTER ONG, S.J. This new field of study raised awareness of the importance of media in understanding the Bible, both in its original contexts and in the contexts of its reception history in subsequent communication cultures.

Early applications of media criticism to the study of the Bible focused on two sets of concerns. Those with a more historical interest sought to uncover new perspectives on the media dynamics of the origins of the Bible and its individual books. Traditionally, the Bible had been conceived as a collection of texts written to be read by readers, similar to modern print book culture. The underlying assumption had generally been that the reader was an individual with a manuscript in hand reading in silence, or sometimes reading aloud alone or to a group. A sign of the pervasiveness of this conception of the Bible has been the ubiquitous reference in biblical commentaries and monographs to the reader and the text.

An important factor in the shaping of research on the media history of the Bible was FORM CRITICISM, which studied the oral traditions that preceded the written biblical texts. Form criticism was itself a response to the underlying tendency of Source Criticism to conceive of the origins of the Pentateuch and the Gospels, for example, in terms of ancient authors pasting together written source documents to produce their own books. By contrast, early form critics like HERMANN GUNKEL, RUDOLF BULTMANN, and MARTIN DIBELIUS argued that the originators of biblical writings were editors who produced their works by collecting and arranging pre-existing oral traditions into written texts. A common metaphor for describing the tradition history of the Gospels was a 'string of pearls', the pearls being individual units of oral tradition and the string being the process of linking them in written order.

While the form critics had made major contributions to the understanding of the oral traditions as sources for the final manuscripts of the Bible, Form Criticism as a discipline tended to reinforce the picture of the Bible in its final written form as a library of texts read by readers. In effect, for form critics, once the oral forms of the tradition were incorporated into written manuscripts, the orality of the tradition came to an end and the Bible became a fully literate tradition with its texts, editors, and readers. The later development of Redaction Criticism, which sought to identify the distinctive contributions of the redactors of the earlier oral and written traditions, reinforced this concept of the Bible as documents formed by editors for readers.

A second stream of early media criticism of the Bible related to the growing impact of modern electronic communications technology on the interpretation of the Bible in contemporary cultures. At the time that BAMM was formed, little scholarly research had been done on the interaction of modern technologies (e.g. film/TV, computers) and the Bible. This absence is perhaps unsurprising when viewed in the larger context of the origins and stated purpose of the Society of Biblical Literature. SBL was formed in 1880 to support the non-sectarian, historical-critical study of the Bible emerging in the late nineteenth century. The most powerful force in the media culture of that period was the mass distribution of printed books and pamphlets. Reflecting this aesthetic, a mandate in the formation of the Society was that the only medium of discourse at its annual meetings would be the reading of scholarly papers. This preference continued in the Society over the ensuing century, even as the media systems of the broader culture radically changed.

Overall, the broader theoretical context of the formation of BAMM was the absence of systematic research on the media of the Bible in biblical scholarship. The framework of Aristotle's *Poetics* highlights the significance of this black hole in biblical scholarship. Aristotle identifies four causes for the meaning of poetry: the form, the content, the final impact, and the medium. While biblical scholars had conducted extensive research on the forms, contents, and meanings of the biblical texts, little had been done to consider the medium of the Bible in antiquity and modern times. More focused research on the media of the Bible, both in its original context and in contemporary contexts, was needed.

Formation of the Bible in Ancient and Modern Media Section

Initial conversations about the need for a research unit focused on the Bible and media took place at the annual meeting of the Society of Biblical Literature in 1979 (Dallas), first between Tom Boomershine and David Rhoads and then between Boomershine and WERNER KELBER, who was then working on his groundbreaking study, *The Oral and the Written Gospel*. With their input and encouragement, Boomershine submitted proposals in 1980 and 1981 for the formation of a new Consultation at the ensuing annual meeting, both of which were rejected by the SBL Program Committee. At the 1982 annual meeting in New York City, Boomershine discussed the possibility once again with Krister Stendahl, president of SBL that year, who encouraged the resubmission of the proposal and offered to recommend it to the Program Committee. A new proposal was hastily written on a borrowed typewriter in the lobby of the hotel and approved, with Stendahl's support, at the end of the meeting; the new Consultation was launched the following year (1983), with Boomershine as chair of the research group. Most of the initial participants in BAMM were veterans of the exploration of new methodological approaches to biblical study, having been previously involved in the Literary Aspects of the Gospels and Structuralist Criticism research units.

David Rhoads presided over the Consultation's initial session in 1983, which featured papers by Werner Kelber, James Sanders, and Tom Boomershine. Kelber's paper, 'Biblical Hermeneutics and the Art of Communication in Antiquity', was a prequel to *The Oral and the Written Gospel*, which was released that same year. Sanders' paper, 'Voice, Vellum, and Vision' was a further development of his research on the transition from voice to manuscript and the history of the canon. Boomershine's paper, 'The Bible in Oral Tradition and Electronic Media', outlined the basic theoretical framework and mission of the group. Though attendance at the first meeting was good (ca. 50), the Consultation's subsequent petition to achieve more permanent status within the Society was denied. BAMM therefore continued as a Consultation into its second year.

At the 1984 annual meeting, Walter Brueggemann chaired a session of papers by Martin Marty and Robert Jewett on the Bible in television, while a second session featured papers by Walter Ong and Tom Boomershine with a response by Werner Kelber. This latter session was the first to explore the scholarly exegesis of a biblical text on the basis of its performance in the ancient world. Boomershine's paper included a dramatic recitation of the story of Peter's denial from memory, the first performance of a biblical story in a BAMM session and, likely, the first in the history of SBL. Both sessions were well attended, and the structure of the programme initiated a pattern that would guide BAMM for the next several decades, with some sessions focusing on the Bible in ancient media and others on the Bible in more modern media (e.g. film/TV, visual arts, and digital media).

Based on attendance at these initial sessions, the stature of those in attendance and those involved in the programme, and the immediate prospect of a volume of Semeia dedicated to the unit's work (edited by Lou Silbermann; Semeia 39, 1987), a proposal for the establishment of BAMM as an SBL Group was accepted and the BAMM research programme at SBL was launched. In 1985, Joanna Dewey became co-chair of the Group along with Boomershine.

Performances and Partnerships

As noted above, the original leadership of BAMM was interested in the research potentials of the performance of biblical compositions and sought to include these in the meetings of SBL. David Rhoads and Tom

Boomershine performed parts of the Gospel of Mark in the first years of the Group, but the goal was a full-length performance of a biblical book for the wider community of SBL. Once again, discussions of this possibility with the Program Committee met with initial resistance. The underlying philosophical issue was whether writings of the Bible were ever performed in their entirety in single settings in the ancient world, rather than recounted in brief oral traditions, as implied by the conclusions of Form Criticism and by the modern practice of reading short portions of Scripture in synagogues and churches. Appealing to the work of scholars such as MILMAN PARRY and ALFRED LORD and a variety of ancient sources, Rhoads, Boomershine, and others contended that long oral performances were common in antiquity. For example, very long stories such as Homer's *Iliad* were performed at festivals, oratorical competitions, and all-night celebrations in ancient Greece. Initial performances of the Gospel of Mark as a whole further confirmed that such performances should be considered both feasible and compelling.

After five years of deliberation, the SBL Program Committee approved a BAMM proposal for the performance of an entire biblical book at the 1988 annual meeting. David Rhoads performed Hans Dieter Betz's translation of Galatians for over two hundred scholars, the first performance of an entire biblical book at SBL. Since that initial venture, BAMM has sponsored performances of many books of the Bible in their entirety, including Mark, John, Galatians, Philemon, and Revelation in the meetings of SBL. The vitality of these performances has inspired the growing practice of the performance of the Scriptures from memory in other academic settings and in modern worshipping communities (see PERFORMANCE CRITICISM).

A further initiative of BAMM that required permission from the structures of SBL was the establishment of partnerships with scholars in related fields outside of biblical studies. The first of such partnerships was with JOHN MILES FOLEY, the pre-eminent scholar in the field of oral tradition. The multifaceted investigation of the interactions between the Bible and communication systems also led BAMM to embrace multidisciplinary partnerships with a wide range of other groups within the community of biblical scholarship, including, among others, research units focused on Structuralist Criticism, the Gospels of Mark and John, the Apocalypse of John, the Bible and Computers, SOCIAL MEMORY, the Historical Jesus, and Translation Studies. This interdisciplinary research has seeded a wide range of groups in SBL that have pursued specific aspects of the BAMM agenda: for example, Performance Criticism; the Bible and Popular Culture; the Bible and Visual Art (see VISUAL CULTURE); Rhetoric and the NT; the Bible and Emotion; Digital Humanities; and Speech and Talk in the Mediterranean World.

Impact of BAMM

Over the past three decades, BAMM's focus on the study of the Bible in ancient and modern media has helped to pioneer a series of research initiatives that have introduced biblical scholars to new fields of study. These new fields have included LITERACY, SOUND MAPPING, Performance Criticism, the media history of biblical interpretation, social memory, the Bible and Film, TRANSLATION for oral cultures, and the Bible and Computers. Overall, the research of BAMM and of scholars involved in its programme has established that the traditional picture of the Bible as a series of texts written and edited by authors and read by individual readers in silence should be significantly nuanced. Literate culture in antiquity was limited to a small elite minority in positions of privilege and power that occurred within the larger context of an overwhelmingly non-literate culture. Oral culture remained the dominant context of a highly complex synthesis of the practices and cultural interplay of orality and literacy.

The recognition of the character of the Bible as performance literature has also generated interest in new approaches to biblical pedagogy. Traditionally, the teaching of the Bible in colleges, universities, and seminaries has been almost completely comprised of the study of the Bible as written texts. The curriculum for introductory courses to both Testaments has typically dealt with the documentary hypothesis (J, E, P, D) for the formation of the Pentateuch and the Two (Mark and Q) or Four (Mark, Q, L, and M) Source theories for the formation of the Synoptic Gospels. BAMM has sponsored an ongoing series of papers and workshops that have introduced a new generation of teachers to strategies and practices for teaching the Bible as performance literature in undergraduate and postgraduate education.

Thomas E. Boomershine (United Theological Seminary, USA)

Further Reading

Silberman, Lou, ed. 1987. *Orality, Aurality, and Biblical Narrative*. Semeia 39. Atlanta: Scholars Press.

Blessings and Curses Blessings and curses are pronouncements of boon and doom enforced by divine or supernatural power. The content of blessings and curses is strongly related to the social function and settings in which they are pronounced. In the biblical world, blessings and curses were invoked primarily in liturgical WORSHIP, the making and breaking of covenant law, the establishment of patriarchal inheritance rights, and in prophetic oracles. Blessings and curses were decreed upon individuals as well as larger communities. Both blessings and curses were an important part of the formation of the identity of a covenant people in the Bible.

Contexts and Functions of Blessings and Curses

In the Bible, two types of blessings are pronounced in liturgical contexts: people blessing God, and people invoking God's blessing upon other people. The act of blessing God occurs primarily in the context of public gatherings when a call is made to bless God's name in conjunction with a call for the community to extol God's divine powers and remember God's salvific acts (see Pss. 104.1; 103.22; 1 Chron. 29.20; Neh. 9.5; Mt. 11.25; Lk. 10.21; 1 Pet. 1.3). The act of blessing others also occurs in liturgical contexts, such as Lev. 9.23, where Moses and Aaron bless the Israelites, as well as in the Priestly Blessing: 'May the Lord bless you and keep you …' (Num. 6.24-26). Some NT epistles include benedictions of divine favour over the recipients that were also used in liturgical settings (2 Cor. 13.14; 1 Thess. 3.12-13; Heb. 13.20-21; Jude 24–25). Imprecations also occur in liturgical prayer. Ps. 68.2 is an example of formulaic curse language: 'As wax melts before the fire, so may the wicked perish before God.' These curses in the psalms invoke calamity or God's vengeance upon enemies (e.g. Pss. 69; 109; 137.9).

Divine pronouncements of blessing and curse form a central feature of God's covenant with the ancient Israelites in the Bible, particularly in Deuteronomy. In these contexts, blessings and curses function to reinforce community boundaries and norms. The laws and statutes of the covenant were sealed in an oath ceremony (Deut. 27–29) in which the ancient Israelites swore allegiance to God and agreed to the terms of the covenant. This oath includes blessings to be meted out upon those who abide by the terms of the oath, and curses upon those who violate its statutes (Deuteronomy 28; Leviticus 26). This covenant is rooted in the election of God's chosen people to act as God's representatives in the world, as servants who return God's blessings back upon the nations (Gen. 12.2-3; 18.18). The Apostle Paul interprets this Abrahamic blessing upon all nations as a reference to the blessing imparted on followers of Jesus, whether Jews or Gentiles (Gal. 3.7-9). Paul also views the work and death of Jesus as a fulfilment of the terms of the covenant, including its curses, so that believers are redeemed from the curse of the abrogation of the law while still receiving its blessings (Gal. 3.10-14).

The paternal blessing upon a son (or a daughter, as in Num. 27) by a father was a means of transmitting legal inheritance rights in the family (Gen. 27; Heb. 11.20; 12.16-17). However, a paternal curse could be given to a son instead of a blessing (Gen. 27.12; 40), thus revoking a son's inheritance prerogative. Similarly, the blessing of Moses upon the tribes of Israel invokes divine favour upon each of the twelve tribes as clans with inherited ancestral lands within the southern Levant (Deuteronomy 33).

Pronouncing oracles of blessing or curse is one of the roles of the prophet in the Bible (see PROPHECY). For example, Balaam the Seer was hired by the ruler of Moab to curse the Israelites, but blesses them instead (Numbers 22–24; Deir 'Alla inscription). Jesus prophetically curses the fig tree as a metaphor for the TEMPLE (Mk 11.12–25). While the terms *blessing* or *curse* may not be used specifically, the metaphorical idea of invoking divine favour or punishment is a central feature of prophetic pronouncements (see Isa. 60–62 for an example of oracle of blessing, and Amos 1–5 for an example of an oracle of punishment). Similarly, in the Sermon on the Plain, Jesus pronounces both blessings and woes upon the poor and the rich respectively (Lu. 6.20-26), closing with a call to 'bless those who curse you' (Lk. 6.28).

Blessings and Curses in the Material Record of the Biblical World

As noted above, the biblical narratives portray primarily oral pronouncements of blessings and curses, often in ritualized settings or prophetic discourse. However, some passages suggest that the act of writing blessings and curses was a factor in their perceived effectiveness. Prior to the eighth century BCE, there is no material record of inscribed curses in ancient Israel or Judah, a fact that may suggest that blessings and curses were exclusively an oral genre in early Israel. However, the practice of inscribing curses on dedicatory inscriptions and treaty oath texts, including accompanying curses, was common in the ancient Near East, flourishing particularly in the ninth through seventh centuries BCE. For example, the instructions to write 'very clearly' the statutes of the law on stelae in Deut. 27.1-2, 8 show striking parallels with the ancient Near Eastern practice of inscribing covenants on stone tablets and stelae. Similarly, the ritual for the case of a suspected adulteress in Numbers 5 stipulates that the curse be written down and ingested by the accused.

From Iron Age Israel into the Late Antique period the writing of curses and blessings flourished in Jewish and Christian communities. The *Ketef Hinnom* amulets, for example, are a set of seventh-century BCE necklaces found in a tomb that contain tiny silver scrolls with inscribed prayers, including a blessing with striking similarity to the Priestly Blessing of Num. 6.24-26. Inscriptions invoking blessings and curses have also been found in tombs, in caves, at cultic sites, and upon cultic artefacts from Iron Age Israel (Khirbet el-Qom, Ein Gedi cave, Kuntillet 'Ajrud, Khirbet Beit Lei). Coptic Christians wrote on papyri and crafted amulets featuring blessings and curses from the first through the twelfth centuries CE. The curses of Deuteronomy 27–28 are invoked in Greek funerary inscriptions found in Phyrgian tombs from the third century CE. Jewish and Christian incantation bowls from the Antique period also feature quotations from Scripture with blessings and curses. Such artefacts were employed for apotropaic and healing purposes.

Melissa D. Ramos (University of California, Los Angeles, USA)

Further Reading

Aitken, J. K. 2007. *The Semantics of Blessing and Cursing in Ancient Hebrew*. Ancient Near Eastern Studies 23. Louvain: Peeters.

Levene, Dan. 2013. *Jewish Aramaic Curse Texts from Late-Antique Mesopotamia*. Boston: Brill.

Meyer, Marvin and Richard Smith. 1999. *Ancient Christian Magic: Coptic Texts of Ritual Power*. Princeton: Princeton University Press.

Sanzo, Joseph. 2014. *Scriptural Incipits on Amulets from Late Antique Egypt: Text, Typology, and Theory*. STAC 84. Tübingen: Mohr Siebeck.

Smoak, Jeremy. 2015. *The Priestly Blessing in Inscription and Scripture: The Early History of Numbers 6:24-26*. New York: Oxford.

Urbrock, William. 1992. 'Blessings and Curses'. In *Anchor Bible Dictionary*, vol. 1. Edited by David Noel Freedman. New York: Doubleday, pp. 755–761.

van der Horst, Pieter W. 2014. *Studies in Ancient Judaism and Early Christianity*. Boston: Brill.

Weinfeld, Moshe. 1992. *Deuteronomy and the Deuteronomic School*. Eisenbrauns: Winona Lake.

Zevit, Ziony. 2001. 'Writ on Rock – Script on Stone.' In *The Religions of Ancient Israel: A Synthesis of Parallactic Approaches*. New York: Continuum, pp. 350–438.

Biosphere (oral) In media criticism, the term *biosphere* refers to the total physical, human, and social context in which an oral utterance (of any length) is delivered and received. The biosphere model highlights the impact of the physical presence of the audience of an oral communication (or other live performance, including, e.g. an oral reading of a written text) on the structure, presentation, and meaning of the message. The term was popularized in biblical studies by WERNER KELBER (e.g. 1983; 1990: 77–8), who referred to the interactive contexts in which ancient Israelites and early Christians exchanged traditions and other information as 'biosphere[s] in which speaker and hearers live … an invisible nexus of references and identities from which people draw sustenance …. and in relation to which they make sense of their lives' (Kelber 1995: 159).

The biosphere model, as conceived by Kelber and integrated more broadly into discussions of ORAL TRADITION and the performative nature of the biblical texts, emphasizes two distinct characteristics of the medium of speech: the event nature of oral words, and the immediate physical presence of the listening audience. Unlike words preserved in WRITING, print, or digital media, spoken words have no physical substance or existence beyond the moments in which they are uttered and are thus best conceived as events rather than objects. As events involving individuals, spoken words may be understood as a form of social transaction, an observation that significantly impacts three aspects of oral communication.

First, the form, presentation, and content of any oral communication are shaped by the homeostatic balance achieved between speaker and audience in the moment of live performance. Because the audience is immediately present and responsive, allowing for a real-time assessment of the success of the communication, speakers engage in 'a continuous process of adjustment of language to communal expectations, of social to linguistic realities' (Kelber 1983: 19, 92). Put another way, the specific wording and delivery of an oral communication may have less to do with the contents of the words or what the author hoped to communicate than with the total human context in which the words were delivered, including not only the intentions of the speaker but also the immediate physical and social environments in which the audience received and reacted to the message.

Second, because oral speech adapts itself to its context not only in its presentation but also in its actual specific content (the specific words being communicated are tailored to the audience in real time), Kelber views the social biosphere as a sort of human intertext, a part of the referential field from which spoken words derive their meaning (Kelber 1990: 77–8). Put another way, the meaning of spoken words is derived not simply from their lexical value, grammatical context, and GENRE, but also from the total human situation in which they are uttered. This observation is particularly helpful in the analysis of performative genres that regularly manipulate the normal lexical meanings of words and idioms – such as PROVERBS, RIDDLES, and PARABLES – and also for understanding special in-group language that may not align with the broader lexical REGISTER.

Third, in view of the above considerations, the biosphere model weighs heavily against the notion of an ORIGINAL version of words that have been communicated in multiple contexts/situations. Because every individual act of oral communication is an event in space and time, and because the precise human contexts of individual events can never be fully reduplicated, and because the meaning of any utterance is tied to the moment of its production and reception, it would be impossible for any two performances of the same content to be identical, even if the words were repeated verbatim. Thus, for example, if an early Christian read aloud a copy of 1 Corinthians in a dozen different house churches, the meaning of each of these performances would be a function of the individual circumstances in which it was delivered. In Kelber's view, any adequate model for understanding the development and transmission of *tradition* must account for this reality.

Tom Thatcher (Cincinnati Christian University, USA)

Further Reading

Kelber, Werner. 1983/1997. *The Oral and the Written Gospel: The Hermeneutics of Speaking and Writing in the Synoptic Tradition, Mark, Paul, and Q*. Bloomington, IN: Indiana University Press.

Kelber, Werner. 1990. *In the Beginning Were the Words: The Apotheosis and Narrative Displacement of the Logos*. *JAAR* 58: 69–98.

Kelber, Werner. 1995. 'Jesus and Tradition: Words in Time, Words in Space'. In *Orality and Textuality in Early Christian Literature*. Edited by Joanna Dewey. Semeia 65. Atlanta: Scholars Press, pp. 139–67.

Bultmann, Rudolf Rudolf Bultmann (1884–1976) was a German NT scholar who ranks among the most influential intellectuals of the twentieth century. His historical-critical biblical work has profoundly shaped NT scholarship. In addition to his impact on biblical studies, Bultmann is also one of the most important theologians of the twentieth century.

Life

Born into a pious Lutheran household, Bultmann was the grandson of missionaries and the son of a pastor (Hammann 2013). Though prohibited from military service by a hip problem, Bultmann lived through both world wars, an experience that had a notable impact on his thinking (Standhartinger 2013; Hamman 2013: 96–104). One of his brothers, Arthur, was killed in France during the First World War (1917), and his other brother, Peter, died in a Nazi concentration camp in 1942. Theologically, Bultmann's existentialism sought to 'establish faith as an attitude of resistance to experiences and entanglements in unjust world affairs' (Standhartinger 2013: 253). Thoroughly a man of his time, Bultmann embraced historical-critical biblical research, and articulated his Lutheran faith with existentialist philosophy.

Bultmann studied theology at universities in Tübingen (1903), Berlin (1904), and Marburg (1905). In the course of his education, the young Bultmann studied under giants of German scholarship, including Hermann Gunkel (1862–1932) and Johannes Weiss (1863–1914). Bultmann's early academic training was heavily influenced by the *Religionsgeschichtliche Schule* (History of Religions School), which analysed early Christianity and the NT not in terms of doctrines but evolutionary historical developments.

Bultmann produced his doctoral dissertation, published in 1910 as *Der Stil der paulinischen Predigt und die kynische-stoische Diatribe* (*The Style of Pauline Preaching and the Cynic-Stoic Diatribe*), under Weiss' supervision. The central thesis of the book was that the oral style of diatribe common to popular philosophers was also Paul's style of preaching and could be identified in his letters, particularly Romans. Although never translated into English, the monograph was reissued in 1984 and remains a seminal work on diatribe in Paul's letters (Stowers 1981: 17–26). This was the first of his many significant contributions to biblical scholarship.

Bultmann's first teaching appointment was at Freidrich-Wilhelms University at Breslau, where he served from 1916 to 1920. During this time, Bultmann wrote what would become a pioneering work in NT scholarship, *Die Geschichte der synoptischen Tradition* (*The History of the Synoptic Tradition*). Although virtually complete in 1919, the book was not published until 1921 and then significantly revised and expanded in a second edition released in 1931. It is the expanded second edition that became a classic. The original manuscript helped secure Bultmann's advancement to the University of Giessen in 1920, succeeding the recently deceased Wilhelm Bousset (1865–1920). Bultmann's time in Giessen was short-lived. He taught there for only two semesters before accepting a position at his alma mater, Marburg, where he taught until his retirement in 1951 and lived until his death in 1976.

Research

Bultmann's life in the small university town of Marburg afforded him a productive research career. In the early part of his career, Bultmann engaged with Karl Barth's commentary on Romans and dialectical theology. He also formed an important friendship with Martin Heidegger (1889–1976), who taught in the philosophy department at Marburg from 1923 to 1928. The middle part of Bultmann's career (1933–45) was marked by a clash with Nazi Socialism, the publication of his commentary on the Gospel of John, and an important lecture, *Neues Testament und Mythologie* (*The New Testament and Mythology*). In this lecture, Bultmann articulated his existential hermeneutic of *Entmythologisierung* (demythologizing). His goal was to reinterpret the myth of the NT, which he considered unbelievable in the twentieth century, to make the Christian message acceptable in the modern world (Congdon 2015). The latter third of Bultmann's career (1945–53) involved him in teaching in the post-war university and saw the publication of his *Theologie des Neuen Testaments* (*Theology of the New Testament*). In terms of lasting impact, Bultmann's most significant contributions to biblical studies were *The History of the Synoptic Tradition* (1921), *The Gospel of John* (1937–41), and his two-volume *Theology of the New Testament* (1948–53).

Bultmann's most important contribution to media criticism of the Bible is certainly *The History of the Synoptic Tradition*, a groundbreaking work in Form Criticism. His stated goal was 'to give an account of the history of individual units of the [synoptic Jesus] tradition, and [of] how the tradition passed from a fluid state to a fixed form' (Bultmann 1968: 3). Following Julius Wellhausen, Bultmann believed that the synoptic tradition consisted of the aggregate accumulation of oral stories, adapted by early believers, and later edited into the static literary frame of the Gospels. Before their literary solidification, these fluid oral stories were retold to meet the particular needs of the earliest communities in which the stories circulated (Byrskog 2007: 5–6). Sayings of Jesus, for example, were often collected for instructional purposes, and miracle stories for apologetics. Individual oral stories were adapted to suit these purposes, causing them to become encrusted with secondary material over time. Bultmann's Form Criticism sought to separate the original oral stories from later editorial layers.

To reconstruct the earlier layers of Jesus tradition (and, ultimately, the message of Jesus himself), Bultmann developed a method of analysis based on the emerging Two-Source Theory for the composition of the Gospels, which argued that Matthew and Luke used Mark and the hypothetical document Q (a Sayings Gospel) as sources of material for their own books. Significantly, Bultmann saw no distinction between the oral and literary stages of the tradition, and therefore utilized observable tendencies in the literary relationships between the extant written Gospels as a template for speculating on ways that traditional units developed and were transmitted orally (Bultmann 1968: 6, 48, 87–8, 321). By observing ways Matthew and Luke appropriated material from their sources, the form critic could identify patterns in the development of Jesus tradition that were likely to have been in effect prior to the composition of written Gospels. Following this approach, Bultmann concluded that the earliest identifiable oral traditions were collections of Jesus' sayings without references to their context. These sayings were altered as they were inserted into narratives, some of which also emerged from early stages of the tradition and some of which were fabricated to provide a context for the saying (Bultmann 1968: 329). The driving force behind the development of tradition was the proclamation of Easter faith.

Although Bultmann's form-critical paradigm dominated Gospels research in the mid-twentieth century and significantly impacted the Second and Third Quests for the historical Jesus, his influence has waned as scholars have developed more nuanced approaches to oral tradition and COLLECTIVE MEMORY. BIRGER GERHARDSON (1926–2013) and WERNER KELBER (b. 1935) significantly challenged Bultmann and other form critics for misconstruing the process of transmission (Gerhardson 1998) and failing to recognize the profound differences between oral and literary media (Kelber 1997: 2–8). While Gospels scholarship has moved beyond Bultmann's form-critical approach, his focus on the development of oral Jesus tradition and the media transition from speech to WRITING in early Christianity has had a lasting impact, and biblical media critics continue to look to him as an important predecessor.

Tyler A. Stewart (Marquette University, USA)

Further Reading

Bultmann, Rudolf. 1931. *Die Geschichte der synoptischen Tradition*. FRLANT 29. 2nd edn. Göttingen: Vandenhoeck & Ruprecht (1st ed. 1921).

Bultmann, Rudolf. 1960. *Existence and Faith: Shorter Writings of Rudolf Bultmann*. Translated by Schubert Miles Ogden. New York: Meridian Books.

Bultmann, Rudolf. 1951–5. *Theology of the New Testament*. Translated by Kendrick Grobel, 2 vols. New York: Scribner.

Bultmann, Rudolf. 1984. *Der Stil der paulinischen Predigt und die kynisch-stoische Diatribe*. FRLANT 13. Göttingen: Vandenhoeck & Ruprecht, (1st ed. 1910).

Bultmann, Rudolf. 1968. *The History of the Synoptic Tradition*. rev. ed. Translated by John Marsh. Oxford: Basil Blackwell.

Bultmann, Rudolf. 1984. *New Testament and Mythology and Other Basic Writings*. Translated by Schubert Miles Ogden. Philadelphia: Fortress Press.

Byrskog, Samuel. 2007. 'A Century with the Sitz im Leben: From Form-Critical Setting to Gospel Community and Beyond'. *ZNW* 98: 1–27.

Congdon, David W. 2015. *The Mission of Demythologizing: Rudolf Bultmann's Dialectical Theology*. Minneapolis: Fortress Press.

Congdon, David W. 2016. *Rudolf Bultmann: A Companion to His Theology*. Eugene, OR: Cascade Books.

Gerhardson, Birger. 1998. *Memory and Manuscript: Oral Tradition and Written Transmission in Rabbinic Judaism and Early Christianity*. Acta Seminarii Neotestamentici Upsaliensis 22. Translated by E. J. Sharpe. Lund: CWK. Gleerup.

Hammann, Konrad. 2013. *Rudolf Bultmann: A Biography*. Translated by Philip E. Devenish. Salem, OR: Polebridge Press.

Kelber, Werner. 1983. *The Oral and Written Gospel: The Hermeneutics of Speaking and Writing in the Synoptic Tradition, Mark, Paul, and Q*. Philadelphia: Fortress Press.

Longenecker, Bruce W. and Mikeal C. Parsons, eds. 2014. *Beyond Bultmann: Reckoning a New Testament Theology*. Waco, TX: Baylor University Press.

Morgan, Robert. 1997. 'Rudolf Bultmann'. In *The Modern Theologians: An Introduction to Christian Theology in the Twentieth Century*. Edited by David F. Ford. 2nd edn. Malden, MA: Blackwell, pp. 68–86.

Schmithals, Walter. 1968. *An Introduction to the Theology of Rudolf Bultmann*. Translated by John Bowden. London: SCM Press.

Standhartinger, Angela. 2014. 'Bultmann's Theology of the New Testament in Context'. In *Beyond Bultmann: Reckoning a New Testament Theology*. Edited by Bruce W. Longenecker and Mikeal C. Parsons. Waco, TX: Baylor University Press, pp. 233–55.

Stowers, Stanley K. 1981. *The Diatribe and Paul's Letter to the Romans*. SBLDS 57. Chico, CA: Scholars Press.

C

Canon/Scripture The word *canon* (Greek *κανών*) originally meant a device that kept other things straight, a measuring stick, or a norm or rule (Gal. 6.16), but it could also denote a normative list or a catalogue. When the early church applied the term to the Scriptures, they appealed to the normative aspect of the term as well as the understanding of *canon* as an authoritative collection, or delimited list, of regulative writings. In the latter sense(s), the word *canon* and its cognates were used by fourth-century church teachers, and have commonly been employed by scholars to describe the formation of the Jewish and the Christian Bible. While the 'Sacred Books' (1 Macc. 12.9) or 'Scripture(s)' (Rom. 1.2; 1 Clem. 53.1; Greek *γραφή*) could have a similar or overlapping denotation, on a basic level, *Scripture* signifies authoritative written revelation of divine origin, whereas *canon* may be understood as a property of sacred Scripture – designating its literary arrangement and delimitation, as well as normative address, as a corpus of Holy Writ.

Although the Jewish and Christian notions of *Scripture* and *canon* share some commonalities with other religious and secular *canons*, several distinctive features within the Jewish-Christian textual tradition set its scriptural canon(s) apart as a unique literary formation. Whereas the literary canons of revered writers of classical Greece (and later literary canons providing benchmarks of excellence in their respective field) are largely priority lists that are in principle open or arbitrary and with little indications of censorship (Hägg 2010: 109), the Jewish and Christian scriptural canons often stress the grouping and ordering of the texts and tend to draw a sharp distinction between books being included and books excluded from the collection of sacred Scriptures. Characteristically these Scriptures – made up of various literary GENRES and composed by numerous authors over a long period of time – are perceived as sacrosanct (Josephus, *Against Apion* 1.37-43; *m. Yadayim* 4.6) or 'God-breathed' (1 Tim. 3.16; cf. Origen, *First Principles* Pref. 8).

Beginning in ancient Israel, crucial moments in the transmission of the biblical material are the points of transition from mainly oral communication to written text. While in its oral phases the material is largely mediated through religious experts; when codified as WRITING, the written text tends to become 'a source of authority by itself' (Van der Toorn 2007: 206–7, 232). Already in the First Temple period, the copying of such authoritative texts was carried out by highly skilled SCRIBES affiliated with the TEMPLE and/or (less likely) the royal palace (Van der Toorn 2007: 82–9). The orally and textually transmitted traditions that gradually took shape as the text and canon of the Jewish Scriptures were here closely associated with the Israelite-Judaean scribal culture. Characteristic of both Jewish and, later on, Christian transmission of central portions of the biblical material was the mutual interaction between oral and written textual means of transmission in which also memorization played a decisive role (Carr 2011: e.g. 25–34, as applied to the book of Proverbs; Kelber and Byrskog 2009). Even though earlier oral and written stages of the biblical text continue to receive scholarly attention, in recent years, and in connection with a desire to apply a more holistic approach to the biblical literature, scholarship has shown renewed interest in the final form of the text, which the Jewish and Christian communities received and canonized as their authoritative text (Barton 2007: 185–91).

Pre-Christian designations of the Jewish Scriptures that indicate an emerging two- or threefold textual structuring include 'the Law and the Prophets' (2 Macc. 15.9) or 'the Law and the Prophets and the other ancestral Books' (variously repeated thrice in the prologue of Ben Sira; cf. Philo, *On the Contemplative Life* 25). To this we may add later the first-century references, such as 'the Law and the Prophets' (Mt. 22.40; Lk. 16.16; Jn 1.45; Rom. 3.21), 'the Law of Moses and the Prophets and Psalms' (Lk. 24.44), and Josephus' famous account of the twenty-two divinely inspired books claimed to be embraced by 'every Jew', and underlined by the canonical formula 'no one has ventured to add to or to take away from them or to alter them'(*Against Apion* 1.37-43). Of the twenty-two Scriptures (Josephus does not enumerate individual writings), five books of Moses, thirteen prophets (cf. *Jewish Antiquities* 10.35) and four remaining books are mentioned. Arguably these twenty-two books are the same as the ones embraced by the twenty-four-book canon lists in the contemporary 4 Ezra 14.45-48 and the rabbinic enumeration in b. Baba Batra 14b–15b (listing 8 books of the Prophets and 11 of the Writings), in which Judges and Ruth on the one hand, and Jeremiah and Lamentations on the other hand, are counted separately. In addition to twenty-two – the number of letters of the Hebrew alphabet – or twenty-four, Jerome indicates that the Jewish Scriptures can be numbered as twenty-seven (the five Hebrew *double letters* counted separately and linked to five books reckoned as double; Prologue to the books of Samuel and Kings). As to the closing of the Jewish canon, scholarship is divided between those who hold that a delimited canon was formed in the Persian or Maccabean period and those who think that it remained open well into the first centuries of the Common Era (Lim 2013: 17).

Interestingly, the shape of the Jewish canon (twenty-two books), in sections of five books (Moses), thirteen books (Prophets), and four books (Writings), as presented by Josephus in the late first century CE, appears to have left traces in the textual arrangement of the Christian Scriptures as well. Several early church teachers adhere, in theory, to a twenty-two-book OT (e.g. Origen, Athanasius and Jerome), and a threefold division is found in Lk. 24.44. We may also notice some parallels in the structuring of the emergent NT: for example, our earliest extant Four-Gospel CODEX, P45 (early third century), contains five books – Gospels and Acts – and an early appearing arrangement of the Pauline letter corpus includes thirteen writings (excluding Hebrews; e.g. *Canon Muratori*, Tertullian, and Gaius). The Jewish-Christian twenty-two-book structure seems to resonate again in Eusebius' enumeration of twenty-two NT writings among the Recognized Books (*ἐν ὁμολογουμένοις*): the four Gospels, Acts, fourteen Pauline epistles, 1 Peter, 1 John, and Revelation (*Ecclesiastical History* 3.25; cf. 3.3). The NT of the Syriac Peshitta, and most likely that of John Chrysostom, represent twenty-two-book corpora similar to that enlisted by Eusebius (preceding his list of five Disputed Books).

From the first and second century on, the codex format – which was the characteristic Christian medium for the Scriptures – in addition to liturgical practice and theological reflection, helped organize the Church's NT as a twofold Gospel–Apostle configuration (cf. Bovon 2002); and, before long, as four-literary-part-volumes that became the ecclesiastical standard up to the present (Trobisch 2000: 24–9, 103). In early canonical ordering, the whole was comprised of: the fourfold Gospel (cf. Irenaeus' emphasis on the number 'four', *Against Heresies* 3.11.8), the eight books of Acts and seven Catholic epistles, the Pauline fourteen-letter corpus ('twice seven Epistles', Amphilochius of Iconium, *Iambics to Seleucus*) and the book of Revelation (which also includes seven epistles, Rev. 2-3). As part of this NT canon – embracing twenty-seven writings ($= 3 \times 3 \times 3$), which Bishop Athanasius in 367 CE (*Thirty-Ninth Epistle*) combined with a twenty-two-book OT canon ($22 + 27 = 7 \times 7$) – a form of numerology seems to have played a role associated with the number of letters in the Hebrew alphabet (twenty-two and twenty-seven; Lim 2013, 41) and with the notion of completion (as to the significance commonly attached to the numbers three, four and seven (see Labuschagne 2000: 1–19, 69–70;

and Bokedal 2014: 318–20). In this connection it is worth noting that to date we have no MANUSCRIPTS in which *apocryphal* Gospels have been bound together with any of the canonical four (Elliott 1996: 107, 110).

By ca. 150–250 CE (Lim 2013: 180), or arguably considerably earlier (Beckwith 1985: 165), the numeration of books in the canon of most Jews had become fixed as twenty-two, or as twenty-four: the tripartite Tanakh (the Law, the Prophets and the Writings) made up of twenty-four Sacred Books (*b. Baba Batra* 14b-15a; a number known also to the author of Gospel of Thomas 52, Victorinus, and Jerome, and perhaps alluded to in Rev. 4.4, 10).

When we consider the reception history of the Jewish and Christian canon formations, it appears that the Jewish twenty-four-book corpus (corresponding to the thirty-nine books of most Protestants), the wider Christian OT canon including Apocrypha or Deuterocanonical books (embraced e.g. by Augustine and the Roman Catholic Church), and a Christian NT comprising twenty-seven books have crystallized as the widely accepted canonical shaping within these respective community contexts.

Integral to the canon formation process, some unique textual and ritual qualities may be noticed. Perhaps the most conspicuous feature contributing to the textual sacredness in Second Temple Judaism, and onwards, relates to the divine name, the Tetragrammaton, which Jewish scribes marked off reverentially in written forms (Barton 1997: 106–21). When the early Christians began producing their own Greek Scriptures this scribal practice was modified and expressed in the so-called *nomina sacra*, particularly sacred words such as God, Jesus, and Spirit written in contracted form in OT and NT manuscripts. Selections from the Jewish Scriptures – not in SCROLL, but in codex format – supplied with *nomina sacra*, obtained a particular Christian IDENTITY (Hengel 2000: 118–19; cf. Barn. 9.7-9; P. Yale 1) and were in this way put side by side with the new Christian Scriptures for liturgical (Justin, *1 Apology* 67; Hengel 2000: 96) and other usage roughly from the time of the composition of the four Gospels, or a little later. In Theodor Zahn's phrasing, 'What was later named "canonical" was originally called "read in corporate WORSHIP"' (Bokedal 2014: 243).

Tomas Bokedal (University of Aberdeen, UK)

Further Reading

Barton, John. 1997. *The Spirit and the Letter: Studies in the Biblical Canon*. London: SPCK.

Barton, John. 2007. *The Old Testament: Canon, Literature and Theology: Collected Essays of John Barton*. Society for Old Testament Study Series. Edited by Margaret Barker. Aldershot, Hampshire: Ashgate.

Beckwith, Roger. 1985. *The Old Testament Canon of the New Testament Church and Its Background in Early Judaism*. Grand Rapids, MI: Eerdmans.

Bokedal, Tomas. 2014. *Formation and Significance of the Christian Biblical Canon. A Study in Text, Ritual and Interpretation*. London: Bloomsbury T&T Clark.

Bovon, François. 2002. 'The Canonical Structure of Gospel and Apostle'. In *The Canon Debate*. Edited by Lee Martin McDonald and James A. Sanders. Peabody, MA: Hendrickson, pp. 516–27.

Elliott, Keith J. 1996. 'Manuscripts, the Codex and the Canon'. *JSNT* 63: 105–23.

Hägg, Tomas. 2010. 'Canon Formation in Greek Literary Culture'. In *Canon and Canonicity: The Formation and Use of Scripture*. Edited by Einar Thomassen. Copenhagen, Denmark: Museum Tusculanum Press, University of Copenhagen, pp. 109–28.

Hengel, Martin. 2000. *The Four Gospels and the One Gospel of Jesus Christ: An Investigation of the Collection and Origin of the Canonical Gospels*. London: SCM Press.

Kelber, Werner H., and Samuel Byrskog, eds. 2011. *Jesus in Memory: Traditions in Oral and Scribal Perspectives*. Waco, TX: Baylor University Press.

Labuschagne, Casper J. 2000. *Numerical Secrets of the Bible: Rediscovering the Bible Codes*. North Richland Hills, TX: Bibal Press.

Lim, Timothy H. 2013. *The Formation of the Jewish Canon*. AYBRL. New Haven: Yale University Press.

Toorn, Karel van der. 2007. *Scribal Culture and the Making of the Hebrew Bible*. Cambridge, MA and London, England: Harvard University Press.

Trobisch, David. 2000. *The First Edition of the New Testament*. Oxford: Oxford University Press.

Catechism See Early Christian Catechism.

Chirograph A *chirograph* is a handwritten document. Like its Latin equivalent MANUSCRIPT (*manus*/'hand' + *scriptus*/'writing'), *chirograph* is loanword to English from the Greek adjective *cheirographos* (*cheir*/'hand' + *graphos*/'writing'). Broadly speaking, *chirograph* is synonymous with manuscript, both terms referring to an individual handwritten text. In media criticism, however, the less common *chirograph* is sometimes employed to draw attention to the medium of handwriting and its related scribal activity, in contrast to oral discourse and print (Rodríguez 2014: 17; see also SCRIBES).

In the ancient world, chirographs were the only written texts and they functioned within a broader culture characterized primarily by orality. It is not surprising, then, that chirographs were perceived as both extremely useful and potentially misleading. As H. Gregory Snyder has pointed out, in the ancient world 'written texts were brought to life by readers or teachers addressing an audience, just as music is brought to life by musical performers' (2000: 2). Chirographs were not detached texts, designed to be easily accessible for a wide audience of silent, individual readers. Just as sheet music in the contemporary world is not typically read apart from a context in which it is played, ancient chirographs required performers who were able to bring the text to life (see PERFORMANCE OF THE GOSPELS, LECTOR). For this reason, Plato protested that the written word is a mere image of true oral discourse (*Phaedrus* 274C–278D). Similarly, in the early church, Papias claimed to investigate Jesus, when possible, by seeking oral testimony rather than focusing on books (Eusebius, *Church History* 3.39.4). To return to the analogy of music, Plato and Papias elevated the performers who played the tunes above the sheet music. Chirographs served a vital function in the ancient world, a function primarily aimed at oral performance.

Although not always using the theory-laden term chirography, biblical scholars are increasingly coming to the realization that the books of the Bible were composed as handwritten texts in an oral culture. The significance of this insight is profound. In Hebrew Bible studies it has led to the re-evaluation of the documentary hypothesis (J, E, D, P), a theory that attempts to reconstruct sources of the Hebrew Bible based on a 'cut and paste' mentality characteristic of typographic cultures but not oral ones (Carr 2005). Similarly, among NT scholars, there has been a movement away from a GREAT DIVIDE approach that assumes a sharp contrast between orality and textuality. Chris Keith, for example, cautions against referring to written texts as 'fixed', 'frozen', 'static', and 'stable' in contrast to 'fluid' and 'free-floating' orality (2011). Keith uses the example of the Pericope Adulterae (Jn 7.53–8.11) to illustrate how chirographic textual traditions could also be fluid. Biblical scholarship is currently in the process of rethinking many of its typographic assumptions as it continues to grapple with the Bible as a collection of chirographs produced in oral cultures.

Tyler A. Stewart (Marquette University, USA)

Further Reading

Carr, David M. 2005. *Writing on the Tablet of the Heart: Origins of Scripture and Literature*. New York: Oxford University Press.

Keith, Chris L. 2011. 'A Performance of the Text: The Adulteress's Entrance into John's Gospel'. In *The Fourth Gospel in First-Century Media Culture*. Edited by Anthony Le Donne and Tom Thatcher. European Studies on Christian Origins/Library of New Testament Studies 426. London: T&T Clark, pp. 49–69.

Rodríguez, Rafael. 2014. *Oral Tradition and the New Testament: A Guide for the Perplexed*. New York: T&T Clark.

Snyder, H. Gregory. 2000. *Teachers and Texts in the Ancient World: Philosophers, Jews and Christians*. New York: Routledge.

Chronotope The term *chronotope* was borrowed from Einsteinian physics by Russian literary theorist M. M. Bakhtin to call attention to the intrinsic connectedness of temporal and spatial relationships artistically expressed in literature. In Bakhtin's theoretical model, a chronotope is composed of what happens (where and when) and how the happening is told (when and where); it calls attention to how a particular blend of time/space opens up a huge category of insight crucial for understanding. For example, the nineteenth-century Paris salon embeds and communicates considerable culturally specific information about art, social values, and class; similarly, when the action of a murder mystery is set in a British stately home in the midst of a snow-bound week, the reader is cued to a larger set of pertinent physical and social factors. A chronotope can be considered at different levels of abstraction (e.g. the road can also be the crossroads, the exodus journey) or from different angles (how the road is glimpsed and experienced variously by different participants). More complex than setting, a chronotope can be a device, a motif, or a plot function. The point of noting chronotopes is the ability to discuss multiple types of relatedness in an orderly way as well as the challenge of recognizing distinctive chronotopes; these remind us what is necessary (though not likely sufficient) for responsible reading.

Barbara Green (Dominican School of Philosophy and Theology, USA)

Circumcision Male circumcision (from the Latin *circumcidere*, 'to cut around') refers to the removal of the foreskin, or prepuce, from the penis, as instructed in the biblical priestly sources (Gen. 17.1-21; Exod. 12.44, 48; Lev. 12.3) for newborn males aged eight days old. In the patriarchal narratives, circumcision marks Abraham's legitimate male successors as recipients of an enduring covenant and is associated with procreation, fertility, genealogy, hereditary succession, and the promise of land. In this context, circumcision validated male membership in the covenantal community; the reciprocal consequence for non-compliance, being 'cut off', is evoked in Gen. 17.14: 'And if any man fails to circumcise the flesh of his foreskin, that person shall be cut off from his kin; he has broken my covenant.' This requirement is distinct from the J/E tradition in Exod. 4.24-26, which highlights the role of circumcision as an apotropaic rite to secure protection from harm.

While circumcision is associated in the Hebrew Bible with Israelite identity, the practice is more broadly attested. Historically, the rite is first represented in Egypt, where it was implemented upon puberty, possibly also upon marriage, and as an initiation into the priesthood. However, there is no extra-biblical evidence that circumcision was practised by Jewish males prior to the post-exilic period. Subsequently Hellenistic sources indicate that epispasm (a surgical procedure disguising the appearance of the cut foreskin) occurred in the Greco-Roman period, at a time when public nudity was socially acceptable. It is also not clear when precisely male circumcision became the identifying ethnic mark of a Jew, given its prevalence in the ancient Levant (see Jer. 9.24-25; Herodotus, *Histories* 2.104; Philo, *Questions and Answers on Genesis* 3.47–48), and also because the abrogation of its requirement for early Christians in the Pauline literature cannot be definitively dated prior to the destruction of the Second Temple.

Sandra Jacobs (King's College London, UK)

Further Reading

Cohen, Shaye J. D. 1995. *Why Aren't Jewish Women Circumcised? Gender and Covenant in Judaism*. Berkeley: University of California Press.

Eilberg-Schwartz, Howard. 1990. 'The Fruitful Cut: Circumcision and Israel's Symbolic Language of Fertility, Descent and Gender.' In *The Savage in Judaism: Anthropology of Israelite Religion and Ancient Judaism*. Bloomington: Indiana University Press, pp. 141–76.

Jacobs, Sandra. 2014. 'The Priestly Requirement of Circumcision'. In *The Body as Property: Physical Disfigurement in Biblical Law*. LHBOTS 582. London: Bloomsbury Press, pp. 28–67.

Codeswitching Codeswitching is generally defined as the intentional alternate use of language codes (two or more languages, dialects, or varieties) in the same utterance or conversation (Lee 2012: 335–41; cf. Bullock and Toribio 2009: 2–5). Codeswitching as a literary device implies the author's intention to emphasize the words or phrases given in the other language. This emphasis occurs naturally in texts that are orally performed because the alien terms are phonetically prominent. This emphasis may be for the purpose of creating vividness, politeness, intimacy, or solidarity (Lee 2012: 346–9). In this respect, codeswitching is 'an important means of conveying linguistic and social information and an indicator of the speaker's momentary attitudes, communicative intents, and emotions' (Grosjean 1982: 152).

The authors of the Hebrew Bible used codeswitching as a literary device for emphasis and dramatic effect. For example, when Rabshakeh, the chief spokesman of Assyria, calls out to the leaders of Hezekiah's government as they stand on the walls of the besieged Jerusalem, the leaders entreat him to speak Aramaic, the language of international diplomacy, so that the larger public gathered there would not understand. Rabshakeh, however, intentionally delivers his speech in the Jews' own language rather than in the Assyrian language for the express purpose of demoralizing the populace and shaming their leaders (2 Kgs 18.26-28; Isa. 36.11-13), a move that adds dramatic intensity to the scene. As another example, the book of Ezra includes two long sections written in Aramaic (4.8–6.18; 7.12-26). Both are literary representations of official correspondence about the rebuilding of the JERUSALEM TEMPLE under the aegis of Darius and Artaxerxes. The author intended to show that the Aramaic correspondence preserved the original decrees declared by the kings and that the decrees were authoritative. Obviously, the change in language would stand out to SCRIBES reading the text of Ezra or to audiences who heard it read aloud.

Similarly, the authors of the Greek NT sometimes use Semitic words as codeswitchings (Lee 2012: 349–90). The introductory amen (*amen*)-formula, for example, which the canonical Jesus sometimes uses to introduce his own pronouncements, would have been phonetically prominent to those listening to oral recitations of the Gospels in Greek (see PERFORMANCE OF THE GOSPELS). In this case, the switch to the Hebrew '*amen*' would have reminded the audience of dominical usage in the OT, thus adding acoustic emphasis to stress the authority of the marked sayings of the Lord.

The writer of the Gospel of Mark occasionally uses codeswitching by inserting Semitic words into the flow of his narrative (e.g. *abba*, *talitha koum*, *ephphatha*). These terms generally heighten the drama and tend to increase the vividness of the portrayal of Jesus and his speech. Jesus' reference to God as '*abba*' rather than the Greek '*pater*' at Mk 14.36, for example, underscores the intimate relationship between Jesus and his 'father', God. Paul uses '*abba*' in a similar way in Rom. 8.15 and Gal. 4.6 to emphasize Christian IDENTITY by portraying all Christians as children of God. When these texts were read aloud in early Christian assemblies, the use of '*abba*' would draw the Greek-speaking audience's attention to that term, thus highlighting the theme of common identity and solidarity. Mark also employs codeswitching in narrating miracle stories; thus, Jesus gives commands in Aramaic when healing a little girl (*talitha koum*; 5:41) and a deaf man (*ephphatha*; 7:34). The use of these Aramaic imperatives in the midst of Greek stories must have been phonetically prominent to the audience, thus adding vividness to the description of the scenes.

Luke employs codeswitching in three ways. First, Luke plays on the connection between language and identity. Thus, immediately after his arrest at the temple, Paul speaks Greek to the Roman captain while addressing the Jewish crowd in Aramaic (Acts 21.37–22.2). The change in language draws the audience's attention to the nuances of Paul's intention and dual identity: speaking stylish Greek to the Roman tribune makes him focus his attention on Paul and portrays Paul as a citizen of a prominent Roman city (21.39); speaking Aramaic to the Jewish crowd in the temple emphasizes Paul's Jewish identity and credentials. Second, Luke uses codeswitching of personal proper nouns to add prestige, pride, identity, or intimacy to a character in the narrative. Thus, James refers to Peter as 'Simeon' at Acts 15.14 to stress his Jewish identity in the context of the Jerusalem Council proceedings. Similarly, Luke purposely changes Paul's name from Saulos to Paulos and vice versa to reflect nuances of the context of Paul's activity. Thus, at Acts 13.9 Saul's name becomes the Latin 'Paul' at a point from which the narrative consistently portrays him as a missionary to Gentiles; at the same time, when Paul narrates the visionary experience in which his calling was delivered, the risen Jesus uses the Semitic 'Saul' (Acts 22.7, 13; 26.14). When Paul's conversion accounts were read aloud by Christians in Greek, the indeclinable Semitic spelling would have attracted the audience's attention to Paul's former identity as a prominent Jew. Third and finally here, Luke sometimes uses codeswitching in naming places. For example, the Semitic spelling *Hierosolyma* would acoustically identify Jerusalem as a distinctly Jewish setting for a scene. Similarly, Luke intentionally codeswitches from the more usual spelling *Nazareth* to the less usual *Nazara* in Lk. 4.16, an acoustic marker that emphasizes the role of this pericope as a turning point in the narrative and that fits the overall theme in that passage of Jesus' rejection in his 'homeland' (4.24).

Similarly, Paul uses codeswitching when he calls Simon/Peter *Kephas* eight times in 1 Corinthians (1.12; 3.22; 9.5; 15.5, Gal. 1.18; 2.9, 11, 14) and *Petros* two times in Gal. 2.7, 8. The codeswitching in calling Peter *Kephas* implies Paul's insinuation to Christians in Corinth and Galatia that he is personally conversant with Peter, one of the pillars of the Jerusalem church, and that he thereby shows solidarity with the Mother Church in Jerusalem. In Galatians 2, Paul calls Peter both *Petros* and *Kephas* in narrating the results of his negotiations with the Jerusalem pillars because the agreement is made for the benefit of Greek-speaking Galatians and because Paul intends to deliver an official and authoritative report of the Jerusalem resolution.

Sang-Il Lee (Chongshin University, South Korea)

Further Reading

Bullock, Barbara E., and Almeida Jacqueline Toribio eds. 2009. *The Cambridge Handbook of Linguistic Code-switching.* Cambridge: Cambridge University Press.

Grosjean, F. 1982. *Life with Two Languages: An Introduction to Bilingualism.* Cambridge: Harvard University Press.

Lee, S.-I. 2012. *Jesus and Gospel Traditions in Bilingual Context: A Study in the Interdirectionality of Language.* BZNW 186. Berlin and Boston: Walter Mouton de Gruyter.

Codex The codex (Latin *cōdex*; also *caudex*, *ĭcis*, m.) as a form of literate media derived from tablets that Romans used to record official documents such as contracts, edicts, and legal proceedings or formal (yet relatively impermanent) household accounts such as ledgers, economic arrangements, and inventories. In terms of physical form, codices were made of wood and sometimes had a wax surface that could be easily smeared to create a fresh writing surface. The tablets could be bound together with string or leather in multiples, but *codex* primarily refers to the object that contemporary observers would identify as a *book*. As opposed to a SCROLL or bookroll, a codex was a collection of thin sheets of material such as PARCHMENT or PAPYRUS, folded and cut into quires (leaves, usually of four, eight, or sixteen), stacked together, bound along the long edge to form a spine and protected with covers of thicker, more durable material such as wood or leather. Writing in the late first century CE, the Roman orator Quintilian describes a parchment codex as a kind of 'notebook' using the term *membranae* (*Institutes* 10.3.31–2). This word shows up also in 2 Tim. 4.13, where it is juxtaposed with 'books' (*ta biblia*), a term that likely refers to the conventional literary medium of the bookroll/scroll, still the 'proper' form of literature at that time.

Emerging around the second century CE, the codex gradually replaced the scroll or bookroll as the dominant textual format, particularly in Christian contexts. Early Christians seem to have privileged the codex over the roll; the literature of the wider Mediterranean world preserved in the archaeological record up until the late third and early fourth century CE is overwhelmingly in roll format, while almost all surviving Christian texts, the earliest being a fragment of the Gospel of John from the second century CE, are codices. A distinguishing feature of Christian IDENTITY from very early on, therefore, was the use, in multiple situational and behavioural contexts, of the codex. This preference may link to the socioe-conomic status of early Christians, though, as Harry Y. Gamble suggests, it is more likely due to the practicality of the medium (Gamble 1995: 66).

The codex has implications for the study of the development of the Christian CANON since the codex form facilitated the collection of diverse texts into a single physical volume. Diversity in content and the ordering of this content within codices can provide insight into the emergence of a canon of authoritative or normative Christian literature, as well as the emergence of a GENRE of holy writing. Textual critics use early codices such as Sinaiticus and Vaticanus to reconstruct primary readings of the biblical texts based on disagreements among MANUSCRIPTS. The codex is tied to constructions of honour, status, and power in terms of their commissioning, possession, use, disposal, or destruction. More recent scholarship examines contexts in which a codex was not approached primarily as a text or texts to be read, but as a material object, separate from any act of reading though with a tacit or acknowledged content, with its own set of healing, ritual, or apotropaic abilities and purposes (Vearncombe 2016).

Erin K. Vearncombe (Princeton University, USA)

Further Reading

Gamble, Harry Y. 1995. *Books and Readers in the Early Church: A History of Early Christian Texts*. New Haven and London: Yale University Press.

Klingshirn, William E., and Linda Safran, eds. 2007. *The Early Christian Book*. CUA Studies in Early Christianity. Washington, DC: Catholic University of America Press.

Roberts, Colin H., and T. C. Skeat. 1983. *The Birth of the Codex*. London: Oxford University Press for the British Academy.

Szymanski, Terrence. 2004. 'The Pauline Epistles'. *Reading the Papyri*. The University of Michigan Papyrus Collection; The Regents of the University of Michigan. Online: http://www.lib.umich.edu/reading/Paul/index.html.

Vearncombe, Erin K. 2016. 'On Headaches, Gospel Codices, and the Interpretation of "Literate Media"'. In *Scribal Practices and Social Structures Among Jesus Adherents: Essays in Honour of John S. Kloppenborg*. Edited by William E. Arnal, Richard S. Ascough, Robert A. Derrenbacker Jr., and Philip A. Harland. Bibliotheca Ephemeridum Theologicarum Lovaniensium 285. Leuven: Peeters, pp. 387–404.

Cognitive/Personal Memory The term *cognitive* or *personal memory* refers to the capacity of individuals to recall and describe events, individuals, and experiences from the past, either the personal past or the collective past of a larger group, the latter including events and pieces of information not directly experienced by the individual. Memory enables humans to recollect and learn from past experiences, and thereby to understand the circumstances of their lives, to construct meaning, and to have a basis for sensible action in the future.

Human memory is a product of many different subsystems of the brain that work with apparent seamlessness to provide a wide range of different types of recall. At a macro-level, it is possible to distinguish memory subsystems for recollections of life incidents (episodic memory), general knowledge (semantic memory), and motor skills (procedural memory). At a micro-level, visual and verbal memory contribute to each of these broader categories of memory, and have different rates of persistence and reliability. Verbal memory can be the memory either of exact words (VERBATIM MEMORY) or of the general meaning of what was said (gist memory). Verbatim and GIST MEMORIES are formed simultaneously from what is heard (auditory input), which is retained by the brain in a phonological loop – an exact representation of sound that lasts for approximately two seconds. Verbatim and gist memory are both parts of a short-term memory system, and gist memory tends to persist longer than verbatim memory. Unconscious processes select certain memories for storage in long-term memory systems.

Medical practitioners and psychologists have long appealed to observable deficits of memory (and other brain functions) in patients whose brains have been damaged by injury, war wounds, or stroke to identify which parts of the brain are associated with which memory subsystems. The development of various techniques for imaging brain activity has allowed a rapid growth in understanding the components of memory and where they might be located in the brain and has revealed additional complexity in the various memory subsystems. For example, memories of rewards, punishments, and stimulus-reinforcer associations are located in the orbitofrontal cortex and amygdala; the temporal cortical visual area is involved in learning invariant representations of objects; and, the hippocampus is implicated in episodic memory. The ability to use language is distributed in different areas of the brain: 'Broca's area is necessary for the production of syntax, [and] grammatical formations involving verbs … whilst Wernick's area is relevant for semantics, the meaning of words, especially nouns' (Rose 2005: 129).

Not everything experienced and observed is retained in memory. It is sometimes exact (e.g. verbatim memory), but is usually an incomplete gist version of what happened. Because not everything can be remembered, humans use SCHEMAS to flesh out their incomplete memories in individual acts of recall. For example, a schema of what usually happens when eating in a cafeteria might be used to flesh out fragmentary memories of a specific meal. Most personal memories are reconstructed from a combination of gist memory, other fragmentary remembered features, and a schema of what usually happens in certain types of circumstances.

Because it is reconstructive, memory is prone to a number of frailties, which include the frailties of transience, absent-mindedness, blocking, misattribution, suggestibility, bias, and (sometimes unwelcome) persistence (Schachter 2001). Memories are transient because they fade over time, to be replaced by memories that correspond to more current concerns. Memories of matters and events to which careful attention is given are more likely to persist. Sometimes not enough attention is given to something that later proves important, and a memory has not formed (absent-mindedness). Some memories are blocked for one reason or another, so that the individual cannot recall them (e.g. personal trauma). Some recollections are misattributed to an individual or circumstance that belongs to another individual or circumstance. The suggestions of others (including misinformation) can be incorporated into personal memories. Human memory tends to make adjustments to take account of what was later understood to have happened in light of an ultimate outcome, a process called *hindsight bias*. Furthermore, because the selection of which memories to preserve in long-term memory is unconscious, sometimes things persist in long-term memories that an individual would much rather forget, such as memories of horrific events. Post-traumatic stress disorder grows out of some such memories.

Yet despite its frailties, human memory is remarkable for its adaptability and functional durability. For example, frailties such as hindsight bias, suggestibility, and transience allow an individual to adjust better to changing circumstances and to work together with others on the basis of commonly agreed upon conceptions of important events. Absent-mindedness assists in preventing the memory capacity of an individual from being overwhelmed. The formation of gist memories that are based largely on schemas helps to provide meaningful information about the environment by assisting in the selection and ordering of specific data.

In the field of biblical studies, memory has been invoked as an important element in the transmission and preservation of JESUS TRADITIONS. For example, RUDOLF BULTMANN and MARTIN DIBELIUS considered human memories to be inadequate to the task of remembering the words and deeds of Jesus over the 30 to 60 years between the events of his ministry and the writing of the Gospels. They concluded that little of the Gospel accounts could be based on memories of actual events. By way of contrast, arguing on the analogy of the teaching practices of rabbis contemporary to Jesus, Harald Reisenfeld, BIRGER GERHARDSSON, and Rainer Riesner all invoked personal memory as a mechanism for ensuring the accurate transmission of the traditions taught to his disciples by Jesus. Robert K. McIver has explored the potential impact that memory frailties might have had on the transmission of memories of Jesus' teachings and activities, and concludes that, like other personal memories, the memories of Jesus found in the Gospels are likely to have a first-order faithfulness to what he did and said. There is a continuing and lively debate in academic scholarship on the Gospels about how much the fact that the teachings and activities of Jesus were remembered over 30 to 60 years before being written in the Gospels has influenced the accuracy and completeness of the Gospel accounts.

Robert K. McIver (Avondale College of Higher Education, Australia)

Further Reading

Baddeley, Alan D. 2001. 'Levels of Working Memory'. In *Perspectives on Human Memory and Cognitive Aging*. Edited by Moshe Naveh-Benjamin, Morris Moscovitch, and Henry L. Roediger III. New York: Psychology Press, pp. 111–23.

Bultmann, Rudolf. 1968. *The History of the Synoptic Tradition*. Oxford: Blackwell.

Dibelius, Martin. 1971. *From Tradition to Gospel*. Cambridge: Clarke.

Dunn, James D. G. 2003a. 'Altering the Default Setting: Re-envisaging the Early Transmission of the Jesus Tradition'. *NTS* 49: 139–75.

Dunn, James D. G. 2003b. *Jesus Remembered*. Grand Rapids, MI: Eerdmans.

Gerhardsson, Birger. 1998. *Memory and Manuscript*. Grand Rapids, MI: Eerdmans.

McIver, Robert K. 2012/2011. *Memory, Jesus, and the Synoptic Gospels*. SBLRBS. Leiden/Atlanta: Brill/Society of Biblical Literature.

Riesenfeld, Harald. 1957. *The Gospel Tradition and its Beginnings: A Study in the Limits of 'Formgeschichte'*. London: Mowbray.

Riesner, Rainer. 1988. *Jesus als Lehrer*. 3rd edn. Tübingen: Mohr.

Roediger III, Henry, James S. Nairne, Ian Neath, and Aimée M. Surprenant, eds. 2001. *The Nature of Remembering*. Washington, DC: American Psychological Association.

Rose, Steven. 2005. *The Future of the Brain*. Oxford: University Press.

Schacter, Daniel L. 2001. *The Seven Sins of Memory: How the Mind Forgets and Remembers*. Boston: Houghton Mifflin.

Schacter, Daniel L., Anthony D. Wagner, and Randy L. Buckner. 2000. 'Memory Systems of 1999'. In *The Oxford Handbook of Memory*. Edited by Endel Tulving and Fergus I. M. Craik. Oxford: University Press, pp. 627–43.

Schubotz, Ricarda I. and Christian J. Fiebach. 2006. 'Integrative Models of Broca's Area and the Ventral Premotor Cortex'. *Cortex* 42: 461–63.

Coins Coins were one of the most prolific tools of mass communication, ideology, and propaganda in the ancient Mediterranean world, and as such represent an important primary source for studying the historical background and sociocultural dynamics of biblical texts, particularly of the NT. Coins bore both images and inscriptions to communicate a wide range of messages, similar in many respects to modern-day billboards. To those in power, they were a potential lens through which their world of honour, power, and divinity could be projected and viewed. One could describe ancient coins as *cultural texts* with meaningful images and inscriptions that call for interpretation.

Coins can inform the study of biblical texts in a number of ways. As physical artefacts, coins serve as primary texts from antiquity, and also engage secondary sources from the areas of history, art, and classics. Coins further provide data for relating the biblical text to other forms of archaeological evidence, and provide artistic and factual depictions of people, items, places, and events from the ancient world. Their imagery may also provide a framework for understanding complex political relationships in antiquity, controversies over ancient rituals, and etymological and philological questions. Obviously, coins also provide information that assists in understanding direct references to coinage and money in the Bible, and can also assist in determining the accuracy of biblical portraits of individuals, places, and events.

Coins were a form of media that was easily distributable and broadly circulated and that could survive extensive handling. Because coins are durable, they often circulated for decades, and sometimes centuries, after their production. Their communicative power thus reached people long after the original audience was gone. As such, coins have their own reception history, particularly those that remained popular for long stretches of history. One solution to this problem is to carefully identify the archaeological context in which the coins were discovered (Krmnicek 2009: 47), but this is only possible in those rare cases in which archaeologists have preserved the coins and provided documentation about their related artefacts. For the large majority of coins, and for coinage as a category of media, coins are best interpreted by situating them within a broader historical context and analysing their imagery from the perspectives of multiple academic disciplines (Elkins 2012: 95).

In a system of fiduciary currency, the government decrees what a coin is worth. This does not mean that the weight of a coin and its type of metal were not important, but rather emphasizes the fact that, in a fiduciary system, the importance of metal merged with the dictums of the political powers, local or otherwise, in the form of a civic stamp (Kurke 1999: 300). The stated value of a coin was reflective of the ruler who was often pictured on one side of the coin – in other words, the symbols and markings on coins implicitly or explicitly guaranteed that the coin had value. Roman coinage from the NT era relied upon both governmental decrees and the weight of metallic content (bullion) to determine market value (Howgego 1995: 128). Markets relied upon a system wherein governmental decrees were considered alongside the purity of gold, silver, or bronze/copper in any given denomination. Where elements of fiduciary currency are found, one will find that the public had some amount of trust in the stability and power of the government; when this power or stability weakened due to war, death, or other types of transitions, value would be based on weight and the value of the metal that composed the coin. At that point, a coin could be melted down for production of more coins or even weapons of war. Fiduciary coinage was particularly important in Judaea because small pieces of bronze/copper coins were sometimes worth more than their weight.

The connection between coins and the ruling powers meant that participation in the economic system could be viewed as defilement, impurity, or sin. Speaking of the NT context, Warren Carter observes that 'economic activity [inherently] means participation in this [Roman] political-military-religious power' (2006: 106). This reality is illustrated by the book of Revelation, which suggests that some early Christians were wary of the present economic system. To participate in Rome's economic successes might mean that one has capitulated the purity of the faith and given in to idolatry. The well-known references to the 'mark of the beast' in Rev. 13.16-17; 16.2, and 19.20 portray a situation in which true believers cannot ethically buy, sell, or trade in the marketplace. This 'mark of the beast' that appears on the body of a person in Rev. 13.16 might have originated from the use of countermarks or small stamps on coins that established their authenticity for use in the marketplace (May 2009: 84). In the apocalyptic worldview of Revelation, faithfulness to Christ might have meant forsaking certain types of transactions and the use of certain coins because of their idolatrous images and inscriptions.

Viewing coins as media, it is important to note that not all images are created equal. In other words, not all coinage would have possessed the same communicative force. In politically explosive contexts such as Judea (especially Jerusalem), it has been suggested that some images were designed to be ambiguous so that neither Jews nor non-Jews would have been offended by the images on the coin. This seems to be the case with Herod the Great (37–4 BCE; see Meshorer 1967: 66). Some images on coins will inevitably remain a mystery because those in power intentionally sought images that communicated ideas that were non-offensive, politically savvy, and religiously sterilized.

Roman Coins

Roman coins often encouraged participation in a patron–client relationship. As such, while the imagery of these coins can and should be studied from the perspective of aesthetics and art, they were also powerful tools of propaganda. The patron–client relationship had two parties: a patrician or wealthy citizen and a client who was dependent practically and financially upon the patron. At the top of the patronage pyramid was Caesar, the great dispenser of land, food, money, gifts, wisdom, and peace. Roman coins thus often included thematic elements emphasizing victories provided by the emperor, including the eagle, the laurel wreath, and the four-horse chariot. Coins with these images projected a world in which Caesar was always victorious and brought his people safety. Coins also often included images of gods (or items associated with them) and Roman temples, with personal portraits appearing on coins after 44 BCE. Religion and politics were often inseparable and, once Caesar was identified as or associated with divinity, coinage served to support the popular connection. Following ancient conceptions of physiognomy (the belief that physical features reflect moral and ethical qualities), personal portraits on large coins that could depict facial qualities such as the nose or forehead were used to communicate power.

For purposes of NT studies, it is helpful to note the difference between Roman imperial coins and provincial coins. These two terms are used by numismatics to classify coinage following the death of Julius Caesar in 44 BCE. Imperial coins are defined as those coins minted directly under imperial authority, mostly at Rome, for empire-wide distribution. Provincial coins are defined as those coins minted for use in a single province of the empire, and as such are often identified by references to the name of a significant city.

Jewish Coins

Like Roman coinage, Jewish coins in the Late Second Temple/NT era are reflective of larger social and political agendas and values. For this reason, Jewish coins are characterized by a lack of human and animal imagery – Herod the Great is the one exception that proves the rule, minting a small bronze lepton with an eagle on it. This broad refusal to picture animals and humans of course reflects deference to the Mosaic Law regarding images. In some instances, Jewish coins included images suggestive of messianic ambition. Symbols of palm branches and clusters of dates suggest economic success and fertility in the land. Jewish coins minted during the period of Roman domination communicated military power. Thus, for example, the images on coins from the reign of Herod Archelaus included a military helmet and a warship with a battering ram called an *aphlaston*. Even images of peace, such as the *caduceus*, were suggestive of a peace that came through Roman rule. Finally, Jewish coins sometimes used images that communicated agricultural fertility because productivity in the promised land was bound up with God's covenantal promises and Jewish IDENTITY (Deut. 8.7-10).

One of the dominant themes of the earliest Christians was the Jewish concept of idolatry. The earliest Christians such as Paul viewed the pagans around them as idolaters. In order to address this problem, Paul is keen to lay out a series of negative and positive propositions about what the God of Israel is truly like. One of these statements is made in his speech to the unconverted at the Areopagus: 'Being then God's offspring, we ought not to think that the divine being is like gold or silver or stone, an image formed by the art and imagination of man' (Acts 17.29). Of all the materials used to make physical idols or artistic images of God, Paul selects 'gold and silver' and stone. What this demonstrates is that a widely travelled Jew such as Paul was able to identify these metals as being associated with the divine in the minds of those attending the Areopagus. In addition to pagan statues that served as gods, the historical context of coinage suggests that the audience may have understood Paul to be referring to coins with their various images of gods as portraying the idolatry he sought to undermine.

David H. Wenkel (Moody Bible Institute, USA)

Further Reading

Carter, Warren. 2006. *The Roman Empire and the New Testament: An Essential Guide*. Nashville: Abingdon.

Elkins, Nathan T. 2012. 'The Trade in Fresh Supplies of Ancient Coins: Scale, Organization, and Politics'. In *All the King's Horses: Essays on the Impact of Looting and the Illicit Antiquities Trade on Our Knowledge of the Past*. Edited by P. K. Lazrus and A. W. Barker. Washington, DC: Society for American Archaeology Press, pp. 91–107.

Harris, William V. 2008. *The Monetary Systems of the Greeks and Romans*. New York and Oxford: Oxford University Press.

Hendin, David. 2013. 'Current Viewpoints on Ancient Jewish Coinage: A Bibliographic Essay'. *CBR* 11: 246–301.

Howgego, Christopher. 1995. *Ancient History from Coins. Approaching the Ancient World*. New York and London: Routledge.

Kreitzer, Larry J. 1996. *Striking New Images: Roman Imperial Coinage and the New Testament World*. JSNTSup 134. Sheffield: Sheffield Academic Press, 1996.

Krmnicek, Stefan. 2009. 'Das Konzept der Objektbiographie in der antiken Numismatik'. In *Coins in Context I: New Perspectives for the Interpretation of Coin Finds*. Edited by H. V. Kaenel and F. Kemmers. SFMA 23. Mainz: Philipp Von Zabern, pp. 47–59.

Kurke, Leslie. 1999. *Coins, Bodies, Games, and Gold: The Politics of Meaning in Archaic Greece*. Princeton: Princeton University Press.

May, David M. 2009. 'The Empire Strikes Back: The Mark of the Beast in Revelation'. *Revenue Experts* 106: 83–98.

Meshorer, Ya'akov. 1967. *Jewish Coins of the Second Temple Period*. Tel Aviv: Am Hassefer.

Metcalf, William E., ed. 2012. *The Oxford Handbook of Greek and Roman Coinage*. New York and Oxford: Oxford University Press.

Reiser, Marius. 2000. 'Numismatik und Neues Testament'. *Biblica* 81(4): 457–88.

Zanker, Paul. 1988. *The Power of Images in the Age of Augustus*. Jerome Lectures 16. Translated by Paul Shapiro. Ann Arbor: University of Michigan Press.

Cold Memory/Hot Memory The terms *cold memory* and *hot memory* were developed by WERNER KELBER to identify the two complementary functions of recollections of the past in a group's COLLECTIVE MEMORY. SOCIAL MEMORY theorists argue that memory works both 'to resurrect the images of the past so as to transport them into the present, and to reconstruct the images of the past so as to integrate them into the present context' (Kelber 2005: 234). Memory, in other words, is concerned both with the preservation and recall of past events ('to resurrect') and with the presentation of the past in ways that are relevant to, and meaningful within, present circumstances ('to integrate'). Both functions are essential as groups appeal to the past as a means to define their identities and corresponding values and lifeways. Kelber, and now other media scholars, refer to the repetitive, preservative element of memory as *cold memory*, while calling the integrative, situational element of memory *hot memory* (see Kelber 2002: 61; 2005: 228–9, 232).

It is important to stress that the hot/cold memory model describes functions of remembering and social memorial processes that cross various media. As noted above, *cold memory* refers to the physical and social processes behind memory storage and recall, while *hot memory* refers to the impact of recollection on groups and individuals, thus emphasizing memory's community-forming dimension. From the perspective of social memory theory, these two functions – recall and IDENTITY formation/maintenance – cannot be strictly differentiated, since every act of remembering ultimately involves both. Further, it is not the case that references to the past in oral speech, rituals, and other live media are *hot* simply because they are explicitly performative in nature, nor that history books or digital databanks are *cold* simply because they encode words and images in hard technologies. Kelber thus insists that both early Christian preaching and the written Gospels were forms of *hot memory*, invoking the past in service of present needs.

The hot/cold memory model provides a helpful framework for understanding the origins and roles of the texts that now appear in the biblical canon. Books such as Proverbs or the Gospel of John need not be understood simply as hard-storage databanks or aides-memoire to support oral performances, but can themselves be seen as dynamic attempts to structure and present traditional material in community-forming ways. In this respect, the hot/cold memory model serves as a corrective to the GREAT DIVIDE approach, which posits inherent and substantial differences between the media dynamics of ORALITY and written texts.

Tom Thatcher (Cincinnati Christian University, USA)

Further Reading

Kelber, Werner. 2002. 'The Case of the Gospels: Memory's Desire and the Limits of Historical Criticism'. *Oral Tradition* 17: 55–86.

Kelber, Werner. 2005. 'The Works of Memory: Christian Origins and Mnemohistory – A Response'. In *Memory, Tradition, and Text: Uses of the Past in Early Christianity*. Edited by Alan Kirk and Tom Thatcher. Semeia Studies. Atlanta: Society of Biblical Literature, pp. 221–48.

Thatcher, Tom. 2008. 'Beyond Texts and Traditions: Werner Kelber's Media History of Christian Origins'. In *Jesus, the Voice, and the Text: Beyond The Oral and the Written Gospel*. Edited by Tom Thatcher. Waco, TX: Baylor University Press, pp. 1–26.

Collective Memory/Social Memory COLLECTIVE MEMORY is a broad rubric under which are often gathered a number of aspects of memory considered as a social and cultural phenomenon (see CULTURAL MEMORY). Properly understood and defined, these aspects cast light on the emergence of early Christianity as a social and cultural movement grounded in a distinctive set of traditions and associated commemorative practices.

The rubric has been criticized for an excessive generality that blunts its analytical utility, and also for its potentially reifying and mystifying effects: it might be taken as hypostasizing an intangible group memory while rendering indistinct what are in fact discrete, empirically tractable cultural phenomena such as myth, history writing, tradition, commemorative ritual, MONUMENTS, and the like. It is best therefore to follow MAURICE HALBWACHS in his use of the term to describe, first, the shaping of individual memories by the social and cultural frameworks of the groups to which persons belong, and second, the shared cultural representations and artefacts (= *traditions*) that emerge from a community's commemorative activities (see Olick 1999). A shared past, perpetuated in a community's collective memory, founds and sustains the IDENTITY of that community and its members. To speak of collective memory is to speak of the emergence and cultivation of a media-based cultural tradition, and its associated practices, grounded in a formative past. This is what makes it pertinent to the study of the biblical literature, the history of Israel, and early Christianity: the bodies of theory that go under the rubric collective memory, to be more precise social memory and cultural memory approaches, are significant because they illuminate our understanding of the formation and history of the early Christian tradition, and, accordingly, of the emergence of early Christianity as a social and cultural movement.

PERSONAL MEMORY and social frameworks of memory exist in close interaction with each other. Society and culture are necessary for the very possibility of individual remembering, for they give coherence and intelligibility to memories, plotting them within cultural symbol systems of meaning. Individual memories receive form and coherence as they are communicated in social interaction. They take expression in communicative GENRES that are drawn from a cultural repertoire of genres that have been learnt through socialization. Memory therefore is bound to cultural media and forms; it is the shaping of memory upon the lineaments of these media and forms that renders it communicable and externalizes it into the social sphere. Moreover, it is in the course of sharing and rehearsing memories in the groups for which they hold pertinence, that is, in commemorative remembering, that the standardized forms of a shared tradition emerge, bearing the shared meanings and norms of a community. Conversely, the tradition thus formed is apt for cognitive assimilation into the individual memory of members of a community, the effect of which is to ground individuals in a social and cultural identity.

Memory therefore exists in essential, reciprocal interaction with an encompassing cultural and social matrix. The latter is itself profoundly shaped by commemorative enterprises, through which a community marks certain elements of its past as being of constitutive significance. Genuine communities are grounded in a formative past, and remembering in these contexts is a high-stakes activity. Research has shown that groups employ effective strategies to subsume individual memories into shared representations. These shared representations display emergent rather than additive properties: they more clearly, integrally, and fully distil out the significance of experienced events than could the mere aggregation of disconnected individual recollections. Commemorative remembering therefore converges on salience – on elements from a community's past crucial to its social and moral identity. In so doing, it taps deep into the encompassing cultural matrix of symbols, narratives, genres, and traditions. Commemorative activities, in other words, occur within an ambient, already existent field of cultural traditions circulating in a variety of media. These clothe emergent representations in traditional forms and infuse them with rich cultural signification. A community's memory work in relation to its foundational events distils out the narratives, shared meanings, and values that ground its identity, constitute it as a moral community, and enable the transmission of its cultural identity across time. Through the ritual rehearsal of its MASTER NARRATIVES and other commemorative traditions, a group constantly reconstitutes itself as a moral community and reproduces its cultural identity in ever-changing social and historical circumstances.

Collective memory is therefore something quite tangible: it exists and is cultivated in media-based traditions and associated practices that emerge out of commemorative enterprises. These traditions and practices function as cultural symbols, that is, as dense concentrations of social and moral signification that have been distilled out of formative and landmark events, freed of all but the barest historical contextualization, and stabilized in expressive media forms. Tradition artefacts are symbolic entities that express and disseminate, or as JAN ASSMANN puts it, make 'visible … permanent, and transmittable' the defining elements of a community's moral universe (Assmann 2006: 70). As already noted, these are apt for assimilation into individual memory, and thus they ground an individual in a specific cultural and social identity. This occurs through the re-enactment, often in ritual contexts, of foundational narrative and moral traditions. To take a pertinent illustrative case, the death of Jesus was an originating, formative event for early Jesus communities. Accordingly, it took commemorative form in master narratives that circulated as traditions enacted in ritual as well as in oral and written media.

Collective memory, properly understood as commemorative artefacts and practices that define and enable the reproduction across time of a community's cultural and moral identity, is dynamic rather than static, for it always exists in close engagement with the community's changing historical and social realities. Collective memory is always being reconstituted at the charged point where a community's salient past, laid down in its normative tradition, intersects with its exigent present realities. It is through constantly bringing the images and representations of its salient past into alignment with its ever-changing present, and vice versa, that a community maintains its continuity across time.

The effect of present social and historical realities in shaping and reshaping representations of the past, and by the same token the utilization of the past to legitimize present social, political, and moral enterprises, leads some theorists to argue that collective memory is mostly the ideological projection of social and political forces of the present and is to be deconstructed as such. This is the strong presentist or radical constructionist position. Other theorists argue that PRESENTISM in this strong form is untenable, the outcome of a theoretical perspective fixated on present factors, one that a priori excludes inquiry into how the past, transmitted in commemorative traditions and practices, informs, shapes, and constrains the dispositions and actions of agents and subjects situated in the present. The social frameworks and cultural symbol systems that permeate the present are themselves products of commemorative enterprises, and they provide the framework for the cognition and interpretation of present realities. The salient past, immanent in the narrative patterns in which it has become engrained in collective memory, supplies the cognitive framework by which a group perceives and orients itself within the present. It makes available the conceptual and moral resources for framing and mastering present realities and thereby ensures the transmission of a cultural identity. This framing occurs through the cultural dynamic that BARRY SCHWARTZ calls 'keying', namely, the signifying of present experiences and realities by connecting them to archetypal images and narrative representations of the salient past. Thus, the salient past, both generating and subsumed into resilient commemorative media, flows in a determinative manner into the ongoing formation of the life of the commemorating community.

Correspondingly, the effect of collective memory is to mobilize action, individual and collective, in the present. The formative past has an exemplary character that provides norms for action in the present. Halbwachs noted that commemoration focuses upon the normative dimension of foundational persons and events. In other words, collective memory has a pronounced ethical complexion; its representations of archetypal persons and events embody a community's moral order. It is by virtue of this normativity that the past lays programmatic moral imperatives upon a community. This accounts for the essential connection that exists between commemorative activities and instructional activities. Schwartz uses the dual imagery of 'mirror' and 'lamp' to describe this dynamic: 'As a model of society, collective memory reflects [= acts as a mirror] past events in terms of the needs, interests and aspirations of the present. As a model for society, collective memory … embodies a template that organizes and animates behavior as a frame within which people locate and find meaning for their present experience [= acts as a lamp]' (Schwartz 2009: 18). Tradition, as the vehicle of collective memory, operates as a system of normative symbols, the elements of which are capable of being brought into new configurations and applications and mobilized to meet new challenges that arise with shifts in a community's historical and social horizons.

Collective memory theory's essential connection with the tangible media realities and dynamics of tradition is what gives it its pertinence to the study of early Christianity as a social movement with an emerging cultural identity and history. This is what makes it more than just an interesting body of social and cultural theory that never finds empirical traction with the classic research problems in the origins of Christianity and its literature. Though much detailed work of this sort needs still to be done, a few areas can be mentioned by way of representative examples in which memory theory throws new light on classic problems.

First and foremost, collective memory studies have raised new questions on the origins and history of the synoptic and Johannine tradition. As BIRGER GERHARDSSON (and others) have argued, the gospel tradition originated in Jesus' own practice as a teacher of memorable *meshalim* in the framework of the master–disciple relationship, an important and historically grounded cultural setting for the cultivation and transmission of tradition in sapiential and prophetic circles. This is a case of the ambient cultural tradition and its repertoire of GENRES providing the framework for the emergence of a new tradition, cultivated in a community's commemorative practices, and assimilated into individual memory. Memory analysis also would predict the appearance of the tradition in various genres, or forms, for example, the *chreiai* or pronouncement stories, and correspondingly, the absence of the characteristic features of individual testimony from the generic profile of the synoptic tradition. Correspondingly, it accounts for the pronounced normative complexion of the tradition, visible, for example, in its density in dominical sayings and narrative genres such as the pronouncement story, in which historical and circumstantial detail radically recedes to support the normative appropriation. As early Jesus-followers coalesced into communities, the major impetus for efforts at remembering Jesus would have been the quest for comprehensive sets of norms. The diffuse actualities of foundational events have been converted into transmissible linguistic artefacts that bear the axiomatic meanings and norms of the tradent Jesus communities.

Collective memory theory also accounts, to a significant extent, for one of the most distinctive features of the synoptic tradition, namely, its curious patterns of variation and agreement, which have been the starting point for the classic source-critical hypotheses and debates. Tradition is enacted in the framework of the contemporary realities of a tradent community, but the converse is also true: a community cognitively apprehends its contemporary realities through the lens of its tradition as it *keys* its contemporary realities to the normative narratives and patterns laid down in its tradition. Hence the tradition's characteristic multiformity and its transformation in different contexts as the tradent communities anchor themselves to their core identity and norms in changing circumstances and in confrontation with new challenges. As with any cultural object, the tradition in its various media realizations leads a cultural life of its own as it reacts with the historical contingencies of its tradent communities. Moreover, as an approach attuned to ancient media realities and to the phenomenology of tradition, memory analysis has the potential to cast light on vexed problems such as the shift from oral to written media, the relationship between epistolary paranaesis and tradition, and how canonization or scripturalization trajectories might be latent in the memory function of tradition.

The concept of collective memory brings one into the sphere of cultural genres, media, artefacts, and practices. But there is also the matter of the *memory/history problematic*, and hence its obvious relevance for historical Jesus research, the field where its impact has in fact so far been most felt and debated. Owing to the wide interest in historical Jesus studies and the charged debates that make it a high-stakes field of inquiry, one sometimes observes a tendency to move directly back and forth between memory theory and historical analysis in a way that risks bypassing what seems the prior and more fundamental question of the origins of the tradition and its history. One of the leading services that memory approaches perform for historical Jesus scholarship is to clarify the phenomenology of the tradition, that is, to clarify for critical historiography its proper object of analysis. The question that memory analysis raises for historical Jesus inquiry is the following: What sort of historiographical approaches are requisite for dealing with tradition – a media-based artefact with a commemorative and representational relationship to historical realities?

Alan Kirk (James Madison University, USA)

Further Reading

Assmann, Jan. 2011. *Cultural Memory and Early Civilization: Writing, Remembrance, and Political Imagination.* Cambridge and New York: Cambridge University Press.

Assmann, Jan. 2006. 'Form as Mnemonic Device: Cultural Texts and Cultural Memory'. In *Performing the Gospel: Orality, Memory, and Mark.* Edited by Richard A. Horsley, Jonathan A. Draper, and John Miles Foley. Minneapolis: Fortress, pp. 67–82.

Bartlett, F. C. 1993/1995. *Remembering: A Study in Experimental and Social Psychology.* Cambridge: Cambridge University Press.

Byrskog, Samuel. 2000. *Story as History – History as Story: The Gospel Tradition in the Context of Ancient Oral History*. WUNT 123. Tübingen: Mohr Siebeck.
Connerton, Paul. 1989. *How Societies Remember*. Cambridge: Cambridge University Press.
Fentress, James, and Chris Wickham. 1995. *Social Memory*. Cambridge: Blackwell.
Halbwachs, Maurice. 1980. *The Collective Memory*. Translated by Frances J. Ditter Jr. and Vida Yazdi Ditter. New York: Harper & Row.
Halbwachs, Maurice. 1992. *On Collective Memory*. Edited and translated by Lewis A. Coser. Chicago: University of Chicago Press.
Kirk, Alan. 2014. 'The Tradition-Memory Nexus in the Synoptic Tradition: Memory, Media, and Symbolic Representation'. In *Keys and Frames: Memory and Identity in Ancient Judaism and Early Christianity*. Edited by Tom Thatcher. Semeia Studies. Atlanta: SBL Press, pp. 131–60.
Kirk, Alan, and Tom Thatcher, eds. 2005. *Memory, Tradition, and Text: Uses of the Past in Early Christianity*. Semeia Studies. Atlanta: SBL Press.
Keith, Chris, and Anthony Le Donne, eds. 2012. *The Demise of Authenticity*. London: T&T Clark, 2012.
Olick, Jeffrey K. 1999. 'Collective Memory: The Two Cultures'. *Sociological Theory* 17: 333–48.
Olick, Jeffrey K., and Joyce Robbins. 1988. 'Social Memory Studies: From "Collective Memory" to the Historical Sociology of Mnemonic Practices'. *American Sociological Review* 24: 105–40.
Rubin, David C. 1995. *Memory in Oral Traditions: The Cognitive Psychology of Epic, Ballads, and Counting-out Rhymes*. New York and Oxford: Oxford University Press.
Schröter, Jens. 1997. *Erinnerungen an Jesu Worte: Studien zur Rezeption der Logienüberlieferung in Markus, Q und Thomas*. WMANT 76. Neukirchen-Vluyn: Neukirchener Verlag.
Schwartz, Barry. 2009. 'Collective Forgetting and the Symbolic Power of Oneness: The Strange Apotheosis of Rosa Parks.' *Social Psychology Quarterly* 72: 123–42.
Schwartz, Barry. 1998. 'Frame Image: Toward a Semiotics of Collective Memory'. *Semiotica* 121: 1–38.
Schwartz, Barry. 1996. 'Memory as a Cultural System: Abraham Lincoln in World War II'. *American Sociological Review* 61: 908–27.
Schwartz, Barry. 1982. 'The Social Context of Commemoration: A Study in Collective Memory'. *Social Forces* 61: 374–402.
Yerushalmi, Yosef. 1982. *Zakhor: Jewish Memory and Jewish History*. Seattle: University of Washington Press.
Zerubavel, Yael. 1995. *Recovered Roots: Collective Memory and the Making of Israeli National Tradition*. Chicago: University of Chicago Press.

Colon A colon (*kōlon*; plural, cola) is the basic unit of Greek prose, measured by the length of a breath (Demetrius *Elocution* 1). A colon is incomplete; the Greek word connotes a member, a component of a larger whole (Aristotle, *Rhetoric* 3.9.7; Demetrius, *Elocution* 1; Quintilian, *Institutes* 9.4.123; *Rhetorica ad Herennium* 4.19.26). Cola are combined into PERIODS (Aristotle, *Rhetoric* 3.9.5, 8-10; Demetrius, *Elocution* 1.5-7, 16). The colon and period comprise the building blocks of Greek prose and thus the basic components of a SOUND MAP. They serve as the prose analogues to the metric line and the verse in Greek poetry (Aristotle, *Rhetoric* 3.8; Demetrius, *Elocution* 1). Cola comprise a single grammatical assertion, containing at least a finite verb, either expressed or implied, and all grammatically related words. The term may also be extended to discuss a phrase of poetry; see POETRY IN THE HEBREW BIBLE.

Margaret E. Lee (Tulsa Community College, USA)

Commemorative Narrative See MASTER COMMEMORATIVE NARRATIVE.

Communicative Economy The term *communicative economy* was coined by JOHN MILES FOLEY both to denote a metaphorical *economy* of communication and also to describe the *economical communication* of oral performance and oral-traditional works. In the first sense, an 'untextualized network of traditional [semantic] associations' acts as the goods and services of a metaphorical economy; in the second, an efficient exchange (between performer and audience) of this network of meaning is *economical* communication (Foley 1995: 54). For example, under the proper social and performative conditions, the introductory phrase 'once upon a time' instantly activates 'an enormous wellspring of meaning' originating from bedtime stories and fairy tales (Foley 1995: 54). The economical manner in which 'once upon a time' elicits this wellspring for both performer and audience is an example of communicative economy.

Communicative economy is enabled by 'word power' or 'the ability of traditional words, phrases, and THEMES to transcend their textual, denotative significance and engage their contextualizing tradition efficiently and effectively' (Rodríguez 2014: 31). In oral performance, words evoke associations that transcend their literal meaning. These associations are relatively stable across multiple performances because they are ensconced in the traditional REGISTER of language (Rodríguez 2014: 31; Foley 1995: 49–53). When both the performer and the audience have access to the same register of language and PERFORMANCE ARENA, 'signals are decoded and gaps are bridged with extraordinary fluency, that is, economy' (Foley 1995: 53). *Register* here refers to 'the configuration of semantic resources that the member of a culture typically associates' with recurrent types of situations (Halliday 1978: 111; Hymes 1989: 440). If both the audience and the performer do not have access to the same cache of semantic resources, then economical communication is stymied because the audience cannot readily decode traditional associations. Likewise, if both the audience and the performer do not enter the same literal or figurative place of oral performance, then economical communication is hampered because the audience cannot easily understand the performance's interpretive frame.

Communicative economy, in the sense that Foley and others have used the term, should be carefully delineated from MILMAN PARRY's and ALBERT LORD's model of *economy*. In oral-formulaic theory, economy characterizes a paucity of phrases in an oral-traditional work that have the same metrical value or express the same idea (Parry 1971: 276). Parry's and Lord's economy describes a 'thrifty' formulaic system, whereas Foley's communicative economy 'speaks to the dedicated, focused relationship between the register and its traditional, performance-centered array of meanings' (Foley 1995: 53). Communicative economy should also be disassociated from the term *economy of language* (concise linguistic expression). 'Once upon a time' is superfluous to any story's introduction, but the formula 'brings into play' traditional associations 'that can be tapped in no other way, no matter how talented or assiduous the performer may be' (Foley 1995: 54). Precisely because everything in the ensuing story 'depends upon engaging the cognitive fields linked by institutionalized association to the phrase', the introduction 'once upon a time' is economical communication (Foley 1995: 54).

Shem Miller (University of Mississippi, USA)

Further Reading

Foley, John Miles. 1995. *The Singer of Tales in Performance*. Bloomington: Indiana University Press.

Halliday, Michael. 1978. *Language as Social Semiotic: The Social Interpretation of Language and Meaning*. Baltimore: University Park Press.

Parry, Milman. 1971. *The Making of Homeric Verse: The Collected Papers of Milman Parry*. Oxford: Oxford University Press.

Hymes, Dell. 1989. 'Ways of Speaking'. In *Explorations in Ethnography of Speaking*. Edited by Richard Bauman and Joel Sherzer. Cambridge: Cambridge University Press, pp. 433–52.

Joubert, Annekie. 2004. *The Power of Performance: Linking Past and Present in Hananwa and Lobedu Oral Literature*. Trends in Linguistics 160. Berlin: Walter Mouton de Gruyter.

Rodríguez, Rafael. 2014. *Oral Tradition and the New Testament*. London: Bloomsbury T&T Clark.

Communicative Memory The expression *communicative memory* was introduced by the German Egyptologist Jan Assmann and initially denoted a subcategory of Maurice Halbwachs' collective memory. It refers to the recent past and delineates a vivid, communicated, and identity-forming memory which spans a temporal framework of 80–100 years (or three to four generations). In biblical studies, communicative memory is rarely referred to, but could be applied to the investigation of oral tradition and to the interpretation of NT texts.

Communicative memory is based on oral communication or other forms of direct interaction and thus limited both in time and in space to the initial period of a group's existence. Without external storage media, it has a temporal horizon of approximately 80–100 years (as is also commonly held in oral history). Within that temporal frame, episodic and (auto-)biographical memories are told, retold, and shared. These narratives remain vivid as long as the storytellers live on as members of the community. Once they pass away or leave the community, their contribution to the group's memory and identity begins to fade if it is not transformed into another form or medium. The transition from communicative memory to the more enduring cultural memory has to bridge what Jan Vansina called a 'floating gap' at the end of the 80–100 years. This process involves selection, modelling, and canonization. The identity-constituting social framework that had been created and established in collective memory becomes institutionalized and no longer limited in time.

According to Assmann's theory, alongside the floating gap, there is another moment of crisis within communicative memory, which he dates forty years after the event. This threshold (*Epochenschwelle*) marks the point when those who have experienced a meaningful event as adults retire from the future-oriented professional life to the age when not only memory grows but also the wish to assure its fixation and transmission. Breakdowns in tradition (*Traditionsbrüche* [Assmann 2000: 88]) are accelerating shifts in memory media which often means that, with scribal societies, writing becomes more and more important. The forty years mentioned by Assmann for the Epochenschwelle are drawing heavily from biblical texts (especially Deuteronomy) and the question might arise whether this is a historicist reading. Thus, it is less confusing to speak of a generational threshold (*Generationenschwelle* [Assmann 2000: 29]) and allow a span of 30–50 years.

Though externalization processes, by which the group memory takes a physical or visual form, can (already) take place in communicative memory, the transition from communicative to cultural memory is not to be confused with the shift from orality to writing (Assmann 1992: 59). It seems quite logical that textualization begins at this stage and provides initial fixed forms for the different composures of the recalled events. Surely, these initial forms can still be subject to alterations, while in cultural memory this is much more difficult. In principle, the formation of communicative and cultural memory operates according to the same underlying processes, even in oral societies. In both cases, the vivid and manifold stream of traditions is narrowed into a single perspective. This also makes clear that the role of writing and texts in the formation and maintenance of memory is complex and that the existence of written media alone does not indicate a certain type of memory.

Aleida and Jan Assmann's latest publications altered their initial idea that communicative/cultural memory represent subsets of collective memory. This shift in theory allows an extended alliance between the different concepts, linking Halbwachs' and Assmann's approach into a threefold concept consisting of social and cultural memory with collective memory as the middle ground. In this process, the term *communicative memory* was abandoned and its artefacts now pass as collective memory (Assmann [Erll/Nünning] 2008: 110; cf. Hubenthal 2014: 142–4).

Sandra Hubenthal (Universität Passau, Germany)

Further Reading

Assmann, Jan. 2011. *Cultural Memory and Early Civilization: Writing, Remembrance, and Political Imagination.* Translated by David Henry Wilson. Cambridge: University Press [Original German Version: 1992].

Assmann, Jan. 2006. *Religion and Cultural Memory: Ten Studies.* Translated by Rodney Livingstone. Stanford: University Press. [Original German Version: 2000].

Erll, Astrid and Ansgar Nünning, eds. 2008. *Cultural Memory Studies: An International and Interdisciplinary Handbook.* Berlin: Walter Mouton de Gruyter, esp. 109–118, 285–298.

Gudehus, Christian, Ariane Eichenberg, and Harald Welzer, eds. 2010. *Gedächtnis und Erinnerung: Ein interdisziplinäres Handbuch.* Stuttgart: Metzler, esp.102–108.

Hubenthal, Sandra. 2014. *Das Markusevangelium als kollektives Gedächtnis.* Göttingen: Vandenhoeck und Ruprecht.

Conversation Analysis Conversation analysis is the study of talk-in-interaction in naturally occurring situations and, as such, resists using data collected from experiments. Conversation analysis has its beginnings in the work of sociologist Harvey Sacks, who applied the insights of ethnomethodology to conversation.

Conversation analysis is driven by four basic assumptions. First, conversation is a meaningfully organized social activity; second, because of its economy, there is 'order at all points' (Sacks 1984: 22) – that is, even elements of talk-in-interaction that have been dismissed in other linguistic approaches (for example, gaze, discourse markers, interjections, intonation, gestures) are assumed to have meaning. Third, conversational utterances occur within sequences in which each utterance is shaped by what came before it (context-shaped) and influences what comes after it (context-renewing). Fourth, everyday conversation is so fundamental to human communication that the study of talk in institutional contexts must occur in comparison to everyday conversation, since the structures and organization of institutional talk are adapted from the structures and organization of everyday conversation.

The two most basic observations of conversation analysis concern turn-taking and sequence organization. In their seminal article of 1974, Harvey Sacks, Emanuel Schegloff, and Gail Jefferson observed the following about conversation: 1) turn-taking occurs; 2) usually only one speaker talks at a time; and, 3) turns often occur with little or no gaps. Taken together, these three observations strongly suggest a set of practices that provide a systematic way of determining when a turn at talk begins and ends and who has the floor to produce the next turn. Sacks, Schegloff, and Jefferson outline the turn-taking system that operates in conversation so that speakers can take turns at speech with little or no gap between turns and little overlapping speech.

Turns at talk occur in sequences. The most basic sequence is called *adjacency pairs*, such as question/answer and offer/refusal. Adjacency pairs may be characterized as follows: '(a) composed of two turns, (b) by different speakers, (c) adjacently placed; that is, one after the other, (d) … differentiated into "first pair parts" … and "second pair parts" …, and (e) pair-type related; that is, not every second pair part can properly follow any first pair part' (Schegloff 2007: 13). For example, in its basic unexpanded form, an assessment by one speaker is typically followed immediately by a second speaker in the form of agreement or disagreement. However, this basic form can be greatly expanded: for example, before a disagreement with an assessment the second speaker may initiate a series of questions, thereby delaying the production of the second pair part of disagreement.

Conversation analysis provides an excellent basis for understanding better what Albert Lord called the 'special grammar' of oral traditions as a type of institutional talk based on adaptations of practices in everyday conversation, as well as for understanding oral traditions as a form of institutional storytelling. Conversation analysis has played a limited role in discussions of literature, including the Bible (Person 2012).

Raymond F. Person, Jr. (Ohio Northern University, USA)

Further Reading

Arminen, Ilka. 2005. *Institutional Interaction: Studies of Talk at Work.* Aldershot: Ashgate.

Hutchby, Ian and Wooffitt, Robin. 2008. *Conversation Analysis: Principles, Practices and Applications.* Cambridge: Polity.

Person, Raymond F., Jr. 2012. 'Conversation Analysis'. In *Dictionary of the Old Testament: Prophets.* Edited by Mark J. Boda and J. Gordon McConville. Downers Grove, IL: InterVarsity, pp. 86–90.

Person, Raymond F., Jr. 2016. *From Conversation and Oral Tradition: A Simplest Systematics for Oral Traditions.* London: Routledge.

Sacks, Harvey. 1984. 'Notes on Methodology'. In *Structures of Social Action: Studies in Conversation Analysis.* Edited by J. Maxwell Atkinson and John Heritage. Cambridge: Cambridge University Press, pp. 21–7.

Sacks, Harvey, Emanuel A. Schegloff, and Gail Jefferson. 1975. 'A Simplest Systematics for the Organization of Turn-Taking for Conversation'. *Language* 50: 696–735.

Schegloff, Emanuel A. 2007. *Sequence Organization: A Primer in Conversation Analysis 1.* Cambridge: Cambridge University Press.

Silverman, D. 1998. *Harvey Sacks and Conversation Analysis.* Cambridge: Polity Press.

Countermemory Countermemory is best understood in opposition to, or as a form of and/or subset within, a group's COLLECTIVE MEMORY. Whereas *collective memory* denotes the social frameworks within which an individual locates and interprets his or her memories, a countermemory is 'an individual's resistance against the official versions of historical continuity' (Foucalt 1977: 160). In other words, an individual or group may choose to emphasize forgotten or marginalized elements of their society's collective memory, essentially creating a new or reconfigured interpretation of history that runs counter to that collective memory. The function of countermemory is to challenge official versions of the past, to give voice to suppressed experiences, to create a cohesive identity for a marginalized group and, in the most positive cases, to urge society towards positive transformation. In these respects, countermemories may act as significant challenges to a society's GREAT TRADITION and its 'official' version of the past.

Groups that develop and promote countermemories often posture their vision in terms of truth-telling and exploring the 'politics of truth', where that truth is contingent, subjective, and transformative (Foucalt 2007). Its very contingency and subjectivity mean that knowing who remembers and what the context of that memory is are both key to understanding the countermemory. In addition, because the role of countermemory is transformative at heart, identifying what it opposes is a further clue not only to understanding the countermemory itself but also to grasping its intended and particular role in society. For example, postcolonial emphasis on the suppression of IDENTITY by colonial powers has created a countermemory movement in which the former colonies remember in freedom individual experiences under colonial power. These countermemories oppose official colonial accounts, seeking to understand the impact of colonial subjugation on their national and ethnic identities so that the former colonies may recover who they were, understand who they are, and avoid extending the influence of the colonial experience to who they will become in the future. In much the same way, Germany today fosters a collective countermemory process in their public memorializations of Holocaust victims in order to transform how Germans respond to the persecution of foreigners among them today (Young 1999).

In the field of biblical studies, countermemory can be used as a model for understanding the development and distribution of perspectives opposed to mainstream ways of remembering and the power structures they support. The NT documents, for example, can be read as alternative ways of remembering Jesus' life, ministry, and death over against the predominant Roman and Jewish political establishments, thus reinforcing a distinct Christian identity over against mainstream society. Similarly, the texts of the Hebrew Bible frequently allude to traces of marginal voices and groups within Israelite society and portray the prophets articulating alternative (for their own times) interpretations of current social realities based on alternate memories of Israel's history and Law.

Judith Odor (Asbury Theological Seminary, USA)

Further Reading

Foucalt, Michel. 1977. *Language, Counter-memory, Practice: Selected Essays and Interviews*. Edited by Donald F. Bouchard. Translated by Donald F. Bouchard and Sherry Simon. Ithaca, NY: Cornell University.

Foucalt, Michel. 1997. *The Politics of Truth*. Edited by Sylvère Lotringer. Translated by Lysa Hochroth and Catherine Porter. Los Angeles: Semiotext(e).

Young, James. E. 1999. 'Memory and Counter-Memory: The End of the Monument in Germany'. *Harvard Design Magazine* 9: 1–10.

Culley, Robert Charles Robert Charles Culley (1932–2013) was professor of Hebrew Bible/OT at McGill University and Presbyterian College from 1967 to 1997. He is the author of several monographs on oral-formulaic language and patterns in biblical literature and of numerous articles on ORAL TRADITIONS, structuralism, and the Psalms. Culley was co-founder, in 1972, of *Semeia*, a journal (now book series) dedicated to biblical studies and contemporary theory. This abbreviated list sums up well the trajectory of his work, which moved from tracing ORALITY in Hebrew Bible texts through a structuralist exploration of patterns in texts and into the testing of the usefulness of various forms of contemporary critical theory for the Bible.

Culley began his career in biblical studies with an interest in oral traditions. This work was relatively new to the field at the time, having only been tentatively explored by Mowinkel, Nielson, and others. Initially (1963), Culley began to think through how to recognize and analyse types and patterns in formulaic language. This work was pursued more fully with his PhD dissertation, subsequently published in 1967, on variations in the language of the Psalms, which worked as crucial signals about the way traditional material was being adapted for the written context. His work was influenced particularly by Vladimir Propp's studies of Russian folktales and ALBERT LORD's investigations of Homeric literature. FOLKLORE studies provided Culley a useful resource to explore the fluid transitions between oral and written language and literature, particularly addressing the question of whether or not one might discern the marks of oral practices in written biblical texts.

After the publication of his dissertation, Culley continued intermittently to comment on the state of the field of oral-formulaic studies and its usefulness for biblical scholarship. He also shifted his interests, however, to consider the patterns and structures of various narratives in the Hebrew Bible. Here again he used Propp and a structuralist approach to inform his work. He did not so much favour the deep structure models of Greimas or Levi-Strauss, but conceived of a textual model that recognized the text's considerable role in establishing the structures in it, as opposed to passively providing evidence of those imposed upon it. Unlike Propp, Culley did not perceive a single, uniform pattern for all the narratives of the Hebrew Bible, but preferred to isolate distinct story types, patterns, and transitions along with the variations that may be found in those patterns. He devoted two monographs and a series of essays to these explorations.

At the same time, Culley developed an interest in what he called, in 1993, the 'newer' approaches to the Bible, such as Ideological Criticism, Feminist Criticism, and post-structuralism, which offered 'substantial challenges' to prior literary and historical approaches (1993: 4). Though he himself did not undertake work using these approaches, they were for him emblematic of the question of the relation between reader and text in the determination of meaning. This was something that would occupy Culley in his work for some time; his book *Themes and Variations* (1992) sought in part to trace where he thought reader and text might be foremost in the interpretive process. Culley also, together with Robert Robinson, presided over the foregrounding of this question in the field via two important issues of *Semeia* dedicated to the subject of textual determinacy (1993; 1995).

Never satisfied to settle this question definitively, Culley continued to explore it in his later work, along with the matter of the conventional and rhetorical aspects of literary texts. He returned to the Psalms in various articles to identify literary patterns of rescue; his supposition was that the psalms balanced individual concerns of speakers (subjects) with stock language that drew on a repertoire of imagery that would have been familiar to all who used the GENRE. Conference papers and unpublished work up to the time of his death were dedicated to exploring the figure of the sufferer in the Complaints, tracing once again the conventions of the language of suffering, but also their unique applications in a variety of psalms.

Fiona C. Black (Mount Allison University, Canada)

Further Reading

Black, Fiona, Roland Boer, and Erin Runions, eds. 1999. 'Introduction: The Work of Robert Culley'. In *The Labour of Reading: Desire, Alienation, and Biblical Interpretation.* Atlanta: SBL Press, pp. 1–12.

Culley, Robert C. 1963. 'An Approach to the Problem of Oral Tradition'. *VT* 113(2): 114–25.

Culley, Robert C. 1967. *Oral Formulaic Language in the Biblical Psalms.* Toronto: University of Toronto Press.

Culley, Robert C. 1972. 'Oral Tradition and Historicity'. In *Studies on the Ancient Palestinian World.* Edited by J. Wevers and D. B. Redford. Toronto: University of Toronto Press, pp. 102–16.

Culley, Robert C. 1976. 'Oral Tradition and the OT: Some Recent Discussion'. *Semeia* 5: 1–33. Atlanta: Society of Biblical Literature.

Culley, Robert C. 1976. *Studies in the Structure of Hebrew Narrative.* Atlanta: Scholars Press.

Culley, Robert C. 1980. 'Orality and Writtenness in the Prophets'. In *Writings and Speech in Israelite and Ancient Near Eastern Prophecy.* Edited by E. Ben Zvi and M. Floyd. Atlanta: SBL Press, pp. 45–64.

Culley, Robert C. 1985. 'Exploring New Directions'. In *The Hebrew Bible and Its Modern Interpreters.* Edited by D. Knight and G. Tucker. Philadelphia: Fortress Press, pp. 167–200.

Culley, Robert C. 1986. 'Oral Tradition and Biblical Studies'. *Oral Tradition*, 1(1): 30–65.

Culley, Robert C. 1992. *Themes and Variations: A Study of Action in Biblical Narrative.* Semeia Studies. Atlanta: Scholars Press.

Culley, Robert C. 2010. 'David and the Psalms: Tithes, Poems and Stories'. In *The Fate of King David: The Past and Present of a Biblical Icon.* LHBOTS 500. Edited by T. Linafeldt, C. Camp, and T. Beal. New York: T&T Clark, pp. 153–62.

Culley, Robert C., and Robert Robinson, eds. 1993. *Characterization in Biblical Literature.* Semeia 63. Atlanta: Society of Biblical Literature.

Culley, Robert C., and Robert Robinson, eds. 1995. *Orality and Textuality in Early Christian Literature.* Semeia 65. Atlanta: Society of Biblical Literature.

Cultural Memory The term *cultural memory* was introduced by the German Egyptologist JAN ASSMANN as a subcategory of MAURICE HALBWACHS' COLLECTIVE MEMORY. The term refers broadly to a community's canonized memory of the remote past, as such memory normatively and formatively presents and defines the group's self-image. In biblical studies, texts from the Hebrew Bible and the NT – as well as related literatures such as some Qumran documents and RABBINIC materials – are read and interpreted as artefacts of cultural memory. References to cultural memory as a hermeneutical concept have predominantly been made by German-speaking scholars following Assmann's theoretical foundation.

The notion of memory as a social process and the question of how IDENTITY is built up and preserved within a memory group provided the basis for Assmann's development of Halbwachs' concept. Assmann distinguishes between COMMUNICATIVE MEMORY and *cultural memory* as subsets of Halbwachs' collective memory. Whereas communicative memory refers primarily to a current generation's shared past, in cultural memory recollections are stabilized and maintained across generations. Thus, cultural memory is organized, formed, and conveyed by social practices and rites of passage and manifests in texts, rites, MONUMENTS, commemorations, and observances (see cultural memory/SOCIAL MEMORY).

Cultural memory is focused on central points of the past that are preserved for the present without being a mere re-presentation of an objective past. Past events are turned into symbolic figures that serve as carriers for remembrance; cultural memory does not memorialize history as such, but rather a community's memory construct insofar as it has actual relevance for the members of the group. It can be understood as the canonized cultural frame that provides a mnemonic group with categories, rules, norms, and symbolic figures to actualize and semanticize the past. In cultural memory, not only the past but also its understanding is canonized.

In Assmann's theory, WRITING and textuality create the possibility of canonization, which is a special form of textualization. The canonical text is not simply written down, but its obligation is enhanced: it becomes normative and authoritative. As biblical CANON formulas indicate (e.g. Deut. 4.2; 13.1; Rev. 22.18), canonical texts cannot be adjusted, but only arranged and explained (Assmann 2000: 82; 1992, 87–103). Often the interpretation also becomes canonized, as can be seen in RABBINIC LITERATURE, where the Gemara is part of the normative text of the Talmud. Assmann's cultural memory theory thus highlights the fact that canonization is a social process: the manifestation of memory in a canon is IDENTITY-forming and linked to the needs of the mnemonic group that refers to it (Assmann 1992: 127). In this sense, a canon produced by the process of canonization can be understood as an artefact of cultural memory (Hubenthal and Handschuh 2013: 109–13).

Regarding media, almost everything that refers to the remote past and has already lasted for more than a century relative to the event recalled can be understood and interpreted as an artefact of cultural memory. This includes texts (e.g. books and steles), buildings (e.g. houses, TEMPLES, arches), and traditions (e.g. rites, calendars, festivity). Generally, in biblical studies only Hebrew Bible/OT texts are read as cultural memory, while systematic theology and liturgy also regard NT texts as artefacts of cultural memory. The difference lies in the distance to the events recalled in the texts: for the authors of the Hebrew Bible/OT, the events they mentioned were mostly of the remote past (cultural memory), whereas the NT authors recall events and situations less than a century old at the time of writing (communicative or collective memory). Today, of course, both the Hebrew Bible and the NT are part of the remote past, and can thus be referred to as normative and formative traditions of cultural memory.

As is also the case with social memory, there is a German/English language barrier that impacts the conception of cultural memory. In addition to the difference between *Gedächtnis* and memory, there is also a semantic difference between *Kultur* (understood as the intellectual, artistic, and creative achievements of a community) and *culture* (a collective term for ideas, customs, and arts in contexts of society and civilization). As *cultural memory* and *kulturelles Gedächtnis* denote slightly different understandings of the issue, it is important to reveal one's theoretical foundation when working with the concept.

Sandra Hubenthal (Universität Passau, Germany)

Further Reading

Assmann, Jan. 2006. *Religion and Cultural Memory: Ten Studies*. Translated by Rodney Livingstone. Stanford: University Press [Original German Version: 2000].

Assmann, Jan. 2011. *Cultural Memory and Early Civilization: Writing, Remembrance, and Political Imagination*. Translated by David Henry Wilson. Cambridge: University Press. [Original German Version: 1992].

Erll, Astrid, and Ansgar Nünning eds. 2008. *Cultural Memory Studies. An International and Interdisciplinary Handbook*. Berlin: Walter Mouton de Gruyter.

Gudehus, Christian, Ariane Eichenberg, and Harald Welzer, eds. 2010. *Gedächtnis und Erinnerung: Ein interdisziplinäres Handbuch*. Stuttgart: Metzler, esp. 93–102.

Hubenthal, Sandra, and Christian Handschuh. 2013. *Der Trienter Kanon als kulturelles Gedächtnis*. In *Formen des Kanons: Studient zu Ausprägungen des biblischen Kanons von der Antike bis zum 19. Jahrhundert*. Edited by Thomas Hieke. Stuttgart: Katholisches Bibelwerk, pp. 104–50.

Cylinder Seals Cylinder seals represent an ancient technology of mark-making whereby a spool-shaped object is rolled across a pliable surface, usually clay, in order to leave an impression (or sealing). As visual media, cylinder seals and sealings communicate systems of accountancy, regulation, protection, IDENTITY, social power, or artistic display.

This technology is associated with the culture of the ancient Near East in general, and the region of Mesopotamia in particular. Temporal contexts align this technique with the OT world and beyond.

Cylinder seals and sealings appeared in the mid-fourth millennium BCE (Uruk period) and diminished by the fifth century BCE (Achaemenid period). Between these margins, thousands upon thousands of these tiny 'rolling pins' were produced. The seals themselves are usually made of worked stone, although wood, bone, or ivory were also used. Seal barrels typically measure two to four centimetres (about one inch) in length and vary in diameter. Many are perforated longitudinally, likely to receive a string or dowel. Some cylinder seals are unperforated and have a knob on top; others are mounted between ornamental metal caps. These furnishings allowed for the seal to be carried or displayed as part of a personal kit of necklace, bracelet, or bead pendant. It also made it possible for the seal to be deployed when needed and rolled evenly across a receptive surface.

Biblically, the *hotam* of Judah the patriarch mentioned in Gen. 38.18 may refer to a cylinder seal. The syntax of the phrase 'seal-and-cord' has the feel of a hendiadys. In the hands of Tamar, this unit has enough social power to identify (and in this case, embarrass) its owner. Cuneiform clay tablets often display sealings in the Mesopotamian world. Such tablets record commercial or legal transactions. The seal ostensibly adds the personal mark of authority or identity to the document. Before tablets, at the dawn of human WRITING systems, cylinder sealings cover clay balls containing tokens. The effort may represent a receipt or guarantee that exchanged goods are of a desired quantity and quality. Finally, unfired clay globs carry sealings and are used to close doors, baskets, or jars.

The barrel face of the cylinder seal is carved intaglio; shapes are carved from the stone in a mirrored reversal. When spooled out, figures, symbols, written signs, or abstract decorations are presented properly, rising from the surface of the sealing. In some cases, scenes flow in a repeating continuum. Others are panelled or bordered. In rare cases, two registers appear, one above the other.

Designs involving figures are popular on cylinder seals. These can be quite intricate, especially when considering the scale of execution: worshippers grovel, boats float, animals dance, horses gallop, charioteers hunt, men labour. Above all else, the gods rule. Such glyphs offer windows into the life- and thought-world of those who produced and used them.

Inscriptions also appear on cylinder seals and sealings. These are, of necessity, concise and formulaic. They communicate divine names, personal names, titles, professions, and/or relationships. Extended inscriptions may detail a blessing, dedication, or commemoration.

The provenience of this technology dictates the use of cuneiform (or wedge-writing) as the language system carrier. However, Hittite and Egyptian hieroglyphic inscriptions are known, as are rare alphabetic inscriptions using Phoenician script. The parallel trajectories of Mesopotamian tablet technology, cuneiform language systems, and the use of cylinder seals for mark-making is hardly accidental. They wax and wane together. The reason is mechanical: the clay that receives the stylus also receives the seal. These tactics of manipulation do not transfer easily into harder venues where ink, PAPYRUS, or vellum (see PARCHMENT) dominate.

Mark Ziese (Johnson University, USA)

D

Dance *Dance* appears in the Hebrew Bible and NT as one of many embodied expressions of emotion, including particularly praise and WORSHIP to God. Throughout Scripture, dance is admonished as a form of praise (e.g. Pss 149; 150; Eccl. 3), and the Bible and early Christian literature portray a variety of characters dancing in a wide range of contexts. These contexts suggest that dance should be viewed as a medium of communication, the bodily expression of a wide range of feelings appropriate to differing occasions.

Dance and/as Worship

Because dance is an embodied action frequently associated with contexts of worship, it should be understood within a larger complex of similar terms and actions described in the Bible. For example, the word *yadah* occurs over seventy times in the Hebrew Bible; it is generally translated as 'praise', but literally means 'to confess with outstretched hands'. Another word translated as 'praise', *barak*, literally means, 'to kneel, bless, praise'. In other words, virtually every occurrence of the word 'praise' in English translations has an embodied connotation, envisioning either outstretching of the hands or kneeling. Similarly, the Hebrew term *shachah*, which appears over 170 times in the Hebrew Bible and is typically translated worship, literally means 'to prostrate, bow down, do reverence to'. A similar pattern is evident in the NT: the Greek word *proskuneo*, translated over fifty times as worship, literally means 'to fall down, kneel, bow low, fall at another's feet'. If we can safely assume that the literary portrayal betrays a common cultural practice, the ancient Israelites and early Christians did not envision worship and praise as activities that occurred in the mind or heart alone, but instead infiltrated the entire body. Put another way, worship was a physical embodiment of faith.

Within the larger complex of terms that describe worship and praise as embodied action, the Hebrew Bible uses eleven different terms to describe activities that are typically translated 'dance' in English: *rekad*, *pazez*, *mahol*, *gul*, *chagag*, *kirker*, *dillug*, *chul*, *sabab*, *pasah*, and *siheq*. The sheer number and distribution of these terms suggests that dance was deeply ingrained in the culture and worship of Israel. The ancient Israelites were an embodied people, dancing in the grip of God's joy, in the face of oppression, and for the purpose of lament. Similarly, the Greek word *aggallio*, which literally means 'leap/jump for joy', is translated as 'exceedingly glad or joyful' and appears over fifteen times in the NT. When 'joy' is read, therefore, dancing is understood, for rejoicing and dancing are synonymous.

Dancers and Dancing

Aside from the wide range of terms that allude to bodily expressions of worship or other emotions, the Bible includes an array of episodes involving dancers and dancing. In Exodus 15, Miriam dances on the shores of freedom after crossing the Sea of Reeds. Upon their escape from slavery, Miriam and the other Israelites chose to celebrate their liberation with dance and song, their bodies affirmed and free. In Judges 11, Jephthah's daughter dances at the doors of her house to greet her father, apparently a customary practice by women and girls in ancient Israelite culture upon the return of men from battle. Yet Jephthah's daughter's dance morphs from a dance of greeting to a dance of lamentation as her father sacrifices her because of his foolish vow. Scripture also portrays dancers in ecstatic episodes of wild abandon. In 2 Samuel 6, King David dances as the Ark of the Covenant is delivered into his city, leaping wildly and, apparently, exposing himself indecorously. In Jdt.15, Judith and other women dance to celebrate the defeat the enemy after she decapitates the oppressor. Her beautiful body, faithful heart, and wise mind combine subversively so that her dance undermines a male custom and instead empowers women to affirm their bodies as agents of worship, victory, and liberation.

Episodes involving dance also appear in early Christian literature. In Mark 6, Herodias' daughter dances to the delight of her stepfather, who then beheads John the Baptist at her request. While later artistic interpretations of the scene have portrayed this dance as seductive and sexually manipulative, the text describes the dancing dalliances of a little girl who plays, leaps, and skips like many young children when given the spotlight. The Gnostic Acts of John (94–97) describe Jesus himself as a dancer, who gathers in a circle to sing a hymn with his disciples and proclaims, 'Grace dances, dance ye all … the number twelve dance on high … all on high have part in our dance … those who dance not, know not what is to come'.

The diversity of figures portrayed as dancers – Miriam, Jephthah's daughter, David, Judith, Salome, and Jesus – and the contexts in which they are shown dancing highlight the primacy of the body in worship. Dance is seen as a way to express liberation and celebration, while also functioning as a form of lament. Abandon and passionate love are invoked through worshipful dances. Subversion and innocence are embodied by these scriptural dancers. And Jesus' dance teaches worshippers of the power of community to gather hand in hand, celebrating and honouring the bodies within the circle and beyond.

Angela Yarber (Wake Forest University, USA)

Further Reading

Adams, Doug, and Diane Apostolos-Cappadona, eds. 1990. *Dance as Religious Studies*. New York: Crossroads Press.

Gagne, Ronald, Thomas Kane, and Robert VerEecke. 1999. *Introducing Dance in Christian Worship*. Portland: Pastoral Press.

Manor, Gloria. 1980. *The Gospel According to Dance: Choreography from the Bible from Ballet to Modern*. New York: St. Martin's Press.

Meyers, Carol. 1999. 'Mother to Muse: An Archaeomusicological Study of Women's Performance in Ancient Israel'. In *Recycling Biblical Figures: Papers Read at a Noster Colloquium in Amsterdam 12-13 May 1997*. Edited by Athalya Brenner and Jan Willem Van Henten. Studies in Theology and Religion 1. Leiden: Deo, pp. 50–77.

Morganstern, Julian. 1916. 'The Etymological History of the Three Hebrew Synonyms for "To Dance"'. *JAOS* 36: 321–32.

Yarber, Angela. 2013. *Dance in Scripture: How Biblical Dancers Can Revolutionize Worship Today*. Eugene: Wipf and Stock.

Dead Sea Scrolls and Other Judean Desert Texts The Dead Sea Scrolls (DSS) comprise a collection of approximately 900 MANUSCRIPTS discovered in caves near the Wadi Qumran on the northwest shore of the Dead Sea beginning in 1947. The documents are composed in Hebrew, Aramaic, and to a much lesser extent, Greek and Latin. They were produced between the third century BCE and the first century CE. The term DSS is sometimes also used to refer to other texts found in the Judean Desert, such as those from Wadi Muraba'at, NAḤAL ḤEVER, Wadi ed-Daliyeh, and Masada. These texts typically date later than the Qumran texts, though those from Wadi ed-Daliyeh date to the fourth century BCE. Among the approximately 900 SCROLLS from Qumran, around 25 per cent are copies of 'biblical' books. The collection provides the oldest and best witnesses to the texts of the books of the Hebrew Bible by more than a millennium as well as copies of some non-canonical texts, including some not previously known.

In assessing the importance of the DSS for understanding the Bible it is imperative to clarify that *Bible* is an anachronistic term when applied to Qumran: neither a Bible nor a list of authoritative books was discovered among the DSS. Nevertheless, the contribution of the DSS towards our understanding of the writing, editing, translating, and transmission of the books of the Hebrew Bible cannot be overstated. Before the discovery of the scrolls, the oldest Hebrew witnesses to the texts of biblical books were medieval Masoretic manuscripts (MT). The DSS allow us to peer behind the medieval Hebrew manuscripts and see a far more diverse and pluriform picture of biblical texts in ancient times. This essay considers the role of the DSS in understanding the Bible in ancient media by concentrating on the following topics: Materials; 'Biblical' Manuscripts; Text Types; Text Collections; Exegetical Literature; Para-texts/Affiliated Compositions; Translations; Tefillin and Mezuzot; and Script Types.

Materials

The vast majority of the DSS are written on parchment (leather), while some are composed on papyrus, ostraca (potsherds), and other mediums. The manufacture of all parchment was expensive, but some manuscripts were more costly than others, so it is noteworthy which literary works were copied on the most expensive materials. Emanuel Tov has found evidence of approximately 30 deluxe manuscripts, characterized by large top and bottom margins (large amounts of intentionally uninscribed leather indicates these were luxury products). A disproportionate number of these deluxe manuscripts (ca. 73%) were used to copy biblical books, the vast majority of which are books of the Torah (Pentateuch). The Qumran manuscripts vary widely in length from single sheets containing one column to scrolls that were more than 20 metres long, containing more than 100 columns. Most texts are poorly preserved, sometimes surviving as little more than a few scraps of leather.

Biblical Manuscripts

Approximately 200 of the 900 scrolls discovered at Qumran can be referred to as biblical manuscripts. But designating a scroll as biblical is no straightforward matter when analysing the DSS. Many of the manuscripts are highly fragmentary. Only one biblical scroll preserves a complete book according to the shape in which it is found in the Masoretic Text (1QIsa[a]). It is not only possible but likely that some manuscripts labelled biblical did not include the entire contents (or the same form of the contents) that we associate with biblical books from the Masoretic Text. For example, it is likely that the Genesis manuscript 4QGenesisd was never a manuscript of chapters 1–50, but only of chapters 1–4 or 1–5 (Brooke 2012: 51–70); therefore, it is inaccurate to describe it as a manuscript of Genesis. At the least, manuscripts like 4QGenesisd make clear to us that the shape and contents of most biblical books were still in a state of flux during Hellenistic times. Texts like 4QReworked Pentateuch present even more complex challenges and scholars have actively debated whether or not it is a biblical text for decades.

Another lesson we learn from the physical manuscripts of biblical books is derived from the number of manuscript witnesses recovered for each book: not all books were of equal value (chart adapted from VanderKam 2010: 48).

Manuscript Count for Biblical Books at Qumran:

Psalms:	**34–36**
Deuteronomy:	**30–32**
Genesis:	**20–21**
Isaiah:	**21**

Exodus:	**16**
Leviticus:	**12–13**
Daniel:	**8**
Twelve Prophets:	**8**
Numbers:	**6–7**
Jeremiah:	**6**
Ezekiel:	**6**
Judges:	**4**
1–2 Samuel:	**4**
Proverbs:	**4**
Job:	**4**
Song of Songs:	**4**
Ruth:	**4**
Lamentations:	**4**
1–2 Kings:	**3**
Joshua:	**3**
Ecclesiastes:	**2**
Ezra:	**1**
Nehemiah:	**1**
1–2 Chronicles:	**1**
Esther:	**0**

Some books, such as Psalms, Genesis, Exodus, Deuteronomy, and Isaiah, are represented in many more copies than the others books. One might reasonably deduce that these books had more authority than the other for the community that collected and produced them. It is noteworthy in this regard that quotations and allusions from the Hebrew Bible in the NT also privilege the same five books. This commonality between the Qumran library and the NT suggests the relative authority of their favourite books was a widespread feature of ancient Judaism. But the significance of the biblical manuscript counts also leads to other important conclusions about authoritative literature in ancient Judaism. For example, several non-biblical books are represented at Qumran in large numbers. JUBILEES is preserved in 14 or 15 copies, suggesting it enjoyed a more authoritative status than most of the biblical books.

Another lesson we learn from the biblical manuscripts is that some of our research methodologies have been inadequate to understand ancient Jewish Scriptures and have perhaps re-inscribed erroneous ideas about how and when they were produced. For example, scholars like Julio Trebolle Barrera have called attention to how the manuscript evidence from Qumran has in many ways collapsed the once distinct methods and theories related to TEXTUAL CRITICISM and literary criticism of the Hebrew Bible (cf. Trebolle Barrera 1999). In other words, we might have in the past made too much of a strict distinction between the roles of author, editor, and copyist in our reconstructions of the biblical texts. A parade example of this problem is found in the manuscripts of the book of Jeremiah. Some of the inconsistencies between the Masoretic Text and SEPTUAGINT of Jeremiah that were previously understood as textual variants now seem more likely to represent distinct or parallel literary editions in light of the Qumran manuscripts: manuscripts that represent the Vorlage of the Septuagint at Qumran are just as old as those that represent proto-MT (Tov 2012: 286–94). This crisis in understanding the stages of composition and editing of biblical texts leads us to discussion of the text types represented by the biblical manuscripts.

Text Types

Before the discovery of the DSS, three primary sources existed for understanding the history of texts of Jewish scriptural books: 1) the Masoretic Text, 2) the Septuagint, and 3) the SAMARITAN PENTATEUCH. Other sources such as translations in Aramaic, Syriac, Coptic, Latin, and Arabic also provide useful, even if limited, data. Before the discovery of the DSS, there was a general consensus that the Masoretic Text represented the text of the Hebrew Bible par excellence and that Septuagint and Samaritan Pentateuch texts primarily represented later corruptions of the Masoretic Text. The DSS have erased this perception. Hebrew manuscripts that correspond roughly to all three text types (as well as entirely unknown text types) have been discovered among the scrolls. The presence of these Vorlagen at Qumran indicates that many of the distinctions between the versions could go back to Persian times.

	Pentateuch (%)	Prophets and Writings (%)
Semi-Masoretic	5	35
Proto-Masoretic	5	10
Pre-Samaritan Pentateuch	5	
Masoretic and Samaritan Pentateuch	27	
Vorlage of LXX	5	4
Independent Traditions	52.5	51

As the table above (adapted and translated from Lange 2009: 19) shows, diverse forms of the biblical texts were found at Qumran. The most instructive feature of the chart may be the last row: most of the biblical manuscripts from Qumran do not align with any previously known form of the books. In other words, the data from Qumran definitely rules out older text-critical models that imagined pristine, ORIGINAL biblical texts that were created by authors only subsequently corrupted over time to produce the distinctions found between the Masoretic Text, Septuagint, and Samaritan Pentateuch. Instead, the differences between versions seem to have originated, in many cases, in the very processes by which the texts were created. Undoubtedly, SCRIBES continued to make intentional and unintentional changes in manuscripts of all text types. But the DSS would seem to disqualify the notion of an Urtext for most biblical books. The DSS also allow us to track trends among text types, in particular, the initial stages of the Masoretic Text's rise-to-prominence.

While there is clearly no dominant textual tradition represented at Qumran, a different picture emerges from the *biblical* texts recovered at other sites in the Judean Desert. The manuscripts from Wadi Muraba'at, Naḥal Ḥever, and Masada tend to be younger than the Qumran manuscripts by one or two centuries and they all belong to the proto-Masoretic tradition. While one must allow for the fact that far fewer manuscripts were recovered from non-Qumran sites, it seems nevertheless that the proto-Masoretic tradition quickly became dominant at the end of the first century CE. One explanation for this transition may be that after the Roman destruction of Jerusalem in 70 CE, those responsible for the proto-Masoretic form of the Hebrew text were the only ones who survived with the ability to transmit their version of biblical books (Tov 2012: 74–80).

Text Collections

The manuscripts from Qumran and other locations in the Judean Desert provide crucial data for understanding the developing relationships between biblical books. For example, from Wadi Muraba'at, Naḥal Ḥever, and

Masada, we have clear evidence that the books of the so-called 'Minor Prophets' were collected and transmitted together in one scroll. This practice might have originated out of practical concerns; that is, in order to make the most efficient and cost-effective use of the media (parchment scroll), small books of the same GENRE were copied together. This practical concern ultimately shaped the meaning of the individual books (since they are read together) and bore directly on their later canonical shape and status. At Qumran some similar practices can be observed. Genesis and Exodus are copied together in two manuscripts: 4Q1 and 4Q11. Exodus and Leviticus are copied together in one manuscript, 4Q17. Leviticus and Numbers are copied together in 4Q23 and Deuteronomy and Exodus might be copied together in 4Q37. Leviticus and Numbers might be copied together in 1Q3. 4QReworked Pentateuch contains portions of Genesis, Exodus, and Deuteronomy, though its status as a biblical text is a matter of dispute. Since books such as Genesis and Exodus are considerably larger than the constituents of the Minor Prophets scroll, one is left to conclude that their relationships are not based on convenience, but instead reflect deliberate choices. And it is interesting that not all of these deliberate choices place books of the Torah in the order that they exist in the Hebrew Bible.

Exegetical Literature

The biblical manuscripts from Qumran are not the only ones that enhance our understanding of the Hebrew Bible. A large number of texts from Qumran serve an exegetical (interpretive) function. They make use of a wide range of exegetical techniques, many of which are also key features of biblical texts. Thus, the Qumran exegetical texts enlarge the data set by which we can evaluate exegetical techniques within the books of the Hebrew Bible. Moreover, exegetical texts give us great insight into some of the earliest interpretations of biblical texts.

One of the largest groups of exegetical texts from Qumran are the PESHARIM, so called because of their highly formulaic use of the Hebrew root *p/sh/r* 'interpret, solve'. What distinguishes the Pesharim from other types of exegetical literature is the way that literary formulas are used to distinguish sharply between the *lemma* (base text) and its interpretation. For example, a pesher might 1) quote a passage of Scripture, 2) declare *pishro 'al* ('its interpretation concerns'), and then 3) offer an authoritative interpretation of the passage. The continuous Pesharim offer interpretations on a verse-by-verse basis throughout large portions of biblical books (in some cases, the Pesharim may have commented upon entire books). The subjects of continuous Pesharim include Habakkuk, Nahum, Hosea, Micah, Zephaniah, Isaiah, and Psalms. Thus, in addition to providing data about ancient interpretations of these biblical books, the generic features of Pesharim also provide textual witnesses to biblical books.

While some Pesharim interpret single scriptural books systematically, other pesher commentaries were produced thematically. Multiple scriptural passages were drawn from different sources in order to produce a treatise on a theme rather than a book. These themes included the restoration of the JERUSALEM TEMPLE and the end of days (e.g. 4Q174 Florilegium). The commentaries draw primarily, though not exclusively, on *biblical* texts.

In addition to the relatively straightforward Pesharim, the DSS bear witness to numerous exegetical traditions that are more difficult to separate strictly from their *lemmata*. Unlike the Pesharim, these texts do not necessarily distinguish the base text from its interpretation. One of the largest groups of these texts is often referred to as REWRITTEN SCRIPTURE. Perhaps what is most important about these texts for understanding the Bible in ancient media is the way in which they provide scholars with external data for constructing theoretical models of the formation of the biblical books.

By the eighteenth century CE, it became increasingly clear to scholars that the process by which the biblical books were written was complex. A critical approach to the texts virtually demanded that one conclude that the texts were produced by many people over a long period of time. Many books (even individual chapters) must have had multiple sources or possibly multiple authors/editors. Before the discovery of the DSS, however, these theories were difficult to test. Did ancient Jewish scribes really work in this way? Would a scribe alter an existing authoritative text by rewriting it? Texts like Jubilees, the Genesis Apocryphon, and the Temple Scroll from Qumran answer this question affirmatively and provide a wide range of external evidence for the scribal techniques that were used to compose many texts of the Hebrew Bible. Certainly, this type of evidence for rewriting already existed in the Hebrew Bible in the form of books like Chronicles, which probably rewrites large portions of Samuel and Kings. But the DSS allow scholars a clearer vista on the scribal techniques since they exist external to biblical texts. For example, the intricate weaving together of two 'battle at the sea' stories in Exodus 14 may reflect the same (or, similar) processes of harmonization that one can observe in the interweaving of Exodus 24 and Deuteronomy 31 in Jubilees 1.

In addition to helping us to understand biblical texts better, rewritten Scripture also problematizes our notions of Scripture and authoritative literature. It is not a simple matter to determine if Jubilees was meant to replace, supersede, augment, or merely interpret its base texts from the Pentateuch. And it is unclear if some ancient readers might have treated Jubilees as interchangeable with or even superior to Genesis. One could reasonably ask the same questions about the Temple Scroll.

Para-Texts/Affiliated Compositions

In addition to exegetical literature that treats biblical texts as authoritative *lemmata* (Pesharim) or attempts to rewrite them in some way (e.g. Temple Scroll), there exist many other manuscripts that are related to biblical texts (or important persons or concepts from biblical texts) in less obvious ways. This group of texts has thrown centuries-old generic categories into disarray. These texts are sometimes referred to as *para-biblical*. The term has a certain utility, but since the very concept of Bible is an anachronism at Qumran, others have opted for more neutral terms, such as *para-text* or *affiliated composition*. Examples of these texts would include Apocryphon of Jeremiah C and 4QPseudo-Daniela–b. These works bear some relationship to the books, characters, or traditions of Jeremiah and Daniel, but it is difficult to understand the character of that relationship and much more research is needed. Precedent for this type of literature is probably found in the biblical book of Jonah, which may have been developed based on the figure named in 2 Kgs 14:25.

Translations

The scrolls from the Judean Desert demonstrate that Jewish scribes were actively translating biblical texts from Hebrew into both Aramaic and Greek in Hellenistic times. Scholars have long assumed that this practice was underway as early as the third century BCE, but the DSS provide our first physical evidence. In Qumran cave 4, Aramaic translations of Leviticus (4Q156) and Job (4Q157) were discovered. In addition, caves 4 (4Q119–122), 7 (7Q11), and the 'Cave of Horrors' from Naḥal Ḥever preserve Greek translations of Hebrew Scriptures. These Greek translations are highly fragmentary, but centuries older than the great fourth-century CE codices (e.g. Codex Sinaiticus and Codex Vaticanus).

Tefillin and Mezuzot

Among the witnesses to the biblical texts at Qumran, we must also include *tefillin* (phylacteries) and *mezuzot*. *Tefillin* are small leather boxes that are secured to the left arm or head with leather straps and used during prayer. They may have been used during other times of the day in the ancient world. A *mezuzah* is a small box that is traditionally secured to the doorpost of a Jewish home. Both of these items contain tiny scrolls with brief passages from the books of Exodus and Deuteronomy. These items were (and still are) used to fulfil the command in Deut. 6.8–9: 'Bind them as a sign on your hand, fix them as an emblem on your forehead, and write them on the doorposts of your house and on your gates' (NRSV). The *tefillin* and *mezuzot* from Qumran are the oldest that have ever been found and thus provide the earliest exemplars for study. The small scrolls reflect the same diversity of text types found among the Qumran biblical scrolls. Since the tiny scrolls in *tefillin* and *mezuzot* were permanently sealed in their capsules and not taken out for reading, this media type indicates another important function for scriptural texts. One may refer to this function as symbolism or as magic, but the media of *tefillin* and *mezuzot* indicate that Exodus and Deuteronomy were far more than significant literary texts. The texts did not necessarily require reading or interpretation in order to confer benefits to the user. They were potent tools – perhaps enchanted objects – that connected users to deity.

Script Types

The vast majority of the scrolls from Qumran are copied in some version of the Aramaic (or 'Square') script. A small number are copied in a paleo-Hebrew script that would have been used more regularly before Jerusalem fell to the Babylonians in 586 BCE. The only scrolls copied in this *paleo-Hebrew* script are Genesis, Exodus, Leviticus, Numbers, Deuteronomy, and Job. Four of these texts are among those that are 1) found in at least 15 copies at Qumran and 2) copied on deluxe manuscripts. So the use of paleo-Hebrew is almost certainly another sign of their importance. The use of the paleo-Hebrew script also provides important information about the owners of the scrolls. Even if the Essenes/sectarians) did not themselves copy the paleo-Hebrew scrolls, they seem to have been capable of reading them. It is tempting to view the inhabitants of Qumran as marginal figures in Jewish society. But the use of both square script and paleo-Hebrew script, as well as the use of both Hebrew and Aramaic languages, indicates that the Essenes must have been welleducated. These scribes were not merely minimally proficient. Moreover, since we know that the Hasmoneans attempted to reinvigorate use of the paleo-Hebrew script in the second century BCE (cf. the inscriptions on their COINS), a relationship with the Hasmoneans (even if a broken one) may be implied.

Bennie H. Reynolds III (Medical University of South Carolina, USA)

Further Reading

Bowley, James. 2011. 'Bible'. In *The Oxford Encyclopedia of the Books of the Bible* vol. 1. Edited by Michael Coogan. Oxford: Oxford University Press, pp. 72–84.

Bowley, James, and John Reeves. 2003. 'Rethinking the Concept of "Bible": Some Theses and Proposals'. *Henoch* 25: 2–18.

Brooke, George. 2005. *The Dead Sea Scrolls and the New Testament*. London: SPCK.

Lange, Armin. 2009. *Handbuch der Textfunde Vom Toten Meer. Band 1: Die Handschriften biblischer Bücher von Qumran und den anderen Fundorten*. Tübingen: Mohr Siebeck.

Tov, Emanuel. 2004. *Scribal Practices and Approaches Reflected in the Texts Found in the Judean Desert*. STDJ 54. Leiden/Atlanta: Brill/SBL.

Tov, Emanuel. 2012. *Textual Criticism of the Hebrew Bible*. 3rd Revised and Expanded Edition. Minneapolis: Fortress Press.

Trebolle Barrera, Julio. 2009. 'Redaction, Recension, and Midrash in the Books of Kings'. In *Reconsidering Israel and Judah: Recent Studies on the Deuteronomistic History*. SBTS 9. Edited by G. Knoppers and J. G. McConville. Winona Lake, IN: Eisenbrauns, pp. 12–35.

Ulrich, Eugene. 1999. *The Dead Sea Scrolls and the Origins of the Bible*. Grand Rapids, Eerdmans.

Ulrich, Eugene. 2010. *The Biblical Qumran Scrolls: Transcriptions and Textual Variants*. VTSup 134. Leiden: Brill.

Ulrich, Eugene. 2011. 'Clearer Insight into the Development of the Bible – A Gift of the Scrolls'. In *The Dead Sea Scrolls and Contemporary Culture*. Proceedings of the International Conference held at the Israel Museum, Jerusalem (6–8 July 2008). Edited by Adolfo D. Roitman, Lawrence H. Schiffman, and Shani Tzoref. STDJ 93. Leiden: Brill, pp. 119–37.

VanderKam, James. 2012. *The Dead Sea Scrolls and the Bible*. Grand Rapids: Eerdmans.

Dialogism *Dialogism* is widely recognized as the signature concept in the theoretical work of Russian literary theorist M. M. BAKHTIN. Though Bakhtin himself did not use the term, his late writings allude briefly and impressionistically to 'dialogical relations'. For Bakhtin, the concept suggests more than simple disagreement, dialectical process, or casual alternation of speakers. Rather, it evokes a spectrum of interrelatedness, along which three types of dialogue can be identified. First, all utterances (speech, a work of art, or a life) are fundamentally responsive to other utterances, always shaped to some extent in terms of other speech. Second, and because of the first point, as speech (or art or life) is composed and performed, multiple voices can be heard in the utterance of a single speaker, for example, as when one quotes another or refers allusively to what another has said, perhaps re-intonating it in a sarcastic tone. A third nuance of the dialogic situates one's speech (or art of life) in relation both to what is asserted impersonally, dogmatically, and authoritatively and to what is available in radically relativistic terms, with the expectation that the utterance (speech, art, life) emerges as authentically and responsibly chosen in view of all obligative and pertinent circumstances.

Barbara Green (Dominican School of Philosophy and Theology, USA)

Dibelius, Martin Martin Dibelius (1863–1947) was a German NT scholar whose pioneering work on JESUS TRADITION, the Gospels, and the historical Jesus was foundational to the development of FORM CRITICISM. Dibelius also significantly contributed to the study of the Acts of the Apostles by applying a Thucydidean model to the composition of the speeches/dialogues in Acts. His approach to Jesus tradition, which focused on the evolution of speech forms and of individual units of tradition in various life settings (see SITZ IM LEBEN) of the early church, in many ways anticipated later research on the development and distribution of SPEECH GENRES.

Dibelius' *From Tradition to Gospel* (1933; 1971) was a milestone work in understandings of the development and transmission of Jesus tradition in the early church. In Dibelius' view, the typical 'forms' of the oral tradition, as evident now from the written Gospels, developed within the contours of the social contexts in which early Christians remembered and discussed Jesus' message and activity. As a result, Dibelius placed a high emphasis on the functional use of language in the development and propagation of those speech genres through which material about Jesus was transmitted.

Dibelius envisioned and described three communicative functions, each tied to a specific social context, as primary to the formation and transmission of early Jesus tradition: 'mission preaching, preaching during worship, and catechumen instruction' (1971: 15). 'Mission preaching' was performed by Christian evangelists with a target audience of non-believing Jews and Gentiles and with a view to their conversion. 'Preaching during worship' was conducted by leaders of Christian communities with a target audience of believers and with a view to ethical exhortation and spiritual formation. 'Catechumen instruction' was performed by Christian teachers with a target audience of recent converts and with a view to their religious education and integration into the community. Each of these situations, and its corresponding audiences and rhetorical functions, created a communicative BIOSPHERE with distinct and inherent 'laws of form construction'; these 'laws', in turn, caused aspects of the tradition to become fixed in their 'outer and inner structure', thus producing the various 'forms' now evident in the written Gospels (quotes 1971: 4, 10).

In Dibelius' view, certain types of gospel material were naturally more applicable to the rhetorical needs of each of the three social settings noted above. The PASSION NARRATIVE, which explained and rationalized the circumstances of Jesus' death against the backdrop of Israel's Scriptures, was particularly useful in contexts of evangelistic preaching. The Passion Narrative took a fixed form at a relatively early date for apologetic purposes, as Christian evangelists needed a viable explanation of the cross and events surrounding it. Similarly, the teachings of Jesus were particularly useful for the instruction of catechumens, and therefore tended to develop along trajectories related to the needs of teachers. Stories of Jesus' deeds were helpful to preachers in their exhortations to Christian congregations because they provided moral examples and pastoral comfort while reinforcing conceptions of Jesus' identity. In each case, then, Dibelius tended to view the development and transmission of both the content and forms of Jesus material as a function of the situations in which such material tended to be used and the rhetorical purposes typical of those situations.

For Dibelius, just as individual forms emerged from typical contexts within the life of the early church, the totality of the oral Jesus tradition, and its eventual incorporation into written Gospels, should be understood in terms of the theological evolution and institutional expansion of early Christianity. In the early days of the tradition, Palestinian and Hellenistic Jewish Christians framed Jesus' words and deeds in distinctly Jewish terms, with emphasis on his role in the fulfilment of Israel's traditional messianic hopes. Later, as the church became more ethnically diverse and included more Gentiles, the tradition was gradually reshaped to portray Christ as a more distinctly divine figure, so that his words and deeds were recast as epiphanies of God's presence. The various written Gospels, and individual units with them, could be located chronologically in reference to this paradigm, with those reflecting a more 'Jewish' outlook representing more primitive stages of the tradition and those more overtly portraying Christ as a divine figure representing its later stages. Mark's Gospel, the first produced, epitomizes the earlier perspective, while Matthew and, especially, John reflect its later evolution.

Significantly, Dibelius, like RUDOLF BULTMANN and other pioneers of Form Criticism, both did and did not attribute particular significance to the media transition from oral tradition to written Gospel. The transition was significant in the sense that the appearance of written Gospels, especially the first written Gospel, Mark, served as a watershed in the transition between the earlier Palestinian stage of the Jesus tradition and its evolution towards Hellenistic terms and concepts. In this respect, Dibelius viewed the written Gospels, and the literary aspirations that they reflected, as important moments in the evolution of the Church's message and perspective. At the same time, the transition was hermeneutically insignificant in terms of understanding the nature of the contents of the written Gospels and their relationships to the oral traditions that preceded them. Dibelius did not view the evangelists as creative authors in the modern sense of the term, but rather as 'principally collectors, [themselves] vehicles of tradition, editors', whose work was 'handing down, grouping, and working over' the oral-traditional units that they inherited (1971: 1, 3). As a result, Dibelius viewed the contents of the written Gospels as essentially identical to the oral traditions that preceded them, did not view Mark or the other evangelists as significant contributors to the value of the story of Jesus, and did not judge the location of oral episodes in fixed written narratives as particularly significant to their meaning (see also NARRATIVITY).

Finally, Dibelius' approach, again similar to other first-generation form critics and typical of the broader interdisciplinary approach to oral tradition in the early twentieth century (see ORAL TRADITION, COMPARATIVE STUDY OF), diminished the significance of individual speakers and authors in the development and transmission of Jesus tradition. Because the individual forms of the gospel tradition developed in response to rhetorical situations that were typical and trans-cultural, these forms and their contents should be viewed as products of an anonymous process rather than of the creative genius of individuals. Thus, 'the personal peculiarities of the composer or narrator have little significance' for understanding the formation and evolution of Jesus tradition, for in fact 'the tradition is cast by practical necessities, by usage, or by origin' to such an extent that 'the individuality of an original writer played no part' (1971: 1, 4). This judgement extended to the evangelists, 'lowly people' representing 'that lower [social] stratum which accords no place to the artistic devices and literary tendencies of polished writing', and to their written Gospels, which Dibelius categorized as 'unliterary' works (1971: 1, 7).

Within more recent media-critical research on the nature and origins of the Jesus tradition and the production and place of written Gospels within that tradition, Dibelius' work is widely viewed as pioneering for its impact on Form Criticism and the study of the historical Jesus, but inadequately nuanced. While Dibelius' model in many respects anticipated later work on the close relationship between social settings and speech genres by emphasizing the functional nature of oral communication, his portrayal of the evangelists as essentially passive and of the Gospels as repositories of largely unprocessed oral tradition has been significantly challenged (see GREAT DIVIDE). Further, Dibelius' notion that 'the Jesus tradition' can be conceived as an essentially monolithic entity evolving from a 'Jewish' perspective towards a more universal 'Greek' outlook has fallen in the face of a more nuanced understanding of the diversity of early Christian belief. Finally, Dibelius' failure to account for the potential hermeneutical significance of the media interfaces between speech/tradition and WRITING/Gospel in early Christianity has been significantly criticized, and in fact served as an impetus for the work of early media critics of the Bible such as WERNER KELBER.

Tom Thatcher (Cincinnati Christian University, USA)

Further Reading

Dibelius, Martin. 1926. *Geschichte der urchristlichen Literatur*. English: *A Fresh Approach to the New Testament and Early Christian Literature*. New York: Scribners, 1936.

Dibelius, Martin. 1933. *Die Formgeschichte des Evangeliums*. English: *From Tradition to Gospel*. Translated by Bertram Lee Wolf. Greenwood, SC: Attic Press, 1971.

Dibelius, Martin. 1935. *Gospel Criticism and Christology*. London: I. Nicholson and Watson.

Dibelius, Martin. 1956. *Studies in the Acts of the Apostles*. Edited by Heinrich Greeven. Translated by Mary Ling. New York: Charles Scribner's Sons.

Discourse Analysis Discourse analysis (sometimes referred to as *textlinguistics*) refers to any of various means of examining discourse using a range of linguistic tools. Such analysis usually involves study of language elements at or above the level of the clause or sentence and often focuses upon the ways in which texts are structured, such as their organization, how they fit together, and patterns of emphasis. Discourse analysis can be applied to either oral or written texts, although in the field of biblical studies all such examinations are of written texts, whether or not they originated in oral performance. To date, relatively less emphasis has been placed upon the oral origins of any of the written biblical documents.

Major Types of Discourse Analysis

Within the field of linguistics, there are a number of different types of discourse analysis. Some early forms of discourse analysis grew out of what is called, in linguistic circles, *pragmatics*. Much linguistic theory differentiates between sentence meaning (or semantics) and utterance meaning (or pragmatics). The philosopher H. P. Grice analysed what he called conversational implicature, that is, what is implied when people converse. These implications include, for example, the cooperative principle – people are trying to cooperate when they converse. Grice's summary of such maxims of communication is usually equated with pragmatics-based discourse analysis, in which the various 'rules' of conversation are used to examine what happens in human discourse.

Akin to Grice's principles is Speech-Act Theory, developed by the philosophers J. L. Austin and John Searle. Speech-Act Theory, which is related to natural language philosophy, focuses upon the aspect of language that does not try to make propositions but is instead used to perform functions. Language is not necessarily, and certainly not always, concerned with relating facts so much as with doing things with words – for example, 'naming', 'promising', 'introducing', etc. Grice's conversational implicature also has some similarities to Relevance Theory, which claims that the most important feature of discourse is the notion of relevance. This theory has been increasingly used in some biblical studies, especially in TRANSLATION theory. A few biblical scholars (e.g. Anthony Thiselton) have utilized Speech-Act Theory as a means of understanding the performative nature of language, but without necessarily developing a full-blown discourse model.

Another stream of discourse analysis is SOCIOLINGUISTICS. *Interactional Sociolinguistics* is a broad sociological approach to discourse analysis that also draws upon other intellectual disciplines. John Gumperz examines the interaction between participants in a communication, recognizing that dialogue is situated in a social context and that the social situation is responsible for the construction of the verbal interaction involved. Another significant sociologically based approach to discourse is CONVERSATION ANALYSIS. This type of discourse analysis grew out of ethnomethodology, a sociological discipline that analyses how people go about knowing and doing things. The analysis of conversation as a creator and reflector of culture was developed by Harvey Sacks, Emanuel Schegloff, and Gail Jefferson. They focus upon how conversation is adjusted in anticipation of and response to one's conversational environment, including in this environment those with whom one converses and the subjects discussed, among others.

Related to Conversation Analysis is *ethnography of communication*, a form of anthropological discourse analysis developed by the anthropologist DELL HYMES to focus upon communication as an important part of culture. With influence from the functionalist Prague School of linguistics, Hymes breaks down communication into various contextual factors: setting/scene, participants, ends, act sequence, key, instrumentalities, norms, and GENRE (speaking). There have been a number of recent efforts to utilize insights from all three of these perspectives – Interactional Sociolinguistics, Conversation Analysis, and ethnography of communication – in biblical studies, although so far the results are relatively small.

Variation analysis was pioneered by the linguist William Labov as a means of understanding how speakers vary their language for different purposes. In that sense, all language is social and functional. Labov is especially concerned to examine language variation related to ethnicity, and he disputes the notion that language deficiency in an ethnic group is caused by anything but social situation.

Another linguistic form of discourse analysis is *Systemic Functional Linguistics*. Michael Halliday, building on the work of the linguist John Firth and the anthropologist Bronislaw Malinowski, examines language according to its function in context. Halliday differentiates three different (meta-)functions of language, related to its progression of thought (ideational metafunction), positioning of the participants (interpersonal metafunction), and means by which the text itself is constructed and held together (textual metafunction). The metafunctions enable examination of how one conveys the What, Who, and How of a text.

Related to Systemic Functional Linguistics is *Critical Discourse Analysis*, which also draws heavily upon a variety of other disciplines, including critical theory (e.g. Jürgen Habermas), politics, and economics. Critical Discourse Analysis is concerned with language and its relationships to power, identity formation, and social construction and deconstruction. Also drawing directly upon the work of Halliday is *Multimodal Discourse Analysis*. Multimodal Discourse Analysis, as advocated by Gunther Kress, encompasses the communicative potential of a wide variety of social semiotic systems, including such media as music, art, and electronic media. Multimodal Discourse Analysis focuses less upon particular media, which may be quite diverse, than their overall meaning function. For biblical scholars, *Systemic Functional Linguistics* has probably been the most productive of the discourse approaches that originated in linguistics, with the insights of Labov being utilized in some studies.

These types of discourse analysis (and many others, depending upon how they are defined) are routinely used in contemporary discourse studies. However, as noted above, not all of these have been widely used within biblical studies.

Major Types of Discourse Analysis in Biblical Studies

The field of biblical studies has the intriguing characteristic of sometimes drawing directly (and even uncritically) upon a variety of critical frameworks and sometimes developing its own approaches based upon the unique characteristics of the biblical literature itself. Although a number of discourse analysis frameworks have been adapted by biblical scholars, there are also a number of developments that are unique to the field of biblical studies. Further, discourse analyses of the Hebrew Bible and the NT have tended to develop along separate lines, probably due to differences in the respective languages of Greek and Hebrew and the distinct specializations of biblical scholars.

OT/Hebrew Bible discourse analysis has readily adopted the work of secular linguistics within its purview. This may be because of the perceived 'foreignness' of the Hebrew language itself, a disposition that perhaps allows Western scholars to more readily draw upon categories from outside the sphere of western Indo-European languages. Thus, discussions of such categories as verbal aspect were a part of Hebrew language research long before they were a part of study of NT Greek. As a result, there is a longer tradition of the use of discourse analysis within Hebrew Bible studies than there is in NT studies. At the same time, however, the approaches to discourse in Hebrew Bible studies are more limited. There are three approaches that have been generally used within Hebrew Bible discourse analysis: grammatical, functional, and cognitive approaches. However, there is also significant overlap among these three approaches (unlike in NT discourse studies), perhaps because of the relatively few practitioners involved.

The *grammatical approach* is influenced by the work of the linguist Robert Longacre that was in turn based upon Kenneth Pike's model of tagmemics. Tagmemics has not been widely received within the wider field of discourse analysis (no doubt because of its complexity and comprehensiveness), but it has been utilized in Hebrew Bible studies as a means of narrative analysis. In Hebrew Bible the emphasis in discourse studies is often upon the function of the verb, and Longacre's approach to discourse, including his theories on verbal semantics, has had a major impact upon the wider field of Hebrew discourse analysis. The resulting studies often emphasize his hierarchy of text types or their related patterns of verbal usage, as in the early work of Francis Andersen and the later work of David Allan Dawson and Roy Heller.

The *functional approach* is based upon the continental functionalist linguistics pioneered by the linguist Simon Dik. Functionalism in Hebrew Bible studies encompasses a wide variety of approaches to the language, to the point that some would include the grammatical approach above, as well as a variety of studies that draw upon more particular theories of Hebrew syntax. Nevertheless, what is characteristic of continental functionalism in Hebrew discourse analysis is the assessment of distributional patterns found in language, often differentiated according to their semantic, pragmatic, or contextual functions. The practitioners of such approaches include scholars who work on particular issues, but also those who are concerned with discourse as a whole. The variety is represented in the work of Jean-Marc Heimerdinger on foregrounding and Christo van der Merwe on syntax.

The *cognitive approach* is the most recent development in Hebrew discourse analysis, and draws upon earlier work that utilized and built upon some of the theories of Noam Chomsky. Whereas Chomskyan linguistics has limited its scope to the clause, cognitive discourse analysis attempts to go beyond such limitations by shifting from the examination of fixed linguistic signs to the way that the mind processes contextually fluid symbols. As a result, conceptual frameworks are essential to understanding whether that understanding is concerned with other semiotic systems or with the language of texts. The use of cognitive discourse models is relatively recent, but gaining in recognition in the work of such scholars as van der Merwe and Ellen van Wolde.

As noted above, NT scholars have come later to the use of modern linguistics. Nevertheless, within the field of NT studies, there are five approaches to discourse analysis that are regularly employed: *tagmemics*, *Systemic Functional Linguistics*, *continental discourse analysis*, *South African colon analysis*, and an eclectic approach that draws upon literary criticism. Save for the last, each of these approaches is relatively distinct.

The Summer Institute of Linguistics (SIL, a sister organization of Wycliffe Bible Translators) has often used a form of *tagmemics* in their discourse analysis. Tagmemics is a functional, hierarchical (it has a recognizable hierarchy of units of language), and stratal (it recognizes various levels within language) model of language based upon slots and their fillers, developed by the linguist Kenneth Pike. Robert Longacre has probably been the major figure in developing such a discourse model that has been applied to the study of the Bible, including the NT. Longacre's approach to discourse is sometimes called *grammatical*, in that he sees units at various levels as primarily grammatical in structure even if they have semantic functions. The result is what is often called a supersentential view of discourse, in which larger discourse units are seen as based upon the analogy of the construction of a sentence. This approach is also often characterized as a top-down model, which moves from larger context to text types to analysis of smaller units.

The second approach is based upon Hallidayan *Systemic Functional Linguistics*, and so has some similarities to tagmemics in its functional and stratal orientation. This approach probably represents the most active group of discourse analysts within contemporary NT studies, including scholars such as Jeffrey Reed, Cynthia Long Westfall, and Stanley Porter. Reed has outlined a direct application of the categories of Systemic Functional Linguistics to the NT, while more recent work has recognized that Greek must provide the parameters for development of its own functional categories. The OpenText.org project, which has linguistically analysed and tagged the entire Greek NT up to the clause complex level, is based upon the system and structure approach of Systemic Functional Linguistics. This includes equating the various systems and structures with elements of the three metafunctions noted above (ideational, interpersonal, textual).

Continental discourse analysis encompasses a wide range of approaches to discourse. Such discourse analysis is still often referred to as *textlinguistics* because of its focus upon specific elements found in the text. Such discourse analysis includes much work done by Scandinavian scholars, such as Birger Olsson, who constitute their own identifiable group within this wider continental approach. Characteristic of continental discourse analysis is the distinction between semantics and pragmatics, a standard distinction within much general linguistics including continental functionalist linguistics. Continental discourse analysis, especially the Scandinavian variety, often also includes rhetorical criticism within its scope. Communication theory based upon the work of Roman Jakobson is also often found incorporated into such a discourse model. The result is an amalgamation of various linguistic categories.

The *South African colon analysis* of discourse is attributed to the work of J. P. Louw and constitutes a unique contribution of South African NT scholarship. Louw defines the COLON, which consists of a subject and its verb, as the minimal unit of discourse structure. Louw's approach to language draws heavily upon early phrase structure grammar developed by Chomsky and then attempts to find larger relationships among these phrase structure units, called cola. These cola are identified and analysed, and then seen in their conceptual relationships to each other. These groupings of cola form meaning units that are then further linked together to constitute the entire discourse.

The final approach to NT discourse analysis is an eclectic catch-all for a variety of approaches. George Guthrie characterizes this eclectic approach by drawing upon different types of discourse analysis, such as

Halliday and Ruqaiya Hasan's work on *cohesion*, and then supplementing it by drawing upon interpretive tools in areas such as RHETORIC and especially literary criticism. The result, for the most part, is an assemblage of various interpretative techniques used according to textual interpretative necessity. There is also a resulting focus upon what might be called the *textual dimension* of language, as many of the interpretative techniques address questions of what makes a text a text, such as its cohesion or how it holds together. Other eclectic approaches, illustrated by the work of Stephen Levinsohn, draw upon cognitive and functional categories, emphasizing how the mind processes language and the functions that language performs.

Most discourse studies of the Bible (both the Hebrew Bible and the NT) are concerned with written texts, rather than oral discourse. Even those that utilize such approaches as Conversation Analysis or ethnography of communication tend to focus upon written texts. This does not have to be the case, although discourse analysis by nature tends to concentrate upon extant texts and not upon hypothetical reconstructions. Nevertheless, discourse analysis of the Bible is in its relatively early stages and will no doubt continue to develop in a variety of ways.

Stanley E. Porter (McMaster Divinity College, Canada)

Further Reading

Bodine, Walter R., ed. 1995. *Discourse Analysis of Biblical Literature: What it is and What it Offers*. SemeiaSt. Atlanta: Scholars Press.
Gee, James Paul, and Michael Handford, eds. 2012. *The Routledge Handbook of Discourse Analysis*. London: Routledge.
Merwe, Christo H. J. van der. 1994. 'Discourse Linguistics and Biblical Hebrew Grammar'. In *Biblical Hebrew and Discourse Linguistics*. Edited by Robert D. Bergen. Dallas: Summer Institute of Linguistics, pp. 13–49.
Merwe, Christo H. J. van der. 2003. 'Some Recent Trends in Biblical Hebrew Linguistics: A Few Pointers Towards a More Comprehensive Model of Language Use'. *Hebrew Studies* 44: 7–24.
Partridge, Brian, and Ken Hyland, eds. 2011. *The Bloomsbury Companion to Discourse Analysis*. London: Bloomsbury.
Porter, Stanley E., and Andrew W. Pitts. 2008. 'New Testament Greek Language and Linguistics in Recent Research'. *CBR* 6(2): 214–55.
Schiffrin, Deborah. 1994. *Approaches to Discourse*. Oxford: Blackwell.
Schiffrin, Deborah, Deborah Tannen, and Heidi E. Hamilton, eds. 2001. *The Handbook of Discourse Analysis*. Oxford: Blackwell.
Wolde, Ellen van, ed. 1997. *Narrative Syntax and the Hebrew Bible*. Biblical Interpretation Series 29. Leiden: Brill.

Drama (Greco-Roman) Drama is an event, not a GENRE: it is a mode of presenting a story in a performance format. The word drama is derived from the Greek verb *draō* ('to do' or 'to act') and entails the enactment of a plot through gestures and/or speech and the impersonation of characters by actors. The word is often appropriated in theological studies to describe the enactment of God's plan for humanity or action in a narrative that is particularly fraught with tension, violence, or twists and turns. In the context of the present discussion, *drama* refers more narrowly to biblical research that draws on the study of theatre and performance texts, the scripts for drama, particularly those of ancient Greece and Rome.

Literary Criticism

While dramatic texts do not rank among the genres initially recognized by biblical form critics, students of biblical narrative often turn to Aristotle's *Poetics* as a starting point for plot analysis. Aristotle identified the elements of plot largely with reference to Sophocles' tragedies, particularly *Oedipus Tyrannus*; since *Poetics* has been foundational to Western literary criticism, Greco-Roman drama has inherently played a significant role in the study of narrative. Aristotle's delineation of *anagnorisis* (the sudden recognition of the identity or situation of the protagonist by the protagonist or another character with power over his or her fate), *peripateia* (a reversal of fortune and/or relationships), and *pathos* (an action that causes distress or leads to destruction) as central plot elements have influenced the way that many scholars read biblical narrative (e.g. Culpepper 1983; Sternberg 1987). Given their tight economy, dramatic pieces are foundational for distilling the ingredients that produce suspense and evoke powerful emotions such as fear and pity.

The application of the study of Greek tragedy to the study of the Bible need not be limited to plot. For example, scholars of the Gospel of John have found an affinity between Greek tragedy and the way the Fourth Evangelist frames his work with a prologue (Jn 1.1-18) and epilogue (John 21), structures his action around exits and entrances, and punctuates action with the comments of the narrator and crowds. The study of the role of the tragic chorus provides insights into the function of crowds in the Synoptic Gospels and the chorus of angels and elders in the book of Revelation. James L. Blevins even suggests that the setting of the seven acts through which the action of the book of Revelation unfolds was informed by the physical layout of the theatre in Ephesus, where the book was presumably written (1984: 393–408).

At least three Hebrew Bible texts – Job, Song of Songs, and Psalm 118 – bear close affinity to plays. The earliest dates for the book of Job place its composition before the flowering of Greek drama, but scholars have long recognized that its structure is very much that of a play, with the dialogue of the characters as the central action. References to gestures, such as Job's statement 'I lay my hand on my mouth' (40.4), are perhaps performance cues, and the thematic focus on suffering makes conversation with scholarship on Greek tragedy meaningful. Origen (ca. 185–254 CE), and subsequently other Christian readers, finds unity in the Song of Songs by seeing its structure as a nuptial poem in dramatic form. While this conclusion may have been influenced by familiarity with Greco-Roman dramatic literature, Marvin Pope agrees that the work's narrator serves as a character within a drama comprised of dialogue without 'introductory statements or transitional directions' (1977: 35).

The action of Greco-Roman theatre is found in speech, frequently in a battle of words known as an *agōn*. Study of the debates between Jesus and his antagonists in the Gospel of John has benefited from comparison to classical performance texts, and biblical scholars have also turned to the form of Greek dialogue in order to understand the progression of prophetic discourse (see PROPHECY). For example, the long monologues of prophets such as Jeremiah lend themselves to dramatic analysis. Students of biblical RHETORIC who seek to school themselves in the techniques of ancient rhetoric find verbal duels of the Greco-Roman stage instructive.

Scholars have resisted arguments based upon a direct genetic relationship between Greek drama and the biblical literature, but beginning with the Renaissance recovery of Attic drama, scholars and theologians have read the biblical narratives against the backdrop of tragedy. Tragic plots expose the fragility of the façade of public life and delve into the private realm of the household and inner life of individuals from Greek history and myths. Readings of Euripides' *Iphigenia at Aulis* awoke a propensity to see parallels with the story of Jephthah's daughter (Judges 11) that was translated successfully for the stage by George Buchanan in 1554. Similar intertextual readings of Sophocles' *Antigone* draw attention to the pathos in the action and speech of characters such as Saul in 1 Sam. 14.24-15.35 and Rizpah in 2 Sam. 21.10.

The absence of the distinctive metre of Greek tragedies and comedies in Hellenistic Jewish and Christian literature speaks against a direct linguistic relationship. Yet abundant evidence exists to suggest that Late Second Temple Jews and early Christians were well aware of the Greco-Roman theatrical tradition. Polemics against going to theatre abound in the writings of the church fathers and Talmudic rabbis. Rabbi Akiba (ca. 40–137 CE) comments that 'he who trills his voice in the chanting of the Song of Songs in the BANQUET halls and makes it like an ordinary song has no share in the world to come' (*t. Sanh.*12.10; quoted in Pope 1977: 19). Tertullian devoted his treatise *de Spectaculis* (ca. 197–202 CE) to dissuading Christians from attending public entertainments, but polemics such as these become evidence that Jews and Christians did partake of such entertainment. One Jewish play from the Second Temple period survives, albeit only in fragments – Ezekiel the Tragedian's *Exagōgē* (ca. second century BCE). Philo of Alexandria notes that he attended the theatre with some frequency (*On Drunkenness* 177) and reports having seen one of Euripides' plays (*That Every Good Person is Free* 141).

Even if one abstained from attending performances in the theatres that Roman engineering supplied to nearly every population centre in its empire, the average person would be well acquainted with images from the plays on decorated vases and walls. Tragedy even supplied content to funerary inscriptions that compared the virtues of individuals to those of characters such as Euripides' *Alcestis*. Any early Jewish or Christian author with a HELLENISTIC EDUCATION would have read selections from the Greek tragedies in their study of rhetoric. Louis Feldman (1999: 179–85) has detected Josephus' dependence upon Greek tragedy in his rewriting of the biblical narrative for a Hellenistic audience, particularly in his treatment of men who 'once they attain to power and sovereignty, then, stripping off all those qualities and laying aside their habits and ways as if they were stage masks, they assume in their place audacity, recklessness, contempt for things human and divine' (*Antiquities* 6.264; LCL). Feldman notes Josephus' distinctive use of the word 'hubris' to describe humanity's essential flaw (e.g. *Antiquities* 5.200) increased emphasis upon dramatic expression of emotion, frequent infusion of irony, representation of Solomon as a Jewish Oedipus through the appropriation of elements of Sophocles' play in the narrative of the two prostitutes (*Antiquities* 8.30), as well as dependence upon *Oedipus at Colonus* in the portrayal of the disappearance of Elijah (*Antiquities* 9.28).

Performance and Ritual Studies

Theatre criticism has evolved into a new school of analysis called *performance studies* that has broadened our understanding of what constitutes drama and encourages the application of the descriptive tools from various methodologies such as structuralism and ritual analysis to a wide array of social and cultural events. The increased awareness that the biblical literature was published and disseminated within an oral culture (i.e. the majority of people would have heard Scripture read or recited rather than reading it themselves) has led to the recognition that biblical works, like drama, are performance pieces (see PERFORMANCE OF THE GOSPELS; TORAH READING). Familiarity with the conventions of plays helps silent readers become mindful of the elements in biblical literature of all genres that facilitate oral reception. Whitney Shiner's *Proclaiming the First Gospel: First-Century Performance of Mark* (2003) is a landmark study of the cues within the Gospel and the social context, including Hellenistic theatre, for its performance. Attunement to the Scripture as a text to be read or recited aloud to an audience expands the focus upon the meaning of words to their sound and persuasive power.

Western theatre's origin lies in ritual. Greek tragedies and comedies were performed beginning in the seventh century BCE during festivals in honour of the god Dionysius. Roman plays seem to have first been performed in honour of Jupiter at the Etruscan festival of Ludi Romani, also in the seventh century. The earliest Christian theatre, the passion plays, began as tropes inserted into the Easter liturgy by the Benedictines of St. Gallen in the tenth century CE. Beyond this historical relationship, scholars of ritual studies such as Victor Turner have turned to theatre studies to inform their language of analysis. Israelite liturgy is inherently dramatic insofar as it is a performance piece in a cultic drama. Psalm 118 functions as a script that guides a performance. The principal performer, the priest, directs other participants to recite their lines (see Ps. 118.2-4) and to enact the directions given in his lines: 'Open to me the gates of the righteous that I may enter through them. … This is the gate of the Lord; the righteous shall enter through it' (118.19-20; see also 27b). A number of other psalms, including Psalms 18, 89, and 101, have comparable elements. Similarly, scholars such as

Larry Hurtado (2003) have drawn attention to how Christian ritual practices may have shaped NT texts, suggesting that the intersection between dramatic performance and Christian Scripture remains a promising avenue of research.

Social History

Illustrations of ancient Israelite dramatic performances lie embedded within the biblical narratives, particularly prophetic narratives. The Prophets contain examples of what might best be called 'street theater', in which the prophet enacted his oracle. God instructs Ezekiel to perform a play in which he lays siege to a brick that represents Jerusalem (4.1-3; see also Jer. 13.1-7; 19.1-13; 27.1-7; Ezek. 5.1-4; 12.1-6). Similarly, Elisha, on his deathbed, tells King Joash to enact his message of victory over Aram by shooting an arrow through an open window (2 Kgs 13.15-19). While Hebrew authors provide very little evidence with which to reconstruct the games and entertainments of Israelite society, these prophetic dramas suggest that something like modern pantomimes were not unknown – otherwise the prophet's audience would have been perplexed by descriptions of dramatizations.

Another fruitful avenue of study that is just beginning to open up is the examination of the Roman comedies, not so much because of their form (although this may yet prove fruitful) but because of what the comedies reveal about the attitudes and understanding of Greco-Roman society. Scholars of Roman social history often contend that Roman comedy and the popular mimes (short sketches, some of which parodied Christian stories and rituals) not only reflected but also influenced society's morals. Paul's language of the fool and the representation of slavery, wives, widows, and homosexuality have been illuminated by examining the plays of Plautus and Terence. Reading the PASSION NARRATIVES in concert with Roman comedy, the only other body of literature that gives as much attention to crucifixion has become requisite to understanding the mocking of the crowds and the reception of the story of Jesus' death within the Greco-Roman world. Biblical scholarship has much to learn from what these plays reveal about Roman legal, political, and religious institutions.

Jo-Ann A. Brant (Goshen College, USA)

Further Reading

Blevins, James L. 1984. *Revelation as Drama*. Nashville: Broadman.
Culpepper, R. Alan. 1983. *Anatomy of the Fourth Gospel: A Study in Literary Design*. Philadelphia: Fortress.
Feldman, Louis H. 1999. *Josephus's Interpretation of the Bible*. Hellenistic Culture and Society 27. Berkeley: University of California Press.
Hurtado, Larry W. 2003. *At the Origins of Christian Worship: The Context and Character of Earliest Christian Devotion*. Grand Rapids: Eerdmans.
Pope, Marvin. 1977. *Song of Songs*. Anchor Yale Bible Commentary 7C. Garden City: Doubleday.
Shiner, Whitney. 2003. *Proclaiming the First Gospel: First-Century Performance of Mark*. Harrisburg: Trinity Press International.
Sternberg, Meir. 1987. *The Poetics of Biblical Narrative: Ideological Literature and the Drama of Reading*. Bloomington: Indiana University Press.

Dundes, Alan Alan Dundes (1934–2005) was an internationally acclaimed American folklorist and anthropologist at the University of California at Berkeley whose vast array of studies was informed to a large degree by the application of Freudian psychology to the interpretation of a wide range of FOLKLORE GENRES among such diverse peoples as Native Americans, African Americans, Germans, Italians, Turks, Christians, Muslims, Jews, and Indians. He was especially influential on his numerous students and generations of folklorists throughout the world who looked at him as a master instructor, a major theoretical and pragmatic scholar, and a champion of engaged and at times controversial scholarship based on multilingual and comparative work. Again and again Dundes made the point that folklore studies need to be based on cross-cultural identification of folklore items followed by an analytical interpretation of these multifaceted references.

His voluminous oeuvre can best be divided into three major categories:

1. Structural analysis, including studies on the relationship of folklore and culture, literature, folktales, stereotypes, folk speech, PROVERBS, investigations informed by structuralism which also include innovative interpretations based on a plethora of folklore references from different times, cultures, languages, and ethnicities;
2. Worldview, resulting in studies on the lineal (future-oriented) worldview in American folk speech, the attitudes expressed in fairy tales, sexuality as underlying motifs in folktales, the view of others in jokes, and the outlooks of certain folk groups (physicians, lawyers, scholars, sailors) on life in general and their social realms and IDENTITY in particular;
3. Symbolism, including contributions on the psychological significance of the cockfight, American football, *latrinalia*, the blood libel legend as a traditional expression of anti-Semitism, the motif of the wandering Jew, the flood myth, arguing that folklore references more often than not can be interpreted from a psychoanalytical point of view as a sign of projective inversion.

All of this led Alan Dundes quite naturally to a look at ancient WISDOM literature and folklore as it is expressed in the Bible, the Qur'an, and other religious accounts, especially creation myths. His major argument is that the multiple books of the Bible, for example, the Synoptic Gospels, fit perfectly well into the definition of folklore, that is, that any originally orally transmitted text exists in a number of variants (see PLURIFORMITY). As is typical for Dundes' meticulous scholarship, he amasses numerous narratives and proverbs and shows how they frequently reappear in varied form in both the Hebrew Bible and NT. Some texts, especially proverbs, also are part of the Qur'an, indicating clearly that the holy books are at least in part based on traditional wisdom literature of the Middle East. With these investigations, it is not Dundes' intent to question the religious messages and beliefs of Christianity, Islam, and Judaism, but rather to show that the established textual approach of FORM CRITICISM is not enough with its comparative analysis of these similar texts. After all, the components of traditional folklore were being transmitted orally and in written form long before they found their all-pervasive written expression in these Scriptures.

Wolfgang Mieder (University of Vermont, USA)

Further Reading

Dundes, Alan, ed. 1988. *The Flood Myth*. Berkeley: University of California Press.

Dundes, Alan, ed. 1989. *Folklore Matters*. Knoxville: University of Tennessee Press.

Dundes, Alan, ed. 1990. 'The Hero Pattern and the Life of Jesus'. In *In Quest of the Hero*. Edited by Robert A. Segal. Princeton: Princeton University Press, pp. 179–223.

Dundes, Alan, ed. 1991. *The Blood Libel Legend*. Madison: University of Wisconsin Press.

Dundes, Alan, ed. 1999. *Holy Writ as Oral Lit: The Bible as Folklore*. Lanham: Rowman & Littlefield.

Dundes, Alan, ed. 2002. *The Shabbat Elevator and Other Sabbath Subterfuges: An Unorthodox Essay on Circumventing Custom and Jewish Character*. Lanham: Rowman & Littlefield.

Dundes, Alan, ed. 2003. *Fables of the Ancients? Folklore in the Qur'an*. Lanham: Rowman & Littlefield.

Dundes, Alan, ed. 2007. *The Meaning of Folklore: The Analytical Essays of Alan Dundes*. Edited by Simon J. Bronner. Logan: Utah State University Press.

E

Early Christian Catechism A *catechism* is a manual used for teaching or learning Christian faith, and the word is derived from the Greek *katechein,* meaning 'to teach' or 'to instruct'. While no manual could have existed in the first generation or two of those who followed Jesus, Paul and the other apostles attempted to bring into their faith the Jews and Gentiles that they met, and they did this by teaching and preaching. The word *catechumen,* in the technical sense of one who receives instruction in Christian faith, first appears in the second century in the writings of Clement of Alexandria (*Stromata* 2.95.3-96.2) and numerous times in the writings of Tertullian.

In the first century, there may have been very little catechesis prior to BAPTISM. Acts 8:20-40 tells of the baptism of an Ethiopian eunuch, which followed almost immediately upon his expression of faith. Paul writes that believers should 'present your bodies as a living sacrifice … which is your spiritual worship … [and] be transformed by the renewing of your minds' (Rom. 12.1-2). The connection between spiritual transformation of body and sacrifice may be based on Isa. 1.10-20, but Paul emphasizes faith in the meaning of Christ's life and death more than knowledge of particular texts.

The earliest written guide to Christian faith is the Didache ('Teaching of the Apostles'), probably written in the first century CE. The first six chapters teach of the 'Two Ways: one of life and one of death', specifying the acts that epitomize the way of life and thus are to be emulated, as well as those sins that lead one to the way of death. These chapters may have originated separately from the rest of the *Didache,* which includes instructions about Christian rituals (baptism, FASTING, prayer, and EUCHARIST) and leadership roles (teachers, prophets, Apostles, bishops). The final chapters of the Epistle of Barnabas (18-20) offer a parallel version of the Two Ways, and an earlier version can be found in the DEAD SEA SCROLLS (1QS 3.13–4.26). The Didache's placement of the teachings of the Two Ways as a prelude to baptism suggests that these teachings constituted a form of catechesis in the early church. This model is confirmed by a reference to catechesis preceding baptism in the writings of Justin Martyr (*Apology* 61). Scripture certainly informed the composition of the teachings in the first six chapters of Didache; while there is little direct quotation of Scripture, most of the teachings are expansions and interpretations of biblical commandments.

Even in the early church, there may have been more than one way of teaching about Christian faith. In the Shepherd of Hermas (Vision 2.4.3), Hermas sees a vision of an old woman, representing the Church. She tells him:

> But when I finish all the words, all the elect will then become acquainted with them through you. You will write therefore two books, and you will send the one to Clemens and the other to Grapte. And Clemens will send his to foreign countries, for permission has been granted to him to do so. And Grapte will admonish the widows and the orphans. But you will read the words in this city, along with the presbyters who preside over the Church.

In other words, there may have been different catechetical groups for different people, at least in Rome.

For the earliest Christians, a life 'in Christ' (to use Pauline terminology) was probably expressed in action and ritual. Thus, Didache begins, 'The way of life, then, is this: First, you shall love God who made you; second, love your neighbor as yourself, and do not do to another what you would not want done to you. And of these sayings the teaching is this: Bless those who curse you, and pray for your enemies, and fast for those who persecute you.' These teachings clearly parallel Mt. 22.37-39 (Mk 12.30-31; cf. Deut. 6.4-5; Lev. 19.18), Mt. 7:12 (Lk. 6.31), and Mt. 5.44 (Lk. 6.27-28), although Didache does not explicitly quote any written sources. Tertullian, writing in the late second century, used Scripture to explain the process of preparing for baptism (*On Baptism* 20):

> Those about to enter on Baptism should supplicate with frequent prayers, fastings, genuflections and vigils, and with confession of all their past sins, that they may set forth the baptism of John also: 'they were baptized,' we are told, 'confessing their sins' (Mt. 3:6). We must be congratulated if we now in presence of the congregation confess our iniquities or meannesses. For we are at one and the same time both making an apology for the past with a struggle between flesh and spirit, and raising up beforehand defences against the trials that are to follow. 'Watch and pray,' he says, 'lest ye fall into a testing situation' (Mt. 26:40-56). And the reason, I believe, why they were tested was that they fell asleep, with the result that they failed the Lord after His arrest, and that he who continued with Him and made use of a sword, actually denied Him thrice; for the saying also had preceded, that no untried person would attain the heavenly realms.

Most early Christian teaching would have been experienced orally, in private teaching or through preaching in the church setting. Still, the experience of catechesis would have been physical and emotional as well as intellectual.

A more detailed curriculum of study can be found in the *Apostolic Tradition*, a collection associated with Hippolytus of Rome (170–235 CE), though including traditions from the third and possibly fourth centuries. This text was used to compose several later church orders, including the *Apostolic Constitutions*, the *Canons of Hippolytus*, and the *Testamentum Domini*. The *Apostolic Tradition* begins the instruction of new catechumens with Scripture: 'Those who are newly brought forward to hear the Word shall first be brought before the teachers at the house, before all the people enter' (15.1). Similarly, according to the *Canons of Hippolytus*, Christian education begins as one is 'instructed in the Scriptures' (10.1). No early Christian text offers a curriculum of study, though the *Apostolic Tradition* has a three-year catechumenate, perhaps to afford enough time to hear the whole Bible read aloud and discussed. Later texts spell out the proper steps for a catechumen, including credal statements, Exorcisms, and renunciations of Satan, as well as lists of vices forbidden to a baptized Christian. The earliest formal collection of catechetical instruction is by Cyril of Jerusalem (313–386 CE).

Marcie Lenk (Shalom Hartman Institute, Israel)

Further Reading

Bradshaw, Paul F. 2002. *The Search for the Origins of Christian Worship*. 2nd edn. Oxford: Oxford University.

Dujarier, Michel. 1979. *The Rites of Christian Initiation: Historical and Pastoral Reflections*. Edited and translated by Kevin Hart. New York: Sadlier.

Whitaker, E. C., and Maxwell E. Johnson. 2003. *Documents of the Baptismal Liturgy Revised and Expanded Edition*. Collegeville, MN: Liturgical Press.

Early Christian Literature Early Christian texts offer many insights into the intersection between written documents and other means of communication in the early Christian movement(s). This entry concentrates on texts traditionally considered *Christian literature* – that is, written documents produced by people who would have considered themselves to be followers of Jesus, even if they did not use the term *Christian* as a self-designation. Further, although any text written by such a person could be considered *Christian literature* (including, e.g. love LETTERS, bureaucratic documents, copies of Homer, and grocery lists), the following examples are drawn from texts whose content or reception history suggests that they would have resonated particularly with Jesus-followers in connection with that aspect of their IDENTITY.

Intersections between Written and Oral/Aural Communication

In the early second century, PAPIAS, the bishop of Hierapolis, had access to both written and oral accounts of the teachings of Jesus and his followers. A statement from the preface of one of his works is included in Eusebius' *Ecclesiastical History* (fourth century CE).

> I do not hesitate to arrange for you, along with the interpretations, everything I have ever carefully learned from the presbyters and carefully recalled, affirming their truth. For I have not taken pleasure in those who have a lot to say, like most people, but in those who teach the truth; nor in those who recall the commandments of others, but in those [who recall the commandments] the Lord has given to the faith, which derive from truth itself. Whenever anyone came who had been a follower of the presbyters, I inquired about the words of the presbyters, what Andrew or Peter had said, or Philip or Thomas or James or John or Matthew or any of the Lord's other disciples, and about what is said by Aristion and the presbyter John, the disciples of the Lord. For I did not think that things from books would benefit me as much as things from a living and surviving voice. (*Ecclesiastical History* 3.39.3-4)

Writing around 120 CE, Papias knows of 'books' – perhaps Gospels – that discuss matters of interest to 'the faith', and has also had personal contact with 'presbyters' who had themselves met apostles and first-generation disciples of Jesus. He considers 'a living and surviving voice' more beneficial than written texts, although he expresses concern that not all 'voices' faithfully transmit 'the truth'. Despite his preference for oral/aural communication, however, Papias seems to feel that the accessibility of a reliable ORAL TRADITION about Jesus is fading as time passes, or at least that it is not as universally available as he would like. He therefore chooses to write down his own 'interpretations' and the things he has learnt (orally) from the presbyters in books.

Texts from earlier Jesus-followers also demonstrate the essential fluidity between written and oral communication in the emerging Christian movement. For example, Paul recalls 'the gospel' concerning Christ's death and resurrection that he had received and passed on to the Corinthians, reciting it once again for their benefit. His letter preserves in written form what may have been an oral formula used by early Jesus-followers: 'Christ died for our sins according to the Scriptures. He was buried and raised on the third day according to the Scriptures. He appeared to Cephas (and then to the twelve) (1 Cor. 15:3-5).'

Based on similar formulaic elements in other NT letters, it seems that short memorized statements played an important role in the emerging movement. Among them, 1 Cor. 15.3-5 is particularly illustrative of the complex interplay between oral and written communication among early Jesus-followers. Paul's letter reminds the Corinthians in writing about a confession he had transmitted to them in person. Nor is Paul's letter itself a purely written phenomenon. He seems to have composed by speaking aloud to SCRIBES, and his letters were delivered by 'living voices' like Phoebe (Rom. 16.1-2) who presumably ensured that they were read aloud to gathered communities and who were in a position to explain their contents. Furthermore, the orally transmitted 'gospel' Paul refers to in 1 Corinthians 15 connects Christ's death and resurrection with earlier written 'Scriptures' (Paul is no doubt thinking about Greek versions of Israel's Scriptures) and Paul's letter itself, as soon as it was penned, included a written expansion on the oral 'gospel' statement referenced above: 'Last of all he appeared even to me, as if to one untimely born. For I am the least of the apostles, not fit to be called an apostle, because I persecuted the church of God. … So whether it is I or they (who preach), this is what we proclaim and what you have accepted' (1 Cor. 15.8-11).

These comments in the first-person singular can hardly have been part of a traditional confession used by Jesus-followers, and thus represent an expansion – initially oral as Paul spoke the words, then written down by a scribe, and then oral again as the letter was read aloud – on a formula that probably existed both in oral and, at least in Paul's letter, in written form.

Interplay between written and oral communication is also evident in narrative texts like the Gospels and Acts that attribute direct speech to Jesus and the apostles. The 'speeches' given by these protagonists, especially in apostle narratives, tend to be new creations rather than precise records of speeches given by historical figures. They signal the importance of oral communication in the early Christian movement, but do so in a medium that involved WRITING. In fact, while some of these 'speeches' would have had an oral life when the texts were read aloud or their stories were retold in oral form, others, especially those now extant in extra-biblical texts with a more limited circulation, may have had little existence off the written page.

One such narrative text, the Vercelli Acts of Peter, is especially intriguing because it shows ambivalence about written Gospel accounts. In the story, Peter sees a group of people reading from a 'Gospel' text. He rolls it up and says to them, 'Men who trust and hope in Christ, know how the holy Scriptures of our Lord must be proclaimed. We wrote these things by his grace, to the extent we understood. Even if they still seem feeble to you, nevertheless [we wrote] the things expressed intelligibly [as far as it was possible] to bring [them] to human flesh (Acts of Peter 20)'. In this fascinating scene, an apostle in a fictional oral dialogue acknowledges the limitations of a written account produced by the apostles. Although the larger point is that human beings cannot fully understand 'the Lord' (and not that a 'living voice' would have been better than a written account), Peter's words illustrate the complex intersection between oral and written communication in the early Christian movement. This was a movement whose members reflected consciously on the media employed in the ongoing Christian conversation, and their texts demonstrate the futility of distinguishing sharply between oral and written forms.

Intersections between Texts and Stories

Peter's 'speech' in the Acts of Peter continues with a (fictional) oral explanation of the Transfiguration story that has just been read from the Gospel SCROLL.

> Our Lord wanted me to see his majesty on the holy mountain, but when I saw the splendor of his glory, together with the sons of Zebedee, I fell down as though dead, and closed my eyes and heard his voice, such as I cannot describe. I thought I had been blinded by his splendor. Recovering my breath a little, I said to myself, 'Maybe my Lord wanted to bring me here to deprive me of my sight'. And I said, 'If that is your will, Lord, I won't object'. Giving me his hand, he raised me up, and when I had stood up I saw him again in a form I could grasp. (Acts of Peter 20)

This passage illustrates a common practice among early Jesus-followers: stories about Jesus and other figures from the past were creatively retold in new ways for new contexts. Writers and storytellers sometimes referred back to written texts (thus the Gospels of Matthew and Luke show literary dependence on Mark) and probably sometimes drew from memory on stories they had heard, read, or recounted, without consulting written documents (see STORYTELLING).

In practice, it is often difficult to tell whether a text like the Vercelli Acts of Peter reflects creative rewriting of an earlier written source (e.g. an account of the Transfiguration story from a Synoptic Gospel), recourse to a tradition that had existed from its earliest stages in oral form, or SECONDARY ORALITY, in which the producer had heard an oral version of a story that had itself been inspired by a written one (e.g. if people who had read written Transfiguration stories had begun repeating them orally). Regardless of the exact process, texts like this show the influence of a general fluidity between oral communication, written communication, and memory in the early Christian movement. Producers of such texts seem to have been thinking at the level of *stories* – that is, about basic plot outlines that had already become part of COLLECTIVE MEMORY – rather than about the details of the specific written texts in which those stories had previously been instantiated.

Another example of a text that may reflect recurrence to a story that was part of collective memory rather than active perusal of written documents is the so-called 'Unknown Gospel' of Papyrus Egerton 2, which may have originated in the middle of the second century (another fragment of the same MANUSCRIPT is known as P. Cologne 255). This narrative recounts the healing of a leper and bears some resemblance to Mk 1.40-45, Mt. 8.2-4, Lk. 5.12-16, and Lk. 17.11-19. The version in P. Egerton 2 is shorter than the Synoptic vignettes, however, and does not mention physical contact between Jesus and the leper. It also offers a more detailed explanation of how the leper contracted his illness than the Synoptic accounts and includes an injunction that he sin no more. This combination of similarities and differences presents a challenge for the conventional maxims of Redaction Criticism and FORM CRITICISM, which struggle to explain relationships between texts where each has details the other lacks. This challenge is quickly overcome, however, if one interprets the vignette in P. Egerton 2 not as a *rewriting* of a written document (or documents) but rather as a retelling of a basic storyline – that is, of a 'story' in the technical sense – and if one understands the new text as being produced without consultation of written or at least without concern for mimicking them in every detail.

Other texts also show that Jesus-followers felt free to retell stories about Jesus in new ways, drawing creatively on stories (plotlines) that were part of collective memory. The Gospel of Peter, known primarily from a fragmentary manuscript of the sixth or seventh century, probably traces in its earliest form to the second century and contains an account of Jesus' death and resurrection whose precise relationship to the canonical Gospels remains a matter of debate. Rather than referring slavishly to written Gospel texts, the producer of the Gospel of Peter seems to have taken the basic plot of the PASSION NARRATIVE, which was already part of the collective memory of Jesus-followers in the second century, and put it into a new written form. This explains why some details that overlap with the canonical Gospels seem to have no real function in the Gospel of Peter. In Peter 24, for instance, Joseph (of Arimathea) buries 'the Lord' (Jesus) in his own grave, which is called 'Joseph's garden'. The motif of Jesus' being buried in a garden is probably inspired, indirectly via secondary orality, by the Gospel of John (Jn. 19.41-42), where it serves as the backdrop for Mary Magdalene's memorable encounter with the resurrected Jesus, whom she mistakes for a gardener (Jn. 20.11-18). In the Gospel of Peter, however, the garden element has no recognizable function, nor is it evidence of a more general interest in providing these sorts of details. By including the garden motif, the producer of the Gospel of Peter is simply acknowledging the collective memory on which he or she is drawing while composing this new work.

Intersections between Texts and the Landscapes of Memory

The fluidity between early Christian media extended beyond overlap between different forms of verbal communication. Extant texts also point to regular intersection between the verbal and visual realms, including topography. By associating persons and events from the past with specific places (real or imagined) within what one might call 'landscapes of memory' (*Erinnerungslandschaften*; cf. Pierre Nora's *lieux de mémoire*), early Christian texts contributed to the development of a collective memory that was pegged to a shared cultural geography. Places like 'Joseph's garden' probably existed only on the mental map of most early Jesus-followers, especially outside of Palestine, but nevertheless would have had considerable evocative power: anytime a Jesus-follower familiar with the story entered a garden, it might remind him or her of the Passion story.

In other cases, writers associated memories with specific places known to their addressees, as indicated by a snippet from the Roman presbyter Gaius, who wrote at the turn of the third century: 'I can point out the trophies [i.e. MONUMENTS] of the apostles. For if you go to the Vatican or the Ostian Way, you will find the trophies of those who founded this church' (Eusebius, *Ecclesiastical History* 2.25.7). In this remark, Gaius ties a shared memory about the apostles to known places in Rome. Similarly, in the middle of the third century, Origen sought to connect places mentioned in biblical texts with real-world Palestine as he knew it. Unable to discover a 'Bethany beyond Jordan' (Jn. 1.28) in his own day, he decided that John the Baptist must have been baptizing in 'Bethabara' (Origen, *Commentary on the Gospel of John* 6.24). Later manuscripts of the Gospel of John that contain this reading probably reflect Origen's influence.

The *Martyrdom of Polycarp*, which dates to the same period, illustrates even more clearly the complex way in which texts intersected with a shared cultural geography in the early Christian movement. This text describes the site of Polycarp's relics as a place where his martyrdom and the deaths of other martyrs were remembered through an annual ritual.

> We took up his [Polycarp's] bones, which are more valuable than precious stones and finer than refined gold, and deposited them where it was appropriate. When we are able to gather together there with joy and rejoicing, the Lord will make it possible [for us] to observe the anniversary of his martyrdom, both in remembrance of those who have already contended and as training and preparation for those who will do so in the future. (*Martydom of Polycarp* 18.2-3)

The text mentions an annual ritual that takes place in an actual location in the 'real world' (probably Polycarp's grave or *Martyrium*), which perpetuates both his memory and that of others.

In later texts, references to known locations become increasingly frequent. Many manuscripts of the Acts of Thecla end with the announcement that Thecla 'went to Seleucia, and after having enlightened many with the word of God, slept a noble sleep' (3.43). This report, which has little to do with the preceding narrative, reflects a later stage in the development of COLLECTIVE MEMORY about Thecla, when that memory had become tied to a specific location. According to a travelogue written by a pilgrim named Egeria, there was an active cult in honour of Thecla at a site in Seleucia (today's Silifke in Turkey) in the 380s. Egeria reports that she visited the martyrium of Thecla on the way back from a visit to the Holy Land: 'When I had arrived in the name of God and a prayer had been made at the martyrium, and the Acts of St. Thecla had been read, I gave endless thanks to Christ our God' (*Itinerary of Egeria* 23.5). Extant manuscripts of the Acts of Thecla thus show how the development of a memorial to Thecla in a specific location fed back into written texts (see PILGRIMAGE).

Other stories about the apostles also mention locations where they were honoured. The version of Peter's martyrdom recounted by Pseudo-Linus, which may go back to the fourth or fifth century, mentions Peter's imprisonment in the infamous Mamertine prison, where a spring appeared, allowing him to conduct baptisms (*Martyrdom of Blessed Peter the Apostle* 5). This scene is frequently depicted on late antique sarcophagi in Rome. The Acts of Titus, which also trace to the early Byzantine period, likewise describe Titus' grave and indicate that miracles continued to occur there: 'His precious grave is an altar. Handcuffs are there with which those afflicted by unclean spirits are bound, and everyone who is found worthy to embrace the resting place of the holy one receives healing there' (Acts of Titus 11, according to Par. gr. 548). The ruins of a cathedral dedicated to Titus can still be visited in Gortyn, Crete, in the location referenced in the text.

All of these texts attest to a dynamic interaction between verbal communication and spatial *landscapes of memory* in the early Christian movement.

Intersections between Texts, Rituals, and Miracles

Early Christian texts also intersect in a complex manner with actions, both ritual and miraculous. The above citations from the *Martyrdom of Polycarp* and Egeria's travelogue illustrate two different ways in which early Christian texts intersected with the practice of ritual. The *Martyrdom of Polycarp* reports about a ritual, while Egeria's account suggests that the Acts of Thecla were themselves read aloud in a context with ritualistic overtones.

The same interplay between texts and rituals is evident in other texts. Some, like the Didache and the Syriac *Doctrine of Addai*, discuss proper ritual practice, while others incorporate material that may have been used in ritual contexts. The DANCE hymn of the Acts of John (94–96) is an example of the latter, as are NT stories of the Last Supper. In Mk 14.22, Jesus distributes bread and tells the disciples, 'Take (this). This is my body'. In Lk. 22.19, his words are elaborated: 'This is my body, which is given for you. Do this in remembrance of me'. Luke's addition shows that the Last Supper was not only remembered as a past event, but accounts of it had begun to play into a repeated ritual. This is also suggested by 1 Corinthians 11, where Paul urges the Corinthians to celebrate the Lord's Supper in a manner in keeping with the memory of Jesus, likewise mentioning the words, 'Do this in remembrance of me' (1 Cor. 11.24) (see EUCHARIST).

In other texts, miraculous deeds come to the fore. In stories about Jesus and the apostles, the protagonists' words are almost always accompanied by deeds of power that corroborate and contribute to their message. Some texts, like the Vercelli Acts of Peter, even ascribe more persuasive power to miracles than to words. The (fictional) crowds of the Acts of Peter are not persuaded by Peter's preaching, but instead by his deeds of power that Jesus is the living god (see, e.g. Acts of Peter 7, 23). Stories like this reflect the ancient conviction that seeing is a better guarantor of reliability than hearing, and ironically do so in a verbal medium, illustrating the complex interaction between verbal and visual (in this case, performative) communication in the early Christian movement.

This was an interaction that went both ways, as a story about Andrew found in a sixth-century version produced by Gregory of Tours demonstrates. The vignette recounts how a Christian woman condemned to a brothel fended off men via incessant prayer and a Gospel book placed on her chest. The book served a talismanic function and prevented potential customers from violating her (Gregory of Tours, *The Book of the Miracles of Saint Andrew the Apostle* 23).

Intersections between Texts and Other Types of Visual Communication

By discussing landscapes of memory, rituals, and miracles, we are already in the realm of visual communication, and there are also other ways in which visual and written communication intersected in the early Christian movement (see VISUAL CULTURE). Texts frequently employed visual imagery, from striking metaphors such as the church as the body of Christ (1 Cor. 12.12-31; Rom. 12.4-5) to the powerful word-pictures that populate apocalyptic texts such as the Revelation of John or the Apocalypse of Peter with its grotesque depictions of hell (see Apocalypses, early CHRISTIAN). Meanwhile, texts also influenced art. As a prominent example, among the earliest images found in Christian catacombs is the 'Good Shepherd', which was probably at least sometimes inspired by the account of Jesus' words in John 10 or a CULTURAL MEMORY that developed out of it.

Conclusion

As all these examples show, texts did not exist in a media vacuum in the early Christian movement, but were simply one aspect of a diversified, multimedia cultural discourse to which the texts themselves attest. References in texts to conversations, personal encounters, geographical locations, rituals, actions, and visual imagery witness to a fluid interplay between communicative media, a context in which 'the book' was not privileged as the only or ultimate means of communicating 'truth' even by the writers of books themselves. This could illuminate the question of why some early Jesus-followers felt free to retell stories so creatively that it sometimes takes modern persons by surprise. With such a wealth of communicative options for transmitting collective memory and 'truth' at their disposal, the early Christians did not always feel the need to privilege and protect the written word.

Tobias Nicklas (Universität Regensburg, Germany) and Julia Snyder (Universität Regensburg, Germany)

Further Reading

Davies, Stephen J. 2014. *Christ Child: Cultural Memories of a Young Jesus*. Synkrisis. New Haven: Yale University Press.

Gamble, Harry Y. 1995. *Books and Readers in the Early Church: A History of Early Christian Texts*. New Haven: Yale University Press.

Markschies, Christoph, and Hubert Wolf, eds., with Barbara Schüler. 2010. *Erinnerungsorte des Christentums*. Munich: Beck.

Nicklas, Tobias. 2016. 'New Testament Canon and Ancient Christian "Landscapes of Memory"'. *Early Christianity* 7: 5–23.

Nicklas, Tobias. 2016. 'Neutestamentlicher Kanon, christliche Apokryphen und antik-christliche "Erinnerungskulturen"'. *NTS* 62: 588–609.

Nora, Pierre, and Lawrence D. Kritzman, eds. 1996–8. *Realms of Memory: The Construction of the French Past*. Translated by Arthur Goldhammer. 3 vols. New York: Columbia University Press. (Revised and abridged translation of Pierre Nora [ed.]. 1984–92. *Les lieux de mémoire*. 7 vols. Paris: Gallimard.)

Early Christian Preaching Preaching, or public proclamation and teaching, was one of the most common ways that early Christians would have encountered the Scriptures and scriptural interpretation. While the formal structure of sermons was not developed until the fourth century or later, there is evidence that Scripture was read and interpreted publically from the very beginnings of Christianity. Preaching served to instruct believers, bring in new members, and was sometimes part of the liturgy itself. Obviously, the extant evidence of ancient preaching is literary, challenging us to reconstruct oral performances from later edited texts.

Philo refers to scriptural reading and interpretation in the synagogue (*Apology* 7.12), though it is likely that this interpretation was more of a translation than an independent discourse (see TARGUMS). According to the Gospels, Jesus taught groups large and small, but there are a number of methodological challenges to including these teachings in the category of Christian preaching. First, Jesus was a Jew speaking to mostly Jewish audiences. The term *Christian* was not used until at least a generation after his death. Second, it is notoriously difficult to distinguish between Jesus' own words and the words put into his mouth decades later by the writers of Gospels. Third, even in cases where the Gospels might accurately record sayings of Jesus, often the same teaching is preserved differently in each Gospel, making it difficult to ascertain the form of these sermons as Jesus himself would have delivered them. One of the best examples is the so-called 'Sermon on the Mount' (Matthew 5–7): most of the teachings in Matthew's Sermon on the Mount are found scattered in different parts of the other Gospels (cf. Mk 4.21-25; Lk. 6.17-7.1; 11.2-4, 33-34; 12.22-34;14.34-35), and none of the others have a story of Jesus preaching on a mountain.

The Gospels are therefore better used as evidence of preaching practices from the latter decades of the first century, reflections of the ways that early Christian preachers themselves taught and also envisioned Jesus teaching. For example, in the 'antitheses' in the Sermon of the Mount (Mt. 5.21-48), Jesus begins with biblical laws and proceeds to insist that his ethic and expectation is much stricter. Similarly, rabbis in the second and third centuries spoke of 'building a fence around the Torah' to ensure that the scriptural laws would not be violated (*m. Avot* 1.1). In this way, the Sermon on the Mount reflects a form of biblical interpretation best known from the end of the first century and later. Similarly, Lk. 4.16-30 (cf. Mk 6.1-6) tells of Jesus reading Isa. 6.1-2 from a scroll in the synagogue in Nazareth, and interpreting those verses by saying, 'Today this scripture has been fulfilled in your hearing'. Listeners are thus instructed to properly interpret the Scripture, in this case as being fulfilled in their own times. This type of interpretation was also found in the PESHER scrolls at Qumran, where prophecies of Nahum, Habakkuk, and Isaiah, among others, were interpreted as referring to events in the lifetimes of the Qumran community.

While the act of proclamation did not always include reference to Scripture, it often did, whether through explicit quotation, paraphrase, or allusion. Paul's LETTERS, which are full of preaching and proclamation, were intended to be read aloud to the community. Though there is no evidence of Paul's words following formal reading of Scripture, this collection of letters is a valuable source of scriptural interpretation through the medium of preaching. For example, in Rom. 10.5-10 Paul quotes and interprets Deut. 30.12-13 to teach that faith and the proclamation of Christ will bring true salvation (the context in Deuteronomy 30, as well as rabbinic interpretation in *b. Bava Metzi'a* 59b, would lead to a different interpretation of those verses). In Gal. 4.21–5:1, Paul alludes to the story of Sarah and Hagar in Genesis 16 and 21 to argue that those in Christ are 'children of the promise, like Isaac', while those who insist on the obligation of the Law are children of Hagar, the slave woman, born into slavery (see PAULINE LITERATURE).

Preaching appears to have had a place in early Christian liturgical contexts (see WORSHIP, EARLY CHRISTIAN). For example, in Phil. 2.6-11 Paul appears to be citing an earlier liturgical poem (the *kenosis*/self-emptying hymn) that evokes the scriptural motifs of the creation of Adam and Eve (Genesis 1–3), the Suffering Servant (Isa. 52.13-53.12) and pre-existent divine Wisdom (Prov. 1.20-33; 8-9) to develop the image of a humble Christ who 'emptied' himself of all honour and power (see also HYMNS).

As early Christian community practice developed, preaching came to be explicitly referenced and discussed in written texts. The Pastoral Epistles instruct leaders to connect public reading of Scripture to exhortation and teaching (1 Tim. 4.11-16; 2 Tim. 4.2), and these practices are mentioned in the writings of Justin Martyr (*1 Apology* 67): 'Then when the reader has finished, the Ruler in a discourse instructs and exhorts to the imitation of these good things.' Similarly, Ignatius of Antioch (*Magnesians* 14.1) refers to himself as 'preacher', and Tertullian (*Apology* 39.3) writes of *exhortio* in the assembly, based on the Scriptures and intended to build up the faith, hope, and Christian practice of the hearers. The Acts of John mentions a liturgy that includes a homily, addressed 'to the brothers'.

Other early Christian texts seem to be written versions of preaching. Thus, *2 Clement* is an exhortation to repentance, combining and interpreting verses from the prophets, Gospels, and Acts in order to bring readers and listeners to leave worldly values to achieve repentance and purity. Melito's *Peri Pascha* is a liturgy that would have been performed at Easter vigil, using the story and text of Exodus to reject Jewish practices and recognize the meaning of Christ's death and resurrection.

In Syriac-speaking churches in the East, there was a blurring of categories between a chanted liturgy and a formal sermon. Lessons might have been experienced in song or in the spoken word. Thus one must be cautioned against applying easy categories to texts that may have been used in various ways, or assuming that the lack of reference to a sermon or homily means that Scripture was not used for instruction. Only by the third and fourth centuries, Greek rhetorical training was applied by Christian preachers in the West, and the formal sermon or homily began to take shape.

Marcie Lenk (Shalom Hartman Institute, Israel)

Further Reading

Christopher, A. Hall. 1998. *Reading Scripture with the Church Fathers*. Downers Grove, IL: InterVarsity Press.

Hays, Richard B. 1989. *Echoes of Scripture in the Letters of Paul*. New Haven, CT: Yale University Press.

Mayer, Wendy. 2008. 'Homiletics'. In *The Oxford Handbook of Early Christian Studies*. Edited by Susan Ashbook Harvey and David G. Hunter. Oxford: Oxford University Press, pp. 565–83.

Stewart-Sykes, A. 2001. *From Prophecy to Preaching: A Search for the Origins of the Christian Homily*. Vigiliae Christianae Supplements 59. Leiden: Brill.

Early Jewish Literature The term *early Jewish literature* typically refers to writings that can be approximately dated to the period between the conquests of Alexander the Great in the fourth century BCE and the first or second century CE, that is, before the codification of the MISHNAH around 200 CE.

This literature was composed in Hebrew, Aramaic, and Greek, in both Palestine and the Diaspora, and comprises virtually every imaginable GENRE, including texts considered divine revelation, poetic and pedagogical material, history, exegetical commentary, theological tractates, popular fiction, and even tragic drama. Studying this material brings significant challenges, particularly the risk of anachronism: there was no fixed biblical CANON at the time, and our modern concepts of books and authors, shaped by print culture, do not necessarily correspond to the way these texts and their tradents were conceived. In addition, many of the texts survive only in much later Christian contexts.

Roughly, the corpus of early Jewish literature comprises Jewish writings composed after most of the texts later collected in the Hebrew Bible and before the rise of rabbinic Judaism. However, this periodization is not exact. The biblical book of Daniel, written in the second century BCE, falls in this era (it is definitely later than important examples of early Jewish literature such as the earliest Enochic books, and contemporary with the book of JUBILEES; see also ENOCHIC TRADITIONS); and the textual forms of other biblical books (e.g. Psalms, Exodus, Jeremiah) were still in flux, so this ongoing work should be considered part of the world of early Jewish literary production. The Greek translation of the Hebrew Scriptures, completed in Alexandria during this time, may also be considered an example of early Jewish literature in its own right (Law 2013), as could parts of the NT (see SEPTUAGINT). But the term is usually used to refer to texts that are not found in most modern biblical canons. Instead, they fall into several overlapping categories: Apocrypha (e.g. Sirach, Judith, Tobit, 1 and 2 Maccabees, and the Greek additions to Esther and Daniel); Pseudepigrapha (e.g. 4 Ezra, 1 and 2 Enoch, 2 Baruch), which survive largely in Christian contexts of translation and transmission; works preserved among the DEAD SEA SCROLLS, a cache of ancient Jewish manuscripts found by the shores of the Dead Sea in 1947 (including sectarian texts, visionary literature in Aramaic, sapiential texts, collections of previously unknown psalms and prayers, and Hebrew and Aramaic originals of some Pseudepigrapha); and a large, multi-generic corpus of Greek literature by Diaspora Jews (such as Philo, Josephus, Aristobulus, the Letter of Aristeas; see Collins 2012; Feldman, Kugel, and Schiffman 2013).

This survey will consider what can be known about the early Jewish media context of these documents, including material media, languages and TRANSLATION, scribal ideology, and performance contexts and audiences.

Before Bibles and Books

It is important to note that the division between *biblical* and *non-biblical* texts is a later scholarly and theological category, and was not meaningful for early Jewish communities until at least the end of the period under consideration here. Although we encounter most early Jewish literature in books that are not included in modern print Bibles, early Jewish literature was not a group of texts distinct from the Hebrew Bible from the perspective of people living in the Hellenistic and Early Roman periods. The Hebrew Bible was not gathered into a specific, fixed collection until after the first century CE, so the literary world could not yet be divided into biblical texts and the non-biblical writings that we usually classify as early Jewish literature (Bowley and Reeves 2003; Kraft 2007; Stone 2011). Before the boundary between canonical and non-canonical texts existed, these texts participated in a differently organized literary culture.

Further, texts that we now call *biblical* were not always at the top or in the centre of the ancient literary repertoire. Texts that are not found in later canons, such as the books of Enoch or Jubilees, were highly valued in Second Temple Judaism, and there is evidence that they were received as divine revelation, no less authoritative than, for example, Genesis or Isaiah – and probably more so than some less influential texts in later biblical canons. Traditionally, much early Jewish literature that draws on older traditions is studied as biblical interpretation or REWRITTEN BIBLE. With few exceptions, however, these texts do not present themselves as rewritings or interpretations; rather they present themselves as new literature, sometimes new Scripture. Thus, we must question the seemingly self-evident hierarchies that privilege the Bible and consider non-biblical texts as its derivations, emanations, or interpretations. Instead, we can ask if biblical and non-biblical texts should instead be considered alongside one another in horizontal, rather than hierarchical, relationships to one another from the perspective of their early Jewish audiences (Reeves 2010: 139–52, especially 147; Stone 2011).

If *Bible* is an anachronistic concept for this time period, we must also question other literary concepts that are more appropriate for print culture than for early Judaism: books and AUTHORSHIP. Rather than stable textual units that we associate with the print book, we instead have evidence of fluid textual forms and collections that were rearranged and expanded over time (see Ulrich 2012). Many scholars have now abandoned the search for either an ORIGINAL or a final text for many ancient Jewish texts, considering instead, as Breed illustrates, that the processes of composition, transmission, and interpretation are not separable from one another, but part of a continuum (Breed 2014). This is not only because of the messy text-critical history of transmission, but also because of a conceptual difference in how writing was imagined: not as a product of an individual author, but as a collaborative project that draws on past heritage and holds itself open for future development (cf. discussion of the book of Ben Sira in Mroczek 2016: 103–10).

Similarly, modern concepts of authorship and intellectual property do not hold for early Judaism, or any other sector of the ancient world. Much early Jewish literature, like canonical literature, is pseudepigraphic – that is, attributed to ancient figures such as Moses, Enoch, Ezra or David. But this should not be considered forgery on the part of these texts' creators, nor as a claim about the literal, historical authorship of them by heroes from the past. The practice confers authority on new writings by placing them in the mouths of revered figures. It is also an honorific move to expand the figure's perceived legacy, and a practice in which a writer effaces his own identity to emulate an exemplary figure (Najman 2003; Reed 2008). Prominent figures like

Moses, Enoch, and David came to be the ideal figureheads of particular genres (respectively, law, visionary/apocalyptic material, and liturgy) that continued to expand in association with these patron characters (see Apocalypses, Early Jewish). The first example of a Jewish writer who placed his own name on his textual creation is Ben Sira (50:27; second century BCE), but this is not a claim to individual authorship in the modern sense. He does not appear to consider the text to be the coherent, original creation of his intellect; instead, he presents himself as a collector and teacher of a moving tradition that he compares to flowing rivers and canals, and his own text – which exists in diverse recensions – joins this dynamic process (Mroczek 2016: 90–103).

Whose Media? Problems of Mediation

A key problem in reconstructing the media life of early Jewish literature is its history of transmission. With the exception of texts found among the Dead Sea Scrolls, we do not possess a single original manuscript or early version for many of these writings. They are mediated to us through secondary means: many have survived only in much later Christian contexts, for instance, in translations that reveal extensive textual development and redaction (e.g. 4 Ezra in Syriac and Latin versions; 2 Enoch only in Slavonic); in short quotations by patristic writers, whose goal was not to preserve this literature, but to use portions of it for their own theological purposes (see Berthelot 2012: 228–53, esp. 230); or, in Christian liturgical material, such as lectionaries (e.g. 2 Baruch in Syriac manuscripts; Lied 2013: 403–28). Thus, in their extant forms, these texts may tell us less about early Judaism than about writing, reading, and reception in late antique and medieval Christian contexts (Kraft 2009; Davila 2005). Thus, scholars of early Judaism confront a different situation from, for example, Assyriologists, where the large quantity of extant material remains makes it possible to say more about scribal culture, education, and the use of texts in their ancient contexts.

The Dead Sea Scrolls and Material Forms of Writing

A major exception to the above principle is the Dead Sea Scrolls, the cache of about 1000 manuscripts in various states of preservation found in eleven caves by the shores of the Dead Sea. These manuscripts were copied between the third century BCE and the first century CE, and, according to scholarly consensus, were collected and deposited by the sectarian community who inhabited the Qumran settlement. Although some of the texts were composed and copied at Qumran, the sheer number of different scribal hands and wide range of dates for the manuscripts show that most were brought in from elsewhere, so that they can tell us about textual practices in early Judaism beyond the sect.

Judging from the scrolls, the most common writing material for literary texts in the land of Israel was parchment, while in Egypt and the Greco-Roman world, papyrus was the preferred writing material for texts of various kinds. While some literary texts written on papyrus exist among the scrolls, the medium was more common for documentary material. Tov has speculated that literary texts on papyri, considered less durable, could have been private copies for an individual's personal use (Tov 2004: 30). The most surprising writing material was copper, used for the Copper Scroll (3Q15), a list of locations where (probably legendary) treasure is hidden.

Even within the corpus of parchment sheets or scrolls, the physical forms of writing vary greatly in size, quality, and apparent purpose. On one end of the spectrum is what Tov calls 'deluxe' editions (Tov 2004: 118–22) – large format scrolls with wide margins and careful professional calligraphy, many containing scriptural texts but also works not contained in the later canon, such as the War Scroll and the Temple Scroll (the latter of which is about 9 metres long, the longest extant scroll preserved at Qumran). A few were wrapped in linen, and some of these carefully prepared and highly valued scrolls were likely stored in the ceramic jars found at Qumran (cf. Jer. 3:14 and Testament of Moses 1.17 for literary references to storing writings in jars). On the other end of the spectrum, we find poorly written scraps that may have been scribal exercises. We also find tiny scrolls, like 4QIncantation (4Q444) which is only four lines tall, as well as *tefillin* and *mezuzot*.

Soon after the time period under consideration here, a new writing technology emerged: the CODEX, which was quickly adopted by Christians – but not by Jews in this period – for their Scriptures. People have often thought of the history of writing as an evolution from cumbersome, limiting scrolls to convenient, flexible codices, with Jews retaining the inferior scroll form for nostalgic or ritualistic reasons. According to this model, the scroll imposed linear reading, and made finding specific passages impossible. With the birth of the codex, these physical limitations were overcome, replaced by new possibilities for textual manipulation (e.g. Vandendorpe 2009: 28–9). This model is sometimes used to explain why Christians were quick to adopt the new form: the codex supported and enabled early Christianity's deployment of fragments of Jewish Scriptures for exegesis and liturgy. But studying the scroll-based literary culture of early Judaism on its own terms complicates this evolutionary narrative. Selective, non-linear citation and rearrangement of textual units was not only possible but ubiquitous in early Jewish literature: the scroll form did not prohibit segmented and selective reading practices, and was not a constraining medium from the perspective of Jewish writers who produced sophisticated, deeply intertextual, dynamically developing literature (Mroczek 2011).

Languages and Script

Early Jewish literature is composed in three languages: Hebrew, Aramaic, and Greek. Since languages are themselves media, it is worth considering how these languages of composition function as modes of communication in different ways. We can begin with the multilingual milieu of ancient Palestine (Greenfield 1978; Schniedewind 2006; Fraade 2012). During the Persian period, the lingua franca of the empire was Aramaic, which had edged out Hebrew as the primary vernacular of Judaea and was the language of administrative and economic communication as well as scribal education. Aramaic (square) script had also replaced the ancient Hebrew alphabet (palaeo-Hebrew) as the usual way to write both Hebrew and Aramaic (see ORTHOGRAPHY). As the palaeo-Hebrew script became archaic and symbolic and remained morphologically static, the letter-forms of the Aramaic script, the system in constant use across the empire, continued to develop.

During the Hellenistic period, when Aramaic was no longer the language of the empire, Hebrew enjoyed a revival, especially with the rise of greater sovereignty under the Hasmonean dynasty and during the Bar Kokhbah revolt (130s CE), with Hebrew (including palaeo-Hebrew script) used on COINS. In the second century BCE, as texts now considered biblical were being copied and revised, important and sophisticated new literature was also being composed in Hebrew, including Ben Sira, Jubilees, prayers and HYMNS, and all the sectarian literature from Qumran. Aramaic texts were also composed and transmitted: the texts in 1 Enoch, the earliest of which date to at least the third century BCE, and Daniel 2–7 are perhaps the most prominent examples, but the list also includes the Genesis Apocryphon, a first-person account of the lives of Enoch, Abraham, and Noah; texts describing the visionary revelations given to ancient patriarchs; and the New Jerusalem text, a vision of a heavenly city. Many of the Aramaic texts are interested in visions, dreams, and events before the Noahic flood, perhaps suggesting a literary preference for the use of particular languages for different themes, although the distinctions are not exact or consistent (see Berthelot and Ben Ezra 2010). Multilingualism was the norm in Palestinian Judaism. Despite scholarly attempts to label one language *vernacular* and another *literary*, there is literary and epigraphic evidence for both Hebrew and Aramaic being used in both ways. The book of Daniel, for instance, switches between Hebrew (1–2.4a and 8–12) and Aramaic (2.4b–7.28) for reasons that remain unexplained.

While the vast majority of texts from Qumran, both Hebrew and Aramaic, are written in the standard square (Aramaic) script, twelve biblical texts (from the Pentateuch and Job) and three non-biblical texts are written in palaeo-Hebrew. The use of the archaic script is a highly marked communicative decision, perhaps meant to represent legitimacy and antiquity. Twenty-eight or twenty-nine manuscripts, both biblical and non-biblical, use the palaeo-Hebrew script for only the Tetragrammaton (the four-letter name of God, YHWH, usually rendered as 'Yahweh' in English translations) or the word Elohim ('God'), as a way to visually distinguish the name of God from other words. A few texts are written in even more marked ways – three different kinds of cryptic script unknown before the Qumran finds seem to reflect an attempt to limit the accessibility of texts to an even smaller initiated group.

Texts in Greek were also found among the Dead Sea Scrolls, although they make up a small minority of the corpus. Greek was the language of the Jewish Diaspora in Hellenistic Egypt and the Mediterranean basin, the former of which produced a large corpus of sophisticated literature. It was in Egypt, in the shadow of the ALEXANDRIAN LIBRARY and Hellenistic textual scholarship, that the Hebrew Scriptures were translated into Greek and that Philo of Alexandria (first century CE) wrote his philosophically inflected theological treatises and allegorical scriptural exegesis (see SEPTUAGINT). How well Philo knew Hebrew, if at all, remains a matter of debate. But, by his time, Jewish identity and literary production did not seem to necessitate a commitment to Hebrew: Greek was the language of Jewish Scripture, prayer, and theology. This valorization of Greek is reflected in the second-century BCE Letter of Aristeas, which, in its legendary account of the translation of the Law into Greek, presents the Greek translation as exactly equal in meaning and value to the Hebrew. It is deepened even more in Philo's account of the translation as a miraculous event where every translator's independent version was identical – a new divinely inspired revelation of Scripture in Greek, repeating Sinai on the Island of Pharos.

Translation in Practice and Ideology

TRANSLATION, then, was a key part of early Jewish literary production. It is in the Second Temple period that the tradition of TARGUM – Aramaic translation and embellishment of Hebrew Scriptures – began. Scholars cite Nehemiah 8, which portrays Ezra reading the scroll of the Law that is then 'translated' by his assistants, as evidence that there was a need for translation into Aramaic after the return from exile. In the later SYNAGOGUE liturgy (see LECTIONARY), the targum was recited alongside the reading of the Torah and *haftarah* (selections from prophetic books that are paired with readings from the Torah), and its role in liturgy was governed by *halakhah* (Jewish law) (see TORAH READING). Aramaic translation did take place: a fairly straightforward Aramaic translation of Job and a fragment of a targum of Leviticus was found among the Dead Sea Scrolls, and at least the Book of Tobit has survived in both Hebrew and Aramaic (as well as Greek). But there is otherwise no manuscript evidence that can be linked directly to the extant targums, whose earliest manuscripts are centuries later, and no Second Temple textual evidence of targumic recitation as a liturgical practice.

Greek translation offers important evidence for how early Jews saw the relationship between languages in practice and ideology. As mentioned above, the legendary account in the Letter of Aristeas, and later by Philo, elevate the status of the Septuagint translation to a divinely inspired text equal to the Hebrew original. But this is a later ideological development, not a description of the translation's original motivations and context. The translation itself is literalistic, attempting to mirror the formal elements of the Hebrew original. This produces an inelegant Greek document that may have originally been used in Jewish education (see EDUCATION, HELLENISTIC) to help non-proficient readers of Hebrew access the original Hebrew source – the way an interlinear Bible translation might do today – rather than to produce a stand-alone Greek composition meant to replace the Hebrew text (Pietersma 2002: 337–64; Wright 2003: 1–27). As the Greek version was disseminated and entrenched, however, ideological accounts like those in Aristeas and Philo developed, valorizing it as identical in authority and meaning to the Hebrew and an inspired version of Scripture in its own right.

Another indication of how translation was practised and theorized is found in the Greek translation and prologue to Ben Sira, studied most prominently by Wright (1989). The translator, who claims to be translating his grandfather's Hebrew text so that diaspora Jews can benefit from his wisdom, asks readers to excuse the infelicities of his translation: he says that expressions in Hebrew do not have the same kind of force when rendered into another language. Beyond his own work, he says, 'also in the case of the Law itself and the Prophets and the rest of the books the difference is not small when these are expressed in their own language'. Although the prologue is written in sophisticated Greek style, the translation itself is a somewhat clunky, unidiomatic attempt to reproduce the Hebrew.

Scribes in Myth and Ideology

We possess little evidence for the social location of SCRIBES and for the institutional contexts of their training and employment. Much of what we know about scribes comes from literary accounts, so it tells us less about social history on the ground than about ideological and legendary constructions of scribalism.

Actual scribes must have been employed in a range of functions, from preparing everyday administrative and legal documents in villages and towns to copying and composing religious texts (Schams 1998). The texts from the Judean Desert yield a few ABCEDARIES and some poorly written sheets that some scholars suggest come from scribes-in-training, but they do not tell us much about the context or curriculum of scribal education (Tov 2004). The one text adduced as evidence for a scribal school in Jerusalem is Ben Sira 51:23: 'Turn to me, you uneducated, and lodge in my house of instruction.' This line has been interpreted to mean that Ben Sira had his own school where he trained scribes. Many scholars view this reference in line with the rest of Ben Sira's text, where he praises the ideal scribe for being pious and divinely guided and presents his own version of Israel's history, to speculate on the kind of curriculum this school may have had. But Ben Sira's reference to the 'house of instruction' appears in an acrostic poem in praise of personified wisdom, a composition that also circulated independently of the book of Ben Sira (it is also found in a Psalms scroll from Qumran, 11QPsalmsa). Its poetic imagery resonates with descriptions of Wisdom and the 'house' she built in Prov. 9.1. The reference to a *beit midrash* in this poem, shot through with poetic imagery and also found in a different literary context, cannot be used to make historical claims about a specific scribal school connected to Ben Sira (Mroczek 2016: 100–3).

While the precise details of ancient Jewish scribal education are unclear, we do have a rich record of how the figure of the scribe and the act of writing functioned in the literary imagination and ideology of early Jewish writers – that is, the tales scribes told about their legendary heroes. Scribes are associated with prophetic revelation and divine contact (Sanders 2016). Ben Sira praises the scribe, the caretaker and compiler of ancestral knowledge, as a pious, divinely inspired man, and says that he himself will 'pour out teaching like prophecy'. The most prominent legendary scribe was Enoch, the seventh antediluvian patriarch who is mentioned only briefly in Genesis but who becomes a hero in the apocalyptic and astronomical texts collected as 1 Enoch and in the narrative of Jubilees. Enoch is the first human scribe, taught to write by angels and instructed to record the movements of the stars. Deathless, he is placed in the Garden of Eden, where he continues to write the deeds of humanity until the end of time. In Jubilees, almost every major character is also elevated to the status of a scribe who speaks with angels: Noah writes down medical and anti-demonic knowledge he learnt from angels; an angel teaches Abraham Hebrew, which had been lost in the confusion of tongues, and he copies the ancestral books; Jacob writes down the content of tablets of history that an angel shows him in a dream. Moses is the amanuensis of Jubilees' frame story: the entire narrative is framed as dictation by the Angel of the Presence, which Moses writes down on Sinai.

In one Qumran text, a part of a Psalms collection (11QPsalmsa col. 27), King David is described as an enlightened scribe who recites and writes thousands of psalms through the spirit of prophecy. In the first-/second-century CE apocalypse 4 Ezra, the character Ezra – a transformed version of Ezra the Scribe in Ezra-Nehemiah – drinks a cup of fire and dictates the Scriptures to a group of five scribes (who write them down without understanding the characters) in an ecstatic performance that lasts forty days and forty nights. He is then taken up into heaven. Indeed, in many texts of the Second Temple period and beyond, ancient figures associated with scribal revelation – Enoch, Moses, Baruch, Ezra, and even David – are also believed, in some traditions, to escape death, gaining a superhuman celestial existence. This motif reflects a deep ideology about writing in the early Jewish imagination – the intertwining of writing with immortality (Thomas 2001: 1.573–88).

Performance and Audience

If there was a mythical ideology connected to writing in early Jewish literature, no similar such ideology seems to exist for orality or memory. That is, there was no discourse comparable to the rabbinic idea of oral Torah vs. written Torah, or prescriptions for which texts should be preserved in writing and read from a text and which (in terms of ideology, if not practice) should be memorized and recited (see Jaffee 2001) (see Reading culture). Though there is no extended thematization or privileging of orality, a few sources present scenes where texts are recited out loud in community. In Nehemiah 8, dating from the Persian period, Ezra stands on a wooden platform and reads from a scroll of the Law all day before the entire people, including women and children, while his Levite assistants go around explaining (or translating) the reading so the people could understand. Later, in the Letter of Aristeas' account of the translation of the Law into Greek on the island of Pharos, the completed translation is read out to the entire Jewish population (Letter of Aristeas 308). In these legendary accounts, the act of reading out loud in front of the whole population entrenches the text as authoritative for and constitutive of that community.

Early Jewish writers also imagined texts being used in less grandiose ways, for communal reading, study, and discussion. In the Genesis Apocryphon's account of Abraham and Sarah's sojourn in Egypt, the Egyptians ask Abraham to share his great wisdom, and in response, he reads to them from the 'books of Enoch' (19.25). Moving from legend to instructions for community practice, the Qumran Community Rule (1QS) requires members to read (unspecified) Scriptures in nightly group sessions: they shall 'be on watch together for a third of each night of the year in order to read the book, explain the regulation, and bless together' (1QS 6:7-8). Greek Jewish writers also speak of group study of texts, including Philo in his description of the Essenes (*That Every Good Person is Free* 12.82) and a report of an adversary complaining that Jews would 'sit in [their] gatherings ... and read in security [their] holy books, expounding any obscure point and in leisurely comfort' (*On Dreams* 2.127) even in times of crisis; Josephus also mentions Sabbath gatherings at which people listen to the Law being read and explained (*Against Apion* 2.175). In his account of the Theraputae, a legendary community of pious men and women, Philo describes Sabbath gatherings that include the recitation and interpretation of texts (*Contemplative Life* 75), but also private study and composition in solitude (25, 29) on the remaining six days. While these are idealized scenarios rather than reports, they are written based on these authors' assumptions about actual reading practices.

If early Jewish literature often represents itself as revelation and education, it is also sometimes clearly marked as entertainment. One example is the genre scholars have called 'the ancient Jewish novel'. Popular novelistic literature began with Hebrew and Aramaic tales but flourished in the Greek-speaking world, with both translations and new compositions (Wills 2002; 2015). Works like Judith, Tobit, Daniel and Susannah, and Joseph and Aseneth hearken back to the characters and settings of more ancient traditions found in biblical texts but participate in the genre of Hellenistic romance writing. They have high adventure, romance, and melodrama, and often feature prominent female characters. As Wills has argued, a rise of LITERACY in Hellenistic cities among entrepreneurs, merchants, and bureaucrats – a class of literate, but not scholarly people – created a market for 'popular' literature connected to oral STORYTELLING traditions, but now circulating in written form (2015: 4). The large number of such tales and the variety of textual forms in which they survive testify to their popularity and flexibility, as these texts did not remain in any one official version but developed over time and from audience to audience.

One question broached in scholarship on ancient novels is the extent of their female readership. On the one hand, the connection between women and the ancient novel may seem to rest on stereotypical assumptions that popular, melodramatic writing must be women's literature. On the other hand, we must consider that there were educated upper-class women in the Hellenistic Jewish world and that they could have constituted a significant part of the audience for such literature, whose compelling female protagonists, unusually prevalent in these texts, would have resonated with them. In addition to these entertaining narratives, there is evidence for one Greek Jewish tragic drama: the *Exagoge* of Ezekiel the Tragedian (perhaps second century BCE?), 279 lines of which survive as fragments quoted in Christian texts. Following the conventions of Greek tragedy, it is a five-act play in iambic trimeter about the exodus from Egypt, including a mystical vision in which Moses is seated on God's throne (Jacobson 1983).

Conclusion

Early Jewish literature presents us with some key challenges. Since most of our sources exist only in much later manuscripts, often in translation, there is a significant and sometimes unbridgeable gap between the material evidence we have and the time period we seek to reconstruct. It is also tempting to interpret this literature through anachronistic media categories, allowing later concepts of canon, textual fixity, and authorship to shape our understanding. At the same time, this corpus contributes to our picture of the materiality and ideology of ancient media in unique ways. The Dead Sea Scrolls, for example, constitute a substantial corpus for the study of scribal practices and material texts, showing great variety in the size, quality, and presumed function of manuscripts, while also presenting examples of ancient liturgy and descriptions of community reading practices. Studying early Jewish literature also brings us face to face with a culture where multilingualism – in Hebrew, Aramaic, and Greek – was the norm, and where writers reflected self-consciously on the nature of translation. Finally, we can trace a recurring motif in early Jewish texts about the centrality of writing as a medium and scribes as mediators and ideal figures, providing an ideological context for the production and reception of literature.

Eva Mroczek (University of California-Davis, USA)

Further Reading

Berthelot, Katell, and Daniel Stökl Ben Ezra, eds. 2010. *Aramaica Qumranica: Proceedings of the Conference on the Aramaic Texts from Qumran in Aix-en-Provence, 30 June – 2 July 2008*. STDJ 94. Leiden: Brill.

Berthelot, Katell. 2012. 'Jewish Literature Written in Greek'. In *Early Judaism: A Comprehensive Overview*. Edited by J. Collins. Eerdmans: Grand Rapids, pp. 228–52.

Bowley, James E., and John C. Reeves. 2003. 'Rethinking the Concept of "Bible": Some Theses and Proposals'. *Henoch* 25: 3–18.

Breed, Brennan W. 2014. *Nomadic Text: A Theory of Biblical Reception History*. Indiana Studies in Biblical Literature. Bloomington: Indiana University Press.

Collins, John J. 2012. *Early Judaism: A Comprehensive Overview*. Eerdmans: Grand Rapids.

Davila, James A. 2005. *The Provenance of the Pseudepigrapha: Jewish, Christian, or Other?* JSJS 105. Leiden: Brill.

Feldman, Louis H., James L. Kugel, and Lawrence H. Schiffman. 2013. *Outside the Bible: Ancient Jewish Writings Related to Scripture*. Lincoln: University of Nebraska Press.

Fraade, Steven. 2012. 'Language Mix and Multilingualism in Ancient Palestine: Literary and Inscriptional Evidence'. *Jewish Studies* 48: 1–40.

Greenfield, Jonas. 1978. 'The Languages of Palestine, 200 B.C.E.-200 C.E'. In *Jewish Languages: Theme and Variations*. Edited by Herbert H. Paper. Cambridge, MA: Association for Jewish Studies, pp. 143–54.

Jacobson, Howard. 1983. *The Exagoge of Ezekiel*. Cambridge: Cambridge University Press.

Jaffee, Martin. 2001. *Torah in the Mouth*. New York: Oxford University Press.

Kraft, Robert A. 2008. 'Early Jewish and Early Christian Copies of Greek Jewish Scriptures'. http://ccat.sas.upenn.edu/rs/rak/earlylxx/jewishpap.html.

Kraft, Robert A. 2007. 'Para-mania: Before, Beside and Beyond Biblical Studies'. *JBL* 126: 5–27.

Kraft, Robert A. 2009. *Exploring the Scripturesque: Jewish Texts and Their Christian Contexts*. JSJS 137. Leiden: Brill.

Law, Timothy Michael. 2013. *When God Spoke Greek: The Septuagint and the Making of the Christian Bible*. New York: Oxford University Press.

Lied, Liv I. 2013. 'Nachleben and Textual Identity: Variants and Variance in the Reception History of 2 Baruch'. In *Fourth Ezra and Second Baruch: Reconstruction after the Fall*. Edited by Matthias Henze and Gabriele Boccaccini with Jason M. Zurawski. JSJS 164. Leiden: Brill, pp. 403–28.

Mroczek, Eva. 2011. 'Thinking Digitally about the Dead Sea Scrolls: Book History Before and Beyond the Book'. *Book History* 13: 235–63.

Mroczek, Eva. 2016. *The Literary Imagination in Jewish Antiquity*. New York: Oxford University Press.

Najman, Hindy. 2003. *Seconding Sinai: The Development of Mosaic Discourse in Second Temple Judaism*. JSJS 77. Leiden: Brill.

Pietersma, Albert. 2002. 'A New Paradigm for Addressing Old Questions: The Relevance of the Interlinear Model for the Study of the Septuagint'. In *Bible and Computer: The Stellenbosch AIBI-6 Conference. Proceedings of the Association Internationale Bible et Informatique 'From Alpha to Byte'. University of Stellenbosch 17–21 July* 2000. Edited by J. Cook. Leiden: Brill, pp. 337–64.

Reed, Annette Yoshiko. 2008. 'Pseudepigraphy, Authorship and the Reception of "the Bible" in Late Antiquity'. In *The Reception and Interpretation of the Bible in Late Antiquity: Proceedings of the Montreal Colloquium in Honour of Charles Kannengiesser, 11–13 October 2006*. Edited by L. DiTommaso and L. Turcescu. Leiden: Brill, pp. 467–90.

Reeves, John C. 2010. 'Problematizing the Bible … Then and Now'. *JQR* 100: 139–52.

Sanders, Seth L. 2016. *From Adapa to Enoch: Scribal Culture and Religious Vision in Judea and Babylon*. TSAJ 167. Tübingen: Mohr Siebeck.

Schniedewind, William. 2006. 'Aramaic, the Death of Written Hebrew, and Language Shift in the Persian Period'. In *Margins of Writing, Origins of Cultures*. Edited by Seth L. Sanders. OIS 2. Chicago: Oriental Institute, pp. 135–52.

Stone, Michael E. 2011. *Ancient Judaism: New Visions and Views*. Grand Rapids, MI: Eerdmans.

Thomas, Samuel I. 2011. 'Eternal Writing and Immortal Writers: On the Non-Death of the Scribe in Early Judaism'. In *A Teacher for All Generations: Essays in Honor of James C. VanderKam*. Volume 1 of 2. JSJ 153. Edited by Eric F. Mason et al. Leiden: Brill, pp. 573–88.

Tov, Emanuel. 2004. *Scribal Practices and Approaches Reflected in the Texts Found in the Judean Desert*. STDJ 54. Leiden: Brill.

Ulrich, Eugene C. 2012. 'The Jewish Scriptures: Texts, Versions, Canons'. In *Early Judaism: A Comprehensive Overview*. Edited by J. Collins. Grand Rapids: Eerdmans, pp. 121–50.

Wills, Lawrence. 2015. *The Jewish Novel in the Ancient World*. Eugene, OR: Wipf and Stock. First published by Cornell University Press, 1995.

Wright, Benjamin G. 2003. 'Access to the Source: Cicero, Ben Sira, The Septuagint and Their Audiences'. *JSJ* 34: 1–27.

Wright, Benjamin G. 1989. *No Small Difference: Sirach's Relationship to Its Hebrew Parent Text*. SBLSCS 26. Atlanta: Scholars Press.

Vandendorpe, Christian. 2009. *From Papyrus to Hypertext: Toward the Universal Digital Library*. Translated by Phyllis Aronoff and Howard Scott. Chicago: University of Illinois Press.

Early Jewish Preaching Early Jewish preaching served as the forerunner of Christian and Islamic preaching and provided the gateway to a tradition that survived, with some interruptions, through the Medieval period and on into the present day in sermons given in contemporary SYNAGOGUES. It has been argued that early Jewish preaching was the invention of Hellenistic Judaism (e.g. Siegert). Indeed, some of the earliest evidence for preaching in the synagogue comes from the NT (see Lk. 4.16-21; Acts 13.14-41).

Throughout the classical rabbinic period (70 to 500 CE), the main instrument of popular education and interpretation of the Hebrew Bible was the sermon, given in the synagogue on SABBATHS and festivals. The speaker who fulfilled this function was known as the *darshan*, from the Hebrew root *d-r-sh*, meaning to 'interpret or explicate' Scripture. The compiler of the MISHNAH, the earliest rabbinic code of Jewish law, at the end of the Tannaitic period (early-third century CE) is reported to have been an inventive preacher, as the following story indicates.

> Once when Rabbi Yehudah HaNasi was sitting and preaching, he realized that the congregation was beginning to doze off. In order to awaken them he said: In Egypt, a woman gave birth to six hundred thousand at one time! There was a student there by the name of Rabbi Yishmael berabbi Yosi who asked: Who was that? He replied to him: That was Jochebed who bore Moses who was equivalent to all the six hundred thousand of Israel! (*Song of Songs Rabbah* 1.15.3).

Notably, the preacher is here described as sitting while giving his sermon. It seems that the preacher in rabbinic times normally was seated (see Lk. 4.20). It may be that in some synagogues the *darshan* was seated facing the congregation on a kind of special throne. This may well have been the function of the 'Seat of Moses' mentioned in the NT (Mt. 23.2) as occupied by 'scribes and Pharisees'. Examples of such thrones have been discovered in the excavations of ancient synagogues in Israel at Hammat Tiberias and Chorazin and in the synagogue on the Aegean island of Delos, and are thought to date from the first century BCE.

One of the most well-attested forms of the rabbinic sermon, the *proem* (Hebrew *Petiḥah*, Aramaic *Petiḥta'*) began to develop in the Tannaitic period (by the third century CE). In this form of the sermon, which may have been used to introduce the scriptural reading (see LECTIONARY; TORAH READING), the *darshan* opened [*pataḥ*] with a verse not found in the scriptural lection itself and, through a series of midrashic interpretations, linked this verse to the beginning of the scriptural reading. A prime example of the early use of the proem form is ascribed to the late-first-century CE sage, Rabbi Eleazar ben Azariah in the Babylonian Talmud, Hagigah 3a-b: 'He opened, "The words of the wise … are given from one shepherd"' (Eccl. 12.11). This opening verse is eventually linked to the verse from Exodus that began the biblical lection on the day this sermon was preached: 'All of the words of Torah are given from one shepherd – One God gave them … for it is written, "And God spoke all these words"' (Exod. 20.1).

Another example of a sermon preached in Tannaitic times is found embedded in the exegetical flow of the early midrashic interpretation to the book of Exodus, in the *Mekhilta de-Rabbi Yishmael* to Exod. 13.19: 'And Moses took the bones of Joseph with him because Joseph had made the Israelites swear an oath. He had said, "God will surely remember you, and then you must carry my bones up with you from this place."' The successive parts of this verse serve as the scriptural backbone of the sermon. First, Moses is praised above other Israelites for remembering the duty of reinterring Joseph in the promised land – this despite the fact that, at the time of Joseph's death hundreds of years earlier, the Egyptians had hidden Joseph's body to prevent the Israelites from leaving Egypt. The sermon proceeds to describe how Serah, the daughter of Asher, who survived from the generation of Joseph, told Moses how to locate and recover Joseph's coffin in order to take it on the exodus. While progressing through the Sinai Desert, the Israelites are depicted as carrying the coffin of Joseph along with the Ark containing the Tablets of the Covenant on which were inscribed the Ten Commandments. This leads to a midrashic tour de force that demonstrates how Joseph fulfilled each of these commandments. For example, Joseph is said to have obeyed the commandment 'You shall not commit adultery' (Exod. 20.14) by not having done so with Potiphar's wife despite her attempts to seduce him. The sermon concludes with a beautiful example of a messianic peroration typical of rabbinic homiletics, here inventively directed to the preacher's audience.

> God will surely remember you [the Hebrew verb *p-q-d*, 'redeem', is repeated first in what looks like a past tense for emphasis and then in the future tense]. He redeemed you in Egypt, and so He will also redeem you at the crossing of the Red Sea. He redeemed you at the Red Sea and so He will also redeem you in the Desert. He redeemed you in the Desert and so He will redeem you at the rivers of Arnon (when crossing the Jordan into the Promised Land). Just as God redeemed you repeatedly in this world, so too will He redeem you in the World to Come.

Marc Bregman (University of North Carolina, Greensboro, USA)

Further Reading

Bregman, Marc. 1982. 'The Darshan – Preacher and Teacher in Israel'. *The Melton Journal*. Spring 1982: 14, Sivan 5742.
Heinemann, Joseph. 1971. 'Preaching'. *Encyclopaedia Judaica*. 2nd revised edition, 2007. Jerusalem: Keter.
Heinemann, Joseph. 1975. *The Literature of the Synagogue*. New York: Behrman House.
Siegert, Folker. 2008. 'The Sermon as an Invention of Hellenistic Judaism'. In *Preaching in Judaism and Christianity*. Edited by Alexander Deeg et al. Studia Judaica 41. Berlin: Walter Mouton de Gruyter, pp. 25–44.

Education, Hellenistic Education in schools throughout the Greco-Roman world was a luxury that only a small percentage of families could afford. Of those receiving formal education, most completed only primary school, and only a few progressed to intermediate and advanced education. Parents unable to afford formal schooling would have taught their children the most basic elements at home, to the extent that they were able, so that the vast majority of the population received little to no formal education. Some Jews, especially those in the Diaspora, participated in Hellenistic education, while others educated their children, especially in the Scriptures, at home and possibly through the SYNAGOGUE.

Greco-Roman Education

During the Greek period, some evidence exists for educational foundations that subsidized teachers in select areas, though this trend had waned by the second century BCE (Harris 1989: 130–6). In the Roman period, the Emperor Vespasian (ruled 69–79 CE) was the first to provide funding for teachers of RHETORIC, though this subsidy does not appear to have been widespread. Generally speaking, then, families paid the fees for their children to receive education, which resulted in attendance primarily by the wealthy. Attrition rates between boys and girls varied greatly, with few females (primarily the most elite) advancing to the higher stages of education (Cribiore 2001: 74–101; Morgan 1998: 48–9). Even among male students, when considered in relation to the overall population of the empire, few advanced to the intermediate stage and even fewer to the advanced stage. More commonly, children learnt a trade through an apprenticeship. Because so few advanced through the educational process, illiteracy was widespread throughout the empire. LITERACY was thus often accompanied by power and influence, though a fair sector of the literate population was comprised of slaves who served as copyists.

It is difficult to know exactly when children began their education, as theorists recommended anywhere between ages three and ten (Morgan 2010). The gymnasium was a primary setting for Greek education, but evidence also shows instructors teaching in private homes or outside. Students practiced WRITING using various writing materials such as wooden or wax tablets, PAPYRUS, OSTRACA, and occasionally PARCHMENT (Morgan 1998: 39).

In contrast to classical Greece, which strongly emphasized MUSIC and gymnastics in education, education from the fourth century BCE accentuated literacy, though not to the exclusion of other subjects. Within the context of Alexander the Great's hellenizing campaign and the need to unify the greatly expanded Greek world after his death, literacy was a means of spreading Greek culture. The Romans largely adopted the educational models developed during the Hellenistic period (Morgan 1998: 21–5).

The various aspects of education became known as the *enkyklios paideia*, 'the cycle of education', which, at its fullest, included reading, writing, grammar, geometry, astronomy, literature, music theory, philosophy, and rhetoric (Morgan 1998: 6–7). Justification for all these subjects, at least from the perspective of an elite educator like Quintilian, stemmed from the conviction that only a good or virtuous man could be an orator, and that these subjects contributed to virtue (*Inst.* 12.1-4). Greco-Roman education also included athletic education; as the gymnasium was a marker of Hellenicity, being one of the first buildings constructed in newly established Greek colonies, the bodily training practiced there was viewed as a basic component of civilized life.

By the time of the Roman empire, education was basically a three-stage process, though recent studies have shown that the divisions between these stages were somewhat permeable, due possibly in part to educators' teaching students of differing abilities in the same classrooms (Cribiore 2001: 40–1). Each stage of education was built on the previous one and provided the foundation for the next.

The primary stage provided foundational material and skills: the alphabet (see ABECEDARY), syllables, basic reading and memorization, counting, recitation, and signature literacy. This content was relatively stable, though the order in which students learnt the material varied. Of the three stages of education, this one was the most commonly attended.

In the intermediate stage, students learnt punctuation and the parts of sentences by studying the classical poets and writers. They also began composing short texts based on what they had read. The authors with whom students interacted (as evident from the rhetorical handbooks and the remains of school text papyri) included Homer, Menander, Hesiod, Euripides, Demosthenes, Isocrates, Virgil, and Horace (Morgan 1998: 99). At this stage, students began to work through a series of preliminary exercises, or *progymnasmata*, which gradually increased in difficulty in preparation for speech composition or HISTORIOGRAPHY. Aelius Theon, author of a first-century CE *progymnasmata*, describes the exercises as 'the foundation of every kind of discourse' (*Progymnasmata* 70). Types of exercises included *chreia*, fable, narrative, maxim, refutation and confirmation, *topos* or commonplace, *ecphrasis*, *encomion* and invective, *prosopopoeia*, *ethopoeia*, *synkrisis*, thesis, law, paraphrase, and elaboration. Though Theon's *progymnasmata* is the earliest extant set of exercises, similar sets were used as early as the fourth century BCE (cf. *Rhetoric to Alexander* 28.1436a25; cf. *Rhetorica ad Herennium* 1.8.12; 4.42.54–4.44.58; Cicero, *On Rhetorical Invention* 1.19.27) and remained a part of the educational curriculum into the Middle Ages. Beyond the wide chronological distribution of the *progymnasmata*, evidence from Rome, Egypt, Alexandria, Antioch, and Constantinople shows their wide geographic distribution among both Latin and Greek writers. Evidence from school papyri also shows exercises in arithmetic, geometry, and algebra alongside grammar and literature (Morgan 1998: 6).

The use of the *progymnasmata* likely continued into the early stages of rhetorical training, which was the final stage of education. Rhetorical handbooks such as those written by Aristotle, Cicero, and Quintilian demonstrate the type of material that more advanced students studied in preparation for civic life. While hundreds of rhetorical handbooks were written in antiquity, only a handful survive today in both Greek and Latin. The handbooks centred on the five components of speech-making: invention, arrangement, style, delivery, and memory (see MEMORY, GRECO-ROMAN THEORIES OF). Rhetorical training culminated with declamation, the practice of composing and delivering speeches based on legal cases. Though declamation was a primary focus, the orators encouraged students to study other subjects in order to be a well-rounded, and thus good, orator, prepared for various jobs in public life.

Jewish Education

A paucity of evidence prior to the rabbinic period makes the reconstruction of Jewish education in the early centuries of the Common Era difficult. The later rabbinic sources suggest that students, almost exclusively male, could receive primary and secondary instruction at a synagogue, study house, or possibly the teacher's house (Hezser 2001: 59); primary instruction included study of the Jewish Scriptures, while secondary instruction included study of the oral law. Some Jews opted to educate their children at home rather than participate in Hellenistic education, though education outside of the home became more popular later in the fourth and fifth centuries CE (Hezser 2001: 59). Whether or not this portrait accurately reflects typical practices in later centuries, it must be viewed as tentative at best or idealistic and anachronistic at worst for understanding Jewish education during the Late Second Temple period, for which Philo and Josephus are among the few sources.

The father often began the education at home with focus on Torah reading. Josephus notes that the Law commands children be taught letters (*paideuein grammata*) and that they should learn the laws and deeds of their forefathers (*Against Apion* 2.204; cf. *Testament of Levi* 13.2), but he offers no clarity on if or how this instruction happened. Philo maintains that children are taught 'by parents and tutors and instructors' (*Embassy to Gaius* 6.115-16), but evidence for such training is lacking outside of the elite; his description clearly would require both literacy and leisure time from the teaching father or the wealth to hire a literate person as an instructor (Keith 2011: 77, 82). Jewish education seems to have included a heavy emphasis on memorization of the Torah, which more likely occurred through hearing the Law read aloud in the SYNAGOGUE than through private reading (Josephus, *Against Apion* 2.175; Keith 2011: 103, 117). Those able to read the text aloud to others were generally among the scribal elite – SCRIBES, Pharisees, Sadducees, and priests. Part of their training entailed studying with famous rabbis or scholars (Acts 22:3). The most common form of education in first-century Judaism, however, was not training in literacy but in a trade through an apprenticeship. Unlike Greco-Roman education, Jewish education did not seem to have an athletic component.

Heather Gorman (Johnson University, USA)

Further Reading

Cribiore, Raffaella. 2001. *Gymnastics of the Mind: Greek Education in Hellenistic and Roman Egypt*. Princeton, NJ: Princeton University Press.

Harris, William V. 1991. *Ancient Literacy*. Cambridge, MA: Harvard University Press.

Hezser, Catherine. 2001. *Jewish Literacy in Roman Palestine*. TSAJ 81. Tübingen: Mohr Siebeck.

Keith, Chris. 2011. *Jesus' Literacy: Scribal Culture and the Teacher from Galilee*. Library of New Testament Studies. New York: T&T Clark.

Levine, Lee I. 2000. *The Ancient Synagogue: The First Thousand Years*. New Haven: Yale University Press.

Marrou, Henri I. 1982. *A History of Education in Antiquity*. Translated by George Lamb. Madison, WI: University of Wisconsin Press.
Morgan, Teresa. 2010. 'Education'. *The Oxford Encyclopedia of Ancient Greece and Rome*. Edited by Michael Gagarin. Oxford: Oxford University Press.
Morgan, Teresa. 1998. *Literate Education in the Hellenistic and Roman Worlds*. Cambridge Classical Studies. Cambridge: Cambridge University Press.
Porter, Stanley E., ed. 1997. *Handbook of Classical Rhetoric in the Hellenistic Period, 330 B.C.-A.D. 400*. Leiden: Brill.
Too, Yun Lee, ed. 2001. *Education in Greek and Roman Antiquity*. Leiden: Brill.
Watson, Duane F. 2000. 'Education: Jewish and Greco-Roman'. In *Dictionary of New Testament Background*. Edited by Craig A. Evans and Stanley E. Porter. Downers Grove, IL: InterVarsity, pp. 308–13.

Education in Ancient Israel Throughout history, education has always begun in the home, where children learn from elders and siblings basic language skills and culture in the course of daily tasks, especially during meals and the process of food preparation. Such was the case in ancient Israel even more so than for modern society, because most households in ancient Israel were agrarian and therefore had little or no use for formal education and required the labour of everyone according to their abilities. Even most urban households required little or no formal education – for example, those whose primary livelihoods came from trades associated with artisan and craftsman guilds (such as ceramics and metallurgy) learnt their trade within the guilds, which were often family businesses (Meyers 1999). Therefore, the home and its near environs were the typical locations for education, and the teachers were often family members. The instruction occurred naturally in the context of the daily activities of the household and its larger social context, whether that was, for example, the rural village or an urban guild. For most occupations, including farming in rural villages and most specialized professions in the city, education was an integral part of everyday life and was oral, lacking any need of LITERACY. Some craftsman may have learnt to sign their names or to reproduce some letters without acquiring the skills of reading and WRITING, but even this minimal level of literacy would not have required formal education by professional teachers.

An elite minority within the urban bureaucracy related to the TEMPLE and palace received a formal education that included reading and writing (Crenshaw 1998; Rollston 2010). However, even their education was primarily oral in nature and written texts served the curriculum mainly as mnemonic aids for the internalization of the culture (Carr 2005; Person 2011). Thus, even ancient Israelite SCRIBES – the most literate members of their society – approached the task of reading, writing, and copying texts in ways that differ remarkably from how moderns understand these same activities (Person 1998).

As the literate members of their society, scribes would have played an important role in the public education of the people by serving as TEXT BROKERS who were responsible for the recitation of texts by memory and/or the public reading of traditional texts at various events, such as religious festivals. Thus, even the illiterate masses, especially in the cities, may have come into contact with literary texts at such occasional communal events. Such public readings of texts are represented in the Hebrew Bible – for example, Moses (Deut. 32.45), Joshua (8.32-35), Josiah (2 Kgs 22-23//2 Chron. 34-35), and Ezra (Neh. 8.2-8) all read the Law to the people, interpreted its meaning, and then led the people in the proper ritual responses to the reading.

We know little about the formal education of ancient Israelite scribes, due to the paucity of evidence. However, most scholars accept that some form of scribal training probably occurred as early as the monarchy based on the following types of evidence:

1. The Hebrew Bible refers to professional scribes (e.g. Jeremiah 36) and written sources, presumably from royal ARCHIVES (e.g. 1 Chron. 27.24) and uses a technical vocabulary related to scribalism (e.g. Eccl. 12.9-12).

2. The complexity of the monarchic bureaucracy required scribal skills.
3. Scribal schools existed throughout the ancient Near East, so by analogy Israel may have had scribal schools.
4. Archaeological evidence, especially epigraphic sources, strongly suggests a professional class of scribes who had undergone standardized formal education (Crenshaw 1998; Davies 1998; Rollston 2010). However, even such specialized formal education most likely occurred within the scribal guilds – that is, within the context of scribal families. Thus, for scribal training, like that of other artisans, the primary context for education appears to be within the family, as suggested by 1 Chron. 2.55: 'the families of the scribes that dwell at Jabez: the Tirathites, the Shimeathites, and the Sucathites' (Rollston 2010: 122–6).

The formal training of scribes would have been designed to meet the administrative needs of the central bureaucracy. Scribes would learn about record-keeping and letter writing, including standardized writing scripts and layouts that facilitated communication. An important part of their training would also be the knowledge of how to produce their own WRITING MATERIALS, including pen and ink. Furthermore, common administrative tasks often required the recording of quantitative data; therefore, the scribes had to learn some formal, standardized numeric system, such as the Egyptian hieratic numeric system. Thus, the well-educated scribe would be someone who had mastered 'the production of Old Hebrew texts in the standard script of the period, the standard ORTHOGRAPHY of the period, the capability of using a dominant numeric system, and the capability of employing a standard format (e.g. for letters, deeds, and so on)' (Rollston 2010: 113). Some scribes must also have been proficient in other languages and scripts, in order to facilitate official correspondence with other nations (see, e.g 2 Kgs 18.17-37; Ezra 4–6).

Despite the widespread acceptance that scribal training occurred in ancient Israel, little epigraphic evidence of the training itself exists. Nevertheless, Christopher Rollston has discussed two texts that he is convinced provide some epigraphic evidence (2010: 111, 120–2). The first is an ABECEDARY, a text that is simply the Hebrew alphabet listed in its standard order. Abecedaries are widely regarded as having an educational function to teach the alphabet, including the form of the standard script. The second, an inscribed stone from the City of David, is what he interprets to be a student exercise text – that is, a text upon which a student learnt to write by copying a standardized example made by the teacher. Although such epigraphic evidence is generally lacking in earlier periods, Emanuel Tov has described such scribal exercises among the Qumran materials and concluded that similar practices probably occurred earlier, including during the monarchy (Tov 2004: 14, 261).

Based upon comparative evidence from Egypt and Mesopotamia, Leo Perdue concluded that the sages and scribes 'comprised a professional social class of intellectuals, composers, officials, and clerks' (Perdue 2008: 3). Since scribes served in various capacities, their education probably consisted of a basic curriculum (emphasizing reading, writing, and arithmetic) followed by more specialized studies to prepare them for the different leadership roles within the temple and royal complexes. That is, which texts were memorized by the advanced students may have differed, depending on what specific leadership roles the students were preparing for within the different family guilds.

Although scribal education required specialized training, it nevertheless probably occurred within the family setting, as suggested by the 'father'/'son' imagery in Prov. 1-9. Just as raising children is portrayed in Proverbs as involving corporeal punishment (13.24), difficult students may have been beaten. In order to keep the students' interests, pedagogical strategies may have included debate and dialogue. Furthermore, since scribal students and their teachers were almost exclusively male, teachers probably spiced things up a bit with gender-based humour, as suggested by the stereotypical dichotomy of foolish and wise women (Crenshaw 1998: 117). In addition to the memorization of literary texts, students were encouraged to learn from their observations of nature and human culture and to apply these insights to new situations (Crenshaw 1998: 120–6).

The administrative scribal skills of record-keeping and writing correspondence would have easily transferred to the preservation and transmission of literature, even if this was a secondary concern of the state. Even though the primarily oral character of ancient Israelite society continued long after the introduction of writing and professional scribal guilds, professional scribes may have functioned to some extent as cultural arbiters on behalf of the central administration in their roles as LECTORS and text brokers, thereby explaining why so much of the Hebrew Bible reflects the perspective of the urban elite.

Raymond F. Person, Jr. (Ohio Northern University, USA)

Further Reading

Carr, David M. 2005. *Writing on the Tablet of the Heart: Origins of Scripture and Literature*. Oxford: Oxford University Press.

Crenshaw, James L. 1998. *Education in Ancient Israel*. New York: Doubleday.

Davies, Philip R. 1998. *Scribes and Schools: The Canonization of the Hebrew Scriptures*. Louisville: Westminster John Knox.

Meyers, Carol L. 1999. 'Guilds and Gatherings: Women's Groups in Ancient Israel'. In *Realia Dei: Essays in Archaeology and Biblical Interpretation in Honor of Edward F. Campbell, Jr. at His Retirement*. Edited by P. H. Williams, Jr. and T. Hiebert. Atlanta: Scholars Press, pp. 154–84.

Perdue, Leo G. 2008. 'Sages, Scribes, and seers in Israel and the Ancient Near East: An Introduction'. In *Scribes, Sages, and Seers: The Sage in the Eastern Mediterranean World*. Edited by Leo G. Perdue. Göttingen: Vandenhoeck & Ruprecht, pp. 1–34.

Person, Raymond F., Jr. 1998. 'The Ancient Israelite Scribe as Performer.' *JBL* 117: 601–9.

Person, Raymond F., Jr. 2011. 'The Role of Memory in the Tradition Represented by the Deuteronomic History and the Book of Chronicles'. *Oral Tradition* 26: 537–50.

Person, Raymond F., Jr. 2016. 'Education and Transmission'. In *Companion to Ancient Israel*. Edited by Susan Niditch. Oxford: Blackwell, pp. 366–78.

Rollston, Christopher A. 2010. *Writing and Literacy in the World of Ancient Israel: Epigraphic Evidence from the Iron Age*. SBL Archaeology and Biblical Studies 11. Atlanta: SBL Press.

Tov, Emanuel. 2004. *Scribal Practices and Approaches Reflected in the Text Found in the Judean Desert*. STDJ 54. Leiden: Brill.

Elephantine Papyri Opposite the city of Syene (modern Aswan), on the east bank of the Nile, lies the island of Elephantine. In the fifth century BCE, when Egypt was under Persian rule (Dynasty 27), an Aramaeo-Jewish Diaspora community lived on the island. This famous so-called 'Jewish colony' of Elephantine has been the subject of numerous studies, especially in the fields of Jewish studies. The existence of a Jewish Diaspora in Egypt was already attested in biblical sources (Jer. 41.16-18; 42; 43; 44:1ff; cf. 2 Kgs 25.22-26). A sensational discovery of fifth-century documents on papyri and OSTRACA found on the island confirmed the presence of Jews at Egypt's southern border.

Since the beginning of the nineteenth century several pieces from this PAPYRUS discovery have made their way through various dealers to Europe, including today's papyrus collection of the Egyptian Museum in the National Museums of Berlin. The texts of this find are all written in Aramaic, the lingua franca of the western Persian empire and therefore also of Egypt. They explain in detail the life of the Aramaic-speaking Jewish community, which was stationed on the border between Egypt and Nubia as a military colony. The Aramaic papyri from Elephantine were all written over a period of less than one hundred years. Many texts are precisely dated. Some are dated in accordance with the Babylonian Jewish calendar. Some are dated with the Egyptian calendar. Most of them more specifically provide the regnal year of the current Persian ruler. The oldest document to bear its own date is from year 27 of Darius I (494 BCE). The latest document dates from the year 5 of Amyrtaeus (399 BCE), the first post-Persian ruler of Egypt (Dynasty 28).

Today the documents on papyri and ostraca are scattered all over the world in various museums. The following groups of texts can be found:

(1) The communal archives of the leader of the community, Jedaniah. LETTERS report on, for example, the destruction of the Jewish temple at Elephantine by Egyptians.

(2) The private family ARCHIVES of the temple official Ananiah, who was married to an Egyptian slave woman. The archive consists mainly of legal contracts.

(3) The private family archives of Mibtahiah, the aunt of Jedaniah. These documents cover a period of three generations and sixty years, and also reflect private law.

(4) Numerous letters of an administrative and private character.

(5) Lists and catalogues of persons or goods (often on ostraca, rather than papyrus).

(6) Literary and historical works: the Story of Ahiqar and the so-called Behistun Inscription of Darius I.

Next to the Aramaic texts thousands of additional papyri have been found at Elephantine using different languages and scripts like Hieratic, Hieroglyphs, Demotic, Greek, Coptic, or Arabic. The Aramaic texts of the Diaspora community of Elephantine were mainly written by its members. They are contemporary with the events they describe, without there being – as is common in biblical texts – any major time lapse, textual corruption, or even later editorial intervention. These documents are the oldest non-biblical evidence of any such community in Egypt. They also give evidence of a YHWH Temple outside of Jerusalem or Palestine on Elephantine Island and thus have sharpened scholarly awareness of both the geographic specificity and the particular ideological perspective. According to these texts in the fifth century there was no single centralized temple cult.

Verena Lepper (Ägyptisches Museum und Papyrussammlung, Staatliche Museen zu Berlin & Humboldt University of Berlin, Germany)

Further Reading

Lepper, Verena M. 2012. 'Die ägyptische und orientalische. Rubensohn-Bibliothek: 4000 Jahre Kulturgeschichte einer altägyptischen Insel'. In *Forschung in der Papyrussammlung: Eine Festgabe für das Neue Museum*. Edited by Verena M. Lepper. Ägyptische und orientalische Papyri und Handschriften des Ägyptischen Museums und Papyrussammlung Berlin 1. Berlin: Akademie, pp. 497–509.

Porten, Bezalel, with J. J. Farber, C. J. Martin, G. Vittman et al., eds. 1996. *The Elephantine-Papyri in English: Three Millenia of Cross-Cultural Continuity and Change*. Documenta et Monumenta Orientis Antiqui 22. Leiden: Brill.

Porten, Bezalel and Ada Yardeni. 1986–99. *Textbook of Aramaic Documents from Ancient Egypt*. 4 vols. Jerusalem: Hebrew University of Jerusalem.

Rohrmoser, Angela. 2014. *Götter, Tempel und Kult der Judäo-Aramäer von Elephantine: Archäologische und schriftliche Zeugnisse aus dem perserzeitlichen Ägypten*. Alter Orient und Altes Testament 396. Münster: Ugarit.

Enchiridion *Enchiridion* is an Anglicized Latin term (derived in turn from the Greek *enkheiridion*, 'that which is held in the hand') that refers to a personal manual or handbook. As a GENRE of ancient literature, handbooks functioned as central locations for amassing essential information about a particular subject and were frequently used as memory aids or teaching tools. For example, rhetorical training (such as that offered in

Quintilian's *Institutes*) stressed the value of creating short sayings (*gnomai*) and stories (*chreiai*) that, gathered in a manual of rhetoric (such as *progymnasmata*), could be used to teach students the basic skills and systematic knowledge essential to a lawyer or other public speaker (Albl 1999: 77–9; see EDUCATION, HELLENISTIC). The orator Quintilian also recommends that students take notes on speeches as part of the memorization process, warning in nearly the same breath of the dangers of becoming too dependent upon such notes in performance (Quintilian, *Institutes*, 11.2.2, 24-26, 44-49). In other words, personal handbooks were useful tools for memorizing material and for jogging one's memory, but were in no way a replacement for the flexibility of the mind and the drama of a skilled performer. In a similar vein, there is evidence of Jewish students recording their rabbi's words in 'scrolls of secrets' which they then memorized (*b.Shab*. 6b, 96b, 156a).

In addition, audience members who took notes on a speech may have done so to reproduce the speech later, either for educational purposes (Quintilian, *Institutes* 11.2.2, 24-26) or to ensure that a faithful account of the speech was recorded, possibly for publication later. For example, Arrian published his notes of the lectures of Epictetus (*Enchiridion of Epictetus*), observing that 'Whatever I heard him say I used to write down, word for word, as best I could, endeavouring to preserve it as a memorial, for my own future use, of his way of thinking and the frankness of his speech' (Epictetus, *Diatribe* 1, pref). Members of the Greco-Roman literary elite also frequently used notebooks (*hypomemata*, *commentarii*) not only as an aid in the learning process (Kennedy 1978) but also to record information for use in later publication (e.g. Pliny, *Letters* III.5). In fact, 2 Tim. 4:13 records Paul's request of parchments from Timothy that may actually have been a form of notebook or enchiridion he drew from in his communications with various churches.

Judith Odor (Asbury Theological Seminary, USA)

Further Reading

Albl, Martin C. 1999. *And Scripture Cannot Be Broken: The Form and Function of the Early Christian Testimonia Collections*. *NovT* Supplements. Leiden: Brill.

Kennedy, George A. 1978. 'Classical and Christian Source Criticism'. In *The Relationship among the Gospels: An Interdisciplinary Dialogue*. Edited by W. O. Walker. San Antonio: Trinity University Press, pp. 130–7.

1 Enoch/Enochic Traditions 1 Enoch is a Jewish text written from the early third century BCE to the first century CE that contains a variety of revelations attributed to Enoch, the antediluvian patriarch briefly mentioned in Gen. 5.24. While the text is often referred to as a single 'book', scholars are now widely agreed that its various sections were composed by a variety of authors over time. These authors exhibit a broad range of knowledge from the ancient Near East and the Greco-Roman world, knowledge they would have initially acquired through multiple media sources, and have adapted for their own purposes. While the Enochic traditions contain a rich array of materials, especially prominent are speculations about the structure and functioning of the cosmos and explanations of the origins of evil and its eventual eradication.

In its current form, the book of 1 Enoch primarily divides into five major sections: The Book of the Watchers (1–36); the Astronomical Book/Book of the Luminaries (72–82); the Animal Apocalypse (83–90); the Epistle of Enoch (92–105); and the Book of Parables (37–71). The only extant text is in Ethiopic, but Aramaic fragments of the book, except for the Parables, have been discovered among the DEAD SEA SCROLLS, and Greek fragments also exist.

The Book of the Luminaries, one of the oldest sections, concentrates on the structure of the cosmos. While the Hebrew Bible reflects some interest in this subject (e.g. Genesis 1; Job 38), VanderKam has shown that 1 Enoch draws on Babylonian astronomical traditions and that Enoch himself in some ways resembles the Babylonian king Enmeduranki (Nickelsburg and VanderKam 2012: 383). For example, reference to 'the gates' through which the sun passes (1 Enoch 72) has parallels in a Hymn to the Sun-God (Shamash), the *Enuma Elish* V, 9-10, and the *Epic of Gilgamesh* IX, 42-45 (Nickelsburg and VanderKam, 2012: 420). All these Akkadian texts were publicly performed in ritualized settings. For 1 Enoch, this astronomical science especially confirms the validity of a 364-day solar calendar, which is essential in the Enochic traditions.

The myth of the Fall of the Watchers (1 Enoch 6–11), which appears in the Book of the Watchers (1 Enoch 1–36), is also foundational to much of the Enochic tradition. An expansion of the enigmatic Gen. 6.1-4, the myth tells of the rebellion of angelic beings called 'Watchers', who descend to earth, have sex with human women, and reveal illicit knowledge. Their rebellious actions transgress divinely established boundaries and throw the cosmos into chaos. Their half-human, half-divine offspring wreak violence on the earth, and, in some texts, after their deaths their spirits continue to cause illnesses and other problems for humans. As Nickelsburg (2001: 191–3) has noted, similarities between the Fall of the Watchers and the Prometheus and demise of the Titans myths suggest that the text is playing with the Hellenistic myths in order to critique the claims of Alexander's successors, the Diadochi. In inscriptions, pronouncements, titles, buildings, statuary, and on COINS, Hellenistic rulers promoted themselves as demi-gods; 1 Enoch 1-36, by contrast, portrays them as the offspring of demons. This critique continues into the final section of 1 Enoch, the parables, which attaches the fate of the 'kings and the mighty' to the punishment of the Watchers and their offspring (67.4-12). In an ironic twist, instead of constructing 'spectacles' of their power for the masses, the kings and the mighty become 'a spectacle for the righteous and [the] chosen ones' (62.12) and are tortured in the hot springs in which they formerly sought health and relaxation (67.8-13).

As Nickelsburg (2001: 238–47) notes, 1 Enoch may reflect knowledge of the religious geography and cultic structures of the Upper Galilee. Prominent geographical locations in the region are mentioned in 1 En. 13.7-9: waters of the Dan, Mt. Hermon, Abel-Main, Lebanon, and Senir. Further, the Watchers bind one another in a curse on Mt. Hermon (6.4-6), which rises to 2814 m. (about 9232 ft.) at the southernmost point of the Anti-Lebanon chain. References to this area as the dwelling place of deities reach as far back as the *Epic of Gilgamesh*. The Hebrew Bible also knows of religious interest attached to the area (cf. 1 Chron. 5.23). Archaeological work has uncovered several cultic centres in the area. At the base of the southwest slope is a cave considered sacred to Pan, an active site from the third century BCE to the sixth century CE. Many idols of gods and goddesses from the Greco-Roman pantheon have been found at the site. If the Enochic traditions did indeed arise in northern Galilee, those responsible for its transmission may have constructed the character of Enoch and his encounters with the divine to compete with local pagan media.

Features of 1 Enoch also indicate that the SCRIBES responsible for the production and growth of the tradition sought to provide a lively and engaging text that, when performed orally, could captivate an audience. Enoch's visionary world is filled with visual, oral, aural, and olfactory media. Journeys and explorations of cosmic geography convey spatiality and movement. Reports of these sensory stimuli combine to provide the audience with a vivid experience that in turn shapes the members' lived experiences and perceptions of reality. The narratives sparkle with the pageantry of ritual behaviour appropriate for a heavenly court, which imitates human decorum (e.g. 9.4-11; 12.1-3; 40.1-10). Angels and the visionary praise God, approach God with ritualized deference (e.g. 14.24), deliver formal petitions (e.g. 9.1-11; 13.4-7; 47.2; 104.1-6), and are commissioned for action (e.g. 10.2, 4, 9, 11; 12.4; 13.1). Enoch and the narrator sound prophetic when issuing pronouncements of judgement, woes, and curses upon the wicked (e.g. 5.4, 5; 12.6; 13.1; 16.4; 94.6-11; 95.4-7; 96.4-8; 98.9–99.2; 99.11-16) and oracles of blessing and hope on the righteous (e.g. 5.8; 58.1-6; 95.3; 96.1; 102.4-5). Dramatic, grotesque, and fascinating beings – various kinds of angels, Watchers, giants, antediluvian patriarchs (e.g. 81.5; 82.1; 91.1; 106.1–107.3), animals (chaps 83–90), and the mysterious Head of Days and Son of Man (46.1-8; 62.9, 14; 71.1-13) – inhabit the world of the text. The audience constantly hears echoes of its own liturgical and textual traditions (e.g. 1.8; 5.8; 22.14; 25.7; 36.4; 39.9-13; 61.11-13; 84.1-6). The people's SOCIAL MEMORY, as well as its hoped-for collective future, is in part portrayed through animal actors in the Animal Apocalypse (chaps. 83–90). This allegorical interpretation of history instructs the audience how to locate itself within Israel's story, to identify opponents, and to recognize the gravity of the community's special teachings and interests. Further, in the TESTAMENT language of the opening lines of the entire corpus, the audience immediately becomes the recipients, guardians, and tradents of the visionary traditions (1.1-3). Through these devices, the tradition asserts the reality of God's rule and promotes a cosmic vision that challenges any rivals.

The complexity of the Enochic traditions suggests that the texts were produced by highly educated scribes, who drew on a wide range of ancient cultural knowledge and media in order to construct texts that could, at times, compete with, critique, or subvert the propaganda and narratives of the ruling classes (see TEXTUAL COMMUNITIES). These scribes had also received extensive training in Israel's traditions and forms of literature and speech, and they had learnt how to apply this knowledge to the ever-changing situations in Second Temple Judaism. The polyvalent features of their key foundational mythology, as well as Israel's traditions, also presented continuous possibilities for reinterpretation, even if on occasion scribes created tensions and inconsistencies within the tradition.

Rodney A. Werline (Barton College, USA)

Further reading

Kim Harkins, Angela, Kelley Coblentz Bautch, and John C. Endres, eds. 2014. *The Watchers in Jewish and Christian Traditions*. Minneapolis: Fortress.

Nickelsburg, George W. E. 2001. *1 Enoch 1: A Commentary on the Book of 1 Enoch, Chapters 1-36, 81-108*. Hermeneia. Minneapolis: Fortress.

Nickelsburg, George W. E. and James C. VanderKam. 2012. *1 Enoch 2: A Commentary on the Book of 1 Enoch, Chapters 37-82*. Hermeneia. Minneapolis: Fortress.

Epigraphy The corpus of epigraphic texts (written inscriptions on physical objects, ranging from small HOUSEHOLD ITEMS to large public buildings) from the ancient Near Eastern and Mediterranean worlds is vast, dwarfing many times over the amount of material in the Hebrew Bible, OT Apocrypha, and Greek NT combined. These inscriptions often broaden our understanding of the ancient biblical world, including facets of that world such as daily life (e.g. marriage, divorce, adoptions, purchases, sales); the nature of EDUCATION; levels of LITERACY among elites and non-elites; ancient bureaucracies; ethnic and linguistic diversity of populations; the nature and diversity of religion; as well as trade, travel, legal practices, and diplomacy.

The languages and scripts of these inscriptions are numerous, ranging from Sumerian, Akkadian, Egyptian, Eblaite, Ugaritic, Phoenician, Hebrew, and Aramaic to Palmyrene, Nabatean, Greek, Latin, Syriac, Coptic, Safaitic, and Ethiopic. It is also important to emphasize that scripts and languages are related yet distinct: an inscription may use the text of one language but be written in the script of another (see ORTHOGRAPHY). For example, many early Aramaic inscriptions are written in the Phoenician script. Similarly, the Coptic language prominent in ancient Egypt (e.g. the Nag Hammadi Papyri) is written in the Greek script (with the addition of six letters borrowed from the Demotic script). Analogous to this is the fact that the script used to write the English language is, of course, the Latin script. Clearly, in the ancient world as today, language and script are not the same thing.

Within the field of Hebrew Bible and Northwest Semitic inscriptions, *epigraphy* is a broad term referring especially to the study of ancient inscriptions, regardless of the medium or the WRITING instrument (e.g. chiselled into stone, incised into pottery with a stylus, ink written with a reed pen on pottery or plaster, ink written with a reed pen on PAPYRUS, PARCHMENT, or vellum, with the latter being a finer quality of parchment). Modern scholars who work on epigraphic texts are referred to as *epigraphists* (or *epigraphers*). Within the field of Hebrew Bible and Northwest Semitic inscriptions, the term *palaeography* refers to a sub-field of epigraphy that focuses on discerning and documenting the diachronic development of the letters of a script series (e.g. the Hebrew script, Phoenician script, Aramaic script) through time as well as the synchronic variation that is present within a script series during a particular chronological horizon, ultimately with the dating of inscriptions as a primary focus. The modern scholar who does palaeographic analysis is referred to as a *palaeographer*. Thus, for the field of Northwest Semitic and Hebrew Bible, *epigraphy* is a general term for the field of inscriptions (regardless of the medium upon which the text is written) while *palaeography* is a precise term that refers especially to the diachronic development of the letters of a script series through time (regardless of the medium).

For classical scholars (i.e. those focusing on Greek and Latin inscriptions), the terms *epigraphy* and *palaeography* have slightly different meanings. Namely, the term *palaeography* refers especially to the style of writing and refers in particular to the different styles of writing that are used on different media. Thus, Metzger has stated that 'palaeography is the science that studies ancient writing, preserved on papyrus, parchment, or paper, occasionally on potsherds, wood, or waxed tablets. Epigraphy deals with ancient inscriptions on durable objects, such as stone, bone, or metal' (Metzger 1981: 3). The study of texts on papyri, especially those of the Greco-Roman period, is often referred to as *papyrology*, while the study of coinage is referred to as *numismatics*. *Epigraphy* is thus a broad term that has been defined in a variety of ways, but the focal point of the field is the study of ancient texts (Bodel 2001; Horbury and Noy 1992).

Media and Content

Often the texts that garner the most scholarly interest are monumental inscriptions (see MONUMENTS). A prominent example from the Late Second Temple period is the much-studied JERUSALEM TEMPLE Mount Warning Inscription (written in Greek, dating to the first century CE) that warns foreigners against proceeding beyond the Court of the Gentiles and states that those who trespass will be guilty for their own deaths. As was typical of monumental inscriptions, this inscription was carefully chiselled into a dressed stone, with a very finely executed script, with precise spacing and letter formation. Also from the Jerusalem temple is the Place of Trumpeting Inscription (written in Hebrew, first century CE), arguably an inscription intended to convey the fact that the Shophar (horn) was blown to signal certain WORSHIP times. Similar in quality is the Theodotos Synagogue Inscription (written in Greek, found in Jerusalem, and hailing from the first century CE as well), a dedicatory inscription that was commissioned by Theodotos son of Vettenos, a priest and ruler of the SYNAGOGUE. Among the most important monumental inscriptions from the First Temple period is the famed Siloam Tunnel Inscription that commemorates the completion of an 1800-foot water tunnel under the city of Jerusalem, an inscription dating to the late eighth century BCE (and written in Hebrew).

A particularly common type of ancient inscription is the burial inscription. These were normally not considered public display inscriptions, nor were they normally monumental. Those from the First Temple period are often chiselled into the walls of a tomb, such as that of the Khirbet el-Qom Tomb. Burial inscriptions often mention the name of the deceased, and sometimes also the name of a god. The Khirbet el-Qom Inscription is particularly important because it mentions not only the Israelite God Yahweh but also a consort of his named Asherah. Sometimes the inscription is chiselled into a sarcophagus, as is the case with the famous Phoenician Ahiram Inscription from the tenth century BCE.

Burial inscriptions from the Second Temple period are especially common. The majority of those preserved are chiselled into the ossuary itself (a small stone box used for secondary burial of the bones after the flesh had decayed), or etched into the ossuary with an incising tool or nail. These often contain just the name of the deceased and a patronymic (that is, the name of the deceased's father), but sometimes 'wife of', 'daughter of', or a place name also occur. On occasion, these inscriptions also contain statements about the manner of death or the religious hopes of the deceased.

Among the additional kinds of inscriptions are seals, which were used like modern stamps to create impressions on documents (see CYLINDER SEALS). Seals were normally made of stone and were typically small (about the size of a COIN) and fairly round. Many seals bore written inscriptions (and thus are called *epigraphic*), while some do not (and so are referred to as *anepigraphic*). Epigraphic seals normally contained the name of the seal-owner, the name of his father, and on occasion also a title. Seals were used as part of the process of authorizing ancient papyrus documents, especially those relating to agreements on purchases, sales, marriages, divorces, and adoptions. After a document was written up on papyrus, it would be rolled, then string would be wrapped around it, and a wet piece of clay would be intertwined with the string; parties to the agreement would impress their seals into the wet clay, similar to the modern practice of signing contracts and other legal documents. The process is beautifully described in the Hebrew Bible (Jer. 32.9-15), and the NT also contains reference to sealed documents (Revelation 5–8).

Papyrus was a popular medium not only for business and legal documents but also for sacred texts as well, including those that were eventually included in the NT and extra-canonical writings such as the Nag Hammadi Coptic Texts (Hurtado 2006). For these texts, a reed pen and ink were used (Metzger 1981: 14–19). For sacred Hebrew writings transmitted within ancient Judaism, ink on parchment (or vellum) was particularly common (Tov 2009). Furthermore, plaster could also be a common writing surface, especially widely used on interior wall of buildings; these inscriptions were often written in ink, after the plaster had dried. Among the most famous biblical references about writing on plaster is that of the narratives of Belshazzar the Babylonian king (Dan. 5). Among the most famous epigraphic texts on plaster are those of Deir Alla that mention Balaam son of Beor, a figure also known in the Bible (Num 22-24). The Deir Alla Inscriptions (see Rollston 2010: 61–2) are interesting not only because of their content but also because black ink is used for the body of the material while red ink is used as a rubric for the titles. Although metal was not a very common medium for writing, it too was used, as evidenced by the famous Copper Scroll from Qumran (3Q15) and the Silver Amulets from Ketef Hinnom, which are inscribed with a portion of the Aaronic Benediction (Num. 6.24-26).

Pottery was also often used a medium for ancient inscriptions. Sometimes the writing would be incised into the clay immediately prior to the firing of that pot, while in other cases the pottery was incised after firing. Sometimes the writing on pottery was added with ink and a reed brush rather than with an incising tool. Writing was sometimes added to complete pottery vessels and sometimes to broken pieces of pottery; ink inscriptions on broken pottery shards are referred to as OSTRACA (sing. *ostrakon*). Thousands of ostraca have been found in excavations throughout the ancient Near East, including sites from Israel, Judah, Moab, Ammon, Greece, and Anatolia. Particularly striking is the fact that many inscriptions on pottery have survived to the modern period (especially those that are incised), although in antiquity writing on pottery would normally have been done for documents of an ephemeral nature (e.g. LETTERS to military officers, field recording of harvested and delivered crops).

In sum, various media were used for writing in antiquity, and the specific instruments used for marking or inscribing were determined by the medium: chisels and incising tools for stone and pottery, ink and pen for papyrus and vellum (see PARCHMENT). The contents of these ancient texts provide important windows not only into scribal culture but also into society as a whole. Finally, it should be emphasized that the quality and quantity of epigraphic texts are critically important components of modern discussions about the percentage of the ancient population that was literate (see LITERACY). Thus, some scholars have used the epigraphic material to argue that only educated elites were capable of reading and writing sophisticated texts, while others appeal to the same evidence to argue that the non-elite populace (e.g. agriculturalists, pastoralists, blacksmiths, carpenters) was capable of reading and writing at a fairly sophisticated level.

Christopher A. Rollston (George Washington University, USA)

Further Reading

Bodel, John, ed. 2001. *Epigraphic Evidence: Ancient History from Inscriptions*. London: Routledge.

Horbury, William, and David Noy. 1992. *Jewish Inscriptions of Graeco-Roman Egypt*. Cambridge: Cambridge University Press.

Hurtado, Larry W. 2006. *The Earliest Christian Artifacts: Manuscripts and Christian Origins*. Grand Rapids: Eerdmans.

Metzger, Bruce M. 1981. *Manuscripts of the Greek Bible: An Introduction to Greek Palaeography*. Oxford: Oxford University Press.

Rollston, Christopher A. 2010. *Writing and Literacy in the World of Ancient Israel: Epigraphic Evidence from the Iron Age*. SBL Archaeology and Biblical Studies 11. Atlanta: Society of Biblical Literature.

Tov, Emanuel. 2009. *Scribal Practices and Approaches Reflected in the Texts Found in the Judean Desert*. STJD 54. Leiden: Brill.

Equiprimordiality *Equiprimordiality* refers to the equality of ORIGINALS that is characteristic of oral culture, as opposed to the concept of a singular original archetype characteristic of print culture. The principle of equiprimordiality indicates that each instantiation of a tradition is equally ('equi'-) original or authentic ('-primordial'). The term has been especially important in the work of WERNER KELBER, who borrowed it from Martin Heidegger's philosophical concept *Gleichursprünglichkeit* and popularized it in the field of biblical studies.

According to WALTER ONG, print differs from oral speech in that it endows texts with a fixed physical existence. In print cultures, words are external and material realities, and the first printing of a text is generally viewed as the singular original from which all others are reproduced, redacted, and copied. In oral cultures, in contrast, words exist only as fleeting vibrations of vocal cords and in memory. The first utterance of a speech act is not considered the single and lone original because the utterance has no permanent physical existence. Every instantiation of an oral proclamation is equiprimordial because each speech act is dependent on, and unique to, the shared context of the producer and receiver of that discourse (called by Kelber the 'BIOSPHERE' of oral communication).

Equiprimordiality is not necessarily a defining characteristic of oral literature alone. The concept often remains influential in textual traditions that have been transferred into a written medium from vibrant ORAL TRADITIONS. This is particularly true of texts produced chirographically, as it was only with the advent of the printing press that exact textual fixity was possible (see CHIROGRAPHS).

Nicholas A. Elder (Marquette University, USA)

Further Reading

Kelber, Werner. 2013. 'In the Beginning were the Words'. In *Imprints, Voiceprints, and Footprints of Memory: Collected Essays of Werner Kelber*. SBLRBS. Atlanta: SBL Press, esp. 77–80, pp. 57–101.

Ong, Walter. 2012. *Orality and Literacy: The Technologizing of the Word.* 30th Anniversary Edition with additional chapters by John Hartley. London: Routledge, esp. 115–33.

Ethnography of Speaking The ethnography of speaking is a hybridizing approach to the study of human speaking that draws together and employs an unrestricted range of theories and methods from FOLKLORE, linguistics, anthropology, psychology, and sociology. It also seeks to gather and extend undeveloped strands of inquiry about human speech implicit in the histories of these various disciplines. As a style of investigation, it studies how speaking both shapes and is shaped by particular personalities, societies, and cultures and how speaking contributes to the maintenance of particular languages and communities. Its theoretical basis was developed initially in the 1960s by linguistic anthropologist DELL HYMES. Because of its multidisciplinary approach, it is also called SOCIOLINGUISTICS and the ethnography of communication. In spirit and style, it is closely related to ETHNOPOETICS and to newly developing cognate forms of analysis called PERFORMANCE CRITICISM.

The fundamental role of language in human existence is and has long been acknowledged in the study of things human and in particular by the disciplines listed above. However, the ways the particular disciplines define and investigate language have often obscured this fundamental character in actual investigative practice. Bringing into conversation the many different kinds of study can provide a richer understanding of the pervasive importance of language and the multidimensional effects of speech. Furthermore, anchoring this multidimensional study ethnographically (i.e. in the speaking that occurs in actual linguistic communities) can expose general structural patterns in the character and role of language that do not readily appear in single discipline inquiry. At the same time, the results of a huge range of particular and disparate studies in the many fields can be brought together and coordinated.

For example, effective speakers in particular social settings must not only abide by laws of grammar and appropriate phonetic schemes, but they must also appreciate and observe a host of particular social and cultural codes shared with their hearers. Individual speakers will exhibit cognitive and expressive functions in their speaking, but they will also communicate in a context of complex linguistic, non-linguistic, and behavioural functions dependent on social and cultural relationships. These in turn demonstrate that the meaning of speech is not achieved only by considering abstract habits of speaking or characteristics of speech. Meaning is also established by reference to contexts, environments, settings, milieus, as well as by reference to how, where, when, and by whom speech events occur. Moreover, analysis that examines many such particular and distinct instances in many different settings and contexts can manifest roles and functions of speaking that would otherwise remain unobserved.

This multipronged approach of the ethnography of speaking is aimed less at comprehensive explanation and more at an ongoing, open-ended, inductive, comparative description of the roles and functions of speaking in human society generally and in particular situations. Generalization and particularity have to be held in tension. Methodological variety is seen as an asset for discovery rather than as a competition for or a reduction to an all-encompassing theory or a single comprehensive way of proceeding. At the same time, no responsible line of inquiry is ruled out a priori. What remains basic is that any actual economy of speaking is always in relation to an actual population or community that cannot be left out of the analysis.

Nevertheless, as Hymes has clearly shown, any speech event will exhibit a complex of component factors, variable features that analysts will observe, describe, list, enumerate, and label. Though seemingly obvious, each represents a broad and complex area of inquiry. They are best understood as pointers towards kinds of questions and tactics of approach. For example, components can include attention to 1) speaker(s); 2) audience; 3) forms or GENRE of communication, such as report, recitation, SONG, exhortation, or story; 4) channel, such as live speech, sound recording, or written text; 5) sociocultural code(s) that affect meaning, as when the speaker is wearing a uniform or a judge's gown; 6) topic; and 7) situation or setting (Hymes, 'Ethnography Part. 1'). As Hymes also demonstrates, corresponding to component factors in speech events are types of function: 1) expressive or emotive function, which includes intensity of feeling in the speaker; 2) directive/rhetorical/persuasive function, which registers the speaker's purpose and anticipated effect on the audience; 3) poetic function, which registers or echoes traditional forms of expression, perhaps shaped in terms of conventional metre or lines; 4) contact, the way in which speaker and hearer(s) are connected; 5) metalinguistic referencing, such as an appeal to external authority; 6) referential functioning, such as associating what is said to matters of relevance to the audience; and 7) contextual/situational functioning, the circumstances that give rise to and situate the particular speech event (Hymes, 'Ethnography Part. 2'). Despite their generality, such factors and functions will always appear and interact in very particular and concrete ways. Culturally traditional events can even include non-human elements such as animals, weather, or other environmental phenomena that a community regards as significant. When these factors operate in multi-language contexts or cross-culturally, effective communication and understanding may depend on successful alignment of the diverse semantic factors.

Like ETHNOPOETICS, the ethnography of speaking has actual and potential applications wherever speaking occurs, ranging from events like traditional STORYTELLING, teaching, and learning language in elementary classrooms, and bureaucratic encounters such as diplomatic exchanges, immigration interviews, court hearings, police interrogations, job interviews, and political processes. They can also be important in contexts involving such relational similarities and differences in and among age groups, generations, and genders as well as different levels of authority, education, expertise, economic status, or social standing in casual, formal, or ritual occasions. There is also the burgeoning realization of ways in which spoken composition is not a one-way act but, as performance, its products are co-created by audiences in settings.

Growing awareness of the radical and pervasive role of speech in biblical literature offers unlimited opportunity for exploring the ethnographic depths of both the Hebrew Bible and the NT. Certainly a sense of the spoken word is foundational in texts such as Genesis 1 ('And God said, 'Let there be …") and John 1 ('In the beginning was the Word …'). Furthermore, there has long been reference to ORAL TRADITION as a complement to the biblical text. Nevertheless, the capacity to probe and describe effectively what this means in particular has largely eluded commentators. The radical shaping effect of speech on the composition of the literary texts and the semantic riches residually embodied in the sociolinguistic settings has been thinly appreciated.

The twentieth-century discovery of ORALITY has flowed from many different directions and from many previously disparate disciplines. These currents have mixed complexly and have become increasingly complementary rather than competitive in both method and particular exploration. They have thus stimulated applications as varied as reconstructing the oral settings of Franz Boas' accounts of Native American stories (Hymes 1981), graphically re-oralizing Zuni narrative poetry (Tedlock 1999) and exposing the political consequences of certain European attitudes towards language use (Bauman and Briggs 2003). Within biblical studies, the use of the techniques of the ethnography of speaking and allied strategies to unveil the oral, speech-based factors and functions embedded in biblical literature has been limited, though in keeping with trends in other fields, varied mixings of approaches are appearing.

A notable exception in the study of the Hebrew Bible is in the work of SUSAN NIDITCH, who has built on the work of WALTER ONG and JOHN MILES FOLEY. For example, she employs the idea that the form and meaning of oral-traditional material – what Foley and Hymes call its REGISTER – references the entire tradition of expression in which it occurs. That is, competent performance implies that performers of traditional material embody and employ sensitivity to the sociocultural world of their audiences.

Randy F. Lumpp (Regis University, USA)

Further Reading

Bauman, Richard, and Joel Sherzer eds. 1989. 2nd edition. *Explorations in the Ethnography of Speaking* Studies in the Social and Cultural Foundations of Language. Cambridge and New York: Cambridge University Press.

Bauman, Richard, and Charles L. Briggs. 2003. *Voices of Modernity: Language Ideologies and the Politics of Inequality*. New York: Cambridge University Press.
Hymes, Dell H. 1981. *'In vain I tried to tell you': Essays in Native American Ethnopoetics*. Philadelphia: University of Pennsylvania Press.
Hymes, Dell H. 'The Ethnography of Speaking'. Parts 1 and 2. http://www.ohio.edu/people/thompsoc/Hymes.html (part 1); http://www.ohio.edu/people/thompsoc/Hymes2.html (part 2). This two-part online article is an updated version of Hymes, Dell H. 1962. 'The Ethnography of Speaking'. In *Anthropology and Human Behavior*. Edited by Thomas Gladwin and William C. Sturtevant. Washington, DC: Anthropological Society of Washington, pp. 15–53.
Niditch, Susan. 1996. *Oral World and Written Word: Ancient Israelite Literature*. Louisville: Westminster John Knox Press.
Niditch, Susan. 2008. *Judges: A Commentary*. Louisville: Westminster John Knox Press.
Tedlock, Dennis. 1999. *Finding the Center: The Art of the Zuni Storyteller*. 2nd edn. Lincoln: University of Nebraska Press.

Ethnopoetics Ethnopoetics is a collective term for a variety of perspectives on, and approaches to, the study of relationships between non-Western oral verbal performances and their renderings in written texts. It is especially aimed at capturing or restoring the qualities of such material as living oral performances. As such, the field of ethnopoetics represents a radical paradigm shift in the treatment of texts rooted in oral composition and performance.

The term *ethnopoetics* is attributed to Jerome Rothenberg, who first used it in the 1960s. Rothenberg recognized the inadequacies of written renderings of oral materials from Native American and other cultures. These renderings often impose Western, literate, Greco-Roman-European poetical assumptions, expectations, and/or formats on materials from other ethnic worlds, or obscure their characteristics as oral performances, or both. Rothenberg observed that each culture has its own POETICS, and effective interpretation depends on identifying and describing aesthetic and poetical assumptions and expectations embodied in specific sociocultural forms of expression. Rothenberg's work demonstrated that if each and every ethnic setting brings its own poetics to its forms of expression, rendering originally spoken materials into textual form requires careful attention to the particular cultural, linguistic, and nonverbal stylistic economy in which the material is embodied, whether in the original language or in TRANSLATION.

DENNIS TEDLOCK, who collaborated with Rothenberg, highlighted the qualities of oral performance in textual renderings of Native American verbal art. He stressed the essentially performative origins and qualities of traditional materials and argued that written renderings of traditional texts should enable re-performances of them, treating them in the manner of musical scores. Transcripts of oral performance should thus include instructions for reading aloud – including notes on expressive elements like intonation, stress, silence, pitch, repetition, formulaic expressions, gestures, and props – so as to bring to life the fuller dynamic and semantic power not only of narratives and stories but also of PROVERBS, RIDDLES, curses, laments, praises, prayers, prophecies, and public announcements. While such notations may fall short of the richness of the original performances on which these texts are based, they can nevertheless provide valuable insights into aesthetically distant worlds, even some that may no longer be accessible otherwise.

DELL HYMES devoted considerable effort to reworking the field notes and translations of Native American narratives, especially those of the northwest American coast. Using field notes by earlier anthropologists (including pioneer anthropologist Franz Boas), Hymes worked to restore the poetic and stylistic qualities of the original oral performances on which the transcripts were based. This approach reveals that the original performances embody more than mere ideological content, THEME, or story line. Rather, these performances invoke and express aspects of the specific sociocultural traditions in which they originate. Hymes identified a number of salient characteristics in oral performance that reveal both structure and meaning. RICHARD BAUMAN, who studied anthropology under Hymes, explored the role and character of performance in verbal art. Bauman has been particularly influential through his study of language ideology (how people's understanding of the function of language shapes the ways they use it).

Since the 1960s, a variety of scholars and methodological approaches have applied and expanded ethnopoetics and its connections to other kinds of studies and to collaborations among scholars of diverse backgrounds and interests. Thus ethnopoetics may be seen less as a single, distinct academic discipline than as a meeting place for the interrelations of materials and questions from disparate academic fields, including anthropology, FOLKLORE studies, linguistics, and aesthetics. Further, the boundaries of ethnopoetics are blurred by numerous terms used to identify its concerns, or concerns derived from or related to it (e.g. ETHNOGRAPHY OF SPEAKING, ethnography of communication, SOCIOLINGUISTICS, linguistic anthropology, performance studies, tradition and memory studies). Methodologically, ethnopoetics connects to work on oral-formulaic theory by ALBERT LORD, ERIC HAVELOCK, JOHN MILES FOLEY, and their students. The scope of inquiry includes poetry from sources as diverse as Homeric, Old English, South Slavic, West African, and Egyptian Bedouin epics to Asian-American poetry and African American and Pentecostal women's sermons.

Ethnopoetics arose with the budding awareness of ethnocentricity in academia as well as in society generally. Additionally, it has contributed in a germinal and concrete way to the recognition of the biases in interpretation generated by text and print sensibilities when the expressive forms of non-Western or oral cultures are encountered. While critics have registered concerns about the difficulty of the work, the dangers of lurking biases and perpetuated stereotypes, and the qualitative variability of the performances on which the ethnographical record may rest, key practitioners stress the crucial importance of thorough knowledge of the languages and cultures expressed in poetical forms.

The challenge posed by ethnopoetics and its allied forms of inquiry is less centred in the study of new contents than in the development of radically new questions and approaches to cultural objects that have long been objects of research. The modern discovery of ORALITY and oral cultures and their distinctive forms of thought and expression has proceeded especially by working back through long-known literatures shaped by oral modalities. The net effect is to require a thorough, ongoing re-envisioning of critical approaches to nearly all written texts from ancient worlds. The immensity of this reexamination and the appropriation of its consequences are becoming increasingly apparent.

Appropriating these consequences is not a matter of simply regarding all earlier studies of the 'classic' materials as wrong, whether the studies be of ancient epics, traditional narratives of indigenous peoples, or canonical narratives in the Hebrew Bible; more subtly, it is a matter of coping with an explosion of new insights into these materials. Further, from a methodological standpoint, since earlier investigators were unaware of their literate biases, ethnopoetics can help reveal unperceived yet crucially important dimensions of meaning that are embodied in orally grounded forms of expression. What is involved is the interplay between orality and LITERACY, between the worlds of oral thought and composition and the effects of rendering them into WRITING. It must be emphasized that this work is far from systematic. The range of materials, the particular subjects of study, the particular assemblies of disciplines and methods, and the particular preferences of individual scholars add up to widely disparate investigations of widely varied materials. Nevertheless, despite the disparity, significant convergences and overlappings are emerging.

Although the potential of ethnopoetics and related approaches to problems in biblical studies have not been fully realized, significant work has been done. As early as the 1960s and 1970s, biblical scholars had begun to glimpse the relevance of the work of Albert Lord, RUTH FINNEGAN, and other major voices in the field, and applications of this theoretical spectrum have more recently gained considerable momentum. Among the most notable efforts, SUSAN NIDITCH has begun to draw together and apply work by scholars of orally rooted literatures – particularly Albert Lord, WALTER ONG, Dell Hymes, and John Miles Foley – to the study of the

Hebrew Bible. Similarly, Raymond Person, working from a familiarity with Bauman, Hymes, and Tedlock, has applied perspectives from John Miles Foley to the complex oral-textual interplay in parallel narratives in the Deuteronomic History and Chronicles. Building particularly on the work of Walter Ong and John Miles Foley, Werner Kelber began a fundamental deconstruction of Form Criticism and other hyper-textualist forms of analysis. His *The Oral and the Written Gospel: The Hermeneutics of Speaking and Writing in the Synoptic Tradition, Mark, Paul and Q* (1983) has stimulated a growing body of NT scholars and scholars of Judaica and early Christianity to explore the synchronic and diachronic dynamics of oral-text interplay in biblical, rabbinic, and other ancient literatures.

A recent experimental embodiment of the impulses ethnopoetical and oral-textual approaches bring to biblical hermeneutics is biblical performance criticism, which, like its predecessors, includes an eclectic array of questions, methods, and foci. A major component of this approach is the use of multimedia performance of biblical material as a supplement to more conventional attention to written text alone.

Randy F. Lumpp (Regis University, USA)

Further Reading

Bauman, Richard. 1977. *Verbal Art as Performance*. Prospect Heights, IL: Waveland Press.

Bauman, Richard. 1986. *Story, Performance and Event: Contextual Studies of Oral Narrative*. New York: Cambridge University Press.

Bauman, Richard and Charles Briggs. 2003. *Voices of Modernity: Language Ideologies and the Politics of Inequality*. New York: Cambridge University Press.

Biblical Performance Criticism. http://biblicalperformancecriticism.org/

Blommaert, Jan. 2006. 'Applied Ethnopoetics'. *Narrative Inquiry* 16(1): 181–90.

Horsley, Richard A., Jonathan A. Draper, and John Miles Foley, eds. 2006. *Performing the Gospel: Orality, Memory and Mark*. Fortress Press: Minneapolis.

Hymes, Dell. 1981. *'In vain I tried to tell you': Essays in North American Ethnopoetics*. Philadelphia: University of Pennsylvania Press.

Hymes, Dell. 2003. *Now I Know Only So Far: Essays in Ethnopoetics*. Lincoln: University of Nebraska Press.

Long, Burke O. 1976. 'Recent Field Studies in Oral Literature and Their Bearing on OT Criticism'. *VT*, 26: 187–98.

Kelber, Werner H. 1983. *The Oral and the Written Gospel: The Hermeneutics of Speaking and Writing in the Synoptic Tradition, Mark, Paul and Q*. Philadelphia: Fortress Press.

Kelber, Werner H. 2013. *Imprints, Voiceprints, and Footprints of Memory: Collected Essays of Werner H. Kelber*. SBLRBS. Atlanta: Society of Biblical Literature.

Niditch, Susan. 1996. *Oral and Written Word: Ancient Israelite Literature*. Louisville: Westminster John Knox, 1996.

Niditch, Susan. 2008. *Judges: A Commentary*. Louisville: Westminster John Knox, 2008.

Person, Raymond F., Jr. 2011. 'The Role of Memory in the Tradition Represented by the Deuteronomic History and the Book of Chronicles'. *Oral Tradition* 26 (2011): 537–50.

Rothenberg, Jerome, ed. 1968. *Technicians of the Sacred: A Range of Poetries from Africa, America, Asia and Oceania*. Garden City, NY: Doubleday.

Tedlock, Dennis. 1983. *The Spoken Word and the Work of Interpretation*. Philadelphia: University of Pennsylvania Press.

Tedlock, Dennis. 1999. *Finding the Center: The Art of the Zuni Storyteller*. Lincoln: University of Nebraska Press. 2nd ed.

Eucharist The Eucharist, or Lord's Supper, is a symbolic community consumption of food and drink (normally bread and wine) that has served as a 'ritual of remembrance' in Christianity since its beginnings. The memorial aspect of the ritual is already evident in the formulation, 'Do this in remembrance of me [Jesus]', in the Pauline and Lukan versions of the so-called 'words of institution' (1 Cor. 11.23-25; Lk. 22.14-20). The literary character of these words in all of the four versions in which it appears in the NT (see also Mt. 26.26-28; Mk 14.22-24) can be described as a consciously shaped tradition tracing the origin of the ritual meal of the Christian community back to Jesus' Last Supper in Jerusalem the night before his death.

Several aspects of the tradition regarding the origins of the meal suggest that the NT texts should not just be regarded as a historical report, but rather as an early Christian explanation of the origin and meaning of the meal celebrated in the Christian community. This is not to deny the historicity of the Last Supper as such (cf. Pitre 2015; Marshall 2009). The central gestures of that meal – the breaking of the bread and passing of the cup – are, however, related to the life and death of Jesus by way of an early Christian interpretation: the broken bread is designated as Jesus' body, and the cup is interpreted as his blood. In all probability, in early Christian communities the 'words of institution' were not spoken at the celebration of the meal itself, but rather served as an aetiological tradition, explaining the origin and meaning of the Christian meal. This conclusion is supported by the observation that there are other traditions and interpretations of this meal in early Christian texts. The Didache, for example, includes prayers that should be spoken, first concerning the cup and afterwards concerning the broken bread (chaps. 9 and 10); the Gospel of John refers to Jesus as the 'bread from heaven' and declares that the flesh of the Son of Man must be eaten and his blood must be drunk in order to participate in his life (6.53); Ignatius refers to the broken bread as the 'medicine of immortality, the antidote we take in order not to die but to live forever in Jesus Christ' (Ephesians 20.2).

As these examples demonstrate, the Eucharist was the central ritual in early Christianity. It symbolized the unity of the community and its relationship with Jesus Christ. Therefore, its interpretation in early Christian texts was not the only dimension in which this ritual became part of the foundational history of Christianity; of at least equal importance was the actual celebration of that meal in community gatherings. The breaking of the bread and the passing of the cup formed its distinctive features, visualizing the equality of all members of the community. At the same time, these characteristic features of the Christian meal distinguished it from other cultic or communal meals in antiquity (see BANQUETS). A second important aspect is the representation of Jesus Christ in the midst of the community. In sharing the bread and the cup, the members of the community participated symbolically in Jesus' Last Supper with his disciples in Jerusalem, just before his death. Therefore, Paul can call the Lord's Supper a 'proclamation of the Lord's death until he comes' (1 Cor. 11.26).

The Eucharist can therefore be regarded as a ritual representation of the exalted Lord within the community. The Greek term *remembrance* (*anamnēsis*) in 1 Cor. 11.24-25 and Lk. 22.19 might therefore be translated as 're-presentation'. The ritual aims to connect the past life and death of Jesus with the time and the actual situation of the community. Therefore, the Eucharist is a prime example of the conception of remembrance or memory as the relationship between present and past, or, put another way, as the perception of the present in light of a meaningful past (see COLLECTIVE MEMORY; CULTURAL MEMORY).

The conclusion that the Eucharist serves to ritually connect present experience with Jesus' past is supported by several aspects of the interpretation of the meal in early Christian texts. In addition to the points noted above, it is striking that the accounts of the Last Supper in Jerusalem are consciously integrated into the PASSION NARRATIVES in the Synoptic Gospels. In this way, the connection between this meal and important aspects of Jesus' activity is highlighted: his communion with the crowds, the sinners, the sick and the poor, including communal meals with them; his life for others, as well as his death as the confirmation of the new covenant between God and mankind ('blood of the covenant'). Justin Martyr, explaining the meaning of the Eucharist for his Roman readers, interprets it as 'not common bread or common drink … but as food … from which our blood and flesh are fed by transformation' (*1 Apology* 66). With this complex and difficult sentence Justin expresses an important characteristic of early Christian perception of the Eucharist that can be found also in the Gospel of John, Ignatius, Irenaeus, and the Gospel of Philip: the Eucharist conveys the new life in Jesus Christ because it is not just ordinary food and drink, but contains God's Spirit, invoked by the Eucharistic prayers. The participants in the Eucharistic meal therefore not only share food and drink with each other but also partake in the resurrection and the eternal life mediated through Jesus Christ as the incarnate Word of God.

Aside from the Eucharistic ritual itself and those early Christian texts that interpret it, a third significant consideration for understanding the Lord's Supper comes from the liturgical tradition (see WORSHIP, EARLY CHRISTIAN). Although the development of liturgy in early Christianity is a thorny field, some aspects may be mentioned. Texts such as 1 Cor. 11.23-36, Didache 9–10, and Justin's *1 Apology* 65 suggest that the Christian meal started with prayers of the assembly or a 'head of the community', followed by the distribution of the bread and the sharing of the cup. According to Pliny's letter to Emperor Trajan (10.96), this meal took place in the evening and was separated from the morning service at sunrise. The liturgical tradition therefore adopted elements of Jewish meals as well as of cultic meals of Greco-Roman assemblies and interpreted them in a distinctive way.

The Eucharist has several dimensions demonstrating its meaning for the remembrance of Jesus Christ in early Christianity. It relates Jesus' earthly activity, including his suffering and death, to the actual situation of the Christian community in later periods of history. It symbolizes the connection between the community that celebrates that meal and the Lord Jesus Christ, his life and death as well as his resurrection and exaltation. This connection is made visible and 'testable' through the shared bread and wine. The Eucharist has a special importance for the development and shape of the Christian communities because it has been the centre of the community gatherings from the earliest days of the church.

Jens Schröter (Humboldt University of Berlin)

Further Reading

Bradshaw, Paul F. 2004. *Eucharistic Origins*. London: SPCK.

Hellholm, David, and Dieter Sänger, eds. 2016. *The Eucharist – Its Origins and Contexts: Sacred Meal, Communal Meal, Table Fellowship in Late Antiquity, Early Judaism, and Early Christianity*. WUNT 1. 3 vols. Tübingen: Mohr Siebeck.

Marshall, I. Howard. 2009. 'The Last Supper'. In *Key Events in the Life of the Historical Jesus: A Collaborative Exploration of Context and Coherence*. Edited by Darrell L. Bock and Robert L. Webb. WUNT 247. Tübingen: Mohr Siebeck, pp. 481–588.

Pitre, Brant. 2015. *Jesus and the Last Supper*. Grand Rapids: Eerdmans.

Schröter, Jens. 2006. *Das Abendmahl: Frühchristliche Deutungen und Impulse für die Gegenwart*. Stuttgarter Bibel-Studien 210. Stuttgart: Katholisches Bibelwerk.

Exorcism The Greek term *exorkismos* ('binding by oath') derives from the verb *exorkoō* ('cause to swear, adjure'). These words can designate 1) the act of driving out, or deterring, demonic beings from persons and places believed to be possessed by them; or, (2) the means employed for this purpose, the solemn and authoritative adjuration addressed to the demon. Exorcism is performed in the name of a god or of God, who is considered the source of the magical exorcizing power. Exorcisms conclude with the *defixatio*, which binds the demon and renders it inoffensive. Exorcism rituals were central to ancient Near Eastern medicine, with demonic possession seen as the cause of certain diseases and exorcism as the cure.

Narrative Portrayals of Exorcisms

Exorcism rituals are portrayed in several ancient Jewish and Christian narrative texts. In the Hebrew Bible, for example, King Saul is tormented by an evil spirit sent by God (1 Sam. 16.14) and David soothes him by playing his lyre (1 Sam. 18.10). Tobit, a deuterocanonical (apocryphal) book extant in Greek translation and found in fragmentary form in Aramaic at Qumran (4Q196-199 = Tobita-d; 4Q200 = Tobite), describes the exorcism of the demon Asmodeus, who has tormented a woman by killing seven of her husbands in the bridal room. The exorcism, which is directed by the angel Raphael, consists of prayer and fumigation of a fish's liver (Tobit 8.1-9). Following the exorcism, Raphael binds the demon (Tobit 8.3). In the narrative the demon functions to impede Sarah's non-endogamic marriages; her marriage to Tobit is a victory of the endogamic marriage over the demonic.

Genesis Apopcryphon (1Q20 = 1QapGen), a narrative interpretation of Genesis traditions found at Qumran, mentions a 'baneful spirit' (*rwḥ mktyš*) that causes impotence in Pharaoh's court after the Egyptians take Sarai from Abram (1Q20 20.16, cf. Gen. 12.10-20). This pestilential spirit (*rwḥ mktš*, *rwḥ b'yš'*) was sent by God in response to Abram's prayer (1Q20 20.16-17) and is exorcized by Abram through further prayer and the laying on of hands (1Q20 20.26-27). The exorcism concludes with the formula 'that he may live' (*whyh*) (1Q20 20.22), which also appears in the healing narrative at Mk 5.23. In this text, the story of the demon and its exorcism fills a gap in the narrative logic of the biblical pericope and offers undeniable proof that neither Pharaoh nor any other Egyptian could have had sex with Sarai while she was in the Egyptian court (1Q20 19.10–20.11; cp. Gen. 12.12-20). The demon was sent by God to Pharaoh's court in response to Abram's prayer.

The NT Gospels contain several stories of demonic possession and exorcism by Jesus. These stories demonstrate Jesus' power over impurities as represented by demons. Jesus' ability to exorcise demons in his own name and by his personal authority and power is portrayed as a sign of his messiahship (Mt. 12.23, 28; Lk. 11.20). As such, Jesus' exorcisms serve a parallel function to the healing stories that also demonstrate Jesus' power over impurity.

The Gospel of Mark contains thirteen healing stories, four of which are exorcisms. Mark 1:21-8 (cf. Lk. 4.31-37; omitted in Matthew) relates the healing of the man with an unclean spirit in the synagogue at Capernaum. Mk 5.1-20 (cf. Mt. 8.28-34; Lk. 8.26-39) reports the case of the Gerasene demoniac (Mt. 8:28 says two demoniacs) who lived among the tombs and could not be restrained. In this episode, Jesus first asks the name of the demon, who is called 'Legion'. The demons beg Jesus not to send them out of the country, so he permits them to enter a herd of swine; the swine rush down the steep bank into the sea and drown. Mk 7.24-30 (cf. Mt. 15.21-28; omitted in Luke) reports the healing of the daughter of the Syrophoenician woman possessed by an unclean spirit (*pneuma akatharton*). Jesus performs this exorcism from a distance. Finally, Mk 9.14-29 (cf. Mt. 17.14-21; Lk. 9.37-42) relates the exorcism of a spirit that renders an epileptic boy mute. Jesus commands the spirit to leave the body of the boy and never enter him again. A similar symptom of possession (inability to speak) is described in Mt. 12.22, where Jesus casts a demon out of a mute and blind man. Luke 11.14 mentions the exorcism of a demon who renders another man mute. Summary references to Jesus' exorcistic ministry appear in Mk 1.32-4, 39, 3.11; Lk. 7.l, 13.32, suggesting that the specific instances noted above were understood to be typical of his ministry.

Practical Texts

Alongside the narrative descriptions noted above, other ancient Jewish texts illuminate ancient understandings of exorcism by containing instructions and scripts for the performance of exorcisms. 4Q560 (4QExorcismar) is a fragmentary Aramaic text from Qumran that was probably intended as a medical text and provides instructions for the remedy of illnesses caused by demons called rwḥ (4Q560 1.ii.5). Epithets for the agents of the illness are the 'evil visitor' (*pqd b'yš*) who 'enters the flesh' (*'ll bbśr'*; 4Q560 1.i.2-3), 'the male penetrator' (*ḥlhy'dkr'*), and 'the female penetrator' (*ḥlhlyt nqb'*; 4Q560 1.i.3). These demonic agents transmit fever (*'š'*), chills (*'ry'*), and pain in the heart (*'št lbb*; 4Q560 1.i.4). The text also mentions a demonic midwife (*yldn*; 4Q560 1.i.2) which might refer to Lilith, the baby-killing female demon who poses as a midwife in several Mesopotamian incantations.

11Q11 (11QapocrPs) contains four apotropaic Hebrew compositions that refer to God as the source of ritual power and close with '*selah*'. These are undoubtedly identical with the four songs composed by David 'for charming the demon-possessed with music' mentioned in 11Q5 (11Q5/11QPsa 27.10). The fourth composition (11Q11 6.3-14) is Psalm 91, (with only minor textual changes and additions), attributed here to David (*šyr ldwyd*). This psalm is an apotropaic blessing for the righteous against a sequence of twelve threatening dangers. Among these, the terms *qeteb* and *deber* refer to demonic representatives of the pestilence, which is also described in metaphorical form as the 'arrow which flies by day' (*ḥṣ y'wp ywmm*; Ps. 91:5). The rest of the terms refer to animal attacks and physical dangers (Ps. 91:12-13). Songs 1-3 are preserved in a highly fragmentary form. Attributed to David and labelled as 'incantation' (lḥš), they show the structure of exorcistic texts. Song 3 (11Q11 5.4–6.3) describes an encounter with a horned and human-faced demon that is rendered inoffensive (11Q11 5.7). The exorcistic formula refers to the origin of the demon 'from humans and from the seed of the holy ones' (… *m*]*'dm wmzr' hqd*[*wšy*]*m*, 11Q11 5.6), recalling the ENOCHIC TRADITION of the origin of demons. Song 2 (11Q11 2.1–5.3) mentions Solomon's name, in a context of incantations, together with spirits and demons (11Q11 2.2-3). YHWH is evoked as the creator God of the universe and examples are cited of his almighty power. The term *adjuring* (*mšby'*;11Q11 3.4; 4.1) introduces the *defixatio*, the binding of the demon and its casting into the nether world. The mention of the name of the angel Raphael (11Q 5.3) suggests that the incantation was written against an illness caused by spirits or against a demonic attack.

These four songs 'for the stricken' were recited, in all probability, at the four liminal days (the equinoxes and solstices of the solar year) as communal prayers intended to avert demonic attacks materialized in seasonal plagues and demonic attacks.

Ida Fröhlich (Pázmány Péter Catholic University, Hungary)

Further Reading

Fitzmyer, Joseph A. 2004. *The Genesis Apocryphon of Qumran Cave I: A Commentary*. 3rd edn. Rome: Pontificio Instituto Biblico, 2004

Fröhlich, Ida. 2012. 'Healing with Psalms'. In *Prayer and Poetry in the Dead Sea Scrolls and Related Literature. STDJ* 98. Edited by Jeremy Penner, Ken M. Penner and Cecilia Wassen. Leiden and Boston, MA: Brill, pp. 197–215.

Fröhlich, Ida. 2013. 'Evil in Second Temple Texts'. In *Evil and the Devil*. Edited by I. Fröhlich and E. Koskenniemi. The Library of New Testament Studies 481. London: Bloomsbury T&T Clark, pp. 23–50.

Ego, Beate. 2003. 'Denn er liebt sie (Tob 6,15 Ms. 319): Zur Rolle des Dämons Asmodäus in der Tobit-Erzählung'. In *Die Dämonen – Demons*. Edited by Armin Lange. Tübingen: J.C.B. Mohr (Paul Siebeck), pp. 309–17.

Sorensen, Eric. 2002. *Possession and Exorcism in the New Testament and Early Christianity*. WUNT 2. 157, Tübingen: Mohr Siebeck.

Wahlen, Clinton. 2004. *Jesus and the Impurity of Spirits in the Synoptic Gospels*. WUNT 2. 185, Tübingen Mohr Siebeck.

F

Fasting Fasting is an ascetic ritual practice that entails the voluntary abstention from food and drink for a finite period of time. Since the physical body requires nourishment to survive, fasting is a form of self-denial that negates one's bodily needs in an effort to bring about spiritual change. While the only compulsory fast mandated in the Hebrew Bible is associated with Yom Kippur, fasting as a means of atoning for sins is an important measure of piety in Second Temple and early RABBINIC LITERATURE.

Given the significance of meal fellowship in antiquity, fasting represented a temporary rejection of both life and community (see BANQUETS). In biblical texts, ritual fasting is a spiritual practice that functions as a response to mourning (1 Sam. 31.13; 2 Sam. 1.12; Pss. 35.15), a means of intensifying one's prayer (2 Sam. 12.16; Est. 4.3; 16) and a preparation for divine revelation (Dan. 9.3; 10.2-3).

In the Second Temple period, fasting developed as a personal spiritual discipline and religious ideal. In Judith, the protagonist fasts daily all year (with the exception of SABBATHS and festivals), and her asceticism is a hailed as mark of her dedication to Judaism (8.6). Both 1 and 2 Maccabees contain references to fasting during wartime: 1 Macc. 3.47 says that Judean soldiers would fast before battle during the Hasmonean war, while 2 Macc. 13.10-12 reports that fasting was customary during heightened military activity. 4 Ezra and 2 Baruch are apocalyptic narratives which each mention the practice of fasting for seven days in order to receive a divine vision (4 Ezra 5.20; 6.31; 2 Bar. 9; 12.5; 20.50).

Philo's description of the THERAPUTAE and their ascetic practices in *The Contemplative Life* suggests that this group saw fasting as a means to achieve a level of purity comparable to that of the priests. The sectarian community at Qumran was also preoccupied with achieving a level of purity only accessible by withdrawing from the general community to create their own ascetic fellowship; for this community, ascetic practice was linked to atonement from sin (see PURIFICATION RITUALS).

In the NT, Jesus' forty-day temptation by Satan is marked by a period of fasting in the wilderness (Mt. 4.2; Lk. 4.2), suggesting that Jesus practised fasting as a form of personal piety. In the Sermon on the Mount, Jesus advises that fasting should be practised with humility (Mt. 6.16-18) and not for show. Although there are other isolated examples of personal fasts (e.g. following Paul's conversion in Acts 9.8-11, and in the context of the ordination of Paul and Barnabas in Acts 14.23), it is not until the apostolic period that regular, communal fasts were instituted in the Christian community, such as Lent or the fast of Good Friday, which marks Jesus' crucifixion prior to Easter Sunday.

Rabbinic Judaism continued to develop the practice of fasting as a mechanism for personal and collective atonement. In *Berakhot* 17a, fasting is a form of ritual sacrifice: the fat and blood 'burned' by fasting is likened to the fat and blood offered by priests upon the temple altar. The rabbis, however, discouraged private fasts, and instead established a litany of additional fast days to be observed by the community. Some fast days were instituted to mark catastrophic events in Jewish history, such as the 17th of Tammuz, the 9th of Av, the Fast of Gedaliah, and the 10th of Tevet. The fast day prescribed in the book of Esther (9:16) also became normative practice during this time.

Megillat Ta'anit, an early rabbinic source devoted to fasting, notes that communal fasts were often instituted during times of drought (*Ta'anit* 18a). Prayers for rain were intensified by the custom of fasting on successive Mondays and Thursdays, especially in the early fall, if the rainy season was slow to begin. The apostolic text Didache suggests that the early Christian community was also influenced by this custom: they preserved the tradition of twice-weekly fasting, but switched the customary fast days to Tuesdays and Fridays in an effort to differentiate their practice from those they viewed as 'hypocrites'.

Andrea Lieber (Dickinson College, USA)

Further Reading

Diamond, Eliezer. 2004. *Holy Men and Hunger Artists: Fasting and Asceticism in Rabbinic Culture*. New York: Oxford University Press.

Finn, Richard Damien. 2009. *Asceticism in the Graeco-Roman World.* Cambridge: Cambridge University Press.

Smit, Peter-Ben. 2014. 'Reaching for the Tree of Life: The Role of Eating, Drinking, Fasting, and Symbolic Foodstuffs in 4 Ezra'. *JSJ* 45(3): 366–87.

Finnegan, Ruth Ruth Finnegan is a social anthropologist with an interest in many aspects of human communication. Her original fieldwork was among the Limba people of Sierra Leone, and she has continued to write on African oral literature throughout her career. She has also written on (among other things) oral poetry, LITERACY and ORALITY, urban STORYTELLING and MUSIC-making in Britain, the practice of quoting, research outside universities, and NONVERBAL aspects of communication. Within the larger scope of her research, biblical scholars have been most attracted to Finnegan's approach to oral communication.

Finnegan's work is characterized by a suspicion of essentialist categorizations, binary oppositions, and elitist or ethnocentric perspectives. She has been consistently critical of GREAT DIVIDE theories that contrast orality and 'oral cultures' with literacy and 'literate cultures', especially where these terms are used as surrogates for traditional/primitive and modern/Western societies. In her view, empirical evidence does not support the kind of distinctions between oral and literate mentalities and societies propounded by scholars such as WALTER ONG. It is overly simplistic to attribute major cultural and historical shifts solely to developments in communication technology, let alone to subscribe to a Western intellectual master narrative that correlates alphabetic literacy and printing with advances in civilization.

Finnegan is also critical of any monolithic view of orality that tends to treat this medium as if it were a unitary phenomenon with universal characteristics in all societies, whether a romantic view of FOLKLORE and ORAL TRADITION, a structural-functionalist sociological perspective, or an unjustified extension of PARRY and LORD's oral-formulaic theory to all forms of oral literature. Her surveys of African oral literature and worldwide oral poetry indicate that oral verbal art can take many forms and can be composed and performed in a great variety of ways. While composition in performance may characterize some oral literature, composition in advance and memorization can also be found, along with free improvisation and other modes.

Finnegan frequently points out that there are in fact very few examples of pure orality to be studied, since in most human societies spoken and written communication have interpenetrated each other for centuries. This problematizes what is meant by *oral poetry*, for example, since much of what would normally count as oral poetry may well have passed through WRITING at some stage. At the same time, Finnegan recognizes that oral literature tends to be more flexible than written material, and that performance is especially important to its realization. Moreover, what might be regarded as the nonverbal aspects of performance (gesture, intonation, expression, tempo, the visual appearance of the performer, the context of performance, the audience's reaction and participation, and many more such factors) may often be as important, if not more important, to the meaning of a performance than the reduction of that performance to words on a printed page, which may also give a wholly misleading impression of the artistry involved.

Eric Eve (Oxford University, UK)

Further Reading

Ruth Finnegan. 1977. *Oral Poetry: Its Nature, Significance and Social Context*. Bloomington: Indiana University Press, 1992.

Ruth Finnegan. 1988. *Literacy & Orality: Studies in the Technology of Communication*. Oxford: Blackwell.

Flashbulb Memory The term *flashbulb memory* was coined by Roger Brown and James Kulik to describe 'memories for the circumstances in which one first learned of a very surprising and consequential (or emotionally arousing) event' (1977: 73). The metaphor derives from the use of a bright pulse of light to illuminate a scene being photographed; as the light adds depth of detail to the image, intense social or emotional trauma can add a sense of heightened awareness to the circumstances in which a particular PERSONAL MEMORY was encoded. Brown and Kulik noted that many in their generation had formed flashbulb memories of the assassination of American president John F. Kennedy in November 1963: still today, many individuals who were alive at that time can remember where they were and what they were doing when they first heard the news of the assassination. From their investigation of the memories that eighty students retained of ten events that had the potential to form flashbulb memories, Brown and Kulik concluded that there are six 'abstract canonical categories' typically associated with flashbulb memories: individuals remember 1) the place in which the news was heard; 2) 'the "Ongoing Event" that was interrupted by the news, [3] the "Informant" who brought … the news, [4] the "Affect in Others" upon hearing the news, [5] as well as "Own Affect" and finally [6] some immediate "Aftermath"' (1977: 80). Based on the sense of vividness self-reported by respondents, Brown and Kulik hypothesized that flashbulb memories might be exempt from normal patterns of MEMORY PERSISTENCE AND DECAY and thus form a highly reliable set of memories.

Since the initial work of Brown and Kulik, memories of many events having the potential to form flashbulb memories have been studied, including memories of the beginning of the American bombing of Iraq under President George W. Bush, the O. J. Simpson trial verdict, the death of Princess Diana, the resignation of Margaret Thatcher, the loss of the space shuttle Challenger, and the terrorist destruction of the twin towers in New York on 11 September 2001. The results of these studies have revealed that while individuals generally consider their own flashbulb memories to be highly accurate, perhaps due to their vividness and sense of personal significance, in actual practice these memories are about as accurate as other memories not associated with such traumatic events. It is hypothesized that the emotional impact of the flashbulb memory tends to lead to its being assessed as accurate.

David Pillemer has characterized flashbulb memories as a subset of a wider category that he describes as 'personal event memories'. For Pillemer, memories of personal trauma, flashbulb memories, memories of critical incidents, and moments of insight are all varieties of personal event memories. Such events evoke a strong emotional response and are likely to form memories of the personal circumstances occurring at the time of the formation of the memory, together with vivid sensory memories that enable the reliving of the event in the imagination.

Robert K. McIver has argued that while none of the pericopes in the Gospels or accounts in the Acts of the Apostles exhibit all six of the abstract canonical categories identified by Brown and Kulik, many of them fit the criteria of personal event memories as outlined by David Pillemer. He has further argued that the accuracy of the personal event memories that found their way into the Gospel accounts should be evaluated in the light of what is known of the accuracy of flashbulb memories, given that flashbulb memories are a type of personal event memory.

Robert K. McIver (Avondale College of Higher Education, Australia)

Further Reading

Brown, Robert, and James Kulik. 1977. 'Flashbulb Memories'. *Cognition* 5: 73–99.
McIver, Robert K. 2011/2012. *Memory, Jesus, and the Synoptic Gospels*. SBLRBS. Atlanta: SBL Press; Leiden: Brill.
Pillemer, David B. 1998. *Momentous Events, Vivid Memories*. Cambridge, MA and London: Harvard University Press.
Talarico, Jennifer M., and David C. Rubin. 2003. 'Confidence, not Consistency, Characterizes Flashbulb Memories'. *Psychological Science* 14: 455–61.

Foley, John Miles John Miles Foley (1947–2012) was the W. H. Byler Endowed Chair in the Humanities at the University of Missouri, where he held appointments in the Departments of English, Classical Studies, Anthropology, and Germanic and Slavic studies. His specialization was the comparative study of ORAL TRADITIONS and literature with roots in oral tradition, especially Serbo-Croatian oral traditions, Homer, and Old English literature. He founded the journal *Oral Tradition* and edited a number of collections that demonstrated the far-reaching implications of the comparative study of oral traditions in the study of literature (see especially Foley 1998; 2005). For example, he corrected the earlier emphasis on composition by demonstrating that the same structures that have compositional utility for oral poets also provide meaning for their reception by the traditional audience.

In addition to his various edited works, Foley's primary scholarly contributions include the most thorough history to date of the Parry-Lord approach to oral traditions (1988) and a series of monographs that extended the Parry-Lord approach in important ways. Using his knowledge of linguistics, Foley extended ALBERT LORD's notion of a SPECIAL GRAMMAR for oral traditions into what Foley calls the 'traditional REGISTER', demonstrating that oral poets use a special traditional language that acts as a medium within individual oral performances for conveying meaning from the performer to the audience (1990; 1991; 1995; 1999). Although MILMAN PARRY and Lord focused almost exclusively upon composition, Foley drew from reception studies, especially the reader-response theory of Wolfgang Iser, to emphasize how the structures in oral traditions also facilitate the audience's reception of performances (1991). For example, Foley extended the discussion of how noun-epithet formulas have a compositional function by demonstrating that, through the use of METONYMY ('a mode of signification wherein the part stands for the whole'; 1991: 7), these same noun-epithet FORMULAS recall in the mind of the audience all of the actions of the individual who is described by a specific formula.

Foley also combined the insights of the Parry-Lord approach with other theoretical models in order to extend their implications. *The Singer of Tales in Performance* (1995) brings the performance approaches of RICHARD BAUMAN, DELL HYMES, and DENNIS TEDLOCK into the conversation, thereby explaining further the PERFORMANCE ARENA of oral traditions. In *Oral Tradition and the Internet: Pathways of the Mind* (2012), Foley uses electronic media as an analogy for oral traditions, arguing that neither of these media follow carefully scripted, linear trajectories but instead provide a multitude of pathways which the internet surfer and the oral poet can choose as they move forward. These observations are emphasized in the parallel website, The Pathways Project (http://www.pathwaysproject.org), in which registered users can visually see the pathways that they have chosen as they move from one topic to another on the website.

Although biblical studies was not one of his primary areas of research, Foley nevertheless has had a significant impact on the field and directly contributed to its dialogue. He participated numerous times in meetings of

The Bible in Ancient and Modern Media Section of the annual meeting of the Society of Biblical Literature, often providing helpful critiques to others' papers as well as presenting his own insights. While most of his contributions in biblical studies concern the Gospels and their underlying Jesus traditions (1994; 2006; with Horsley and Draper 2005), Foley's work also has been influential in the study of the Hebrew Bible and ancient Near Eastern literature (see especially Foley 2005), the NT, Qumran, and rabbinic literature. For example, Foley's understanding of the traditional register has been applied to the biblical book of Judges (Niditch 2008) and to proverbs (Fontaine 2002), prophetic literature (Hays 2002), and the Gospels (Kelber 1997; Horsley 2008).

Raymond F. Person, Jr. (Ohio Northern University, USA)

Further Reading

Foley, John Miles. 1988. *The Theory of Oral Composition: History and Methodology*. Bloomington: Indiana University Press.

Foley, John Miles. 1990. *Traditional Oral Epic: The Odyssey, Beowulf, and the Serbo-Croatian Return Song*. Berkeley: University of California Press.

Foley, John Miles. 1991. *Immanent Art: From Structure to Meaning in Traditional Oral Epic*. Bloomington: Indiana University Press.

Foley, John Miles. 1994. 'Words in Tradition, Words in Text: A Response'. *Semeia* 65: 169–80.

Foley, John Miles. 1995. *The Singer of Tales in Performance*. Bloomington: Indiana University Press.

Foley, John Miles, ed. 1998. *Teaching Oral Traditions*. New York: Modern Language Association.

Foley, John Miles. 1999. *Homer's Traditional Art*. University Park: Pennsylvania State University Press.

Foley, John Miles, ed. 2005. *A Companion to Ancient Epic*. Oxford: Blackwell.

Foley, John Miles. 2006. 'The Riddle of Q: Oral Ancestor, Textual Precedent, or Ideological Creation?' In *Oral Performance, Popular Tradition, and Hidden Transcript in Q*. Edited by Richard A. Horsley. Semeia St. 60. Atlanta: Society of Biblical Literature, pp. 123–40.

Foley, John Miles. 2012. *Oral Tradition and the Internet: Pathways of the Mind*. Urbana, IL: University of Illinois Press. See also http://www.pathwaysproject.org

Foley, John Miles with Richard A. Horsley, and Jonathan A. Draper, eds. 2005. *Performing the Gospel: Orality, Memory, and Mark: Essays Dedicated to Werner Kelber*. Minneapolis: Fortress Press.

Fontaine, Carole. 2002. *Smooth Words: Women, Proverbs and Performance in Biblical Wisdom*. LHBOTS 356. New York: T&T Clark.

Hays, Katherine M. 2002. *'The Earth Mourns': Prophetic Metaphor and Oral Aesthetic*. SBL Academia Biblica 8. Atlanta: Society of Biblical Literature.

Horsley, Richard A. 2008. *Jesus in Context: Performance, Power, and People*. Minneapolis: Fortress Press.

Niditch, Susan. 2008. *Judges: A Commentary*. Louisville: Westminster John Knox.

Folklore/Folkloristics Folkloristics is the study of folklore. Folklore, however, like many categories of communication and human behaviour, is difficult to define precisely – Funk and Wagnalls' classic *Standard Dictionary of Folklore, Mythology, and Legend*, for example, listed nineteen different definitions of folklore (Leach 1959). Patricia Kirkpatrick (1998), noting the variety of ways in which the term *folklore* has been utilized by scholars, observes that most formal definitions share two central criteria, an emphasis on 1) the means of its transmission and 2) the concept of tradition. Her model is similar to that of Robert A. Georges and Michael Owen Jones, who assert in their introduction to folkloristics that the term *folklore* 'denotes expressive forms, processes, and behaviors' that are 1) learnt, taught, utilized, and displayed during customary interactions; and, that 2) are deemed traditional (1995: 1). Both definitions stress the role of tradition and transmission as crucial aspects of folklore.

According to most folklorists, true *folklore* is usually defined as 'lore in process or performance' (Niditch 1993: 3). 'Lore' entails a range of genres (e.g. folktales, oral histories, legends, myths, ballads,

PROVERBS, RIDDLES, jokes), rituals, and games, as well as material cultural artefacts, such as folk art. 'Process or performance' entails the 'work's living currency in a social context' both during its creation and in its experience by the audience (Niditch 1993: 3). SUSAN NIDITCH, however, cautions against formulating a definition of folklore that too restrictively focuses on ORALITY or oral transmission, observable performance settings, or indigenous living contexts (Niditch 1987; Niditch 1993). Rather, Niditch favours the description of folklore as 'the traditional', by which she means lore, either written or oral, that conveys a patterned repetition wherein symbols, words, syntax, content, structure, thoughts, THEMES, and forms recur, at times in a novel and flexible manner (Niditch 1993). Similarly, ALAN DUNDES maintains that patterns and variations are the most crucial aspects of folklore, as evidenced by variations in both written folklore (e.g. flyleaf inscriptions, GRAFFITI, book verses, xerography) and orally transmitted folklore (myths, folktales, legends, proverbs, riddles, superstitions, curses, charms, tongue-twisters, and games; Dundes 1999). For Dundes, the two most 'salient characteristics of folklore' are multiple existence and variation (Dundes 1999: 18) (see PLURIFORMITY).

Folkloristics and the Bible

The view that folklore can be found in the biblical texts and, indeed, that the biblical texts are folklore was often disavowed by folklorists and biblical scholars in the past, partly due to the ambiguity of the meaning of the term as described above. On the biblical studies side, the possible presence of folklore in the Bible was viewed as theologically problematic because folklore was widely viewed as old-fashioned, uneducated, remedial, or otherwise unsophisticated in its presentation and as (therefore) untrue in its content. HERMANN GUNKEL's seminal monograph *The Folktale in the Old Testament* (1917) opens by addressing the question, 'What has the Bible to do with folklore?' Gunkel likens the comparison of the Bible to such 'subordinate' forms as folklore as tantamount to 'an attack on the prestige of the holy book'. He declares, therefore, that 'the Bible hardly contains a folklore anywhere … and [the] near total eradication [of folklore] from the holy tradition is one of the great acts of biblical religion' (1987: 33). At the same time, it 'seems hardly credible to us' that any ancient people would exist without a folklore; therefore, one may posit that the OT contains folkloric remnants and motifs (1987: 33).

Gunkel proceeds to elucidate the importance of folkloric elements in the biblical corpus by comparing sections of the Hebrew Bible to folklores from different parts of the world. Indeed, for Gunkel, the folkloric aspects of the biblical text served a significant exegetical function: by peeling back the layers of OT narratives, especially the narratives about Israel's patriarchs, and by isolating the ancient, folkloric motifs embedded in these oral legends, Gunkel believed that the ORIGINAL form of the narrative as well as its SITZ IM LEBEN (the primitive social context of these legends) could be revealed (Kirkpatrick 1988).

Unlike Gunkel, who wanted to search for 'sublimated myths' in the OT in order to elucidate an original oral core, the classicist James George Frazer attempted to identify and catalogue the various folklores and folkloric themes in the Hebrew Bible. Frazer's multivolume *Folklore in the Old Testament* (1918; and subsequently expanded and revised by Theodore Gaster) is the first study to seriously consider the presence of folklore in the biblical text. Using a comparative anthropological approach, Frazer methodically lists the customs, stories, beliefs, motifs, and themes found in other traditions throughout the world that exhibit parallels with the OT (Gaster 1981). As Alan Dundes notes, Frazer's subscription to the view that folktales represent primitive and less sophisticated forms of communication perhaps explains why his study focused only on the Hebrew Bible rather than including the NT (Dundes 1999).

Though modern scholars would no longer ascribe to Frazer's evolutionary view of cultures, his impressive work served as a precursor to later, and more sophisticated, compendia of folkloric themes and variants, such as those that emerged from the Finnish or Historical-Geographic School. One of the best known, and still utilized, representatives of this category is Antti Aarne and Stith Thompson's catalogue and classification system of various types of folkloric motifs and storylines (the Aarne–Thompson Indexes). The Aarne–Thompson Type Index offers an ordering and classifications of particular types of tales (e.g. 'animal tales') and their variations. Smaller components of folktales, such as specific motifs, are also catalogued in the multivolume *Motif–Index of Folk Literature* by Thompson and his students.

Susan Niditch (1987) argues that such works of folkloric taxonomy had a particular purpose that reflected a larger research aim: by collecting and collating as many examples of various folktales from around the world as possible, the Finnish school believed that the development of a tale could be delineated and traced. By comparing the stories, and by studying patterns of shared motifs in specific regions or periods of time, the evolution of a tale from its earliest form could be revealed. As Niditch rightly notes, however, such an understanding not only presumes a particular vision of a tale's development, but also the existence of an earlier, unchanged form of a folktale – put another way, these methods tended to assume the existence of an ORIGINAL form. While this approach is now widely viewed as problematic, the Aarne–Thompson Type Index still remains a useful aid in biblical studies, elucidating both the unique aspects of biblical narratives as well as the ways in which they fit into a larger spectrum of traditional literature (Niditch 1993).

Other studies in folkloristics have also attempted to classify and clarify components, building blocks, and features of traditional literature by taking a comparative approach. For example, Axel Olrik has outlined the essential characteristics of traditional narratives. According to Olrik, a piece may be identified as a folk narrative if it includes such features as a clear opening and closing, repetition, the presence of no more than three or four characters, the use of character contrast, the presence of twins or two of a kind, and marked patterning or climatically used tableau scenes, among others (Olrik 1965). Vladimir Propp, the well-known Russian Formalist, in his classic work on the morphology of folk tales, dissects and lays out the typical action sequences or functions of fairy tales and folklore (Propp 1960). By setting out the sequence and organization of a form or the structure of a tale, Propp sought to lay the groundwork for a deeper historical analysis. While Propp's work examined 'the diachronic patterns of folktales' (Niditch 1987: 9), the research of Claude Levi-Strauss, the famous structural anthropologist, centred on the synchronic, deep structures within folklore and myths. In particular, Levi-Strauss, applying the structuralist linguistic theories of Ferdinand de Saussure to anthropological studies, hypothesized that humans understand the world in terms of binary dichotomies. These binarisms, which are reflected and present in myths and folklore, are a means by which societies attempt to resolve and ameliorate the contradictions that make up human existence. Hence, folktales, for Levi-Strauss, perform a necessary social function.

Despite this history of scholarship on folklore, the Bible, for a variety of reasons, was not widely envisioned or accepted as traditional literature. Alan Dundes argues that this was the case because, aside from the assumption that folklore was somehow inherently primitive, some folklorists equated folklore exclusively with ORAL TRADITION. Under this model, folklore is no longer truly 'folklore' once it is recorded in writing. The Bible, as a written text, was therefore viewed not as folklore per se, but rather as a fixed, fossilized remnant of it (Dundes 1999) (see GREAT DIVIDE). According to Dundes, however, the presumption that oral tradition once written down disappears underestimates the 'tremendous tenacity of tradition' (1999: 9–10). Even after folkloric productions such as SONGS are written down, they still continue to be transmitted and sung and, therefore, still function as a folklore. Kirkpatrick similarly stresses that orality simply identifies the medium through which some folklore is transmitted, not the transmitted thing itself (Kirkpatrick 1988).

Earlier generations of biblical scholarship were also generally less open to the oral processes that lie behind the biblical texts. Kirkpatrick (1988) notes that biblical scholars have long wondered about the trustworthiness of oral transmission (Kirkpatrick 1988), and Dundes observes that the twin mischaracterizations of folklore as unhistorical and as primarily oral have led to an unawareness of the biblical text as folklore (Dundes 1999). Niditch notes further that an overemphasis on historicity, Ur-forms, and original versions in biblical studies has distracted scholars from a recognition of the biblical text as traditional literature, much of which emerged from an 'oral mindset' context (1987; 1996).

Recent recognition of the folkloristic aspects of the biblical texts has thus gone hand in hand with a renewed interest in orality and oral transmission. Scholars who have long recognized the link between folklore and the Bible have turned with renewed interest to models of orality and oral transmission processes in hopes that they can shed light on the transmission history of biblical texts. As noted earlier, Gunkel, the father of FORM CRITICISM, believed that Israelite literature began as short, simple, folksy oral productions that were performed in particular life settings (see *Sitz im Leben*), and he therefore set out to uncover this original oral core. So also the Scandinavian Uppsala School maintained that biblical traditions were orally transmitted for a long period of time before being set down in WRITING (Engell 1969; Nielson 1954). A notable member of this school, Ivan Engnell, posited that many of the variations in the Pentateuch can be explained as the product of oral transmission (Engnell 1969). Moreover, NT scholars such as RUDOLF BULTMANN, noting the thin line separating oral and written traditions, have argued that both need to be taken into account when discussing the formation of the Gospels.

Recent scholarship has offered a more nuanced understanding of the oral context that informed the writing, composition, and transmission of the biblical text. For example, biblical scholars, using the works of Albert LORD and MILMAN PARRY on formulaic language in Homeric literature (Lord 1968), have uncovered the presence of similar formulaic language in the Bible and thus have elucidated the performative background of certain biblical texts (Culley 1967; Gunn 1974). Most importantly, there has been a movement away from regarding the biblical literature from a binary written/oral – and thus, relatedly, history/folklore – viewpoint, reflecting a general move away from the GREAT DIVIDE approach. Scholars such as SUSAN NIDITCH have effectively shown that orality and LITERACY are mutually interactive and that a written work, such as the Bible, can still be highly influenced by the oral culture from which its compositions emerged. Indeed, the presence of vestiges of orality in the biblical text, such as formulaic phrases, epithets, intertextuality, and repetition, clearly indicate that the Bible is the product of a complex transaction between orality and literacy.

Dundes (1999) argues that the biblical text itself testifies to the importance of oral transmission and learning. For example, in Deuteronomy 31, Moses is instructed to speak and orally teach God's Laws and commandments to the elders and the people, and Deut. 6.6-7 suggests that Israelites were expected to memorize songs and texts. Malachi 2.7 reminds the reader that knowledge comes from oral tradition and learning, not written texts. Dundes argues that a similar preference for orality underlies NT texts as well, citing Eusebias of Caesarea (Dundes 1999). For some early Christians, unlike in the modern context, written texts were deemed less important and less trustworthy than the *living voice*, and thus in need of oral testimonial confirmation (see EARLY CHRISTIAN LITERATURE; PAPIAS) . According to Dundes, the lack of appreciation for the orally centred ancient environment of the biblical texts has led to a misunderstanding of the importance of orality in the formation, composition, and transmission of the Bible.

Repetition and Variation in Folklore

The growing cognizance of the oral background of the biblical texts is intimately intertwined with a recognition of the Bible as traditional literature. Relatedly, this realization is crucial to an understanding of the variety of patterns and repetitions found in biblical and related literatures. In biblical studies, recurring motifs, stories, THEMES, or language have usually been explained as the result of redactional accretions or editorial emendations. When reframed as folklore, however, these patterns can be explained as the creative products of a shared, interrelated, traditional culture.

The recurring, patterned repetition that epitomizes folklore is varied and diverse. Depending on the type of folklore, these repetitions can encompass themes, language, and/or motifs or, in material folk works (e.g. art), be exemplified in decorative patterns or similar designs. Niditch notes that that these traditional patterns can be present in a single work or be shared by a number of works; they can occur in one culture or across cultures; and, they can be synchronic, appearing at one time, or diachronic and therefore present over a lengthy period of time (Niditch 1987).

Building on this principle, Dundes details the presence of similar types of variations, repetitions, and duplications in the Bible. These patterns, according to Dundes, clearly indicate the Bible's traditional background and reveal its oral origins. He notes, for example, the use of variations of number in the flood myth in Genesis, in which Noah is instructed to take into the ark two different numbers of animals (cp. Gen. 6.19-20 with 7.2-3). Moreover, two different numbers of bread and fishes are noted before Jesus' multiplication miracle in the book of Matthew (Mt. 14.15-22; 15.32-39). Another common variation, according to Dundes, is that of nomenclature, in which two different names are utilized for the same character in variations of the same tale. For example, the three wife-sister tales in Genesis (12.10-20; 20.1-18; 26.1-17) utilize two different names for the same character (Pharaoh/Abimelech). Indeed, the folkloric, structural, and literary aspects of these three wife-sister tales have been thoroughly investigated and elucidated by Niditch, who has also pointed to the presence of the trickster-underdog motif in all three variations (Niditch 1987). Finally, patterns in sequence can be detected in texts, such as the two variant versions of the story of Jesus' temptations in Matthew and Luke (Mt. 4.1-11; Lk. 4.1-13; see Dundes 1999).

For Dundes, these patterns and variations clearly indicate the oral roots of the biblical text. For others, such as Niditch, a clear understanding of the origins and cultural contexts of the biblical narratives remains a complicated and uncertain endeavour (Niditch 1993). Instead of a precise determination of oral origins, she argues that the value of the folkloric approach lies in the kinds of questions it raises about the biblical narrative. For example, folklorists ask how the context and social location of the audience are reflected in works of folklore, and how works of folklore, in turn, affect the social dynamics of the audience and their community. By utilizing the folkloric lens, biblical scholars can ask similar questions of the biblical text and its ancient audience. In so doing, the various cultural settings reflected in the text and which led to the composition of these traditional narratives can be more fully elucidated. Relatedly, the ways in which context affects and transforms the meanings of these texts can be detected and explored (Niditch 1993: 25–6). Thus, folkloric studies or folkloristics, by examining the underlying cultural context, the developmental process, and the meaning of patterns and variations found in traditional literature, provides a crucial interdisciplinary model of analysis for the biblical text.

Suzie Park (Austin Presbyterian Theological Seminary, USA)

Further Reading

Culley, Robert. 1967. *Oral Formulaic Language in the Biblical Psalms*. Near and Middle East Series 4. Toronto: University of Toronto Press.

Culley, Robert. 1986. 'Oral Tradition and Biblical Studies'. *Oral Tradition* 1: 30–65.

Dundes, Alan. 1999. *Holy Writ as Oral Lit: The Bible as Folklore*. Lanham, MD: Rowman & Littlefield.

Engell, Ivan. 1969. *A Rigid Scrutiny: Critical Essays on the Old Testament*. Translated and edited by John T. Willis. Nashville: Vanderbilt University Press.

Gaster, Theodor H. 1981. *Myth, Legend, and Custom in the Old Testament. A Comparative Study with Chapters from Sir James G. Frazer's Folklore in the Old Testament*. 2 vols. Gloucester, MA: Peter Smith.

Georges, Robert A., and Michael Owen Jones. 1995. *Folkloristics: An Introduction*. Bloomington and Indianapolis: Indiana University Press.

Gunkel, Hermann. 1987. *The Folktale in the Old Testament*. Translated by Michael D. Rutter. Sheffield: Almond Press.

Gunn, David. 1974. 'Narrative Patterns and Oral Tradition in Judges and Samuel'. *VT* 24: 286–317.

Kirkpatrick, Patricia A. 1988. *The Old Testament and Folklore Study*. JSOT Supp. 62. Sheffield: JSOT Press, 1988.

Leach, Maria, ed. 1959. *Funk and Wagnalls Standard Dictionary of Folklore, Mythology and Legend*. San Francisco: Harper & Row.

Lord, Albert Bates. 1968. *The Singer of Tales*. New York: Atheneum Publishers.

Nielsen, Edward. 1954. *Oral Tradition: A Modern Problem in Old Testament Introduction*. London: SCM Press.

Niditch, Susan. 1993. *Folklore and the Hebrew Bible*. Minneapolis: Fortress Press.

Niditch, Susan. 1987. *Underdogs and Tricksters: A Prelude to Biblical Folklore*. San Francisco: Harper & Row.

Niditch, Susan. 1996. *Oral World and Written Word*. Louisville: Westminster John Knox.

Olrik, Axel. 1965. 'Epic Laws of Folk Narrative'. In *The Study of Folklore*. Edited by Alan Dundes. Englewood Cliffs, NJ: Prentice-Hall, pp. 129–41.

Propp, Vladimir. 1960. *The Morphology of the Folktale*. Austin: University of Texas Press, 1960.

Form Criticism *Form criticism* is an English rendering of the German *Formgeschichte*, an influential twentieth-century interpretive model for analysing both Hebrew Bible and NT texts that are grounded in ORAL TRADITION. The term *form* translates the two words *Form* and *Gattung*, where the former denotes the literary shape of an individual passage while the latter identifies, on the basis of this literary shape, the literary GENRE to which the unit belongs. The term *criticism* is a modification of the German *Geschichte*, 'history', and indicates this method's focus on the history of forms. Form Criticism includes analysis of the literary shape or pattern of speech of an individual textual unit (*Form*); when comparison with other units suggests a common pattern, the units can be classified according to general literary genres (*Gattung*). Form-critical analysis also has a diachronic dimension (*Geschichte*), tracing the forms/genres evident in a tradition back to their oral origins by determining how such forms come into being and develop in particular speech situations.

The Emergence of Form Criticism

The origins of Form Criticism may be traced to the work of German OT professor HERMANN GUNKEL (1862–1932). Although not working with an elaborate method of form-critical analysis, Gunkel advanced a history of Israelite literature that focused on the conventional rather than the individual and defined the scholarly task as the reconstruction of the history of literary genres (*Gattungen*). In Gunkel's view, the individual genres now evident in the biblical text originated in specific social settings of the Israelite people (*Sitz im Volksleben* or SITZ IM LEBEN). The speaker/singer chose the genre to follow as the occasion presented itself but was then restricted by its established pattern, a situation that placed primary control on composition with conventional elements while limiting individual variations (Gunkel 1906, 1909, 1917). Gunkel applied his approach to Genesis and the Psalms and traced the earliest source material back to pre-literary stages of ethnological, aetiological, and ceremonial legends aiming to explain local phenomena and to the cultic life of Israel (Gunkel 1901, 1985). European scholars such as Albrecht Alt, Georg Fohrer, Sigmund Mowinckel, Martin Noth, Gerhard von Rad, and Claus Westermann developed Gunkel's approach for the study of a broad range of material in the Hebrew Bible.

Gunkel's students MARTIN DIBELIUS (1883–1947) and RUDOLF BULTMANN (1884–1976) developed the standard view of NT Form Criticism that came to dominate scholarship in Germany and elsewhere up to the end of the twentieth century (Byrskog 2007). Dibelius was first to use the term *Formgeschichte* programmatically in the 1919 edition of his *Die Formgeschichte des Evangeliums*, perhaps under the influence of Franz Overbeck's

1882 article on the origin of patristic literature and Eduard Norden's 1913 study of religious speech (Overbeck 1882: 423; Norden 1913). The revised editions of Dibelius' and Bultmann's studies of Form Criticism from the early 1930s came to influence NT scholarship in terms of the method of analysis of the synoptic tradition (Dibelius 1933; Bultmann 1931). Influenced by Julius Wellhausen's argument that the Synoptic Gospels built on oral traditions and Karl Ludwig Schmidt's separation of the editorial framework of the Gospel of Mark from the individual units within it that had been transmitted orally (Wellhausen 1905; Schmidt 1919), Dibelius and Bultmann developed a form-critical method that classifies the units of the Gospels into literary forms and traces each individual form to its period of oral transmission and origin.

Two premises were crucial to early Form Criticism, one relating to the oral origins of the biblical material and another relating to the relationship between oral form and social setting. First, it was assumed that the forms were shaped orally, not in WRITING, with the result that Form Criticism was viewed as a method for tracing oral patterns of communication and transmission. For Gunkel, the literary genres of the Hebrew Bible represented brief utterances with a simple style produced in speaking or singing; for Dibelius and Bultmann, the oral materials behind the Gospels were folkloristic and rooted in the life of the illiterate people, with the Greek of the Gospels reflecting the spoken language of the early uneducated Christ believers. Dibelius and Bultmann developed different taxonomies of oral forms in the Gospels based partly on analogies in the Jewish and Greco-Roman literature, but the written Gospels did not, in their view, conform to any contemporary literary genre. The Gospels were instead considered as folk literature (*Kleinliteratur*) and as expanded Hellenistic cult legends based on the early Christian kerygma. Since both the synoptic tradition and the Gospels were popular and unliterary entities, the transition from ORALITY to textuality involved no significant media shift.

Second, it was assumed that each individual form corresponded to a particular situation in the early Christian community, the so-called *Sitz im Leben*. This expression denotes not any specific historical setting for the composition/writing of a text or the individual units within it, but rather a recurrent situation in the collective life of a community that shapes tradition according to oral patterns peculiar to the social dynamics of that situation. Gunkel and other scholars of the Hebrew Bible focused on communal functions and offices in ancient Israel, such as the priest, the wisdom teacher, the singer, and the narrator. These individuals, and the speech forms they utilized, functioned in the settings of liturgy, law courts, EDUCATION, or other recurrent, collective activities of the people. For Dibelius the *Sitz im Leben* for early JESUS TRADITIONS were preaching to non-Christians (evangelism), Christians (exhortation), and recent converts (catechism), and for Bultmann they consisted of preaching, apologetics, polemics, edification, discipline, and the scribal work of the Christian community. Each of these recurrent situations, they assumed, exhibited definite social characteristics and needs that fostered particular styles, forms, and types of literature according to general laws of transmission, making 'form' a sociological rather than a purely aesthetic entity.

Form Criticism Today

From its early days (e.g. Fascher 1924), Form Criticism has been critiqued by scholars, and the discipline has undergone significant changes over the years. Scholars of the Hebrew Bible continue to utilize Form Criticism, sometimes taking up James Muilenburg's (1969) programmatic call to move beyond Form Criticism and attend to the aesthetics of larger literary units and the interrelationship between texts and their audiences. Despite its changes and challenges, however, Form Criticism is still used broadly as a method for analysis of the origin and development of the Israelite traditions recorded in the Hebrew Bible (Koch 1989; Sweeney and Zwi 2003). The debate has been more intense in NT circles, where Form Criticism has been significantly modified and occasionally abandoned. Most significantly, Form Criticism's conception of oral tradition has been questioned due to its narrow focus on folkloristic modes and its neglect to include discussion of individual and SOCIAL/COLLECTIVE MEMORY as aspects of transmission (Kirk and Thatcher 2005).

BIRGER GERHARDSSON (1926–2013) brought attention to both issues in 1961, arguing that early Christian oral transmission was in some ways similar to the rabbinic ideal of transmitting the oral Torah through deliberate memorization (Gerhardsson 1998). Ed Sanders (1969) questioned the tendencies of transmission that both Dibelius and Bultmann thought governed the changes of tradition in settings of folkloristic orality and argued that, where changes do occur in the post-canonical synoptic tradition, no consistent 'laws' governing the development of the synoptic tradition are evident (Sanders 1969). WERNER KELBER (1983) focused on less advanced forms of ORALITY and argued against Gerhardsson that transmission takes place in the act of performance (Kelber 1997). Influenced by Erhardt Güttgemanns' (1970) critique of the form-critical assumption of a linear transition between orality and writing, Kelber was profoundly critical of the form-critical model of an accumulative and organic growth of traditions leading inevitably to written texts (the Gospels), and has more recently nuanced his model with theories of scribal orality and memory (Kelber 2008, 2009). Gerhardsson, Sanders, and Kelber have, in their own distinct ways, questioned the basic tenets of traditional Form Criticism and have initiated a new critical discussion of its possibilities and limits.

The new scholarly landscape has stimulated revised form-critical programmes and applications. Form criticism assumes that human verbal communication is expressed in well-defined patterns, and the insight that there existed in antiquity advanced forms of orality evident in the narrative and rhetorical dimensions of the Gospels has led to a more nuanced form-critical cataloguing that replaces the old taxonomies. Newer classifications consider comparative Greek and Roman forms and GENRES that accord with ancient rhetorical terminology (see RHETORIC). Influenced by Vincent Taylor's (1935) modification of traditional form-critical terminology and indirectly developing Muilenburg's (1969) vision of Form Criticism, Burton Mack, Vernon Robbins, and Klaus Berger initiated a new phase of research by studying patterns of persuasion in the Gospel texts and identifying rhetorical forms as they function for different social purposes (Mack and Robbins 1989; Berger 1984, 1987, 2005). Rather than being a unique folkloristic genre, the Gospels are examples of Greek biography and include forms used in contemporary Greek and Roman literature for persuasive communication. This rhetorically oriented Form Criticism pays more attention to classifying units in the Gospels in terms of their pragmatic function than to tracing the history of the forms.

The recent introduction of theories of social/collective memory, combined with rhetorical analysis, has re-directed attention to the history of forms and maintains that the biblical traditions originated and developed for particular communicative purposes evident in the rhetorical elaboration of mnemonic forms (Byrskog 2010). Dibelius and Bultmann did not engage MAURICE HALBWACHS' seminal discussions of memory as socially conditioned in their form-critical programme, despite its strong influence on French sociology in the early 1930s and its potential relevance to the form-critical emphasis on the creative remembering community (Schwartz 2005: 47–50; Byrskog 2014).

Although recent attention to social/collective memory does not follow the paths of traditional Form Criticism, the discovery of inherently rhetorical and mnemonic forms (such as the *chreia* and the *apomnēmoneuma* in the Synoptic Gospels) allows comparison with ancient rhetorical handbooks to trace how the memory of the past became formalized in the process of adapting it to various situations and of textualizing it as historicizing biography. The impact of what was said and done on witnesses to the originating events of the Gospels and the construction of a mnemonic past by those who were not present take on verbal forms of tradition that accord with available patterns of communication. Rather than assuming that activities in the early Christian communities automatically moulded the tradition into certain patterns, this rhetorically and mnemonically oriented method argues that the SITZ IM LEBEN embodied a recurrent situation within the life of the communities when certain people remembered the Jesus tradition. The future prospect of NT Form Criticism lies in the combination of insights concerning the rhetorical and mnemonic dimensions of the origin and development of the Jesus tradition.

Samuel Byrskog (Centre for Theology and Religious Studies, Lund University, Sweden)

Further Reading

Berger, Klaus. 1984. 'Hellenistische Gattungen und Neues Testament'. ANRW 2.25.2: 1031–1432.

Berger, Klaus. 1987. *Einführung in die Formgeschichte*. UTB 1444. Tübingen: Francke Verlag.

Berger, Klaus. 2005. *Formen und Gattungen im Neuen Testament*. UTB 2532. Tübingen: Francke Verlag.

Blank, Reiner. 1981. *Analyse und Kritik der formgeschichtlichen Arbeiten von M. Dibelius und R. Bultmann*. Basel: Friedrich Reinhardt Kommisionsverlag.

Bultmann, Rudolf. 1931. *Die Geschichte der synoptischen Tradition*. FRLANT 29. 2nd edn. Göttingen: Vandenhoeck & Ruprecht (1st ed. 1921).

Byrskog, Samuel. 2007. 'A Century with the Sitz im Leben: From Form-Critical Setting to Gospel Community and Beyond'. *ZNW* 98: 1–27.

Byrskog, Samuel. 2010. 'The Transmission of the Jesus Tradition: Old and New Insights'. *Early Christianity* 1: 1–28.

Byrskog, Samuel. 2014. 'The Message of Jesus'. In *Reckoning a New Testament Theology*. Edited by Bruce W. Longenecker and Mikeal C. Parsons. Baylor: Baylor University Press, pp. 3–22.

Dibelius, Martin. 1933. *Die Formgeschichte des Evangeliums*. 2nd edn. Tübingen: Mohr Siebeck. First edition 1919.

Fascher, Erich. 1924. *Die formgeschichtliche Methode. Eine Darstellung und Kritik. Zugleich ein Beitrag zur Geschichte des synoptischen Problems*. BZNW 2. Gießen: Alfred Töpelmann.

Gerhardsson, Birger. 1961/1964. *Memory and Manuscript: Oral Tradition and Written Transmission in Rabbinic Judaism and Early Christianity*. Reprint of 2nd edn. The Biblical Resource Series. Grand Rapids: Eerdmans, 1998.

Güttgemanns, Erhardt. 1970. *Offene Fragen zur Formgeschichte des Evangeliums. Eine methodologische Skizze der Grundlagenproblematik der Form- und Redaktionsgeschichte*. BEvT 54. München: Kaiser Verlag.

Gunkel, Hermann. 1901. *Die Sagen Genesis*. 2nd ed. Göttingen: Vandenhoeck & Ruprecht.

Gunkel, Hermann. 1906. 'Die Grundprobleme der israelitischen Literaturgeschichte'. *Deutsche Literaturzeitung* 27: 1797–1800, 1861–6.

Gunkel, Hermann. 1909. 'Bibelwissenschaft: Literaturgeschichte Israels'. *RGG* 1: 1189–94.

Gunkel, Hermann. 1917. 'Formen der Hymnen'. *ThR* 20: 265–304.

Gunkel, Hermann. 1985 [1933]. *Einleitung in der Psalmen. Die Gattungen der religiösen Lyrik Israels*. 4th edn. Göttingen: Vandenhoeck & Ruprecht.

Keith, Chris. 2012. 'The Indebtedness of the Criteria Approach to Form Criticism and Recent Attempts to Rehabilitate the Search for an Authentic Jesus'. In *Jesus, Criteria, and the Demise of Authenticity*. Edited by Chris Keith and Anthony Le Donne. London: T&T Clark, pp. 25–48.

Kelber, Werner H. 1997. *The Oral and the Written Gospel: The Hermeneutics of Speaking and Writing in the Synoptic Tradition, Mark, Paul*, and *Q*. Voices in Performance and Text. Bloomington: Indiana University Press (Reprint of the 1983 ed.).

Kelber, Werner H. 2008. 'The Oral-Scribal-Memorial Arts of Communication in Early Christianity'. In *Jesus, the Voice, and the Text: Beyond the Oral and the Written Gospel*. Edited by Tom Thatcher. Baylor: Baylor University Press, pp. 235–62.

Kelber, Werner H. 2009. 'Conclusion: The Work of Birger Gerhardsson in Perspective'. In *Jesus in Memory: Traditions in Oral and Scribal Perspectives*. Edited by Werner H. Kelber and Samuel Byrskog. Baylor: Baylor University Press, pp. 173–206.

Kirk, Alan and Tom Thatcher. 2005. 'Jesus Tradition as Social Memory'. In *Memory, Tradition, and Text: Uses of the Past in Early Christianity*. Edited by Alan Kirk and Tom Thatcher. SemeiaSt. Atlanta: SBL Press, pp. 25–42.

Koch, Klaus. 1989 [1964]. *Was ist Formgeschichte? Methoden der Bibelexegese*. 5th edn. Neukirchen-Vluyn: Neukirchener Verlag.

Mack, Burton L., and Vernon K. Robbins. 1989. *Patterns of Persuasion in the Gospels*. Foundations & Facets: Literary Facets. Sonoma, CA: Polebridge Press.

Muilenburg, James. 1969. 'Form Criticism and Beyond'. *JBL* 88: 1–18.
Norden, Eduard. 1913. *Agnostos Theos. Untersuchungen zur Formengeschichte religiöser Rede*. Leipzig: Teubner.
Overbeck, Franz. 1882. 'Über die Anfänge der patristischen Literatur'. *Historische Zeitschrift* 48: 417–72.
Sanders, Ed P. 1969. *The Tendencies of the Synoptic Tradition*. SNTSMS 9. Cambridge: Cambridge University Press.
Schmidt, Karl Ludwig. 1919. *Der Rahmen der Geschichte Jesu. Literarkritische Untersuchungen zur ältesten Jesusüberlieferung*. Berlin: Trowitzsch & Sohn.
Schwartz, Barry. 2005. 'Christian Origins: Historical Truth and Social Memory'. In *Memory, Tradition, and Text: Uses of the Past in Early Christianity*. Edited by Alan Kirk and Tom Thatcher. SemeiaSt. Atlanta: SBL Press, pp. 43–56.
Sweeney, Marvin A., and Ehud Ben Zwi, eds. 2003. *The Changing Face of Form Criticism for the Twenty-First Century*. Grand Rapids: Eerdmans.
Taylor, Vincent. 1935 [1933]. *The Formation of the Gospel Tradition: Eight Lectures*. 2nd edn. London: Macmillan.
Tuckett, Christopher. 2009. 'Form Criticism'. In *Jesus in Memory: Traditions in Oral and Scribal Perspectives*. Edited by Werner H. Kelber and Samuel Byrskog. Baylor: Baylor University Press, pp. 21–38.
Wellhausen, Julius. 1905. *Einleitung in die drei ersten Evangelien*. Berlin: Georg Reimer.

Formulas The term *formula* is a technical definition given for certain linguistic repetitions found in early Greek epic poetry by Homeric scholar Milman Parry in the late 1920s. The term was soon linked to the study of oral elements in various literary texts and has belonged to oral tradition studies since, though vigorous debate regarding the term's meaning and application continues. Parry's fullest definition was 'a group of words which is regularly employed under the same metrical conditions to express an essential idea' (Parry 1971: 272). In Parry's formulation, 'a group of words' refers to a syntactically bound collocation of words in a verse; 'regularly employed' indicates that the group repeats within the corpus; 'same metrical conditions' refers to the group's prosodic size as limited by definite metrical boundaries; and 'to express an essential idea' indicates, according to Parry, that the group of words, when taken as a whole, would signify a single name, hero, god, or other semantic unit. The last point is considered particularly controversial – how to define and measure the formular presentation of an 'essential idea' has never reached consensus. An example of a formula from Serbo-Croatian is the following in which different three-syllable verbs meaning 'mount' are paired with different three-syllable words meaning 'horse', which occurs in the last six syllables of the ten-syllable poetic line.

posede đogina	he mounted the white horse
posede dorata	he mounted the brown horse
sede na dorina	he mounted the brown horse
zasede hajvana	he mounted the animal (Lord 1960: 48)

Versions of the formula, formularity, and other permutations were later developed and adapted by scholars (including Parry) for the analysis of poetries in ancient, medieval, and modern traditions, especially for works and traditions thought to be oral-connected, folklore-related, or performance-derived. The term was stimulated in particular by Albert Lord's presentation and analysis of oral-traditional epic (specifically, ancient Greek, Anglo-Saxon, South Slavic, and modern Greek) in *The Singer of Tales* (1960). Variant renditions of the term are still used today by traditional philologists and by fieldworkers studying living and deceased genres such as oral epic, lyric, ballad, praise poetry, prosimetric forms, and folk prose. Despite the variety found in the history of the term's usage, there is general agreement that any discussion of a formula will require calibration of the term to the specific linguistic structures and formal elements present within the tradition under analysis. Any formal elements – such as the particular oral tradition's metrical rules, genre-based constraints, performance practices, and musical parameters – must be specified and discussed in relation to the phonological and grammatical structures of the language itself.

Parry developed the term *formula* in order to create a methodological test for solving what he perceived to be a fundamental problem in the Homeric scholarship of his day: failure to separate the poetic material inherited by tradition from the poetic material contributed by the individual poet (Parry 1971: 6). Today this distinction would be considered highly problematic by some, dubious by others, and in any case enormously complex; since the advent of Lord's work, most scholars agree that in oral epic traditions comparable to the South Slavic one, each performance is better understood as a recomposition-in-performance, where both traditional and individual elements are fused at the moment of singing.

From today's point of view, it is clear that the notion of the formula was at times used by scholars for misguided purposes. In early and mid-twentieth-century research, for example, enthusiasm for ORALITY led some to argue that the mere presence of formularity in an ancient or medieval text could be used to prove its oral provenance. The philological awareness eventually emerged, however, that the presence of formulaic items alone does not demonstrate the existence of even partial oral origin. One piece of proof came when Lord explained that two of the most famous works in the Yugoslav literary tradition were clear examples of literate authors borrowing explicitly and obviously from the oral epic language: 1) Andrija Kačić Miošić's *Razgovor ugodni naroda slovinskoga* (*Pleasant Conversation of the Slavic People*), composed c. 1755, and 2) Petar Petrović Njegoš *Gorski vijenac* (*The Mountain Wreath*), composed c. 1846, were both written by using the traditional South Slavic oral epic decasyllabic language, for clear and important literary reasons, but neither works were presented, received, or interpreted as 'oral' (Lord 1986: 19–64; 1995: 212–37). These examples (and many others since) have made clear that writers working at their desks, in any historical period, can possess multiple reasons and capacities to borrow, adapt, mould, and transform traditional oral poetic languages for deployment within written literary works. One consequence of this finding is that the mere presence of formulaic language in a text can never be used as the single criterion to prove the oral origin of that text.

With this caveat in mind, however, it is clear that the tradition of formulaic and oral-formulaic analysis that followed in the wake of Parry and Lord, and was later practised by scholars such as JOHN MILES FOLEY, Lauri Honko, Lauri Harvilahti, and others, has provided essential resources for better understanding oral performance and oral-traditional singing techniques. Perhaps the most important point about formular semantics comes from Foley's work on (what he called) 'immanent referentiality'. As Foley demonstrated, oral traditions make regular use of formular items whose literal meaning, if sought from a dictionary, would never yield the same results as those items' meanings when used by the poets and audiences fluent in the tradition (see TRADITIONAL REFERENTIALITY). For example, Foley argued that 'green fear' in the Homeric corpus has nothing to do with green'; rather, it is a semantic item that occurs only in the presence of a supernatural threat (1999: 216–8). When Homeric audiences heard 'green fear', they were being cued that a supernatural force was present, rather than being told that there was anything particularly 'green' about that fear. Foley has further demonstrated that comparable tradition-immanent and internal modes of signification are pervasive in the South Slavic and Anglo-Saxon poetic traditions as well. Foley's observation demonstrates that oral traditions can acquire specialized meanings arising from tradition-internal linguistic repetitions and that these specialized formulas enhance rather than diminish the communicative range of the poetry. Oral traditions develop their own idiomatic usages, meanings, and tradition-immanent references, whose meanings must be discovered through the tradition instead of modern lexical resources. As a result, obscure textual passages must be studied by collecting similar instances of the language within that particular genre, corpus, and tradition. This insight is relevant to an array of philological and hermeneutical problems, be they the interpretation of archaisms, obscure phraseology, or other perceived problems of textual coherence and unity.

Rather than rote memorization of an archive of formulas, Egbert Bakker, Foley, Honko, Harvilahti, and others have also asserted that mastery of an oral epic language (or *idiolect*, as an individual singer's poetic language is sometimes called) frequently comes to resemble the mastery of a spoken dialect or second language. Fluency in an oral epic language and tradition usually means that skilled singers have internalized the epic language much like one internalizes a second language and therefore involves what Lord called the SPECIAL GRAMMAR. The idea that singers perform by stringing together various memorized formulas or immobile pieces of diction is almost certainly false. Fluency in an epic linguistic idiom is much like fluency in spoken speech, provided that the additional parameters of MUSIC, metre, archaism, dialect admixture, and metrically bound traditional phraseology, as well as other parameters typical of oral SONG traditions, are considered as additional factors constraining and constituting that particular specialized language.

Aaron.P. Tate (University of Wisconsin, USA)

Further Reading

Bakker, Egbert. 1997. *Poetry in Speech: Orality and Homeric Discourse*. Ithaca: Cornell University Press.

Edwards, Mark. 1986. 'Homer and Oral Tradition: The Formula, Part I.' *Oral Tradition* 1/2: 171–230.

Edwards Mark. 1988. 'Homer and Oral Tradition: The Formula, Part II.' *Oral Tradition* 3/1–2: 11–60.

Foley, John Miles. 1988. *The Theory of Oral Composition: History and Methodology*. Bloomington: Indiana University Press.

Foley, John Miles. 1990. *Traditional Oral Epic: The Odyssey, Beowulf, and the South Slavic Return Song*. Berkeley and Los Angeles: University of California Press.

Foley, John Miles. 1991. *Immanent Art: From Structure to Meaning in Traditional Oral Epic*. Bloomington: Indiana University Press.

Foley, John Miles, ed. 1999. *Hebrew Oral Traditions. Oral Tradition* 14.

Foley, John Miles. 2000. *Homer's Traditional Art*. University Park: Pennsylvania State University Press.

Foley, John Miles. 2002. *How to Read an Oral Poem*. Chicago: Illinois University Press.

Lord, Albert B. 1960. *The Singer of Tales*. Reprint Cambridge, MA: Harvard University Press.

Lord, Albert B. 1986. 'The Merging of Two Worlds.' In *Oral Tradition in Literature: Interpretation in Context*. Edited by John Miles Foley. Columbia: University of Missouri Press, pp. 19–64.

Lord, Albert B. 1986. 'Perspectives on Recent Work on the Oral Traditional Formula'. *Oral Tradition* 1/3: 467–503.

Lord, Albert B. 1995. *The Singer Resumes the Tale*. Ithaca: Cornell University Press.

Harvilahti, Lauri (in collaboration with Zoja Sergeevna Kazagaceva). 2003. *The Holy Mountain: Studies on Upper Altay Oral Poetry*. Helsinki: Suomalainen Tiedeakatemia.

Honko, Lauri. 1998. *Textualising the Siri Epic*. Folklore Fellows Communications 264. Helsinki: Academia Scientiarum Fennica.

Niditch, Susan. 1995. 'Oral Register in the Biblical Libretto: Towards a Biblical Poetic'. *Oral Tradition* 10: 387–408.

Parry, Milman. 1987. *The Making of Homeric Verse. The Collected Papers of Milman Parry*. Oxford and New York: Oxford University Press.

G

Genealogies Genealogies are a specific form of cultural recall, characterized by the core structure of ancestor trees and using a highly formalized language. Genealogies fulfil various sociopolitical functions, among them the construction of IDENTITY/alterity and the support of economical, political, and religious power claims. Genealogies do not logically result from a given past, but are constructed and ideological acts of memory.

Defining genealogies as acts of memory accommodates the fact that genealogies do not logically result from the past in a predefined way. Instead, genealogies reflect complex cultural processes of interpretation, negotiation, and choice, in which meaning is applied to particular names, places, and relationships while others are forgotten or repressed. Conceptualizing genealogies as a form of CULTURAL MEMORY highlights the performative quality of genealogy composition, where the notion of performance encompasses both wilful acts and unconscious patterns of action. Further, the characterization of genealogy as cultural memory draws attention to the location of genealogies in the present time of their composition. In their contexts, genealogies provide particular interpretations and appropriations of the past that correlate the past with the present and future (Bal, Crewe, and Spitzer 1999). Both their performative quality and the location in the present of their composition account for the fluidity of genealogies. Genealogies emerge at the intersection of commitments to previous generations and particular legacies on the one hand, and deliberate compositions on the basis of actual needs on the other. They are open for actualization, changeable, and fluid in view of their particular aims and contexts.

Segmented Structures

Genealogy composition is a form of cultural recall that prioritizes relationships. Genealogies are not only lists of names, but accounts of nuanced nets of relationships. In fact, only the indication of relationships turns a list of names into a genealogy. Relations in genealogies are primarily expressed in terms of kinship, but the scope of genealogies is typically much broader. Genealogies recall origins and the emergence of individuals, communities, and cultures; they refer to groups, places, and literary traditions; and they concern geo-political, ethnic, sociopolitical, economical, and religious matters. Beyond merely mirroring blood ties, genealogies reflect, propose, and support various forms of relations.

In terms of form, genealogies depict relations in linear or in segmented structures. *Segmentation* refers to the branching out of a genealogy to the end of establishing and communicating affiliations, demarcations, and hierarchies. Segmentation implies highlighting some names and relations while overshadowing or excluding others. Creating a segmented genealogy is thus intimately linked to defining affiliations and demarcations – in other words, to constituting both identity and alterity. In addition, segmented genealogies establish hierarchies between particular genealogical segments, for example, by means of determining main lines and side lines on the basis of segmentation through first or secondary wives. The creation of identity by means of establishing belonging and difference is often rendered in us/them language. However, collective identity is not homogeneous and fixed. Instead, collective identities are generally multidimensional and fluid. They include alterity. In consequence, difference needs to be located both inside and outside collective identities

(Baumann and Gingrich 2004). The biblical genealogies achieve integration, othering, and ethnic and/or social stratification in the context of the multidimensional, fluid, and dialogical identities of ancient Israel and Second Temple Judaism. Patterns of belonging and othering through segmentation, which ostensibly concern the differentiation between the internal 'we' and the external 'they', may have pertained to hierarchies and demarcations within the 'us' group itself.

Genealogies' potential to construct and enunciate identity/alterity does not mean that a given genealogy necessarily maps its sociopolitical context. A genealogy is not a mirror of a past or present identity situation, but a constructed account of the past. This account of the past is not necessarily identical with the implied programme for the present. The analysis of a genealogy needs to reckon with a difference between the agenda of the memory performance and the agenda pursued in the present. Acknowledging the past in a certain way does not mean that the present should remain the same; the opposite might be the case. Assigning the importance of a place, person, or literary tradition to the past may be a first step in forgetting it/her.

Linearity and Fissure

Along with segmentation, genealogies depict relations in linear forms. Linear structures come with particular rules of succession, for example, patrilinearity. Building on these key notions of transfer, linear structures trace successions through the generations and constitute the depth of a lineage. The depth of a genealogy conveys continuity. It involves notions of inheritance and legacy, thereby working towards legitimating religious, political, and socio-economical claims and offices. The legitimating functions of genealogies are especially palpable in the case of priestly genealogies and their support of claims to priestly offices and privileges (e.g. 1 Chron. 5.27–6.66 MT).

In the biblical genealogies, the legitimation of offices and power claims is closely related to the notion of patrilineal succession. As a key notion of transfer, patrilinearity designates males (fathers, sons, brothers) as central agents for the continuation of a lineage. By doing so, these genealogies communicate and sustain the ideals of a patriarchal society that reserves central sociopolitical and economical positions for the autochthonous adult male. This male-centred perspective has an important implication: female-gendered fragments hold potential for deviation. Thus, in the biblical genealogies, the many references to women are an important means to complicate the genealogy, to indicate fissures and complexity, and to subvert primary rules of succession. Instances of this dynamic are the differentiation of Jacob's children and grandchildren according to their mothers Leah, Silpah, Rachel, and Bilhah (Gen. 46.8-27), and the reference to Tamar and Bath-shuah in 1 Chron. 2.3-4, which indicates a fissure in the patriarchal succession and brings forward genealogical agents who engage gendered, ethnic, and social complexity. However, fissures and complexity also occur in the male matrix of the genealogies. In both cases, male matrix and female fragments, deviations, fissures, and complexity are critical inroads for tapping into the potential of the genealogy GENRE to perform meaningful acts of memory.

For deviations, fissures, and complexity in genealogies, form is a major concern. As a rule, genealogies come with FORMULAS and a strongly formalized language. Aside from its basic value as a mnemonic aid, the use of formalized language is an important agent in advancing interests in a genealogy and in constituting a normative past. For example, the *toledoth* formula, which introduces most of the Genesis genealogies, establishes a succession from the creation of humankind to the ancestral narratives and into the emergence of the priesthood (see Exod. 6.16-25; Num. 3.1-4) and monarchy (Ruth 4.18-22). In this way, the formula functions as a structuring device, while at the same time lending authority to identity conceptions, which draw on continuity with the ancestral narratives, and legitimating the institutions of priesthood and monarchy (Hieke 2003).

At the same time, the formalized language of genealogies invites variation in and play on established form and formulas. In this context, form is also a means to challenge or even subvert the dominant layer of a genealogy. The biblical genealogies are masterpieces in playing on form, using variation and deviation as strategies for making a point. For example, the list of *toledoth* in Genesis 5 enfolds a succession from father to firstborn son in an iterative and rhythmic structure. After the narrative of the fratricide in Genesis 4, the rhythmic form reassures that the line of life was not broken but is still passed on from generation to generation. However, the text includes some minor deviations. For example, Gen. 5.3 does not list the firstborn son Cain, but instead traces the lineage through the substitute son Seth. This deviation modifies the basic principle of primogeniture the moment it is installed and, by doing so, nuances the character of the lineage, which now includes the motif of the younger, ostensibly less important, son as the one who carries on the line.

The biblical genealogies often combine a play on form with a strong engagement of the literary traditions to which they belong. Genealogies often provide a reduced skeletal structure. Still, they are a form of narrative memory: names and relational terms tell stories and pool literary and/or historical traditions. The biblical genealogies also draw heavily on the biblical narratives in which they are generally embedded. They live by their audience's ability to 'read' the stories behind the names and make their arguments implicitly by engaging and linking them.

Interrelating literary traditions and historical events is a characteristic feature of the biblical genealogies. This interrelation can be best accommodated by a notion of cultural recall that understands cultural memory as a broad umbrella concept, such as that proposed by Mieke Bal or Astrid Erll. This model integrates conceptions of cultural memory (e.g. that of JAN ASSMANN), COLLECTIVE/SOCIAL MEMORY, and PERSONAL MEMORY. By doing so, it is able to account for the characteristic ways in which the biblical genealogies combine myth, history, and literature to the end of creating identity-driven performances that are relevant at the time of their composition and beyond.

Ideology and Politics

In conclusion, genealogies are an inherently ideological genre. Involving decisions, inclusion and exclusion, rules of succession, and the power to legitimate offices and claims, they are a highly political form of recall. This potential can be engaged in different directions. On the one hand, genealogies are an apt means to constitute a normative past in acts of memory that negotiate territorial, cultural, and religious claims to the end of establishing a monopoly in the definition of present and future identities. On the other hand, genealogies are able to perform counter-present memory acts (see COUNTERMEMORY), which recall the past against or in addition to mainstream memories (e.g. by means of drawing on alternative archives, recalling repressed threads, or bringing marginalized ancestors into focus). As counter-present memory acts, genealogies may serve as tools for a pluralistic identity construction. Either way, genealogies provide a potent and often intriguing way of performing past and present.

Ingeborg Löwisch (Universiteit Utrecht, Netherlands)

Further Reading

Bal, Mieke, Jonathan Crewe, and Leo Spitzer, eds. 1999. *Acts of Memory: Cultural Recall in the Present*. Hanover: University Press of New England.

Baumann, Gerd, and Andre Gingrich, eds. 2004. *Grammars of Identity/Alterity: A Structural Approach*. Oxford: Berghahn Books.

Erll, Astrid, and Ansgar Nünning, eds. 2008. *Cultural Memory Studies: An International and Interdisciplinary Handbook*. Berlin: W. Walter Mouton de Gruyter.

Foucault, Michel. 1977. 'Nietzsche, Genealogy, History.' In *Language, Counter-Memory, Practice: Selected Essays and Interviews*. Edited by Donald F. Bouchard. New York: Cornell University Press, pp. 139–64.
Hieke, Thomas. 2003. *Die Genealogien der Genesis*. HBS 39. Freiburg: Herder.
Johnson, Marshall D. 1969. *The Purpose of the Biblical Genealogies with Special Reference to the Setting of the Genealogies of Jesus*. SNTSMS 8. Cambridge: Cambridge University Press.
Labahn, Antje, and Ehud Ben Zvi. 2003. 'Observations on Women in the Genealogies of 1 Chronicles 1–9.' *Biblica* 84.4, pp. 457–78.
Löwisch, Ingeborg. 2009. 'Gender and Ambiguity in the Genesis Genealogies: Tracing Absence and Subversion through the Lens of Derrida's "Archive Fever"'. In *Embroidered Garments: Priests and Gender in Biblical Israel*. Edited by Deborah W. Rooke. Sheffield: Sheffield Phoenix Press, pp. 60–73.
Löwisch, Ingeborg. 2014. *Trauma Begets Genealogies: Gender and Memory in Chronicles*. Sheffield: Sheffield Phoenix Press.
Lux, Rüdiger. 1995. 'Die Genealogie als Strukturprinzip des Pluralismus im Alten Testament.' In *Pluralismus und Identität*. Edited by J. Mehlhausen. VWGT 8. Gütersloh: Gütersloher Verlagshaus, pp. 242–58.
Sparks, James T. 2008. *The Chronicler's Genealogies: Towards an Understanding of 1 Chronicles 1-9*. SBL Academia Biblica 28. Atlanta: Society of Biblical Literature.
Wilson, Robert R. 1977. *Genealogies and History in the Biblical World*. New Haven: Yale University Press.

Genre Genre, the forms that speech and WRITING might take, is a crucial aspect of communication. Members of a culture typically possess a shared repertoire of genres and a knowledge of how these different forms convey meaning. Over the past century of research, genre studies has come to be viewed less as an exercise in the classification of texts and their subunits and more as a comprehensive discussion of texts in terms of their communicative function, historical development, and the cognitive models that allow people to group things together in the first place. These questions have enriched discussions of genre in biblical studies.

Within the field of biblical studies, serious investigation of genre arose alongside the development of FORM CRITICISM. Pioneered by HERMANN GUNKEL in a series of early twentieth-century studies on Genesis and the Psalms, Form Criticism attempts to isolate the pre-literary stages in the development of a biblical text. Gunkel posited a history of simple ORAL TRADITIONS, *Gattungen*, that could be identified behind the extant biblical texts on the basis of content, mood, and linguistic form. These *Gattungen* originated in particular social contexts (see SITZ IM LEBEN) governed by particular formal conventions. Gunkel's analysis was partially based on the presupposition that the older, oral forms of speech were pure and simple, as opposed to the more complex genres now evident in the Hebrew Bible and NT. The presumed purity of these types was based on the inherent tie between oral forms of speech and the life settings within which they were typically spoken. According to this theory, these simple forms developed into the more complex literature preserved in the Hebrew Bible when they were committed to writing. Form criticism is not primarily concerned with literary genres but with discerning the traces of oral *Gattungen* and the social settings in which they originated.

Gunkel's concern for the evolution of oral forms in their originating contexts was shared by MIKHAIL BAKHTIN, an influential theorist in research on SPEECH GENRES. Gunkel distinguished between genres in their 'pure' forms and the later mixing of types that occurs when simple speech forms evolve in writing. Bakhtin similarly posited a division between primary (simple) genres that take form in 'unmediated speech communication' and secondary (complex) genres, which adopt and adapt various primary genres. The primary genres lose their immediate relation to actual reality and to 'real utterances' in their absorption into secondary genres (Bakhtin 1986: 62).

The perception that a *Gattung* was originally simple, pure, and rigidly tied to its *Sitz im Leben* was a central tenet of Form Criticism. Gunkel stressed the purity of oral forms: when altered, they become impure. Bakhtin, on the other hand, represents a later development in genre criticism: genres are dynamic, submitting naturally to change. Both theorists distinguished between simple and complex genres. Simple genres can be identical with a single speech act (e.g. a single PROVERB), while complex genres incorporate a variety of simple genres into more elaborate literary works (e.g. biblical wisdom literature). More recent evaluations of the status of Form Criticism in biblical studies have emphasized the inherent fluidity of genres, and are as concerned with the transformation of genres as with elucidating the typical features of a presumed ORIGINAL simple form (Sweeney and Ben Zvi 2003; cf. Newsom 2005).

Models of Genre

A new interest in genre theory emerged with the 'literary turn' in biblical studies in the 1970s. The Society of Biblical Literature's Genres Project, launched by Robert Funk, produced influential studies on miracle stories, APOCALYPSES, LETTERS, pronouncement stories, and PARABLES (published in Semeia volumes 11, 14, 20, 22, 29, and 36). These studies illustrate the tendency of biblical scholarship to classify or define each biblical genre on the basis of observable shared traits. The Apocalypse Group of the SBL, for example, viewed their task as the identification of a 'group of written texts marked by distinctive recurring characteristics which constitute a recognizable and coherent type of writing' (Collins 1979a:1). This approach to genre takes as its ideal the taxonomic models created in the sciences, subject to explicit, formalized and verifiable rules.

The centrality of classification in genre studies has not wholly disappeared. Despite (or in response to) disparagement of a simplistic understanding of genre as a series of rigidly defined classes, Adena Rosmarin has sought to revive classification as a pragmatic 'theory of explanation' necessary to 'enable[e] criticism to begin' (1995: 21–2). One reads a text 'as if' it belonged to a particular genre. Genre serves as a heuristic tool for the critic, allowing her to relate these texts to others of a similar type. John Collins also defends genre classification as a basic tool for biblical studies, noting that 'without classification there is not generic analysis, and all classification depends on noting features that are shared by a group of texts' (Collins 2010: 419).

Since the 1970s, several alternative models have been presented as a framework for discussions of biblical genres (Newsom 2005). Alistair Fowler popularized Wittgenstein's concept of family resemblance as an alternative to traditional classification models (Fowler 1982). The family resemblance model follows a genetic analogy, in which members of a class are not connected by one single identifiable feature but instead by a series of overlapping similarities. Following this approach, no single trait may be characteristic of all individual members of a genre family. This model acknowledges the often fluid boundaries of genre categories.

Extending the genetic analogy, some theorists have adopted the metaphor of evolutionary biology to explain the development of genre. This model attends particularly to the evolution of, and interrelationships between, different genres. In biblical studies, F. W. Dobbs-Allsopp has used this model to discuss the evolution of the Israelite city-lament genre and its relationship to Mesopotamian city laments (Dobbs-Allsopp 2000). Evolutionary approaches analyse generic survival in terms of productivity and environment: do traditions continue to produce new similar texts over time? This characteristic is defined as *primary productivity*, in contrast to *secondary productivity*, in which related texts are produced according to *fixed formulas*, taking the shape of imitation or parody of earlier genres. The evolutionary approach to genre also attends to environmental factors that affect the influence of particular genres. Returning to the example of ancient Near Eastern city laments, these environmental factors can include the prominence of urban culture, and the relationship between a city's demise and the survival of its related culture.

Other approaches focus on the social function of genres as modes of communication (Newsom 2005; 2010). Genre shapes the expectations of a reader or hearer, providing several clues to meaning that might remain implicit in the content of the texts themselves. In this understanding of genre, questions of function are central. Emphasizing this social function also draws attention to the crucial role of genre analysis in the interpretation of ancient texts. A modern critic lacks an inherent shared cultural knowledge with the author or intended audience of the ancient documents she analyses. This cultural knowledge must be carefully cultivated as a primary task of scholarship. One challenge to this approach relates to the overlap (or not) of form and function. For example, though one might accept that both Proverbs and Ecclesiastes are both examples of ancient *wisdom literature*, their communicative functions differ quite radically. Thus, recognizing genre as a mode of communication is less a question of replacing one model of genre with another as placing important emphasis on the way genres enable communication itself.

One of the remarkable things about genre as a social phenomenon is the way that individuals acquire this cultural knowledge. For the most part, people successfully recognize and communicate in a variety of spoken and literary genres. Recent insights from cognitive science demonstrate empirically how such categories are formed and tested (Frow 2005: 54–5; Newsom 2010: 245). Within this prototypical model of genre, categories are constructed around typical concrete instances of communication. Beyond the typical, there is a spectrum of membership in the category based on characteristic but not defining features. For example, any domesticated animal might be considered a 'pet', but modern Westerners typically think of particular typical members of the pet category before others: a dog or cat would be *typical* members of the category, whereas a tarantula or snail would be *atypical*. Similarly, there are *highly typical* and *less typical* texts within a particular genre: the book of Revelation might be considered a *typical* apocalypse, while Proverbs, Job, and Ecclesiastes would be *typical* examples of wisdom literature. Such concerns are illustrated by the discussion surrounding the labelling of Genesis 1 as a *myth*. This discussion often centres on comparison with other typical representatives of the category myth in the ancient Near East, such as *Enuma Elish*. Various definitions are given to myth, largely on the basis of describing these prototypical examples.

Prototype theory also challenges the often binary nature of genre assignment: is a given text 'in' or 'out'? A prototypical model of genre encourages an understanding of texts as existing along a continuum of membership to particular genre categories. Genres are instead viewed as fuzzy categories constructed by analogy from the most typical exemplars.

Theorist John Frow describes genres as 'worlds', with 'effects of reality and truth, authority and plausibility, which are central to the different ways the world is understood' (Frow 2005: 2). These effects are determined by the relationship between textual structures and the situations that occasion them. In this way, the social setting in which a genre is created, so central for biblical Form Criticism, re-emerges within a new concept of genre. Within this rubric, the genres of *history* or *philosophy*, for instance, rely on various modes of proof that are acceptable to establish 'truth'. What counts as evidence or an acceptable argument within philosophy and history differs. It is not a collection of formal features that defines a genre, but rather the frame through which the genre sees and conceptualizes reality.

However defined, genre is an essential element in the understanding of both ancient and modern texts. As genre theory evolves, so too does our understanding of the role of form in biblical studies. Questions of function, of historical development, and of cognitive models of categorization encourage new types of inquiry into systems of biblical and ancient media, as well as methodological clarity in formal analysis.

Aubrey E. Buster (Emory University, USA)

Further Reading

Bakhtin, Mikhail M. 1986. 'The Problem of Speech Genres.' Translated by Vern W. McGee. In *Speech Genres and Other Late Essays*. Edited by Caryl Emerson and Michael Holquist. Austin, TX: University of Texas Press, pp. 60–102.

Collins, John, ed. 1979. *Apocalypse: the Morphology of a Genre*. Semeia 14. Missoula, MT: SBL Press.
Collins, John. 2010. 'Epilogue: Genre Analysis and the Dead Sea Scrolls.' *DSD* 17: 418–30.
Dobbs-Allsopp, F. W. 2000. 'Darwinism, Genre Theory, and City Laments.' *JAOS* 120: 625–30.
Fowler, Alistair. 1982. *Kinds of Literature: An Introduction to the Theory of Genres and Modes*. Cambridge, MA: Harvard University Press.
Frow, John. 2005. *Genre: The New Critical Idiom*. Abingdon: Routledge.
Gunkel, Hermann. 1998 [1933]. *Introduction to the Psalms. The Genres of the Religious Lyric of Israel*. Translated by Joachim Begrich. Göttingen: Vandenhoeck & Ruprecht.
Newsom, Carol. 2005. 'Spying Out the Land: A Report from Genology.' In *Seeking Out the Wisdom of the Ancients: Essays Offered to Honor Michael V. Fox on the Occasion of his Sixty-fifth Birthday*. Winona Lake, IN: Eisenbrauns, pp. 437–50.
Newsom, Carol. 2010. 'Pairing Research Questions and Theories of Genre: A Case Study of the Hodayot.' *DSD* 17: 241–59.
Rosmarin, Adena. 1985. *The Power of Genre*. Minneapolis: University of Minneapolis Press.

Gerhardsson, Birger Birger Gerhardsson (1926–2013) was a Swedish NT scholar whose publications focused on ORAL TRADITION and transmission in Rabbinic Judaism and early Christianity. Gerhardsson explicitly postured his work as an alternative to German FORM CRITICISM, and his research has made a lasting impact on discussions of the nature and reliability of the gospel tradition. He participated in numerous international conferences and attended regularly the annual meetings of the *Studiorum Novi Testamenti Societas* (SNTS), serving as its president in 1990. Gerhardsson was an ordained priest in the Lutheran Church of Sweden and was professor of exegetical theology at Lund University, Sweden, from 1965 to 1992. In addition to his influential publications on tradition and transmission, he wrote extensively on the Gospel of Matthew and on ethics, early Jewish and Christian confessions, the resurrection, and the Lord's Prayer.

Gerhardsson began his doctoral studies in Uppsala in 1952 under Anton Fridrichsen and continued from 1953 under Harald Riesenfeld, but his earliest interest in oral tradition was peaked by Professor Ivan Engnell's work on the Hebrew Bible. Already in his unpublished *Licentiatenarbeit* from 1956 (*Studier i Jakobsbrevets uppkomstmiljö*), Gerhardsson argued, contra MARTIN DIBELIUS, that the sayings of Jesus alluded to in the letter of James had been transmitted independently of their use in paraenesis.

Gerhardsson's doctoral dissertation, revised and later released as *Memory and Manuscript* (1961/1964), turns attention to the profoundly mnemonic character of written and oral tradition, introducing neglected diachronic aspects into the form-critical programme. Gerhardsson focuses on the technical procedures that were implemented by the early church in its transmission of the gospel tradition, drawing analogies from the use of Torah in the Tannaitic and Amoraic RABBINIC materials, in particular the situations in which a text was reproduced through memorization. Gerhardsson also reckons with efforts to relate that which was memorized to new situations. Being cautious not to impose the methods of the rabbinic movement on early Christianity, Gerhardsson also considers evidence from the early Fathers and the importance they attached to discipleship and memory as a point of departure for his investigation of the JESUS TRADITION, and infers from Luke and Paul the existence of an apostolic collegium in Jerusalem that grouped Jesus' sayings in memorable units and formulated episodes about Jesus' actions. Gerhardsson realizes that the tradition was used in many situations, but pays special attention to a distinct SITZ IM LEBEN of transmission in which a teacher passed on material to his students by means of rote repetition followed by interpretation. Jesus himself initiated this process by teaching his disciples in word and deed – occasionally repeating the same material several times in various forms – and requiring them to remember what they heard and saw.

Gerhardsson elaborated his view in several subsequent publications. His study of the Temptation (Mt. 4.1-11) argues for the crucial importance of the Shema (Deut. 6.4-5) as a means of understanding how the

Pharisaic followers of Jesus worked with the Scriptures and the tradition. Other studies dealt extensively with the PARABLES ('narrative *meshalim*') and the mighty acts of Jesus in Matthew, explicating how Gerhardsson's seminal thesis on oral transmission is reflected in the gospel tradition and the Gospels. In a 1983 paper entitled 'The Path of the Gospel Tradition', Gerhardsson identifies ten weaknesses of the model of oral tradition that informed Form Criticism: 1) the distinction between Palestinian and Hellenistic streams of tradition; 2) the notion that form may be taken as a sociological fact; 3) the presumed link between form and *Sitz im Leben*, the 'life setting' in the early church in which tradition was used; 4) the search for a pure form of oral-traditional material; 5) the view that Jesus and the early Christians were 'unliterary'; 6) the notion that the work on tradition took place separately from the Evangelists' work of redaction; 7) the separation of narrative entities in the tradition; 8) the minimization of individual traditionists/tradents in the transmission and development of gospel material; 9) the neglect of written tradition; and 10) the significance of Mark's achievement in producing a complete written narrative of Jesus' career (see NARRATIVITY).

Gerhardsson offered further major contributions to the study of tradition and transmission in *The Gospel Tradition* (1986). Here he presents a model of tradition that distinguishes between 'inner' and 'outer' tradition. The former are fundamental convictions that express themselves in fellowship and that generate tradition for the next generation. The latter is the outward form of the inner tradition, externalizing itself in verbal tradition, behavioural tradition, institutional tradition, and material tradition. When the tradition is new and permeates existing realities, it may be labelled *programmatic* tradition. When it is old but still exists without being consciously accepted or rejected, it may be called de facto tradition. Gerhardsson also explicates his view on orality and textuality, mainly in dialogue with the work of WERNER KELBER.

In 2009, Samuel Byrskog and Werner Kelber released a collection of essays that explore the significance of Gerhardsson's approach, both in the larger history of NT scholarship and in its potential relevance to specific critical/exegetical problems. This collection of essays explores the significance and impact of Gerhardsson's work on NT studies.

Samuel Byrskog (Centre for Theology and Religious Studies, Lund University, Sweden)

Further reading

Gerhardsson, Birger. 1966. *The Testing of God's Son (Matt 4:1-11 & Par): An Analysis of an Early Christian Midrash*. ConBNT 2.1. Lund: Gleerup.

Gerhardsson, Birger. 1986. *The Gospel Tradition*. ConBNT 15. Lund: Gleerup.

Gerhardsson, Birger. 1996. 'The Path of the Gospel Tradition.' In *The Gospel and the Gospels*. Edited by Peter Stuhlmacher. Grand Rapids: Eerdmans, pp. 75–96.

Gerhardsson, Birger. 1996. *The Shema in the New Testament: Deut 6:4–5 in Significant Passages*. Lund: Novapress.

Gerhardsson, Birger. 1998. *Memory and Manuscript: Oral Tradition and Written Transmission in Rabbinic Judaism and Early Christianity, with Tradition and Transmission in Early Christianity*. ASNU 22. Lund: Gleerup: 1961; 2nd edn. 1964; reprint. Grand Rapids: Eerdmans.

Kelber, Werner, and Samuel Byrskog, eds. 2009. *Jesus in Memory: Traditions in Oral and Scribal Perspectives*. Waco, TX: Baylor University Press.

Gist Memory
Memory, Gist and Verbatim

Gist memory and verbatim memory are two aspects of the human COGNITIVE/PERSONAL MEMORY system that captures recollections of meaningful words, whether they be heard or read. *Verbatim memory* refers to recollections of the exact wording of something that was heard or read; *gist memory*, by contrast, refers to recollections of the meaning or conceptual substance of what was heard or read, but not necessarily the exact sounds or words. While individuals sometimes believe that their recollections represent what was heard or read *verbatim*, individual acts of memory are normally reconstructions of the gist of what was communicated.

Short-term verbatim memory is somewhat limited in scope and relies on the brain's phonological loop, which can remember exact words and sounds (see LONG-TERM/SHORT-TERM MEMORY). While it was once widely believed that gist memory formed from short-term verbatim memory as a sort of distillation of details (i.e. exact recollections being sorted into more general categories), C. J. Brainerd and Valerie Reyna (2004), among others, have demonstrated that gist memory and verbatim memory are formed in the brain at exactly the same time. Brainerd and others have described this particular model of verbal memory formation as 'fuzzy trace theory', which is now one of the standard explanations of a set of verbal memory errors that derive from the fact that the adult human brain generally remembers meaning/gist rather than exact words. Although both verbatim and gist memory function at every stage in human development, in early childhood individuals tend to rely mostly on verbatim memory, with a transition to greater dependence on gist memory as they grow older (and thus have a larger bank of data to recall).

Without constant rehearsal, verbatim memory tends to be shorter-lived than gist memory, so most LONG-TERM memory is gist memory. Some genres of communication, however, seem to be more resilient in one memory type than another, generally corresponding to their length and/or complexity. Thus, aphorisms and PROVERBS, which depend heavily on the surface text for the communication of meaning, tend to be remembered verbatim, while stories, which draw their effect from the total sequence of the presentation, tend to be remembered in gist. If the story is attached to a joke that has a punchline, for example, the punchline tends to be remembered verbatim, while the story is remembered in gist form.

The effects of gist memory are clearly evident in the biblical documents, and the concept has been particularly significant in considerations of the preservation of Jesus' sayings and JESUS TRADITION in the Gospels. Much of the teachings of Jesus in the Synoptic Gospels is preserved either as short aphoristic sayings or as parables with a story line. The aphorisms of Jesus would have been remembered verbatim by those that first heard them, but quickly forgotten unless they were repeated regularly. Jesus' parables would have been remembered in gist form, with the exception that it is likely that a parable's punchline would have been remembered verbatim, or near verbatim. It is to be expected that parables would have been remembered for a longer time than aphorisms, but even so, for parables to be remembered with reasonable accuracy over the several decades that are thought to have passed between Jesus' telling them and their being written in the Gospels, it would have been necessary for parables to have been rehearsed or repeated from time to time.

Robert K. McIver (Avondale College of Higher Education, Australia)

Glossolalia/'Speaking in Tongues' Glossolalia (from the Greek *glossa* 'tongue' and *lalein* 'speak') is the term given to the charismatic gift or practice of speaking in tongues, namely in a linguistic form that is foreign or alien to the speaker. If such tongues are comprehensible or recognizable to others, however, *xenolalia* is the more appropriate term, inasmuch as a genuine 'foreign' (*xenos*) language is being uttered.

The Hebrew Bible offers no formal mention of the glossolalic phenomenon (1 Sam. 10.10, e.g. is no equivalent). Explicit NT references are restricted primarily to two books, Acts (2.1-13; 10.44-45; 19.6) and 1 Corinthians (14.1-40), with significant variation between their respective portrayals. Acts depicts glossolalia as fundamentally an initiatory experience, whereas Paul's Corinthian discourse portrays it as a regular, if contested, feature of church life. Paul conceives of the practice as benefiting the individual, whereas Luke ascribes it a more communal or public function, especially at Pentecost. Luke associates glossolalia with the prophetic gifting, again quintessentially at Pentecost, while Paul distinguishes the two practices, affirming their fundamental difference. While the glossolalia of Acts 2 are actually comprehensible xenolalia (2.6; 2.8), Paul emphasizes the very incomprehensibility of tongues, stressing their subsequent need for interpretation (1 Cor. 14.27). Both authors concur, however, that glossolalia involves speaking in a linguistic form unknown to the speaker, and that it incorporates some form of divine praise. The 'groaning' of the Spirit in Rom. 8.26 may reflect a further allusion to glossolalia, but Paul does not name it as such. More explicit is the reference to 'new tongues' as an accompaniment to missionary proclamation in the disputed longer ending of Mark (16.17).

Paul declares that he can speak in tongues (1 Cor. 14.18) and expresses his desire that all might exercise glossolalic practice (14.5). However, there would seem to be an over-enthusiasm for tongues at Corinth, perhaps derivative from the factionalism alluded to elsewhere in the LETTER (1.10-12), with the tongue-speakers asserting their spirituality – and, by extension, their power and influence – within the congregation. Not all the Corinthians exercised glossolalia, but those who did may have been consequently invested with special authority because of the particular divine presence or insight they would have been perceived to bring; they may have seemed able to engage a power beyond themselves, and tap into the spiritual/divine accordingly. Paul therefore expresses some reticence about glossolalic practice, averring that tongues are directed to God (14.2) rather than to other humans, and are perceived as mystery (14.2). He gravitates towards the use of PROPHECY rather than tongues (14.5), with the effect of each communicative act of particular significance. The unbeliever will be brought to faith and worship by exposure to prophecy, whereas s/he would perceive the tongue-speaker as merely exhibiting 'madness' (14.23). Such madness would seem to be a negative consequence or sign of glossolalia (14.22), dissuading them from participation in the believing community, though Paul may actually have intended a more positive rendering, with 'madness' contextually indicative of the divine presence or activity within the assembled congregation (Chester 2005).

The phenomenon of glossolalia attests not just to the inherent ORALITY of liturgical practice in Corinth, but also to the perception that divine communication was mediated primarily through oral means. Paul himself observes that (genuine) communication occurs only through shared language, and that the 'otherness' of glossolalic discourse precludes such (oral) communication. In an essentially oral/aural culture, language functions as a marker of IDENTITY and culture, and the utilization of an unknown, 'mystical' language places the tongue-speaker(s) in a position of power over those who did not have access to, or knowledge of, that language. Hence the (performative) mode of communication is as important as the content, reflecting MARSHALL MCLUHAN's observation that 'the medium is the message' (McLuhan 1964).

Scholarship has speculated on connections between the Corinthian glossolalia and other contemporary religious phenomena, the most commonly noted parallel being the Pythian oracle at Delphi, whose priestly utterances required subsequent prophetic interpretation. There are some notable differences in function (e.g. the Pythia may well have spoken in comprehensible language), and if they are to be classified in any sense as *glossolalic*, it is in their cryptic dimension (i.e. they need interpretation) rather than any linguistic similarity. An absolute point of comparison between glossolalia and other Hellenistic religious practice is therefore lacking (Forbes 1997) and glossolalia is likely 'a Christian neologism' (Esler 1994). A stronger parallel, however, may be with the affective aspect of the glossolalic discourse, namely that the oracle speaks with, or possesses, an authority beyond themselves.

Paul offers no information on the origins of the practice of speaking in tongues, nor does he assume or assert its demise. Neither does he comment on the linguistic pattern of the glossolalic utterance (beyond their incomprehensibility), though Goodman's work on the rhythm of contemporary glossolalic utterances may be germane (Goodman 1972). Debates continue as to whether Corinthian glossolalia possessed some form of linguistic consistency or were rather merely formularized babbling. The practice of interpretation (cf. 1 Cor. 14.13) may imply some form of translation (i.e. rendering the unknown language into familiar Greek). Alternatively, the interpretive process may actually turn the tongue into language itself, and thereby into some form of intersubjective human communication. More positively, glossolalia manifest pre-textualized authority; their very otherness precludes their being textified as in so doing they would lose their very essence. They resist textification (Smith 1997): they cannot be written or repeated, and struggle even to be encapsulated in words (cf. Rom. 8.29).

As to the visual aspect of glossolalic utterance, one must be careful not to jump to behavioural conclusions. It is not clear whether glossolalic practice invited or necessitated audience participation (beyond the interpretive function), though other manifestations of inspired speech (e.g. Lucian's *Alexander of Abunoteichos* [*Alexander the False Prophet*]) seem to have involved audience interaction. The Pentecost accusation of drinking excessive wine (Acts 2.13) need imply little about glossolalic manifestation, and – 1 Cor. 14.23 notwithstanding – there is no Pauline imperative to view glossolalia as necessarily invoking ecstatic or wild behaviour. However, some form of accompanying physical activity or nonverbal communication seems plausible; Lucian, for example, can speak of Apollo forcing his way into the Pythia's body, presumably indicative of significant physical manifestation.

David M. Allen (Queen's Foundation for Ecumenical Theological Education, UK)

Further Reading

Cartedge, Mark, ed. 2006. *Speaking in Tongues: Multi-disciplinary Perspectives*. Milton Keynes, UK: Paternoster Press.

Goodman, Felicitas. 1972. *Speaking in Tongues: A Cross-Cultural Study of Glossolalia*. Chicago: University of Chicago Press.

Hovenden, Gerald. 2002. *Speaking in Tongues: The New Testament Evidence in Context*. JPTSup 22. London: Sheffield Academic Press.

McLuhan, Marshall. 1964. *Understanding Media: The Extensions of Man*. Cambridge, MA: MIT Press.

Goody, Jack John (Jack) Rangine Goody (1919–2015) was a British anthropologist and historian who taught for most of his career at Cambridge. Although his primary fieldwork was conducted in Africa, his writings display wide comparative interests. An important aspect of his research concerned the comparison of non-literate and literate cultures and the transition from non-literate to literate, especially considerations of how media transitions impact economics, religion, and human cognition in general. His work in this area was influenced by Milman Parry, Albert Lord, Walter Ong, Eric Havelock, and Maurice Halbwachs, and Goody's own writings have, in turn, influenced biblical studies. This research path began in an important article he coauthored with Ian Watt, an English professor at the University of California, Berkeley, entitled 'The Consequences of Literacy', which focused on a proposed 'dichotomy between non-literate and literate societies' (1963: 305). Throughout his career, Goody particularly sought to challenge ethnocentric assumptions regarding the cultural uniqueness (= superiority) of the West (1977), the long-term effects of writing on social organization (1986), and the 'interface between the written and the oral' in literate societies (1987).

Goody's earlier work is now often associated with the Great Divide approach, which posits a categorical and monolithic opposition between oral and literate modes of thought and communication, despite the fact that Goody himself strove to resist such binary thinking (e.g. 1977: 1–18, 146–62). While highlighting the potential differences between media and the cultural appropriation of them, Goody expressed a desire 'to maintain a balance between the refusal to admit of difference in cognitive processes or cultural developments on the one hand and extreme dualism or distinction on the other' (1977: 16–17). Today Goody's work, like that of Walter Ong, is viewed as an important, if now somewhat obsolete, early stimulus to greater reflection on the interfaces between ORALITY and LITERACY in the biblical world.

Raymond F. Person, Jr. (Ohio Northern University, USA)

Further Reading

Goody, Jack. 1977. *The Domestication of the Savage Mind.* Cambridge: Cambridge University Press.
Goody, Jack. 1986. *The Logic of Writing and the Organization of Society*. Cambridge: Cambridge University Press.
Goody, Jack. 1987. *The Interface between the Written and the Oral.* Cambridge: Cambridge University Press.
Goody, Jack. 1991. 'Toward a Room with a View: A Personal Account of Contributions to Local Knowledge, Theory, and Research in Fieldwork and Comparative Studies.' *Annual Reviews of Anthropology* 20: 1–23.
Goody, Jack, and Ian Watt. 1963. 'The Consequences of Literacy.' *Comparative Studies in Society and History* 5: 304–45.
Pallares, Burke, and Maria Lúcia. 2002. 'Jack Goody.' In *The New History: Confessions and Conversations.* Cambridge: Polity Press, pp. 7–30.

Graffiti Thousands of graffiti, or 'wall writings', from the ancient world have been discovered, often comprising little more than crude drawings and a word or two. Some date to the First Temple period, thousands more date to the Second Temple period and later. They can be found throughout the Middle East and the Roman empire. A great number of Latin graffiti have been preserved at POMPEII and Herculaneum thanks to the eruption of Vesuvius in 79 CE. A considerable number of Greek graffiti have been found in the lower section of Smyrna's *agora* (market place), buried when the upper section collapsed (probably from an earthquake). These graffiti date from the second to the fourth centuries CE.

Graffiti are usually etched into the plaster or paint on walls, in both public and private locations. They appear as words, sentences, or brief paragraphs. Some contain personal names, abbreviations, symbols, numbers, or drawings. Most graffiti are explicit, though some are cryptic. Every conceivable GENRE is represented among the graffiti, including RIDDLES, moralizing maxims, poetry, threats, warnings, curses, political propaganda or satire, social comment, prayers, vulgarities, erotic expressions – sometimes accompanied by crude illustrations – and expressions and drawings related to athletes and gladiators. The graffiti were produced by people from all walks of life – affluent and poor, free and slave, the educated and the barely literate.

What precisely counts as *graffiti*, as opposed to something commissioned by a homeowner or the proprietor of a business, is not always easy to determine. This is especially true in cases where the writing is well executed, sometimes bordering on calligraphy, and the artwork is professional in appearance. In any case, not all graffiti should be viewed as vandalism in the modern sense. Some of it is well intentioned, even if impulsive and crudely executed, for example the names and messages left on the walls of family tombs (either etched into the stone or drawn with charcoal). A tomb at Beth She'arim, Galilee, includes a word of comfort addressed to members of a family: 'Good luck in your resurrection.'

A few graffiti have been found that relate to John the Baptist and Jesus of Nazareth. In reference to the former, a faint inscription was recently observed on the east side of the so-called Tomb (or Pillar) of Absalom in the Kidron Valley at the foot of the Mount of Olives. Above the robber's hole, the Byzantine-era graffito reads: 'Here is the tomb of Zachariah, martyr, old, very pious, father of John.' To the right of the robber's hole, written sideways, is another graffito, which reads: 'The tomb of Simeon who was a very just man and a very devoted old (one), and for the consolation of the people was waiting.' Both graffiti allude to Luke's infancy narrative. In 2000, archaeologist Shimon Gibson discovered a crudely etched figure on the wall of a cave in Shuba, about three miles west of Ain Karim, a region associated with John the Baptist. Although the cave itself dates as far back as the exilic period, there is evidence that Byzantine Christians (fourth to sixth centuries CE) made use of it, perhaps for BAPTISM and footwashing. Gibson and others believe the beardless figure on the wall was meant to depict John.

Jesus is depicted in the Roman catacombs, mostly dating from the third and fourth centuries CE. One drawing shows a beardless Jesus in a Roman tunic, while another portrays a fully bearded Jesus. The latter image closely resembles portraits of Jesus on fifth-century and later Byzantine COINS. Perhaps the most interesting depiction of Jesus is found in the well-known Palatine Graffito (also known as the Alexamenos Graffito). This late second/early third-century graffito depicts a crucified human figure with the head of a donkey. The figure's hands and arms are outstretched, evidently nailed to the cross beam, or *patibulum*. The figure is wearing a short-sleeved *colobium*, or undershirt (typical dress of slaves), that extends from the shoulders to the waist. The feet rest on a short, horizontal plank. The crucified figure is looking at another figure who stands near him with one arm upraised; the upraised hand and arm are either a salute or, as one scholar has suggested, the act of throwing a kiss. Between and beneath the two figures, etched in four lines, are the words *Alexamenos sebete Theon*. Taken at face value, these words mean, 'Alexamenos, worship God!', but the imperative is unlikely. Most interpreters think *sebete* is probably a misspelling of the indicative form *sebetai*, which would make the saying descriptive of the image: 'Alexamenos worships (his) God.'

The cross shape of the Palatine Graffito is also attested in the similar late-second-century Puteoli Graffito. The hands and feet of the naked victim are nailed to the *patibulum* and the upright stake. There is, however, no reason to think that the Puteoli Graffito was in reference to Jesus. Some graffiti allude to crucifixion in curses upon enemies. For example, one reads: 'May you be nailed to the cross!' (CIL 2082: *in cruce figarus*). Another reads: 'Samius (says) to Cornelius, "Get hung!"' (CIL 1864: *Samius Cornelio suspendre*).

The myriads of graffiti at Herculaneum, Pompeii, and Smyrna – sites in which acts of nature preserved painted and plastered surfaces and thereby preserved the graffiti – may suggest that LITERACY rates were higher than some recent studies have suggested. Because they are directed towards and generally emerged from general audiences, graffiti provide important glimpses into everyday life in antiquity.

Craig A. Evans (Houston Baptist University, USA)

Further Reading

Baird, J. A., and C. Taylor, eds. 2011. *Ancient Graffiti in Context*. London and New York: Routledge.

Cook, J. G. 2008. 'Envisioning Crucifixion: Light from Several Inscriptions and the Palatine Graffito.' *NovT* 50: 262–85.

Cook, J. G. 2013. 'John 19:17 and the Man on the Patibulum in the Arieti Tomb.' *Early Christianity* 4: 427–53.

Gibson, S. 2004. *The Cave of John the Baptist*. New York: Doubleday.

Milnor, K. 2014. *Graffiti and the Literary Landscape in Roman Pompeii*. Oxford: Oxford University Press.

Morstein-Marx, R. 2012. 'Political Graffiti in the Late Roman Republic: "Hidden Transcripts" and "Common Knowledge"'. In *Politische Kommunikation und öffentliche Meinung in der antiken Welt*. Edited by C. Kuhn. Stuttgart: Steiner, pp. 191–218.

Naveh, J. 2001. 'Hebrew Graffiti from the First Temple Period.' *Israel Exploration Journal* 51: 194–207.

Puech, É. 2004. 'Le tombeau de Siméon et Zacharie dans la vallée de Josaphat.' *Revue biblique* 111: 563–77 + plates II–IV.

Squire, M. 2009. *Image and Text in Greco-Roman Antiquity*. Cambridge and New York: Cambridge University Press.

Varone, A. 2002. *Erotica Pompeiana: Love Inscriptions on the Walls of Pompeii*. Rome: 'L'Erma' di Bretschneider.

Zias, J. 2005. 'The Tomb of Absalom Reconsidered.' *Near Eastern Archaeology* 68: 148–65.

Great Tradition/Little Tradition The term *great tradition* refers to the total set of values that operate within a complex society's COLLECTIVE MEMORY to rationalize and maintain the homogeneous outlook necessary for that society, and its individual members, to maintain a distinct identity and the common lifeways that follow from that identity. While a great tradition is always particular to the history, circumstances, and social configuration and values of the society that promotes it, its abstract values are perceived by members of the group as universal truths. Because they serve a global social function, great traditions are broadcast through mass media channels, including both physical channels such as public MONUMENTS, the layout of buildings and cities, and written texts, and also less visible social channels, such as the annual calendar with its cycle of commemorative events (e.g. SABBATH, Passover).

While great traditions are experienced by the individuals who subscribe to them as aspects of the natural order and rhythm of life, they are constructed and maintained by an intellectual elite who are expert in the historical, religious, or technical knowledge on which a society depends (e.g. Jeroboam's construction of a new political/religious identity and cult for the northern tribes; Ezra's reconstruction of the Judahite community through appeal to a canon of sacred texts). In reference to the concerns of biblical studies, great traditions are often grounded in and maintained by traditions, texts, and institutions that the society considers sacred, such as the written Torah and the JERUSALEM TEMPLE and its cult – a fact that granted considerable social power to the post-exilic and Late Second Temple Jewish scribal, priestly, and rabbinic classes.

Within any complex society, the unifying homogeneity of the great tradition operates above and alongside local variations that modify or in some cases overtly defy its values and content. In the process of dissemination, as the elite theoretical vision is filtered through local circumstances and the practicalities of everyday life, 'some themes are lost, new ones are added, symbols acquire new meanings and are put to new purposes' (Scott 1977: 2). The contents of these popular appropriations of the official policy or party line are called *little traditions*. Little traditions represent the translation of the broad social vision, the 'official' version of things, into the FOLKLORE and folk life of individual groups within the larger society, and as such generally involve a shift from abstract principles to identification with immediate personal experience. It is important to stress the plural – *little traditions* – simply because little traditions are always local and therefore multiple, while the great tradition is by definition universal and singular.

Religious great traditions are represented by the creeds of the world's major faith systems (e.g. Judaism, Islam, Christianity), while political great traditions take the form of theories of government and economics (e.g. communism, colonialism, democracy, capitalism) and are represented in key legal documents (e.g. the US Constitution). In many cases, and in every case in antiquity relevant to the field of biblical studies, the religious and political contents of a great tradition are explicitly intertwined, especially when it serves the interests of the elite to do so. Notable examples include the consolidation of religious and political power in Jerusalem under David and Solomon, the alliance between Ezra and Nehemiah in the parallel culture-constructing activities of publicly reading sacred texts and building city walls, and the Roman appropriation of the Jerusalem priestly aristocracy as a vehicle for the management of the Judean population.

Biblical scholars who utilize the great/little tradition model have been heavily influenced by the formulations of sociologists Robert Redfield and, particularly, James C. Scott. Scott's model is characterized by the premise that the relationship between great and little traditions is often conflictual. Because they are maintained and disseminated by cultural elites and scribal experts (e.g. SCRIBES, scholars, priests, lawyers) who have special access to foundational social documents that are not widely available to the masses, great traditions are inherently embedded in, and structured to maintain, current structures of power and privilege. The *public transcripts* – codes of value, speech, and behaviour that unify regular social interactions – that derive from a great tradition are thus inherently reflective of elite interests, even if not formulated as such. Against this privileging homogeneity, little traditions support subversive *private transcripts*, coping mechanisms that allow the underprivileged masses to act out in ways that provide psychological (and sometimes physical) relief without rising to the level of outright rebellion or otherwise disrupting the unifying normalcy of everyday life that the great tradition makes possible. Scott refers to these intentional folk challenges to the official version of things as 'profanations' because they often involve parodies or/and manipulations of the language and symbols of the great tradition.

In normal circumstances, profanation of the great tradition is confined to folk texts, rituals, and genres of communication in which the current social order is 'symbolically negated', often through a motif of reversal that stands the real-world hierarchy of power on its head and suspends deference to the norms of the great tradition (quote Scott 1977: 241). When these social strategies fail and the masses can no longer emotionally or materially sustain the systems supported by the great tradition, profanation may evolve into protest or outright revolt, often with an attack on the symbols, institutions, and individuals through/by which the great tradition was disseminated (e.g. the takeover of the Jerusalem temple and burning of the high priest's house during the early days of the first Jewish Revolt in 66 CE).

The great/little tradition model has been widely applied in biblical studies as a framework for explaining the relationship between popular and institutional religious and social forms in ancient Israel, including the Jesus movement and the rise of the early church in the Late Second Temple period. The biblical texts themselves – while serving as foundational documents in support of the Judahite monarchy, the restored post-exilic temple state of Jerusalem, and the priestly and scribal classes that managed Israel's civic and religious lifeways – give frequent testimony to the ongoing tensions between the great tradition they encode and the beliefs and practices of non-elites, both populist beliefs that worked against homogeneity (e.g. Baalism and inter-ethnic marriage and commerce) and prophetic movements that called for a return to a more pristine expression of Israel's faith and identity than that sanctioned by the priests and scribes and the kings who supported them (e.g. Jeremiah and Jesus).

Tom Thatcher (Cincinnati Christian University, USA)

Further Reading

Horsley, Richard, ed. 2004. *Hidden Transcripts and the Arts of Resistance: Applying the Work of James C. Scott to Jesus and Paul.* Semeia St. Atlanta: SBL Press.

Redfield, Robert. 1956. *Peasant Society and Culture: An Anthropological Approach to Civilization.* Chicago: University of Chicago Press.

Scott, James C. 1977. 'Protest and Profanation: Agrarian Revolt and the Little Tradition.' *Theory and Society* 4 (1977) 13. Part I of this essay appears on pp. 1–38; Part II (from a later number of the same year and volume of the journal) appears on pp. 211–46.

Scott, James C. 1990. *Domination and the Arts of Resistance: Hidden Transcripts.* New Haven, CT: Yale University Press.

Great Divide Media criticism is the 'analysis of the function and dynamics of various media of communication (speech, writing, ritual, etc.), and especially of the significance of shifts from one medium to another (e.g. from oral to written expression)' (Rodríguez 2014: 22). This analytical approach takes as a given that media shifts are, in fact, significant, that 'medium matters', and even that, citing MARSHALL MCLUHAN, 'the medium is the message' (McLuhan 1964). The emphasis on differences between communication media has frequently led to the impression, rightly or wrongly, that media critics assume categorical distinctions between media, especially ORALITY, handwritten texts (see CHIROGRAPHS) printed texts, and electronic media (in addition to ritual, ICONOGRAPHY, art, sculpture, etc.). The term *Great Divide* (frequently with capitals) refers to this widely discredited assumption: namely, that oral and written media are fundamentally different and distinct. Nearly every media critic distances her- or himself from the Great Divide theory, but it remains influential among some biblical scholars. For example, although WERNER KELBER rightly acknowledges the unhelpfulness of 'the great divide thesis' with respect to the JESUS TRADITION (1995: 159; see also Kelber and Thatcher 2008: 29–30), he also hesitates to dismiss it out of concern for denying altogether media 'distinctions and tensions' (Kelber 2015). Joanna Dewey goes so far as to endorse a strong distinction between oral and written media: 'the Gospel of Mark was composed in an oral style and performed orally. The gospel remains fundamentally on *the oral side of the oral/written divide*' (2008: 86; emphasis added). Even so, the majority opinion, inasmuch as there is any consensus in such matters, agrees that, 'if research over the past quarter-century has shown anything, it's that the so-called Great Divide of orality versus literacy amounts to an illusion that has outlived its usefulness' (Foley 2012: 18–19; see also p. 221).

Rafael Rodríguez (Johnson University, USA)

Further Reading

Dewey, Joanna. 2008. 'The Gospel of Mark as Oral Hermeneutic.' In *Jesus, the Voice, and the Text: Beyond The Oral and the Written Gospel*. Edited by Tom Thatcher. Waco, TX: Baylor University Press, pp. 71–87.

Foley, John Miles. 2012. *Oral Tradition and the Internet: Pathways of the Mind*. Urbana, IL: University of Illinois Press.

Kelber, Werner H. 1995. 'Jesus and Tradition: Words in Time, Words in Space.' In *Orality and Textuality in Early Christian Literature. Semeia* 65. Edited by Joana Dewey. Atlanta: SBL Press, pp.139–67.

Kelber, Werner H. 2015. Review of Rafael Rodríguez, *Oral Tradition and the New Testament: A Guide for the Perplexed*. RBL [http://www.bookreviews.org].

Kelber, Werner H. and Tom Thatcher. 2008. '"It's Not Easy to Take a Fresh Approach": Reflections on The Oral and the Written Gospel (An Interview with Werner Kelber).' In *Jesus, the Voice, and the Text: Beyond The Oral and the Written Gospel*. Edited by Tom Thatcher. Waco, TX: Baylor University Press, pp. 27–43.

McLuhan, Marshall. 1964. *Understanding Media: The Extensions of Man*. Cambridge, MA: MIT Press.

Rodríguez, Rafael. 2014. *Oral Tradition and the New Testament: A Guide for the Perplexed*. London: Bloomsbury T&T Clark.

Gunkel, Hermann Hermann Gunkel (1862–1932) was a German OT scholar significant for his influence on biblical interpretation in the twentieth century. The founder of FORM CRITICISM, Gunkel's work heavily influenced subsequent generations of biblical scholars.

Gunkel began his studies at Göttingen in the summer of 1881, and there he was exposed to the historical focus of Adolf von Harnack and Ulrich von Wilamowitz-Müeollendorff, as well the systematic theology of Albrecht Ritschl (Wonneberger 1985: 297). Gunkel resisted Ritschl's doctrinal and dogmatic approach to faith and history and, influenced by Bernhard Duhm, instead became interested in the experiential aspects of religion (Hammann 2014: 15–19). The desire of Gunkel and some of his like-minded colleagues to acknowledge both the spiritual and developmental nature of religious history led to the formation of the *Religionsgeschichtliche Schule* ('History of Religions School'). This approach endeavoured to refine the analyses of historical criticism by reaching past the literary origins of the biblical texts to their pre-literary religious influences and sources. Along with Gunkel, the school included Duhm, Albert Eichhorn, Alfred Rahlfs, Ernst Troeltsch, Wilhelm Wrede, and Rudolf Otto.

Gunkel's academic career was unremarkable, yet advantageous to his scholarship. Initially beginning as lecturer of NT at Göttingen, his approach to history was unpopular, running counter to the entrenched thinking that approached religious history dogmatically (Buss 2007: 499). He was ultimately transferred to Halle, where he taught OT studies. This new focus provided the context for Gunkel's comparative analysis of Genesis and Babylonian literature and his development of Form Criticism, expressed in the first of three editions of his commentary on Genesis. He then spent more than a decade as a low-status affiliate professor in Berlin before finally gaining a full professorship at Giessen in 1907, where he produced his third volume on Genesis in 1910 and a volume on the Prophets in 1917. He transferred to Halle in 1920, producing his volume on the Psalms in 1926 (Buss 2007: 499). Gunkel retired in 1926, and died in 1932 after several years of ill health (Hammann 2014: 377–81).

While Gunkel's teaching career was ordinary, his scholarly output was prolific. One obituary described 'Gunkel's literary labors [as] enormous and a bibliography of his works is appalling' (Easton 1932: 238). Consistent with the *Religionsgeschichtliche Schule*, Gunkel argued that the cyclical perspective of ancient Near Eastern literature also applied to the OT. This approach to the text through comparative religion is most evident in his 1895 *Schöpfung und Chaos in Urzeit und Endzeit* (*Creation and Chaos in the Primeval Era and the Eschaton*), in which he traced similar themes and symbols in Genesis, Revelation, and Babylonian literature.

Gunkel's 1901 *Die Sagen der Genesis* (*The Legends of Genesis*) honed his comparative religious method through a pioneering use of Form Criticism, an interpretive technique that assumes biblical texts are rooted in ORAL TRADITIONS and attempts to trace the development of those traditions into their latter written forms. Gunkel considered the GENRE of a text to be rooted in its SITZ IM LEBEN ('setting in life'), a phrase he coined to describe the sociological context behind the production of a particular text or unit of tradition. Broadly, oral tradition refers to a society's oral transmission of its own heritage, including the transition from oral to literary forms and their resulting interactions.

Gunkel's development of Form Criticism also expanded the conventional understanding of psalm types to include their use as liturgical forms rooted in the Israelite cult (see PSALMS IN WORSHIP). Begun with a partial treatment in 1903, his comprehensive work on the Psalms was completed in 1926. His treatment gave rise to a genre-based approach to Psalms, in which the psalms came to be understood as enduring forms that influenced faith across Israelite history. That the GENRE aspects of the Psalms seem obvious to modern interpreters is attributable to Gunkel's careful application of his methodology to the text.

Similar to his work with the Psalms, Gunkel's 1917 *Die Propheten* classified various types of PROPHECY and their function in Israelite society. He also emphasized the oral prehistory of the prophetic literature, noting that the prophets were primarily preachers who delivered oral messages that were only committed to writing later. The *Sitz im Leben* for the prophetic writings not only involved the political and socio-religious context of the individual prophet, but also reflected the mechanism by which oracles were delivered. Ecstatic experience, then, became a central component of the prophetic material.

Gunkel's 1917 work *Das Märchen im Alten Testament* (*The Folktale in the Old Testament*) engaged the presence of FOLKLORE in the Old Testament. While he resisted the idea that folklore was present in the final form of the biblical next, Gunkel nevertheless perceived folkloric elements as underlying the patriarchal accounts. By isolating those elements, folklore serves as a mechanism for determining the ORIGINAL tradition and the *Sitz im Leben* behind particular narratives.

Gunkel's works, together with the companion efforts of the *Religionsgeschichtliche Schule*, shaped biblical studies for the twentieth century. Gunkel's work came to define mid to late twentieth-century biblical studies as it inspired scholars such as RUDOLF BULTMANN, MARTIN DIBELIUS, Sigmund Mowinckel, Gerhard Von Rad, and Martin Noth to broaden the role of the oral traditions behind biblical literature.

Gunkel's methodology also firmly established the dominance of comparative religious studies that filtered biblical interpretation through the lens of oriental religious history and ethnology. His understanding permanently removed religion from an exclusively divine origin, acknowledging instead the effect of its socio-religious and historical context. While one significant ramification of such comparative studies has been the deepening of the divide between historical-biblical and theological studies as separate academic endeavours, Gunkel's approach has proved invaluable in its contribution to the larger historical-crucial disciplines through its illumination of the biblical text.

Rob Fleenor (Johnson University, USA)

Further Reading

Bultmann, Rudolf, and K. Kundsin. 1962. *Form Criticism*. New York: Harper.
Buss, Martin. 1999. *Biblical Form Criticism in Its Context*. Sheffield, England: Sheffield Academic Press.
Buss, Martin J. 2007. 'Gunkel, Hermann.' In *Dictionary of Major Biblical Interpreters*. Edited by D. K. McKim. Downers Grove, Ill.: IVP Academic; Nottingham, England: InterVarsity Press, pp. 499–503.
Buss, Martin J., and Nickie M. Stipe. 2010. *The Changing Shape of Form Criticism: A Relational Approach*. Sheffield, England: Sheffield Phoenix Press.
Easton, Burton Scott. 1932. 'Gunkel, Hermann, 1862-1932.' *Anglican Theological Review* 14(3): 237–38.
Gunkel, Hermann. 1917. *Die Propheten*. Göttingen: Vandenhoeck & Ruprecht.
Gunkel, Hermann. 1967. *The Psalms: A Form-Critical Introduction*. Philadelphia: Fortress Press.
Gunkel, Hermann. 1987. *The Folktale in the Old Testament*. Sheffield: Almond.
Gunkel, Hermann, and William Herbert Carruth. 1964. Th*e Legends of Genesis, the Biblical Saga and History*. New York: Schocken Books.
Gunkel, Hermann, and K. C. Hanson. 2009. *Israel and Babylon: The Babylonian Influence on Israelite Religion*. Eugene, OR: Cascade Books.
Gunkel, Hermann, and Heinrich Zimmern. 2006. *Creation and Chaos in the Primeval Era and the Eschaton: A Religio-Historical Study of Genesis 1 and Revelation 12*. Grand Rapids, MI: Eerdmans.
Hammann, Konrad. 2014. *Hermann Gunkel: eine Biographie*. Tübingen: Mohr Siebeck.
Wonneberger, Reinhard. 1985. 'Gunkel, Hermann.' *Theologische Realenzyklopädie* 14: 297–300.

Guslar The term *guslar* (pl. *guslari*) is used to describe the oral poets of the former Yugoslavia (now Bosnia-Herzegovina, Croatia, Macedonia, Montenegro, Serbia, Slovenia, and Kosovo) whose performances of traditional epic material significantly informed the development of the Parry-Lord model of ORAL TRADITION and composition. Scholars of MILMAN PARRY and ALBERT LORD's generation referred to *guslari* and their performance tradition as 'Serbo-Croatian', but the currently preferred designation for the language in which they perform is 'South Slavic'. The title *guslar* derives from the fact that these performers accompany their STORYTELLING by playing the *gusle*, a sonorous single-stringed instrument typically played with a bow.

Having learnt of the existence of the *guslari* from the Slovenian scholar Matija Murko, Milman Parry and his student Albert Lord were primarily responsible for introducing the *guslari* and their techniques to Western scholarship as possible modern analogies to ancient bards like Homer (see HOMERIC QUESTION) and, more broadly, as a model for undertaking the comparative study of oral traditions. As such, the *guslari* significantly impacted the formation and evolution of the oral-formulaic theory. The impact of Parry and Lord's work continues in the form of the Milman Parry Collection at Harvard University, which is the largest library of recordings of *guslari* (both epics and interviews) in the world and which includes the original field recordings collected by Parry and Lord that influenced their research. The Milman Parry Collection is currently curated by Stephen Mitchell and Gregory Nagy and is easily accessible with an open online presence (http://chs119.chs.harvard.edu/mpc/). JOHN MILES FOLEY also contributed much to our understanding of the *guslari* and their craft.

Through the work of Parry, Lord, and Foley, the *guslari* and their verbal art have significantly impacted the study of the Bible and oral tradition, particularly the understandings of the transmission of oral traditions and the performative nature of traditional texts.

Raymond F. Person, Jr. (Ohio Northern University, USA)

Further Reading

Alan, D. Baddeley 2001. 'Levels of Working Memory.' In *Perspectives on Human Memory and Cognitive Aging*. Edited by Moshe Naveh-Benjamin, Morris Moscovitch, and Henry L. Roediger III, 111-23. New York: Psychology Press, 111–23.

Brainerd, C. J., and V. F. Reyna. 2004. 'Fuzzy-trace Theory and Memory Development.' *Developmental Review* 24: 396–39.

Flegel, Kristen E., and Patricia A. Reuter-Lorenz. 2014. 'Get the gist? The Effects of Processing Depth on False Recognition in Short-term and Long-term Memory.' *Memory & Cognition* 42: 701–11.

H

Halbwachs, Maurice Maurice Halbwachs (1877–1945) was a French sociologist who is widely regarded as the founder of the field of COLLECTIVE MEMORY: the study of how groups remember and how their memories condense and transcend those of their members. Viewed from the perspective of contemporary scholarship, Halbwachs' work reflects a presentist/constructionist approach (see PRESENTISM/CONSTRUCTIONISM), in which the content of social memory is viewed primarily as a construct in service of present social needs rather than a record of the ACTUAL PAST.

For Halbwachs, collective memory and history warrant the clearest possible distinction. History is objective, stable, and independent of the social conditions in which it is composed. Collective memory is cultivated in groups and remains even when group members die, move away, and are replaced by others. When groups themselves disperse and disappear, moreover, their memories are preserved only by former members, and these memories vanish when the last member dies. Further, because every individual is entangled in a web of group affiliations, all personal memory operates within a social frame (see COGNITIVE/PERSONAL MEMORY). The calendar, religion, family, community, state symbols and rituals – these and other entities provide a framework by which individual memories can be mapped, located, and accessed.

Religious communities and religious memory are prominent among the topics of Halbwachs' investigation. Claiming to bear witness to eternal truths, religious groupings are communities of memory, for the essence of their beliefs must remain stable as society changes. Such communities typically distinguish themselves from other religions of origin, out of which they developed, but they also maintain continuity with them. Christians, for example, stressed continuity with Judaism, whose Scripture played a definite role in portrayals of Jesus, Paul, and the early church in the documents that came to form the NT.

Halbwachs' *Social Frameworks of Memory* (1925) and *Collective Memory* (1950) contain theoretical essays on religious memory, while *The Legendary Topography of the Gospels* (1941) is an analysis of the commemorative sites that early Christian pilgrims established in Palestine. Halbwachs also published *The Origins of Religious Sentiments*, an interpretive summary of his mentor Emile Durkheim's *Elementary Forms of the Religious Life*. In these works, Halbwachs' main observations concern the relation among belief, ritual, physical sites, and memory, again with an emphasis on the reasons for, and shape of, memory constructions, apart from the purported content of those memories (the actual past). The locations of Christian holy sites in Jerusalem, for example, bear no established relation to the career of the historical Jesus, but individuals need concrete places and objects in order to maintain and articulate their religious worldview and ethos. This universal need for tangible objects to stand for the intangible is always felt in the present, which takes one directly to Halbwachs' views on the constructionist character of religious beliefs and rites. If people adapt the realities of the past to the beliefs and spiritual needs of the present, then the reality of the past ceases to be located in the past. Instead, the past becomes a screen on which individuals project their present concerns. Halbwachs' approach, which draws from his other great teacher, Henri Bergson, makes provision for memory as a vehicle for mental images of the past, but not for memory as a route to past realities.

In recent years a more subtle relation between history and memory has emerged. Some scholars assert that history reflects the collectivity's memory of events, but that memory is no longer as valid as it was when its media were chiefly oral. Some claim that memory is invariably warped and that history corrects it in the very process of drawing upon it. Others claim that memory is the only antidote for historical error. In each case, debate is grounded in Maurice Halbwachs' pioneer writings.

Barry Schwartz (The University of Georgia, USA)

Further Reading

Halbwachs, Maurice. 1992. *On Collective Memory*. Translated by Lewis A. Coser. Heritage of Sociology Series. Chicago: University of Chicago Press.

Hallel The term *Hallel* refers to the liturgical recitation of Psalms 113–118 on each day of the festivals of Hanukkah and Sukkot, the first day of Passover and on Shavuot (*t. Suk* 3.2). The Hallel is also recited during the Passover seder. An abridged version of the anthology which omits Pss. 115.1-11 and Ps. 116.1-11 is recited on New Moon festivals. In addition, the term *Hallel ha-gadol* (the great Hallel) refers to the liturgical recitation of Psalm 136 on SABBATHS and festivals. According to *m. Ta'an* 3.9, this psalm was also recited to celebrate the end of severe draughts.

According to the tannaitic rabbinic texts, recitation of Hallel is an obligation for all adult male Jews. *T. Sotah* 6.3 states that schoolchildren learnt Hallel through a call-and-response repetition of the verses. However, as was the case with most commandments that required LITERACY, the rabbinic sages made accommodations for men who did not have the necessary skills or knowledge to carry out the commandment. *M. Suk* 3.10 states that if a woman, slave or minor (who are not obligated to recite Hallel) is reciting Hallel on a man's behalf, he must repeat each word after the reciter. The text concludes with a statement disapproving of this practice. If an adult man is reciting for him, the man in question can discharge his obligation by answering 'Hallelluyah'. These practices, which allow for the antiphonal recitation of the psalms, demonstrate how early rabbinic Judaism attempted to institutionalize obligations that required either literacy or knowledge of Scripture within an adult male population in which literacy and scriptural knowledge were not universal.

As described in the RABBINIC LITERATURE, the practice of Hallel serves to connect the experience of Jewish WORSHIP to the COLLECTIVE MEMORY of Israel's exodus from Egypt and to the defunct TEMPLE cult. The earliest ascription of origin (*m. Pes* 5.7) states that Hallel was recited as the Paschal lambs were being slaughtered in the Temple on the eve of Pesach. The Talmud preserves additional traditions: in a debate in *b. Pes*. 117a, one authority states that the prophets mandated that the Israelites should recite it before major events threatening collective misfortune and on every occasion of rescue from misfortune. A debate ensues between two other opinions. According to one, the Israelites and Moses first recited Hallel at the Red Sea while the second ascribes the Psalms to David and identifies them with the Temple rituals of Passover and Sukkot (Tabernacles). These two myths of origin for the practice of Hallel serve to reinforce the rabbinic construction of early Jewish prayer in general (see WORSHIP, ANCIENT JEWISH). The association with exodus forges a mimetic connection between contemporary worshippers and Israel's formative event. According to this position, when contemporary Jews recite Hallel, they are re-enacting the exodus. The association with the Temple cult reinforces a second prominent theme in the rabbinic construction of Jewish prayer, in which the statutory prayers become a substitute for the rituals of the Temple cult.

Elsie R. Stern (Reconstructionist Rabbinical College, USA)

Havelock, Eric Alfred Eric Alfred Havelock (1903–88) was a British-trained classicist whose career was mostly in North America, including appointments at Toronto, Harvard, and Yale. Influenced by MILMAN PARRY's oral-formulaic thesis, Havelock explained the shift in ancient Greek linguistics and thought from Homer and the pre-socratic philosophers to PLATO as a product of a corresponding shift in communications media from ORALITY to LITERACY. Havelock first proposed this groundbreaking thesis in his influential *Preface to Plato* (1963), and it continued to be the subject of his work in later publications. In his introduction to the published collection of his essays, Havelock describes the Greek alphabet as 'a piece of explosive technology, revolutionary in its effects on human culture, in a way not precisely shared by any other invention' (1982: 6). Havelock's final book provided what he understood as a 'unified picture of a crisis that occurred in the history of human communication, when Greek orality transformed itself into Greek literacy' (1986: 1), this time tracing the media shifts from ancient orality to literacy through to modern oral communications media, including the radio.

Havelock's work – like that of WALTER ONG, JACK GOODY, and others – significantly impacted early work on the media dynamics behind biblical literature, including a heightened sensitivity to the interfaces between orality and WRITING. At the same time, more recent studies have adopted a more nuanced approach, and most scholars today would view Havelock's model as an illustration of the GREAT DIVIDE, which posits an overly universal and monolithic view of the relationship between oral and written modes of communication.

Raymond F. Person, Jr. (Ohio Northern University, USA)

Further Reading

Havelock, Eric A. 1963. *Preface to Plato.* Cambridge, MA: Harvard University Press.

Havelock, Eric A. 1978. *The Greek Concept of Justice: From Its Shadow in Homer to Its Substance in Plato.* Cambridge, MA: Harvard University Press.

Havelock, Eric A. 1982. *The Literate Revolution in Greece and Its Cultural Consequences.* Princeton: Princeton University Press.

Havelock, Eric A. 1986. *The Muse Learns to Write: Reflections on Orality and Literacy from Antiquity to the Present.* New Haven: Yale University Press.

Hexapla The Hexapla, a synopsis of texts of the OT in different languages laid out in six parallel columns, was produced by Origen of Alexandria (ca. 185–254) in the third century CE. Columns one and two included the Hebrew consonantal text in Hebrew letters and a vocalized Hebrew text in Greek transliteration, respectively; column five included the text of the Greek SEPTUAGINT. In columns three, four, and six, Origen placed the Jewish revisions of the Septuagint produced by Aquila, Symmachus, and Theodotion, respectively. For some books, such as the Psalter, Origen found other Greek versions, which he called Quinta (Fifth), Sexta (Sixth), and Septima (Seventh), because he did not know the names of the revisers. His reasons for undertaking the project were apologetic, harmonizing, and exegetical.

Evidence for the existence of the Hexapla, the composition of which is mentioned by Eusebius (*Ecclesiastical History* VI.16) and Epiphanius (*On Weights and Measures* 7, 19), survives in four kinds of sources: 1) extant MANUSCRIPTS containing the synopsis or columnar arrangement of texts (Ra 86 [Hos. 11:1]; Ra 113 [two lines of the heading of the book of Psalms]; Ra 1098 [ca. 148 verses from Psalms]; Ra 2005 [13 verses from Psalms]); 2) colophons in Greek, and especially Syro-Hexapla, manuscripts; 3) marginal notes in copies of the Septuagint, especially *catena* (verse-by-verse commentaries constructed from excerpts from earlier biblical commentators), that include readings from the Hexapla; and 4) brief descriptions of the Hexapla in Origen, Eusebius of Caesarea, Epiphanius, Jerome, Rufinus, and Theodoret of Cyrrhus.

Probably before the final books of the Hebrew Bible were translated into Greek, some Jewish groups had already begun to revise the Old Greek version of the OT, in part to bring the translation into closer quantitative alignment with the Hebrew text (e.g. 8ḤevXII gr dated to ca. 25 BCE). This revisionary activity is known as the *kaige* tradition since one of the characteristics of the revisions, and even the new translations of this tradition (e.g. Song of Songs), was to use Greek *kaige* for the Hebrew *gam/wəgam* ('and also'). The Jewish *recentior* Theodotion (30 BCE–30 CE or 180 CE) was a member of this tradition, which culminated in the recension of Aquila (ca. 120 CE). These two *recentiores* revised the Old Greek translations and brought the Greek version into more formal alignment with the Hebrew text. Symmachus' recension (ca. 200 CE) was a response to these two versions and evinces a functional and less literal translation technique.

Origen describes his own work on two occasions but nowhere calls it the Hexapla (*Comm. Matt.*, XV.14; *Ep. Afr.*, 3–7). He describes his method for 'healing' the disagreements between the Septuagint manuscripts as follows: 1) passages not appearing in the Hebrew but in the Septuagint are marked with an obelus (÷); 2) passages not appearing in the Septuagint but in the Hebrew, which he added from one of the recentiores, are marked with an asterisk (※). He also used a metobelus (↙) to mark the end of the word or phrase marked with an asterisk or obelus.

An open question among researchers concerns how the fifth column (the Septuagint text) appeared. Did Origen apply the signs to the fifth column of the original Hexapla (thus creating his recension within the fifth column of the Hexapla)? Or did Origen himself, or Pamphilus (ca. 240–310) and Eusebius, create a recension corrected with the signs separate from the synopsis (Dines 2004: 100–2)? Epiphanius (ca. 315–403) may describe both Origen's Hexapla in columns and his later recension with signs when he describes Origen's synopsis (*On Weights and Measures* 7, 19; *Refutation of All Heresies* 64.3.5–7) and Origen's use of the signs (*On Weights and Measures* 2–3, 7–8). Epiphanius does not mention the signs in his description of the Hexapla. Probably, Epiphanius saw the Hexapla and it did not have signs, for he would almost certainly have mentioned this feature (cf. *Refutation of All Heresies* 65.4.4–6). Also according to Epiphanius, Origen inserted the asterisk beside the Greek word or phrase added from the recentiores, which the Septuagint omitted (*On Weights and Measures* 2). This process probably describes not the crafting of the Hexapla but a later corrected text with signs, for in these contexts he nowhere mentions the Hexapla. Furthermore, Epiphanius (as well as Eusebius and many colophons of the Syro-Hexapla) describes a Tetrapla as the four Greek versions without the Hebrew versions. Epiphanius describes the Tetrapla ambiguously as to whether these four Greek versions were in columns or not (*On Weights and Measures* 19.526–529). Perhaps the Tetrapla was Origen's corrected text both with signs and with the readings of the three recentiores in the margin, where they differed markedly from the Septuagint. In this way the Tetrapla furnished four versions of the text.

The work of Theodotion, Aquila, and Symmachus survives primarily in fragmentary marginalia due to Origen's Hexapla and the later recension. These versions mainly attest the proto-Masoretic Text, but sometimes they preserve interesting variants. For example, in Job 28.11a ('He dams up the streams'), MT reads *ḥibbēš* ('to dam up'); Theodotion, however, reads *exēreunēsen*, which presupposes the Hebrew original *ḥippēś* ('to search') in his *Vorlage*. Theodotion uses this equivalent also in Ps. 64.7. The change in sibilants is accounted for by the graphemic identity of the respective phonemes /ś/ and /š/, which was not differentiated before the Masoretes. The interchange between *b* and *p* is explained by dialect interference in North West Semitic (e.g. *npš*//*nbš* 'life'). Theodotion and the Old Greek (*bathē de potamōn anekalupsen*; 'And he uncovered rivers' depths') probably preserve the original text, for the passage describes humanity's search for or uncovering of the sources of the rivers ('The sources of the rivers they probe'; NRSV). At least, Theodotion provides an important variant to the MT in this instance.

The Hexapla as Ancient Media

In the third century CE, the roll book or SCROLL was still the dominant form of book technology, and examples of the CODEX book form were rare. Normally, a codex contained one column of text per page, but there are examples of third-century codices containing multiple columns per page. Christians had already made more use of the codex than their pagan contemporaries, so Origen's use of the codex form would not have been unusual. Even his use of multiple columns per page was not unique. However, the use of the columns and the multilingual nature of the work probably brought significant advance to book technology.

Origen used columns, but not primarily for the purpose of reading down one column and continuing at the top of the next one, though the Hexapla could also have been read productively this way. Rather, if the extant manuscripts are closely representative of the Hexapla, Origen placed one word in each parallel column, which would have aided the ancient scholar reading across the columns for the purpose of comparing the different versions word by word. This layout would help Christian scholars discern the differences between the Hebrew version, the *recentiores*, and the Septuagint. Ancient sources describe a Hebrew column in Hebrew letters and words and a column in Greek letters but Hebrew words (i.e. Greek transliteration of the Hebrew), respectively. The layout and contents of the Hexapla are best understood if we assume that Origen and later scholars could read some Hebrew but needed much help. Indeed, Epiphanius says that scholars who were ignorant of the Hebrew letters could discern their phonetic value by looking at the Greek transliteration (*On Weights and Measures* 7.179-80). As special kind of media, the Hexapla reveals that only a few ancient Christians in the third and fourth centuries could read the Hebrew version, and these readers were mainly aided by the Greek transliteration and the other Greek versions in the synopsis.

John D. Meade (Phoenix Seminary, USA)

Further Reading

Dines, Jennifer M. 2004. *The Septuagint*. London: T&T Clark, 95–103.

Gentry, Peter J. 2016. '1.3.1.2 Pre-Hexaplaric Translations, Hexapla, post-Hexaplaric translations.' In *Textual History of the Bible*. General Editor Armin Lange. Brill Online, 2016.

Grafton, Anthony, and Megan Williams. 2006. *Christianity and the Transformation of the Book: Origen, Eusebius, and the Library of Caesarea*. London: Harvard University Press.

Law, T. Michael. 2008. 'Origen's Parallel Bible: Textual Criticism, Apologetics, or Exegesis?' *JTS* 59(1): 1–21.

Marcos, Natalio Fernández. 2000. *The Septuagint in Context: Introduction to the Greek Version of the Bible*. Translated by Wilfred G. E. Watson. Leiden: Brill, pp. 206–22.

Historiography, Ancient The field of historiography has within its purview the study of techniques and methods used to write about the past. Historiographers attend to both overarching developments within the discipline of history itself and to investigations into how those individuals who engage in interpreting and preserving accounts of events, people, places, and cultures make use of source material, perceive the flow of time, select subject matter, and determine the scope of their projects (among other similar considerations). To that end, historiographers also tend to look for the overt as well as unstated assumptions and philosophical frameworks that underlie how historians approach their craft.

Study of ancient Jewish and Greco-Roman historiography in relation to the biblical texts and the wider culture in which the CANON took shape is important for at least two reasons. First, several biblical documents fall within the GENRE of *history*. For example, a text such as Chronicles in the Hebrew Bible is clearly focused on recording events from the past, as demonstrated by the fact that it begins with genealogical material for which the source of the historian's information is specifically identified (1 Chron. 9.1). Similarly, the Gospels of the NT may be described as biographies that highlight the actions and words of Jesus of Nazareth. Luke, for instance, is clear that he is undertaking a project designed to set down an orderly account of events for his readers (Lk. 1.1-4), while the author of the Fourth Gospel cautions his audience that he had to be selective about the number of Jesus' signs that he was able to record in his text (20.30). Second, beyond the issue of genre, historiographical considerations are vital because the entire Judeo-Christian tradition has at its core the presupposition that God acts in history and that the record of God's interactions with and on behalf of humanity is instructive for how adherents to the faith should structure their worldview and model their behaviours and actions.

Given these two considerations, questions about how, for example, the conventions of first-century Greco-Roman histories informed the composition of NT documents of that period, or whether ancient Jewish historians portray the Canaanites in ways that reflect a desire to encourage a sense and understanding of Jewish IDENTITY among their ancient Jewish readers, fit well with approaches related to ancient historiography. Furthermore, historiographers' curiosity about the types of oral and written sources that might have been used by any given historian, how histories reflect perceptions of memory and IDENTITY, and whether or not historical compositions were read aloud once published, are points where the field of historiography naturally intersects with investigations into ancient media culture.

With regard to ancient historiography more generally, the first point to make in the broad discussion is that rather than speaking of *ancient historiography*, it is perhaps better to refer to *historiographies*. Ancient sources indicate that vastly more ancient authors were engaged in the field of history than is suggested by the scant number of texts that have survived from the period. Further, ancient historians employed many varied methodologies. Indeed, the modern practice of compiling lists of the primary characteristics found in ancient histories obscures nuances from author to author and from region to region. For instance, this practice disguises the fact that Greco-Roman history-writing spans a period that stretches from Herodotus' composition of his *Histories* (ca. 450s–420s BCE), with its focus on the Persian Wars, to the latter half of the fourth century CE when Europus, Festus, Ammianus Marcellinus, and Aurelius Victor were writing imperial histories for Rome. The timeline might even be stretched to the sixth century when Procopius (born ca. 500 CE) recorded the wars during the reign of Justinian. Given these factors, generalizations are difficult.

As an illustration of the dangers of oversimplification, one might examine the modern presupposition that Greek historians' conception of time is cyclical rather than linear, a view that was popularized by R. G. Collingwood (1956: 25–29) and an assumption that is often contrasted with a Judeo-Christian linear progressive view of time as represented by the Hebrew canon (cf. Momigliano 2012: 182). Granted, a cyclical view of history is evident in Thucydides' assertion that past events are similar to future ones and thus may serve as a template (*Peloponnesian War* 1.22). The 'wheel of time' is also apparent in Polybius' digression in Book VI on the stages and cycle of life from birth to death for cities and constitutions. Yet in the remaining portion of Polybius' work, the Second Punic War is treated as a single rather than a repeated event. Furthermore, another Greek historian, Timaeus (born ca. 350 BCE), a section of whose extant work focused on careful linear chronology and division of time based on Olympic events, does not share a cyclical outlook at all. Leaving aside Greco-Roman historiography for Jewish, it is also difficult to make the case that the progression of history in the Hebrew text is linear without exception. To cite a notable example, an explicit narrative cycle of apostasy, punishment, repentance, forgiveness, and deliverance is characteristic of the book of Judges.

Perhaps another aspect of oversimplifying the complexities of ancient history involves the tendency of scholarship, both in the classical and modern eras, to concentrate on a canon of great ancient historians.

Attention to the triads of Herodotus (fifth century BCE), Thucydides (born 460/455 BCE), and Polybius (born ca. 200 BCE) for the Greeks, and Sallust (born ca. 86 BCE), Livy (born 64 or 59 BCE), and Tacitus (born ca. 56 CE) for the Romans, with occasional nods to Xenophon (born ca. 430 BCE) and Caesar (born 100 BCE), relegates other historians and genres of history to the margins, contributes to denigrating their contributions, and downplays divergent methodologies. Josephus (born 37/38CE) and Cassius Dio (born 164 CE) themselves are often treated as second-tier writers. Further, the list of 'greats' tends to exclude biographers like Plutarch (born ca. 50 CE), Suetonius (born ca. 70 CE) and, of course, local historians and genealogists of which there were many but of whom there are only fragmentary remains. Clearly these writers were contemporaries of early Christian authors or, in the case of Cassius Dio, wrote texts dealing with events in the early first century CE, in which biblical scholars are interested. They consequently merit study. In addition, both biography and local history are genres that are strikingly important given that gospel texts concentrate on a specific region and focus on a key personality.

The good news is that a desire to expand the canon of sources for study of ancient historiography is one of several new moves that modern scholars have been making in recent decades. Rather than merely including Josephus, Cassius Dio, and others, however, the current impulse is to go much further. Since an interest in the past evidenced by ancient authors appears not only in classical texts that have been traditionally labelled *historical* but also in other genres, the move now is to examine ancient poetry, DRAMA, and other literature. Essentially, there is no need to privilege historical texts over other sorts of documents (Marincola 2011: 6). The implications of this sort of thinking for Jewish texts like Esther, where there is debate concerning whether the document is history or historical fiction, open up new avenues of thinking. As a result, scholars may assume that the details of everyday life presented in a text have veracity (or at least verisimilitude), and can then approach a document with an eye towards what it reveals about women, religious persecution, economics, the dynamics of power, and other social realities without bogging down on questions of its genre. Likewise, a text such as the Fourth Gospel – which has often been sidelined in discussions of the historical Jesus because of its divergence from the Synoptics and its perceived theological character – can now be examined with fresh eyes.

This broadened inclusion of texts considered to contain historical material is, in part, the result of two factors. First, at the end of the twentieth century the postmodern turn in approaches to history called into question the existence of objective history and blurred the lines between historical and non-historical texts for modern researchers. This was a departure from the ancient practice of historiography, where practitioners in the Greco-Roman world did distinguish between genres and understood historiography as a mode of writing that intentionally addressed the past (as they comprehended it) in ways that other types of writing did not. This was the case despite granting some affinities between history and other literature, such as poetry (Quintillian, *Institutes* X.1.31).

Second, there has been a move to focus on different aspects of history, so that economic causes of events, social relationships, power structures, and cultural or ethno-history have become popular in present-day historiography. While ancient Jewish historiography did not shy away from sprinkling historical texts with personal details (hence stories such as David and Bathsheba, or the detailed descriptions of some aspects of religious life), such details were not necessarily thick on the ground in Greco-Roman histories. Indeed, aside from Herodotus' fascinating description of the culture, MONUMENTS, and customs of Egypt, they did not focus on the subject matter of everyday life, social institutions and relationships, and economics. Instead, the canonized Greco-Roman histories tended to centre on significant men, wars, and politics. This no doubt explains why Josephus, when recording the story of Ruth in his rendition of his nation's past, apologizes to his readers for including the episode about an insignificant woman in his text (Josephus, *Antiquities* 5.9.1-4).

In the case of Greek histories, this limited focus was due to the fact that Herodotus, who is known as 'the father of history' (despite being preceded by the genealogist Hecataeus in the late sixth century BCE), set the course for most Greek history writing by relying on Homer. He followed the bard's lead not only by deciding to start with the Trojan War, but also by emulating Homer's tendency to highlight the activities of heroic men. For their part, Roman histories were written by members of the senatorial class and were narrowly focused on Roman interests and political manoeuvers. In short, there is a break between what the ancient authors of Greco-Roman histories and what present-day historians value as subject matter. Thus, to unearth glimpses of everyday life, rituals, and other matters, modern researchers now turn to ancient documents outside the traditional histories, including, ironically, the biblical documents themselves. Indeed, the NT Gospels, no doubt reflecting the influence of Jewish historiography as well as Greco-Roman, do not hesitate to talk about fishermen and common people and make mention of everyday goods and services that reflect the economic situation of the era.

Another recent move in twenty-first-century scholarship of ancient historiography, particularly Greco-Roman historiography, is to take seriously the role of RHETORIC in the ancient educational system. As a result, efforts to examine how reliable ancient histories might be and how any given author might have collected and used sources, though still of interest in the field of biblical studies, has given ground to an interest in how ancient histories function rhetorically. Attention to matters of style and eloquence to some degree place histories on the same plane as poetry, drama, and other types of literature. Cicero commended the Greek historians as exemplars of eloquence, so indicating there is a desirable link between rhetoric and history (*On Oratory* 2.12.51; 2.13.55-58; *On the Laws 1.2.5*). In addition, ancient writing made extensive use of embedded speeches, a sign of how ubiquitous rhetoric was in the culture. But a current question faced by historians is how far rhetoric influenced the field of ancient historiography. Granted, Thucydides confesses to embroidering the speeches of generals based on what he supposed might have been said in a given circumstance (*Peloponnesian War* 1.22.1), but does this negate the veracity of his material in total? John Marincola finds a middle ground by viewing historical texts as works of literature with individual structures and themes, but written by authors who appear concerned with veracity as demonstrated by the fact that they castigate predecessors for errors of fact (Marincola 2011: 8). Indeed, Polybius, a century after Timaeus, criticizes his historical forebear for not evaluating the accuracy of witnesses and for working solely in Athens rather than travelling to make historical discoveries (*Histories* 12.4; 12.25, 27).

Criticism of one's predecessors such as that offered by Polybius was a common motif in ancient histories and was designed to demonstrate the superiority of one's own work. It is even evidenced by Josephus (*Against Apion* 1.3), who points out that Greek histories and genealogies are contradictory and also extols the care the Jews took to produce written records (*Against Apion* 1.6-8) in order to promote his *Antiquities*. When it comes to other ancient historians, however, the use and value accorded to written sources varied. For instance, Thucydides was sceptical about written records (*Peloponnesian War* 1.21) and privileged oral accounts and his own eyewitness expertise as a participant in the war. In a similar vein, regardless of whether he consulted written sources such as one of the other Synoptics or a text of the OT, the author of Luke/Acts mentions an ORAL TRADITION about the life of Jesus that was handed down from eyewitnesses (Lk. 1.2). Livy, for his part, was known to convey the same incident multiple times and slavishly reported from his written sources, which may prove an enlightening parallel to the presence of doublets in biblical texts. Furthermore, written sources, when used by the most well-known ancient historians, were rarely quoted but were freely adapted for artistic ends (Grant 1995: 34), a practice which raises interesting issues in relation to Revelation, which is awash with allusions to the OT but lacks direct quotations.

Even though Josephus, Livy, and others had recourse to written materials, use of oral tradition as a source during the early empire was common. In fact, Seneca (born ca. 4 BCE–1 CE), a statesman and author of a satire and tragedies, plays on the ubiquity of oral testimony when he mocks its potentially arbitrary and fictitious nature, subject to a witness' perception of the audience (*Apocolocyntosis* [*The Pumkinification of the Divine Claudius*] 1.1).

The issue of oral sources brings us to the last paradigm shift in the modern analysis of ancient historiography in recent decades and, finally, to the point where interest in ancient media culture and ancient historiography intersect: an acknowledgement that society during the biblical era was significantly more attuned to aural/oral culture than is modern civilization. For instance, it is increasingly acknowledged that histories were in all likelihood meant to be read or performed aloud, a fact alluded to by Lucian of Samosata (born 120 CE) when he derides Herodotus for obtaining renown by peddling his histories on a public tour of major cities in Greece (*Herodotus and Aëtion* 1-3; see also Zelnick-Abramovitz 214: 176–81). In terms of Hebrew texts, there are indeed clear traditions for public reading of the Torah and other specific SCROLLS, like Esther, during festival celebrations (Mishnah, *Megillah* 1.1-2.4), although provisions are made for silent reading of or for copying out the texts to fulfil one's obligations for the celebration (see READING CULTURE).

This emerging perspective has generated new interest in how oral history, or the history preserved by witnesses, differs from oral tradition, for which there are no longer contemporary observers. It also raises questions about how memory shapes a society's relationship to its past (Von Ungern in Marincola 2011: 124–30) and how myth and facts can be combined to create community identity. Investigating along these lines, Raymond Person, for instance, has recently hypothesized that the interplay between written and oral culture, along with scribes writing with an eye towards texts being read in public should be considered in analyses related to the relationship between Samuel-Kings and Chronicles (Person 2010).

Clearly there are now new frontiers for modern scholars to consider in evaluating biblical texts, their historicity, transmission, and what keys they may hold for understanding the past.

Beth M. Sheppard (Duke University, USA)

Further Reading

Collingwood, R. G. 1956. *The Idea of History*. Oxford: Oxford University Press.

Dignas, Beate, and R. R. R. Smith, eds. 2012. *Historical and Religious Memory in the Ancient World*. Oxford: Oxford University Press.

Grant, Michael. 1995. *Greek and Roman Historians: Information and Misinformation*. London: Routledge.

Kraus, C. S., and A. J. Woodman. 1997. *Latin Historians*. New Surveys in the Classics 27. Cambridge: Cambridge University Press.

Marincola, John. 2001. *Greek Historians*. New Surveys in the Classics 31. Cambridge: Cambridge University Press.

Marincola, John, ed. 2011. *Greek and Roman Historiography*. Oxford Readings in Classical Studies. Oxford: Oxford University Press.

Mehl, Andreas. 2011. *Roman Historiography: An Introduction to Its Basic Aspects and Development*. Translated by Hans-Friedrich Mueller. Chichester, UK: Wiley-Blackwell.

Momigliano, Arnaldo. 2012. *Essays in Ancient and Modern Historiography*. Chicago: University of Chicago Press.

Na'aman, Nadav. 2006. *Ancient Israel's History and Historiography: The First Temple Period*. Winona Lake, IN: Eisenbrauns.

Person, Raymond F., Jr. 2010. *The Deuteronomic History and the Book of Chronicles: Scribal Works in an Oral World*. SBL Ancient Israel and Its Literature 6. Atlanta: SBL Press.

Zelnick-Abramovitz, Rachel. 2014. 'Look and Listen: History Performed and Inscribed.' In *Between Orality and Literacy: Communication and Adaptation in Antiquity*. Edited by Ruth Scodel. Mnemosyne. Leiden: Brill, pp. 174–96.

The Homeric Question *The Homeric Question* denotes the scholarly debate regarding the origin, composition, and AUTHORSHIP of the Homeric poems, the *Iliad* and the *Odyssey*. There is ongoing uncertainty and debate surrounding those works over authorial identity, compositional technique, geographical location, original form (textual, oral, combined), single or multiple composers, single or multiple editors, cultural context, forms of transmission, early reception, and more.

Some of these questions date back to antiquity. Herodotus refers to the question of authorial attribution. There is Hellenistic evidence for the problems, solutions, and methods adopted by scholars for handling the poems circa-250 BCE and after. Cicero, Plutarch, and Aelian refer to questions of authorship, attribution, and transmission. Josephus asserts that the Homeric poems are inferior to the Mosaic Torah because the former were collected after diffusion in oral form (thus scattered and degenerate, allegedly). Luigi Ferreri has shown that the question was already known and discussed by textual editors in the early Renaissance (Ferreri 2007).

The modern form of the question addresses: 1) the unreliability of the evidence for a historical composer; 2) crucial questions concerning the relationship between alphabetic WRITING, SONG traditions, and the original forms of the poems; 3) ignorance regarding the respective roles of singers, writers, transcribers, audiences, editors, private wealth and/or civic support in composition and textualization; 4) effects of early transmission on the form and language of the poems as preserved in medieval MANUSCRIPTS; and, 5) new insights about form, length, dialectology, and performance arising from the study of living oral epic song traditions.

The question enjoys its own tradition within Homeric studies and intellectual history. F.A. Wolf, in the *Prolegomena ad Homerum* (1795), was one of the earliest modern scholars to address the question. Influenced by biblical scholarship (see Grafton 1981), Wolf suggested that oral transmission ceased prior to the editing of the poems in Alexandrian Egypt. Wolf argued that the ORIGINALS, which were composed before alphabetic writing, were impossible to recover. Therefore modern editors should strive to reconstruct Alexandrian editions. Centuries of debate followed, and continue to this day, with two primary camps emerging: Analysts, who believe in multiple hands, and Unitarians, who argue for a single composer. The question has also served as a measure for European literary and cultural modernity: the *querelle des Anciens et des Modernes* at the end of the seventeenth century, the vogue for folk poetry after Ossian, and the rise of romantic nationalisms have each made use of the question. Archaeological discoveries and Indo-European linguistics (esp. Greek dialectology and Homeric linguistics) have also contributed. Important breakthroughs came when MILMAN PARRY compared the language of the Homeric poems to the epic songs he recorded from illiterate singers in the former Yugoslavia in the 1930s; global comparative work in this vein continues to this day, as does intensive discussion of the question.

A. P. Tate (University of Wisconsin, USA)

Further Reading

Davison, J. A. 1963. 'The Homeric Question.' In *A Companion to Homer*. Edited by Frank Stubbings and Alan Wace. London: Macmillan, pp. 234–65.

Luigi Ferreri. 2007. *La questione omerica dal cinquecento al settecento*. Pleiadi 10. Rome: Edizioni di storia e letteratura.

Grafton, Anthony. 1981. 'Prolegomena to F.A. Wolf.' *Journal of the Warburg and Courtauld Institutes* 44: 101–29.

Simonsuuri, Kirsti. 1979. *Homer's Original Genius: Eighteenth-Century Notions of the Early Greek Epic (1688-1798)*. Cambridge: Cambridge University Press.

Turner, Frank. 1997. 'The Homeric Question.' In *A New Companion to Homer*. Edited by Ian Morris and Barry Powell. Leiden: Brill, pp. 123–45.

Household Items (media aspects of) Household items are those utilitarian objects necessary for survival in nearly every agrarian household of the Iron Age (ca. 1200–586 BCE) and later. Many items (e.g. ceramic objects, stone tools and vessels, metal implements and weapons, textile tools) are known because whole or fragmentary examples have been recovered in archaeological excavations; others (e.g. baskets, mats, textiles, leather containers) are made of organic materials (plant fibres, animals hairs and skins) and are known only because they are mentioned in biblical texts or depicted in ancient ICONOGRAPHY. Embedded in these items were aspects of ethnicity, gender IDENTITY, and value that would have been intuitively understood by those who saw or used them but are more difficult for us to discern. Yet several examples lend themselves to consideration in ways that suggest their communicative aspects.

The most common household items in antiquity were ceramic vessels. Once fired, the ceramic will not disintegrate, yet the vessels are easily broken and must constantly be replaced. Potsherds are thus ubiquitous at archaeological sites of the biblical period. Pottery forms and decorative elements are expressive of ideas, ethnicity, and cultural contact, and they are a common de facto cipher of aesthetic and other values. Because the shapes of most vessels were related to their function, particular forms would connote specific foodstuffs or drinks. A cooking pot, for example, likely signified a stew, probably meatless, whereas a jug would indicate the water within. A large storage jar would denote the grain it held and also food and survival, for grain-based comestibles constituted about seventy per cent of the daily calorie intake of agrarians in the biblical world. A jar overflowing with grain would mean survival and even prosperity, whereas an empty jar would conjure up the all-too-common famines, thereby signifying death and destruction (e.g. Ps. 31.12; Jer 19.1-11). One particular Israelite storage-jar form – the collared-rim jar, so named because of the ridge at the bottom of its neck – may represent ethnicity. Because it seems to be a continuation of a Canaanite form, it suggests Canaanite ancestry for at least some Israelite groups. Commonly found at Israelite sites, it a possible marker of Israelite ethnicity. However, as a form suited to agrarian households, it could just as easily, or also, have had functional value. Decorative elements, however, are more likely to signify ethnicity. Philistine wares, for example, are noted for their graceful birds and geometric designs, but they are rarely found at Israelite sites, even those close to Philistia. This suggests Israelite reluctance to use vessels made by others, and the virtual lack of imported wares at Israelite sites gives a similar impression. Yet economic factors may be implicated in this situation, for imported wares were probably more costly. The same may be true for another feature of Israelite ceramics: they rarely have painted decorations, perhaps because of the more costly nature of decorated vessels. Highly burnished vessels do appear, but mainly in the wealthier northern kingdom. Still, the preponderance of plain wares bespeaks functionality as well as separation from other peoples and, less likely, an avoidance of material ostentation.

Stone items are also frequently found in households. An important example is the basalt grinder, the upper stone used with a lower stone (quern) for grinding grain into flour for bread, the sine qua non of food. (Note that the Hebrew word for 'bread' [*leḥem*] is sometimes used more generally for food.) Because bread in premodern societies is an economic substance as well as a physical one, grinding tools would readily connote bread or food as an economic commodity. They would also signify the gender of those who used them, as grinding was usually a woman's task. For millennia – until the introduction of more efficient milling machines in the Greco-Roman period – women spent two to three hours each day grinding, usually in the company of other women doing the same. Grinding was thus a process of social interaction as well as one that produced an essential component of the Israelite diet. The identification of a tool essential for bread production with women thus connoted their position at the nexus of household social and economic processes.

Some household items likely had religious or ritual meanings in addition to functional ones. Terracotta oil lamps, for example, provided light for household tasks and also had apotropaic value. Light was believed to ward off the dangers of the dark, for terror and pestilence as well as evil forces were linked with night and darkness (Ps. 91.5-6). The light of oil lamps signified divine protection (e.g. Job 29.2-3), and thus lamps were imbued with both religious significance and utilitarian value. A similar confluence is associated with metal blades. These household items were used for food preparation and perhaps protection against enemies. But they might also be brandished near parturient mothers and their newborns to fend off the demons believed to threaten women and their infants. The high infant and childhood mortality rates, with only half of newborns surviving to age five, were attributed to malevolent supernatural beings. A knife would thus take on theological meaning as a household item that could deal with problems that are handled today by medical personnel. Just as prayer might accompany medical interventions, incantations likely accompanied the use of protective items in biblical antiquity.

In the aggregate, most household items likely transcended their functionality. They connoted aspects of the interrelated social, economic, ethnic, gendered, and religious dynamics of household life.

Carol Meyers (Duke University, USA)

Further Reading

Dever, William G. 1997. 'Syro-Palestinian Ceramics of the Neolithic, Bronze, and Iron Ages.' In Volume 1 of *The Oxford Encyclopedia of Archaeology in the Near East*, 5 volumes. Edited by Eric M. Meyers. New York: Oxford University Press, pp. 45–71.

Meyers, Carol. 2013. *Rediscovering Eve: Ancient Israelite Women in Context*. New York: Oxford University Press.

Rowan, Yorke M. 2013. 'Stone Tools, Bronze and Iron Age.' In Volume 1 of *The Oxford Encyclopedia of the Bible and Archaeology*, 2 volumes. Edited by Daniel M. Master. New York: Oxford University Press, pp. 369–72.

Hymes, Dell Folklorist, linguist, and anthropologist Dell Hymes (1927–2009) was a major contributor to the aesthetical movement called ETHNOPOETICS, especially in extended and often lively exchanges with the parallel work of anthropologist DENNIS TEDLOCK. He is also known for his distinctive linguistic anthropology, which itself contributed to the development of another interdisciplinary sub-field called SOCIOLINGUISTICS where linguistics, anthropology, and sociology meet. Hymes founded and edited the journal *Language in Society*.

Perceiving that culture and community come to life in language as spoken, Hymes saw that the ways people actually speak provide rich environments for exploring the meanings of individual and collective human life. Not only is this true in contemporary speech events, but it can be at least partially recovered from more distant environments by careful reading of the ethnographic record of earlier investigators.

Hymes devoted considerable effort to reworking the field notes and translations of Native American narratives, especially those of the Northwest coast. Using field notes by earlier researchers, including pioneer anthropologists Franz Boas and Edward Sapir, he worked to restore the poetic and stylistic qualities of the ORIGINAL oral performances on which they were based. This approach reveals that the original performances embody more than mere ideological content, THEME or story line, let alone mere entertainment or instruction. Rather, these performances embody, invoke, and express aspects of the entire sociocultural traditions in which they originate. The meaning of speech is not limited to abstract rules of vocabulary and grammar but encompasses the whole context of social relations in which its performance occurs.

Hymes identified salient characteristics in oral performance that reveal both structure and meaning and developed an analytic model with sixteen characteristics that he then incorporated into the acronym 'S-P-E-A-K-I-N-G' as a tool for holistic analysis of performance and text. In this model, 'S' stands for 'setting and scene', 'P' for 'participants', 'E' for 'ends', 'A' for 'acts sequence', 'K' for 'key' (tone, manner, spirit), 'I' for 'instrumentalities' (stylistic factors such as formality or informality), 'N' for 'norms' (social rules, audience effects), and 'G' for GENRE (the kind of speech event).

Hymes contributed significantly to the development of an interdisciplinary sub-field labelled variously as Ethnography of Speaking, Ethnography of Communication, and Sociolinguistics. Attention to the social context of spoken performance links it to ethnopoetics by paying special attention to the specific performative qualities of particular speech communities.

Hymes ascribed the character of his approach to studying oral performance to his musicologist mentor Kenneth Burke, who insisted that the investigator should use all there is to use. 'The point of method is not to look for any single feature, but to look for what counts in the text and tradition' (Hymes 2003: 37). Hymes explicitly connected his own work with that of John Miles Foley and oral-formulaic theory.

Randy F. Lumpp (Regis University, USA)

Further Reading

Hymes, Dell. 1981. *'In vain I tried to tell you': Essays in Native American Ethnopoetics*. Philadelphia: University of Pennsylvania Press.

Hymes, Dell. 1994. 'Ethnopoetics, Oral-Formulaic Theory and Editing Texts.' *Oral Tradition* 9/2: 330–70.

Hymes, Dell. 2003. *Now I Know Only So Far: Essays in Ethnopoetics*. Lincoln and London: University of Nebraska Press.

Hymes, Dell. 'The Ethnography of Speaking.' Parts 1 and 2. http://www.ohio.edu/people/thompsoc/Hymes.html (part 1); http://www.ohio.edu/people/thompsoc/Hymes2.html (part 2).

Hymns *Hymn* is a transliteration of the Greek *hymnos*, a broad term referring, in the Hellenistic world, to a song of praise to the divine. Used interchangeably with *psalm* and *ode*, *hymnos* also translated various Hebrew generic terms for song, like *shir*, *mizmor*, and *tehillah*. The term was used both for scriptural Psalms and for praise and hymn-singing in general. In modern scholarly usage, *hymn* may refer to any song of praise (including Hebrew songs of praise not explicitly referred to as *hymns* in Greek) but typically excludes the compositions in the canonical Psalter. In the ancient imagination, though, biblical psalms and other hymns were not strictly separated before the canon was fixed. In several Qumran collections (e.g. 11QPsa; 11QPsb; 4QPsf), non-canonical hymns are found side by side with psalms that became biblical, with no difference in presentation, and traditions about David present him as the singer of hymns beyond the canonical psalms (e.g. 11QPsa 27; Josephus, *Antiquities* 7.305).

In the Hebrew Bible and early Judaism, hymn-singing was identified as a key activity of the heavenly beings (e.g. Ps. 103; Sir. 42.16-17; Jub. 2; ShirShabb; Rev. 5.8-10). While the precise context in which hymns were performed in ancient communities remains obscure, a variety of sources grant insight into the transmission and performance of hymns. Hymns embedded in prose texts; actual collections of hymns, especially Qumran manuscripts; and, ancient references to practices of hymn-singing richly illustrate the affective, sensory, and sometimes ecstatic dimensions of singing praises to the divine.

Hymns Embedded in Prose

Hymns embedded in biblical narratives represent some of the oldest biblical Hebrew poetry. The Song of the Sea (Exodus 15) celebrates the divine warrior's great power and victory over the Egyptians, and represents an older layer of tradition than the prose narrative version of the crossing of the Sea of Reeds. In its narrative context, the song is placed in the mouth of Moses, who leads the men in praise, while his sister Miriam – whose song does not appear in the biblical text – leads the women. Other early songs of praise embedded in narrative texts include the songs of Moses (Deut. 32.1-43), Hannah (1 Sam. 2.1-10), and David (2 Samuel 22). In their contexts, these hymns are presented as spontaneous, occasional outpourings of praise. The practice of placing such hymns in the mouth of characters in a narrative continues in Hellenistic Jewish texts, such as Daniel (Song of the Three Children, at 3.23 in Greek), Judith (16.1-17), and Tobit (13.1-8), where characters sing hymns to celebrate overcoming a crisis, as well as in early Christian writings. For example, in Lk. 1.46-55, a hymn reminiscent of the Song of Hannah is placed in Mary's mouth. The tenuous connections with the narratives in which they appear suggest that these hymns originated independently. Elsewhere in the NT, scholars have isolated a number of short Christological hymns embedded in the Pauline and Pseudo-Pauline epistles (Eph. 2.14-16; Phil. 2.6-11; Col. 1.15-20; and 1 Tim. 3.16).

Liturgical Performance and Music

While the embedded texts noted above may represent hymns that were performed in liturgy, there is little concrete evidence for how these and other hymns were used in early Jewish and Christian WORSHIP. Many biblical psalms have headings that suggest a liturgical setting, such as headings that mention a worship leader, or enigmatic terminology that suggests musical notation whose meaning has long been lost. The earliest manuscript of a Christian hymn with words and Greek vocal musical notation is P. Oxy. XV 1786, from the late third century CE (see Cosgrove 2011).

Despite these hints, the precise place of hymnody within ancient liturgical practice is difficult to pin down. While psalms and other hymns (e.g. the later *piyyutim*) became a key part of fixed Jewish liturgy after 70 CE, and while some passages in Paul suggest their use in the communal liturgies of early Christian communities (e.g. 1 Cor. 14.26; Col. 3.16), it is unclear to what extent either biblical psalms or other hymns were part of fixed daily Jewish liturgy outside the TEMPLE in earlier times. Manuscripts from Qumran testify to developing practices of fixed daily liturgy that contained petitionary prayers and blessings for specific days, but are not forthcoming about the precise place of hymns in these liturgical complexes (see Schuller 2003).

Similarly, Hebrew Bible texts, Qumran manuscripts, and other Hellenistic Jewish texts refer to the performance of hymns accompanied by musical instruments (e.g. Exod. 15.20; 1 Chron. 15.16; Jdt. 16; Sir. 47.8-11; Josephus, *Antiquities* 7.305; 1QS 10.9). However, it is not clear whether hymns were actually performed with musical accompaniment in early Jewish and Christian worship. For example, the Qumran *Community Rule* (1QS) mentions musical instruments in a first-person song about praising God, but the references are more likely reusing scriptural language and are best read as poetic images and metaphors rather than indications of actual liturgical practice.

Perhaps the most significant corpus of hymns at Qumran is the *Hodayot* (Thanksgiving Hymns), which exist in eight different manuscripts dating from the middle Hasmonean period (like 4QHb) through the Herodian (like 1QHa). The *Hodayot* are traditionally divided into *Community Hymns* and *Teacher Hymns*; earlier scholarship identified the latter as the autobiographical writings of a specific historical individual, the Teacher of Righteousness, who appears as a persecuted and divinely favoured figure in many Qumran sectarian texts. More recently, however, scholars have noted that the first-person material draws on traditional figures and imagery. These scholars identify the first-person voice as a literary strategy that enables subsequent readers and reciters of the texts to identify with the speaker's intensely described experiences of suffering and enlightenment.

Since there are no rubrics or any other paratextual instructions for specific liturgical recitation, many scholars have interpreted the *Hodayot* as devotional poetry, not communal liturgy. However, some indications of communal performance, such as extended communal calls to praise (e.g. 4QHa frag. 7, 13–18), do exist, and it is possible to imagine multiple contexts of use. Some manuscripts have more liturgical features, while others, such as the very small manuscript 4QHc, might be copies for private use (cf. also small, possibly personal copies of the Words of the Luminaries, 4Q504, and Songs of the Sabbath Sacrifice, 4QShira; see

Schuller 2003). Although we cannot tell precisely how or when the *Hodayot* were performed, the number of manuscripts and their variety testifies to the importance of these texts to the life of the community. Scholars suggest that performance of the *Hodayot* could foster indoctrination into sectarian identity (Newsom 2004), or that their ritualized reading generated religious experience as the reader followed the compositions in sequence, from evocations of abject physical and emotional distress to their culmination in claims to angelic transcendence (Harkins 2012).

Angelic Liturgy, Ecstatic Hymnody, and Writing

Angelic transcendence is also central to the Songs of the Sabbath Sacrifice, extant in nine manuscripts from Qumran and one from Masada. These thirteen compositions contain rubrics specifying the context of performance: they are dated to thirteen successive Sabbaths (we may speculate that the cycle was meant to be repeated four times to complete the year) and include the phrase 'for the Maskil', presumably a liturgical leader. The texts call themselves 'songs', but they challenge common expectations for this genre. The Songs describe the heavenly temple and the praise of the angelic hosts, but they do not give the words of the praises, and do not follow any formal conventions of parallelistic poetry. Their poetic power comes from the repetition of words and key motifs, and from the richly evocative, sensory descriptions of celestial sights and sounds. Through performance of the songs, the worshipping community could simulate the experience of joining the angels in praise.

The Testament of Job (1st c. BCE – 1st c. CE?) gives more evidence that the singing of hymns was imagined as an ecstatic, angelic activity. Near the end of the narrative, each of Job's three daughters is transformed, and sings hymns in the angelic language and 'in accord with the hymnic style of the angels' (48.3). Here, as in the Songs of the Sabbath Sacrifice, the angelic hymns are described, but not quoted; instead, the reader is directed to two fictional books where they are written, and the text states that Job's brother, Nereus, writes down 'most of' the hymns in a book to preserve them (51.4). This reflects an ideological concern with written preservation, but strikingly, the words of the hymns are not transmitted, perhaps to preserve the otherworldly elusiveness of their divine words. The same may pertain to Rev. 14.2-3, which describes the sound of the heavenly odes that only the redeemed could learn (see TESTAMENT).

Philo of Alexandria's account of the THERAPEUTAE includes a rare description of communal hymnody and its musical and ecstatic elements (*Contemplations* 80-89), although it is a moralistic and literary creation, not an eyewitness report. Philo describes male and female choruses, each with its own leader, which are structured in imitation of Moses and Miriam's songs in Exodus 15. Before finally uniting into a single choir, the choruses sing hymns of many musical styles, accompanied by ecstatic cries, movement, and dancing that Philo compares to a Bacchic festival. A similar comparison between drunkenness and hymn-singing appears in Eph. 5.18-20, where the community is enjoined not to be drunk with wine, but rather to be 'filled with the Spirit as [they] sing psalms and hymns and spiritual songs'. The Therapeutae, Philo writes, not only contemplate the writings of the ancients, but also compose their own songs and hymns in various metres and melodies. Such metrical variety seems to have been considered a value of hymns as a genre: it also appears in Josephus, who reports that David 'composed songs and hymns to God in varied meters; some he made in trimeters, and others in pentameters' (*Antiquities* 7.305).

In these references to the composition and performance of hymns, Philo, Josephus, and the author of Ephesians, as well as 1 Cor. 14.26, Col. 3.16, and 1QS, remain vague: they do not mention the precise words of the hymns or refer to specific collections. At the same time, these texts clearly testify to the importance of hymn-singing as a devotional practice.

Eva Mroczek (University of California-Davis, USA)

Further Reading

Chazon, Esther G., Ruth Clements and Avital Pinnick, eds. 2003. *Liturgical Perspectives: Prayer and Poetry in Light of the Dead Sea Scrolls*. STDJ 48. Leiden: Brill, 2003. See esp. Schuller, Eileen M., 'Some Reflections on the Function and Use of Poetical Texts Among the Dead Sea Scrolls,' pp. 173–90.

Cosgrove, Charles H. 2011. *An Ancient Christian Hymn with Musical Notation. Papyrus Oxyrhynchus 1786: Text and Commentary*. STAC 65. Tubingen: Mohr Siebeck.

Harkins, Angela K. 2012. *Reading with an 'I' to the Heavens: Looking at the Qumran Hodayot through the Lens of Visionary Traditions*. Berlin: de Gruyter.

Leonhardt, Jutta. 2001. *Jewish Worship in Philo von Alexandria*. TSAJ 84. Tubingen: Mohr Siebeck.

Newsom, Carol A. 2004. *The Self as Symbolic Space: Constructing Identity and Community at Qumran*. STDJ 52. Leiden: Brill.

Penner, Jeremy, Ken Penner and Cecilia Wassen, eds. 2012. *Prayer and Poetry in the Dead Sea Scrolls and Related Literature: Essays in Honour of Eileen Schuller on the Occasion of her 65th Birthday*. STDJ 98. Leiden: Brill.

Weitzman, Steven P. 1997. *Song and Story in Biblical Narrative: The History of a Literary Convention*. Bloomington: Indiana University Press.

I

Iconography in the Hebrew Bible Research into the iconography of the Hebrew Bible has received less attention in the study of biblical themes and motifs than might be expected, given the plethora of supporting materials from surrounding cultures excavated over the last three centuries. Several factors may be cited to explain this relative lack of interest. Scholars of the biblical text have become increasingly specialized in their approaches and, often, philological and theological data is privileged over evidence from material culture, which is considered the province of archaeologists and art historians. Further, the Hebrew Bible's second commandment against 'graven images' (Exod. 20.4; Deut. 5.8) has predisposed scholars to view ancient Israel as an aniconic society, one in which images that might appear in the textual and physical evidence could be considered merely decorative. Until very recently, this view was largely consistent with the personal religious preferences of the majority of biblical scholars, most of whom were elite, white, European Protestant clerical males nourished on the *sola scriptura* mindset of the Protestant Reformation. However, more recent approaches incorporate the realization that the legitimacy of iconographic images was extremely fluid in ancient Israel, as early features became outlawed (e.g. Nehustan, the bronze serpent of 2 Kings 18.4) and later features were reassigned to a much earlier provenance to provide legitimation.

The rich images found in Jewish Greco-Roman SYNAGOGUES in the Holy Land, as well as the stunning wall paintings of the Dura-Europos Synagogue in Syria, along with an increased focus on minor arts in the form of functional items like CYLINDER SEALS, pottery, furniture, carvings, and textiles, all of which were surely used and handled, has led to new interest in iconographical studies of the supposedly aniconic biblical text. As a secondary society, biblical Israel recycled images from the primary cultures of the great river valleys, and because of its more rough-and-ready material culture context the arts of Syro-Palestine seldom achieved the sophisticated level of its upscale parents Egypt and Mesopotamia. With less monumental and high art available to analyse, archaeologists eventually became interested in domestic installations, with all of their small artefacts (see HOUSEHOLD ITEMS). An unintended consequence of the study of small finds has been a relatively greater focus on provenance for the origin of images and the traditions about them, rather than a sustained interest in their changes over time as later offshoots of the core tradition. However, in the current climate of Postcolonial Studies, interest in Empire's appropriation and distribution of visual media has brought iconography into the larger theological and historical conversation.

Increasingly sophisticated iconographical studies make use of the latest findings concerning media of various types. Ignoring the world of images and their role in creating consensus for the communities that see and use them is no longer an option, although the work is increasingly interpretive rather than simply descriptive. The work of Edwin R. Goodenough and Joseph Gutmann in the mid-twentieth century and, currently, the massive analytical undertakings of Othmar Keel and Christoph Uehlinger, along with their students at the University of Fribourg, is particularly noteworthy. Such work has shown that there was a clear progression of images and shifting interpretations as history and culture moved from the Bronze to the Iron Ages and later. Assessment of the role of mass media during the first millennium BCE, as biblical states were dissolved into provinces of various empires, has emerged as a critical element in interpretation of the role of iconography as an imperial strategy of control. Finally, the development of digital study tools like OCHRE (Online Cultural and Historical Research Environment; http://ochre.uchicago.edu) means that scholars are on the edge of an explosion of knowledge as cross-cultural collections of materials become more readily available.

Images and Words: The Textualization of the Visual

To be sure, the visual motifs and themes that constitute biblical Israel's canonical images do not come to modern readers with a contextual key to decode their meanings. In fact, given that the Bible is most basically a written text, visual elements do not appear in the text as images. Rather, the visual image is rendered into a word picture – a transformation of the key motifs from visual to auditory (if we take seriously that many biblical passages originated orally and went through long stages of transmission and editing).

This transition from image to word begins in the very first chapters of Genesis, which alludes to iconic images that were common in the surrounding cultures but which take on a new meaning when transposed to the biblical narrative. For example, the image of the Sacred Tree (Genesis 3) flanked by one or two royal figures – sometimes same sex, but also as a heterosexual pair – occurs frequently in the ancient Near Eastern materials, but with no hint of naïve nakedness marking the characters. Similarly, images of trees were sometimes shown with a snake, but there are no extant images portraying only two trees, nor do we find snakes as threats to trees (although the Sumerian myth of 'Inanna and the Huluppu Tree' tells us that Inanna's rescued tree is later afflicted by a 'snake that would not be charmed,' and in the Gilgamesh Epic a snake steals the plant of rejuvenation from Gilgamesh). Materials from Egypt, such as tomb paintings, often show a 'goddess tree,' usually associated with Hathor or Isis, feeding liquids to the deceased – an image that is suggestive of the role that the Asherah, or stylized sacred tree of Canaan's Mother-goddess, might have played for royal women during biblical times.

These strategies of reuse and reinterpretation of images from other cultures form a matrix in which biblical images (related in the text) must be situated and against which they must be interpreted. For example, while very few non-elites would have had access to the interior of the JERUSALEM TEMPLE, Isaiah 6 recounts the prophet's mystical experience in the Holy of Holies, where he sees the decorative images in the Temple come to life. The seraphim are identified as the poisonous winged cobra (the Uraeus of Egyptian Pharaohs) stationed over the royal throne (or on Pharaoh's headdress). Associated with the goddesses Wedjat, Hathor, or Tefnut, and thought to spit fiery poison at Pharaoh's enemies, by the time this image comes to life in the temple its gendered aspect has been fully submerged in Israel, providing a ready example of how biblical interpreters and artisans incorporated what modern scholars might consider alien theological data.

Minor Arts and the Cultural/Textual Distribution of Images

Looking at the biblical text, throughout the Torah there are intriguing hints of the influence of the minor arts – hints that have persisted through the centuries of remembrance and reshaping of various episodes. It is impossible to overestimate the importance of these 'lesser' arts, because they were arguably more widely distributed than any text or inscription. In ancient societies, where LITERACY was largely limited to the elite, everyday objects delivered their media messages to many more people than written texts could have. While the biblical text is seldom explicit, by adding in comparative archaeological materials we can begin to see a broader picture with respect to the ways in which iconography travelled and was disseminated geographically and cross-culturally.

For example, Cain has a mark (probably a tattoo rather than a birthmark) placed on his face after he is driven out for the murder of his brother (Genesis 4), a visual motif that harkens back to the practice of tattooing runaway slaves in Mesopotamian societies. While we cannot know the exact image of the mark, it was clearly a visual communication in the form of an image that carried and conveyed meaning to all who viewed it, and the text indicates God was its Maker/Creator.

Similarly, in Gen. 35.4, Jacob collects from his family 'all the foreign gods that they had, and the rings that were in their ears' and buries them beneath a terebinth tree near Shechem. This episode is of interest not least because it provides a first-hand ancient narrative of something archaeologists are always pursuing: plausible reasons for the deposition of a hidden hoard! The 'foreign gods' are most certainly either metal or clay (most likely the former, as metal had to be buried; clay would have been shattered, which is not reported here), with some shape or incised symbol (often of an astral or vegetal motif) that had been standardized to betoken the numinous. Further, it would not be uncommon for the earrings mentioned to bear some sort of meaningful decorative work or beads (cf. on jewellery and textiles: Gen. 24; Judg. 8.21, 25; 2 Sam. 12.30; Isa. 3.16 [anklets 'tinkling']; Ezek. 16.10-12, 17). All these texts indicate that the possessor of the object was not of the lowest status, or at least was perceived as worthy in the eyes of a gift-giver or was more powerful as the one taking booty, inasmuch as luxury items were usually used by elite classes.

In Genesis 37, the much-prized *ketonet-passim*, a long tunic with sleeves, flamboyantly translated by the King James Bible as a 'coat of many colors,' is given by Jacob to his first son, Joseph (by his favourite wife), and it functions as an important plot motif in the novella about the first 'court Jew'. This can happen only because the textile carried implications of preference and honour, and was recognized and interpreted as such by Joseph's brothers in the narrative (for an opposite use of textile as signifier, see the reference to torn clothing in Lev. 13.45-46). Paintings from the nineteenth-century BCE Egyptian Tomb of Beni-Hasan point to an even deeper set of cultural meanings. Here, Asiatic figures from Canaan are portrayed bringing tributes of people and goods to the Pharaoh in Egypt. Among them is a child, and also a musician (?) holding the classic *kinnor*, a small hand-held harp specific to the less wealthy regions of the Levant. The envisioned delegation of tributes, entertainers, and guards all wear the richly patterned textile tunics that the Egyptian painters routinely used to identify characters as members of the Canaanite ethnic group. Reading the wall painting and the Genesis narrative in parallel, the patterned textiles carry meaning for all to see: 'Canaanite'. From comparative studies of textiles and metalwork among medieval European Celtic groups, it is also likely that there was a mutual interpenetration of motifs like knot-work or intricate weavings which regularly appear in both textiles and on metals. The full meaning of these media will likely not be unlocked until we juxtapose the two types of creations, metal and cloth, in order to see which version developed first.

The classic biblical portrayal of the Hebrew God as manifested in a 'Savior' theology also draws on well-known, and apparently well-loved, images from the Levantine encyclopedia of the divine. God delivers the Hebrew people from slavery in Egypt with a host of miracles, all summarized in the epithet 'a mighty hand and an outstretched arm' (e.g. Deut. 5.15). This is in fact the typical position in which the Canaanite weather god Ba'al is portrayed on cult stands and folk art objects from the region. While YHWH competed against Ba'al for the exclusive fidelity and WORSHIP of the Chosen People, YHWH's media team was fruitfully absorbing all the attributes of Ba'al into the verbal portraits of YHWH's most important activities on behalf of Israel (Hos. 2). It should be noted that the transposition of Ba'al's visual theology into YHWH's verbal theology was a smashing success: the visual image of the 'Hand of God/Fatima/Hamsa' encircles countless necks as a popular motif in modern jewellery, while Ba'al has vanished into obscurity.

Many more examples of the Hebrew Bible's rich tapestry of transposed iconography could be enumerated. The images gracing the Jerusalem temple and the high priest's robes are steeped in widely distributed artistic representations. The Song of Songs is redolent with the iconic produce of the natural world, whether Egypt, Mesopotamia, or the Levant, which lends itself easily to paeans in praise of love and the Beloved. In the screeds of Hosea, Isaiah, Jeremiah, and Ezekiel against the biblical women of their day, one finds a wealth of information about the minor arts: the 'fashion-forward' dress of the elite women of Jerusalem clearly symbolized a luxurious wealth, which may well have included imported, foreign items whose colours, motifs, and manufacture speak to a thriving world of trade where the images on both useful and decorative items passed through many hands. Even the 'cakes for the Queen of Heaven' that so outraged Jeremiah as a practice of popular family religion were not image-free: cake moulds have been found in Syrian excavations that show that such items were baked into a suggestive fertility shape, normally resembling the female body or some portion thereof.

The Creation and Distribution of Images

One of the more interesting questions in the study of iconography in the Hebrew Bible relates to the very few references in the text to the creation of artefacts bearing images (especially in relationship to building the wilderness Tabernacle and the Jerusalem temple; Exod. 31; 35; 1 Kgs 4-11), although many of the more upscale items were apparently produced by Phoenician artisans (2 Sam. 5.11). In the Babylonian exile of the sixth century BCE, Nebuchadnezzar II deported one thousand Israelite artisans and smiths (2 Kgs 24.16), indicating their high worth as human booty.

Some villages may have specialized as a group in a particular craft, based on the local availability of raw materials and/or trade route location. Similarly, certain industries were gathered into craft quarters (e.g. the 'bakers' street' in Jer. 37.21) in order to manage noxious fumes or byproducts, a practice well attested in the Bronze Age. Extant economic records indicate that such enterprises were usually family-run. Could others from outside the family line enter the trade, and was that considered a good or bad fate? Were women excluded from such production work, or might they work on certain tasks in the process, or take over certain ancillary duties? It is clear that family women constituted a work group that pooled its work on textile and food production, and made their own sales of their produce (Proverbs 31). Finally, given the enormous importance of glyphic evidence, what should we look for in trying to pinpoint the locus, method, sale, and distribution of seals or small metal decorative objects, and does this paradigm change over time?

Other questions might be added with respect to the use of iconography by the conquering empires. If Jewish exiles were employed in foreign workshops, what kind of work did they do, and what iconographical changes did their new context demand? How did officials of the empires commission works, and were they personal commissions or mass orders intended for some ideological purpose among colonial servants from conquered populations?

Malachi 4.2, added as a finale to the book by a later editor concerned with foreign influence during the Persian period, states that 'YHWH will rise like a Sun of Righteousness with healing in his wings', causing the Jews to skip out of their stalls like calves. Does the co-option of the winged solar disk of the high gods of empires as a sigil of the Hebrew God and his compassionate intent speak of the absorption of foreign iconography to reinterpret needs of the present, or does it actually represent a complete capitulation to the tragedies of history, as depicted on the Black Obelisk of Shalmaneser III? There 'Jehu, son of Omri' crouches before the Assyrian conqueror beneath a winged solar disk, and the use of the image there is certainly oppressive. By Malachi's time, however, things have changed (or, rather, conquerors have), from the coercive brutality of the Assyrians to the enlightened management and home rule of the Persians.

Similarly, when the Song of Song's Beloved wants to be a seal 'set upon (the lover's) heart', does that reflect the heart of the commissioner, the maker, or the user, and does its appearance there also betoken the elite Jew as author, now happily in the service of Persian overlords? A dizzying array of questions have yet to be formulated, much less researched, leaving the curious scholar in anticipation of a veritable lifetime of iconographic immersion.

Carole R. Fontaine (Andover Newton Theological School, USA)

Further Reading

Goodenough, Edwin R. 1953–4. *Jewish Symbols in the Greco-Roman World.* 4 Vol: Bollingen Series XXXVII. New York: Pantheon Books.

Gutmann, Joseph, ed. 1971. *No Graven Images*. New York: KTAV.

Gutmann, Joseph, ed. 1976. *The Temple of Solomon: Archaeological Fact and Medieval Tradition in Christian, Islamic, and Jewish Art.* Religion and the Arts 3. Missoula, MT: Scholars Press.

Gutmann, Joseph. 1988. 'The Dura Europos Synagogue Paintings and Their Influence on Later Christian and Jewish Art.' *Artibus et Historiae* 9(17): 25–9.

Keel, Othmar. 1977. *Jahwe-Visionen und Siegelkunst*. Stuttgart: Verlag Katholisches Bibelwerk.

Keel, Othmar and Christoph Uehlinger. 1998. *Gods, Goddesses and Images of God in Ancient Israel*. Minneapolis: Fortress.

King, Philip J. and Lawrence E. Stager. 2001. *Life in Biblical Israel*. Library of Ancient Israel, ed. Douglas A. Knight. Louisville: Westminster John Knox.

Lurker, Manfred. 1980. *The Gods and Symbols of Ancient Egypt: An Illustrated Dictionary*. London: Thames and Hudson.

Sass, Benjamin, and Christoph Uehlinger, eds. 1993. *Studies in the Iconography of Northwest Semitic Inscribed Seals.* Orbis Biblicus et Orientalis 125. Fribourg and Goettingen: Vandenhoeck & Ruprecht.

Schloen, J. David and Sandra R. Schloen. 2012. *OCHRE: An Online Cultural and Historical Research Environment.* Winona Lake, Indiana: Eisenbrauns.

Uehlinger, Christoph, ed. 2000. *Images as Media: Sources for the Cultural History of the Near East and the Eastern Mediterranean (1st millennium BCE).* Orbis Biblicus et Orientalis 175. Fribourg and Goettingen: Vandenhoeck & Ruprecht.

Identity Identity refers to the distinctive characteristics belonging to an individual or shared by all members of a particular category/group. From an individual perspective, the core of identity is the categorization of the self into a particular role. From the group perspective, the core of identity is in the categorization of the individual within the group, and/or of the entire group, into a particular role (Stets and Burke 2000). While there is significant overlap between these two ways of viewing the self, this entry will focus on the group perspective, particularly the ways that individuals and groups use the resources of MEMORY to construct a sense of identity.

Memory and Social Identity

Social identity refers to that part of an individual's sense of identity that comes from belonging to a particular group and serves as the line of interaction between personal and group identity. Social identity encompasses three important factors: the individual's recognition of belonging to the group; the individual's recognition of the value attached to the group; and the attitudes of group members towards insiders and outsiders. Social identity theories focus on the ways group members understand themselves as part of the group and differentiate their group from other groups in order to achieve a positive identity.

Categorization takes place, in part, by creating distinctions between the in-group and out-groups. One way that these distinctions are created and sustained is by referencing a group prototype that represents the identity of the group. Group prototypes can be understood as vague attributes of the group's identity that serve to prescribe how group members should think, feel, and behave. Through this self-categorization process, one begins to see her/himself and the world through the lens of the group prototype. Individual perceptions, attitudes, feelings, and behaviours are dictated by the group's prototype (Hogg, Hohmann, and Rivera 2008: 1273–4). Perhaps most often, a group's prototype is a representation of a person who is remembered as embodying the identity of the group, though the prototype does not necessarily have to be an actual or current member of the group but rather is an ideal image of the group's character (Smith and Zarate 1990) (see REPUTATION). Group prototypes, however, are not fixed characters that group members are to imitate, since later group members may reinterpret the group's prototype according to the current needs of the group. Prototypes from the past must be remembered and commemorated in meaningful ways in order for their prototypical status to remain effective. This ongoing process of reinterpreting a group's prototype, and thus the group's identity, raises the matter of the role of SOCIAL MEMORY in the identity (re)making process.

The connection between social memory and social identity has been highlighted by JAN ASSMANN, who describes a transition between two phases in the development of a COLLECTIVE MEMORY. The first phase, COMMUNICATIVE MEMORY, is characterized by the face-to-face circulation of foundational memories shared among those who experienced a group's originating events ('eyewitnesses'). This type of memory, however, 'cannot sustain group-constitutive remembrances beyond the three to four generations able to claim living contact with the generation of origins' (Kirk 2005: 5–6), simply because the eyewitnesses eventually die. This limitation forces the emergent community into a second phase that is characterized by what Assmann calls CULTURAL MEMORY, a common image of the originating past that 'comprises that body of reusable texts, images, and rituals specific to each society in each epoch, whose "cultivation" serves to stabilize and convey that society's self-image. Upon such collective knowledge, for the most part (but not exclusively) of the past, each group bases its awareness of unity and particularity' (1995: 132).

As the period of communicative memory passes, groups employ strategies for remembering their prototype(s) in ways that meet the need of the group in its current situation. Thus, prototypes are remembered/reinterpreted according to the current needs of the group, including needs relating to solidarity and normativity. This phenomenon is illustrated by BARRY SCHWARTZ's study of the post-Civil War characterization of George Washington (Schwartz 1991) and the depiction of Abraham Lincoln during the Second World War (Schwartz 1996). Similarly, McIver describes how the first-century Judean group who committed suicide at Masada was presented by Josephus and then reinterpreted by twentieth-century Zionists (McIver 2011), and Damgaard notes ways that Moses was remembered in narratives from ancient Judaism through fourth-century CE Christianity (Damgaard 2013). These studies show that just because prototypes are essential to identity, the present context may be as determinative as the ACTUAL PAST in collective memory. There are limits, however, to these reinterpretations. Rather than being completely fabricated, the memories of past historical figures remain 'a stable image upon which new elements are intermittently superimposed' (Schwartz 1991: 234.). That is, memory of a group's prototype is not so much a fixed content as a series of 'ongoing processes of construction [of the past] in narrative form' (Olick and Robbins 1998: 122).

Narrative, Memory, and Identity

Paul Ricoeur defines narrative identity as 'the kind of identity that human beings acquire through the mediation of the narrative function' (1991: 188). According to Ricoeur, the development of an individual's identity takes place through interaction with a narrative in a threefold process: 1) prefiguration (the pre-understanding the reader/hearer brings to the text, an understanding that may also be conceived as a pre-existing identity); 2) configuration (the author's construction of the text and the readers' interaction with the narrative world of the text); and 3) refiguration (the fusion of the world of the text and the world of the reader). Narrative identity, then, is constructed as an individual (or group) engages a narrative with a certain pre-existing identity and reconfigures that identity based upon interaction with the narrative (see COMMEMORATIVE NARRATIVE.

Narrative and memory work together in the (re)construction of social identity as groups 'create shared life stories or narratives of the group which tie past, present and predicted futures into a coherent representation' (Cinnirella 1998: 235). Thus, group members reinterpret the group's past to make its identity more compatible with new situations and future directions. This reinterpretation may be accomplished by appealing to stories surrounding a group prototype from the past. Thus, group prototypes and a group's developing memory of that prototype play an important role in the construction and maintenance (including future reconstructions) of group identity. In this way, cultural memory is crucial for the construction of narrative identity. 'It is the continuity of memory which contributes to the certainty of one's self, even though that self can exist only in relation to others. The continuity of memory operates through narrative to construct a coherent identity, appropriating the past and anticipating the future … narrative identity is developed in interaction with its social and cultural contexts' (Kirkman 2002: 32). Thus, identity can be formed through narratives in the same manner in which readers come to know characters in literature: by interacting with the narrative in combination with cultural memory, that is, with their own experience and knowledge.

Similarly, Liu and László stress the identity-forming function of narrative, noting that social representations of the past are 'stories of events with a temporal structure that can be related thematically from a particular point of view' and thus should be 'approached as narratives'. Thus, 'in the case of historical narratives, these stories reflect group identity on the one hand, and connect individuals to the group on the other' and may be revised according to the identity needs of the group (2007: 95). Narrative perspective and the ability to generate empathy help to illustrate the relationship between the recipients of the narrative and the culture that generated the narrative. Narrative perspective is viewed as a 'relational concept between the producer and the recipient of narrative' that 'establishes a surface structure empathy hierarchy that influences how the reader or listener constructs the meaning of the narrated event and opens the way for participatory affective responses' (2007: 96). The hope is that 'the reader, viewer, or listener … participates vicariously in the narrative to the extent that [s]he shows empathy for the point of view expressed and the characters and situations depicted' (2007: 98). In this way, 'narrative connects individuals to a collective through symbols, knowledge and meaning'. This collective memory 'goes back to the supposed origins of the group' and 'objectifies memories that have proven to be important to the group, encodes these memories into stories, preserves them as public narratives, and makes it possible for new members to share group history' (2007: 87–8).

To summarize, social identity is constructed by differentiating between in-groups and out-groups and is often rooted in group norms that consist, in part, of shared beliefs and practices. To embody their identity, groups attribute the role of prototype to some ideal person(s) from the past through the vehicle of social memory. Group prototypes, and thus the identity of the group, are not static but are capable of change depending upon the evolving situation of the group as the group remembers its prototypical figures in new ways. The memory of this prototype becomes the chief character in the group's formative narrative history and personifies the shared identity of that group. As new situations emerge, the group may remember/reinterpret the prototype in a new light in order to address the new context.

Coleman A. Baker (Texas Christian University, USA)

Further Reading

Assmann, Jan and John Czaplicka. 1995. 'Collective Memory and Cultural Identity.' *New German Critique* 65: 125–33.

Baker, Coleman A. 2012. 'Social Identity Theory and Biblical Interpretation.' *Biblical Theology Bulletin* 42(3): 129–38.

Baker, Coleman A. 2011. *Identity, Memory, and Narrative in Early Christianity: Peter, Paul, and Recategorization in the Book of Acts*. Eugene, OR: Wipf and Stock.

Cinnirella, Marco. 1998. 'Exploring Temporal Aspects of Social Identity: The Concept of Possible Social Identities,' *European Journal of Social Psychology* 28(2): 227–8.

Damgaard, Finn. 2013. *The Memory of Moses in Biographical and Autobiographical Narratives in Ancient Judaism and 4th-Century Christianity*. New York: Peter Lang.

Hogg, Michael, A., Zachary P. Hohmann and Jason E. Rivera. 2008. 'Why Do People Join Groups? Three Motivational Accounts from Social Psychology.' *Social and Personality Psychology Compass* 2(3): 1273–4.

Kirk, Alan. 2005. 'Social and Cultural Memory.' In *Memory, Tradition, and Text: Uses of the Past in Early Christianity.* Edited by Alan Kirk and Tom Thatcher. Semeia St. Atlanta: SBL Press, pp. 1–24.

Kirkman, Maggie. 2002. 'What's the Plot? Applying Narrative Theory to Research in Psychology.' *Australian Psychologist* 37(10): 32.

Liu, James H., and Janos László. 2007. 'Narrative Theory of History and Identity: Social Identity, Social Representations, Society and the Individual.' In *Social Representations and Identity: Content, Process, and Power.* Edited by Gail Moloney and Iain Walker. New York: Palgrave Macmillan, pp. 85–107.

McIver, Robert K. 2011. *Memory, Jesus, and the Synoptic Gospels.* SBLRBS, Atlanta: SBL Press.

Olick, Jeffrey K. and Joyce Robbins. 1998. 'Social Memory Studies: From "Collective Memory" to the Historical Sociology of Mnemonic Practices.' *Annual Review of Sociology* 24.

Ricoeur, Paul. 1991. 'Narrative Identity.' In *On Paul Ricoeur: Narrative and Interpretation.* Edited by David Wood. London: Routledge, pp. 188–200.

Schwartz, Barry. 1991. 'Social Change and Collective Memory: The Democratization of George Washington.' *American Sociological Review* 56(2): 221–36.

Schwartz, Barry. 1996. 'Memory as a Cultural System: Abraham Lincoln in World War II.' *American* Schwartz, Barry. *Review* 61(5): 908–27.

Smith, Eliot R. and Michael A. Zarate. 1990. 'Exemplar and Prototype Used in Social Categorization.' *Social Cognition* 8 (3): 243-62.

Stets, Jan E., and Peter J. Burke. 2000. 'Identity Theory and Social Identity Theory.' *Social Psychology Quarterly*, 63(3): 224–37.

Tucker, J. Brian, and Coleman A. Baker. 2014. *The T&T Clark Handbook to Social Identity in the New Testament.* London: T&T Clark/Bloomsbury.

Initiation Rituals Initiation rituals, which mark or enact an individual's entrance or acceptance into a group, have played an important role in societies both ancient and modern. While virtually every culture has practices that could fit the definition, the term *initiation ritual* itself is artificial. In the Bible, for example, there is no term for *ritual*, let alone *initiation ritual*. Consequently, identification of initiation rituals depends on how the interpreter draws the boundaries.

The initiation rituals described in the Bible served multiple functions corresponding to the group or role into which an individual was entering. Circumcision in the Hebrew Bible and baptism in the NT are the Bible's quintessential rituals marking entrance into a community. The circumcision ritual enacts an individual's entrance into YHWH's covenant community (Gen. 17; Lev. 12.2; cf. the blood ritual initiating Israel into the covenant with YHWH at Mt. Sinai at Exod. 24.3-8), while baptism plays a similar role for Christian initiation (Col. 2.11-12; cf. Acts 2.41; Rom. 6.4; Eph. 4.5). Other rites, such as anointing with oil, initiate an individual into an office or a particular role, including kings (1 Samuel 9; 16), priests (Exodus 29; Leviticus 8), prophets, and, in the NT, the appointment of individuals to oversee food distribution (Acts 6.1-6). The Nazirite ritual (Numbers 6) functions as an initiation rite, in the sense that, after undergoing the ritual, an individual is (temporarily) elevated to holy, priest-like status and becomes part of the Nazirite group. Atonement (*kipper*) in the priestly texts of the Pentateuch may also be classified as an initiation rite (Exodus 29–30; throughout Leviticus, especially chapters 4-16) in that it grants re-admission to the covenant community. As a consequence of the ritual, individuals burdened by sin or impurity receive atonement and forgiveness or cleansing, allowing them to rejoin the worshipping community and regain limited access to the divine abode.

In most cases, in both ancient and modern times, initiation rites are one-time events (e.g. Israelites need not be circumcised twice). However, in certain cases, most notably with the Nazirite and atonement rites, group membership is contingent on fulfilment of subsequent obligations. If a Nazirite fails to uphold the strict regulations, he must undergo a re-initiation rite to re-consecrate him as a Nazirite. At the end of the specified period, a Nazirite also undergoes a de-initiation rite that returns him to common status. Likewise, individuals are continually beset by sin and impurity and are continually barred from and readmitted to the worshipping community after the appropriate re-initiation rituals.

In many cases, the transition from outside to inside a group is a social construct that cannot be verified through normal empirical means – there may be no significant tangible change in the individual or the community once the ritual is accomplished. Initiation rituals serve to concretize the abstract aspects of these changes in status and to mark events and their results as important by ceremonializing them. The effectiveness of initiation rituals derives from the fact that authorities within the community prescribe the rite, and the participants agree that it accomplishes the desired goal. For example, in a modern context, there is no clear cause-effect way to achieve the abstract concept known as marriage; a wedding ceremony, with all its attendant rituals, concretizes marriage and marks it as an important transition in life, as the couple changes status from single to married. A wedding works not intrinsically, but because the participants agree that it does and an authority recognizes its validity, just as monetary currency has real, quantifiable value only because an authority declares that it does and the people agree. In the same way, sprinkling blood does not logically lead to people and objects becoming clean, but does provide a concrete set of actions that represent the symbolic aspects of the experience.

In initiation rites, like other rituals, ritual authorities commonly leave the rationale for the individual elements undefined, defining instead the goal of the larger ritual complex. For the participants, the mechanics of the ritual are largely irrelevant as long as they achieve the desired result. In turn, while the overall outcome is clear, there is room for significant variability in explaining the details and their effects. For example, while all would agree that circumcision clearly marks entrance into the Israelite covenant community and that anointing marks the entrance into the office of a king or a priest, interpretations vary regarding how and why they work and what else they might achieve. In fact, this ambiguity benefits the ritual system. Once fully defined, a system cannot easily expand to fit new circumstances. Fixed rites with flexible explanations, however, possess both the authority of antiquity and the freedom to change.

Just because initiation rituals are social constructs that tap into a group's COLLECTIVE MEMORY and guiding sense of values and identity, most initiation rituals only work within a specific community. For example, a typical modern American wedding would not signal marriage for an ancient Israelite. Rituals thus promote group solidarity and bind the individuals who participate more firmly to the group, while at the same time differentiating the particular group from others.

In several cases, rather than simply marking a change in community status, biblical initiation rituals enact transformation in an individual. In the case of the Nazirite and priest, the initiation rituals impart holiness to an individual, while in the case of the atonement rituals, the rites themselves grant atonement and forgiveness or cleansing. In other cases, like circumcision and baptism, it is less clear what transformation, if any, occurs, though baptism is associated with the reception of the Holy Spirit (Acts 2.38). In these cases, ritual functions to achieve something that could not be achieved through ordinary means alone. It brings the divine power to bear on the mundane, addresses otherwise intangible concepts like holiness and sin, and achieves transformation.

Michael B. Hundley (Syracuse University, USA)

Further Reading

Bernat, David A. 2009. *Sign of the Covenant: Circumcision in the Priestly Tradition.* SBL Ancient Israel and its Literature 3. Atlanta: SBL Press.

Eliade, Mircea. 1958. *Rites and Symbols of Initiation.* New York: Harper and Row.

Hundley, Michael B. 2011. *Keeping Heaven on Earth: Safeguarding the Divine Presence in the Priestly Tabernacle.* FAT 2/50. Tübingen: Mohr Siebeck.

Kavanagh, Aidan. 1978. *The Shape of Baptism: The Rite of Christian Initiation.* New York: Pueblo.

Van Gennep, Arnold. 1960. *The Rites of Passage.* Chicago: University of Chicago Press.

Inscriptions See EPIGRAPHY.

Intersemeiotics See TRANSLATION.

J

Jamnia See Yavneh.

Jesus Tradition The term *Jesus tradition* describes one of the most foundational concepts in Gospels and historical Jesus research. Broadly stated, 'Jesus tradition' refers to the stories about, and the teachings attributed to, Jesus in early Christianity and, more narrowly, to the recording of those stories and teachings in written texts ('Gospels'). Jesus and Gospels scholars, however, do not usually offer any clear definitions of what they mean when they refer to the Jesus tradition. For example, although the term *Jesus tradition* appears 106 times in the second edition of the *Dictionary of Jesus and the Gospels* (Green, Brown, and Perrin 2013), none of the *Dictionary*'s entries offers an explicit definition of the term, and there is no entry for 'Jesus tradition'. The entry 'Tradition' (Green, Brown, and Perrin 2013: 966) refers the reader only to the entries on 'Orality and Oral Transmission' and 'Rabbinic Traditions and Writings', neither of which offers a definition of '(Jesus) tradition'. Clearly, the *Dictionary*'s editors and contributors expect readers to know, even if only intuitively, what is meant by 'Jesus tradition'.

Unfortunately, things are not always sufficiently clear to help the would-be reader. This lack of clarity allows scholars to mean more than one thing by 'Jesus tradition' and to slip from one meaning to another without comment. This phenomenon is illustrated, for example, in the work of prominent NT scholar James Dunn. 'What we have done in the present chapter is, in effect, to work backward from the character of the *Jesus tradition* as it still appears in the *Jesus tradition*' (2005: 53–4; emphases added). In the first instance, 'Jesus tradition' refers to the sum total of stories about Jesus (sayings, narratives, etc.) that might be preserved in a written Gospel or text; in the second instance, it refers to the written Gospels themselves, especially the Synoptic Gospels (and perhaps to a lesser extent, John). Dunn elsewhere notes that 'our starting point [in a "quest for the historical Jesus"] will almost always be the Jesus tradition preserved in the Synoptic Gospels' (Dunn 2003: 328). Here, 'Jesus tradition' refers to an abstract phenomenon that might be preserved in one or more written texts; the tradition, in other words, originates outside written texts and provides the raw materials comprising those texts. Dunn appeals to the 'impact' Jesus made on his contemporaries and implicitly defines the Jesus tradition in terms of that impact: 'The initial formulation of the tradition, we may say, was itself the impact made by Jesus. That which grasped and shaped their lives is what they put into verbal form in what we now call the Jesus tradition' (2005: 30). At the same time, Dunn, like many other biblical scholars, does not offer an explicit, programmatic definition of this crucial term.

John Miles Foley's work in oral performance and oral-derived texts helps to fill in this lacuna. Foley takes a semiotic approach to tradition, which he defines not in terms of content (e.g. 'the sum total of stories about Jesus [sayings, narratives, etc.] that might be preserved in a written gospel or text') but as 'a dynamic, multivalent body of meaning' (1995:xii). As a 'body of meaning', tradition refers to the contextualizing field to which individual texts in any medium (written, oral, ritual, and others) refer and which enables individual texts to convey meaning between an author/speaker/performer and a reader/listener/audience. In other words, tradition identifies 'the context that renders a verbal message (oral or written) meaningful' (Rodríguez 2014: 79). Tradition as context extends Dunn's implicit definition of tradition as an abstract collection of content (or stories) centring on Jesus to incorporate the totalizing function of images of Jesus as the ground against which sayings or narratives from or about Jesus, as figures, are recognized and interpreted. In other words, the Jesus tradition is not simply the bits from which accounts of Jesus' life and teachings are built, but rather comprises the entire set of assumptions and understandings that guided audiences' and readers' receptions of individual sayings or narratives about Jesus. This broader understanding of the Jesus tradition includes, but is not limited to, the content that contributed to an account of Jesus' life and teaching.

Werner Kelber describes tradition as 'a circumambient contextuality … an invisible nexus of references and identities from which people draw sustenance, in which they live, and in relation to which they make sense of their lives' (1995: 159). This broadened understanding of tradition cannot be reduced to strictly textual relationships, nor does it preclude the literary relationship between textual expressions of the tradition. Rather, as a multivalent body of meaning, the Jesus tradition provides the field within which Jesus' followers recounted, transmitted, or expressed accounts of Jesus' life and teaching (including interpretations of those accounts and applications to the later contexts; e.g. Paul's unattributed echoes of/allusions to Jesus tradition in 1 Thess. 5.2-3, 13; Rom. 12.14; 14.14; 1 Cor. 13.2).

The discussion to this point has aimed at reconfiguring the concept *Jesus tradition*. Jesus' tradents lived within the Jesus tradition and were shaped by it. In this sense, the Jesus tradition is a cultural analogue, and analysing the Jesus tradition is analogous to analysing culture, a process Clifford Geertz describes as 'sorting out the structures of signification … and determining their social ground and import' (1973: 9). Unfortunately, analyses of the Jesus tradition for over two centuries have focused narrowly on questions of composition (source and redaction criticism) and, consequently, have reduced the Jesus tradition to the raw materials comprising our written sources. Scholarship in this vein has focused on compositional questions such as: Did an author find this saying/narrative in one of his sources or create it himself? If text *b* is a parallel of text *a*, was the author of *b* influenced by (or did he copy from) *a*? When we encounter the Jesus tradition as written text, our analyses should turn towards efforts to explain the texts within the contextualizing field of the tradition and address broader questions of expression and reception in addition to composition. Such questions include: What has this Evangelist accomplished by expressing the tradition in precisely this way? How might this Evangelist's readers (or audience) have experienced and interpreted this expression of the tradition? How does this text convey meaning between author/speaker/performer and reader/listener/audience?

The point is to recover not just how Jesus' tradents shaped the Jesus tradition but also to illumine how they were themselves shaped by it. If, to take one widely discussed example, Luke has greatly expanded his account of Jesus in Nazareth, which he encountered at least in Mk 6:1-6a but probably not only in his reading of Mark (see Lk. 4.16-30), can we explain Luke's expansions in terms of the tradition(s) he inhabited? In fact we can (see Rodríguez 2010: 138–73): Luke does not merely create his Nazareth scene out of whole cloth but rather incorporates images and ideas he found in the Jesus tradition (cp. Lk. 7.18-23) as well as in Isaianic and other Israelite traditions (Isa. 61.1-2; 1 Kgs 19; 2 Kgs 5). In so doing, he does more than simply redact (or alter) the Jesus tradition he inherited; Luke utilizes resources already latent within the tradition to bring the tradition to bear on a new situation in innovative ways (see Keith 2011: 142–5). The challenge of media criticism is to recapture a sense of tradition in this larger, more encompassing sense, and by so doing to resist the ever-present temptation to reduce the Jesus tradition to its textual detritus.

Rafael Rodríguez (Johnson University, USA)

Further Reading

Dunn, James D. G. 2003. *Jesus Remembered. Christianity in the Making 1*. Grand Rapids: Eerdmans.
Dunn, James D. G. 2005. *A New Perspective on Jesus: What the Quest for the Historical Jesus Missed*. London: SPCK.
Foley, John Miles. 1995. *The Singer of Tales in Performance. Voices in Performance and Text*. Bloomington, IN: Indiana University Press.
Geertz, Clifford. 1973. *The Interpretation of Cultures*. New York: Basic Books.
Green, Joel B., Jeannine K. Brown and Nicholas Perrin, eds. 2013. *The Dictionary of Jesus and the Gospels*. 2nd edition. Downers Grove, IL: InterVarsity Press.
Keith, Chris. 2011. *Jesus' Literacy: Scribal Culture and the Teacher from Galilee*. Library of Historical Jesus Studies 8/ LNTS 413. London: T&T Clark, 2011.
Kelber, Werner H. 1995. 'Jesus and Tradition: Words in Time, Words in Space.' In *Orality and Textuality in Early Christian Literature*. Edited by Joana Dewey. Semeia 65. Atlanta: SBL Press, pp. 139–67.
Rodríguez, Rafael. 2010. *Structuring Early Christian Memory: Jesus in Tradition, Performance, and Text*. European Studies on Christian Origins/LNTS 407. London: T&T Clark.
Rodríguez, Rafael. 2014. *Oral Tradition and the New Testament: A Guide for the Perplexed*. London: Bloomsbury T&T Clark.

Jesus Tradition and Memory Form criticism conceived memory as individual reminiscence (see personal/cognitive memory). Understood as such, memory hardly fit the generic profile of the synoptic tradition. Form criticism therefore made a sharp distinction between memory and tradition and assigned memory a very marginal role in the tradition's origins and development. Other approaches at times reacted against this standard model with attempts to bring the synoptic tradition into close phenomenological alignment with eyewitness memory. Memory theory calls in question the respective ways that both these approaches model the relationship between memory and the tradition. It shows that tradition is a memory artefact, forming at the interface of cognitive and cultural operations of memory (see cultural memory). But it also accounts for the evident autonomy of tradition, its leading a life of its own as it interacts with the historical and social contingencies of a tradent community.

Tradition forms along a memory continuum that runs from the cognitive to the cultural. Neural-biological research shows that human memory is a cognitive artificer that massively condenses raw perceptual input, conforming emergent memories to formulaic types, schemas, and standard narrative patterns drawn from a cultural repertoire of genres learnt through socialization. These give memories durability and coherence while foregrounding the existential salience of remembered experiences for the remembering subject. They also render memories capable of externalization into the social world, for the genres and narrative schemas for memory are also pragmatic media for its communication.

This cognitive convergence upon salience gives memories a normative and affective density. Under certain conditions these cognitive artefacts have the potential to be taken up into wider cultural and moral formation projects and their various media. Orientation to a salient past is constitutive of authentic communities, and it is through sociocultural processes of commemoration that memory is transmuted into bodies of normative tradition (see Identity). Communities fashion their foundational memories collaboratively, in face-to-face communication. These shared representations display emergent properties: they more clearly, integrally, and fully distil out and express the significance of an experienced event than could a mere aggregation of disconnected individual recollections. The resulting tradition comes thereby to transcend the limitations of unreflective and unstable eyewitness memories with their idiosyncratic perspectives. The normative charge of tradition is intensified, moreover, by its formative alignment with archetypal narratives, persons, and motifs of the epic past; it takes shape in the matrix of a more ancient cultural tradition. Accordingly, it is in the course of sharing and rehearsing memories in the groups for which they hold salience that they can come into sharper relief as standardized forms of a shared tradition bearing a community's shared meanings and norms that ground its IDENTITY, constitute it as a moral community, and enable transmission of cultural identity across time.

This accounts for a number of the features of the synoptic tradition, such as its high density of dominical sayings and pronouncement stories, its shaping and deep tincturing by the ambient biblical narrative and moral tradition, and its generic uniformity (i.e. the absence of distinguishing features of individual episodic memory). It also accounts for the autonomy of tradition vis-à-vis the actual occurrences that are its grounds. Already in memory formation salient elements and patterns of meaning are abstracted from the flux of experience and configured in symbolically concentrated cognitive artefacts that are mediated in various genres and schemas. In the words of evolutionary biologist Terrence Deacon, the effect is an 'increasingly indirect linkage between symbolic mental representation and its grounds of reference' (Deacon 1997: 424). Tradition, emerging out of commemorative remembering within communities, amounts to symbolic mediation of the past: it subsumes salient elements of the past freed from all but the barest historical and social contextualization. Its coalescing in mnemonically efficient, durable representational forms, grounded in, yet loosened from, originating historical contexts, is what makes a tradition capable of ongoing normative engagement with the present realities of its tradent community. Like any cultural object, tradition leads a life of its own as it interacts with the changing social and historical contexts of its tradent communities.

This in turn helps account for the MULTIFORMITY of the synoptic tradition (i.e. its property of variability), evident in the residues of its oral expression but also propagating to a significant extent into the written medium of the Gospels. A community is able to remember, inculcate, and transmit its formative past to the extent that that past has been mnemonically consolidated in the schematic media forms of a tradition. In its actual enactment tradition is refracted through the contemporary realities of its tradent community, but at the same time a community refracts and thereby cognitively apprehends its contemporary realities through the lens of its tradition. This is the major factor in the dynamism of the tradition, its transformations in different contexts. It is precisely in its transformations that the normative memory function of tradition for its tradent community comes to expression. ORAL TRADITION genres, specimens of which are still partially visible in the Gospels, are themselves strategies to maximize the memorability and therefore the stability of tradition, while simultaneously enabling the flexibility that renders tradition responsive to new situations.

In sum, one sees the convergence of memory – properly understood as a tangible set of practices on a cognitive and cultural continuum – with the phenomenology of the tradition. This includes the shift from the oral to more durable forms in the written medium, which brings scribal media and memory practices into play (see SCRIBAL MEMORY).

Alan Kirk (James Madison University, USA)

Further Reading

Assmann, Jan. 2011. *Cultural Memory and Early Civilization: Writing, Remembrance, and Political Imagination.* Cambridge and New York: Cambridge University Press.

Assmann, Jan. 2006. 'Form as Mnemonic Device: Cultural Texts and Cultural Memory.' In *Performing the Gospel: Orality, Memory, and Mark.* Edited by Richard A. Horsley, et al. Minneapolis: Fortress, pp. 67–82.

Bauckham, Richard. 2006. *Jesus and the Eyewitnesses: The Gospels as Eyewitness Testimony*. Grand Rapids and Cambridge: Eerdmans.

Bruner, Jerome, and Carol Fleisher Feldman. 1996, 'Group Narrative as a Cultural Context of Autobiography.' In *Remembering Our Past: Studies in Autobiographical Memory.* Edited by David C. Rubin. Cambridge: Cambridge University Press, pp. 291–317.

Byrskog, Samuel. 2000. *Story as History – History as Story: The Gospel Tradition in the Context of Ancient Oral History*. WUNT 123. Tübingen: Mohr Siebeck.

Deacon, Terrence W. 1997. *The Symbolic Species: The Co-Evolution of Language and the Brain.* New York and London: W. W. Norton.
Erll, Astrid, and Ansgar Nünning, eds. 2010. *A Companion to Memory Studies.* Berlin: Walter Mouton de Gruyter.
Foley, John Miles. 2006. 'Memory in Oral Tradition.' In *Performing the Gospel: Orality, Memory, and Mark.* Edited by Richard A. Horsley, et al. Minneapolis: Fortress, pp. 83–96.
Kirk, Alan. 2014. 'The Tradition-Memory Nexus in the Synoptic Tradition: Memory, Media, and Symbolic Representation.' In *Memory and Identity in Ancient Judaism and Early Christianity: A Conversation with Barry Schwartz.* Edited by Tom Thatcher. Semeia Studies. Atlanta: SBL Press.
McIver, Robert K. 2011. *Memory, Jesus, and the Synoptic Gospels.* SBLRBS. Atlanta: SBL Press.
Rubin, David C. 1995. *Memory in Oral Traditions: The Cognitive Psychology of Epic, Ballads, and Counting-out Rhymes.* New York & Oxford: Oxford University Press.
Schwartz, Barry. 1996. 'Memory as a Cultural System: Abraham Lincoln in World War II,' *American Sociological Review* 61: 908–27.
Schwartz, Barry. 1998. 'Frame Image: Towards a Semiotics of Collective Memory,' *Semiotica* 121: 1–38.
Schwartz, Barry. 2009. 'Collective Forgetting and the Symbolic Power of Oneness: the Strange Apotheosis of Rosa Parks', *Social Psychology Quarterly* 72: 123–42.
Paul Thompson. 2000. *Voices of the Past: Oral History.* 3rd edition; Oxford and New York: Oxford University Press.
Zimmermann, Ruben. 2010. 'Memory and Form Criticism: The Typicality of Memory as a Bridge between Orality and Literality in the Early Christian Remembering Process.' In *The Interface of Orality and Writing.* Edited by Annette Weissenrieder & Robert B. Coote. Tübingen: Mohr Siebeck, pp. 13–43.

Jousse, Marcel Marcel Jousse (1886–1961) was a French scholar who, along with MILMAN PARRY, ranks among the pioneers in the study of oral style and orally based cultures. A thinker of global ambitions, he aspired to achieve a grand synthesis of anthropology, ethnology, psychology, linguistics, biblical exegesis, and pedagogy. The publication of *Le Style oral rythmique et mnémotechnique chez les Verbo-moteurs* (1925) (The Oral Style (1990)) launched Jousse's career, which took him to a number of prestigious academic positions in Paris. For roughly a quarter of a century, he delivered over 1,000 lectures, mostly without the assistance of script, at the Sorbonne, the École des Hautes Études, and the École d'Anthropologie. Following his death, he rapidly faded from scholarly attention, and until recently has remained virtually unacknowledged in English- and German-speaking scholarship. Thanks to the efforts of Edgard R. Sienaert during the last twenty-five years, Jousse's work is now being made available in English translation (1990; 2000; 2001a,b; 2004; 2005; 2006; 2016).

Jousse's research was based on his theory of oral style, a groundbreaking innovation at the time. He was among the first to identify oral style, composition, and structures of thought as distinct from those characteristic of WRITING cultures. A Jesuit priest, he paid particular attention to the Hebrew Bible and the Aramaic TARGUMS, NT texts, and the ancient Galilean ethnic milieu, viewing all as reflecting a verbomotoric culture that managed life verbally, interactively, and communally. Writing extensively on the Gospels and the language of Jesus, Jousse viewed the Greek gospel texts as palimpsests that had been superimposed upon the Aramaic voice of the 'Rabbi Iéshoua de Nazareth'.

The core of Jousse's theory was encapsulated in three anthropological laws: rhythmo-mimicry, which stated that from childhood humans learn, remember, and repeat by way of imitation in accord with rhythmic oral patterns; bilateralism, which posited that human language originated in binary fashion and was grounded in the need for balance;[1] and formulism, which connoted language in fixed formulas for the purpose of supporting MEMORY, easy access, and ready replay of information. The anthropological profile of these three laws was not meant to refer to the academic discipline of anthropology but – quite literally – to their rootedness in human corporeality. In societies without or with only minimal alphabetic writing, he observed, language, remembrance, and reading are fully embodied (rather than purely mental) activities.

For this reason, Jousse viewed the oral style governed by the three anthropological laws as a phenomenon of worldwide validity. Fully acknowledging that writing has the cultural effect of overriding anthropological oral style features and often relegating them to near-forgetfulness, Jousse insisted that many residually oral texts signal recognizable roots in a once dominantly oral culture. There exist, in Jousse's view, definable similarities between means of communication, techniques of memorization, and faculties of imitation among peoples in continents as different as Asia, Africa, and the Americas sufficient to warrant the premise of universal anthropological laws.

Jousse perceived his life's work as being in tension with a humanistic scholarship that was almost exclusively based on written texts. He viewed himself as 'a resistance fighter' against human sciences, which in their bookish ethnicity and Eurocentrism had cancelled out a large amount of human history and knowledge. Not surprisingly, therefore, current ORALITY studies exhibit often strained relations with text-focused humanistic disciplines, above all classical philology and biblical studies.

Werner H. Kelber (Rice University, USA)

Further Reading

Jousse, Marcel. 1990. *The Oral Style*. Translated by Edgar R. Sienaert and Richard Whitaker. Columbia, MO: Garland.

Jousse, Marcel. 2000. *The Anthropology of Geste and Rhythm*. Translated by Edgard R. Sienaert and Joan Lucy Conolly. Durban: Mantis.

Jousse, Marcel. 2001a. *The Parallel Rhythmic Recitatives of the Rabbis of Israel*. Translated by Edgard R. Sienaert and Joan Lucy Conolly. Durban: Mantis.

Jousse, Marcel. 2001b. *Memory, Memorization and Memorisers in Ancient Galilee*. Translated and edited by Edgard R. Sienaert and Joan Lucy Conolly. Durban: Mantis.

Jousse, Marcel. 2004. *Holism and Education: Seven Lectures by Marcel Jousse*. Translated and edited by Edgard R. Sienaert and Joan Lucy Conolly. Durban: Mantis.

Jousse, Marcel. 2005. *The Fundamentals of Human Expression and Communication. Seven Lectures by Marcel Jousse*. Translated and edited by Edgard R. Sienaert and Joan Lucy Conolly. Durban: Mantis.

Jousse, Marcel. 2006. *Be Your Self! Seven Lectures on Colonisation, Self-colonisation and Decolonisation*. Translated and edited by Edgard R. Sienaert and Joan Lucy Conolly. Durban: Mantis.

Jousse, Marcel. 2006. *In search of coherence: Introducing Macel Jousse's Anthropology of Mimism*. Translated and edited by Edgard R. Sienaert. Eugene, OR: Pickwick.

Jubilees Jubilees is a second-century BCE Jewish text that serves as a prime example of REWRITTEN SCRIPTURE. The narrative follows closely the contents of Genesis and Exodus 1–19, sometimes apparently quoting these biblical texts verbatim but more often paraphrasing and interweaving them with material from other authoritative literary traditions or with new original material. Jubilees also strategically downplays or ignores some content from its base texts. This method of (re)presenting authoritative religious literature has been described by Géza Vermes as 'applied exegesis' (Vermes 1975). In other words, although Jubilees is strikingly similar to its base texts, it is evident that the purpose of the composition of Jubilees was not primarily to preserve the base texts, nor even to provide an interpretation that would resolve their philological or theological problems, but rather to affirm contemporary ideas and perspectives that could be best amplified by using those particular base texts.

The only extant complete copies of the book are recorded in Ge'ez, or ancient Ethiopic. Manuscript discoveries among the DEAD SEA SCROLLS have confirmed scholars' long-held suspicion that the text was first written in Hebrew. It was later translated from Hebrew into Greek and from Greek into Ethiopic and

Latin. VanderKam has concluded that Jubilees utilized Hebrew base texts that do not closely align with any of the known major manuscript traditions of the Hebrew Bible (e.g. MASORETIC Text, SEPTUAGINT, SAMARITAN PENTATEUCH). He has also determined that the Ge'ez translator(s) were conservative in their rendering of the Greek version (VanderKam 1977; 1989; 2000).

Jubilees was probably written between 170 and 150 BCE. A date much later in the second century is ruled out by the physical manuscript 4QJubileesa (dated 125–100 BCE on paleographical grounds) and by the fact that Jubilees is cited in the Damascus Document (CD). A date much earlier in the second century is probably ruled out by references to texts such as 1 ENOCH (particularly the Book of Dreams, 1 Enoch 83–90).

Jubilees as Rewritten Scripture

Notably, Jubilees claims the same level of divine inspiration as its base texts. The book purports to comprise the contents of the heavenly tablets dictated to Moses by the Angel of the Presence on Mt. Sinai. The first chapter actually claims to present a first-person address from the deity. This feature of the text is perhaps one of the reasons it enjoyed scriptural status in the Dead Sea sect, and possibly among other Jewish and Christian groups. Further evidence that Jubilees was treated as Scripture is evident from the fact that it is one of the most well-represented texts at Qumran (fourteen, possibly fifteen manuscripts) and is widely distributed among the caves (1, 2, 3, 4, and 11). Moreover, the text is cited as an authoritative source in the Damascus Document and may have served as an authoritative base text for other compositions such as 4QPseudo-Daniela–b and the Apocryphon of Jeremiah C. Jews and Christians continued to use the book in medieval times, though it only achieved canonical status in the Abyssinian (Ethiopic) Orthodox Church, where it remains a biblical book.

Several tendencies illuminate Jubilees' purpose in retelling large portions of Genesis and Exodus. First, Jubilees emphasizes the centrality of the Law revealed at Sinai. One way it does this is to rewrite patriarchal narratives in order to demonstrate that the patriarchs followed the Law even before it was revealed to Moses. For example, in *Jub.* 6.17-18, Noah observes *Shavu'ot*. Second, the writer(s) emphasize the righteousness of the patriarchs at points where Genesis and Exodus may leave some doubt about their character. For example, whereas Genesis implies that Abraham sold his wife to the Pharaoh (Gen. 12.10-16), Jubilees' version of the story claims that the Pharaoh stole Sarai (*Jub.* 13.10–15). Third, Jubilees uses similar strategies to emphasize the righteousness of God, again at points where Genesis and Exodus may have left some doubt. For example, while Genesis seems to imply that the deity's plan to blot out wickedness in Genesis 6 was a failure (despite the extreme measure of drowning nearly all living things, human wickedness returns in a matter of days), Jubilees emphasizes that the return of wickedness was brought about by demons, not humans (10.1-14).

Fourth, Jubilees repeatedly underscores the importance of chronology, a theme reflected in the central structure of the narrative and the source of the book's name. The text argues conspicuously for the use of a 364-day solar calendar (6.32-38), and the entire story is organized around a chronological scheme of Jubilee cycles (49-year periods). Fifth, Jubilees emphasizes the role of the priesthood. In the same way that the Sinaitic Laws are placed deep in Israel's prehistory, the central role of priests is traced all the way back to the first human being, Adam (3.27). A related emphasis concerns the identities and roles of female characters. On several occasions, the writer highlights the righteousness of the patriarchs and the integrity of the priestly family lines by providing detailed information about the wives of the patriarchs, including their names, genealogies, and acts of piety. Sixth, unlike its base texts, Jubilees tells its story with a specific end in mind. While eschatology is not as prominent as in the Hellenistic-era APOCALYPSES, it plays a role in Jubilees. For example, chapter 23 looks forward with anticipation to a utopian future in which the righteous will find peace, drive out their enemies, rejoice forever, see judgements against their enemies, and know that the Lord is an executor of judgement (cf. 23.29-31).

Jubilees and Scribal Skills

Aside from the insights the text provides as a premier instance of rewritten scripture, Jubilees provides important insights into conceptions of literate skills in at least some sectors of ancient Hellenistic Judaism. For example, while one presumes that the writer(s) of Jubilees did not think God would need written records to preserve information, the text nevertheless suggests that all events of human history (past and future) are recorded on tablets in heaven. A special human is given access to these tablets with the help of an angel.

Similarly, while the canonical biblical books clearly portray Moses as a lawgiver, Jubilees also highlights his skills as a SCRIBE. Neither Genesis nor Exodus make an explicit claim for Mosaic authorship, but Jubilees leaves no doubt that Moses is responsible for recording its content from the dictation of the heavenly tablets (e.g. 2.1-2). Indeed, Jubilees draws attention to the various patriarchs' prowess in the scribal arts on several occasions, including Enoch (4.16-26), Cainan (8.1-4), Abraham (11.14-17), and Jacob (19.14). The esteem in which literate skills were held can be seen in the writer's contrast of Jacob and Esau: 'Jacob learned writing, but Esau did not learn because he was a rustic man … he learned war, and all of his deeds were fierce' (19.14). The writer(s) also highlights how the power of the scribal arts can lead to danger. For example, Cainan learnt to sin by transcribing a stone that was inscribed by the Watchers before the flood. So literate skills were understood as a powerful and double-edged sword. They formed the primary means to unlock illicit powers of divination, but they also provided the means for the most righteous humans to serve the deity faithfully. For the writer(s) of Jubilees, the written word had the power to transcend time, a heavenly technology transferred to earth.

Bennie H. Reynolds, III (Medical University of South Carolina, USA)

Further Reading

Collins, John J. 2012. 'The Genre of the Book of Jubilees.' In *A Teacher for All Generations: Essays in Honor of James C. VanderKam*. Edited by Eric F. Mason. JSJS 153. Leiden: Brill, pp. 737–55.

Endres, John C. 1987. *Biblical Interpretation in the Book of Jubilees*. Catholic Biblical Quarterly Monograph Series 18. Washington, DC: Catholic University of America Press.

Kugel, James L. 2012. *A Walk through Jubilees: Studies in the Book of Jubilees and the World of Its Creation*. JSJS 156. Leiden: Brill.

Segal, Michael. 2007. *The Book of Jubilees: Rewritten Bible, Redaction, Ideology and Theology*. JSJS 117. Leiden: Brill.

VanderKam, James C. 1977. *Textual and Historical Studies in the Book of Jubilees*. HSM 14. Missoula: Scholars Press.

VanderKam, James C. 1989. *The Book of Jubilees*. 2 vols. Corpus Scriptorum Christianorum Orientalium 510–511; Scriptores Aethiopici 87–88. Louvain: Peeters.

Vermes, Géza. 1975. *Post-Biblical Jewish Studies*. SJLA 8. Leiden: Brill.

K

Kelber, Werner Werner Kelber is an NT scholar whose interests have ranged from NARRATIVITY in the Gospels to the implications of ancient media studies, through a consideration of ORAL TRADITION, scribality, and COLLECTIVE MEMORY theory. He has been a pioneer in introducing the interdisciplinary study of aspects of ORALITY to NT scholarship and in stimulating interest in this area. In *The Oral and the Written Gospel* (1983), Kelber challenged the form-critical paradigm of a process of an inevitable linear evolution of the JESUS TRADITION from simple, isolated oral units to the written Gospels (in particular Mark), demonstrating that such a model fails to appreciate the substantial media difference between oral tradition and written Gospel. Although Mark's Gospel shows a high degree of residual orality (as Kelber illustrates in some detail), the fact that it was committed to WRITING resulted in something fundamentally new. The written text allowed both a distancing from the immediate constraints of a live audience and novel narrative emplotment that resulted in a fundamental break with the preceding oral tradition. The act of writing constituted a deliberate decision by Mark to silence the voice of oral tradition, both through undermining the standing of the principal bearers of that tradition and by including only a minimal amount of sayings material and strictly subordinating them to his narrative design. In contrast, both Q and Paul sustained primarily oral sensibilities. In the course of making his case, Kelber identified several shortcomings in FORM CRITICISM's understanding of oral tradition. Such notions as *original form* and *laws of transmission*, on which the form-critical enterprise depended, have no place in the dynamics of the spoken word, since each fresh performance of the tradition is ORIGINAL.

Responding to criticism that his early work leaned too heavily on the now-discredited GREAT DIVIDE thesis, Kelber's subsequent research has emphasized the interaction between the oral and written media in ancient culture, while continuing to insist on the difference between them. While writing imparts a certain degree of fixity to a text, ancient MANUSCRIPTS were also subject to MOUVANCE (fluidity) in the process of transmission and copying. Kelber has also more explicitly embraced recent work on social memory (although it was already effectively present in the discussion of HOT MEMORY and preventive censorship in *The Oral and the Written Gospel*), as well as embracing JOHN MILES FOLEY's ideas on metonymic referentiality and the enabling reference of tradition, coining the term BIOSPHERE as a metaphor for the cultural-memorial-traditional environment in which acts of speaking and writing take place. Finally, Kelber has continued to argue that the dominant historical-critical paradigm in biblical studies remains too fettered by print culture assumptions, too ignorant of developments in other fields, and in urgent need of reform into an oral-scribal-memory-performance paradigm better suited to the media realities of the era it purports to study.

Eric Eve (Oxford University, UK)

Further Reading

Kelber, Werner. 1997. *The Oral and the Written Gospel*. Bloomington: Indiana University Press.

Kelber, Werner. 2013. *Imprints, Voiceprints and Footprints of Memory: Collected Essays of Werner Kelber*. SBLRBS. Atlanta: SBL Press.

L

Lector The term *lector* (Latin *lector*; Greek *anagnōstēs*) refers to a trained reader, usually of servile status, who performed public reading from a MANUSCRIPT. 'Public reading' denotes a reading event in which a text is read aloud directly from a manuscript with fitting vocal expression for one or several listeners (see READING CULTURE).

Lectors of servile status – either slaves or freedmen – regularly performed public readings in the Greek and Roman world. Such readings occurred in a number of settings, including lectors reading aloud for their masters (private settings), performances of public readings at literary gatherings and dinners (semi-private settings), and readings in recital halls and theatres (public settings). Lectors were highly specialized and performed public readings of literary prose and poetry writings, but rarely of DRAMA.

Although the manner in which lectors read aloud varied, some conventions of public reading are identifiable in literary and pictorial sources from the Greco-Roman world. The lector commonly was seated, held a manuscript in his hands, and read aloud from it with fitting vocal expression, yet without gestures and mimicry. Contemporary customs also called for a clear, faultless, and appropriate pronunciation of the text.

There were several good reasons for using a lector, even for those who could potentially manage a successful public reading. First, the task of deciphering close-knit, *scriptio* continua manuscripts and giving an appropriate vocal expression of the texts found in them was both complicated and laborious, calling for advanced EDUCATION and recurrent practice. Second, since audiences were unforgiving towards mistakes in delivery, public reading was always characterized by risk, even among friends. This risk may have been accentuated in early Christian communities (see PAULINE LITERATURE), in which mispronunciation and misinterpretation could result in expulsion or charges of heresy. Third, the act of reading someone else's composition aloud could be considered physical labour, which was best left to servants, such as lectors. Fourth, lectors were among the few who focused almost exclusively on performing professional, faultless, and pleasing public reading according to contemporary conventions. They thus provided wealthy men and women the means to enjoy literary writings in various settings without exposing themselves to exertion, risk, labour, or the need for regular practice.

Few people could manage public reading in early Christian communities. Next to lectors, who could either be members of the community in their own right or servants of a wealthy member, only a small group of well-educated upper-class men could perform the task. Community leaders, among whom such upper-class men were probably overrepresented, sometimes not only interpreted the text, but also performed the public reading of it. Early Christian communities managed without officially appointed readers until the late second century CE, when the function of public reading was turned into a church office.

Dan Nässelqvist (University of Gothenburg, Sweden)

Further Reading

Nässelqvist, Dan. 2015. *Public Reading in Early Christianity: Lectors, Manuscripts, and Sound in the Oral Delivery of John 1–4*. NovTSup 163. Leiden: Brill.

Starr, Raymond J. 1991. 'Lectores and Roman Reading.' *CJ* 86: 337–43.

Letters The twenty-one letters included in the NT make up a significant proportion of the earliest literary evidence of emerging Christianity. These letters relate to different groups and locations, the diversity of their cultures, their IDENTITIES and COLLECTIVE MEMORIES, and their disputes and conflicts. Although the NT traditions suggest that the Jesus movement emerged within the Palestinian working class, something about their experience and ancient media culture inspired fishermen and artisans to become authors who wrote or dictated impressive oratories and persuasive arguments, as we have letters attributed to Peter, John, James, Jude, and Paul. This letter writing bears witness to early developments in the literary culture of the Jesus movement, highlights the inter-connectedness of Christian communities, and provides insights into early Christian culture and WORSHIP.

Literary and Cultural Environment

Although the Greek word *epistolē* (epistle), was originally used for oral communications delivered by messengers, by the first century CE it was widely used for written communications, including military reports, communications between Roman officials in different parts of the empire (see VINDOLANDA), personal letters, art, and extended philosophical treatises. The Romans developed an early postal system that provided a support network for couriers. Similarly, the NT letters were delivered to their recipients by associates in ministry. These letters provide early literary evidence for communicative efforts by early Christian leaders, advising and encouraging communities of believers. It is unlikely that many of Jesus' earliest followers would have been able to read and write fluently (see LITERACY), but the apostolic leaders hired SCRIBES to help them with the task of letter production. For example, Paul's letters make reference to Tertius (Rom. 16.22) and Sosthenes as scribes, or co-authors (1 Cor. 1.1-2), and also mention his occasional personal handwriting for special emphasis (Gal. 6.11; see PAULINE LETTERS).

The NT letters, as written texts designed in many cases for mass delivery to presumably illiterate audiences, blur the boundaries of ORALITY and textuality, reading, and interpretation, as the written material was to be published and supplemented orally (cf. the roles of Phoebe in Rom. 16 and Tychicus in Eph. 6). Reflecting this mixed milieu, Paul's letter to the Galatians illustrates the incorporation of performance elements into written documents, such as metaphors and oratorical techniques (e.g. Gal. 3.19-20). The letters illustrate the early Christian use of both literature and oral communication, as letters endorse oral discourse (Eph. 4.20-24) and provide textual evidence for the extensive networking of early Christian communities and the circulation of epistolary literature (see 1 Pet. 1.1; Col. 4.16). Letters provide interesting evidence for early Christian media culture and how letter writing was received, including cases where the receipt of a letter led to a dispute. For example, 2 Pet. 3.15-16 refers to Paul's letters, their circulation, and interpretive disputes arising from their contents and complicated style.

While scribes were crucial for letter production, the messengers crucial to their delivery to different destinations, as well as their reading and exposition to different communities, were pivotal for these literary works and their literary history. It is because of their assumed apostolic origin that communities circulated and preserved these texts, leading ultimately to their canonization. Although their production, reading, and interpretation were probably fluid and contextualized, these texts became important for post-NT church fathers and their theological debates.

Despite the typical use of fragile PAPYRUS as a medium, considerable literary evidence of ancient letter writing has survived. The letters of PLATO and Aristotle give insights into ancient letter writing, which could combine autobiographical materials and personal concerns with philosophical ethics and persuasion. Like the letters of the NT, the writings of, for example, Cicero, Pliny the Younger, and Seneca not only provide insights into the epistolary genre but also serve as significant sources on social history. See, for example,

Pliny's *Letters* X.96, an exchange between Pliny, a provincial governor, and the Emperor Trajan that famously discusses the liminal legal status of Christians in the early second century. The literary fluidity of the genre is illustrated by Ovid's poetic *Letters of Heroines*, which would be of interest to students of gender in antiquity. The letters of Greco-Roman philosophers to their pupils provide material for comparison with the New Testament letters, particularly in their use of protrepsis and paraenesis (interchangeable terms for moral exhortation, of which the former is often thought to be aimed at conversion), rhetorical devices that are applied in the NT to calls for the re-socialization of 'nations' and a pious life of devotion to Israel's God and his Son, Christ. Another important feature of the NT epistles is their intertextuality, seen in allusions and quotations of authoritative traditional materials. This is seen most prominently in the use of Jewish Scriptures in the Pauline letters and Hebrews, as well as in the inclusion of early Christian HYMNS (Phil. 2.6-11), creeds (Eph. 4.4-6), and some colloquial sayings (Tit. 1.12).

Letters and/as Exhortation

Structurally, the NT letters follow contemporary literary conventions, including references to the credentials of their supposed authors in the beginning and acquaintances in different communities in the final greetings. The NT letters bear the names of reputable apostolic figures, but these individuals clearly relied on scribes (see Rom. 16.22; 1 Pet. 5.12) and their personal writing would have been an exception rather than the rule (see Gal. 6.11; 1 Cor. 16.21). The role of the amanuensis (a scribe) may explain some of the features typically assumed to indicate pseudonymity, such as differences in grammar and vocabulary between letters presumably produced by the same author. The concept of apostolic authorship (even if pseudonymous) is important, as the letters claim to pass on the legacy of apostles, giving their contents a stamp of authority rooted in association with Jesus himself. Most of the NT letters were written to communities of Jesus-followers of diverse ethnicities and are thus concerned with shaping and correcting their collective values, rituals, or behaviours. Others are more personal and aimed at individual recipients, like Philemon and the 'Elect Lady' mentioned in 2 John.

The NT letters sought to reduce cultural difference as they devalued polytheism and indigenous cultures, promoting instead a lifestyle that mimicked Jewish culture and its values. In the process, the belief that Jesus was Israel's promised messiah became gradually centralized in early Christian identity and COLLECTIVE MEMORY. While some of Paul's letters are critical of Jewish ritual praxis and challenge the validity of Jewish boundary markers such as Torah observance and CIRCUMCISION, Hebrews and James offer important data on the diversity of early Christian faith. Letters witness early Christianity's conservative social orientation in the diverse Roman empire, instructing believers to maintain established social conventions and hierarchies (cf. 1 Pet. 2–3; Col. 3–4; Eph. 5–6) and to respect authorities, even enduring hostility (Romans 13; 1 Pet. 2.11-17).

Recent studies on the Roman empire and Christian discourse have demonstrated how early Christians mimicked imperial language, developing a subaltern discourse that borrowed and played upon imperial concepts and terms like *lord*, *savior*, and *salvation* in counter-political rhetoric, promoting Jesus as the peaceful, yet ultimately superior, king. Although such concepts are today widely viewed as 'theological', their origins were political. Recent interdisciplinary scholarship drawing on the social sciences and literary theory offers vital perspectives for understanding social influences in the NT letters (both in the antiquity and present day), and their contribution to complex questions of class, ethnicity, gender, and sexuality.

Minna Shkul (University of Sheffield, UK)

Further Reading

Ascough, Richard S., Philip A. Harland, and John S. Kloppenborg. 2012. *Associations in the Greco-Roman World: A Sourcebook.* Waco: Baylor University Press.

Jenkins, Thomas E. 2006. *Intercepted Letters: Epistolarity and Narrative in Greek and Roman Literature*. Lanham: Lexington Books.
Klauck, Hans-Josef. 2006. *Ancient Letters and the New Testament: A Guide to Context and Exegesis*. Waco: Baylor University.
Marshall, Howard, Stephen Travis and Ian Paul. 2011. *Exploring the New Testament: Letters and Revelation*. Volume 2. 2nd edn. London: SPCK.
Muir, John, 2008. *Life and Letters in the Ancient Greek World*. London: Routledge.
Reasoner, Mark. 2013. *Roman Imperial Texts: A Sourcebook*. Minneapolis: Fortress.
Stowers, Stanley K. 1986. *Letter Writing in Greco-Roman Antiquity*. Library of Early Christianity. Philadelphia, PA: Westminster.
Segovia, Fernando F., and R. S. Sugirtharajah, eds. 2009. *A Postcolonial Commentary on the New Testament Writings*. Bible & Post-colonialism. London: T&T Clark.
Taplin, Oliver, ed. 2000. *Literature in the Greek and Roman World: A New Perspective*. Oxford: Oxford University.
Tucker, J. Brian, and Coleman A. Baker, eds. 2014. *T&T Clark Handbook to Social Identity in the New Testament*. London: T&T Clark.

Libraries See ARCHIVES.

Literacy In general terms, literacy refers to the skills of reading and WRITING. Although largely taken for granted in modern industrialized societies, these skills were rare in antiquity. Ancient cultures lacked anything like a widespread, publicly funded elementary EDUCATION system that could reach a majority of the populace, whose agrarian lives largely did not require the abilities to read and write. Reflecting on these cultural conditions and allowing for minor fluctuations at different locations and times, William Harris famously proposed a 10 per cent overall literacy rate for the Greek and Roman worlds (1989: 22, 272, 328–9). Others have critically evaluated and, offering their own nuances to the arguments and conclusions, generally affirmed Harris' proposal for majority illiteracy in detailed studies on ancient Israel (Carr 2005: 116, 270n.51; Niditch 1996: 3940, 58–9; Rollston 2010: 127–35, esp. 128n.1) and Second Temple, Bar Kokhba era, and rabbinic Judaism (Hezser 2001: 496; Jaffee 2001: 15 n. 8; Keith 2011: 72–85; Wise 2015: 345–55), as well as early Christianity (Gamble 1995: 4–6; Keith 2009: 54–94). The majority opinion among scholars of the Bible and its cognate disciplines is therefore firmly that the biblical cultures were overwhelmingly illiterate. These findings contradict the claims of Josephus and Philo for universal Jewish literacy and education in the first century CE (Josephus, *Against Apion* 1.12 §60; 2.25 §204; Philo, *Embassy to Gaius* 16.115-16). One must, however, consider both the apologetic nature of their claims and the upper-class lifestyle that Josephus and Philo experienced as educated individuals. There is little evidence to suggest that their upbringings were the common experience for most Jews (or any other groups) in the ancient world.

Also differing markedly from the modern context, reading and writing skills were separately acquired and separately utilized in antiquity. Reading instruction preceded writing instruction (Manilius, *Astronomica* 2.755–761), while intricate copying and compositional writing were introduced at the further stages of literate education (Dionysius of Halicarnassus, *On Literary Composition* 2.229). Since education was not compulsory or subsidized, students remained in school only as long as needed to acquire specific skills required by their position in life. Even among the privileged minority, very few attained the capacity to write for themselves. As a result, formal writing ability was even rarer than reading ability, limited primarily to those with advanced scribal training. Yet, as the extant Greco-Roman Egyptian school papyri (see PAPYRUS) and OSTRACA show, a more rudimentary form of writing instruction sometimes preceded reading instruction, wherein students learnt to copy mechanically letters of the alphabet and their personal names (Cribiore 2001: 167; see ABECEDARY). Quintilian and Seneca both refer to this method, by which students were taught to trace letters that they could not recognize as syllables or words (Quintilian, *Institutes* 1.1.27; Seneca, *Letters from a Stoic* 94.15). As Cribiore notes, this evidence reveals that one of the clear aims of ancient education – in full knowledge that most students would not progress beyond initial instruction – was simply to enable the student to sign his or her own name and to participate in literate culture in at least a marginal way (1996: 4–5, 7, 10).

Documentary papyri frequently reveal the lacunae that such a meagre literate education could fill. For example, one may consider the Babaṭha cache from the time of the Bar Kokhba Revolt (early second century CE), which was discovered in a cave alongside several bodies, one of which was presumably Babatha herself. These MANUSCRIPTS include frequent statements that a SCRIBE had to sign Babatha's name for her because she was illiterate (P. Yadin 15.35–36; 16.35; 22.34). Similar examples occur in the Bar Kokhba documents with which Babatha's documents were found (see Wise 2015: 1–7, 36–61), in the Oxyrhynchus papyri (e.g. P. Oxy. 1636.45-46), and elsewhere throughout the papyrological record (see further Kraus 2007: 107–26).

Since very few students progressed through all the stages of literate education, literacy existed in shades and gradations that reflected the time and depth of the individual student's learning. At the lower end of the spectrum were those whose education did not progress beyond the acquisition of signature literacy, the capacity to reproduce their names. Similar to these individuals were a group, identified in the papyri with the term *slow writer* (*bradeōs graphōn*), who could mechanically reproduce letters without being able to read what they were writing (see especially Kraus 2007: 131–45). Perhaps the most famous of these is Petaus, a late-second-century CE Egyptian village scribe. While practising his formula for document reception by copying it over and over, Petaus omitted an initial vowel on a verb and then repeated the mistake thereafter, suggesting that he was reproducing mechanically each line from the previous but could not read well enough to catch the error (P. Petaus 121 [P. Köln inv. 328]). Slow writers fell into a broader class that scholars refer to as *semi-literate* because they are neither strictly literate nor illiterate. Another semi-literate slow writer is the early Christian author of the Shepherd of Hermas, who claims he must copy a little book letter by letter since he cannot identify syllables (*Vision* 2.1.4). More advanced than Petaus or Hermas are Spintharo and Tiro, the scribes of Cicero. The former could follow dictation syllable by syllable while the latter could follow whole sentences (Cicero, *Letters to Atticus* 13.25).

Another type of literate skill is craftsman's literacy, which refers to the literate abilities a given labourer needed in order to conduct his or her trade. Petaus' ability to reproduce his reception formula in his capacity as a village scribe represents a type of craftsman's literacy, though this term also refers to actual labourers who could not have read Homer or Torah but could follow alphabetic/numeric building instructions, such as the masons at Herod's palace at Masada (see Millard 2001: 122, 125). In the Hebrew Bible, the master-craftsmen Bezalel and Oholiab are portrayed as displaying craftsman's literacy when they carve 'Holy to the Lord' on the holy diadem (Exod. 39.30 MT).

No matter how advanced a craftsman's literate skills became, however, they could not rival the social authority granted to those individuals in the Jewish and Christian tradition whose education focused upon Scripture and thus secured for them scribal literacy. Scribal literacy refers to the ability to read, compose, copy, and revise an authoritative, sacrosanct text and thus serve as a TEXT-BROKER for the majority of illiterates who revered that text. Scribal literacy in the biblical periods was the possession of scribes, priests, Pharisees, Sadducees, and other teachers who provided the masses points of access to the holy texts. Many biblical leaders are portrayed in scribal-literate terms, and these examples indicate that scribal literacy in the Jewish context revolved primarily (though not exclusively) around the public reading and interpretation of the law, which seems to have been the focus of scribal-literate JEWISH EDUCATION (Hezser 2001: 68, 474). A very clear example is Ezra, who reads publicly the Law while Levites interpret for the audience (Neh. 8:1-8). Sir.

3.24–39.1 praises the scribe who studies the Law in contrast to the craftsman and other manual labourers who work with their hands. In his prologue, Sirach provides one of the clearest images of scribal literacy enabling the educated to serve as text brokers: 'Now, those who read the Scriptures must not only themselves understand them, but must also as lovers of learning be able through the spoken and written word to help the outsiders' (Sir. 1.1 NRSV). Significantly, the Gospels portray Jesus contradictorily as both a craftsman who is rejected as a SYNAGOGUE teacher (Mk 6.3//Mt. 13.55) and as a scribal-literate teacher who reads publicly in a synagogue (Lk. 4.16-20). John 7.15 indicates that some of Jesus' audiences were confused as to whether he held scribal literacy (see further Keith 2011). Reading abilities, like writing abilities, existed in gradations, and the evidence reveals that public reading of Scripture was a particularly valued skill that undergirded one's reputation as a textual authority (see TORAH READING). This was especially the case in the Second Temple and rabbinic periods, when biblical Hebrew was no longer a daily language for most Jews. At Qumran, public reading was so significant that 4Q266 prohibits a member of the assembly from reading Torah publicly unless he can do so without stumbling over the words (5.2.1-4).

Several social facets of literacy in the biblical periods raise a number of implications for modern interpreters of ancient Jewish and Christian texts, four of which will be highlighted here. First, the evidence reveals a literate division not only between social classes, but also between genders. The literate individuals who appear in the evidence are overwhelmingly male, reflecting the patriarchal societies of the biblical periods. Female literacy is not unknown; Origen, for example, was said to employ highly literate female scribes capable of calligraphic writing (Eusebius, *Ecclesiastical History* 6.23; Jerome, *On Illustrious Men* 61). Nevertheless, female literacy was rare compared to male literacy and, where evidence is available, it is clear that males served as the authors and editors of the texts that came to form the Jewish and Christian Scriptures. When considering those texts, therefore, modern readers must be aware that their portrayals of women – laudatory and misogynistic alike – inherently reflect the perspective of the masculine authors and the cultures from which they wrote, wherein women were often treated as property.

Second, one must keep in mind the multilingual nature of all periods of biblical history. Individuals could hold various literate abilities in different languages. Thus, for example, it is not entirely clear whether the reference to the early Christian LECTOR Aurelius Ammonius as 'illiterate' in P. Oxy. 2673 indicates that he could not read Greek (but could read Coptic), could not write Greek, or was entirely illiterate, all of which have been suggested by scholars.

Third, literate skills intertwined with social class in a multifaceted way depending upon the specific community in which those skills were used. For example, the ability to write in one's own hand was prized by some members of the elite class (Cicero, *Letters to Atticus* 2.23; Quintilian, *Institutes* 1.1.28–29), perhaps the reason that Paul sometimes calls attention to writing Greek in his own hand (1 Cor. 16:21; Gal. 6:11; Phlm. 19; cf. also Col. 4:18; 2 Thess. 3:17). Nevertheless, as these examples show – by implicitly drawing attention to Paul's use of an amanuensis for the rest of the writing task – writing was a prized skill that the educated could avoid by dictating to a scribe, which was normal practice (see Jer. 45.1; Cicero, *Letters to Atticus* 13.25; Pliny the Younger, *Letters* 3.5; Eusebius, *Ecclesiastical History* 6.23; Augustine, *The Retractions Prologue* 2). That is, the true mark of the educated elite was the possession of rare literate abilities that they employed only when they chose to do so, but could readily assign to others when they wished. In this sense, the act of writing, and especially rote copying, was often viewed as the work of slaves or freedmen copyists and thus disparaged (*Rhetorica ad Herennium* 4.4.6). Both Jewish and Christian scribes, however, came to differ starkly from this opinion, viewing the act of copying their holy texts as divine work (b. *Soṭah* 20a; see also Philo, *On the Special Laws* 4.160, 163) or even salvific work

(*Martyrdom of Polycarp* 22.3), no doubt reflecting the fact that their tasks consisted of scribal literacy and thus the growing sacralization of Scripture.

Fourth, literacy is not textuality (Stock 1983: 7), which is to say that the simple presence of written texts in antiquity was not necessarily a measure of the number of people who could read them, nor that the ability to read them was essential to their social value. A majority of the populace was illiterate throughout biblical history, but that does not mean that people were unfamiliar with texts, their contents, or their social power. Scholars have frequently confused textuality and literacy in claiming that esteem for sacred texts led to higher literacy rates among Jews than other ancient populations, a claim that cannot be substantiated. Frequent liturgical reading of the texts, particularly in the later periods in synagogues and churches, familiarized communities with their traditions. Furthermore, numerous pieces of evidence exist to indicate that illiterate individuals regularly came into contact with texts. For example, Babatha likely could not read, and certainly could not write, the contracts she held in her possession, but valued them to the extent that she literally took them to her death. Similarly, from an earlier period, Isa. 29.12 imagines a scenario whereby a text is presented to an illiterate person, who responds, 'I do not know a book'. In this sense, modern scholars should not confuse knowledge about texts and their contents with ability to read those texts oneself.

Overall, scholars should consider the biblical cultures highly illiterate but also highly textual. This reality underscores the important social role of scribal-literate text brokers in these societies and thus the important manners in which literacy intertwined with sociopolitical power in ancient Judaism and Christianity. It is no coincidence that the most authoritative interpreters in these communities, with very few exceptions, were from the educated class.

Chris Keith (St. Mary's University, UK)

Further Reading

Cribiore, Raffaella. 1996. *Writing, Teachers, and Students in Graeco-Roman Egypt*. American Studies in Papyrology 36. Atlanta: Scholars Press.

Cribiore, Raffaella. 2001. *Gymnastics of the Mind: Greek Education in Hellenistic and Roman Egypt*. Princeton: Princeton University Press.

Carr, David M. 2005. *Writing on the Tablet of the Heart: Origins of Scripture and Literature*. New York: Oxford University Press.

Gamble, Harry Y. 1995. *Books and Readers in the Early Church: A History of Early Christian Texts*. New Haven: Yale University Press.

Harris, William. 1989. *Ancient Literacy*. Cambridge, MA: Harvard University Press.

Hezser, Catherine. 2001. *Jewish Literacy in Roman Palestine*. TSAJ 81. Tübingen: Mohr Siebeck.

Jaffee, Martin S. 2001. *Torah in the Mouth: Writing and Oral Tradition in Palestinian Judaism, 200 CE–400 CE*. New York: Oxford University Press.

Keith, Chris. 2009. *The Pericope Adulterae, the Gospel of John, and the Literacy of Jesus*. New Testament Tools, Studies, and Documents 38. Leiden: Brill.

Keith, Chris. 2011. *Jesus' Literacy: Scribal Culture and the Teacher from Galilee*. Library of Historical Jesus Studies 8/ LNTS 413. London: T&T Clark.

Kraus, Thomas J. 2007. *Ad fontes: Original Manuscripts and Their Significance for Studying Early Christianity*. Texts and Editions for New Testament Study 3. Leiden: Brill.

Millard, Alan. 2001. *Reading and Writing in the Time of Jesus*. The Biblical Seminar 69. Sheffield: Sheffield Academic Press.

Niditch, Susan. 1996. *Oral World and Written Word: Ancient Israelite Literature*. Louisville: Westminster John Knox.

Rollston, Christopher A. 2010. *Writing and Literacy in the World of Ancient Israel: Epigraphic Evidence from the Iron Age*. SBL Archaeology and Biblical Studies 11. Atlanta: SBL Press.
Stock, Brian. 1983. *The Implications of Literacy: Written Language and Models of Interpretation in the Eleventh and Twelfth Centuries*. Princeton: Princeton University Press.
Wise, Michael Owen. 2015. *Language and Literacy in Roman Judaea: A Study of the Bar Kokhba Documents*. AYBRL. New Haven: Yale University Press.

Long-Term/Short-Term Memory The categories short- and long-term memory are used to differentiate the temporary holding of information in personal awareness (short-term memory) from its storage for later recall (long-term memory). Knowing the processes, capacities, and limitations of these types of memory can help us form a realistic picture of how biblical material was remembered and transmitted (orally and in WRITING) in the ancient world, and how memories of the information behind and within biblical texts were transformed in the process of storage, recall, and transmission.

Overall, human personal memory (see COGNITIVE/PERSONAL MEMORY) is not structured to function as an archive that preserves individual items of information unchanged. Instead, experiences are integrated into an associative map of reality that helps individuals interpret later events and respond efficiently and appropriately to them. In the integration process, memories tend to be biased in the direction of what we already know, and general memories tend to be more reliable than specific ones (e.g. we are more likely to retain an accurate general impression of our total secondary school experience than to retain accurate knowledge of the details of any particular event).

Neurobiological research has illuminated many of the physical processes by which interpretation, consolidation, and storage of experience take place, but its implications remain subject to empirical validation: can/do individuals actually perform acts of memory in ways that neurobiological assumptions would imply? Thus, classic studies of memory remain relevant.

Short-Term Memory

Sensory recall is the shortest-term form of memory, with impulses lasting less than a second in the brain before being converted to a form that allows more permanent storage and manipulation. This form of memory is utilized in a functional way, as, for example, when we belatedly decode a sentence that we did not understand as we first heard it.

Short-term memory proper is illustrated by the process of remembering an unfamiliar telephone number as we dial it. The sensory impulse of seeing or hearing the number normally fades in seconds, but can be extended if we focus attention and mentally rehearse the material, as in repeating a phone number to ourselves, thus giving it a more permanent form. Short-term memory is closely related to *working memory*, in which the brain holds an image of what we are consciously thinking about. Its capacity has been estimated at 7 ± 2 items, but this varies between persons and with the type of material and how it is organized. The precise neurological mechanisms of short-term memory probably vary with modality (e.g. visual and auditory short-term memory may not be exactly the same).

Deliberate memorization techniques use association and rehearsal in short-term memory to facilitate storage in long-term memory. Practice trains the brain in ways that facilitate the conversion of inputs to long-term storage.

Long-Term Memory

Long-term memories emerge as the impulses and formations of short-term memory are sorted for more permanent storage. Long-term memory takes several forms. *Implicit memory* is formed and functions outside of consciousness, although we may be conscious of its effects. It includes procedural memory (e.g. how to ride a bicycle), associations learnt in very early childhood, and some aspects of traumatic memory. *Semantic memory* contains consciously accessible general information about the world. It allows us to understand language, name the current prime minister, find our way through familiar neighbourhoods, and know that apples are edible. *Episodic memory* pertains to particular events, including those of our own lives. Semantic and episodic memory can be grouped together under the heading of consciously accessible *declarative memory*. As with short-term memory, different modalities may be processed in slightly different ways.

Implicit memories are the most durable over time, while episodic memory is the least reliable and the most subject to change. Episodic memories are subject to cross-contamination of details from similar events or/and from information imported from general knowledge of the world – if three similar experiences took place in a movie theatre, the details of all three tend to blend together, along with general semantic memories of all movie theatres. The power of suggestion, as when an attorney asks leading questions, is an example of how episodic memories can be modified: details suggested in the cross-examination become attached to the original episodic memory.

Neurobiologically, the formation of declarative memories is a complex and long-term process involving multiple brain areas. The hippocampus plays a critical role in the earlier stages of storage and recall, but well-established memories seem accessible in the cortex even when the hippocampus is damaged.

Emotional tagging plays an important role in the establishment and functioning of several types of long-term memory. In general, the stronger the emotional associations, the more easily we form and recall memories. However, extreme physical or emotional stress (trauma) may enhance implicit learning while interfering with normal episodic memory, so that a person later experiences profound anxiety in certain situations but cannot remember why, or suffers flashbacks in which past events seem to be occurring in the present.

Memory and Biblical Studies

While biblical scholars have only recently begun to engage research on PERSONAL/COGNITIVE MEMORY (e.g. McIver 2011), its concerns are significant to a number of key problems in understanding the relationships between events, ORAL TRADITIONS about them, texts produced on the basis of them, and manuscript traditions (involving SCRIBAL MEMORY). Studies of personal memory also overlap at many points with the concerns of COLLECTIVE MEMORY, inasmuch as collective memories are formed in dialogue with, and significantly influence, the ways that individuals recall their personal and group past. The following questions seem particularly fruitful for future research.

First, how do the biases of short- and long-term memory affect oral transmission? Concerns here include ways that categorical biases (e.g. the tendency to confuse similar-sounding words) might affect the transmission of information in both oral and manuscript traditions; how an individual's existing cognitive maps (which naturally differ for individuals with different cultural backgrounds and personal histories) influence their initial hearing/sorting of information; and, how the individual's existing mental maps modify material at both the point of storage in long-term memory and the point of recall.

Second, how do the biases of short- and long-term memory affect scribal transmission? Concerns here include ways that reading mistakes, whether of the eye or ear, impact the entry of data into a SCRIBE's short-term memory; and, the types of writing mistakes (memory shifts between intake and inscription) that might emerge in the course of 'copying' a manuscript.

Third, how do the mechanisms and characteristic errors of verbatim learning (which will presumably be invoked at the point when a tradition has come to be regarded as authoritative) vary from those of simply recalling something because we found it interesting (the most likely approach in earlier phases of transmission)? For example, how would oral accounts of a traditional story of one of Israel's heroes, performed from memory, vary mnemonically from instances where a scribe recalls a clause from the Law of Moses that was memorized from a manuscript?

Fourth, and finally here, how does the assimilation of scriptural tradition into memory affect interpretation and the memory of other events in history and personal life? As a related concern, one might ask how Jesus' associates and the early Christians interpreted his life and teachings within cognitive SCHEMA heavily influenced by the Scriptures of Israel.

Marti J. Steussy (Christian Theological Seminary, USA)

Further Reading

Baddeley, Alan D. 1999. *Essentials of Human Memory*. Hove, UK: Psychology Press.
LeDoux, Joseph. 2002. *The Synaptic Self: How Our Brains Become Who We Are*. New York: Viking Penguin.
McIver, Robert K. 2011. *Memory, Jesus, and the Synoptic Gospels*. SBL RBS. Atlanta: SBL Press.
Schacter, Daniel L. 2001. *The Seven Sins of Memory: How the Mind Forgets and Remembers*. Boston: Houghton Mifflin Company.

Lord, Albert Albert Bates Lord (1912–91) was an American scholar whose work in FOLKLORE and comparative literature was central to the development of the methodological approach now commonly known as oral-formulaic theory. He initially worked alongside his teacher MILMAN PARRY, who had himself earlier laid the philological foundation for this approach through his examination of Homeric poetry. Lord later expanded oral-formulaic theory far beyond his mentor's original ideas so that it would eventually become applicable to the study of hundreds of ancient, medieval, and modern traditions.

Shortly after completing his AB in classics at Harvard, Lord accompanied Parry to Yugoslavia, where from June 1934 to September 1935 he acted as Parry's assistant during the collection of hundreds of performances by GUSLARI, singers of South Slavic epic who were for the most part illiterate yet able to produce SONGS that were sometimes several thousand transcribed verses in length. By means of these performances and also through conversations with the singers themselves, Parry hoped to provide real-world, comparative evidence for the ORAL TRADITION he had hypothesized to be on display in Homer's *Iliad* and *Odyssey* – perhaps most apparently within its recurrent and stylized phraseology that he had termed 'formulaic'. However, Parry's untimely death late in 1935 occurred before he could complete a full analysis of the collected materials, and it fell largely to Lord to carry out Parry's intended comparative programme.

Lord began this work by producing a series of articles addressing specific features of Homeric poetry (including possible performance units, narrative inconsistencies, and enjambement tendencies) that could be productively compared to their South Slavic oral epic counterparts. But it was his dissertation – originally produced in 1949 in conjunction with his PhD in comparative literature from Harvard – that was to become the centre around which a new discipline focused on oral tradition would ultimately form. Published in 1960 as *The Singer of Tales*, this seminal work is broken into two parts: 'The Theory' and 'The Application'. The first of these two sections is often assessed as the more important; in it, Lord draws primarily from his fieldwork among the South Slavic singers in order to establish many key features and practices found within oral-traditional poetry. Lord's focus throughout is on the ways in which the ambient tradition enables the individual singer's composition in performance. Among detailed explanations of structural units such as the FORMULA AND THEME (with both of these concepts taken from Parry's work but greatly expanded upon by Lord in relation to the South Slavic poetic arena in particular), Lord discusses how singers train over time to learn their craft, the ways in which textualization of a song may or may not affect its tradition-bearers, and the variation allowable within a traditional system that might at first glance seem rather rigid and overly systematic.

However, as significant as these theoretical explorations and observations were – not least because they demonstrated how singers could perform their lengthy epics without the influence of LITERACY or a need for verbatim memorization – it is arguably the second section of *The Singer of Tales* and the methodology it espouses that gave rise to Lord's most enduring legacy. Here, he takes the knowledge obtained from the South Slavic evidence (much of which Lord published along with collaborators as parts of Harvard University Press' Serbo-Croatian Heroic Songs series and in a volume entitled *Serbo-Croatian Folk Songs*) and applies it directly towards understanding several other European epics that survive only in textualized rather than oral form: Homer's *Iliad* and *Odyssey*, the Old English *Beowulf*, the Old French *Song of Roland*, and the medieval Greek *Digenis Akritas*. Though previous scholars had already undertaken specific analyses of individual elements within many of these poems in terms of their possible oral and/or traditional nature (see Foley 1988, esp. chaps. 2 and 4), Lord was the first to commit wholeheartedly to the comparative method in order to explicate how larger narrative elements such as THEMES and story patterns contribute not only to the compositional structure of these epics but also to the meanings contained within them.

The lasting effect of this commitment to comparative analysis cannot be overstated, as it was the primary force that drove Lord's scholarship – and in turn that of others – for many years to come. Lord's own work would eventually touch on dozens of traditions from around the world. His two later volumes, published in 1991 (*Epic Singers* and *Oral Tradition*) and posthumously in 1995 (*The Singer Resumes the Tale*), include discussions of central Asian, Finnish, and Bulgarian epic – in addition to the epics already explored in *The Singer of Tales* – as well as non-epic traditions such as Anglo-American folk balladry and Latvian *dainas*. Lord also helped broaden the field's focus to include even non-poetic, literary texts such as the Gospels (see, for instance, Lord 1978) that retain multiple connections to oral tradition. Through these efforts that lasted for more than half a century, Lord's work provided a theoretical framework and comparative model useful to countless scholars for the interpretation and analysis of an ever-widening array of texts and traditions from around the world.

R. Scott Garner (Rhodes College, USA)

Further Reading

Culley, Robert C. 1986. 'Oral Tradition and Biblical Studies.' *Oral Tradition* 1(1): 30–65.

Foley, John Miles. 1988. *The Theory of Oral Composition: History and Methodology*. Bloomington: Indiana University Press.

Grey, Morgan E., Mary Louise Lord and John Miles Foley. 2010. 'A Bibliography of Publications by Albert Bates Lord.' *Oral Tradition* 25(2): 497–504.

Lord, Albert B. 1960. *The Singer of Tales*. Cambridge, MA: Harvard University Press.

Lord, Albert B. 1978. 'The Gospels as Oral Traditional Literature.' In *The Relationships among the Gospels: An Interdisciplinary Dialogue*. Edited by William O. Walker, Jr. San Antonio, TX: Trinity University Press, pp. 33–91.

Lord, Albert B. 1991. *Epic Singers and Oral Tradition*. Ithaca, NY: Cornell University Press.

Lord, Albert B. 1995. *The Singer Resumes the Tale*. Edited by Mary Louise Lord. Ithaca, NY: Cornell University Press.

Lord, Albert B., and Béla Bartók, eds. and trans. 1951. *Serbo-Croatian Folk Songs*. New York: Columbia University Press.

Parry, Milman, Albert B. Lord and David E. Bynum, colls., eds., and trans. 1953-present. *Serbo-Croatian Heroic Songs (Srpskohrvatske junačke pjesme)*. Cambridge, MA: Harvard University.

M

Manuscript A manuscript is a handwritten copy of an ancient literary or documentary text. Whereas the term *text* may refer to a recognizable tradition that occurs in multiple copies (e.g. the Gospel of John), the term *manuscript* refers to an individual copy of that work (e.g. P^{66}). Scholars sometimes use the term CHIROGRAPH when referring to a manuscript when they wish to emphasize the dynamics of transcribing the tradition by hand. Manuscripts occurred in the bookroll (SCROLL) and CODEX format and could be written on PAPYRUS or PARCHMENT.

Manuscripts serve an important role in ancient media studies, especially as they relate to the study of the Bible and the cultures surrounding it, for at least two reasons. First, in earlier generations of scholarship, manuscripts served as a foil for scholars who emphasized the oral nature of ancient transmission. From this perspective, the textualization of a tradition – the WRITING of a tradition on a manuscript – was viewed as the end of an interactive process of oral communication that featured storytellers who performed the tradition before a live audience. Because the act of writing was understood as a way of replacing the living oral storyteller with an inanimate bookroll or codex, manuscript tradition was understood as fixed or stable in contrast to more free and fluid ORAL TRADITION. To cite an influential example, WERNER KELBER's seminal study *The Oral and the Written Gospel* (1983) juxtaposed the 'written regimentation of textualization' (1983: 146) with 'the fluid medium of orality' (1983: 202) and 'free-floating oral speech' (1983: 209), an approach now sometimes referred to as the GREAT DIVIDE model of the relationship between ORALITY and writing. More recent studies, however, have problematized this characterization of manuscript tradition. Keith (2011), for example, argues that manuscripts can also function in a performance mode, whereby the writing author is influenced by a perceived audience. Similarly, Kirk (2008) has argued that manuscript tradition exhibits a necessary degree of instability, alongside a relative stability, due to the fact that it is embedded in particular historical and social contexts. In the very least, the numerous textual variants attested in manuscript tradition of the Hebrew Bible and NT point to the fact that manuscripts never fixed the traditions they encoded in an ultimate sense.

As these more recent developments demonstrate, a second manner in which manuscripts have featured prominently in media-critical studies relates to contemporary understandings of the sociological and hermeneutical dimensions of manuscript culture. Egyptologist JAN ASSMANN (2006), for example, has highlighted what manuscripts contribute hermeneutically to the transmission process that oral tradition alone cannot provide: written texts, unlike spoken words, enable tradents to pass the tradition over space and time, with the inscriber of the manuscript eventually connecting with a reader who may live centuries after the initial textualization of the tradition and on the opposite side of the globe. In this respect, the written manuscript allows the tradition to detach temporally from the oral performer and her/his immediate listening audience and resonate in a broader context that Assmann refers to as the 'extended situation' (2006: 103) (see CULTURAL MEMORY). The potential of manuscripts to speak to extended situations plays a primary role in the development of CANONS of holy texts. In a slightly different vein, Hurtado has argued for studying manuscripts as the earliest artefacts of Christianity (2006). He demonstrates that various features of the early Christian manuscripts, such as the width of their margins or their employment of *nomina sacra* and other readers' aids, offer clues to the social realities of the Christians who created or used this medium.

Manuscripts are thus now viewed by media critics of ancient Israel and early Christianity as material artefacts in their own right, whose significance includes, but extends beyond, the texts they transmitted.

Chris Keith (St. Mary's University, UK)

Further Reading

Assmann, Jan. 2006. *Religion and Cultural Memory*. Translated by Rodney Livingstone. Cultural Memory in the Present. Stanford: Stanford University Press.

Hurtado, Larry W. 2006. *The Earliest Christian Artifacts: Manuscripts and Christian Origins*. Grand Rapids: Eerdmans.

Keith, Chris. 2011. 'A Performance of the Text: The Adulteress's Entrance into John's Gospel.' In *The Fourth Gospel in First-Century Media Culture*. Edited by Anthony Le Donne and Tom Thatcher. European Studies on Christian Origins/Library of New Testament Studies 426. London: T&T Clark, pp. 49–69.

Kelber, Werner H. 1983. *The Oral and the Written Gospel: The Hermeneutics of Speaking in the Synoptic Tradition, Mark, Paul, and Q*. Voices in Performance and Text. Bloomington: Indiana University Press.

Kirk, Alan. 2008. 'Manuscript Tradition as a tertium quid: Orality and Memory in Scribal Practices.' In *Jesus, the Voice, and the Text: Beyond The Oral and the Written Gospel*. Edited by Tom Thatcher. Waco: Baylor University Press, pp. 215–34.

Masoretic Text The Tiberian Masoretic tradition (MT) is the source of the medieval MANUSCRIPTS that form the base of today's editions of the Hebrew Bible (e.g. BHS). Though there are thousands of medieval Masoretic manuscripts, the principal witnesses to this tradition are Codex St. Petersburg (Leningrad), National Library of Russia, Firkovitch I, B 19a (dated 1009 CE) and the Aleppo Codex (tenth century CE; the text selected by Maimonides as the model codex of Ben Asher). The Masoretic tradition consists of the consonantal text, the vocalization of the text, the accent system, specific layouts of the text, and other paratextual features in and around the text. Collectively, these features reveal the MT's status as a written text developed in the context of, and attempting to codify and support, an ongoing tradition of oral reading and public performance of the biblical content.

The consonantal text (text written with only consonant letters, no vowels) is the base layer of the MT (i.e. proto-MT) and its date of origin can only be hypothesized, with suggestions ranging between the fifth and third centuries BCE. The earliest evidence of biblical manuscripts (ca. 250 BCE) from around the Dead Sea attest to the proto-MT. Forty-three fragments found at Masada, Wadi Sdeir, Wadi Murabba'at, Naḥal Se'elim, and NAḤAL ḤEVER (twenty fragments are unprovenanced) attest the proto-MT almost identically and exclusively (e.g. MasPs[a]). The texts from Masada are dated between 50 BCE and 30 CE, while texts from the other sites date between 20 BCE and 115 CE. Of about two hundred and twelve biblical manuscripts found at Qumran (250 BCE–68 CE), fifty-seven exhibit an exclusive agreement to MT (e.g. 1QIsa[b]). Five texts from the third to eighth centuries CE evidence the consonantal text of MT, along with tens of thousands of biblical fragments discovered in the Cairo Genizah dating from the ninth century CE. Furthermore, the pre-hexaplaric and hexaplaric Greek versions (see HEXAPLA), Aramaic TARGUMS, Syriac Peshitta, and the Latin Vulgate attest this consonantal text. The SEPTUAGINT mainly attests MT, but it also attests other versions.

In the ninth century BCE, the Hebrew letters *hê*, *wāw*, and *yôd* (and occasionally *'ālep*) were used in written texts to indicate long vowels and, later in the Qumran SCROLLS, short vowels as well. But this system was not consistent and did not represent all the vowels. The Masoretes, like other groups of their period, invented a written vocalization system to indicate the correct pronunciation of the orally transmitted text. For example, from 411 CE Syriac manuscripts began to utilize dots that provided queues for oral pronunciation, thereby specifying the meaning of certain words by distinguishing them from other words with a similar consonant structure. Syriac shows evidence of the vowel sign for [*a*] prior to the seventh century, and the full vocalization system came to exist by the eighth century. The MT exhibits vowel signs (written above, below, and sometimes within consonants) in all of its codices datable to the ninth century. MT is thus the sum of a complex of written and oral components, symbolized in the vowels, accent marks, and the *qərê*.

The consonantal text preceded the vowel system, and the latter complemented the former, though not perfectly. At times the vowels do not harmonize with the consonantal text, resulting in alternate readings: the *kətîb* ('what is written', the consonants in the manuscript) and the *qərê* ('what is read', the suggested pronunciation of words using the proposed vowel sounds). The manuscripts and most editions of the Hebrew Bible do not provide the vocalization of the *kətîb* but only the *qərê*, which is found in the margin of manuscripts and editions (e.g. Josh. 6.13 *kətîb*: *hāwlōk*; *qərê*: *hlwk* [= *hālôk*]). The MT includes approximately fifteen hundred *kətîb*/*qərê* notes. The most common instance is the Tetragrammaton *YHWH*, which is read either as *'ădōnāy* or as *'ĕlōhîm*. In some situations, the *qərê* arose as a euphemism for the *kətîb* (e.g. 1 Sam. 5.9 *kətîb*: *'plym* 'haemorrhoids?'; *qərê*: *təḥōrîm* 'tumors'). Instances such as these are, however, relatively rare and the majority of the *qərê* are not intentional changes to the written text.

The Masoretes also developed a system of accents or cantillation marks above and below the consonants in the text in order to preserve the traditional reading of the text. These accents basically function as punctuation marks, joining or dividing words, phrases, and clauses. The system of accents is uniform for all books except Job, Proverbs, and Psalms, which have a different system. The system of disjunctive and conjunctive accents probably added a solemnity to the public reading and exegesis of the text. The disjunctive accents mark syntactic divisions. The Masoretes did not invent the chant itself, only the system of accents that would preserve it. Some manuscripts (Greek and Hebrew) from the Second Temple period exhibit spaces between sense units and these correspond to the disjunctive accents in the Masoretic codices. There may have been different layers to the cantillation tradition as evidenced in places where two different accents are placed on the same words (e.g. Exod. 20.13-16).

The Masoretes generally followed tradition in the layout of text in manuscripts, although there was some development to this feature of the text. Each folio of the principal witnesses has three columns of text, while the poetic books (Psalms, Proverbs, and Job) have two wider columns of text per folio. The Masoretes adopted traditional methods for laying out poetic texts. In Exodus 15 and Judges 5 they used 'a half-brick over a whole brick, and a whole brick over a half-brick' format – 'space over text and text over space'. In Deuteronomy 32 they used 'half-brick on top of half-brick' – 'space over space and text over text'. Both layouts are traced back to rabbinic sources (e.g. *Soferim* 12.10). The chief codices show a system of spaces intended to divide poetic stichs, a layout reminiscent of MasPs[a], in which each column of text contains one stich divided into two halves or hemistichs by a space. However, in the Aleppo Codex the system of spaces does not preserve the syntactic or sense unit divisions with precision (e.g. Ps. 81.8c has a large space dividing bound form and free form, which is not correct). Pausal forms and accents became the key terminal markers used in the Masoretic codices, and the system of spaces appears to be a memory of a past scribal technique.

Finally here, the MT evidences a number of other paratextual features that reflect its identity as the written codification of an ongoing scribal dialogue and performance tradition. These paratextual features include: 1) division into verses; 2) division into paragraphs; 3) raised letters (e.g. suspended *nun* in Judg. 18.30); 4) inverted *nuns* to mark misplaced passages (e.g. Num. 10.35-36); 5) *puncta extraordinaria* or supralinear dots that mark elements to be deleted or which are uncertain (e.g. Gen. 33.4); 6) The *Tiqqune Sopherim* or the 'corrections of the scribes' (e.g. Num. 11.15 'your wickedness' is changed to 'my…'); and 7) *Litterae Minusculae* and *Majusculae*, which drew attention to details important for the Masoretes (e.g. Deut. 6.4).

More paratextual features were supplied around the text, providing a sort of scribal commentary on its mechanics. The *Masora Parva* contained notes, written in the spaces between the columns, recording observations about the number of times a word or phrase occurs, grammatical peculiarities, *Qərê*, and especially ORTHOGRAPHY. *Masora Magna*, written above and below the columns (and sometimes in the margins) describe the phenomena in *Masora Parva* in more detail. *Masora Finalis* contain lists for which there was no space in the *Masora Parva* and *Masora Magna*. *Sebirin* is an abbreviation for *sebirin wematin*: 'One might think that X must be read instead of Y, but that is a wrong assumption' (e.g. Judg. 11.34). Textual variants are also indicated between Western/Tiberian and Eastern/Babylonian readings.

John D. Meade (Phoenix Seminary, USA)

Further Reading

Khan, Geoffrey. 2012. *A Short Introduction to the Tiberian Masoretic Bible and its Reading Tradition*. Piscataway, NJ: Gorgias Press.

Tov, Emanuel. 2012. *Textual Criticism of the Hebrew Bible*. 3rd rev. Minneapolis, MN: Fortress Press.

Barthélemy, Dominique. 2012. *Studies in the Text of the Old Testament: An Introduction to the Hebrew Old Testament Text Project*. Translated by Stephen Pisano, Peter A. Pettit, Joan E. Cook, and Sarah Lind. Winona Lake, IN: Eisenbrauns.

Yeivin, Israel. 1980. *Introduction to the Tiberian Masorah*. Translated by and edited by E. J. Revell. Masoretic Studies 5. Missoula, MT: Scholars Press.

Master Commemorative Narrative A *master commemorative narrative* is a metanarrative that operates as an organizing principle for recollections of the past within a group's COLLECTIVE MEMORY. *Metanarrative* stresses that master commemorative narratives do not consist of a fixed content and do not represent a database of all cultural knowledge; they are, rather, patterns of remembering – often tied to significant rituals, places, or people – that organize the ways that groups and the individuals within them understand the past. The term was coined by Yael Zerubavel in her 1995 study *Recovered Roots*, which explores memorial strategies adopted in the construction of a national identity for the modern nation of Israel, and is widely applicable to a number of critical issues in the study of ancient Israel and Christian Origins.

Zerubavel notes that most members of a group experience the collective past through established patterns of commemoration associated with significant events, places, or people – for example, birthday parties, wedding anniversaries, or the celebration of religious or national holidays like Passover, American Thanksgiving, or Guy Fawkes Day. 'Each [individual] act of commemoration reproduces a commemorative narrative, a story about a particular past that accounts for this ritualized remembrance and provides a moral message for group members' (1995: 6). To cite two obvious examples, the Jewish Passover celebration, particularly as envisioned in Exod. 12 and Deut. 16, is a memorial meal in which members of the Jewish community ritually rehearse events associated with the deliverance from Egypt; similarly, the Christian EUCHARIST, since its earliest observances, has been associated with a particular understanding of the events surrounding Jesus' arrest, trial, and death (1 Cor. 11.23-26; Mk 14.12-25). Memorial occasions of this kind may or may not explicitly involve STORYTELLING – Passover often does, but a modern Western family's Christmas celebration may not – but the stories behind these events could be told by the individuals involved. While the precise wording and contents of individual accounts would vary, such stories would generally follow observable patterns and plotlines; these patterns, viewed collectively, are the substance of commemorative narratives.

Zerubavel's reference to the 'moral message' that commemorative narratives convey emphasizes the key role played by collective memory in the establishment and maintenance of group IDENTITY and norms related to that identity. Because group (and individual) identity relies heavily upon the shared remembered past, knowledge of commemorative narratives and participation in those rituals in which such narratives are rehearsed significantly impacts the value systems of groups and their individual members. The PAULINE LITERATURE of the NT, for example, regularly appeals to this function of collective memory in the context of moral discourse, referring Christian readers to events from the life of Christ that they should emulate (e.g. Phil. 2.4-13; 1 Tim. 6.11-16) or locating Paul's and/or the readers' conversion experience(s) within a narrative framework that implies a particular lifestyle (e.g. Rom. 6.1-14; Eph. 2.1-21; Col. 1.21-23; 3.1-11; 1 Tim. 1.12-17).

By their very nature, individual memorial rituals – a family Hanukkah or Easter celebration, a community fireworks display on American Independence Day (4th of July), or a visit to the grave of one's grandparents – are fragmentary in the sense that they preserve and communicate commemorative narratives relating to specific complexes of events. 'Yet [all] these commemorations [observed by a particular group] together contribute to the formation of a master commemorative narrative that structures collective memory' (Zerubavel 1995: 6). Because they connect many smaller storylines in a larger nexus of meaning, master commemorative narratives create a 'broader view of history … that is culturally constructed and provides the group members with a general notion of their shared past' (1995: 6). Even though the master narrative may be rarely, or never, rehearsed in full, it serves as a unifying frame that provides context and meaning for the smaller commemorative rituals that inhabit it.

Both individual commemorative narratives and the master narratives that unify them may become encoded in institutional expressions of the historical past, including, significantly, literature and educational systems. The canonization of particular narrative representations of past events indicates an attempt on the part of a group, or of powerful literate individuals within the group, to define and manage identity and related norms. Obvious examples include the canonization of a particular scribal vision of Israel's historical past during the post-exilic period, and the composition of NARRATIVE GOSPELS that offer a definitive account of Christ's activity and teaching. As both artefacts and containers of collective memory, canonical narratives authorize particular understandings of a group's origins and identity, and their capacity to do so is enhanced in cultural settings where WRITING imbues its contents with a numinous quality.

Tom Thatcher (Cincinnati Christian University, USA)

Further Reading

Zerubavel, Yael. 1995. *Recovered Roots: Collective Memory and the Making of Israeli National Tradition*. Chicago: The University of Chicago Press.

McLuhan, Marshall Marshall McLuhan (1911–1980) was a pioneer researcher on the pervasive impact of communication technology in the formation of culture and author of the proverbial summary of media research, 'The medium is the message'. McLuhan grew up in Manitoba, Canada, and graduated first from the University of Manitoba and later from Cambridge University. He served as professor of English at several American universities, most notably St. Louis University (1937–44), where he taught and mentored the highly influential authority on communication, technology, and religion, WALTER J. ONG, S.J. McLuhan suggested that Ong do his dissertation on Peter Ramus, which was in turn the seminal step in Ong's engagement with media studies. McLuhan joined the faculty of St. Michael's College in the University of Toronto in 1946 where he established the Center for Culture and Technology (1963) and taught until 1979. While at Toronto, McLuhan worked with Harold Innis and joined ERIC A. HAVELOCK, Northrop Frye, and Edmund Carpenter in the formation of the Toronto School of Communication Theory.

McLuhan was one the most influential scholars of media theory and the interaction between communication technology and culture in the twentieth century. His major works – *The Mechanical Bride*, *The Gutenberg Galaxy*, *Understanding Media*, *The Medium is the Message: An Inventory of Effects* – were all successful publications, with the last two selling more than a million copies each. McLuhan became a leading public intellectual of his generation, appearing frequently on television talk shows and news programmes as a commentator and provocateur. He was a prophet of the new age of electronic and now digital communication technology who, for example, predicted the World Wide Web thirty years before it appeared.

While he never engaged in biblical research, his theories and concepts have impacted biblical interpretation in at least three key areas. First, McLuhan advocated the importance of the training of perception. In biblical studies, the dominant training of perception of the Bible is the silent reading of the text with the eyes by an isolated individual. The perception of the Bible in ancient media was based on the training of audiences who heard and interacted with the sounds of compositions with their ears. The recognition of this discontinuity paved the way for a revision of the training of perception in biblical performance (see Performance Criticism) and pedagogy.

Second, McLuhan's most provocative proverb – 'the medium is the message' – was a counter to the assumption in literary criticism that the meaning of a text is contained solely in its content. Historically, biblical interpretation has focused on the identification of the content of biblical tradition, with particular attention to theology as the 'message' of the Bible. This definition of the biblical message is based on the anachronistic assumption that the medium of the Bible was a collection of texts read by readers looking for ideas implicit in the text. The foundational conclusion of recent research on the Bible in ancient media is that the media culture of the ancient world was a predominantly oral culture that only gradually became a predominantly literate culture over the ensuing 2,000 years. In that cultural context, the dominant medium of the Bible was the performance of compositions for audiences. This change in the conception of the original medium of the Bible transforms the perception of its meaning in its original context and potentially in its contemporary context.

Third, McLuhan's most important historical work was *The Gutenberg Galaxy*, which traces the literary and cultural impact of the printing press in the centuries after its invention. McLuhan concluded that the shift from manuscript to print as the dominant technology of communication was the cause of major changes in the literature, religion, economy, and culture of Europe. When McLuhan's advocacy of the pervasive impact of media change is tested in relation to the history of biblical interpretation, a direct correlation can be identified between the major changes in communication technology and the paradigm shifts in biblical transmission and interpretation from oral to Manuscript to print to silent text. Furthermore, the implication of McLuhan's prescient descriptions of the effects of electronic/digital communication technology is that the medium of biblical transmission and interpretation needs to be reformed for the culture of the digital age.

Thomas E. Boomershine (United Theological Seminary, USA)

Further Reading

Elizabeth Eisenstein. 1979. *The Printing Press as an Agent of Social Change*. Cambridge: Cambridge University Press.

McLuhan, Marshall. 1962. *The Gutenberg Galaxy: The Making of Typographic Man*. Toronto: University of Toronto Press.

McLuhan, Marshall. 1964. *Understanding Media: The Extensions of Man*. New York: McGraw-Hill.

McLuhan, Marshall, and Quentin Fiore. 1967. *The Medium is the Message: An Inventory of Effects*. Middlesex: Penguin Books.

Memory, Greco-Roman Theories of In media criticism of the Bible, research into ancient theories of memory has focused primarily on the Greco-Roman context, where PERSONAL MEMORY was viewed as an essential element in the composition and performance of philosophical and rhetorical discourses and one of the five canons of RHETORIC. Building upon the seminal writings of the Greek philosophers PLATO (420s–348 BCE) and Aristotle (384–322 BCE), Latin rhetorical theorists such as Cicero (106 BCE–46 BCE) and Quintilian (35–100 CE) developed complex memory systems that supported lengthy and spontaneous public speeches. The close connection drawn in antiquity between performance and memory is reflected in the popular portrayal of Mnemosyne (memory personified), a consort of Zeus, as the inventor of language and mother of the nine Muses (Hesiod, *Theogony* 53–74; Pindar, *Paeans* 6, 7).

Personal Memory

Although the ancient philosophers and rhetors viewed memory as a pillar of speech, they understood its cognitive operations to be primarily visual in nature. Plato popularized the widespread notion that memory is a form of mental script, in which sensory data 'write words on our souls' (*Philebus* 34A, 35A–D, 39A; LCL). Writing on behalf of/as Socrates, Plato compared the acquisition of memory to engravings on a block of wax, a metaphor that portrays recall as a form of inner reading and forgetting as a form of erasure. 'Whenever we wish to remember anything we see or hear or think of in our minds, we hold this wax under the perceptions and thoughts and imprint them upon it, just as we make impressions from seal rings; and whatever is imprinted we remember and know as long as its image lasts, but whatever is rubbed out or cannot be imprinted we forget and do not know' (*Theaetetus* 191D, also 193C; LCL).

Aristotle, Plato's pupil, further popularized the WAX TABLET model. Aristotle's theory of memory is grounded in the premise that images precede words in all human thought (*On Memory* 449b30–31; 450b20–451a1; see also *On the Soul* 431a14–19; 432a5–9). Sensory impressions, including the sounds of words, are converted to images and imprinted in the tissues or fluids of the physical body; attempts at recall initiate a mental process that locates and reviews stored impressions – a fact that easily explains, for Aristotle, why age or other physical limitations may impact memory capacity (i.e. some body types do not hold impressions as well or as long as others; see *On Memory* 450a32–450b11; 453a14–453b6). To differentiate genuine memories of the past from other mental processes (e.g. to distinguish the memory of an idea or concept from a new idea), Aristotle explains that the act of recall requires the remembrancer to evoke and unite two mental images: one image representing the thing or concept being remembered and another representing the passage of time (e.g. to remember what one ate for lunch yesterday, one must locate a stored impression of the lunch and combine it with an image representing 'yesterday'; *On Memory* 452b23–453a3). Consistent with this mechanical conception of memory's operations, Aristotle followed his mentor in comparing memory to imprints (*tupoi*) and signet rings (see, e.g. *On Memory* 450a25–31).

For purposes of the present discussion, the wax tablet/stylus model of memory is significant for its impact on Roman rhetorical theory and practice in the first centuries BCE and CE. Cicero, adopting a visual model of cognition and recall, refers to memory as 'the twin sister of writing' (*gemina litteraturae*; *Divisions of Rhetoric* 26). Observing that 'the keenest of all our senses is the sense of sight', Cicero conjectured that the mind converts all sensations, as well as abstract concepts, to visual images, which are then imprinted in the body; in recall, one peruses these stored images to reproduce the past (*On the Orator* 2.357; LCL). Reflecting the same approach, Quintilian reminds aspiring orators that 'the most important factor in Memory is mental concentration, a sharp [inner] eye, as it were, never diverted from the object of its gaze' – to remember, one must literally be able to look inside herself (*Institutes* 11.2.11; LCL).

Memory and Performance

Reflecting the popular view of memory and recall as primarily visual operations, ancient models of composition and live performance were based on strategies for ordering mental images. In the NT period, the most significant of these strategies, often referred to as the MEMORY THEATRE method, was associated with the earlier Greek poet SIMONIDES of Keos (550s–460s BCE). Simonides' system, as interpreted by the Latin rhetorical theorists, required the orator to develop and arrange two types of mental images in advance of live performance, *loci* ('places') and *imagines* ('images' of things/people). As indicated by the anonymous author of *Rhetorica ad Herennium* (80s BCE), an 'image' is 'a figure, mark, or portrait of the object we wish to remember' (3.29; LCL) – that is, a visual symbol that represents a concept, fact, or person one wishes to recall in delivering a speech or telling a story. *Loci* are mental images of real or imaginary places that are easily recalled, such as the rooms of a house or a theatre. In preparing for a speech, the orator would assign images to the individual facts, people, themes, illustrations, etc. that he would need to recall; these visual symbols would then be located within the *locus* and their positions carefully remembered. In performance, the speaker would simply walk through the *locus* in his mind's eye and discuss the points associated with each mental object he encountered there. A speaker might, for example, assign each fact or point to be addressed to a piece of exercise equipment, then locate these items in a familiar gymnasium; to perform the speech, the rhetor would walk through the gym to recall aspects of the argument. This system would thus help performers remember not only the content of their messages, but also the order of the presentation (see, e.g. Cicero, *The Orator* 2.355; Quintilian, *Institutes* 11.2.21).

Obviously, to be practical, the memory theatre model required the oral performer to command a large repertoire of flexible and functional memory images. *Rhetorica ad Herennium* advises aspiring speakers to develop a solid base of *loci* that could be filled with any number of images specific to a given speech (3.31–32). More memorable images would clearly be easier to recall; therefore, the images that represent specific facts and arguments should be unusual rather than mundane: 'base, dishonorable, extraordinary, great, unbelievable, or laughable … striking and novel'. In the real world, when walking through a room one is much more likely to notice a snarling dog than a common household object; similarly, one's memory theatre should be filled with items that are difficult to forget, and bear some quality that will remind the performer of the points associated with them (3.38–39). Since standards for what is 'striking' vary from person to person, none of the ancient theorists advocate a one-size-fits-all approach to the development of memory images, instead advising performers to develop a system that suits their own tastes and memories.

The popularity of the place system model of memory in live speech performance supports the notion that ancient rhetorical productions were not fixed at the surface level. Put another way, the content of a prepared discourse would consist primarily in its mnemonic substructure, with the actual words spoken reflecting the performer's adaptation of the remembered material to the dynamics of the immediate performance context. Cicero thus might know what he planned to say and in what sequence before entering the court, but would not know ahead of time or afterwards exactly what words would/had come from his mouth.

Memory and Writing

As noted earlier, ancient memory theorists often compare the act of remembering to imprinting images or characters on a wax tablet, and correspondingly conceive of recollection as a form of reading. This logic readily translates into situations where a performer may wish to recall a written text verbatim, as when citing a personal LETTER or an imperial decree in court. In these situations, Quintilian advises that the speaker visualize the remembered text as words written on a page and then simply read what he sees to the audience (*Institutes* 11.2.32).

Quintilian's discussion of the relationship between memory and writing helpfully illustrates the social dynamics of ancient composition in performance and the relationship between written texts and prepared speech. Unlike some ancient theorists, Quintilian places a high value on rote memorization – composing speeches, or at least key movements, in advance, orally or in writing, and then reciting them verbatim before the audience (see *Institutes* 11.2.45). This approach, he observes, is superior to the memory theatre model in that it assists the oral performer in the recall of language elements that are not easily assigned to visual images (conjunctions, transitions, critical strings of words, etc.; 11.2.24–25). At the same time, rote memory is impractical and, in some settings, may even be counterproductive. Most obviously, writing out a composition and then memorizing it for recitation can take a great deal of time; in most cases, the speaker is better served to invest preparation time in developing a solid grasp of the facts and the line of argument (11.2.48). Further, public presentation and debate require continuous real-time adjustment: the speaker must continually adapt the discourse to audience response and counterargument, an impossibility with a memorized discourse (11.2.2, 11). Finally, and somewhat the reverse of modern expectations, the memory theatre model, which creates a spontaneous composition on the basis of a general framework, is more persuasive than verbatim recitation: 'The judge admires more, and fears less, things which he does not suspect of having been prepared in advance to outwit him' (11.2.47; LCL translation).

Tom Thatcher (Cincinnati Christian University, USA)

Further Reading

Cicero. *On the Orator*. 1959. Translated by E. W. Sutton and H. Rackham. LCL. Cambridge, MA: Harvard University Press.

Quintilian. 2001. *Institutes of Rhetoric*. Translated by Donald A. Russell. LCL. Cambridge, MA: Harvard University Press.

Sorabji, Richard. 1972. *Aristotle on Memory*. Providence, RI: Brown University Press.

Yates, Francis. 1966. *The Art of Memory*. Chicago: University of Chicago Press.

Memory, Persistence and Decay of Impressions of events, things, and people persist in human memory for variable periods of time (see COGNITIVE MEMORY). Some persist (remain memorable) for a very long time, while others decay (fade from memory) almost immediately. Which memories persist the longest is determined by unconscious processes, although it is possible for individuals to ensure that specific memories are more likely to endure by giving close attention to the events which formed the memory and to the frequent rehearsal of those events.

Modern psychological research has determined that memories decay according to predictable patterns, a phenomenon first investigated systematically by Hermann Ebbinghaus. Published in 1885, Ebbinghaus' study of the rate at which he himself forgot memorized lists of nonsense syllables is credited as the first experimental investigation into the performance of human memory. Ebbinghaus reported that his memories of the lists initially decayed at a very fast rate, but that this rate slowed over time – in other words, memories that passed the initial phases of sudden decay tended to become gradually more stable. Subsequent investigation has shown that many types of memories, not only lists of items, follow a decay pattern similar to that discovered by Ebbinghaus. Wixted and Ebbesen (1991; 1997), for example, have shown that Ebbinghaus's data yielded a *forgetting curve* very similar to those they obtained for human memories of lists of high-frequency nouns, visual memory, and the length of time that a pigeon remembered a learning task. They found that forgetting curves are approximated more closely by the power curve, $b = 184/((\log t)1.25 + 184)$ (where b is the saving of work evident in relearning, and t is the time in minutes counting from one minute before the end of the learning period), rather than by the logarithmic curve suggested by Ebbinghaus.

A large volume of publications describing the results of experiments investigating human memory appears every year, but almost all of these report experiments that produce results show memory decay over very short periods of time (seconds, minutes, or sometimes days at most). Controlled experiments that trace memories over periods of time as long as months or years are difficult to conduct and consequently are infrequent, but some experiments have covered periods as long as five years, and a few have explored the quality of memories that have persisted for as long as thirty to fifty years.

Willem A. Wagenaar, for example, devoted six years to an experiment to determine how well he remembered events in his own life. At the end of each day, Wagenaar wrote down one event that was in some way distinguishable from all other memories he had accumulated over his lifetime. He noted details of who, what, where, and when each day's recorded event occurred, and a critical detail in the form of a cue question. At intervals, sometimes as long as five years, he tried to remember these memories after being given one of the cues, 'who, what, where and when' (in random order), followed by a second cue, then a third. He then used the cue question to determine whether he was really remembering a specific event, or only one like it. Wagenaar discovered that his memories over a period of five years followed the general decay curve that has been found to be typical of shorter-term memories: much was lost initially, but the rate of decay slowed, and some memories persisted over the longest periods he tested.

Harry P. Bahrick investigated very long-term persistence of Spanish language skills among English-speaking individuals in the United States who had studied Spanish in high school or college. His results showed that the decay of individuals' memories of the Spanish language followed closely a logarithmic decline for the first three to five years. This decline is enough to extinguish the knowledge of Spanish in those who studied Spanish for only a short time period, or who had not performed well from an academic standpoint. But those who had studied Spanish for a longer period and to a certain level of proficiency were able to retain a substantial residual of knowledge of Spanish over the first three to five years, despite the decay of their memory of the language. Language skills that had persisted for three to five years remained relatively constant from that time until twenty-five years had elapsed, after which time proficiency declined further. Similarly, Harry P. Bahrick, P. O. Bahrick, and R. P. Wittlinger studied very long-term memories of faces and names by using photos in high school yearbooks. They discovered that students were able to distinguish with great reliability photographs of their high school peers from photos of other students who were from classes that they had not attended even after periods as long as fifty years. Teachers, however, were not very proficient at the task of identifying students in classes they had taught after periods of this length.

Robert K. McIver has argued that these experimental results can be used to provide an assessment of the persistence of memories of Jesus' teaching and other activities for the thirty to sixty years that elapsed between the events of his ministry and the composition of the Gospels. While many memories of Jesus would have decayed by the time the Gospels were written, experimental and other evidences suggest that a significant proportion of memories about Jesus would have persisted over the time that had elapsed by the time the Gospels were written. McIver further argues that memories that persisted over the first five years after the crucifixion would likely persist in human memories for the next thirty or forty years. This would be particularly true if these memories were repeated and rehearsed, as memories of Jesus almost certainly were in conversations between Christians and in preaching and teaching activities in the early church.

Robert K. McIver (Avondale College of Higher Education, Australia)

Further Reading

Bahrick, Harry P. 2000. 'Long Term Maintenance of Knowledge.' In *The Oxford Handbook of Memory*. Edited by Endel Tulving and Furgus I. M. Craik. Oxford: University Press, pp. 247–362.

Bahrick, Harry P., P. O. Bahrick and R. P. Wittlinger. 1975. 'Fifty Years of Memory for Names and Faces: A Cross-sectional Approach.' *Journal of Experimental Psychology* 104: 54–75.

Ebbinghaus, Herman. 1885. *Über das Gedächtnis*. Leipzig: Duncker and Humblot. Translated into English and published as *Memory: A Contribution to Experimental Psychology.* New York: Dover, 1964.

McIver, Robert K. 2011/2012. *Memory, Jesus, and the Synoptic Gospels*. SBLRBS. Atlanta: SBL Press.

Wagenaar, Willem A. 1986. 'My Memory: A Study of Autobiographic Memory over Six Years.' *Cognitive Psychology* 18: 225–52.

Wixted, John T., and Ebbe B. Ebbesen. 1991. 'On the Form of Forgetting.' *Psychological Science* 2: 409–15.

Wixted, John T., and Ebbe B. Ebbesen. 1997. 'Genuine Power Curves in Forgetting: A Quantitative Analysis of Individual Subject Forgetting Functions.' *Memory and Cognition* 25: 731–9.

Memory Theatre A *memory theatre* is a mnemonic device used in place system techniques for the recall of information in live performance. Ancient (and modern) place systems facilitated the recall of both individual pieces of information and the interrelations between them by associating data points with familiar physical locations. By the Medieval and Early Renaissance periods, and especially in esoteric traditions, these physical locations were sometimes described as *theatres* (see, e.g. Guilio Camillo's *The Idea of the Theater*, published in 1550), although earlier Greco-Roman rhetorical theorists envisioned a wide range of real or imagined locations as helpful frameworks for organizing ideas (see MEMORY, GRECO-ROMAN THEORIES OF). Memory theatres, and place systems generally, figure prominently in ancient discussions of rhetorical theory and practice, since they allowed individuals to deliver lengthy prepared remarks from memory before live audiences.

Ancient mnemotechnique, and models of public speaking based on such techniques, highlighted strategies for arranging and ordering mental images in ways that would facilitate recall in oral performance. By the NT era, these strategies were largely associated with a legendary episode from the life of the Greek poet SIMONIDES (556–468 BCE), who purportedly developed a memory system based on the interior visualization of two types of pictures, which the Latin rhetors would later call *loci* and *imagines* (see Cicero, *The Orator* 2.355; also Quintillian, *Institutes* 11.2.11-21). An *image* is 'a figure, mark, or portrait of the object we wish to remember' (*Rhetorica ad Herennium* 3.29) – essentially, a symbolic visual representation of an individual fact, idea, or illustration that one needs to recall when delivering a speech. Loci are mental snapshots of real or invented places, such as the rooms of a house or the sections of a local theatre (hence the later *memory theatre* model noted above). In preparing for a speech or debate, the orator/performer would place the images representing the individual points within the imagined location; in performance, the speaker would simply peruse the memory site in her/his mind's eye, discussing the points/issues/events/individuals associated with each item as she/he encountered it. Cicero assures his students that this method will enable them to easily recall the facts of the case, the outline of the arguments, points of style in delivery, and precedents from other settlements (*The Orator* 2.355).

Because place system techniques were generally purely functional, at least in the NT era, they were not standardized or encoded with particular esoteric value. Aspiring speakers were encouraged to develop a system of places and images that would be highly memorable to them personally, even if meaningless to others. Aristotle, for example, suggested the use of *midpoints*, a technique in which the remembrancer places images in a linear sequence, perhaps based on a series of numbers or letters that could serve as a visual indexing system for recalling the point/issue/event associated with each number/letter (*On Memory* 451b18-452b6; 452a17-24). The anonymous author of *Rhetorica ad Herennium* proposes the use of memory images that are 'base, dishonourable, extraordinary, great, unbelievable, or laughable … striking and novel' – anything that will make them easy to recall (3.35-37).

Aside from their purely functional value as aides-memoire, place systems reflected and reinforced the media aesthetic of antiquity. Even literate orators, who could prepare notes and even entire speeches or treatises in WRITING before delivering them, were not encouraged to consult written MANUSCRIPTS in live performance, nor even to memorize them for verbatim recitation. According to Quintillian, the ability to deliver a well-structured speech spontaneously 'gives a reputation for quickness of wit', especially if 'we are believed to have made the speech up on the spot, instead of bringing it ready made from home; and this impression is very valuable both to the orator and the Cause, because the judge admires more, and fears less, things which he does not suspect of having been prepared in advance to outwit him' (*Institutes* 11.2.47).

Memory theatre/place system techniques are helpful for biblical scholars in understanding the interfaces between memory, speech, and writing in ancient live performances of remembered material. For example, early Christian performers may have utilized place system techniques to assist in the recall and articulation of traditional stories about Jesus, or may have developed visual strategies for arranging and delivering complex concepts for public and private discussions of points of faith.

Tom Thatcher (Cincinnati Christian University, USA)

Further Reading

Thatcher, Tom. 2006. *Why John Wrote a Gospel: Jesus–Memory–History*. Louisville: Westminster John Knox.
Yates, Francis. 1966. *The Art of Memory*. Chicago: University of Chicago Press.

Metonymy Metonymy is the term applied by JOHN MILES FOLEY to the basic aesthetic of oral-traditional composition. In Foley's definition, *metonymy* is a figure of speech by which 'a part stands for the whole' (Foley 1991: 7). For example, popular English regularly uses the term 'the stage' to represent the theatre in full, including actors, performances, and repertoire. By analogy, *metonymy* refers to the way elements of language and content in individual oral and oral-influenced texts evoke a wider range of traditional usage. Recurrent phrases, motifs, and structural patterns (categories comparable to FORMULA, THEME, and STORY PATTERN) act as metonymic signals of a span of literary expression that is both continuous and multiform (see PLURIFORMITY). Oral and oral-influenced literary traditions are multiform in that basic compositional elements are configured and expanded differently in different contexts or 'performances', both live and written (Foley 1995). Metonymy introduces an extensive, variegated extratextual dimension into individual oral texts through phrases, motifs, and patterns bearing an 'inherent' meaning that transcends the particular literary expression while investing it with depth and breadth (Foley 1991).

The Homeric epics, for example, use the same formulaic epithets for major characters whenever and however they are portrayed. Achilles is called 'swift-footed Achilles' over thirty times in the *Iliad*, not only when he is in combat but also when he has withdrawn from battle to his tent (*Iliad* 1–17) or is seated to receive Priam's appeal for the body of his son Hector (*Iliad* 24). Such epithets may seem awkward or extraneous to the modern reader, but they function metonymically to remind an audience of who Achilles is in all his movements and responses throughout the epic (Foley 1998).

Metonymy pertains to the processes of both composition and reception, or interpretation of a work by an audience. It presumes shared knowledge of the literary tradition by both composer and audience. In a metonymic aesthetic, literary works are shaped in relation to traditional language and content so as to shade individual compositions with the resonance and range of the tradition as a whole. This aesthetic is predominantly an art of allusion or association rather than of linear sequence (Foley 1991), as traditional elements may appear intrusive or contradictory in their immediate contexts.

Metonymy in Biblical Texts

Examples of metonymic referencing of larger complexes of tradition are evident throughout the Bible. Titles can often evoke meanings that go beyond the immediate literary context. In the Hebrew Bible, the frequently used title 'the Lord, the God of hosts' or 'Lord of hosts' conveys the prevailing power of God in different contexts, including the acclamation of God as creator (Amos 4.13), God's transcendent presence in the TEMPLE (Isa. 6.5), and his roles as teacher (Isa. 5.24), triumphant warrior (Isa. 1.24; 2.12; 3.1), and executor of judgement (Amos 5.14-16; Isa. 5.7, 16; 28.22). Similarly, in the Gospel of Mark, the title 'Son of Man' for Jesus recalls both his mortal embodiment and prophetic mission (Mk 8.31; 9.31; 10.33, 45; 14.21) as well as his divine authority and return in glory at the end of the age (Mk 2.10, 28; 8.38; 13.26; 14.62). These meanings, in turn, enfold the occurrences of the phrase in Ezekiel and in Daniel 7.

On the level of motif, the scenario of the unusual birth of a hero runs through both Testaments, implicitly linking the birth stories of Jesus to those of John the Baptist, Samuel, Samson, Moses, Jacob, and Isaac (cf. Jer. 1.5), so that each can be read in relation to the others. The broad story pattern of the vindication of the servant of the Lord who remains faithful through suffering recurs in the laments of the Psalms, Job, and Jeremiah, in the servant songs of Isaiah, in the exaltation of the wise and just in Daniel and in Wisdom 2–5, and in the PASSION NARRATIVES of the Gospels. Each usage of this motif adds to and receives richness and complexity from the whole body of tradition. On a broad scale, the shaping of the Gospels according to language, motifs, and structural patterns that are manifested in the Hebrew Bible is itself an illustration of the use of metonymic reference to intensify and expand meaning beyond the immediate compositional context.

Metonymy and Creativity

Metonymic use of traditional patterns diminishes neither the creativity of the composer nor the active participation of the recipient in interpretation, but has been compared to the Saussurean dynamic of *langue* and *parole* (Nagy 1996). Flexibility, selection, and innovation are evident in the ways individual compositions reflect the broad lines of traditional patterns yet break new ground by introducing new configurations and articulations into the body of tradition. An illustration from the Hebrew Bible is the motif of rivalry between brothers in the Genesis narratives of Cain and Abel, Jacob and Esau, and Joseph and his brothers. Each rivalry narrative entails a different outcome (murder, amicable separation, reunion) and each also incorporates unique compositional elements (which may themselves be traditional), among them the phrase 'sin is lurking at the door' (Gen. 4.7), Jacob's dream of a heavenly ladder and his wrestling with God (Gen. 28.10-22, 32.22-32 [Hebrew 32.23-33]), and Joseph's strategic plan to bring his brothers to self-recognition (Gen. 42–45). The four NT Gospels illustrate the role of selection and shaping of the traditions about Jesus. Each Gospel manifests fundamental continuity with a common narrative tradition, yet each contributes to this shared structure a distinct compositional design, marked theological emphases, and unique expansions.

The gaps and inconsistencies created by metonymic use of traditional patterns compel the involvement of audiences in interpretation. Knowledge of the larger oral or oral-influenced tradition in its multiformity enables an audience to discern the many shades of meaning conveyed by familiar language and content and allows for multiple interpretive possibilities.

Metonymy and Methodology

Lack of knowledge of the full range of traditional language and content poses a challenge to identifying and interpreting metonymy in ancient texts. Creating a referential background for a text begins with grouping phrases, motifs, and structural patterns that show kinship, tracing consistent threads within each group, and observing the way compositions weave these threads variously in different contexts. Comparisons across GENRES (as well as with works outside the CANON or literary tradition) can help in sketching a background for an individual text as well as highlight its distinctive foreground, revealing the warp and woof of metonymic art.

Katherine M. Hayes (Saint Joseph Seminary, USA)

Further Reading

Foley, John Miles. 1991. *Immanent Art: From Structure to Meaning in Traditional Oral Epic*. Bloomington: Indiana University Press.

Foley, John Miles. 1998. 'The Impossibility of Canon.' In *Teaching Oral Traditions*. Edited by John Miles Foley. New York: The Modern Language Association, pp. 13–33.

Foley, John Miles. 1995. *The Singer of Tales in Performance*. Bloomington: Indiana University Press.

Hayes, Katherine M. 2002. *'The Earth Mourns': Prophetic Metaphor and Oral Aesthetic*. Academica Biblia 8. Atlanta: SBL Press.

Nagy, Gregory. 1996. *Poetry as Performance: Homer and Beyond*. Cambridge: Cambridge University Press.

Niditch, Susan. 1996. *Oral World and Written Word: Ancient Israelite Literature*. Louisville: Westminster John Knox.

Slatkin, Laura M. 2011. *The Power of Thetis and Selected Essays*. Hellenic Studies 16. Cambridge, MA: Harvard University Press.

Mishnah The Mishnah is the first document of rabbinic Oral Law, assumed to have been edited around 200 CE. It constitutes the basis of the later Palestinian and Babylonian Talmuds, which are commentaries on the Mishnah and follow its structure into orders and tractates. The Mishnah is mostly legal (halakhic) in content and highly stylized in its formulation. Its relationship to the Hebrew Bible is very complex: biblical ideas inspired rabbis, and biblical quotes are used as proof texts. The Mishnah is not an interpretation of the Bible, however, but an exposition of rabbinic law as it developed after the destruction of the Second TEMPLE in 70 CE. Rabbinic law (halakhah) of the first two centuries CE was mostly transmitted orally and comprised all areas of ancient Jews' daily life, ranging from family issues (e.g. marriage and divorce) to property law (e.g. damages and sales) and religious holidays and rituals. As part of the so-called oral Torah it constitutes a second body of holy writings after and besides the Hebrew Bible (the so-called written Torah).

Among the main issues of scholarship on the Mishnah are the nature of its sources and the processes of its redaction. To what extent did the editors rely on traditional material and to what extent did they formulate or even create the texts themselves? This question is also related to the transmission of the material: is the highly stylized form in which the texts came down to us related to the oral transmission of the sources or an aspect of its written presentation? The concise formulation of halakhic rules, opinions, and case stories, which eliminates all but the most relevant details, may have served memorization and transmission from one generation of scholars to the next. The formulaic pattern could also have been imposed on the source material by the editors, however, at the time when they created a written collection of traditional rabbinic law (see RABBINIC LITERATURE). The elliptical style in which the texts are formulated makes them applicable to a variety of situations and encourages further discussions among scholars. Tannaitic rabbis are unlikely to have actually spoken in this style, an issue which impedes the use of the texts for historical and historiographical purposes.

The processes of the Mishnah's redaction and PUBLICATION are similarly obscure. It is generally assumed that the first patriarch Rabbi Yehudah ha-Nasi was the editor, perhaps together with a group of rabbinic colleague-friends who supported him in the collection, presentation, and arrangement of material retrieved from his contemporaries. Due to his central place within the rabbinic network, Rabbi Yehudah ha-Nasi would have been well suited to collect traditions from contemporary scholars at various locations of Roman Palestine. These traditions had probably been transmitted to them orally from their respective teachers and teachers' teachers. In the process of oral transmission they may have been changed and adapted to different circumstances, discussed and commented upon. Specific details would have been lost and tradents' names confused or forgotten. Only the rudiments of cases may have been considered memorable and useful to later generations. At the same time, some stories and teachings may have been transmitted as written lists, associated with particular rabbis or arranged thematically. Yet the written transmission would not necessarily have been closer to the 'original' voice of the teacher: the texts would have been formulated by those later scholars who initiated the writing and/or by the SCRIBES themselves (who may or may not have been identical with the collectors). In any case, the editors would have been responsible for choosing the traditions preserved in the Mishnah with which they created a perpetual memorial for themselves and their colleague-friends.

Throughout the Amoraic period (200-mid-fourth century CE) the Mishnah may have been transmitted mostly orally, through recitation in scholarly circles followed by discussions and applications to new cases and circumstances. Several versions of written tractates may have circulated as well. These versions probably differed from the Mishnah MANUSCRIPTS which came down to us and represent a later textual stage. What is important is the interplay between ORALITY and WRITING, between memorization, discussion, and adaptation of the text to new circumstances, a process which still continues today.

Catherine Hezser (SOAS University of London, UK)

Further Reading

Alexander, Elizabeth Shanks. 2006. *Transmitting Mishnah: The Shaping Influence of Oral Tradition.* Cambridge: Cambridge University Press.

Hezser, Catherine. 2002. 'The Mishnah and Ancient Book Production.' In *The Mishnah in Contemporary Perspective*. Edited by Alan J. Avery-Peck and Jacob Neusner. Leiden: Brill, pp. 167–92.

Jaffee, Martin. 1994. 'Writing and Rabbinic Oral Tradition: On Mishnaic Narrative, Lists and Mnemonics.' *JJTP* 4: 123–46.

Samely, Alexander. 2007. 'Oral and Written Texts.' In *Forms of Rabbinic Literature and Thought*. Edited by Alexander Samely. Oxford: Oxford University Press, pp. 116–40.

Monuments Many civilizations, though not all, create monuments. Certainly the major empires that span the biblical writings – Egypt, Assyria, Babylon, Persia, Macedonia (Syria and Egypt), and Rome – engaged in monumentalizing, constructing palaces, TEMPLES, gates, tombs, statutes, various civic buildings, and numerous other monuments. The following discussion concentrates not so much on construction materials, techniques, and designs for monumental media, but rather on their functions and societal resonances as expressions of the identities and ideologies of ruling powers and their subjects. The monumentalizing practices of individuals and groups will be addressed before noting several techniques all monuments employed to gain attention and communicate their claims.

Monuments and Individuals

One dimension of *monumentality* concerns their import for those who created them. Some monuments expressed and defined the identities of individuals and provided a means of asserting their place in society and the cosmos as persons of significance. Constructing monuments also provided individuals with a means of resisting the impulse of time and the fragility of human existence that readily consigned them to oblivion after death. With a commemorative function, monuments, especially but not exclusively funerary monuments that lined the roads into cities, preserved and provoked memory, linking past and future generations by memorable deeds and lives.

For rulers, monuments memorialized their lives, ideologies, and accomplishments. In celebrating key accomplishments such as military victories, they highlighted occasions that foregrounded elite societal values and commitments. Monuments embraced and defied space in displaying and celebrating rule over subjugated land and people. In relation to time, monuments commemorated past victories and asserted a future of domination, thereby framing the present and seeking to secure the ruler's permanence. Often monuments aligned such events, rulers, and subjugated peoples with the gods. They acknowledged and constructed success as the blessing of the gods who sanctioned rule and sought their continued favour. Monuments thereby set individuals and communities in relation to the gods and located them in cosmic contexts, while expressing social, political, and religious identities and priorities. They could assert stability and vision in times of social change, and formulate afresh ruling ideology in times of contest and conflict.

To take several oft-cited examples relating to the biblical period, the Black Obelisk from the Assyrian capital Kalhu or Nimrud, dating to ca. 825 BCE, celebrated King Shalmaneser III's political success and military power. The obelisk, a black limestone monument just over six feet high, included scenes of conquered peoples paying tribute. One scene comprising both pictures and writing probably depicted the Israelite king Jehu submitting to Assyrian rule and paying tribute of silver and gold (ca. 841 BCE). In commemorating a significant person and events, monuments like this one unified a society by marking focal points deemed (by ruling elites) to be societally constitutive and memorable. They performed a visionary function in identifying and honouring (elite) societal priorities (see Great Tradition). In a similar display of political power and military prowess, the Behistun inscription, in three languages, narrates the accomplishments of King Darius the Great (522–486 BCE) in subduing rebellion in the Persian empire. The inscription (15 m × 25 m [approximately 49 ft × 82 ft]) is positioned on a limestone cliff above a road connecting the cities of Babylon and Ecbatana. It is accompanied by an image of the victorious Darius. His left foot holds down a subjugated figure lying on his back. Nine other figures have bound hands and rope around their necks.

Some five centuries later, in 9 BCE the Roman Senate dedicated the *Ara Pacis Augustae*, the Altar of Augustan Peace. This marble monument, whose walls were decorated with friezes depicting mythological scenes and religious processions, celebrated the emperor Augustus' military victories in Gaul and Hispania. The working altar acknowledged the divinely sanctioned establishment of Roman rule/domination (peace and prosperity) throughout its empire.

Monumentalizing provided provincial elites with a means of asserting their place in the world, securing imperial favour, and displaying wealth, power, and prestige. So the very wealthy and powerful Plancia Magna of Perge in Anatolia, high priestess of Artemis and of the imperial cult, financed the rebuilding of gates for the city. The gate complex comprised towers, a horse-shoe shaped courtyard, a two-tiered triumphal arch with three entrances, and statues of Greek and Roman deities and emperors. Her tomb was located near the gates. As a natural extension of this function, monuments also provided provincial elites with a means of competing with one another and with other cities for civic and imperial honours. Late in the first century CE in Ephesus, free cities in Asia dedicated a temple to the Flavian *Sebastoi* comprising the emperor Domitian and the deified emperor Titus, and their deceased father the deified Vespasian. The temple seems to have displayed images of some 35-40 deities, only two of which have been identified for certain as Isis and Attis. The temple not only signified religious sanction and provincial deference, but also brought honour to Ephesus among other cities in the province, identifying it as a *neokorate* city, a warden or keeper of the imperial temple. Monuments thus also participated in and emerged from the competitions among elites and cities for honour and status. Inhabitants of cities were beneficiaries of this competitive euergetism or civic good works of generosity. The result was numerous civic amenities, memorials with active roles and pragmatic functions in their communities, such as temples, theatres, aqueducts, stadia, and fountains.

Non-elites also constructed monuments to assert their place in the world, defy time, and preserve memory of their lives. About the middle of the first century BCE, for instance, a baker in Rome named Marcus Vergilius Eurysaces built a large tomb for himself. Not much is known about Eurysaces, though it is possible that he had been a slave of Greek origin who had been freed. Whatever his origin, he had gained significant wealth and status as a baker. His tomb monument ostentatiously celebrates his successful life and, like other Romans, memorializes him against time and death in a visually distinctive manner. Eurysaces' tomb clearly indicates that monuments did not emerge only top-down at the initiative of rulers; they were also initiated from below. To cite another example, late in the first century (4-2 BCE), in Ephesus, the capital city of the province of Asia, two imperial and wealthy freedmen, Mazaeus and Mithridates, financed prominently located monumental or triumphal gates constructed from marble that lead into the commercial agora. They dedicated the gates to their patron, the emperor Augustus, and other members of the imperial family. The triple-arched complex included statues of Augustus and his designated heirs Gaius and Lucius Caesar, accompanied by inscriptions of dedication to the emperor in Latin and to the inhabitants of Ephesus in Greek. The freedmen clearly had both audiences in view in declaring, as did other freedmen, their gratitude to their imperial patron, displaying their socio-economic success and seeking lasting glory for themselves by ingratiating themselves into and imposing themselves upon the consciousness of future generations. This monument may also have been the burial place of both freedmen.

Monuments and Groups

Like individuals, various groups in antiquity used monuments to define and assert their place in society, at times competing with other groups. A guild or association of fish-catchers and sellers in Ephesus, for example, constructed a customs building near the harbour in the mid-first century CE. They dedicated it to the emperor Nero, his mother and wife, and to the people of Rome and Ephesus, thereby participating in the common provincial activity of negotiating Roman presence and power by exhibiting allegiance and presenting themselves as loyal but important societal contributors. The Ephesus customs building also listed, in descending order of levels of contribution to its construction, some 100 males (plus some women and children). The building thus functioned, as did other monuments, to render eternal the name/s of their builder(s), patron(s), and subject(s). This naming attested societal membership, participation, and contribution; it also expressed aspirations to status, commemorating the loyalty and appreciation of the contributors, who presented themselves as successful and/or influential members of their societies. Such monuments honoured individuals and groups who upheld societal virtues, benefited other inhabitants, and sought to defy SHORT-TERM MEMORIES.

Monumental Rhetoric

Monuments garnered attention in various ways. Often (though not always) they were of large scale. Commonly they were positioned in prominent locations, employed distinctive and beautiful materials such as coloured marbles and mosaics, were carefully designed, and exuded permanence. Enhancing their visibility, they used particular geometric forms, such as columns to represent divine and state power, arches for military victory, and temple-like triangular pediments for divine blessing. They featured statues of emperors, gods, and successful figures, along with friezes of, for instance, mythical or battle scenes. The panels at the Sebasteion temple complex at Aphrodisias, for example, presented subjugated peoples as women. These panels upheld not only the importance of military power and domination but also the qualities of desirable (imperial) masculinity such as courage, leadership, and victory that ensured domination.

Some monuments employed writing, sometimes in bronze lettering or tablets (e.g. Augustus' *Res Gestae*). In societies with a significant range of degrees of LITERACY, such writing announced to educated passers-by the occasion of the monument and identity of its providers with a level of detail not always possible in images or design. For those unable to read, the mystifying presence of letters attested power and status. Accompanying images clarified at least the broad contours of the message.

Monuments thus performed various functions. They carried and stimulated important memories. They memorialized deceased persons, especially the great but also those of lesser status, highlighting accomplishments, relationships, and virtues. They honoured definitive events such as military victories. They utilized yet transcended particular historical frameworks linking past, present, and future. They prioritized, celebrated, and inculcated societal values and norms such as success, wealth, status, and power. They expressed and secured personal identities and aspirations, the ideologies and accomplishments of rulers and ruled, the social attainments and ambitions of monument-builders, the political identities of communities, and the sacral identities of a cult and/or community.

Warren Carter (Brite Divinity School, USA)

Further Reading

Alcock, Susan E. 2002. *Archaeologies of the Greek Past: Landscapes, Monuments, and Memories*. The W. B. Stanford Memorial Lectures. Cambridge: Cambridge University Press.

Armayor, O. Kimball. 1978. 'Herodotus' Catalogues of the Persian Empire in the Light of the Monuments and the Greek Literary Tradition.' *Transactions of the American Philological Association* 108: 1–9.

Bradley, Richard. 1993. *Altering the Earth: The Origins of Monuments in Britain and Continental Europe*. The 1992 Rhind Lectures. Society of Antiquaries of Scotland Monograph Series Number 8. Edinburgh: Society of Antiquaries of Scotland.

Carter, Warren. 2014. 'Masters of the Sea? Ephesian Fishermen, John 6:16-21, and John 21.' In *But These Are Written ... Essays on Johannine Literature in Honor of Professor Benny C. Akers*. Edited by Craig S. Keener, Jeremy S. Crenshaw and Jordan Daniel May. Eugene: Wipf and Stock, pp. 65–79.

Güven, Suna. 1998. 'Displaying the Res Gestae of Augustus: A Monument of Imperial Image for All.' *Journal of the Society of Architectural Historians* 57(1): 30–45.

Hesberg, Henner von. 2008. 'The Image of the Family on Sepulchral Monuments in the Northwest Provinces.' In *Role Models in the Roman World: Identity and Assimilation*. Vol. 7 of Memoirs of the American Academy in Rome. Edited by Sinclair Bell and Inge Lyse Hansen. Ann Arbor, MI: University of Michigan Press, pp. 257–72.

MacDonald, William. 1986. *The Architecture of the Roman Empire*. Vol. 2: *Urban Reappraisal*. New Haven: Yale University Press.

MacMullen, Ramsay. 1982. 'The Epigraphic Habit in the Roman Empire.' *American Journal of Philology* 103(3): 233–46.

Petersen, Lauren Hackworth. 2003. 'The Baker, His Tomb, His Wife, and Her Breadbasket: The Monument of Eurysaces in Rome.' *The Art Bulletin* 85(2): 230–57.

Smith, Roland R. R. 1987. 'The Imperial Relief from the Sebasteion at Aphrodisias.' *Journal of Roman Studies* 77: 88–138.

Smith, Roland R. R. 1988. 'Simulacra Gentium: The *Ethnē* from the Sebasteion at Aphrodisias.' *Journal of Roman Studies* 78: 50–77.

Thomas, Edmund. 2007. *Monumentality and the Roman Empire: Architecture in the Antonine Age*. Oxford: Oxford University Press.

Woolf, Greg. 1996. 'Monumental Writing and the Expansion of Roman Society in the Early Empire.' *The Journal of Roman Studies* 86: 22–39.

Mouvance Mouvance is a term that originally described the instability and flexibility of oral poetry, but was then applied to the MANUSCRIPT culture of oral traditions and literature with roots in ORAL TRADITIONS, originally medieval poetry.

Medievalist Paul Zumthor (1981; 1983; 1990) introduced the term *mouvance* to discussions of the differences between oral and written discourse. Drawing from comparative evidence, Zumthor described the instability and variability between particular oral performances of traditional narrative poetry at two levels: 1) the flexibility evident within stanzas that appear in multiple performances; and 2) the variations of which stanzas might be included or excluded in any particular oral performance (1990: 207). Reflecting on these observations, Zumthor used the term *mouvance* to describe the relationship of any particular performance to the broader tradition in which it participates. 'Thus the performance of a poetic work finds the fullness of its meaning in the rapport that connects it to those [performances] that have gone before it and to those that will follow it. Its creative force results, in fact, in part from the mouvance of the work' (1990: 203). Although he understood that WRITING changes culture significantly (e.g. especially in legal settings), Zumthor insisted that the mouvance of oral poetry means that oral poetry resists such change, even better than everyday oral discourse (1990: 203).

Although some of the oral poetry Zumthor studied only existed in written texts, he seemed to understand mouvance as primarily a characteristic of oral discourse that nevertheless might be evident at times in written manuscripts. John Dagenais more explicitly applied mouvance to the copying of manuscripts of medieval literature, thereby broadening what appears to be narrower application in Zumthor's work. Dagenais defined mouvance as 'the peculiar way in which handwritten texts "move" about each other and about a presumed originary center' (1994: 130). Before the invention of the printing press, all ancient and medieval literary texts were handwritten and, therefore, all 'moved' about the originary center as SCRIBES performed the literary text in their copying of one manuscript to another.

The application of mouvance to manuscript culture has been somewhat influential in biblical studies, most notably in the work of WERNER KELBER (2013: 414–30). Kelber and Alan Kirk (2008) have applied mouvance to observations from NT TEXTUAL CRITICISM. Similarly, Shem Miller (2015) applied mouvance to the textual plurality found in the DEAD SEA SCROLLS (see MULTIFORMITY). However, this rich term from medieval studies has more to contribute to discussions of biblical texts.

Raymond F. Person, Jr. (Ohio Northern University, USA)

Further Reading

Kelber, Werner. 2013. *Imprints, Voiceprints and Footprints of Memory: Collected Essays of Werner Kelber*. SBLRBS. Atlanta: SBL Press.

Kirk, Alan. 2008. 'Manuscript Tradition as Tertium Quid: Orality and Memory in Scribal Practices.' In *Jesus, the Voice and the Text: Beyond the Oral and the Written Gospel*. Edited by Tom Thatcher. Waco: Baylor University Press, pp. 229–34.

Miller, Shem. 2015. 'The Oral-Written Textuality of Stichographic Poetry in the Dead Sea Scrolls.' *DSD* 22: 162–88.

Zumthor, Paul. 1981. 'Intertextualité et mouvance.' *Littérature* 41: 8–16.

Zumthor, Paul. 1983. *Introduction à la poésie orale*. Paris: Éditions du Seuil.

Zumthor, Paul. 1990. *Oral Poetry: An Introduction*. Translated by Kathryn Murphy-Judy. Foreword by Walter Ong. Minneapolis: University of Minnesota Press.

Multiformity The term *multiformity* describes the thematic variation, narrative fluidity, and semantic polyvalence of ORAL TRADITIONS. As RUTH FINNEGAN observes, 'by its very nature oral literature is changeable' (1988: 69). Oral traditions therefore 'exist in multiple forms at the same time, so that no one form of the tradition represents a more "authentic" or "ORIGINAL" form of that tradition' (Rodríguez 2014: 24). Multiformity is akin to the term MOUVANCE: the essential indeterminacy of an oral text and its MANUSCRIPT tradition (Dagenais 1994: 17–24, 130; Zumthor 1990: 203–9). In oral-formulaic theory, multiforms are 'repeatable and artistic expressions of variable length which are constitutive for narration and function as generic markers' (Honko 1998: 100).

ALBERT LORD first described the variation of oral traditions as multiformity; more importantly, he proposed that multiformity permits the recreation of oral traditions in performance (2000: 99–102; 133). Lord observed that singers create divergent performances of an oral tradition, yet they consider each performance to represent the same oral tradition. These recreations are possible because each performance only presents a portion of the full tradition, and oral traditions exist in several authentic forms (2000: 100–1; 120–3). The ostensible paradox of inexact replicas, according to Lord, results from transposing the fixity of print into oral traditions. Consequently, Lord preferred 'multiformity' to 'variants': whereas 'multiformity' distances one from a text-based understanding of oral traditions, the term 'variants' portrays divergent oral traditions as alterations of an ideal text (2000: 100–1, 125). Variations are not invasive (to a putative original idea or text) because oral traditions are predominantly multiform.

Multiformity and mouvance are rooted in the operation of three oral-traditional dynamics: context, memory, and scribal practices. First, multiformity is 'a response to the exigencies of specific enactment contexts' (Kirk 2008: 216) because 'the performer/composer is aware of the need to speak in accordance with the demands of his audience rather than some authenticated but remote prototype' (Finnegan 1988: 69). Second, the power of the performer's memory generates multiformity. As FOLEY notes, memory in oral tradition is 'a kinetic, emergent, [and] creative activity' that in many cases 'is linked to performance' (Foley 2006: 84). While an oral-traditional manuscript provides a reference point for recitation, the 'primary existence and transmission' of an oral text is 'in the medium of memory' (Kirk 2008: 219). Third, multiformity stems from scribal performance. By incorporating their understanding of the oral REGISTER of language, SCRIBES re-perform as they copy (Doane 1994: 420–3). Some of the synonymous readings, additions, and scribal corrections found in the Hebrew Bible and the DEAD SEA SCROLLS, for example, are evidence that ancient Israelite scribes copied written texts with an oral mindset (Person 1998: 603–8). Indeed, scribes integrate the linguistic and paralinguistic repertoires of spoken communication into written copies, thereby changing the manuscript tradition according to variations in oral performance (O'Keeffe 1990: 4–6).

Shem Miller (University of Mississippi, USA)

Further Reading

Dagenais, John. 1994. *The Ethics of Reading in Manuscript Culture: Glossing the Libro de buen amor*. Princeton: Princeton University Press.

Doane, A. N. 1991. 'Oral Texts, Intertexts, and Intratexts: Editing Old English.' In *Influence and Intertextuality in Literary History*. Edited by Jay Clayton and Eric Rothstein. Madison: University of Wisconsin Press, pp. 75–113.

Doane, A. N. 1994. 'The Ethnography of Scribal Writing and Anglo-Saxon Poetry: Scribe as Performer. *Oral Tradition* 9: 420–39.

Finnegan, Ruth. 1988. *Literacy and Orality: Studies in the Technology of Communication*. Oxford: Basil Blackwell.

Foley, John Miles. 1995. *The Singer of Tales in Performance*. Bloomington: Indiana University Press.

Foley, John Miles. 2006. 'Memory in Oral Tradition.' In *Performing the Gospel: Orality, Memory, and Mark*. Edited by Richard Horsley, Jonathan Draper and John Miles Foley. Minneapolis: Fortress Press, pp. 83–96.

Honko, Lauri. 1998. *Textualizing the Siri Epic*. Helsinki: Academia Scientiarum Fennica.

Kirk, Alan. 2008. 'Manuscript Tradition as A Tertium Quid: Orality and Memory in Scribal Practices.' In *Jesus, the Voice, and the Text: Beyond the Oral and Written Gospel*. Edited by Tom Thatcher. Waco: Baylor University Press, pp. 215–34.

Lord, Albert. 2000. *The Singer of Tales*. 2nd edn. Edited by Stephen Mitchell and Gregory Nagy. Cambridge: Harvard University Press.

Nagy, Gregory. 2001. 'Homeric Poetry and the Problems of Multiformity: The "Panathenaic Bottleneck".' *Classical Philology* 96: 109–19.

O'Keeffe, Kathleen O'Brien. 1990. *Visible Song: Transitional Literacy in Old English Verse*. Cambridge: Cambridge University Press.

Person, Raymond F., Jr. 1998. 'The Ancient Israelite Scribe as Performer.' *JBL* 117: 601–9.

Rodríguez, Rafael. 2014. *Oral Tradition and the New Testament*. London: Bloomsbury T&T Clark.
Zumthor, Paul. 1990. *Oral Poetry: An Introduction*. Translated by Kathryn Murphy-Judy. Minneapolis: University of Minnesota Press.

Music The Bible and its related ancient literature witness to a concept of music in which organized sound was not an independent medium, but was always allied with what modern Western culture regards as non-musical elements. Those elements might be functional (directing, warning, signalling), verbal (uttered liturgy, poetry, PROPHECY, prose), visual (DANCE, drama), or symbolic (ritual). The concept of music as a discrete, aural phenomenon, the content, form, and performance of which could be appreciated for their own sake, is unknown in the Bible.

The widespread ancient belief that the sound of certain instruments possessed magical powers added a further functional element. The sound of the lyre (*kinnor*), for example, was regarded as 'sweet' or 'gentle' (e.g. Ps. 81.2 [Hebrew 81.3]) and as having apotropaic properties. Skilled and sensitive players could release the magical powers to influence the human psyche. Such beliefs lie behind the young David's playing the lyre to calm Saul's troubled soul (1 Sam. 16.16-23; 18.10), Elisha's calling for a 'musician' (most likely a lyre-player) to play while he prophesied (2 Kgs 3.15-16), and Job's playing a psaltery to placate his maidservants (*Testament of Job* 14.4).

The Hellenization of the Near East in the fourth and third centuries BCE extended the concept of 'music' to include organized sound as a discrete phenomenon. Nevertheless, the prevalent Near Eastern conception remained in place alongside the Greek. In biblical Hebrew and Aramaic there is no word meaning 'music' in the modern sense, and although the Greek term *mousikē* (from which the word 'music' is derived) is used in the SEPTUAGINT and related ancient literature in Greek, it always means a combination of sound and one or more 'non-musical' elements.

No musical notation is extant from the ancient Israelites, early Jews, or early Christians. Knowledge of their music is therefore dependent on historiographical and archaeological evidence. The musical idiom is a matter of speculation based on comparisons with music elsewhere in the ancient Near East (especially Anatolia and Mesopotamia) and cautious extrapolation backward in time from the earliest known Arab, Jewish, and Christian traditions. It is perhaps best envisaged as approximating a mix of Arab *maqām* and Jewish cantillation, the essential features of these being: 1) traditional melodic figures as structural elements; 2) microtonal intervals; 3) monophonic style; 4) improvised ornamentation following accepted conventions; 5) unison or random parallel intervals in communal song; and, 6) semi-melodic motivic recitative for formal reading or reciting to an audience. The last of these features would have been especially evident in the recitation of liturgy and the oral transmission of traditional laws, narratives, poetry, and teachings. Such solo delivery of verbal material in a semi-melodic style produced several noteworthy results: it set the text apart from ordinary speech; it carried the text in a way which made it clearly audible (advantageous in large assemblies and in the open air); and, it rendered the text more memorable. At the same time, a recitative style was rhythmically and tonally flexible, allowing the oral delivery to follow the natural rhythm of the words and to underline their syntax. In antiquity, this style of oral delivery would have been regarded as 'reading', 'reciting', 'saying', or 'uttering', even in the case of material formed as poetry, which was likely to have been delivered in a more melodic style than prose.

Many of the features listed above would also have applied to melodic instruments – pipes and plucked strings. It is known that strings of the lyre were tuned and retuned as required to make available a variety of melodic figures.

Exactly how voices and instruments meshed when sounding together is not known. It cannot be taken for granted that there was any requirement for the two to begin and end simultaneously, to use the same melodic figures, or for melodic instruments to follow vocal pitches exactly, or in heterophony, or at all.

Music in Ancient Israel and Judah

In ancient Israel/Judah, music is evinced in both religious and non-religious contexts. In religious contexts, five areas are pertinent: sacrifices and other rites; processions; sacred dance; prophetic ministry; and, warfare.

Music was intrinsic to the performance of sacrifices and other rites at TEMPLES and high places (see WORSHIP, ANCIENT ISRAELITE; WORSHIP, ANCIENT JEWISH). During burnt offerings music consisted primarily of two elements of equal importance, performed simultaneously: the singing (*shir*) of sacred texts and the playing (*zmr*) of plucked-string instruments (*kinnor* and *nevel*, the latter probably a large lyre but often translated 'harp'). Those elements were not *accompaniment*, either to each other or to the rites; they belonged together and to the rites as ritual music. Divine commands in Num. 10.1-10 specify that two metal trumpets (*hatsotserot*) were to be blown by Aaronide priests for signalling and to invoke the deity at whole burnt offerings and sacrifices of well-being. This practice was also intrinsic to the rites. The *cultic shout*, a loud acclamation to the deity by voices and instruments, was a customary interjection during rites on holy days at centres of worship.

Sources imply that the musicians at sacrifices and other rites were male. Closer identification is not made, except for the priestly trumpeters. It is possible that the musicians were prophets (Smith 2011: 55–9). Some prophets were associated with centres of worship (Gibeah: 1 Sam. 10.5; Bethel and Jericho: 2 Kgs 2.3, 5; Jerusalem and the Temple: Isa. 29.10; 30.10; Jer. 2.2; 4.5; 7.1-2; 17.19-20; 19.1-2; 26.2, 7-10; 30.19; Amos 1.2), and it is possible that oracles preserved in biblical books attributed to prophets were uttered as ritual music (see especially Isa. 5.1-7; 12.1-6). Several prophetic oracles are laments or dirges (e.g. Ezek. 19.1-14; 27.2; 32.2-16; Amos 5.1-17; Mic. 2.4), which were poetic forms delivered as song or chant. However, reconsideration of the biblical and extra-biblical accounts of Hezekiah opens for the possibility that a Levitical musical service, similar to that at the Second Temple, existed before the exile (2 Chr. 29.25; see Young 2012). In 2 Chr. 8.14 and 35.15 Solomon and Josiah respectively are credited with instituting a Davidic Levitical musical service.

The musical repertory at temples and high places may have included prophetic oracles, particularly laments, as mentioned above. The likelihood that laments belonged to the repertory is reinforced by notices at 2 Sam. 1.18; Ezek. 19.14; and 2 Chr. 35.25. Several pre-exilic psalms refer to music in worship and imply or specify settings in important centres (Pss. 7; 18; 21; 30; 40; 43; 61; 66; 68; 75; 81; 89; 95; 137; 144). It is not known whether any of those psalms was sung in worship; they may nevertheless give an idea of the kind of material employed. This may also be the case with cultically significant early biblical poetry from outside Psalms (see POETRY IN THE HEBREW BIBLE), some of which carries suggestions of having been sung while instruments were played (Smith 1998; 2011: 50–1).

Processions were associated with worship at religious centres (1 Sam. 10.5; 2 Sam. 6.3-5, 15–17; 1 Kgs 1.40; Isa. 30.29b; Ps. 68.24[25]). The instrumentation comprised percussion, shakers, winds, plucked strings, and the human voice, in various combinations. Ps. 68.25[26] places young women (*alamot*) playing hand drums (*tuppim*/*tofefot*) among the instrumentalists.

The Hebrew Bible shows sacred DANCE as typically allied with song or the sound of instruments, or both. Dance could be an element in processions (2 Sam. 6.5, 14). Settings in communal worship and in Jerusalem/Zion are sometimes implied (Exod. 32.19; Pss. 30.4[5]-12[13]; 87.7; 149.3; 150.4).

The exercise of prophetic ministry may have included reciting oracles during rites at main places of worship, as implied above. Be this as it may, in 1 Sam. 10.5 and 2 Kgs 3.15-16, prophesying is described as taking place to the sound of instruments. The simile in Ezek. 33.32 suggests that prophecy could be uttered as a song and that a prophet personally might play to provide the instrumental sound.

In warfare, shofars were blown to muster armies (Judg. 3.27; 6.34), and priests with metal trumpets and singers praising the deity accompanied troops into battle (Num. 31.6; 2 Chr. 20.21). Trumpet blasts invoking the deity's aid, battle hymns, and rallying shouts gave encouragement during the fray (Num. 10.9, 35; 2 Chr. 13.14-15; 20.22). Victors were welcomed home by women singing, dancing, playing hand drums (*tuppim*: Exod. 15.20-21), and shaking sistrums (*shalishim*: 1 Sam 18.6-7). The remarkable story of the Battle of Jericho (Josh. 6.1-27) further illustrates belief in the apotropaic properties of certain instruments (shofars in this case), especially when used in ritually controlled sacred contexts.

Outside the sphere of religion, wealthy Israelite households employed male and female musicians who, as singers, players, and dancers, provided entertainment and pleasing aural ambience (Gen. 31.27; 1 Kgs 10.12; 2 Sam. 19.35[36]; Eccl. 2.8; Ps. 45.8[9]). HYMNS and other utterances over infants and on the birth of children are well attested (Gen. 30.6-24; 1 Sam. 2.1-10). Funerary rituals included wailing and the utterance of laments. Lamentation and wailing were also responses to the destruction of cities; the book of Lamentations, for example, preserves five laments over Jerusalem. At weddings, a wedding song was customary, perhaps sung by the bride and groom (Jer. 7.34; 16.9; 25.10; 33.11a). The text of a work song, the Song of the Well, is provided at Num. 21.17-18 and introduced into its context with a command to sing. The strong, regular rhythm of the Hebrew would be effective in coordinating a team of workers using the regularly repeated movements that digging a well would require.

Music in Second Temple Judaism

Sources from the Second Temple period add nothing new to the concept of music defined at the beginning of this article, or to the occasions for music and the genres employed. However, they provide grounds for supposing that the melodic style was overall more varied than earlier as a result of the increasing influence of Hellenistic culture on Diaspora Judaism in areas distant from Israel/Palestine.

Sources also provide greater detail and deeper insights. The musical service at the Second Temple was highly organized. It was the prerogative of mature adult male members of specific Levite families and clans, following traditions believed to have been instituted by David. The heads of the pertinent Levite families are characterized as 'seers' and their musical service is described as 'prophesying'. The Levite musicians sang as a group and played plucked-string instruments (*kinnor* and *nevel*), and occasionally paired cymbals (*metsiltayim*) and single cymbals (*tseltsilim*). Two groups of Levitical instruments are identified: 'instruments of song' (*kele shir*, namely 'harps' and lyres; 1 Chr. 16.5, 42;; 42; 2 Chr. 5.13; Smith 2011: 64–5); and 'instruments of David' (*kele dawid*, namely 'harps', lyres and cymbals; 1 Chr. 23.5; 25.1; cp. 2 Chr. 7.6; 29.26, 27).

The repertory of ritual music consisted primarily of psalms. At the twice-daily sacrifices Levites recited eight daily proper psalms (one on each day of the week, SABBATH to Sabbath); at the Passover sacrifices they recited the HALLEL (Pss. 113–118). Biblical poetry from outside Psalms may also have been recited: a late source (*b. Rosh Hash.* 31a) proposes the Song of the Sea (Exod. 15.1b-19) and the Song of the Well (see POETRY IN THE HEBREW BIBLE).

Already at the end of the pre-exilic period there was a sense that music at sacrificial and other rites at the temple was sacred to the temple itself as well as to worship of the deity. This finds retrospective expression in Pss. 40.1[2]-3[4] and 137.2-6. In the Second Temple period the exclusiveness of the temple music is a strong feature underlined by two factors: the sanctity of the Levites' instruments (like the Levites themselves, they had to be ritually clean for service in the temple), and the location of the Levites' dwellings in or near Jerusalem.

Away from the temple, SYNAGOGUES were local centres of religious assembly. However, there is no evidence of a temple-style musical service in the early synagogue, since temple music, being sacred to the temple, had no legitimacy elsewhere. However, the shofar and the Hallel were not exclusive to the temple, so that shofar signalling and the paschal recitation of the Hallel took place in synagogues. There is no evidence of the use of daily proper psalms in synagogues at this time, but psalms in addition to the Hallel were recited occasionally.

In humbler settings, and while the temple still stood, the Passover meal took place in 'households' outside the temple. The meal had its own ritual, which included recitation of the Hallel by the 'head of the household', the remaining members contributing the 'hallelujah' refrain. Otherwise, the prevalent concept of music is aptly exemplified in a children's taunt quoted in the NT: 'We piped for you and you would not dance, we wailed for you and you would not mourn' (Mt. 11.17). A sacred ring dance with song (text provided) and implications of pipe playing is described in the Acts of John 94. Concerning customs of mourning, a remark in the MISHNAH says, 'Even the poorest man in Israel should not hire fewer than two pipes and one professional wailing woman' (*m. Ketub* 4.4).

Music in Early Christianity

The NT witnesses only to vocal music among the early Christians. The terms *hymn*, *psalm*, and (*spiritual*) *song* (Eph. 5.19) cannot automatically be taken to identify specific items or genres since they are typically used in a general, undifferentiated sense to refer to religious poetic texts. Acclamations and short poetic passages in the NT may represent material sung by the earliest Christians; some may have been used liturgically.

From the mid-second century CE onwards, sources use terminology more precisely and inform about the use of different genres. Two genres were paramount: hymnody and psalmody. Hymnody – melodic song to free religious poetic texts in free and strict metre – was at first used extra-liturgically for didactic purposes, but later primarily liturgically. Psalmody – the recitation of items from the book of Psalms – was a prominent constituent of corporate and private daily prayer, which typically took place on waking, in the middle of the day, and before sleeping.

An early substantial hymn fragment with musical notation has been preserved: the late-third-century CE Oxyrhynchus Hymn (Cosgrove 2011). The earliest reference to the use of an item from the book of Psalms in a Christian context occurs in the Acts of Paul 9 (late second century CE). The earliest extra-biblical reference to probable Christian song in worship occurs in Pliny the Younger's report of his interview with Christians in Bithynia (*Letters to Trajan* 10.96:7; 111–112 CE), which records that they used to gather before dawn 'and utter a song among themselves [*carmenque … dicere secum invicem*] to the Christ as to a god'.

John Arthur Smith (Church of Norway)

Further Reading

Brown, William P., ed. 2014. *The Oxford Handbook of the Psalms*. Oxford: Oxford University Press.
Burgh, Theodore W. 2006. *Listening to the Artifacts: Music Culture in Ancient Palestine*. London: T&T Clark.
Cosgrove, Charles. 2011. *An Ancient Christian Hymn with Musical Notation: Papyrus Oxyrhynchus 1786: Text and Commentary*. STAC 65. Tübingen: Mohr Siebeck.
Giles, Terry, and William J. Doan. 2009. *Twice Used Songs: Performance Criticism of the Songs of Ancient Israel*. Peabody MA: Hendrickson.

Kolyada, Yelena. 2009. *A Compendium of Musical Instruments and Instrumental Terminology in the Bible*. London: Equinox.

Smith, John Arthur. 1998. 'Musical Aspects of Old Testament Canticles in their Biblical Setting.' *Early Music History* 17: 221–64.

Smith, John Arthur. 2011. *Music in Ancient Judaism and Early Christianity*. Farnham: Ashgate.

Young, Robb Andrew. 2012. *Hezekiah in History and Tradition*. VTSup 155. Leiden: Brill.

N

Naḥal Ḥever Naḥal Ḥever is a stream in the Judean Desert that runs towards the Dead Sea, about 3 km (approximately 2 mi) south of En Gedi. The stream became famous because of important MANUSCRIPT finds in two caves at the head of the stream. During an initial survey in 1953, Yohanan Aharoni found ten caves and two Roman siege camps above two of them (Caves 5/6 and 8). The Bedouin had already searched these caves before the archaeologists excavated them. Nevertheless, Aharoni found fragments of the Greek Minor Prophets scroll in Cave 8, which indicates that the main section of this scroll discovered by the Bedouin came from this cave. In 1991, David Amit and Hanan Eshel found an eleventh cave in the western part of Naḥal Ḥever. The Seiyal texts are now regarded as coming from Naḥal Ḥever, but their exact cave provenance cannot be established (hence the use of X before the siglum *Hev/Se* for these manuscripts).

Cave 5/6, in which nineteen skeletons were found, is situated on the northern bank of Naḥal Ḥever. It is also called the Cave of Letters, because in 1960 Yigael Yadin found there a leather flask containing fifteen LETTERS sent by Shimon bar Kosiba (Bar Kokhba). Cave 8 lies opposite Cave 5/6 on the southern bank of Naḥal Ḥever. It is called the Cave of Horror because Aharoni found there more than forty skeletons. Three OSTRACA were found bearing names of the deceased placed on top of the skeletons. The evidence – two Roman camps and skeletal remains of men, women, and children – evidently points to violence and refuge as the context of deposition for the manuscripts at the caves in Naḥal Ḥever.

The texts from the Cave of Letters that were found in controlled excavations point to at least four different collections, representing private ARCHIVES: thirty-five legal papyri belonging to Babatha and written in Greek, Aramaic, and Nabatean-Aramaic; six legal papyri written in Greek, Aramaic, and Nabatean of Salome Komaise; six legal papyri in Hebrew and Aramaic of Eliezer bar Shemuel; and fifteen papyri in Hebrew, Aramaic and Greek from Bar Kokhba. These documentary texts are extremely important because they shed new light on various historical, social, and cultural aspects of Jewish society during the first and second centuries CE. In addition, two fragmentary biblical texts – one from Numbers in a late Herodian book hand dated to the middle of the first century CE) and another from Psalms (dated by Ada Yardeni to the early first century CE) – were found and later were matched with fragments that the Bedouin had purportedly found at Seiyal (Naḥal Ṣeʾelim), but the original deposition context of the two biblical manuscripts remains unclear. From the Cave of Horror comes the important Greek Minor Prophets, whose two SCRIBES are dated to the latter half of the first century BCE. Apart from a few other very small fragments, three small fragments of PARCHMENT of a prayer text (8Ḥev 2) were found during the excavation of an untouched grave; it is possible that this text was placed next to the dead.

Although the texts from the caves at Naḥal Ḥever are predominantly of a documentary nature, they also attest to the spread of literary texts across different strata of ancient Jewish society, albeit at different levels of engagement. Regional or local elites, wealthy families from villages such as those of Babatha or Salome Komaise, may indeed have owned some of the literary manuscripts found in the caves at Naḥal Ḥever. This means that access to and possession of literary texts was not limited to urban centres such as Jerusalem. Babatha and Salome seem to have been illiterate, as was Salome's brother. However, Babatha's second husband was literate and apparently also had the practised hand of an experienced writer. Perhaps those who were literate read from the texts to those who were not able to read, perhaps in the social context of family or friends, or even in the larger social context of the village, as we know from anthropological evidence. However, we may assume that the manner in which such people engaged with these literary texts was different from some of those behind the DEAD SEA SCROLLS from Qumran, or from Ben Sira or Flavius Josephus. Josephus' level of engagement was particularly of a different nature: studying, commenting, copying, and writing texts. Thus, we must reckon with different levels of LITERACY.

Finally, the texts, documentary and literary, also throw important light on the level of multilingualism or bilingualism. The private ARCHIVES from Naḥal Ḥever show a multifaceted engagement with different languages in the different settings of everyday life. For example, with regard to the Bar Kokhba LETTERS there is the famous letter in Greek (5/6Ḥev 52) in which the writer, Soumaios, apologizes for not having written it in Hebrew, which, scholars suggest, may have been expected from him. The manuscript finds from Naḥal Ḥever seem to agree with recent research on bilingualism in the Roman Near East and Egypt that argues for stable bilingualism in the countryside, where local languages were used alongside Latin and Greek, and a monolingual urban context, with speakers proficient in Latin or Greek (or both) but often not in the local vernaculars.

Mladen Popović (Groningen, Netherlands)

Further Reading

Clackson, J. 2012. 'Language Maintenance and Language Shift in the Mediterranean World during the Roman Empire.' In *Multilingualism in the Graeco-Roman Worlds*. Edited by Alex Mullen and Patrick James. Cambridge: Cambridge University Press, pp. 36–57.

Hezser, Catherine. 2001. *Jewish Literacy in Roman Palestine*. Tübingen: Mohr Siebeck.

Popović, Mladen. 2012. 'Qumran as Scroll Storehouse in Times of Crisis? A Comparative Perspective on Judaean Desert Manuscript Collections.' *JSJ* 43: 551–94.

Wise, Michael O. 2015. *Language and Literacy in Roman Judaea: A Study of the Bar Kokhba Documents*. New Haven: Yale University Press.

Narrative Gospels Historical Jesus and Gospels scholarship has typically differentiated the origin and transmission of reputed sayings of Jesus from stories about him. This differentiation closely mirrors the generic distinction between Sayings and Narrative Gospels. Scholars often read this latter distinction back into earliest Christianity, with the implication that SAYINGS GOSPELS and Narrative Gospels represent different streams of early Christian belief. Typically in such schemes, Sayings Gospels (e.g. Q, Gospel of Thomas) exhibit special interest in Jesus' wisdom and teachings and place little to no significance on accounts of Jesus' death, while Narrative Gospels (e.g. Gospel of Mark) feature apocalyptic traditions and emphasize the events and meaning of Jesus' passion.

In addition to the four canonical Narrative Gospels (and any of their hypothetical narrative sources), scholars generally categorize a number of extant non-canonical Gospels as Narrative Gospels on the basis of their primary literary form, including the Gospel of Peter, the Egerton Gospel (P. Egerton 2 and P. Köln 255), and a fragmentary PAPYRUS from Oxyrhynchus (P. Oxy. 840). In addition to these, two late second-century texts purport to narrate events of Mary's birth and upbringing or of Jesus' childhood, the Infancy Gospel of James and the Infancy Gospel of Thomas, respectively. This category would also include the so-called 'Jewish-Christian Gospels', none of which survive but which modern scholars have reconstructed from fragments quoted in various patristic sources. Though the precise number of Jewish Christian Gospels remains a matter of debate, scholars typically identify three: the Gospel of the Ebionites, the Gospel of the Hebrews, and the Gospel of the Nazarenes (see introductory discussion in Foster 2008).

The form critics postulated a written PASSION NARRATIVE that provided a significant source for the account of Jesus' death in the Gospel of Mark, the earliest of the canonical Gospels. John Dominic Crossan called this narrative the 'Cross Gospel', which he also identified as a significant source behind the second-century Gospel of Peter (Crossan 1988). Historians also propose collections of miracle stories, called 'miracle catenae', as early written narratives, which the author of Mark used in the composition of his Gospel (Koester 1990: 201–5). Although pre-Markan narrative texts exist only as conjecture from other written texts, these conjectures continue to exert influence over our understanding of the development of the Narrative Gospel tradition.

The author of the Gospel of Mark is typically credited with creating the narrative framework behind the Synoptic Gospels and, to a lesser extent, the Gospel of John. Potential sources for this framework include various ORAL TRADITIONS, written notes (and/or WAX TABLETS; see Poirier 2012), and narrative texts. WERNER KELBER especially popularized the hypothesis that the Gospel of Mark radically transformed the JESUS TRADITION by narrativizing it, thereby creating 'a novel unity' (1997: 91) out of the pre-written 'unorganized oral lore' (1991: 79). In other words, Mark transformed the Jesus tradition from episodic units that could be contextualized in any number of ways to a story with its own narrative logic (beginning, middle, and end), established connections between episodes, and a diminished capacity to adapt individual pericopae to new or multiple contexts. The appearance of the first narrative Gospel, according to Kelber, radically transformed the ways the earliest Christians used and understood the Jesus tradition (see NARRATIVITY).

According to both of the currently most popular source-critical hypotheses (the Two-Source hypothesis and the Farrer hypothesis), the Gospels of Matthew and Luke both followed Mark's narrative framework and expanded it with additional narrative materials (including birth narratives and post-resurrection appearances of Jesus) as well as extensive teaching materials (PARABLES, discourses, etc.). However, Matthew's and Luke's developments of the Narrative Gospel GENRE qualify Kelber's thesis that the narrativization of the Jesus tradition radically restricted its malleability and fluidity. Both Gospels consistently demonstrate a willingness to combine Markan traditions with additional materials (e.g. Mt. 12.22-32||Lk. 11.14-23; 12.10; cf. Mk 3.22-30) and to transpose Markan traditions from one context to another (e.g. Mk 11.25||Mt. 6.14-15).

The relationship between the Synoptic Gospels and the Gospel of John is complex and has been explained in various ways, ranging from John's literary dependence on one or more of the Synoptics to John's literary independence, with innumerable proposals in between (see Smith 2001). Johannine scholars often identify two major sources behind the Fourth Gospel – a Signs Source behind the seven signs/miracles of John 1–12, and a Passion Narrative – as well as various other sources. Whatever the precise contours of the relationship between the Fourth Gospel, the Synoptic Gospels, and whatever hypothetical sources may have actually existed, John clearly demonstrates the continued flexibility of the Jesus tradition even after the development of written Narrative Gospels. The striking features of this Gospel include, among other things, the dramatic recontextualization of the Temple Incident to the beginning of Jesus' ministry (Jn. 2.13-22), the 'Johannification' of the Feeding of Five Thousand and the Miraculous Sea-Crossing (Jn 6), and a distinctive account of Jesus' passion. In other words, many of the very same features media critics attribute to the oral Jesus tradition also characterize the written Narrative Gospels.

The narrative impulses behind the Jesus tradition show themselves even in our very earliest evidence. The hypothetical source Q, which comprises primarily sayings material preserved in the Gospels of Matthew and Luke, begins with an account of Jesus' BAPTISM by John and his temptation experience in the wilderness (Q 3.7-22; 4.1-13) and includes other narrative episodes (e.g. the Beelzebul Controversy; Q 11.14-20). Two of the earliest Jesus traditions preserved in Paul's LETTERS take a basic narrative form: the story of Jesus' Last Supper (1 Cor. 11.23-25) and stories of Jesus' death and resurrection/vindication (1 Cor. 15.3-8; Phil. 2.6-11) (see EUCHARIST). The development of written Narrative Gospels certainly had tremendous effect on the Jesus tradition itself, not least in its largely – but not totally – successful portrayal of Jesus as a Galilean prophet who journeys to Judea and Jerusalem once, at the end of his earthly ministry. However, we should not underestimate the tradition's narrative impulses from the very beginning, so that even individual or independent episodes were performed, received, and interpreted against a basic understanding of the chronology of Jesus' life, beginning with the baptism of John and continuing through his death and resurrection outside Jerusalem (see Acts 1.22; 10.37–41).

Rafael Rodríguez (Johnson University, USA)

Further Reading

Crossan, J. Dominic. 1988. *The Cross that Spoke: The Origins of the Passion Narrative*. San Francisco: Harper & Row.
Foster, Paul, ed. 2008. *The Non-Canonical Gospels*. New York: T&T Clark.
Kelber, Werner H. 1997 [1983]. *The Oral and the Written Gospel*. Bloomington, IN: Indiana University Press.
Koester, Helmut. 1990. *Ancient Christian Gospels: Their History and Development*. Philadelphia: Trinity Press International.
Poirier, John C. 2012. 'The Roll, the Codex, the Wax Tablet and the Synoptic Problem.' *JSNT* 35: 3–30.
Smith, D. Moody. 2001 [1992]. *John among the Gospels*. Columbia: University of South Carolina Press.

Narrativity Narrativity is the quality of coherent structure and story-like articulability that individuals and social groups bestow upon PERSONAL MEMORIES, the ACTUAL PAST, traditions, history, and discourses. Narrative serves as a memorial tool that aids the storage and communication of cultural texts. The verbal form of the word 'narrativity', 'to narrativize', refers to the process of endowing raw data (historical, memorial, or otherwise) with an intelligible narrative frame that supports the remembrance and re-articulation of that data in service of COLLECTIVE MEMORY.

Memory is only social if it is communicable and capable of being transmitted. Memory can be articulated in a variety of media, including calendars, rituals, MONUMENTS, GENEALOGIES, maps, and lists, among others. These media are, in and of themselves, non-narrative in form. Narrative, however, is another natural container, if not the most instinctive medium, for memory's storage and articulation. David Carr emphasizes that life is largely experienced as narrative; this being the case, the articulation of the past in narrative form is not an imposition of a foreign medium on raw historical or memorial data, but rather a re-articulation of memory in its most organic mode. Because humans experience the world as narrative and naturally narrativize their own experiences, narrativity is simultaneously a quality of human understanding and a means of human expression.

Hayden White contends that, like memory, history must be narrativized if it is to be communicable. In his view, historical narrativity is the inevitable process of endowing real events from the actual past with the coherence, integrity, fullness, and closure that is foreign to those events as raw historical data. To speak of *history* is therefore to speak of narrative. Interpreting narratives does not require bracketing off history altogether; the two are intrinsically connected.

Narrativization, the process of endowing memories or history with narrativity, is a selective process. Narrativizers determine which memories will be filtered out of their memorial, oral, or written narrative, which will be included, the order in which they will be presented, and how they will be interconnected. In the process, individual episodes from the remembered past are fixed within a particular linear framework that provides a larger interpretive context for establishing their significance. JAN ASSMANN emphasizes the importance of forgetting and repression in the process of transforming raw memories into a meaningful narrative. The narrativization process will inevitably be informed by both the historical past and the present exigencies of the producer's own social context. The process naturally acquires some degree of PRESENTISM/

CONSTRUCTIONISM. While narrativity's role in the storage and articulation of memory, history, and cultural texts is the object of the memory theorist's inquiry, what exactly narrativity consists of is the subject of the narratologist's attention. Narratologists are concerned with what elements constitute narrativity and what media forms possess it.

Biblical narrative critics have been attuned to the basic literary features of narrativity since the early 1980s: character, plot, setting, point of view, and RHETORIC. More recently, literary critics, influenced especially by poststructuralist theory and following the influential work of Monika Fludernik, have redefined narrativity and its constituent elements based largely on the characteristic of experientiality – whether or not a text or medium evokes real-life experience. Within the field of narratology, narrativity is considered a fuzzy category rather than a binarial one. As H. Porter Abbott defines it, narrativity is not a property that a text does or does not have, but rather a felt quality that exists in degrees or gradations. Marie-Laure Ryan has proposed eight conditions for determining the level of a medium's narrativity. Because of the proliferation of definitions of narrativity in the field of narratology, she offers these criteria as a toolkit for do-it-yourself descriptions of narrativity. While experientiality is a significant condition for judging narrativity, there are other variables that carry weight when considering the phenomenon: sequentiality, eventfulness, tellability, and narrative competence are especially important. According to some narratologists, most media, including oral stories, literature, visual art, and even architecture, possess these qualities and so also narrativity.

In the end, the greatest significance of narrativity for biblical media studies is how it supports the capacity for individuals and social groups to store and re-articulate memories, history, and cultural texts in a coherent, structural form that supports individual and collective memory.

Nicholas A. Elder (Marquette University, USA)

Further Reading

Abbott, H. Porter. 2009. 'Narrativity.' In *Handbook of Narratology*. Edited by Peter Hühn. Berlin: Walter Mouton de Gruyter, pp. 309–28.

Assmann, Jan. 2006. *Religion and Cultural Memory: Ten Studies*. Translated by Rodney Livingstone. Stanford: Stanford University Press, esp. 1–4; 85–7; 105–8.

Carr, David. 1986. *Time, Narrative, and History*. Bloomington: Indiana University Press.

Cubitt, Geoffery. 2007. *History and Memory*. Manchester: Manchester University Press, esp. 96–109.

Denton, Donald. 2004. *Historiography and Hermeneutics in Jesus Studies: An Examination of the Work of John Dominic Crossan* and *Ben F. Meyer*. Journal for the Study of the Historical Jesus Supplement Series 262. London: T&T Clark, esp. 168–92.

Fentress, James, and Chris Wickham. 1992. *Social Memory*. Oxford: Blackwell Publishing Company, esp. 47–51.

Fludernik, Monika. 1996. *Towards a 'Natural' Narratology*. London: Routledge, esp. 20–38.

Ryan, Marie-Laure. 2007. 'Toward a Definition of Narrative.' In *The Cambridge Companion to Narrative*. Edited by David Herman. Cambridge: Cambridge University Press, pp. 22–36.

White, Hayden. Oct. 1980. 'The Value of Narrativity in the Representation of Reality.' *Critical Inquiry* 7: 5–27.

Niditch, Susan Susan Niditch (b. 1950) is an American religious scholar, Biblicist, and folklorist whose research has surveyed a variety of aspects of ancient and early Judaism. Her work centres on the interdisciplinary study of early literature from the ancient Near East and the Hebrew Bible. She trained under the folklorist ALBERT BATES LORD as well as the biblical scholar Frank Moore Cross at Harvard University.

Niditch's research has focused on three main areas of study: 1) FOLKLORE and folkloric topics, such as the interplay between oral and written, as well as the elucidation of particular traditional motifs in the Hebrew Bible; 2) religious ethics, in particular, the nature of war and violence in the Hebrew Bible; and 3) the notion of the body in ancient Judaism, especially as it relates to issues of gender. Niditch is best known for bringing the methods and conclusions of folkloristics into the study of the Hebrew Bible. Examining the presence of folkloric elements in the Hebrew biblical text, Niditch has sought to show that biblical literature should be understood and read as traditional literature. One of her best known works, *Underdogs and Tricksters: A Prelude to Biblical Folklore*, includes an introductory essay that outlines a coherent folkloric approach to the study of the biblical text. The monograph also traces and examines the presence of the 'trickster and underdog' motif – a motif frequently found in traditional literatures from around the world – in the stories in Genesis as well as in the later text of Esther.

Aside from authoring several books on the folkloric study of the Hebrew Bible, her work has also focused on the related issue of ORALITY as reflected in the Hebrew Bible. *In Oral World and Written Word*, Niditch elucidates the ways in which the written Hebrew biblical text emerges out of a largely oral world. Noting that scholarship has largely dismissed the oral background of the biblical text as primitive and defunct, she argues that the biblical text should more accurately be viewed as an interplay between oral and written or as reflecting an oral-literary continuum. Her work examines features in the biblical text, such as repetition, epithets, and formulaic patterns (see FORMULAS), that form the oral aesthetic of this ancient text.

Niditch is also well-known for her research on issues of religious ethics, and, in particular, on the topic of war in the Hebrew Bible. Her monograph, *War in the Hebrew Bible*, delves into the problematic depictions of violence and warfare in various biblical texts. Tracing the different ideologies of war found in the Hebrew text, Niditch illuminates the complicated and multivocal vision of violence and war in ancient Israel. Related to her interest in violence and warfare, Niditch's works have also focused on issues concerning the body in ancient Judaism. Her most recent monograph, *My Brother Esau is a Hairy Man*, looks at the ways in which hair is utilized in the stories in the Hebrew Bible to reflect complex ideas about religion and identity. Continuing her interest on the body in ancient Israel, Niditch's commentary on the book of Judges surveys the ways in which concerns about the body, gender, sexuality, and identity reverberate in the stories in Judges.

Suzie Park (Austin Presbyterian Theological Seminary, USA)

Further Reading

Niditch, Susan. 1980. *The Symbolic Vision in Biblical Tradition.* Harvard Semitic Monograph Series 30. Chico: Scholars Press, 1980.

Niditch, Susan. 1984. *Chaos to Cosmos: Studies in Biblical Patterns of Creation.* Studies in the Humanities. Chico: Scholars Press, 1984.

Niditch, Susan. 1987. *Underdogs and Tricksters: A Prelude to Biblical Folklore*. New York: Harper and Row, 1987.

Niditch, Susan. 1990. *Editor, Text and Tradition: The Hebrew Bible and Folklore*. SemeiaSt. Atlanta: Scholars Press. 1990.

Niditch, Susan. 1993. *War in the Hebrew Bible: A Study in the Ethics of Violence*. New York: Oxford University Press, 1993.

Niditch, Susan. 1993. *Folklore and the Hebrew Bible*. Minneapolis: Fortress/Augsburg, 1993.

Niditch, Susan. 1996. *Oral World and Written Word.* Ancient Israelite Literature. Louisville: Westminster.

Niditch, Susan.1997. *Ancient Israelite Religion.* New York: Oxford University Press.

Niditch, Susan. 2008. *Judges: A Commentary*. Old Testament Library. Louisville: Westminster/John Knox.

Niditch, Susan. 2008. *'My Brother Esau is a Hairy Man': Hair and Identity in Ancient Israel*. New York: Oxford University Press.

Nonverbal Communication in Performance In considerations of performance, nonverbal communication is communication that takes place without words in the context of oral speech or live presentation. In a live exchange, any form of communication that does not involve words may be considered nonverbal, including tone and modulation of voice, rate of speech, facial expression, eye contact, gestures, posture, proximity to others, appearance, and dress. Nonverbal communication operates in cooperation with spoken words to provide additional information and meaning, often (but not solely) of an emotional nature. Nonverbal communication was a critical aspect of the performance of ancient texts, including presumably texts of Scripture.

Both the Hebrew Bible and the NT were produced in gesticular and nonverbally expressive societies. A study in the gestures of the ancient Arabs reveals that gestural communication was ordinary and not exceptional (Kruger 1998: 142). The ancient Greeks used 'the language of head, hands, and torso everywhere' (Household 1999: 6). The Latin orator Cicero (first century BCE) speaks of using the 'voice and gesture; and the entire body of a man, all his facial and vocal expressions … .' Cicero also speaks of the language and eloquence of the body, meaning the whole performance of the speech including voice, posture, and gesture (*The Orator* 3.216, 3.222; Graf 1992: 37). Likewise, the Latin orator Quintilian (first century CE), in a detailed textbook on speech composition and delivery, states that one should use the 'voice, look, and the whole carriage of the body' (*Institutes* 11.3.2). Indeed, gesticulation and body language were key to communicating to large crowds where distant members of the audience may not have been able to see a person's facial expressions nor hear clearly.

Nonverbal Communication and the Hebrew Bible

Unlike the Greco-Roman texts, we do not have ancient Hebrew rhetorical textbooks or descriptions of how Hebrew Bible texts were performed. Yet the biblical texts themselves provide clues to the nonverbal communications culture in which they were produced. First, the Hebrew Bible reflects the performative culture in which it was produced, one where legal realities were demonstrated by gesture or action, such as the removal of a sandal to indicate the failure of a brother-in-law from keeping his duty to his dead brother's widow (Deut. 25.5-10) or the striking of the hands together to seal an agreement (Prov. 17.18; 22.26). Publicly witnessed actions were as binding as modern written contracts, a necessity in the low LITERACY cultures of antiquity (Kruger 1998: 147).

As a second clue, the Hebrew Bible is full of allusions to nonverbally expressive behaviour. Joy or happiness is expressed by leaping (Mal. 4.2), hand clapping (Isa. 55.12; Ps. 98.8), foot stomping (Ezek. 25.6), dancing (Ps. 30.12), and skipping (Ps. 114.4). Disdain, disgust, contempt, or mocking is shown by waging or tossing the head (2 Kgs 19.21/Isa. 37.22); spitting (Num. 12.14; see also Deut. 25.9; Job 30.10); hissing (1 Kgs 9.8; Zeph 2.15; Job 27.23; Lam. 2.16); sticking out the tongue (Isa. 57.4); clapping the hands (Ezek. 25.6; Neh. 3.19; Job 27.23; Lam. 2.15); shaking the hand or fist (Isa. 10.32; Zeph. 2.15); gaping the mouth at/against (Job 16.9); or/and gnashing or grinding the teeth (Job 16.10; Ps. 35.16; Lam. 2.16). Sadness, despair, or dejection is indicated by a fallen or drawn face (Gen. 4.5). Mourning or grief is indicated by gashing the body (forbidden in Lev. 19.27-28; Deut.14.1, but apparently practised in Jer. 16.6; 41.5; 47.5; 48.37); pulling out the beard and hair (Ezra 9.3); beating the breast (Isa. 22. 12; Jer. 6.26; Mic. 1.8); not eating (2 Sam. 3.35; 12.17); and/or tearing one's garments (Gen. 37.34; 2 Sam. 1.11; 3.31;13.31; Job 1.20). Anger could be expressed by striking the hands together (Num. 24.10). Apparently, hand clapping of various sorts was a versatile nonverbal expression, given its use for communicating joy, contempt, or anger.

While the Hebrew Bible refers to a wide range of nonverbal communication practices, it is difficult to know precisely the role played by gestures and expressions in performances of the biblical narratives and prophetic oracles. Did Isaiah actually shake his fist when uttering 10.32, or toss his head to mimic the action spoken of at 37.22? Would a storyteller mimic the tearing of garments when relating the events of Gen. 37.34, or draw the hand across the body like a blade to indicate gashing at Lev. 19.27-28? Given the expressiveness of ancient Israelite culture noted above, it seems likely that performers of these texts would utilize at least some of their encoded nonverbal cues in performances of the material.

Nonverbal Communication and the New Testament

Indicative of its significance in Greco-Roman communications culture, the renowned orator Demosthenes was quoted as saying that delivery was the first, second, and third most important aspect of the speech. This was true not only in view of the impact of nonverbal communication on audience reception of the message, but also for assisting memory. Quintilian lists memorization and delivery as the fourth and fifth parts of oration (*Institutes* 1.3.1) and ancient rhetorical theorists collectively emphasize the importance of memory in the composition and performance of speeches (see MEMORY, GRECO-ROMAN THEORIES OF). In oral cultures, the memorization and recitation of large blocks of material was not uncommon, including full speeches and whole stories, perhaps including epics such as the *Iliad* or *Odyssey* (or at least lengthy sections thereof). Competitions among educated friends were held in which each would take a turn citing the next line of an epic (Shiner 2003: 121–2). Arranging specific gestures to go along with parts of a narrative or speech was part of the memorization process and was understood to aid in memorizing (Quintilian, *Institutes* 1.11.14). Both Quintilian and Cicero indicate that poor delivery could ruin a good message, while good delivery could strengthen a poorly worded speech (Quintilian, *Institutes*, 3.3.3; Cicero, *The Orator* 3.54.213).

The Greek word *hypokrisis* is used for the delivery of a speech, a stage actor performing, and for expressively reading a text (Shiner 2003: 83; see also LECTOR). The children of those who could afford EDUCATION were taught to read with expressiveness, receiving instruction about tone of voice, breath control, when and when not to pause, speed and volume of diction, and using greater or lesser expressiveness and energy (Shiner 2003: 100; see Quintilian, *Institutes* 1.8.1; see EDUCATION, HELLENISTIC).

Ancient orators used body language not only for sake of memory and more effective delivery, but also to recommend themselves to their audiences. This self-recommendation was accomplished by strong voice, posture, and gesture. Physiognomy, where one assesses character and intelligence based on physical appearance, was a common practice in antiquity. The dignified voice and appearance of the orator served to add credibility to the speaker and words spoken (Graff 1992: 45). Reflecting this cultural norm, Quintilian advises would-be orators to adopt a style of delivery that is 'manly, combining dignity with charm' (*Institutes* 1.8.2). This cultural aesthetic may lie behind the Corinthians' apparent accusations of Paul: 'For they say, "His letters are weighty and strong, but his bodily presence is weak, and his speech contemptible"' (2 Cor. 10.10; NRSV).

The refined style espoused by Cicero and Quintilian was conservative, yet the popular practice was likely much more dynamic, as can be seen from Quintilian's cautions against the style of other orators and teachers. This more dynamic style was thought by Quintilian to be 'designed to charm the ears of the uneducated majority' (*Institutes* 10.1.43), more appropriate for actors than serious orators (*Institutes* 11.3.183). The highly expressive, almost bombastic, style of popular oratory is also criticized by other ancient writers, including Plutarch, Cicero, and Tacitus. These negative assessments by leading theorists may suggest that more physically expressive performances were the norm among the masses, perhaps representing what the earliest Christians would have expected and regularly experienced.

Specific gestures and other nonverbal performance techniques mentioned in Greco-Roman sources include (see further Aldrete 1999; Shiner 2002 chapter 6):

> Argumentation: Join the tip of the middle finger and thumb palm up, move the hand right and left (*Institutes* 11.3.92). This gesture is used for narration of facts with slower movement and for refuting with faster movement. This technique is often used at the beginning (*exordium*) of a speech, and may be alluded to at Acts 26.1.

Exhortation: Cup the hand with fingers slightly spread and extend the arm with the hand raised slightly above the head (*Institutes* 11.3.103).

Insistence: Point with the index finger towards the ground in front of the speaker (*Institutes* 11.3.94).

Sorrow: Turn the head slightly to the right while bringing the right hand up towards the temple with the palm open.

Restraint: Extend the right arm slightly to the side, palm down and fingers out.

Compliance: Extend the arm to the front bent at a right angle with the hand towards one's face and the index and middle fingers extended.

Disagreement or dissent: Extend the arm to the side, palm down and fingers outstretched.

Approval: Extend the forearm in front of the body and make a circle with the thumb and index finger with the other fingers extended.

Puzzlement: Point to the face with the index finger.

Love: Raise the open hand palm down above the head.

Fear: Raise the hands to the side with the palms forward.

Thinking: Raise a partly closed fist to the side of the jaw with all the fingers and thumb closed enough to make a small circle.

The norms of ancient media culture and comments from its leading rhetorical theorists provide clues for the earliest performances of the NT texts and/or the traditional materials behind them. Depending on the genre of literature (LETTER, NARRATIVE GOSPEL, APOCALYPSE), the performance might range from that of expressive reading from a MANUSCRIPT to stage acting from memory. The narratives and the Apocalypse may have been memorized, and given time, letters may have been memorized in order to be delivered/performed for a gathered congregation. The dialogue in narratives would be spoken and gestured as if the various characters involved were speaking. We know that differing tonal modulations were sometimes given to the various characters in the narrative portion (*narratio*) of a speech (see Shiner 2003: 92). Speed would be modulated depending on the particular events being narrated or, in the case of a letter, the issues being discussed. While some gestures were stylized and specific to speech making and to the stage, others may have mirrored common and conventional gestures and physical mannerisms from daily life (Quintilian, *Institutes* 11.3.85-86, 102-3; see Hall 2004: 149).

Overall, modern interpreters of the Bible should keep in mind that silent reading of manuscripts was not the norm in antiquity, as it is today (see READING CULTURE). For the kinds of texts present in both Testaments, the design and audience expectation was often for performance. While PERFORMANCE CRITICISM has capitalized on this observation, it is important to note that simply reproducing an ancient performance with nonverbal communicative gestures would confuse a modern audience. Keeping in mind that performance gestures may sometimes have mirrored ordinary gesticulation, a good approach may be to discern the effect of specific gestures and reproduce these in a modern gesticulation at the appropriate portions of the text. Also, given the difference of gesticulation among various cultures, culturally appropriate gesticulation must be discerned for the target audience.

Britt Leslie (United Theological Seminary, USA)

Further Reading

Aldrete, Gregory S. 1999. *Gestures and Acclamations in Ancient Rome*. The Johns Hopkins University Press.

Bremmer, Jan. 1992. *A Cultural History of Gesture*. Edited by Herman Roodenburg. Cornell University Press.

Graf, F. 1992. 'Gestures and Conventions: The Gestures of Roman Actors and Orators.' In *A Cultural History of Gesture*. Edited by J. Bremmer and H. Roodenburg. Ithaca, NY: Cornell University Press, pp. 36–58.

Hall, Jon. 2004. 'Cicero and Quintilian on the Oratorical Use of Hand Gestures.' *Classical Quarterly* 54(1): 143–60.

Household, A. J. 1999. *When Gesture Was Expected: A Selection of Examples from Archaic and Classical Greek Literature*. Princeton: Princeton University Press.

Kruger, Paul A. 1998. '"Nonverbal Communication" in the Hebrew Bible: A Few Comments.' *Journal of Northwest Semitic Languages* 24(1): 141–64.

Kruger, Paul A. 2009. 'Nonverbal Communication and Narrative Literature: Genesis 39 and the Ruth Novella.' *Biblische Notizen* 141: 5–17.

Matthews, Victor H. 2012. 'Making Your Point: The Use of Gestures in Ancient Israel.' *Biblical Theology Bulletin* 42(1): 18–29.

Shiner, Whitney. 2003. *Proclaiming the Gospel: First Century Performance of Mark*. Harrisburg, London and New York: Trinity Press International.

O

Oaths In the biblical world, oaths (Hebrew *shevca*; Greek *horkos*) occurred in human or divine discourse, and typically consisted of a promise reinforced by a curse invoking a deity or king who could enforce the curse. Oaths typically referenced one's own behaviour, as with, for example, Jehoram's pledge to assassinate Elisha: 'So may God do to me, and more, if the head of Elisha son of Shaphat stays on his shoulders today' (2 Kgs 6.31). Less often, the curse could be directed towards another; Eli, for example, adjured young Samuel, 'May God do so to you and more also, if you hide anything from me of all that he told you' (1 Sam. 3.17b). The biblical authors also portray God making oaths, swearing by God's self (Isa. 45.23; Jer. 49.13; 51.14), by God's own holiness (Ps. 89.35 [MT 36]), by God's right hand (Isa. 62.8), or by God's name (Jer. 44.26). In other cases, simple declarative statements are understood to be divine oaths (Ps. 89.3-4 [MT 4-5]; 132.11, cf. Heb. 6.13-18).

Oaths became so stereotyped through popular usage that the curse portion of the formula ('Thus and more may God do to me/you') was often dropped or abbreviated to something like 'As Yahweh lives', leaving only the promise, introduced by *'īm* ('If I/you do/do not'), which becomes a negative asseveration. King Saul thus says, in vowing to preserve David's life, 'As Yahweh lives, if he is put to death', but the meaning, as indicated by the NRSV, is 'As Yahweh lives, he [David] shall not be put to death' (1 Sam. 19.6b; see also Gen. 14.23, 42.15; Num. 14.23; 1 Sam. 3.14; 2 Kgs 2.2, 3.14; Isa. 22.14; Ps. 132.3-4, Job 6.28, Heb. 4.3). Oath-taking was so common that laws were developed to regulate the practice, requiring persons who swore falsely to confess their wrongdoing, pay a financial penalty, and offer sacrifices for expiation (Lev. 5.20-26).

Oath-taking persisted into the first century, when NT writers recalled with favour God's solemn oaths (Lk. 1.73; Acts 2.30; Heb. 6.13-17). In the NT, forceful assertions are sometimes called oaths, as when Peter swore that he did not know Jesus (Mt. 26.74; Mk 14.71) or when Herod swore to give his dancing daughter whatever she requested (Mk 6.23). Jesus, however, seems to take a generally negative posture towards oaths, charging his followers to speak with such integrity that their 'yes' or 'no' should be sufficiently binding (Mt. 5.34-37; see also Jas 5.12). This restriction extended to oaths that appealed to something valuable other than God as 'witness'. Thus, Jesus warned his disciples not to swear by their heads (Mt. 5.33), and criticized rabbis who debated whether oaths were more binding if sworn by the temple, its gold, the altar, or the gift on the altar (Mt. 23.16-20).

Functions of Oaths

In the oral milieu, and in the absence of binding written contracts (or sometimes within the context of, or alongside, a written document), the oath added a sense of permanence, solemnity, and consequence to speech, extending the force of what was said beyond the moment of the utterance. Oaths functioned orally to reinforce the veracity of a promise by invoking punishment from a higher power if one's word proved false. Because they involved serious matters, oaths were typically located in informal but intense settings of social interaction, as when Abraham swore he would not take anything from Sodom's king because 'I have raised my hand to

Yahweh, to the Most High, creator of heaven and earth' (Gen. 14.23), or when Joseph swore (by Pharaoh) that his brothers could not return without Benjamin (Gen. 42.15). This intensity, and the implication of consequence for breaking one's word, is sometimes harnessed in biblical narrative portrayals of oaths to heighten the drama of a story. Despite the self-imprecations, oath-takers could also be oath-breakers, especially regarding conflict situations that reflect negatively on the oath-taker. Saul (1 Sam. 14.44), David (1 Sam. 25.22), Jezebel (1 Kgs 19.2), Ben-hadad (1 Kgs 20.10), and Jehoram (2 Kgs 6.31) all made oaths that they failed to keep. More positively, oaths could be used to pledge loyalty. Ruth swore that she would never leave her mother-in-law Naomi (Ruth 1.17), even as Jonathan and David swore fealty to each other (1 Sam. 20.13-17).

Oaths on a national scale were commemorated in official documents designed for public viewing. Treaties from Hittite, Neo-Assyrian, and Neo-Babylonian sources typically required defeated nations to swear fealty to the new suzerain, who then published the covenant in various ways as a public record. Such oaths were considered serious: when Judah's king Zedekiah rebelled against his Babylonian overlords, the prophet Ezekiel excoriated him for breaking the treaty oath that he had sworn by Yahweh (Ezek. 17.11-21; 21.23-29). Scholars have often perceived in the covenant ceremony of Deut. 27–29 a reflection of ancient suzerainty treaties, with Yahweh proscribing conditions for a peaceful and productive relationship while Israel swears loyalty to God. In place of the ambiguous 'May God do thus and so to me' of more informal oaths, the covenant oath includes stated rewards for obedience and curses for disobedience.

Material exemplars of Hebrew oaths from the biblical period are rare, but their PUBLICATION is well attested by the ORAL TRADITIONS that found their way into the written record. Moses instructed the Israelites to erect plastered stones and write on them the words of their sworn covenant with God when they came into the land (Deut. 27.1-8). The tablets containing the commandments were kept in the Ark of the Covenant, symbolic of the covenant Israel had sworn to uphold (Deut. 10.1-5; 1 Kgs 8.9; 2 Chr. 5.10). Oaths are implied rather than spelt out in Samuel's solemn institution of kingship in Israel, during which he explained the 'rights and duties of kingship' and then 'wrote them in a book and laid it up before the LORD' (1 Sam. 10.25). These examples highlight the interface between ORALITY and WRITING by showing how written texts could serve as memorial artefacts of prior acts of speaking.

The prevalence of oath-taking in daily conversation can be illustrated by two examples from the Lachish LETTERS, a collection of OSTRACA recording messages sent between military leaders prior to the Babylonian destruction of Jerusalem in 587 BCE. Having been accused of not reading recent orders, a soldier named Hoshayahu wrote to defend himself with an oath, 'As Yahweh lives, I do not need a SCRIBE to read your orders for me' (Letter 3; a similar oath occurs in Letter 6).

Tony W. Cartledge (Campbell University, USA)

Further Reading

Cartledge, Tony W. 1992. *Vows in the Hebrew Bible and the Ancient Near East*. Sheffield: JSOT Press.

Lehman, Manfred R. 1969. 'Biblical Oaths'. *ZAW* 81: 1, 74–92.

Matthews, Victor H., and Don C. Benjamin. 2006. *Old Testament Parallels: Laws and Stories from the Ancient Near East*. 3rd edn. Mahwah, NJ: Paulist Press.

Thiselton, Anthony C. 2009. 'Oaths,' in *The New Interpreter's Dictionary of the Bible*, Vol. 4. Nashville: Abingdon.

Ziegler, Yael. 2007. '"So Shall God Do ...": Variations of an Oath Formula and Its Literary Meaning.' *JBL* 126: 59–81.

Ong, Walter J., S.J. Walter Jackson Ong, S.J. (1912–2003) was a prolific and polymathic twentieth-century scholar whose professional publishing and teaching career spanned over six decades and numerous academic disciplines. In addition to his over four hundred published works, the Ong Archives at Saint Louis University contain a comparable number of unpublished writings. Ong's academic home-base was English literature, but it extended beyond that in fundamental ways. His publications included studies on John Milton, Gerard Manley Hopkins, Joseph Conrad, and T.S. Eliot and analyses of literary criticism and critiques of the textual biases of the New Criticism. Yet his interests and writings sprang from and flowed into a panoramic interplay of academic fields including history, language, philosophy, theology, communication and media, psychology, biology, anthropology, and education, among others.

It is tempting to approach Ong as an expert in one or more academic fields, most notably in Renaissance and early modern European intellectual history. While true enough, this approach would miss what is most distinctive and valuable about his thought and work. A central characteristic of his way of proceeding in scholarship is to correlate analogous patterns from a wide range of disciplines rather than to reduce multiple sources into a single perspective. The effect of this is to continuously enlarge the horizon of inquiry and understanding rather than to narrow it to a few explanatory coordinates. Ong's persistent urge to challenge reductionist assumptions leads to more open-ended inquiry than to closed-system thinking.

The sheer mass and variety of Ong's works makes it hard to summarize their contents or generalize their sweep. However, there are several works that singly and together both illustrate the character and scope of Ong's work generally and offer valuable resources and perspectives for biblical studies. *Ramus, Method and the Decay of Dialogue: From the Art of Discourse to the Art of Reason* (1958) is Ong's foundational work, which coalesces his insights into intellectual history and the shaping role of attitudes towards verbal expression on human sensibility. It traces meticulously the transit from the oral disputational milieu of the medieval university to the flat, diagrammatic, depersonalized, visualist dialectic of Peter Ramus and associates that took hold of education beginning in sixteenth-century Europe, precisely the century that saw the beginnings of the modern, historical-critical study of the Bible.

The Presence of the Word: Some Prolegomena to Cultural and Religious History (1966) greatly deepened and extended what Ong had discovered about how shifts in verbal communication generate characteristic biases in human cultural history. Founded on studies from a wide range of disciplines, Ong investigates how the human 'word' is 'present' under the complex and varying circumstances from primary oral culture, through phonetic manuscript literacy to typographic and into electronic processing. He discussed themes such as the cultural and religious significance of the orally based Hebrew word *dabar* (= spoken 'word-event') and its transformation into various forms of text and textual hermeneutics.

Fighting for Life: Contest, Sexuality and Consciousness (1981) is a somewhat more specialized embodiment of Ong's relationist hermeneutic that takes as an impulse a response to E.O. Wilson's biological reductionism. It examines the multifaceted relationships of 'contest and other adversatives' to the formation of human masculine and feminine identities and the role of I–Thou relationships in a wide range of settings and issues that connect with the formation and interpretation of biblical literature and other religious phenomena.

Orality and Literacy: The Technologizing of the Word (1982) is perhaps his most popular and most widely read work. This modest-sized study gathers and distils Ong's long-term investigation of relationships between human knowing, orality-literacy, and communications technology. It addresses both the historical and cultural contributions of orality-literacy studies as well as the history of those studies themselves. As such the book can be seen in part as an extension of the hermeneutical tradition of Milman Parry, Albert Lord, Eric Havelock, and Marcel Jousse. Ong offers suggestions about the value of this approach for the study and interpretation of biblical literature. It should be noted that reading this book apart from Ong's wider corpus risks missing the fuller scope of Ong's relational approach.

Although Ong explored some of the biases built into modern biblical scholarship, he did not pursue them extensively himself. While he is often read and cited by biblical scholars, there has been little serious application of the remedies he suggests for the '... disability [that] has interfered with our understandings of the Bible, with its massive oral underpinnings, and that of the very nature of language itself' (1967: 20–21).

The clearest and most developed demonstration of Walter Ong's relevance for biblical studies is the work of WERNER H. KELBER. His *The Oral and The Written Gospel: The Hermeneutics of Speaking and Writing in the Synoptic Tradition, Mark, Paul and Q* (1983), with a foreword by Ong, challenges systemically the text-bound myopia of FORM CRITICISM. Kelber applies Ong with full force by showing how form-critical hermeneutics assumes that ORAL TRADITION functions comparably to textual composition and transmission, and why this assumption radically distorts the process by which biblical literature came about and how it should be understood.

Randy F. Lumpp (Regis University, USA)

Further Reading

Kelber, Werner H. 1983. *The Oral and The Written Gospel: The Hermeneutics of Speaking and Writing in the Synoptic Tradition, Mark, Paul and Q*. Foreword by Walter J. Ong, S.J. Philadelphia: Fortress Press.

Kelber, Werner H. 2013. *Imprints, Voiceprints, and Footprints of Memory: Collected Essays of Werner H. Kelber.* SBLRBS. Atlanta: SBL Press.

Farrell, Thomas J., and Paul A. Soukup, eds. 2002. *An Ong Reader: Challenges for Further Inquiry*. Cresskill NJ: Hampton Press, 2002.

Farrell, Thomas J. 2015. *Walter Ong's Contributions to Cultural Studies: The Phenomenology of the Word and I-Thou Communication*. Revised Edition. New York: Hampton Press, 2015.

Ong, Walter J. 1958. *Ramus, Method, and the Decay of Dialogue: From the Art of Discourse to the Art of Reason.* Cambridge, MA: Harvard University Press.

Ong, Walter J. 1967. *The Presence of the Word: Some Prolegomena for Cultural and Religious History*. New Haven and London: Yale University Press.

Ong, Walter J. 1977. 'Maranatha: Death and Life in the Text of the Book.' In *Interfaces of the Word: Studies in the Evolution of Consciousness and Culture*. Ithaca and London: Cornell University Press, pp. 230–71.

Ong, Walter J. 1981. *Fighting for Life: Contest, Sexuality, and Consciousness*. Ithaca and London: Cornell University Press.

Ong, Walter J. 1982. *Orality and Literacy: The Technologizing of the Word.* London and New York: Methuen.

Ong, Walter J. 1986. 'Text as Interpretation: Mark and After.' In *Oral Tradition in Literature: Interpretation in Context.* Edited by John Miles Foley. Columbia: University of Missouri Press, pp. 147–69.

Oral Tradition, the Comparative Study of The term *oral tradition* encompasses three interrelated topics of research relevant to biblical studies. First, it denotes ways in which societies and individuals carry information, organize themselves, and make sense of their lives via oral communication. Thus defined, oral tradition manifests itself in speech and dialogue; makes use of stories and SONGS; carries laws and instructions; imparts political, religious, and medical knowledge; transmits edicts and proclamations; revels in HYMNS and acclamations; defines itself in lists and genealogies; excels in epic poems of monumental proportion and also in aphoristic sayings of succinct brevity; thrives on ballads and PARABLES; narrates myths and rituals; recites prayers and blessing; pronounces cures and curses; and much more. For the longest time in the history of homo sapiens, oral tradition has been the primary medium for the planet's inhabitants. WRITING systems developed relatively late. Oral tradition predated chirographic technologies, but was by no means confined to primary oral cultures. In numerous manifestations, it extended deep into MANUSCRIPT cultures, coexisted with print technology, and in the current digital revolution experiences a revival as electronically mediated SECONDARY ORALITY. Thus, oral tradition dwarfs literature both in output and complexity. Owing to its adaptability and durability, it is a phenomenon of global dimensions.

Second, the term/concept *oral tradition* may be used more expansively with the recognition that it is not limited to verbal communication transmitted without written texts, but that written texts themselves interface with speech in numerous and complex ways. What further amplifies the worldwide presence of living traditions is a myriad of so-called oral-derived or traditional texts that variously interact with oral communication. Intermediality designates written texts that are in some ways related to, or derived from, an oral or oral-scribal performance tradition and that were, therefore, partially or in toto in place prior to their present existence. Recognition of this reality has prompted scholars to extricate oral, traditional elements embedded in written texts so as to make them the object of focused studies. Today the realization prevails that the notion of detachable speech is problematic because spoken words are sound, so that they are un-representable and therefore irretrievable in textual form. Nonetheless, a very large number of texts in the ancient media world are examples of intermediality. Irrespective of the extent to which they drew on tradition, they were part of a *Rezitationskultur* (JAN ASSMANN), destined to be read out loud so as to be internalized in people's hearts and minds. The key to the analysis of oral-derived texts lies in an interpretive reorientation from the textual to the aural, performative arena (see READING CULTURE). This can be accomplished by identifying rhythmically shaped diction, repetitive techniques, parallelisms, audience cues, TYPICAL SCENES, stock phrases, epithets, and countless other features that were fashioned in response to performative imperatives and memorial needs. In short, oral-derived or traditional texts require the cultivation of a new set of sensibilities that include attention to a grammar of sound, the recognition of mnemonic devices, and an appreciation of emotional effects.

Third, the term *oral tradition* may connote not only the medium and content of texts themselves but also the context shared by performer and hearers. Used in this broad sense, oral tradition includes written texts, or more often knowledge imparted via re-oralized texts, as well as oral communications, but it entails more than both. Oral tradition as context is an often invisible nexus of information, memories, and identities from which people draw sustenance and in relation to which they make sense of their lives. This invisible BIOSPHERE is at once tradition's most elusive and foundational manifestation. Tradition as context for performance is once again difficult to understand for the contemporary interpreter, even though it shares certain analogies to modern receptionist theory (Wolfgang Iser; Hans Robert Jauss). What oral tradition as context suggests is that texts in themselves do not carry the full meaning: part of the work of understanding is accomplished by the informing context, and the other part by the event of textual recitation. Word-power in the full sense emerges from the interface of textual performance and traditional context. In this contextual sense, tradition is the oxygen of interpretation.

The Study of Oral Tradition

The intellectual apprehension of the phenomenon of oral tradition owes much to MARCEL JOUSSE (1886–1961) and MILMAN PARRY (1902–35), who were instrumental in laying the foundation of what was to become an academic discipline in its own right. The work of both scholars was grounded in extensive fieldwork, Jousse conducting research in the Middle East and Parry in the former Yugoslavia. Jousse, in addition to his fieldwork, mentioned three experiences that had shaped his oral sensibilities: his childhood in the deeply rural Sarthe region southwest of Paris, his study of oral structures in the Hebrew Bible and Aramaic TARGUMS, and his acquaintance with Native American people groups. His fame rests on his theory of oral style, which was programmatically developed in *Le Style oral rhythmique et mnémotechnique chez les verbo-moteurs* (1925; English 1990). The technical term *verbomotoric* was Jousse's choice to describe oral style and culture as being word-focused rather than object-directed, interactive more than strictly mental as well as rhythmic, formulaic, and grounded in the bilaterality of the human body. What was radical about Jousse's theory was the claim that oral traditions and communication were not, as Western humanities had been inclined to imply, a form of writing, but a phenomenon *sui generis* and distinguishable from writing cultures. Jousse's theoretical ambitions aspired a *grande synthèse*, reaching far beyond a theory of communication. His explorations encompassed a wide variety of linguistic, biological, and cultural features; compositional techniques and performance activities; learning processes; anthropological laws; the human propensity for miming; connections between utterance and gestures; memorial processes; and many more. In the first half of the twentieth century, therefore, Jousse's oral style theory stood out as an all-encompassing, interdisciplinary phenomenology of speech, human nature, and action. Despite his impact on the study of oral tradition, Jousse's work has remained largely unacknowledged in biblical scholarship.

The academic standing of Milman Parry, the second founding figure of what came to be the modern discipline of oral tradition studies, is closely allied to the Oral-Formulaic Hypothesis, which conceptualized oral compositioning techniques of the Homeric epics. This theory asserts that the highly patterned, formulaic diction of the two monumental Homeric epics, the *Iliad* and the *Odyssey*, were fashioned under the pressure of oral performance, rather than representing the work of literate 'authors' in the modern understanding of that term. A number of insights advanced by Parry had been proposed by others before him. Some historical critics, for example, had explicated Homer's metrically fashioned language in ways that came close to Parry's concept of FORMULA. Others, observing that a developed technology of WRITING was not available in Homer's time, surmised that the poet must have been drawing on traditional lore. Three individuals exercised a particular impact on Parry. From his own teacher at the Sorbonne, the French linguist Antoine Meillet, he adopted the idea that Homeric language 'was entirely composed of formulae handed down from poet to poet'. The Slovenian ethnographer and comparative linguist Matija Murko familiarized Parry with the tradition of South Slavic singer-poets, and suggested to him the possibility of compositional analogies with the Homeric epics. A third influence was Jousse himself. Parry attended Jousse's lectures in Paris, read his seminal 1925 book, repeatedly cited from it, and advised ALBERT LORD, then his student, to read it.

Given this extensive scholarly prehistory, Parry's distinct achievement was the combination of the fruits of his own extensive anthropological fieldwork with an exacting philological analysis of the *Iliad* and *Odyssey* into a comprehensive theory of the oral, traditional nature of Homeric language. The analogies he observed between early twentieth-century South Slavic SONGS and ancient Greek epics enabled him to develop the concept of Homer as an oral, and not merely traditional, poet. Up to ninety per cent of Homer, in Parry's estimation, was constructed on formulaic diction of the kind he had identified in the districts and outlying regions of the western Balkans – both on the level of individual phrases and expressions, and on the level of thematic and scenic parallelisms. The explanation for the massively formulaic language, Parry argued, lay in the word processing of oral tradition: ancient bards had employed pre-formulated elements handed down by previous singers and made them fit into the metrical design of the hexameter, all in the interest of serving the requirements of memory. None of this entailed rote memorization of the content of texts; rather, in all instances, the singers exercised freedom to engage traditional building blocks creatively. Thus, the Homeric epics, while thoroughly traditional, were enacted via composition in performance, with each performance constituting a unique creation. Tradition was thus a process not of repetitions, but of recreations. The challenge Parry's thesis posed to the text-centred, literary approach was to come to terms with the reality that *Iliad* and *Odyssey* were not the first in a long line of great books in the literary civilization of the West, but the fossilized remnant of a once living performance tradition.

Along with Jousse and Parry, Albert Lord ranks as a co-founder of what was to become the modern discipline of oral tradition. In his classic study *The Singer of Tales* (1960), a follow-up volume, *Epic Singers and Oral Tradition* (1991), and in a host of articles, Lord defended and expanded the validity of the Oral-Formulaic Hypothesis, which came to be known as the Parry-Lord thesis. With regard to the production and consumption of oral-traditional literature, Lord reiterated Parry's concept of composition in performance, renounced the notion of a single ORIGINAL version of oral texts, and advocated the concept of multiple originals (see PLURIFORMITY). He also expanded the boundaries of the oral-compositional formula to include larger syntactic units, blocks of lines, and even whole sentences. Lord also expanded the scope of the comparative database, reaching beyond the Homeric poems and Muslim cycles from South Serbia, Bosnia, and Herzegovina to encompass Old English, Old French, Byzantine, and Bulgarian literature, as well as epic traditions from Central Asia. He also moved beyond Parry in treating the media transition from performance to scribality, an issue hitherto largely ignored by Homeric scholars. To resolve the problem of how the profoundly oral-formulaic Homeric epics had become textualized, he introduced the idea of dictation: Homer, a bard unskilled in the new technology of writing, depended on competent SCRIBES to record his work. Lord conceded that the texts of the *Iliad* and *Odyssey* 'suggest some reliance on writing' (1991: 45) and are not exact representations of oral performance. Homer's works as we have them are thus neither direct autographs of oral processes of composition in performance nor products of developed scribal technologies, but 'oral dictated texts' – something of a middle voice, a media category *sui generis*.

The Parry-Lord thesis met with little acceptance in the authors' home discipline of classical philology, with the noteworthy exception of ERIC HAVELOCK (1903–88). A classical philologist, Havelock was puzzled by the linguistic and conceptual gap that separated Homer and the Pre-socratics from PLATO and much of subsequent Greek philosophy. Why were Plato and post-Platonic philosophers inclined towards metaphysical and abstract thought, while pre-Platonic thinkers, at least as described in the extant written sources, seemed to represent a very different state of mind? Havelock's widely acclaimed *Preface to Plato* (1963) answered this question by advancing a new approach to Platonic philosophy: Homer and Plato belonged to two different cultural phases, their respective approaches illustrating the technological shift that occurred from the fifth to the fourth centuries BCE with the introduction of writing. At that time, Greece experienced a medium change from 'the 'poetic', or 'Homeric', or 'oral' state of mind' (1963: 47) to a new conceptual discourse that had grown out of alphabetized, stored knowledge and LITERACY. Parry's thesis of Homer's oral, formulaic style, Havelock acknowledged, along with insights offered especially by Martin P. Nilsson and other philologists, enabled him to find 'the outline of the answer' (1963: x) in the medium shift from an oral to a literate stage in Greek civilization (1963: x).

Havelock demonstrated his thesis through a close analysis of the Platonic attack on the poetic tradition in Book 10 of the *Republic*. Why, Havelock asked, this focus on epic poetry in a treatise largely devoted to political theory, and why was Plato passionately committed to excluding the poetic experience from education? In a perceptive rendering of the psychosomatic dynamics of oral performance and auditory response mechanisms, Havelock described *poetry* as standing for the whole system of Greek education, which was exemplified in the emphasis on Homeric recitations, reenactments, repetitions, mnemonics, metrics, the hypnotic power of spoken words, bodily reflexes, and the audience's sympathetic identification – a whole performative apparatus which, in Plato's eyes, crippled the intellect and indoctrinated the young. Plato's 'main enemy' was 'the oral state of mind' (Havelock 1963: 41), as epitomized by the core of the Greek *paideia* manifested in the performance of epic poetry and its effects on hearers. Plato's tirade was thematized from the perspective of a developing literacy that encouraged the kind of mental and emotional distances required for more objective critical thinking. This preferred educational aim is explicit in Book 10 of *Republic*: readers should think about poetry instead of identifying with it, and they should conceive of themselves as subjects apart from the object.

Havelock's thesis was significant for at least two reasons. First, it located Platonic thought squarely in ancient communications history, explicating Plato's repudiation of the poetic performance culture as a result of a paradigm shift from oral to written culture. Second, Havelock not only documented the practice of oral tradition in uniquely sensitive prose, but also explained Plato's profound hostility towards it as a defining feature in ancient philosophical history.

The Parry-Lord thesis scored its greatest success outside the fields of classics and philosophy, impacting and unifying a wide range of disciplines; John Miles Foley has rightly described the comparative study of oral tradition as 'one of the most far-reaching research programs in the humanities over the last century' (2002: 109–10). Driven by a wide-ranging comparative relevance and near-universal applicability, the Parry-Lord thesis impacted, and often deeply affected, research in over one hundred language areas, extending from Sumerian to ancient Greek to Old English to medieval Spanish, and including languages from the Indian subcontinent and the South Pacific to the Americas and Africa. Viewed through the Parry-Lord lens, oral-traditional structures were found everywhere. Over time, the rapidly growing exploration of oral cultures evolved into a separate field of knowledge with a subject matter, history, and methodology uniquely its own. Perhaps most importantly, the range of new data and insights encouraged a growing awareness that the new discipline required 'a wholesale shift in perception and awareness' (Foley 1987: 189) that differed from the conventional apprehension of literacy as the medium through which all human communication should be interpreted.

In the nineteenth and twentieth century, the three overlapping disciplines of ethnopoetics, folkloristics, and anthropology created an intellectual climate that was favourably disposed towards oral tradition and orality studies. Although this work was not directly derived from or dependent on Jousse's oral style theory or the Parry-Lord thesis, all three fields, in varying degrees, explored issues related to oral composition and performance. Ethnopoetics came closest to bringing oral tradition to the forefront of scholarly imagination. Along with folkloristics, this new discipline devoted its efforts to the recording and examination of a vast amount and wide variety of indigenous traditions in their authentic social contexts. From the study of these data emerged an ever-growing awareness of blind spots and visual biases in the dominant textual criticism, and a cultivation of long-suppressed, oral-based sensibilities. The principal conclusion of the work of Jerome Rothenberg, Dennis Tedlock, Dell Hymes, and others was that many of the syntactical structures, poetic patterns, and aesthetic qualities of the majority of folkloric materials are in fact performance features that require special appreciation as such. As a result, ethnopoetics, along with branches of anthropology, was directly confronted with the two key issues of transcription and performance. Keenly attuned both to the oral quality of the materials under review and to typographic ways of constructing written texts, the problem was how to capture oral poetics on the uniformly linearized, meticulously formatted, voiceless page so as to retain their performative quality. Lurking beneath the dilemma of ethnopoetic writing was the larger hermeneutical issue of the representation of the Other, in this case the oral performer as other than the highly literate scholarly analyst. How does one understand performative texts not as the Same through conventional literary categories, but as the authentically Other through categories that are germane to an ethnography of speaking?

Anthropology's most significant contributions to oral tradition were delivered by scholars working in African studies. Widely regarded as a work of pioneering significance, Jan Vansina's *Oral Tradition: A Study in Historical Methodology* (1961) singled out oral tradition as a defining category worthy of serious academic treatment. First published in French in 1961, it was written at a time when Western historiography lacked an adequate conceptual framework for the analysis of the history of peoples without writing and when African verbal art was tacitly (or explicitly) viewed as 'primitive literature'. Drawing on fieldwork in the Central African countries of the Congo, Rwanda, and Burundi, Vansina thematized oral tradition by means of an elaborate theoretical framework in which the concept of testimony occupied a central position, with *tradition* conceived as a chain of testimonial transmissions. Vansina sought to frame and answer the question of whether and to what extent largely unwritten traditions, many of which relied on memory, were dependable sources for a reconstruction of a people's history. The issue, as Vansina saw it, was to test the reliability of oral tradition so as to make it safe for the historian. His follow-up volume, *Oral Tradition as History* (1985), substantially reiterated this approach: oral tradition remains 'on probation' (160) so long as it is not independently confirmed.

It is worth noting that not all Africanists share Vansina's position, as subsequent research has demonstrated. Scholars such as Jeff Opland, Liz Gunner, and Annekie Joubert do not view oral tradition, purified from historical errors, as an aid in historical reconstruction, but instead regard the unqualified integrity of oral tradition itself as an essential component of the people's history. Two rather different approaches to oral tradition are observable: the historical school, which scrutinizes memory (see COGNITIVE PERSONAL MEMORY) and oral tradition from the perspective of historical accuracy, and the ethnopoetic approach, which values oral tradition as cultural asset and verbal artistry sui *generis*, which can expose flaws in the historical paradigm.

With RUTH FINNEGAN's *Oral Poetry* (1977), a classic in the study of oral tradition, a new level of globalism and comparative analysis was accomplished. An Africanist by training, Finnegan discussed an unprecedented and dazzling array of traditions, genres, and topics from across the world, ranging from Tibet to Oceania and from the Fiji Islands to Uzbekistan, including praise songs and Moorish poetry, chanted sermons, and Texas prison tunes, all of which treat love, heroic deeds, mourning, political elections, and many more topics. Taking serious account of the vast pluralism of oral tradition, she adopted a stance of scepticism towards the notion of 'universal laws' of tradition and any kind of monolithic theory. For example, while she endorsed and demonstrated the basic correctness of the Parry-Lord thesis, she discounted its universal applicability. Both in *Oral Poetry*, and more so in *The Oral and Beyond* (2007), Finnegan moved the study of oral tradition onto a stage of critical self-reflection. Challenging what she viewed as part of the Romantic strand in orality studies, she dismissed notions such as the anonymous roots of tradition; communal compositional processes; word-perfect memorization; an evolutionary transmission of traditions; intrinsic links between oral genre and social setting; *la pensée sauvage* of primitive, oral society; and the glamourizing and nationalizing of 'the folk'. Perhaps most importantly, she objected to the notion of a 'pure' oral tradition untrammelled by scribal interference. Increasingly weary of the 'radical divide between "oral" and "written" modes' in scholarly paradigms (1977: 258), Finnegan focused on the productive interfacing of the two media modalities. She also steadily distanced herself from a purely linguistic conceptualization of oral tradition and sought to capture its intrinsic multisensory and paralinguistic features. On the whole, her work exhibits a trajectory from the linguistic turn to intermediality and on to multisensory performance qualities.

The work of WALTER ONG (1912–2003) is distinctive for its integration of a number of theoretical and historical concerns into a sweeping phenomenology of communication, culture, and consciousness. Central to this phenomenology was Ong's premise of a media development from primary orality through scribality to typography, now more recently followed by the electronic revolution and an electronically facilitated secondary orality. Far from being strictly evolutionary, these communications media are reinforcing and undermining, displacing and transmuting, supplementing and overlying one another, all the while affecting the mind and cognitive processes and generating a broadly successive, yet variable, reorganization of the human sensorium.

Although Ong is perhaps best known for his concise, and extremely influential, summary of his model in *Orality and Literacy* (1982), his earlier *Ramus, Method, and the Decay of Dialogue* (1958) perhaps represents his pivotal scholarly achievement. Ong here offers an exhaustive study of the French philosopher/theologian, educational reformer, and logician Pierre de la Ramée (1515–72), and of Ramism, the intellectual movement that contributed to a shift in Western intellectual history from the more vocal world of ancient (and medieval) culture to the progressively visual and spatial model of knowledge in pre-modernism. This shift, Ong observed, owed much to print technology, and to the sense of order and control it imposed upon human intelligence. Nowhere in his magnum opus did Ong develop oral tradition as a phenomenon *sui generis*. Yet implications of orality are present from start to finish, and the premise is evident throughout that deep knowledge of vocally sounded and living words is crucial if one is to grasp written words and the transition towards the chirographically and typographically controlled spatialization of words.

Following his work on Ramus, Ong ceaselessly endeavoured to understand what spoken words actually are, and to come to terms with an economy of processing knowledge that is distinctive of dominantly and residually oral texts, thought, and cultures (1967; 1977b). Absorbing the insights of Jousse, Parry, Lord, and numerous others, and based on his own work in Renaissance literature, Ong became convinced that 'our entire understanding of classical culture now has to be revised – and with it our understanding of later cultures up to our own time' (1967: 18) and that the decisive breakthrough in biblical studies was 'yet to come' (1977: 231). All his efforts to conceptualize an 'oral noetics' culminated in *Orality and Literacy* (1982), a work frequently cited and widely translated. What aroused particular interest was Ong's listing of nine universal 'characteristics of orally based thought and expression' (1982: 36–49). Not since Jousse had there been a conceptualization of oral tradition of such precision and uncompromising explicitness. This aspect of Ong's work has since provoked the most controversy and invited the charge of a technological/cultural Great Divide mentality driven by a too-crude distinction between oral and written. But it has to be kept in mind that Ong's thinking was of a relational kind: even though oral tradition could be viewed as standing alone in all its distinctiveness, it never lived apart from the continuum of a communications history in which all media shaped the cultures in which they operated and were in turn subject to constant shifts and realignments.

It is, finally, to the credit of John Miles Foley to have energized the study of oral tradition with a never before achieved theoretical and interpretive sophistication. One of the world's foremost experts on comparative oral traditions, Foley was the founding director of the Center for Studies in Oral Tradition (1986) as well as the founding editor of the journal *Oral Tradition* (1968). The latter exploded from an annual rate of 1200 readers in the paper format to ca. 18,000 readers representing 167 countries and territories in the open source electronic format in 2014. In his capacity as a classicist, Foley defined and demonstrated the idiomatic quality of Homeric language, which dictionaries in their focus on lexical accuracy were ill-equipped to capture. In a significant advance beyond Parry and Lord, he reevaluated the concept of formulaic diction, which functions, Foley argued, not as a convenient, serviceable 'filler' in the metered language of Homer, but as 'metonymic referentiality' or traditional referentiality (1991: 10), which reached out of immediate textual surroundings and tapped larger traditional contexts (see Metonymy). *Meaning* in this process was generated not by the text alone, but in the interface of textual performance and hearers fluent in the tradition. In many ways the heir to Parry and Lord, Foley appropriately served as editor of the two voluminous *Festschriften* in honour of Lord (*Oral Traditional Literature*, 1981) and in memory of Parry (*Comparative Research on Oral Traditions*, 1987). Moreover, he proved himself an expert in Old English literature. Rather than elaborating the similarities of oral-traditional literatures, he explored the specifics of the formulaic diction and thematic structure in the heroic poem Beowulf and other tradition-dependent Anglo-Saxon literature. And in the field of Slavic studies he edited a 1030-line version of the South Slavic epic, *The Wedding of Mustajbey's Son Becirbey* (2004), comprised of the original-language transcription, an English translation, and a performance-based commentary. Foley was also the first to devise a media taxonomy that categorized the vast array of oral traditions under four headings: oral performance, voiced texts, voices from the past, and written oral texts.

Foley's last book moved orality studies beyond anything ever undertaken in the new discipline. *Oral Tradition and the Internet* (2012), a study in media criticism, is meant to be a challenge more than a definitive solution. Situating oral tradition within the global media universe, the book endeavoured to illustrate the fundamental homology between oral tradition and the internet as well as their basic dissimilarities with the print medium. Notwithstanding obvious disparities, numerous similarities between oral tradition and the internet are indisputable, including, most conspicuously, non-proprietariness, open access, fluency, and networking. Both belong to the public domain and are not owned by a single author or publisher, whereas print authorship is usually identifiable and strictly regulated. The two media practice a communicative democracy, while the linearized 'brick-and-mortar book' entails a built-in program of exclusion. Both derive authority from limitless updating, whereas the trump medium of textuality is often viewed as an anchor of stability that is immune to the chaos of historical contingencies. And both oral tradition and the internet navigate knowledge through pathways and via networks, whereas textual thinking prefers one-track trajectories. Foley's comparative media study demonstrated uncanny affinities between the oldest and the most recent communications technologies, and in turn sharpened our consciousness of the comparatively static, unchangeable nature of the textual medium.

Werner H. Kelber (Rice University, USA)

Further Reading

Finnegan, Ruth. 1977. *Oral Poetry*. Cambridge: Cambridge University Press.

Finnegan, Ruth. 2007. *The Oral and Beyond: Doing Things with Words in Africa*. Chicago: University of Chicago Press.

Foley, John Miles. 1981. *Oral Traditional Literature: A Festschrift for Albert Bates Lord*. Columbus, OH: Slavica Publishers.

Foley, John Miles. 1987. 'Reading the Oral Tradition Text: Aesthetics of Creation and Response.' In *Comparative Research on Oral Traditions: A Memorial for Milman Parry*. Edited by John Miles Foley. Columbus, OH: Slavica, pp. 185–212.

Foley, John Miles. 1988. *The Theory of Oral Composition: History and Methodology*. Bloomington: Indiana University Press.

Foley, John Miles. 1991. *Immanent Art: From Structure to Meaning in Traditional Oral Epic*. Bloomington: Indiana University Press.

Foley, John Miles. 2002. *How to Read an Oral Poem*. Champaign, IL: University of Illinois.

Foley, John Miles, Trans. 2004. *The Wedding of Mustabey's Son Becirbey as performed by Halil Bajgoric*. Suomalainen Tiedeakatemia. E-Edition: http://oraltradition.org/zbm.

Foley, John Miles. 2012. *Oral Tradition and the Internet: Pathways of the Mind*. Champaign, IL: University of Illinois Press. See also http://www.pathwaysproject.org

Havelock, Eric. 1963. *Preface to Plato*. Hoboken, NJ: Blackwell.

Jousse, Marcel. 1990. *The Oral Style*. Translated by Edgard R. Sienaert and Richard Whitaker. Abingdon, UK: Taylor & Francis.

Lord, Albert B. 1960. *The Singer of Tales*. Cambridge, MA: Harvard University Press.

Lord, Albert B. 1991. *Epic Singers and Oral Tradition*. Ithaca, NY: Cornell University Press.

Ong, Walter. 1958. *Ramus, Method, and the Decay of Dialogue: From the Art of Discourse to the Art of Reason*. Cambridge, MA: Harvard University Press.

Ong, Walter. 1967. *The Presence of the Word: Some Prolegomena for Cultural and Religious History*. New Haven, CT: Yale University Press.

Ong, Walter. 1977. *Interfaces of the Word: Studies in the Evolution of Consciousness and Culture*. Ithaca, NY: Cornell University Press.

Ong, Walter. 1982. *Orality and Literacy: The Technologizing of the Word*. London: Methuen.

Vansina, Jan. 1961. *Oral Tradition: A Study in Historical Methodology*. Translated by H. N. Wright. Abingdon: Routledge.

Vansina, Jan. 1985. *Oral Tradition as History*. Madison, WI: University of Wisconsin.

Oral tradition and the New Testament See Jesus Tradition; Jesus Tradition and Memory

Orality In discussions of biblical media, the term *orality* is used in at least two senses: first, and more narrowly, to denote human communication by word of mouth; second, and more broadly, to describe the media status of cultures in which oral communication predominates, with an emphasis on ways that orality produces a mindset and cultural orientation different from those characteristic of modern literary or print cultures. While the latter description may be legitimate as a way of drawing attention to the differences between ancient/biblical and modern media contexts, there is some danger in portraying orality in an essentialist fashion as something fundamentally opposed to literacy, particularly if orality is associated with 'primitive' communal cultures while literacy is associated with 'advanced' scientific cultures. Different media play important roles in enabling different kinds of societies, but it is important to avoid generalizations based on a monocausal social determinism (= a single factor determines the characteristics of a society) or a simplistic binary opposition that fails to recognize the continuous and complex spectrum of modes of interaction between oral and written media in all cultures (see Great Divide).

In view of the above concerns, current scholarship, more so than previous generations, is cautious about generalizations regarding orality and oral cultures, particularly any notion that a universal set of laws governs all forms of oral communication. For example, orality should not be universally equated with folklore or oral tradition, as if all forms of oral verbal art had been handed down from some primitive past where they had emerged from some mysterious collective. Similarly, no single oral performance tradition should be treated as absolutely representative of orality in all times and cultures, such as, for example, the South Slavic epic poetry studied by Milman Parry and Albert Lord as the basis of their highly influential oral-formulaic theory (although certain aspects of that theory, such as the notion of composition in performance, the variability of oral tradition, and the lack of an original oral text, while by no means universal, have application beyond South Slavic or Homeric epic poetry).

Noting the above cautions, there do tend to be differences between oral and written media. An oral 'text' can be more readily adapted to the needs of the moment, the context of performance, or the reaction of the audience. Thus, while written texts can be memorized and passed on more or less intact by purely oral transmission, oral texts are typically more flexible than written ones, and thus often pluriform – there may not be a fixed original of which successive performances are 'variants', as would be the case with manuscripts. This does not mean that oral texts are completely subject to homeostasis (conformity to present social needs by dropping or adapting anything that is no longer relevant or serviceable), not least because certain oral genres often retain seemingly archaic modes of expression; it does mean that oral texts are generally more capable of adapting to changing needs than are written ones, especially when the process of writing out a new version by hand would be relatively time-consuming and laborious.

A central feature of oral communication is that it is actualized only in performance: although speech can be said to exist potentially in social and individual memory, any specific act of speech exists only in the moment when words are articulated. The nature of an oral performance may, however, vary enormously from one social setting to another, and according to the occasion, the genre, the audience, and the skill and style of the performer. Moreover, the actual words spoken by an oral performer may be only one aspect of the performance, and not necessarily the most important. Even when the performance is centred on the spoken word, the tempo, intonation, mimicry, and similar aspects of delivery style will greatly contribute to its meaning, as well as the facial expressions, gestures, bodily movements, and deportment of the speaker (see Nonverbal Communication in Performance). Where a performance also includes music, dance, or active audience participation, these too may greatly contribute to the significance of the performance event.

The context of oral performance is also important to its content and meaning. Context includes such factors as the social standing of the performer and audience and the relationships between them, the nature of the occasion, the expectations surrounding the genre being performed, and the social function of the performance, which may vary, for example, from almost pure entertainment to a significant rite of passage to a political protest to a sermon or missionary proclamation. Context also includes what JOHN MILES FOLEY has called 'the enabling referent of tradition' or what WERNER KELBER calls the 'BIOSPHERE', aspects of the COLLECTIVE and CULTURAL MEMORY of performer and audience that allow the meaning of a performance to resonate far beyond the literal sense of the words actually spoken (or sung) as they conjure up a web of associations (which may, of course, also be evoked by other aspects of the performance, such as any music used). Performance may also be marked off from everyday speech by use of a special REGISTER (such as the employment of poetic, archaic, or other special language) and the use of introductory formulas (e.g. 'once upon a time'; 'unaccustomed as I am to public speaking') to signal the nature of the performance that is about to follow.

There is no universal way in which oral transmission takes place. Composition in performance based on a stock of traditional THEMES and motifs is found in many kinds of oral transmission, but is by no means universal. More or less fallible memorization can also play a role, and there may be other factors, such as frequent repetition of a notionally fixed text in a liturgical setting that further stabilizes particular oral texts. These possibilities are by no means mutually exclusive: all may have a role in any particular oral performance or tradition, and there is no way of knowing in advance of studying a particular tradition which will predominate. Moreover, oral and written modes of transmission often intermingle. Thus, in the case of the ORAL TRADITIONS supposedly underlying some biblical literature, where there is no longer any living available oral tradition to study, it may be impossible to determine what the processes of transmission were. It seems reasonable to suppose that material deemed religiously significant and important for group IDENTITY would have been subject to some kind of social control, but such control could theoretically act to adapt the material to changing circumstances as much as to preserve it, so it is hard to postulate much more than some combination of continuity and change, while making cautious use of comparative literature and the surviving written evidence to make informed guesses about the likely nature and extent of each.

Eric Eve (Oxford University, UK)

Ordeals An *ordeal* is a form of ritual in which a person accused of wrongdoing is subjected to a physical test, such as drinking an unpleasant concoction or being plunged into a river, the result of which determines his or her guilt or innocence. Ordeals were a widespread ancient Near Eastern phenomenon and especially prominent in cases where a human court might be incapable of reaching a verdict, such as when there were no witnesses to a crime (e.g. in proving a young woman's virginity). In such cases, the court often opted to transfer the case to the divine court, following the widespread assumption that nothing escaped the divine gaze (Prov. 15.3; cf. Ps. 19.13; 139.1-12; Zech. 4.10; 2 Chron. 16.9).

Ordeals, along with other rituals such as divination and OATHS, were widely viewed as channels for determining the divine verdict. In contrast to divination, which often preceded a trial and was used to justify bringing a person to trial, ordeals were typically featured at the climax of a court case and could be viewed as proof of guilt or innocence. Whereas an oath transferred both jurisdiction and punishment to the divine court, an ordeal was designed to reveal the person's guilt or innocence yet left the sentence and, especially, its execution to human judges. Issues like potential marital infidelity, which typically had no witnesses, were particularly suited to trial by divine appeal.

Unlike divination and oaths (e.g. 1 Sam. 14.41 and Exod. 22.11, respectively), it is difficult to definitively identify ordeal rituals in the Bible. Further, although distinct in theory, in biblical antiquity the ritual boundaries between divination, oaths, and ordeals often blurred in practice. Numbers 5.11-31 envisions such a hybrid ritual, one involving an ordeal element and an oath. Here, an enraged husband who suspects his wife of adultery brings her to the sanctuary (cf. CH 131; 132). Since divorce without compensation theoretically requires proof of wrongdoing (e.g. sexual infelicity), and because the requisite two witnesses required to convict in civil court (Num. 35.30; Deut. 19.15) are lacking, the husband appeals to the cult for a verdict. For the ordeal itself, the priest takes holy water, mixes in it earth from the floor of the divine abode (cf. ARM 10.9), writes a curse and washes it in the water; the woman then makes an oath and drinks the potion (cf. *Šurpu* III 62). If she is innocent, no harm will come to her; if guilty, the bitter water will cause something like a prolapsed uterus with the result that she loses her fertility. Rather than an unspecified divine punishment, the punishment here is found in the text of the oath placed in the water itself and follows as a result of the ordeal at an unspecified time. In effect, a future pregnancy will prove her innocence.

Resolving a complex social and legal issue in this manner brings closure on multiple levels to an otherwise complicated and volatile situation. Through the ordeal and its outcome, the people of Israel are assured that they have done their duty, will not be punished for adultery committed in their midst (cf. Deut. 21.1-9), and that the woman will be punished if guilty. Positively for the accused, the ordeal protects the woman from immediate and excessive retribution and gives her a way to regain her honour. Since it is presumed that a guilty woman would not willingly undergo the ordeal, it satisfies the husband's suspicions, clears his name, and removes the stigma from his family (cf. LU 14; CH 127). Thus, ordeals and the ordeal-oath hybrid in Numbers 5 fill a necessary legal gap and serve to promote justice and the solidarity of the nuclear family.

Various biblical texts employ ordeal language metaphorically, such as the 'cup of wrath' passages that use the motif of a drinking trial to refer to coming judgement (see Pss. 60.5; 75.9; Isa. 51.17-23; Jer. 25.15-29; 49.12; 51.7, 39; Lam. 4.21; Ezek. 23.31-34; Obad. 16; Hab. 2.15-16; Zech. 12.2). Some scholars have suggested that the 'Psalms of the Accused' (Pss. 3; 4; 5; 7; 11; 17; 23; 27; 57; 62) refer to an actual drinking trial, but here again, the language may simply be metaphorical. Similarly, in the NT, Paul employs an ordeal motif to stress the significance of reverence in participation in Eucharistic meals: 'Anyone who eats and drinks in an unworthy manner eats and drinks judgment upon himself' (1 Cor. 11.27-34). Here, the consumption of a consecrated substance subjects the participant to divine testing, with the threatened verdicts including weakness, illness, and possibly death ('many of you are weak and ill, and some have died'; 11.30).

Michael B. Hundley (Syracuse University, USA)

Further Reading

Frymer-Kensky, Tikva. 1977. *The Judicial Ordeal in the Ancient Near East*. 2 vols. Ph.D. Diss. Yale.
Levine, Baruch A. 1993. *Numbers 1-20*. AB 4. New York: Doubleday.
Johnston, Philip. 2005. 'Ordeals in the Psalms?' In *Temple and Worship in Biblical Israel*. Edited by J. Day. LHBOTS 422. London: T&T Clark, pp. 271–91.

Original The term *original* is primarily used in the field of Gospels studies to refer to the form of a pericope that chronologically precedes all of its other attested forms and, as such, is the one upon which other, later versions are based. It is also used more broadly to identify the first versions of written manuscripts of the Bible (see textual criticism) and to identify source texts in the field of translation studies. The discussion here will focus on the implications of the term for the study of oral tradition, particularly Jesus tradition.

The idea that there was an *original* form of any given gospel pericope was central to the work of the early NT form critics, in particular, that of its most influential practitioners, Rudolf Bultmann (1884–1976), and Martin Dibelius (1883–1947). These early pioneers of *Formgeschichte* ('Form Criticism') worked from the premise that it was possible to recover an original form of any given tradition through the application of appropriate 'laws' that were thought to govern the development of tradition from its earlier to later forms. Traditions were typically thought of as developing from original, shorter, simpler forms to longer, more complex forms over time. As such, it was argued that one could recover the original form of a tradition by removing the additions and modifications made to the text over time.

Form criticism served as a foundation for subsequent work in historical Jesus research. Original forms of Jesus tradition were thought to be more useful than later, less reliable traditions when engaging in the process of historical reconstruction. Much of the work in the area of historical Jesus research during the late twentieth and early twenty-first centuries was built on form-critical work that established the original form of gospel traditions.

Although the term *original* has held a prominent place within the work of form-critical scholarship, there have been several lines of critique that have raised questions regarding the usefulness of the term and its associated underlying assumptions. The concept of an *original* took shape prior to the publication of recent studies in ancient media. Form critics studied the Gospels and the ORAL TRADITIONS underlying them with methods derived from a literary paradigm, which assumed that pre-inscribed traditions were shaped and formed by processes not unlike those that shaped and formed texts – in other words, observable tendencies in the development and transmission of written Gospels could be retrojected backward to explain the evolution of the oral traditions that preceded them. Media scholars now emphasize that the gospel tradition was birthed within a highly oral media context and was shaped and formed by non-literary processes of tradition formation and transmission. Numerous insights derived from studies in ORALITY and LITERACY, oral performance, and FOLKLORE have challenged, each in their own way, the very concept of an *original* form of any tradition. For example, oral performance theory has shed light on the way in which tradition is shaped and formed by both a performer and an audience, and folklore research has illustrated, among other things, the variable character of non-literary traditions. Rather than speaking of an original form of any given Jesus tradition, tradition such as that found in the Gospels is perhaps best described as being PLURIFORM in nature.

Terence C. Mournet (Ashland Theological Seminary, USA)

Further Reading

Bultmann, Rudolf K. 1963. *The History of the Synoptic Tradition*. 2nd edn. Translated by John Marsh. New York: Harper and Row.

Dibelius, Martin. 1971. *From Tradition to Gospel*. Translated by Bertram Lee Woolf. Cambridge: James Clarke.

Orthography *Orthography* literally means 'correct writing'. As a technical term, it refers to a broad constellation of the components of a WRITING system, including the graphemes (the signs or letters in a writing system) used to represent the phonemes (the smallest meaningful units of sound) of a language, as well as aspects of a writing system such as word division, line-breaks, punctuation, the demarcation of sentences, and the demarcation of paragraphs. In earlier generations of research, the term orthography was prescriptive rather than descriptive, in the sense that it was assumed that there were 'correct' writing conventions and 'incorrect' writing conventions. Often the term orthography is understood in its narrowest sense to refer to spelling conventions in a written language, and as such it is a subset of phonology.

The world's writing systems can be subdivided into two major categories: alphabetic and non-alphabetic. An *alphabetic* writing system is (broadly) one in which a single grapheme (written character) is used to represent a single phoneme (meaningful sound) – for example, the written Greek letter δ (delta) represents the 'd' sound, the Greek letter θ (theta) represents the 'th' sound, etc. Alphabetic writing systems normally have between twenty and forty graphemes/letters which can stand individually or in combination for all the meaningful phonemes utilized by the languages they represent. Familiar examples include Hebrew, Aramaic, Greek, Latin, Coptic, Spanish, English, Arabic, German, and French. Some alphabetic writing systems can be described as having a *shallow orthography*, meaning that the writing system conveys the represented sounds with precision (e.g. German), while others have a *deep orthography*, meaning that the writing system and modes of spelling convey the indicated phonemes with less precision (e.g. French and English).

A *non-alphabetic* writing system, by contrast, does not use characters that represent individual sounds of the spoken language. Instead, the signs used by a non-alphabetic writing system are logographic (a single written character can visually represent an entire word), syllabic (a single written sign can represent an entire syllable), and determinate (a written sign signifies something about the nature of the preceding or following word, such as the determinative for 'metal' before the word 'silver' or the determinative for 'woman' before the word for 'maidservant'). Because their signs generally represent words or concepts instead of the individual sounds that make up words, non-alphabetic writing systems typically have hundreds of signs (e.g. Sumerian, Akkadian, Mandarin Chinese).

This entry will focus on spelling conventions in the writing systems used in the biblical languages (ancient Hebrew, Aramaic, and Greek), all of which have alphabetic writing systems (letters/characters represent spoken sounds). In addition, there will be some reference to conventions relating to word division and line-breaks within these ancient languages.

Pre-Masoretic Hebrew and Aramaic

The Hebrew and Aramaic alphabets consist of twenty-two graphemes (letters). Originally these letters represented consonants only, not vowels (following the Phoenician writing system, from which the Hebrew and Aramaic derived). During the early period of usage, however, both Hebrew and Aramaic began to use certain consonants also to represent certain final long vowels (but not final short vowels), as evidenced in the corpus of extant Hebrew and Aramaic inscriptions (some of which are as early as the ninth century BCE). Soon after, Aramaic and, sometime slightly later, Hebrew also began to use certain consonants to represent certain medial long vowels (but not medial short vowels), as evidenced in inscriptions (Cross and Freedman 1952; Rollston 2006: 61–5). This usage of consonants to represent vowel sounds is referred to as *mater lectionis*. The Hebrew and Aramaic consonants that could be used as matres lectionis were *heh*, *waw*, and *yod*. Adding to the complexity of this early orthographic system, the consonants that were sometimes used as *matres lectionis* to represent vowels also continued to be used as consonants as well, with the result that several early Aramaic/Hebrew characters could represent more than one sound from the respective languages.

Inscriptional data yields several important details about written Hebrew and Aramaic. First, the earliest attested inscriptions written in the Hebrew language and in the Old Hebrew script (as opposed to the Phoenician script, for example) hail from the ninth century BCE. The earliest attested Aramaic inscriptions of any length also hail from the ninth century BCE, although these are still written in the Phoenician script (i.e. they use Phoenician characters to represent the sounds of the Aramaic language). The distinctive Aramaic script emerged in the eighth century BCE.

Second, throughout the Pre-Masoretic period, the orthographic practices used for Old Hebrew and Aramaic inscriptions differed from those of Phoenician inscriptions in multiple ways, especially in the usage of *matres lectionis* (consonants representing vowel sounds) in Old Hebrew and Aramaic and the non-usage of *matres lectionis* in Phoenician. Old Hebrew and Aramaic inscriptions consistently used *yod* as a *mater lectionis* to mark final long /i/; *waw* to mark final long /u/; and *heh* variously to mark a final long /o/, a final long /a/, or a final long /e/. For Old Hebrew, there is no evidence for the use of internal *matres lectionis* before occasional usages in the late eighth century BCE (e.g. the Royal Steward Inscription). The usage of internal *matres lectionis* in Old Hebrew becomes even more common during the seventh and sixth centuries and this continues through the centuries, with heavy usage in the Dead Sea Scrolls (Qimron 1986: 17–24; Tov 2004). Aramaic, by contrast, began usage of internal *matres lectionis* earlier than in Old Hebrew, a practice attested as early as the ninth century BCE (e.g. in the Tel Fakhariyeh Bilingual Inscription) and persisting throughout the centuries before the Common Era.

In Hebrew inscriptions, dividers were normally (although not always) used to separate words. These word dividers followed the word and were normally either a short vertical stroke or a dot. Over the course of time, word division was often indicated simply by the presence of a space between words, rather than by the use of a vertical stroke or dot. For early Aramaic inscriptions, there is often no word division (e.g. the Sfire Treaty Inscription of the eighth century BCE), but rather *scriptio continua* (continuous writing without word division); gradually, word division came to be indicated in Aramaic (as in Hebrew) by the presence of a space (e.g. the Aramaic Behistun Inscription from Elephantine). For the Hebrew and Aramaic Dead Sea Scrolls, the use of a space between words is the norm. In both Hebrew and Aramaic texts of antiquity, it was common for words to be split across lines, with a word beginning at the end of a line while the final letters appeared on the following line. Finally, it should be emphasized that doubled consonants were normally not indicated in the Pre-Masoretic orthographic conventions of Hebrew or Aramaic.

Masoretic Hebrew and Aramaic Orthography

The Masoretes were Jewish tradents of the received text(s) of the Hebrew Bible, working especially from ca. 600–1000 CE (see Masoretic Text). The Masoretes worked primarily in three geographical regions: Tiberius, Babylon, and Jerusalem ('Palestine'). Thus, the various manuscripts produced by these three groups of Masoretes are classified as Tiberian, Babylonian, and Palestinian (Saenz-Badillos 1993: 86–111). The major manuscripts that form the basis of the modern Hebrew Bible are Tiberian.

Although these three Masoretic manuscript traditions differ, they share a common methodology for representing short and long vowel sounds with precision (the consonants, of course, had long been represented with precision by the twenty-two letters of the Hebrew alphabet). Thus, the Masoretic system of vowel pointing – inserting dot characters below consonants to represent the vowel sounds between them – built on the Pre-Masoretic system of matres lectionis in multiple ways, especially by marking the short vowels (rather than just the long vowels). Moreover, the Masoretic vowel pointing subdivided the long and short vowels, so as to more precisely reveal the exact length of the long and short vowels. In addition, the Masoretic vowel system included a mechanism for showing doubled consonants (namely, the usage of the *dagesh forte*) as well as a method for indicating whether a *begadkefat* letter was a stop or spirant. Naturally, even the Masoretic vocalization system reflects some variation, as the Hebrew Bible is a large corpus with a long history of transmission in antiquity (Barr 1989). Finally, it should be emphasized that although Hebrew and Aramaic are distinct Northwest Semitic languages, the Masoretic system was employed for the entire Hebrew Bible, including those portions written in Aramaic (Dan. 2.4b-7.28; Ezra 4.8-6:18, 7.12-26; Jer. 10.11).

Early Greek Orthography

Greek inscriptions are attested as early as the eighth century BCE and were continuous from that point on during antiquity. The corpus of extant Greek inscriptions is vast, pervading not only the Mediterranean world but also the ancient Near East (Bodel 2001), and provides a wide range of data on ancient Greek orthography over time and in different regions.

The Greek language is Indo-European, but the script used to write Greek was derived from a Semitic script, namely, the Phoenician script (McCarter 1975: 65–102). Since the Greek script was (largely) borrowed from the Phoenician script, the letters of that alphabet were used to represent similar sounds in Greek. For example, Semitic *bet* (used to represent the 'b' sound) became Greek *beta*; Semitic *gimel* (used to represent the 'g' sound) became Greek *gamma*; Semitic *kap* (used to represent the 'k' sound) became Greek *kappa*; and, Semitic *taw* (used to represent the 't' sound) became Greek *tau* (for pronunciation of Greek, see Metzger 1981: 11–13). The important point here is that the names for the letters of the Greek alphabet were borrowed from pre-existing Semitic names. It should also be emphasized that the script used during the early centuries was the majuscule script (all capital letters). The minuscule script (all lower-case letters) seems to have become fully developed and more widely used during and after the ninth century CE (Metzger and Ehrman 2005: 18).

Among the more interesting orthographic features of the Greek writing system, some letters that had been used only for consonants in Phoenician were employed in Greek to write only vowels. For example, Semitic *heh* was used to represent the Greek vowel *epsilon*, while Semitic *yod* was used to represent the Greek vowel *iota*. Arguably, the phenomenon of *matres lectionis* (attested in Aramaic and Hebrew, but not in Phoenician) can account, at least in part, for these innovations in Greek. But Greek orthographic innovations were not only confined to letters that could serve as *matres lectionis*. Thus, for example, Semitic *het* was used only as a consonantal letter in Phoenician, Aramaic, and Hebrew, but this letter was the basis for the shape (but not the sound) of Greek vowel *eta*. Similarly, Semitic *'ayin* was used only as a consonantal letter in Phoenician, Aramaic, and Hebrew, but this letter was the basis for the shape (but not the sound) of the Greek vowel *omicron*. Finally, it should be emphasized that the Greek alphabet also included some letters that were not present at all in Semitic, such as, *phi* and *psi*.

Regarding other aspects of Greek that fall under the broader category of orthography, it should be emphasized that Greek inscriptions are normally written in *scriptio continua* (no breaks between words), and words can begin on one line with the remainder of the same word written on the succeeding line.

Hellenistic ('Koine') Greek Orthography

Various dialects of Greek are attested in the epigraphic and literary corpus, including Homeric, Attic, Doric, and Ionic. The discussion here will focus on Hellenistic Greek, since the SEPTUAGINT, the NT, and much of the Greek corpus of EARLY CHRISTIAN LITERATURE is written in the Hellenistic dialect.

Hellenistic Greek has twenty-four letters (note that an additional early Greek letter called *digamma* was not used in Hellenistic Greek, except as a symbol for the numeral six). Seven of these letters are vowels: *alpha*, *epsilon*, *ēta*, *iota*, *omicron*, *upsilon*, and *ōmega*; *epsilon* and *omicron* are always short; *ēta* and *ōmega* are always long; and *alpha*, *iota*, and *upsilon* may be long or short. Diphthongs are also present in Greek and can be described as the combination of two adjacent vowels in the same syllable so as to approximate a single sound (two written vowels together representing a single phoneme). The standard diphthongs in Hellenistic Greek are *ai*, *au*, *ei*, *eu*, *oi*, *ou*, and *ui*.

A number of orthographic variations are attested in Hellenistic Greek, some of them revolving around the reflexes of consonants, but most revolving around the writing of vowels (Blass, Debrunner, Funk, 1961: 7–8, 13–20). Moveable *nu* (the insertion of the letter *nu* at the end of some words that end with vowels when they appear in a line before another word that begins with a vowel) is very well attested in Hellenistic Greek, though also present in earlier dialects (e.g. Attic, Ionic). Moveable *sigma* is also attested in Hellenistic Greek, especially in the case of certain words (e.g. *outōs*, *euthus*). Among the most interesting features of early Christian Greek MANUSCRIPTS is the presence of certain abbreviations, particularly in the use of *nomina sacra*, that is, 'sacred names' (Hurtado 2006: 95–134). Because Hellenistic Greek includes many personal names, place names, and some technical terms (e.g. military) of foreign origin (primarily Hebrew, Aramaic, and Latin, but some Persian, etc.), the varied transliteration(s) of these foreign nouns into Greek is an important component of Hellenistic orthography (Blass, Debrunner, Funk, 1961: 20–24).

Various diacritical marks were used in ancient Greek. The Greek accent marks are the acute (´), the grave (`) and the circumflex (˜), characters that appear above vowels to represent changes in pitch or/and emphasis in the spoken version of the language. Accent marks were developed by grammarians in Alexandria in the centuries before the Common Era. Greek also utilizes two breathing marks, rough breathing (ʽ) and smooth breathing (ʼ), with the former signalling the presence of an 'h sound' before the letter and the latter signalling the absence of this sound. Diaeresis (¨) is a diacritical mark (consisting of a pair of supralinear dots) that is often used to indicate that an initial vowel (especially an *iota* or *upsilon*) is not to be combined with a preceding vowel (i.e. diaeresis is used to indicate that the two vowels are not a diphthong, but rather two separate phonemes).

Word division was not the norm in ancient Hellenistic Greek (Metzger and Ehrman 2005: 22), though it is sometimes attested. *Scriptio continua* was the norm, a fact that has sometimes complicated the understanding of texts (in cases where multiple different word divisions can be constructed from the same string of letters, depending upon where one inserts the breaks). Elision (abbreviating by dropping letters) can occur in Greek, and is well attested when a word that ends in a short vowel is followed by a word that begins with a vowel. Elision is particularly well attested with the Greek propositions *dia* (e.g. *di' upomonēs*) and *de* (e.g. *d'an*). Similarly, crasis (combination of words into a single term) is also attested in Hellenistic Greek, especially with *kai* (e.g. *kan* for *kai ean*).

Although punctuation was used by the Alexandrian grammarians before the Common Era, it is impossible to determine whether there were punctuation marks in the original autographs of the Septuagint, NT, or early christian literature since there are no extant autographs of these corpora. Paucity of punctuation was probably the norm (e.g. Metzger and Ehrman 2005: 41), but some of the earliest manuscripts of the NT (e.g. P45, P46) do contain some basic punctuation, as does also Codex Vaticanus (Blass, Debrunner, Funk, 1961: 10).

Christopher A. Rollston (George Washington University, USA)

Further Reading

Barr, James. 1989. *The Variable Spellings of the Hebrew Bible: The Schweich Lectures of the British Academy 1986*. Oxford: Oxford University Press.

Blass, F., Debrunner, A., and Robert W. Funk. 1961. *A Greek Grammar of the New Testament and Other Early Christian Literature*. Chicago: University of Chicago Press.

Bodel, John. 2001. *Epigraphic Evidence: Ancient History from Inscriptions*. Approaching the Ancient World series. Abingdon: Routledge.

Cross, Frank Moore, and David Noel Freedman. 1952. *Early Hebrew Orthography: A Study of the Epigraphic Evidence*. AOS 36. New Haven: American Oriental Society.

McCarter, P. Kyle. 1975. *The Antiquity of the Greek Alphabet and the Early Phoenician Scripts*. HSM 9. Missoula, Montana: Scholars Press.

Metzger, Bruce M. 1981. *Manuscripts of the Greek Bible: An Introduction to Greek Palaeography*. New York: Oxford University Press.

Metzger, Bruce M., and Bart Ehrman. 2005. *The Text of the New Testament: Its Transmission, Corruption, and Restoration*. 4th edn. New York: Oxford University Press.

Qimron, Elisha. 1986. *The Hebrew of the Dead Sea Scrolls*. HSS 29. Atlanta: Scholars Press.

Rollston, Christopher A. 2006. 'Scribal Education in Ancient Israel: The Old Hebrew Epigraphic Evidence.' *BASOR* 344: 47–74.

Saenz-Badillos, Angel. 1993. *A History of the Hebrew Language*. Translated by John Elwolde. Cambridge: Cambridge University Press.
Tov, Emanuel. 2004. *Scribal Practices and Approaches Reflected in the Texts Found in the Judean Desert*. STDJ 54. Leiden: Brill.

Ostraca The term *ostraca* (plural; sg. *ostrakon*) is a Greek loanword often used to describe pieces of pottery bearing a written message. As broken pottery is ubiquitous across the biblical landscape, discarded shards, usually smaller than a human hand, could be picked up and recycled as tablets for recording short notes, receipts, lists, and even drawings. The nature of the medium lends itself to inking and scratching, graphic technologies common to the Levant in the first millennium BCE. Unlike more perishable materials, ostraca form a durable part of the archaeological record of the ancient Near Eastern and Classical worlds. They continue to be recovered and studied for clues regarding not just the development of WRITING but other aspects of literary, social, economic, military, and even artistic systems.

The use of pottery shards or limestone chips as tablets may have originated in second millennium BCE Egypt. At the workman's village of Deir el-Medina, ostraca detail daily life in the New Kingdom period. Literary and non-literary (or figural) shards have been recovered. Some of these have been linked to educational contexts and may be school texts. Others appear to be receipts, pay stubs, and rosters. Egyptian figural ostraca are quite diverse and present graphic images, scenes to be transferred to tomb walls, and even portable architectural plans. Ostraca, it seems, could function as ancient sticky notes.

More relevant to students of the Hebrew Bible are ostraca recovered from first millennium BCE contexts in Israel/Palestine. Here, well-known collections from Samaria, Lachish, and Arad are joined by isolated finds such as those from Khirbet Qeiyafa and Tell es-Safi. These illuminate daily life in monarchical Israel. As in Egypt, such notes suggest immediate use in the form of lists, receipts, rosters, and brief LETTERS. Ostraca finds intensify in the period from the ninth to sixth centuries BCE. Phoenician, Hebrew, Aramaic and other local dialects are attested.

When considered within the context of ancient media culture, ostraca invite analysis at several levels, including media, concept, and code. At the level of media, ostraca are written messages, or better, message snippets. These are frozen artefacts in a largely oral society. Senders and receivers worked within the restrictions of simple strokes applied to the face of a disposable potsherd. At the level of concept, ostraca frequently present economic 'moments'. Interpreting these moments in terms of commodities, quantities, or workmen can be difficult. Historical 'moments', such as those captured on the Lachish Letters, are no less challenging, but perhaps more dramatic. Embedded theological phrases cast light on contemporary religious vernacular. Finally, at the level of code, ostraca demonstrate the use of linear alphabetic West Semitic conventions. While debate lingers, it is likely that the ability to encode and decode such messages was limited to trained elites. As such, ostraca evince the development of the apparatus of state; they give testimony to the immediate needs of local authority and control.

Mark Ziese (Johnson University, USA)

P

Papias (on writing) Papias of Hierapolis (fl. ca. 110–135 CE) was one of the earliest Christians to write on the Jesus tradition outside of the NT. His five-volume work, *The Explanation of the Lord's Oracles*, has unfortunately perished, but fragments survive (Norelli 2005; Holmes 2007). One fragment, particularly important for the study of orality in early Christianity, is a quotation from the prologue by the fourth-century church historian Eusebius.

> Now I [Papias] will not hesitate to supplement the interpretations for you with whatever I carefully learned from the elders and carefully remembered, since I am confident in the truth on their account. For I did not delight in those who say a lot, as many delight, but in those who teach the truth. Nor did I delight in those who remember the commandments of others, but in those who remember the commandments given by the Lord to the faith and derived from truth itself. Whenever someone who had also followed the elders came along, I would examine the elders' words – 'What did Andrew or what did Peter say? Or Philip? Or Thomas or James? Or John or Matthew or any other of the disciples of the Lord?' – just as I examined what Aristion and the elder John, disciples of the Lord, were saying. For I did not assume that whatever comes from books is as helpful to me as what comes from a living and lasting voice. (Eusebius, *Eccl. History* 3.39.3-4)

Papias' statement opens a window into the mechanics of oral transmission in the early second century. Clearly, transmission involved travelling tradents. Papias' home of Hierapolis was located in the well-travelled Lycus valley of Phrygian Asia Minor, so when Christian itinerants passed through town, he could ask them about what the disciples of Jesus said. This process involved hearsay, but it was not anonymous hearsay. Papias asked for information by name, and Eusebius tells us that he often mentioned his sources by name (Eusebius, *Eccl. History* 3.39.7).

Yet there is a noticeable tension in Papias' expressed preference for the 'living voice' and his own writing of five volumes on Jesus's sayings (Walls 1967). To be sure, expressions of preference for oral instruction were commonplace in antiquity (Alexander 1990), and book learning was often faulted for being incomplete, useful mainly as a reminder of what had been taught (Mansfeld 2004, citing Galen among others). To a certain extent, such a lack of completeness is a criticism underlying Papias' account of the composition of the Gospel according to Mark: though it was written by someone who followed Peter, it merely contains what Mark remembered of Peter's teaching. By contrast, Papias justifies his own written work by appealing to his diligence in collecting oral traditions from a variety of sources in a line of succession that goes back to Jesus.

According to Papias then, both written accounts and oral traditions about Jesus existed side by side in his lifetime. Books were only as authoritative as their authors and even then they were not complete (cf. Jn 20.30). Oral traditions were still available but they were dispersed among various individuals and needed both diligence to collect and judgement to evaluate. Nevertheless, Papias' preference for the 'living and lasting voice' should not be taken as privileging of orality per se over writing. He claims, after all, to discriminate between 'those who teach the truth' and 'those who say a lot'. Rather, it is only among those sources he already considers authoritative in their connection to Jesus that Papias treasures orality for its capacity to provide a fuller picture of Jesus' teaching than what books can provide.

Stephen C. Carlson (Australian Catholic University, Australia)

Further Reading

Alexander, Loveday. 1990. 'The Living Voice: Scepticism towards the Written Word in Early Christian and in Graeco-Roman Texts.' In *The Bible in Three Dimensions: Essays in Celebration of Forty Years of Biblical Studies in the University of Sheffield*. Edited by David J. A. Clines, Stephen E. Fowl, and Stanley E. Porter. JSOTSup 87. Sheffield: Sheffield Academic Press, pp. 221–47.

Holmes, Michael W. 2007. *The Apostolic Fathers: Greek Texts and English Translations*. 3rd edn. Grand Rapids: Baker Academic.

Norelli, Enrico. 2005. *Papia di Hierapolis: Esposizione degli oracoli del Signore: I frammenti*. Letture cristiane del primo millennio 36. Milan: Paoline.

Mansfeld, Jaap. 2004. 'Galen, Papias, and Others on Teaching and Being Taught.' In *Things Revealed: Studies in Early Jewish and Christian Literature in Honor of Michael E. Stone*. Edited by Esther G. Chazon, David Satran, and Ruth A. Clements. JSJS 89. Leiden: Brill, pp. 317–29.

Walls, A. F. 1967. 'Papias and Oral Tradition.' *Vigiliae Christianae* 21: 137–40.

Papyrus Papyrus is a tall, fibrous reed plant that grew along the shallow banks of the Nile River in Egypt. Papyrus was used for a variety of purposes in the ancient world (e.g. for making sandals, mummy wrappings, rope, nets, sails, basketry), but it came to be used most predominantly as a WRITING surface. *Papyrus* is the Latinized form of the Greek word *papuros*, from which the English word 'paper' is derived. The papyrus that grows in Egypt today is not the ancient plant (*Cyperus papyrus*) but another kind of specimen.

A detailed account of the production of writing papyrus appears in Pliny the Elder's (23–79 CE) *Natural History* (xiii 74-82). Although historians have noted several problems with minor details of Pliny's account, most agree on the general process of production on the basis of observation and modern experimentation. To make a papyrus sheet, thin strips were cut from the inside of the reed (the pith) and aligned vertically on a hard surface, slightly overlapping to create one layer. Another series of thin strips was placed on top of the first, with these strips being aligned horizontally. Both layers were then pressed and hammered, and the papyrus' juices caused the layers to coalesce into a single, durable sheet. The surface was then smoothed and polished with perhaps a stone or ivory and its frayed edges were cut to make them straight. The side of the sheet that features the fibres running in a horizontal direction is known as the *recto*, while the side featuring the fibres running in a vertical direction is known as the *verso*. Usually, papyrus took writing on the *recto*, since the vertical fibres on the *verso* created resistance to the direction of writing.

The most common book form in the ancient world was the papyrus scroll (or bookroll), which consisted of a series of already constructed papyrus sheets pasted together at their overlapping edges (known as a *kollēsis*). There is good deal of debate over the standard dimensions of papyrus sheets (Pliny's account speaks only of the width of the sheets and their trade names), how many sheets came in a unit, whether the sheets could be sold separately, and the price of purchase. Papyrus was imported from Egypt into regions all across the Mediterranean basin and remained in use until the time of the Arab conquest (seventh century CE). Ultimately, papyrus was replaced by PARCHMENT, though we know from the historical record that many ancient authors preferred papyrus. For example, Augustine apologizes to Romanianus for having to use vellum instead of papyrus (Letter 15.1; P.L. xxxiii 80).

There are a few biblical references to papyrus. Of special importance is Job's reference to the marshy areas in which papyrus is known to have grown: 'Can papyrus grow where there is no marsh?' (Job 8:11; cf. 40:21). In an oracle concerning Egypt in the book of Isaiah, it is prophesied that 'papyrus will rot away' (Is 19:6). In most versions of the SEPTUAGINT, Moses' mother places him in a basket made with 'bitumen' (*asphaltopissa*), but Aquila's version states explicitly that the basket is made of papyrus (*papureōn*).

Brice C. Jones (University of Louisiana at Monroe, USA)

Further Reading

Bülow-Jacobson, Adam. 2009. 'Writing Materials in the Ancient World.' In *The Oxford Handbook of Papyrology*. Edited by Roger S. Bagnall. Oxford: Oxford University Press, pp. 3–29.

Hendriks, I. H. M. 1980. 'Pliny, Historia Naturalis XIII, 74-82, and the Manufacture of Papyrus.' *ZPE* 37: 121–36.

Hendriks, I. H. M. 1984. 'More about the Manufacture of Papyrus.' In *Atti del XVII Congresso Internazionale di Papirologia*, vol. 1. Naples: Centro Internazionale per lo Studio dei Papiri Ercolanesi, pp. 31–7.

Lewis, Naphtali. 1974. *Papyrus in Classical Antiquity*. Oxford: Oxford University Press.

Skeat, T. C. 1995. 'Was Papyrus Regarded as "Cheap" or "Expensive" in the Ancient World?' *Aegyptus* 75: 75–93.

Parables (of Jesus) The term *parable* is a transliteration of the Greek word *parabolē*, a word found in the NT throughout the Synoptic Gospels (17 times in Matthew, 13 times in Mark, and 18 times in Luke) and twice in the Book of Hebrews. The term is also found in ancient Greek RHETORIC, as Aristotle (*Rhetoric* 2.20), for example, divides the means of persuasion into enthymeme and example. The latter is further divided into historical examples and fictional examples, where the two types of fictional examples are identified as fable (*logoi*) and parable (*parabolē*). In the SEPTUAGINT, *parabolē* often renders the Hebrew term *mashal* and it has often been observed that both *mashal* and *parabolē* are utilized to identify various types of figurative speech. For this reason, although the importance of parables in the JESUS TRADITION is universally recognized, the precise definition and identification of a parable, not to mention the interpretation of particular parables, has been the subject of intense scholarly discussion and debate.

In recent scholarship, there has been running debate over whether parables should be understood on the basis of modern, scholarly definitions of discrete literary GENRES or upon the broad, ancient use of the term. Most of the definitions that have been offered for parables focus on the elements of *narrative* and *metaphor*, though Klyne Snodgrass voices the lingering suspicion that 'possibly no definition of parables will do, for any definition that is broad enough to cover all the forms is so imprecise that it is almost useless' (Snodgrass 2008: 7). Ruben Zimmermann, however, has followed the recent shift in literary studies from understanding genre as a correspondence with a narrowly defined set of supra-historical linguistic norms to viewing genre as a function of and deriving from a shared recognition within the communication taking place in a particular era. For this reason, he has proposed a six-part definition of a parable as 'a short narratival (1) fictional (2) text that is related in the narrated world to known reality (3) but, by way of implicit or explicit transfer signals, makes it understood that the meaning of the narration must be differentiated from the literal words of the text (4). In its appeal dimension (5) it challenges the reader to carry out a metaphoric transfer of meaning that is steered by contextual information (6)' (Zimmermann 2015: 137). Zimmermann's definition reflects the work of nearly four dozen scholars in the *Kompendium der Gleichnisse Jesu*, the most significant collaborative study of the parables to date.

The parables of Jesus have garnered significant attention in NT studies, in particular in historical Jesus studies. From David Friedrich Strauß to Adolf Jülicher to C. H. Dodd to Joachim Jeremias to John Dominic Crossan, scholars have consistently viewed parables as belonging to, and being especially characteristic of, the preaching and teaching of Jesus. At the same time, however, under the influence of FORM CRITICISM the parables were often studied in order to uncover the ORIGINAL and pure oral form of the parable as well as their SITZ IM LEBEN at an earlier stage than the one reflected in their written forms as found in the Gospels. Despite the many helpful insights garnered since the groundbreaking work on the parables by Adolf Jülicher at the end of the nineteenth century, criticism of the form-critical presuppositions and the more recent shift in Jesus studies involving memory and the 'remembered' Jesus in the works of, for example, James D. G. Dunn and Jens Schröter, have led to new approaches to considering the parables as media of early Christian memory. In a series of articles, Ruben Zimmermann has examined the parables as media used in early Christian communities to remember Jesus. Drawing on the CULTURAL MEMORY theory of JAN ASSMAN, Astrid Erll, and Kaludia Seibel, he contends that the parable can be understood as one of the *Wiedergebrauchs-Formen* ('forms of re-use') employed in the process of remembering Jesus. Specifically, there are three functions connecting the parables, along with other forms, to the process of remembering. These functions are the tradition-creating function (*traditionsstiftende Funktion*), the community-creating function (*gemeinschaftsstiftende Funktion*), and the meaning-creating function (*sinnstiftende Funktion*).

First, the parables function in constructing and developing early Christian tradition. This function can clearly be seen in the variation found in the transmission of the parables in different contexts. The historical question of primary interest in considering the parables as media for remembering Jesus, however, is not the goal of recovering the 'authentic kernel' behind, for example, the Parable of the Lost Sheep in Q 15.1-7, Mt. 18.12-14, Lk. 15.1-7, or Gospel of Thomas 107. Rather, the goal is to understand the manner in which such variation contributed to the creation and reception of the memory of Jesus in various early Christian communities. In this example, it becomes evident that even as the parable creates certain traditions in its various versions, its prominent characteristics and structures are largely fixed. In this sense the form-bound memory is not completely free. At the same time, despite certain unchanging characteristics and structures, the parable's linguistic form and certain emphases are not set in stone.

Second, the collection and utilization of parables is also formative in the development of the communities in which they were employed. On the one hand, many parables reflect the social roots of the early Jesus movement and the concrete life circumstances in which the theological message of Jesus was advanced. Here it is particularly significant to observe, for example, the manner in which the memory of the parables of Jesus and Jesus' message of the kingdom of God developed. In our oldest sources, Mark and Q, there are only two instances in each text where the kingdom of God is expressly referenced in their many parables (Mk 4.26-29, 30-32 and Q 13.18-19, 20-21). In Matthew, however, the parables become the constitutive speech used for Jesus' preaching about the kingdom.

Finally, the memory of the parables creates meaning in that, for example, in the Parable of the Wicked Tenants (Mk 12.1-12) the death of Jesus is interpreted or in the Parable of the Wedding Banquet (Mt. 22.1-14) the destruction of Jerusalem is reflected upon. The parables not only describe a reality (*mimesis*) but actually contribute to the creation of it (*poiesis*) through the medium of language. The memory of the parable genre is thus both a recollection of past events in the early Jesus movement and an interpretive context in which those movements' own experiences and history find expression and meaning.

From the perspective of parables as media of memory, it can also be observed that the written parables did not bring a memory culture in early Christianity to an end but rather set it in motion. The texts are not merely historical sources but present and re-present the memory of Jesus. As such, the medium and the message are interrelated, as already expressed in the famous dictum of Eberhard Jüngel that the Kingdom comes to expression 'in parable as parable'. Or, as Eduard Schweizer expressed it, Jesus as the preacher of parables is himself the 'parable of God'. The parables are not simply the expression of one ethical maxim or an aspect of soteriological reflection, they relate to the remembering community in a much more holistic manner and with a view towards the entirety of existence. The memory of Jesus and his parables invited early Christian communities to reflect upon the significance of both the preacher and his parables and thus shaped the media in which the remembered Jesus has been passed down to us today.

Dieter T. Roth (Johannes Gutenberg Universität Mainz, Germany)

Further Reading

Hultgren, Arland J. 2000. *The Parables of Jesus: A Commentary*. Grand Rapids: Eerdmans.

Scott, Bernard Brandon. 1989. *Hear Then the Parable: A Commentary on the Parables of Jesus*. Minneapolis: Fortress.

Snodgrass, Klyne. 2008. *Stories with Intent: A Comprehensive Guide to the Parables of Jesus*. Grand Rapids: Eerdmans.

Zimmermann, Ruben. 2007. 'Formen und Gattungen als Medien der Jesus-Erinnerung: Zur Rückgewinnung der Diachronie in der Formgeschichte des Neuen Testaments.' In *Die Macht der Erinnerung*. Edited by Martin Ebner et al. *Jahrbuch für Biblische Theologie* 22. Neukirchen-Vluyn: Neukirchener, pp. 131–67.

Zimmermann, Ruben. 2010. 'Memory and Form Criticism: The Typicality of Memory as a Bridge between Orality and Literality in the Early Christian Remembering Process.' In *The Interface of Orality and Writing: Speaking, Seeing, Writing in the Shaping of New Genres*. Edited by Annette Weissenrieder and Robert B. Coote. WUNT 260. Tübingen: Mohr Siebeck, pp. 130–43.

Zimmermann, Ruben. 2015. *Puzzling the Parables of Jesus: Methods and Interpretation*. Minneapolis: Fortress.

Zimmermann, Ruben, in collaboration with Gabi Kern, eds. 2008. *Hermeneutik der Gleichnisse Jesu: Methodische Neuansätze zum Verstehen urchristlicher Parabeltexte*. WUNT 231. Tübingen: Mohr Siebeck.

Zimmermann, Ruben in collaboration with Detlev Dormeyer, Gabi Kern, Annette Merz, Christian Münch, and Enno Edzard Popkes, eds. 2007. *Kompendium der Gleichnisse Jesu*. Güttersloh: Güttersloher Verlagshaus.

Parchment/Vellum Parchment was an ancient WRITING material typically made from the skins of sheep or goats. The terms *parchment* and *vellum* are often used interchangeably, but the latter designation refers strictly to the finer skins of a smaller animal, such as a calf or kid. In Latin, parchment was usually called *pergamena* or *membrana*, and in Greek, *diphthera* or *derma*. As evident from the Latin name indicated above, the word *parchment* is derived from the name of the city Pergamon/PERGAMUM in Asia Minor where, according to popular tradition, this form of writing material was developed.

Pliny the Elder reports (*Natural History* 13.11, quoting Varro) that parchment was 'invented' (Latin, *repertas*) as a result of a rivalry between King Eumenes II of Pergamon (197–159 BCE) and King Ptolemy V ('Epiphanes') of Egypt (205–180 BCE) over who had the best LIBRARY. To secure the reputation of his own collection, Ptolemy stopped the exportation of PAPYRUS; the Pergamenes resourcefully responded by inventing parchment as an alternate writing material. Most scholars agree that this story is legendary in nature, since parchment was in use centuries prior to the reigns of Ptolemy and Eumenes.

Unlike papyrus, parchment took a considerable amount of time to produce. Parchment manufacturers would choose an unblemished skin of an animal and dehair it by soaking it in a lime solution for several days and then scraping away the hairs with a hand tool. The skin would then be stretched taut, left to dry, and later treated with alum and chalk. Finally, the manufacturer would cut the skin to a particular dimension (most parchment codices tended towards a square shape) and would then sell it, most likely in a series of sheets.

The advantages of parchment over papyrus are several. It is on the whole a superior writing surface, more durable (although papyrus was also durable), and lacks fibre resistance as with the *verso* of a papyrus sheet.

The main disadvantages were that parchment was more expensive and took longer to manufacture, which is why everyday documents were written on papyrus rather than parchment. Even though papyrus continued to be used, the material evidence demonstrates that parchment ultimately became the standard WRITING material; it was used consistently for book production throughout Late Antiquity up until recent centuries, when it was replaced by paper. The increase in the use of parchment in the fourth century CE was largely contemporaneous with the widespread use of the CODEX, the preferred written medium of the early Christians.

The majority of NT MANUSCRIPTS are written on parchment, and there is a direct reference to parchment at 2 Tim. 4:13, where the author asks for the recipients of the letter to bring his 'cloak', 'the books', and 'especially the parchments' (*membrana*). Most scholars today agree that this request refers to a type of Roman parchment notebook. In his letter to Amphilochius in 376 CE, Basil of Caesarea claims that his fellow clergy prevented him from sending his treatise *On the Holy Spirit* on papyrus, demanding instead that it be written on parchment (Letter 231).

Brice C. Jones (University of Louisiana at Monroe, USA)

Further Reading

Metzger, Bruce M., and Bart D. Ehrman. 2005. *The Text of the New Testament: Its Transmission, Corruption, and Restoration*. 4th edn. Oxford: Oxford University Press.

Thompson, Edward Maunde. 1912. *An Introduction to Greek and Latin Palaeography*. Oxford: Clarendon Press.

Turner, Eric G. 1980. *Greek Papyri: An Introduction*. 2nd edn. Oxford: Clarendon Press.

Parry, Milman Milman Parry (1902–35) was an American classicist whose work on Homeric poetry provided the foundation for the methodological approach that is now termed *oral-formulaic theory*. His untimely death prevented Parry himself from bringing to fruition the fuller comparative studies he envisioned; nevertheless, his work on the formulaic language of Greek epic changed the landscape of Homeric scholarship, and the extension of his ideas by others (such as his student ALBERT LORD) would eventually lead to an entire field of comparative research into the world's ORAL TRADITIONS.

The seeds of Parry's revolutionary views towards Homeric poetry were already on display within his MA thesis (completed in 1923 at the University of California at Berkeley), in which he investigated the regularized diction of Homer as compared with that of other ancient Greek poets. Here Parry first mentions the idea of complicating the so-called HOMERIC QUESTION – that is, the identity of Homer and his relationship to the origins of the *Iliad and Odyssey* – by inserting considerations of the 'traditional element in the style' of these works (A. Parry 1971: 422). At the time of Parry's research, most Homeric scholars had fallen into one of two camps with regard to this question. The 'Analysts' maintained that the epics were compilations of smaller poems (perhaps by different authors or even from different periods) edited together in a fashion that sometimes gave rise to the inconsistencies observable in the texts we have today. The opposing view was held by the 'Unitarians', who argued that the *Iliad* and *Odyssey* derive from a single poetic genius and display an overall artistic and narrative unity that transcends individual narrative or stylistic infelicities. Parry's work, however, would make this centuries-old debate more or less irrelevant: both the unity and the inconsistencies of the epics could be understood as products of a long-lived tradition of verse-making passed down through multiple generations of Greek poets who employed a particularized idiom to create and then re-create their SONGS.

Parry's MA thesis went on to mention a few aspects of this specialized idiom – for instance, the usage of 'ornamental epithets' (426) and the systematic metrical positioning of certain types of phraseology (422-23) – but it was in his two doctoral theses (available in English translation in A. Parry 1971), produced at the University of Paris in 1928, that Parry would take on the challenge of actually trying to prove that traditional techniques of composition were at the heart of the Homeric poems. The starting point for this proof was the phraseological unit that Parry called a 'FORMULA' and defined as 'an expression regularly used, under the same metrical conditions, to express an essential idea' (13). Through detailed analysis of a subset of these recurring phrases known as 'noun-epithet formulas', Parry showed that units such as 'swift-footed Achilles' and 'the white-armed goddess Hera' had been shaped over time by tradition in order to mesh with the complex metrical requirements of the dactylic hexameter; as a result of this process, efficient systems of noun-epithet formulas had developed so that poets could easily combine them with other similarly structured phraseological units to create traditionally idiomatic, whole-line verses. In general there was an economy of expression such that phrases having the same metrical and semantic values were rare, but flexibility and innovation within the system were still possible as poets created new formulas by means of analogy. By demonstrating that a very large percentage of metrical anomalies occur at precisely the points in the epic hexameter where formulaic elements were being joined together, Parry provided additional evidence to show that such patterned language lay at the root of Homeric composition.

Throughout Parry's early work, the focus had always been upon the traditional nature of Homeric poetry; however, under the influence of the philologist Antoine Meillet and the Slovenian ethnographer Matija Murko, Parry gradually came to believe that the features he had been detailing were not only traditional, but also oral in origin. If early Greek poets had been composing under the constraints of oral performance, it was clear why the regularized system of diction would have been necessary in the first place. In addition, other poetic characteristics such as the additive nature of Homeric verse and its dialectal variation became much more easily understandable. Thus, over the next few years as he was embarking on his teaching career (spending a year at Drake University before moving on to take a position in the Classics Department at Harvard University), Parry produced a series of essays (all collected in A. Parry 1971) that expanded upon his original ideas to include this new perspective and convincingly argue the case for an oral-traditional Homer.

In order to further validate his hypotheses, Parry determined to test the results of his analysis of ancient epics against field evidence from living oral traditions in the modern world. Having learnt from Murko of a thriving oral epic tradition in Yugoslavia, Parry travelled to the area in the summer of 1933 to lay the groundwork for a return visit that would stretch from June 1934 until September 1935. During this second trip, Parry – along with his student Albert Lord and their native assistant, Nikola Vujnović – recorded hundreds of performances from GUSLARI, singers who were for the most part illiterate yet able to produce epic poems that were sometimes several thousand transcribed verses in length. Unfortunately, Parry's untimely death late in 1935 prevented him from completing the full comparative analyses he had planned. However, continued work by Lord and others in publishing and analysing these materials extended the comparative methodological framework embodied by oral-formulaic theory into the study of hundreds of ancient, medieval, and modern traditions as well as into disciplines as varied as history, anthropology, philosophy, and religious studies.

R. Scott Garner (Rhodes College, USA)

Further Reading

Foley, John Miles. 1988. *The Theory of Oral Composition: History and Methodology*. Bloomington: Indiana University Press.

Parry, Adam, ed. 1971. *The Making of Homeric Verse: The Collected Papers of Milman Parry*. Oxford: Clarendon Press.

Parry, Milman, Albert B. Lord, and David E. Bynum, colls., eds., and trans. 1953-present. *Serbo-Croatian Heroic Songs (Srpskohrvatske junačke pjesme)*. Cambridge, MA: Harvard University Press.

Passion Narrative The phrase *passion narrative* refers narrowly to the extended stories of Jesus' suffering and death found in each of the canonical Gospels (Mt. 26.1-27.61; Mk 14.1-15.47; Lk. 22.1-24:56: Jn 18.1-19.42), as well as in the non-canonical Gospel of Peter, and more broadly to the early Christian ORAL TRADITIONS and rituals underlying these accounts that preserved the story of Jesus' death. *Passion* here derives from the Greek *paskhô*, 'I suffer', via the Latin *passio*, 'suffering'. Containing a series of episodes extending from Jesus' prayer and betrayal in Gethsemane through his burial, the passion narrative comprises a single story upon which each individual episode depends. The episode of Jesus' empty tomb is probably also integral to the passion narrative. In scholarship on the formation and transmission of the memory of Jesus' suffering and death, *passion narrative* may designate this story in whatever medium of narrative utterance it exists, as well as the form or pattern of performance in general.

The composition of the passion narrative presents particular questions in terms of ancient media. Of the passion narratives in the canonical Gospels, Matthew and Luke can be shown to be dependent upon Mark; Mark, John, and Peter thus represent three accounts of Jesus' suffering and death that are similar to but independent of one another. Such a story must then belong to an early stage in the formation of the gospel tradition, but attempts to find a single written source for these three accounts have proved unconvincing. Paul, despite his focus on Jesus' death and resurrection, apparently did not know a written text similar to the gospel passion narratives. It is therefore necessary to look beyond the written medium to understand the formation of the passion narrative.

A further consideration is that the passion narratives are not *reportage* – they were not mechanically fashioned from eyewitness material, but rather can be demonstrated to be the product of use and interpretation of the Scriptures of Israel. As such, the development and transmission of the passion narrative(s) serve as a case study in the interplay of the ACTUAL PAST and its subsequent representations in early Christian COLLECTIVE MEMORY. Raymond Brown (1994) argued that the passion narrative was 'history remembered' through the vehicle of scriptural prophecy, while John Dominic Crossan (1988) characterized the passion narrative as 'prophecy historicized', arguing that the passion narrative arose out of a process of searching the Scriptures of Israel to explicate the death of Jesus. Crossan emphasized the ancient scribal and exegetical context in which the passion narrative developed, rather than the ritual practices of early Christian communities, as constitutive of the narrative memory of Jesus' passion. Approaches of this kind did not explicitly engage the question of the medium for composition and transmission or the role of CULTURAL MEMORY in the generating narrative.

Other examinations of the passion narrative have hinted at questions of media. Nickelsburg, for example, analysed Mark's passion narrative and argued that the motif of 'the suffering and vindicated righteous' found throughout the Scriptures of Israel was a major influence on the shape of the passion narrative. Nickelsburg focused attention on how such a storytelling tradition might provide a medium for the construction narratives about Jesus' death. A turn towards early Christian cultic life as a medium of memory can be observed in the proposals of form critics such as Georg Bertram, Gottfried Schille, and Ludger Schenke, who identified the passion narrative as a cultic legend for early celebrations of Jesus' death and resurrection. Their work, however, shows little concern for the workings of cultic practice or the processes of cultural memory to account for the generation of narrative.

Viewed through the lens of the work of MILMAN PARRY, ALBERT LORD, and Gregory Nagy, the cultic dimensions of the story of Jesus' death become clearer, particularly in light of Lord's insight that ORAL TRADITION is characterized primarily by composition in performance. This approach seeks to identify the traditional POETICS by which early Christians came to speak of Jesus' passion. Considering the early Christian memories of Jesus' death evident in sources that do not obviously depend on the accounts in the NARRATIVE

GOSPELS (e.g. 1 Corinthians, Hebrews, 1 Peter, Epistle of Barnabas), the story of Jesus' passion may be viewed as an aspect of the cultic practices of various early Christian communities, through the generative medium of cultural memory. These practices included the use of the Scriptures of Israel, especially the narrative of the exodus, wilderness, and entry into the land of promise, together with the songs and stories of the suffering righteous who were vindicated by God (e.g. the Psalms and Deutero-Isaiah).

These Scriptures, available in the cultic practices of the community as story and song, provided a performance medium for telling a new story and singing anew Jesus' death. At every point of such memory of the passion, significant markers of cultic practice and the context of the reenactment of memory also appear. Such cultic practices (BAPTISM, EUCHARIST, covenant renewal) in which Jesus' death was remembered thus constituted a generative medium. The formation of a story of Jesus' suffering and death must then include the dimension of ritual practice. Stories were told, songs sung, and rituals performed such that Jesus' death became the central point in the reenactment of the cultic life of the community and integral to its self-definition and constitution. The poetics of cultural memory point to the interrelation of narrative, ritual, and social IDENTITY as media for the formation and transmission of the passion narrative.

Such a process accounts for the multiformity and independence of the passion narratives in the written Gospels, as well as the indications of an ongoing narrative tradition of Jesus' passion apart from the Gospels. The passion narratives in Mark, John, and Peter can thus be regarded as distinct outcroppings of a continuing performative process. The techniques and media by which the written medium of the Gospels draws upon the ongoing performative medium for the passion narrative require further investigation.

Ellen Bradshaw Aitken (McGill University, Canada)

Further Reading

Aitken, Ellen Bradshaw. 2004. *The Poetics of the Passion: Jesus' Death in Early Christian Memory*. Göttingen: Vandenhoeck & Ruprecht.

Brown, Raymond. 1994. *The Death of the Messiah*. 2 vols. New York: Doubleday.

Crossan, John Dominic. 1988. *The Cross that Spoke: The Origins of the Passion Narrative*. San Francisco: Harper & Row.

Nickelsburg, George. 1980. 'The Genre and Function of the Markan Passion Narrative.' *Harvard Theological Review* 73: 153–84.

Pauline Literature Nearly half of the NT literature claims to have been written by Paul, a Jewish artisan who went from being a violent pursuer of Jesus' disciples to one of his foremost champions and a leading rhetorician of the earliest church, following a religious experience that he believed to be a radical encounter with the risen Christ (see Galatians 1; 1 Corinthians 15). On the basis of this experience, Paul became a self-proclaimed apostle who assumed the role of a scribal teacher of the Law, a posture that allowed him to challenge even the viewpoints of some of the apostles commissioned by Jesus (see Galatians 2). Although the Pauline LETTERS suggest that he worked with a number of other individuals, such as Barnabas, Timothy, Titus, and the lesser known Sosthenes and Tertius, Paul's name that is most often associated with the shaping of distinctive Christian IDENTITY.

As indicated by numerous references in letter openings and closing statements, the Pauline literature arose in the context of Paul's extensive travels and the leadership he exercised in establishing early Christian communities. Paul's mission was both a part of the rapid growth of the movement as well as a driving force in its cultural evolution. In terms of numeric growth, Paul's letters are related to, and reflect, the expansion of the Palestinian Jesus movement into urban areas across the ancient Mediterranean world. Additionally, Paul's REPUTATION grew through his extensive correspondence, as he interacted with communities he had visited or aspired to visit, such as that in Rome. In terms of social influence and cultural reforms, Paul's letters bear witness to a renegotiation of Jewish culture in the service of multi-ethnic association. The most substantive contribution of the Pauline literature to understandings of early Christian media culture is the evidence these letters provide for inter-communal networking, the expansion of the movement, and insights gained from Paul's responses to social–ideological pressures facing the minority group, particularly issues arising from the recruitment of non-Israelites (Gentiles). Paul's literary reputation focuses upon inclusion of diverse ethnicities among Jewish Christ-followers, benefiting from Judaism's imperial approval as well as its literature, culture, and the recruiting base provided by its already-established social networks.

Social Positioning of the Christ-movement

Like any reading process, interpretation of the Pauline literature is, and has always been, influenced by particular sociopolitical contexts and (sub)cultural meta-narratives at particular times and circumstances. Traditionally, it was thought that Paul left behind his Jewish culture when he joined the Jesus movement. More recently, however, the scholarly debate described as the 'new perspective on Paul' has rejected the assumption of an early 'parting of the ways', providing a more critical appreciation of Paul's Jewish culture and heritage. Furthermore, recent scholarship has demonstrated that the Pauline epistles are not so much articulations of an overarching 'Pauline theology' as occasional communications addressing different circumstances, a perspective that allows the apparent contradictions in Pauline thought to be contextually explained.

Pauline epistolary writing typically intertwines the interpretation of Jewish texts with moral exhortation (compare, for example, Gal. 1–3 and 4–6). For example, in Galatians 3 Paul offers an allegory on Abraham's offspring that prioritizes his views and devalues the Jewish custom of CIRCUMCISION for Christ-followers. The letters also illustrate some of the controversies relating to readings of Jewish texts, as for Paul, Christ signalled a new era of interpretive freedom and intertextuality legitimated by the Spirit. Paul asserts authority, and his wielding of social power can be extremely rigid (Gal. 1.6-9). In 2 Corinthians, Paul allegorizes early Christian disputes, placing an interpretive veil over the face of Moses and his followers and arguing that the Spirit of God authorizes his own hermeneutical attempts to relativize the Law (2 Cor. 3). While Paul himself refuses the personal need for 'letters of recommendation' (2 Cor. 3.1), he clearly used epistolary correspondence to bolster his reputation (see also Gal. 1–3; Philippians 3; 2 Corinthians 11). Paul's interaction with Jewish Scriptures illustrates how formative Jewish traditions were to Paul, and earliest Christian discourse, as well as how crucial it was for him to be regarded as a legitimate interpreter of these traditions in the early Christian movement. Paul's letters interact with Jewish traditions, providing some of the earliest literary evidence for inclusion of ethnic others and relativizing the importance of Jewish ritual culture among Jesus' followers from a non-Jewish background. Jewish traditions, in Paul's reinterpretation, provide the key components for early Christian identity and worldview, which was used to re-socialize polytheistic Greco-Romans. This included worship of a monotheistic God, anchoring their identity in the story of Israel, and developing a theology of prophetic fulfilment of Jewish traditions portraying Jesus as the promised messiah, and eschatological Saviour of all ethnicities.

Authorship and Cultural Evolution

The authorship of 2 Thessalonians, Colossians, Ephesians, and the Pastoral Epistles to Timothy and Titus is widely disputed on linguistic and cultural grounds, as it has been argued that the evident differences in syntax and writing style between these documents and the other Pauline letters may be indicative of different authors. It is also possible, however, that these variations reflect the work of differing amanuenses, the SCRIBES who transcribed Paul's letters, presumably by dictation. For example, Romans is often considered to be the best example of Paul's thought (and writing), but it was transcribed by the otherwise unknown Tertius (Rom. 16.22). Occasional references to Paul's own handwriting indicate his basic competence to read and write (see 1 Cor. 16.21; Gal. 6.11; Col. 4.18; 2 Thess. 3.17; Phlm. 19), thus placing Paul among the grapho-literary elite who could hire the services of professional scribes as needed for the more extended task of writing out a lengthy correspondence (see LITERACY). However, although we know Paul used an amanuensis to do his writing we do not know what level of freedom these scibes may have exercised from minute choices of terminology to representing Pauline thought more freely, or whether it was even possible for his associate to complete some works following his death, summarizing, or recording some of his thoughts posthumously.

At the same time, it is commonly argued that the differences within the Pauline corpus cannot be fully explained in terms of scribality alone. For instance, these letters noted above lack expressions and themes typical of Paul (e.g. *charismata*; *parousia*) while including novel concepts, such as the depiction of the universal church in Ephesians. Additionally, differences in the cultural positioning of these letters include issues surrounding Jewishness, leadership, and gender, moving from the early egalitarianism of Gal. 3:28 towards more institutionalized, hierarchical communal structures. Moreover, changes in ritual life, a diminishing charismatic orientation, and a greater desire for accommodation of the movement within Greco-Roman society indicate that a different mode of religion was evolving, causing a lasting shift in the cultural orientation of Christianity. This shift is seen, for example, in the inclusion of the household codes in Col. 3–4 and Eph. 5–6. To many Pauline scholars such sociocultural accommodation may be best explained by a later date and differences in authorship, with the pseudonymous letters emerging at a time when Christians were becoming less concerned with divine intervention in history than ensuring that the movement would fit well into Roman society. According to this view, pseudonymity offers a literary disguise for a later writer to offer an interpretation of an earlier tradition. While Paul himself was able to stress the importance of his personal experience of revelation to legitimate his writings (despite not being an eyewitness of Jesus), the Christian movement seemed to reject similar claims later, as apostolic authority became decisive.

It is possible that Paul's attitudes shifted as he neared the end of his life, and many of the disputed letters bear reference to Paul's chains and imprisonment. For many interpreters of Paul, the disputed letters are too different, and the shift of attitudes they display is perhaps going in a direction different from what we would expect – moving further away from his Jewish traditions towards a more independent Christian movement. The disputed letters provide literary evidence for devaluation of Jewish culture and traditions. For example, Ephesians 2 refers to a law-abolishing Christ, Titus discredits 'Jewish myths', and Colossians 2 denounces Jewish law while explicitly promoting reformist counter-rituals such as BAPTISM, which is portrayed as a 'spiritual CIRCUMCISION'. Similarly, the lack of urgency to explain God's ongoing covenant with Israel makes these letters puzzling, at least to their 'new perspective' readers. It is quite possible that these letters emerged later, shaping early Christian SOCIAL MEMORY and identity by mimicking Pauline letter writing, giving more novel community praxis (such as rejection of Torah observance) historical roots anchored in the legacy of Paul while simultaneously embellishing his reputation as the apostle par excellence. The use of a scribe may well provide the continuity with Paul and his later followers, addressed in the disputed letters. One way or another, the use of a scribe blurs the idea of authorship, and complicates the contemporary quest for tracing the authentic Paul and assessing his legacy in early Christian thought.

Minna Shkul (University of Sheffield, UK)

Further Reading

Elliott, Neil, and Mark Reasoner, eds. 2010. *Documents and Images for the Study of Paul*. Minneapolis: Fortress.
Keith, Chris. 2008. '"In My Own Hand": Grapho-Literacy and the Apostle Paul.' *Biblica* 89: 39–58.

Marchal, Joseph A. 2012. *Studying Paul's Letters: Contemporary Perspectives and Methods*. Minneapolis: Fortress.
Nanos, Mark D., ed. 2002. *The Galatians Debate: Contemporary Issues in Rhetorical and Historical Interpretation.* Grand Rapids: Baker Academic.
Richards, E. Randolph. 2004. *Paul and First-Century Letter Writing: Secretaries, Composition and Collection.* Downers Grove: InterVarsity.
Stanley, Christopher D. 2008. *Paul and the Language of Scripture: Citation Technique in the Pauline Epistles* and *Contemporary Literature*. SNTSMS 74. Cambridge: Cambridge University Press.
Wilder, Terry L. 2004. *Pseudonymity, the New Testament, and Deception. An Inquiry into Intention and Reception.* Lanham: University Press of America.
Westerholm, Stephen. 2004. *Perspectives Old and New on Paul*. Grand Rapids: Eerdmans.
Zetterholm, Magnus. 2009. *Approaches to Paul. A Student's Guide to Recent Scholarship*. Minneapolis: Fortress.

Performance Arena The term *performance arena* designates the literal and figurative place of oral performance – both a geographical site (possibly with ritualistic overtones) and a metaphorical area where performers and audience go to experience an oral text. In living traditions, a performance arena is a 'series or collection of actual physical sites', such as the royal court, SYNAGOGUE or mosque (Foley 1999: 23). The performance defines the space rather than vice versa, since the same space may be used for other speech events at different times. For example, the words exchanged within a marriage ceremony can transform a courtroom or a church into a wedding. Even when the performance is closely connected to a specific geographic locale, the speech event produces the performance arena.

Obviously, in the case of ancient texts the original performance arena cannot be directly observed; instead, one must reconstruct it based on narrative portrayals and comparative ethnographic data. Because speech defines the site, there is no 'dislocation when the performance arena changes from a 'real' site to a rhetorically induced forum in a text' (Foley 1999: 23). The same arena is invoked by read/written performance and by heard/spoken performance.

Drawing on the work of RICHARD BAUMAN, JOHN MILES FOLEY coined the term *performance arena* and defined it as 'the locus where the event of performance takes place, where words are invested with their special power' (1995: 47). The source of the word-power is the ambient traditions surrounding the performance arena, where a 'specialized form of communication is uniquely licensed to take place' (1995: 8). Upon entering the arena, modes of expression become idiomatic – namely, ways of speaking are made coherent with 'preselected, emergent kinds of meaning' (1995: 47). The performance is 'intelligible on its own terms' because performers and audience credit 'each act or verbal transaction with the context they have learned to provide' (1995: 48).

In Richard Bauman's words, the language of performance is charged with an 'interpretive frame'. Associative values particular to the performance event form a framework from which words derive special meanings (1975: 8–10). Performance thus transforms 'the basic referential uses of language' and encodes a set of connotations that are not accessible from the literal meaning of words (1975: 9–11). The further the audience is – culturally and temporally – from the traditions underlying an oral-derived text, the more difficult it is to identify the interpretive frame, simply because the performance arena is summoned solely by rhetorical signals, and each community has its own culturally specific ways to key oral performance (Foley 1995: 79–80; Bauman 1978: 15–24). The comprehension of verbal art nonetheless requires incorporating its oral context: an oral text or performance can only be correctly understood within its interpretive frame or performance arena.

The EUCHARIST in early Christianity provides an illuminating illustration of a performance arena. In this ritual context, men and women gathered in specific places to recite prayers and partake in the presence of

Christ's body and blood in bread and wine. Romans such as Minucius Felix (a third-century Latin apologist), however, did not attend the arena of this traditional oral performance and therefore misunderstood this rite as a cannibalistic orgy (cf. *Octavius* 9.5-9). The word-power surrounding the performance arena of the Eucharist, however, vested the 'drinking' and 'eating' with idiomatic connotations that made the performance intelligible in its own terms solely for those who grasped the interpretive frame.

Shem Miller (University of Mississippi, USA)

Further Reading

Bauman, Richard. 1977. *Verbal Art as Performance*. Rowley: Newbury House Publishers.
Foley, John Miles. 1995. *The Singer of Tales in Performance*. Bloomington: Indiana University Press.
Foley, John Miles. 1999. *Homer's Traditional Art*. University Park: Pennsylvania University Press.

Performance Criticism (Biblical) Biblical performance criticism is the study of the biblical writings as witnesses to oral performances that were either told from memory or presented as prepared readings before communal audiences in the context of the predominantly oral cultures of the ancient world. Such performances might have occurred in informal conversations or as STORYTELLING in a house or a market place or in more formal settings, such as after a meal or in WORSHIP or at the temple. Performances would have ranged from brief stories and sayings to lengthy presentations, such as the Joseph cycle, the story of the Exodus, a Gospel, or a Pauline letter. The performed texts may have been repeated in a somewhat rote fashion or, perhaps more commonly, retold loosely from memory or improvised to fit different situations. Performance criticism seeks to (re)imagine such performances. In so doing, it shifts the focus of our understanding from what a written text *means* to the *impact* a performance of that text's content has on an audience.

As an interpretive method, biblical performance criticism seeks to change the paradigm for biblical studies from a print mentality to that of a predominantly oral culture; to view the biblical writings as performance literature; to re-imagine the media dynamics of the ancient world in terms of cultures that were predominantly oral and memorial; to construct imaginative scenarios of ancient performances as means to interpret anew the traditions of the Bible; to reconsider the disciplines used to study the Bible so as to take account of orality; and to develop steps towards a disciplined, scientific performance analysis of biblical texts. Many strands of research and experience have come together to comprise performance criticism. Since the 1980s, scholars have been exploring the orality of the biblical world in several ways: analysis of ancient Israel, Greece, and Rome as predominantly oral/memorial cultures; media studies; performance studies of narrative; explorations of PERSONAL and COLLECTIVE MEMORY; theatre studies; and the experience of performing biblical writings in TRANSLATION from memory to contemporary audiences.

The Shift from Print to Performance

Since the invention of the printing press, the Bible has been read and studied primarily within the context of the print medium, although it was of course already in print form in the MANUSCRIPT medium in antiquity. The print-age communications model of today envisions an unchangeable biblical text designed to be the same in all printed copies and formatted to facilitate modern reading practices. The assumption is that most people are able to read and that books are inexpensive and readily available. Overwhelmingly, people today read the Bible individually and silently or hear short passages read aloud to them in a church or a classroom. When scholars study the Bible, they usually work alone and silently, and they interpret meaning in terms of the dynamic aesthetics of a printed text. Accompanying these cultural realities is a tendency to assume that the ancient Israelites and early Christians encountered the writings/content now in the Bible in much the same way. In fact, however, the print-age media model of an autonomous text and an isolated reader may not have been typical of the predominantly oral cultures of the ancient Mediterranean world (see READING CULTURE). In these contexts, communication of traditions was relational – vocal, dynamic, changing, emotive, transformative, and communal. Meaning was embodied and negotiated in interactions, often highly ritualized, between performer and audience.

In ancient oral cultures that have WRITING (manuscript cultures), it is likely that only a very small minority comprised of the powerful and their retainers could read and/or write with any fluency (see LITERACY). The overwhelming majority could not read or write at all. An oral/aural medium predominated, even for the very limited number who could read or write with facility. Manuscripts were expensive and few. Much of what people knew was learnt through face-to-face, word-of-mouth communication. Traditions were passed on in memory through informal conversations and formal presentations. Speeches and stories were sometimes composed in memory by ear and performed orally, sometimes without recourse to writing. Oral dictation to a SCRIBE was the primary means to get speech transcribed into writing. Manuscripts typically facilitated memory and served public reading (see PERFORMANCE OF THE GOSPELS; TORAH READING).

In such cultures, performances were central. An 'author' could compose orally in mind and memory, in performance, or through dictation. The composition was not repeated verbatim but was somewhat fluid as the performer responded to live audiences in real-time in the course of performing. Whether performed from memory or read aloud, the composition-as-performance would be lively and animated, and might have manifested features typical of ancient arts of oral speech as well as arts of performance. The audiences for performances would be communal; texts were not normally experienced alone or in private. People respond to texts differently in communal settings as opposed to private readings, particularly in reference to the lively interactions that take place between the performer and the audience. Also, performances are inherently embodied by and in their human communications contexts, bringing the past of a story into the immediacy of the here and now. The ancient performer could have expressed emotions in the act of performing and sought to evoke emotions in the audience. A performance provides sights and sounds and movement that engage the imagination. The audience is drawn into a different world as they encounter characters and places and events (see NONVERBAL COMMUNICATION IN PERFORMANCE). In these ways, performance has the power to create a powerful impact on an audience that cannot be reduced entirely to the content of the words being communicated.

The goal of performance criticism is to change the model of the scholarly study of the Bible from communication in print to communication in performance. This goal represents a foundational paradigm shift from author to composer, from silence to sound, from fixed text to more fluid composition, from printed text to manuscript and embodied performance, from reading silently to reading aloud and expressively, from a passive individual reader to an active communal audience, from private reading to public engagement, and from a focus on lines and passages in a text to presentations of lengthy sequences. Above all, the new paradigm represents a shift in focus from what a text *means* so as also to encompass what a performance *does* in order to create an impact upon an audience.

The Bible as Performance Literature

The writings collected in the Bible may be viewed as examples of ancient *performance literature*, as remnants of what were once living performances. That is, the ancient texts could have reflected an originating oral performance or they could have been composed in writing in order to be performed – like musical scores or theatre scripts. In music and theatre studies, it would be unusual for scholars to study scores and scripts without also experiencing performances of these texts. Yet biblical scholars have worked for centuries without experiencing performances of biblical psalms or prophecies or wisdom or gospel stories or LETTERS.

Of course, we cannot recover any actual performances from ancient times. Nevertheless, we can get some sense of what performances were like from ancient sources. Rhetorical handbooks by Aristotle, Cicero, Longinus, Quintilian, and the author of *Rhetorica ad Herennium* describe the dynamics of the delivery of speeches. Many ancient histories, novels, letters, and satires, as well as the biblical materials, contain descriptions of rituals, SONGS, STORYTELLING, orations, theatrical events, and entertainment at meals. Artistic representations on vases as well as from paintings and sculptures also demonstrate characteristics of ancient performances. In addition, we are able to infer much from the ancient texts themselves about how a particular composition, or portions of one, may have been performed and what impact it may have had on audiences. We are also learning about the nature of performance through comparative studies of performers in modern cultures that are predominantly oral. In addition, some modern interpreters are getting in touch with the dynamics of performance by doing their own performances of biblical compositions from memory in contemporary languages.

The choice of the word *performance* in the designation of performance criticism is salutary because, unlike the implications of a term like *recitation*, ancient performances were animated and often dramatic and artful, engaging and emotional, powerful and transformational. Also, unlike prophecy or storytelling or oration, *performance* is a term that can encompass many GENRES of biblical literature.

Performance in the Media Culture of Antiquity

Re-imagining the ancient Mediterranean world broadly and the biblical world narrowly as predominantly oral cultures involves a consideration of four dynamics of ancient media culture: the predominance of orality; the centrality of memory; the nature and functions of manuscripts; and the dynamics of performances. The interrelationships between these four components were dynamic and shifting, depending on the culture, the era, and the geographical location, as well as whether the audience was urban or rural, elites or peasants, and male or female or mixed.

The Predominance of orality

Performance criticism appropriately re-conceives the biblical worlds as predominantly oral cultures, with varying dynamic interactions between writing and orality in different eras and regions (e.g. Palestine, Greece, Rome, Egypt). Ancient pre-industrial agrarian cultures were typically comprised of a small ruling elite, generally representing about 2 per cent of the total population, with some retainers, no middle class, about 90 per cent peasants or slaves, and a small number on the margins of society.

The rates of those who could read generally reflected this configuration. LITERACY rates might be as high as 15 per cent among urban males and as low as 2 per cent or less in rural areas. Estimates of percentages of those who could read vary in relation to different locales and reflect different levels of proficiency, beginning, at the lowest level, with the simple capacity to write one's name or copy letters. Most scholars now think that there was no general educational system for the populace, either for Greco-Romans or in Israel. The advanced stage of Greco-Roman EDUCATION for the elite focused on training for rhetorical oration in public life. Reading and writing with facility was limited almost exclusively to this group of wealthy and powerful men and some women along with some of their trained slaves and retainers. Some merchants of long-distant trade may have had a limited capacity to read and write for their work, or they hired literate employees to carry out these functions. For the most part, writing and reading were sometimes considered physical labour and bore little or no prestige, though they could also be viewed as intrinsic, and in certain contexts, prestigious oral performances were sometimes the main means to pass on stories and traditions to and among the populace. In these cases writing, when available, generally supported oral traditioning.

Elites used writing as a way to exert and maintain their political and economic power. Writings on MONUMENTS and buildings, in decrees and administrative letters were often means to intimidate peasants with mysterious scripts that they could not understand and that could be used against them. The elites also used performances of their GREAT TRADITIONS – stories, laws, rituals, and other foundational texts committed to writings with enduring cultural status – as means to exert dominance. As a means of resistance, the populace had their own little traditions that supported their struggles. Furthermore, they used subtleties in oral speech to express their point of view through irony, exaggeration, understatement, dissimulation, and doublespeak. Their lower class perspectives in this covert language were hidden from elites but evident to fellow peasants. Appreciating the complex dynamics of these manifestations of language enables us to understand better the hegemony of the oppressors and the methods of resistance by the weak. Embedded traces of these power dynamics are evident in the extant biblical texts.

In predominantly oral cultures, there were many features of language designed to make speech engaging and memorable, traces of which are embedded in our written Scriptures: stories told in patterns (similar to the variable structures of jokes), maxims, PROVERBS, FOLKLORE, among others. The rhythmic sounds and parallel structures of words were catchy and easily remembered. Short stories, parables, and pithy sayings now embedded in the biblical writings may have circulated individually before being incorporated into clusters of sayings and larger narratives. The oral traditions that eventually made their way into the collection of biblical writings were but a tip of the iceberg of all the oral traditions.

Lengthy performances were important in predominantly oral cultures. Oral presentations of Israelite traditions, often contextualized in ritual settings (e.g. the Passover festival, SABBATH observance, CIRCUMCISION of a newborn family member), were a way to strengthen community, to create/solidify/modify/or subvert COLLECTIVE MEMORIES, and to forge a common identity. So too, in the early church throughout the latter part of the first century and well into the second century, there were likely sustained performances of Gospels, letters, and the Apocalypse even after written texts of these compositions became widely available.

In their earliest expressions, many of the NT texts could have been performed in their entirety. It is hard to imagine, for example, that a community would receive a letter of Paul and hear only part of it. While such an experience might not fit the aesthetic sensibilities of modern audiences, lengthy storytelling events, long oral speeches, and extended readings of literary works were common in the Greco-Roman world. The Gospels of Mark and John take modern storytellers about two hours or less to tell; Matthew and Luke take from three to four hours; with the exception of Romans and what we now call 1 and 2 Corinthians and Hebrews, the letters in the NT would each have taken less than a half hour to present; Revelation takes about an hour and a half. In ancient cultures, none of these times for performance events were prohibitive for performers to perform (from memory or by reading) or for audiences to experience in one sitting.

Also, many Hebrew traditions, on certain occasions, could have been presented in their entirety, especially at feasts celebrated in the TEMPLE. Many Israelite traditions, such as the Joseph cycle, the giving of the Law, the Exodus stories, or the exploits of David, would have circulated from memory with little direct connection with the writings themselves. Some have suggested that Hebrew writings considered to be Scripture in the first century CE were sometimes divided into passages for brief readings in SYNAGOGUE gatherings. However, this practice is unlikely to have been applied to compositions now collected in the NT, at least not at first, because they were not viewed as Scripture. Rather, they were possibly told as a whole in the genre of storytelling in the market places, in house churches, in community gatherings, and around meals (see BANQUET/MEALS).

Furthermore, since these early Christian writings were not yet viewed as Scripture, there may have been greater freedom to improvise on the compositions, as witnessed by the use of the Gospel of Mark by the authors of Matthew and Luke. Storytellers were expected to put their own stamp on the compositions and to shape their stories to particular audiences. Stories were changed also by the back-and-forth nature of the movement from performance to scribal copying and back again to performance. As performance literature in oral cultures, the manuscripts now collected in the Bible may represent a single occasion or the results of many occasions of the telling of a Gospel or a letter (or portions thereof) in the history of its performance.

The Centrality of Memory

In the predominantly oral cultures of antiquity, memory more than writing was considered to be the 'storehouse of knowledge'. It is impossible to overstate the centrality, both actual and perceived, of memory in these memorial cultures. Memory capabilities were part of the dynamics of the society for everyone. People with exceptional memories naturally came to the forefront as bearers of tradition (see MEMORY, GRECO-ROMAN THEORIES OF). For educated elites, memory was the subject of rhetorical training in mental techniques designed to aid recall. While rote memorization was not unknown, for example in reciting short poems or sections of prepared speeches, most performances of tradition were somewhat fluid and creative. Stories and orations were composed using language, style, and structures that facilitated recall by the performer and recollection by the audience. Traces of these memory arts are evident throughout the Bible in features such as chiastic structures, various forms of parallelism, catch words, recurring motifs, TYPE SCENES, multiple patterns of repetition, verbal FORMULAS, and sounds that signal structural shifts, all devices that might help a performer remember what to say and do next.

A fundamental purpose of performing was to shape the communal IDENTITY of the society or group through collective memory. Ancient performers were able to hold lengthy compositions, such as the epics of Homer, in memory. Rabbinic tradents of Israel knew great swaths of Scripture and tradition from memory. Many biblical traditions, even lengthy compositions like Gospels and letters, may have gone from oral performance to oral performance without writing. When writing occurred, it supported memory as well as the preservation of traditions through performances of public reading. It is necessary for us to rethink the nature of consciousness in order to grasp the dynamics of memory in predominantly oral cultures, especially in an electronic world where information is at our fingertips with little need for human memory.

The Nature and Function of Manuscripts

Writing was often accomplished by dictation to a scribe or by a scribe writing from memory. Apart from the elite, most people had indirect access to texts and information recorded on scrolls, the contents of which they experienced either through personal memory, by having the information told to them from memory, or by having the texts read to them.

Writing in ancient cultures was quite different from modern book culture. Writing was done on SCROLLS comprised of sheets made from PAPYRUS reeds and pasted together or, on treated animal skins (see PARCHMENT), or on hard physical objects such as monuments or OSTRACA (pottery shards). SCRIBES wrote in a cross-legged position on the floor or seated on a stool with the scroll draped across the thigh. In Greek and Latin scrolls, the writing was formatted in narrow columns, with lines comprised of one letter after another from beginning to end, sometimes, though not always, with no spaces between words or sentences, and or no punctuation. There were no divisions into chapters and verses. These alphabet sounds were comprised of syllables that denoted sounds, and when ancient scrolls were read, they were sounded out to form words and phrases (see ORTHOGRAPHY).

With limited reading aids in the earliest manuscripts, scrolls did not facilitate reading aloud with ease before a communal audience. Some elites in Roman culture (or slaves in their service) were able to read manuscripts easily and silently, a skill that is rarely noted in the sources and usually cited as evidence of the unusual intellectual ability of the silent reader. For public performances, readers would need extensive preparation and practice (see LECTOR). There is a difference of opinion among scholars about whether public performances involved prepared reading from a scroll or were presented from memory; it is likely that both commonly occurred. Those who were able to read and those who could not read passed on the traditions, repeating and explaining them as they told and retold them. Writing was thus not a substitute for memory and speech; rather, writing was integrally intertwined with the dynamics of both.

The Dynamics of Performance

Performances were the dominant way in which traditions were passed on, communities were shaped, and social identity was formed. The techniques of oral speech, the strength of memory, and the presence of manuscripts all fed into and served performances.

The modern experience of Scripture as silent print text naturally strips the biblical writings of some of their power and emotion. By contrast, performances in antiquity could be embodied in forceful ways, incorporating expressive voice inflection, volume, pace, pitch, and tone along with bodily gestures, facial expressions, posture, and movement. Ancient storytellers and orators knew how to generate suspense and irony, how to represent characters, and how to build the plot to a climax. Performances were designed to demonstrate the meaning of a story, arouse emotion, and generate an effect on an audience.

In some cases, we can infer from the extant biblical stories and letters themselves what features may have characterized live performances of these texts. For example, when a Gospel says that Jesus 'laid hands on' someone for healing, or when Paul describes the leaders in Jerusalem offering him 'the right hand of partnership', these imply certain gestures that would likely have been physically enacted by performers as they spoke the relevant words. Similarly, when a demon 'screams' or someone 'pleads' with Jesus or a crowd 'is astonished', these are clues for the performer to mirror the volume or inflection or tone of those characters in the story. Although we can never determine specifically how voice and gesture were expressed in antiquity, descriptions of what were considered to be contextually appropriate gestures and bodily postures are available in the ancient rhetorical handbooks and in portrayals of orators and storytellers in ancient works of art.

Public reading involved the same dynamic as performances from memory, although the expressions were limited by the skill of the reader and the need to manipulate a scroll. Nevertheless, as in contemporary readers' theatre, a composition could have been read powerfully through various vocal dynamics, accompanied by posture changes, some limited gestures, and head movement, as well as facial and eye expressions. Some readers may have been skilled enough to go back and forth between reading and presentation from memory. However, reading may not have been as animated as performing from memory; performing without a scroll left the body free to engage in movement, gestures, and greater audience interaction. In some cases, a scroll may simply have been held closed in the left hand as a sign of the authority of the composer, while the right hand remained free for gestures.

To fully grasp the nature of performance, it helps to imagine a scenario involving a composite construction of the content and dynamics of the performance, the place in which the performance took place, the social and cultural location of performer and audience, the dynamics in the community being addressed, and the specific historical circumstances. The goal is to imagine what range of meanings/impacts the composition may have conveyed and the potential outcomes it may have had on a specific communal audience in a particular time and place.

Reading the Bible as Performance Literature

Re-imagining ancient Israel and the cultures of the early church as predominantly oral cultures leads us to rethink the methods by which we study the Bible. Performance Criticism involves a reorientation of scholarly disciplines in light of the shift in medium from print to performance. For example, Source Criticism is rethinking the literary solutions to the documentary hypothesis and the synoptic problem by taking into account multiple oral originals for the fluidity of Israelite traditions and the sayings of Jesus. FORM CRITICISM and genre criticism are exploring ways'in which PARABLE, gospel, APOCALYPSE, epistle, wisdom tradition, and ethical exhortation functioned in the temporal and emotional experience of oral performances. Some textual critics are rethinking the fluidity of the earliest manuscript traditions in light of interaction of scribes with the flexibility of oral performances and by attending to the role of memory variants. Rhetorical Criticism is starting to take account of the importance of memory and the arts of delivery in the study of the NT epistles. Narrative Criticism is rethinking narrative traditions as they were embodied in a performer and received by a communal audience. Ideological/ethical criticism is shifting its focus to make explicit the power dynamics of performance events and of the social implications of the presence of authoritative texts. Performance Criticism itself is an eclectic field that brings together – and in turn realigns – the concerns and conclusions of a wide range of disciplines and models, including some fields that are relatively new to biblical studies, such as media studies, speech-act theory, theatre studies, performance studies, oral tradition research, and TRANSLATION studies.

In addition, the contemporary act of performing biblical traditions, either in the original or in contemporary translations, proves to be a fruitful means of research. Unlike an analysis of print, the exegete-as-performer not only assesses the potential meanings of a line but must also make choices about how each line can be delivered. Furthermore, a performer is acutely attuned to the composition primarily as a rhetorical act designed to have an impact on an audience. The performer also gains a sense of the comprehensive impact of an entire composition, say of a psalm or the Wisdom of Solomon or a Gospel or letter, as it may work to bring change and transformation to a listening community from the beginning to the conclusion of the composition in performance.

The following steps are typical elements of a performance-critical analysis of a biblical book or passage, particularly an analysis involving an actual performance of a biblical text.

- *Select a passage that has integrity as a speech-unit.* This may involve either the composition as a whole or units within the composition, such as episodes, stories, parables, speeches, sayings, and thematic units, etc. These are usually identified by content, linguistic structures, and sound markers. For example, a performance critic might consider the Genesis creation story, the book of Jonah, the discourse of the Sermon on the Mount in Matthew, the Gospel of Mark or a healing story within Mark, a discrete passage from a letter of Paul or the vision of the New Jerusalem in the book of Revelation.
- *Complete a DISCOURSE ANALYSIS of the language and translate it.* This involves an analysis of grammar, syntax, and potential meanings of words in context, using the language patterns to trace the way in which one line would lead to the next and interconnect with other lines to give coherence to a composition in performance.
- *Do an oral/aural analysis of the passage.* Note patterns and structures: series of three, parallel statements, ring compositions, repetition of words or lines with variation. Consider also metaphors, analogies, allegories, exaggeration, forceful language, and unusual words. Performance critics give particular attention to SOUND MAPPING, analysing the structure of the Hebrew or Greek text to identify oral/aural patterns that would be evident to the ear, such as alliteration, assonance, onomatopoeia, rhythm, rhyme, repetition, and structural markers. This analysis may involve listening to the text in the original language. Following this analysis, the translation is revised with a view to communicating these aural features, where possible, in a contemporary language.

- *Analyse the genre of the passage, with a view to considering how generic features might be communicated in a live performance.* A performance of a biblical narrative, for example, would consider the settings, characters, plot, role of the narrator, emotive flow, and point of view of the biblical text. Consider how theses dynamics may be embodied in action, emotion, and characterization so as to impact audiences. For example, how could ironic elements of the book of Jonah be communicated so as to impact a modern audience in a way similar to what ancient Israelite audiences may have experienced?
- *Conduct an analysis of the performance features of the passage.* Here the performance critic looks for clues within the text itself as to how it may have been performed in antiquity, including possible allusions to vocal expressions such as inflection, volume, emphasis, and pace; bodily expressions such as gestures, movement, facial expressions; and, emotions. Such features are not add-ons to what is written, but are integral to the expression of meaning. For example, the portrayal of the dying Jesus as one who '*cried out loudly,* My God, my God, why have you forsaken me?' (Mk 15.33) is by no means incidental to the meaning of that verse. Similarly, a facial expression can show that a line is to be taken ironically or humorously.
- *Identify the associations that ancient audiences may have had with this passage.* In what ways do the content, verbal style, plot dynamics, and characters in the unit recall other biblical traditions or cultural realities? How do these associations affect the meaning and impact of the unit?
- *Imagine an ancient performance in a specific context.* How would the following factors influence interpretation: the physical setting of time and place; the social location of the performer and the audience; geographical location; cultural context; and, the history of the community?
- *Memorize a translation and do a performance for an audience.* Recognize that your embodied performance is now a 'version' or translation of the biblical composition you are performing. Performance critics typically use feedback from the viewing audience to gain further interpretive insights on the meaning and impact of the biblical text.

While individual performance critics emphasize different aspects of the interpretive process outlined above, the overall methodology seeks to open the biblical text to live performances and to use the results of live performances to gain further insights into the text. The limited possibilities of a single text fixed in print are thus expanded by the realization that a given composition can take many embodied forms in performance events; the performer chooses one of these potentials and uses it to inform a new performance that creates a coherent meaning and a coherent impact – that is, a *coherent interpretation* – for a modern audience. Typically, performances are built around one potential overall outcome of a biblical composition. Put another way, the performance enacts the text in a way that reflects the researcher's conclusions about its primary or potential meaning. For example, if a performance critic determined that the purpose of Paul's letter to Philemon was to persuade Philemon to release Onesimus from slavery and treat him as a brother and for the whole house church to embrace relationships of mutuality, the critic would consider how to bring together the content of the epistle, the techniques of ancient letter writing, the original social context of the communication and its power dynamics, and performance strategies in relation to the audience as means to demonstrate that particular interpretation in and through the act of performing the letter.

There were many potential impacts of different biblical compositions in antiquity. At minimum, common understanding involves persuading an audience to agree with a certain point of view. But there are many more potential rhetorical impacts: telling a story or performing a prophecy or reading a letter may change the course of a community or even a nation, evoke the capacity for compassion, lead people to be generous, give the courage to be faithful in the face of oppression or persecution, bestow honour where there is shame, open faith to new possibilities, reconcile relationships, and so on. When one reconsiders the act of performing in terms of outcome, one is able to bring all the elements to bear on telling the story in such a way as to have a particular interpretive impact.

The goal of Performance Criticism is thus not to determine one 'correct' interpretation of an ancient composition. In fact, performance multiplies possibilities for interpretation, because each performance expresses a composition in different ways. Performance criticism increases our imagination about ancient compositions, changes our relationship to the text in an oral medium, enables us to discern the power dynamics of performance, and teaches us anew what these writings of the Bible may possibly have meant in diverse ancient settings.

David Rhoads (Lutheran School of Theology at Chicago, USA)

Further Reading

Boomershine, Thomas. 2015. *The Messiah of Peace: A Performance-Criticism Commentary on Mark's Passion-Resurrection Narrative.* Biblical Performance Criticism Series 12, Eugene: Wipf and Stock.

Botha, Pieter J. J. 2012. *Orality and Literacy in Early Christianity.* Biblical Performance Criticism Series 5. Eugene: Wipf and Stock.

Carr, David. 2005. *Writing on the Tablets of the Heart: Origins of Scripture and Literature.* Oxford: Oxford University Press.

Dewey, Joanna. *The Oral Ethos of the Early Church: Speaking, Writing, and the Gospel of Mark.* Biblical Performance Criticism Series 8, Eugene: Wipf and Stock, 2013.

Doan, W., and T. Giles. 2005. *Prophets, Performance, and Power: Performance Criticism of the Hebrew Bible.* New York: T&T Clark.

Hearon, Holly E., and Philip Ruge-Jones, editors. 2009. *The Bible in Ancient and Modern Media: Story and Performance.* Biblical Performance Criticism Series 1, Eugene: Wipf and Stock.

Kelber, Werner. 2013. *Imprints, Voice prints, and Footprints of Memory: Collected Essays of Werner H. Kelber.* SBLRBS. Atlanta: SBL Press.

Lee, Margaret Ellen, and Bernard Brandon Scott. 2009. *Sound Mapping the New Testament.* Salem: Polebridge Press.

Scott, James. 1985. *Weapons of the Weak: Everyday Forms of Peasant Resistance.* New Haven: Yale University Press.

Shiner, Whitney. 2003. *Proclaiming the Gospel: First-Century Performance of Mark.* Harrisburg: Trinity Press International.

The website for Biblical Performance Criticism: http://www.biblicalperformancecriticism.org. Accessed 12 August 2016.

Performance of the Gospels (in antiquity) The original medium of the Gospels was the sounds of stories performed for audiences either with or without a MANUSCRIPT in hand. This conclusion is based on the descriptions of performances of similar works in ancient Greco-Roman culture such as the Homeric epics, field research on existing oral cultures, and the verbal structures of the Gospel documents. The significance of the recognition of the sounds of the stories as the original medium of the Gospels is twofold: 1) these works were designed to be heard rather than read in silence; and 2) these writings were usually performed for audiences rather than read in private by individual readers.

The practice of the public performance of writings for audiences in the early churches is evident in the NT (see LETTERS). Paul urges the Thessalonians to read his letter 'to all the brothers' (1 Thess. 5.27) and exhorts the Colossians, 'When this letter has been read among you, have it read also in the church of the Laodiceans' (Col. 4.16). The composer of Revelation opens the book with a blessing of readers and audiences: 'Blessed is the one who reads aloud the words of the prophecy and blessed are those who hear and who keep what is written in it' (Rev. 1.3). Instances of private reading undoubtedly occurred, but even when reading in private, the reader would typically read aloud and experience the sounds of the story. Thus, in the Acts story of the Ethiopian eunuch, the Ethiopian dignitary is reading aloud from an Isaiah scroll in his chariot and Philip hears him reading (Acts 8.30) (see READING CULTURE).

The performance of the Gospels served the practical function of making the stories available for the 85–90 per cent of persons in the Greco-Roman world who were illiterate (see LITERACY). Public proclamation of the Gospels in the first century is reflected in the account of the composition and first PUBLICATION of the Gospel of Mark by Eusebius (early fourth century), who cites PAPIAS the bishop of Hierapolis (early second century) as his source. Eusebius states that Papias and Clement report that Mark composed his Gospel at the urgent request of the Roman community after they had heard Peter's oral stories about Jesus, and then notes a general understanding that 'they say that this Mark was the first that was sent to Egypt, and that he proclaimed the Gospel which he had written, and first established churches in Alexandria' (*Eccl. History* 2.16.1). Regardless of the uncertain historicity of this specific account, the notion that Mark proclaimed the Gospel he had composed made sense to Eusebius as a description of first-century performance of the Gospels.

The purposes of the performance of the Gospels would have varied with their specific settings. There may have been occasions when the followers of Jesus gathered together in homes to tell and hear the stories of Jesus, whether from memory or read to them from manuscripts, as well as proclamations for a more general public. The Gospels were probably performed in a variety of lengths, as is reflected in the varying lengths of the extant canonical Gospels. Mark is the shortest Gospel and takes two to two-and-a-half hours to recite verbatim, while Luke is the longest and requires approximately three and a half hours. Since STORYTELLING was a form of entertainment in the predominantly oral cultures of antiquity, a story of two to four hours was a good evening of entertainment.

Memory played a central role in performances of the Gospels. In the context of the centrality of memory in ancient EDUCATION and cultural formation, it is likely that many performances of the Gospels were done from memory, while others would have involved reading from a written manuscript. On those occasions when the storytellers read from a manuscript, extensive preparation and familiarity with the text would have been required beforehand. Performance from memory made it possible for the storytellers to use a full range of gestures and to interact more directly with the audience.

In many cases, these early proclamations of the Gospels may have been far more demonstrative and emotional than the traditional liturgical readings to which contemporary churches are accustomed. Gospel performances could have included major variations in volume from soft and intimate to very loud – for example, 'Jesus cried out in a loud voice' (Mk 15.34). Oral performers and readers could also change tempo for dramatic effect. Since the stories were composed in breath units, a common pattern was that long Greek COLA and PERIODS (English phrases and sentences) were fast, while short cola and periods were slow and, therefore, emphatic (see SOUND MAPPING). In contrast to ancient DRAMA, there was only one person in the performances of the Gospels who presented all of the characters.

The audiences of performances and readings of the Gospels could be addressed directly by the storyteller and by the characters the storyteller embodied for dramatic effect (see AUDIENCE ADDRESS). In speeches of more than two cola, the audiences were addressed by the characters speaking, usually Jesus, to the characters in the story, such as 'the Pharisees' or 'the disciples'. This created a high degree of interaction between the storyteller and the audience. Audiences could respond to the content with applause, expressions of approval and disapproval, and encouragement for the storyteller.

The writings of what we now call the NT were not Scripture in the first century and were not treated as Scripture until the late second and third century. In these later centuries, the Gospels began to be read in short passages by readers for gathered Christian communities in worship settings (see WORSHIP, EARLY CHRISTIAN). But in those readings the fundamental continuity of the medium of sound continued to be the medium in which the Gospels were experienced. The implication of the importance of the original medium has been stated well by Harry Gamble: 'no ancient text is now read as it was intended to be unless it (is) also heard, that is, read aloud' (1995: 204).

Thomas E. Boomershine (United Theological Seminary, USA)

Further Reading

Foley, John Miles. 1988. *The Theory of Oral Composition: History and Methodology*. Bloomington, IN: Indiana University Press.

Gamble, Harry. 1995. *Books and Readers in the Early Church: A History of Early Christian Texts*. New Haven, CT: Yale University Press.

Lee, Margaret Ellen, and Bernard Brandon Scott. 2009. *Sound Mapping the New Testament*. Salem, OR: Polebridge Press.

Shiner, Whitney. 2003. *Proclaiming the Gospel: First-Century Performance of Mark*. Harrisburg, PA: Trinity Press.

Pergamum Pergamum/Pergamon (modern Bergama) is a city located approximately 16 miles (26 kilometres) inland from the Aegean Sea in the Caicus river valley of present-day Turkey. One of the seven letters to the cities of Asia Minor found in the book of Revelation is addressed to a first-century Christian congregation located in the city (Rev. 2.12-17). Pergamum was significant in antiquity as a manufacturing centre for PARCHMENT and as the home to a major LIBRARY.

Pergamum likely had its origins as early as the eighth century BCE as a small fortified city located on a high promontory or pergamus, from which its name is thought to derive. Visited by Xenophon in the fourth century BCE (*Anabasis* 7.8.7-24), the hilltop town blossomed in the wake of Alexander the Great's death when Philetairos (alt. Philetaerus), a garrison commander, was assigned by Lysimachus to guard a treasury stored in the fortress. Instead, Philetairos staged a coup in the general's absence, seizing the stronghold and the bullion for himself (Strabo, *Geography* 13.4.1). Rumoured to have been a eunuch, Philetairos bequeathed the city and its local environs in 263 BCE to his nephew Eumenes I and, under what became known as the Attalid Dynasty, the independent Pergamene kingdom eventually grew to encompass a significant region that included the cities of Ephesus, Smyrna, Sardis, and Melitus. The Attalids became supporters of Rome and ruled their kingdom from the city of Pergamum until Attalus III willed the realm to Rome upon his death in 133 BCE. At that point, the Roman senate restructured the kingdom as the province of Asia and established judicial circuits to facilitate its governance (Evans 2012: 78). While Ephesus eventually became the administrative seat of the province due to its convenient location as a harbour city, Pergamum retained considerable prestige as the former capital and regional centre of culture and learning. Indeed, during the Roman era it benefited from euergetism that was manifested in a number of public works that included construction of a temple to Serapis (popularly known as the 'Red Hall' and likely built during the Hadrianic age), modification of a second-century BCE gymnasium (the largest known from antiquity), and renovation of the temple of Asclepius and an accompanying ancient health centre (or Asclepeion) that served as the home-base for the famous physician Galen (born 129 CE).

The building programme of the Roman period, however, did not overshadow the public works that were characteristic of the earlier Hellenistic era. Perhaps to counteract their rather inauspicious beginnings, the Attalids had used the canvas of the city and its public architecture as a medium to communicate the image of the city's rulers as a highly sophisticated, cultured elite. For instance, a notable school of sculpture developed under Attalus I and Eumenes II (rulers between 241 and 159 BCE) that created a series of figures to commemorate the defeat of the Galatians in 233 BCE. During that same period, Attalus I began construction of the Altar of Zeus, which features an inner frieze depicting the myth of Telephus, son of Heracles, who was linked to the founding mythology of the city. Although this is sometimes associated with the 'throne of Satan' mentioned in Revelation (2.13), it is more plausible that the author of Revelation is referencing the fact that in 29 BCE Augustus made Pergamum a *neokoros* or host city for a temple dedicated to the imperial cult (Wilson 2012: 285). This shrine to Roma and Augustus, though commemorated in coinage, has not yet been located. Although other Asian cities eventually came to serve as *neokoroi*, Pergamum was unique in that it became host to temples for two other emperors, Trajan (early second century CE) and Caracalla (early third century).

Like the Altar of Zeus, the Library of Pergamum provides further evidence of the Attalids' support of the educational and media culture of their era. Although there are detractors, it is generally thought that the library, founded by Eumenes II (197–160 BCE), occupied four rooms that were part of the complex of the sanctuary of Athena on the acropolis; three of these rooms housed books, while the fourth and larger space permitted public debates and readings, possibly similar to the *recitationes* popularized later at the library of Rome during the era of Augustus by Gaius Asinius Pollio (Staikos 2000: 94; see also Pliny the Younger, *Letters* 1.13; Quintillian, *Institutes* 10.1.102, Koester 1998, 18). Second only to the great LIBRARY OF ALEXANDRIA, Pliny reports that the Library of Pergamum housed over 200,000 volumes (*Natural History* 13.70), although the remains of the facility on the acropolis would have been able to house only about 20,000 books. The library was pillaged during the Roman Civil War by Antony, who gifted its holdings to Cleopatra in recompense for the destruction of the library at Alexandria (Plutarch, *Antonius* 58.5-59). Since Pergamum retained its reputation as a centre of learning into the first century CE, some attempt must have been made to restore the collection, though it likely remained modest. Pergamum also supported the broader book trade by functioning as a centre for the manufacture of parchment, with Rome as a primary market (Casson 2001: 52). The Pergameme librarian and Stoic philosopher Crates (second century BCE) is credited with devising a method to produce high quality parchment (John the Lydian, *The Months* 1.28; Wünsch edition numbering).

The vibrancy of Pergamum's media culture is further attested by its many performance and entertainment venues. In addition to the Hellenistic theatre on the acropolis (construction began under Philetairos), which is the steepest theatre in Asia and had a capacity to seat 10,000 spectators, the plain below the hill was home to a Roman-era hippodrome, a Roman-style theatre, and a coliseum/amphitheatre (all presently unexcavated). The amphitheatre is one of only three in Asia Minor, and could be filled with water to accommodate mock nautical battles and entertainments. The Asclepeion boasts an additional small theatre able to seat 3,500, while the gymnasium and bath complex located on the middle acropolis included an Odeon for musical performances and poetry readings.

Finally, discussion of Pergamum's ancient media culture would not be complete without a brief nod to its mint. Continuously in operation from the time of Philetairos through the early Byzantine era, coinage was produced with symbols and inscriptions conveying messages and images that served the propaganda interests of the city and region's rulers (see COINS).

Beth M. Sheppard (Duke University, USA)

Further Reading

Casson, Lionel. 2001. *Libraries in the Ancient World*. New Haven: Yale University Press.

De Grummond, Nancy T., and Brunilde S. Ridgeway, eds. 2000. *From Pergamon to Sperlonga: Sculpture and Context*. Berkeley: University of California Press.

Evans, Richard. 2012. *A History of Pergamum: Beyond Hellenistic Kingship*. London: Continuum.

Fant, Clyde E., and Mitchell Glenn Reddish. 2003. *A Guide to Biblical Sites in Greece and Turkey*. Oxford: Oxford University Press, especially pp. 273–99.

Koester, Helmut, ed. 1998. *Pergamon, Citadel of the Gods: Archaeological Record, Literary Description and Religious Development*. Harvard Theological Studies 46. Harrisburg, PA: Trinity Press International.

Radt, Wolfgang. 1999. *Pergamon. Geschichte und Bauten einer antiken Metropole (mit bildern von Elisabeth Steiner)*. Darmstadt: Primus Verlag.

Staikos, Konstantinos. 2000. *The Great Libraries: From Antiquity to the Renaissance (3000 B.C. to A.D. 1600)*. Translated by Timothy Cullen. New Castle, DE: Oak Knoll Press.

Sutherland, C. H. V. 1973. 'Augustan Aurei and Denarii Attributable to the Mint of Pergamum.' *Revue Numismatique* 6(15): 129–51.

Wilson, Mark. 2012. *Biblical Turkey: A Guide to the Jewish and Christian Sites of Asia Minor*. Istanbul: Ege Yayinlari, especially pp. 279–92.

Personal Memory See Cognitive/Personal Memory.

Period A period (*periodos*) is a unit of Greek prose, composed of cola. The period and colon comprise the building blocks of Greek prose. They serve as the prose analogues to the verse and metric line in Greek poetry (Aristotle, *Rhetoric* 3.8) and comprise the basic components of a sound map. Both are defined as breath units in Hellenistic literary criticism (Cicero, *The Orator* 3.46.181; Quintilian, Institutes 9.4.125; Aristotle, *Rhetoric* 3.9.5). The term may also be extended to discuss a sentence of poetry (see poetry in the Hebrew Bible).

Margaret E. Lee (Tulsa Community College, USA)

Pesharim The *pesharim* (singular: *pesher*) are 'a type of biblical interpretation found in the Qumran scrolls in which selected biblical texts are applied to the contemporary sectarian setting by means of various literary devices' (Berrin 2000: 644). A prominent example may be found in the *Pesher Habakkuk* (1QpHab), which cites lines from the book of Habakkuk and then applies these directly to the experiences of the community and its founding figures.

Writing Pesher, Making the Bible

At the time of the composition of the pesharim, no Bible as such (a fixed, universally recognized canon of sacred books) had yet come into existence. Nevertheless, the authors of the pesharim considered a wide variety of writings, including some of the books that would later become part of the biblical canon, to be authoritative. The way in which prophetic Scripture (including the Psalms and possibly some other visionary texts such as Gen. 49 [4Q252]) was treated in the pesharim both emphasized and contributed to its authoritative status. By using these writings to build a communal identity, the authors of the pesharim implied their authority as divinely inspired Scripture (cf. 1QpHab 3.12–7.5). At the same time, in this formative period the use of these writings in the pesharim – and also in the NT, whose authors by and large cite the same set of writings – actively contributed to their prominence within the communities behind these writings and, eventually, to their inclusion in the canon.

The scriptural texts quoted in the pesharim cannot simply be identified as a forerunner of the later Masoretic Text. In a notable number of cases, the pesharim bear witness to other text forms. In some instances, the pesharim appear to be familiar with more than one reading of the scriptural text, underscoring the polymorphous nature of Scripture as quoted in these commentaries. An oral division of the scriptural text into verses and half-verses may be reflected in the pesharim, although the scope of their lemmata is in all likelihood due to the aims of the commentator (Tov 2004: 135–42). Some Masoretic divisions of Scripture into sections seem to be paralleled in the pesharim, but this, in itself, is not conclusive evidence for an established tradition of scriptural section divisions in this period (Tov 2004: 143–63). On the other hand, lemmata and interpretations are often distinguished by means of vacats, which point in a more general sense to the scribal practice of indicating sense divisions. Some pesher scrolls (1Q14, 1Q15, 1QpHab, 4Q161) have the divine name written in paleo-Hebrew script (Tov 2004: 218–21). Some pesher scrolls (1QpHab, 4Q163) contain marginal marks, although their significance is largely unknown (Tov 2004: 178–218).

Pesher, Identity, and History

It has long been held that the pesharim provide a unique window onto the actual history of the movement in which they were composed. Today, however, scholars are more cautious, and the concept of historical memory plays an important role in assessments of the pesharim. In the pesharim, Scripture is not simply read through the lens of the history of the movement, but a communal identity, history, and hope for the future are constructed through the interpretation of Scripture (Davies 2010).

The pesharim exhibit a 'we/you' perspective, favouring an in-group referred to by a variety of terms and denoting the movement in which the pesharim originated, over against a variety of out-groups (Jokiranta 2013: 134–48, 173–5). This we/you perspective often emphasizes dichotomies in the base text, such as that between the Assyrians and God's people (1QpHab) or the righteous and the wicked (4Q171). In other cases, threats directed to Israel's enemies are applied to the contemporary opponents of the movement behind the pesharim (4Q169). This we/you perspective also has a personal side: some of the pesharim refer to a conflict between the 'Teacher of Righteousness' (portrayed in some texts as a founding figure of the movement) and his various opponents. In these pesharim, the image of a righteous teacher who is persecuted by wicked opponents is likewise developed from the base text. Of course, this portrayal should not be taken *prima facie* as historical evidence: the pesharim display the historical memory of the movement, not plain historical fact. The memory of the Teacher plays an important role in the pesharim and in the movement behind them: he is considered a major source of authority (García Martínez 2010) and functions as a prototype (Jokiranta 2013: 175–82) in which various features of the movement as a whole are united (Brooke 2010).

The pesharim not only attest to the historical memory of the movement in which they originated, but also to its construal of the future. It is well known that the authors of the pesharim conceived of themselves as living in the latter days. Hence, the judgement of the wicked and the vindication of the righteous were expected to occur presently. The way in which this judgement and vindication would take place, are, again, often described by picking up on elements in the base text. In 4Q171 2.9-12, for instance, the movement behind the pesharim – referred to here as *'ēdat ha-'ebyônîm* ('the counsel of the poor ones') – is said to be rescued, after a period of distress, from the snares of Belial, so as to possess the land and enjoy abundance; these themes are taken from Ps. 37.11 ('and the poor shall possess the land and enjoy peace in plenty'). In sum, the pesharim provide a unique window onto the way in which past and future were remembered and expected by the authors of these commentaries, who, through their use of Scripture to construct their historical memory and expectations of the future, aimed at creating a communal identity.

Performing Pesher

As commentaries, the pesharim quote and employ Scripture with a particular aim in mind. However, it can safely be assumed that the pesharim themselves also fulfilled one or several purposes within the life of the movement in which they were composed. Unfortunately, the pesharim themselves contain few clues as to what this purpose may have been. Signs in the MANUSCRIPTS may point to oral performance (Snyder 2000), but this is not certain. Some scholars have implied a communal or even liturgical setting for the pesharim by describing some of the thematic commentaries as homiletical or by situating the pesharim within the context of the study of the Law as prescribed in 1QS 8.14-16. Others, however, have pointed to the fact that only one manuscript of each pesher seems to have been preserved, and conclude that they are individually executed studies of prophetic Scripture. Hence, it is hard to determine with certainty what role the pesharim played within the community. Nevertheless, it is plausible that the pesharim were a 'method of instruction' (Nitzan 1991), and that they originated and were employed either within a liturgical or a study context (the two are not mutually exclusive), possibly also being used in the instruction of new members.

Pieter B. Hartog (Kathlolieke Universiteit Leuven, Belgium)

Further Reading

Berrin, Shani L. 2000. 'Pesharim.' *EDSS* 2: 644–7.

Brooke, George J. 2010. 'The "Apocalyptic" Community, the Matrix of the Teacher and Rewriting Scripture.' In *Authoritative Scriptures in Ancient Judaism*. Edited by Mladen Popović. JSJS 141. Leiden: Brill, pp. 37–53.

Davies, Philip R. 2010. 'What History Can We Get from the Scrolls, and How?' In *The Dead Sea Scrolls*. Edited by Sarianna Metso, Hindy Najman, and Eileen M. Schuller. Leiden: Brill, pp. 31–46.

Fraade, Steven D. 1993. 'Interpretive Authority in the Studying Community at Qumran.' *Journal of Jewish Studies* 44: 46–69.

García Martínez, Florentino. 2010. 'Beyond the Sectarian Divide.' In *The Dead Sea Scrolls*. Edited by Sarianna Metso, Hindy Najman, and Eileen M. Schuller. STDJ 92. Leiden: Brill, pp. 227–44.

Jokiranta, Jutta. 2013. *Social Identity and Sectarianism in the Qumran Movement*. STDJ 105. Leiden: Brill.

Nitzan, Bilha. 1991. 'The Pesher and Other Methods of Instruction.' In *Mogilany 1989: The Teacher of Righteousness*. Cracow: Enigma, pp. 209–220.

Snyder, H. Gregory. 2000. 'Naughts and Crosses.' *DSD* 7: 26–48.

Stuckenbruck, Loren T. 2010. 'The Legacy of the Teacher of Righteousness.' In *New Perspectives on Old Texts*. Edited by Esther Chazon, Betsy Halpern-Amaru, and Ruth Clements. STDJ 88. Leiden: Brill, pp. 23–49.

Tov, Emanuel. 2004. *Scribal Practices and Approaches Reflected in the Texts Found in the Judean Desert*. STDJ 54. Leiden: Brill.

Pilgrimage Pilgrimage is the practice of making a journey attributed with ritually symbolic meaning to a destination attributed with complementary meaning. The scale of the practice ranges from visits to a grave to travels to a long sequence of sacred sites. Pilgrimage is a natural byproduct of cognitive capacities that emerged in human evolution for assigning meaning to locomotion and place. This suggests that pilgrimage should be studied with an awareness of how it is shaped by tendencies rooted in cognitive evolution.

One evolutionary dynamic active in pilgrimage is creativity. Pilgrimage traditions can be generated anytime a site is attributed with appropriate meaning. This often happens during reflection on emotional events, such as death. In ancient Israel, sites identified with the tombs of ancestors, legends such as the sacrifice of Jephthah's daughter, and deceased prophets attracted cultic activities. Pilgrimages to tombs became especially popular when the benefits were extended beyond the dead person's kin. This trend is epitomized by Byzantine Christian cults of saints and contemporary Jewish veneration of rabbis who had been buried at Beth She'arim from the second to fourth centuries CE. Both practices include promised healings and other miracles.

A second feature in an evolutionary approach to pilgrimage rituals is adaptations to changing situations. Often this occurs by appropriation. Beginning with the Israelite monarchies, proponents of the cult of Yahweh in Jerusalem appropriated older traditions associated with El, Baal, Asherah, and other deities worshipped at Shechem, Dan, Bethel, and other centres. They also appropriated agricultural festivals by attaching them to the emerging exodus tradition and centralizing three annual festivals in Jerusalem (Passover, Weeks, and Booths). Later Christian pilgrimage to Palestine appropriated Jewish history to obtain the legitimating aura of antiquity. This perceived antiquity informed Byzantine Christian interest in Jewish sites in the *Bordeaux Itinerary* and perhaps also the *Lives of the Prophets*, which is probably a Christian work. Christian emperors and church leaders further encouraged creation of a Christian 'Holy Land' by superimposing distinctively Christian legends over other sacred sites.

A third evolutionary dynamic is growth in complexity. Increasing variety in forms, meanings, and functions can result from negotiating symbiotic and parasitic relationships. Complexity in pilgrimage traditions emerged from integration with food and medicine sourcing, trade, war, tourism, education, and other social practices. The antiquity of such patterns is attested by a ritual centre used in the 10th–9th millennia BCE at Göbekli Tepe in Turkey. The energy required for the site's construction suggests that its ritual functions were complemented by political roles. Later kings exploited the political potential of pilgrimage. In the eighth and seventh centuries BCE, the Judean kings Hezekiah and Josiah consolidated power by promoting cult centralization in Jerusalem. Herod the Great pursued a similar strategy in the first century BCE by transforming the TEMPLE mount into a nationalistic showcase. Contrary to efforts at centralization were social and psychological forces that assured the vitality of local centres. Personal relationships, finances, and health were conveniently addressed in nearby oracle sanctuaries, healing shrines, and the homes of neighbourhood magicians. In the early Roman period, Strabo and Pausanias show that improved transportation infrastructure was transforming many ritual centres into tourist attractions and way stations. Complementary inscriptions at El-Kanais, Egypt, record the gratitude of Jews for the favour of the local deity (Pan-Min) while on a caravan route in the second and first centuries BCE. The commercial potential of pilgrimage was exploited by Byzantine Christian tour guides like those mentioned in *Egeria's Travels*, who created new pilgrimage traditions by linking biblical stories to sites with dubious credentials.

Fourth, pilgrimage was also shaped by the same economy of energy consumption that paleoanthropologists cite when discussing biological constraints on early human social practices. For example, the costs of a long pilgrimage could include ship fare, lodging, and time away from employment. The appeal of a long journey was also diminished by local SYNAGOGUES and churches, holy men and women, and domestic cults that promised similar blessings. Perhaps the most parsimonious form of pilgrimage was advocated by Philo of Alexandria and early Christian Platonists, who applied pilgrimage imagery to education, contemplation of heavenly worlds, and other journeys that were merely symbolic. These safer and less costly alternatives made it difficult to sustain more ambitious forms of pilgrimage through periods of war, plague, and famine. The preservation of a pilgrimage tradition in literary memory is no guarantee of its survival in actual practice.

The methodological implication of the previous four points is that any pilgrimage tradition must be studied with appreciation of its formation. Traditions associated with Mt. Sinai provide an illuminating case study. Archaeology suggests the Israelites gradually emerged from indigenous Canaanite groups and small bands of immigrants. One of these groups may have come from Midianite territory in northwest Arabia or southwest Jordan, bringing with them CULTURAL MEMORIES of one or more sacred mountains there (see Exod. 3.1; Deut. 1.2; 33.2; Judg. 5.4; Hab. 3.3, 7). But pilgrimage to this region was probably eclipsed by the convenience of ritual centres in the new homeland. Information that might have supplemented biblical references to Mt. Sinai also may have been completely forgotten in subsequent demographic and cultural upheavals. In consequence, one cannot assume the reliability of details in later authors such as Philo and Josephus, who identify Mt. Sinai with a high peak in northwest Arabia or southwest Jordan. They may have been trying to connect contemporary geography with biblical interpretation. Some scholars argue that Josephus identified Mt. Sinai with Jabal Katrina, but this is based on a strained inference from a passage in which Josephus summarized the fictions of an Alexandrian critic (*Against Apion* 2.20-27). The identification of Jabal Katrina with Mt. Sinai must be attributed to homiletic creativity in early Christian monastic communities. Tales about sites from exodus traditions in the Talmud and Midrashim originated in a similar way.

In view of the factors above, legends associated with pilgrimage sites are routinely undermined by archaeological excavation and critical reading of texts. The greatest value of these traditions is not their claims about the past, but what they reveal about individual transmitters and the creators of COLLECTIVE MEMORY.

Allen Kerkeslager (Saint Joseph's University, USA)

Further Reading

Albertz, Rainer, and Rüdiger Schmitt. 2012. *Family and Household Religion in Ancient Israel and the Levant*. Winona Lake, IN: Eisenbrauns.

Elsner, Jas, and Ian Rutherford, eds. 2005. *Pilgrimage in Graeco-Roman and Early Christian Antiquity*. New York: Oxford University Press.

Frankfurter, David, ed. 1998. *Pilgrimage and Holy Space in Late Antique Egypt*. Religions in the Greco-Roman World 134. Leiden: Brill.

Henshilwood, Christopher, and Francesco d'Errico, eds. 2011. *Homo Symbolicus*. Philadelphia: John Benjamins.

Kerkeslager, Allen. 2000. 'Mt. Sinai – in Arabia?' *BRev* 16/2 (April): 32–9, 52.

Smith, Mark S., with Elizabeth Bloch-Smith. 1997. *The Pilgrimage Pattern in Exodus*. Sheffield: Sheffield Academic.

Plato (on writing and memory) Plato (ca. 428–348 BCE) was an Athenian philosopher and founder of the school known as the Academy. While he is the most well-known author to have produced dialogues featuring his teacher Socrates, he is not the only one to have done so; the historian Xenophon, for example, also wrote dialogues featuring Socrates. In Plato's earlier dialogues, such as the *Apology* and the *Euthyphro*, some historians of philosophy have attempted to discern a 'Socratic philosophy', one that Plato later departed from in his so-called middle dialogues, including the *Republic*, *Phaedo*, and *Symposium* (Vlastos 1991). This approach to Plato's corpus is far from unanimously adopted among modern interpreters, however, many of whom have argued that the figure of Socrates should be considered as a fictional character created by Plato throughout his works (Kahn 1998; Annas and Rowe 2002; Gerson 2006).

Plato's relevance to research in ancient media culture emerges particularly from his discussions of the value of various forms of WRITING, which occur prominently in his explorations of moral psychology, metaphysics, epistemology, and political philosophy. Particular attention has been given to Plato's somewhat ironic ambivalence towards writing as a medium. In the *Phaedrus*, where Socrates and Phaedrus explore the moral benefits of RHETORIC, Socrates declares that written works are not as beneficial to the reader as a teacher is to a student, for only a teacher can provide a student with personal engagement (276a-278b; cf. 341c-345c). In the *Republic*, on the other hand, Plato castigates the tragic poets for creating works that confuse the non-rational part of the soul by presenting images of the mundane events of human life as instances of true misfortune (601e-608b). Plato's own myths, such as the *Myth of Metals* and the *Myth of Er*, appear to be examples of alternative written works intended to benefit the reader. Writing is explored yet again in the political context of the *Laws*, where Socrates argues that written laws, in virtue of their generality, are limited in that they cannot attend to the specific contexts of circumstances requiring legislation, as only a human lawgiver can (875c3–d5). At the same time, the dialogue's discussions of how the written preludes of the laws explain the rationale behind punishments indicate that Plato in this period was more inclined to think that the general populace could be instructed in knowledge of the good, a departure from the *Republic* (885c8-e5; Bobonich 2002).

Such discussions played an important role in ERIC HAVELOCK's analysis of Plato's significance for the development of LITERACY, and literate culture, in ancient Greece (Havelock 1963). In contemporary media studies, Plato's explorations of the difference between appearance and reality have provided important intellectual background for the role of the senses in cognition. His allegory of the cave in *Republic* 7 has been a 'foundational instance of the anxious primacy of sight' for informing the work of theorists such as Jacques Derrida and Paul De Man (Jones 2010: 88–9; cf. De Man 1971, Derrida 1993).

Kathleen Gibbons (Washington University, USA)

Further Reading

Annas, Julia, and Christopher Rowe, eds. 2002. *New Perspectives on Plato, Ancient and Modern*. Cambridge, MA: Harvard University Press.

Bobonich, Christopher. 2002. *Plato's Utopia Recast: His Later Ethics and Politics*. Oxford: Oxford University Press.

Carone, Gabriela Roxana. 2005. *Plato's Cosmology and Its Ethical Dimensions*. Cambridge: Cambridge University Press.

De Man, Paul. 1971. *Blindness and Insight: Essays in the Rhetoric of Contemporary Criticism*. New York: Oxford University Press.

Derrida, Jacques. 1993. *Memoirs of the Blind: The Self-portrait and Other Ruins*. Chicago: University of Chicago Press.

Gerson, Lloyd. 2006. *Knowing Persons: A Study in Plato*. Oxford: Oxford University Press.

Havelock, Eric. 1963. *Preface to Plato*. Cambridge, MA: Harvard University Press.

Jones, Catherine. 2010. 'Senses.' In *Critical Terms for Media Studies*. Edited by W. J. T. Mitchell and Mark Hansen. Chicago and London: University of Chicago Press, pp. 88–100.

Kahn, Charles. 1996. *Plato and the Socratic Dialogue: The Philosophical Use of a Literary Form*. Cambridge: Cambridge University Press.

Nightingale, Andrea. 1993. *Genres in Dialogue: Plato and the Construction of Philosophy*. Cambridge: Cambridge University Press.

Vlastos, Gregory. 1991. *Socrates: Ironist and Moral Philosopher*. Cambridge: Cambridge University Press.

Pluriformity The term *pluriformity* is typically used in Gospels studies to refer to the existence of the Jesus tradition in multiple forms. It is an implicit rejection of earlier form-critical work that sought to recover the original form of any given tradition or unit of tradition (see Form Criticism).

There are two primary uses of the term *pluriformity* within the context of Gospels research. First, pluriformity is used to highlight the existence of multiple forms of the same tradition within the gospel tradition. The canonical Gospels (Matthew, Mark, Luke, John) contain many parallel, shared traditions that can vary significantly in terms of verbatim agreement. Earlier form-critical scholarship approached such parallel traditions with a view towards discerning which Gospel, if any, preserved the original form of the tradition, of which the others represent more or less faithful 'variants'. From that perspective, there was a single original and subsequent derivation from this original could be explained in terms of secondary literary or editorial activity. However, in light of recent studies on ancient media, the term *pluriformity* is used as a way to describe the existence of these divergent parallels without privileging the so-called original version over the others. Describing individual parallels as pluriform attestations of the Jesus tradition affirms that, in the world of oral performance, it is not possible to speak of an original version but only of multiple performances of any particular tradition. The tradition itself was likely multiform from its earliest stages.

Further, folklorists have provided additional insight into the pluriform nature of both oral and written traditions. In particular, they have shown how the Bible is replete with parallel but divergent traditions. Rather than succumb to the temptation to label one as original and all others as secondary, folklorists suggest that these multiform traditions illustrate the extent to which the Bible can be situated within the genre folklore. Pluriformity is the norm for folkloristic traditions and recognizing the Bible as such helps readers avoid potential pitfalls associated with any attempt to distinguish between original and secondary tradition.

Second, pluriformity is used in a broader sense in some discussions on the extant inscribed canonical Gospels of Matthew, Mark, Luke, and John. Here, the term is used to emphasize the distinctive shape and character of each respective Gospel as a whole, and its presentation, or portrait, of Jesus. Pluriformity of the gospel tradition was affirmed early by the church in its rejection of Tatian's *Diatessaron*, a second-century CE harmonization of the four Gospels that presented a singular portrait of Jesus, woven together by compiling material from Matthew, Mark, Luke, and John together into a single, cohesive narrative. In rejecting Tatian's *Diatessaron*, the church affirmed the pluriform nature of the gospel tradition, and in affirming all four canonical Gospels, embraced the diversity inherent in the tradition itself.

Terence C. Mournet (Ashland Theological Seminary, USA)

Further Reading

Dundes, Alan. 1999. *Holy Writ as Oral Lit: The Bible as Folklore*. Lanham, MD: Rowman & Littlefield.

Lord, Albert B. 1978. 'The Gospels as Oral Traditional Literature.' In *The Relationships Among the Gospels: An Interdisciplinary Dialogue*. Edited by William O. Walker Jr. San Antonio: Trinity University Press, pp. 33–91.

Mournet, Terence C. 2005. *Oral Tradition and Literary Dependency: Variability and Stability in the Synoptic Tradition and Q*. WUNT II 195. Tübingen: Mohr Siebeck, especially 69–73.

Poetics The term *poetics* can carry a wide range of meanings, from the study of all human activity (based on the Greek verb *poieo*, 'to do or make') to the modern study of theories of literature. In the context of media studies, poetics refers to a range of theoretical models that seek to define the term *literature* and ways that literature differs from other 'non-literary' forms of communication. The term *poetics* may also be used to identify the compositional processes that underlie, and the results of these processes as evidenced in, literary texts. While the study of poetics has a long history in the Western philosophical tradition, going back at least as far as Aristotle, the present entry will focus on major concerns that animate modern discussion.

Comparative Poetics

Comparative poetics concerns the effort to understand literature in general by analysing diverse instances of literatures from various cultures, both those closely related to each other but also, and more importantly, those distant from each other in time and space. Every culture has its own implicit poetics – that is, its own understanding of what is and is not literature as reflected in its literary productions. Some cultures also have an explicit form of poetics that can be understood as *originative* or *foundational* – that is, specific critics within these cultures define the nature and function of literature based on what they view to be the most popular or most prestigious literary GENRE. For example, Aristotle's famous study of poetics was based on the genre of drama rather than epic (Miner 1990: 7).

Various schools of thought, reflecting differing approaches, are evident within the modern comparative study of poetics. Two prominent schools that have been influential on poetics in biblical studies are Russian formalism (for example, the work of Roman Jakobson) and structuralism (for example, the work of Jonathan Culler). Poetics also influenced the work of MILMAN PARRY, ALBERT LORD, and JOHN MILES FOLEY as they strove to understand Homeric epic better from the perspective of Serbo-Croatian epic poetry (see GUSLAR), other living ORAL TRADITIONS, and orally derived literature. Foley has explicitly been influenced by ETHNOPOETICS, a form of poetics based on anthropological fieldwork on oral verbal performance.

Cognitive Poetics

Since Aristotle, poetics has included discussions of the cognitive and affective dimensions of how literature functions in society. Modern cognitive poetics draws from the cognitive sciences to understand better how readers make meaning in their interactions with literature and draws from literary studies as a way of providing data concerning how meaning in general is organized cognitively (see further Stockwell 2002; Brône and Vandaele 2009). A recent volume entitled *Oral Poetics and Cognitive Science* (Pagán and Antović 2016) combines for the first time cognitive science and the comparative study of oral traditions in the Parry-Lord school, thereby producing a cognitive oral poetics.

Poetics and the Bible

Comparative poetics as applied to the Hebrew Bible has mostly been limited to comparisons within the Semitic languages and other ancient Near Eastern languages. Its application to Hebrew poetry can be found in the work of, for example, Robert Culley, who drew extensively from the work of Parry and Lord, and James Kugel (see also poetry in the Hebrew Bible). Its application to Hebrew narrative can be found in the work of, for example, Robert Alter, Adele Berlin, and Meir Sternberg, whose influence in poetics transcends biblical studies as the long-time editor of the journal *Poetics Today*. The relative lack of poetry in the NT may have influenced the relative lack of studies applying comparative poetics with an assumption that poetics had little to contribute to the study of narrative. Therefore, the influence of poetics in NT studies has been primarily through its influence on Narrative Criticism, especially of the Gospels (Rhodes 1982). An important exception is the work of Petri Merenlahti (2002).

Cognitive poetics has just begun to have an influence in biblical studies as well. Some recent scholars of the Hebrew Bible who have used cognitive poetics in their publications are Albert Kamp (2004), Ellen van Wolde (2009), Job Jindo (2010), and Raymond Person, Jr. (2016). Van Wolde explicitly attempts to transform the methodologies used in biblical studies by taking seriously cognitive approaches to literature. However, cognitive poetics remains underutilized in biblical studies, especially since those specialists of other literatures have made good use of biblical and other related literatures in their own analyses. For example, Reuven Tsur (2008) specializes in medieval Hebrew literature and Michael Burke (2003) has discussed briefly NT parables as important examples of literature that forces cognitive changes.

Raymond F. Person, Jr. (Ohio Northern University, USA)

Further Reading

Alter, Robert. 1981. *The Art of Biblical Narrative*. New York: Basic Books.
Berlin, Adele. 1983. *Poetics and the Interpretation of Biblical Narrative*. Sheffield: Almond.
Berlin, Adele. 1992. *The Dynamics of Biblical Parallelism*. Bloomington: Indiana University Press.
Brône, Geert, and J. Vandaele, eds. 2009. *Cognitive Poetics: Goals, Gains and Gaps*. Berlin: Walter Mouton de Gruyter.
Burke, Michael. 2003. 'Literature as Parable.' In *Cognitive Poetics in Practice*. Edited by Joanna Gavins and Gerard Steen. Abingdon: Routledge, pp. 115–28.
Jindo, Job Y. 2010. *Biblical Metaphor Reconsidered: A Cognitive Approach to Poetic Prophecy in Jeremiah 1-24*. Biblical Interpretation Series 68. Winona Lake, IN: Eisenbrauns.
Kamp, Albert. 2004. *Inner Worlds: A Cognitive-Linguistic Approach to the Book of Jonah*. Translated by David Orton. Leiden: Brill.
Kugel, James. 1998. *The Idea of Biblical Poetry: Parallelism and Its History*. New Haven: Yale.
Merenlahti, Petri. 2002. *Poetics for the Gospels? Rethinking Narrative Criticism*. New York: T&T Clark.
Miner, Earl. 1990. *Comparative Poetics: An Intercultural Essay on Theories of Literature*. Princeton: Princeton University Press.
Pagán, Cristóbal Cánovas, and M. Antović, eds. 2016. *Oral Poetics and Cognitive Science*. Berlin: Walter Mouton de Gruyter.
Person, Raymond F., Jr. 2016. *From Conversation to Oral Tradition: A Simplest Systematics for Oral Traditions*. Abingdon: Routledge.

Preminger, Alex, and T. V. F. Brogan, eds. 1993. *The New Princeton Encyclopedia of Poetry and Poetics*. Princeton: Princeton University Press.
Rhodes, David M. 1982. 'Narrative Criticism and the Gospel of Mark.' *JAAR* 50: 411–34.
Sternberg, Meir. 1985. *The Poetics of Biblical Narrative: Ideological Literature and the Drama of Reading*. Bloomington: Indiana University Press.
Stockwell, Peter. 2002. *Cognitive Poetics: An Introduction*. Abingdon: Routledge.
Tsur, Reuven. 2008. *Toward a Theory of Cognitive Poetics*. Brighton: Sussex Academic Press.
van Wolde, Ellen. 2009. *Reframing Biblical Studies: When Language and Text Meet Culture, Cognition, and Context*. Winona Lake, IN: Eisenbrauns.

Poetry in the Hebrew Bible Biblical Hebrew poetry shares features with a range of oral-traditional poetry. These features include the recurrent use of similar phrases, motifs, and structural patterns that parallel the categories of formula, THEME, and STORY PATTERN developed in the study of ancient Greek epic poetry by MILMAN PARRY and ALBERT LORD. The characteristics of oral-traditional style have been linked to the expectations of oral performance. The dynamic of live performance, captured by the phrase PERFORMANCE ARENA, entails a traditional mode, or REGISTER, of poetic language and content that is familiar to an audience through repeated use and is thus weighted with inherent meaning. Traditional patterns are re-articulated and reconfigured in individual performances, but each instance of a pattern calls to mind the whole range of expression.

In poetic compositions that have been fixed or even composed in WRITING, the dynamic of performance in a live, physical setting shifts to a rhetorical setting akin to literary GENRE. HERMANN GUNKEL's early twentieth-century delineation of the biblical psalm types in relation to an occasion of WORSHIP (SITZ IM LEBEN) as well as to distinctive content and language anticipated more recent comprehensive studies on the oral-traditional character of biblical Hebrew poetry. Consideration of the rhetorical settings of poetic texts in oral performance enhances the significance of textual signs of traditional modes of composition and reception, or interpretation by an audience. The following discussion of biblical Hebrew poetry will illustrate the oral aesthetic that underlies many poetic compositions in the Hebrew Bible.

Traditional Patterns in Hebrew Poetry

The patterns of oral-traditional poetry vary widely, depending on the parameters of the particular poetic tradition. Biblical Hebrew poetry, as opposed to ancient Greek epic poetry, is generally non-narrative, but displays a wide range of formats. The Psalms and Song of Songs include lyric poetry; PROVERBS, gnomic poetry; the prophetic books, rhetorical poetry (see RHETORIC); 2 Sam. 1.19-27 is elegiac; Exod. 15.1-18 and Judges 5 contain epinician poetry; Job, poetic dialogues. In Hebrew poetry as a whole, Albert Lord's category of theme (a typical scene or episode) can be applied as a descriptive set of elements, a topos or motif: for example the corruption of Judah and Jerusalem, the physical wasting of the lamenter, or the comparison of wisdom (and its qualities) to silver, gold, and other precious treasures. Story pattern can be seen as an overarching thematic pattern, such as the divine reckoning with Israel and Judah in prophetic oracles of judgement, the petition for and expectation of deliverance in lament psalms, or the suffering and vindication of the blameless and faithful in Job, Daniel, and Isaiah 53.

Phrases take shape within the limits of the Hebrew poetic line, which is short and generally self-contained (without enjambment), yet not strictly defined in terms of length or metre. Prosodic flexibility makes possible compact formulaic phrases that allow for variation, e.g. 'Blessed be the Lord, the God of Israel' (Ps. 41.13a [Hebrew 41.14a]; 106.48a), 'Blessed be the Lord God, the God of Israel' (Ps 72.18a), and 'Blessed be the Lord forever, amen and amen' (Ps. 89.52 [Hebrew 89.53]). Variation is also displayed through the prominent division of the poetic line into two or three discrete yet connected parts (cola) and the related structural element of parallelism among cola. These prosodic features are conducive to different combinations of phrases within poetic lines. Thus, in the psalms cited above, Pss. 41.13 [Hebrew 41.14] and 106.48 pair 'Blessed be the Lord, the God of Israel' with 'from forever to forever' in the second COLON. The second colon of Ps. 72.18 offers a different thought: 'who alone does wonders' (which itself echoes the first colon of Ps. 136.4, 'who alone does great wonders'). Psalm 136 exemplifies the fluid architecture of traditional phrases in Hebrew poetry. The first three lines of this psalm intersperse appellations for God (from 'Lord' to 'God of Gods' to 'Lord of Lords') in the first colon with the phrase 'his mercy endures forever' in the second colon. This phrase recurs in each subsequent line of the psalm. In all these instances, exact replication of phrases, parallel phrases, or phrase clusters is rare. Rather, related elements are re-articulated in new contexts with changes in wording, syntax, and structure – see, for example, the variations of the phrase 'inherit the earth' in Pss. 25.12-13; 37.28-29; Prov. 2.20-22; and Isa. 57.13. In this case, traditional language crosses poetic genres (lyric, gnomic, and rhetorical).

Another notable characteristic of oral-traditional poetry is the occurrence of archaic words and phrases to create a mode of speech distinct from ordinary speech – that is, a different linguistic REGISTER. Biblical Hebrew poetry displays a number of distinctive syntactical and lexical usages. These include use of the prefixal form of the verb, which may reflect an archaic *yaqtul* preterite, to convey the simple past.

The Poetry of Psalms

The designation of numerous psalms as SONGS (*šîr* and *mizmôr*), often with reference to musical accompaniment, envisions a context of public performance (see MUSIC). In Pss. 40.3 [Hebrew 40.4] and 149.1, the phrase 'new song' (*šîr ḥādās*) is paralleled by 'praise' (*tĕhillâ*), thus folding another major designation for psalms into the arena of song and communal worship. Frequent references to Zion and the TEMPLE also evoke this setting, as depicted in narrative form in 1 Chro. 15–16.

The recurrent language, images and motifs, and thematic structures of the Psalter bespeak a shared aesthetic and also highlight the originality of particular expressions of praise, lament, thanksgiving, wisdom, and their subtypes. The basic psalm types reflect common structural elements and content, including phraseology. For example, the comparison of adversaries to wild animals is frequent in individual laments. This motif is intricately developed in some psalms and briefly alluded to in others, with different animals named (Pss. 7.1-2; 17.11-12; 22.12-21 [Hebrew 22.13-22]; 35.17; 57.4 [Hebrew 57.5]; 58.4-6 [Hebrew 58.5-7]). Phraseology that is similar yet PLURIFORM is also illustrated in the parallelism of Ps. 25.4 ('Make known to me your ways, O Lord/teach me your paths') and the related formulations in Pss. 27.11; 86.11; 119.12, 35; and 143.8-10. Here the poetic language moves across psalm types (for more examples, see Culley 1967).

The Poetry of Proverbs

The poetic sayings of Proverbs are rhetorically framed in a context of parental instruction (Prov. 1–9; 23.15, 19, 22-26; 31.1). Familiar phrases and motifs as well as patterns of comparison and contrast appear in ever-shifting constellations throughout the book. For example, the motif of wisdom as a 'path', opposed to the disastrous path of the wicked and obtuse, is recurrent. The predominance of antithetic parallelism in Proverbs generates repeated patterns of contrast between the wise and foolish, the just and wicked, the diligent and lazy, the restrained and unrestrained. Yet variation in the pairing of qualities, in imagery, and in phrasing is frequent. Thus Prov. 15.16, 'Better a little with fear of the Lord/than a great fortune with turmoil' is reformulated in 15.17 as 'Better a dish of greens where love is/than a fattened ox and hatred with it.' Even contradictory sayings built on familiar oppositions are possible (Prov. 10.15; 11.28; 13.8; 26.4-5). The contrast between what is recurrent and what changes gives such sayings their provocative force (see further Fox 2009).

Prophetic Poetry

The prophetic speeches presume a rhetorical setting of public oral delivery and draw on a common repertoire of phrases, motifs involving clusters of phrases and images, and overarching thematic patterns. Prophetic oracles that reflect the broad pattern of accusation and judgement use traditional imagery to depict desolation, as in the reversion of the land to a wilderness overrun by wild animals (Isa. 13.20-22; 34.10-15; Jer. 9.10; 10.22; 49.33; 50.39; 51.37; Zeph. 2.13-14), frequently 'a dwelling place of jackals'. The desiccation of the land and extinction of life is captured in the motif of the earth, or a related subject, mourning (*ʾābal*) in Hos. 4.3; Joel 1.10; Amos 1.2; Isa. 24.4, 7; 33.9; Jer. 4.27-28; 12.4; 12.10-11; 23.10 (see Hayes 2002). Obversely, oracles of salvation that convey the thematic pattern of restoration after judgement employ images of the fertility of the land, including the motif of planting and cultivating vineyards (Amos 9.13-15; Joel 3.18 [Hebrew 4.18]; Zech. 8.12; Isa. 65.21-22; Jer 31.5). Although the presentation and context of such phrases and motifs vary, the affinities among occurrences both intensify and modulate the poetic power of each expression across the prophetic corpus.

Katherine M. Hayes (Saint Joseph Seminary, USA)

Further Reading

Culley, Robert C. 1967. *Oral Formulaic Language in the Biblical Psalms*. Toronto: University of Toronto Press.

Culley, Robert C. 2000. 'Orality and Writtenness in Prophetic Texts.' In *Writings and Speech in Israelite and Ancient Near Eastern Prophecy*. SBL Symposium Series 10. Edited by Ehud Ben Zvi and Michael H. Floyd. Atlanta: SBL Press, pp. 45–64.

Culley, Robert C., ed. 1976. *Oral Tradition and Old Testament Studies*. *Semeia* 5. Missoula: Scholars, 1976.

Fox, Michael V. 2009. 'Reading a Proverb.' In *Proverbs 10–31*. Anchor Yale Bible Commentary 18B. New Haven: Yale University Press, pp. 484–98.

Gevirtz, Stanley. 1963. *Patterns in the Early Poetry of Israel*. Studies in Oriental Civilization 32. Chicago: University of Chicago Press.

Hayes, Katherine M. 2002. *'The Earth Mourns': Prophetic Metaphor and Oral Aesthetic*. Academica Biblia 8. Atlanta: SBL Press.

Pompeii (writing/literacy in) Nowhere does the ancient world come alive more than in the archaeological sites of Pompeii and Herculaneum, two Greco-Roman towns destroyed and (ironically) preserved in large measure by the eruption of Mount Vesuvius in 79 CE. Within their tomb-like remains are realia that impact greatly on our understanding of LITERACY and media in the ancient world.

Written artefacts are numerous in the two towns, primarily in the form of wall inscriptions or GRAFFITI. More than 11,000 specimens have been recorded from Pompeii and Herculaneum. Beyond graffiti, a few literary treasures emerge from Pompeii, although nothing to compare with the nearly 1,800 PAPYRUS SCROLLS discovered in Herculaneum's luxurious VILLA OF THE PAPYRI (themselves highly charred and largely unreadable). One corpus of written material comprises the legal and financial documents belonging to a leading Pompeian banker, Lucius Caecilius Jucundus. Stored in his house, they record the business dealings of many ordinary residents, especially the sale of property and slaves. Most of these WAX TABLETS are signed, with as many as ten people (often slaves) adding their marks of identification, evidently in sequence according to their status on the social hierarchy. Also beyond graffiti, wine amphorae have been found that are marked by labels listing their origin and delivery destination. A fresco depicts a man (probably Terentius Neo) holding a scroll and his wife holding a stylus in her right hand to inscribe the wax tablets that she holds in her left hand. A mosaic at the entryway of one house (the House of the Faun) advertises a greeting, 'Welcome'. Another reads 'Profit is joy' (CIL X.875); another, 'welcome, profit' (X.874); still another, 'Beware of the dog' (X.877).

But Pompeii's wonders of literacy lie with its graffiti. The external walls of houses, commercial properties, and public spaces provided shared space used by the populace in general, fostering discourse of all kinds within public arenas. Included in that discourse were *dipinti*, graffiti painted in red over white on external walls. These were painted by sign writers who often worked at night and sometimes even put themselves in the picture: 'Aemilius Celer wrote this on his own by the light of the moon' (IV.3884); 'Unico writes, without the rest of the team' (IV.3529); 'Onesimus was the whitewasher' (IV.222). One painter excoriated his partner: 'Lantern carrier, hold the ladder' (IV.7621). Over 2,500 of these *dipinti* were *programmata* – political endorsements in which individuals (usually well-placed men, but occasionally women) or groups (including even an undetermined group called the 'dice throwers') advertise their support for a candidate running for civic office. Others were announcements of forthcoming gladiatorial games.

The majority of Pompeii's graffiti were either etched into plaster with a hard object or drawn with simple charcoal. These graffiti occur on external walls as well as internal walls, and in properties covering the whole of the socio-economic spectrum. They engage virtually every area of life and thus, through them, the first-century town comes alive.

A good number of inscriptions, for instance, cite sentences from 'high literature', such as Homer, Ovid, Seneca, and most of all, Virgil (48 occurrences; one citation of Virgil was even inscribed into the wall of Pompeii's leading brothel). Many of these might have been written by young students learning to write, their teachers giving them exercises from Greco-Roman classic literature (see EDUCATION, HELLENISTIC). Some graffiti are simply the letters of the alphabet written out in order, as if students were practising their WRITING assignments (see ABECEDARIES). At other times, the graffiti contain complex palindromes in alluring word-squares.

More frequently, however, Pompeii's inscriptions capture moments of life. Some are life-changing moments: '23rd January, Ursa gave birth on a Thursday' (IV.8820). Some are mundane moments: 'It took 640 paces to walk back and forth between here and there ten times' (IV.1714). Devoid of any puritanical sentiment, their inscribers often state things bluntly. 'I screwed many girls here' (IV.2175); 'If anyone wants a screw, he should look for Attice – she costs four sesterces' (IV.1751); 'Apollinaris, the doctor of emperor Titus, shit well here' (IV.10,619). Sometimes inscriptions simply state that their inscriber 'was here', advertise premises for rent, note that the inscriber made 'a vow to the household deities' in that place, or offer 'good wishes and good health' to members of the imperial family. Sometimes the graffiti tease: 'Epaphra, you are bald!' (IV.1816); 'This is Rufus' (IV.9226, in which an elite figure is caricatured as a bald man with a large, swollen-finger type nose and a protruding chin). On the wall of the slave latrine we read the playful ribbing of a slave named Martha: 'This is Martha's dining room; she shits in [her] dining room' (IV.5244). Sometimes they chide: 'Basilica Chios, I hope your piles become sore once again, so that they hurt even more than they hurt before' (IV.1820). Consider also this extended taunt between two men in love with the same barmaid: 'Successus the weaver loves Iris, the barmaid of the inn. She doesn't like him, but he asks [for sex?] and she feels sorry for him. A rival wrote this. Farewell.' Then the following appears, written by Successus himself: 'You're jealous, bursting out with that comment. Don't try to muscle in on someone who's better-looking, and is a wicked and charming man.' Then the 'rival' reinscribes, now listing his name. 'I have written and spoken. You love Iris, who doesn't care for you. Severus to Successus.'

As indicated by the above examples, the graffiti sometimes include touching references to friendship or love. 'Pyrrhus to his colleague Chius: I am in sorrow because I hear you have died; and so, farewell' (IV.1852). 'I don't want to sell my husband, not for all the gold in the world' (IV.3061). 'I would rather die than be a deity without you' (IV.1928). 'Methe from Atella, slave of Cominia, loves Chrestus. May Pompeian Venus be dear to both of them and may they always live in harmony' (IV.2457). Often, however, they speak poetically of love gone wrong. 'Nothing can last forever. When the Sun has shone brightly, it returns to Ocean. The Moon wanes, which recently was full. Even so the fierceness of Venus [the goddess of love] often becomes a puff of wind' (IV.9123). Sometimes their references to love are less than poetic, however, as in this angry tirade against the same goddess: 'I wish to break the ribs of Venus with sticks and maim the goddess's loins! If she can rip apart my tender heart, why can't I break her head with a stick?' Sometimes the graffiti offered words of wisdom. 'A small problem gets larger if you ignore it' (IV.1811). 'While I live, you are coming, hateful death' (IV.5112). 'He who disdains life will easily despise god' (IV.5370).

This short survey provides only a sample of the writing on display in the first-century town of Pompeii. But even a small sampling offers significant insight into the contours of ancient literacy. Pompeii was awash with a low-grade form of literacy that included a breadth of GENRES targeted for readerships across a broad spectrum of the populace. This does not mean, of course, that everyone was literate; far from it. For vast swathes of the population, most inscriptions on Pompeian walls must have been little more than lines and curves joined together that meant something to others within the town. But neither is it the case that literacy pertained only to the Pompeian elite and/or their retainers. Pompeii's literary remains problematize any attempt to distinguish between 'literate' and 'non-literate' in relation to general sectors within the populace. The walls of Pompeii instead display a spectrum of literate competencies or *literacies*.

Bruce W. Longenecker (Baylor University, USA)

Further Reading

Cooley, Alison E., and M. G. L. Cooley. 2004. *Pompeii: A Sourcebook*. London: Routledge.
Hartnett, Matthew. 2012. *By Roman Hands: Inscriptions and Graffiti for Students of Latin*. 2nd edn. Newburyport, MA: Focus Publishing/R. Pullins Co.
Keegan, Peter. 2014. *Graffiti in Antiquity*. London and New York: Routledge.
Milnor, Kristina. 2014. *Graffiti and the Literary Landscape in Roman Pompeii*. Oxford: Oxford University Press.
Wallace, Rex E. 2005. *An Introduction to Wall Inscriptions from Pompeii and Herculaneum*. Wauconda IL: Bolchazy-Carducci Publishers, Inc.

Postmemory Marianne Hirsch's work on postmemory participates in ongoing and developing theoretical discussions in Holocaust and genocide studies, while extending to other fields addressing trauma, memory, and inter/transgenerational acts of transfer. She defines postmemory as 'the relationship of the second generation to powerful, often traumatic, experiences that preceded their births but that were nevertheless transmitted to them so deeply as to seem to constitute memories in their own right' (2008: 103). Through this mnemonic process, 'less-directly affected participants' can be impacted by the persistence of events that occurred before their birth, even after victims and survivors of a trauma have passed on (Hirsch 2008: 111).

Hirsch describes the process of postmemory and the affective impact on the descendants of victims and survivors as one in which later generations 'remember' via stories, bodily mannerisms, and images that are transmitted deeply and affectively. Thus, the connection of postmemory to the past is not facilitated by 'recall' but rather by imagination, projection, and creation. The affective force of postmemory may even displace the memories of later generations as the past haunts the present (Hirsch 2008: 106–7). According to Hirsch, postmemory illumines the problem of mnemonic transmission through both collective and personal trauma, catastrophic events, and other ruptures, including exile (2008: 104) (see CULTURAL MEMORY).

Hirsch primarily applies postmemory to the ways in which the traumatic memories of Holocaust victims and survivors are transferred to (through family photographs in particular) and represented in second-generation fiction, art, memoir, and testimony. With that said, Hirsch's concept of postmemory can be a valuable heuristic device in analysing inter/transgenerational transmissions of trauma. Because Hirsch's work is read in various ways, postmemory has turned out to be a fruitful and malleable concept that can inform new approaches to biblical studies.

In Second Temple Judaism, the Babylonian destruction and exile of Jerusalem was transmitted inter/transgenerationally through the processes of ORAL TRADITION, textual production, and textual performance. The Hebrew Bible and Second Temple literature are infused with post-memories of the Babylonian destruction and exile, from Ezra-Nehemiah (especially Ezra 3.11-13) to Chronicles, Lamentations, prophetic literature, and Psalms, as well as much later texts like Daniel, Damascus Document, 4 Ezra, and 2 Baruch. These later Second Temple texts imagined Israel in a state of exile that continued well into the Second Temple period. For some mnemonic communities, exile was not overcome during the Second Temple period and was reactivated as a site of trauma by later Second Temple communities. Here, the affective force of postmemory is evident as the memories of later generations are displaced by memories of exile. In this sense, the affective impact of trauma on later generations can be reactivated by and reactivate earlier traumas. Moreover, in the cases of Daniel, 4 Ezra, 2 Baruch, and Josephus' *Jewish War*, the postmemory of an earlier trauma is reactivated by a second (later) trauma. This mnemonic process is facilitated by aesthetic, symbolic, and institutional structures and tropes that transmit postmemory (Hirsch 2008: 107).

Tim Langille (Arizona State University, USA)

Further Reading

Hirsch, Marianne. 2008. 'The Generation of Postmemory.' *Poetics Today* 29(1): 103–28.

Potmarks/Potter's Marks The term *potmark* is used to describe a non-decorative sign or symbol on the surface of a ceramic vessel. This mark may be painted, scratched, incised, stamped, or applied (as a clay addition). Potmarks take a variety of shapes, ranging from a simple slash across the handle of an Iron Age cooking pot to a more complex design, such as a human figure of clay appliqué on the body of an Aegean jar. Patterns of dots, chevrons, crescents, fingernail scratches, or fingerprints are common potmarks. It is assumed that many of these are signifiers, perhaps akin to a brand stamp or signature found on the bottom of a coffee mug today.

For sake of clarity, it is helpful to separate the more general term *potmark* from the more specific term *potter's mark*. The former includes pre-fired as well as post-fired markings. These may be made at any point along the life of a container, including the time of manufacture, transmission, use, or deposition. However, because some post-fired marks come about as a result of accidental contact with another object, or may have been executed on a stray sherd apart from the life of the vessel, these are more difficult to assess. Potter's marks, on the other hand, are pressed into the soft surface of a vessel before firing and as part of the production process. That said, distinguishing between pre-fired and post-fired marks is often difficult in the field and virtually impossible from published archaeological reports.

Potmarks are as old as the ceramic craft. Archaeological excavations in Egypt, Mesopotamia, the Aegean, and the Levant have yielded tens of thousands of exemplars. These appear several millennia before the time of Abraham on vessels of various sizes and shapes. Both élite and common ware carry such marks. While the practice of pot-marking surges in time and place, it continues to and through the Greco-Roman periods. Without a doubt, Biblical-era personalities handled marked containers on a daily basis.

Those who handled these containers likely would have found potmarks in specific vessel zones. Shoulders, loop handles, or bases are ready targets for marking. This may be for display purposes or, in the case of potter's marks, a reflection of how pre-fired or 'leather-hard' pieces were sorted, handled, or loaded into a kiln.

Despite the frequent appearance of potmarks, there is no consensus on how to interpret them. In many cases, it is difficult to align these enigmatic dots and slashes with known systems of WRITING. This incongruity has led most modern interpreters to consider the potmark not as a linguistic sign to be 'read' per se, but as some other kind of signifier. Proposals range from decoration to trademarks, location indicators, time stamps, content or capacity markers, counters, signatures, pre-writing expressions, or some kind of production device. Unfortunately, no single proposal can adequately explain the entire corpus of material evidence across time and space.

Ethnographic analogies drawn from modern cultures in Peru and Mali may provide helpful clues on the purposes of potter's marks. In these contexts, where pot-marking traditions continue, potmarks link specific vessels to specific producers. Individual artisans work cooperatively with others to conserve fuel in the firing process. Hence, the potter's marks function as a production code for use in a shared workspace. Outside of that workspace, they have no meaning.

Mark Ziese (Johnson University, USA)

Presentism/Constructionism Presentism (or *constructionism*) is the position that memory is a mental state or shared experience that is constructed primarily according to the needs and strategies of the present (rather than generated primarily from past realities). Scholars who approach COLLECTIVE MEMORY from this perspective would generally oppose themselves to advocates of CONTINUITISM/TRADITIONALISM. Presentists emphasize the creativity, fluidity, and utility of commemoration and emphasize the synchronic conditions of the social present.

Presentism is in many respects consistent with the theoretical model of the widely-acknowledged 'father' of collective memory studies, sociologist MAURICE HALBWACHS (1877–1945). Halbwachs argued that memory is entirely social in nature and imaginatively built in the cognitive present. Halbwachs did allow for an enduring impression of the past, but argued forcefully against a necessary correspondence between the ACTUAL PAST and present memory. Extreme presentists argue that memory is always constructed in the present, so the past has no leverage against commemorative activity (including the writing of history). Applied to ORAL TRADITION and performance, presentists argue that 'the individual narrators are in fact responsible for the final composition of the story (at least in large part) when they are actually performing it for their audience' (Finnegan 1988: 92). Applied to political history, presentists emphasize the tendency of groups/societies to promote and distort history in ways that prove advantageous, while suppressing the disadvantageous elements (cf. Zerubavel 1995; Hobsbawm 1983). Thus, memories and commemorations tell us a great deal more about the individuals/groups who distort the past and much less about past figures and objects. In this view, history is a structured version of collective memory.

An alternate expression of the presentist approach to collective memory is represented by the work of Pierre Nora (1931–). Nora argues that memory and history are at odds: memory is absolute because it upholds the present with integrity; history is always incomplete, always relative (1989: 8–9). For Nora, memory is pure and fluid until historians attempt to utilize and concretize it. In this way, Nora represents a full turn away from Halbwachs, who argued that memory is relative while history is objective and concrete. It is important to note that most social memory theorists do not advocate extreme presentism (memory has no relationship to the past) or extreme continuitism (memory always accurately represents the past). Even so, many theorists betray tendencies towards one of these two polarities.

Anthony Le Donne (United Theological Seminary, USA)

Further Reading

Finnegan, Ruth. 1988. *Literacy and Orality: Studies in the Technology of Communication.* Oxford: Blackwell.
Halbwachs, Maurice. 1925. *Les Cadres sociaux de la mémoire*. Paris: F. Alcan.
Hobsbawm, Eric. 1983. 'Introduction: Inventing Traditions.' In *The Invention of Tradition.* Edited by E. Hobsbawm and T. Ranger. Cambridge: Cambridge University Press, pp. 1–14.
Nora, Pierre. 1989. 'Between Memory and History: Les Lieux de mémoire.' *Representations* 26: 7–25.
Zerubavel, Yael. 1995. *Recovered Roots: Collective Memory and the Making of Israeli National Tradition.* Chicago: University of Chicago Press.

Prophecy Prophecy is an oral phenomenon that includes four necessary components: 'the divine sender of the message, the message itself, the human transmitter of the message and the recipient(s) of the message' (Nissinen 2003: 2). Prophets are one type of non-inductive intermediary between the divine and human worlds. In contrast to inductive intermediaries, such as astrologers, who interpret something in the material world as a divine sign, prophets receive special messages (audible and/or visible) directly from a deity. Although prophecy is a phenomenon found in many cultures throughout history and into the contemporary world, the focus here is on prophecy in the ancient Near East, especially in Israel up to the late Second Temple period. Of course, the only reason we know anything about ancient prophecy is because of written texts. Some of these written texts are GENRES that were simply used to facilitate communication of the prophetic message from the prophet to the recipient over significant distance (for example, LETTERS); others are genres that suggest some later reinterpretation of earlier prophetic messages in which various prophetic messages were edited together into one collection for a new application.

The English word 'prophet' derives from the Greek word *prophētēs* (*pro + phemi*), which means 'one who speaks for another'. Thus, the Greek and English words reflect the definition given above. This is also the case with some of the other terms used for prophets in the ancient Near East, including the following: the Babylonian *āpilum/āpiltum* (from *apālu*, 'to answer'), the Assyrian *raggimu/raggintu* (from *ragāmu*, 'to shout'), the Hebrew *nabi* (from *nabu*, 'to announce'), and the Hebrew *ḥōzê* (from *ḥazah*, 'to see'). Other prophetic titles refer to ecstatic behaviour sometimes associated with prophecy (for example, the Babylonian *muḫḫû(m)/muḫḫûtu(m)* and the Assyrian *maḫḫû/maḫḫūtu*, from *maḫû*, 'to become crazy') or to other types of crossing social boundaries (for example, the Babylonian *assinnu*, 'man-woman') (Nissinen 2003: 5–8).

Prophecy in the Ancient Near East

We have considerable epigraphic evidence of prophecy in the ancient Near East and ancient Mediterranean Sea basin from ancient Mari in the eighteenth century BCE to the Roman period oracles at Delphi (see EPIGRAPHY). Here I will focus on materials from Mari and Nineveh, especially since the primary sources are now easily accessible in one volume in transliteration and English translation (Nissinen 2003).

Mari was the capital of an ancient kingdom on the banks of the Euphrates River in modern Syria, not far from the Iraqi border, that flourished in the late third and early second millennium BCE. During archaeological excavations, over twenty thousand cuneiform tablets were discovered. Most of these tablets came from the reigns of the last two kings, Yasmaḫ-Addu and Zimri-Lim, who ruled just prior to Mari's destruction by Hammurabi, the king of Babylon in 1760 BCE. Some of the cuneiform tablets include references to prophets, especially some of the Mari letters addressed to Yasmaḫ-Addu and Zimri-Lim and some administrative documents (Nissinen 2003).

In these Mari documents, prophets and prophetesses are closely connected with TEMPLES. The deities from which prophetic messages originate include both gods (Dagan, Adad, Šamaš, Marduk) and goddesses (Ištar, Belet-ekallim, Diritum, Ninḫursag). The recipient of the message – as would be expected in a royal

ARCHIVE – is consistently the king. As such, the messages often concern military campaigns, promising victory or giving warnings, but in some cases the deity complains that the king has not paid proper attention to the care of a temple and its cult. As noted by the different prophetic titles, there is some diversity among the Mari prophets. Thus, the prophetic message may be communicated in a vision or dream, the deity may be portrayed as speaking directly to the prophet, the prophet may exhibit ecstatic behaviour, and/or the message may be induced by a strong drink. The Mari prophets are clearly part of the professional temple bureaucracy as can been seen by their payment (including a donkey, garment, weapon, and silver) and their close relationship to other cult professionals, especially musicians and chanters. The Mari letters strongly suggest the oral character of prophecy, in that the reason that the prophetic message was written down was simply to facilitate communication over long distances between the prophet and the king. In other words, many prophetic oracles were probably never written down and were communicated orally when it was possible for a messenger to go the short distance from the temple to the palace in a short period of time to deliver the message orally. Furthermore, the prophets are not the senders of the letters, but are mentioned and quoted by the royal officials who sent the letters (Nissinen 2000b).

The Neo-Assyrian evidence, which comes primarily from a royal archive that was buried during the destruction of Nineveh in 612 BCE by the Babylonians and Medes, is mostly limited to the reigns of Esarhaddon and Assurbanipal in the seventh century BCE. The deity most commonly referred to in this material is Ištar of Arbela and her other manifestations; however, other deities speak through prophets as well. For example, the raggimu La-dagil-ili prophesies in the name of both Aššur and Ištar (##84-88 in Nissinen 2003) and one document (#71 in Nissinen 2003) has prophecies from three deities, Bel, Ištar, and Nabû. As should be expected in a royal archive, the recipient of the messages is consistently the king and the messages include military matters, succession of the throne, and the importance of attending to the deities' needs by proper WORSHIP.

The Neo-Assyrian materials include three collections of prophetic oracles, demonstrating a heightened interest in prophecy during the reign of Esarhaddon. The First Collection (##68-77 in Nissinen 2003) consists of oracles from different prophets 'proclaimed during Esarhaddon's victorious war against his brothers before his rise to power in the year 681' (Nissinen 2003: 101), all of which includes the deities' support for Esarhaddon's victory. The Second Collection (##78-83 in Nissinen 2003) consists of oracles from different prophets that 'deal with the stabilization of Esarhaddon's rule and the reestablishment of the cult of the gods of Babylon' (Nissinen 2003: 101). Esarhaddon's father, Sennacherib, had destroyed Esaggil, the main temple of Marduk in Babylon, in 689 BCE, when the city of Babylon had rebelled against him. Now Esarhaddon is being urged by the prophets to reestablish the temple in Babylon (##78, 80 in Nissinen 2003). The Third Collection (##84-88 in Nissinen 2003) contains oracles from the same prophet, La-dagil-ili, all of which are connected to 'Esarhaddon's enthronement ritual in Ešarra, the temple of Aššur in Assur, which took place in Adar (XII), 681' (Nissinen 2003: 101). This collection expresses the deities' assurance of peace, but also expresses that Ištar is upset with the lack of proper ritual offerings. These three collections are unusual among non-biblical materials in the ancient Near East in that they provide evidence of scribal editing of prophetic oracles into larger collections, presumably for later cultic purposes.

Prophecy in the Hebrew Bible

Prophecy is a topic of discussion throughout the Hebrew Bible – that is, not only in the Prophets, but also in the Law and Writings. In the Law, Abraham (Gen. 20.7), Moses (Deut. 18.15; 34:10), Aaron (Exod. 7.1), and Miriam (Exod. 15.20) are all identified as prophets. In the Writings, there are references to prophecy in Psalms (51.0; 74.9) and Proverbs (29.18) as well as the portrayal of prophets in many places in Chronicles paralleling that of Samuel-Kings and references to Haggai and Zechariah in Ezra 6.14. Of course, the majority of references to prophets and prophecy occurs in the section of Prophets, both the Former and Latter Prophets. Given the diversity of literary genres and historical periods portrayed in the literature as well as the long literary history of the prophetic books, it is difficult to summarize the portrayal of prophecy in the Hebrew Bible. However, the above definition of prophecy reflects this diversity, both for the YHWH prophets and their opponents, the 'false' prophets. Although at one time there might have been some distinction between a *prophet*, a *seer*, and a *man of God*, such a distinction is now lost – for example, in 1 Samuel 9, Samuel is referred to by all three prophetic titles. Nevertheless, despite such difficulties, we can conclude that the prophets of ancient Israel and Judah fit well within their larger cultural context; they are often identified with cultic activities and their recipients are often the king or other political leaders (especially when there was no king).

In contrast to prophetic literature of other ancient Near Eastern cultures, references to prophets and prophecy in the Hebrew Bible were incorporated into a greater number of literary genres and the resulting prophetic literature underwent extensive revision over many centuries. These revisions made relevant the earlier prophetic messages to later and later times (Nissinen 2014). This certainly represents a scribal reinterpretation that transforms the definition of prophecy beyond what probably would have been recognizable by actual prophets. That is, the immediacy of the prophetic message from the deity to the recipient through the prophet is so determinative of prophecy that the prophet and recipients most probably would not imagine that the message would prove useful for predicting some distant future that they themselves could not envision. Although it is true that the Neo-Assyrian collections reused oracles for a different situation, this reuse was within the lifetime of the original recipient and only implied that the earlier oracles remain true for Esarhaddon and his son, Assurbanipal. In contrast is the rewriting of the earliest Israelite prophets and their prophecies with their messages containing predictions of the later Babylonian exile, something that would have been nonsense to the prophets and their contemporary audiences who are portrayed as living centuries earlier in the narratives about prophets (for example, Moses in Deut. 4.25-31; Isaiah in 2 Kgs 20.16-18; Isa. 39.5-8). This scribal intervention through narrative imagination probably also expanded the definition of *prophet* to include others, especially those who were not 'professional' prophets. For example, both Samuel-Kings and Chronicles portray what might be called 'ad hoc prophets' – that is, individuals who receive messages directly from YHWH because the 'spirit' possesses them, even though they are not prophets, such as Israelite kings (Saul in 1 Sam. 19.23; David in 2 Sam. 23.2), foreign kings (Sennacherib in 2 Kgs 19.7; Necho in 2 Chr. 35.20-22; Cyrus in 2 Chr. 36.22-23), and laypersons (Saul's messengers in 1 Sam. 19.20) (Person 2013: 193–7). In fact, various scholars have argued that some SCRIBES (especially the 'Chronicler') may have understood themselves as some type of 'writing prophet' (Person 2013: 197–9), even though it is unlikely that prophets themselves wrote anything (Nissinen 2014). Despite such scribal interventions, we can still see through the prophetic literature of the Hebrew Bible well enough to conclude that prophets played an important role in ancient Israel and Judah and it was because of this role that the Hebrew Bible, a product of the scribal elite, contains so many references to prophets and prophecy.

Prophecy in the NT

The Greek word *prophētēs* was used in the SEPTUAGINT to translate the Hebrew *nabi* and occurs frequently in the Apocrypha; therefore, it is not surprising to find it in the NT. Although *prophētēs* refers to the prophets of the Hebrew Bible (for example, Elijah and Jeremiah in Mt. 16.14) and even to other characters in the Hebrew Bible (for example, Abel in Lk. 11.50-51), its use is not limited to these prophets of old and includes NT figures as well (for example, Jesus in Mt. 21.11; Anna in Lk. 2.36; Agabus in Acts 21.10). In fact, the portrayal of

Jesus in the Synoptic Gospels has led many scholars to suggest that the historical Jesus was an eschatological prophet who preached about the impending Kingdom of God (for example, Witherington 1999).

In his important work on Christian prophecy, M. Eugene Boring used the following definition: 'The early Christian prophet was an immediately inspired spokesperson for the risen Jesus, who received intelligible messages that he or she felt impelled to deliver to the Christian community or, as a representative of the community, to the general public' (1991: 38; emphasis removed). His definition has much in common with the above definition from Nissinen, especially when we consider that Boring did 'not intend to draw any sharp distinction among Christian prophets who portray themselves, or are portrayed, as speaking for God, the risen Jesus, or the Holy Spirit' (1991: 38). In other words, Christian prophets simply prophesy according to their understanding of the deity, significantly influenced by the idea of the resurrected Jesus. Boring also understood Christian prophecy as primarily an oral phenomenon that was later written down. In fact, he concluded that the Christian prophets both repeated sayings of the historical Jesus that they heard in the ORAL TRADITION as well as sayings of the risen Jesus directly speaking through them in ways that were not distinguished from one another, because their faith perspective understood that the same Jesus was speaking. Consequently, they all were 'words of the Lord'. When the Christian prophets' words were later written down, the Gospel writers also did not make any distinction (and probably could not have, even if they wanted). Therefore, the distinction between the historical Jesus and the resurrected Jesus who spoke through the prophets is an anachronism that some modern scholars apply to the Gospel sayings in their quest for the historical Jesus. Although Boring's focus is on the Synoptic Gospels, he nevertheless discussed the widespread influence of Christian prophecy in the Pauline and deutero-Pauline epistles, Acts, the Gospel and Letters of John, Revelation, the Didache, and Hermas. He thus concluded, 'Early Christianity was a prophetic movement' (1991: 17). As such, early Christianity was an oral movement that later wrote down its traditions as the first generation of Christians were dying out or, in the case of Paul's letters, was written down for practical necessities rather than preserving the tradition for future generations.

Prophecy in Other Late Second Temple Literature

Early Christianity was a prophetic movement significantly influenced by the emphasis on prophecy in the Hebrew Bible and this was also the case with other late Second Temple literature. That is, early Christianity reflected an early Jewish emphasis on prophecy. Ben Sira not only retold stories about the prophets in the Hebrew Bible (for example, Samuel in Sir. 46.13-20 and Isaiah in Sir. 48.17-25), but also understood himself as an interpreter of the Law engaging in prophecy, when he wrote 'I will again pour out teaching like prophecy' (24.33; see also 39.1; Beentjes 2006). Philo of Alexandria was well versed in his knowledge of the prophets of the Hebrew Bible through his knowledge of the Haftarah, a liturgical cycle of readings from the Prophets, and he referred to the allegorical interpretation of the 'great mysteries' of the prophets within a specific school of thought (Cohen 2006). As an initiated member of this school, Philo understood himself as participating in the persistence of prophecy through the study and interpretation of Scripture (Levison 2006). Josephus likewise referred to both biblical and contemporary prophets and understood himself as 'a latter-day Jeremiah, giving advice in the Second Temple period similar to that given by his predecessor at the time of the destruction of the first Temple' (Feldman 2006: 239; see also Grabbe 2006). The Qumran community had a heightened interest in prophecy and prophetic literature. The Prophets are included in the biblical SCROLLS found in the nearby caves (especially Isaiah) and the sectarian literature prominently includes references to prophets and prophecy, most notably the *Habakkuk Pesher* (see PESHARIM). The Qumran community saw itself in continuity with the biblical prophets, including understanding the Teacher of Righteousness as a prophet like Moses in both form and function, even though he is described by none of the biblical prophetic titles. Furthermore, the Qumran community understood that the Teacher was a forerunner of the coming eschatological prophet, who would immediately precede the coming of the priestly messiah and the royal messiah (Jassen 2007; Brooke 2006).

In short, we can see how both the scribal intervention and redefinition of prophecy that began with the initial writing down of the classical prophets and continued with the long history of revision of the prophetic literature of the Hebrew Bible influenced the understanding of prophets and prophecy in early Christianity and Judaism. Although oral prophets continued to speak divine messages, as is evidenced by references to them in the NT, Josephus, and other literature, we know little about these prophets. Rather, we know somewhat more about the 'writing prophets', those who defined prophecy in such a way so that it included the reinterpretation of past prophetic messages in the composition, revision, and/or transmission of texts by SCRIBES such as the Chronicler, Ben Sira, the author of the *Habukkuk Pesher*, Josephus, Philo, and the author of Matthew.

However, despite such scribal intervention, we can nevertheless discern an oral aesthetic within the prophetic literature of the Hebrew Bible and later literature. For example, Katherine Hayes (2002) has demonstrated the metonymic qualities of the metaphor of the earth mourning in prophetic literature – that is, she has successfully argued that we must read the nine passages that contain this metaphor together in order to reconstruct the extratextual references that each of the texts depend on for their communicative force (see METONYMY). Similarly, SUSAN NIDITCH (2011) analysed the apparent contradictory understandings of 'good blood' and 'bad blood' in Zechariah 9, demonstrating that a fuller understanding of this text can only occur when one looks at the metonymic meaning of 'blood' within the broader tradition that provides the context of this text. As these two examples demonstrate, a better understanding of prophecy as an oral phenomenon and what changes may have occurred in its being written down, especially when the prophetic literature undergoes centuries of revision, are necessary for understanding more fully the TRADITIONAL REFERENTIALITY of prophecy and prophetic literature.

Raymond F. Person, Jr. (Ohio Northern University, USA)

Further Reading

Beentjes, Pancratius C. 2006. 'Prophets and Prophecy in the Book of Ben Sira.' In *Prophets, Prophecy, and Prophetic Texts in Second Temple Judaism*. Edited by Michael H. Floyd and Robert D. Haak. LHBOTS 427. London: T&T Clark, pp. 135–50.

Ben Zvi, Ehud and Michael H. Floyd, eds. 2000. *Writings and Speech in Israelite and Ancient Near Eastern Prophecy*. SBL Symposium Series. Atlanta: Society of Biblical Literature.

Boring, M. Eugene. 1991. *The Continuing Voice of Jesus: Christian Prophecy and the Gospel Tradition*. Louisville: Westminster John Knox.

Brooke, George J. 2006. 'Prophecy and Prophets in the Dead Sea Scrolls: Looking Backwards and Forwards.' In *Prophets, Prophecy, and Prophetic Texts in Second Temple Judaism*. LHBOTS 427. Edited by Michael H. Floyd and Robert D. Haak. London: T&T Clark, pp. 151–65.

Cohen, Naomi G. 2006. 'The Prophetic Books in Alexandria: The Evidence from Philo Judaeus.' In *Prophets, Prophecy, and Prophetic Texts in Second Temple Judaism*. LHBOTS 427. Edited by Michael H. Floyd and Robert D. Haak. London: T&T Clark, pp. 166–93.

Feldman, Louis H. 2006. 'Prophets and Prophecy in Josephus.' In *Prophets, Prophecy, and Prophetic Texts in Second Temple Judaism*. LHBOTS 427. Edited by Michael H. Floyd and Robert D. Haak. London: T&T Clark, pp. 210–39.

Floyd, Michael H., and Robert D. Haak, eds. 2006. *Prophets, Prophecy, and Prophetic Texts in Second Temple Judaism*. LHBOTS 427. London: T&T Clark.

Grabbe, Lester L. 2006. 'Thus Spake the Prophet Josephus … The Jewish Historian on Prophets and Prophecy.' In *Prophets, Prophecy, and Prophetic Texts in Second Temple Judaism*. LHBOTS 427. Edited by Michael H. Floyd and Robert D. Haak. London: T&T Clark, pp. 240–7.

Hayes, Katherine. 2002. *'The Earth Mourns': Prophetic Metaphor and Oral Aesthetic*. Academia Biblica 8. Atlanta: Society of Biblical Literature.
Jacobs, Mignon, and Raymond F. Person, Jr., eds. 2013. *Israelite Prophecy and the Deuteronomistic History: Portrait, Reality and the Formation of a History*. Ancient Israel and Its Literature. Atlanta: Society of Biblical Literature.
Jassen, Alex P. 2007. *Mediating the Divine: Prophecy and Revelation in the Dead Sea Scrolls and Second Temple Judaism*. STDJ 68. Leiden: Brill.
Levison, John R. 2006. 'Philo's Personal Experience and the Persistence of Prophecy.' In *Prophets, Prophecy, and Prophetic Texts in Second Temple Judaism*. LHBOTS 427. Edited by Michael H. Floyd and Robert D. Haak. London: T&T Clark, pp. 194–209.
Niditch, Susan. 2011. 'Good Blood, Bad Blood: Multivocality, Metonymy, and Mediation in Zechariah 9.' *VT* 61: 629–45.
Nissinen, Martti, ed. 2000a. *Prophecy in Its Ancient Near Eastern Context: Mesopotamian, Biblical, and Arabian Perspectives*. SBL Symposium Series. Atlanta: Society of Biblical Literature.
Nissinen, Martti. 2000b. 'Spoken, Written, Quoted, and Invented: Orality and Writtenness in Ancient Near Eastern Prophecy.' In *Writings and Speech in Israelite and Ancient Near Eastern Prophecy*. Edited by Ehud Ben Zvi and Michael H. Floyd. SBL Symposium Series. Atlanta: Society of Biblical Literature, pp. 235–71.
Nissinen, Martti, ed. 2003. *Prophets and Prophecy in the Ancient Near East*. Atlanta: Society of Biblical Literature.
Nissinen, Martti. 2014. 'Since When Do Prophets Write?' In *In the Footsteps of Sherlock Holmes: Studies in the Biblical Text in Honour of Anneli Aejmelaeus*. Edited by Kristin De Troyer, T. Michael Law, and Marketta Liljeström. Leuven: Peeters, pp. 585–606.
Person, Raymond F., Jr. 2013. 'Prophets in the Deuteronomic History and the Book of Chronicles.' In *Israelite Prophecy and the Deuteronomistic History: Portrait, Reality and the Formation of a History*. Edited by Mignon Jacobs, and Raymond F. Person, Jr. Ancient Israel and Its Literature. Atlanta: SBL Press, pp. 187–99.
Witherington, Ben, III. 1999. *Jesus the Seer: The Progress of Prophecy*. Peabody: Hendrickson.

Proverb(s) A proverb is a short, pithy saying that makes an observation by aligning (sometimes unrelated) images, often in the service of a moral point and with the aim of forming character. A proverb usually contains a contrast between different types of people – for example, 'the righteous' vs. 'the wicked'; the 'wise person' vs. 'the fool' – to make a contrast between extremes of behaviour, the consequences of which are then spelt out. The biblical book of Proverbs is the largest single collection of proverbs within the CANON, but examples of the GENRE may also be found throughout the Bible's narrative, poetic, prophetic, and epistolary texts (see POETRY IN THE HEBREW BIBLE; PROPHECY).

There are two stages in the formation of proverbs, the first oral and the second written. It is likely that most proverbs originated in oral culture. The form is short and memorable and the content is predictable inasmuch as it features a contrast between two options – good behaviour that will lead to good outcomes and bad behaviour that will result in disadvantage or moral decline. Our knowledge of proverbs in ancient Israel is largely confined to the book of Proverbs, although there are proverbs elsewhere in the Hebrew Bible (e.g. Eccl. 7:1-13) and also in the NT (e.g. Mt. 6:19-20; Jas 4:6). One indicator of the oral origin of proverbs is their repetition within Proverbs, rarely identically but often with the repetition of one line and the addition of a new second line. This indicates that proverbs were easily varied to suit different contexts and occasions. Many proverbs betray an agricultural background, mentioning phenomena from the natural or animal world that are compared/contrasted with human behaviour – for example, the rain brought by the north wind is compared to the gloom brought by a person's backbiting tongue (Prov. 25.23), and meeting a she-bear robbed of her cubs is better than consulting a fool (Prov. 17.12). Proverbs act as a warning against becoming a certain type, such as a fool, a lazy person, a member of 'the wicked' or an angry person. Many topics are covered – relationships with others (masters and servants, friends, relatives and neighbours); the dangers of falling into poverty through laziness; the importance of carefully chosen words; warnings against false loans, bribery and the 'smooth-tongued'; and, praise of hard work and well-acquired wealth.

The coining of proverbs is a worldwide phenomenon known across many different cultures and periods of time. In relation to biblical proverbs, important work has been done on modern-day cultures, notably on tribal wisdom in Africa (Golka). Looking at the role of proverbs in such cultures may give us insight into their use in the past – for example, some modern cultures use proverbs in educational settings or legal contexts, providing helpful models for understanding the origins and social function of biblical proverbs. We also have proverbs from ancient times, notably ancient Sumer and Egypt, that considerably predate biblical proverbs. In Egyptian proverbs the main contrast is not between the wise person and the fool but between the silent person and the 'heated'. It is difficult to determine the specific original contexts of some ancient proverbs, but again oral circulation is likely for the purposes of educational instruction before they were written down into collections.

An important distinction needs to be made between the oral stage and the written stage of proverb development, largely because of the change of context. Those who wrote down proverbs were the educated, the *literati*, the wise at the court of kings. Scribal collectors may have used proverbs developed originally in oral contexts for educational purposes, mainly in schools where young men would learn to read and write and train for positions in the court and state. This educational model clearly existed in Egypt, so it is plausible that it existed in Israel also, albeit on a smaller scale. The court of King Solomon, a king renowned for his wisdom and for the coining of proverbs, is one suggestion for an early context (ninth century BCE) for the development of written collections of proverbs, and this king is mentioned in superscriptions in the book of Proverbs (1.1; 10.1). Another possibility, not exclusive of the first, is the court of King Hezekiah (ninth century BCE), who is mentioned in Prov. 25.1. This kind of WRITING down probably occurred over a long period of time, and may have found a fresh context during and after the exile in the family unit (see Camp 1985). Arguably, the family unit was always a source of proverbial activity in the oral stage (e.g. the references to teaching by father and mother in Prov. 1.8), but it probably endured and gained fresh momentum in later contexts after the collapse of the Jerusalem monarchy and its court.

There are debates about whether 'one-limbed' sayings that involve no contrast (e.g. Prov 14.10) subsequently gave way to two-limbed (the majority) and three-limbed sayings that contrast two like or unlike phenomena. In this model, the more complex, multi-lined sayings that appear in the book of Proverbs were essentially a literary phenomenon rather than a product of ORALITY (McKane). However, the balance of probability lies with the opposite scenario, with elements of catchword and wordplay serving as magnets for drawing otherwise dissimilar proverbs together.

One interesting question is how individual sayings came to form larger clusters and then whole sections of literary collections (Heim). The biblical book of Proverbs is put together in sections, with an introduction in chapters 1–9 that contains few proverbs but more theological profundity; a major sayings section (10.1–22.16) made up of a miscellany of sayings and topics; a section (22.17–24.22) that contains sayings which closely parallel the structure of an Egyptian prototype, the Instruction of Amenemope (which was used in educational circles to teach reading and writing); a further section of sayings, often including repeats (chapters 25–29); and, finally, some short, individually ascribed sections (chapters 30–31). Within the main sayings collections it is hard to find thematic clusters; the topics seem very mixed. There are small thematic sections, e.g. 16.10-15 on the king, but there is also the sense of a very jumbled whole, which would fit a largely oral origin. The proverbs have a wide thematic spread, including everything from advice on table manners at court to observations on how lazy people prefer to spend the whole day in bed. Proverbs on table manners are more likely to have a courtly origin rather than a more general societal one, given that only courtiers would need to worry about table manners in front of the ruler (Prov. 23.1). There are a number of king sayings, especially warning against inciting the anger of the king, which can lead to bad consequences (Prov. 16.14).

A related question is the role of redactors in bringing clusters together. In particular, are the references to God/the Lord and the fear of the Lord in Proverbs an original aspect of the individual proverbs themselves, or are they a later addition by a pious redactor who wished to bring the collection into line with more theological parts of the canon? There is a cluster of 'God proverbs' in Prov. 15.25–16.1, but explicitly theological references are often sprinkled among proverbs on other topics. Were the proverbs then originally without such divine reference? In a culture in which there was no split between the secular and the religious worldviews, such a division seems false. It is likely that mention of God is more primary, harking again from the earlier oral stage.

When addressing the development of individual proverbs and literary collections, it is helpful to speak of an oral/literary continuum (see Niditch 1996). It is not as if an entirely oral culture suddenly gave way to a completely literary one. Rather, the process was probably piecemeal and took place over a long period of time. It is because we have a book of Proverbs that we can see it as a finished whole, but until the time of the fixation of the book in a canon, the process of collection and placing into the present literary context was probably a fluid one. The cumulative wisdom of these proverbs leads Proverbs to feature the more developed theological idea of a path to Wisdom (represented by a female figure in Proverbs 8) which is contrasted with a path to Folly (represented by a prostitute or foreign woman). This epitomizes the element of choice contained in each proverb – these are choices that ultimately determine whether one is on the path to 'life' or to 'death'. The educational task is at the heart of reciting and writing proverbs – young people need to learn right from wrong through the accumulated experience of their elders. Such wisdom is enshrined in each and every proverb, formulated to make a witty observation or a moral point, to be memorable but also to be acted upon in dealings with others in everyday life.

Katharine J. Dell (University of Cambridge, USA)

Further Reading

Camp, Claudia V. 1985. *Wisdom and the Feminine in the Book of Proverbs.* Sheffield: Almond Press.

Dell, Katharine J. 2006. *The Book of Proverbs in Social and Theological Context.* Cambridge: Cambridge University Press.

Fontaine, Carole. 2002. *Smooth Words: Women, Proverbs and Performance in Biblical Wisdom.* LHBOTS 356. London: T&T Clark.

Golka, Friedemann. 1993. *The Leopards' Spots: Biblical and African Wisdom in Proverbs.* Edinburgh: T&T Clark.

Heim, Knut M. 2001. *Like Grapes of Gold Set in Silver: Proverbial Clusters in Proverbs 10:1-22:16.* BZAW 273. Berlin and New York: Walter Mouton de Gruyter.

McKane, William. 1970. *Proverbs: A New Approach.* Old Testament Library. London: SCM.

Niditch, Susan. 1996. *Oral World and Written Word: Ancient Israelite Literature.* Louisville: Westminster John Knox.

Witherington III, Ben, 1994. *Jesus the Sage: The Pilgrimage of Wisdom.* Minneapolis: Fortress Press.

Psalms in Worship The biblical psalms have nurtured the public and private faith of Jews and Christians through the centuries, yet we have almost no knowledge of how they were originally used. In searching for evidence, the best place to start is actually outside the Psalter, looking at both archaeological data and the biblical witness. The NT, the MISHNAH, and EARLY CHRISTIAN LITERATURE together show that the psalms, whose poetic medium allows for great freedom of interpretation, had become the backbone of both Jewish and Christian prayer and WORSHIP by the fifth century CE.

A number of important artefacts and paintings from the ancient Near East portray figures singing, playing musical instruments, DANCING, and moving in procession. At Ur in Mesopotamia, archaeologists have discovered pipes, rattles, and drums dating as early as the second millennium BCE (see MUSIC). A seventh-century BCE alabaster relief from Nineveh (Assyria) shows four figures playing a tambourine, cymbals, and two kinds of lyre. In Egypt, the walls of the tombs in which Pharaohs of the New Kingdom were buried frequently depict harpists and musicians playing silver and bronze trumpets. Similarly, the thirteenth-century BCE Abydos Stele portrays a ritual procession of women playing tambourines with a female harpist at the rear.

Archaeological evidence from Syro-Palestine includes, for example, a twelfth-century BCE painting on an ivory handle from Megiddo of a figure playing a lyre; an eleventh-century BCE ceramic incense stand from Ashdod of a singer and four other figures playing the lyre, drums, cymbals, and double pipe; and, a fifth-century BCE terracotta figure from Achsiv of a woman playing a tambourine.

The Use of Psalms in the Hebrew Bible and Other Jewish Sources

Because the culture of the Bible cannot be set apart from that of the ancient Near East at large, biblical references to ritual/liturgical performance should be understood in light of the archaeological record. No images of ancient worship exist from sites in ancient Israel, but the Bible speaks of women dancing and playing tambourines (Exod. 15.20-21; Judg. 11.30-40; 1 Sam. 18.6-7) and of cultic prophets using musical instruments to evoke ecstatic experience (e.g. 1 Sam. 10.5). Similarly, references in the book of Psalms to musical instruments and cultic processions (e.g. Ps. 47.5-7; 81.1-3; 150.1-6; 68.24-27; 132.8-10) should be understood as describing the music and rituals that accompanied the words themselves.

While it seems clear that the Psalms refer to liturgical activities, the challenge is determining precisely what kind of liturgical activity is being described. Israelite religion and its liturgy developed over three very different historical contexts, and the 150 psalms included in the biblical book of Psalms must belong to one of these. During the earliest period (ca. 950–587 BCE), during the monarchy and before the destruction of the TEMPLE OF JERUSALEM by the Babylonians, the psalms served a developing 'state religion', and thus emphasize themes relating to Israel's king, national enemies (e.g. 2, 20, 21, 72, 89, 110 and 132) and God's protection of Zion (46, 48). These psalms may have been used for state occasions, accompanied by music and dance. During the second period, that of the 'templeless cult' during the period in which the people were taken into exile in Babylon (587–520 BCE), all that was left of psalmody was the act of singing in memory of the past. Psalms such as 137 likely reflect this period. The third period began with the restoration of the temple in ca. 520 BCE and ended with its destruction by the Romans in 70 CE. Throughout the majority of this period, the Israelites were under the foreign rule of the Persians, the Greeks, and then the Romans, and during this time the psalms would not only have been used for communal worship but also for individual prayer. On the latter, Psalms 1 and 119 are good examples of psalms composed for more private reflection. Throughout this period, many psalms would have accompanied music and ritual, especially in the Jerusalem temple. In diaspora communities, which worshipped regularly in SYNAGOGUES far away from Jerusalem and its rituals, the psalms would usually have been read and sung without any elaborate musical or ritual accompaniment.

If individual psalms were sung and recited in different liturgical occasions, is there other biblical evidence that can point to their use? The Torah may seem like an obvious source of information, but here there are difficulties. The three main Law codes (Exod. 20.23–23.9; Deut. 12–26; and the priestly codes in Exod. 21–31, 35–40, Lev. 1–27, and Num. 1–10), discuss SABBATH-keeping, annual festivals, sacrifice, and the priesthood, but these legal texts do not mandate the performance of psalms. At the same time, the Psalter expresses little interest in any of this cultic legislation: the only obvious reference to Sabbath appears in the superscription over Psalm 92, and there are no explicit references to festivals such as Passover or Tabernacles. References to specific sacrifices stipulated in the Torah are also minimal: for example, a frequent technical term, *minḥâ*, is used only in Pss. 72.10 and 90.8. Unlike the legislation in the Torah, the Psalter tells us little about how animal sacrifices might have been used, and at times actually seems to minimize their significance. For example, psalms about guilt and penitence seem to reject the idea of sacrifice (40.5-8; 51.16-17; 141.2) and some (often called 'songs of thanksgiving') refer instead to spiritual sacrifices (Pss. 40.5,8; 50.14-15; 69.30-31; 116.17-19). Further, the Psalms say almost nothing about priestly mediation: Aaron is remembered in just eight psalms (77, 99, 105, 106, 115, 118, 133, 135), and the only other priest to be honoured is Melchizedek (Ps. 110:4), who is not even of Israelite ancestry. The Psalms do mention temple singers, for example the guilds of Korah (42–49; 84; 85; 87; 88), and Asaph (50; 73–83), and Ethan (89). Overall, whereas the Torah is concerned with the rituals of liturgy, the Psalter focuses on the words themselves, through prayer and song.

1 Chronicles 16 offers important insights here. Probably written some seven centuries after the time it narrates, this text ascribes specific psalms to the occasion when David moved the Ark of the Covenant to Jerusalem. Four psalms from the Psalter are cited (1 Chron. 16.8-22//Ps. 105.1-15; 1 Chron. 16.22-33// Ps. 96.1-13; 1 Chron. 16.34//Pss. 106.1 and 136.1; 1 Chron. 16.35-36//Ps. 106.46-47), suggesting that the Chronicler is describing how psalms such as these would have been sung at public occasions during his own time. The presence of Levitical singers in the narrative (1 Chron. 15.11–16:6) also confirms references to their role in the Psalms.

The destruction of the temple and its liturgy in 70 CE had a profound effect on the use of the psalms. As a sign of mourning for the loss of the temple, some later rabbinic authorities forbade musical instruments and others even forbade the singing of psalms, advising that they should only be read instead. Nevertheless, public reading of psalmody was a vital and important part of synagogue practice, with certain psalms allotted to specific days of the week and to particular liturgical occasions.

One extra-biblical Jewish source that provides important information about the use of psalms in Jewish worship is the Mishnah. This is a much later compendium of rabbinic legal material (late second century CE or later), but it may well preserve traditions from the Second Temple period (pre-70 CE). Like the Torah, the Mishnah is primarily concerned with cultic legislation, indicating, for example, that certain psalms were to be used on Sabbath days (Psalms 19, 33, 90, 91, 92, 93, 135, 136, 145–150), or at annual festivals (e.g. Psalms 113–118 for Passover). Even here, like the Chronicler, the Mishnah may well point to uses of these texts some centuries after the Psalter as a whole was compiled. One strand of continuity is seen in the references to the prominence of the Levitical singers. *Tāmîd* 7.4 speaks of seven psalms (24, 48, 81, 82, 92, 93, 94) that were supposedly sung by the Levites at the daily sacrifices of the temple; *Pĕsāḥîm* 5.7 states the Levites sang the Hallel psalms (113–118) during Passover; in *Bikûrîm* 3.4, the Levites sing Psalm 30; and, in *Sukâ* 5.4 and *Midôt* 2.5 the Levitical singers are described as reciting the Songs of Ascents (120–134) on the fifteen steps of the temple.

The Use of Psalms in the NT and Other Christian Sources

While the NT is much older than the Mishnah, it obviously also emerged from a period after the Psalter was compiled. This is evident from the fact that the NT authors cite the Septuagint version of the Psalms, which was itself produced in the second century BCE. The NT suggests that psalms were sung by early Christians (Eph. 5.19; Col. 3.10) but provides little clear evidence on the specifics of how they were used. Luke 1 and 2 include texts that imitate the biblical psalms composed for personal use, and Rev. 18–22 also uses the language of psalmody to describe the singing of a heavenly choir. Therefore, although the role of the Levitical singers disappears from Christian worship, it is clear that the singing of psalms, probably to musical accompaniment, still played a vital role.

In later Christian reception, the first two centuries of the church also offer very little evidence of musical accompaniment in worship, perhaps as a counter to pagan practices. Even as late as the fourth century CE, Ambrose of Milan, although well known for promoting the chanting of psalms, nevertheless advised that singing should sometimes be a private affair in defiance of pagan revelries at BANQUETS with their wine, music, and song (*Exposition on Psalm* 118 xix, 32). At the same time, and corresponding to evolving Jewish practices, set hours for prayer began to emerge in church practice and particular psalms were prescribed for these. For example, Psalm 141 became associated with evening prayer and Psalm 63 with morning prayer. In the fifth century CE, Pseudo-Chrysostom observes that psalms were memorized, prayed, and sung everywhere, by clergy and lay, educated and illiterate alike. 'David is first, middle and last … in the singing of early morning hymns … in the tents of funeral processions … in the houses of virgins … in the fields and deserts … in the monasteries … the convents … David is first and middle and last … David alone stands by, turning earth to into heaven and making angels of men' (*On Repentance*, taken from *Patrologia Graeca*, LXIV, 12-13).

The Psalms in Corporate and Personal Liturgy

What, then, are the implications of this brief survey of psalmody for modern understandings of the place of psalms in worship? Several key points may be cited.

The first and most obvious point is that the poetic medium of the psalms has created a great freedom in the way they can be used. This is evident in the way that individual psalms were composed for different worship settings and, later, in the ways they were adapted for use in Jewish and Christian liturgy and private devotion. Within the Bible, psalms sometimes accompanied sacrificial rituals, and at other times they were independent of them. Outside the Bible, psalms sometimes were sung and accompanied by music, but at other times they were read and used as public and private prayers. As noted above, while it is clear that the psalms played a key role in ancient Jewish and Christian prayers and hymnody, it is currently impossible to know precisely how they were used in worship. At the same time, however, the fact that these texts have survived so many vicissitudes and that they are still, next to the Gospels, the most popular book of the Bible to be read and used today suggests that they have a common universal appeal. Through the medium of poetry they speak of a shared human experience that overrides the particularities of their ancient origins (see POETRY IN THE HEBREW BIBLE).

A second important point to note is that Jews and Christians have read and used, and always will read and use, the psalms in distinctive ways. David (and to some extent, Moses) is an important lens in Jewish approaches to the psalms, while Christ is the lens through which Christians approach them. This calls for mutual appreciation between faith traditions, rather than negation, and should make us more aware of 'the other'.

A third point is to see just how much the ongoing liturgical appropriation of the psalms in each faith tradition has produced a vast array of aesthetic responses. One example may be taken from artistic representations of themes from the psalms, especially in illuminated MANUSCRIPTS dating from the ninth to fifteenth centuries CE. Another example, again arising from the link of psalmody to worship, is the prolific number of musical arrangements of psalms. The fifteenth and sixteenth centuries CE bear testimony to the many ways in which the psalms inspired the creative spirit, whether in psalms still in Latin composed for the royal courts or psalms in the vernacular set in metrical rhythm and paraphrased in rhyme. Whether through art, music, or poetic imitation, there are many ways we can appreciate the reception history of the psalms through the ages.

Overall, modern readers need to be better versed in psalmody in order to appreciate the origin of the biblical psalms and their historical place(s) in Jewish and Christian worship and devotion. Jewish rabbis and

Christian monks and nuns through the ages have known the entire Psalter (whether in Hebrew or in Latin) by heart. It is no cliché to observe that the more we read the psalms, the more we will remember, and the more we remember, the greater their impact will be on our hearts and minds.

Susan Gillingham (University of Oxford, UK)

Further Reading

Eaton, John. 1984. *The Psalms Come Alive: Capturing the Voice and Art of Israel's Songs*. Downers Grover, IL: InterVarsity Press.

Gillingham, Susan E. 2008. *Psalms through the Centuries*. Oxford: Wiley-Blackwell.

Gorali, Moshe. 1993. *The Old Testament in Music*. Jerusalem: Maron Publishers Ltd.

Holladay, William L. 1993. *The Psalms through Three Thousand Years*. Minneapolis, MN: Augsburg.

Human, Dirk. 2011. 'Cultic Music in the Ancient Orient and in Ancient Israel/Palestine.' *Verkündigung und Forschung* 56: 45–51.

Keel, Othmar. 1978. *The Symbolism of the Biblical World: Ancient Near Eastern Iconography and the Book of Psalms*. Translated by Timothy J. Hallett. New York: Seabury Press.

Stapert, Calvin. 2007. *A New Song for an Old World. Musical Thought in the Early Church*. Grand Rapids: William B. Eerdmans.

Wieder, Laurence, ed. 1995. *The Poets' Book of Psalms. The Complete Psalter as Rendered by Twenty-Five Poets from the Sixteenth to the Twentieth Centuries*. New York and Oxford: Oxford University Press.

Publication (in antiquity) The act of WRITING and disseminating a literary text in the Greco-Roman world was a process involving at least three steps: composition, revision, and publication. Publication frequently involved retracing previous steps as a text was revised and disseminated among widening circles of acquaintances. It was also an activity with both social and private dimensions. Each step could include several participants beside the author and could be characterized by oral delivery, whereas copying and circulation frequently proceeded privately rather than through a commercial book trade.

Composition-Revision-Publication

The act of composing a first draft could take several forms. The most common procedure was for an author to dictate the text to a secretary, who turned it into a draft ready for revision. Some writers preferred to write in their own hand, however, and Quintilian urged his students to avoid 'the luxury of dictation' (*Institutes* 10.3.19) and thus compose better texts at a slower pace. Such autograph copies could become collectibles; Lucian mentions 500-year-old MANUSCRIPTS written by Demosthenes that were still in circulation (*The Ignorant Book-Collector* 4). LETTERS comprised the only literary GENRE that was written in the author's own hand with any level of frequency. Writers such as Cicero, Pliny the Younger, and Quintilian took pride in drafting their own correspondence.

The process of revision, which Quintilian deemed to be 'by far the most useful part of study' (*Institutes* 10.4.1), was regularly conducted in a social setting. The draft was read aloud, either by a LECTOR or the author himself, to a small group of gathered friends. These then discussed the text, gave their opinion, and suggested improvements. Pliny the Younger often held such readings for revision purposes and stresses that one should observe the reactions of the listeners, since 'facial expressions, eyes, nods, applause, murmurs, and silences' (*Letters* 5.3.9) reveal their true opinions. The revision could also take place in a more confined setting, in which a lector or a secretary read the rough draft aloud for the author, who decided upon changes and additions that the servant included in a new draft. In most cases, authors remained in control of a text during the revision process and did not distribute copies. Occasionally, however, they sent the draft of a work in progress to a friend and asked for his or her opinion, which could result in it being copied and circulated without the consent of the author. To Cicero's fury (*Letters to Atticus* 13.21a), Atticus, a close friend, once forwarded such a draft to a mutual friend.

Although it is rarely possible or even relevant to identify a single publication event for an ancient literary writing, circulation of a text in a circle wider than the author's close friends functioned as its 'release'. Such circulation was frequently communal in character. Authors had copies made and disseminated them through personal and social networks. They could also stage public recitals to make the composition (and themselves) known. Herodotus is said to have made a name for himself by reading his *Histories* aloud during the Olympic Games, and Lucian commented that this case proved the impact of public recitals as 'the short-cut to glory' (*Herodotus* 1–3). Some authors deposited a copy in a public LIBRARY or with a book dealer, from which strangers could access it and have copies made. Publication thus meant that the author irrevocably had let the text out of his/her control. The first disseminated version continued in circulation even if the author revised it further. Someone could also distribute a text based on previous oral delivery – Quintilian, for example, found that some of his oral lectures on RHETORIC had been published by his students, albeit in his name (*Institutes* 1, preface, 7). Such instances accentuate that it is not always relevant to point to a single ORIGINAL text in antiquity.

Authorship and Publication in Early Christianity

Early Christian writings spread more rapidly and over wider areas than many other literary writings in antiquity. Texts were circulated through networks of individuals and communities, in which they were copied and read aloud. The steps of composing, revising, and publishing are evidenced in early Christian sources. Paul seems to have dictated his letters to a secretary, but he also added sections in his own hand (1 Cor. 12.21; Gal. 6.11; Phlm. 19; cf. Col. 4.18; 2 Thess. 3.17). The letters were then 'published' by being received and read aloud in the communities to which they were addressed, and spread into wider circles by being copied, forwarded, and read aloud in other early Christian communities. The Shepherd of Hermas describes how the publication of a Christian literary writing could have taken place: 'You shall write two small book rolls and send one to Clement and one to Grapte. Clement will send his to the foreign cities, since he is permitted to do so, and Grapte will admonish the widows and the orphans. But you shall read it aloud in this city together with the elders who have been put in charge over the community' (*Visions* 2.4.3). Public reading in the local community as well as distribution of written copies to other communities through networks of Christians thus played a role in the publication of early Christian writings.

Dan Nässelqvist (University of Gothenburg, Sweden)

Further Reading

Gamble, Harry Y. 1995. *Books and Readers in the Early Church: A History of Early Christian Texts*. New Haven: Yale University Press.

Haines-Eitzen, Kim. 2013. 'The Social History of Early Christian Scribes.' In *The Text of the New Testament in Contemporary Research: Essays on the Status Quaestionis*. Edited by Bart D. Ehrman and Michael W. Holmes. New Testament Tools, Studies, and Documents 42. Leiden: Brill, pp. 479–96.

Hurtado, Larry W. 2014. 'Oral Fixation and New Testament Studies? "Orality," "Performance," and the Reading of Texts in Early Christianity.' *NTS* 60: 321–40.

Hurtado, Larry W., and Chris Keith. 2013. 'Writing and Book Production in the Hellenistic and Roman Periods.' In *The New Cambridge History of the Bible: From the Beginnings to 600*. Edited by James Carleton Paget and Joachim Schaper. Cambridge: Cambridge University Press, pp. 63–80.

Nässelqvist, Dan. 2015. *Public Reading in Early Christianity: Lectors, Manuscripts, and Sound in the Oral Delivery of John 1–4*. NovTSup 163. Leiden: Brill.

Starr, Raymond J. 1987. 'The Circulation of Literary Texts in the Roman World.' *Classical Quarterly* 37: 213–23.

Purification Rituals The purification rituals described in the Hebrew Bible are cultic actions, primarily ablutions, that remove ritual impurity from persons and objects in Israel. According to the priestly traditions, ritual impurity stems from particular conditions of the human body, including death, scale disease, and sexual discharges (Lev. 11–15). The purpose of these rituals is primarily to protect the sanctuary; consequently, anyone affected by impurity is ineligible for participation in cultic WORSHIP and must first purify themselves. Archaeologists confirm the reality of this phenomenon by the large number of ritual baths found in close proximity to the JERUSALEM TEMPLE mount. While the primary concern of the priestly purification rituals is cultic, according to Deuteronomy, the people of Israel form a holy people (Deut. 7.6). Thus, purification rituals are meaningful even without the presence of the temple (4Q174 1.6; 1 Cor. 6.19). In Second Temple times, many Jews (e.g. Essenes, Pharisees) washed before meals as if they were eating holy food.

Broadly speaking, rituals are a way of expressing group values and constraining social behaviour and there is often a rich density of meaning behind them (Bell 1997: 81–2). Ritual purification is universally associated with death and rebirth. Jacob Milgrom uses this insight to uncover symbolism behind ritual purification in the Hebrew Bible (1991: 766–8, 960–2). First, the corpse is the most potent impurity bearer; it cannot be purified and those who touch it require ritual purification. Second, scale disease, with its visual deterioration of the body, seems to reflect the dead among the living and thus the person is excluded from human habitation. Third, sexual discharges not only concern the loss of life-giving fluids but, along with death, they emphasize the contrast between human mortality and the divine essence, which shares no sexual processes and is not subject to the life/death cycle. Water is the universal cleanser and works well as a symbolic purgative for what is unacceptable on the metaphysical level (e.g. 'Wash me and I shall be whiter than snow', Ps. 51.7b). Contact with water brings dissolution, fertilization and regeneration. Thus, the forces of impurity and death threaten to overcome the people of holiness and life, but through ritual purification Israel removes hindrances to divine access and expresses hope in the life-giving Creator.

Later Jewish and early Christian texts continue to associate purification with life. NT authors compare Jesus' gift of eternal life to 'living water', a strong purgative in the cultic system (Jn 4.14; 7.37-39; Rev. 7.17; 21.6; cf. Lev. 14.5; Num. 19.17). For the MISHNAH, the most effective ablutions are performed in 'living water' or that which derives directly from a natural, God-given source (e.g. rain, a spring) and has not been subject to human intervention (*m. Miq.* 1.8; *Sifra shemini sheratzim* 9.1; 11.7). Archaeology has confirmed that ritual baths were supplied by rain and sometimes adjoining reservoirs.

Ritual is both symbolic and operative. In addition to the simple reincorporation of a temporarily impure individual into the community, ritual purification can also initiate an individual into a new status (Turner 1977: 36–52). In the priestly texts of the Hebrew Bible, priests and Levites are also ritually purified when they are inaugurated into service (Lev. 8.6; Num. 8.6-7). Among the Essenes, the borders of group IDENTITY were marked, reinforced, and penetrated by ritual ablutions. A member of lower standing would defile a superior simply by touching him (Josephus, *War* 2.150). After the first year of training the Essene novitiate is 'made a partaker of the waters of purification' although still not fully integrated into the community (Josephus, *War* 2.138). According to the Talmud, proselytes enter Judaism through ritual ablutions, CIRCUMCISION and sacrifice (*b. Ker.* 8b).

In many cases, ritual purification was performed in order to invite supernatural activity. The classic example is the ablutions Israel performs before receiving the Sinaitic revelation (Exod. 19.14). In some Second Temple texts, the penitent immerses in water as a plea for forgiveness (Life of Adam and Eve 6–7; *Sibylline Oracles* 4.165–68; Test. Levi 18.7). According to the Community Rule, new members are cleansed by their humble repentance and purification in cleansing waters (1QS 3.6–9). The act of immersion expresses the need for divine grace and spiritual renewal by putting the individual's prayer into physical form.

The anticipated supernatural activity sought during ritual ablutions was not limited to atonement. While standing in the water during his BAPTISM, Jesus experiences divine manifestation and affirmation of his ministry (cf. Mt. 3.16-17). The Dead Sea sect required superogatory purifications in order to retain angels for the eschatological battle (1Q28a 2.3–11; 1QM 7.3-6; cf. 1QH 19.10–14). Essenes purified themselves in expectation of prophetic revelation (Josephus, *War* 2.159). Nevertheless, like Leviticus, most Jewish texts focus on the correctness of the ritual rather than on its supernatural benefits. The rabbis, in fact, express concern that these rituals will be used as magical tools (*Num. R.* 19:4).

In early Christianity, ritual ablutions are both symbolic and initiatory. Christian BAPTISM functions not only to symbolize life and death with Jesus Christ but also identifies who is legitimately part of the community. John the Baptist immerses those who would repent from sin and join his disciples (Mk 1.3-4), a process described by Josephus as 'joined together by means of baptism' (*Antiquities* 18.116–17). Paul asserts that baptism is the mechanism for putting off the old sinful creature and 'putting on Christ' (Gal. 3.27; cf. Rom. 6.4; Tit. 3.5).

Hannah K. Harrington (Patten University, USA)

Further Reading

Baumgarten, Joseph M. 2006. 'The Law and Spirit of Purity at Qumran.' In *The Bible and the Dead Sea Scrolls: The Second Princeton Symposium on Judaism and Christian Origins. II. The Dead Sea Scrolls and the Qumran Community*. Edited by James Charlesworth. Waco: Baylor University Press, pp. 93–168.

Bell, Catherine. 1991. *Ritual: Perspectives and Dimensions*. Oxford: Oxford University Press.

Milgrom, Jacob. 1991. *Leviticus 1–16.* AB 3. New York: Doubleday.

Turner, Victor. 1977. 'Variations on a Theme of Liminality.' In *Secular Ritual*. Edited by Sally F. Moore and Barbara G. Myerhoff. Assen: Van Gorcum, pp. 36–52.

Q

'Q' (The Sayings Source) Within the Two-Source Hypothesis approach to the solution of the Synoptic Problem, 'Q' is the name given to the second major source (the Gospel of Mark being the first) utilized by the authors of the Gospels of Matthew and Luke. Thus, Q is generally understood as designating the so-called *double tradition* material common to Matthew and Luke that is not found in Mark. Most of this material, though there are a few notable exceptions, is sayings material. The name *Q* is drawn from the German word *Quelle*, meaning 'source'. In the history of research, in addition to the simple designation Q, one also finds scholars referring to this source with terms such as *Logienquelle* ('Sayings Source'), SAYINGS GOSPEL, or *Halbevangelium* ('Half-Gospel').

When considering Q within its ancient media environment, three issues are of particular relevance. The first of these is the question of whether one should consider the Q source as a set of ORAL TRADITIONS, a written document, or some combination of oral and written traditions. Armin D. Baum, for example, contends that the Q material should not be traced back to a written sayings collection, but rather to a relatively flexible oral tradition. James D. G. Dunn and Terence C. Mournet, though not presenting a purely oral paradigm for Q, have nevertheless questioned the assumption that the entirety of the Q material was accessed by Matthew and Luke in written form. They have been particularly concerned with the manner in which our post-Gutenberg world of scholarship has been shaped by a literary paradigm that inclines towards viewing all sources as written sources. Nevertheless, most Q scholars remain convinced that Q was a written document based upon the concurrence of Matthew and Luke in verbal and sequential aspects in the double tradition. As John Kloppenborg points out, these similarities include the almost verbatim agreement between Matthew and Luke in certain double tradition pericopae, the shared use of unusual words or phrases in double tradition material, and the significant sequential agreement in portions of the double tradition.

If one follows the majority scholarly view that Q, at least in part, was a written document, the second significant issue relates to the medium through which Q was transmitted. Taking up the suggestion of Ulrich Luz and Migaku Sato that Q should be envisioned as a type of *Ringbuch* (loose-leaf notebook), Robert A. Derrenbacker, Jr. has argued for the medium of Q being a proto-CODEX. Such a proto-codex could very well have functioned as an aide-memoire for its contents, and as such, Q, in both its medium and its function, would have occupied a transitional place in the developing JESUS TRADITION. Derrenbacker concludes that this type of written document should be located on a trajectory between orally transmitted logia and a written, narrative bios of Jesus. For this reason, the study of Q as a source for Matthew and Luke may allow unique insight into a written text functioning in the transitional space between oral and written traditions as classically conceived.

Finally, given that presently there are no material remnants of Q, and thus no MANUSCRIPT evidence for its wording or citations in early Christian literature, the third question to consider is the manner in which one seeks to access this document. The reigning paradigms in the study of Q have been built upon the principles of Source and Redaction Criticism and have led to attempts at ever-increasing precision regarding the written text of Q. This trend culminated in the extensive work and discussions of the International Q Project (published in a series of notices in the *Journal of Biblical Literature* from 1990 to 1997) and the publication of the *Critical Edition of Q* in 2000. Recently, however, some Q scholarship has revisited the challenges of reconstructing the Q source and have questioned our ability to do so, and even the necessity of doing so. Instead of approaching Q as a reconstructed text behind Matthew and Luke, perhaps it would be more fruitful to approach it as an intertext between Matthew and Luke. Ruben Zimmermann has observed that Q as an intertext remains a text, at least in the sense of a *textus* ('structure'), and that this textual structure is composed of narratival and metaphorical elements, both of which can be considered apart from a verbatim reconstruction of the source. The focus of this approach to Q falls upon the manner in which Matthew and Luke reflect the images, characters, PARABLES, preaching, and other aspects of Q. In other words, the study of Q may be able to move forward and beyond certain reconstruction impasses by analysing the figurative world, constellation of characters, or other narratival and metaphorical aspects through a literary, intertextual analysis of the Q source.

Dieter T. Roth (Johannes Gutenberg Universität Mainz, Germany)

Further Reading

Baum, Armin D. 2008. *Der mündliche Faktor und seine Bedeutung für die synoptische Frage: Analogien aus der antiken Literatur, der Experimentalpsychologie, der Oral Poetry-Forschung und dem rabbinischen Traditionswesen.* TANZ 49. Tübingen: Francke.

Dunn, James D. G. 2003. 'Altering the Default Setting: Re-envisaging the Early Transmission of the Jesus Tradition.' *NTS* 49: 139–75.

Kloppenborg, John S. 2000. *Excavating Q: The History and Setting of the Sayings Gospel.* Minneapolis: Fortress.

Mournet, Terence C. 2003. *Oral Tradition and Literary Dependency: Variability and Stability in the Synoptic Tradition and Q.* WUNT II/195. Tübingen: Mohr Siebeck.

Roth, Dieter T., Ruben Zimmermann, and Michael Labahn, eds. 2014. *Metaphor, Narrative, and Parables in Q.* WUNT 315. Tübingen: Mohr Siebeck.

Schröter, Jens. 1997. *Erinnerung an Jesu Worte: Studien zur Rezeption der Logienüberlieferung in Markus, Q und Thomas.* WMANT 76. Neukirchen-Vluyn: Neukirchener.

R

Rabbinic Literature Medium was a central theological concept for the ancient rabbis, and thus the question of biblical media has long occupied students of rabbinic Judaism. The early rabbis (*Tannaim*, 1st–3rd c. CE) were great champions of canonization and conservators of a written Hebrew Bible (*torah she bi-ktav*), but they also altered the landscape of the biblical by developing a notion of an unwritten/oral Torah (*torah she be'al peh*), understood to operate alongside the written text and expressly not to be written down. Oral Torah was, for them, a necessary component of their conception of the revealed Bible and came to sanction the written version's proper interpretation. In early rabbinic literature, the halting emergence of this notion (an idea that would not, according to Jaffee [2001], be fully articulated before the 4th c.) is evident in the landscape of competing biblical communities and in a world of vying written cultures.

Scripture and Canon

The earliest rabbinic literature emerges in the third century CE, and is part of a literary-religious landscape of increasingly scriptural communities. Rival communities with a shared authorizing Scripture (Torah) of necessity generated a range of strategies for reifying the central text, patrolling its boundaries, and authorizing its own elites as sole brokers of its meaning (see TEXT-BROKER). For many, the writtenness of Scripture was a key component of its claim to authority: it was written by God and transmitted by his most important prophets, priests, and deputies. The rabbis' own investment in the medium of Scripture is evident in a range of data, which cannot be easily separated from their work of canonization (see CANON). For example, the prominence of a fixed biblical text is evident in their regular use of citation formulas to introduce biblical verses. Such formulas are rare in Second Temple Jewish literature and signal the rabbis' evolving desire to prioritize the Bible in its scriptural form and make distinct their own voices in relationship to it. This distinguishes their literature from translations and paraphrases, among other strategies for Scripture-based literary development.

Also significant is the way the rabbis present Torah in their own writings. *Midrash* (rabbinic biblical interpretation) is especially useful in providing clues to the centrality of a fixed and written Scripture. The rabbis embed clearly marked biblical lemmas in interpretive frameworks that both highlight scriptural fixity and claim mastery over its meaning. In the excerpt below from a *midrash* on Deuteronomy (11.32), the italics indicate the biblical verse and the roman script the rabbinic interpretation. Rabbinic priorities insinuate themselves into the plain meaning of the verse and claim it unequivocally for their own sanctioned curriculum and pious regimen. In this example, in a verse ostensibly demanding unalloyed obedience to God's Law (written Torah), the rabbis interweave glosses according to which study and interpretation (oral Torah), under rabbinic aegis, set the terms for subsequent performance and obedience.

> *And ye shall observe* – this refers to study – *to do* – this refers to performance – *all the statutes* – these are the interpretations – *and the ordinances* – these are the regulations – *which I set before you this day* (Deut. 11:32) (*SifreDt* § 58, trans. Hammer)

The above example also illustrates how citation formulas serve to set the biblical lemma off from the commentarial apparatus and grant it special authority, even as the rabbis direct its interpretation. Despite the uniquely rigid distinction between Scripture and interpretation evidenced here, the end point, ironically, is that oral Torah blurs the line between text and interpretation. This highlighting of Scripture in its fixed writtenness was secondarily accomplished through language. Rabbinic literature occurs in a non-biblical set of languages: Mishnaic, Hebrew, and Aramaic. A keen ear would have heard clearly how the Hebrew of the rabbis differed from the Hebrew of the Bible (see CODESWITCHING).

Citation is a powerful tool in rabbinic canon formation in another way as well: the Torah (Pentateuch) was perhaps the most widely agreed upon set of books for early Jews, and by linking Torah citation with proof texts from more distant books (for example, Habakkuk and 2 Samuel below) the rabbis circumscribe a canonical library in practice.

> *The Lord is a Man of War, the Lord is His Name* (Exod. 15:3). … It also says (*va'omer*), *Draw out also the spear and battle axe* (Ps. 35:3). He appeared to them with bow and arrows, as it is said (*shene'amar*) Thy bow is made quite bare (Hab. 3:9). And it also says (*va'omer*), *He sent out arrows and scattered them* (2 Sam. 22:15) … . I might understand that He has any need of any of these measures, it therefore says *The Lord is His Name*. (*Mekhilta de-Rabbi Ishmael, Shirata 4*, trans. Lauterbach)

Proof-texting, in short, was a way to elevate a set of works (what we know as Prophets and Writings) to the level of Torah (which remained first among equals) – asserting a CANON through usage and effectively effacing or silencing a cadre of rival documents, some of which may well have had canonical claims or aspirations in their own right (i.e. ENOCH or JUBILEES, or even the SEPTUAGINT). It is worth noting that this work of fixing occurred in a world of biblical versions (see TEXT CRITICISM; Reeves 2010). The rabbis neither label extant canons nor simply freeze-frame a linear development, but instead actively choose and construct. Taking a more frontal approach, the rabbis also explicitly address the topic of the list of sanctified books (cf. *m. Yadayim* 5.5) and, in cognate measure, explicitly forbid all books not on their list (*m. Sanhedrin* 10.1).

The rabbinic categories of oral and written Torah, though ideologically vital, are themselves misleading. 'Written' Torah circulated in memory and voice while the 'Oral' Torah was in cases committed to writing. That said, concern for the materiality of the Torah made Scripture, despite being engaged largely orally and archived in memory, an iconic and obdurately written thing in rabbinic culture, and hand in hand with the centrality of a fixed written Scripture came attention to its iconic form. Perhaps the fullest example appears in the medieval tractate *Soferim*, which mandates every aspect of the production of the biblical SCROLL, from materials to margins. However, this thorough treatment is foreshadowed in the less systematic tannaitic corpus. The earliest rabbinic literature makes clear that the scroll as scroll was not like other material objects – it could render impurity, had distinctive sets of punishments tied to its abuse, and was the only text allowed to be read domestically on SABBATH. The obligation to save it from fire overrode Sabbath prohibitions against carrying, and the physical scroll appears prominently in the choreography of liturgical ritual (i.e. *m. Shabbat* 24.26–28; *m. Yoma'* 7.1; *m. Sotah* 7.8; see WORSHIP, JEWISH; TORAH READING). Certain fragments of text had amuletic power and animated ritual objects (*mezuzot* and *tefillin*) by being encased inside them.

Oral Torah

As noted above, *oral Torah* names a set of traditions that stand beside the written Torah. They are not identical to it, but share its authority. In its classic iteration, oral Torah was mythologized to have been revealed to

Moses on Sinai along with the written, and then handed down through chosen curators from that time until the rabbis themselves become its inheritors and generators (*m. Avot* 1.1). As concretized in the extant literary corpus, tannaitic oral tradition is preserved in a set of texts, the most important of which is the MISHNAH, a collection of laws arranged topically (ca. early third century CE). A cognate corpus known as the Tosefta preserves both later and earlier material arranged according to the Mishnah's ordering. In addition, there are lemmatic exegetical commentaries on the Torah known as the *halakakhic midrashim* connected to each of the Pentateuchal books excluding Genesis.

Oral Torah usefully blurs any line that might too facilely be drawn between *Bible* and *interpretation*, even as a biblical text becomes bounded and fixed. By claiming the written Torah was only part of God's full revelation, the notion of oral Torah allowed the rabbis to assert their control over revelation – and, in the process, their ownership of a Scripture that was claimed by a wide range of religious communities, both Jewish and, increasingly, Christian (Yuval 2011).

The apparent paradox that oral traditions come down to us in writing serves to point out the distinctive nature of rabbinic ORALITY. What is not distinct to the rabbis is that they lived and operated in an oral REGISTER for nearly all their scholarly work, as did intellectual elites throughout the ancient Mediterranean basin. They learnt, taught, recited, and analysed texts orally. This is as true for what they deemed the written Torah as it was for the oral Torah. As Jaffee (2001) notes, what is distinctive about oral Torah is not that it is oral, nor that the rabbis worked predominantly in oral media, but that they theorized orality explicitly and made medium an explicit ideological and theological priority. Oral Torah, in short, was not to be written down – it did not happen to be oral; it was so mandated.

Media Context

While the phenomenon of oral Torah becomes a distinguishing feature of rabbinic Judaism, it strongly reflects and responds to cultural patterns typical of the ancient Roman East. As one strategy in an atmosphere marked by a range of gestures towards canonization happening in other Jewish and nascent Christian communities, rabbinic oral Torah seems to draw from a number of cultural streams, prominent among them the apparently discordant drives of mimesis and separation. Oral Torah mirrors the educational and social organizations of Greek elite learning, especially philosophical and rhetorical education. Techniques of oral pedagogy, mastery, and performance are shared between certain Greek, Roman, and rabbinic learnt elite. In addition, the privileging of the master–disciple relationship, and the importance of teachers in authorizing genealogies, are practices shared between the rabbis and their Greek neighbours (Tropper 2005; Jaffee 2001; see EDUCATION, HELLENISTIC).

Yet while the structure of transmission shared cultural elements, it does in many cases the work of segregation. Oral Torah, especially as it pertained to its core concern, Law, may also have served as a particularly rabbinic recusal from the overwhelming textuality of the Roman East, and the expanding power of Rome in the early centuries of the Common Era (Woolf and König 2013; Dohrmann 2016). The cities in which the rabbis thrived were also characterized by a highly visible world of legal writing – the sages would have had much opportunity to encounter Rome in the form of legal writing, as the cities were literally plastered with posted decrees (Ando 2000) (see POMPEII). Written laws, publically displayed, in ARCHIVES, contracts, rescripts, and court, were common features of the landscape, and awareness of them was vital for successfully navigating everyday life. This legal urban space in stone, PAPYRUS, and PARCHMENT also signalled the incursion of Roman imperial power. An oral law could circulate both beneath the nose of Roman power and out of its sight.

Natalie B. Dohrmann (University of Pennsylvania, USA)

Further Reading

Ando, C. 2000. *Imperial Ideology and Provincial Loyalty in the Roman Empire*. Berkeley: University of California Press.

Bagnall, R. S. 2011. *Everyday Writing in the Graeco-Roman East*. Berkeley: University of California Press.

Dohrmann, N. B. 2016. 'Means and end(ing)s: Nomos versus narrative in early rabbinic exegesis.' *Critical Analysis of Law* 3: 30–49.

Dohrmann, N. B. 2015. 'Can "Law" be private? The mixed message of rabbinic oral law.' In *Public and Private in Ancient Mediterranean Law and Religion*. Edited by Clifford Ando and Jörg Rüpke. Religionsgeschichtliche Versuche und Vorarbeiten 65. Berlin: Walter Mouton de Gruyter, pp. 187–216.

Hezser, C. 2001. *Jewish Literacy in Roman Palestine*. Tübingen: Mohr Siebeck.

Jaffee, M. S. 2001. *Torah in the Mouth: Writing and Oral Tradition in Palestinian Judaism 200 BCE–400 CE*. Oxford: Oxford University Press.

Lapin, H. 2011. 'Epigraphical Rabbis: A reconsideration.' *JQR* 101: 311–46.

Naeh, S. 2008. 'The Script of the Torah in Rabbinic Thought, (a)' (Hebrew). *Leshonenu* 70: 125–41.

Reeves, J. C. 2010. 'Problematizing the Bible ... Then and Now.' *JQR* 100: 139–52.

Sussman, Y. 2005. '"Torah shebe'al peh": Peshutah ke-mashma'ah.' *Mehqerei Talmud* 3. Edited by Y. Sussman and D. Rosenthal. Jerusalem: Magness. 209–384.

Tropper, A. D. 2004. *Wisdom, Politics, and Historiography. Tractate Avot in the Context of the Graeco-Roman Near East*. Oxford: Oxford University Press.

Tropper, A. D. 2005. 'Roman Contexts in Jewish Texts: On Diatagma and *Prostagma* in Rabbinic Literature.' *JQR* 95: 207–27.

Yadin-Israel, A. 2004. *Scripture as Logos: Rabbi Ishmael and the Origins of Midrash*. Philadelphia: University of Pennsylvania Press.

Yadin-Israel, A. 2015. *Scripture and Tradition: Rabbi Akiva and the Triumph of Midrash*. Philadelphia: University of Pennsylvania Press.

Yuval, Y. I. 2011. 'The Orality of Early Jewish Law: From Pedagogy to Ideology.' In *Judaism, Christianity, and Islam in the Course of History: Exchange and Conflicts*. Edited by L. Gall and D. Willoweit. Munich: R. Oldenburg Verlag, pp. 237–60.

Woolf, Greg, and Jason König, eds. 2013. *Encyclopaedism from Antiquity to the Renaissance*. Cambridge: Cambridge University Press.

Ras Shamra Tell Ras Shamra, situated in northwestern Syria, contains the remains of the city of Ugarit, which flourished during the Middle and Late Bronze Age. It has become famous due to the excavations undertaken there since 1929, during which about 5000 clay tablets inscribed with WRITING were uncovered – one of the largest collections of documents currently known from antiquity. All in all, nine languages in five scripts are attested in the various Ras Shamra ARCHIVES. Among these tablets are the earliest West Semitic texts written in Ugaritic and in an alphabetic cuneiform script (see ORTHOGRAPHY). This alphabetic cuneiform is an invention of Ugaritic scholars that combines writing on clay tablets with the principle of an alphabetic script consisting of twenty-seven (thirty) consonants. The earliest cuneiform texts date to the middle of the thirteenth century BCE. Texts written in Ugaritic cuneiform have also been found outside the kingdom of Ugarit in Greece, Cyprus, Lebanon, Israel, and Syria.

The alphabetic cuneiform texts comprise different literary GENRES, including myths, epics, rituals, hymns, prayers, oracles and omen texts, LETTERS, legal and economic texts, lists, alphabets (see ABECEDARIES), medical texts, scribal exercises, and inscriptions on different objects. The texts written in Babylonian cuneiform are mostly letters, economical and juridical documents, and lexical lists.

Among the most important archives and LIBRARIES found are those in the Royal Palace, the House of the High Priest, the House of the Hurrian Priest, and the houses of Rashapabu and Urtenu. Of special interest is the House of the High Priest because its library was divided into two parts, with ritual texts housed in room 1 and tablets containing myths and epics in room 7. This indicates a clear separation of rituals on the one hand and myths and epics on the other, presumably due to the different uses and audiences of these texts.

The best known literary piece of Ugaritic mythology is the Baal cycle (KTU 1.1-1.6), which narrates how the weather god Baal defeated the sea god Yammu, built his royal palace, and defeated the god of the underworld, Motu. The Hebrew Bible contains some remnants of West Semitic mythological texts but no complete myths or epics (cf. e.g. Gen. 6.1-4; Job 37–41; Pss. 29, 48, 93, 104).

Since Ugarit was destroyed in 1185 BCE, it is difficult to establish any direct relationship between the Ras Shamra tablets and the Bible. Nevertheless, there is a continuity of civilization, literature, and religion between them. This becomes especially visible in the poetic sections of the Hebrew Bible (see POETRY IN THE HEBREW BIBLE) and, in a somewhat distorted manner, in its religious texts, which contain polemics against the deities Asherah, Baal, Reshep, and Mot.

Oral communication was, on the whole, dominant in the culture of Ugarit, with LITERACY restricted to the kingdom's upper and scribal classes. Myths and epics were fixed in written form on clay tablets that served as aides-memoire for recitals. Even the ritual texts limit themselves to the most essential information and refrain from giving detailed explanations on their execution/performance.

Herbert Niehr (Universität Tübingen, Germany)

Further Reading

Dietrich, Manfried, Oswald Loretz, and Joaquin Sanmartín. 2014. *Die keilalphabetischen Texte aus Ugarit, Ras Ibn Hani und anderen Orten*. AOAT 360/1. Münster: Ugarit-Verlag.

Niehr, Herbert. 1999. 'Zu den Beziehungen zwischen Ritualen und Mythen in Ugarit.' *Journal of Northwest Semitic Languages* 25: 109–36.

Olmo Lete, G. del. 1999. *Canaanite Religion according to the Liturgical Texts from Ugarit*. Bethesda, MD: CDL Press.

Pardee, Dennis. 2012. *The Ugaritic Texts and the Origins of West Semitic Literary Composition*. Oxford: Oxford University Press.

Smith, Mark S. 2001. *Untold Stories. The Bible and Ugaritic Studies in the Twentieth Century*. Peabody, MA: Hendrickson Publishers.

Reading culture Classicist William A. Johnson coined the phrase *reading culture*, as well as the similar term *reading community*, to emphasize that reading in the ancient context was primarily a social phenomenon rather than an individual phenomenon. Johnson was particularly reacting against a lengthy history of research concerning whether ancient people could read silently. Although affirming that ancient people did occasionally read silently, Johnson insisted that the amount of scholarly effort directed at this research question had missed the opportunity to ask larger sociological questions about ancient reading practices and the cultural realities in which they were located (Johnson 2010: 9). He thus advocated a shift in scholarly focus, stating: 'Reading is not, in my view, exclusively or even mostly a neurophysiological, cognitive act – not in fact an individual phenomenon, but a sociocultural *system* in which the individual participates' (2010: 11; emphasis original).

Working from this perspective, Johnson focused on ways in which aspects of ancient book culture were embedded in larger constructions of reality and identity among various ancient readers. Those aspects could range from the specific citation practices of obscure authors to the realia of ancient book culture. As one example, Johnson argued that certain features of ancient bookrolls/SCROLLS (see also CODEX and MANUSCRIPT), such as their usage of *scriptio continua* (no breaks between words), size of their margins, or costs of production, reflect their connection with the educated class. 'The bookroll seems … an egregiously elite product intended in its stark beauty and difficulty of access to instantiate what it is to be educated' (2010: 21).

Although Johnson primarily focused on elite literary culture in the high Roman empire (see LITERACY), his research has clear significance for the distinct reading cultures of Second Temple Judaism and early Christianity, among others, and scholars of Christian Origins have begun to apply his approach to these reading cultures. Larry Hurtado (2012), for example, has applied Johnson's approach to early Christian manuscripts, and Chris Keith (2015) has applied them to the textualization of the Gospel of Mark.

Chris Keith (St. Mary's University, UK)

Further Reading

Hurtado, Larry W. 2012. 'Manuscripts and the Sociology of Early Christian Reading.' In *The Early Text of the New Testament*. Edited by Charles E. Hill and Michael J. Kruger. New York: Oxford University Press, pp. 49–62.

Johnson, William A. 2010. *Readers and Reading Culture in the High Roman Empire: A Study of Elite Communities*. Classical Culture and Society. New York: Oxford University Press.

Keith, Chris. 2015. 'Early Christian Book Culture and the Emergence of the First Written Gospel.' In *Mark, Manuscripts, and Monotheism: Essays in Honor of Larry W. Hurtado*. LNTS 528. Edited by Chris Keith and Dieter T. Roth. London: Bloomsbury T&T Clark, pp. 22–39.

Realism Realism, in its simplest and most fundamental sense, refers to the belief that the world's qualities exist independent of how one perceives them. Anti-realism, by contrast, conceives the observer's perception of the world to be constructed by his or her own preconceptions, standpoints, problems, and interests. In the context of biblical media studies, the term *realism* may be used to define approaches to COLLECTIVE MEMORY and ORAL TRADITION that emphasize the rootedness of the content of tradition in events of the ACTUAL PAST. In this sense, *realism* contrasts with PRESENTISM/CONSTRUCTIONISM, which tends to view not only the form but also the content of memory primarily as a social construct.

Without qualification, both perspectives, realism and constructionism, lead to untenable theories of knowledge. Real entities and events cannot be known simply 'as they are' because different observers must perceive them in different ways. A house, for example, appears differently depending on whether one stands in front of it, behind it, or on the side of it, and all three views differ from that looking down from an airplane. Constructionist theories, however, are untenable because they annihilate reality by reducing it purely to the life situations in which it is conceived and imply the existence of multiple truths.

Realists deny that truth is relative to the manifold situations of life. There is only one truth – the entity as it is – but it takes the synthesis of different observations to grasp it. On the other hand, when treating unobservable entities, including ancient events and persons, realists cannot claim that knowledge depends exclusively on concrete entities inscribing themselves on the senses. Instead, they rely on evidential traces from which they draw what philosophers of science call 'inference to the best explanation'.

To no question in epistemology are realism issues more relevant than to the veracity of the Scriptures. For example, the writers of the Gospels may never have seen Jesus or witnessed his sermons and actions directly; rather, their knowledge reflected ideas about him that were produced and transmitted mainly by word of mouth. Obviously, the Gospel accounts are dependent upon, and artefacts of, the collective memories of Jesus among early Christians, not unmediated transcriptions of the actual past. Here the question is whether the oral communication of eyewitnesses passed on to non-witnesses can be treated as 'evidence' and, if so, in what sense. A realist view would tend to suggest that, while the Gospels obviously reflect the interpretive biases of their authors and their sources, their presentation of Jesus is in some way grounded in the actual past of his career. In fact, much of what we know of the past is based on precisely this transmission process, which, in BIRGER GERHARDSSEN's well-documented view, is more reliable than it might be today because of the common ancient practice of rote memorization, a practice required by oral tradition.

A realist approach to the Gospels would also consider ways that the assumed actual past is refracted through the different existing sources for Jesus, with a view to establishing their overall reliability and validity. The reliability of Gospel sources is indexed by several criteria, including agreement on what the four Evangelists independently attest (= ways that a common actual past has been shaped to reflect distinct commemorative interests). Similarly, the validity of Gospel content is indexed by its correspondence to oral tradition and external writings, including the Q source, the LETTERS and impressions of Paul, Tacitus, Pliny the Younger, Josephus, and the messianic and apocalyptic preoccupations of Jewish culture. From a realist perspective, historical authenticity is generally warranted by conformity to such external criteria.

Barry Schwartz (The University of Georgia, USA)

Register *Register* is a sociolinguistic term that refers to the different types of speech styles used by the same person in different social settings and, by extension, the major speech styles associated with recurrent types of situations. DELL HYMES made an important distinction between two types of language variation: 'Major speech styles associated with social groups can be termed variants, and major speech styles associated with recurrent types of situations can be termed registers' (Hymes 1974: 440). That is, linguistic variants may be due to historical change and/or regional dialects, but even people within the same social group may use different linguistic registers based on the social setting that they are participating in at any given moment. For example, lawyers speak differently when they are in the courtroom than when playing with their young children.

An important illustration of register appears in the work of Joel Sherzer, who reported on the linguistic varieties among the Kuna people of Panama and Colombia, identifying four formal registers within the language: 1) *tule kaya* (the person language), 2) *sakla kaya* (chief language), 3) *suar nuchu kaya* (stick doll language), and 4) *kantule kaya* (*kantule* language) (Sherzer 1983: 22). *Tule kaya* is the everyday Kuna register. *Sakla kaya* (chief language) is also called the 'gathering house language' or 'God's language' and refers to the 'chiefs' who know how to use this register in the context of making official decisions on behalf of the community. *Suar nuchu kaya* refers to the anthropomorphic figures that represent the spirit world of animals, plants, and other natural objects that communicate using this register to address the *ikar wismalat*, those human specialists who know how to use this register in their healing charms. *Kantule kaya* is named after the *kantule*, the women specialists who chant using this register in their roles as leaders in the puberty rites marking girls' transition to adulthood. Sherzer demonstrated the variation in vocabulary, phonology, morphology, and syntax among these four registers (see also SPECIAL GRAMMAR).

Drawing from linguistic studies by Hymes, Sherzer, RICHARD BAUMAN, and others, JOHN MILES FOLEY extended ALBERT LORD's understanding of the special grammar of ORAL TRADITIONS to describe an 'oral traditional register' (Foley 1995: 82–92). Foley defined oral traditional register as 'an idiomatic version of the language that qualifies as a more or less self-contained system of signification in the act of traditional oral performance' (Foley 1995: 15). Foley also noted that those features in the Parry-Lord approach to oral traditions – FORMULA, THEME, and STORY PATTERN – contribute to oral-traditional registers (Foley 1995: 52–3). Foley illustrated his understanding of oral traditional registers in discussions of Serbo-Croatian charms (1995: 110–15) and Homeric hymns (1995: 150–75) (see GUSLAR).

Foley's understanding of oral traditional register has had a significant influence in some discussions of biblical texts. For example, SUSAN NIDITCH concluded that, 'In the Hebrew Bible, traditional style or oral register emerges in the following features: (1) The presence of repetition … (2) The use of formulas and formula patterns to express similar ideas or images throughout the tradition. … (3) The use of conventionalized patterns of content that recur throughout the tradition' (1996: 10–11). Niditch illustrated these features in a variety of ways, including a discussion of the victory-enthronement pattern throughout the ancient Near East and how the creation imagery in Genesis 1, Genesis 2–3, and Ezekiel 28 are variations that required some familiarity with this pattern and its related oral register (see also PERFORMANCE ARENA; POETRY IN THE HEBREW BIBLE).

In the study of the NT, Rafael Rodríguez noted the utility of Foley's notion of register and illustrated this with a discussion of *ekballō* ('cast out') in Mark. 'In the Exodus tradition, *ekballō* summons the entire narrative of Israel's cries from Egypt, the confrontation between YHWH and Pharaoh, the escort out into the wilderness, and God's promise that he would clear the land as the people advanced. Mark taps this much larger narrative with extreme economy, indeed by simply using one unexpected word' (Rodríguez 2014: 93) (see METONYMY). This 'extreme economy' is possible only because of the word-power of words and phrases in an oral traditional register to recall metonymically larger components of the broader tradition (see METONYMY and COMMUNICATIVE ECONOMY).

Raymond F. Person, Jr. (Ohio Northern University, USA)

Further Reading

Foley, John Miles. 1995. *The Singer of Tales in Performance*. Bloomington: Indiana University Press.
Hymes, Dell. 1974. 'Ways of Speaking.' In *Explorations in the Ethnography of Speaking*. Edited by Richard Bauman and Joel Sherzer. Cambridge: Cambridge University Press, pp. 433–51, 473–4.
Niditch, Susan. 1996. *Oral World and Written Word: Ancient Israelite Literature*. Louisville: Westminster.
Rodríguez, Rafael. 2014. *Oral Tradition and the New Testament: A Guide for the Perplexed*. London: Bloomsbury T&T Clark.
Sherzer, Joel. 1983. *Kuna Ways of Speaking: An Ethnographic Perspective*. Austin: University of Texas Press.

Reputation *Reputation* refers to a person's publicly available persona, the Gestalt that enables individuals, groups, and whole societies to perceive, appraise, and evaluate that individual, whether or not they have ever directly encountered this person and sometimes across great historical or geographical distances. Reputation arises out of social interaction and the discursive efforts of 'entrepreneurs' who have invested themselves in establishing a particular image of a given person. A reputational entrepreneur is 'a self-interested custodian' (Fine 2001: 63) who proposes and defends a reputational narrative.

Broadly speaking, two factors contribute to the social construction and deployment of a person's reputation: 1) data, images, and narratives from the ACTUAL PAST of a person's life; and 2) the adaptation and application of these data, images, and narratives to express and/or address present needs and circumstances. The dynamics of a person's reputation are thus one specific application of Barry SCHWARTZ's model of 'keying/framing' as a function of COLLECTIVE MEMORY, according to which a reputation functions as both a model *of* and a model *for* the remembering community or society.

The texts of both the Hebrew Bible and the NT engage in reputational entrepreneurial processes, and extra-canonical texts engage, manipulate, extend, and/or transform the reputations of many of these same figures (e.g. Abraham, Enoch, Peter, or Paul). The analysis of reputational dynamics has the potential to illumine the social and historical significance of both famous and infamous figures from a group's past (historical as well as mythical).

The Formation of Reputation

Reputations depend on the efforts of interested agents to propose a particular image for the reputed individual. A person may function as his or her own reputational entrepreneur. However, others – friends, family, followers, opponents, etc. – often play a crucial role in determining a person's historical reputation. A reputational entrepreneur has two fundamental tasks: 'to propose early on a resonant reputation that is linked to the cultural logic of critical "facts" and then to make that image stick, diverting other interpretations' (Fine 2001: 78). Fine identifies three dynamics that are constitutive of the production and reception of a person's reputation: motivation, narrative facility, and institutional placement.

Motivation. Every historical event and figure is capable of multiple interpretations. Consequently, someone has to perceive the opportunity to advance their interest (or the interest of their larger group or society) by proposing or defending a particular interpretation of a given figure. As a figure's reputation becomes more controversial, the challenges involved in linking a reputational narrative to the larger cultural logic become more imposing. In such cases, continuing entrepreneurial efforts on behalf of a given reputation requires more motivation. For example, both Josephus (*War* 2.261–63; *Antiquities* 20.169–72) and Luke (Acts 21.38) mention an Egyptian who at one point enjoyed the reputation of 'a prophet' and led a large crowd out to the Mount of Olives. After Felix, the Roman procurator, attacked the crowd and the Egyptian fled, only one reputation would survive for this man: a 'false prophet' (Josephus) and rebel leader (Luke). Understandably, no one found sufficient motivation to counter this interpretation of the Egyptian's flight from Felix. At the same time, early Christians found sufficient motivation and resources to promote and maintain Jesus' messianic reputation even in the face of the circumstances of this death.

Narrative facility. As reputational entrepreneurs propose and/or defend a reputation, it must be sufficiently plausible to be convincing, both to the entrepreneurs and to their audience(s). Pontius Pilate affixed the notice of the charge against Jesus to the cross, lampooning the claim that this person might be (or be acclaimed) 'King of the Jews'. This charge, hung over this man's head, depended on the utter implausibility of this particular reputation for its rhetorical effect. Some historians still find it implausible that Jesus ever claimed any title or role similar to 'King of the Jews', though others counter that something about Jesus's message must have rendered it sufficiently plausible (to Pilate, at least) that Jesus and/or his followers made some such a claim on Jesus' behalf. Whether or not the historical Jesus – the Jesus of the actual past – made any such claims, his early followers redoubled their efforts to cast Jesus in royal hues, often in direct connection with his crucifixion (Rom. 1.3-4; Jn 18.36; Rev. 5.5-6; *Martyrdom of Polycarp* 9.3).

Institutional placement. Finally, the successful construction of reputation depends in some measure on the credibility of the reputational entrepreneur and their ability to facilitate the spread of a reputational narrative. This dynamic comprises two variables. First, successful reputational entrepreneurs must have (or must be able to convince others they have) plausible access to accurate information. Second, successful entrepreneurs must be able to disseminate a reputation to the public. A number of NT texts speak to this dynamic. The author of Luke does not claim to be an eyewitness to Jesus' life and teachings, but he has 'investigated everything carefully from the beginning' (plausible access) and he writes to Theophilus (dissemination; Lk.1.3). Luke also emphasizes the apostles' institutional placement. Despite being 'illiterate and uneducated', Peter and John spoke 'boldly' (dissemination) and 'had been with Jesus' (plausible access; Acts 4.13). The final form of the Fourth Gospel similarly claims direct access to eyewitness testimony (Jn 21.34).

In addition to the production and reception of reputational narratives, analyses of historical reputations consider how reputations function in social contexts. 'Reputations are not only *made*, they are *used*' (Fine 2001: 76). The debate about the source of Jesus' exorcistic prowess – whether from Beelzebul or from the finger/Spirit of God – provides one interesting example of the ideological manipulation of reputational narratives (Mk 3.22-27; Mt. 12.22-30; Lk. 11.14-23). Jesus' opponents did more than offer an alternative explanation of Jesus' power; they also advocated an alternative response to him. Jesus' followers were not merely interested in advocating a particular reputation for Jesus; they sought to establish the grounds for deciding other issues, including IDENTITY, the interpretation of Israel's Scriptures, the response to Roman political hegemony, etc. in reference to this understanding of his activity and message.

Rafael Rodríguez (Johnson University, USA)

Further Reading

Fine, Gary Alan. 2001. *Difficult Reputations: Collective Memories of the Evil, Inept, and Controversial*. Chicago: University of Chicago.

Fine, Gary Alan. 2012. *Sticky Reputations: The Politics of Collective Memory in Midcentury America*. New York: Routledge.

Rodríguez, Rafael. 2010. *Structuring Early Christian Memory: Jesus in Tradition, Performance, and Text*. ESCO/LNTS 407. London: T&T Clark.

Schwartz, Barry. 2000. *Abraham Lincoln and the Forge of National Memory*. Chicago: University of Chicago.

Schwartz, Barry. 2008. *Abraham Lincoln in the Post-Heroic Era*. Chicago: University of Chicago.

Reputational Entrepreneurs See Reputation.

Reworked Pentateuch *4QReworked Pentateuch* (4QRP) refers to a collection of five manuscripts found among the Dead Sea Scrolls in cave 4 at Qumran: 4Q158, 4Q364, 4Q365, 4Q366, and 4Q367. Scholars disagree about whether and to what extent the manuscripts are formally related, but recent studies indicate that the manuscripts are not individual copies of the same book (Bernstein 1998; Segal 2000; Brooke 2001; Zahn 2011). The contents of the manuscripts are generally consonant with the books of the Torah (Pentateuch), though they include numerous unique elements. Some manuscripts are similar to the Samaritan Pentateuch, sometimes even demonstrating a formal relationship with the Samaritan Pentateuch. But the 4QRP manuscripts also bring together disparate Torah material in new textual constructions far more freely than the Samaritan Pentateuch does. Unique readings in 4QRP are typically the product of rearrangements/harmonizations and expansions/additions. Four of the 4QRP manuscripts contain material from multiple books of the Torah, but only one (4Q365) contains material from all five books of the Torah. Meanwhile, 4Q367 has only material from Leviticus.

The 4QRP manuscripts might seem at first an unlikely locus for a major debate among Dead Sea Scrolls specialists, not least because they are highly fragmentary and many of their readings differ little from other copies of Pentateuchal books. But a close examination of the unique features of the texts reveals significant insights on how scriptural texts were written, edited, copied, and transmitted in the Late Second Temple period. Thus, the debates over categorizing 4QRP are really debates over the very nature of the 'biblical' texts in antiquity.

An example that helps to illustrate this point is found among the additional material of 4QRP (that is, material that is not found in any other form of the books of the Torah). The largest example is a set of instructions for a wood offering to be made at the temple (see 4Q365 23). These instructions form part of Leviticus 24 in 4Q365. No notice or formal exegetical markers are used by the scribe to draw attention to the new material. Indeed, the scribe's use of the literary formula, 'And YHWH spoke to Moses, saying', which is found throughout Leviticus, has the effect of camouflaging the addition. Put another way, the scribe responsible for the instructions about the wood offering clearly believed that the instructions were or should be a part of Leviticus.

Why was the material about the wood offering inserted by the scribe of 4Q365? Many scholars view the addition of the wood offering as a means by which a scribe 'corrected' the text of Leviticus in order to anticipate contemporary festival traditions. Following this reading, the addition aligns Moses' intentions/instructions with Hellenistic-era cultic procedures. We know from numerous sources that some form of a wood offering was envisioned as part of the normal operation of the temple cult (Neh. 10.35, 13.31; Jubilees 21; Temple Scroll 23–24; Josephus, *Jewish War* 2.425; *Meg. Ta'an.* 4.5). Should this unique material (and other similar examples) lead us to classify 4Q365 as something other than Leviticus?

Some scholars think ancient readers would have made a clear distinction between 4QRP and the text of Leviticus. But it is possible to point to more extensive textual additions within the medieval Masoretic manuscripts of Leviticus itself. Many scholars view Leviticus 17–26 (the Holiness Code) as a late addition to the core priestly stratum of Lev. 1–16. The addition of the Holiness Code to Leviticus seems to have served some of the same purposes as the addition of the wood offering passage found in 4Q365. For example, Lev. 16.7-10 contains provisions for the sacrifice of one goat to YHWH and one goat to Azazel (possibly a goat demon). This procedure appears to be corrected in order to account for contemporary concerns in Lev. 17.6-7, which explicitly forbids offering sacrifices to goat-demons. Thus, if the internal editorial/exegetical features within Leviticus are to be any guide, it is difficult to use additional material like the instructions for the wood offering in 4Q365 to categorize it as something other than a version of Leviticus.

The exegetical features of the text, however, may not be the only issues of concern for understanding 4QRP. Molly Zahn has analysed 4QRP in light of Michael Segal's criteria for discerning the difference between *biblical* and *rewritten biblical* texts (cf. Zahn 2008; Segal 2005) (see REWRITTEN SCRIPTURE). These categories include literary voice, scope, and coverage. Zahn shows that, just as the exegetical strategies found in 4QRP do not distinguish it from Leviticus, neither does the literary voice. For example, we may contrast the approach found in the 4QRP manuscripts with the approach found in the Temple Scroll, which modulates the literary voice of Deuteronomy from Moses to God himself (i.e. YHWH narrates the text in the first-person).

The related criteria of scope and coverage do appear to reveal differences between 4QRP manuscripts and the books of the Torah. Sadly, the fragmentary nature of the texts gives us a fractured view of their scope. It is impossible to know how 4QRP marked its beginning and its end. A similar situation applies to the coverage of the text. Just how much of what we now call 'the Pentateuch' was or could have been included in the 4QRP manuscripts? It strains the evidence to assume that 4QRP could have contained the majority of the contents found in all five Torah books (in more or less their form in the MASORETIC TEXT): the size of the SCROLL would be unprecedented by Qumran standards and vastly larger than the Temple Scroll. Overall, the state of the evidence currently disallows precise conclusions about what, exactly, 4QRP represents. One firm conclusion that 4QRP does help us reach, however, is that the process of WRITING, editing, and transmitting what later became biblical texts was far more complex than we could have guessed before the discovery of these texts.

Bennie H. Reynolds, III

Further Reading

Brooke, George. 2001. '4Q158: Reworked Pentateucha or Reworked Pentateuch A?' *DSD* 8: 219–41.

Segal, Michael. 2000. '4QReworked Pentateuch or 4QPentateuch?' In *The Dead Sea Scrolls Fifty Years After Their Discovery*. Edited by Lawrence H. Schiffman, Emanuel Tov and James C. VanderKam. Jerusalem: Israel Exploration Society, pp. 391–99.

Tov, Emanuel, and Sidnie A. White. 1994. 'Reworked Pentateuch.' In *Qumran Cave 4, VIII: Parabiblical Texts, Part 1*. Edited by Harold Attridge et al. DJD 13. Oxford: Oxford University Press; see particularly plates XIII-XXXVI, pp. 187–351.

Zahn, Molly. 2011. *Rethinking Rewritten Scripture: Composition and Exegesis in the 4QReworked Pentateuch Manuscripts*. *STDJ* 95. Leiden: Brill.

Rewritten Scripture *Rewritten scripture* is a term of convenience used primarily by specialists who work on the DEAD SEA SCROLLS. It refers to works of literature that appear to rewrite already existing works recognized as SCRIPTURE/CANON, especially for exegetical reasons. The term does not name a GENRE of literature so much as a mode of presentation used to communicate one's exegesis of a text. An example of rewritten scripture is the second century BCE JUBILEES. This text retells many stories from the book of Genesis in the same order that Genesis tells them, but introduces important changes to the Genesis version of the stories. For example, Jubilees emphasizes different ideas, such as the solar calendar, and reinterprets passages that might seem to impugn the character of important figures such as Noah or Abraham.

After the discovery of the Dead Sea Scrolls beginning in 1947, standard categories for describing ancient Jewish literature were rendered inadequate. In order to describe accurately the contents of texts like the Temple Scroll, the Genesis Apocryphon, 4QREWORKED PENTATEUCH, and Jubilees, scholars first used terms like 'rewritten Bible'. But continued research has made clear that *Bible* is an anachronistic term when applied to Qumran: no official (or informal) list or collection of authoritative books has been discovered there. Moreover, examples of 'rewritten Bible' can be found inside the Bible itself: Deuteronomy reworks material from Exodus, and Chronicles reworks material from Samuel and Kings. Thus, many have adopted the more neutral expression 'rewritten scripture'. The Dead Sea Scrolls have been helpful to research into these canonical biblical texts by allowing scholars to see and understand more clearly the processes behind the rewriting of Scripture.

Rewritten scriptural texts make use of a variety of methods and forms of exegesis. Its constituents are, however, distinct from forms of exegetical literature such as the PESHARIM, which distinguish sharply between their lemma (base text) and its interpretation. Because rewritten scriptural texts have a less formal relationship with their base texts, it is sometimes difficult to know if a work was intended (or used) as an interpretation, a version, or a replacement for the underlying work(s) of Scripture. For example, one can observe that Temple Scroll 25–27 harmonizes Leviticus 23, Numbers 29, and Leviticus 16. Similarly, Jubilees 1 harmonizes Exodus 24 and Deuteronomy 31. But one can observe the very same type of harmonization in the two interwoven 'battle at the sea' stories in all versions of Exodus 14. Thus, scholars are only beginning to develop the language and categories needed to understand the exegetical texts from Qumran. Despite its inherent ambiguities, however, most still find significant utility in the term *rewritten scripture*: it facilitates critical comparisons of ancient Jewish literature and the scribal modes that were used to produce them. These critical comparisons can be seen in the scholarly debate over whether or not 4QREWORKED PENTATEUCH (4QRP) represents an expansive version of the Pentateuch or a distinct, extra-biblical literary work (see Zahn 2008: 315–39). Most agree that the methods of reworking Scripture (or, presenting exegesis) found in 4QRP are no different than the methods found in the SAMARITAN PENTATEUCH (a text that was used as an official version of the Pentateuch by some Jewish communities). Indeed, literary criticism indicates that the scribal modes of exegesis one can observe in 4QRP are no different than those that were used to construct every version of every book of the Pentateuch (e.g. one can compare the harmonistic combination of two flood stories in all known versions of Gen. 6–9). Whereas scholars previously distinguished between the scribal roles of WRITING, editing, and copying (because these tend to be distinct roles in the modern world), Dead Sea Scrolls specialists have used the trope of rewritten scripture to gain a better view of the implications of the creation and growth of Scriptures as texts. Ultimately, it is true that the recognition of the scribal modes associated with rewritten scripture make it more difficult to determine what was and was not *scripture* (based on internal criteria). Fortunately, however, this means we now know more, not less, about the texts as they existed in their ancient environments.

Bennie H. Reynolds III (Medical University of South Carolina, USA)

Further Reading

Bernstein, Moshe. 2005. '"Rewritten Bible": A Generic Category which has Outlived Its Usefulness?' *Textus* 22: 169–96.

Brooke, George. 2000. 'Rewritten Bible.' *EDSS* 2: 777–81.

Brooke, George. 2002. 'The Rewritten Law, Prophets, and Psalms: Issues for Understanding the Text of the Bible.' In *The Bible as Book: The Hebrew Bible and the Judean Desert Discoveries*. Edited by Edward D. Herbert and Emanuel Tov. London: British Library, pp. 31–40.

Crawford, Sidnie White. 2008. *Rewriting Scripture in Second Temple Times*. Grand Rapids: Eerdmans.

Vermes, Géza. 1961. *Scripture and Tradition in Judaism*. Studio Post-Biblica 4. Leiden: Brill.

Zahn, Molly. 2008. 'The Problem of Characterizing the 4QReworked Pentateuch Manuscripts: Bible, Rewritten Bible, or None of the Above?' *DSD* 15: 315–39.

Zahn, Molly. 2011. *Rethinking Rewritten Scripture: Composition and Exegesis in the 4QReworked Pentateuch Manuscripts*. STDJ 95. Leiden: Brill.

Rhetoric in Antiquity Rhetoric is the art of verbal persuasion. Although attempts to communicate persuasively are universal, Greeks in the classical period sought to classify and describe rhetoric formally. Republican Rome prohibited both rhetoric and philosophy as idleness, but their usefulness was recognized by Cicero's time (first century BCE; see Suetonius, *Rhetoricians* 1). Well before the Christian movement reached Rome, rhetoric was pervasive among the elite.

Ancient rhetorical handbooks, written as primers for aspiring public speakers on best practices for the preparation and delivery of speeches, differ in emphasis, varying according to author, period, and location. Despite differences, however, many features of Greek and Roman rhetoric remained fairly stable. This entry offers illustrative samples from various handbooks and speeches. The degree of influence on early Christianity is debated, but points of contact are evident.

While some valued the skill of speaking extemporaneously (e.g. Seneca the Elder, *Controversies* 4. pref. 7), rhetoricians generally constructed speeches through a process involving *invention* (collecting resources), arrangement (organizing the speech), finding the most appropriate wording and expression, memorizing the speech (see MEMORY, GRECO-ROMAN THEORIES OF), and finally delivering it. Delivery included matters such as voice intonation, gestures, and even personal appearance (see NONVERBAL COMMUNICATION IN PERFORMANCE). Much current interest in ancient rhetoric focuses on the types, arrangement, and strategies in speeches.

Rhetoric and Education

Some villages offered elementary education to those who could afford it, and towns could have gymnasia, but advanced rhetorical training was available only in larger cities (see EDUCATION, HELLENISTIC). Despite some geographical variation, study with a *grammatikos* usually began around ages ten to twelve; this could include some elementary rhetorical exercises (Suetonius, *Grammarians* 4). Studies at this stage included memorizing maxims (*gnomai*) and anecdotes (*chreiai*). Starting from a maxim, one could develop essays or speeches by praising the speaker, paraphrasing the maxim, supporting its verity, citing different authorities for confirmation, and offering a concluding exhortation.

Advanced education usually began in the mid-teens (e.g. Quintilian, *Institutes* 2.2.3). Studies at this stage focused on philosophy or, more often, rhetoric. Some who could afford it continued with exceptional teachers for many years (Seneca, *Moral Letters to Lucilius* 108.5), but many completed formal training by age eighteen (e.g. Pliny, *Letters* 5.8.8). Students memorized passages from famous orators, valuing imitation, and practised declamation. The elite used rhetoric in politics and, at a higher level, in courts (Dio Chrysostom, *Discourse* 18.1-2, 5).

Although only the elite received tertiary training in rhetoric, and while very few went on to become professors of rhetoric, the influence of rhetoric and rhetorical training was pervasive in Hellenized and/or Romanized urban centres. Urban citizens were regularly exposed to rhetoric in civic assemblies, members of the elite sometimes spoke at festivals and competitions, and some speakers with lesser status practised their skills in markets.

Following Socrates, philosophers often criticized rhetoric for its amoral stance – to the philosophers' dismay, students were trained to argue both sides of a case rather than simply asserting a single 'true' position (Cicero, *Orator* 14.46; Dio Chrysostom, *Discourse* 51.2; Ps.-Quintilian, *Declamations* 331.14). Elites despised some orators as populist demagogues (Lucian, *A Professor of Public Speaking* 20). Refined persons would persuade fellow members of the elite rationally and passionate speeches were designed for popular consumption, but the most effective speakers took a middle ground (Dionysius of Halicarnassus, *Demosthenes* 15). By the early empire, however, philosophers (e.g. Seneca) often used rhetoric, and orators (e.g. Dio Chrysostom) often developed philosophic topics. Philosophy provided moral content, while rhetoric empowered one to persuade others to embrace it (cf. Cicero, *On Rhetorical Inventions* 1.1.1; Fronto, *Eloquence* 1.18).

Types of Rhetoric

Although the standard division of ancient rhetoric into three categories – deliberative, forensic, and epideictic – neglects the frequent mixing of types and does not encompass all speeches, it offers a starting point. In general, the different types of rhetoric were judged to be appropriate to different social contexts. *Deliberative* rhetoric sought to persuade hearers concerning some course of action and was common in public assemblies or councils; *forensic* (judicial) rhetoric dominated courts; and *epideictic* rhetoric (praise and sometimes blame) dominated funeral orations, festivals, and similar occasions (Dionysius of Halicarnassus, *Isocrates* 20; Theon, *Progymnasmata* 1.74-76 [Butts]; Menander, *Rhetor* 1.1.331.4-9). Reflecting their respective contexts, forensic rhetoric preferred a plain style, whereas epideictic rhetoric often preferred a more lavish or grand style (Fronto, *Letters to Marcus Caesar* 3.16.1); praising a deity could invite sublime prose. Some of the proposed Christological hymns in Paul's writings might reflect such grand rhetoric, although much of Paul's argumentation seeks to persuade deliberatively.

Starting especially in Paul's era (although perhaps not dominant before the second century CE), the Second Sophistic ushered in a revival of Attic rhetorical style, imitating earlier, classical models. Typically reserved, it welcomed little ornamentation and few figures of speech. Rhetoricians contrasted this style with the flowery, bombastic, highly emotive Asianic style, the dominant Hellenistic style in Koine Greek. Some, however, found the Attic style too severe and continued to prefer more passion and repetition (e.g. Pliny, *Letters* 2.96.1-12), as practised by some earlier orators (Cicero, *Orator* 39.135). Early Christian texts such as Ephesians and 2 Peter might resemble Asianic style, which may have been more appreciated in cities of western Asia Minor in this period. Some saw value in both extremes, as well as a middle approach (Aulus Gellius 6.14). Whereas forensic rhetoric valued plain style, epideictic emphasized ornamentation (Fronto, *Letters to Marcus Caesar* 3.16.1).

Rhetorical Arrangement, Strategies, and Devices

Rhetoricians valued arrangement for optimum persuasion. A speech typically began with a *proem* (Latin *exordium*), or introduction. This exordium helped set the speech's tone and concisely introduced themes (Cicero, *On Rhetorical Inventions* 1.15.20; Quintilian, *Institutes* 4.1.5, 35).

Many kinds of speech then proceeded to a *diēgēsis* (Latin *narratio*), a narration of circumstances leading up to the speech event. They then offered a thesis (Latin *propositio*), briefly summarizing one's argument, or a division into points of agreement and disagreement with opponents. (Technically, a *thesis* addresses a general theme, whereas a *hypothesis* addresses a specific case.) In a speech's *probatio*, many (especially deliberative or judicial) speeches would then develop proofs, sometimes also divided into confirmation of one's own position and refutation of the opposing one.

Speeches normally concluded with an *epilogos* (Latin *peroratio*), often meant to rouse the audience, although extant speeches occasionally ended abruptly. Recapitulation or summary of one's case was typical in such conclusions and, in long speeches, also at the end of individual sections (*Rhetoric to Alexander* 36, 1444b.21-35). Orators sometimes cited a maxim to conclude their argument (cf. Acts 20.35). Transitions between sections were common (*Rhetorica ad Herennium* 4.26.35).

While the above elements are commonly discussed in the handbooks and are evident in extant speeches from antiquity, skilled orators exercised considerable flexibility in actual speeches. A few speeches, in fact, even used random order (Menander, *Rhetor* 2.4, 391.19-28, 392.9-14). Extant speeches do not always follow the forms prescribed in rhetorical handbooks (see e.g. Cicero, *Orations to Brutus* 46.156; *To Quinctio* 10.35). Genuine debates in courts differed from the tamer discipline of the schools (Tacitus, *Dialogues* 31; Ps.-Quintilian, *Declamations* 338.4).

Clarity was essential to good style (*Rhetoric for Alexander* 25, 1435a.24–1435b.22; Quintilian, *Institutes* 8.2.22), although digression and returning to the point were common. Orators amplified points consistent with their arguments and could even embellish speeches during delivery (Dionysius of Halicarnassus, *Demosthenes* 53). They could amplify or elaborate narrative by adding information gleaned from inference or other sources (Theon, *Progymnasmata* 3.224-40). They could develop a case through extensive *synkrisis*, or comparison, whether of analogous or unequal matters (e.g. 2 Cor. 11.22-23).

Following Aristotle's penchant for classification, rhetorical handbooks developed a range of broad strategies and specific devices for effective persuasion. Speakers could appeal to *êthos* (character), *logos* (reason), or *pathos* (emotion; *Rhetorica ad Herennium* 4.50.63; Quintilian, *Institutes* 6.2.8-9). Forensic appeals to character argued that the alleged actions contradicted or cohered with what was known of the person. Orators aroused emotion when needed (Cicero, *The Orator* 2.46.189; Quintilian, *Institutes* Bk. 5). Some orators were better at fiery rhetoric, others at reasoning with hearers (Cicero, *Orator* 5.20–6.21); fēamous speakers did not all prefer the same style (Polybius 33.2.10; Cicero, *Letters to Brutus* 56.204). Stoics, naturally, eschewed emotional rhetoric (*Seneca Lucil.* 108.7). Many valued the ability to vary one's style (e.g. Pliny, *Letters* 6.33.7-8).

Orators designed speeches to communicate with their designated audiences (Dionysius of Halicarnassus, *Demosthenes* 15). Building rapport with audiences was essential (e.g. *Rhetoric to Alexander* 29, 1436b.17-19, 38-40; 1437a.1-1438a.2; 1442a.22-1442b.27). Orators naturally would dwell on points advantageous to their case with a particular audience, while hurrying over those that could prove disadvantageous (Theon, *Progymnasmata* 5.52-56). Persuasion appealed to the audience's sense of honour and advantage; regular forms of argument included appeals to what was necessary, legal, advantageous, and so forth.

Orators regularly cited concrete examples (*paradeigmata*), whether historical or invented. Rhetoric valued vividness (*enargeia*), presenting something as if before the eyes of the audience (Theon, *Progymnasmata* 7.53-55; Quintilian, *Institutes* 6.1.31; cf. Gal. 3:1). A common rhetorical exercise, valuable especially in epideictic rhetoric, was *ekphrasis*, vivid and detailed description, often of a work of art. Declaimers also practised *ēthopoiia*, composing speeches in character (imitating a person) and *prosōpooiia*, composing them as personifications (Demetrius, *Elocution* 5.265; Hermogenes, *Progymnasmata* 9).

Over the centuries, various rhetorical handbooks described a range of specific devices. For example, speakers attempted to hold the audience's attention by using devices such as

- personification (*Rhetorica ad Herennium*. 4.53.66; Hermogenes, *Inventions* 4.10.199-200);
- *antonomasia* (also called *epitheton*, substituting an epithet for a name; e.g. *Rhetorica ad Herennium* 4.31.42);

- *aporia* (feigning not knowing what to say; e.g. Isocrates, *Antidosis* 140, 310);
- *catachresis* (using a normally inappropriate expression; *Rhetorica ad Herennium* 4.33.45);
- *epanorthosis* (also called *metabolê*, self-correction; *Rhetorica ad Herennium* 4.26.36);
- hyperbole (*Rhetorica ad Herennium* 4.33.44);
- various forms of irony;
- METONYMY and synecdoche (applying one image to another with which it is associated; *Rhetorica ad Herennium* 4.32.43–4.33.45; cf. 'Christ' in 1 Cor. 12.12; Col. 3.11);
- *paradoxon* (surprising the hearers with something unexpected);
- *paralipsis* (claiming to pass over a point, and thereby mentioning it in the process; *Rhetorica ad Herennium* 4.27.37; cf. e.g. Phlm. 19; Heb. 11.32);
- *paronomasia* (wordplays; *Rhetorica ad Herennium* 4.21.29–4.22.31; cf. Jn 3:8);
- *prodiorthosis* (preparing hearers for a shocking statement; e.g. Dio Chrysostom, *Orations* 38.7; Hermogenes, *Inventions* 4.12.202-3; 2 Cor 11.1);
- *prokatalepsis* (answering objections in advance; *Rhetoric to Alexander* 18, 1432b.11–1433b.16).

Speakers often employed humorous wit at others' expense, though this practice risked creating enmity. They might also engage the audience with rhetorical questions of various sorts (e.g. Maximus of Tyre, *Orations* 1.1).

Speakers especially roused their audiences with repetition. In oral communication, repetition creates a sense of rhythm and emphasis, while also making content more memorable. Forms of repetition included

- climax, or *sorites*, in which one point builds on another (*Rhetorica ad Herennium* 4.34-35; Demetrius, *Elocution* 5.270; cf. Wisdom 6:17-20);
- anaphora (repeating a word at the beginning of successive clauses; x.../x...; roughly the same as *epibolē*; e.g. Demetrius, *On Style* 5.268; Fronto, *To Marcus Caesar* 2.3.1, 3; 3.3);
- antithesis, contrasting opposites (*Rhetoric to Alexander* 26, 1435b.25-39; Dionysius of Halicarnassus, *Lysias* 14);
- *homoeoptoton* (often repeating a grammatical case) and *homoeoteleuton* (end-rhyme).

Many rhetorical devices emphasized repetition of sounds, phrases, or word-endings and word-beginnings. These repetitions both 'pleased the ear', providing emotional appeal, and aided memorization.

Rhetoric and Early Christianity

Many observers through history (e.g. Augustine and Melanchthon) have interpreted the NT in light of ancient rhetoric, and this practice flourished in the late twentieth century. Critics of Rhetorical Criticism question whether it is relevant to impose Greco-Roman rhetorical outlines on letters or collections of Jesus' sayings. As noted above, since many ancient speeches did not follow strictly the model categories and outlines suggested in rhetorical handbooks, the imposition of such outlines on the NT LETTERS can be problematic – evident in the fact that attempts to provide rhetorical outlines of Paul's letters often vary widely. Only rhetorical handbooks much later than Paul's time address letters. Further, rhetorical features evident in some NT writings, such as narrative introductions (cf. Gal. 1.11–2.14), appear not only in rhetoric per se but in a range of genres (e.g. Rev. 1.9-20), as do theses (cf. Acts 1.8; Rom. 1.16-17) and summarizing conclusions (Matt 28.18-20).

Nevertheless, most of Paul's letters, in contrast to ordinary (and usually quite short) ancient business letters, include substantial argumentation, and thus naturally reflect argumentative patterns of the wider rhetorical culture, particularly those typical of deliberative rhetoric. Moreover, numerous rhetorical devices appear. Scholars debate the level of Paul's exposure to rhetoric; probably his tertiary training focused in the SEPTUAGINT, but his letters reveal that, whatever his exposure to rhetoric at an earlier level, he developed argumentation well. The speeches in Acts 24.10-21 and 26.2-29 naturally develop elements of forensic rhetoric. The former speech (24.18-19) may include the practice of returning charges against accusers (see e.g. Lysias, *Orations* 3.1, §96; Cicero, *Orations to Brutus* 40.137; *The Orator* 3.204).

Not limited to speeches, rhetorical patterns and concerns affected writing in many genres. For example, an orator might critique the rhetoric even of an edict (Fronto, *Speeches* 12). Sensitivity to ancient rhetorical practice thus sheds some light on a range of NT passages.

Rhetorical devices described in the handbooks appear frequently in the NT, including, for example, alliteration (2 Tim. 3.3-4; Heb. 1.1); *anaphora* (Heb. 11.3-31); *antimetabole* (repeated words with inverted sense; Mk 2.27; probably Gal. 2.20); *antistrophe* (also known as *epiphora*; ...x/...x; Mk 13.31; 1 Cor. 1.27-28; 13.11); *antonomasia* or *epitheton* (substituting a title for a name; Jn 19.11; 2 Cor. 8.18); *apostrophe* (turning from one's audience to single out a hearer; Mt. 20.13; Rom. 2.3); chiasm (inverted parallelism; probably in Acts 2.22-36; Rom. 2.6-11; 8.35-39; 1 Pet. 3.16–4:5); climax (Rom. 5.3-5; 8.29-30; 10.14-15; Js 1.14-15; 2 Pe.t 1.5-8); correction (Gal. 4.9; and perhaps 1 Cor. 1.16); and, *catachresis* (possibly Mt. 6.27). Of course, these instances do not all require that the authors were trained in Greek rhetoric – some of these patterns/devices are evident in the OT and would have been typical of ancient Near Eastern oral communication. They do, however, illustrate the sorts of devices circulating in ancient Mediterranean speech and provide a vocabulary for describing them.

Scholars familiar with Greco-Roman rhetorical devices recognize some of these in Paul's letters, just as rhetorical traits of Jewish sages surface in Jesus's teachings and apocalyptic devices appear in Revelation. For example, Paul appeals to pathos as needed (2 Cor. 6.11-13; Gal. 4.12-20; Phlm. 9–12), and frequently utilizes a number of widely recognized rhetorical devices, including *dilogia* (repeating a word) or *anadiplosis* (a word or phrase ending one clause also begins the next; Rom. 3.25-26; 8.16-17; 1 Cor. 2.6; Gal. 1.8-9; Phil. 4.4), *anaphora* (1 Cor. 1.12, 20, 26; 12.4-6; 15.39-41; 2 Cor. 7.2; 11.20, 26; Phil. 3.2), *symplochê* (x...y/x...y; 1 Cor. 10.21; 15.42-44; 2 Cor. 9.6), antithesis (Rom. 5.12-21; 1 Cor. 1.18; 15.40, 42-49, 53-54; 2 Cor. 3.7-11; 4.8-10; 6.7-10), and rhetorical questions. Again, whether Paul knew the technical names and formal academic discussions surrounding these devices, he clearly had mastered their use. Ironically, even orators' letters (such as those of Cicero and Pliny the Younger) used ornamentation and rhetorical devices relative sparingly, simply because letters were not speeches (cf. Cicero *Friends* 9.21.1; Senec, *Letters to Lucilius* 75.1-3).

Overall, Greco-Roman rhetoric's influence was widespread. Although probably few if any NT writers had tertiary training in rhetoric, its forms in popular culture helped shape their communication strategies. This was especially important for writers seeking audiences that expected such conventions.

Craig S. Keener (Asbury Theological Seminary, USA)

Further Reading

Anderson, R. Dean, Jr. 2000. *Glossary of Greek Rhetorical Terms Connected to Methods of Argumentation, Figures, and Tropes from Anaximenes to Quintilian.* Leuven: Peeters.

Aune, David E. 2003. *The Westminster Dictionary of New Testament and Early Christian Literature and Rhetoric.* Louisville: Westminster John Knox.

Kennedy, George A. 1972. *The Art of Rhetoric in the Roman World: 300 B.C.–A.D. 300*. Princeton: Princeton University Press.

Porter, Stanley E., ed. 1997. *Handbook of Classical Rhetoric in the Hellenistic Period, 330 B.C.–A.D. 400*. Leiden: Brill.

Russell, D. A., and M. Winterbottom, eds. 1972. *Ancient Literary Criticism: The Principal Texts in New Translations*. Oxford: Oxford University Press.

Watson, Duane F., ed. 1991. *Persuasive Artistry: Studies in New Testament Rhetoric in Honor of George A. Kennedy*. JSNTSup 50. Sheffield, UK: Sheffield Academic.

Riddles A *riddle* is an ambiguous interrogative statement that intentionally hides its referent and asks the audience to name it. An *ambiguous* statement is one that could reasonably refer to more than one thing, depending on the frame of reference. While speech is often accidentally ambiguous (= unclear), riddles are intentionally ambiguous, strategically blurring the boundaries between established conceptual categories. For example, the question 'What has four wheels and flies?' is ambiguous in the sense that it could reasonably refer to a wide variety of items (e.g. an airplane); it is intentionally ambiguous in that it challenges the audience to identify the 'correct' referent, 'a garbage truck', by recognizing that the description combines terms that are normally assigned to different conceptual domains (in this case, 'things with wheels'/trucks and 'things that fly'/airplanes). While many Western riddles take the form of questions, all riddles, despite their grammatical form, are interrogative in the sense that they seek an 'answer' – the riddler offers a descriptive statement, and the audience is asked to reply with the name of the correct referent. Beyond this basic dialogic structure, the formal features of riddles can vary widely from culture to culture and even within a single culture, a fact that riddlers exploit to further confuse their audiences.

In many traditional cultures, *wit* – the ability to ask and/or answer difficult ambiguous questions – is significant because it demonstrates command of three types of cultural knowledge. First, the witty person evidences content knowledge, awareness of the attributes of the subject of the riddle (e.g. the garbage truck from the sample riddle above). Second, the witty person demonstrates taxonomic knowledge, mastery of the classification schemes that a group uses to order the world. These first two types of intelligence are illustrated by the famous 'Riddle of the Sphinx', supposedly solved by Oedipus: 'What goes on four legs in the morning; two legs in the afternoon; and three legs in the evening?' To provide the correct answer, 'a human being', one must possess content knowledge, basic information about human anatomy and the fact that elderly people in some cultures walk with canes ('three legs'). But one must also understand the riddle's underlying taxonomic system: that the developmental stages of life can be defined in terms of physical capabilities; that the stages of life can be compared to the phases of a day; and, that a 'day' may be conceived as consisting of three distinct periods of time (morning, afternoon, evening). A person who lacks this information (e.g. a person from a culture that did not use canes) and understanding (e.g. a person from a culture that divided the day into four phases instead of three) would not be able to answer.

Third and finally here, *wit* demonstrates intellectual prowess through knowledge of cultural traditions, which most often simply means that one knows the 'right' answer in advance through prior experience or training. By definition, riddles rarely 'admit to [purely] logical solutions where one and only one answer satisfies the descriptive grid imposed on the riddle topic', and therefore typically cannot be answered on 'rational grounds'. Instead, 'most riddles depend for their solution on either inspired guessing or simply knowing the riddle – which is to say, knowing traditions' (quotes Slotkin 1990: 154). For example, the popular children's riddle 'What's black and white and red all over?' can reasonably refer to more than one thing; content knowledge and taxonomic knowledge may point to several possible solutions (e.g. 'a newspaper';

'a zebra with a diaper rash') but cannot discriminate between them, thus requiring the riddlee to know the answer to the joke in advance.

Because wit reflects command of group knowledge, logic, and traditions, in many cultures riddling plays a key role in the establishment of social IDENTITY and intellectual status. While modern Western societies typically relegate riddles to leisure-time settings (e.g. jokes, nursery rhymes, crossword puzzles), cross-culturally they are often performed in contexts that emphasize the group's solidarity and continuity: greetings; rituals 'involving initiation and death'; courtship and wedding ceremonies; and, 'the educational encounter between teacher and student' (Burns 1976: 145). As a corollary to this principle, riddles may function as the 'underdog's channel', a means of defining a subgroup within the dominant culture on the basis of a shared but 'secret' common knowledge. Riddles are thus often utilized by individuals who occupy marginal positions in a society (e.g. women, peasants, children), sometimes as a vehicle to challenge the assumptions and taxonomies of the dominant GREAT TRADITION. Riddles can thus be used to maintain a sense of group identity or to create a new group with a distinct identity on the basis of shared knowledge that is not available to outsiders.

Because everyday speech depends upon clarity of communication and therefore avoids ambiguity, riddles, which are intentionally ambiguous and seek to confuse, are typically performed in controlled social environments that signal to the audience the nature of the exchange (see PERFORMANCE ARENA). In these 'riddling sessions', one person plays the riddler who poses ambiguous questions, while the audience plays the role of the riddlee who must provide the answer. The rules of riddling sessions are as localized, and therefore as diverse, as the forms of riddles themselves. A riddling session may include only one question, a series of questions posed by one riddler, or a back-and-forth exchange. These rules must be observed even when they are not explicitly stated. To take a well-known example from the Hebrew Bible, Samson clearly thinks that the Philistines have cheated him by forcing his fiancée to tell them the answer to his riddle about the 'sweet eater'. He protests by killing thirty Ashkelonites, yet still satisfies the rules of engagement by paying on his earlier bet to the survivors (Judg. 14.18-19). The settings and rules of riddling sessions are intuitive to members of the groups that exchange them orally, but may also be embedded in literary contexts (such as the Samson narrative just noted) where they may be less obvious to readers from other cultures.

Research on riddles and riddling can inform biblical studies at several points. First, and most obviously, the Bible contains a number of statements that are explicitly delivered as riddles, including Samson's riddle noted above and Jesus' famous statement, 'Give Caesar what is Caesar's and God what is God's' (Mk 12.17). Second, awareness of the riddling session as a traditional social form may provide insights for understanding the narrative structure of passages of Scripture that portray this form of exchange. To cite an obvious example, Mk 12.13-34 portrays a riddling session in which Jesus establishes his superior wit by answering the difficult questions of the Pharisees, Sadducees, and a scribe, and then by proffering a riddle of his own to the crowds that assumes his expertise on the interpretation of the Scriptures.

Third, and perhaps more significantly, riddles illustrate one of two ways of establishing and maintaining intellectual prestige and credentials in traditional cultures such as ancient Israel and Late Second Temple Judaism. In settings where the great tradition of a society depends on foundational sacred texts, the power of the scribal class rests in their expertise in using these texts to define and manipulate values and lifeways. A great tradition can be challenged indirectly, however, by witty individuals who are capable of identifying cracks in its taxonomies or/and who demonstrate an innate capability to deconstruct the tradition by highlighting its apparent contradictions. This riddling/parabolic, revisionist approach is typified by Israel's prophetic tradition and by Jesus and his movement. Both Jesus and the prophets challenged the hegemony of the priestly/scribal outlook by posing questions that could not be easily answered from within the framework of typical scholarly discourse simply because it manipulated the taxonomic categories from which that discourse proceeded.

Tom Thatcher (Cincinnati Christian University, USA)

Further Reading

Burns, Thomas A. 1976. 'Riddling: Occasion to Act'. In *Journal of American Folklore* 89: 139–65.
Crenshaw, James. 2005. *Samson: A Secret Betrayed, A Vow Ignored.* Eugene, OR: Wipf & Stock.
Pepicello, W. J., and Thomas A. Green. 1984. *The Language of Riddles: New Perspectives*. Columbus, OH: Ohio State University Press.
Slotkin, Edgar. 1990. 'Response to Professors Fontaine and Camp.' In *Text and Tradition: The Hebrew Bible and Folklore*. Edited by Susan Niditch. SBL Symposium Series. Atlanta: Scholars Press, pp. 153–9.
Thatcher, Tom. 2006. *Jesus the Riddler: The Power of Ambiguity in the Gospels*. Louisville: Westminster John Knox.

S

Sabbath Within the Hebrew Bible, observation of the Sabbath, or seventh day of the week (Saturday), is identified as a central and critical religious practice for ancient Israelite and Judean worshippers of YHWH. By the Second Temple period, there is ample evidence of widespread Jewish observance of the Sabbath, consisting mainly of abstention from work and communal gathering for WORSHIP and study in the land of Israel and in the Diaspora. In the centuries around the turn of the first millennium CE, both Jews and non-Jews viewed Sabbath observance as a central marker of Jewish IDENTITY, and differences regarding Sabbath practice functioned as flashpoints and boundary markers in intra-Jewish sectarian conflict and competition.

Sabbath in the Hebrew Bible

The commandment to observe the Sabbath through cessation of work appears in several pentateuchal texts, including both iterations of the Ten Commandments (Exod. 20.8-11; Exod. 31.12-17; Exod. 34.21; Lev. 19.3; Deut. 5.14-15). In addition to this central mandated practice of abstention from work, the biblical texts identify other practices with the Sabbath. Numbers 28.9-10 mandates additional sacrificial offerings for the Sabbath, and Hos. 2.3 identifies the Sabbath as a day of joy. The superscription of Psalm 92 identifies it as a song for the Sabbath. In the Hebrew Bible, the Sabbath and its observance function as powerful mnemonic devices that function to remind YHWH worshippers of two central theological tenets, God's creation of the universe and YHWH's deliverance of his people from Egypt. As an example of the former, Exod. 20.11 connects the Sabbath and its observance to God's role as creator by noting that, 'For in six days the Lord made the heaven and earth and sea, and all that is in them, and He rested on the seventh day; therefore the Lord blessed the Sabbath day and hallowed it.' In this context, the Sabbath is a testimony to, and consequence of, God's role as creator and master of the world. As an example of the latter, Deut. 5.11 links Sabbath observance to remembrance of the exodus: 'Remember that you were a slave in the land of Egypt and the Lord your God freed you from there with a mighty hand and an outstretched arm; therefore the Lord your God has commanded you to observe the Sabbath day.' The centrality of the Sabbath as a sign of God's role as creator and redeemer is also reflected in the concentric cycles of Sabbath, sabbatical year, and year of jubilee which, in their various biblical iterations, attest to God's ownership of the created world and to God's insistence that the Israelites have no master, human or divine, other than YHWH.

The theological weight and mnemonic function of the Sabbath resonate with the seriousness attributed to both its transgression and observance in biblical texts. Exodus 31.14 states that transgression of the Sabbath commandment is punishable by death, and Neh. 13.15-22 identifies profanation of the Sabbath as one of the behaviours that led to the devastation of Jerusalem by the Babylonians. In this passage, Nehemiah identifies his establishment of strict Sabbath practice throughout Jerusalem as one of the acts that should accord him divine merit. The universalistic oracle in Isa. 56.3-7 twice identifies observance of the Sabbath as one of the central practices that can testify to a foreigner's allegiance to YHWH and establish eligibility to offer sacrifices in the TEMPLE.

Sabbath in the Late Second Temple Period

Late Second Temple era texts testify to the centrality of the Sabbath for Jewish practice and identity in this period. Both Josephus (*Against Apion* 2.175) and Philo (*Life of Moses* 2.216) testify that Jews gathered on the Sabbath to study the Torah. This portrait is supported by the Gospels, which attest that Jesus 'went to the synagogue, as his custom was, on the Sabbath day' (Lk. 4.16). This synagogue episode from Luke also describes a scriptural recitation followed by a sermon. Texts from the MISHNAH also describe and mandate communal prayer and scriptural recitation in synagogues on the Sabbath (see TORAH READING). The Songs of the Sabbath Sacrifice from Qumran bear witness to the composition of elaborate liturgies for the Sabbath and the belief that the Sabbath was a propitious time for prayer.

Non-Jewish sources identify the cessation of work on the Sabbath as a peculiarity of Jewish custom. Both 1 Macc. 2.33-38 and Josephus' *Antiquities* 12.274-77 state that the Seleucids took advantage of Jewish Sabbath observance by attacking on the Sabbath. Whether or not these accounts are historically true, they reflect the degree to which Jews in this period identified Sabbath observance as critical to their identity and practice.

While there was agreement on the centrality of Sabbath observance, there was significant variation in Jewish understandings of the details and parameters of appropriate Sabbath practice, and the proper observance of the Sabbath became a point of contention and marker of identity in the intra-Jewish sectarian conflicts of the period. Both the residents of Qumran and the early rabbis elaborated on the prohibition against work by delineating different lists of prohibited and permitted activities. The Gospels also reflect the role of the Sabbath in Jewish sectarian self-definition. In Mark 2, a series of episodes in which Jesus challenges Pharisaic interpretations of Jewish law culminates in a challenge to what is identified as a Pharisean interpretation of the Sabbath law. This passage demonstrates how interpretations and enactments of Sabbath practice in the early first century CE served as markers of sectarian difference.

Elsie R. Stern (Reconstructionist Rabbinical College, USA)

Further Reading

Blidstein, Gerald, ed. 2004. *Sabbath: Idea, History, Reality*. Beersheva: Ben Gurion University of the Negev Press, 2004.

Eskenazi, T. C., D. J. Harrington and W. H. Shea, eds. 1991. *Sabbath in Jewish and Christian Traditions*. New York: Crossroad.

Graetz, Michael J., Jacobs, Louis, Gottlieb, Efraim and Fraiman, Susan Nashman. 2007. 'Sabbath.' In *Encyclopaedia Judaica*. Edited by Michael Berenbaum and Fred Skolnik. 2nd edn. Vol. 17. Detroit: Macmillan Reference USA, pp. 616–22.

Samaritan Pentateuch The Samaritan Pentateuch is the version of the first five books of the Hebrew Bible – Genesis, Exodus, Leviticus, Numbers, and Deuteronomy (the *Torah*) – regarded as canonical by the Samaritan Israelite community. These five books constitute the entire canon of Scripture for the Samaritans. The Samaritan Pentateuch preserves a text of the Torah that differs in significant ways from the MASORETIC TEXT (the canonical Hebrew Jewish text). It is copied in a particular version of the paleo-Hebrew or ancient Israelite script, and is a consonantal, unvocalized text (no vowel points) (see ORTHOGRAPHY).

History of Scholarship

Western biblical scholars first learnt of the Samaritan Pentateuch in 1616, when a complete manuscript was brought to Europe by Pietro della Valle. Comparison with the Masoretic Text revealed numerous variants between the two texts, often in the direction of expansion; for many of these variants, the Samaritan Pentateuch agreed with the SEPTUAGINT (the ancient Greek translation of the Torah) over the Masoretic Text, although a particular group of large-scale editorial changes were unique to the Samaritan Pentateuch. Also, the Samaritan

Pentateuch exhibited a particular Samaritan theological bias, for example arguing for the choice of Mount Gerizim as the place selected by God for God's unique sanctuary. This is manifest in the Samaritan Pentateuch version of the Ten Commandments in Exodus and Deuteronomy, in which the final commandment enjoins the Israelites to build a sanctuary on Mount Gerizim. In light of these characteristics, many scholars dismissed the Samaritan Pentateuch as a secondary or vulgar text, not useful for TEXTUAL CRITICISM.

This assessment changed, however, with the discovery of the DEAD SEA SCROLLS in the 1940s and 1950s. Of the biblical manuscripts found in the Qumran caves, four in particular, 4QpaleoExod^{m}, 4QNum^{b}, 4QExod-Lev^{f}, and 4QREWORKED PENTATEUCH^{b}, exhibited the same large-scale editorial changes found in the Samaritan Pentateuch. Since these manuscripts were found in a clearly Jewish milieu (Qumran), it could not be argued that they were Samaritan texts; thus the label *pre-Samaritan* was adopted. It is now understood that the Samaritan Pentateuch is one exemplar of an ancient text of the Torah, in circulation in Palestine in both the Samaritan and Jewish communities during the Second Temple period. A single exemplar of this ancient text was chosen by the Samaritans as their canonical text, probably in the early first century BCE after the destruction of their sanctuary by the Hasmonean ruler John Hyrcanus in c. 110 BCE.

The Nature of the Text

As noted above, the most distinct characteristic of the Samaritan Pentateuch, and of the pre-Samaritan text tradition on which it is based, is the large-scale editorial changes made to an earlier text of the Pentateuch, changes not shared with the Masoretic Text or the Septuagint. These changes do not occur in the legal section of the Pentateuch (Exod. 21–23 and Leviticus), but rather in certain narrative sections. These sections may be grouped as follows.

- Genesis 5 and 11: The changes resolve chronological problems between the genealogical lists and the narrative passages, making sure that none of the antediluvian patriarchs (i.e. Jared, Methuselah, and Lamech) survived the flood.
- Exodus 7–11: In the story of the Ten Plagues, the pre-Samaritan version makes sure that each time God gives a command to Moses (and Aaron) its fulfilment is narrated with the exact detail of the command. Thus there can be no question that Moses fulfilled all of God's instructions exactly.
- Deuteronomy 1–3: The scribe(s) responsible for the pre-Samaritan version compared the details of Moses' speech in Deut. 1–3 with the corresponding narratives in Exodus and Numbers to make certain that they agreed in all their details. If a detail from the speech was missing in the narrative, it was retrojected back into its proper place in the narrative. For example, Num. 10.11 is preceded by Deut. 1.6-8; Num. 13.33 is followed by Deut. 1.27-33; and, Num. 14.41 is preceded by Deut. 1.42. Much less frequently, Deuteronomy borrows from Numbers. The aim was to eliminate disagreements between the books.

In addition to these major blocs, numerous local changes of the same type were made. For example, in the pre-Samaritan version of Gen. 30.36, Jacob actually dreams the dream which he later recounts to Rachel and Leah in Gen. 31.11-13 (missing in the Masoretic Text and the Septuagint).

The purpose of these large-scale editorial changes is not obvious. Although they do remove infelicities in the text, the scribe(s) was not systematic; that is, incongruities remain that were not corrected. The changes that were made generally involve, in one way or another, the figure of Moses, and may seek to highlight his role and importance.

Once the Samaritans had adopted one of these pre-Samaritan manuscripts as their canonical text, they introduced changes to make it conform more closely to their theology concerning Mount Gerizim as the place chosen by God as the proper place of WORSHIP. The clearest example of this change is the insertion, at Exod. 20.17 and Deut. 5.18, of a commandment to build an altar on Mount Gerizim.

> When the LORD your God has brought you into the land of the Canaanites that you are entering to possess, set up some large stones for yourself and cover them with plaster. Write on the stones all the words of this law. And when you have crossed the Jordan, set up these stones on Mount Gerizim, as I command you today. Build there an altar to the LORD your God, an altar of stones. Do not use any iron tool upon them. Build the altar of the LORD your God with unhewn stones and offer burnt offerings on it to the LORD your God. Sacrifice whole offerings and eat them there and rejoice in the presence of the LORD your God.
>
> This mountain is across the Jordan, westwards towards the setting sun, in the territory of the Canaanites, who dwell in the Arabah facing Gilgal, near the large tree of Moreh, facing Shechem.

The elevation of Mount Gerizim is also in view in the Samaritan version of passages in which God's choice of an appropriate place of worship is mentioned. In these contexts, the Samaritan Pentateuch uniformly uses the past tense of the verb 'to choose', indicating that God's choice was known to Moses and made before the entry into the promised land. For example, at Deut. 12.5 the Samaritan Pentateuch reads, 'But you shall seek the place that the Lord your God *has chosen* out of all your tribes as his habitation to put his name there'; 'has chosen' refers back to Gerizim, identified in 11.29-30. By contrast, the Masoretic Text reads, 'But you shall seek the place that the Lord your God *will choose* out of all your tribes as his habitation to put his name there.' Thus the place is unnamed and unknown to Moses; in the Jewish tradition, the unnamed place was later revealed to be Jerusalem, a city that did not fall until Israelite rule under the time of David and Solomon. Thus the Samaritan Pentateuch reflects the understanding of the Samaritan community, while the Masoretic Text reflects the understanding of the Jewish community. It is likely that the Samaritan Pentateuch is a revision of some form of the base text underlying the Masoretic Text.

Sidnie White Crawford (University of Nebraska-Lincoln, USA)

Further Reading

Anderson, Robert T., and Terry Giles. 2012. *The Samaritan Pentateuch*. SBLRBS. Atlanta: SBL Press.

Kartveit, Magnar. 2013. *The Origin of the Samaritans*. VTSup 128. Leiden: Brill.

Knoppers, Gary N. 2013. *Jews and Samaritans: The Origins and History of their Early Relations*. New York: Oxford University Press.

Purvis, James D. 1968. *The Samaritan Pentateuch and the Origins of the Samaritan Sect*. Cambridge, MA: Harvard University Press.

Sayings and Dialogue Gospels Sayings and Dialogue Gospels are early Christian texts that present Jesus as a speaker of sayings or that show him in dialogue with others, with the implicit assumption that such was his primary, or sole, activity. Sayings Gospels differ structurally and conceptually from NARRATIVE GOSPELS, such as Matthew and John, which locate Jesus' teachings and dialogues within the framework of a larger narrative of his life and activity. Some Sayings Gospels, such as the Gospel of Thomas, include almost no narrative material beyond very rudimentary human contexts for the exchange of Jesus' words. As a result, the presentation of Jesus' message in Sayings Gospels is not impacted by the principle of NARRATIVITY, specifically in the sense that the apparent meaning of Jesus' words is not influenced by their location within the framework of a larger story, as would be the case in a Narrative Gospel. Perhaps the most well-known Sayings Gospel is Q, a presumed sayings source for the NT Synoptics that currently exists only as a hypothetical reconstruction based upon source-critical examination of Matthew, Mark, and Luke.

While the extant examples of Sayings and Dialogue Gospels share a common interest in preserving alleged sayings and speeches of Jesus (some of which have parallels in the extant Narrative Gospels or other ancient sources), they vary greatly in terms of their provenance. The character of the extant Sayings and Dialogue Gospels also varies greatly, illustrating the diversity of the Jesus tradition during the first several centuries of the Common Era. Dates of composition range from mid-first century CE to the third century CE. Some of these texts are complete documents, while others are fragmentary. In terms of theology, some of the Sayings and Dialogue Gospels align with the canonical Gospels (all of which are Narrative Gospels) while others represent theological trajectories that differ significantly from the canonical Jesus tradition.

The Sayings and Dialogue Gospels also vary greatly in terms of their genre. Some, such as the Coptic Gospel of Thomas, which consists of 114 sayings of Jesus, lack any narrative framework or apparent organizational structure. This has led some scholars to suggest that Thomas is a prototypical example of the pure form of a Sayings Gospel and to cite this text as evidence for the possible existence of the Q source. Q itself was originally envisioned in the eighteenth century as a pure Sayings Gospel containing little to no narrative material. However, more recent Q scholarship has argued that Q included both sayings and narrative material and as such should be viewed as a mixed-genre text.

With the possible exception of Q, most extant Sayings and Dialogue Gospels display a broadly Gnostic theological character, with the revelatory sayings of Jesus providing insights essential to the reading community's access to salvation. To cite several notable examples, the Gospel of Philip, Gospel of Thomas, Dialogue of the Saviour, and the Apocryphon of James (all discovered in Nag Hammadi, Egypt in 1945) reflect Gnostic theological interests that are, for the most part, not shared by the authors of the Synoptics or Q. The Gnostic character of these Gospels would tend to date their composition between the first and third centuries CE, the period in which Gnosticism developed as a distinct (at least in comparison to the emerging 'orthodox' perspective) system of thought. Beyond this general observation, however, the dates of specific Sayings or Dialogue Gospels must be determined on a case-by-case basis. While early research on these texts tended to assume that expressions of a 'more developed' Gnostic theology indicated a later date of composition, more recent research has been hesitant to assume clear, linear, and uniform trajectories in the evolution of early Christian thought. Since Q is, by definition, a source utilized by the authors of the canonical Gospels, this text must have been in circulation prior to the composition of Matthew and Luke (mid–late first century CE), suggesting that the genre itself originated at a very early period in Christian history.

In terms of form and genre, the method of presentation of the sayings of Jesus found in the extant texts differs on a case-by-case basis. Often the narrator prefaces a saying with a short introductory titular phrase, such as 'Jesus said/He said …' (e.g. Thomas), 'the Savior answered …' (e.g. Apocryphon of James), 'the Master …', or other similar formulas. When included within the literary structure of a dialogue, the narrator often presents Jesus' sayings as responses to questions posed by other individuals, such as Mary, Peter, Matthew (e.g. Thomas 21), or to collective groups of individuals, such as the disciples (e.g. Thomas 22; Dialogue of the Savior). The structure of the dialogue often follows the general pattern illustrated by Thomas 21:

> [individual or group] Mary said to Jesus:
>
> [question directed to Jesus] 'Whom are your disciples like?'
>
> [response/saying of Jesus] He said: 'They are like servants who are entrusted with a field that is not theirs.'

In some Dialogue Gospels, as the name of the genre suggests, the conversation may include extended answers on the part of Jesus, or/and several rounds of exchange, a pattern reflecting the Farewell Address of Jesus in Jn 13–17.

In some cases, ancient Christian texts that fall into other genres (e.g. Narrative Gospel, LETTER, APOCALYPSE) included sayings material and dialogue sections. To cite the most notable example, the canonical Gospels of Matthew, Mark, Luke, and John all include sayings material within the framework of their larger presentations of Jesus' ministry. The Gospel of John in particular frames Jesus' teaching within a number of extended dialogues/discourses involving both friends (e.g. the disciples) and enemies (the Pharisees; 'the Jews'). John utilizes the dialogue form to provide plausible literary contexts for the presentation of sayings and longer teachings to his own audience. The author of John regularly uses misunderstandings on the part of Jesus' dialogue partners as opportunities to interject clarifying teachings of Christ within the narrative framework of his larger presentation.

Jesus scholars have often shown interest in Sayings Gospels as potential sources for Jesus' message, sometimes arguing that these texts preserve more primitive or authentic versions of Jesus' teaching. Much attention has been focused on the question of the extent to which these sayings and dialogues reflect the *ipssisma verba Jesu* – the literal words that Jesus himself spoke. However, from a perspective informed by studies in ancient media, it is necessary to question the very idea that any tradition is capable of capturing the 'exact words of Jesus'. All sources for Jesus, including Q, Thomas, and other Sayings Gospels, reflect both individual and COLLECTIVE MEMORIES of him and, as such, have been shaped by both the conscious and subconscious processes associated with human cognition. Put another way, the lack of a narrative framework does not suggest that the sayings material preserved in these sources is any less stylized than sayings materials found in narrative presentations of Jesus' career.

In sum, the Sayings and Dialogue Gospels offer readers a glimpse into the diversity of Christian tradition during the first three centuries of the Common Era and illustrate the various ways in which Jesus was remembered during the early stages of the Christian movement.

Terence C. Mournet (Ashland Theological Seminary, USA)

Further Reading

Gathercole, Simon. 2014. *The Gospel of Thomas: Introduction and Commentary*. Texts and Editions for New Testament Study II. Leiden: Brill Academic Press.

Goodacre, Mark. 2012. *Thomas and the Gospels: The Case for Thomas's Familiarity with the Synoptics*. Grand Rapids, MI: Eerdmans.

Kloppenborg, John S. 2000. *Excavating Q: The History and Setting of the Sayings Gospel*. Minneapolis, MN: Fortress Press.

Koester, Helmut. 1990. *Ancient Christian Gospels: Their History and Development*. Harrisburg, PA: Trinity Press International.

Schema The term *schema*, originally introduced to developmental psychology by Jean Piaget (1928) and applied to COGNITIVE/PERSONAL MEMORY by Frederick Bartlett (1932), refers to a learnt cognitive framework that enables one to organize past experience and to make sense of new information. Narratives, scripts, stereotypes, models, perspectives, and frames are common examples of schemata, which allow individuals and groups to quickly identify and distinguish things and events as these are connected to or keyed into them. In studies of COLLECTIVE MEMORY, schemata are viewed as critical elements of the frameworks of memory, provided by groups to allow individuals a common framework for recalling and discussing the meaningful past.

The function of a schema is evident in the example of two individuals watching a baseball game. One person knows nothing about the game's rules and how it is played; the other is an avid fan. When questioned afterward about important performances of the game, the spectator unfamiliar with baseball will remember less because he lacks a schema to organize his perceptions and comments; the fan, however, will be more readily able to discuss what happened because he possesses a stable schema, or grid, on which he can store his memory of events from the game and from which he can recover them when needed. A schema, then, works by mediating between the perception of an entity and its comprehension. Without such mediation, events and their participants remain without structure and meaning.

A single schema can be applied to multiple sources of information. For example, after Jesus died and Jews began to form Christian communities, stories about Apollonius of Tyana (a contemporary of Jesus) appeared and proliferated. Keyed by its proponents into the life of Jesus, the narrative began with Apollonius' virgin birth and sacrificial death. Jesus and Apollonius were two real yet different historical figures, but the (probably competing) carriers of their stories used a comparable schema to define their relative significance, thereby producing the oft-noticed similarities between their respective biographies. On the other hand, multiple schemata can be applied to the same object. During the Late Second Temple period, when anticipation of the end of days was widespread, at least three messianic schemata existed: the *warrior messiah* who would drive Rome from Judea; a *priestly messiah* to supply the theology of deliverance from the world of evil; and the *prophet messiah*, who would announce the arrival of God's new kingdom, over which he would preside. Jesus' prophetic mission – to announce the coming apocalypse – satisfied the prophetic messiah schema, but his suffering and death on the cross contradicted all messianic schemata. To render Jesus' death comprehensible, early Christians developed a new *suffering messiah* schema, which was accomplished by keying the events of his death into motifs and passages from the Jewish Scriptures.

Barry Schwartz (The University of Georgia, USA)

Schwartz, Barry Barry Schwartz (b. 1938) is an American sociologist and historian whose recent work has focused on collective memories of significant figures from the American past, including most notably former US Presidents George Washington (1732–99) and Abraham Lincoln (1809–65). Schwartz's work has been influential in research on early Christian CULTURAL MEMORY, and he has participated in several meetings of the Society of Biblical Literature and has contributed to several published collections on biblical studies, focusing particularly on the historical Jesus.

Schwartz's most substantive contributions emerge from two key elements of his theoretical paradigm: 1) a strong preference for TRADITIONALIST/REALIST approaches to COLLECTIVE MEMORY (see REALISM); and, 2) the principle of *keying/framing*, which describes ways that groups use the past as a template for interpreting current experience.

On the first point above, Schwartz is widely associated with the 'traditionalist' approach to collective memory, a view that emphasizes the reciprocal relationship between the ACTUAL PAST and its subsequent commemorations. Resisting constructionist approaches that view the content of collective memory as a product of power structures – that is, the past is fabricated in service of ideological interests, and thus cannot be distinguished from these interests – Schwartz insists that originating events play a key role in collective memory, both because memory originates from the actual past and because past events contribute to the shape and constituency of remembering communities and also to the content of the personal memories of individuals (for the contrasting perspective, see PRESENTISM/CONSTRUCTIONISM). Past events change both the lives of remembering individuals and the physical and social landscapes of remembering groups, and in this way the past not only contributes content to collective memory but also impacts the social frameworks in which collective memory develops and is articulated.

On the second point above, Schwartz helpfully explains the complex relationships between the actual past and collective memory in terms of *keying* and *framing*. A memory *frame* is a person, event, place, institution, or situation from the past that is remembered by a particular group; *keying* is the process by which the group maps a current circumstance to features of a frame as a means of integrating present realities into past experience. Keying is critical to a group's sense of IDENTITY and continuity: interpreting the present through the lens of the past offers resources for integrating current challenges into a larger sense of heritage. Because, again, the actual past and the present are linked in a reciprocal relationship, the value of a frame may change over time as the same precedent is successively keyed to new situations. In biblical scholarship, keying/framing is illustrated by the adaptation of exodus motifs in the prophetic literature, by the interplay between Israel's Torah traditions and the narrative texts of the Hebrew Bible, and by the NT's adaptation of themes and texts from the Hebrew Bible as a lens for understanding Jesus' life and significance.

Following the above principles, Schwartz's analysis typically proceeds from a broad scholarly consensus on the basic content of the past to considerations of the ways that this past has been represented in response to changing social circumstances over time. This approach is reflected, for example, in Schwartz's two-volume study of Abraham Lincoln. The argument of both volumes opens with an overview of the scholarly consensus on major themes and issues in Lincoln's life and career, then proceeds to trace shifts in popular collective memory of Lincoln over time, comparing his commemoration in each new generation with the actual past. Such analysis demonstrates that the remembered past 'is both a model of society and a model for society' (Schwartz 2000: 18): a 'model of' in the sense that the past is continually reshaped so that its content can speak to present circumstances in a meaningful way; a 'model for' in the sense that the actual past constrains its subsequent representations to the extent that it emerged from real-world circumstances that differ from present realities.

Tom Thatcher (Cincinnati Christian University, USA)

Further Reading

Schwartz, Barry. 2000. *Abraham Lincoln and the Forge of National Memory*. Chicago: University of Chicago.

Schwartz, Barry. 2005. 'Christian Origins: Historical Truth and Social Memory.' In *Memory, Tradition, and Text: Uses of the Past in Early Christianity*. Edited by Alan Kirk and Tom Thatcher. SemeiaSt. Atlanta: SBL Press, pp. 43–56.

Schwartz, Barry. 2008. *Abraham Lincoln in the Post-Heroic Era*. Chicago: University of Chicago.

Schwartz, Barry. 2011. 'What Difference Does the Medium Make?' In *The Fourth Gospel in First-Century Media Culture*. Edited by Anthony Le Donne and Tom Thatcher. ESCO/LNTS 426. New York: T&T Clark, pp. 225–38.

Scribal Memory The term *scribal memory* refers narrowly to the knowledge of traditional texts held in the COLLECTIVE MEMORY of SCRIBES and, more broadly, to the impact of such knowledge on the biblical writings and their MANUSCRIPT traditions. Scribal memory may influence how an individual scribe 'copies' a manuscript of a biblical text, producing readings that may differ from others but are not 'new' simply because they reflect the scribe's conscious or subconscious appropriation of other versions of the same text, of other texts, or even of the broader tradition. In Alan Kirk's words, 'scribal memory was the interfacial zone where WRITING and oral-traditional practices converged and interacted' (2008: 219). As such, the concept is helpful for understanding the interfaces between memory, ORALITY, and writing in antiquity, and the impact of these interfaces on the biblical manuscript tradition.

While the term *scribal memory* has been used infrequently by biblical scholars (see, e.g. Carr 2005: 38; DeConick 2006: 24; Kirk 2008: 218–20, 222; Horsley 2010: 22; Horsley 2013: 282; Brooke 2013: 57; Miller 2015: 179), the concept of scribal memory has informed a number of studies as a model for explaining the existence of variants in the biblical literature, which existed in antiquity in a context of textual plurality (see

Pluriformity). These variants may be evident within the text of a single biblical book, between biblical books that touch on similar events or themes, or between the extant manuscripts of a single or multiple biblical books (= within the manuscript tradition).

David Carr's *Writing on the Tablet of the Heart* (2005) has been widely influential in conceptions of the workings of scribal memory. Drawing extensively from comparative evidence from throughout the ancient Near East and the ancient Mediterranean worlds, Carr argues that literary texts like the Gilgamesh Epic, the *Iliad*, and the Bible functioned primarily as memory aids, because 'the focus was as much or more on the transmission of texts from mind to mind as on transmission of texts in written form' (2005: 5). Carr located the use of these written texts within educational contexts in which the goal was the internalization of the literary tradition. For example, in Mesopotamia, 'by the first millennium, texts increasingly serve … as authoritative reference points for the checking of scribal memory' (2005: 38). Although this is the only place Carr uses the term 'scribal memory', the educational process he describes focused on the creation and maintenance of scribal memory for the transmission of texts in the context of the broader community.

Carr extended his arguments in *The Formation of the Hebrew Bible* (2011) to include a model for 'memory variants', which are 'the sort of variants that happen when a tradent [= scribe] modifies elements of texts in the process of citing or otherwise reproducing it from memory' (2011: 17). These modifications may include, for example, 'exchange of synonymous words, word-order variation, [and the] presence and absence of conjunctions and minor modifiers' (2011: 33). Carr provides numerous examples of memory variants in the transmission processes of Gilgamesh, the Qumran Temple Scroll (11Q19), the biblical books of Chronicles, and parallels in the biblical book of Proverbs.

Building upon Carr's understanding of memory variants, Raymond Person has utilized the concept of scribal memory in a number of studies that challenge the consensus model for understanding the relationship between Samuel-Kings and Chronicles, biblical books that describe the same or similar events and thus include a significant amount of overlapping content. Person argues that these parallel texts are best understood not in terms of literary dependence or variants, but rather as two faithful reproductions of the broader tradition preserved in the communal memory of the people (2010; 2011; 2015). As such, these written texts were never static retrieval mechanisms, but rather devices that facilitated 'the creative activity of remembering (not memorizing) the broader tradition so that it can continue to live on in the oral-aural communication of the ongoing performances' (Person 2011: 549). Person's approach explains not only the relationship between Samuel-Kings and Chronicles, but also other literary relationships within the biblical manuscript tradition – for example, the relationship between MT-Samuel, LXX-Samuel, and 4QSam[a]. 'Each manuscript represents the broader tradition as an imperfect instantiation of the broader tradition that existed, on the one hand, in the interplay of coexisting parallel written texts, none of which alone can possibly represent the fullness of the tradition, and, on the other hand, in the mental text in the collective memory of the people' (2015: 197). Although Person does not use the term 'scribal memory', his reference to the 'collective memory of the people' would include scribal memory, since scribes were responsible for both the written transmission and public reading or recitation of these literary texts.

Both Carr and Person appeal to the evident textual plurality found in the Dead Sea Scrolls to illustrate the works of scribal memory, and some Qumran scholars have adopted a similar model. George Brooke, drawing significantly on the work of Maurice Halbwachs and Jan Assmann, concludes that 'individual scribes use their memories in the transmission process, a factor that sometimes lies behind the emergence of some variant readings, but they also pay attention to wider issues of cultural memory as they contribute to the creative adaptation of those compositions on which they work for their own contemporary purposes' (2013:xvii). Thus, although there is *individual scribal memory* – individual scribes do remember things, and these memories may impact their work – such memory 'is in large part socially and culturally constructed' (2013: 57) in the sense that each scribe remembers in the context of his/her role as a member of a larger community. Drawing on the work of Carr and Person on memory and performance, Miller analyses the layout, or 'stichography', of selected poetic texts in the Dead Sea Scrolls. 'Stichography is a scribal practice that renders the written format of poetry more convenient for oral performance' (2015: 165), such as the common practices of printing poetic texts in inset lines in modern English translations of the biblical psalms and of printing scripts of Shakespeare's plays in lines that reflect the iambic pentameter inherent in the compositional style. After noting that the formatting of the Song of the Sea in two different Dead Sea Scrolls texts varies, Miller concludes that the varying stichography may reflect different scribal memories of the oral performance of the text (see 2015: 179 for explicit use of the term 'scribal memory').

Alan Kirk, drawing widely from studies of ancient and medieval manuscript culture, has provided an excellent summary of the role of orality and memory in scribal practices (2008), with particular emphasis on the implications of scribal memory for biblical TEXT CRITICISM. Quoting Carr, Kirk asserts that, for scribes, 'the manuscript was ancillary, it was the visual, material support – an external "reference point" – for the primary existence and transmission of the text in the medium of memory' (2008: 219). The performance of a text was often based on the scribe's memory of the text, and the copying of the text was influenced significantly by the scribe's memory of the text – both the SHORT-TERM MEMORY of what the scribe had just read on the manuscript being 'copied' and also the scribe's LONG-TERM MEMORY of the literary text(s) the particular manuscript represented. 'As the manuscript text was activated in scribal memory in recitation and transcription, it has the potential to intersect and react with this traditional repertoire at many points' (2008: 222). Borrowing from Paul Zumthor, Kirk characterizes the affect of scribal memory on the transcription of any particular manuscript as an instance of manuscript MOUVANCE, a term that refers to the indeterminacy of manuscripts within the oral manuscript culture of ancient and medieval literature, which always existed in a state of textual plurality. In Kirk's view, mouvance is a helpful model for understanding NT textual criticism since it provides a more nuanced understanding of the ways that individual Christian scribes both influenced, and were influenced by, the collective memories of the communities of which they were members.

Like Kirk, Chris Keith has stressed that, in an oral manuscript culture, 'a manuscript's significance or "meaning" often extends beyond its content' (2014: 170) because of its relationship to scribal memory. This principle is illustrated by Keith's detailed discussion of the insertion of the story of the Woman Caught in Adultery into some ancient manuscripts of the Gospel of John (Jn 7.53-8:11). In Keith's view, this phenomenon 'suggests [that], at least for some scribes, the limits of the "Johannine" tradition were not quite as rigid as they are for modern scholars' (2011: 54). Put another way, while modern scholars would tend to view this passage as an 'intrusion' or 'interpolation' into a more pristine ORIGINAL text, the passage was placed there because, in the collective memory of some scribes, it belonged there as a part of the Johannine expression of the JESUS TRADITION. Although Keith does not use the term scribal memory, his model illustrates how scribal memory could understand a tradition to be broader than any one manuscript, an observation which in turn provides a framework for understanding why and how early Christian texts existed in a state of fluidity.

As noted in the brief review above, the term *scribal memory* can be used to describe the impact of ancient media, both written/visual and oral/aural, on the work of ancient and medieval scribes in any act of the transmission of the biblical tradition. Scribal memory is active in every form and at every stage of transmission, whether the first textualization of an ORAL TRADITION (when a tradition is first committed to WRITING), the transcription of one written manuscript to another manuscript, the recitation of a literary text recorded in multiple manuscripts, or the reading aloud of a single manuscript. In each of these scribal acts, the collective memory embodied in a particular scribe influences the transmission of the selected instantiation of the broader tradition in that single time and place.

Raymond F. Person, Jr. (Ohio Northern University, USA)

Further Reading

Brooke, George J. 2013. *Reading the Dead Sea Scrolls: Essays in Method*. SBL Early Judaism and Its Literature 39. Atlanta: Society of Biblical Literature.

Carr, David M. 2005. *Writing on the Tablet of the Heart: Origins of Scripture and Literature*. Oxford: Oxford University Press.

Carr, David M. 2011. *The Formation of the Hebrew Bible: A New Reconstruction*. Oxford: Oxford University Press.

DeConick, April D. 2006. *The Original Gospel of Thomas in Translation with a Commentary and New English Translation of the Complete Gospel*. LNTS 376. London: T&T Clark.

Horsley, Richard A. 2010. *Revolt of the Scribes: Resistance and Apocalyptic Origins*. Minneapolis: Fortress.

Horsley, Richard A. 2013. *Text and Tradition in Performance and Writing*. Eugene: Cascade Books.

Keith, Chris. 2011. 'A Performance of the Text: The Adulteress's Entrance into John's Gospel.' In *The Fourth Gospel in First-Century Media Culture*. Edited by Anthony LeDonne and Tom Thatcher. LNTS 426. London: Bloomsbury, pp. 49–69.

Keith, Chris. 2014. 'Prolegomena on the Textualization of Mark's Gospel: Manuscript Culture, the Extended Situation, and the Emergence of the Written Gospel.' In *Memory and Identity in Ancient Judaism and Early Christianity: A Conversation with Barry Schwartz*. Edited by Tom Thatcher. SemeiaSt. Atlanta: SBL Press, pp. 161–86.

Kirk, Alan. 2008. 'Manuscript Tradition as a tertium quid: Orality and Memory in Scribal Practices.' In *Jesus, the Voice, and the Text: Beyond The Oral and the Written Gospel*. Edited by Tom Thatcher. Waco: Baylor University Press, pp. 215–34.

Miller, Shem. 2015. 'The Oral-Written Textuality of Stichographic Poetry in the Dead Sea Scrolls.' *DSD* 22: 162–88.

Person, Raymond F., Jr. 2010. *The Deuteronomic History and the Book of Chronicles: Scribal Works in an Oral World*. SBL Ancient Israel and Its Literature 6. Atlanta: Society of Biblical Literature.

Person, Raymond F., Jr. 2011. 'The Role of Memory in the Tradition Represented by the Deuteronomic History and the Book of Chronicles.' *Oral Tradition* 26: 537–50.

Person, Raymond F., Jr. 2015. 'Text Criticism as a Lens for Understanding the Transmission of Ancient Texts in Their Oral Environments.' In *Contextualizing Israel's Sacred Writing: Ancient Literacy, Orality, and Literature Production*. Edited by Brian Schmidt. SBL Ancient Israel and Its Literature 22. Atlanta: SBL Press, pp. 197–215.

Scribes/scribality Scribes were the professional writers of MANUSCRIPTS and documents in antiquity. WRITING was primarily a technical skill that required special training and was done to earn a living. Throughout First and Second Temple times scribes would have been associated with the TEMPLE. After the destruction of the temple in 70 CE some of these specialized scribes may have continued writing Torah SCROLLS whereas others would have offered their services on the open market, writing documents, LETTERS, and other types of texts required by private individuals and businessmen. Some scribes were hired as private secretaries or functioned as intermediaries between the Jewish populace and the Roman administration. From Hellenistic times onwards, bi- or even tri-lingualism in Hebrew, Aramaic, and Greek would have been an advantage. Greek-educated slaves would have been employed for scribal purposes by the wealthy. They also seem to have functioned as tutors and pedagogues who could instruct children of the Jewish upper strata in the Greek language and the reading of Homer. Torah scribes, on the other hand, seem to have sometimes taught Jewish boys elementary TORAH READING skills. Both the writing of texts and the teaching of elementary reading skills, sometimes carried out by one and the same person, were paid professions, which did not confer a higher social status on the scribe. On the contrary, scribes were commonly looked down upon in both Greco-Roman and rabbinic society. As writing technicians they were considered unable to compete with the higher intellectual skills claimed by rabbis and philosophers whose discussions and transfer of knowledge were conducted orally.

Little is known about the roles and functions of scribes in the First Temple period (approximately 950–587 BCE). Obviously, the role of scribes as writers of religiously relevant texts is related to the development of the text of the Hebrew Bible, concerning which scholars have put forth various theories. Wisdom traditions may have circulated orally before they were put into writing. It is also imaginable that written collections existed alongside ORAL TRADITIONS until versions of the book of Proverbs were created. The complex interplay between various types of written texts and orally transferred material is also likely for the developmental history of other biblical books. Besides being associated with the wisdom tradition, scribes would also have been linked to prophets (cf. Jeremiah's scribe Baruch) and were responsible for the written transmission of prophetic speech (see PROPHECY), visions, and divination.

Their intervention would have ranged from record-keeping to editing and formulating texts. They would have been active at the various stages between first rudimentary note-taking of oral traditions to the PUBLICATION of fully fledged literary works. Whereas some scribes were mere technicians of the written word, others were intellectuals who thought about the texts they wrote and interpreted them before, during, or after their writing practice. It is therefore difficult, if not impossible, to distinguish between composition and writing and between editors and scribes of ancient religious documents. These functions could have been carried out by one and the same person, or the composers of the texts hired scribes and instructed them to write down the partly oral and partly written material in the way in which they produced it. Since biblical literature distinguishes between wise men, prophets, and scribes, one may assume that certain differences between their respective roles existed. Editors or composers of mostly orally transmitted material may have functioned as intermediaries between the practitioners of wisdom and prophecy on the one hand and scribes on the other – that is, they may have taken the initiative in creating the biblical texts.

During the monarchic period scribes would also have been needed for bureaucratic purposes. They would have been in charge of keeping various types of official records relating to the Israelite kings, the royal court, and the monarchy. Scribes would have drawn up friendship contracts with other nations, written official treaties and agreements, circulated laws and edicts, and kept records of tax payments. The more complex the monarchic system became, the more administrative scribes and secretaries would have been needed. Perhaps scribes wrote short histories of the respective kings or created collections of anecdotes and stories relating to them. Whether and to what extent they composed the biblical book of Kings and the book of Chronicles remains uncertain, for reasons already mentioned.

Scribes are commonly assumed to have been trained in scribal schools or guilds, but different types of training must have existed for the various forms of scribal activity. Court historians would have received a different training than administrative secretaries and writers of prophetic visions. Although a strict distinction between the religious and secular domains seems unlikely for ancient Israelite society, different scribal specializations and expertise would have pertained to the various contexts and requirements. Therefore a variety of scribal 'schools' would have existed, depending on the contexts and locations where scribes were needed. Since Jerusalem was the capital of the monarchy and the location of the temple, the most important scribal training would have taken place there. Royal and temple-related scribes would have had the highest status within the scribal profession, since they had the most important tasks to fulfil.

One of the major changes brought about in the Second Temple period was Hellenism and the use of Greek as the major administrative and literary language used by Diaspora Jews. In Palestine, too, Hellenistic influence would have been widespread. Scribes knowledgeable in Greek and bilingual scribes would have been needed at least within the administrative sphere and as writers of documents that could be deposited in official Greek ARCHIVES. Again, various types of scribal skills and specializations have to be reckoned with. Scribes who wrote Aramaic sales documents and Hebrew marriage contracts would have needed different skills than scribes who wrote Greek novels or Hebrew Torah scrolls. The language as well as the social context and type of writing would have determined the training requirements and expertise. Within the Palestinian-Jewish religious context scribes of holy texts would have been held in high esteem, especially when a culture of Torah study developed in Pharisaic circles. In the Greek-speaking Diaspora, scribes with a Greek literary EDUCATION would have written various types of Greek Jewish literary texts. Whether and to what extent they also composed such texts is unclear and has to be examined on a case-by-case basis, although certainty cannot be achieved. The authors of wisdom texts, for example, may have been both sages and scribes. More likely, however, sages dictated their thoughts to scribes or scribes recorded their oral discussions, as was the case with Greek philosophical texts, where authors and scribes were not identical. There is no reason to assume that the situation was different in Jewish intellectual circles.

The relationship between ancient Jewish intellectuals, who would have read and discussed the written text of the Torah but usually lacked the technical skills to write Torah scrolls, and professional scribes who were trained in the copying of the texts would have been complex and competitive. As Torah interpreters post-70 CE rabbis generally look down on scribes who are mainly associated with the more mundane task of writing the texts. Some rabbinic narratives suggest, however, that some scribes may have given advice to people based on their Torah knowledge (see RABBINIC LITERATURE). Scribes may have claimed – and often possessed – close familiarity with the texts, which they could interpret and comment upon. Some intellectuals, who were engaged in discussions based on their reading of the Torah, may have possessed writing skills themselves and created written drafts of traditions which were subsequently amended by scribes. Authors, editors, and scribes may have worked in close cooperation with each other. A similarly complex interplay may be assumed for the creation of the Greek Jewish texts.

In the Gospels of the NT Pharisees and (Torah-)scribes are often mentioned side by side but at the same time distinguished from each other. Both groups were probably seen as scholarly and text-oriented by outsiders, so that they could easily be associated with each other. Their actual roles and activities would have differed but also overlapped. Some Pharisees may have been scribes but not all scribes were Pharisees. Pharisees were religious intellectuals who were experts in Torah knowledge on the basis of memorization and oral discussion, whereas scribes were trained to copy the text with ink on PARCHMENT. In an oral cultural context higher level intellectual activity consisted of the oral discussion, explanation and application of a largely memorized text. The mere technical skill of writing was not considered sufficient by intellectuals and did not confer a higher prestige on scribal professionals. In contrast to those who 'merely' copied the text of the Torah, Pharisaic and rabbinic sages incorporated the text themselves. They functioned as corporeal representations of Torah knowledge, which became the main focus of Jewish IDENTITY after the destruction of the Second Temple in 70 CE.

After the destruction of the temple, temple-related scribes would have entered the open market. They may have offered their services as writers of religious texts, but also as document and letter writers. In the administrative sphere bi- or tri-lingual scribes would have been in demand, especially in locations where (branches of) the Roman provincial administration existed. Another scribal function mentioned in rabbinic sources is the elementary teaching of TORAH READING to boys (see EDUCATION IN ANCIENT ISRAEL). Such teaching was not institutionalized, however, and would have taken place only where a certain public demand for such teaching existed. In a largely agricultural society, where at least ninety per cent of the population worked as farmers, such a demand is unlikely to have been high. Especially in the first two centuries when rabbis were not yet able to convince many of their male coreligionists of the necessity of Torah study, only the most religiously committed (i.e. rabbinic) and sufficiently well-off fathers would have been willing to spend time and money on their sons' Torah reading skills, skills which had no practical work-related value. The Torah memorizing and reading skills taught by Torah scribes and supported by rabbis were meant to create a pool of males who could read the Torah aloud in public gatherings, a practice that was probably seen as honourable. Boys who had gained such education could proceed and become the disciples of rabbis – that is, engage in a specifically Jewish form of higher learning comparable to philosophy in Greek and Roman society – but only a small number of them would have taken this step. Like scribes who wrote documents, letters, and Torah scrolls, scribal elementary teaching was a (probably rather lowly) paid profession, which may have been advertised by word of mouth.

Scribal elementary teachers are rarely mentioned in tannaitic sources, which suggests that private education in Torah reading became more common from the third century CE only, when rabbis were more prominent in the cities and could serve as role models. Another reason for an increase in elementary Torah teaching in late antiquity is the emergence of the SYNAGOGUE as the religious centre of the local Jewish community. From the fourth century onwards these lavish buildings with in-built Torah shrines would have required males who could read the Torah aloud during SABBATH services. The teaching of (Torah) writing to scribal apprentices is not discussed in rabbinic sources, though. Perhaps rabbis were not interested in this skill or it was taught in different contexts to scribal apprentices only. Scribal skills may have been transmitted within families from one generation to the next. Or scribes formed guilds that introduced novices to the scribal arts. Wherever scribal training was carried out, specialization would have been welcomed to avoid too much competition.

Rabbis needed scribes as writers of Torah scrolls and elementary Torah teachers, since Torah scrolls and boys who could read the Torah were the basis of their own higher education. At the same time, they looked down on scribes and considered themselves intellectually superior to them qua being sages. A few Amoraic texts state that particular rabbis 'instructed' scribes, but this oral instruction consisted in halakhic teachings rather than in technical writing skills. The very fact that rabbis presented themselves as instructors of scribes in rabbinic learning shows that rabbis considered them deficient in this regard but at the same time receptive. In Amoraic sources scribes are also sometimes portrayed as students of sages, who asked them halakhic questions and approached them on their own initiative. Some statements directly or indirectly subordinate scribes to rabbis and one text even claims that scribes are among those professionals who 'have no share in the world to come' (ARNA 36). Such a harsh criticism may have been due to seemingly high salaries scribes requested for their services or errors they might introduce into the Torah text. It seems that scribes sometimes competed with sages in the interpretation and application of the Torah, another reason for contention.

Rabbinic texts provide few details on the location and activities of scribes. In Tannaitic texts scribes are associated with Jerusalem only. It may have taken some time until the former temple- and court-related scribes adjusted themselves to the new situation and diversified their skills and locations. One may assume that from the third century onwards scribes were more widely available at least in the major cities of Roman Palestine. Some rabbis would have employed them to write LETTERS, notes, and documents. At some stage scribes may have been commissioned to put rabbinic rules and stories about rabbis in writing, texts which may have circulated as collections and formed the basis of later rabbinic documents such as the MISHNAH. Throughout the first to fifth centuries CE the writing of halakhic notes, collections of traditions, and versions of Tannaitic tractates would have coincided with rabbinic oral teaching, discussion, and transmission. In all likelihood, rabbis and scribes interacted closely in the creation and development of rabbinic documents. Various scribal manuscript versions of these documents would have circulated in Byzantine times, which were reinterpreted and discussed orally by subsequent generations of Torah scholars.

Catherine Hezser (SOAS University of London, UK)

Further Reading

Carr, David M. 2005. *Writing on the Tablet of the Heart: Origins of Scripture and Literature*. Oxford: Oxford University Press.

Demsky, Aaron, and Meir Bar-Ilan. 1988. 'Writing in Ancient Israel and Early Judaism, Part One: The Biblical Period.' In *Mikra. Text, Translation, Reading and Interpretation of the Hebrew Bible in Ancient Judaism and Early Christianity*. Edited by Martin Jan Mulder. CRINT II.1. Assen: van Gorcum, pp. 1–20.

Hezser, Catherine. 1997. 'Scribes.' In *The Social Structure of the Rabbinic Movement in Roman Palestine*. Tübingen: Mohr Siebeck, pp. 467–75.

Hezser, Catherine. 2001. 'The Costs and Availability of Scribes.' In *Jewish Literacy in Roman Palestine*. Tübingen: Mohr Siebeck, pp. 118–26.

Jamieson-Drake, David W. 1991. *Scribes and Schools in Monarchic Judah: A Socio-Archeological Approach*. The Social World of Biblical Antiquity Series 9. Sheffield: Sheffield Academic Press.

Kelber, Werner. 2004. 'Roman Imperialism and Early Christian Scribality.' In *Orality, Literacy, and Colonialism in Antiquity*. Edited by Jonathan A. Draper. SemeiaSt. Atlanta: SBL Press, pp. 135–54.

Perdue, Leo G., ed. 2008. *Scribes, Sages, and Seers: The Sage in the Eastern Mediterranean World*. Göttingen: Vandenhoeck & Ruprecht.

Rollston, Christopher A. 2010. *Writing and Literacy in the World of Ancient Israel: Epigraphic Evidence from the Iron Age*. SBL Archaeology and Biblical Studies 11. Atlanta: SBL Press.

Saldarini, Anthony J. 1989. *Pharisees, Scribes and Sadducees in Palestinian Society: A Sociological Approach*. Edinburgh: T&T Clark.

Schams, Christine. 1998. *Jewish Scribes in the Second Temple Period*. JSOTSup 291. Sheffield: Sheffield Academic Press.

Toorn, Karel van der. 2007. *Scribal Culture and the Making of the Hebrew Bible*. Cambridge, MA: Harvard University Press.

Tov, Emanuel. 2004. *Scribal Practices and Approaches Reflected in the Texts Found in the Judean Desert*. STDJ 54. Leiden: Brill.

Scriptoria Scriptoria were areas designed for SCRIBES to copy write documents, particularly in SCROLL or CODEX form. Through scriptoria, broadly defined, have come the majority of extant premodern versions of the Bible, as well as a great deal of extant ancient and medieval literature.

The term *scriptorium*, which has no known equivalent in classical Greek or Latin, stems from an eleventh-century neologism for a generic Latin word that simply meant WRITING or writing instrument. The anachronism (used in this article for convenience) does not imply there were no such spaces before the medieval period; rather, the act of copying was so inseparable from the host institution (ARCHIVES, LIBRARIES, and booksellers) that a separate term was usually unnecessary. This proximity of function, as well as its portability, explains why so little unambiguous material evidence survives.

Very early scriptoria have been identified across the ancient world in places such as the palace complex of Knossos, Crete (based on Middle/Late Bronze clay tablets), the lower city of Ḫattuša from the late Hittite empire, and throughout ancient Egypt in a type of facility known as *per-ankh* ('House of Life'). In the Hellenistic world, Greek archives and libraries, which would procure book loans from other institutions, had the facilities to make copies on site (Galen, *Hippocrates Epidemics* 3; Kühn 607). Ink residues in a room at Qumran and patterns of editorial marks on scrolls found at the near-contemporary library at Herculaneum (first century CE) have been interpreted as evidence of scriptoria (see VILLA OF THE PAPYRI). Although tenuous, the conjectures fit with what one would expect of facilities used by communities devoted to creating and preserving written texts.

The host facility and its corresponding priestly or clerical culture greatly influenced the kinds of texts that were copied, how they were copied (by dictation or inspection), and how they were used. As public literary tastes expanded beyond the central concerns of cult or state, so too books began to be commissioned and created independent of these institutions. In the marketplace in fifth-century Athens, vendors sold books in demand (Plato, *Apology of Socrates* 26d; Eupolis fragment 327). As LITERACY and literary culture spread, so too did book selling and its requisite scribal services. The types of scribes varied – from slaves to freemen, from skilled to pedestrian, from those who worked (aurally or visually) phrase by phrase to those who could work only letter by letter (cf. Cicero, *Atticus* 13.25; Shepherd of Hermas, *Vision* 2.1.3–4). The diversity is seen in handwriting styles on extant MANUSCRIPTS, which fall on a spectrum ranging from highly polished literary hands to documentary ones.

The rise of the scribe for hire altered the nature of the scriptorium, which, in the service of private networks and booksellers, could be temporary and portable and could include other professionals such as illuminators and bookbinders. Anyone who had access to a secretary or a literate slave, or had the means to hire a professional copyist, thereby also had the potential to reproduce any text. Equipment and furnishings for a personal scriptorium could be as minimal as a bench, an inkwell, and some writing materials. A shelf might be required for written exemplars, whether dictated or directly copied (Biblioteca Medicea Laurenziana, Codex Amiatinus, folio 5r; early eighth century CE). Baruch probably served the prophet Jeremiah in such a setting, as did Tertius (Rom. 16.22) and other scribes the Apostle Paul.

The confluence of institution and private scribal network shaped the book trade in the ancient West, which first arose in the Roman Late Republic. Cicero (106–43 BCE), for example, depended upon his friend Atticus and his staff of *librarii* to publish and copy literary works, to publicize, circulate, and correct them, and to perform other scribal services. Such private ventures coincided with the establishment of permanent libraries and archives in Italy, along with the necessary scriptoria.

Writing from the oldest surviving Christian and Jewish documents show hands that have features that come from both sides of the documentary/literary spectrum, indicating production primarily through private networks of scribes, and therefore outside permanent, high-end scriptoria attached to institutions (Qumran being the exception that proves the rule). As Christianity developed, so too did a more sedentary and refined scribal culture. Origen's enormous literary output, first in Alexandria but especially in Caesarea in Palestine, was facilitated by scribal services underwritten by private and institutional patronage (Eusebius, *Church History* 7.23-36). Emperor Constantine commissioned at extravagant expense fifty deluxe Bibles, executed under the direction of Eusebius, in the same city Origen had worked (Eusebius, *Life of Constantine* 4.36-37). Christian literature became commercially viable and suitable for mass copying, illustrated by the *Life of St. Martin* (fourth century CE), whose quick popularity required numerous copies and brought sizeable profits to booksellers in Rome (Sulpicius Severus, *Dialogues* 1.23).

Christian monasteries, which emerged in the fourth century CE, immediately attracted scribal culture, and therefore joined libraries, archives, and booksellers in providing the services of a high quality scriptorium (e.g. Palladius, *Lausiac History* 38.10). The first attested monastic scriptorium was located in Cassiodorus' Vivarium (mid-fifth century CE; *Institutes* 1.15, 30). The first depiction of a scriptorium, from a plan of the Benedictine Abbey of St. Gall (Stiftsbibliothek Sankt Gallen, manuscript 1092; ca. 820 CE), places it beneath the library. As monasteries increased in size, structure, and influence, so too did activities in the scriptorium, with changes in the thirteenth century, both East and West, leading to professionalized specialization and a commercial book industry.

Scriptoria had detectable influence on both the aesthetics and content of biblical texts. Computing techniques that match manuscripts to specific scriptoria promise new insights on the reception and transmission of the biblical text.

Joel Kalvesmaki (Dumbarton Oaks, USA)

Further Reading

Gardiner, Alan H. 1938. 'The House of Life.' *Journal of Egyptian Archaeology* 24(2): 157–79.
Gordin, Shai. 2010. 'Scriptoria in Late Empire Period Ḫattuša: The Case of the É GIŠ.KIN.TI.' In *Pax Hethitica: Studies on the Hittites and Their Neighbours in Honour of Itamar Singer*. Edited by Yoram Cohen, Amir Gilan and Jared L. Miller. Wiesbaden: Harrassowitz Verlag, pp. 158–77.
Haines-Eitzen, Kim. 2000. *Guardians of Letters: Literacy, Power, and the Transmitters of Early Christian Literature*. Oxford; New York: Oxford University Press.
Mugridge, Alan. 2004. 'What Is a Scriptorium?' In *24th International Congress of Papyrology*, vol. 2. Helsinki: Societas Scientiarum Fennica, pp. 781–92.
Reynolds, L. D., and N. G. Wilson. 2013. *Scribes and Scholars: A Guide to the Transmission of Greek and Latin Literature*. 4th edn. Oxford: Oxford University Press.
Staikos, K. 2004. *The History of the Library in Western Civilization*. 5 vols. 1st English ed. New Castle, DE: Oak Knoll Press.

Scrolls A scroll consists of a series of PAPYRUS, PARCHMENT, or leather sheets sewn or glued together for the purpose of being inscribed. Often referred to as a *roll* or *bookroll*, the scroll was the most common book form in antiquity, but was eventually replaced by the CODEX.

In the Greco-Roman period, most scrolls were made out of papyrus sheets called *kollēmata* (sing. *kollēma*) that were glued together at their edges, resulting in an overlap of the papyrus known as a *kollēsis*. A certain number of narrow columns of text would be written on the *recto* side of the papyrus (the side where the papyrus fibres run in a horizontal direction). This side of the papyrus constituted the inside of the scroll, thereby safeguarding it from damage. Generally, the backside of a scroll, known as the *verso*, was left blank, but there are numerous examples where SCRIBES also inscribed the verso. A scroll that has text on both the recto and verso is known as an *opisthograph* (cf. Rev. 5.1). In contradistinction to many images of scrolls in medieval and modern art that depict scrolls being unrolled vertically (a format known as a *rotulus*), most ancient scrolls were unrolled horizontally (although there are exceptions, such as the rotulus scrolls among the ELEPHANTINE PAPYRI). One may point to the Great Isaiah Scroll (1QIsa) among the DEAD SEA SCROLLS, which can be seen unrolled horizontally at the Shrine of the Book in Jerusalem. Very few rollers upon which scrolls would have been wound have survived. In an effort to protect the scroll when it was rolled up, most scribes added a blank sheet at the beginning called a *protocollon*. Sometimes scribes, booksellers, or readers would add tags made of papyrus or parchment that served as book titles; examples of these tags have survived and are also depicted in Greco-Roman art.

The length of scrolls varied. According to Pliny the Elder (*Natural History* 13.23), there were never more than twenty sheets to a roll, but the evidence speaks against this claim: many extant scrolls exceed twenty sheets. Pliny's statement most likely pertained to the standard number of sheets in a manufactured roll sold on the market. Scribes were always at liberty to extend the length of a pre-manufactured scroll: they could shorten the scroll by cutting off the superfluous material, or lengthen it by simply pasting (or in the case of parchment and leather, sewing) on additional sheets. In non-literary or documentary scrolls, such as legal documents, private LETTERS, and contracts, the scroll would often be rolled, tied up with a string, and sealed with a clay seal.

It seems that operating a scroll sometimes posed inconveniences, as depicted in some Athenian vase paintings. In the well-known story told by Pliny the Younger (*Letters* 2.1.5), Verginius Rufus dropped a scroll because 'its weight caused it to slip from his hands'; while bending down to pick it up, he broke his hip. It has been suggested that the inconvenience of unrolling and rolling up a scroll served as one of motivating factors for transitioning to the codex, but this may or may not have been the case. T. C. Skeat has demonstrated, on the basis of a modern experiment, that the process was not as difficult as previously assumed. Nevertheless, working with scrolls (producing them, inscribing them, reading them, storing them, handling them, etc.) required skills that perhaps not all people possessed, and this underscores the importance of scribes and public readers in antiquity (see LECTOR).

Scrolls are mentioned throughout the Bible. The Hebrew word for scroll is *sefer*, and the Greek word *biblion*. In the Gospel of Luke, an attendant brings Jesus a scroll of Isaiah to read in the SYNAGOGUE at Nazareth (4.17-20). Jesus unrolls the scroll, reads from Isaiah, then rolls it back up and gives it to the attendant. In Revelation, John sees a scroll 'written on the inside and on the back', a description of an opisthograph (5.1).

Brice C. Jones (University of Louisiana at Monroe, USA)

Further Reading

Johnson, William A. 2009. 'The Ancient Book.' In *The Oxford Handbook of Papyrology*. Edited by Roger S. Bagnall. Oxford: Oxford University Press, pp. 256–81.

Skeat, T. C. 1981. 'Two Notes on Papyrus: I, Was Rerolling a Papyrus Roll an Irksome and Time-Consuming Task?' In *Scritti in onore di Orsolina Montevecchi*. Edited by Edda Bresciani. Bologna: Clueb, pp. 373–6.

Second Temple See TEMPLE, JERUSALEM.

Secondary Orality The term *secondary orality* was developed by Walter ONG to describe the use and reuse of material included in written texts within an oral culture/context. Ong used the term *primary orality* to describe the use and reuse of oral materials in cultures 'totally untouched by any knowledge of writing or print'; *secondary orality*, by contrast, emerges in contexts such as 'present-day high-technology culture in which a new orality is sustained by telephone, radio, television, and other electronic devices that depend for their existence and functioning on writing and print' (2007: 11). As indicated by the preceding quote, the term *secondary* is not qualitative, but rather describes the place of ORALITY in social contexts where communications culture is dominated by forms of WRITING (manual, print, or digital). In such a context, orality interacts with, and is to some extent dependent upon, the experience of written texts and their contexts.

At first glance, it seems anachronistic to apply Ong's model to the biblical literature, inasmuch as written texts were not as widely distributed or accessible in antiquity as they are today. Biblical scholars, however, have adapted the concept of secondary orality as a helpful tool in discussing the relationship between passages in biblical texts that show parallels and differences in setting, structure, and wording. In this context, the term *secondary orality* names the shift from written back to oral in the transmission of material (material drawn from a written document is re-incorporated into ORAL TRADITION/performance), and thus has expanded traditional discussions of literary dependence in ways that acknowledge the relationships between written texts while also accounting for the dynamics of oral performance and PUBLICATION in antiquity.

The concept was first applied to problems in biblical studies by WERNER KELBER, who observed that when a written 'text enters the world of hearers by being read aloud [as was typically the case in antiquity], it functions as secondary orality. But now the story narrated is one that was never heard in primary orality, for it comprises textually filtered and contrived language' (1983: 217–18). Kelber illustrates the concept by using secondary orality as a model for explaining the appropriation of the Jewish Scriptures in the NT writings. In the predominantly oral world in which the Gospels were written, the written texts of the OT were typically experienced through reading aloud and normally cited orally from memory – the contents of the written texts of Scripture were thus encountered primarily as oral content, even though this oral material was dependent upon writing. 'The existence of allusions and influences, in addition to quotations, suggests that much of Scripture, like much literature in antiquity, was mentally accessible to an oral mode of appropriation. Obviously, orality derived from texts is not the same as primary orality, which operates without the aid of texts. The PASSION NARRATIVE is largely built on texts and texts recycled into the oral medium, that is, secondary orality' (1983: 197).

More recently, the concept of secondary orality has been helpfully applied to a number of problems relating to the composition of, and relationships between, biblical texts, particularly the early Christian writings. Here it helps to understand and to describe the change from written to oral media which could be found in a written text. Michael Labahn uses the concept to explain the relationship between the miracle stories in John and in the Synoptics, arguing that similarities between the texts may not indicate direct borrowing of one author from another, but rather the re-entry of material included in one written Gospel into the stream of oral tradition utilized by another (Labahn 1999; cf. 2000; 2006; 2016).

Similarly, Samuel Byrskog, following Margaret Mills (1990), refers to the 're-oralisation' of material in written texts under the creative impulse of the oral performer. Byrskog's model seeks to nuance the traditional Two Source approach to the composition of the Gospels by acknowledging both the relationships between written Gospels and the creative adaptation of material found in written texts in an oral milieu. He thus portrays the author of Matthew as a hearer and re-teller of Mark's story, drawing material from Mark to develop his own unique PERFORMANCE OF THE GOSPEL in conjunction with an 'oral hermeneutic' (2000: 348), one that allowed Matthew to engage Mark's material in an 'empathetic and participatory' fashion typical of oral composition (2000: 338). According to Hans-Josef Klauck, secondary orality is a helpful tool for the study of apocryphal texts that were 'brought to light in recent scholarship' (Klauck 2003: 3). He claims:

> The narrative in the canonical gospels enters a phase of new, secondary orality, where these texts are exposed to a free reformulation and above all to a harmonizing assimilation of the various versions. This too may be a route which permitted the canonical gospels to exercise indirect influence on the composition of apocryphal texts.

Secondary orality can also be applied as a more adequate model for understanding the relationships between apocryphal Gospels and parallel material in the canonical Gospels (see Uro 1998; DeConick 2006; Czachesz 2007; Frey 2008; Gathercole 2012).

Michael Labahn (Martin Luther Universität Halle-Wittenberg, Germany)

Further Reading

Byrskog, Samuel. 2000. *Story as History – History as Story. The Gospel Traditions in the Context of Ancient Oral History.* WUNT 123. Tübingen: Mohr Siebeck.

DeConick, April D. 2006. *The Original Gospel of Thomas in Translation. With a Commentary and New English Translation of the Complete Gospel.* LNTS 287. New York: T&T Clark.

Frey, Jörg. 2008. 'Die Lilien und das Gewand: EvThom 36 und 37 als Paradigma für das Verhältnis des Thomasevangeliums zur synoptischen Überlieferung.' In *Das Thomasevangelium: Entstehung – Rezeption – Theologie*. Edited by J. Frey, E. E. Popkes, and J. Schröter. BZNW 157. Berlin: Walter Mouton de Gruyter, pp. 122–80.

Gathercole, Simon. 2012. *The Composition of the Gospel of Thomas: Original Language and Influences.* SNTSMS 151. Cambridge: Cambridge University Press, particularly 155–9, 209–24.

Kelber, Werner H. 1983. *The Oral and the Written Gospel. The Hermeneutics of Speaking and Writing in the Synoptic Tradition, Mark, Paul, and Q.* Philadelphia: Fortress Press.

Klauck, H.-J. 2003. *Apocryphal Gospels: An Introduction.* London: T&T Clark.

Labahn, Michael. 1999. *Jesus als Lebensspender: Untersuchungen zu einer Geschichte der johanneischen Tradition anhand ihrer Wundergeschichten*. BZNW 98. Berlin: Walter Mouton de Gruyter.
Labahn, Michael. 2000. *Offenbarung in Zeichen und Wort. Untersuchungen zur Vorgeschichte von Joh 6,1-25a und seiner Rezeption in der Brotrede*. WUNT 2/117. Tübingen: Mohr Siebeck.
Labahn, Michael. 2006. 'Fishing for Meaning. The Miraculous Catch of Fish in John 21.' In *Wonders Never Cease: The Purpose of Narrating Miracle Stories in the New Testament and Its Religious Environment*. Edited by Michael Labahn, and B. J. Lietaert Peerbolte. LNTS 288. London: T&T Clark, pp. 125–45.
Labahn, Michael. 2016. '"Secondary Orality" in the Gospel of John: A "Post-Gutenberg" Paradigm for Understanding the Relationship between Written Gospel Texts.' In *The Origins of John's Gospel*. Edited by Stanley E. Porter and Hughson T. Ong. Johannine Studies 2. Leiden, Boston: Brill, pp. 53-80.
Mills, M. A. 1990. 'Domains of Folkloristic Concern. The Interpretation of Scriptures.' In *Text and Tradition. The Hebrew Bible and Folklore*. Edited by S. Niditch. SemeiaSt. Atlanta: SBL, pp. 231–41.
Ong, Walter J. 2007. *Orality and Literacy. The Technologizing of the World.* New York: Routledge.
Uro, Risto. 1998. 'Thomas and Oral Gospel Tradition.' In *Thomas at the Crossroads. Essays on the Gospel of Thomas*. Edited by Risto Uro. Studies of the New Testament and its World. Edinburgh: T&T Clark, pp. 8–32.

Septuagint The term *Septuagint* (typically abbreviated LXX) refers to the ancient TRANSLATION of the Hebrew Torah into Greek. According to the *Letter of Aristeas*, seventy(-two) translators journeyed from Jerusalem to Alexandria at the request of Ptolemy II Philadelphus (285–247 BCE) to render only the Mosaic Law into Greek. In time, other ancient authors (e.g. Justin Martyr) extended the scope of the work of the seventy(-two) to all of the Hebrew Scriptures, and this use of the term is found in scholarly literature today. However, Septuagint scholars make a distinction between the Septuagint translation of the Torah and the later Old Greek translations of the other books, which may have been translated by the end of the second century BCE, as the Greek Prologue to Ben Sira (ca. 132 BCE) suggests.

While the word *Septuagint* gives the impression that the translation is a monolith produced by something akin to a modern translation committee, a different translator was responsible for each book or perhaps part of a book (as might be the case in Samuel-Kings) and earlier translations were sometimes revised by a later reviser. Translation types have been analysed on a continuum from literal to free approaches. The text-critical value of each book will vary based on the kind of translation it is.

Septuagint as Translation

Consistent with the traditional perspective noted above, the Pentateuch was translated first. Comparing the Septuagint to its presumed Semitic precursors, Genesis and Exodus exhibit a free type of translation technique, while Leviticus, Numbers, and Deuteronomy exhibit a more literal approach. Both approaches, therefore, are present in the first five books. The rest of the books show these two tendencies to greater and lesser degrees. A more literal approach is seen in Psalms and a still more literal translation is observed in Ecclesiastes. Isaiah demonstrates a free approach, and Job shows still a freer technique. A few short examples will show the different approaches.

- LXX Ecclesiastes represents a highly literal approach. It oftentimes uses the same Greek root for each Hebrew root, displaying a concordance principle of translation (e.g. *peri/parapherō/hll* III 'madness'). Furthermore, each Hebrew word has a corresponding Greek word. For example, the translator rendered the definite direct object marker in Hebrew (*'ēt*) – normally left untranslated – with *sun*, the preposition meaning 'with'.
- LXX Isaiah varied its approach from transliteration (cf. *seraphin/m* in 6:2) to expansive and exegetical renderings of the Hebrew source. For example, the word *ləbēnîm* ('mudbricks') in Isa. 9.9 triggered an allusion to the *ləbēnîm* in Gen. 11.3. LXX Isa. 9:10 includes the phrase 'come … and

let us build a tower for ourselves', which is absent from the Hebrew text of Isaiah but alludes to the story of the Tower of Babel in Gen. 11.4.

- LXX Job has been sometimes called a paraphrase since the translation is some one-sixth shorter, or approximately 390 lines shorter, than the Hebrew source. For example, the original translator shortened the text of Job 28 by half, so that only vv. 1–3a, 4b, 9b–13, 20–21a, 22b–26a, and 27b–28 should be considered the Old Greek version. Origen of Alexandria added vv. 3b–4a, 5–9a, 14–19, 21b–22a, and 26b–27a in order to bring the Greek text into closer alignment with the Hebrew source (see HEXAPLA). However, the work could also be characterized as an epitome of the longer original, since most of the shortening and expanding (cf. LXX Job 2.9a–d; though perhaps the extended diatribe of Job's wife arose through scribal transmission) serves to make the message of the longer Hebrew original relevant to a Jewish-Hellenistic audience.

These few examples show that not every translation in the corpus is equally valuable for TEXTUAL CRITICISM of the Hebrew source (i.e. freer translations) or for discerning the exegesis or theology of the translator (i.e. literal translations). Focus on the Septuagint as a translation causes one to analyse the character of the translation of each book so that, before one engages in text-critical work or attempts to discern the exegesis or theology of a translation, one must ask, 'What kind of translation is this?'

The Septuagint and the Text of the Hebrew Bible

Before the recent focus on study of the Septuagint as a translation that exhibits multiple tendencies, biblical scholars often used the Septuagint as a source for reconstructing the ancient Hebrew Bible. That is, scholars have been able to reconstruct the underlying Hebrew text of the Greek translation, and this reconstructed text often preserves a better and more original text than the Hebrew MASORETIC TEXT. Even though the translation is now studied for its own sake, the Septuagint may still be used with good success as a textual witness to the Hebrew Bible, so long as one discerns actual textual differences from both apparent and insignificant ones (for more explanation of the following issues, see Gentry 2006: 194–206).

- *Inner Greek Corruptions*. If one uses the Septuagint as a witness to the Hebrew Bible, one must use the actual translation, not a variant of the translation. For example, 2 Chron. 31.6 has *qadašîm* '[tenth] of holy things'. LXX 2 Chron. 31.6 reads *aigōn* '[tenths] of goats', but two witnesses, 93 ArmII, read *hagiōn* ('of holy things'). Early in the transmission of the Septuagint text, a Greek SCRIBE read *ΑΙΓΩΝ* instead of *ΑΓΙΩΝ*, since letters of the square series were easily confused in papyri and uncials. Mention of herds and flocks earlier in the verse also led the scribe to write 'goats' instead of holy things, thus causing an accidental variation from the Hebrew.
- *Differences Due to Factors in Translation*. Many differences between the Hebrew text and the Septuagint arose due to translation technique, but these differences do not constitute genuine textual variants. The examples noted above from Job illustrates this phenomenon. Furthermore, differences due to interference from late or post-biblical Hebrew or Aramaic do not constitute true variants. For example, LXX Eccl. 2.12c has *boulē* ('counsel') for Hebrew *melek* ('king') from *I mlk*. In Aramaic, *II mlk* 'to consult, ask for advice' is well attested, and this meaning influenced LXX Ecclesiastes in this case. Although the difference appears significant, the Greek version still attests the same Hebrew consonants as the Masoretic Text.
- *Different Reading Traditions*. The vocalization of the Hebrew Scriptures was not represented graphemically at the time of the Greek translations except for some of the *plene* spelling traditions

represented in some of the Dead Sea Scroll manuscripts. Much of the reading tradition of the Greek translators agreed with the later Masoretic tradition, but the Greek translators also had their own reading tradition at times. For example, in Isa. 3.12, the Hebrew consonantal root is *nšm*, which could be read in two different ways, depending on which vowel points are implied by the reader. The Masoretic Text has *nāšîm* ('women'), whereas the Septuagint has *hoi apaitountes* ('creditors'), a rendering of *nōšîm* ('creditors') from *nš'* or I *nšh*. That is, both the Masoretic Text and Septuagint read the same Hebrew consonantal text, but supply different vowels based on different reading traditions.

- *Confusion of Similar Letters*. Oftentimes a Septuagint translator renders a variant text that arose through an error caused by similar letters in the square script, such as d/r (ד/ר), b/k (ב/כ), h/ḥ (ה/ח), y/w (י/ו) etc. Although technically the translator is rendering a different text than that of the more original Hebrew, these kinds of variants are not too significant and more often witness indirectly to the better textual tradition of the Masoretic Text (e.g. Prov. 23.7 *šā'ar* 'calculates' in the Masoretic Text vs. *śā'ēr* 'hair' in the Septuagint). That is, the text critic interprets the readings of the Septuagint in these cases as secondary and as indirectly attesting to the Hebrew text of the Masoretic Text.
- *Different Vorlage*. In Isa. 53.8, the Masoretic Text and Septuagint differ significantly. For the last word in the verse, the Masoretic Text has *lāmô* ('his/theirs'), while the Septuagint has *eis thanaton* ('to death'), which probably represents a different Hebrew Vorlage that had *lamāwet* ('to death'). The best explanation of this problem is that the Hebrew Vorlage of the Septuagint preserves the more original text, while the text of the Masoretic Text and all other witnesses transmitted a secondary text without the final *taw* due to accidental mutilation. This difference between the texts cannot be explained sufficiently without recourse to positing that the Septuagint rendered a different Hebrew text than the Masoretic Text, which is now lost.
- *Large-Scale Differences between the Septuagint and the Masoretic Text*. There are situations where a group of real textual differences between the Masoretic Text and Septuagint form a pattern, so that the only explanation is that one or the other of these represents a variant edition or recension in the history of a biblical book. Most scholars would agree that this premise is validated by the following instances:

  a. LXX Jeremiah is a translation of a shorter Hebrew version than the Masoretic Text;

  b. LXX Ezekiel translates a shorter version than the Masoretic Text;

  c. LXX 1 Samuel 16–18 translates a shorter version than the Masoretic Text;

  d. the literary shape of several chapters of 1 Esdras is older than the Masoretic Text edition of the parallel chapters in Ezra-Nehemiah and Chronicles;

  e. LXX Joshua and LXX Judges probably show a pattern of textual variants that attest a different stage in the redactional history of the books of Joshua and Judges;

  f. As noted above, few scholars still hold to the older viewpoint that LXX Job represents a translation of a shorter Hebrew text than the one observed in the Masoretic Text. Most scholars now posit that the shorter Greek version arose from translation technique, not textual factors.

Different explanations for this pluriformity are available. Most scholars believe that these different versions represent different literary editions, and therefore represent different stages in the literary history of individual books. Sometimes the Masoretic Text represents the earlier edition of a book and the Septuagint a later, more final stage, and sometimes the Septuagint represents the earlier edition while the Masoretic

Text represents the later, more final form of a book. Some scholars hold that the relationship of these variant editions is not to be envisioned as a linear, historical development, but rather these variant editions arose from two different but concurrent tendencies during the transmission of the text: 1) many of the manuscripts and ancient translations demonstrate that scribes tended to copy texts as received in a straightforward or conservative manner; 2) while other manuscripts and ancient translations demonstrate that scribes revised and updated the text, perhaps to make it relevant to the current circumstances.

John D. Meade (Phoenix Seminary, USA)

Further Reading

Cox, Claude. 2014. 'Some Things Biblical Scholars Should Know about the Septuagint.' *ResQ* 56(2): 87–100.

Gentry, Peter J. 2006. 'The Septuagint and the Text of the Old Testament.' *BBR* 16(2): 193–218.

Marcos, Natalio Fernández. 2000. *The Septuagint in Context: Introduction to the Greek Version of the Bible*. Translated by Wilfred G. E. Watson. Leiden: Brill.

Tov, Emanuel. 2012. *Textual Criticism of the Hebrew Bible*. 3rd rev. Minneapolis: Fortress Press.

Short-Term Memory See Long-Term/Short-Term Memory.

Simonides Simonides (c. 556–468 BCE) was an acclaimed Greek poet from Keos, an Aegean island near Attica. He served as protagonist of a legendary account that earned him a reputation as the father of memory arts. The story, recorded by Cicero (*Orator* 2.351-54) and Quintilian (*Institutes* 11.2.11-17), was well-known in antiquity and underscored the visual and spatial natures of memory. It informed the Greek mnemonic system of *topoi* ('places') and paved the way for the development of the Roman architectural or *memory palace* system of *loci* ('places') and *imagines* ('images') (see MEMORY, GRECO-ROMAN THEORIES OF). These approaches shed light on how ancient texts were organized for the purposes of interior mastery, rumination, and recitation (see MEMORY THEATRE).

The intriguing story narrates Simonides' recital of lyric poetry during a BANQUET in Thessaly celebrating the boxing victory of the aristocrat Scopas. Scopas became offended when Simonides chanted a passage to the twin gods, Castor and Pollux, who were highly regarded for their boxing prowess. After Scopas declared that he would only pay half of Simonides' fee for the victory ode, he informed him that he needed to procure the remaining payment from the two gods. When Simonides later left the building to meet two men reportedly waiting outside for him, the building's roof collapsed, crushing the occupants beyond recognition. Simonides, however, was able to identify the mangled remains by recalling the guests' prior seating arrangement at the table, demonstrating the importance of placing images into carefully ordered spaces as a mnemonic technique.

Jeffrey E. Brickle (Urshan Graduate School of Theology, USA)

Further Reading

Small, Penny J. 1997. *Wax Tablets of the Mind: Cognitive Studies of Memory and Literacy in Classical Antiquity*. London: Routledge.

Thatcher, Tom. 2011. 'John's Memory Theatre: A Study of Composition in Performance'. *In The Fourth Gospel in First-Century Media Culture*. Edited by Anthony Le Donne and Tom Thatcher. ESCO/LNTS 426. London: T&T Clark, pp. 73–91.

Yates, Frances A. 1966. *The Art of Memory*. Chicago: The University of Chicago Press.

Sitz im Leben *Sitz im Leben* ('life setting') is a German phrase coined by HERMANN GUNKEL (1862–1932) to describe the 'typical situation or occupation in the life of a community' (Bultmann 1968: 4) in which a unit of ORAL TRADITION emerged and was transmitted. In Gunkel's view, traditional units, including those eventually incorporated into the biblical texts, emerge out of a particular social context and carry a particular function and purpose derived from that situation. Further, the form in which the text is communicated – its genre or *Gattung* – is based on and directly linked to its *Sitz im Leben*. In other words, the genre of a text is determined by the social/traditional contexts in which the material was rehearsed, so that identifying the *Gattung* or GENRE of a biblical passage could reveal the life setting in which the traditional material underlying the text developed and/or was used. Gunkel's model was particularly significant to the development of biblical FORM CRITICISM, which relied heavily on assumed life settings to explain the origin, form, and contents of biblical pericopae.

The concept of *Sitz im Leben* has been applied particularly to texts such as the Pentateuch and the Gospels, which were probably transmitted orally before they were written down. Traditional form critics sought to discern the original life setting behind individual biblical stories and sayings based on their final forms (Bultmann 1968: 4; Travis 1977) (see BULTMANN, RUDOLF; DIBELIUS, MARTIN). More recently, however, scholars have become less confident in the notion that individual biblical passages can be traced back through tradition to single points of origin, and also more sceptical of the assumption that traditional units within the biblical narratives can be isolated from their larger contexts and 'reconstructed' (see NARRATIVITY). In oral cultures, the genre of a text emerging out of oral tradition is not simply a mathematical product of original setting, style, and form, but develops under the influence of multiple aspects of community, culture, and belief systems within a performative setting. In fact, a given genre may be expressed within many different settings and still retain its distinctive form and content, rendering pointless any search for an original *Sitz im Leben* (Long 1976: 34–5).

For these reasons, the use of *Sitz im Leben* as a framework for analysing a biblical text has moved from historical and theological emphases to primarily sociological uses – to exploring the relationship between a text's social function and its interpretation (Rendtorff 1985). Thus, scholars who identify WORSHIP as the primary oral context of the Pentateuch explore the implications of worship as the contextual backdrop to interpreting the Law of Moses, while NT scholars seek to identify the *Sitz im Leben* of the church or of Jesus' ministry in order to engage the dynamic between community life and textual interpretation revealed by the various sayings and stories of Jesus in the Gospels.

Judith Odor (Asbury Theological Seminary, USA)

Further Reading

Black, David Alan, and David S. Dockery. 2001. *Interpreting the New Testament: Essays on Methods and Issues*. Nashville: Broadman & Holman.

Bultmann, Rudolf. 1968. *The History of the Synoptic Tradition*. Translated by John Marsh. Second Edition. Oxford: Basil Blackwell.

Byrskog, Samuel. 2007. 'A Century with the Sitz im Leben: From Form-Critical Setting to Gospel Community and Beyond.' *ZNW* 98: 1–27.

Rolf Rendtorff. 1983. *The Old Testament: An Introduction*. Translated by John Bowden. Philadelphia: Fortress Press.

Travis, Stephen H. 1977. 'Form Criticism.' In *New Testament Interpretation: Essays on Principles and Methods*. Edited by Howard I. Marshall. Milton Keynes, UK: Paternoster, pp. 153–62.

Social Memory The concept of social memory was introduced by the French sociologist MAURICE HALBWACHS (Halbwachs 1992) and refers to the influence of a given social framework on the individual's memory processes. In biblical studies, social memory theory is often referred to in discussions of the memory and recollection processes of groups, and is predominantly used by English-speaking scholars.

Halbwachs first introduced the idea that every form of memory is a social phenomenon. Every act of remembering needs a social framework to enable the individual to (re-)construct the past in intelligible and communicable terms. This social framework consists of a COLLECTIVE MEMORY in which the individual localizes his or her PERSONAL MEMORIES in order to be able to understand, explain, and communicate them, and thus to build up his or her IDENTITY. Aware of the fact that it is not groups, but only individuals, who remember, Halbwachs did not simply transfer the act of remembering from the individual to the group but concluded that the group provides a socially-constructed framework for the perception and estimation of individual memories.

Halbwachs' theory distinguished two different categories of memory: social and collective memory. *Social memory* refers to the influence of the social framework on the individual's memory processes, while collective memory denotes the process of the group establishing a framework to semanticize and actualize events as memories. In both concepts, memory is thoroughly social. The difference lies in the perspective: social memory interprets events in the light of certain categories; collective memory delivers the categories by which this interpretation is made. In daily life, both categories of memory constantly overlap and cannot easily be distinguished. One difference is that whereas social memory tends to be ephemeral, collective memory tends to be stable. Inasmuch as collective memory operates beyond the experiences and perceptions of individual.

Media of social memory are usually more of an oral nature and not created in order to shape tradition, although they draw from the past and transport history. A personal diary would be regarded as a medium of social memory, while a family chronicle would be a medium of collective memory, the distinctive criterion being the intention to create a tradition. From biblical times, OSTRACA and private LETTERS could be regarded as artefacts of social memory, for they bear witness to the ephemeral and everyday communications and practices. Biblical texts might contain traces of social memory, and thus (oral) tradition can be fruitfully understood in terms of social memory. But according to Halbwachs' categories, no biblical text can be understood as an artefact of social memory.

A stumbling block in the international discussion is posed by linguistic differences between English and German terminology. Not only do *social* and *sozial* describe different ideas, the German terms *Gedächtnis* and *Erinnerung* refer to two different concepts, while the English 'memory' does not make this distinction. The difference is further complicated by the fact that memory is most often understood to designate a process, a force, or a repository, whereas *Gedächtnis* denotes rather the storage capacities, sensory impressions, and mental processes.

Sandra Huebenthal (Universität Passau, Germany)

Further Reading

Gudehus, Christian, Ariane Eichenberg and Harald Welzer, eds. 2010. *Gedächtnis und Erinnerung: Ein interdisziplinäres Handbuch*. Stuttgart: Metzler, esp.109–14.

Halbwachs, Maurice. 1992. *On Collective Memory*. Edited and translated by Lewis A. Coser. Chicago: University of Chicago Press.

Huebenthal, Sandra. 2012. 'Social and Cultural Memory in Biblical Exegesis. The Quest for an Adequate Application.' In *Cultural Memory in Biblical Exegesis*. Edited by Pernille Carstens et al. Piscataway, NJ: Gorgias, pp. 175–99.

Kirk, Alan. 2005. 'Social and Cultural Memory.' In *Memory, Tradition, and Text*. Edited by Alan Kirk and Tom Thatcher. SemeiaSt 52. Atlanta: SBL Press, pp. 1–24.

Sociolinguistics *Sociolinguistics* is a term that covers a variety of theoretical approaches to the relationship between language and society, both why we vary our speech depending on different social contexts and how language has different social functions. Sociolinguistics encompasses a variety of approaches to the study of language and society that differ in how they collect linguistic data and how they employ quantitative and/or qualitative analytic traditions to interpret the data (for some specific examples, see CONVERSATION ANALYSIS; DISCOURSE ANALYSIS; ETHNOGRAPHY OF SPEAKING; ETHNOPOETICS). Some sociolinguists collect their data using anthropological and ethnographic approaches; some use data from controlled experiments. Topics of sociolinguistic study often include how speakers choose different linguistic variants and REGISTERS based on their social interactions as influenced by gender, age, ethnicity, and geographical region and how these linguistic choices influence our constructions of social reality as well as our cognitive abilities to interpret our surroundings. Thus, emphasis is often placed on contrasts between formal and informal forms within a particular language. Since individuals participate in various speech communities, each with its own linguistic norms, individuals must develop their own sociolinguistic competence, so that they know which language (or variation of a language) to use in any particular social situation (see CODESWITCHING).

In her *Introduction to Sociolinguistics*, Janet Holmes lists four 'sociolinguistic universals'.

First, 'All speech communities have linguistic means of distinguishing different social relationships' (Holmes 2013: 450). Feminist approaches have emphasized the different social relationships based on gender (Newsome, Ringe, and Lapsley 2012) and postcolonial approaches have focused on race, ethnicity, and class (Sugirtharajah 2006). For example, the biblical character Ruth is variously identified by the following, all of which are loaded with meaning concerning her (conflicting) social relationships: 1) by the narrator as 'the Moabite' (1.22; 2.2) and Naomi's 'daughter-in-law' (1.22); 2) by Naomi as 'my daughter' (2.2); 3) by Ruth herself as 'a foreigner' (2.10) and 'your [Boaz's] servant, even though I am not one of your servants' (2.13; see also 3.9); 4) by the elders as 'this young woman' (4.12); 5) by the women as 'your [Naomi's] daughter-in-law who loves you, who is more to you than seven sons' (4.15); and 6) by Boaz as 'young woman' (2.5), 'my daughter' (2.8), 'worthy woman' (3.11), 'the woman' (3.14), 'the Moabite, the widow of the dead man' (4.5), and 'my wife' (4.10). As is evident in the Ruth narrative, certain rituals can alter one's social status – in this case, marriage altered Ruth's social status relative to Boaz from 'young [marriageable] woman' to 'my wife' (see also INITIATION RITUALS; BAPTISM; CIRCUMCISION).

Second, 'All speech communities have linguistic means of distinguishing different contextual styles' (Holmes 2013: 450). A variety of studies have argued that the various forms of Hebrew, Aramaic, and Greek in the Bible can be understood as having been influenced by different registers – for example, formal versus informal speech or standard versus nonstandard (Rendsburg 1990; Porter 2000a,b,c). Biblical narrative includes characters who participate in codeswitching – for example, Rabshakeh speaks in Hebrew, while Hezekiah's officials speak in Aramaic, both of whom are trying to influence the Hebrew-speaking public of Jerusalem (2 Kgs 18.26-28//Isa. 36.11-13).

Third, 'All speech communities have linguistic means of expressing basic speech functions: ... [both] referential and affective functions' (Holmes 2013: 450). Referential functions include means of referring to or marking social status – such as ethnicity, gender, and class – in ways that may also communicate either solidarity and empathy with others or maintaining some social distance from the Other. The affective functions include expressive utterances of emotion, such as laments (Pss. 12-13; Jer. 11.18-20; Matthew 23) and directives, such as admonitions (Prov. 1.8-19; Mk 1.15; 1 Corinthians 7). Both referential and affective functions are often combined – for example, in blessings and curses and in OATHS – and may find expression in poetry (see POETRY IN THE HEBREW BIBLE).

Fourth, 'In all speech communities language change implies language variation, with social variation an important contributing component' (Holmes 2013: 450). The biblical languages are not linguistically uniform and this observation has been interpreted as implying social variation. In fact, although generally ignored, a few biblical narratives emphasize such linguistic variation (Genesis 11; 2 Kgs 18.26-27; Judg. 12.2-6) (Person 2007). Of course, social variation may be due to different factors, the two most important for the study of the biblical languages being historical variation (for example, early versus late; see Joosten and Rey 2008; Schniedewind 2013; for a criticism of this approach in Biblical Hebrew, see Young, Rezetko, and Ehrenvärd 2008) and geographical variation (regional dialects; see Garr 1985; Rendsburg 1990; Porter 2000a,b,c). Unfortunately, due to the dearth of epigraphic Hebrew materials from ancient Israel, it is often difficult methodologically to distinguish the cause of the language variation (for example, historical versus geographical). Despite such limitations, Holmes' four sociolinguistic universals clearly apply to the biblical languages and literature.

Raymond F. Person, Jr. (Ohio Northern University, USA)

Further Reading

Bayley, Robert, Richard Cameron and Ceil Lucas, eds. 2013. *The Oxford Handbook of Sociolinguistics*. Oxford: Oxford University Press.

Garr, W. Randall. 1985. *Dialect Geography of Syria-Palestine, 1000-586 B.C.E.* Philadelphia: University of Pennsylvania Press.

Holmes, Janet. 2013. *An Introduction to Sociolinguistics*. London: Routledge.

Holmes, Janet, and Kirk Hazen, eds. 2014. *Research Methods in Sociolinguistics: A Practical Guide*. Oxford: Wiley-Blackwell.

Joosten, Jan, and Jean-Sébastien Rey. 2008. *Conservatism and Innovation in the Hebrew Language of the Hellenistic Period.* STDJ 73. Leiden: Brill.

Martin, Dale B. 1990. *Slavery as Salvation: The Metaphor of Slavery in Pauline Christianity*. New Haven: Yale University Press.

Miller, Cynthia L. 1996. *The Representation of Speech in Biblical Hebrew Narrative: A Linguistic Analysis*. Atlanta: Scholars Press.

Newsom, Carol A., Sharon H. Ringe, and Jacqueline E. Lapsley, eds. 2012. *Women's Bible Commentary*. Louisville: Westminster John Knox.

Person, Raymond F., Jr. 2007. 'Linguistic Difference Emphasized; Linguistic Difference Denied.' In *The Archaeology of Difference: Gender, Ethnicity, Class and the 'Other' in Antiquity. Studies in Honor of Eric M. Meyers*. Edited by Douglas R. Edwards and C. Thomas McCullough. Boston: American Schools of Oriental Research, pp. 119–27.

Polak, Frank. 2006. 'Sociolinguistics: A Key to the Typology and the Social Background of Biblical Hebrew.' *Hebrew Studies* 47: 115–62.

Porter, Stanley E. 2000a. 'Dialect and Register in the Greek of the New Testament: Theory.' In *Rethinking Contexts, Rereading Texts: Contributions from the Social Sciences to Biblical Interpretation*. Edited by M. Daniel Carroll. Sheffield: Sheffield Academic Press, pp. 190–208.

Porter, Stanley E. 2000b. 'Dialect and Register in the Greek of the New Testament: Application with Reference to Mark's Gospel.' In *Rethinking Contexts, Rereading Texts: Contributions from the Social Sciences to Biblical Interpretation*. Edited by M. Daniel Carroll. Sheffield: Sheffield Academic Press, pp. 209–29.

Porter, Stanley E., ed. 2000c. *Diglossia and Other Topics in New Testament Linguistics*. Sheffield: Sheffield Academic Press.

Rendsburg, Gary A. 1990. *Diglossia in Ancient Hebrew*. AOS 72. New Haven: American Oriental Society.

Rezetko, Robert, and Ian Young. 2014. *Historical Linguistics and Biblical Hebrew: Steps Toward an Integrated Approach*. SBL Ancient Near East Monograph 9. Atlanta: SBL Press.

Schniedewind, William M. 2013. *A Social History of Hebrew: Its Origins through the Rabbinic Period*. New Haven: Yale University Press.

Sugirtharajah, R. S. 2006. *The Postcolonial Biblical Reader*. Oxford: Blackwell.

Young, Ian, Robert Rezetko, and Martin Ehrensvärd. 2008. *Linguistic Dating of Biblical Texts*. 2 vols. London: Routledge.

Song In media studies, the term *song* typically refers to traditional texts that have informed the oral-formulaic approach to the comparative study of ORAL TRADITIONS and to literature with roots in oral tradition, based originally on MILMAN PARRY's and ALBERT LORD's fieldwork with South Slavic bards (see GUSLAR). These texts are identified as songs simply because they are typically sung or chanted by their composers before live audiences, in some cases accompanied by instrumentation.

In epic traditions of singing compositions, the epic singer's notion of a song resides in 'the stable skeleton of narrative' (Lord 1960: 99) that provides the basis for any specific performance. Although this skeleton must be maintained, no two performances of a song will be identical in wording. Instead, the wording of a song will vary from performance to performance, even between performances by the same singer, and other changes will occur as well, such as elaboration or simplification of various THEMES within the song or a different order of items in a series (Lord 1960: 119). Building on these observations, Lord concluded that 'our concept of "the original," of "the song", simply makes no sense in oral tradition', so that '"oral transmission," "oral composition," "oral creation," and "oral performance" are all one and the same thing' (1960: 101). In fact, in some genres the same 'song' can include different heroes as the main character, because 'the type of hero is more significant than the specific hero' (1960: 120).

Lord's understanding of song has had some influence in biblical studies, beginning with the work of his Harvard colleague, Frank Moore Cross, especially in his essay 'The Song of the Sea and Canaanite Myth' (1973: 112, 117; see also MUSIC; POETRY IN THE HEBREW BIBLE). More generally, Lord's fieldwork on traditional songs has significantly challenged the notion of a single ORIGINAL text in contemporary models of both ORAL TRADITION and TEXTUAL CRITICISM.

Raymond F. Person, Jr. (Ohio Northern University, USA)

Further Reading

Cross, Frank Moore. 1973. *Canaanite Myth and Hebrew Epic: Essays in the History of the Religion of Israel.* Cambridge, MA: Harvard University Press.
Lord, Albert B. 1960. *The Singer of Tales*. Cambridge, MA: Harvard University Press.

Sound Mapping Sound mapping is an interpretive technique that analyses speech sounds in Hellenistic Greek literature to discern a composition's organizational structure as determined by audible patterns. Because sound mapping reveals a composition's inherent structure based on sound clues, its results can critique conventional structural proposals based on the analysis of a biblical text's theological ideas or abstract literary themes.

Sound mapping recognizes that literature in the Greco-Roman world was communicated primarily through spoken performance rather than silent reading (see PERFORMANCE OF THE GOSPELS; READING CULTURE; TORAH READING). Unlike silent reading, which permits re-reading at will and thus the mental abstraction of logical concepts and literary themes, spoken performance of a written work requires listeners to process sounds sequentially in real time. Sound mapping serves as a tool to discern meaning-making strategies appropriate to the auditory and time-bound character of spoken, public performances experienced by the first audiences of NT compositions. Its analytical processes rest on the premise that sound creates structure and furnishes fundamental interpretive clues in literature composed for spoken performance.

A *sound map* is a graphic display of the sound patterns and distinctive acoustic features that organize a literary composition in Hellenistic Greek. Sound mapping begins with a printed or electronic version of a Greek composition from which the organizing marks that accommodate silent reading have been removed, including titles, paragraphing, punctuation, and conventional versification. The passage is then analysed in breath units, thus detecting audible patterns as they would be enunciated in spoken performance. A sound map graphically displays audible patterns as linear streams of sound, replicating the inductive mental process practised by fluent listeners in real time.

Sound mapping analyses acoustic clues according to conventions and criteria active in the cultural environment that produced the NT. Sound mapping techniques derive from ancient reflections on Greek grammar, which ancient Greek literary critics regarded as the science of spoken sound (Dean 1996). Since Greek is an inflected language, grammatically related words with rhyming endings cluster together. Flexible word order in Greek permits the arrangement of sounds for auditory effect. Similar sounds can be elided, expanded, repeated, contrasted in parallel, or concatenated in elongated sequences to form larger sound patterns. Such effects shape a listener's construction of meaning and imbue a composition with unique sound signatures that entail specific associations. Sound mapping displays such patterns graphically to depict a composition's organic structure.

The breath units recognized in ancient Greek grammar and Hellenistic literary criticism are the COLON (*kōlon*) and the PERIOD (*periodos*). Ancient Greek critics defined 'colon' as a component part and 'period' as a complete utterance. A colon is necessarily incomplete; the Greek word connotes a member, a component of a larger whole (Aristotle, *Rhetoric* 3.9.7; Demetrius, *Elocution* 1; Quintilian, *Institutes* 9.4.123; *Rhetorica ad Herennium* 4.19.26). Cola are combined into periods (Aristotle, *Rhetoric* 3.9.5, 8-10; Demetrius, *Elocution* 1.5-7, 16). 'Period' implies a circular path: It connotes an utterance that begins in one place, proceeds along a line of discourse and returns at the end to its starting place (Demetrius, *Elocution* 11). Its characteristic features are *rounding* and *balance*. Rounding refers to the similarity of a period's beginning and end; balance refers to the aesthetic equivalence of its various components. Periods are often elongated at the end to signal closure.

Both periods and cola are described as breath units, even though periods consist of cola (Aristotle, *Rhetoric* 3.9.5; Cicero, *Orator* 3.46.181; Demetrius, *Elocution* 1; Quintilian, *Institutes* 9.4.125). According to Greek literary criticism, periods and cola function both as grammatical units and as stylistic features: all prose consists of periods, yet some prose is not very periodic – its periods are not rounded or balanced but consist of several cola strung together. For the purposes of a sound map, a colon consists of a predicate (simple or compound, expressed or implied) or strong verbal element and all words grammatically related to it. A period consists of one or more cola that express a complete, sensible utterance.

In a sound map, a passage is analysed into breath units by identifying its cola and periods. Conventional chapter and verse numbers, titles, and headings are removed, since these elements are extrinsic to the composition and were added later to accommodate silent reading. After a passage is analysed into breath units, repeating sound patterns are discerned. These audible patterns organize sounds for meaning. Unlike silent readers, sensitive to the recurrence of words or phrases surrounded by white space on a printed page or computer screen, listeners interpret sounds in real time as they strike the ear in a linear stream. Unaided by visual clues, a listener's sensitivity to repetition is oriented towards discrete acoustic units, such as phonemes and syllables. Sound mapping plots repetitions of phonemes, syllables and longer audible sequences. This procedure observes patterns not discernable through the normal process of silent reading or by reading a Greek composition in TRANSLATION.

A short passage from the Sermon on the Mount (Mt. 5.13-16) serves as a useful example of sound mapping because of its brevity and clear sound clues. The passage is displayed below, ready for sound mapping. Because sound mapping analyses audible patterns in a Greek composition, sound maps are presented in Greek, making this analytical technique less accessible to interpreters who lack fluency in the Greek language. An English translation appears below. The translation reads awkwardly because it follows the Greek word order so as to align with the sound map. The soundmap below illustrates how speech sounds in Greek organize a passage and reinforce its meaning.

Ὑμεῖς ἐστε τὸ ἅλας τῆς γῆς ἐὰν δὲ τὸ ἅλας μωρανθῇ ἐν τίνι ἁλις θήσεται εἰς οὐδὲν ἰσχύει ἔτι εἰ μὴ βληθὲν ἔξω καὶ καταπατεῖσθαι ὑπὸ τῶν ἀνθρώπων Ὑμεῖς ἐστε τὸ φῶς τοῦ κόσμου οὐ δύναται πόλις κρυβῆναι ἐπάνω ὄρους κειμένη οὐδὲ καίουσιν λύχνον καὶ τιθέασιν αὐτὸν ὑπὸ τὸν μόδιον ἀλλ' ἐπὶ τὴν λυχνίαν καὶ λάμπει πᾶσιν τοῖς ἐν τῇ οἰκίᾳ οὕτως λαμψάτω τὸ φῶς ὑμῶν ἔμπροσθεν τῶν ἀνθρώπων ὅπως ἴδωσιν ὑμῶν τὰ καλὰ ἔργα καὶ δοξάσωσιν τὸν πατέρα ὑμῶν τὸν ἐν τοῖς οὐρανοῖς. (Matt. 5: 13–16)

You are the salt of the earth if salt becomes bland how will it be made salty again for nothing is it useful any more except for throwing out and to be walked on by people You are the light of the world no way is it possible for a city to be hidden [if] on a hilltop [it is] situated nor does one light a lamp and put it under a basket but [they put it] on a lampstand and it illuminates everyone in the house so let shine your light in front of people so that they will see your good works and give glory to your father who is in the heavens

After removing verse numbers, punctuation, and line-breaks, the passage is organized into breath units according to grammatical criteria, based on the functional definition of a colon as a predicate (expressed or implied) or other strong verbal element and all words grammatically associated with it. This definition is 'functional' because it responds to the demands of actual usage. It does not serve as a rigid criterion. For example, cola 5 and 6 below do not contain predicates but they both contain strong verbal elements to which all the other words in their cola are related. Colon 5 contains a participle (βληθὲν/throwing out), and colon 6 contains an infinitive (καταπατεῖσθαι/to be walked on). Cola 4-6 are numbered as three cola but they could also be analysed as a single colon, associated with the predicate ἰσχύει (is useful) in colon 4.

In the illustration below, each colon is placed on a new line. Cola are numbered to facilitate reference. Predicates and strong verbal elements that delineate cola are presented in boldface type. Note that colon 9 contains a compound predicate. The predicate is implied but not expressed in colon 10.

1. Ὑμεῖς **ἐστε** τὸ ἅλας τῆς γῆς
2. ἐὰν δὲ τὸ ἅλας **μωρανθῇ**
3. ἐν τίνι **ἁλισθήσεται**
4. εἰς οὐδὲν **ἰσχύει** ἔτι
5. εἰ μὴ **βληθὲν** ἔξω
6. καὶ **καταπατεῖσθαι** ὑπὸ τῶν ἀνθρώπων
7. Ὑμεῖς **ἐστε** τὸ φῶς τοῦ κόσμου
8. οὐ **δύναται** πόλις κρυβῆναι ἐπάνω ὄρους κειμένη
9. οὐδὲ **καίουσιν** λύχνον **καὶ τιθέασιν** αὐτὸν ὑπὸ τὸν μόδιον
10. ἀλλ' ἐπὶ τὴν λυχνίαν **καὶ τιθέασιν**
11. καὶ **λάμπει** πᾶσιν τοῖς ἐν τῇ οἰκίᾳ
12. οὕτως **λαμψάτω** τὸ φῶς ὑμῶν ἔμπροσθεν τῶν ἀνθρώπων
13. ὅπως **ἴδωσιν** ὑμῶν τὰ καλὰ ἔργα
14. καὶ **δοξάσωσιν** τὸν πατέρα ὑμῶν τὸν ἐν τοῖς οὐρανοῖς

1. You **are** the salt of the earth.
2. If salt **becomes bland**,

3. how will it **be made salty** again?
4. For nothing **is it useful** any more
5. except for **throwing** out
6. and **to be walked on** by people.
7. You **are** the light of the world.
8. No way **is it possible** for a city to be hidden [if] on a hilltop [it is] situated.
9. Nor does one **light** a lamp and **put** it under a basket
10. but [they **put** it] on a lampstand
11. and it **illuminates** everyone in the house.
12. So **let shine** your light in front of people
13. so that **they will see** your good works
14. and **give glory** to your father who is in the heavens.

Once the passage has been organized into grammatical breath units, patterns emerge that are not evident in an English version. In the example above, cola 1 and 7 begin with the same sounds (ὑμεῖς; 'You')and are organized in parallel. This observation provides a primary structural clue: the passage consists of two units with similar components. Emphasis falls on repeated sounds (Ὑμεῖς ἐστε/you are) and parallel elements (τὸ ἅλας/salt; τὸ φῶς/light).

1. Ὑμεῖς ἐστε	τὸ ἅλας	τῆς γῆς	(You are the salt of the earth)
7. Ὑμεῖς ἐστε	τὸ φῶς	τοῦ κόσμου	(You are the light of the world)

The intervening cola (cola 2-6) repeat vowel sounds that echo the portion of colon 1 that is repeated in colon 7 (ε/ει). Note from the example below that this repetition of sound cannot be easily translated into English.

1. **Ὑμεῖς ἐστε** τὸ ἅλας τῆς γῆς
2. **ἐὰν** δὲ τὸ ἅλας μωρανθῇ
3. **ἐν** τίνι ἁλισθήσεται
4. **εἰς** οὐδὲν ἰσχύει ἔτι
5. **εἰ** μὴ βληθὲν ἔξω
6. καὶ καταπατε**ῖ**σθαι ὑπὸ τῶν ἀνθρώπων

1. **You are** the salt of the earth.
2. **If** salt becomes bland,
3. **how** will it be made salty again?
4. **For** nothing is it useful any more
5. **except** for throwing out
6. and to be walked on by people.

All intervening cola also include sounds from the portion of colon 1 that differs from colon 7. (Note that ει and η are analysed as homophones.) The auditory coherence of these cola associate cola 1-6 with each other. The elongation of colon 6 identifies cola 1-6 as a single period.

Colon 7 begins with the same opening sounds as colon 1. Subsequent cola repeat distinctive sounds in colon 7. Cola 8 and 9 employ similar beginning sounds:

1. **Ὑμεῖς ἐστε τὸ** ἅλας τῆς γῆς

...

7. **Ὑμεῖς ἐστε τὸ** φῶς **τοῦ** κόσμ**ου**
8. **οὐ** δύναται πόλις κρυβῆναι ἐπάνω ὄρ**ου**ς κειμένη
9. **οὐ**δὲ καίουσιν λύχνον καὶ τιθέασιν αὐτὸν **ὑ**πὸ τὸν μόδιον
10. ἀλλ' ἐπὶ τὴν λυχνίαν
11. καὶ λάμπει πᾶσιν τοῖς ἐν τῇ οἰκίᾳ

Cola 1-6 and cola 7-11 constitute periods by virtue of their grammatical integrity and the rounding and balance achieved through parallelism. Parallel structure balances corresponding cola. The two periods begin with the same sounds and exhibit similar grammatical arrangements. Both periods open with declarative statements in their initial cola (you are salt/light), followed by an elaboration with rhyming beginning sounds in cola 2-6 and 8-11. Cola are connected by grammatical subordination using a conditional statement in the first period (ἐάν/if, colon 2) and an opposition in the second period (οὐ ... οὐδέ ... ἀλλά/not...neither...but, cola 8-10). Both periods end with a colon that that is connected to the previous colon by parataxis (καί/and).

Because of their parallel structure and repeated opening sounds, these periods can be analysed as discrete units and re-numbered to highlight their parallelism:

1.1 **Ὑμεῖς ἐστε** τὸ ἅλας τῆς γῆς
1.2 ἐὰν δὲ τὸ ἅλας μωρανθῇ
1.3 ἐν τίνι ἁλισθήσεται
1.4 εἰς οὐδὲν ἰσχύει ἔτι
1.5 εἰ μὴ βληθὲν ἔξω
1.6 **καὶ** καταπατεῖσθαι ὑπὸ τῶν ἀνθρώπων
2.1 **Ὑμεῖς ἐστε** τὸ φῶς τοῦ κόσμου
2.2 οὐ δύναται πόλις κρυβῆναι ἐπάνω ὄρους κειμένη
2.3 οὐδὲ καίουσιν λύχνον καὶ τιθέασιν αὐτὸν ὑπὸ τὸν μόδιον
2.4 ἀλλ' ἐπὶ τὴν λυχνίαν
2.5 **καὶ** λάμπει πᾶσιν τοῖς ἐν τῇ οἰκίᾳ

1.1 **You are** the salt of the earth.
1.2 If salt becomes bland,
1.3 how will it be made salty again?
1.4 For nothing is it useful any more
1.5 except for throwing out
1.6 **and** to be walked on by people.
2.1 **You are** the light of the world.
2.2 No way is it possible for a city to be hidden [if] on a hilltop [it is] situated.
2.3 Nor does one light a lamp and put it under a basket
2.4 but [they put it] on a lampstand
2.5 **and** it illuminates everyone in the house.

Three cola remain in this passage:

12 οὕτως λαμψάτω τὸ φῶς ὑμῶν ἔμπροσθεν τῶν ἀνθρώπων

13 ὅπως ἴδωσιν	ὑμῶν	τὰ καλὰ ἔργα
14 καὶ δοξάσωσιν τὸν πατέρα	ὑμῶν	τὸν ἐν τοῖς οὐρανοῖς

12 So let shine your light in front of people
13 so that they will see your good works
14 and give glory to your father who is in the heavens.

Cola 12 and 13 begin with sounds similar to the opening sounds of cola 7 and 8 (ου/ο). Cola 12-14 include frequent repetition of distinctive sounds from the subject of 2.1, τὸ φῶς (light). The second person pronoun (ὑμῶν/your) occurs in the middle of all three cola.

12 **οὗτως** λαμψάτω **τὸ φῶς**	**ὑμῶν**	ἔμπροσθεν τῶν ἀνθρώπων
13 **ὅπως** ἴδ**ωσ**ιν	**ὑμῶν**	τὰ καλὰ ἔργα
14 καὶ δοξάσ**ωσι**ν τὸν πατέρα	**ὑμῶν**	τὸν ἐν τοῖς οὐρανοῖς

12 So let shine [your] light	your	in front of people
13 so that they will see	your	good works
14 and give glory to	your	father who is in the heavens.

Similar sounds associate cola 12-14 with each other. Similar beginning sounds in cola 12-14 also associate these cola with the second period (Ὑμεῖς ἐστε τὸ φῶς τοῦ κόσμου/you are the light of the world, colon 7). Cola 12-14 cohere as a single period. All three periods begin their final colon with καί/and. Cola 12-14 can be analysed as part of the second unit in this passage, since signals of a new unit do not occur but the cola cohere because of similar auditory features.

2.1 **Ὑμεῖς ἐστε** τὸ φῶς τοῦ κόσμου.		
2.2 οὐ δύναται πόλις κρυβῆναι ἐπάνω ὄρους κειμένη		
2.3 οὐδὲ καίουσιν λύχνον καὶ τιθέασιν αὐτὸν	ὑπὸ	τὸν μόδιον
2.4 ἀλλ’	ἐπὶ	τὴν λυχνίαν,
2.5 καὶ λάμπει πᾶσιν τοῖς ἐν τῇ οἰκίᾳ		

3.1 οὗτως λαμψάτω τὸ φῶς	ὑμῶν	ἔμπροσθεν τῶν ἀνθρώπων
3.2 ὅπως ἴδωσιν	ὑμῶν	τὰ καλὰ ἔργα
3.3 καὶ δοξάσωσιν τὸν πατέρα	ὑμῶν	τὸν ἐν τοῖς οὐρανοῖς

2.1 You are the light of the world.	
2.2 No way is it possible for a city to be hidden [if] on a hilltop [it is] situated.	
2.3 Nor does one light a lamp and put it	under a basket
2.4 but [they put it]	on a lampstand
2.5 and it illuminates everyone in the house.	

3.1 So let shine light	your	in front of people
3.2 so that they will see	your	good works
3.3 and give glory to	your	father who is in the heavens.

Thus, a sound map of Matthew 5.13-16 reveals two discrete units with parallel structure and repeated sounds at each unit's beginning. The first unit contains one period. The second unit contains two periods. Cola have been re-numbered below to reflect the division of the passage into periods.

Unit 1 (5.13):

1.1 **Ὑμεῖς ἐστε** τὸ ἅλας τῆς γῆς
1.2 ἐὰν δὲ τὸ ἅλας μωρανθῇ
1.3 ἐν τίνι ἁλισθήσεται
1.4 εἰς οὐδὲν ἰσχύει ἔτι
1.5 εἰ μὴ βληθὲν ἔξω
1.6 **καὶ** καταπατεῖσθαι ὑπὸ τῶν ἀνθρώπων

Unit 2 (5.14-16):

1.1 **Ὑμεῖς ἐστε** τὸ **φῶς** τοῦ κόσμου.
1.2 οὐ δύναται πόλις κρυβῆναι ἐπάνω ὄρους κειμένη
1.3 οὐδὲ καίουσιν λύχνον καὶ τιθέασιν αὐτὸν ὑπὸ τὸν μόδιον
1.4 ἀλλ' ἐπὶ τὴν λυχνίαν,
1.5 **καὶ** λάμπει πᾶσιν τοῖς ἐν τῇ οἰκίᾳ
2.1 **οὕτως** λαμψάτω **τὸ φῶς** ὑμῶν ἔμπροσθεν τῶν ἀνθρώπων
2.2 **ὅπως** ἴδωσιν ὑμῶν τὰ καλὰ ἔργα
2.3 **καὶ** δοξάσωσιν τὸν πατέρα ὑμῶν τὸν ἐν τοῖς οὐρανοῖς

Unit 1 (5.13):

1.1 **You are** the salt of the earth.
1.2 If salt becomes bland,
1.3 how will it be made salty again?
1.4 For nothing is it useful any more
1.5 except for throwing out
1.6 **and** to be walked on by people.

Unit 2 (5.14-16)

1.1 **You are** the **light** of the world.
1.2 No way is it possible for a city to be hidden [if] on a hilltop [it is] situated.
1.3 Nor does one light a lamp and put it under a basket
1.4 but [they put it] on a lampstand
1.5 **and** it illuminates everyone in the house.
2.1 **So** let shine [your] **light** your in front of people
2.2 **so that** they will see your good works
2.3 **and** give glory to your father who is in the heavens.

The sound map demonstrates that speech sounds organize the passage and establish its structure. Further, sound-structure reinforces its meaning. The accent falls on the opening phrases of each unit (Ὑμεῖς ἐστε/you are). The second unit reinforces the emphasis on 'you' with the repetition of ὑμῶν (your) in its closing period. The two component units divide the passage topically (unit 1, salt; unit 2, light). The first unit emphasizes τὸ ἅλας (salt) with repeated, rhyming phonemes. Similarly, τὸ φῶς (light) and rhyming phonemes receive special emphasis.

Biblical interpretation must correctly discern compositional units to properly comprehend a composition's structure and, finally, its meaning. Sound mapping addresses this need by employing Hellenistic guidelines for Greek composition, which privilege the structural clues furnished by spoken sound over those derived from abstract logic or semantic meaning. Compositions differ in the number, type and format of the parts that comprise the whole. For this reason, and because intermediate-sized units are not identified by Hellenistic literary critics, sound mapping does not propose a standard nomenclature or numbering scheme for component units. Rather, a sound map's numbering and typography serve pragmatic ends to depict a biblical composition's organic integrity.

Sound mapping offers interpretive insights based on a composition's inherent structural features. It does not produce a single, authoritative description of a Greek composition. Since sound mapping is an interpretive process, a composition's sounds can be analysed in various ways, just as several conductors might analyse the same musical score differently. Sound mapping admits multiple interpretations. Yet sound's physical character and the consensus that characterizes the analysis of sound in Hellenistic literary criticism establish a firm foundation for interpretation. Because sound reveals a spoken composition's organic structure, sound mapping can critique interpretations that rest on structural proposals that cannot be implemented through sound's unique dynamics.

Margaret E. Lee (Tulsa Community College, USA)

Further Reading

Brickle, Jeffrey E. 2012. *Aural Design and Coherence in the Prologue of First John.* LNTS 465. New York, NY: T & T Clark.

De Waal, Kayle B. 2015. *An Aural-Performance Analysis of Revelation 1 and 11.* New York: Lang.

Dean, Margaret E. 1996. 'The Grammar of Sound in Greek Texts: Toward a Method of Mapping the Echoes of Speech in Writing.' *Australian Biblical Review* 44: 53–70.

Lee, Margaret E. 2013. 'Melody in Manuscript: The Birth Narrative in the Gospel of Matthew.' In *Testimony, Witness, Authority: The Politics and Poetics of Experience*. Edited by Tom Clark, Tara Mokhtari, and Sasha Henriss-Anderssen. Newcastle upon Tyne: Cambridge Scholars.

Lee, Margaret E. 2014. 'Sound and Structure in the Gospel of Matthew.' In *From Text to Performance: Narrative and Performance Criticisms in Dialogue and Debate*. Edited by Kelly Iverson R. Biblical Performance Criticism 10. Eugene, OR: Wipf and Stock.

Lee, Margaret Ellen, and Bernard Brandon Scott. 2009. *Sound Mapping the New Testament*. Salem, OR: Polebridge.

Nässelqvist, Dan. 2015. *Public Reading in Early Christianity: Lectors, Manuscripts, and Sound in the Oral Delivery of John 1-4*. *NovT* Supplements. Leiden: Brill.

Scheppers, Frank. 2011. *The Colon Hypothesis: Word Order, Discourse Segmentation and Discourse Coherence in Ancient Greek*. Brussels: Academic & Scientific.

Special Grammar Albert Lord introduced the term *special grammar* as a way of emphasizing that oral composition is not as mechanical as early critics of Milman Parry and Lord had imagined – that is, the critics mistakenly interpreted oral-formulaic theory as requiring that the oral bard memorized a variety of formulas that they mechanically strung together in ways that denied any real creativity. However, Lord insisted that the *special grammar* of the oral bard was a natural language system with grammatical rules and structures that nevertheless allowed for originality and creativity.

> In studying the patterns and systems of oral narrative verse, we are in reality observing the 'grammar' of the poetry, a grammar superimposed, as it were, on the grammar of the language concerned. Or, to alter the image, we find a special grammar within the grammar of the language, necessitated by the versification. The formulas are the phrases and clauses and sentences of this specialized poetic grammar. The speaker of this language, once he has mastered it, does not move any more mechanically within it than we do in ordinary speech. When we speak a language, our native language, we do not repeat words and

> phrases that we have memorized consciously, but the words and sentences emerge from habitual usage. This is true of *the singer of tales* working in his specialized grammar. (Lord 1960: 35–6)

This special grammar includes the system of formulas, THEMES, and STORY PATTERNS that Parry and Lord discerned as compositional aids for traditional singers (see ORAL TRADITION, COMPARATIVE STUDY OF).

Lord's notion of a special grammar has been widely accepted in Homeric studies, especially the idea that such poetic language is a natural outgrowth of everyday speech. Michael Nagler asserts that, because 'oral-formulaic composition is a language, … the training of the oral bard is more like the acquisition of a linguistic skill than the memorization of a fixed content' (1967: 310). Egbert Bakker concludes that 'meter and formulas entail the stylization of ordinary speech, rather than some inherently poetic principle' (1997: 2). Elizabeth Minchin concludes that 'the Iliad and the Odyssey are instances of "special" storytelling' (2001: 203) and that 'Homer's mimesis of speech acts is an echo of everyday discourse from his own world' (2007: 19). Based on his comparative study of the GENRE of the 'Return Song' in Serbo-Croatian epic, the Odyssey, and Beowulf, JOHN MILES FOLEY described any system of traditional phraseology as 'a complex, heterogeneous, ever-evolving collection of inequivalent elements overseen by rules and processes no single singer ever consciously imagined', an observation that 'allows us to "re-complicate" poetic composition, to take it out of the arena of lockstep simplicity and back into the realm of language – the most complex of human abilities and arts' (1990: 199, 200).

Many scholars of literature, including the Bible, often assume a gulf between oral and written discourse, a theoretical model sometimes called the GREAT DIVIDE. Similarly, poetry (or even literary artistry in general) is often understood as so significantly different from everyday conversation that WRITING is required for such sophistication. Therefore, Lord's notion of a special grammar as applied to something like the hexameter line of Homeric poetry, alliterative verse of Old English, or the parallelism of POETRY IN THE HEBREW BIBLE seems counterintuitive, especially when these poetries are imagined as orally composed – that is, conversation is often assumed to be simplistic and therefore oral discourse is incapable of such complexity, which would be more characteristic of literature. However, this understanding is based on an inadequate understanding of everyday conversation, especially a failure to take seriously what Gail Jefferson called 'the poetics of ordinary talk' (1996).

Based on her analysis of data taken from studies in CONVERSATION ANALYSIS of naturally occurring conversations, Jefferson concluded that 'the poetics of ordinary talk' include what in literary studies would be called assonance and alliteration, and in fact these POETICS influence word selection in everyday conversation. Since words and phrases are made up of sounds and many words belong to more than one category, she identified two kinds of triggering mechanisms: 'sound-triggering' and 'category-triggering'. *Sound-triggering* or *sound-selection* occurs when speakers choose among various options as they select their next word based on the sound of the preceding words, what in literary studies would be called assonance and alliteration. The following quote from a sports commentator illustrates sound-triggering or alliteration based on the sound [f]. Note that Jefferson places the recurring sound in brackets:

> I have heard all this [f]oo[f]aw back and [f]orth about uh couldn't [f]ire the three shots in seven seconds and so [f]orth and so on. I am [f]ascinated by this … (1996: 14)

Here we can ask the question, why did the sportscaster choose the word 'fascinated' rather than 'amazed', 'interested', or 'enthralled'? The answer seems to lie in the recurring [f]-sound.

Category-triggering or *category-selection* occurs when speakers choose among various options as they select their next word based on some category created by a preceding word or words. Below are several examples from three different conversations. Note again that Jefferson places brackets around the words in the same category.

> I wanted to go to an [agricultural] college but my mother [steered] me away from that.
>
> I hope to become more consistent as I get [deeper] into this w[hole] problem.
>
> Russia's the worst. We went twenty four hours once without [eating] a thing. I just got [fed] up waiting. (1996: 17)

Once the poetics of ordinary talk are recognized, Lord's proposal regarding the special grammar for oral epic seems much more plausible. For example, Old English alliterative verse may be an exaggeration of sound-selection, and parallelism in Hebrew poetry may be an exaggeration of category-selection (Person 2016a; 2016b; see POETRY IN THE HEBREW BIBLE). That is, just as no individual speaker created these triggering mechanisms in their everyday conversational language, no single oral poet created the special grammar of their epic tradition. Although most participants in everyday conversation are unaware of the various practices they are using (for example, triggering mechanisms), oral poets are verbal artists who have a heightened awareness of the poetics inherent in language in general and have honed over many generations ways of playfully exploiting the poetics of everyday conversation for aesthetic effect (Person 2015).

Because special grammars are adaptations of poetic resources in everyday conversation, they may not follow some linguistic rules that are based on everyday language use. For example, source and redaction critics generally assume a high degree of linguistic uniformity in written texts by single authors – that is, they assume that the mixing of vocabulary and grammatical forms from different dialects and historical periods points to composite texts, from which sources and redactional layers can be discerned based on the different linguistic forms. However, the special grammar of oral epic allows for such mixing of different dialects and linguistic forms from various historical periods – for example, the traditional REGISTER of Serbo-Croatian epic utilizes two dialects (*ijekavski* and *ekavski*) and includes archaisms (Turkish vocabulary and the aorist verb form), while Homeric epic includes both Ionic and Aeolic forms of Greek (Foley 1999: 76–86). The function of such linguistic mixing in special grammars may be to communicate the traditional nature of the oral epic or the written text as transcending time and space. In fact, the special grammar continues as a contemporary linguistic register, so that the addition of neologisms may occur within such a living language.

Because of this characteristic of linguistic mixing, the application of source and redaction criticism on the basis of linguistic criteria may be based on misunderstandings of the special grammar of biblical texts. For example, what are often understood as Early Biblical Hebrew forms and Late Biblical Hebrew forms are often mixed in texts in the Hebrew Bible (Young, Rezetko, and Ehrensvärd 2008); it is quite possible that this linguistic mixing may be explained, at least in some cases, as a characteristic of a special grammar or traditional register in addition to the explanations given by text, source, and redaction criticism concerning composite texts and scribal corruptions (Person 2016b). If this is the case, then this observation greatly complicates the application of source and redaction criticism to ancient literature, including biblical texts.

Raymond F. Person, Jr. (Ohio Northern University, USA)

Further Reading

Bakker, Egbert. J. 1997. *Poetry in Speech: Orality and Homeric Discourse*. Ithaca, NY: Cornell University Press.

Foley, John Miles. 1990. *Traditional Oral Epic: The Odyssey, Beowulf, and the Serbo-Croatian Return Song*. Berkeley: University of California Press.

Foley, John Miles. 1999. *Homer's Traditional Art*. University Park, PA: Pennsylvania State.
Jefferson, Gail. 1996. 'On the Poetics of Ordinary Talk.' *Text and Performance Quarterly* 16: 11–61.
Lord, Albert B. 1960. *The Singer of Tales*. Cambridge, MA: Harvard University Press.
Minchin, Elizabeth. 2001. *Homer and the Resources of Memory: Some Applications of Cognitive Theory to the Iliad and the Odyssey*. Oxford: Oxford University Press.
Minchin, Elizabeth. 2007. *Homeric Voices: Discourse, Memory, Gender*. Oxford: Oxford University Press.
Nagler, Michael N. 1967. 'Towards a Generative View of the Oral Formula.' *Transactions of the American Philological Association* 98: 269–311.
Person, Raymond F., Jr. 2015. *From Conversation to Oral Tradition: A Simplest Systematics for Oral Traditions*. London: Routledge.
Person, Raymond F., Jr. 2016a. 'From Grammar in Everyday Conversation to Special Grammar in Oral Traditions: A Case Study of Ring Composition.' In *Oral Poetics and Cognitive Science*. Edited by Pagán, Cristóbal and Mihailo Antovic. Stuttgart: Mohr Siebeck, pp. 30–51.
Person, Raymond F., Jr. 2016b. 'The Problem of "Literary Unity" from the Perspective of the Study of Oral Traditions.' In *Empirical Models Challenging Biblical Criticism*. Edited by Raymond F. Person, Jr. and Robert Rezetko. SBL Ancient Israel and its Literature 25. Atlanta: SBL Press.
Young, Ian, Robert Rezetko, and Martin Ehrensvärd. 2008. *Linguistic Dating of Biblical Texts*. 2 vols. London: Equinox.

Speech Genres Speech genre is a term introduced by the Russian literary theorist Mikhail Bakhtin (1895–1975) in a 1952/1953 essay, which appeared in English translation in 1986 as 'The Problem of Speech Genres'. Understanding Bakhtin's use of 'speech genres' depends on understanding his use of 'utterance'. Utterances may be oral or written, and every utterance – which may be as short as a single word or as long as a novel – has theme, style, and structure. Within particular spheres of discourse, specific types of utterances predominate, with similarity of theme, style, and structure between them. This collection of similar utterances is what Bakhtin termed a 'speech genre'. Utterance is the individual unit of communication; speech genre is the class or type. Speech genres are diverse and varied, ranging from 'the single-word everyday rejoinder [to] the multivolume novel' (Bakhtin 1986: 61). Speech genres, like utterances, may be either oral or written.

Bakhtin distinguished between two major categories of speech genres: primary and secondary. Secondary or complex speech genres, including 'novels, drama, all kinds of scientific research, major genres of commentary, and so forth' (1986: 62), are made up of primary speech genres. Primary or simple speech genres are those 'that have taken form in unmediated speech communication' (1986: 62). In a novel where letters have been incorporated, such as the letters between Jane and Elizabeth in *Pride and Prejudice*, the primary speech genre of letter is taken into the secondary speech genre of novel.

Bakhtin argued that primary speech genres do not remain unaltered when incorporated into secondary speech genres. They lose their close relationship to a life context and exist only in a mediated form. Both primary and secondary speech genres should be analysed; Bakhtin called the emphasis on primary speech genres 'a vulgarization of the entire problem' (1986: 62). He emphasized the analysis of interrelationships between primary and secondary speech genres in their historical contexts. He claimed that speech genres are the means to link historical context with linguistic development.

The dynamics of the relationship between a primary speech genre (such as a letter) and a surrounding secondary speech genre (such as a novel) was further explored by Yuri Lotman (1922–93), especially in the parts of his essay published in English as 'The Text Within the Text' (1993). When one text is placed within another, both the inserted text and the surrounding text are altered. The inserted text (from a primary speech genre) is transformed so that a new meaning is produced, while the surrounding text (comprising a secondary speech genre) also undergoes transformation that makes evident the disruption that has been introduced.

Bakhtin's concept explains why there is variation (sometimes extreme) between utterances even within a single speech genre. Once a genre has been chosen, the uniqueness of every individual and situation leads to differences in the deployment of the genre. He argued that when we learn language, we also learn how to deploy language; we learn the speech genres that are available to us. The basis for communication is not language itself, but speech genres: without speech genres to frame our utterances, we would be unable to communicate. Yet while language is relatively stable (e.g. verb morphology), speech genres are very flexible, suitable for adaptation. 'But to use a genre freely and creatively is not the same as to create a genre from the beginning; genres must be fully mastered in order to be manipulated freely' (Bakhtin 1986: 80).

Speech genres should also be seen within the broader context of Bakhtin's thought. Speech genres are not identical with 'heteroglossia', although there is overlap. *Heteroglossia* is Bakhtin's term for the entry of a variety of voices, linguistic forms and linguistic REGISTERS into a work, primarily the novel. Use of primary speech genres is one way heteroglossia enters the novel: a differing genre with its own theme, style, and structure will bring in a differing a voice. DIALOGISM, another key Bakhtinian term, denotes the interplay between the heteroglossia. Thus the relationship between primary and secondary speech genres may be designated as one form of dialogism.

Bakhtin's concept of speech genres lies behind most contributions to genre theory written in the past two decades: its importance cannot be overstated. Its focus on interrelationship and transformative capacity has moved genre theory from taxonomy to analysis of effect (see Frow 2006).

Whereas the identification of primary speech genres may look like FORM CRITICISM as it has been traditionally practised in biblical studies, the analytical category of speech genres places no value on this identification except inasmuch as the interaction of the primary speech genres with the larger utterance is examined. While Form Criticism sought to identify the SITZ IM LEBEN or life context of primary speech genres, Bakhtin dismissed the possibility of extracting real-life oral speech from within written primary speech genres or from within larger secondary speech genres. 'They [primary speech genres] lose their immediate relation to actual reality and the real utterances of others' (Bakhtin 1986: 62). From this perspective, the form-critical project is misguided.

The applicability of Bakhtin's approach to biblical scholarship may be illustrated through numerous examples. From a Bakhtinian perspective, 1–2 Chronicles is an utterance from a secondary speech genre, while a book like Psalms is a collection of utterances from primary speech genres. In Psalms, the individual utterances may be analysed, and while they still have a context within the book as a whole, that book is not a secondary speech genre. Bakhtin was more interested in the effect of primary speech genres within a secondary speech genre like 1–2 Chronicles: a single utterance that contains within itself a number of speech genres. To use the analytical category of speech genres most usefully, first we identify examples of primary speech genres, and then we see how they operate within the book as a whole. The texts of Genesis through 2 Kings, Esther, Ezra-Nehemiah, Jeremiah, Daniel, Jonah, or Habakkuk in the Hebrew Bible, as well as a few texts from the NT also lend themselves to this kind of analysis.

The clearest example of a primary speech genre in 1–2 Chronicles is the psalm in 1 Chron. 16.8-36. It is a psalm created by fusing Ps. 105.1-15, Ps. 96.1-10, and Ps. 106.1, 47-48. Yet it reads as a complete psalm, with the characteristic style, theme, and structure of the genre. It has no existence outside of 1–2 Chronicles, much as the letters of Jane to Elizabeth have no existence outside of *Pride and Prejudice*; 1 Chronicles 16 is no more a 'real' psalm than Jane's letters are 'real' letters. The author of 1–2 Chronicles, having mastered the speech genre of psalm, creatively generated a new psalm. The speech plan (see Bakhtin 1986: 77) of 1–2 Chronicles determined the choice of genre at this point, and its incorporation into the larger utterance of 1–2 Chronicles. The incorporation of the psalm changes both the psalm and the surrounding narrative. The psalm is read for its thematic links with the surrounding narrative, while the narrative has its themes reinforced by the differing genre of the psalm.

Another clear example of a primary speech genre in 1–2 Chronicles is Abijah's speech in 2 Chron. 13.4-12. It is obviously an insertion when compared to the parallel text in 2 Kings 15, but its nature as its own utterance is also evident from analysis. This text is a royal speech; the narrative claims that 800,000 warriors heard this speech (2 Chron. 13.3), which highlights the artificial nature of the setting and speech. The key Chronistic themes of Davidic kingship, levitical service and seeking God are in the speech, but the exhortatory style and tight rhetorical structure mark the speech as a different speech genre than the surrounding narrative. The speech reinforces the speech plan of 1–2 Chronicles, while the narrative gives the speech a purpose it would otherwise lack.

Other primary speech genres found within 1–2 Chronicles include genealogy, priestly/levitical rota, prophetic speeches, and prayers. In the case of 1–2 Chronicles, utterances from these speech genres are most easily identifiable by their absence from the parallel texts of Samuel–Kings. However, they are also identifiable by the differences in style, theme, and structure from the surrounding text. While the identification of these utterances is important, it is the analysis of the interplay between these utterances and the entire utterance of 1–2 Chronicles that lies at the heart of speech genres.

Christine Mitchell (St. Andrew's College, University of Saskatchewan, Canada)

Further Reading

Bakhtin, Mikhail M. 1986. 'The Problems of Speech Genres.' In *Speech Genres and Other Late Essays*. Translated by V.W. McGee. Edited by C. Emerson and M. Holquist. Austin, TX: University of Texas, pp. 60–102.
Boer, Roland, ed. 2007. *Bakhtin and Genre Theory in Biblical Studies*. Semeia St. Atlanta: SBL Press.
Frow, John. 2006. *Genre*. London: Routledge.
Holquist, Michael. 2002. *Dialogism*, 2nd edn. London: Routledge.
Lotman, Yury M. 1994. 'The Text Within the Text'. Translated by J. Leo and A. Mandelker. PMLA 109: 377–84.

Story Pattern A *story pattern* is a distinct complex of narrative elements that recurs in multiple forms within oral-traditional literature. The *return song*, for example, reflects the pattern of an absent hero, the devastation caused by his absence, and his return to set things right. This pattern typically includes scenes of disguise, deceptive story, and recognition and is often preceded by the crying out of the hero in captivity. The most famous instance of a return song is Homer's *Odyssey*. Yet the basic story pattern and its key components can be applied to a variety of heroes, including Achilles in the *Iliad* (Lord 1960: 186). Differences between forms of the same story pattern include expansion and omission of material, changes in detail and action, changes in the order of events, and substitution of variant forms of a narrative element (Lord 1960: 105, 123).

A particular set of thematic elements indicates a distinctive story pattern, yet shared elements can link different story patterns, evoking a broader generic pattern. For example, the Serbo-Croatian story patterns of return songs, rescue songs, wedding songs, and capture of city songs suggest an overarching narrative pattern of captivity and release/rescue (Lord 1960: 122).

Albert Lord spoke of story pattern in relation to song, one of the three categories of oral-traditional literature (the other two being formula and theme/type scene). In *The Singer of Tales*, Lord's study of Serbo-Croatian songs and Greek epic, the song as a whole 'is the essence of the story' that is told and is 'built on the stable skeleton of narrative' or the story pattern (1960: 99, 158–60). Although the wording and aspects of the content of a story may change in different performances or renditions of a song over time, the basic story pattern remains constant. John Miles Foley extended discussion of the role of story pattern in traditional narrative. In terms of composition, a story pattern often generates new and more complex patterns, such as double cycles and multiple protagonists, which are grounded in the essential pattern (1990: 367–8). In terms of meaning, a story pattern marks a special mode or REGISTER of speech with which a live or reading audience is familiar and which infuses a narrative or performance with heightened significance (1995: 53). The pattern creates expectations in an audience, who then see the particular story unfold in its details in relation to other instances of the pattern.

The audience's knowledge of a story pattern can create a sense of inevitability in a narrative. In the return pattern, for example, the hero's absence or withdrawal leads to devastation and, in time, to return and restoration. This sequence is essential to the pattern, creating expectations in the minds of audiences about how the story will progress – at some point, the hero must return to resolve the devastation. Writing on the origins of Greek tragedy in traditional stories, Richmond Lattimore asserts that 'the story itself, as an ordered series of events, has its own rights' (1964: 6). The consistent parameters of the tale work in dynamic tension with the flexibility of its specific content and wording in any given performance. At the same time, the resonance of the pattern intensifies the impact of the particular narrative (Foley 1995: 177).

To cite an obvious example from the biblical corpus, the broad narrative pattern of exile or absence, rescue/return, and reconciliation is evident in very different forms in the ancestral stories of Jacob and Joseph, the exodus narrative, the prophetic collections (especially the major prophets), and arguably in the psalms of lament, the book of Job, and the PASSION NARRATIVES of the Gospels. This pattern would have set broad parameters and expectations both for the biblical 'authors' as composers and also for audiences familiar with this traditional narrative form.

Katherine M. Hayes (Saint Joseph Seminary, USA)

Further Reading

Foley, John Miles. 1990. *Traditional Oral Epic: The Odyssey, Beowulf, and the Serbo-Croatian Return Song*. Berkeley: University of California Press.

Foley, John Miles. 1995. *The Singer of Tales in Performance*. Bloomington: Indiana University Press, 1995.

Lattimore, Richmond. 1964. *Story Patterns in Greek Tragedy*. Ann Arbor: University of Michigan Press.

Lord, Albert B. 1960. *The Singer of Tales*. Harvard Studies in Comparative Literature 24. Cambridge, MA: Harvard University Press.

Storytelling Storytelling occurs when a speaker or speakers narrate(s) events and characters from a place and time different from the speech event of the story itself. That is, in some sense storytelling transports the storyteller(s) and the hearers from their present setting into a past or future setting, so that they together can overhear and see what happened or will happen in the narrative world. Storytelling occurs often in everyday conversation and in talk in institutional settings. Therefore, in order to understand storytelling in ORAL TRADITIONS and literature, we should first understand how everyday storytelling occurs.

Storytelling in Everyday Conversation

As demonstrated in various studies in CONVERSATION ANALYSIS, storytelling in everyday conversation is a complex phenomenon, requiring all of the participants to pay close attention to the story-in-progress so that they can participate in the co-production of the story from their own unique perspectives. Of course, such close attention is also necessary with all face-to-face talk, but storytelling nevertheless has different qualities due to the necessity of allocating multiple turns to the storyteller(s). That is, participants in everyday conversation use an elaborate turn-taking system to allocate cooperatively who has the right to speak next so as to minimize overlapping speech (Sacks, Schegloff, and Jefferson 1974). Therefore, if a participant in a conversation wants to tell a story, he/she must seek permission from the other participants to suspend the regular turn-taking system, so that he/she can have the floor to speak multiple turns until the story is completed (Schegloff 1997).

Storytelling is sensitive to the broader conversational context in which it occurs. In fact, if the audience of the story changes during the story-in-progress, then the story itself may change in real time (M. Goodwin 1997). Due to such context sensitivity, storytelling occurs within a socially standardized sequence involving a story preface, the story itself, and the story reception (Schegloff 1992). In the story preface, a participant (either the potential storyteller or another participant familiar with the story) proposes a story that is somehow relevant to the ongoing conversation, seeking mutual agreement for a suspension of the regular turn-taking practices, so that the potential storyteller(s) can have multiple turns in which to narrate the events of the story. If successful, then the story itself is produced. The storyteller will construct the story so that it fits within the conversational context and conforms to his/her presumptions about the level of knowledge of the recipient(s), providing only enough information necessary to achieve a successful storytelling event (C. Goodwin 1986). The story may be constructed in ways that invite the participation of knowledgeable recipients, thus including them in the co-production of the story-in-progress (Lerner 1992). The recipients, both those who know the story and those who do not, likewise orient themselves to the story on the basis of their knowledge. When necessary, they interject comments concerning the level of their knowledge of the story-in-progress. Thus, the recipients' participation in the story-in-progress may facilitate the storyteller's construction of the story itself (Mandelbaum 1993). The recipients' participation, however, is not limited to facilitating the incipient design of the storytelling. In fact, even unknowledgeable recipients may intervene in a story-in-progress in ways that may completely redirect the story and its interpretation (Mandelbaum 1989).

Few studies in conversation analysis compare how a story is retold in different conversational settings; however, a few studies have looked at story retellings (M. Goodwin 1990/1991; Greatbatch and Clark 2010). Since storytelling in everyday conversation is context sensitive, their results should not be surprising. On the one hand, the story itself can change dramatically depending on the audience (M. Goodwin 1990/1991); on the other hand, even when the story itself remains very similar in wording from one storytelling to the next, it can be embedded within a broader sequence so that the story is interpreted for different purposes (Greatbatch and Clark 2010). Thus, much like everyday conversation, storytelling is context sensitive, so that the story may serve different purposes in various conversational settings and, in turn, these diverse settings may effect how the story itself is told (see CONVERSATION ANALYSIS.

Storytelling in Institutional Talk

Talk in institutional settings is an adaptation of practices in everyday conversation with different institutions making variant adaptations, so that in some sense the specific form of institutional talk helps to define the institution – that is, to indicate that the talk is no longer everyday conversation but talk within the institutional setting itself. Storytelling that occurs within institutions is typically not for entertainment alone, but serves other important functions within the institutions (Greatbatch and Clark 2010). For example, storytelling plays a central role in Alcoholics Anonymous meetings in which established members tell their stories as a way of providing mutual support (Arminen 2003). In institutional settings the suspension of the standard turn-taking system for everyday conversation may be highly formalized. For example, at Alcoholics Anonymous meetings, the chair selects the next speaker (the story preface); the storyteller must stay within a carefully monitored time frame (the story itself); the audience is expected to be silent during the storytelling, and at the end the audience is expected to provide supportive applause and comments (the reception sequence). Nevertheless, even Alcoholics Anonymous stories, which are monologic, betray their sensitivity to the social context, in that the opening address provides the topic of discussion for the following stories, all of which are then in some sense part of the reception sequence of the opening address.

Storytelling in Oral Traditions

Epic and HISTORIOGRAPHY, which are clearly forms for storytelling, are important GENRES in oral traditions and literature. Therefore, just as institutional storytelling is an adaptation of conversational storytelling, storytelling in oral traditions is also an adaptation of storytelling in everyday conversation that serves various purposes of socialization. The difference occurs when we consider how spontaneous everyday storytelling and storytelling in institutional settings like Alcoholics Anonymous meetings are in contrast to oral-traditional storytelling that may have strict formal requirements, such as the decasyllable line in Serbo-Croatian epic, the hexameter poetic line in Homeric epic, or the alliterative poetic line in Old English. That is, although institutional storytelling often involves the telling of a new story, at least for many of the hearers, the oral bard performs stories that are understood to be traditional stories from the heroic past that are generally well known to the hearers. As such, oral traditional epics are adaptations of storytelling in everyday conversation that make use of what Albert Lord calls SPECIAL GRAMMAR – that is, a performance language with its own grammatical rules and structures that facilitate the composition and reception of traditional epic but also allow for originality and creativity on the part of the bard (Lord 1960; Person 2016).

Storytelling in the Bible

The Bible contains various genres, many of which are forms of storytelling (epic, history, gospel, apocalyptic) probably with roots in oral traditions. These stories, whether performed orally from memory or read aloud, had their own various ancient contexts and were likely performed and received relative to those varying contexts. This proposition at least finds support in portrayals of storytelling within the Bible, as the examples of Nathan's story to David (2 Sam. 11.27–12-5) and Jesus' PARABLE of The Good Samaritan (Lk. 10.25-35) demonstrate. That is, the literary representation of storytelling within the biblical text itself suggests what some of the contexts were for some of the types of storytelling that became biblical literature.

Because of David's adultery with Bathsheba and murder of Uriah (2 Samuel 11), God was angry and sent Nathan to David with a story about how a rich man who had many sheep and goats stole a lamb from a poor man to prepare a meal for his guest (2 Sam. 11.27–12.4). When David hears the story, he is angry at the injustice and demands that the rich man be punished (2 Sam. 12.5-6). Nathan then reveals that David is that man and that God is angry with him and will punish him accordingly (2 Sam. 12.7-12). David then confesses and God mitigates his punishment (2 Sam. 12.13-15).

When the lawyer asks Jesus the question 'Who is my neighbor?' (Lk. 10.29) Jesus answers with the Parable of the Good Samaritan (Lk. 10.30-35). When he ends the parable, Jesus asks the question 'Which of these three, do you think, was a neighbor to the man who fell into the hands of the robbers?' and the lawyer answers correctly (Lk. 10.36-37).

Both of these stories are excellent literary representations of how stories in conversation fit within their conversational contexts. Both are closely connected to the narrative that precedes them. Nathan's story of the rich and poor man is crafted to reflect David's crimes and Jesus' parable implies an answer to the lawyer's question. Both are followed by a reception sequence. David expresses anger at the injustice of the story, thereby betraying his hypocrisy, so that God through Nathan can exploit his reaction to emphasize his own guilt and the necessity of his forthcoming punishment. When Jesus ends the parable, he asks a question that more directly addresses the topic of the lawyer's own question, so that the lawyer himself interprets the parable accordingly and answers his own earlier question. Furthermore, if the author of Luke is copying the story of the lawyer's question from Mark and adding the parable from some other source, we have further evidence that a story can be retold in a new context, thereby modifying the interpretation of the pre-Lukan source and therefore the story itself.

These two literary representations of storytelling illustrate well the context sensitivity of stories in the biblical world. Therefore, even if we cannot reconstruct the specific contexts in which the various forms of storytelling that comprise the Bible occurred, we can nevertheless conclude that storytelling in the ancient world, whether occurring spontaneously in conversation or from the public reading of texts, was embedded within a context in which the story served purposes in addition to entertainment. Thus, the insights of FORM CRITICISM can be adapted so that the SITZ IM LEBEN is understood as *Sitz im Diskurs*.

Raymond F. Person, Jr. (Ohio Northern University, USA)

Further Reading

Arminen, Ilkka. 2003. 'Second Stories: The Salience of Interpersonal Communication for Mutual Help in Alcoholics Anonymous.' *Journal of Pragmatics* 36: 319–47.

Goodwin, Charles. 1986. 'Audience Diversity, Participation and Interpretation.' *Text* 6: 283–316.

Goodwin, Marjorie H. 1990/1991. 'Retellings, Pretellings, and Hypothetical Stories.' *Research on Language and Social Interaction* 24: 263–76.

Goodwin, Marjorie H. 1997. 'Toward Families of Stories in Context.' *Journal of Narrative and Life History* 7: 107–12.

Greatbatch, David, and Timothy Clark. 2010. 'The Situated Production of Stories.' In *Organisation, Interaction and Practice: Studies of Ethnomethodology and Conversation Analysis*. Edited by Nick Llewellyn and Jon Hindmarsh. Cambridge: Cambridge University Press, pp. 96–118.

Lerner, Gene. 1992. 'Assisted Storytelling: Deploying Shared Knowledge as a Practical Matter.' *Qualitative Sociology* 15: 247–71.

Lord, Albert B. 1960. *The Singer of Tales*. Cambridge, MA: Harvard University Press.

Mandelbaum, Jennifer. 1989. 'Interpersonal Activity in Conversational Storytelling.' *Western Journal of Speech Communication* 53: 114–26.

Mandelbaum, Jennifer. 1993. 'Assigning Responsibility in Conversational Storytelling: The Interactional Construction of Reality.' *Text* 13: 247–66.

Person, Raymond F., Jr. 2015. *From Conversation to Oral Tradition: A Simplest Systematics for Oral Traditions*. Routledge Studies in Rhetoric and Stylistics 10. London: Routledge.

Sacks, Harvey, Emanuel A. Schegloff and Gail Jefferson. 1974. 'A Simplest Systematics for the Organization of Turn-Taking for Conversation.' *Language* 50: 696–735.

Schegloff, Emanuel A. 1992. 'In Another Context.' In *Rethinking Context: Language as an Interactive Phenomenon*. Edited by Alessandro Duranti and Charles Goodwin. Cambridge: Cambridge University Press, pp. 193–227.

Schegloff, Emanuel A. 1997. '"Narrative Analysis" Thirty Years Later.' *Journal of Narrative and Life History* 7: 97–106.

Synagogues The synagogue (in Hebrew *beth knesset*, or 'house of assembly') is the premier institution for Jewish prayer and Scripture reading. It developed first in the diaspora during the exile and much later as a purpose-built structure in Palestine. The idea of prayer taking place outside the TEMPLE in Jerusalem and without sacrifice came to the fore mainly after the Babylonian exile and the destruction of the first temple in 586 BCE.

For biblical scholarship, the experience and importance of the exile extends far beyond the concern for historical details and realia. What has become the consensus communis is that the trauma of exile and displacement forced upon the exiled Jewish leadership a sense of urgency about how best to preserve their historical and literary legacy. This was accomplished firstly in the creation of the synagogue as an alternative place of WORSHIP and secondly in the editing and preserving of their sacred writings, in which were embedded the CULTURAL MEMORIES, sacred values, and texts of the earlier periods. The result of this effort was nothing short of astounding, producing in the Persian period the Pentateuch and the former prophets (Genesis–2 Kings) as well as the later prophets and a good deal of the *Kethuvin* or Writings. With most of Scripture in hand before the Hellenistic period, the stage was set for the rise of the synagogue as a purpose-built structure first in Egypt, then in Palestine, and at various locations in the diaspora in the Roman period.

The Babylonian exiles learnt to pray in what was called a 'little temple' (Ezek. 11.16) or the 'dwelling place' of God (Ps. 90.1). In Egypt, the synagogue was called *proseuchē* or 'house of prayer' from a relatively early date in the Hellenistic period. In Second Temple Judaism the reading of Scripture was often associated with the city gate and other communal activities, such as the septennial reading of Torah on Sukkoth (Deut. 31.9-13), the reading of the law by Ezra before the Water Gate standing on a wooden platform (Nehemiah 8), and the reading of Scripture by priests, Levites and other officials (2 Chron. 11.7-9). All this points to the centrality and significance of biblical literature early in the Second Temple period long before the CANON was a reality.

We have abundant evidence from archaeological investigations for synagogues from the Second Temple period at sites such as Gamla and Herodium. In addition, the well-known Theodotus Inscription from Jerusalem dated to the first century CE states unambiguously that the synagogue to which it refers was built 'for the reading of the Law and for the teaching of the commandments' and served as a kind of hospice or guest-house (Corpus Inscriptionum Judaicarum II: 1410). Since the synagogue was built by 'Theodotus son of Vettenos' the building was probably constructed to serve Jews who originally came from Rome as many as three generations earlier and possibly for pilgrims as well. Theodotus is called priest and *archisynagogos*, which suggests a connection to the temple, though the same term is often used in the diaspora to connote a leadership role. The varied uses of the synagogue implicit in this inscription are also borne out by later literary references and are characteristic of the institution to this day.

The rise of the synagogue while the temple still stood in Jerusalem is part of a larger picture in which alternative ways of approaching God were being implemented. We know from Qumran, the NT, and the MISHNAH that Bible study in small groups (*havurot*) was practised and was a regular feature of life in some circles (Pharisees, Essenes, etc.). Reading the Law and teaching the commandments as mentioned in the Theodotus Inscription, therefore, fits well into what we know from other sources as well. Thus, this literature reinforces the idea of the importance of Scripture in the life of first century Jews in Palestine, including the followers of Jesus. It is no wonder that in the development of the synagogue after the destruction of the Second Temple in 70 CE two architectural features dominate and that most buildings reflect these realities: the symbolic importance of the temple itself and the liturgy and services that were conducted in it; and the centrality of the Bible. The former is manifested in the principle of sacred orientation – that is, facing towards Jerusalem; the latter in the placement of the reader's platform or *bema*. While each of these features is not universally adopted in synagogues for a variety of reasons – often practical ones such as topography – their influence is apparent to any student in the field. Often extreme measures had to be taken to accommodate these principles, one being the so-called awkward 'about-face' – that is, sometimes when a synagogue is oriented in a different direction, the worshippers may need to turn around to face Jerusalem in order to pray or watch and listen to the reading of the Torah.

No consensus exists today on the nature of the liturgy in Second Temple synagogues (see Levine). Some scholars would say there was only the reading of the Law and explanation of it. Others have suggested that, while the earliest liturgical blessings are those of the TORAH SERVICE, other components of prayer were already present as well. To be sure, the more complete liturgy of the synagogue is a product of the post-70 CE reinterpretation of worship that was a major focus of attention after the temple was destroyed. Whatever services were like before 70, the mere existence of so many synagogues and references to them in literature and EPIGRAPHY made the transition to the full development of the Galilean synagogues and their liturgy that much easier.

The earliest evidence for a table on which the Torah scroll was read comes from Magdala on the western shore of the Sea of Galilee just south of Capernaum, also known as the Plain of Gennosar. Preliminary dating has placed the decorated limestone table base in the early first century CE. Its location on the north end of the synagogue shows that it took sacred orientation into account as well, since it faces the Holy City. Hence, the synagogue at Magdala, associated with Mary Magdalene, exhibits both characteristic features noted above – that is, sacred orientation and the centrality of the reading of the Law. The base of the reader's table is decorated with a carved menorah, rosette, ceramic vessels, and architectural members, perhaps suggesting a strong connection with the JERUSALEM TEMPLE. In any event, the synagogue construction is of very high level of artisanship and contains mosaics and frescoes indicative of an affluent community. An adjacent villa and street very close to the harbour, with all sorts of shops, points to a high level of activity in this seaside centre. All together the settlement conveys a strong sense of cultural ties to Jerusalem, while at the same time exhibiting a sense of independence by having such an elaborate, albeit small, synagogue.

Just northeast of Magdala at the northern tip of the lake lies the site of Capernaum associated with Jesus's ministry in the north. Till the excavation at Magdala no other site received so much attention by scholars of early Christianity and the archaeology of the lake region. Capernaum is referred to in all the canonical Gospels as a place in which Jesus preached and worked miracles and some refer to it as his home (Mk 2.1; Mt. 4.13, 9.1). Other NT sources identify it as the hometown of Peter, Andrew, James, John, and Levi/Matthew (Mt. 4.13-22; 9.9; Mk 2.14; cf. Jn 1.44 and 12.21). Archaeologists have identified a domicile there as the House of Peter, venerated for centuries just thirty metres south of the well-known limestone synagogue, which is dated to a much later period. Today a modern, octagonal pilgrim church stands above the ruin. Whether the house below can be understood as a kind of house church in the first century, however, is complicated and not entirely certain. No distinguishing features that we might identify with a church or synagogue can be isolated in it until the fourth century CE, when it was decorated with red and white plaster with floral and geometric designs. The Franciscans, who run Capernuam today, also claim there is a first century synagogue under the great limestone synagogue.

Moving to the post-70 CE situation of synagogues in the north, the architectural details of all the different phases of the synagogues at Nabratein stand out for their excellent state of preservation and the manner in which they convey cultural and religious values in their art and architecture. Located north/northeast of the city of Safed in the Upper Galilee, Synagogue I is a broadhouse and has been dated to the second century CE and is 11.2 × 9.35 metres (36.7 × 30.7 ft). What is most important about the interior is that there are two stone podiums or *bemas* in each of the corners of the southern long wall, where the excavators also posit a Torah shrine in which the biblical SCROLLS were housed. In addition, in the centre of the building, there is a break and imprint in the white plaster flooring indicating the presence of a table of some sort. The excavators have identified this spot as a place for a reader's table, where Scripture was read. So what was significant at Magdala about a century or so earlier is also attested at Nabratein in the mid-second century CE, where a podium is added for the storage of the biblical scrolls on the Jerusalem-facing wall, and in the next century a Torah shrine is added atop the podium or *bema*. These structural changes support the idea that the synagogue over time took over more of the sacrality of the Jerusalem temple.

Synagogue II at Nabratein from the third century produced a beautiful pediment for a Torah shrine that stood on one of the *bemas* on the southern, Jerusalem-orienting wall. Its rampant lions on either side of a demi-dome and place for the hanging of the eternal light show how artistic decoration could greatly enhance the religious and cultural significance of the Torah shrine and what it housed, conveying strength and beauty. The biblical scrolls that were stored in the Torah shrine were rolled scrolls as opposed to what became dominant in the church at this time or a bit later, namely the CODEX. This key difference in how the sacred word was transmitted on PARCHMENT or skin becomes one of the most important signifiers in the synagogue and church.

Once Christianity became the official religion after Constantine and new synagogue construction was forbidden, we have evidence of elaborate redecoration of existing synagogues – for example, mosaic floors with narrative scenes. At this time often an apse was added to house the Torah shrine and offer seating for the clergy or leadership behind a balustrade. The liturgy of the service was now further enriched with the addition of homilies and poetic expansions on the Torah readings, but the overall template for the synagogue had been established earlier and its adaptability to different styles and influences over time made it fit in or stand out wherever it was built. The memory of the destroyed temple and its holiness remained an essential part of every synagogue in the diaspora, signified by sacred orientation or a sign indicating what was east (*mizrach*), a raised platform or *ambol* for reading or interpreting Scripture, a Torah shrine to house the biblical scrolls often adorned with rampant lions, and a seating plan intended to emphasize the centrality of the reading of Scripture in worship.

Eric M. Meyers (Duke University, USA)

Further Reading

Frey, J.-B. 1975. *Corpus Inscriptionum Judaicarum*, 2 vols. Rome: Pontificio Istituto di Archeologia Cristiana, 1936-52. Reprint New York: KTAV, 1975.

Hachlili, Rachel. 2013. *Ancient Synagogues – Archeology and Art: New Discoveries and Current Research*. Handbook of Oriental Studies, Section I: The Near and Middle East. Leiden and Boston: Brill.

Levine, Lee I. 2005. *The Ancient Synagogue: The First Thousand Years*. 2nd edn. New Haven: Yale University Press.

Meyers, Eric. M. 2013. 'Synagogues, Palestine.' In *The Oxford Encyclopedia of the Bible and Archaeology*, vol. 2. Edited by Daniel M. Master. Oxford and New York: Oxford University Press, pp. 249–58.

Meyers, Eric. 2002. 'Jewish Culture in Greco-Roman Palestine.' In *Cultures of the Jews*. Edited by David Biale. New York: Schocken, pp. 135–80.

Meyers, Eric M., and Carol L. Meyers. 2009. *Excavations at Ancient Nabratein: Synagogue and Environs*. Meiron Excavation Series, vol. VI. Winona Lake, IN: Eisenbrauns.

Meyers, Eric M., and Mark A. Chancey. 2012. *Alexander to Constantine: Archaeology of the Land of the Bible*. AYBRL Vol. 3. New Haven: Yale University Press.

T

Targums A targum is a Jewish Aramaic TRANSLATION of a (Hebrew) biblical text. The term applies both to translations of individual passages (especially as they were used in the ancient SYNAGOGUE liturgy) and to translations of biblical books or entire divisions of the Hebrew Bible. Some scholars have pushed for a narrower definition, limiting *targum* to works emerging during the rabbinic era (so as to exclude the Aramaic translations found at Qumran; e.g. Flesher and Chilton 2011: 8). The emphasis within targum studies on the rabbinic context is not misplaced, however, as the targums that have survived from antiquity all appear to be products of rabbinic institutions, and as such preserve numerous rabbinic exegetical traditions. The definition offered by Samely (1992: 180) has rightly met with wide approval: 'Targum is an Aramaic narrative paraphrase of the biblical text in exegetical dependence on its wording.'

Targums exist for all of the books of the Hebrew Bible, with the exception of the two books that are already partly Aramaic: Ezra and Daniel. For most of the Bible, only a single targum is extant, but there are multiple extant targums of the Pentateuch and Esther. There has been considerable debate over why targums were created in the first place, but the most convincing view is that they simply filled a need for translation by congregations that could not understand the Hebrew biblical text that was read aloud during the synagogue liturgy (see *m. Meg.* 2.1). (The need for such a practice is already evident in Nehemiah 8.) The serviceability of this view, of course, depends on questions about what languages were still widely understood, as those scholars who hold that Hebrew was still widely spoken during the rabbinic period (e.g. Abraham Tal, Steven Fraade) typically insist that the rise of the targum must be explained on other grounds.

Although targums ostensibly served as simple translations, many of them expand upon the text of Scripture with clarifying glosses. Almost as a rule, they also remove problematic language in cases where a literal rendering might lead to a misunderstanding. This can be seen in the widespread practice of removing divine anthropomorphisms from the biblical text, or in the practice of multiplying references to the Shekhinah.

Scholars have classified the extant targums primarily by the dialects of Aramaic variously employed (as this gives the clearest indication of possible date ranges and provenience) and secondarily by the targums' individual translational characteristics (e.g. straightforward or expansive renderings). Scholars commonly refer to three relevant dialects, each corresponding to a period in Jewish history: 1) Jewish Literary Aramaic (ca. 200 BCE–200 CE); 2) Jewish Palestinian Aramaic (ca. 200 CE–500 CE); and, 3) Late Jewish Literary Aramaic (see Flesher and Chilton 2011: 8–11, 156–7). One targum to the Pentateuch (Targum Onqelos) and one targum to the Prophets (Targum Jonathan) were written in dialect 1 above, and thus can be dated earlier than all other rabbinic targums. Targum Onqelos, in fact, contains a mixture of western and eastern dialectal aspects, probably suggesting a two-stage composition. The most important targum composed in dialect 2 is Targum Neofiti, a nearly complete Palestinian targum of the Pentateuch discovered in the Vatican library in 1949. Finally, a late date for the Babylonian Targum Pseudo-Jonathan (to the Pentateuch) and for most of the Writings targums is indicated by their having been composed in dialect 3. The earliest targums of all are those found at Qumran (4QTgLev, 4QTgJob, 11TgJob). A number of fragmentary targums were also found in the Cairo Geniza.

Although we tend to read the explanatory glosses in the targums as a layer of commentary separate from the biblical text, it is not unlikely that many of the original readers of targums failed to make that differentiation, and that they received the glosses as a part of 'Scripture'. If they could not read Hebrew, they would have had no way of comparing a reading from a targum to a reading of the text it is based on. Even when readers did recognize the difference, they may have accorded enough authority to the glosses that they also functioned as Scripture. The additions or alterations represented by the targumic text show that the biblical text was not as sacrosanct as it is often envisioned. A certain amount of change seems to have been acceptable, especially for the sake of clarity.

John C. Poirier (Kingswell Theological Seminary, USA)

Further Reading

Flesher, Paul V. M., and Bruce Chilton. 2011. *The Targums: A Critical Introduction.* Waco, TX: Baylor University Press.

Houtman, Alberdina, and Harry Sysling. 2009. *Alternative Targum Traditions: The Use of Variant Readings for the Study in Origin and History of Targum Jonathan.* Studies in Aramaic Interpretation of Scripture 9. Leiden: Brill.

Kaufman, Stephen A. 1994. 'Dating the Language of the Palestinian Targums and their Use in the Study of First Century CE Texts.' In *The Aramaic Bible: Targums in their Historical Context.* Edited by D. R. G. Beattie and M. J. McNamara. JSOTSup 166. Sheffield: Sheffield Academic Press, pp. 118–41.

Samely, Alexander. 1992. *The Interpretation of Speech in the Pentateuchal Targum.* TSAJ 27. Tübingen: Mohr Siebeck.

York, Anthony D. 1974. 'The Dating of Targumic Literature.' *JSJ* 5: 49–62.

Tedlock, Dennis Anthropologist Dennis Tedlock (1930–2016) is recognized especially for his award winning translation of *Popul Vuh: The Mayan Book of the Dawn of Life* and for his performance-based translations of traditional Zuni Pueblo STORYTELLING. His distinctive approach to these materials has made him a major contributor to the theory and method of interpreting spoken arts. In the 1970s, Tedlock collaborated with poet scholar Jerome Rothenberg, with whom he founded the journal *Alcheringa/Ethnopoetics* to explore varied human poetries, to foster experiments in translating oral-traditional materials, and to fight cultural genocide.

With Rosenberg, DELL HYMES, and others, Tedlock gave shape to the aesthetics movement known as ETHNOPOETICS, a multifaceted 'field for experimentation' that studies the performative quality of oral verbal art. He developed ways to produce printed texts that enable readers to treat them like 'musical scores', including such expressive elements as intonation, stress, silence, pitch, repetition, formulaic expressions, gestures, and props to bring to life the fuller dynamic and semantic power not only of narratives and stories but of PROVERBS, RIDDLES, curses, laments, praises, prayers, prophecies, public announcements, and other oral-based texts. Tedlock's transcription techniques are illustrated by the following example.

> He was herding, his sheep were spread out (*sweeping gesture towards the east*)
> when they came along there shouting.
>
> (*chanting*) 'THE------RE SHU-------MEEKULI
> GOES OUR WHITE
>
> WA--------Y
>
> RUNNING A
>
> OUT HELP
> WHOEVER IS THERE PLEASE US
>
> **CATCH HIM FOR US!**'
>
> That is what they were shouting as they kept after him.

(*in a low voice*) 'Ah, yes, there's a Yaaya dance today, something must've happened.' (1983: 27)

Tedlock's approach puts the story back into the world of sound and hearing, allowing the reader to take up the role of the performer, to enter into the performance event. This move radically challenges the way anthropology has approached fieldwork with original sources. Rather than reducing native materials to a supposed objective report, Tedlock proposed a 'dialogical anthropology' that deals with informants as living 'people from the other side of the conversation'. Text renderings become less finished or definitive products than open-ended accounts that foster ongoing revisiting and revision. The approach goes beyond contrast and/or comparison among fixed texts to generate dialogue between and among various peoples and one another as well as with the investigators. It validates both the individuality of particular performers and the humanity of the people(s) whose traditional ways of speaking and telling the performer represents.

The substance of Tedlock's work is conversant with and connected not only to classic and contemporary anthropologists but to a wide range of scholars in related and tangent fields, including ALBERT LORD, Victor Turner, ERIC HAVELOCK, ERVING Goffman, RICHARD BAUMAN, and JACK GOODY and, by implication, to the work of WALTER ONG and JOHN MILES FOLEY. He did extensive collaborative fieldwork and publication with his wife, anthropologist Barbara Tedlock. His influence is evident in the literal translation style found in SUSAN NIDITCH's commentary on Judges, where, for example, she insists on maintaining the verb-noun order of the Hebrew in her English translation.

Randy F. Lumpp (Regis University, USA)

Further Reading

Niditch, Susan. 2008. *Judges: A Commentary*. Westminster: John Knox, 2008.
Tedlock, Dennis. 1983. *The Spoken Word and the Word of Interpretation*. Philadelphia: University of Pennsylvania Press.
Tedlock, Dennis. 1996. *Popul Vuh: The Mayan Book of the Dawn of Life*. New York: Simon & Schuster.
Tedlock, Dennis. 1999. *Finding the Center: The Art of the Zuni Story Teller*. 2nd edn. First published, New York: Dial, 1972. Lincoln and London: University of Nebraska Press.
EPC/Dennis Tedlock Home Page – Electronic Poetry Center. http://epc.buffalo.edu/authors/tedlock/http://epc.buffalo.edu/authors/tedlock/RESUME.htm

Tell El Amarna See AMARNA LETTERS.

Temples The major empires that span the biblical writings – Egypt, Assyria, Babylon, Persia, Macedonia (Syria and Egypt), and Rome – utilized temples as media of communication. Temple buildings provided a physical location for meaning-making through religious ceremonies, but were not the only sacred spaces: altars, sacred precincts and groves, shrines in other buildings, even houses, were also places for religious observance. Reflecting this reality, the Latin term *templum* can signify an area of the sky marked out to observe communicative signs from the gods, an area of ground in which auspices concerning the will of gods might be read, and any place devoted to WORSHIP. In the ancient world, temples expressed meaning and interpretations of life that worshippers experienced through rituals; stimulated significant economic activity; and, secured and sanctioned the societal order and political ideologies of ruling powers. The following discussion, formulated with particular reference to the Roman empire, concentrates not so much on construction materials, techniques, and designs for temples, but on their functions and societal resonances in effecting communication with inhabitants of the empire.

The Social Function of Temples

Temples functioned as cult centres in which worshippers approached deities with requests for benefits, protection, and favours (prayer); with various offerings, sacrifices, and hymns to honour a deity (veneration); to seek messages from a deity (divination); and, to secure favourable interaction with a deity through rituals signifying, for example, initiation or PURIFICATION. Distinctive architecture marked Roman-era temple buildings, often including a raised platform, a colonnaded portico on top of which was placed the triangular pediment that often displayed a relief of the temple's mythology, and the *cella*, the internal central, rectangled room that often contained the cult image or statue of the deity or deities venerated in the temple, along with a plinth or table to receive offerings. Cult images were frequently cared for with much devotion. Altars for sacrifices might be located inside or, commonly, outside the temple building itself. Some altars (such as the Altar of Augustan Peace in Rome, the *Ara Pacis Augustae*) were independent of temples. The provision of finest materials, craftsmanship, and expensive decoration of temples provided elites with opportunities to display wealth, enhance the prestige of local communities, and secure divine blessing.

It should be stressed that ancient temples differed from modern churches, SYNAGOGUES, and mosques in significant ways. Temples were places to honour deities and were not the home-base for worshipping congregations. Further, the cult activities conducted at temples were not scheduled at set times on a weekly basis; individuals could engage in any of these activities at any time. Temples also sponsored civic festivals on a regular calendar that expressed the myths that informed the practices associated with honouring the particular deity. Greco-Roman temples were also places of manumission for slaves. Temples of Asclepius, Apollo, Athena, Dionysos, and Isis, to name a few, were places where slaves were sold to the god and thereby manumitted. The person's identity and status underwent the radical change from slave to freed. The temple was the place of encounter with the transforming power of the god or goddess.

Moreover, while there is plenty of inscriptional and votive evidence for personal, household, and communal requests for divine favours (e.g. success in love and business, healings, safety in travel, triumph in war), religion and politics ('church and state') were usually not separated entities in ancient imperial societies. Often religious systems and rituals enacted in temples were aligned with imperial aspirations and hierarchical societal structures so as to support and sanction those realities. The long-established temple and sanctuary of Asclepius in Corinth, for example, provided a place of encounter with the god through sleep and dreams whereby, it was hoped, the god would prescribe some healing regimen and in response the grateful recipient would make anatomically shaped votive offerings and sacrifices. But the temple did more than provide healing; the temple communicated the presence of Asclepius in Corinth, reflecting the presence of the god in Rome and contributing another link between this Roman colony and the empire's centre to construct Corinth as a mini-Rome. Asclepius was the son of Apollo, a divine patron of Julius Caesar and Augustus; to honour Asclepius at his temple in Corinth was to honour these imperial founders and assert loyalty to Rome.

Elites, with considerable wealth and social networks, usually controlled temples, funding festivals, sacrifices, BANQUETS, cult images and objects, and providing and maintaining buildings, as well as serving as the functionaries and officials necessary for cult. Elites benefited socially from such euergetism (public good work) by gaining honour and securing the gratitude, dependence, and cooperation of non-elites. In doing so, they ensured that temples and their activities served interests of power and control in securing the social order and political alignments of the civic and imperial structures.

Temples and/as Imperial Communication

Evidence for the roles of temples in the intersections and intertwinings of religion and politics is manifold. A prominent example is the long history of the temple of Jupiter Capitolinus that dominated Rome from its commanding position on the Capitoline Hill. It evoked the city's founding, the actions of various leaders, and key events in the city's history. Another starting point is the argument of the architect Vitruvius in insisting that public buildings in Rome, including temples, should express with dignity the ruler's power. This view informed Augustus' programme of constructing and restoring temples in Rome, a key strategy in communicating divine sanction and favour for his power and *auctoritas*. According to his *Res Gestae* 20, Augustus restored at least eighty-two temples in the city and constructed others of considerable significance. For example, he erected a temple of white marble to Apollo, the god who had ensured Octavian/Augustus' victory over Antony at Actium in 31 BCE. In 29 BCE he dedicated the temple of the deified Julius Caesar, who had adopted Augustus as his son and whose death Augustus had avenged. The temple displayed an image of Venus, Caesar's ancestress, and trophies of Augustus' victory at Actium including the prows of captured Egyptian ships mounted on a speaker's platform in front of the temple. The temple aligned Augustus with Julius Caesar and communicated his Julian lineage. It also highlighted the role of temples in impressing on people the divinely sanctioned power of military force.

In part inspired by and emulating the temple of Jupiter Capitolinus as representing Rome's founding, Augustus erected the temple of *Mars Ultor* (Mars the Avenger). The temple was promised at the Battle of Philippi in 42 BCE against Brutus and Cassius, the assassins of Julius Caesar. It underscored Augustus' role in avenging Caesar's death and legitimized his rule. The temple featured images of Mars, father of Romulus, and of Venus, ancestress of the Julian line through the legendary hero Aeneas. It also included statues of Augustus and, not surprisingly, the deified Julius. Images presented genealogical lines of descent from Mars and Venus down to Augustus, thereby legitimizing his rule. Augustus was represented in the piazza driving a chariot. While the image presented a military ruler, the inscription saluted him as father of the nation (*pater patriae*) and the context presented him as both the fulfilment of Roman history and the personification of Roman power. The temple, dominating the Forum of Augustus, communicated the divine power understood to sanction his political rule and auctoritas, his military power, and the empire. Augustus required the Senate to meet in this temple when discussing matters of war and victory, and stipulated that commanders of troops depart from it for battle and return to it with the spoils of victory to be displayed there (Suetonius, *Augustus* 29). It provided space for impressing foreign representatives who were received there and for defining masculinity as young Roman men put on the toga representing manhood (Cassius Dio, 55.10). This temple communicated the empire-sustaining ideological-political-theological-military agenda comprising piety towards the gods that secured divine favour expressed in virtues (manly courage in war) and Roman victory. The result was *pax Romana*, Roman peace, born of the subjugation of the nations.

Temples honouring Roman gods and (deified) emperors performed similar functions of proclaiming and honouring Roman power and culture in provincial centres. Late in the first century BCE, perhaps by the year 10 BCE, Herod, the Roman client king of Judea, dedicated a temple to Augustus and Roma in the newly constructed city of Caesarea Maritima. The temple, covered in white stucco, expressed his loyalty and gratitude to his patron Augustus, and secured his alliance and protection, thereby bolstering Herod's own power. Displaying images of both Augustus and Roma, and impressively located on a platform mound overlooking the harbour, the temple was visible to all as they entered the harbour and communicated both Roman presence as well as the loyalty of Herod and his kingdom to Rome.

The location of Herod's temple to Augustus was typical of imperial temples, which were customarily located in prominent civic spaces where their messages (both overt and implicit) would be regularly communicated to large numbers of people. In PERGAMUM in Asia, the temple dedicated to Augustus and Dea Roma was placed on the highest point of the acropolis. In Aphrodisias, the imperial temple was accentuated by approach through a lengthy porticoed courtyard. Panels bore images of mythological figures related to Aphrodisias and the imperial household, along with various peoples, depicted as women, who had been subjugated by Rome. These panels communicated not only Rome's military power and domination but also the qualities of desirable (imperial) masculinity, such as courage, leadership, and victory, that ensured domination over feminized weaker peoples. In POMPEII in Campania, dominating the forum were two temples, an older Greek temple of Apollo and a temple of Jupiter Capitolinus honouring the deities Jupiter, Juno, and Minerva. These three deities were represented by three statues in the *cella*. This Capitoline temple originated when the town became a colonia in the first century BCE. It was strategically located at the end of the forum, classically marking the city as Roman and visually communicating Rome's authority to all who passed.

In Ephesus, late in the first century CE, free cities in Asia dedicated a temple to the Flavian Sebastoi comprising the emperor Domitian, his deceased brother and the deified Emperor Titus, and their deceased father the deified Vespasian. The temple signified not only religious sanction and provincial deference, but also brought honour to Ephesus among other cities in the province. Ephesus had competed with those cities for honour and prominence, identifying it as a neokorate city, a warden or keeper of the imperial temple and cult. Ephesus was also the site of the temple of Artemis, one of the seven wonders of the ancient world. Temples of varying sizes seem to have existed on the site since the eighth century BCE, with a large marble temple being constructed in the sixth century BCE and further construction in the fourth century. In addition to the massive statue of Artemis, it housed images of some thirty-five to forty deities, including Isis and Attis. This temple was big business for Ephesus, with the honouring of Artemis, a goddess especially associated with fertility, ensuring the well-being of the city along with blessings dispensed in response to individual requests. Games, contests, theatrical performances, and processions were held in the goddess's name, all requiring local resources and skills, providing local employment, drawing crowds to the city, stimulating a market economy, and providing city elites opportunities to compete with each other for social honour and power by associating with the temple and in making gifts to it.

The scene in Acts 19 involving conflict between silversmiths and Paul attests the temple's religious, economic, and civic functions as guarantor of the well-being of Ephesus along with the need to ensure that provincial allegiance to the temple did not disrupt social order and attract Roman attention. The growing presence of imperial honouring in Ephesus secured an alliance between emperors and Artemis. It certainly did not replace the local goddess, but instead allied Rome with this ancient and local deity. Images of emperors and members of imperial families were carried in processions along with those of Artemis, and images of emperors were placed in the temple of Artemis.

The Jerusalem Temple as Mass Medium

The Jerusalem temple performed similar functions, communicating the religious foundations of the Jewish people through festivals and ritual, and effecting both economic reach and sociopolitical control (see TEMPLE, JERUSALEM). Its political alliance was established from the outset with King Solomon's founding of the temple. Babylonian forces destroyed Jerusalem and the temple in the sixth century BCE, but it was later rebuilt by the returned Judean exiles under the auspices of Cyrus the Persian and then dramatically by Herod, puppet king of the Romans. It was administered by professional priests whom Josephus designates as the leaders of Judea (*Antiquities* 20.251). In the first century, the Roman governor of Judea appointed the chief priests and, for a period of time, stored the high priestly garments in the Antonia fortress next to the temple as a symbolic means of control. The temple, along with much of Jerusalem, was destroyed by Roman forces in 70 CE. Subsequently in the 130s CE, the emperor Hadrian signalled Rome's control of Jerusalem by rebuilding the city as a colony (Aelia Capitolina) which included a temple dedicated to Jupiter.

In the pre-70 Jerusalem temple, just as in temples throughout the Greek and Roman worlds, priests offered sacrificial animals, incense, and libations on a daily basis, effecting atonement for the nation as well as blessings on Rome and its emperor. Priests also offered sacrifices for individuals such as those making a sin offering, or mothers after childbirth and lepers who had been healed. Different offerings were acceptable according to the means of the worshipper – for example, mothers after childbirth who could not afford a sheep could instead bring a less costly turtledove or pigeon. The temple thus incorporated those of lesser means even while it reinforced the social hierarchy. Priests also presided at the prominent PILGRIMAGE festivals of Passover, Weeks/Pentecost, and Tabernacles, festivals that commemorated key events in Israel's history such as exodus from slavery in Egypt and secured divine blessing for ongoing agricultural productivity. Priests exerted considerable societal power as the keepers of these traditions and rituals and of the COLLECTIVE MEMORY of the community-forming events that they commemorated.

The Jerusalem temple's economy was vast and far-reaching. Herod's rebuilding provided employment for some eighteen thousand skilled and unskilled workers (Josephus, *Antiquities* 20.219). Its operation utilized extensive supplies of animals for sacrifices, feed for them, oil, flour, wine, cloth for vestments, and other materials, all of which required a market economy and administration and labour to procure. Temple treasurers administered accounts, including payment for offerings, receiving tithes and offerings of first-fruits, and the temple tax of two drachmas/two denarii levied on all Judean males including those in the Diaspora. After the Roman destruction of the temple in 70 CE and refusal to allow its rebuilding, Rome continued to collect this tax but repurposed it as a tax that marked Judeans as a defeated and subjugated people and offensively used it to build the temple of Jupiter Capitolinus. Matthew's Gospel sanctions the payment of this tax post-70 by followers of Jesus but does so by subversively redefining the significance of the payment (Mt. 17.24-27).

Temple treasuries in the Jerusalem temple provided space for storage of building materials as well as the supplies necessary for its daily function. In addition to being a warehouse, the temple was, like many temples in the ancient world, a bank for both public and private funds. In the Roman Forum, for example, the temple of Saturn housed the state treasury in an internal strong room. The temple of Artemis in Ephesus housed great wealth and valuables deposited not only by wealthy provincials from Asia but also from elsewhere (Dio Chrysostom, *Oration* 31.54). The emperor Nero is said to have plundered it. The Jerusalem temple similarly stored private monies and treasured possessions as well as tax income. Such a source of funds was tempting for Roman governors. Pilate appropriated funds from the Jerusalem temple for an aqueduct, provoking a hostile reaction from Jerusalemites that quickly escalated into violence (Josephus, *Antiquities* 18.60). The later governor Florus similarly took temple funds, thereby moving a deteriorating situation closer to the war of revolt of 66-70 CE (Josephus, *Jewish War* 2.293).

Among the various messages ancient temples communicated, we can note the importance of honouring deities in various rituals in order to secure individual and communal well-being, a key role in stimulating economic activity in local centres, and the close connection between control of temple-based religious observances and the exercise of imperial, military, and societal power.

Warren Carter (Brite Divinity School, USA)

Further Reading

Bahat, D. 1999. 'The Herodian Temple.' In *The Cambridge History of Judaism*. Vol. 3. The Early Roman Period. Cambridge: Cambridge University, pp. 38–58.

Beard, Mary, John North, and Simon Price. 1998. *Religions of Rome*. 2 vols. Cambridge: Cambridge University.

Carter, Warren. 1999. 'Paying the Tax to Rome as Subversive Praxis: Matthew 17:24-27'. *JSNT* 76: 3–31. Reprinted in Warren Carter. 2001. *Matthew and Empire: Initial Explorations*. Harrisburg: Trinity Press International, pp. 130–44.
Cooley, Alison, and M. G. Cooley. 2004. *Pompeii and Herculaneum: A Sourcebook*. London: Routledge.
Friesen, Steven. 1995. 'The Cult of the Roman Emperors at Ephesos: Temple Wardens, City Titles, and the Interpretation of the Revelation of John.' In *Ephesos Metropolis of Asia: An Interdisciplinary Approach to Its Architecture, Religion, and Culture*. Edited by Helmut Koester. Harrisburg: Trinity Press International, pp. 229–50.
Friesen, Steven. 2001. *Imperial Cults and the Apocalypse of John: Reading Revelation in the Ruins*. Oxford: Oxford University Press.
Goodman, Martin. 2005. 'The Temple in First Century CE Judaism.' In *Temple and Worship in Biblical Israel*. Edited by John Day. LHBOTS. London: T&T Clark, pp. 459–68.
Hanson, K. C., and Douglas Oakman. 1998. *Palestine in the Time of Jesus: Social Structures and Social Conflicts*. Minneapolis: Fortress.
Kahn, Lisa. 1996. 'King Herod's Temple of Roma and Augustus at Caesarea Maritima.' In *Caesarea Maritima: A Retrospective after Two Millennia*. Edited by Avner Raban and Kenneth Holum. Leiden: Brill, pp. 130–45.
Knibbe, Dieter. 1995. 'Via Sacra Ephesiaca: New Aspects of the Cult of Artemis Ephesia.' In *Ephesos Metropolis of Asia: An Interdisciplinary Approach to Its Architecture, Religion, and Culture*. Edited by Helmut Koester. Harrisburg: Trinity Press International, pp. 141–55.
Price, Simon R. F. 1984. *Rituals and Power: The Roman Imperial Cult in Asia Minor*. Cambridge: Cambridge University.
Richardson, Peter. 1996. *Herod: King of the Jews and Friend of the Romans*. Columbia: University of South Carolina Press.
Rives, James B. 2007. *Religion in the Roman Empire*. Malden and Oxford: Blackwell.
Stamper, John W. 2005. *The Architecture of Roman Temples: The Republic to the Middle Empire*. Cambridge: Cambridge University Press.
Srelan, Rick. 1996. *Paul, Artemis, and the Jews in Ephesus*. Berlin: Walter Mouton de Gruyter.
Wickkiser, Bronwen L. 2010. 'Asklepios in Greek and Roman Corinth.' In *Corinth in Context; Comparative Studies on Religion and Society*. Edited by Steven Friesen, Daniel Schowalter, and James C. Walters. *NovT* Supplements 134 Leiden: Brill, pp. 37–66.
Thomas, Christine. 1995. 'At Home in the City of Artemis: Religion in Ephesos in the Literary Imagination of the Roman Period.' In *Ephesos Metropolis of Asia: An Interdisciplinary Approach to Its Architecture, Religion, and Culture*. Edited by Helmut Koester. Harrisburg: Trinity Press International, pp. 81–117.
Zanker, Paul. 1990. *The Power of Images in the Age of Augustus*. Ann Arbor: University of Michigan Press.

Temple (Jerusalem) The Second Temple of Jerusalem stood from roughly 516 BCE to 70 CE. During that time, it functioned as the central site of cultic WORSHIP and a major ideological focal point for Jews throughout the world. Following its destruction in 70 CE, the Temple became a prominent object of CULTURAL MEMORY for Jews and, to a lesser extent, for Christians.

According to Ezra 1–6, the construction of the Second Temple was initiated by Zerubbabel, a Babylonian Jew commissioned by the Persian King Cyrus I to govern his newly acquired province of Judea following his conquest of Babylon in 539 BCE. Zerubbabel's Temple was completed in the sixth year of the reign of King Darius I, that is, around 516 BCE (Ezra 6.15). The prophets Haggai and Zechariah bear witness to its construction. Its early years of operation provide the historical backdrop of the so-called Third Isaiah prophecies (Isa. 56–66). Ezra 7–10 and Nehemiah attest to the Temple's role as the principal cultic and civic institution of Jerusalem and the administrative seat of Judea in the early to mid-fifth century BCE. The new Temple evidently resumed the function of its predecessor as a site for the collection and production of sacred texts. Priestly SCRIBES working under the authority of the Persian government were likely responsible for the creation and subsequent dissemination of the received form of the Pentateuch, their contributions discernible in the cultic concerns of its final editorial layer.

The scant surviving evidence attesting to the Temple's operation in the decades following Nehemiah's governorship suggests that it continued to function as the hub of Jewish cultic and political activity without pause. It was likely in this era that priestly scribes composed the books of Chronicles, subtly rewriting Israel's history to promote the cultic values of their age. Josephus records what is likely an apocryphal legend of a visit to the Temple by a reverential Alexander of Macedon during his campaign against the Persians c. 333 BCE (*Antiquities* 11.317-45). Regardless of the story's historicity, its obliging tone suggests that subsequent Jewish generations saw the Greek subjugation of Judea as an event of no negative consequence towards their central communal institution. The healthy state of the Jewish cult at the turn of the second century BCE is observed by Jesus Ben Sira, who recounts a festive ritual celebration by a high priest named Simon credited with having renovated and fortified the Temple's sacred precinct (Sir. 50.1-21). A visually sumptuous account of a visit to the Temple in the Letter of Aristeas appears to date to roughly the same period. In contrast, 1 Enoch, Jubilees, and the Damascus Document express dissatisfaction with the Temple's cultic establishment, proffering alternative priestly ideologies to those practised in Jerusalem. Whether supportive or critical of the Temple's leadership, these diverse literary artefacts of the early Hellenistic age appear to attest to the development of an educational apparatus based in the Temple for the scribal training of young men of priestly lineage eligible for service in its cult.

In 167 BCE, the Temple became a site of conflict between rival claimants to the Jewish high priesthood. The dispute prompted the Seleucid Greek King Antiochus IV to send a military force to protect his preferred appointee and his local supporters. The resulting occupation of the Temple's precinct incited a popular rebellion led by the Hasmoneans, a priestly clan offended by what they saw as the illicit administration of their national cult and the sacrileges committed by the heathen soldiers sent to guard the offenders. The apocalyptic visions of Daniel 7–12 allude to the alleged misconduct of the soldiers and the initial outbreak of the revolt.

The ensuing struggle for the Temple between the Jewish rebels and their Seleucid adversaries is documented in the deuterocanonical books of 1 Maccabees and 2 Maccabees, each of which presents a unique perspective on the significance of the events in question. According to 2 Maccabees, the earlier of the two books, God appointed the Seleucids to violate the Temple's sanctity in order to punish the Jews for having allowed their chief priests to corrupt their national cult and, thereby, to endanger the welfare of their people. The triumph of the Hasmoneans in retaking the Temple thus signalled the subsiding of God's anger against his people and, moreover, God's approval of the new cultic order inaugurated by the rebels. That, it seems, was the rationale of the Hasmoneans in instituting the Hanukkah festival to commemorate not their military victory over the Seleucids but their rededication of the Temple. Written decades after the Hasmoneans consolidated their power, 1 Maccabees downplays the cultic ideologies of the rebels by omitting reference to the crooked priests and emphasizing instead the intolerable cruelty of Antiochus.

The ultimate victory of the rebels ushered in what would be nearly a century of Jewish self-rule in Judea. In the years following the revolt, the Hasmoneans gained control of the high priesthood and combined the cultic authority traditionally invested in the office with the civic authority formerly exercised by the Seleucids. The first Hasmonean priest-king Simon (reigned 142–135 BCE) made Jerusalem the seat of his government and enlarged the Temple's sacred precinct. His successors would continue to improve its facilities, welcoming ever-growing numbers of Jewish visitors from throughout Judea and the Diaspora to offer sacrifices at the Temple during their annual pilgrimage festivals. The Temple thus appears as a site of continual activity in the histories of the Hasmonean dynasty in 1 Maccabees and Josephus' *Antiquities*. Certain Jews of the Hasmonean era came to see their Temple as more than just the centre of their national cult. The book of Jubilees intimates that God chose the site of the Temple at the moment of the world's creation, setting it at the very centre of the earth. The Temple Scroll from Qumran envisions a dramatic expansion of its precinct to accommodate the throngs of worshippers its author believed would descend upon Jerusalem at the end of days. The Temple thereby was fashioned into an eternal signifier of Jewish identity transcending the mundane realities of its operation.

In 63 BCE, Jerusalem was taken by the Roman general Pompey. His daring entry into the Temple's inner sanctum, which the Jews deemed forbidden to all but their high priests, became a minor sensation among Greek and Roman authors. In 37 BCE, Rome installed Herod as the client king of Judea, effectively doing away with the remaining vestiges of the Hasmoneans' political influence. Herod refurbished the Temple and further expanded its precinct, creating a sprawling and opulent sacred campus outfitted for high volumes of worshippers. Herod's Temple earned a reputation as one of the most magnificent facilities of its kind in the civilized world. Josephus, a priest raised in Jerusalem, was a regular visitor during his youth, and Philo of Alexandria made the trek to Jerusalem at least once. Both attest to the grand spectacle of the Temple cult at the peak of its operation during the mid-first century CE.

The Temple was commandeered as a stronghold by the Jewish insurgents who rose against Rome in 66 CE. The rebels, whom Josephus accounts as the Zealots, found an early champion in Eleazer ben Ananias, a son of a former high priest who campaigned for the cessation of sacrifices on behalf of Gentiles. The Zealots also reportedly installed their own high priest, one Phannias ben Samuel, to preside over the Temple cult at the start of the rebellion. Control of the Temple thus seems to have been no less a motivation for those opposing the Romans than it had been for those who had opposed the Greeks centuries ago. The war itself did not touch the Temple directly until 68 CE, when a band of Zealots under the leadership of the John of Gischala, having fled the Galilean battlefront, sought refuge in its quarters. According to Josephus, the arrival of the Zealots compelled the former high priest Ananus ben Ananus, who opposed the rebellion, to call upon Jerusalem's citizens to drive John's men from their city. Thus besieged in the Temple, John coordinated an attack against Ananus and his supporters that left the popular priest dead and the Zealots firmly in control of Jerusalem. The Temple remained in the hands of the rebels when the Roman army finally reached the city in 70 CE. Following a brief siege by the general Titus, the walls of Jerusalem were breached and the Temple was summarily razed to the ground. Josephus, at the time a prisoner of war, witnessed the event and recorded it in tragic detail in his chronicle of the conflict. Other Greek and Roman commentators less sympathetic to the Jews exulted in Rome's victory over what they deemed the barbarous rebels. The Temple, recently renowned for its magnificence and for the fervent devotion of its patrons, became in its ruined state a symbol of the Jews' national humiliation.

The Temple as a Site of Memory

The destruction of the Temple sent shockwaves through the world's Jewish population. Gone were the cultic services whereby they presumed to maintain their national covenant with God. Encomia for the Temple appear in such texts as 2 Baruch, 4 Baruch, and 4 Ezra, apocalyptic compositions set in the wake of the Babylonian conquest and meant to inspire hope that the Second Temple would be rebuilt just as Solomon's Temple had been centuries ago. That hope likely inspired the Jewish rebels who once again challenged the Romans during the second Jewish revolt of 132–135 CE under the leadership of Simon bar Kosiba, or Bar Kokhba. Stylized images of the Temple's façade appear on coins issued by his supporters, apparently to advertise their plan to save Jerusalem from a plan to convert it into a Roman military colony.

Memory of the Temple inspired early Christians as well. Herod's Temple appears in the Synoptic Gospels as Jesus' final destination before his arrest and crucifixion and in the Gospel of John as a regular site of pilgrimage for Jesus and his disciples. A narrative sequence unique to Luke depicts a blessing of the infant Jesus in the Temple and a young Jesus later holding court among its teachers (Lk. 2.21-52). The Temple appears in Acts as the site where Jesus' disciples assembled to initiate the apostolic mission (1–5) and where Paul was arrested (21–23). Prophetic visions of the Temple's destruction ascribed to Jesus likely date to the period following its actual demolition, echoing the beliefs of his followers that Rome's eradication of the Jews' place of worship signalled God's rejection of their cult (Mt. 24.1-2; Mk 13.1-8; Lk. 21.5-19; Jn 2.19). These bitter reflections speak to the early development of a theological construction of Jesus as the one true point of meeting between heaven and earth and his self-sacrifice as a functional substitution for the Jewish Temple and its traditional ritual economy. The same sentiment is evidently reflected in the apocalyptic visions of Revelation, which foretell an eschatological Jerusalem with no temple (21.9–22.5).

The rabbinic sages recalled their people's bygone shrine more fondly. The MISHNAH, a legal compilation of the early third century CE, recounts numerous aspects of the Temple's past operation. Tractates in the order *Mo'ed* describe the liturgies and sacrifices performed by the Temple priests during Jewish festivals. Tractates in the order *Qodashim* include procedural details of those sacrificial rites along with information on the Temple's physical features. Later rabbinic texts preserve narrative traditions recounting the highs of its days under the Hasmoneans and Herodians and the lows of its devastation during the First Jewish Revolt (see RABBINIC LITERATURE). Why the sages were so preoccupied with the Temple is unclear. Perhaps they wished to preserve knowledge of its rituals in anticipation of the Messianic age, when they believed the Temple would be rebuilt and its cult reinstated. Perhaps they meant to remind their followers of their nation's cultic constitution in the absence of the functioning cult that once defined their collective sense of purpose. In any case, the sages clearly imagined the Temple as a vital locus of Jewish CULTURAL MEMORY long after hope for its imminent restoration faded (see POSTMEMORY.

The sages were not alone among their fellow Jews in cultivating memories of the Temple. Temple iconography was common in early Jewish VISUAL CULTURE. Wall paintings from the SYNAGOGUE of Dura-Europos in Syria depict the Tabernacle as a colonnaded building in the Greek style, thereby evoking the majestic Jewish sanctuary of more recent memory. One appears to depict the Temple itself encircled by the walls of Jerusalem. Working during the early-third century CE, the artist cannot have had first-hand knowledge of the Temple's appearance, yet the intended object of reference is obvious. Tableaus featuring the Temple's menorah, or lampstand, and other of its ritual implements appear in mosaic carpets and paintings from later SYNAGOGUES and burial facilities throughout the Land of Israel and the Diaspora. Architectural elements from the synagogues of Migdal and Ḥorvat Kur in the Galilee feature images of those vessels carved in stone. Depictions of Torah arks in the same contexts indicate that those reliquaries of sacred SCROLLS often were designed to mimic the Temple's façade. A sculptural fragment from the synagogue of the Galilean town of Capernaum appears to represent the Ark of the Covenant as a wheeled cabinet fashioned as a miniature Temple. All these diverse artefacts seem meant to serve a common commemorative function, namely to impart something of the Temple's renowned holiness to the contemporary Jewish ritual spaces of the synagogue and cemetery.

Depictions of the Temple were rare in early Christian culture, which likely is to be attributed to the disdain for that definitively Jewish institution expressed in the NT. It features in apocryphal writings involving Jesus, Mary, and James, among others. Images of the Temple occasionally appear in visual media depicting stories from the Gospels set on its premises, in which examples it is typically depicted as a generic building in the Greek style. A notable exception is a mosaic from a Byzantine-era chapel on Mount Nebo in Jordan, which features an architectonic rendering of the Temple accompanied by a quotation from Ps. 51.21 expressing hope for the restoration of Jerusalem and its sacrificial cult.

Joshua Ezra Burns (Marquette University, USA)

Further Reading

Carr, David M. 2005. *Writing on the Tablet of the Heart: Origins of Scripture and Literature*. Oxford: Oxford University Press.

Cohn, Naftali S. 2013. *The Memory of the Temple and the Making of the Rabbis*. Philadelphia: University of Pennsylvania Press.

De Silva, Carla Gomez. 1996. 'The Temple in the Iconography of Early Christian Art.' *Assaph: Studies in Art History* 2: 59–82.

Fraade, Steven D. 2009. 'The Temple as a Marker of Jewish Identity before and after 70 CE: The Role of the Holy Vessels in Rabbinic Memory and Imagination.' In *Jewish Identities in Antiquity: Studies in Memory of Menahem Stern*. Edited by Lee I. Levine and Daniel R. Schwartz. TSAJ 130. Tübingen: Mohr Siebeck, pp. 237–65.

Hayward, C. T. R. 1996. *The Jewish Temple: A Non-Biblical Sourcebook*. London: Routledge.

Laderman, Shulamit. 2003. 'Images of the Temple in Jewish Art and Their Parallel Literary Sources.' In *Envisioning the Temple: Stones, Scrolls, and Symbols*. Edited by Adolfo Roitman. Jerusalem: Israel Museum, pp. 97–125.

Regev, Eyal. 2011. 'Josephus, the Temple, and the Jewish War.' In *Flavius Josephus: Interpretation and History*. Edited by Jack Pastor, Pnina Stern and Menahem Mor. JSJS 146. Leiden: Brill, pp. 279–93.

Testaments (Jewish) The ancient Jewish testamentary literature typically embraces the pseudepigraphic voice of a figure known from the Hebrew Scriptures, most often one of the patriarchal or pre-diluvian ancestors presented in the Pentateuch (e.g. Enoch, Abraham). Testaments portray these individuals delivering a farewell address to their kindred prior to their imminent passing, the message of which is often didactically charged on a variety of topics. While the seeds for the genre were sewn in the Hebrew Scriptures (e.g. Gen. 49) and the form eventually came to full bloom in early Christian writings (e.g. *Testaments of the Twelve Patriarchs*), the genre germinated in several key Second Temple period Jewish texts.

The extant ancient Jewish literature include a small selection of formal testaments (e.g. *Testament of Moses*, perhaps also *Testament of Abraham* and *Testament of Job*), testament-like addresses within larger narrative frameworks (e.g. 1 En. 81–82; 1 Macc. 2.49-70; Jub. 7), and works that, while not technically testaments themselves, are integral for tracing the development of the genre (Aramaic Levi Document, Testament of Qahat, and Visions of Amram). A cross-section of these texts offers important insights into early testamentary literature's orientation to media, particularly regarding motifs of scribalism, transmission of ancestral lore in textual form, and the concern for handing down teaching through approved and safeguarded genealogical channels.

The *Testament of Moses* includes a common fixture in the budding testamentary tradition: the transmission of booklore from one generation to the next. In this instance, Moses delivers materials to his successor Joshua, who is charged with safeguarding 'these words and this book' until the end of the ages (10.11; cf. 1.17, 11.1). This two-tiered strategy, therefore, links the discourse to an authoritative figure from scriptural memory and associates the writing in question with a textual artefact located within the narrative.

Arguably the most significant concentration of materials that appears in the evolution of the testament genre is a triad of Aramaic texts at Qumran: Aramaic Levi Document, Testament of Qahat, and Visions of Amram. These texts are again couched in pseudepigraphic perspectives, which are strategically coupled with a broader range of textual modalities.

Thanks to insightful overlaps between the Qumran Aramaic Levi texts and the more complete copies known from the Cairo Genizah it is possible to recover most of Levi's extensive wisdom discourse (Aramaic Levi Document 82–98), which endorses scribalism and the acquisition of knowledge. For example, Levi's list of lauded behaviours and practices emphasizes the instruction of one's sons in 'scribal craft and instruction and wisdom', for in gaining these one acquires glory (Aramaic Levi Document 88; 4Q213 1 i: 9). As the Qumran text becomes increasingly fragmentary and the Genizah text is absent, a likely parallel reference to this threefold body of tradition is found in the context of an additional mention of 'books' (4Q213 2.5, 9). While these instances point to the importance of maintaining traditions and take a cautious approach to their transmission for future generations, Aramaic Levi also makes efforts to associate its teachings with more ancient traditions or even ancestral booklore. For instance, Levi claims to have learnt 'the law of the priesthood' (Aramaic Levi Document 13) from his grandfather, Isaac, who in turn learnt priestly praxis from Abraham's example, who had no less an authoritative source than the book of Noah (Aramaic Levi Document 57).

The so-called Testament of Qahat likewise adds to the chain of tradition by portraying the priestly patriarch as passing 'all my writings' on to his son, Amram (4Q542 1 ii.12), the contents of which apparently represent a conglomerate of traditional materials inherited through Levi (4Q542 1 ii.9-13). While the precise content of the tradition is largely lost in the fragmentary text, it is evident that their core contained items pertaining to the priesthood, stretching back through Levi, Jacob, Isaac, and Abraham (4Q542 1 i.10-13). Given this unique heritage, Qahat admonishes his sons to safeguard the inheritance entrusted and bequeathed by the ancestors, taking special care to protect it from outsiders (4Q542 1 i.4-5).

The idea of the transmission of ancestral lore is at best latent in Visions of Amram, perhaps because Testament of Qahat already achieved Amram's acquisition of the priestly tradition as outlined above. Textual media, however, are integral to the narrative frame of Visions of Amram in a special way. Prior to delving into the first-person narrative, the work commences with a telling title, 'A copy of "The Writing of the Words of the Vision(s) of Amram, son of Qahat, son of Levi"' (4Q543 1a, b, c.1-4; 4Q545 1a i.1-4; 4Q546 1.1-2). This clever authorial strategy is fully appreciated only after Amram's vivid dream-vision revealing the dualistic structure of the cosmos and otherworldly endorsement of the priestly line of Aaron (e.g. 4Q544 1.10-15; 4Q545 4). Immediately following this revelation, Amram relates, 'I awoke from the sleep of my eyes and wrot[e] the vision' (4Q547 9.8). In this way, the incipit and portrayal of Amram as a dream-writer serve to anchor the entire composition in the pseudepigraphic penmanship of Amram, from within the narrative itself.

For all of their contributions to our understanding of the development of the testament GENRE in ancient Judaism, however, none of these three Qumran texts can be considered an exemplar of the testament genre in the truest sense. Rather, they attest to a growing tradition en route to the testamentary genre. These writings thus provide insight into the core ideas, narrative delivery, and inclination to associate such traditions with ancestral discourses often involving the transmission of instruction and knowledge in a scribal product.

Andrew B. Perrin (Trinity Western University)

Further Reading

Collins, John J. 1984. 'Testaments.' In *Jewish Writings of the Second Temple Period.* Edited by Michael E. Stone. Assen: Van Gorcum. Philadelphia: Fortress, pp. 325–56.

Drawnel, Henryk. 2010. 'The Literary Characteristics of the Visions of Levi (so-called Aramaic Levi Document).' *Journal of Ancient Judaism* 1: 303–19.

Frey, Jörg. 2010. 'On the Origins of the Genre of the "Literary Testament:" Farewell Discourses in the Qumran Library and their Relevance for the History of the Genre.' In *Aramaica Qumranica: Proceedings of the Conference on the Aramaic Texts from Qumran in Aix-en-Provence, 30 June–2 July 2008.* Edited by Katell Berthelot and Daniel Stökl Ben Ezra. *STDJ* 94. Leiden: Brill, pp. 345–75.

Parry, Donald W., and Emanuel Tov, eds. 2005. *The Dead Sea Scrolls Reader, Vol. 3: Parabiblical Texts.* Leiden: Brill.

Perrin, Andrew B. 2013. 'Capturing the Voices of Pseudepigraphic Personae: On the Form and Function of Incipits in the Aramaic Dead Sea Scrolls.' *DSD* 20: 98–123.

Testimonia *Testimonia* are collections of OT passages drawn from a (usually thematic) anthology of scriptural passages. They are widely thought to comprise the source of OT quotations in certain instances within the NT, as well as in certain apostolic fathers (esp. Barnabas) and in a number of church fathers (esp. Justin Martyr, Irenaeus, Tertullian, Cyprian, Lactantius, and Ps.-Gregory of Nyssa). The term *testimonia*, when considered interchangeably with 'testimonies' or 'testimony book', goes back to the nineteenth century, being first used by J. Rendel Harris at least as early as 1889 (Falcetta 2003: 283–4). The term has sparingly been applied to oral collections of proof texts as well.

While there is no direct evidence that Christian testimonia sources existed in the first century (there is no specific reference to such in the NT or second-century Christian texts), the GENRE existed among Jews contemporary with the NT writers. As Hodgson (1979: 363) points out, 'excerpt collections' were a commonplace in the ancient world. The theory of the NT writers' use of testimonia sources is an inference, but it is backed by a number of strong indicators. According to the prevailing view, the selection of passages included in a testimonia source was often topical, intended to prove a given doctrine or position, such as the apostolic kerygma or the church's superiority over the SYNAGOGUE. This view of testimonia sources as topically organized is consistent with the nature of texts found at Qumran (cf. 4QTestimonia, 4QFlorilegium) and elsewhere (cf. Papyrus Rylands 3.460). Not all collections of OT passages, however, are meant to be proof-textual. Albl (1999: 7) distinguishes two subtypes: 'testimonia collections' proper (which serve to prove a 'forensic' point) and 'extract collections' (which serve a different purpose). Testimonia sources can also be classified by whether they include other material in addition to the scriptural passages that they quote (such as commentary or explanatory glosses). Some scholars (e.g. Dietrich-Alex Koch and Christopher Stanley) prefer to think of these sources as personal anthologies (especially within the purview of Paul's writing career), created partly for the traveller's convenience and partly to avoid the expense of complete rolls of the books of Scripture.

There is perhaps more disagreement over when the testimonia hypothesis should be invoked to explain the epiphenomenal aspects of a NT passage than over whether such sources existed. For this reason, scholars have worked with tentative lists of potential indicators that a testimonia source lies behind a given OT quotation. The three strongest indicators are 1) an OT quotation's deviance from the SEPTUAGINT version of a saying (especially in an author that prefers the Septuagint); 2) the composite nature of certain OT quotations in the NT; and, 3) a NT writer's ascription of a passage to the wrong OT book. A number of subsidiary indicators have also been suggested, including 4) the independent use of the same passages by different NT authors; 5) the thematic linking of quoted passages; 6) the use of passages contrarily to their original function (cited out of context); 7) the inclusion of exegetical glosses; and, 8) the use of a passage within an anti-Jewish polemic. Indicator 6, emphasized by Wilhelm Bousset, has for the most part fallen out of use, due to a greater awareness of the creativeness with which scriptural passages were employed apart from the testimonia hypothesis. Indicators 7 and 8, which were proposed by Harris, do not apply to the NT writings but rather to the patristic use of testimonia sources (see Albl 1999: 16, 21–2).

Although the testimonia hypothesis enjoyed widespread support in the early twentieth century, its applicability to the NT writings was also often challenged, especially on the grounds of a supposed lack of contemporary parallels (Jewish or Christian). That objection lost its force with the discovery of 4QTestimonia and 4QFlorilegium. In the mid-twentieth century, C. H. Dodd gave the testimonia hypothesis its greatest challenge when he posited that the proof texts lying behind the apostolic *kerygma* circulated in oral rather than in written form, but his thesis probably only cut against a careless extension of the (written) testimonia hypothesis as a universal explanation for OT quotations in the NT. The hypothesis as a whole was also strengthened considerably with the discovery of non-Septuagint-aligned Greek OT texts, including the *kaige* recension posited by Dominique Barthélemy in 1963. The *kaige* Greek OT represents an alternative version to the widely used Septuagint translation of Scripture. It appears to have been widely used in some circles of the early church. As it became clear that the Septuagint text competed in the first century with the *kaige* and other forerunners of the Greek OT texts compiled in the third century by Origen, scholars began to find evidence of these competing OT texts being used in a patterned way in the NT. This allowed clusters of non-Septuagint-aligned OT quotations to serve as a sort of fingerprint for the use of testimonia sources, and helped solidify the case for a testimonia source in general.

We should probably not think of the NT writers as working directly from a written testimonia source every time they quoted a testimonia verse, but rather as working from a fund of memorized verses. They are more likely indebted to a testimonia source when they are made to support aspects of the gospel itself, or when they are connected with other theological set pieces that would have been shared more widely.

John C. Poirier (Kingswell Theological Seminary, USA)

Further Reading

Albl, Martin C. 1999. *And Scripture Cannot Be Broken: The Form and Function of The Early Christian Testimonia Collections. NovT Supplements* 96. Leiden: Brill.
Barnard, L. W. 1967. 'The Use of Testimonies in the Early Church and in the Epistle of Barnabas.' In *Studies in the Apostolic Fathers and their Background.* New York: Schocken, pp. 109–13.
Falcetta, Alessandro. 2003. 'The Testimony Research of James Rendel Harris.' *NovT* 45: 280–99.
Hodgson, Roger Jr. 1979. 'The Testimony Hypothesis.' *JBL* 98: 361–78.
Miller, Merrill P. 1971. 'Targum, Midrash and the Use of the Old Testament in the New Testament.' *JSJ* 2: 29–82.

Text-broker(s) The term *text-broker* refers to an educated individual who serves as a point of contact between written traditions and the constituencies who prize those traditions. The term was coined by Gregory Snyder, who observes that 'the appropriation of texts in the ancient world almost always involved some type of mediation by a trained specialist' (2000: 11). Although the brokering of texts could play an important role in class distinction, such mediation was common for all classes. Pliny the Elder's slaves frequently read to him or took dictation – even while he bathed (Pliny the Younger, *Epistle* 3.5) – despite the fact that he was no doubt educated himself. AUTHORSHIP by dictation was typical among those who could afford SCRIBES (Hurtado and Keith 2013: 71–2), and the privileged status that guaranteed an EDUCATION often simultaneously guaranteed an ability to avoid using literate skills oneself. Tasks such as rote copying could thus be viewed as menial (*Rhetorica ad Herennium* 4.4.6), though some ancients still esteemed literate skills and preferred to read and write for themselves in various circumstances (Cicero, *Atticus* 2.23; Jerome, *On Illustrious Men* 75; Quintilian, *Institutes* 1.1.28–29).

Outside the elite educated classes, however, text-brokerage reflected different power dynamics, because the vast majority of the ancient world was illiterate (Harris 1989; Hezser 2001). Particularly in contexts where a culture revered a text or texts as sacrosanct, the minority literates who were trained to read, copy, interpret, and teach those texts, and thus possessed scribal LITERACY, held tremendous authority vis-à-vis the majority of illiterates who could not directly access those texts themselves (see Sir. 38.24–39.5). This was certainly the case at all points in biblical history. One clear example is the portrayal of Ezra the scribe-priest reading publicly the law in Hebrew while the Levites interpret it for the Aramaic-speaking returnees from exile, who otherwise could not understand (Neh. 8.1-9). Text-brokering was also a central function of the SYNAGOGUE in Second Temple Judaism, as this weekly meeting provided most Jews with direct access to their holy Scriptures in the form of public reading and teaching (Josephus, *Against Apion* 2.17 § 175; Philo, *Hypothetica* 7.12–13; *That Every Good Person is Free* 12.81–82; Lk. 4.16–20; Acts 15.21; Theodotus Inscription; cf. 2 Cor. 3.15).

From this perspective, one may note that the historical sources portray teachers such as Moses, Joshua, Josiah, Ezra, Jesus, Paul, Hillel, Shammai, Akiba, Marcion, Justin Martyr, Augustine and many others as leaders who postured themselves as brokers of authoritative texts, most of which came to form the Hebrew Bible and NT. When conflict with other teachers ensued, these instances often reflected the central issue of who had the authority to speak for those texts. The brokering of texts was a central feature of Judaism and Christianity, for the ideologies and personalities that proliferated could not have done so without this central cultural dynamic (see Textual Community).

Chris Keith (St. Mary's University, UK)

Further Reading

Hurtado, Larry W., and Chris Keith. 2013. 'Writing and Book Production in the Hellenistic and Roman Periods.' In *The New Cambridge History of the Bible: From the Beginnings to 600*. Cambridge: Cambridge University Press, pp. 63–80.

Snyder, H. Gregory. 2000. *Teachers and Texts in the Ancient World: Philosophers, Jews and Christians*. New York: Routledge.

Textual Criticism In general, *Textual Criticism* refers to the study of ancient manuscripts and their texts; *biblical textual criticism*, then, refers to the study of ancient manuscripts of those texts now included in the Bible. As a research model, textual criticism involves the collation of manuscripts in the various biblical languages as well as other types of textual evidence. Textual Criticism is highly important for our understanding of the ancient media environment, as it deals specifically with the reading and writing of ancient manuscripts.

In older formulations within biblical studies, the main goal of Textual Criticism was discovering the original text of a particular book or passage of the Bible – that is, reconstructing the wording of the single first draft of the passage or book as produced by the original author. More recently, however, biblical text critics have abandoned the search for the original text, and instead use the term *Textual Criticism* to refer to the study of the texts of the Hebrew Bible and NT in an effort to identify the earliest written stages of those traditions and to understand how the various ancient textual traditions developed in their variety. In discussions of the Hebrew Bible, this variety includes, for example, the Masoretic Text, the Aramaic targums, the Samaritan Pentateuch, and the Septuagint, while NT textual critics might consider the differences between the Greek text and its ancient translations in Latin, Coptic, and Syriac.

Manuscript Variation and the Mechanics of Sight

Before Gutenberg's invention of the printing press in the fifteenth century, scribes copied the biblical text from previous copies by hand, sometimes providing synonyms or other alterations. As the scribes attempted to fulfil their task of making faithful copies of the text, they nevertheless made textual changes – that is, adding, omitting, substituting, or transposing words. Some of these textual changes were errors of spelling or obvious slips. Some of these textual changes resulted in no real change in the meaning of the text. At times the changes resulted in new meaningful readings, more likely to become perpetuated.

The challenge for the modern text critic is to discern when a textual change was accidental and when it was intentional. This challenge is heightened by the fact that it is quite possible that some changes that are today perceived as theologically significant were not viewed as such by the ancients (Person 1998; Person 2015). As noted above, variants may have entered the manuscript tradition consciously or unconsciously and, even though there may be slight differences in meaning, the modern critic sometimes has little evidence for discerning which reading is the earliest and which represents a later 'change' (Tov 2012: 87, 257-58). An example may be taken from comparison of the Masoretic Text and the Samaritan Pentateuch for Num. 21.5.

MT Num. 21.5: Why did you bring us up (*h'lytnw*) from Egypt?
SP Num. 21.5: Why did you take us out (*hwṣ'tnw*) of Egypt? (Tov 2012: 87)

Similarly, some manuscripts of 1 Cor. 2.1 speak of the 'mystery (*mystērion*) of God' while others refer to the 'testimony (*martyrion*) of God', with the root words in Greek being remarkably similar. Apparently, a scribe substituted one word that looked or sounded like another at some point in the manuscript tradition, though which reading is original is debated. In both of these examples, while the variant readings could imply variant theological perspectives, it is impossible to know for certain whether the ancient scribes would have perceived them as such and, especially, to determine which reading is more likely to be the original and which the variant.

Many variations can be explained as 'misreadings', instances where a scribe simply made a mistake in copying letters or words. For example, if two similar words, or two words with similar beginning or ending letters (*homoioarcton*/*homoioteleuton*), stood near one other in the same line, the scribe's eye could easily jump from the first to the second word or letter(s). This could result in the omission of an entire word or of letters in a word (haplography); conversely, the eye could jump back in the text so that the same sequence of text was copied twice (dittography). For example, the variant manuscripts of 1 Thess. 2.7 suggest that a Greek letter was either accidentally omitted or repeated.

'We were gentle (*egenēthēmen ēpioi*) among you.' (NRSV)
'We were like young children (*egenēthēmen nēpioi*) among you.' (NIV)

Similarly, the Isaiah Scroll from Qumran (1QIsa[a]) appears to include an example of haplography (omission of a phrase) in Isa. 26.3-4.

MT Isa 26.3-4: For in You it trusts. Trust in the LORD
1QIsa[a] 26.3-4: For in You. Trust in the LORD (Tov 2012: 222).

In the PARABLE of the Good Samaritan (Lk. 10.25-37), the fourth-century Codex Sinaiticus omits what is now verse 32 ('So likewise a Levite, when he came to the place and saw him, passed by on the other side' – parallel to the actions of the 'priest' in v. 31), possibly due to a haplography where the scribe skipped several lines by accident because verses 31 and 32 end with the same word: 'passed by on the other side' (*antiparēlthen*).

Other variants among existing manuscripts appear to represent instances where a scribe attempted to improve the text, because it contained an error or was otherwise judged to be lacking in some way. For example, scribes could substitute or add what seemed to be a more appropriate word or form of a word. In the Gospels in particular, scribes frequently changed words to harmonize one account or version of a saying or story with its parallel (Parker 1997: 40–3). A similar phenomenon is evident in parallel texts in the Hebrew Bible (e.g. 2 Kings 18–20//Isaiah 36–39; 2 Kgs 24.18–25.30//Jeremiah 52; see Person 1997). Here again, in some cases, improvements and harmonizations may have entered the textual tradition accidentally. For example, a scribe may have added a note or made a comment regarding a word or phrase in the margin of a manuscript or above a line; later scribes, uncertain of the provenance of the comment or perhaps affirming the earlier scribe's suggestion, may have included it in the biblical text itself (Schmid 2008: 16–23).

After a copy had been made, a different manuscript could be used for comparison to check and correct readings. Corrections could be made by the copying scribe or a different scribe. For example, in the Isaiah Scroll of Qumran (1QIsa[a]), Isa. 38.21-22 appears at the end of a short line, extends into the margin, and is written in a different hand from the remainder of the manuscript – that is, apparently, a different scribe compared 1QIsa[a] to another manuscript in order to make such 'corrections'. Similarly, in Codex Vaticanus (B 03, fourth century CE) a later scribe restored a reading of Heb. 1.3 that had been corrected and reproached the earlier corrector by adding a note in the margin: 'Fool and knave, leave the old reading and do not change it!'

Thus, in the transmission process, words and phrases were sometimes omitted, inserted, substituted, or transposed, and sentences were rewritten. In some instances whole sections were added to manuscripts – note, for example, the additions to Daniel and Esther in the Septuagint, the Long Ending of Mark (Mk 16.9-20), and the story of the woman caught in adultery (Jn 7.53–8.11). In other cases, we have different versions of biblical books that seem to be even more systematic. For example, the Masoretic Text of Jeremiah is generally regarded as an expansion of a much shorter, earlier text, one similar to that preserved in the Septuagint. Similarly, the so-called 'Western' text of Acts, as reflected in Codex Bezae (D 05, early fifth century CE), is an expansive revision that is partly the result of editorial activity. The differences between the Masoretic Text of Daniel and the Septuagint of Daniel are so significant that some scholars have suggested that these texts never had a common written source, but instead reflect two separate textualization processes of an ORAL TRADITION (Young 2016).

However, in spite of such textual changes, we must not necessarily think of the typical scribe as an author or editor who invented new readings in the act of producing manuscripts or someone who consciously thought of himself as participating in the authorship of the text (Schmid 2008). Moreover, what now appear to us as scribal interventions may actually reflect different reading traditions of the texts in their textual plurality. It is nevertheless helpful to make a clear distinction of the various stages and roles in the composition and transmission process (authors, editors, scribes, correctors, readers), so that modern critics can avoid sweeping and unverifiable statements about the intentions of individual scribes. Especially in the case of the Hebrew Bible, these distinctions are often quite difficult to make, given how late the standardization of the text was in many instances. Put another way, a lack of textual stability means that even scribes somewhat removed from the time and place of any purported original composition of the text nevertheless sometimes exerted significant influence on the shape of the text through their additions, omissions, substitutions, and/or transpositions.

Manuscript Variation and the Mechanics of Sound

Obviously, all the books of the Bible were at some point committed to writing by their authors (either directly or, certainly normally, with the assistance of scribes), and these written texts were copied for preservation and broader circulation, a process that produced the manuscripts that exist today. These manuscripts existed, and were read, studied, and copied, alongside the ongoing and vibrant oral traditions and ritual practices of the Israelites and early Christians; to the extent that these oral traditions and rituals impacted scribes, they would also have interacted with, and influenced, the evolving manuscript tradition. Yet it remains the case that scribes certainly read and copied their written exemplars. Such work was often completed by individuals working alone, a reality that is reflected, for example, in the typical Byzantine portrayal of the NT Evangelists sitting alone at a lectern or writing desk (as scribes of that period would have done) with a manuscript in front of them. As noted above, this copying process created a number of variations now evident in the manuscript tradition, reflecting either visual errors or more intentional editorial corrections on the part of individual scribes.

Some variants, however, are best explained not as products of silent reading, but rather as the results of oral/aural processes. Apart from visual copying, scribes could sit together in a room (e.g. a SCRIPTORIUM or a monastery) and transcribe a text as it was read aloud by a dictator. While this process would facilitate mass production of manuscripts, it also raised the possibility of phonetic confusion and other changes created as the scribes wrote down what they thought they had heard, or assumed they must have heard. A prominent example may be taken from the NT's *itacisms*, instances where listening scribes apparently confused vowels and diphthongs that sound like the Greek letter *iota* (*ι*). Thus, some manuscripts of 1 Cor. 15.54-55 read *neikos* instead of *nikos*, so that 'death is swallowed up by controversy' instead of 'by victory'. Another instance is reflected in Codex Sinaiticus (01 א), where one of the scribes apparently spelt many words phonetically, producing a wide range of alternate readings.

In the transmission process of the Hebrew Bible, the reading tradition – that is, the tradition behind the oral pronunciation of the consonantal text – was even more critical, since the Hebrew script does not include vowels and the same consonants can produce different words when different vowels are supplied by the reader (see ORTHOGRAPHY; MASORETIC TEXT). If the alphabet used for English did not have vowels, for example, then the consonants '*br*' could produce the words 'bear', 'bare', 'beer', and 'bier' depending on which vowels are supplied in pronunciation. Although later scribes developed various ways of representing vowels, the Hebrew biblical texts found as late at the DEAD SEA SCROLLS did not have a systematic way of representing the vowels. Therefore, for example, the difference between the Masoretic Text and the Septuagint reading of Gen. 15.11 is best explained by the observation that the consonantal Hebrew text could produce different pronunciations depending on the vowels supplied by the reader (see Schorch 2016).

> MT Gen. 15.11: And when the vultures came down on the carcasses, Abraham drove them away (*wayyaššēb ʾōtām*).
>
> LXX Gen. 15.11: And when the vultures came down on the carcasses, Abraham sat down together with them (*kai sunekathisen autois = wayyēšeb ʾitām*).

It should be noted that the impact of reading aloud on the manuscript tradition is not limited to cases where biblical texts were mass-produced in scriptoria. Silent reading was rare in the ancient world, and scribes working individually from manuscripts may have pronounced words and phrases aloud as they copied them; in the moment of transition from original to copy, the scribe's own pronunciation would have influenced his work. This would be especially true of the Hebrew Bible: since the Hebrew text included only consonants, scribes must have at least imagined how a given word would have been pronounced by supplying the relevant vowels, a cognitive process that would obviously impact the production of manuscripts.

The Textual Evidence: The Hebrew Bible

Historically speaking, the *Hebrew Bible* – that is, the Tanak, the Jewish canon behind the Masoretic Text – did not exist until at least as late as the second century CE. As a result, Textual Criticism of the Hebrew Bible involves the study of a wide range of texts and their various versions in a variety of languages, including a number of texts that are not actually included in the Hebrew Bible as we know it today. Put another way, for purposes of Textual Criticism, the Hebrew Bible refers to the collation and study of manuscripts of numerous literary texts composed and transmitted in multiple languages in the various Israelite and Jewish communities that preceded the canonization of the Tanak. Thus, the textual evidence includes multiple editions of some canonical books, some books that are non-canonical (= that do not now appear in the Hebrew Bible), and earlier translations of these various canonical and non-canonical books.

While an earlier generation of text critics assumed that efforts to reconstruct the original versions of the biblical books could best be supported by focused research on the Hebrew-language texts in the Masoretic tradition, the discovery of the Dead Sea Scrolls has called for a reassessment of the value of the so-called 'sectarian' or 'vulgar' textual traditions and translations. For example, scholars have become much more open to the reality that the Septuagint, although a Greek translation, in some instances may reflect manuscript traditions much older than those represented in the Hebrew Masoretic Text. Modern text critics must therefore work with manuscripts in multiple languages.

Broadly speaking, Textual Criticism of the Hebrew Bible considers manuscript evidence from three major categories: Hebrew-language texts, especially the Masoretic Text but also including the Dead Sea Scrolls and other texts discovered in the Judean Desert; ancient translations of Hebrew texts into other languages, including, for example, the Greek Septuagint; and, quotations of biblical books in other ancient sources, such as the RABBINIC LITERATURE or the writings of the church fathers (the latter normally translations into Greek or Latin).

The primary Hebrew-language text remains the Masoretic Text, a composite collection of thousands of manuscripts produced by medieval Jewish scribes (the 'Masoretes'). The primary witnesses to this tradition are the Leningrad Codex (1009 CE) and the Aleppo Codex (tenth century CE). The Masoretic Text is the textus receptus for the modern Hebrew Bible, the tradition used as the basis of most modern translations and thus the text cited most often in contemporary Jewish and Christian WORSHIP.

The discovery of the Dead Sea Scrolls and other texts from the Judean Desert – all dating from the third century BCE to the first century CE and therefore much older than the Masoretic Text – has significantly expanded the available corpus of ancient Hebrew-language biblical texts. While all the Dead Sea Scrolls were produced centuries after the purported time of composition of the biblical texts, they nevertheless offer tremendous insights into the transmission of the biblical texts in the centuries prior to the canonization of the Hebrew Bible. Some of the Dead Sea Scrolls attest a proto-Masoretic Text textual tradition; others attest different textual traditions. Overall, the evidence from the Dead Sea Scrolls suggests that the transmission process prior to canonization allowed for considerable diversity in copies of authoritative texts, and even for the existence of different editions of the same biblical text preserved within the same scribal community. Thus, the notion of an original text of the Hebrew Bible in the centuries prior to its standardization and canonization now appears to be anachronistic.

The textual plurality suggested by the evidence from the Dead Sea Scrolls (multiple editions of biblical books existing side by side, both with one another and with non-canonical materials) has renewed scholarly interest in Hebrew textual traditions that had previously been dismissed, most significantly the Samaritan Pentateuch.

The discovery of the Dead Sea Scrolls has also renewed scholarly interest in ancient translations as witnesses to the textual history of the Hebrew Bible. Earlier generations of scholars tended to view these translations as *sectarian* or *vulgar* editions of the Bible that served the needs of the particular communities that produced them and, therefore, were useful mainly for understanding these various communities' theological interests, not the early history of the biblical text itself. More recent research, however, has revealed that some of these translations appear to be based on Hebrew precursors that agreed with the Dead Sea Scrolls and other sources that predate the Masoretic Text. This renewed interest is most obvious in the study of the ancient Greek translations (the Septuagint and Old Greek), but is also to be found in the study of the Aramaic targums, the Latin Vulgate, and the Syriac Peshitta.

Finally, in addition to the study of the biblical manuscripts themselves, text critics seek for clues to understanding the textual plurality of the Bible by examining quotations of the Hebrew Bible in other ancient literature. The most important sources for such quotes include rabbinic literature, the NT, the church fathers, and the 'non-biblical' manuscripts of the Dead Sea Scrolls. Especially significant among the Dead Sea Scrolls are the PESHARIM, a genre of writing in which biblical texts are quoted extensively, with the quotes followed by commentary that explains how the passage relates to the Qumran community and its history and practice. Extant pesharim sometimes attest the proto-Masoretic Text and sometimes other textual traditions.

Because of the textual plurality evident in the Dead Sea Scrolls and the broadening of the database for the text-critical study of the Hebrew Bible, the very distinction between 'biblical' and 'non-biblical' texts is now being seriously questioned. For example, when the Psalms Scroll from Qumran (11QPs[a]) was first published, some scholars argued that it should not be considered a manuscript of the book of Psalms in light of its many variations from the Masoretic Text. This approach is now widely viewed as anachronistic, especially since the Psalms manuscripts of the Dead Sea Scrolls collectively suggest plurality, thereby providing additional support to the Greek and Syriac evidence that various editions of the book of Psalms circulated during the Late Second Temple period. Similarly, scholars now argue that the REWORKED PENTATEUCH texts from Qumran should no longer be classified as 'non-biblical', simply because the types of variation between these texts and the Masoretic Text are evident even within the Masoretic canon (e.g. the reworking of material from Leviticus in Deuteronomy; see Person 2015: 203–7). Thus, the modern Hebrew Bible should be viewed as the product of a long and complex history involving the composition and transmission of various literary texts in multiple editions, from which the canonical texts were selected, standardized, and canonized.

The Textual Evidence: The New Testament

The textual tradition for the NT is far richer than that for any other body of ancient literature. Therefore, NT text critics have generally been reluctant to emend the text, assuming that the ORIGINAL reading is present somewhere in the surviving material.

The autographs of the NT are now lost, but over 5000 Greek NT manuscripts of varying age, material, handwriting, and textual character have been preserved. Some of these are quite ancient; for example, one of the earliest NT PAPYRUS fragments, $\mathfrak{P}^{52}$, which includes Jn 18.31-33, 37-38, dates to the middle of the second century, only decades removed from the composition of the Fourth Gospel. Along with these many Greek manuscripts, NT text critics consider other textual witnesses, such as early translations (versions) into Latin, Syriac, Coptic, and other languages and quotations of the NT by early Christian writers (the church fathers).

The primary sources for NT Textual Criticism are the extant Greek manuscripts, now numbering more than 5400. These are classified using several different criteria: 1) by the material on which they are written (papyrus, PARCHMENT, or paper); 2) by the type of script in which they are written (majuscule/uncial or minuscule/cursive); and, 3) by the function of the document (continuous-text, lectionary with church lessons) (see ORTHORGRAPHY). These criteria overlap in the traditional categorization scheme for listing manuscripts.

The NT documents were first written on papyrus. Today there are 131 known papyrus manuscripts, each of which is identified by the letter $\mathfrak{P}$ (P) and a number. Nearly all of these have been found in Egypt, where they were preserved by the dry desert climate. About half are dated prior to or around the turn of the third/fourth centuries, and are particularly significant for our knowledge of the early text of the NT. Virtually all of the papyrus manuscripts are in CODEX (book) form, reflecting the fact that Christians almost immediately adopted this format, whereas the scroll continued to dominate secular literature for centuries. Many of the papyri reflect a widespread tendency among Christian scribes to abbreviate divine names, in particular Jesus/*Iēsous* ($\overline{IC}$), Christ/*Christos* ($\overline{XC}$), Lord/*kyrios* ($\overline{KC}$), and God/*theos* ($\overline{\Theta C}$).

Because of the fragile nature of the material, the vast majority of extant papyri are highly fragmentary, with some notable exceptions. In 1930–1931 the collector Chester Beatty purchased three early and important

TABLE 1 Chester Beatty papyri

Manuscript	*Date (CE)*	*Content*
$\mathfrak{P}^{45}$	200–250	portions of the Four Gospels and Acts (30 leaves)
$\mathfrak{P}^{46}$	200–225	portions of Rom, Heb, 1–2 Cor, Eph, Gal, Phil, Col and 1 Thess (86 leaves)
$\mathfrak{P}^{47}$	200–300	portion of Revelation (10 leaves)

papyri that preserve extensive portions of the NT and that are frequently cited in discussions of the early textual history of the NT books.
Four more PAPYRUS codices acquired in the mid-1950s by Martin Bodmer are also particularly significant.

New papyri come to light in a steady stream, not least from the Oxyrhynchus find in Egypt, which so far has yielded about 60 per cent of the extant NT papyri.

Another major category of Greek NT manuscripts are the 323 known majuscules (texts using all capital letters) written on parchment, which are identified by a number starting from 01 (some also have a letter/siglum stemming from an older classification system). Only three fragmentary majuscules are securely dated to the pre-Constantinian period (before 313 CE) and belong, with the papyri, to the era before the production of the monumental majuscule codices. Six of the extensive majuscules stand out because of their age (fourth or fifth century CE) and are of crucial importance for the history of the biblical text, many including material from both the Septuagint and the NT.

TABLE 2 The Bodmer papyri

Manuscript	*Date (CE)*	*Content*
$\mathfrak{P}^{66}$	200–250	portion of John (75 leaves)
$\mathfrak{P}^{72}$	300–350	1–2 Pet and Jude (95 leaves). Part of a miscellaneous codex with two LXX Psalms and six other non-canonical texts.
$\mathfrak{P}^{74}$	7th cent.	portions of Acts and the General Epistles (124 fragments)
$\mathfrak{P}^{75}$	200–250	portions of Luke and John (50 leaves)

TABLE 3 Six important majuscules

Manuscript	*Date*	*Content and textual character*
Codex Sinaiticus (א 01)	4th cent.	OT (Septuagint), NT, the Epistle of Barnabas, the Shepherd of Hermas. 'Alexandrian' text ('Western' in John 1–8).
Codex Alexandrinus (A 02)	5th cent.	OT (Septuagint), most of the NT, *1–2 Clement*. Akin to the Byzantine text in the Gospels; akin to 'Alexandrian' in the rest of NT (particularly valuable in Rev).
Codex Vaticanus (B 03)	4th cent.	OT (Septuagint), most of the NT. Prime representative of the 'Alexandrian' text, considered by many to be the most valuable MS of the NT.
Codex Ephraemi Syri Rescriptus (C 04)	5th cent.	A palimpsest (biblical text overwritten) preserving parts of the OT (Septuagint) and NT. The text is of mixed quality (particularly valuable in Revelation).
Codex Bezae Cantabrigensis (D 05)	5th cent.	A Greek-Latin codex with the Four Gospels, Acts (nearly 10% longer than the general text), and a fragment of 3 John. Chief Greek representative of the 'Western' text type.
Codex Washingtonianus (W 032), also known as the Freer Gospels	5th cent.	Four Gospels. A mixed text copied from several exemplars. Similar to $\mathfrak{P}^{45}$ in Mark representing a very early type of text.

Most of the later majuscules conform to the mainstream text of the Byzantine church (see below). With the transition to minuscule script (texts using all lower case letters) from the seventh century, the majuscules soon passed out of use. The last twenty or so originate in the tenth century.

The minuscule script arose in the seventh century CE, with the oldest extant NT minuscule, the Uspenski Gospels, dating to 835 CE. During this period, the Byzantine text type came to dominate the Greek manuscript tradition, so that the great majority of the approximately 2930 extant minuscules represent the Byzantine Majority Text. For classification, minuscules are identified with a number starting from 1. For practical reasons, the majority of manuscripts (mostly minuscules) with a similar Byzantine text are subsumed under a common siglum in critical editions (𝔐 or Byz). However, some 10 per cent of the minuscules are known to represent other textual streams and are therefore more valuable in the reconstruction of the text.

In contrast to the continuous-text manuscripts, lectionary manuscripts, identified by the letter *l* (or L) followed by a number, have their NT text arranged in separate pericopes, or lessons, to be read in church on particular days during the ecclesiastical year. Although more research is necessary, by and large the lectionaries, currently numbering to about 2440, reproduce the Byzantine Majority Text, and therefore few are cited in the standard critical editions.

As noted above, NT text critics consider not only the extant Greek manuscripts of the biblical books, but also the earliest translations or versions of these texts in other languages, particularly the Syriac, Latin, and Coptic Versions. Each version evidences a distinct textual tradition with several successive revisions and new translations. Thus, the earliest and most important translations are the Old Syriac, the Old Latin, and, in Coptic, the Sahidic and Bohairic Versions. These earliest translations were prepared by missionaries in the second and third centuries CE and therefore predate many of the extant Greek manuscripts. At the same time, it is often difficult to reconstruct the original Greek reading behind a particular rendering, simply because many features of the Greek language could not be literally conveyed in translation. A sound use of versional evidence therefore requires a detailed knowledge of the possibilities and limitations of each language to express the Greek originals.

In addition to the Greek manuscripts and early versions, NT text critics sometimes appeal to the vast number of scriptural quotations included in the extant works of early Christian writers, including Clement of Alexandria (d. 212 CE), Origen (185–254 CE) (see HEXAPLA), and Eusebius of Caesarea (263–339 CE). One particularly useful feature of patristic quotations is that they serve to date and localize readings geographically, since the provenance of the author is generally known (as opposed to the anonymous scribes who produced most Greek manuscripts of the biblical books). Here again, however, the patristic evidence may only be utilized with awareness of its limitations. First, like the biblical manuscripts themselves, the patristic text may have been modified in the course of transmission, either accidentally or purposefully. Scriptural quotations in particular were subject to changes by scribes. Second, it is sometimes difficult to ascertain whether a church father is citing from an existing manuscript or from memory, or whether the 'citation' of a biblical book is actually a paraphrase. For early Christian authors who quote the Bible in versions (rather than the Greek), these problems are magnified.

The Practice of Textual Criticism

Since no single manuscript, manuscript family, or larger group of manuscripts (a *text type*) can be accepted uncritically as representing the original version of a biblical passage or book, the various extant witnesses must be evaluated passage by passage. The evaluation of variant readings in individual passages is generally based on some guiding principles or criteria (Wasserman 2013). The most widely accepted principle is to prefer whichever reading would best explain the rise of all the others, but beyond this general rule, text-critical choices depend on two types of evidence: 1) external evidence, data relating to the manuscripts themselves (age, provenance, etc.); and, 2) internal evidence. Two categories of internal evidence are particularly helpful: transcriptional probabilities relating to what scribes were more likely to have copied; and, intrinsic probabilities relating to what an author was more likely to have written.

In practically all current methodologies in biblical Textual Criticism, criteria related to external and internal evidence are taken into account in varying combinations. Differing reconstructions of the initial text reflect differing approaches to the question of how to combine the various types of criteria in a given instance. Which criteria should be applied when and what weight should each be given? Very often the various criteria will compete with one another, so that decisions must be based on the balance of probabilities.

For example, text critics have long appealed to the well-established transcriptional criterion that the more difficult reading is to be preferred. As noted above, scribes tended to correct or improve unclear terms and to harmonize texts for smoother reading; therefore, following the principle of *lectio difficilior lectio potior*, one may conclude that a clearer reading is less likely to be original. At the same time, and in practice, it may often be hard to judge the difference between a difficult reading and a reading that resulted from an error in copying. Hence, this criterion does not apply in cases where another more specific transcriptional factor better explains the origin of the difficulty.

Textual Criticism and Ancient Media Culture

Although biblical scholars who specialize in ancient media criticism have often not engaged textual critics (and vice versa), the concerns of biblical Textual Criticism are deeply intertwined with the dynamics of the ancient media environment, such as ancient copying practices, oral and aural influence on copying practices, and the multilingual nature of the socio-historical context in which these texts were transmitted. In light of their overlapping interests, specialists in Textual Criticism and ancient media studies will benefit from further scholarly interaction.

As one clear example of similar emphases, specialists in oral tradition and text critics now routinely question or reject the notion of an ORIGINAL form or original text. For ORALITY specialists, this conviction stems from the fact that each performance of a particular tradition is, in some sense, unique in terms of the slight (or significant) alterations to the traditional material made by a performer in light of the audience's reception of any given performance. Equally, ancient teachers are likely to have given the same oral teaching on more than one occasion. Thus, whereas text critics have historically focused on reconstructing the original version of a written passage by sifting through variants in the textual tradition, media critics have placed emphasis upon the inherent PLURIFORMITY of the tradition, stressing, for example, that Jesus could have delivered the same sayings or sermons on multiple occasions or that the Gospel authors could have created multiple versions of the saying/sermon based on the conviction that Jesus often taught in this way. Writing several decades ago, WERNER KELBER could speak of the idea of an original form of a given tradition as 'a phantom of the literate imagination' (Kelber 1983: 59).

Most text critics are likewise now reluctant to talk about the 'original' text of a biblical passage or book. Even definitions of the term are challenging: does 'original' refer to an intended text, autographic text, authorial text, initial form of text, published text, or something(s) else (Epp 1999)? The issue is complicated further because there was, in the ancient world, no such thing as PUBLICATION in the modern sense. Most books were initially released to a small group of friends in writing or through public reading, after which the author would make improvements prior to releasing a more polished version. Sometimes these earlier 'drafts' were circulated against the author's will, again raising the question of which 'version' should be considered original.

In the case of the NT, one could possibly regard the earliest recoverable stage simply as the point when an individual writing first began to circulate and be copied, and effectively left the author's control (Holmes 2013: 657). However, Paul's letters were collected early on and published as a collection, which further illustrates the complexity of the concept of an original text (see PAULINE LITERATURE). Most scholars now refer to the earliest recoverable text as the initial text (German *Ausgangstext*) and, overall, have welcomed the challenge put forth by David Parker in a now-classic study (Parker 1997: 6–7) to abandon the notion of the 'original' text as the sole goal of study and to embrace the study of the full manuscript tradition.

In the case of the Hebrew Bible, the increased emphasis on media-critical issues is illustrated by comparing the third edition of Emanuel Tov's highly influential *Textual Criticism of the Hebrew Bible* (2012) with the two earlier editions. This comparison clearly reveals that Tov has softened his earlier insistence on the existence of an original text. Moreover, based on his understanding of the characteristic textual instability of the Hebrew Bible, Julio Trebolle has concluded that we need 'another analytical model … that accepts the co-existence of parallel editions. The final process of composition and redaction of a work can give rise to several editions that can co-exist and even intermix' (Trebolle 2006: 98). Thus, many text critics of the Hebrew Bible have abandoned the goal of determining what the original text is and in some cases have rejected the very notion of an 'original' text.

As another instance of the interface between Text Criticism and media studies, scholars now consider ways that manuscripts reveal the sociocultural and intellectual character of the communities who produced and used them (Hurtado 2006). Scholars examine the physical material, the scribal hand, the layout, ORTHOGRAPHY, illuminations and other paratextual features of manuscripts (see WRITING MATERIALS). The textual variants themselves, although most are secondary, may serve as windows on the history, culture and theology of the scribes' communities (Ehrman 2013). Such windows inform scholars on issues such as the political or sociocultural location of transmitters of tradition in stratified ancient societies.

In these ways and more, Textual Criticism and media criticism are creating new perspectives on the ancient world that produced, remembered, performed, and copied the traditions of ancient Judaism and early Christianity.

Tommy Wasserman (Ansgar Teologiske Høgskole, Norway) and Raymond F. Person, Jr. (Ohio Northern University, USA), with Chris Keith (St. Mary's University, UK)

Further Reading

Ehrman, Bart D. 2013. 'The Text as Window: New Testament Manuscripts and the Social History of Early Christianity.' In *The Text of the New Testament in Contemporary Research*. 2nd edn. Edited by Bart D. Ehrman and Michael W. Holmes. New Testament Tools, Studies, and Documents 42. Leiden: Brill, pp. 803–30.

Ehrman, Bart D., and Michael W. Holmes. 2013. *The Text of the New Testament in Contemporary Research: Essays on the Status Quaestionis*. 2nd edn. New Testament Tools, Studies, and Documents 42. Leiden: Brill.

Epp, Eldon J. 1999. 'The Multivalence of the Term "Original Text" in New Testament Textual Criticism.' *Harvard Theological Review* 92: 245–81.

Hill, Charles E., and Michael J. Kruger, eds. 2012. *The Early Text of the New Testament*. New York: Oxford University Press.

Holmes, Michael W. 2013. 'From "Original Text" to "Initial Text": The Traditional Goal of New Testament Textual Criticism in Contemporary Discussion'. In *The Text of the New Testament in Contemporary Research*. 2nd edn. Edited by Bart D. Ehrman and Michael W. Holmes. New Testament Tools, Studies, and Documents 42.Leiden: Brill, pp. 637–88.

Hurtado, Larry W. 2006. *The Earliest Christian Artifacts*. Grand Rapids, MI: Eerdmans.

Kelber, Werner H. 1983. *The Oral and the Written Gospel: The Hermeneutics of Speaking and Writing in the Synoptic Tradition, Mark, Paul, and Q*. Voices in Performance and Text. Bloomington: Indiana University Press.

Parker, D. C. 1997. *The Living Text of the Gospels*. Cambridge: Cambridge University Press.

Person, Raymond F., Jr. 1997. *The Kings/Isaiah and Kings/Jeremiah Recensions*. BZAW 252. Berlin: Walter Mouton de Gruyter.
Person, Raymond F., Jr. 1998. 'The Ancient Israelite Scribe as Performer.' *JBL* 117: 601–9.
Person, Raymond F., Jr. 2015. 'Text Criticism as a Lens for Understanding the Transmission of Ancient Texts in Their Oral Environments.' In *Contextualizing Israel's Sacred Writings: Ancient Literacy, Orality, and Literary Production*. Edited by Brian Schmidt. SBL Ancient Israel and its Literature 22. Atlanta: SBL Press, pp. 197–215.
Schmid, Ulrich. 2008. 'Scribes and Variants – Sociology and Typology.' In *Textual Variation: Theological and Social Tendencies? Papers from the Fifth Birmingham Coloquium on the Textual Criticism of the New Testament*. Edited by H. A. G. Houghton and D. C. Parker. Piscataway: Gorgias Press, pp. 1–23.
Schorch, Stefan. 2016. 'Dissimilatory Reading and the Making of Biblical Texts: The Jewish Pentateuch and the Samaritan Pentateuch.' In *Empirical Models Challenging Biblical Criticism*. Edited by Raymond F. Person, Jr. and Robert Rezetko. SBL Ancient Israel and its Literature 25. Atlanta: SBL Press, pp. 109–28.
Tov, Emanuel. 2012. *Textual Criticism of the Hebrew Bible*. Minneapolis: Fortress.
Trebolle, Julio. 2006. 'Samuel/Kings and Chronicles: Book Division and Textual Composition.' In *Studies in the Hebrew Bible, Qumran, and the Septuagint Presented to Eugene Ulrich*. Edited by Peter W. Flint, Emanuel Tov, and James C. Vanderkam. VTSup 101. Leiden: Brill, pp. 96–108.
Wasserman, Tommy. 2013. 'Criteria for Evaluating Readings in New Testament Textual Criticism.' In *The Text of the New Testament in Contemporary Research: Essays on the Status Quaestionis*. 2nd edn. Edited by Bart D. Ehrman and Michael W. Holmes. New Testament Tools, Studies and Documents 42. Leiden: Brill, pp. 579–612.
Young, Ian. 2016. 'The Original Problem: The Old Greek and the Masoretic Text of Daniel 5.' In *Empirical Models Challenging Biblical Criticism*. Edited by Raymond F. Person, Jr. and Robert Rezetko. SBL Ancient Israel and its Literature 22. Atlanta: SBL Press, pp. 271–302.

Textual Communities The term *textual community* was developed by Brian Stock as a label for a sociological model for explaining the rise of heretical/reformist sects during the medieval period of European history. Stock's *The Implications of Literacy* (1983) explored six such reform movements with a view to identifying common traits and factors that might point to a uniform theory on the causes and conditions of religious innovation. Surprisingly, Stock concluded that these movements did not share 'profound doctrinal similarities or common social[, political, or economic] origins', but instead were all characterized by 'a parallel use of texts [here the Christian Bible and other canonical church documents], both to structure the internal behavior of the group's members and to provide solidarity against the outside world' (Stock 1983: 90, 99). Because such movements crystalize around a vision derived from a reinterpretation of authoritative texts, Stock refers to them as 'textual communities'.

Stock's model is significant to biblical studies because the society from which he drew his samples – Europe at the turn of the millennium – paralleled the media culture of ancient Israel and Late Second Temple Judaism in important respects, particularly in the role that numinous sacred texts and the scribal classes who maintained and interpreted them played in the development and dissemination of the GREAT TRADITION (see SCRIBES). Stock stresses that textual communities do not depend on mass LITERACY, but rather on individuals within the scribal class 'who, having mastered it [the written corpus], then utilized it for reforming a group's thought and action' by 'invoking [written] precedent, [to] demand that society as a whole abandon "customary" principles of moral conduct' (Stock 1983: 90). Put another way, informed scribes can challenge the great tradition by promoting a little tradition based on the authorized CANON, thereby constructing a COUNTERMEMORY that reconfigures elements of the 'official' version of things by appeal to the very documents that are foundational to hegemony. When a sufficient number of non-literate converts gather around the literate teacher(s) and begin to actualize the new interpretation, a *textual community* is born.

Stock's analysis of specific eleventh-century heresies identifies four key stages in the evolution of a textual community. First, as a precondition, the larger society must have an established or emerging great tradition grounded in a canon of texts that support its key doctrines. Second, individuals emerge within the scribal class who are capable of envisioning an alternative to the norms of the great tradition, and who can defend this new vision by appeal to the canon. These individuals proceed to disseminate their new interpretation to the non-literate masses through oral preaching or other mass media vehicles. The scribes may posture themselves, or may be perceived by the masses, as prophetic or charismatic due to the nature of their rhetoric or/and the radical social vision they promote, but this vision is ultimately grounded in readings of texts (see TEXT-BROKER(S).

Third, converts to the new vision form a textual community committed to practising that vision. Since the vision is revisionist, the community's activity is generally counter-cultural, sometimes involving specific acts of resistance to current power structures and thus representing a defined little tradition. At the fourth stage in the cycle, scribal brokers of the established order attack the textual community, accusing it of dangerous innovations and attempting to label it 'heretical'. This suppression often involves a counter-interpretation of the texts and traditions in question that reaffirms traditional understandings and power structures (see examples in Stock 1983: 104–6, 115–20, 124–9).

Stock's model is fruitful for research into the biblical literature simply because it can be applied to such a wide range of instances. Obvious examples include the reform movements surrounding the writing prophets of the Hebrew Bible (e.g. Isaiah, Jeremiah), who often rationalize their alternate vision by appeal to Torah; the Qumran Community that produced the DEAD SEA SCROLLS; early Christianity, which grounded its claims in a revisionist reading of the OT that keyed Jesus and the church to Israel's sacred canon; and, the various reform movements that arose in Judea in the decades leading up to the First Jewish Revolt. Because the Jerusalem great tradition depended heavily on scribal management of a corpus of sacred texts that the masses viewed as foundational to faith and practice, this tradition was particularly vulnerable to innovation by entrepreneurial scribal experts.

Tom Thatcher (Cincinnati Christian University, USA)

Further Reading

Stock, Brian. 1983. *The Implications of Literacy: Written Language and Models of Interpretation in the Eleventh and Twelfth Centuries*. Princeton: Princeton University Press, 1983.

Thatcher, Tom. 1998. 'Literacy, Textual Communities, and Josephus' Jewish War.' *JSJ* 29: 123–42.

Theme (in oral theory) Within oral theory, the term *theme* refers to recurrent narrative units occurring in MULTIFORM and drawing from shared traditional idioms. Specific definitions and usages of the term vary according to academic discipline, cultural tradition, and scholarly method. Examples of tropes that have been identified as themes include arming for battle and feasting patterns in Homeric epic, exile or 'beasts of battle' imagery in Old English poetry, and punishment or rescue sequences in biblical prose. The oral-formulaic theme is best understood as a variable unit offering verbal artists a stable core that can be adapted to suit a wide range of narrative and performance contexts. Thus, the repetition of a given theme is not attributable to a single, ORIGINAL source text, but rather to a shared traditional idiom of expression. Any particular telling of a battle or arming scene, for instance, is always resonant of other such scenes in the audience's wider experience with the narrative tradition.

As Alexandra Hennessey Olsen has observed, one of the potential difficulties with the term THEME lies in the overlap between its 'technical oral-formulaic sense' and its more general use as a recurring idea or element within a narrative (1986: 579). ROBERT CULLEY notes connections with its usage in MUSIC, especially in the sense of 'themes and variations', which 'evokes the double nature of the phenomenon of repeated yet varied patterns in biblical narratives' (1992: 1). The term *theme* also has specialized meaning within rhetoric and writing, as a student might be asked to compose a theme on a given topic as a writing assignment. While none of these senses fully conveys the specialized meaning within oral-formulaic studies, all nonetheless provide important aspects of the concept as applied to a meaningful unit of composition.

The idea of a theme first appears within oral-formulaic studies in MILMAN PARRY's review of Walter Arend's work with 'TYPICAL SCENES'. In his posthumously published notes on 'Ćor Huso', Parry employed the concept of theme, as distinct from the metrically bound 'verse', as a productive way of explaining the relationship of the singer to his tradition: 'the verses and the themes of the traditional SONG form a web in which the thought of the singer is completely enmeshed' (1933–5: 449–50). Of South Slavic singers in particular, Parry asserted that 'the poetry does stand beyond the single singer. He possesses it only at the instant of his song' (450). Ultimately a product of both the individual and the tradition, any orally composed song within this tradition 'must be made of the traditional themes and traditional verses' (450).

Building on Parry's suggestive, but not definitive, remarks on themes, ALBERT BATES LORD offered a more formal definition of the theme as 'a recurrent element of narration or description in traditional oral poetry' (1951: 73), which he later clarified as 'repeated incidents and descriptive passages' in oral epic (1960: 4). In Lord's configuration, the theme was defined against the FORMULA as a unit 'not restricted, as is the formula, by metrical considerations' (1951: 73). Defined in large part by its very flexibility, the theme has therefore always been a more amorphous categorical unit than the formula, which has generally been associated with metrical, and often verbatim, repetition. The theme must thus be understood less as a universal construct than as a concept to be calibrated according to specific cultural and generic contexts (Foley 1990: 8–9). Indeed, the value of the theme as compositional tool lies precisely in its infinite variability within traditionally determined limits.

While attempts at overly precise parsing of the term *theme* have not proven especially useful in and of themselves, the concept has long offered a powerful analytic tool when understood in specific cultural, linguistic, and generic contexts. A case in point of the usefulness of the theme as a tradition-dependent index of meaning in spite of its murkiness as a universal, definable unit is the 'Beasts of Battle', a long-recognized pattern in both secular and biblical verse of Old English literature. Francis P. Magoun first identified the 'Beasts of Battle' as an oral-formulaic theme characterized by 'the mention of the wolf, eagle, and/or raven as beasts attendant on a scene of carnage' (1955: 83). Subsequently, Lord noted a 'difference of emphasis' from that of Magoun: 'I should prefer to designate as motifs what they call themes and to reserve the term theme for a structural unit that has a semantic essence but can never be divorced from its form, even if its form be constantly variable and multiform' (1960: 198). In this configuration, the 'Beasts of Battle' would clearly be a 'motif' rather than a 'theme'. Donald Fry, noting the confusion resulting from such conflation of the terms theme, type scene, and motif, later delineated a theme as 'a recurring concatenation of details and ideas' (1968: 53), as opposed to a narrative-based type scene.

While awareness of these overlapping terms and senses is important for understanding earlier scholarship in oral-formulaic theory, more recent work on the 'Beasts of Battle' and other such patterns reflects a greater ease with multiple systems of classification, the primary focus being placed on the meaning behind the pattern rather than its label. Whether described as a theme or by an alternate term, the 'Beasts of Battle' is most conventionally employed within Old English poetry in martial contexts, as in the *Battle of Maldon* (lines 104b-7) and the *Battle of Brunanburh* (lines 60-65), where the beasts quite logically appear on the side of the losing army. Accordingly, if used effectively, the theme can be a predicator of coming events. In the Old English poem *Exodus*, for example, the Beasts of Battle circle Pharaoh's army (161-69) as the soon-to-be-victorious Israelites prepare for battle. Similarly, the Old English *Judith* depicts a battle without counterpart in the Latin Vulgate (generally understood as the source text) and creatively presents the Beasts of Battle on the side of the

Assyrians, an obvious signal of an upcoming Bethulian victory to audiences familiar with the theme's portent. Such innovations on traditional themes demonstrate that a skilled verbal artist relies on a given theme not only – or even primarily – for its narrative expedience, 'but for its unique significative capabilities; namely, because it indexes the context in which he or she wants the communication to be received' (Foley 1995: 181).

One of the more significant advances in scholarship on the theme relevant to biblical studies in particular has been its application to prose narratives. Offering a fairly loose definition of themes as 'repeated patterns' (1992: 47), ROBERT CULLEY explores the patterns and variations to better understand productive tensions in biblical narrative. In the garden story of Genesis 2-3, for instance, we see a fairly clear-cut example of what Culley calls the 'Punishment Sequence', a pattern shared by a number of stories in the Bible 'that tells about a person or a group doing something which is viewed as wrong by the deity so that divine punishment follows' (1992: 57). Therefore, Adam and Eve's expulsion from the garden after eating the fruit from the prohibited tree resonates meaningfully with other such punishments, such as Lot's wife being turned to a pillar of salt for violating the edict not to look back on her burning city (Gen. 18–19) or the attack by bears against two boys who mock Elisha (2 Kings 2.23-25). However, intertwined with this sequence is another familiar pattern, which Culley terms the 'Achievement Sequence', in which 'something is desired and then acquired' (1992: 124), seen in such episodes as Isaac's procurement of a wife (Genesis 24). As Culley explains it, 'eating the fruit leads to loss of the garden home through expulsion, but over and against this there is the gain of the divine characteristic of knowing good and evil' (126). Culley thus invites readers to explore the tensions produced by the interweaving of multiple traditional patterns and to 'allow the play of perspectives to reveal different angles and aspects of the text' (1992: 126).

Endorsing a similar shift in biblical studies towards 'reception aesthetics', P. J. J. Botha calls for an end to 'debates on what are or are not themes and motifs' (1991: 326). Compositional units such as the theme are indeed better viewed 'not as objective entities in themselves but as necessarily incomplete cues to be contextualized by an audience's subjective participation in the tale-telling process' (Foley 1986: 216). Thus, we do well to understand the theme, like the various units that it designates, as context-specific and multiform.

Lori Ann Garner (Rhodes College, USA)

Further Reading

Botha, P. J. J. 1991. 'Mark's Story as Oral Traditional Literature: Rethinking the Transmission of Some Traditions about Jesus.' *Hervormde Teologiese Studies* 47(2): 304–31.

Culley, Robert C. 1992. *Themes and Variations: A Study of Action in Biblical Narrative*. Atlanta: Scholars Press.

Foley, John Miles, ed. 1986. *Oral Tradition in Literature: Interpretation in Context*. Columbia: University of Missouri Press.

Foley, John Miles. 1990. *Traditional Oral Epic: The Odyssey, Beowulf, and the Serbo-Croatian Return Song*. Berkeley: University of California Press.

Foley, John Miles. 1995. *The Singer of Tales in Performance*. Bloomington: Indiana University.

Fry, Donald. 1968. 'Old English Formulaic Themes and Type-Scenes.' *Neophilologus* 52: 48–54.

Lord, Albert Bates. 1951. 'Composition by Theme in Homer and Southslavic Epos.' *Transactions of the American Philological Association* 82: 71–80.

Lord, Albert Bates. 1960. *The Singer of Tales*. Cambridge, MA: Harvard University Press.

Magoun, Francis Peabody. 1955. 'The Theme of the Beasts of Battle in Anglo-Saxon Poetry.' *Neuphilologische Mitteilungen* 56: 81–90.

Olsen, Alexandra Hennessey. 1986. 'Oral-Formulaic Research in Old English: I.' *Oral Tradition* 1(3): 548–606.

Parry, Milman. 1933–5. *The Making of Homeric Verse: The Collected Papers of Milman Parry*. Edited by Adam Parry. Oxford: Clarendon Press, pp. 437–64.

Therapeutae The Therapeutae were a Late Second Temple Jewish monastic sect mentioned in Philo of Alexandria's (ca. 20 BCE–50 CE) treatise *The Contemplative Life*. According to this text, the Therapeutae lived in a monastic community at Lake Mareotis/Mariout near Alexandria, spending considerable amounts of time in individual private dwellings but regularly coming together for community meetings. Philo expresses uncertainty about the origins of the group or the meaning of their name, noting that it derives from the Greek verb *therapeuō* ('heal'; 'WORSHIP') and as such was consistent with their aesthetic focus on physical health/hygiene and spiritual wellness achieved through the contemplation of divine truth. In other ancient contexts the term *Therapeuate* was used to identify devotees of the healing gods Asclepius and Sarapis, and particularly to identify members of the medical staff associated with temples to Asclepius.

Aside from its value as a source for understanding ancient Jewish monasticism, Philo's description of the Jewish Therapeutae provides a helpful portrait of the interface between texts and ORALITY in ancient Jewish scribal practice and the uses of sacred Scripture in devotional settings. Philo envisions that the daily hermitage of these monks was characterized by meditation upon the sacred writings, many of which must have been known primarily through their memories of earlier readings or their experiences of hearing communal readings, and the teachings of various philosophical sects (*Contemplative Life* 25, 29). These researches were supported by a rigorously ascetic lifestyle and bracketed by a fixed regimen of personal prayer (23-24, 27, 34-37, 68-69, 73); not surprisingly, academic conclusions were often articulated in the form of devotional poems and hymns (29-30). On SABBATH, the monks gathered for group study sessions similar to those envisioned in the Qumran Manual of Discipline (see 1QS 6), with senior scholars expounding principles of the law; these oral teachings, while focused on minute exegetical details of the texts, were intended to 'penetrate from the hearing through to the soul' (30-31). Philo seems to envision that these lectures were followed by general discussion of problem passages from the Scriptures, with various individuals citing relevant texts and proposing questions (76-77), and then by individual and communal singing of hymns (79-88). Clearly in this case, the written words of the physical sacred SCROLLS were activated by, and derived their meaning from, their oral articulation.

Tom Thatcher (Cincinnati Christian University, USA)

Thomas, Rosalind Rosalind Thomas (1959–) is a classicist whose early teaching career was at the University of London and who currently teaches at University of Oxford. Her expertise concerns the democracy of classical Athens, and she has written widely on the interaction between ORALITY and LITERACY in ancient Greece. Her work also expanded the application of the study of ORAL TRADITIONS from epic poetry to other genres, such as HISTORIOGRAPHY (Herodotus and Thucydides).

Influenced by the work of MILMAN PARRY, ALBERT LORD, RUTH FINEGAN, and MAURICE HALBWACHS, Thomas has been extremely critical of the GREAT DIVIDE thesis (including the work of Eric HAVELOCK and the early work of JACK GOODY), which posits significant and categorical cognitive and cultural differences between traditional and literate societies. Referring to the binaries implied in the Great Divide thesis, she observes that 'classical Athens of the fifth and fourth centuries B.C. provides a striking refutation of these ideas and divisions' (1989: 2). She has thus contributed much to understandings of the diversity within oral-traditional and literate cultures, and to the dangers of categorical statements about either of them or the relationships between them.

For example, although Thomas accepted that the term *functional literacy* has some value, she also noted that it nevertheless avoids important questions such as 'what exactly is enough literacy to get by, in what circumstances and for whom?' (2009: 16). Therefore, *functional literacy* is different within *banking literacy*, *citizen literacy* (= the ability to sign one's name), *commercial literacy* (including making lists), and *officials' literacy* (reading and writing bureaucratic documents; 2009). For an example concerning how orality and literacy might interact differently within the classical Greek period, Thomas located and discussed the following forms of communication on a continuum from more oral to more textual: family traditions (including GENEALOGIES), the local traditions of a polis or city (including funeral speeches), and the works of historians like Herodotus who wrote regional or national histories (1989). This continuum approach allowed her to observe that, in ancient Greece, 'oral transmission … could subsist alongside "literacy", and the two were not necessarily incompatible' (1989: 95). Although her own expertise pertained to classical Athens, she nevertheless emphasized the importance of the comparative method to understanding the interaction of orality and literacy. For example, she served as one of the guest editors for a two-volume special edition of the journal *Oral Tradition* entitled 'Performance Literature' that included articles covering various world literatures from the ancient to the modern period (2005).

Thomas has provided an excellent model for understanding how orality and literacy interacted in the ancient world and, thereby, has had a positive impact on biblical scholars who have drawn significantly from the comparative study of orality and literacy (see ORAL TRADITION, THE COMPARATIVE STUDY OF). Her work remains especially pertinent in correcting the lingering effects of the Great Divide thesis in biblical studies.

Raymond F. Person, Jr. (Ohio Northern University, USA)

Further Reading

Gerstle, Drew, Rosalind Thomas, and Stephanie Jones, eds. 2005. Performance Literature. A special issue of *Oral Tradition* 20.1,2.

Thomas, Rosalind. 1989. *Oral Tradition and the Written Record in Classical Athens*. Cambridge: Cambridge University Press.

Thomas, Rosalind. 1992. *Literacy and Orality in Ancient Greece*. Cambridge: Cambridge University Press.

Thomas, Rosalind. 2000. *Herodotus in Context: Ethnography, Science and the Art of Persuasion*. Cambridge: Cambridge University Press.

Thomas, Rosalind. 2009. 'Writing, Reading, Public and Private "Literacies": Functional Literacy and Democratic Literacy in Greece.' In *Ancient Literacies: The Culture of Reading in Greece and Rome*. Edited by William A. Johnson and Holt N. Parker. Oxford: Oxford University Press, pp. 13–45.

Torah Reading/Service Engagement with Scripture was a central element of SYNAGOGUE WORSHIP as early as the Second Temple period. However, the first detailed descriptions of Torah reading in the synagogue come from the early rabbinic period and describe rabbinic practices. According to the MISHNAIC tractate *Megillah* and the corresponding material in the Tosefta, scriptural texts should be performed (read aloud) in the synagogue on SABBATHS, festivals, Mondays, and Thursdays. On Sabbaths and festivals, a pentateuchal portion (Torah portion, *parashah*) was recited, followed by a portion from the Prophets (*haftarah*). On Mondays and Thursdays and Sabbath afternoons, only a pentateuchal portion was recited. Through these weekly portions, the entire Pentateuch was recited, in its canonical order, over the course of approximately three and half years. In later Babylonian custom, the entire Pentateuch was recited over the course of a year.

The Torah portions for festivals corresponded to the themes of the respective festivals, while the prophetic texts were selected to correspond to the theme of the Torah portion or to the theme of the festival or liturgical season. Both the Torah portion and the *haftarah* were recited with intralinear TRANSLATION into Aramaic and were sometimes accompanied by a homily. In the early rabbinic period, the books of Esther and Lamentations were recited on the festival of Purim and the 9th of Av, respectively. By the late rabbinic period, Song of Songs, Ruth, and Ecclesiastes were added to the lectionary as special texts for Passover, Shavuot (Pentecost), and Sukkot (Tabernacles). While translation practices have changed over time, the rest of this structure has remained largely constant in Jewish practice up until today.

In early Judaism, the majority of Jews were unable to read (see Literacy). As a result, the performance of Scripture in the synagogue would have been the primary, if not only, engagement that most Jews had with Scripture. This sociological reality has implications for our understanding of early Jewish Scripture. While the rabbinic sages considered the entire Hebrew Bible to have scriptural status, most Jews would only encounter those texts that were recited in the synagogue (see rabbinic literature). As a result, entire swathes of the biblical collection would have been unknown to most Jews in antiquity. For example, very few texts from Judges or Joshua become part of the lectionary. While some of the stories from these books might have been known in purely oral form, most Jews would never have encountered this scriptural material in textual form. Thus, the synagogue lectionary is central to an understanding of the shape and content of early Jewish Scripture.

Contents and Shape of the Lectionary

As noted above, the lectionary consisted of the Pentateuch, read in canonical order in its entirety over the course of approximately 3 ½ years according to Palestinian practice and over one year according to Babylonian practice. On Sabbath mornings and on festivals, the Torah portion was followed by a portion from the Prophets. It appears that the choice of *haftarah* for Sabbaths remained either entirely flexible or a matter of local custom until the Middle Ages. In addition to these weekly lectionary texts, there were special Torah readings for festivals that corresponded directly to them. For instance, *m. Megilla* 3.5 states that on Passover they read from the 'festivals' portion of Leviticus (Lev. 23.4ff). Unlike the *haftarot* for Sabbaths, the *haftarot* for the festivals were determined by the end of the rabbinic period. These either corresponded to the festival Torah portions or dealt directly with the holiday or its themes as identified by the rabbis. For example, *b. Megilla* 31a identifies Zechariah 4 as the *haftarah* for Hanukkah, presumably because it describes a vision of a menorah (candelabrum) which corresponds to the central ritual object and ritual practice of the holiday. By the end of the rabbinic period, the lectionary collection had come to include the five scrolls (Esther, Song of Songs, Ruth, Lamentations, and Ecclesiastes) that were recited on five festivals during the year (Purim, Passover, Shavuot, the 9th of Av, and Sukkot respectively).

While these are the scriptural texts that comprise the lectionary, they do not fully describe the contents of the lectionary as it would have been experienced by Jews in antiquity. The Mishnah mandates that the recitation of the Torah portions and *haftarot* are to be accompanied by an intralinear translation into Aramaic, which was the vernacular language of Jews in Roman Palestine (see Targums). The rabbinic directions regarding this practice are ambiguous and have generated significant scholarly debate. The Jerusalem Talmud (4th c. CE) states that the translator must recite his translation without referring to a scroll, suggesting that he is delivering a spontaneous translation of the recited Scripture. However, according to *T. Megilla* 6.41, 'R. Yehudah said: One who translates a verse according to its form (e.g. literally) lies and the one who adds to it, blasphemes'. The Babylonian Talmud (*Kid* 49a) resolves this contradiction by stating that legitimate translation conforms to 'our translation' (i.e. *Targum Onkelos*). Thus it is unclear whether those who were following the Mishnah's mandates would have been a) reciting a translation that largely conformed to *Targum Onkelos*, which is a relatively literal translation, or b) generating a spontaneous translation based on their own understanding of the Hebrew text, or c) reciting a translation that reflected a targum other than Onkelos, many of which contain significant amounts of material not reflected in the plain sense of the Hebrew text. Our lack of certainty regarding the nature of contents of the translations limits our ability to understand with certainty the verbatim content of the Scripture received by early rabbinic Jews. If most Jews received the content of Scripture largely through the Aramaic translation, we cannot be sure exactly what words they received and understood.

As noted above, the order and arrangement of texts in the synagogue lectionary is quite different from the canonical order of the texts it includes. For example, on any given Sabbath, synagogue communities would hear a mini-anthology consisting of a portion from the Torah and a selection from the Prophets. These mini-anthologies often convey messages different from those conveyed by the plain sense of their constituent texts when read in isolation or in their canonical contexts. By the medieval period (although there is reason to believe the practice began significantly earlier), Isa. 42.5-43:1 had been designated as the *haftarah* for the first Torah portion of Genesis (Gen. 1.1-6:8). These chapters describe the creation of the world and the events that occur to humans before the emergence of Abraham's line, which will not appear until Genesis 12. Within the biblical canon, the lack of particularist attention to Israel and its forebears in the opening chapters of Genesis is striking. The *haftarah*, however, retrojects Israel's privileged status back to the very beginning of creation: 'Thus said God the Lord, who created the heavens and stretched them out, Who spread out the earth and what it brings forth, Who gave breath to the people upon it and life to those who walk thereon: I, the Lord, in my grace, have summoned you, and I have grasped you by the hand. I created you, and appointed you a covenant people. A light of nations' (Isa. 42.5-6).

Torah Reading and Early Jewish 'Scripture'

There is much we do not know about the composition, transmission and canonization of the biblical texts. However, it is safe to assume that the texts that were eventually granted canonical status reflected the experiences, convictions, and interests of their authors, transmitters, and authorizers. Similarly, the biblical texts that became part of the synagogue lectionary reflect the perspectives of the rabbinic sages and resonate with the broader themes and concerns of RABBINIC LITERATURE. By comparing the contents of the lectionary with the contents of the biblical canon, overlaps and divergences between the perspectives articulated in the larger scriptural canon and those highlighted by the early rabbis in the synagogue lectionary may be identified.

Three major differences emerge in this comparison. First, the lectionary Bible is significantly smaller than the canonical biblical collection. The *haftarot* appearing in the medieval lists comprise approximately 20 per cent of the Prophetic books (Joshua-Malachi in the Jewish Bible) and only 10 per cent of the Prophets and Writings exclusive of the five scrolls. Second, the *haftarot* are not representative of the diversity of the prophetic canon. The *haftarot* draw disproportionately from the books of the latter prophets and draw only selected excerpts from Joshua–2 Kings. A person who read the canonical Bible 'cover to cover' would encounter extensive narratives about the tribal prehistory and political pasts of the kingdoms of Israel and Judah, and would gain the impression that Israel developed from a tribal confederation into two, and ultimately, one, monarchy. Further, in the canonical texts, Israel's history, which unfolds in the land of Israel, is characterized by tales of political realpolitik set within a theological framework and occasionally inflected with explicitly theological ideologies. By contract, a person who encountered these narratives primarily through the context of the synagogue lectionary would experience a very different portrait of Israel. The Israel of the Torah, the focus of the lectionary, emerges as a people outside of the land of Israel and remains there for the duration of the Torah's narrative. In contrast to the narratives contained in the former prophets, the narratives of the Pentateuch are intensely theological. The relationship between God and Israel is the primary determinant of the people's fate. The construction of Israel in the lectionary as a polity defined by its relationship to God rather than through its sovereign political status thus resonated with the status of rabbinic Jews in the Roman empire.

While the lectionary Bible favours the latter prophets in general, Isaiah, and especially Deutero-Isaiah is the most heavily represented. Consequently, when compared to the latter prophets as a whole, the lectionary texts contain a higher concentration of texts in the lectionary cycle that depict YHWH as a loving, comforting, and compassionate God. This reflects the larger context of rabbinic theology that, like late antique Christian theology, sought to amplify the loving and compassionate aspects of the biblical portraits of God. Last and perhaps most important is the privileging of the Pentateuch in the synagogue Bible. By mandating the recitation of the entire Pentateuch, including the cultic laws that had become obsolete centuries earlier, the framers of the rabbinic lectionary asserted the ongoing religious relevance of the laws, either as mandates for practice – either through literal observance or through the construction of analogous practices – or as objects of study. Thus, for its late antique audience, the synagogue Bible would both reflect and buttress central tenets of rabbinic theology and identity that are articulated elsewhere in rabbinic texts. By articulating these perspectives through the biblical texts themselves, the creators of the lectionary demonstrate that these tenets bear the pedigree and the authority of Scripture itself.

Elsie Stern (Reconstructionist Rabbinical College, USA)

Traditional Referentiality JOHN MILES FOLEY developed the term *traditional referentiality*, which 'entails the invoking of a context that is enormously larger and more echoic than the text or work itself, that brings the lifeblood of generations of poems and performances to the individual performance or text' (1991: 7). Drawing in part from work in reception theory by such scholars as Hans Robert Jauss and Wolfgang Iser, Foley's application of traditional referentiality radically and productively reshaped the field of oral-formulaic theory. Much early work in oral-formulaic studies had tended to view traditional units, such as FORMULAS and THEMES, primarily as practical building blocks of composition, not tools for individual artistic expression. As Richard Horsley has explained, the field had become known for examining repeated phraseology and narrative patterns 'often in rather wooden fashion, to test literatures from a variety of cultures for their oral features' (2008: 97). The new focus on traditional referentiality, with its dual attention to reception as well as composition, redressed this false dichotomy between formulaic structure and artistic expression.

As a dynamic means of creating meaning, traditional referentiality is closely linked with the rhetorical device of METONYMY, whereby the part evokes or stands in for the whole. Metonymy as a rhetorical trope traces back to the ancient Greek rhetoricians (see RHETORIC), who considered it as a primarily decorative or ornamental figure, not necessarily integral to content. As understood within an oral-traditional context, however, metonymic referencing becomes far more than ornament, as it 'allows the poet and the audience to access a rich, complex signification inherent in their common experiences' (Quick 2011: 597–8). In this verbal framework, a performance, whether oral or written, in turn becomes 'an opportunity for co-creation of meaning with the poet through the vehicle of the metonymic referent' (598). As Catherine Quick has effectively shown, Foley's work with traditional metonymy 'turned the question around – could the conventions of ORAL TRADITIONS be the *source* of artistic power rather than a limitation to be mitigated? The answer is, of course, yes' (2011: 597).

Representative examples from ancient Greek epic, one of the three traditions through which Foley first demonstrated the concept, illustrate the range of expressive possibilities for even very small phraseological units. A particularly well-known and insightful example is the epithet of 'swift-footed Achilles' (*podas ōkus Achilleus*), which occurs over fifty times in Homeric epic. As a metonym, 'swift-footed Achilles' in any given instantiation resonates with all of the times a listener may have heard the phrase. Thus, this label has the power to evoke 'the mythic entirety of the Achaean hero' (Foley 1996: 210), even at times when the modifier 'swift-footed' may seem incongruous, as when 'swift-foot Achilles' is said explicitly to be seated in his tent. Indeed, it is at such moments when a metonymic trait, in this case reminding audiences of Achilles' larger role as truly the best of the Achaeans, is likely to be most powerful.

Awareness of the metonymic potential of phraseology that might be seen as extraneous, even narratively inappropriate, can often lead to a deeper and clearer understanding of otherwise elusive language. By collating the ten instances of 'green fear' (*chlōron deos*) within the Homeric corpus, Foley was able to discern that in nine of the ten occurrences, the fear is supernaturally inspired; in these cases, the phrase 'green fear' does not evoke a colour but rather serves as 'a coded sign for something beyond mortal control' (Foley 1996: 217). The one seeming exception in Book 22 of the *Odyssey* describes the response of one of Penelope's relentless suitors upon the long-awaited return of her husband Odysseus. Against the backdrop of tradition, where the phrase consistently invokes supernatural sources of fear, the phrase alerts an audience aware of the larger tradition, well before the events unfold, to the fact that the suitors' inexcusable deeds have indeed laid the groundwork for divine vengeance.

The force of traditional referentiality is not limited to noun-epithet formulas and can even apply to such a seemingly insignificant phrase as 'if ever'. In Homeric prayers and supplications, 'if ever' (*ei pote*) is consistently associated with successful requests. For an audience attuned to this extra-lexical meaning, 'if ever' thus functions proleptically as an indicator of success, and through its traditional referentiality, the phrase 'relies upon its metonymically indexed nature to function as an enhanced compositional unit with a greatly extended connotative meaning' (R. Garner 1996: 371). As with many other formulas, it is not the words in and of themselves but, rather, their usage within a particular context – in this case supplication – that activates specialized connotative meanings.

While, as these examples suggest, its original applications were to oral and oral-derived poetry, the concept of traditional referentiality has since been expanded to prose, a direction especially fruitful for biblical studies. Susan Niditch, for example, employs traditional referentiality to better understand the metonymic meaning underlying *ʾăbîr yaʿăqōb*, literally 'bull of Jacob'. Translations that reduce the reference of the bull to an implication of strength and render *ʾăbîr* as 'Mighty One' are 'countermetonymic', 'theologically motivated' to 'invoke only one aspect of the phrase's meaning' (Niditch 1996: 15). The epithet, however, is rich in traditional meaning, the horned crown serving as 'an important symbol of god-power throughout the ancient Near East' (1996: 15). While the image of the bull has likely been diminished in translations due to fears of perpetuating mythologies related to bull iconography, Niditch notes that 'for many, perhaps most Yahweh worshipers, the bull symbol invoked a range of positive aspects of the deity as powerful, youthful bringer of plenty, rescuer from enemies' (1996: 15).

In a more focused application of phraseological patterning, Niditch also explores three biblical instances of the phrase of 'see and it was good' (wattēreʾʿōtôkî ṭôb hû) in relation to one another within an oral-traditional aesthetic.

> 'And God **saw** the [created thing] that **it was good**.' (Gen. 1:12; cf., vv. 4, 10, 18, 21, 25, 31).
>
> 'He [Issachar] **saw** a resting place that **it was good**.' (Gen. 49:14)
>
> 'The woman became pregnant and she [mother of Moses] gave birth to a son and **saw he was good**.' (Exod. 2:2)

While the parallel phraseology is indisputable, the nature of the passages' relationships to one another depends upon one's frame of reference. The more conventional view holds the creation story as a fixed and textualized 'source' invoked by later authors. However, the assumption that Genesis 1 is being quoted in its written form presupposes 'a relative chronology in which Genesis 1 is earlier than Exodus 2, a problem for those who would assign these passages to a sixth-century P source and a tenth-century J source respectively' (Niditch 1996: 18). However, the repetition suggests an alternate scenario when approached within a framework that adequately allows for traditional metonymic meaning. As Niditch explains, 'the phrase "to see and it was good" has to do with creation, procreation, and beginnings': the creation of the world in Genesis 1, the establishment of a new people (the Israelites) in Exodus 2, and the founding of a new settlement on a particular plot of land in Genesis 49. Although it is tempting to assume that the world-creation is invoked in the latter usages, such a view may in the end deprive 'to see and it was good' of its traditional force. Exodus 2, Niditch argues, 'need not be reliant on Genesis 1 or vice-versa, but all three passages may reflect the sort of metonymic or traditional referentiality that so aptly described the workings of epithets' (1996: 18).

Because it relates to meaning that occurs in the exchange with the audience, traditional referentiality has also proven a productive concept within performance studies. In the field of biblical studies in particular, Richard Horsley has advocated an approach that remains 'focused squarely on the historical social context in attempting to understand the work done by an orally performed text *as it metonymically references the tradition*' (2008: 147, emphasis original). In his exploration of Mark in terms of oral performance (see PERFORMANCE OF THE GOSPELS), Horsley explains the significance of the shift: 'we are thus no longer searching for the meaning of the text, but attending to *the work that a text does in a community of people*' (2008: 147, emphasis original). An approach such as this seeks to understand the connotations evoked by metonymic referencing through traditionally-freighted images or phrases. For example, in Mark 5:9, the name of the demon ('Legion') that had wrought such violence against its host as well as the larger community 'would have evoked the experience of being conquered and controlled by the Roman army' (Horsley 2008: 99).

Traditional referentiality has even been discussed productively in terms of material culture. As E. A. Mackay has demonstrated, visual ICONOGRAPHY found on early Greek vase-painting creates meaning in ways similar to formulas and themes in contemporary verbal arts. The lion skin and club closely associated with Herakles, for instance, serve as far more than aids to identification. Like the noun-epithet formulas of the verbal tradition, these images 'regularly signify more than just an essential idea; they seem consistently to resonate with the entire concept of the heroic Herakles, victor in many conflicts, supreme over many monsters' (1995: 294). At times such attributes are relevant to the context, as when the lion's skin is needed to provide protection from attack; but 'they are also to be found in situations where their referentiality is clearly extra-contextual' (1995: 294), activating the story of the Nemean lion and indexing Heracules' ability as a hero to slay monsters of the lion's calibre.

In similar fashion, the notion of traditional referentiality can help us more fully understand the complex relationship between particular architectural features and their connotative meanings. Features of traditional buildings work very much like formulaic phrases, themes, and TYPE SCENES in oral narrative. For example, through repeated exposure in specific contexts, the log cabin of the American frontier has come to be associated with a specific set of ideals, including integrity, perseverance, humility, and pre-industrial simplicity (L. Garner 2011: 24–8). Similarly, extant Old English poetry, viewed in conjunction with the archaeological record, shows that references to features of the Anglo-Saxon hall – specifically timber construction, height, elevated location, prominent gables, and arched structures – had the power to evoke particular connotations of heroic ideals most typically depicted within the Germanic hall. As traditional metonyms, such features could then be activated in innovative and unexpected ways (L. Garner 2011: 28–64). For instance, the Old English *Andreas* relates a story of Jesus speaking in a chapel that was 'high and wide-gabled' ('*heah ond horngeap*', 1.668), characteristics applied in the epic tradition to such legendary halls as *Beowulf's* Heorot (1.82).

In verbal and visual arts, therefore, traditional referentiality 'activates for the audience a field of recollections that are laden with meaning and charged with emotion for the particular culture whose traditions the formulas encode' (Bradbury 1998: 138). The concept differs importantly from literary allusion 'in that an audience experiences a formula not in relation to a specific earlier text from which it is wholly distinct but in relation to the multiform tradition of which it is a part' (138). A metonym references not a specific, identifiable source text, but derives meaning instead from previous experience of the audience, with traditional referential meaning accumulating over the course of many occurrences.

Lori Ann Garner (Rhodes College, USA)

Further Reading

Bradbury, Nancy Mason. 1998. 'Traditional Referentiality: The Aesthetic Power of Oral Traditional Structures.' *Teaching Oral Traditions*. Edited by John Miles Foley. New York: Modern Language Association.

Foley, John Miles. 1999. *Homer's Traditional Art*. University Park: University of Pennsylvania Press.

Foley, John Miles. 1991. *Immanent Art: From Structure to Meaning in Traditional Oral Epic*. Bloomington, IN: Indiana University Press.

Garner, Lori Ann. 2011. *Structuring Spaces: Oral Poetics and Architecture in Early Medieval England*. Notre Dame, IN: University of Notre Dame Press.

Garner, R. Scott. 1996. '*Ei Pote*: A Note on Homeric Phraseology.' *Oral Tradition* 11: 363–73.

Horsley, Richard A. 2008. *Jesus in Context: Power, People, and Performance*. Minneapolis, MN: Fortress Press.

Mackay, E. A. 1995. 'Narrative Tradition in Early Greek Oral Poetry and Vase-Painting.' *Oral Tradition* 10: 282–303.

Niditch, Susan. 1996. *Oral World and Written Word: Ancient Israelite Literature*. Louisville: Westminster John Knox Press.

Quick, Catherine. 2011. 'The Metonym: Rhetoric and Oral Tradition at the Crossroads.' *Oral Tradition* 26: 597–600.

Traditionalism/Continuitism *Traditionalism* (or *continuitism*) is a theoretical position within COLLECTIVE MEMORY research that advocates that memory (variously defined) demonstrates a longitudinal connection between past and present. Scholars who adopt a continuitist/traditionalist approach generally oppose themselves to presentists. In contrast to those who argue that memory is constructed (mostly) according to the needs and dynamics of the present, continuitists argue that the past continues to hold sway over the present and vice versa (e.g. Schwartz 2011: 225–6; Keith 2012: 58).

Like other SOCIAL MEMORY theorists, continuitists conceive of memory as fluid, active, and (often) strategically framed. They argue that memory involves framing and keying within socially conditioned constructs. This approach distinguishes itself from PRESENTISM, however, in its emphasis that continuity and stability between the ACTUAL PAST and its subsequent representations are essential to a group's capacity to reinforce its collective sense of IDENTITY (see Zelizer 1995; Ben-Yehuda 1995). Continuitists emphasize the tendency for memory to uphold individual and collective identities. Without the perception of continuity with previous stages of identity formation, the individual/group will have a difficult time rendering a memory intelligible. In this view, it is the perceived continuity with the past that is important to uphold identity (Le Donne 2009; 2013).

It is important to note that most social memory theorists do not advocate extreme presentism (memory has no relationship to the past) or extreme continuitism (memory always accurately represents the past). Even so, many theorists betray tendencies towards one of these two polarities.

Anthony Le Donne (United Theological Seminary, USA)

Further Reading

Ben-Yehuda, Nachman. 1995. *The Masada Myth: Collective Memory and Mythmaking in Israel*. Madison, WI: The University of Wisconsin Press.

Keith, Chris. 2012. *Jesus' Literacy: Scribal Culture and the Teacher from Galilee*. LNTS 413. London: T&T Clark.

Le Donne, Anthony. 2009. *The Historiographical Jesus: Memory, Typology, and the Son of David*. Waco, TX: Baylor University Press.

Le Donne, Anthony. 2013. 'The Problem of Selectivity in Memory Research: A Response to Zeba Crook.' *Journal for the Study of the Historical Jesus* 11: 77–97.

Schwartz, Barry. 2011. 'What Difference Does the Medium Make?' In *The Fourth Gospel in First-Century Media Culture*. Edited by Anthony Le Donne and Tom Thatcher. ESCO/LNTS 426. London: T&T Clark, pp. 225–38.

Zelizer, Barbie. 1995. 'Reading the Past against the Grain: The Shape of Memory Studies,' *Critical Studies in Mass Media* 12: 214–39.

Traditionsbruch *Traditionsbruch* is a term coined by Jan Assmann to describe the crisis brought about by the breakdown of social/institutional frameworks for the transmission and cultivation of a community's foundational traditions. Assmann also refers to this as the 'crisis of memory'.

In the case of a *Traditionsbruch*, a community, confronted with the loss of its connection to its formative past, and thus with the threat of its own dissolution, must turn towards more enduring media for its formative traditions (see Cultural Memory). Assmann's case studies clarify the phenomenon. The Persian destruction of the Egyptian dynastic succession, the millennia-long framework for the transmission of Egyptian tradition, sparked a countermovement to codify Egyptian tradition in monumental media of temple buildings, which were inscribed inside and out with representations of formative myths and teachings. Similarly, the collapse, in the wake of imperial conquests, of the classical polis framework for rhapsodic cultivation of the Homeric epic tradition led to the intense efforts of the Alexandrian scholars of the Hellenistic age to consolidate and standardize the Homeric tradition. The calamitous *Traditionsbruch* Israel experienced in exile spurred the production of Torah as a written artefact, the consolidation of foundational traditions in the durable medium of writing. The written cultural artefacts that emerge out of a *Traditionsbruch* become the basis for reconstituting the moral and cultural identity of the tradent group, and for ensuring its long-term viability.

One category of *Traditionsbruch* has particular relevance for the study of Christian origins, especially for explaining the appearance of written Gospels in the late first century CE. For emergent communities such as the early church, the passing of the first generation presents a *Traditionsbruch*, for it means the loss of the living memory connection with the charismatic period of origins, the breakdown of the generational framework for the oral cultivation of the tradition. The community, if it is not to dissolve along with its memory, must accelerate the shifting of its normative tradition into more durable media, into the written medium in particular. This ensures the transgenerational transmission and perpetuation of a moral and cultural identity. The *Traditionsbruch* phenomenon described by Assmann helps explain the appearance of the first written Gospel (Mark) at the initial generational transition in early Christianity, the point where the living memory connection to the formative period of origins was breaking down. For its part, the Lukan Prologue (Lk. 1:1–4) explicitly states that the book seeks to consolidate, and thereby secure, the tradition that has been passed down by its living carriers. This programmatic inauguration of a written Gospel tradition opens up a new era characterized by the primary and secondary production of gospel literature that continues through the third century.

The theoretical framework provided by the *Traditionsbruch* concept easily accommodates additional factors that might be adduced to explain the origins of written gospel media in the late first century CE. These additional factors might include the institutional and cultural shock in the wake of the Jewish War and the destruction of Jerusalem, the increasing geographical dispersion of the Christian communities around the Mediterranean, and the ethnic and cultural shift from Jew to Gentile.

Alan Kirk (James Madison University, USA)

Further Reading

Jan Assmann. 2011. *Cultural Memory and Early Civilization: Writing, Remembrance, and Political Imagination.* Cambridge: Cambridge University Press.

Jan Assmann. 2006. *Religion and Cultural Memory.* Stanford: Stanford University Press.

Jan Assmann. 2006. 'Form as a Mnemonic Device: Cultural Texts and Cultural Memory.' In *Performing the Gospel: Orality, Memory, and Mark.* Edited by Richard A. Horsley, Jonathan A. Draper, and John Miles Foley. Minneapolis: Fortress Press, pp. 67–82.

Translation In popular usage, *translation* refers to the transfer of a text and/or its meaning from one language to another. Media-critical perspectives, however, have raised a number of questions that call for a broader definition that understands *translation* not as a mechanical transfer of content but rather as a rewriting or recreation of a text in another medium. Reflecting this trend, recent translation studies – and biblical research based on these models – parallels, and can draw insights and energy from, a broad range of cognate disciplines, including FOLKLORISTICS, ETHNOPOETICS, Theatre Studies (especially dramaturgy), Musicology (especially Ethnomusicoloy), and Film Studies. Each of these disciplines addresses questions relating to the transfer of material not only from one language to another but also across differing media.

Translation in Antiquity

In the ancient Roman world, translation most often involved translating material from Greek into Latin. Cicero discusses different methods of translation according to the types of texts: historical, poetic, and rhetorical. For oratory, he asserts that translation into Latin is not to be word-for-word but should demonstrate an imitation of the figurative beauty of the Greek. At the same time, he insists that the resulting Latin should appear natural while preserving the general style and force of the language. Cicero's approach demonstrates the fluid relationship between the written and spoken word: oration was the goal for delivery, but this did not exclude the role of the written word. Translators in antiquity pursued more than the transfer of information; they understood the cultural contributions of translation. The Romans, for example, wanted to assert their identity through their translations as distinct from that of the Greeks.

Within this context, Bible translation has a long history. The SEPTUAGINT – the Greek translation of the Hebrew Scriptures – often marks the starting point of this history. Philo's dubious description of the origins of this translation envisions that the seventy sages who produced the Greek Bible worked in isolation and, guided by God, produced identical results. More realistic assessments gained from other Jewish sources reveal that methods of Bible translation depended upon what a translation would be used for. A word-for-word approach was abandoned in liturgical settings, and extant TARGUMS (oral interpretations of the Hebrew Bible) demonstrate the interpretive role of translators. This diversity of methods describes an understanding more complex than might be expected from Rabbi Yehuda's warning, 'Who translates one verse literally is a falsifier, who adds anything is a blasphemer' (*t. Megilla* 4.41; *b. Qiddushin* 49a). As for translation and media, two second-century BCE Jewish comments underscore the interface of WRITING and ORALITY. The preface to the Wisdom of Ben Sira discusses differences of meaning from the Hebrew to Greek 'when spoken in the original' (Sir. 1.25). The emphasis seems to be on when the language is spoken. Similarly, Philo's presentation of how the Septuagint came into being describes that once the draft translation was completed it was read aloud to be verified. In other words, speaking aloud a translation was part of the method of checking its quality.

From the start, the Christian movement was integrally linked to translation with its use of the Septuagint and the rewriting of ORAL TRADITIONS into Greek Gospels. The second century continued this understanding with the Peshitta, the Syriac translation of the Bible, along with the fourth-century Latin translation of the Bible, the Vulgate. Through the centuries, Christians understood that the sacred text was a translated text. This ethos of translation was not restricted to languages. Media variation from icons to architecture, from drama to MUSIC, also demonstrate this ethos. The history of the Bible includes its translation from one language to another and from one medium to another. This suggests that the Bible is an ideal place to discuss the relationship of media and translation. Chronologically, with the rise of print, one can trace a shift in priority in the translation of oral performance characteristics of ancient written texts. The following sections pursue this discussion by exploring recent developments in approaches to translation and media and their impact on the translation of the Bible.

Translation and Media

In the mid-twentieth century, Roman Jakobson discussed three types of translation: intralingual, interlingual, and INTERSEMIOTIC. The last two concern our discussion here. *Interlingual* refers to the popular conception of translation noted above, the movement of material from one language to another. *Intersemiotic*, the transition of material from one sign system to another, is equally significant. For example, if a German novel is made into a Hollywood movie, where does translation take place? Is it solely in the act of moving from one language into another? Or is the act of shifting from a book to a film – a change in the medium – also a form of translation? This type of multi-translation is inherent in the Christian Bible. Take, for example, the PARABLES of Jesus. Jesus presented these stories verbally to live audiences in the Aramaic language. When these stories were eventually written down, translation took place as the Aramaic was rendered into Greek, and also as the lively spoken stories were transferred to writing on silent PARCHMENTS. When one sign system (MANUSCRIPT) is used to communicate that which was previously in another sign system (oral performance), we have an instance of Jakobson's intersemiotic translation.

Once semiotics is introduced to the discussion of translation, space is opened to think of translation in all sorts of sign systems, not simply in the move from Hebrew or Greek biblical texts to other texts written in modern languages. Paintings, ICONOGRAPHY, architecture, theatrical performances, DANCE, and music each provide opportunities for intersemiotic translation. If one views one of Jesus's stories, such as The Prodigal Son, in this light, we begin to see the rich contributions of translation through the centuries, from the early oral tradition to written Gospels to wall paintings and mosaics, from printed texts to theatrical renditions and ballet – all 'translations' of a famous parable..

Translation Studies

Although translation has been a human activity for millennia, a systematic investigation into translation – distinct from linguistics or comparative literature – began only in the 1970s. Translation studies recognizes the tremendous contributions of the translation of the Bible to its discipline, but has also made some significant critiques of Bible translation. Translation studies has gone through a series of turns that can be compared to paradigm shifts in its views of translation. Two of these turns are mentioned below.

The first turn in translation studies can be attributed in many ways to Eugene Nida, a Bible translator known for his work on 'dynamic equivalence'. Although his approach introduced many challenges (see below), Nida shifted the focus of translation work to the audience. Nida held the source text and its language and culture in high regard, but believed that translation work should focus on the reception of the translation. Nida's principle of dynamic equivalence reflects this approach, suggesting that the goal of any Bible translation should be to provide today's audiences with an equivalent experience to that which audiences in antiquity experienced.

Translation studies scholars have pursued this focus by recognizing the power of audiences to interpret and appropriate texts for their own purposes.

The second turn in translation studies represents a shift in focus from linguistics to culture. This turn is not a dismissal of the value of linguistics, but an expansion and repositioning of language in the broader cultural contexts in which texts (in a general sense) are created. Aligning the discussion to culture provides opportunity to discuss two significant themes in cultural studies: IDENTITY and power. Translation studies scholars expanded the discussion by making visible the previously invisible translator, a move that recognized that translators bring their own identities into their translations. Translators and translations are not neutral or objective. Also on the theme of identity, translation studies recognizes that translators and translations inform cultural identity. To cite an obvious example, the King James Version became much more than a translation of the Bible but also a powerful influence on the English language and culture. A related aspect of the cultural turn in translation studies is the recognition of how translation is involved in asymmetric power relations. Translation in general has been historically implicated in colonial projects, and so it is natural for translation studies in a cultural turn to be informed by postcolonial studies. The combination of these two points about the cultural turn – identity and power – stresses that the translator can no longer be viewed as a neutral liaison between source and target texts, but rather plays the role of a cultural mediator.

Bible translation in many ways anticipated the cultural turn in translation studies, as it has been carried out in thousands of languages and cultures around the world. Numerous studies have discussed how the translation of the Bible into indigenous languages/cultures has informed identity. At the same time, Bible translation has also been accurately described as embedded within many colonial projects. Postcolonial scholars critique this not only in terms of the ideological content of the Bible but also in the material choices of promoting the print medium and LITERACY over against the aesthetics of traditional oral cultures. Translation has been viewed variously as an instrument of colonial subjugation and as a vehicle of liberation. In recent years, this has also been suggested in the case of non-print media. Tremendous resources have been expended in the past two decades to promote Bible translation beyond print – through film, audio, STORYTELLING, sign language, performance, and many other media. The challenge remains to assess theories and practices that have been assumed with print translation but might not be appropriate for non-print translation. This could be the greatest challenge to Bible translation in the first quarter of the twenty-first century.

Among biblical scholars, the terms *equivalence* and *fidelity* are still often used today in discussions of translation. But these concepts are contested among the broader community of translation research. *Equivalence* carries obvious assumptions about how translation is perceived and sets up a dichotomy with unilateral relationships between source and target texts, languages, and cultures. *Faithfulness* or *fidelity* is the natural extension of this notion of equivalence. In the mid-twentieth century, discussions about equivalence became further nuanced with the terms *literal* and *dynamic* equivalence. In biblical studies, many would define a *literal* translation as one that closely respects the words and syntax of the source text, as opposed to a *dynamic* translation that prioritizes the transfer of the meaning of texts and foregoes when necessary the form or linguistic structures of the source text. This distinction, however, which prioritizes the purely linguistic dimension of translation, can promote a separation of form from meaning and a conduit model of communication – that is, a notion that an 'intended meaning' can be distilled from the language and medium and then reinserted into another language and medium.

Most communication theories today – influenced by post-structuralist and deconstructionist approaches to language – critique several aspects of the notion of equivalence, most particularly ideas that a singular meaning can be located within a source text and that it is possible to separate a 'pure meaning' from its linguistic and medial form. Similarly, media theorists emphasize the impossibility of separating message (content) from medium (see McLuhan, Marshall). In addition, the assertion of the death of the author and the values of receptionalism underscore the agency of those who appropriate translations (audiences and readers) in generating the 'meaning' of the translated text.

Reflecting these concerns, today translation studies scholars question the evaluative concept of equivalence. Many prefer to discuss translation in terms of similarity and difference. These scholars also depart from the traditional concern with what is 'lost in translation' to emphasize what might be gained, an approach that became increasingly popular following the turn towards the model of rewriting and recreation noted above. Viewed from this perspective, translation is a creative act, and its results are not evaluated exclusively in terms of the source text. Poetry remains the strongest case in point with regard to this view of translation. Almost by definition, it is impossible to produce a truly 'equivalent' translation of a poem when the discussion is framed in terms of comparison with the source text, simply because poetry inherently manipulates the rules of language with a view to creating an emotive effect. But poetry translation is possible if viewed as a creative act that has the liberty to bring something new into the world that was not in the source – if translators are viewed as playing a role similar to that of the poets themselves. Given the considerable amount of poetry in biblical material, this discussion is relevant for the translation of the Bible.

Interpretation, Authority, and the Original

Thus far, the term *source* has been used in this discussion when referring to what is translated, in view of increasing theoretical concern with the notion of the original version of a translated text. These concerns reflect several theoretical issues. First, biblical scholars understand that the biblical texts they are translating are actually modern scholarly constructs pieced together from a variety of ancient sources, the results of the work of Textual Criticism. One can question, then, whether the version of Isaiah currently available to translators is the original text of that book, if any. A second and related concern arises from the comparative study of oral tradition. Because the biblical texts were produced in a highly oral milieu with a variety of complex interfaces between speech and writing, it is more helpful, from an orality perspective, to assume a pluriformity of original biblical compositions that were experienced in multiple occasions and contexts – elements of, and perhaps the entirety of, a book such as 1 Corinthians would have been orally composed, recomposed, written down, and published through reading on numerous occasions, each with situational variations. In such a context, each performance of Paul's letter was an original. Third, research in semiotics understands translation as an infinite set of semioses in which there is a continuous play of signified, signifier, and interpretation. As soon as one indicates the original, this original reveals itself as the result of earlier semiosis.

The general decline in confidence in the notion of an original biblical text has had a domino effect, with the result that translation scholars may now assert that there are only translations and no originals or that, in some cases, a translation should be held in higher esteem than the original. Take for example, the earliest renderings of a canonical Gospel text, such as the Gospel of John. This original is already a translation of an (or many) earlier verbal presentation(s), a transition from speech to writing, and these oral presentations have informed the experience and understanding of their hearers, who have in turn translated this experience – interlingually and intersemiotically – into a written Greek Gospel.

The emerging picture of originals and the relationship between source texts and translations raises further issues for the consideration of two important components of Bible translation: interpretation and authority.

Most translation studies scholars accept the premise that 'all translation is interpretation'. This does not mean that 'anything goes' or that there is no such thing as a wrong or bad translation. Rather, the claim underscores what was said above: translation is a series of choices. But if all translation is interpretation at some level, then the translator is no longer neutral or objective, with the result that the translator's agency (visibility) must be recognized. The goal of translation, therefore, is not to be 'objective', but rather to be responsible in one's choices – responsible to the earlier texts and responsible to potential audiences. Translation is a cultural act that negotiates meaning and offers ways to think and act in new ways.

Not all translated sacred texts are viewed as authoritative over their communities, but this is generally held to be the case in modern Christianity, where English, German, Spanish, or other translations are generally viewed as sacred Scripture, just as much (or more so) as their Hebrew or Greek originals. Discussions of authority in Bible translation often revolve around the notion of *inspiration*, and this leads to questions of what or who is inspired. In view of the emerging picture of the role of the translator (see above), translation cannot be excluded from discussions of biblical authority. An *authoritative* translation is one recognized by a community or its representative institutions as somehow reflecting and informing norms of behaviour.

Throughout history, the question of the communications medium has also factored into discussions of the *authority* of biblical translations. Most media scholars today reject broad generalizations about oral versus written media and cultures (see GREAT DIVIDE), focusing instead on the interfaces of speech, writing, and other media in specific historical periods, cultures, circumstances, and genres. From an INTERSEMIOTIC perspective, this interface of media indicates a clustering and interaction of multiple sign systems. This emphasis on media interface with regard to authority was already evident in antiquity. Depictions of oral performances in antiquity often portray the orator holding a scroll – even when the performance was fully memorized or composed impromptu, the visual presence of a written text could function as an instrument or symbol of authority. The question of the relationship between biblical authority and media transitions is particularly relevant in the context of the current digital revolution. Digital reading material is often given characteristics of a printed book, and many digital Bible products present themselves with images of the printed book or visual features of books. These depictions are meant to reinforce the authority of these presentations.

Effectively, then, the notion that a biblical translation – from language to language and/or across media – is authoritative is ultimately a matter of trust. The hearer or user of translations must trust the translation in order for it to be authoritative for them. For this very reason, the Preface or 'note from the translators' at the beginning of most modern print Bibles functions rhetorically to assure the reader of the trustworthiness of the translation. Such rhetoric generally asserts that the most reliable available original texts were used and that the method of translating from these foreign texts was accurate, with fidelity as the result. In addition, a presentation of the translator or committee of translators is made that underscores their expertise, experience, and how they represent the intended audiences. Such trust is essential because, without it, readers will not view a translation as authoritative and therefore will not purchase it. In those religious communities where centralized institutions are authoritative, a seal of approval (*imprimatur*) demonstrates the same rhetorical strategy of trust to assure authority.

In the case of most modern translations, the translator is unknown to the reader. This invisibility is also a strategy to inculcate trust. The publisher asks the translator to translate a text in a way so that it no longer appears foreign to the reader. If successful, the reader might not know, or may choose to forget, that the text is a translation, so that it becomes for this reader an authoritative original. Originality remains a cultural value to support the authoritative nature of a text. This strategy, however, is less successful in cases where the translated biblical text is not written, but instead delivered to its audience through another medium. For example, in cases where a biblical passage is memorized and performed orally before an audience (see PERFORMANCE CRITIZISM, or where an artist is present for a gallery display of depictions of biblical scenes, the physical proximity of the translator to the consumer enhances the awareness that the text is being mediated through another person – a dynamic that biblical performance critics exploit.

These observations come full circle in the consideration of the relationship between interpretation and authority. One of the common strategies used to demonstrate that a translated text is authoritative is declaring the objective and faithful nature of the translation and translators. Although translation is inherently interpretive, objectivity as a predecessor to authority is sought. However, translations that move the biblical text beyond print – music, architecture, drama, fine arts – typically do not seek to make the mediator (interpreter) invisible. The strategy therefore changes to assuring the audience of the trustworthiness of the interpreters.

Overall, translations are done for a purpose. These purposes or functions shape the translation process and product, and theoretical models that highlight these elements may be called *functional* approaches. Functional theories emphasize the need to shape a translation according to the intended audience and, because intended audiences vary, allow for a multiplicity of legitimate translations. This approach takes into consideration the complex network of people and institutions involved in translation beyond the translators themselves. Commissioners of a translation have particular objectives; publishers have their parameters; target audiences demonstrate their interests.

This understanding of functional translation provides a way to evaluate various media translations of the Bible. For example, an interlinear translation of biblical material can be understood as successful if the commissioning agency and targeted audience anticipate such a translation for particular purposes. A film translation of a Gospel parable can prove to be successful if it meets the stated purpose of the initiator of the project and provides the audience with the appropriate communication for those viewers. This should not be understood as the end justifying the means, however. Ethics of translation is often articulated as faithfulness to a source text. The functional approach brings this faithfulness into tension with loyalty to the intended audience. Such a reorientation does not neglect the need to evaluate translations, but the ways to evaluate them changes considerably. If the goal is not equivalence, there nonetheless remains some question of assessment. Terms such as *adequacy*, *similarity*, and *authenticity* are often used in such cases.

Translation and Performance

In its original contexts, much of the biblical material was presented – performed or publicly read – by individuals in the presence of live audiences, and these performers, whether they intended to or not, became embodiments of the message. Gestures, facial expressions, posture, tone of voice, proximity vis-à-vis the audience – all these sign systems were meaningful parts of the communication experience (see NONVERBAL COMMUNICATION IN PERFORMANCE). Now, centuries later when the voices and gestures have faded, the books of the Bible remain as written records of these performances (see PERFORMANCE OF THE GOSPELS; TORAH READING). The translation of these fossils into other media, including back into the original medium of speech, is a challenge that has been taken up by scholars who emphasize the performative dimensions of the biblical texts.

Some biblical scholars are interested in reconstructing historical media translations of the Bible, or/and conduct exegetical work based on close analysis of the soundscape of the language of the biblical texts. Rather than focusing solely on the content of the biblical material, these scholars began to ask what the biblical language sounded like, and how it was experienced as sound when performed or read aloud to ancient Israelite and Christian audiences. This line of scholarship seeks to identify intentional soundscapes, acoustic patterns, and reoccurring phrasings to highlight the oral nature of the biblical material. The emerging discipline of SOUND MAPPING attempts to present the results of this research in a form that allows scholars to closely analyse the acoustic dynamics of the biblical texts and their interpretive implications.

More ambitiously, PERFORMANCE CRITICISM seeks insights into the meanings of the biblical texts by recreating them in spoken performances before live audiences, sometimes in the original language (Hebrew or Greek) but more often in a modern language (English). In order to perform a biblical text, one usually translates a passage or entire book from Hebrew or Greek into the performing language. This is no small feat, inasmuch as the English translation seeks to render not only the words or message of the source but also its perceived oratorical intentions. Plays on words or sounds in the Hebrew or Greek are notoriously difficult to translate. Performance critics also seek to discover implicit 'stage directions' within the biblical texts – clues to how the ancient performers might have used inflection or bodily gestures – and incorporate these into performances. Research into ancient rhetorical manuals provides insight on how one might read into the biblical material allusions to posture, gestures, tonality, etc. (see RHETORIC). However, these rhetorical manuals describe particular culturally-defined performance mannerisms that are not necessarily universal. For example, a gesture or tone of authority in one language and culture (e.g. rules for delivering court speeches in Latin in Italy) may not directly transfer into another language and culture (e.g. telling a story about Jesus in Greek in Ephesus). Therefore, any attempt to determine the meaning of these performance features so as to re-embody them with culturally appropriate gestures or tones follows the translation assumptions of dynamic equivalence, where form (e.g. gestures) can be separated from meaning. The discussions above with regard to translation studies indicate that this approach to translation lacks the theoretical underpinnings to support what happens in practical translation.

If one starts, as suggested in translation studies, with an understanding of translation that is interpretive and creative rather than objective and focused on 'the original meaning', biblical Performance Criticism's understanding of translation can be expanded. Put another way, the high standards of academic rigour that biblical Performance Criticism seeks to achieve depend on a theoretical model that moves beyond a simple dichotomy between *dynamic* and *literal* to the complex discussions of intersemiotics noted above. In many ways, this scenario resembles the tensions between philologists and translation studies scholars. The predominance of linguistics and its traditional emphasis on the original text/meaning is similar to trends in biblical scholarship that have understood translation as primarily language oriented and retrospective. As noted above, translation studies has demonstrated since the 1980 a cultural turn that adjusts the role of linguistics in the process of translation and has changed the translation viewpoint from retrospective to prospective (i.e. from the ancient author and his/her original text and towards the experience of the modern audience of the translation).

Biblical Performance Criticism, like translation studies, values the role of the audience by placing the audience as an important participant in the performance event. The audience does not simply passively receive what a performer provides, but by their presence and interaction with the performer(s) negotiate the meaning that they experience. Biblical Performance Criticism thus depends on several levels of translation work. In cases where the biblical text is performed in a modern language (e.g. English, Spanish), there is the interlingual translation from ancient texts, although here with particular attention to how what the audience hears will impact how they understand and appreciate the wording. At the same time, translation for performance goes beyond wording when it moves the biblical text from the page to the stage. Paralinguistic features of voice (e.g. timber, volume, rhythm) must concord with the words; gestures must likewise correspond, as well as facial features. With a turn to the audience, translators (and performers as translators) must decide whether they will attempt a historical translation-performance (attempting to reproduce the original language and setting more closely) that risks misunderstanding by modern audiences, or will shape the translation-performance so that the modern audience experiences 'something like' what was experienced in antiquity. Foundational to such questions is a turn from focus on the historical source language and culture to the contemporary audience and its norms.

The Bible provides a rich environment to explore its translation into various languages and media. Recent translation studies supports viewing this history as a series of interpretive recreations that link to the past but also express something new. The desired functions of a translation take into consideration the receptive audiences and shape a translation accordingly. The ancient and modern medium of performance demonstrates that translation involves more than languages but includes multiple sign systems.

James Maxey (Nida Institute for Biblical Scholarship, USA)

Further Reading

Bassnett, Susan. 2014. *Translation*. New York: Routledge.

Hodgson, Robert, and Paul A. Soukup, S.J., eds. 1997. *From One Medium to Another: Basic Issues for Communicating the Scriptures in New Media*. Kansas City: Sheed & Ward.

Maxey, James A., and Ernst R. Wendland, eds. 2012. *Translating Scripture for Sound and Performance: New Directions in Biblical Studies*. Eugene, OR: Cascade Books.

Nord, Christiane. 1997. *Translating as a Purposeful Activity: Functionalist Approaches Explained.* Manchester: St. Jerome.

Type Scene A type scene 'may be regarded as a recurrent block of narrative with an identifiable structure, such as a sacrifice, [or] the reception of a guest' (Edwards 1992: 284). Type scenes can be observed for events that repeatedly occur in traditional narratives from a wide range of cultures, including Homeric epic (Arend 1933), biblical narrative (Alter 1981), South Slavic epic, and Anglo-Saxon verse (Foley 1999).

The concept of the type scene was first developed by scholars of Homeric epic, in particular Walter Arend. Arend effectively described the repeated patterns that characterize type scenes, the kinds of variations from these patterns that typically occur, and the ways that such variations can create meaningful artistic effects. Work by Milman Parry and his student Albert Lord, begun about the same time as Arend's study and continued under Lord for several decades thereafter, contextualized type scenes within a traditional system of oral poetics, partly by means of field work in the former Yugoslavia with oral poets whose work displayed many of the same features that characterize Homeric epic (including type scenes, which Parry and Lord called themes). Such oral poetry, Parry and Lord argued, was characterized by a reservoir of repeated forms at every level of composition that grew over time through the accretion of the efforts of many generations of individual poets. Later on, scholars working in various disciplines argued that type scenes could be found in other traditional narratives, including the South Slavic poems that were studied by Parry and Lord and the Hebrew Bible.

Type scenes can be seen as a narrative analogue to traditional formulas for names of particular characters, or for very brief events such as introducing a direct speech. Just as a traditional narrative develops regular, repeated phrasing to name major heroes and to describe frequently occurring events like 'and the Lord said to him', so too it narrates common incidents, such as the arrival of a guest, in repeating patterns. Robert Alter (1981: 95–6) lists five techniques of 'repetitive structuring and focusing devices' in the Hebrew Bible, beginning with the most specific (individual word-roots) and ending with type scenes, which he characterizes as 'the largest and most composite', since they may include all his other devices. Thus, type scenes form one part of narrative systems that rely heavily on repetitive devices both to convey a story and to tell it in a particular way. While type scenes are described primarily as a form of repetition, variation characterizes the individual examples of a given type. This means that no single example of a type scene incorporates every element that is commonly found for a given type: specific instances are 'examples, not standards' (Foley 1999: 85).

Examples of type scenes in biblical narrative include the announcement of a coming child to an infertile would-be mother, encountering a future bride at a well, and the last words of a dying hero. Alter's (1981:

51–62) analysis of different instances of the 'future bride at the well' type vividly conveys the dynamic interplay between the expectations that an audience would bring to any episode featuring a young unmarried girl at a well and the way that such an incident actually unfolded in a given example of the type. For instance, the meeting between Abraham's servant and Rebecca (Gen. 24.10-61) is both the first and the most elaborate example of this type in the Hebrew Bible. This scene plays out in such detail both because it expands on traditional features of the type (e.g. this meeting includes an unusually large quantity of direct discourse, which enhances the characterization of the individuals in the scene) and also through variations on typical elements (only here does a substitute male figure rather than the future groom meet the young girl at the well). This variation from the usual pattern of such type scenes depicts Isaac as an unusually passive character, which is consistent with his behaviour throughout the Genesis narrative. Similarly, only here does the girl herself rather than the visiting male stranger draw water from the well, again consistent with her overall characterization: while Isaac is conspicuously passive as a patriarch, Rebecca consistently takes matters into her own hands, as when she advises Jacob on how to steal the birthright from Esau. In the next example of the 'bride at the well' type scene (Gen. 29.1-20), the story is told largely from the point of view of Jacob, the future groom. These aspects of the characters of Isaac and Rebecca are not conveyed exclusively by the manner in which this example of the 'young man meets bride at well' type treats the major elements of such a scene; at the same time, this particular scene demonstrates how deployment of the aesthetic possibilities of type scenes contributes to the overall depiction of several major characters in Genesis.

As the above example demonstrates, the nature and quality of the variations displayed by a particular instance of a type scene lend emphasis and colour to the narrative in a variety of ways. Variation engages an audience by violating their expectations of what such a type scene 'should' be like, and then requiring them to make sense of these variations: What are the differences from the usual patterns? How do these differences affect the way the story unfolds? A skilled narrator from a tradition that includes type scenes can enrich the quality and interest of his narrative by skilfully balancing repetition and variation in his narration of type scenes.

Deborah Beck (University of Texas at Austin, USA)

Further Reading

Alter, Robert. 1981. *The Art of Biblical Narrative*. New York: Basic Books.

Arend, Walter. 1933. *Die typischen Scenen bei Homer*. Berlin: Weidmannsche Buchhandlung.

Edwards, Mark W. 1992. 'Homer and Oral Tradition: The Type-Scene.' *Oral Tradition* 7/2: 284–330.

Foley, John Miles. 1999. *Homer's Traditional Art*. University Park: Pennsylvania State University Press.

Lord, Albert. 2000. *The Singer of Tales*. Cambridge, MA: Harvard University Press.

Parry, Adam, ed. 1987. *The Making of Homeric Verse: The Collected Papers of Milman Parry*. Edited by Adam Parry. Oxford: Oxford University Press.

V

Verbatim Memory See memory, Gist and Verbatim

Villa of the Papyri, Herculaneum The Villa of the Papyri (*Villa dei Papyri*), just outside the walls of Herculaneum (near modern Naples on the southwest coast of Italy), contained one of the largest ancient LIBRARIES discovered to date. The SCROLLS, which focus particularly on Epicurean philosophy (especially that of Philodemus), were carbonized by the eruption of Vesuvius in 79 CE that destroyed Herculaneum, POMPEII, and many surrounding villages and estates. The Villa is also of broader interest for understanding first-century media because it gives strong indications of a coordination of texts, art, and architecture, revealing an important nexus between power (in terms of wealth), culture, and philosophy.

The Villa was discovered in the eighteenth century and its main floor was extensively explored by means of tunnels into the volcanic overlay. The Villa was mapped by Karl Weber in the mid-eighteenth century and a large number of statues and scrolls were removed, along with a number of mosaic floors. The excavation was then closed and the exact location forgotten until its rediscovery in 1986. Between then and 1990, some of the original tunnels were re-explored (de Simone in Zarmakoupi 2010). From 1994 to 1998, open-air excavations were carried out for the first time on the Villa, exposing the atrium area and discovering three more floors of rooms built into and at the bottom of the slope on which the Villa stood. Further excavation in 2007–8 preserved and gave greater clarity to areas dug in the nineties (Guidobaldi and Esposito in Zarmakoupi). A key point to note is that all studies published up to 1986, and many since, are based solely on the eighteenth-century exploration of the Villa.

Because of the scale of wealth on view, and because of the prevalence of the writings of Philodemus, most scholars have concluded that the Villa was owned by L. Calpurnius Piso Caesoninus, Consul of 58 BCE and a major patron of Philodemus. However, on the basis of analysis from the 2007–8 excavation, Esposito has argued that the main section of the Villa was constructed all at the same time, in the period of fresco production of 'Second Style' types Ic-IIa, namely c. 40–30 BCE, too late for Piso and probably also for Philodemus (Guidobaldi and Esposito in Zarmakoupi). This would not exclude the possibility, however, that Piso commissioned the building, nor that his son (usually distinguished as pontifex) could have been the first owner.

Architecture and Art

There are two key architectural aspects of the Villa. One is provision of an ideal place for leisure. The Villa is spread across four floors, emphasizing the view across the Bay of Naples, especially from the newly discovered 5.5 metre (about 18 feet) high bow window structure. The Villa is space for cultural appreciation and reflection. However, this is not a modest retreat. It is on an epic scale, the most prominent feature being a peristyle garden c. 94 × 32 metre (about 308 × 105 feet), built around a pool running two-thirds of the length – more of what would be expected of a Hellenistic monarch's palace than a private home.

The size of the collection of art matches the architecture. Over 80 sculptures have been recovered. Styles and subjects are very eclectic: many humans, some gods, and other mythical creatures. Of the humans, some are identifiable philosophers, some are Hellenistic rulers. Many statues are unidentified. Scholars have suggested programmatic links to Epicureanism, or the gymnasium, or Hellenistic monarchy. Other decorative art in the Villa ranges from Second to Fourth Style. Sadly, most frescoes seen in recent excavations are extremely fragmentary, often as a result of eighteenth-century removal.

The Library

About 1850 fragments of scrolls (Houston 2014) have been recovered from the Villa so far, and more may be present in unexcavated rooms. About 69 different works have been detected among scrolls that have been at least partly unrolled and read, some in more than one copy. Houston argues that the collection ran to between 600 and 1000 rolls. Continuing work on the scrolls is reported principally in a dedicated journal, *Cronache Ercolanesi*.

The scrolls from the various find spots cohere to give the impression of a library, mainly in Greek and strongly focused on philosophy; most other types of text are absent. Authors identified include Epicurus (several copies of sections of *On Nature*, although no other works) and several Epicureans: Metrodorus and Colotes of Lampsacus, Polystratus, Carneiscus, Demetrius of Laconia, Zeno of Sidon, and Philodemus of Gadara. There are also three works by the Stoic Chrysippus, and possibly works by Caecilius Statius and Ennius (Houston in König et al. 2013).

There are over 30 works by Philodemus of Gadara (c. 110–c. 40 BCE). Apart from the Villa, his limited extant works are poetry, none of which appears in the library. Instead, the collection is mainly ethical, with books on subjects such as flattery, frank speech, gratitude, and anger. There is also a history of philosophers, both Epicurean and from other schools. There are also works on RHETORIC. Sider sees the collection as 'Philodemus' working library' (Sider in Zarmakoupi). This would not be ruled out by the new late proposed date of the Villa, although that does more or less exclude the idea of Philodemus having worked there: the collection could have gone there after his death. However, Delattre demonstrates that the Villa has so far yielded hardly any of the works that Philodemus cites in his own work (Delattre in Cronache Ercolanesi 26 1996). This must raise serious questions about the collection being his working library.

Overall, the Villa of the Papyri is a key resource for understanding the formation of private libraries in the ancient world. The coordination between the textual collection and other elements of the Villa is also of interpretive significance. Wealth, culture, and philosophy are presented as belonging together. The library and its context are preserved at a point in time in the midst of the production of the NT texts. NT interpreters should bear in mind both the overall culture/philosophy/power nexus that the Villa presents, and the range of detail from the Villa's contents, especially the library and what it shows about the philosophical interests and book collecting practices of the Villa's owners.

Peter Oakes (University of Manchester, UK)

Further Reading

Houston, George. 2014. *Inside Roman Libraries: Book Collections and their Management in Antiquity*. Chapel Hill: University of North Carolina Press.

König, Jason, Katerina Oikonomopoulou, and Greg Woolf, eds. 2013. *Ancient Libraries*. Cambridge: Cambridge University Press.

Mattusch, Carol C. 2005. *The Villa dei Papyri at Herculaneum: Life and Afterlife of a Sculpture Collection*. Los Angeles: Getty Publications.

Wallace-Hadrill, Andrew. 2011. *Herculaneum: Past and Future*. London: Francis Lincoln.
Zarmakoupi, M., ed. 2010. *The Villa of the Papyri at Herculaneum: Archaeology, Reception and Digital Reconstruction*. Berlin: Walter Mouton de Gruyter. http://blogs.getty.edu/iris/a-virtual-model-of-the-villa-dei-papiri/

Vindolanda The Vindolanda ARCHIVE takes its name from a Roman fort near Hadrian's Wall in Northern England, just south of the border with modern Scotland, that was occupied from the late first through at least the mid-fourth centuries CE. In 1973, archaeologists discovered hundreds of ink-inscribed wooden leaves that preserved military documents and private LETTERS valuable for reconstructing daily life in a Roman military camp. These texts are also important for the study of WRITING and written media, and for ancient epistolary practices.

Moisture and time are the deadly enemies of archaeological remains. At Vindolanda, however, local clay and happenstance created a waterlogged and anaerobic environment that preserved a good amount of organic material from the Roman period: thousands of pairs of shoes, clothing, leather goods, and to date, some 1500 texts written between 85 and 120 CE. Recovery and preservation is ongoing. Most of the tablets are badly damaged, but several hundred can be partially reconstructed, falling into roughly two main categories: military documents (accounts, lists) and private letters.

The format of the leaves resembles a foldable postcard, with text written on both the left and right halves of the rectangle. A line is scored down the centre and the leaf folded to protect the writing on the inside while the name of the addressee is placed on the outside. When freshly cut, the wood was thin enough (between 1 and 3 millimetres) and flexible enough to avoid breaking. Letters were not incised but written with carbon-based ink. The heavy use of these leaf tablets is significant from the standpoint of writing technology. While PAPYRUS was the writing material of choice in the East, writing with ink on wood seems to have been far more common in this part of the empire than previously assumed. WAX TABLETS are commonly encountered as well – some 180 have been discovered at Vindolanda – but the heavy use of leaf tablets was unsuspected.

Certain features of the documents are important for the study of Latin palaeography. With very few exceptions, the tablets are written in Old Roman Cursive script. Scholars have noted the similarity between the cursive hands at Vindolanda and the (few) Latin papyri from Egypt. The uniformity in writing style from opposite sides of the empire testifies to a surprising degree of cultural homogeneity where written language is concerned. Latin writing from the first century of the Common Era often features an *interpunct*, or medial dot, for purposes of word separation, though the practice died out in the second century. The Vindolanda tablets are consistent with this transitional stage: some texts employ a medial dot between words, but most do not. Spacing between words, generally uncommon in other Latin texts from this period, is found occasionally. Among the tablets has also been found the earliest known example of Latin shorthand writing.

The lists and letters capture the details of quotidian life in a Roman border post ('return the axe'; 'gruel, 5 modii'; 'please send beer'). Tablet 346, a letter from an unknown writer, is often cited as an endearing example: 'I have sent (?) you … pairs of socks from Sattua, two pairs of sandals and two pairs of underpants, two pairs of sandals … Greet … ndes, Elpis, Iu …, … enus, Tetricus and all your messmates with whom I pray that you live in the greatest good fortune.' Roughly a hundred letters can be connected to Flavius Cerialis, the prefect assigned to the fort around the year 100 CE.

From the standpoint of writing and LITERACY, the existence of such tablets does not require a radical shift in estimates of literacy where the general population is concerned. To be sure, military elites demonstrate relatively high literacy; based on the character of his Latin, Cerialis was a fairly elegant stylist. Literacy seems to have extended some distance down the ranks of the centurions and decurions as well, which highlights the importance of literacy within military subculture. Beyond this, the tablets provide a wonderful window on the role that writing and written language played in the organization and running of provincial society. In this Roman fort, on the extreme edge of the empire, writing and written texts were a ubiquitous aspect of life.

Individual tablets offer glimpses of literary and epistolary culture. Tablet 118 has a line from Virgil's *Aeneid*, written in *capitalus rustica* script, perhaps as a writing exercise, since the obverse side contains a letter that was apparently not delivered. This fragment may indicate the use of Virgil in a school context (see Education, Hellenistic). Tablet 660, though fragmentary, is a graceful letter of introduction reminiscent of Pliny the Younger. Tablet 291 is a birthday invitation from Claudia Severa to Sulpicia Lepidina (wife of Flavius Cerialis). The letter was written by a secretary, but contains a few concluding lines from Severa herself, perhaps the earliest known example of Latin writing from a woman's hand. Tablet 611 derives from Haterius Nepos, probably identical with T. Haterius Nepos, who later became prefect of Egypt for the years 120–124 CE. His letter also closes with a note in his own hand, after the fashion of the Apostle Paul in Galatians. Several dozen of the letters show this practice of subscription, along with other epistolary conventions and accidents, such as an error traceable to dictation in Tablet 234. The process of drafting and correcting a letter is on display in Tablet 218. Overall, the archive illuminates many facets of epistolary culture, providing important context for the interpretation of letter-writing practices in the NT.

H. Gregory Snyder (Davidson College, USA)

Further Reading

Bowman, A. K. 1994. *Life and Letters on the Roman Frontier*. New York: Routledge, especially the chapter, 'Letters and Literacy.'

Bowman, A. K., and J. D. Thomas. 1983. *Vindolanda: The Latin Writing-Tablets*. London: Society for the Promotion of Roman Studies. Britannia Monograph 4.

Bowman, A. K., and J. D. Thomas. 1994. *The Vindolanda Writing-Tablets (Tabulae Vindolandenses II)*. London: The British Museum Press. The definitive edition is maintained online: http://vindolanda.csad.ox.ac.uk/

Bowman, A. K., and J. D. Thomas. 2003. *The Vindolanda Writing-Tablets (Tabulae Vindolandenses III)*. London: The British Museum Press.

Bowman, A. K., and J. D. Thomas. 2011. 'The Vindolanda Writing-Tablets (Tabulae Vindolandenses IV, Part 2)'. *Britannia* 42: 113–44 (Tablets 870-889).

Bowman, A. K., J. D. Thomas, and R. S. O. Tomlin. 2010. 'The Vindolanda Writing- Tablets (Tabulae Vindolandenses IV, Part 1)'. *Britannia* 41: 187–224 (Tablets 854-869).

Visual Culture The term *visual culture* refers to the full expanse of images manifested, produced, and consumed by a given culture, as well as the agents, institutions, conceptualities, and practices that put those images to use. The term may also be used more broadly in reference to a defined mode of academic inquiry (i.e. visual culture studies) that seeks to analyse how images, visual practices, and ways of seeing reflect various cultural forces and contribute to the social construction of reality. A consideration of ancient Near Eastern and Greco-Roman visual culture has the potential to advance the study of the Bible and related literature by shedding light on a number of important topics, including the meaning of biblical imagery, the background of biblical theologies concerning divine images, and the history of ancient Israelite and early Christian religions.

The Study of Visual Culture

The study of visual culture first surfaced in the late 1980s and early 1990s, and since then it has been incorporated into a number of different academic fields. The emergence of visual culture studies can be situated with respect to two broader intellectual developments: 1) the rise of interest in cultural studies and visual studies across the humanities and social sciences; and 2) a critical reappraisal of traditional approaches to art history.

At the most basic level, the impetus to study visual culture can be seen as a product of a more general shift towards the academic study of culture. This *cultural turn*, which first surfaced in Britain in the 1950s and then flourished in North America in the 1970s, prompted increased scrutiny concerning the ways in which cultural forces influence everyday life, individual experiences, social relationships, and institutions. The field of culture studies also came to be characterized by a special interest in how new theoretical perspectives (e.g. post-structuralism, deconstructionism, neo-Marxist philosophy, psychoanalysis) could guide the analysis of cultural processes, including the ways in which communities negotiate meaning with respect to class, economics, ethnicity, gender, race, and politics.

Early practitioners of cultural studies were neither exclusively nor even especially interested in visual materials. However, they were concerned with the ways in which all forms of signification – whether texts, images, embodied acts, rituals, or performances – not only reflect social and cultural influences but function to create the worlds people live in and care about. Thus, the cultural turn gave birth, though somewhat belatedly, to the study of visual culture by providing a theoretical framework for thinking about the visual field as a cultural field.

The birth of visual culture studies can also be traced to the groundswell of academic interest in all things visual in the closing decades of the twentieth century. This *visual turn* or 'pictorial turn' (Mitchell 1994) has had an exceptionally wide arc, impacting fields ranging from anthropology to gender studies to history. In these and other fields, methodologies that are solely based on the study of written texts have rapidly given way to those that take seriously the role and importance of images as primary sources in the analysis of history, societies, cultures, and religions. In addition, this turn to images has been marked by a rise of interest in critical theories about the nature of visual representation, and with it, new questions about the power, agency, social function, and cognitive affects of art and everyday visual objects.

In sum, *visual culture* can be understood as a technical term that seeks to identify, categorize, and lend institutional credibility to a broader, interdisciplinary impulse towards critical reflection on the cultural function and effects of the visual realm. Insofar as visual culture studies brings together new developments in cultural studies and visual studies, it can be seen as a mode of academic inquiry 'that regards the visual image as the focal point in the processes through which meaning is made in a cultural context' (Dikovitskaya 2005: 1).

As noted above, a second major impetus for the emergence of the study of visual culture relates to developments in the field of art history. Visual culture studies and art history share a number of related concerns. Both fields, for instance, are interested in the interpretation of visual artefacts; further, in executing these interpretations, both fields give attention to the contexts in which a visual object is produced and viewed. Beyond this, however, significant differences emerge. In fact, while visual culture studies was not developed to supplant traditional approaches to art history, many of its practitioners have attempted to problematize the assumptions that have long guided art historical research. Two such assumptions are particularly notable.

First, the study of visual culture breaks with traditional modes of art history insofar as it is not primarily concerned with questions of style, ICONOGRAPHY, aesthetic value, and connoisseurship. Though such considerations are not altogether abandoned in visual culture studies, more emphasis is placed on what images do as cultural artefacts. That is, how are images responded to in certain social settings? How do visual media function in the formation of values, relationships, ideologies, and religious belief? And in what sense do works of art shape cultural habits and expectations? While it is not impossible to ask such questions from within art history, the study of visual culture undertakes a more systematic appraisal of the cultural dimensions of the visual field.

Second, in comparison to art history, visual culture studies tends to analyse a far more diverse and eclectic array of visual objects. Rather than focusing exclusively on 'high' art or fine art (i.e. paintings, sculptures, or other museum pieces that are primarily meant to be appreciated for their aesthetic quality and/or historical and intellectual significance), scholars of visual culture consider a much broader range of visual media (e.g. TV, film, internet images, etc.) as well as popular art and everyday non-art objects (e.g. GRAFFITI, cartoons, ads, product labels, architecture, landscapes, rituals, clothing, mass-produced kitsch). Moreover, the study of visual culture also looks to images produced in diverse cultural contexts, especially those that lie outside Western canons of art.

By calling into question elitist notions of high culture and Western ideals of aesthetic value, the study of visual culture effectively 'democratize[s] the community of visual artefacts by considering all objects – and not just those classified as art – as having aesthetic and ideological complexity' (Dikovitskaya 2014: 2). However, this does not necessarily suggest that all distinctions between art and non-art or fine art and popular art are heuristically invalid. Instead, the study of visual culture seeks to historicize and contextualize such distinctions, exploring the various ways in which definitions of art and non-art, high culture and popular culture are negotiated by different people and at different periods.

While the earliest articulations of visual culture research were met with some degree of resistance from within art history, more optimistic appraisals of the field began to surface by the mid-1990s. At this time, programmes in visual culture studies were established alongside art history departments at institutions such as Columbia, Cornell, the University of Chicago, the University of Rochester, and UC Irvine; since then, similar programmes have been initiated in a number of other institutions. The topic of visual culture and its accompanying methodologies have also increasingly been integrated into traditional art history survey classes, not to mention courses in film studies, media studies, and cultural studies. Scholarly contributions to this field have also been on the rise since the early 2000s, and now an abundance of journals, handbooks, readers, and specialized monographs are available on this topic.

Visual Culture and/in Biblical Studies

Since the late 1990s, a number of important studies have undertaken the analysis of religious visual culture (Plate 2002; Morgan 1998; 2005; Morgan and Promey 2001). These studies explore the ways in which religion is materialized, mobilized, and maintained through the performances, rituals, spaces, feelings, and responses that emerge from and rely on visual materials. Studying the visual culture dimensions of religion includes understanding how visual materials and practices have the capacity to facilitate belief by cultivating religious feelings and sensibilities, activating shared memories and values, and absorbing one's consciousness in a meditative state of prayer or self-reflection. The steady growth of research on these and related topics suggests that a consideration of visual culture has secured a seat at the table of well-accepted methods in the academic study of religion.

Yet despite these broader trends in religious studies, biblical scholars have been somewhat slower to embrace research on visual culture. Several recent studies have explored the potential intersection of visual culture studies and biblical studies, with some appraisals expressing optimism (Bonfiglio 2016) and others a small degree of caution (Uehlinger 2015). In either case, the reasons for this general lack of engagement of visual culture in biblical studies are several.

First, the study of the Bible has traditionally been a word- or text-centred discipline, with a primary focus specifically on written/printed words. This methodological tendency is not without justification. The Bible is, after all, a collection of books that can be read with text-oriented questions in mind, be they about literary sources, composition history, textual variants, or philological features. In addition, reading the Bible in light of other ancient texts – legal codes, epic poems, LETTERS, royal treaties, wisdom sayings, and the like – can prove exceedingly helpful from a comparative perspective, affording interpreters access to the historical, cultural, and literary background of both OT and NT. Both of these approaches – studying the Bible as a text and in light of other texts – are decidedly logo-centric in their orientation, which is to say they are concerned primarily, if not exclusively, with verbal culture. As such, while some biblical scholars show interest in 'biblical art' (i.e. art that self-consciously displays biblical themes or interprets biblical stories), the field as a whole has not yet undertaken a systematic consideration of the visual dimensions of the cultures in which the Bible was first produced.

However, the methodological gap between biblical studies and visual culture studies is not one-sided. For their part, scholars of visual culture focus primarily, if not exclusively, on contemporary images. Rarely can one find a study of visual culture that examines pre-1950s art, let alone the sort of really ancient art – such as iconography from the Iron Age through the Greco-Roman period – that would be most relevant to biblical scholarship. In fact, some visual culture theorists go so far as to suggest that visual culture itself is a unique characteristic of contemporary culture, saturated as it is with TV, film, electronic billboards, internet images, and other forms of digital media (Mirzoeff 1999: 6).

This view can and should be challenged in light of the fact that images and visual perception are a constitutive component of all cultures past and present. Nevertheless, it remains the case that studying visual culture in ancient contexts is far more difficult than in contemporary ones. In order to analyse visual practices, visual reception, and the social affects of specific ways of seeing, scholars of visual culture routinely rely on ethnographic surveys, interviews, testimonies, photographs, films, and video archives. Comparable data is hard, if not impossible, to come by when dealing with the ancient world. For instance, if one were studying the visual culture of early Jewish SYNAGOGUES, one would have access to a wealth of iconographic artefacts but little direct evidence of how early Jewish worshippers would have interpreted, responded to, or interacted with those artefacts. At best, a scholar of any ancient religion would have to rely on indirect, comparative, and at times analogical evidence when attempting to draw informed conclusions about the nature and affect of visual culture in a given setting.

While some degree of caution is necessary when it comes to integrating biblical studies and visual culture studies, there remain several distinct advantages to a union of the two fields. First and most generally, it would be difficult to conceive of any definition of 'religion', whether ancient or modern, that excluded the visual realm. In fact, historian Colleen McDannell argues that instead of merely being a matter of words and creeds, '"genuine" religion has always been expressed and made real with objects, architecture, art, and landscapes' (1995: 272). It follows that if visual culture matters in the formation and expression of religion, then visual culture necessarily must matter in the study of religion, whatever the historical context may be. Thus, ignoring visual culture in the study of the Bible and related literature would result in a glaring gap, if not a systematic misconstrual, in our understanding of the history and development of ancient Israelite and early Christian religions.

Second, when it comes to studying the cultural contexts of biblical literature, there is simply far more visual evidence to work with than textual evidence. In fact, archaeological discoveries have made it clear that iconographic artefacts, especially in the form of impressions made by stamp or CYLINDER SEALS, outnumber inscriptions and other written records in the material culture of ancient Egypt, Mesopotamia, Persia, Greece, and Rome. Ancient Israel is no exception. However one might interpret the Decalogue's prohibition against making certain types of divine images (Exod. 20.4-5; Deut. 5.8-9), it is unequivocally the case that ancient Israel regularly produced, viewed, and distributed images (Schroer 1987). This is not to suggest that written texts were unimportant, but rather simply to stress that the abundance of images in the archaeological record cannot be ignored. Not unlike other forms of material culture, ancient images constitute an essential, and especially abundant, form of comparative data for biblical research.

Third, biblical scholars should be interested in visual culture in light of how ancient images functioned. In the ancient world, images did not merely serve as decorations. Rather, they were commonly used as media for transmitting information between senders and receivers. In this sense, images, much like texts, should be seen as a constitutive component of a given culture's symbol system. As a type of language, images can be read, and their viewers can be trained to understand visual vocabularies and standard tropes of pictorial syntax. In fact, studies of the 'minor arts' (e.g. CYLINDER SEALS, COINS, amulets, and other forms of miniature, mass-produced visual artefacts) suggest that images functioned as the most widely utilized vehicle of communication in the ancient world (Uehlinger 2000). This observation, coupled with the fact that textual LITERACY rates would have been extremely low in the ancient world, suggests that images were used more often, and by more people, as a way of conveying information and ideas. If ancient images primarily had a communicative function, then it follows that they preserve and reflect knowledge about politics, religion, economics, culture, and other critical social realities of daily life. In this way, ancient images can provide modern researchers with a valuable window into the conceptual world that lies behind the Bible.

In light of these observations, a small but growing number of biblical scholars have begun to turn to ancient art, or iconography, as a crucial comparative resource in the study of the Bible and ancient religion. This approach, which is commonly known as iconographic exegesis, was pioneered by Othmar Keel of the University of Fribourg (Switzerland) in the early 1970s. His groundbreaking study, *Die Welt der altorientalischen Bildsymbolik und das Alte Testament: Am Beispiel der Psalmen* (1972; English, *The Symbolism of the Biblical World: Ancient Near Eastern Iconography and the Book of Psalms* [1978; repr. 1997]), represented the first systematic attempt to compare the conceptual world of an OT book with ancient Near Eastern iconography that exhibits similar motifs.

Since that time, Keel and a loose network of his students and colleagues in Europe, South Africa, Israel, and North America have further developed iconographic exegesis as a way of engaging ancient visual culture. This approach has made a number of important contributions to biblical studies proper. Perhaps most significantly, iconographic exegesis has helped shed light on the meaning of biblical metaphors by showing conceptual correspondences between literary imagery and prominent iconographic motifs (e.g. Strawn 2005; de Hulster 2009). Iconographic evidence has also been brought to bear on the study of Israelite religion, and especially questions about the nature and extent of the image ban and the role of the goddess (Keel and Uehlinger 1998). In addition, other biblical methodologies, including literary analysis, tradition history, and gender studies are also now increasingly drawing on ancient visual evidence to augment their findings. Finally, it should be noted that the rise of iconographic exegesis has resulted in a number of important catalogues of ancient art, most notably Silvia Schroer's multivolume series entitled *Die Ikonographie Palästinas/Israels und der Alte Orient: Eine Religionsgeschichte in Bildern* (IPIAO) and Keel's multivolume *Corpus der Stempelsiegel-Amulette aus Palästina/Israel* (CSAPI).

Iconographic exegesis marks a significant step towards engaging the study of visual culture within the field of biblical studies. However, several caveats should be noted. With few exceptions, iconographic exegesis has been used in service of OT interpretation and related religio-historical research. There remains a need to apply this approach more extensively to the study of the NT and early Jewish literature (see, e.g. Weissenrieder, Wendt, and Gemünden 2005). In addition, there is also a need for further revision of the theory and methods of iconographic exegesis, especially in terms of visual analysis and ways of relating biblical and iconographic data. Several recent studies have taken significant steps in this direction (LeMon 2010; Strawn, de Hulster, Bonfiglio 2015). Third, and most significantly, while iconographic exegesis certainly involves the study of aspects of visual culture, most of its practitioners have yet to apply visual culture theory to their research. That is to say, outside of its interest in images as an object of study, iconographic exegesis rarely reflects the underlying concerns and questions of the field of visual culture studies.

Avenues of Future Inquiry

How, then, might the field of biblical studies more fully engage a visual culture approach? At least three key concerns of visual culture studies might be particularly fruitful to future research.

Visual Practices

The study of visual culture, in contrast to traditional modes of art history or even iconographic exegesis, tends to be practice-centred rather than artist- or object-centred. Put another way, a visual culture approach focuses less on the artist and the art object and more on the broader social, cultural, institutional, and intellectual practices that put these images to use. Underlying this focus on visual practices is the conviction that what an image 'means' is not strictly determined by an analysis of its formal qualities or even the artist's background and intention, but is rather a function of the image's reception and use. What an image 'means' thus cannot be isolated from the liturgical settings, everyday spaces, and embodied performances in which it functions. In the context of biblical studies, this practice-centred outlook would prompt scholars to go beyond an analysis of the theologies conveyed by certain images (e.g. depictions of the resurrection in early Eastern Orthodox iconography) or the way in which particular works of art interpret biblical stories (e.g. Rembrandt's *The Return of the Prodigal Son*). Rather, a visual culture approach would emphasize that what people do with images has everything to do with what those images 'mean', or even why they might be classified as 'religious' in the first place.

To take but one example, a practice-centred focus would open up new questions about the Ark of the Covenant in the OT. From an object- or artist-centred perspective, previous studies have considered the ark's iconographic design, especially in relation to Yahweh's cherubim throne and comparable ancient Near Eastern prototypes (Mettinger 2013). However, it is also possible to consider the implications of how the ark was put to use. Especially in 2 Samuel 6, possessing the ark is crucial to the Israelites' success in battle against the Philistines. While the biblical authors never refer to the ark as an image – let alone a divine image – the Israelites respond to and rely upon the ark in ways that are closely analogous to how divine images were used in ancient Mesopotamia and Egypt. The ark, not unlike the anthropomorphic cult statuary of ancient Israel's neighbours, seems to function as a material manifestation of the deity's power and presence, especially in battle and ritual procession. Thus, even if it were the case that ancient Israelite religion was purely aniconic (without images), a visual culture approach would underscore the fact that the Israelites put material objects to use in and through practices that roughly approximate the 'iconic' religions of other ancient Near Eastern cultures.

The Visual Field as a Cultural Field

A second central concern of the study of visual culture is that visual perception is not merely a biological phenomenon. Seeing, in other words, entails more than just the lens of the eye focusing light on the photoreceptive cells of the retina, which in turn convert patterns of light into neural signals. Rather, visual perception is (also) a cultural phenomenon. In visual culture studies, vision is construed as a culturally shaped habit, and as such, distinct *ways of seeing* are shaped by education, cultural expectations, religious beliefs, and social context. There are two primary implications of approaching the visual field as a cultural field.

First, visual perception can no longer be understood as a stable, natural, or universal phenomenon, and certainly not as an objective one. Vision itself can be said to have a history, one that is informed by social and cultural forces and that fluctuates over time and place. In this sense, a visual culture approach not only recognizes that different viewers see different things in their everyday lives, but that they actually see the same things in different ways. Even subjects such as people, buildings, celestial bodies, and so forth would be seen and understood differently by a given viewer based on the beliefs, customs, and values of their cultural context. As such, a visual culture approach to biblical studies would entail more than just comparing visual motifs from, say, ancient Egypt and ancient Israel-Palestine. Rather, it would include scrutinizing how these motifs participate in the formation of distinct Egyptian and Israelite visualities. In this view, the characteristic ways in which concepts such as kingship, violence, cosmology, the gods, and so forth were depicted would be seen not only as reflecting different cultural and religious sensibilities, but also as shaping a distinct way of understanding and interacting with political, ethical, ecological, and theological realities. Thus a consideration of visuality alongside iconography in biblical studies would help to underscore the ways in which images participate in the social and cultural construction of reality.

Second, understanding the visual field as a cultural field also implies that seeing is a thoroughly engaged, purposeful, and constructive activity. Visual experiences are always structured and organized by a system of epistemological lenses, cultural knowledge, and social experiences that constitute what might be referred to as 'ways of seeing'. Different ways of seeing, then, are a means by which viewers, whether consciously or unconsciously, search for what they hope to see or have been conditioned to look for. This suggests that 'the structure and operation of vision [is] a religious act' and that seeing itself is a 'proactive gesture' that is deeply inflected by prior beliefs, values, and theological commitments (Morgan 2005: 6). Put simply, religious ideas condition viewers to see in an image what they already believe.

Applying this aspect of visual culture to biblical studies would offer a new way of approaching the search for cult images of Yahweh in the material culture of ancient Israel. This line of inquiry is often carried out on iconographic grounds alone, with researchers debating whether certain visual artefacts qualify as Yahwistic iconography. However, from a visual culture approach it would also be possible to ask whether certain images, even if not originally intended to depict Yahweh, would have been seen, responded to, or imagined as images of the Israelite God. In other words, did Israelites see or recognize Yahweh in what were, strictly speaking, non-Yahwistic images? Proving this to be the case with any specific image would, of course, be difficult if not impossible. Nevertheless, it is possible – and potentially fruitful – to analyse conditions of spectatorship in ancient Israel, including the ways viewers would have been accustomed to associating images and texts (as in the case of the 'Yahweh and his Asherah' inscription on Pithos A from Kuntillet 'Ajrud) or to understanding Yahweh as absorbing features of non-Yahwistic deities (as in the case of biblical descriptions of Yahweh as a Baal-like god of the storm). In either case, a visual culture approach would underscore the fact that the oft-debated search for Yahweh's image must take into account the cultural and religious dimensions of visual perception, not just iconographic styles.

The Image–Text Relationship

Third, the study of visual culture is characteristically concerned with the image–text relationship. Such interest is manifest in the impulse towards inter-artistic comparisons, such as those that seek to relate a specific text with a particular piece of art. A similar approach is possible in biblical scholarship, especially in studies of reception history that consider how post-biblical art interprets motifs and stories from the Bible (see INTERSEMEIOTICS; TRANSLATION). Scholars of visual culture are also interested in analysing the conjunction of word and image within the same object, noting how visual and verbal elements interact with one another in the construction of meaning. Attention to the image–text relationship in individual mixed-media objects is also possible in biblical studies, whether in the analysis of illuminated medieval Bible MANUSCRIPTS or Iron Age Israel-Palestine stamp seals that contain both an iconographic design and an accompanying inscription.

In visual culture studies, interest in the image–text relationship often goes beyond a concern for inter-artistic comparisons. Namely, the study of visual culture is also characterized by new theoretical perspectives concerning the interaction between visual and verbal forms of representation. As is evident in the work of visual culture theorist W. J. T. Mitchell (e.g. 1986; 1994) rigid dichotomies between image and texts are often challenged. Specifically, Mitchell posits the existence of an image–text 'dialectic' as a way of accounting for the many ways in which the visual makes its way into the verbal (i.e. the visuality of texts) and the verbal into the visual (i.e. the textuality of images). Working from a similar framework, biblical scholars might call into question the privileging of word over image, whether in interpretive methodology or in theological orientation. This might involve highlighting places in the biblical witness that offer a more positive appraisal of visual experience (e.g. Ps. 34.8 [Heb. 9]; Ps. 17.15) than what is suggested in the Decalogue, or analysing the role and importance of visual materials in early Jewish and Christian WORSHIP practices. Alternatively, a consideration of the role of images as a type of language might help further inform recent debates about rates of textual literacy in the ancient world. Or, finally, a concern for the visual dimensions of texts might lead to research on the ways in which the Bible can function as a type of image or icon – that is, displayed as an object to be seen, contemplated, and meditated upon rather than a text to read (Toorn 1997).

In each of these ways, a critical engagement with ancient visual culture and the methods of visual culture studies promises to offer new insights into the role and importance of images and visual practices in what has traditionally been a text-based field.

Ryan P. Bonfiglio (Columbia Theological Seminary, USA)

Further Reading

Bahrani, Zainab. 2003. *The Graven Image: Representation in Babylonia and Assyria.* Archaeology, Culture, and Society. Philadelphia: University of Pennsylvania Press.

De Hulster, Izaak J. 2009. *Iconographic Exegesis and Third Isaiah.* FRLANT 2/36. Tübingen: Mohr Siebeck.

Dikovitskaya, Margarita. 2005. *Visual Culture: The Study of the Visual After the Cultural Turn.* Cambridge: MIT Press.

Dikovitskaya, Margarita. 'Visual Studies.' *Encyclopedia of Aesthetics.* Vol 2. 2nd edn. Edited by Michael Kelly. London: Oxford University Press.

Elkins, James. 2003. *Visual Studies: A Skeptical Introduction.* New York: Routledge.

Heywood, Ian, and Barry Sandywell. 2012. *The Handbook of Visual Culture.* London/New York: Berg.

Keel, Othmar, ed. 1995-present. *Corpus der Stempelsiegel-Amulette aus Palästina/Israel: Von den Anfängen bis zur Perserzeit.* 4 vols. Orbis biblicus et orientalis. Series archaeologica. Göttingen: Vandenhoeck & Ruprecht.

Keel, Othmar, ed. 1997. *The Symbolism of the Biblical World: Ancient Near Eastern Iconography and the Book of Psalms.* German original 1972; reprint edition Winona Lake, IN: Eisenbrauns.

Keel, Othmar, and Christoph Uehlinger. 1998. *Gods, Goddesses, and Images of God in Ancient Israel.* Translated by Thomas H. Trapp. German original 1992; reprint edition Minneapolis: Fortress Press.

LeMon, Joel M. 2010. *Yahweh's Winged Form in the Psalms: Exploring Congruent Iconography and Texts.* Orbis biblicus et orientalis 242. Göttingen: Vandenhoeck & Ruprecht.

McDannell, Colleen. 1995. *Material Christianity: Religion and Popular Culture in America.* New Haven: Yale University Press.

Mettinger, Tryggve N. D. 2013. *No Graven Image? Israelite Aniconism in Its Ancient Near Eastern Context.* Coniectanea biblica: Old Testament Series 42. Original 1995. Reprint edition Winona Lake, IN: Eisenbrauns.

Mirzoeff, Nicholas. 1999. *An Introduction to Visual Culture.* London and New York: Routledge.

Mitchell, W. J. T. 1986. *Iconology: Image, Text, Ideology.* Chicago: University of Chicago Press.

Mitchell, W. J. T. 1994. *Picture Theory. Essays on Verbal and Visual Representation.* Chicago: University of Chicago Press.

Morgan, David. 1998. *Visual Piety: A History and Theory of Popular Religious Imagery*. Berkeley: University of California Press.

Morgan, David. 2005. *The Sacred Gaze: Religious Visual Cultural in Theory and Practice*. Berkeley: University of California Press.

Morgan, David, and Sally M. Promey, eds. 2001. *The Visual Culture of American Religions*. Berkeley: University of California Press.

Plate, S. Brent. 2002. *Religion, Art, and Visual Culture: A Cross-Cultural Reader*. New York: Palgrave.

Schroer, Silvia. 1987. *In Israel gab es Bilder: Nachrichten von darstellender Kunst im Alten Testament*. Orbis biblicus et orientalis 74. Göttingen: Vandenhoeck & Ruprecht.

Schroer, Silvia, ed. 2005–11. *Die Ikonographie Palästinas/Israels und der Alte Orient: Eine Religionsgeschichte in Bildern*. 4 vols. Fribourg: Academic Press.

Strawn, Brent A. 2005. *What Is Stronger than a Lion? Leonine Image and Metaphor in the Hebrew Bible and the Ancient Near East*. Orbis biblicus et orientalis 212. Göttingen: Vandenhoeck & Ruprecht.

Strawn, Brent A., Izaak J. de Hulster, and Ryan P. Bonfiglio. 2015. *Iconographic Exegesis of the Hebrew Bible/Old Testament: An Introduction to Its Method and Practice*. Göttingen: Vandenhoeck & Ruprecht.

Uehlinger, Christoph, ed. 2000. *Images as Media: Sources for the Cultural History of the Near East and the Eastern Mediterranean* (1st Millennium BCE). Orbis biblicus et orientalis 175. Göttingen: Vandenhoeck & Ruprecht.

Uehlinger, Christoph, ed. 2015. 'Approaches to Visual Culture and Religion: Disciplinary Trajectories, Interdisciplinary Connections and Some Suggestions for Further Progress'. *Method and Theory in the Study of Religion* 27: 384–422.

van der Toorn, Karel, ed. 1997. *The Image and the Book: Iconic Cults, Aniconism, and the Rise of Book Religions in Israel and the Ancient Near East*. Contributions to Biblical Exegesis and Theology 21. Leuven: Peters.

Weissenrieder, Annette, Friederike Wendt, and Petra von Gemünden, eds. 2005. *Picturing the New Testament: Studies in Ancient Visual Images*. WUNT 193. Tübingen: Mohr Siebeck.

W

War Rituals A war ritual is an act (or series of acts) deliberately performed before, during, or after battle in order to affect some aspect of the battle and its consequences. War is a violent clash between two opposing forces, each seeking to impose its will on the other. As such, war is inherently uncertain and chaotic. War rituals seek to bring order to an uncertain reality and foster a sense of control over the uncertainty of battle among the participants of the ritual. These rituals also contribute to group IDENTITY (over against the 'other' of the enemy), inspire and motivate combatants, and solidify the group's motivations for war. Additionally, in the ancient Near East war was a divinely commissioned act, and many rituals attest to the desire to seek permission and assistance from, and to honour, various deities.

Each pre- and peri-war ritual assumes that present actions, often symbolic and conducted according to specific patterns, can have immediate or future direct effects on the outcome of a battle, or can influence the deity to bless those conducting the ritual(s) and to curse their opponents. The protection of one's army and the desire to ensure success on the battlefield are the primary goals of pre-war rituals. Peri-war rituals, conducted during the course of a battle, seek to influence or change the course of a battle, and may serve to inspire combatants in the midst of battle. Post-war rituals seek to memorialize and commemorate the battle and slain comrades, give thanks to the deity, and cleanse those individuals and objects returning from battle. In this way, order is re-established and individuals and objects are (re)integrated into society. Additionally, the society is protected from contamination and its attendant consequences.

War rituals are acts of performance and multimedia, multisensory (visual, oral/aural, olfactory, bodily movement) experiences that seek to persuade (e.g. the deity), inspire, commemorate, and otherwise influence individuals and outcomes. They are usually performed publicly before an audience (human and divine); include scripted speech, actions, body language, and props; and are often symbolic. War memorials, such as victory stelae and iconographic reliefs, are visual media and symbols of power. They seek to communicate information (e.g. the actions and outcome of a particular king's campaign), praise deities, and influence the audience through the power of written and graphic media.

War Rituals in the Hebrew Bible

The Hebrew Bible describes numerous examples of war rituals, almost all of which have ancient Near Eastern parallels. We may categorize war rituals by their temporal relation to battle: pre-, peri- (during), and post-battle.

Pre-battle rituals are conducted to determine whether an army should go to war, to seek the deity's favour for victory, to prepare friendly combatants for battle, and/or to curse the enemy. Before going into battle, the Israelites sought the permission and blessing of YHWH through an active inquiry via an intermediary, such as a priest (e.g. 1 Sam. 14.36-37; 23.9-12), an object (e.g. an ephod, 1 Sam. 30.7-9), or a prophet (e.g. 1 Kgs 22).

In the ancient Near East, diviners were sometimes employed to bless friendly armies and curse opponents. Numbers 22.1–24.25 reports an ironic example of ritual cursing. The Moabite king Balak employs the seer Balaam to curse the Israelites as they travel through Moab to pre-empt a conflict with the Israelites. Unfortunately, this ritual cursing backfires and Balaam ends up blessing Israel, rather than cursing it. Although the story of Balaam is likely a literary construct, the practice of cursing one's enemies through ritual acts is an attested historical practice.

Execration rituals curse and symbolically defeat an enemy prior to battle. In 2 Kgs 13.14-19, the prophet Elisha instructs the Israelite king Joash to shoot an arrow out of a window. As Joash shoots, Elisha utters a spell: 'Yahweh's arrow of victory, and an arrow of victory against Aram.' Elisha then instructs Joash to strike several arrows against the ground to represent the extent to which Israel would defeat Aram (cf. the use of horns in 1 Kgs 22.10-12). In Jer. 19.1-15, Yahweh tells the prophet Jeremiah to break a clay vessel in front of the Jerusalemites to symbolize how Yahweh would destroy Jerusalem. This act parallels Egyptian execration rituals in which Egyptian priests would write the names of Egypt's enemies on a clay vessel or figurine and smash the vessel while reciting an execration formula.

Battle was considered a sacred event and participants were required to be ritually clean to protect them and to ensure the effectiveness of the ritual – in the case of battle, to ensure victory. Cleansing ensured that an individual was ritually pure, and consecration (often with oil) moved an individual from a profane state of being to a state appropriate for battle (see Purification Rituals). According to Josh. 3.5, the Israelites consecrated themselves before crossing the Jordan and beginning their campaign against the Philistines (see also Deut. 23.9-14; cf. 1 Sam. 21.4-5).

Lastly, the Hebrew Bible and other ancient Near Eastern texts depict warriors performing sacrifices or making vows before battle to garner the deity's support for a campaign. Both Samuel (1 Sam. 7.7-14) and Saul (1 Sam. 13.8-12) make sacrifices prior to battle, though Saul's sacrifice was performed improperly. Jephthah makes a vow prior to leading the Israelites into battle with the Ammonites in which he promises, much to his later regret, to sacrifice the first thing that comes through the door of his house after he returns from battle if Yahweh gives him victory (Judg. 11.19-31). In the Ugaritic tale of King Kirta, Kirta purifies himself and offers sacrifices prior to taking his army on campaign. Additionally, on the third day of his march, Kirta stops at the shrine of Asherah in Tyre, the Goddess of Sidon, and makes a vow offering to give silver and gold if he is successful in capturing a princess from a foreign king to be his bride.

Aside from these pre-war rituals, on some occasions rituals are performed during battle, usually to re-direct the course of the battle. In a battle between the Israelites and the Amalekites (Exod. 17.8-16), Moses stands on a hill and raises the 'staff of God' to aid the Israelites' victory (cf. Exod. 14.16-28). 2 Kings 3.27 describes another peri-battle ritual, in which Mesha, the king of Moab, sacrifices his own son to stem the tide of the battle against the Israelites. This action is apparently efficacious, and the wrath of either Chemosh (the Moabite deity) or Yahweh turns against Israel, forcing the Israelites to retreat.

Post-battle rituals serve several purposes. Some thank the deity for victory and give the deity a share of the spoils, while other rituals purify the combatants and their plunder from the stain of battle. In some ancient Near Eastern cultures, battle made warriors unclean (see e.g. Numbers 31, Hittite post-battle rituals, and Mesopotamian royal inscriptions). In order to return to the camp and reintegrate into society, and to participate in further religious rituals, warriors had to purify themselves. Other rituals were done to bring further harm on the defeated enemy.

After defeating the Amalekites (1 Sam. 15.15-15; cf. 1 Sam. 14.31-35), Saul conducts a post-battle sacrifice apparently intended to devote some of the spoils to Yahweh (v. 21). Numbers 31 records that after battle, warriors, spoils, and captives were to be cleansed and purified to (re)integrate them into Israelite society. Numerous royal inscriptions from Mesopotamia, for example, regarding Yahdum-Lim, Sargon II, Ashurnasirpal II, and Ashurbanipal, refer to making sacrifices and washing weapons and soldiers after battle. According to Num. 31.25-47, a portion is given to Yahweh after the objects are purified. Numbers 31.50

states that the Israelite warriors offered a portion of their spoils to Yahweh to make atonement for themselves, perhaps because killing in battle brought guilt upon an individual.

Mourning for the dead, whether slain warriors or civilians, is another post-battle ritual attested several times in the Hebrew Bible. For example, David mourns Saul and Jonathan's deaths by tearing his clothes, weeping, FASTING, and singing a lament (2 Sam. 1.11-27). Mourning rituals were often communal. Laments are also found in, for example, Pss. 44, 60, and 79; Isa. 14.3-20; Jer. 48; Ezek. 32.1-16; and the book of Lamentations.

Lastly, the commemoration of warfare is a multifaceted performative act sometimes involving songs and the construction of victory stelae. After Yahweh defeats the Egyptians in the Red Sea, Moses and Miriam lead the Israelites in song commemorating Yahweh's victory (Exod. 15.1-21). Similarly, the prophetess Deborah and the military commander Barak lead the Israelites in song after defeating the Canaanites in battle (Judg. 5.1-31). Victory stelae were common throughout the ancient Near East and usually included a prose or poetic narrative commemorating the king's victory (or campaign) and often artistic depictions of aspects of the battle (or campaign). War reliefs, such as those found in Mesopotamia and Egypt, provided detailed depictions of warfare. They often told a graphic narrative commemorating victory over one's opponents and were often placed to influence a foreign audience.

Deuterocanonical War Rituals

The books of 1 and 2 Maccabees describe a number of pre-, peri-, and post-battle rituals related to warfare during the Maccabean conflicts in the Hellenistic period. These rituals show both continuity with biblical rituals and developments not depicted in the Hebrew Bible.

A pre-battle ritual depicted in 1 and 2 Maccabees is a ritual complex including prayer, fasting, sprinkling oneself with ashes, tearing one's clothes, wearing sackcloth, and reading the 'book of the law' (see 1 Macc. 3.44-60; 2 Macc. 10.24-28; 13.9-12; 14.15). On other occasions, only prayers are offered prior to battle (e.g. 2 Macc. 12.28; 15.20-27). 1 Maccabees 4.30-33 depicts Judas praying for victory and cursing the enemy, calling for God to fill the enemy with fear. 2 Maccabees 15.11-16 reports that as Judas prepared the Jews for battle, and as Onias the high priest prayed on the behalf of the Jews, the prophet Jeremiah appeared and gave Judas a golden sword, which was a gift from God to strike down his enemies. The divine giving of a sword prior to battle is referred to in numerous ancient Near Eastern texts (Egyptian and Mesopotamian) and may be the background for Joshua's encounter with the divine messenger in Josh. 5.13-15.

One specific peri-battle ritual is recorded in 2 Maccabees. In 2 Macc. 12.36-37, Judas prays in the midst of a long battle, raises a battle cry, and apparently sings hymns, prior to charging the enemy troops unexpectedly. Post-battle rituals in 1 and 2 Maccabees include mourning rituals, singing hymns and laments, and offering prayers for forgiveness (1 Macc. 2.6-14; 4.14; 9.14-21; 2 Macc. 12.39-45). 2 Maccabees 15.28-35 reports the post-battle humiliation of Nicanor, the enemy commander. Judas orders his troops to cut off Nicanor's head and arm and carry them to priests at the altar in Jerusalem. After cutting out Nicanor's tongue and blessing God, Judas hangs Nicanor's head from the citadel as a sign of God's help. This parallels the Philistines' actions in 1 Sam. 31.8-10 in that after finding Saul's body on the battlefield, they behead his corpse and hang his body from the wall of Beth-shan. Similar actions are attested in Assyrian and Egyptian royal inscriptions and war reliefs.

Jason A. Riley (Fuller Theological Seminary, USA)

Further Reading

Bahrani, Zainab. 2008. *Rituals of War: The Body and Violence in Mesopotamia*. New York: Zone Books.

Kelle, Brad E., Frank Ritchel Ames, and Jacob L. Wright, eds. 2014. *Warfare, Ritual, and Symbol in Biblical and Modern Contexts*. SBL Ancient Israel and its Literature 18. Atlanta: SBL Press.
Klingbeil, Gerald A. 2007. *Bridging the Gap: Ritual and Ritual Texts in the Bible*. Winona Lake: Eisenbrauns.
Smith, Mark S. 2014. *Poetic Heroes: Literary Commemorations of Warriors and Warrior Culture in the Early Biblical World*. Grand Rapids: Eerdmans.

Wax Tablet As a medium, wax tablets were widely used in antiquity for occasional, functional WRITING such as school exercises, household lists, or business accounts. Typically consisting of a wooden frame covered with a layer of wax, and often in the Roman period linked together in a two-paged diptych, writers marked the wax by cutting into it with a pointed stylus. The surface could be renewed by heating and/or by applying new wax.

The imagery of the wax tablet served as a dominant metaphor in antiquity to represent the engraving of perceptions and thoughts upon the human soul. The notion that memory making was visually oriented strongly influenced theorists and practitioners of the memory arts. The wax table model helps modern interpreters understand how the ancients viewed the process of recording memories – including the interior inscription of texts – as the mental writing of images (see MEMORY, GRECO-ROMAN THEORIES OF).

For PLATO, memory functioned like impressions left on wax by a signet ring, with the physical senses triggering the writing of images upon the inner self. Just as the size of the tablet and firmness of the wax's surface could compromise the impression's clarity and stability, so could the strength of an impression or the physical/mental condition of the remembrancer impact the depth and clarity of memories. Plato also believed that before birth the soul perceived eternal, non-material Ideas or Forms. While this knowledge was almost completely erased at birth, leaving behind only faint traces, it remained dormant but recoverable to the memory through dialectical inquiry (*Theaetetus*; *Meno*). Plato thus favoured oral speech's dialectical capabilities over writing, which tended to weaken recollection through dependence on external characters that were often ambiguous in meaning and unresponsive to questioning (*Phaedrus*).

Aristotle retained Plato's essential metaphor but emphasized the imprinting's empirical reality rather than recovery of latent knowledge of Forms, thus more closely anchoring memory to the material world. Weakness in memory could be attributed to physiological impairments. Due to memory's past orientation, Aristotle envisioned its creation as a twofold process of converting the perception to a sense-type image, then to a memory image in the soul (*On Memory and Reminiscence*).

Jeffrey E. Brickle (Urshan Graduate School of Theology, USA)

Further Reading

Coleman, Janet. 1992. *Ancient and Medieval Memories: Studies in the Reconstruction of the Past*. Cambridge: Cambridge University Press.
Small, Penny J. 1997. *Wax Tablets of the Mind: Cognitive Studies of Memory and Literacy in Classical Antiquity*. London: Routledge.
Whitehead, Anne. 2009. *Memory*. The New Critical Idiom. London: Routledge.

Wisdom Collections Collections of wisdom literature have come to be identified as the result of ecclesiastical actions, primarily for purposes of canonization, and of academic processes related to literary classification. Evaluation of wisdom materials begins with decisions about individual texts which then are grouped together for a variety of reasons. One identifying characteristic of wisdom literature in the Hebrew Bible is the presence of the term *ḥokmah*. Out of 153 appearances of this term in the Hebrew Bible, 88 are found in the three books considered to be wisdom compositions: Proverbs, Job, and Ecclesiastes. The same case can be made for the presence of *sophia* in Wisdom of Solomon and Sirach.

This is the primary characteristic that has permitted these five compositions to be designated as the biblical 'wisdom books'. Attempts to use these books as a basis for the identification of common themes or even literary forms that then could be used as criteria for the classification of other wisdom literature have not been successful. However, this collection has been the body of literature most frequently employed in the identification of other wisdom materials. This has been true for the evaluation of materials of the ancient Near East prior to the production of biblical literature as well as for post-biblical literature.

From this vantage point, scholars have viewed wisdom compositions as the creations of a scribal class functioning in royal courts and/or temple administrative contexts. For the most part, they have been viewed as instructional materials for younger SCRIBES coming into some type of official service. This literature could be employed in the intellectual and spiritual formation of persons designated for these roles as well as the development of the technical skills of the administrative roles they were expected to fill. The scribe learnt this material as well as how to record it in WRITING. In this sense, the scribe became both the keeper of the record and its authoritative interpreter. In that role, scribes were responsible for developing the religio-intellectual foundations of the ruling class and the society they produced.

The Ancient Near East

The scribal schools that produced wisdom materials in both Mesopotamia and Egypt were established by the third millennium BCE. In Mesopotamia, children from elite families were drawn into a demanding educational process that had already begun in their homes. In these schools, they learnt the mechanical aspects of scribal production and the larger portion of their output was records of business and administrative matters, though some went on to inscribe religious, scientific, and literary works and to engage in intellectual work on these matters. Egypt similarly had its traditions that were transmitted and cultivated in a scribal institution called the 'house of life', related to but not part of the temple. Instructional materials (*sebayit*) concerning matters of living are evident in the collections of both traditions. The cuneiform tablets of Mesopotamia permitted greater preservation of these materials than the pieces of Egyptian OSTRACA and PAPYRUS.

Hebrew Bible

Although there may be multiple origins for the statements found in a composition such as Proverbs, the productions of the scribal class would have occurred in court and school settings, presumably in similar contexts to those discussed with regard to the ancient Near East. The material of Job and Ecclesiastes points to the uncertainty and questioning that will have emerged within these scribal classes with the decline and end of Israel and Judah. At the beginning and conclusion of the Job narrative, one sees an attempt to reach back to earlier mythology while dealing with the disillusionment of the extant.

Apocryphal or Deuterocanonical Books

The Hebrew version of Ben Sira dates to the early second century BCE and gives clear evidence of a composition written for the production and EDUCATION of scribes, as it is instruction transmitted from an elder to a junior. The context has now shifted to a temple context, perhaps a school setting connected to the temple (see TEMPLE, JERUSALEM). Here we see the production of a worldview that includes the identification of wisdom with Torah, which seems to mean here much more than simply the first five books of Hebrew Bible. Torah wisdom becomes the centre for a worldview that negotiates Jewish IDENTITY in the midst of Hellenistic hegemony. From this centre, the priestly families should operate and the scribal functionaries would provide guidance and direction towards that end.

The Wisdom of Solomon deals with a similar issue; however, in this instance wisdom is retained as the centre of attention. That is, the unique combination of Hebrew tradition and Greek thought in the Wisdom of Solomon does not betray a temple context. Scribal schools will certainly have been part of Alexandrian Jewish life, its most likely point of origin.

Dead Sea Scrolls

Wisdom literature is amply represented in the Dead Sea Scrolls. 4QInstruction is the longest composition and the most amply represented with fragments of at least eight manuscripts. The discovery of this composition has reoriented a good deal of scholarly study of wisdom in Hebrew literature of the second half of the Second Temple period. Present within this composition is an explicit integration of wisdom with eschatology and other themes known from apocalyptic literature (see Apocalypses, Early Jewish). Composed probably in the early second century BCE, the primary addressee throughout the composition is the *meybyn* ('the discerning one') who is taught by the *maskylym* ('sages') about the treatment of parents, wives, masters, etc. With regular reference to this figure as being in a state of poverty, issues of debt are a frequent topic. Craftsmen, farmers, women, and slaves are included among the addressees at various points. There is no evidence of a connection with the elites in this composition. With no exterior text such as Torah cited as an authority, the addressee is enjoined to consider the 'mystery of existence' or 'mystery of what will be'. In this case it is necessary to be among the circles of the *mebynym* to appropriate the revelation of this mystery.

Examination of the sectarian compositions from Qumran, such as the various copies of the Community Rule, the Thanksgiving Hymns, and the Damascus Document, suggests that wisdom-related terminology such as *da`at* ('knowledge'), *'emet* ('truth'), *sekel* ('insight'), and *binah* ('understanding') is central to their ideology and rhetorical strategy. 'The sage is to provide understanding and to teach all of the children of light about the generations of all humankind, about their types of spirits …' (1QS 3.13-14). In other words, only members of the group can understand the full scope of human history and the nature of humanity. In this case, the transmission of scribal knowledge is no longer in the service of the aristocracy, but now reserved for those who belong to a group with a specific understanding of the Jewish way of life and belief that is only available to them.

Scribal production of wisdom during the last centuries BCE becomes much more disparate in terms of literary form and genre and it becomes more difficult (and then impossible) to identify compositions consistent with the trajectory established on the basis of the biblical texts. In the production of early Christian texts we no longer recognize explicit wisdom texts, but find interest in wisdom in texts such as Matthew, James, and the Didache.

John Kampen (Methodist Theological School in Ohio, USA)

Further Reading

Clifford, Richard J., ed. 2007. *Wisdom Literature in Mesopotamia and Israel*. SBL Symposium Series 36. Atlanta: SBL Press.

Kampen, John I. 2011. *Wisdom Literature*. Grand Rapids: Eerdmans.

Perdue, Leo. 2013. *The Sword and the Stylus: An Introduction to Wisdom in the Age of Empires*. Grand Rapids: Eerdmans.

Worship, Ancient Israelite Our understanding of ancient Israelite worship is shaped by two sets of media: biblical texts and archaeological evidence. Both describe a range of worship practices, including ritual performances at central and local shrines as well as secular sites, the recitation of psalms and other prayers, and the inscription, consultation and recitation of material understood to be central to the covenant between Israel and YHWH. In addition, both biblical texts and extra-biblical evidence describe Israelite worship of gods other than YHWH. Within the biblical texts, the description of these practices is framed by, and filtered through, an ideological commitment to the exclusive and centralized worship of YHWH. This entry describes the range of religious practices present in both the archaeological and biblical records, concluding with a discussion of the place of these practices in the COLLECTIVE MEMORY of Jews in antiquity.

Archaeological Evidence for Israelite and Judean Worship

Archaeological excavations in the territories of ancient Israel and Judah have yielded substantial data regarding the media and practices of ancient Israelite and Judean worship in the first millennia BCE. Relevant finds include ritual objects such as altars, model furniture, model shrines, libation vessels and stands, figures of humans or animals, and apparatus for burning incense. These have been found at diverse settings, ranging from domestic sites to regional sanctuaries like those at Horvat Qitmit and Arad to the large sanctuary at Dan. In addition, an array of architectural features such as permanent altars and standing stones, that were likely elements of worship, have been found in non-domestic sites throughout the territory. Written artefacts that include personal names, personal and bureaucratic seals, and, in a few cases, explicitly religious inscriptions also contribute to our knowledge of ancient Israelite and Judean religious practice in this period.

While there continue to be scholarly debates about the proper identification of individual sites and the relevance of particular objects or classes of objects, there is growing consensus regarding the overall portrait of worship demonstrated by the material evidence. The presence of unambiguously ritual objects such as libation vessels and human and animal figurines in a range of sites demonstrates that ancient Israelite and Judean worship was highly decentralized. Forms of worship were practised in homes, local communal sites, larger regional sites, and monumental national sites like Dan and, presumably, the JERUSALEM TEMPLE. The material evidence from these sites suggests that the offering of food, drink, and aromatics was a central medium for Israelite and Judean worship. In domestic sites, the ritual objects have been found in areas where food was prepared and often alongside everyday objects used for food preparation. Remnants of food and drink in bowls on stands and in vessels with special pouring spouts, as well as evidence for the burning of aromatic spices, all point to regular offerings of food and drink. In the more public sites, there is evidence for the sacrifice of animals and the burning of meat as well as grain and liquid offerings.

The material evidence also testifies to other religious practices. EPIGRAPHIC evidence from the region of Samaria testifies to the making of vows, and the burial of real and symbolic objects in graves testifies to ritual care of the dead. Evidence of food consumption and offering has also been found in burial sites, suggesting that ancient Israelites and Judeans practised food offerings to, and ritual meals with, their deceased ancestors. The presence of *astragali* (preserved knuckle bones) at shrine sites also testifies to practices of divination. The presence of vessels inscribed with the Hebrew letters *kof-kaf* (for *kodesh kohanim*, 'set apart for priests') at the fortress shrine at Arad bears witness to the dedication of foodstuffs to the cult.

The archaeological evidence also demonstrates that human and animal figurines, regularly referred to in the Bible as 'idols', were also key media for ancient Israelite and Judean worship. Thousands of animal and human shaped figurines have been found throughout the territories of ancient Israel and Judah. Most of the animal figures are shaped like miniature livestock, while the majority of human figures are pillar-based statues of women, usually holding their breasts. These female figurines have been found primarily at domestic sites and burial sites. Scholars debate the nature of these figurines, especially the pillar-based female statues. While some have identified them as figures of goddesses (Keel and Uehlinger 1998: 193–5), others identify them as symbols of fertility and fecundity, representative of the desired outcome of the worship (Frymer-Kensky 1992: 159), and still others identify them as magic talismans (Dever 2008: 187–8).

While the archaeological record clearly points to the widespread offering of food, drink, and incense to the god/s, as well as the use of votive figures in worship, the identity of the deities to whom this worship was addressed is less clear, not least because the precise religious significance of many extant artefacts is difficult to determine. Examples of this ambiguous data include the many seals and bullae that include ICONOGRAPHY identified with ancient Near Eastern gods other than YHWH, such as solar discs or images of bulls. When found in an Israelite or Judean context, it is difficult to determine whether these images were understood as symbols of gods other than YHWH or as more generic representations of divine powers that were also associated with YHWH. Place names that include *ba'al* or *el* as constitutive elements are another example: such names could be relics of an earlier belief in distinct gods, El and Ba'al, signs of ongoing veneration of these gods, or simply generic names for YHWH or his attributes (Zevit 2001: 594–603).

The strongest evidence for the widespread veneration of YHWH comes from the *onomastica* (lists of names). Surveys of personal names that include or invoke the name of a deity predominantly involve YHWH or El (Tigay 1987: 187). These names also point to worshippers' beliefs or desires regarding the deity and suggest that the granters of these names understood God as their personal deity, responsible for the birth of the child so named and holding the power to protect and sustain her/him. The frequency of the element *eli* ('my god') in these names attests to experiences of strong personal relationship between the worshipper and God (Albertz and Schmitt 2012: 485).

There is also material evidence that ancient Israelites and Judeans venerated a female deity. The most commonly cited pieces of evidence include a tenth-century decorated stand found at Ta'anach and eighth-century inscriptions from Kuntillet Aj'rud in the eastern Negev and Khirbet el-Qom in Judah. The Ta'anach stand has four levels of images: the lowest level shows a naked female figure flanked by two lions, which she is touching with her hands; the next level shows two cherubim; the third level shows two lions again, this time flanking a tree; the fourth level shows an animal, probably a calf or horse, topped by a solar disc, flanked by lions and cherubim. Lions and trees were popular symbols of the goddess Asherah, so it is nearly certain that the female figure on the first level is Asherah. Cherubim and sun discs were popular symbols for YHWH, so it is likely that the upper-most level represents that deity. If these interpretations are correct, then the cult stand from Ta'anach testifies to Israelite worship of YHWH and Asherah jointly. This would suggest that, for the makers and users of the cult stand, YHWH and Asherah were a divine couple, just as Asherah was understood to be the wife or consort of El in Ugaritic literature. The inscriptions however, are more ambiguous. Both make reference to 'YHWH's Asherah'. Scholars continue to debate whether the term *Asherah* in this context is a proper name for the goddess or an anonymous divine consort, or a reference to a powerful symbolic ritual object, as suggested by texts such as 1 Kgs 16:33. Whether or not the inscriptions refer to Asherah or another female divine consort, it is likely that, in the early first millennium BCE, some Israelites and Judeans venerated a female deity associated with, but distinct from, YHWH.

Biblical Depictions of Ancient Israelite Worship

The portrait of ancient Israelite and Judean worship offered in the biblical texts overlaps with, but is not identical to, that which emerges from the material evidence. Biblical descriptions of ancient Israelite and Judean worship focus largely on the centralized worship of YHWH at the portable Tabernacle and, later, at the TEMPLE in Jerusalem. The biblical texts also identify more personal practices such as prayer and vow-taking to be legitimate forms of YHWH worship. While the biblical texts frequently allude to the reality of the decentralized worship of YHWH and other gods, it identifies these practices as catastrophically transgressive.

The Jerusalem temple plays a significant role in descriptions of, and normative prescriptions for, worship in the Hebrew Bible. Because the presumed site of the First/Solomon's temple is now located under a Muslim holy site, there has been no archaeological excavation of it and therefore no material evidence to corroborate, challenge, or augment the biblical descriptions. At the same time, the biblical description of the Jerusalem temple and the rituals performed there are largely typical of state-sponsored cults throughout the ancient Near East. In the ancient Near East, temples were the most prominent and vigorous medium for the representation and worship of gods. Temples were understood to be the earthly palaces of the gods, and their architecture and decoration reflected the deity's power and particular characteristics. As dwelling places for the deity, temples were also sites for worship, which largely took the form of rituals of veneration, supplication, and connection between the worshipper and the god.

The descriptions of the first temple in the books of Kings and Chronicles conform to this broader cultural reality. Solomon's temple is described as a massive structure analogous to the king's palace that stood next to it. The layout of the temple consisted of a series of spaces of increasingly greater degrees of holiness and, correspondingly, of increasingly restrictive access. The courtyards were the most public and stood at the border between the profane space of the surrounding city and the sacred space of the temple interior. The interior spaces of the temple progressed from the outermost, that was accessible to priests and Levites, to the innermost Holy of Holies. As in other ancient divine and human palaces, the focus of the inner sanctum is the throne, described in Exodus 25 as the 'mercy seat'. Whereas in human palaces and other divine palaces the king or a physical representation of the god sat on the throne, in the biblical description YHWH does not reside on the throne in physical form but rather dwelt there in the invisible form of the divine presence.

The temple's iconography, as described in the biblical texts, communicated YHWH's role as creator of the natural world and powerful ruler of the cosmos. The other furnishings of the temple, as described in 1 Kings, are also suggestive of God's dominion. The constellation of the menorah with its floral decorations, the vast basin supported by twelve sculpted bulls, and the iconography of seraphim and cherubim within the temple point to the three zones of the universe – land, sea, and sky – over which YHWH claimed dominion. In addition, the iconography of flora, fauna, and celestial beings also designated the categories of beings over whom God claimed sovereignty. Because the temple was understood to be the site of God's manifestation on earth, it was also the most potent site for the worship and veneration of YHWH. The most prominent forms of this worship were sacrifice and PILGRIMAGE.

According to the pentateuchal texts, regular and occasional sacrifice of animals, grains, and liquids was the primary medium in the worship of YHWH in the temple. While Leviticus locates these instructions regarding these sacrifices in the context of the wilderness wanderings and the Tabernacle, they are usually understood to relate to the sacrificial cult that was performed at the Jerusalem temple. These sacrifices were the primary cultic expressions of the ongoing relationship with God and also could serve as more specific expressions and enactments of gratitude, supplication, and atonement. While our primary evidence for Israelite/Judean animal sacrifice is textual, the description of meat, grain, drink, and incense offerings in the biblical texts resonates with the archaeological evidence for the centrality of such practices in domestic, local, and regional worship sites.

The biblical texts, as well as extra-biblical Second Temple literature, also describe pilgrimage and prayer as additional media for the worship of YHWH. The biblical texts mandate three pilgrimage festivals each year for all Israelite men, *Sukkot*/Tabernacles, *Pesach*/Passover, and *Shavuot*/Pentecost (Exod. 23.14-17; Deut. 16.16-17). These pilgrimages were expressions of the pilgrims' allegiance to YHWH and served to sacralize key moments in the annual agricultural cycle (Deut. 26.1-11). They also provided a means for collecting agricultural tithes (Deut. 14.22-26) and served as occasions for enacting and constructing a sense of national community (Nehemiah 8).

The Bible also attributes a significant role to personal and communal prayer in the worship life of Israelites. Solomon's prayer in 1 Kings 8.12-53 identifies the temple as a site of prayer on behalf of the community, and Nehemiah 9 also describes such a community prayer. The book of Psalms attests to the composition and performance of liturgical material by professional cultic poets/singers. Several of the psalms are attributed (probably belatedly) to 'the leader', presumably a choir leader or lead musician (e.g. Ps. 4.1; 5.1; 6.1; 8.1). Psalms 120–134 bear the superscription 'a song of ascents', suggesting that they were performed during the pilgrimages to Jerusalem mentioned above. The antiphonal format of some psalms (e.g. Psalm 118) suggests that they were sung by groups in cultic settings. In addition, scattered biblical texts describe individual prayer both in both cultic spaces (1 Sam. 1.9-12; 2 Kgs 19.14-19) and secular sites (Gen. 24.12-14; 2 Sam. 7. 17-29).

While both personal and communal prayer were central media for Jewish worship in the Second Temple and rabbinic periods, it is difficult to know how widespread this practice was in ancient Israel and what forms it took. Nevertheless, and as noted earlier, the theophoric names that survive in the epigraphic evidence testify to beliefs in YHWH as a personal protector and provider, themes that are also articulated in many of the biblical psalms and narrative instances of personal prayer.

Both legal and narrative material in the biblical corpus describe vow-taking and the dedication of one's person or possessions to God as media of worship. Leviticus 27 contains a series of laws governing the voluntary consecration of people and property to God, and the chapter ends with mention of a mandatory tithe on crops and herds. There are also narrative descriptions of individuals making vows. For example, Gen. 28.20 shows Jacob vowing allegiance to YHWH if YHWH grants him protection; Numbers 6 describes the Nazirite vow; and 1 Samuel 1 describes Hannah's dedication of Samuel to God as a sanctuary servant. These legal and narrative texts resonate with the material evidence for vows and dedications of property.

The Role of Scripture in Ancient Israelite and Judean Worship

For people familiar with the role of sacred writings in contemporary Judaism and Christianity, it is often difficult to internalize the paradoxical fact that the religion described in the scriptural texts of the Hebrew Bible was not a scriptural religion. As mentioned earlier, temples and shrines, not scrolls, were the primary loci of the divine presence in ancient Israel and Judah, and religious professionals like priests and prophets were the primary repositories and arbiters of the divine will. That being said, the biblical texts themselves do testify to the existence of a body of material known as the *Torah* ('authoritative teaching') and these texts enjoin the Israelites to study and obey this teaching. However, this *Torah* was not primarily textual, nor was it identical to any single written text or textual collection in the modern sense. While there is thus no 'bible' in the Bible, the biblical texts do testify to the growth of ideas and practices that laid the groundwork for the emergence of a canonical Jewish Scripture in the Second Temple period. Whether, when, and to what extent this Torah and the written texts that came to encode it were aspects of Israelite worship is less clear.

The book of Deuteronomy and other texts produced by the deuteronomic school (e.g. Psalm 1) insist that knowledge of the *Torah* of God is crucial because this instruction articulates the stipulations of the covenant on which Israel's survival depends. However, in most of the relevant texts, *Torah* is represented as primarily pedagogical – that is, as instruction in how to behave according to the will of the deity. Engagement with *Torah* is not, in and of itself, viewed as an act of worship. For example, in Deuteronomy 6 Moses enjoins the Israelites to recite the divine instructions, 'When you stay at home and when you are away, when you lie down and when you get up'. He further enjoins them to 'bind them as a sign on your hand and let them serve as a symbol on your forehead, inscribe them on the doorposts of your house and on your gates'. In later Judaism, these injunctions were interpreted literally and translated into the practices of thrice-daily prayer (which includes recitations from Scripture) and the affixing of *mezuzot* to doorposts and the binding of phylacteries to one's forehead. But the earliest evidence for these practices, which clearly involve written texts of Scripture, comes from the Second Temple period; Deuteronomy, by contrast, portrays the recitation, inscription, and display of the words of the divine instruction as mnemonic strategies, designed to remind the Israelites of God's will so that they will not deviate from it.

It is only in the Second Temple period text of Ezra-Nehemiah that a *Torah* scroll is portrayed as functioning both as a pedagogical source and as a tool for worship. In Nehemiah 8, the members of Ezra's community of returned exiles gather to hear a ritual recitation of words of *Torah*. In this scene, the Torah scroll is treated as both a locus of the divine and as a source of divine instruction. The people treat the scrolls as objects: when they see them, they raise their hands in prayer and prostrate themselves (Neh. 8:5-8). In this scene and the one that follows, a text of the Torah of Moses/Torah of God serves as a source for divine instruction and access to the divine will. This representation of Torah as both a source for revealed knowledge and a sacred object testifies to the beginnings of the scripturalization of Torah in the Second Temple period. The biblical collection also bears witness to the process by which a diverse array of material became scripturalized, laying the foundations for Judaism and Christianity's understanding of the entire scriptural collection as the 'word of God'. It is likely that the legal material in Deuteronomy as well as material in the early prophets are among the earliest written materials to be identified as God's Torah. When Deuteronomy mandates that the king shall have a 'copy of this teaching written for him' (Deut. 17.18) and that the 'Israelites shall inscribe every word of this teaching' on stones at Mt Ebal (Deut. 27.8), the authors likely had in mind some or all of the laws contained in Deuteronomy.

Reflecting this evolving perspective, in Deuteronomy, Ezra-Nehemiah, a number of Psalms, and passages in Proverbs engagement with God's word as articulated by Levites and other sages is considered a medium for worship. In Nehemiah 8–9, texts of the Torah of Moses are also deployed in worship. Scattered texts in Psalms and Proverbs point in a similar direction. Psalm 1, for example, states, 'Happy is the man who has not followed the counsel of the wicked … the *torah* of the lord is his delight and he recites that teaching day and night'.

Decentralized Worship in/and Scripture

Like the archaeological evidence, the biblical texts testify to decentralized worship of YHWH and other gods throughout Israel and Judah. Various biblical texts describe Ba'al worship as a practice that occurred from Israel's sojourn in the wilderness (Num. 25.1-9) through the pre-monarchic period (Judg. 2.10-13; 1 Sam. 7.2-4) and into the periods of the kingdoms of Israel and Judah (1 Kgs 16.31-33; 2 Kgs 21.3). In addition to Ba'al worship, the biblical texts describe Israelite veneration of Asherah (1 Kgs 18.19; 2 Kgs 23.4). There are also references to Israelite worship of Ashtarot in the pre-monarchic period (e.g. Judg. 2.13). In addition, biblical texts refer to Israelite/Judean worship of Molech (2 Kgs 23.10) and Judean worship of the Queen of Heaven (Jer. 7.17). The texts also describe Israelite worship at cultic sites outside of Jerusalem. 1 Kings 12.25ff derides the construction of a national shrine in the kingdom of Israel. Various texts, primarily those in the deuteronomic history, also admit to non-centralized worship of YHWH and other deities both in Israel and Judah: 'They too built for themselves shrines, pillars, and sacred posts on every high hill and under every leafy tree' (e.g. 1 Kgs 14.21-23). Other texts narrate the use of visual representations of deities in Israelite and Judean worship (2 Kgs 18.4; 2 Kgs 21.7; 23.4-7).

While the archaeological record testifies to the normative and public nature of these decentralized and pluralistic religious practices, the biblical texts, especially those that represent a deuteronomic perspective, decry these practices as heretical and catastrophically transgressive. The biblical collection is overwhelmingly dominated by texts that identify monotheistic worship of YHWH as the original and solely authentic form of Israelite and Judean worship. According to the pentateuchal narrative, Abram/Abraham entered into a covenant with YHWH that established YHWH as the god of Abraham and his descendants (Gen. 17.1-14). Within the narrative of the Pentateuch, this covenant with Abraham's clan becomes the foundation and forerunner of YHWH's covenant with Israel (Exod. 19.11-8). This covenant explicitly demands exclusive worship of YHWH (Exod. 20.3). While the legal texts of the Pentateuch identify extensive terms of this covenant, texts reflecting a deuteronomic perspective (Deuteronomy, Kings, Jeremiah) elevate the exclusive worship of YHWH as the key practice that determines Israel's destiny (e.g. Deut. 6.10; 8.19; 2 Kgs 21.1-15). These deuteronomic texts identify the worship of gods other than YHWH as either foreign practices – most notably practices of non-Israelite people indigenous to the land of Canaan – or as heretical deviations from original and authentic Israelite worship. In addition, the deuteronomic texts assert that the proper worship of YHWH is centralized in a single location (Deut. 12), identified in non-pentateuchal texts as the temple in Jerusalem. The texts of the biblical collection also assert that proper worship of YHWH is aniconic, stressing that there are no, and cannot be, legitimate visual representations of YHWH (Exod. 20.4-6; Exod. 32.1-7; 1 Kgs 12.25-33).

The discrepancy between the material evidence for the normativity of these practices and the biblical condemnation of them can be illuminated by both the presumed authorship of the biblical texts and the role that worship assumed in the CULTURAL MEMORY of post-exilic Judah. While the Bible contains texts from a wide time period and diverse geographical locations, it is likely that most were produced by authors affiliated with the priestly or governmental elite. As such, the portrait of ancient Israelite religion in the Hebrew Bible represents the perspectives and interest of these parties. This perspective is most influential in biblical judgements regarding orthodox and deviant religious practice.

If we assume that the authors of the textual material were affiliated with the court and the temple, then the perspective articulated in the texts makes sense. Scholars have long argued that the paired tropes of monotheism and centralized worship align with the interests of the Jerusalem court (Meyers 1994: 360–1). As was the case in much of the ancient Near East, the national god was understood to be the patron deity of the king, and the king was understood to be the deity's regent on earth. Thus, the YHWH-only monotheism of much of the biblical collection is not only an argument for YHWH's authority but is also an argument for the authority of the Davidic king with whom YHWH is identified (2 Samuel 7; 1 Kgs 9.1-9). In addition, the centralization of worship in Jerusalem concentrated priestly power and the economic engine of tithes and sacrifices in the national cult. Both the biblical narratives and the so-called 'royal psalms' assert that YHWH is the patron god of the Davidic house. Within this royal theology, YHWH both validates the Davidic line and also promises to act on behalf of the Davidic kings (2 Samuel 7; 1 Kgs 9.1-9; Psalm 2, 72, 89, 110, 132). Within a pre-exilic context, the commitment to centralized, exclusive worship of YHWH can be understood as a religious perspective that aligns with the political interests of the likely authors of early strata of the biblical material.

The priestly descriptions of temple worship present a parallel situation. These texts, which not only describe the centralized sacrificial cult but also assert its unique validity, assert a privileged role for the priests and Levites and lay out practices that would provide for their livelihood. If, as is most likely, the authors of the priestly texts were associated with the priesthood either before, during, or after the exile, it is not surprising that these texts would support the crucial role and authority of the Jerusalem priests.

The disavowal of non-centralized, non-exclusive worship assumes a central role in the collective memory enshrined in the later, post-exilic strata of the biblical texts. Whereas in the earlier strata of texts this position aligned with the interests of priestly and royal scribes, after the conquest of Judea by the Babylonians this perspective became a crucial element of the covenantal ideology that was repeatedly asserted to explain the fall of Judah. Within the latest strata of the biblical texts, non-exclusive worship practices are represented not just as religiously 'unorthodox' but as catastrophic transgressions of divine will that led to the demise of the kingdoms of Israel and Judah.

Ancient Israelite Worship in Jewish Cultural Memory

As noted above, it is likely that there are both alignments and divergences between biblical depictions of ancient Israelite and Judean worship and the actual worship practices of ancient Israelites and Judeans. However, by the last centuries of the first millennium BCE, the worship prescriptions and descriptions articulated in scriptural texts became the subjects of interpretive reflection and litmus texts for sectarian debates regarding religious practice. This is true even as Second Temple Era Jews continued to produce texts that make claims to authority similar to those found in the texts that eventually would become canonical for rabbinic Judaism and Christianity. Books included in the DEAD SEA SCROLLS and the NT demonstrate how Jews of the period used textual discourse about practice to justify particular forms of belief and observance.

After the destruction of the Second Temple in 70 CE, the central pillars of the biblical descriptions of ancient Israelite and Judean worship became central elements in the ongoing CULTURAL MEMORY of Jews, even as these practices were necessarily replaced by other modalities of worship. Most crucially, the temple and its cult continued to be vital elements in the Jewish consciousness in late antiquity even centuries after the temple's destruction. Much of the MISHNAH is devoted to discussion of temple rituals and to rules of purity that are relevant only in a context where there is a functioning temple cult. In addition, mishnaic discussions of non-cultic matters, especially marriage and inheritance, perpetuate the special status of members of the priestly (and, in some cases, Levitical) lines. For example, even though the priesthood no longer functioned in a cultic capacity, male members of the priestly line are still forbidden from marrying divorced women and coming into contact with corpses. The sacrificial system is also identified as the basis and rationale for the structure of later Jewish prayer. In addition, the liturgical calendar described in the biblical texts becomes the basis of the Jewish liturgical calendar. While there was dispute among Second Temple Jewish groups regarding whether the calendar was strictly lunar or was lunar–solar, the basic liturgical calendar described in the Pentateuch became the calendrical framework of all forms of Judaism in late antiquity and beyond. All forms of Judaism organized time according to cycles of seven-day weeks (each culminating in a SABBATH), months (each beginning with a festal day), and years, marked by the three pilgrimage festivals and the additional festivals of Rosh Hashana and the Day of Atonement.

The worship practices that are authorized as legitimate within the biblical texts had the greatest impact on Jewish collective memory and worship practice. However, some worship practices that are acknowledged but discredited by the biblical texts, or are hinted at by the archaeological evidence, were also present in later Jewish worship and theology. Most notably, ancient Jewish magical texts and artefacts testify to ongoing belief in supernatural beings other than YHWH, and also to the iconic representation of deities or other supernatural beings on ritual objects. Similarly, while all known forms of early Judaism limit worship to a single deity (YHWH) who is understood to be male, the development of the rabbinic idea of the *shekhinah*, the feminine immanent presence of God, can be understood as the trace and transformation of ancient Israelite/Judean goddess worship.

Elsie R. Stern (Reconstructionist Rabbinical College, USA)

Further Reading

Albertz, Rainer, and Rüdiger Schmitt. 2012. *Family and Household Religion in Ancient Israel and the Levant*. Winona Lake: Eisenbrauns.

Dever, William. 2008. *Did God Have a Wife?: Archaeology and Folk Religion in Ancient Israel*. Grand Rapids: Eerdmans.

Frymer Knesky, Tikva 1992. *In the Wake of the Goddesses*. New York: Free Press.

Keel, Othmar, and Christoph Uehlinger. 1998. *Gods, Goddesses, and Images of God in Ancient Israel*. Minneapolis: Fortress Press.

Meyers, Carol. 1991. *Discovering Eve: Ancient Israelite Women in Context*. New York: Oxford University Press.

Tigay, Jeffrey. 1987. 'Israelite Religion: The Onomastic and Epigraphic Evidence'. In *Ancient Israelite Religion: Essays in Honor of Frank Moore Cross*. Edited by P. D. Miller, P. D. Hanson, and S. D. McBride. Philadelphia: Fortress, pp. 157–94.

Zevit, Ziony. 2001. *The Religions of Ancient Israel: A Synthesis of Parallactic Approaches*. London: Continuum.

Worship, Ancient Jewish *Worship* translates the Hebrew term *'avodah* (lit. 'work, service'). Initially, *'avodah* described the sacrificial rites and ancillary rituals of the temple in Jerusalem, particularly those acts overseen or enacted by the priests (*kohanim*) and Levites, as described initially in the Hebrew Bible and later in rabbinic writings such as the MISHNAH, Tosefta, and Talmuds. In the centuries following the destruction of the JERUSALEM TEMPLE in 70 CE, the term *'avodah* was broadened to include the statutory prayers and rituals that were understood to substitute for temple practices. By the Middle Ages, such prayers were primarily associated with the SYNAGOGUE, but the term may be used more broadly to describe Jewish ritual life and piety in general, including domestic practices that are overtly religious in nature (e.g. lighting SABBATH candles) or less obviously so (e.g. the maintenance of a kosher home). Given the nature of Jewish liturgical sources, most of which postdate the Tannaitic period (= after 220 CE), and the development of Jewish liturgy in the rabbinic context, this article will not only examine early sources (from the mishnaic period and before) but also consider Jewish worship in the synagogue context into the period of late antiquity (see RABBINIC LITERATURE).

Jewish Worship in the Second Temple Period

While the term *Jewish worship* suggests a certain amount of uniformity, in practice Jewish prayer and liturgy reflect the historical diversity of Jews. Like Judaism itself, modes of worship have transformed dynamically over time. Pre-exilic sources stress the importance of the sacrificial cult, but the significance of liturgical (or proto-liturgical) texts should not be underestimated. Such works include not only the brief petitions to the deity found in the Pentateuch (e.g. Gen. 20.17, 25.21; Deut. 9.20-26) but also the paradigmatic prayer of Hannah in 1 Samuel 2 (which became, for the rabbis, the model for the custom of praying *sotto voce*), the lengthy prayer by Solomon at the dedication of the first temple (1 Kgs 8), and the book of Psalms. Persian and Hellenistic Jewish writings, in turn, display a particularly keen interest in prayer and pietistic practices, such as the penitential prayers of Ezra (Ezra 10.1) and Nehemiah (Neh. 1.4-11), the FASTING of Esther (4.16; expanded by numerous prayer-insets in the Greek version of the text), and the depiction of Daniel as one who, with 'his windows … open in his chamber toward Jerusalem … kneeled upon his knees three times a day, and prayed and gave thanks before his God' (Dan. 6.11; see also the confession in Daniel 9). Perhaps most significantly, Nehemiah 8 describes the ceremony of reading from the Torah in the public square with Levites passing among the people to clarify its sense – perhaps indicating the birth of the practice of translating Scripture in the synagogue (see TARGUMS) or explicating its meaning (*midrash*). These sources together create a picture of a Judaism that, by Hellenistic times, was profoundly interested in liturgical rituals beyond the temple.

The liturgical materials from Qumran shed important light on the development of Jewish prayer and ritual during the Second Temple period, as do literary sources such as Philo (e.g. his writings on the THERAPEUTAE) and non-canonical works such as Tobit, 1 ENOCH, 4 Ezra, and JUBILEES. The liturgy of the Samaritan community likewise provides an important counterpoint to what would become mainstream (rabbinic) Jewish liturgy, as do movements such as Hekhalot mysticism within mainstream (rabbinic) Judaism. The dynamic relationship between Jewish worship in antiquity and nascent Christian ritual has also received significant attention from scholars. The overall emerging picture is one of great fluidity and complexity.

Jewish Worship in the Rabbinic Context

Jewish worship cannot be directly equated with the ritual praxis depicted in the Hebrew Bible (see WORSHIP, ANCIENT ISRAELITE). Neither, however, can the study of Jewish worship be separated from biblical studies, in that the rituals most associated with rabbinic Judaism both derive from and deploy biblical texts. Our understanding of the development of Jewish worship and liturgy is complicated by the fact that almost all of our knowledge comes from rabbinic literary sources that reflect a distinctive attitude and agenda. With this caveat, it may be said that, in the biblical context, *worship* primarily describes the cultic offerings associated with the Jerusalem temple or other cultic sites; with the destruction of the temple by the Romans in 70 CE, however, this sacrificial system was suspended. In the absence of the temple, and justified by the biblical statement, 'We will render the bullocks of our lips' (Hos 14.3), the rabbis substituted prayer for sacrifice (see *NumR* 18.21; *PdRK Shuvah* 24; *b. Yoma* 86b). This blurring of prayer into worship is not without precedent in the biblical text itself: the book of Psalms includes passages that favour prayer over sacrifice (40.7-10; 51.19; 69.31-32), while others assert their equivalence (119.108; 141.2). The new status of prayer does not mean that prayer was itself innovative; the rabbis were careful readers of the biblical text and attuned to the contexts and rhetoric of prayer and worship practices as they appeared in Scripture, both as individual practices and communal rituals, independent of the temple cult and alongside it. In addition to prayer, study of the biblical text, a feature of Jewish piety from the time of the Babylonian exile if not earlier (not only Neh. 8, but also throughout Deuteronomy), became a central component of Jewish worship in Second Temple times, with the ceremony for reading from the Torah scroll becoming a centrepiece of synagogue ritual (see TORAH READING).

Furthermore, while the basic framework of the Jewish liturgy was established by the early centuries of the Common Era, and largely codified by the eighth century CE, rabbinic hegemony over matters of worship was challenged by the Karaite ('scripturalist') movement, which also began during the eighth century in Baghdad. While Rabbanite (rabbinical) and Karaite liturgy had much in common (particularly the order and themes of many prayers), the Karaites rejected rabbinic liturgical compositions and favoured instead the use of biblical quotations as prayer texts. Anan ben David (ca. 715–85), one of the founders of Karaism, stipulated that prayers should consist only of Psalms and scriptural passages. Despite this ruling, Karaites eventually began to compose their own original prayer texts, much like their Rabbanite opponents. In the Middle Ages, various localized rites, broadly classifiable as Ashkenazic and Sefardic traditions, developed, and the prayer book was continually adapted to reflect broader religious trends, whether Kabbalistic, rational, or postmodern.

Even within the limits of rabbinic Jewish liturgy, historical development is a crucial factor. Significant uncertainties linger concerning the early period of the development of synagogue liturgy, which began to take shape when the temple in Jerusalem still stood and probably focused on the reading of Torah. Over subsequent centuries, new liturgies were created as additional ritual occasions were created and developed. Materials recovered from the Cairo Genizah highlight the long period of fluidity and liturgical creativity and complicate the portrait, presented in rabbinic literature, of a hierarchical imposition of a statutory liturgy. The claim that Rabbi Simeon ha-Pakuli 'arranged the eighteen benedictions in order before Rabban Gamaliel in

Yavneh' (*b. Berakot* 28b) is an Amoraic memory of a Tannaitic event understood to record the composition of the *'Amidah* – the central prayer of the Jewish service (the existence of which is assumed by the Mishnah); this text was, according to tradition, subsequently promulgated to and accepted by the Jewish community. Yet in all likelihood, the actual process of creation and codification was far more complicated, with some elements of the service being transferred from temple ritual while others were gradually innovated and then codified. Furthermore, the rabbinic structuring of the liturgy would have been one element of the gradual, general spread of rabbinic authority in liturgical matters, a process that has been a subject of much dispute in recent decades. It is likely that in the Tannaitic period the liturgy itself was still quite fluid and that in its fullest form, recognizable today, its use was limited primarily to rabbinic communities – likely a small subset of the Jewish population in the early centuries CE.

At the same time, the existence of fixed prayers (particularly the Shema) seems to have been widespread in Judaism in antiquity. There is evidence for morning and evening liturgies (which, like rabbinic prayers, may have specifically substituted for the temple cult) from Qumran, and the term *proseuchē* – the most common term for a synagogue outside the NT, appearing roughly thirty times in Josephus, Philo, and Egyptian papyri – specifically refers to a prayer space. Likewise, the Mishnah (e.g. the opening of *m. Berakhot*) assumes that prayer rituals existed side by side with the temple's rites. Indeed, it may be that in the post-70 CE Jewish world the 'rabbinic innovation' (reflecting the same impulse as seen at Qumran, if not the direct influence) was the synthesis of extant and evolving prayer structures with the idea of substitution for sacrifice. In any case, the basic framework and language created in the rabbinic period, both in the land of Israel and Babylonia, took hold with sufficient consistency to permit reference to a mainstream Jewish worship by the eighth or ninth century CE, despite the localized differences among communities in the medieval period and in modern Jewish movements.

Rabbinic Liturgy

For all its differences from Israelite worship as depicted in the Hebrew Bible, Jewish worship understands itself as a direct continuation of earlier forms of piety. Just as biblical sources indicate prayers offered at specific times of day (twice a day in 1 Chron. 23.30; three times a day in Dan. 6.11), *m. Ber* 4.1 assumes the existence of thrice-daily prayer rituals (*shacharit* in the morning, *minchah* in the afternoon, and *ma'ariv* in the evening) while connecting other rituals (e.g. the morning Shema) to the temple daily calendar. In rabbinic parlance, prayer is termed 'worship (*avodah*) of the heart' (*b. Ta'an* 2a), transferring the 'worship' of the temple to the synagogue (*m. Ber* 4.1; *b. Ber* 26a). At the same time, the rabbis distinguish the obligation to pray from other scriptural obligations such as sacrifice, noting that 'prayer (*tefillah*) is a rabbinic ordinance' (*b. Ber* 21a).

The first tractate of the Mishnah, on the subject of 'Blessings' and dealing with a variety of liturgical matters, domestic and public, includes a variety of prayer texts and practices, both personal (those of individual sages) and communal. The prayer known as the *'Amidah* ('the standing prayer'; also known as the *Shemoneh Esreh*, that is, 'the eighteen benedictions', or simply *ha-tefillah*, 'the prayer') was specifically understood to substitute for the temple offerings, to be recited fully (first silently and then aloud) in the morning and afternoon each weekday, with an additional recitation on the Sabbath and holidays, in place of the additional (*musaf*) offering. The *'Amidah* is recited silently in the evening, in order to complement the evening recitation of the Shema, a prayer which is a composite of biblical texts (Deut. 6.4-6, 11.13-21; Num. 15.37-41). The association of the *'Amidah* with the temple is underscored by the fact that one faces the temple when praying it (*m. Berakot* 4.5). The absence of the precentor's repetition in the evening derives from the fact that there were not evening sacrifices in the temple. While recitation of the Shema is not part of biblical worship per se, as early as the Mishnah (*m. Ber* 1.1) the timing of its recitation was connected to temple rituals, and after 70 CE that connection continued to forge an IDENTITY between Jews who worshipped in the temple and those who worshipped in its absence.

While the timing and occasion of rabbinic prayer was connected to temple rituals, biblical texts became both a source and resource for the composition of new liturgical texts. Psalms which were associated with Levitical rituals in the temple, such as the daily psalm (see *m. Tāmîd* 7.3-4) and the HALLEL (*m. Pes* 10.5; *m. Sukk* 4.8), were translated into synagogue ritual, while other biblical texts not previously part of temple worship were also incorporated in whole or in part into various stations of the liturgy. Biblical poems such as the Song at the Sea (Exodus 15) became rabbinic liturgical texts. Even more pervasively, biblical allusions texture the language of rabbinic prayer, particularly liturgical poetry (*piyyut*), and lend innovative liturgical language depth and resonance (see POETRY IN THE HEBREW BIBLE). Furthermore, the ceremony for reading from the Torah scroll, along with complementary passages from the Prophets (the *haftarah*) – a custom dating from before 70 CE – forms a central part of synagogue ritual (see TORAH READING). While rabbinic ruling permitted the recitation of prayers in the vernacular (*m. Sot.* 7.1-2), the dominant language of prayer remained Hebrew, in part because it was considered God's own language and thus more effective (see *b. Shabb* 12b) but also because Hebrew was 'the language of the sanctuary' (*Targum Pseudo-Jonathan* to Gen. 31.47) and thus rooted in the world of the temple. Indeed, as Hebrew became less and less readily comprehensible, prayers in Hebrew may have been perceived as more and more numinous and holy. At the same time, the retention of Hebrew underscored the link between synagogue ritual and the world of the Bible and the temple, thus reflecting an impulse to reinforce a sense of continuity with and connection to the political and religious worlds of pre-70 CE and also to forge a Jewish identity unified by a common prayer language even as the diaspora expanded.

Just as the organization and language of prayer in the synagogue reflects both continuity with biblical traditions and accommodations of post-temple circumstances, Jewish liturgical traditions acknowledge the history of priestly leadership in worship while radically democratizing most ritual functions. A number of liturgical poems from late antiquity commemorate the traditions of the twenty-four priestly watches, and the Mishnah states that 'for the sake of peace' a priest receives the honour of reading first from the Torah scroll, a Levite reads after him, and an Israelite third (*m. Gittin* 5.8). Recitation of the Priestly Blessing (Num. 6.24-26), in a ritual known as 'lifting of the hands' (*nesi'at kapayim*), likewise remained a prerogative of the priestly line. At the same time, leadership of the routine liturgy simply required fluency with the prayers. More decisive in many respects was the requirement that many of the key rituals of Jewish worship require a prayer quorum (*minyan*) of ten adult males. Without this critical mass, many rites (including communal recitation of the Shema and *'Amidah*, the priestly blessing, ritual reading of the Torah and *haftarah*, mourner's *kaddish*, wedding liturgy, or the full Grace after meals) could not be conducted (see *m. Meg* 4.3). The practice of requiring a quorum for such rites underscores the fundamentally communal nature of Jewish worship, as opposed to the largely individual and family-based orientation of biblical sacrifice and prayer.

The Jewish liturgy as we now possess it emerged only after centuries of fluidity and development, with distinctive customs differentiating rites in the land of Israel and Babylonia in the Tannaitic and Amoraic eras (as well as Hellenistic and Roman Alexandria) and, in later centuries, localized rites throughout the diaspora. In general, the Palestinian-Jewish rite seems to have been particularly fluid, with the Torah cycle lasting three to three and a half years (the so-called 'triennial' cycle), new liturgical poems embellishing the Sabbath and holiday prayers, and Aramaic translation practices varying widely. Conversely, the Babylonian rite seems to have been typified by a preference for uniformity and hierarchy, as a consequence of the authority of the rabbinic academies located there. Rav Amram ben Sheshna Gaon, the head of the Academy in Sura, authored the first prayer book (*seder*) in the ninth century CE; the academies likewise favoured a single 'authorized' Aramaic translation (*Targum Onqelos*), and they vigorously opposed the inclusion of liturgical poetry, which would have made the service more varied. The Babylonian community read the entire Torah scroll in a single year (the annual cycle), with the result that significantly more time was devoted to the recitation of the biblical text in Babylonian rite synagogues than in their Palestinian counterparts.

The Mishnah assumes the existence of statutory liturgical structures even in temple times (such as the recitation of the morning *Shema*, the opening topic of the MISHNAH), and understands the *'Amidah* to also be very early (*m. Berakot* 4.3). It is unclear precisely how and when the prayer texts became firmly established, however, as the Mishnah also stresses the fluidity and dynamism of prayer (*m. Ber* 4.4). One school of thought, associated with Ezra Fleischer, argues that the dynamic liturgical innovations of Jewish Late Antiquity in the Land of Israel reflect a rebellion against an extant fixed ritual, while another approach, associated with Joseph Heinemann, asserts that the liturgy crystallized slowly over time: first orders of prayers, then fixed benedictions, and finally fully fixed wording. While in modern settings the liturgy is recited from a printed text, in antiquity the liturgy would have been improvised or recited from memory. Likewise, the translation of Scripture (see TARGUMS) would have been an oral performance, perhaps based on a studied script, and a cantor would have performed the liturgical poems, perhaps with participation from the community and/or a choir. The lack of written scripts resulted in significant local variation in medieval Jewish ritual, particularly in terms of the poems selected to embellish various services. For all the significance of textuality in understanding the history of Jewish prayer texts and religious rituals, actual worship ritual would have been largely an oral (and aural) phenomenon.

Texts, Contexts, and Exegesis

Whether encountered in written or spoken form, through sight or by hearing, Jewish worship is deeply grounded in biblical material. While many of the words of the prayer book reflect a post-biblical context and are written in the same Hebrew as the Mishnah and many midrashic compendia, the most powerful words of the liturgy often come directly from the Bible.

The *Qedushah*, which names the combination of Isa. 6.3 and Ezek. 3.12, exemplifies the importance of biblical language in the context of Jewish worship. The potency of these words derives from their origin in the biblical text, where they appear as angelic words overheard by mortal prophets. Due to their heavenly origin, the utterances in these two verses were regarded as superior to mortal compositions. The quotation of Isa. 6.3 and Ezek. 3.12 in the liturgical context permitted the human congregation to join with the heavenly hosts in the act of praising God. These verses played an important part in early Jewish liturgy; Qumran liturgical texts (including the Songs of the Sabbath Sacrifice) allude to Isa. 6.3 in a fashion which seems to preserve its exclusively angelic purview, while Isa. 6.3 also became a standard part of the Christian liturgy, where it was known as the *trisagion* ('thrice-holy') or *sanctus*. In rabbinic Judaism, too, enthusiasm for the *Qedushah* appears to have been widespread; rabbinic rulings limiting its recitation to occasions when a prayer quorum (*minyan*) of ten adults was present underscore an enduring desire on the part of individuals to perform this text more frequently than the statutory liturgy allows.

While the *Qedushah* was particularly significant, a number of other liturgical texts were lifted whole cloth from their original biblical contexts and knitted together into new compositions. These compositions were often structured on the basis of shared themes or, most effectively, common words, in a technique of composition called *florilegia* ('word-bouquets'). *Florilegia* are attested in Judaism very early on: one can consider the *Shema* a kind of *florilegium*, as well as the texts inserted in phylacteries and *mezuzoth*, and the GENRE is also attested at Qumran (4QFlorilegium). In rabbinic Judaism, the *florilegium* was particularly popular as a method for composing penitential prayers, such as *selihot*. While most often *florilegia* quote the language of the Bible verbatim, in some instances the quotations are adapted (e.g. altered from being in the singular 'I' to the plural 'we') to suit the liturgical context. Comparison of MANUSCRIPTS makes it clear, furthermore, that individual compositions could be lengthened, shortened, or rendered more elaborate in different communities even while the same basic structure was retained.

In addition to direct quotation of complete biblical verses, other liturgical texts were composed through a careful knitting of brief phrases or even allusions to biblical texts. In particular, Jewish liturgical poetry (*piyyut*) draws its vocabulary from the biblical text, but not in a straightforward biblicizing style. Whereas the Qumran *Hodayot* hymns follow the biblical psalms closely, Hebrew liturgical poems (*piyyutim*) represent a radical departure in terms of style and form. The classical *Qedushah*, for example, weaves together the language of the weekly Torah portion, the *haftarah*, and the liturgical eulogies of the *'Amidah* into a single composition. As a result, poems shared a roughly similar structure from week to week but also reflected the specific lectionary of that Sabbath's scriptural readings. The language of the Torah portion and *haftarah* inflected the language of these *piyyutim*, but so, too, did the language of other verses which (in a style resembling *florilegia*) were quoted verbatim after specific poetic units. These verses often prove to be midrashic intertexts, associated with the Torah portion by means of rabbinic biblical interpretation, and as a consequence the *piyyutim* firmly wed the language of the Jewish prayer service to the content of Torah study.

In addition to the central prayer rubrics of the Shema (a composition created out of biblical verses) and the *'Amidah* (a rabbinic text recited in place of the biblically mandated sacrifices), reading from the Torah scroll held pride of place in the synagogue as a commemorative ritual. The ceremony surrounding the Torah reading, as presented in the Tosefta (*t. Meg* 3.11) and Palestinian Talmud (*y. Meg*. 4.1-2) and developed during the Middle Ages, can be understood to recreate the revelation at Sinai in a fashion similar to the way that the Christian EUCHARIST enables participants to experience the Last Supper for themselves. As early as the period of the restoration of the Jews to the land of Israel under Persian rule (as seen in Nehemiah 8), however, rehearsal of the Torah text has been accompanied by diverse forms of explication and interpretation, notably translation into the vernacular (as in the Aramaic targums), exegesis and homily (as in the *midrashim*), and liturgical embellishment (as in the *piyyutim*).

The rituals of Jewish worship cannot be separated from the physical and sensory contexts in which they took place, although the non-textual elements of rituals are often difficult to recover and, in the case of Jewish worship, varied significantly depending on the majority culture among whom Jews lived. With regard to the period when the rabbinic liturgy and literatures crystallized, abundant SYNAGOGUE mosaics and frescoes dating from the third to seventh centuries CE depict scenes from the Bible, images of the temple, and cosmological phenomenon such as the zodiac, significantly enriching modern understandings of how the biblical text and liturgical rituals were experienced by and taught to Jews in the rabbinic period. Funerary ICONOGRAPHY has likewise proven an important source of insight into Jewish identity in antiquity, as well as offering insight into the nature of burial rituals among Jews in the Greco-Roman and Byzantine worlds. Other elements of early Jewish worship, however, such as how the liturgical poems were performed, remain far more speculative, with scholars having to work primarily by analogy from non-Jewish sources, including Greco-Roman oratory and theatre and what is known from early Christian ritual. The study of Jewish ritual and liturgy is increasingly recognized as a highly interdisciplinary field.

As the above discussion indicates, Jewish worship emerged from, and developed in, an ongoing dynamic relationship with the biblical text and its ongoing traditions of interpretation. The Bible itself records diverse religious practices, including those of the Jerusalem temple; in turn, the biblical text provided language for articulating the replacement of sacrificial rituals with liturgical prayer and study. Over the centuries, Jewish worship has been typified by patterns of tradition and innovation, with biblical language deeply texturing, enriching, and authenticating new liturgical compositions, ranging from late ancient liturgical hymns to medieval mystical meditations to modern compositions. Jewish worship bears little overt resemblance to worship as described in the Hebrew Bible, but is fundamentally a product of biblical textuality and interpretation.

Laura S. Lieber (Duke University, USA)

Further Reading

Elbogen, Ismar. 1993. *Jewish Liturgy: A Comprehensive History*. Translated by Raymond Scheindlin. Philadelphia: Jewish Publication Society; New York: Jewish Theological Seminary of America.

Fine, Steven. 2005. *Art and Judaism in the Greco-Roman World: Toward a New Jewish Archaeology*. 2nd edn. Cambridge, UK; New York: Cambridge University Press.

Langer, Ruth. 1998. *To Worship God Properly: Tensions between Liturgical Custom and Halakhah in Judaism*. Cincinnati: Hebrew Union College Press.

Levine, Lee I. 2000. *The Ancient Synagogue: The First Thousand Years*. 2nd edn. New Haven: Yale University Press.

Reif, Stefan. 1993. *Judaism and Hebrew Prayer: New Perspectives on Jewish Liturgical History*. Cambridge: Cambridge University Press.

Worship, Early Christian *Early Christian worship* refers to the various expressions of Christian ritual life and piety that spanned the public and private spheres over the course of the first four centuries of the Common Era. While the term suggests a certain amount of consistency, uniformity, and standardization, in practice Christian ritual life was a highly variegated phenomenon across time and space. How converts were initiated into the community, for example, could take on a wide range of practices (see INITIATION RITUALS). In the initiation practices of churches located in Eastern regions of the Roman empire, initiates were often divested of their clothes and anointed with oil, only later to be followed by a water BAPTISM and then a first EUCHARIST (Ps-Clement LXVII). The significance of the pre-baptismal anointing could range from purifying the loins to EXORCISMS, and was often thought to carry revelatory power (Acts of Thomas 27; cf. Jas 5.13-18). According to Hippolytus, the Oil of Exorcism was applied during the pre-baptismal exorcism, while the Oil of Thanksgiving was applied in two subsequent stages; first, upon the initiate's emergence out of the water an elder anointed the naked body; and, second, upon returning to the church the bishop anointed their foreheads (Hippolytus, *Apostolic Tradition* 21). By way of contrast, churches located in the Western regions of the Roman empire maintained a long tradition of refraining from anointing the initiate until after they were baptized (*Didascalia Apostolorum* xlix). This diversity of early Christian initiation practices was due, at least in part, to the lack of any geographical centre or source of authority whereby standards of normativity were dictated, allowing geographically separate communities to develop a wide array of distinct theological and liturgical traditions. The Christian liturgical rite was standardized across regions only after centuries of innovation, adaptation, and development.

Due to the impressive diversity of forms found within early Christian worship, a concise survey simply will not do justice to the impressive range of practices and texts. Therefore, this entry will focus on a central feature of early Christian worship practices, especially as it relates to the multimedia context of antiquity, namely, that early Christian worship provided a context for the communication of information, serving as a medium for the transmission of tradition. As memory theorist Paul Connerton demonstrates, commemorative rituals provide the opportunity for those assembled to invoke and rehabilitate in their present time those major events that played a formative role in the history of their own community (see COLLECTIVE MEMORY; CULTURAL MEMORY). Were we to neglect the commemorative nature of early Christian rituals, we would neglect their mnemonic power and the critical role they played in transmitting traditions of early Christianity. Through COMMEMORATIVE rituals a community is reminded of its own IDENTITY as represented by and communicated through its MASTER NARRATIVE. The following discussion will focus on ways that the master narratives of individual Christian communities was conveyed and sustained by their ritual performances in worship.

Throughout the Hellenistic world, meals played a central role among voluntary associations, including the not-so-easily distinguishable trade guilds, religious groups, political assemblies, and funerary societies. Christ cults were no exception to this trend, which is why issues pertaining to meals, such as dining etiquette and conflict, dietary additions and restrictions, and idealized banqueting motifs and metaphors occur so frequently throughout the surviving literature and art (see BANQUET). Just how such meals may have functioned within each of these settings is an issue of central importance in ongoing scholarly debate. What is clear, however, is that such communal meals served a central role in organizing and facilitating early Christian gatherings.

Two instances in the PAULINE LITERATIVE make explicit reference to meals, Gal. 2.11-14 and 1 Cor. 10–11. Taken together, these passages evidence regular meal-sharing practices in three separate Christian communities – Antioch, Galatia, and Jerusalem. There is further support that the church in Rome also regularly attended such meals (Rom. 14–15). Acts 2.42 ('They devoted themselves to the apostles' teaching and fellowship, to the breaking of bread and the prayers') has long served as the archetype of early Christian worship. While this model may be attractive for modern conceptions of liturgy, it is deemed by many scholars to function as an idealization with more to do with the representational interests of the author than the apostolic age. It does, however, succinctly summarize the interfaces within early Christian gatherings between the practice of eating and the commemoration of tradition ('the apostle's teaching'), which were intricately tied and played a central role in defining a critical aspect of early Christian worship practices. The custom of organizing at table for regular meals provided a common context in which groups told stories, which could serve a variety of ends, not least to engage in the performance of their shared collective memories (see PERFORMANCE OF THE GOSPELS).

In 1 Cor. 10–11, Paul refers to the practice of participating in common meals. The meal commemorates the one Jesus presided over on the night of his arrest and which he admonished the attendees to continue (1 Cor. 10.16-17; 11.20-29). The practice of customary meal-sharing is intricately tied to the commemoration of Jesus' death to such an extent that Paul claims, 'As often as you eat this bread and drink the cup, you proclaim the Lord's death until he comes' (11.26; see EUCHARIST). Memories of Jesus' death, however, seem to be tied to a much broader commemorative narrative that draws on covenantal language, including references to the story of the exodus, wandering in the wilderness, and entrance into the land (10.1-18). Therefore, through the commemorative ritual of sharing a meal together, the Corinthian community is reminded of its own identity as it is represented by, and communicated through, its master narratives (10.1-22). This passage thus illustrates ways in which early Christian worship practices provided believers an occasion to tell stories about their shared past.

According to Paul, these meals were supposed to remind the Corinthians of their collective IDENTITY and shared SOCIAL MEMORY at a time of much division in the community. The Corinthian Christ-followers appear to have been in a state of negotiating issues pertaining to the cult's policies of consuming meat. That there is discord around the discussion seems consistent with the numerous other points of contention evidenced in the letter. The significance of the conflict has absolutely nothing to do with restrictions on eating meat in general, nor does it have anything to do with the meat itself in an ontological sense. Rather, the meat becomes an issue of contention as a result of its symbolic encoding through its affiliation with civic TEMPLE sacrifice. Paul charges the Corinthian Christ-cult to introduce dietary consciousness, which would ritually maintain certain boundaries with sacrificial institutions, and likely construct an identity that was in contradistinction to the civic sphere. Thus, abstaining from certain sources of meat would effectively eliminate all chance of monetarily supporting these organizations, while at the same time performing an alternative identity within the meal setting itself. Paul offers correctives that carry implications beyond the prescription of better eating habits. It is his goal to instil an even more prominent ethos of self-subordination with concern for neighbour as the meta-ethic. He encourages that ritual adjustments be made by having meat-eating occasionally cease whenever anyone from the community raises questions on account of her/his conscience. The community is, in turn, encouraged to respond to the objector with great sensitivity and solidarity. Thus, the determinative factor when it comes to marking dietary boundaries is not Law, cult legends, nor tradition, but the ever-adjusting conscience of cult members.

The process of encoding meals with particular significance was pervasive in the ancient Mediterranean, central to the social life of all groups no matter what class, ethnicity, or religious identification. Food was good to think with. As Mary Douglas famously points out, 'If food is treated as a code, the messages it encodes will be found in the pattern of social relations being expressed. The message is about different degrees of hierarchy, inclusion and exclusion, boundaries and transactions across the boundaries. Like sex, the taking of food had a social component, as well as a biological one' (Douglas 1972: 61).

That ritual meals were generative for the production of early Christian knowledge of self through the performance of commemorative discourses is confirmed later in the letter: following Paul's discussion of the meal in chapters 10–11, he proceeds to address issues pertaining to the assemblies, which were likely connected to the meals and which included formal addresses, prayers, singing, and thanksgiving (14.1-33). This conforms to expectations of the types of activities associated with the symposium that served as the second major component of communal meals in the Hellenistic world. Various modes of discourse characterized early Christian worship, which may have developed in symposia-like settings. The NT attests to these in mentioning prayer (1 Cor. 11.4-5), thanksgiving (Eph. 5.20; Heb. 13.15), hymns and songs (Eph. 5.19), and instruction (1 Cor. 14.26; Col. 3.16). The SEPTUAGINT may have been read as in the developing synagogue liturgies (see TORAH READING), or it could have been performed in some way that it entered into the discursive texturing and composition of Christian prayers. Biblical verses and phrases were regularly taken from their original contexts and put together into new compositions.

One of the most salient characteristics of early Christian communities was that they expressed themselves through songs whenever they assembled together, which could also serve as a method for the transmission of Christian knowledge production and performances pertaining to the recitation of the commemorative narrative (see HYMNS). Communal singing was thought to serve as a witness to an individual's possession of the Spirit and membership in the community. Ephesians provides a glimpse into the musical world of the early Christians, admonishing the community to 'sing psalms and hymns and spiritual songs among yourselves, singing and making melody to the Lord in your hearts; giving thanks to God the Father at all times and for everything in the name of our Lord Jesus Christ' (5.18-20). A number of the songs produced by early Christians were remembered in the church for centuries, some even embedded in the literature of the NT, such as the Christ Hymn of Philippians 2, the Canticle of Mary in Luke 1, and the apocalyptic songs in Revelation 4 and 5. Further references include Mt. 26.30; Acts 16.25; Rom. 15.9; 1 Cor. 14.15; Col. 3.16; Eph. 5.18-20; and, Heb. 2.12.

In conclusion, early Christian texts reflect a significant diversity in the range of embodied practices and discursive modes practised over the first four centuries of the Common Era. There are myriad ways of relating such practices to the multimedia context of antiquity in which the surviving texts were both produced and consumed. After all, early Christian texts were not composed in a media vacuum, nor at a desk by an isolated scribe, but likely grew out of a sensory and physical communal space that proved to be generative for the production of early Christian knowledge and traditions. Early Christian worship possessed a significant amount of commemorative power, as it served as a medium for the recitation of collective memories, which asserted the past's continued relevance over the evolving present.

Drew W. Billings (Hobart and William Smith Colleges, USA)

Further Reading

Aitken, Ellen Bradshaw. 2004. *Jesus' Death in Early Christian Memory: The Poetics of the Passion.* Göttingen: Vandenhoeck & Ruprecht.
Aune, David E. 1992. 'Worship, Early Christian'. In *The Anchor Bible Dictionary*. Vol. 6, Edited by David Noel Freedman. New York: Doubleday, pp. 973–89.
Bradshaw, Paul F. 2010. *Reconstructing Early Christian Worship*. Collegeville, MN: Liturgical Press.
Connerton, Paul. 1989. *How Societies Remember*. New York: Cambridge University Press.
Douglas, Mary. 1972. 'Deciphering a Meal'. *Daedalus* 101: 61–81.
McGowan, Andrew B. 2014. *Ancient Christian Worship*. Grand Rapids, MI: Baker Academic.
Smith, Dennis E., and Hal Taussig, eds. 2012. *Meals in the Early Christian World: Social Formation, Experimentation, and Conflict at the Table*. New York: Palgrave Macmillan.

Writing and Writing Materials Writing is first attested in human history around 3200 BCE, with the evidence suggesting that it began in Mesopotamia at that time and in Egypt a generation or two later. These early Mesopotamian and Egyptian writing systems were non-alphabetic. However, around the eighteenth century BCE, alphabetic writing was invented by Semites familiar with the writing system(s) of Egypt. The first alphabetic writing system is referred to as Early Alphabetic (or Proto-Canaanite, or Proto-Sinaitic; see ORTHOGRAPHY). Linear Early Alphabetic persisted for several centuries before the Phoenicians standardized it during the late second millennium BCE. Although the Phoenician Alphabet was first used in the Phoenician city-states of Lebanon, it soon became the prestige script and is attested widely throughout much of the Levant and the larger Mediterranean world. Therefore, it is not surprising that the script in which the ancient Israelites used to write inscriptions during the tenth century BCE was the Phoenician alphabet. However, by the ninth century BCE, a distinctive Old Hebrew alphabet is attested in both Israel and Judah, with some of the inscriptions from Tel Arad (e.g. Arad Ostracon 76) and Tel Rehov (e.g. the ink and incised jar inscriptions from Stratum IV) hailing from this period and written in the Old Hebrew script (Aharoni 1981; Ahituv and Mazar 2014).

Writing in Ancient Israel and the Early Second Temple Period

Of the extant Old Hebrew inscriptions hailing from Israel and Judah during the First Temple period and the early Second Temple period, most are written on various forms of pottery, though this was not an exclusive writing surface. Sometimes these inscriptions were written on complete (unbroken) pots, either with ink (using a reed pen, cf. Jer. 8.8) or with a sharp incising instrument (normally of metal, cf. Jer 17.1; 19.24). These inscriptions are referred to as 'jar inscriptions'. Sometimes a seal (often with a personal name or place name) would be impressed into the leather-hard clay of a jar during the process of the jar's manufacture. These inscriptions are referred to as *jar impressions* (see also POTTER'S MARKS). Because broken pieces of pottery were so readily available in antiquity, it was common for ancient scribes to use ink to write on potsherds (distinct from writing on complete pots that were subsequently broken, as noted above). The technical term for an ink inscription on pottery is *ostracon* (pl. OSTRACA). Sometimes inscriptions were incised into broken pieces of pottery using a metal instrument. These are referred to as *pottery inscriptions* or *incised pottery inscriptions*. Inscriptions falling into these four categories (jar inscriptions, jar impressions, ostraca, and pottery inscriptions) are the most common types of inscriptions from the First Temple period and the early Second Temple period (Reisner, Fisher, Lyon, 1924; Aharoni 1981; Tur-Sinai, Harding, Lewis, Starkey, 1938; Beit-Arieh 1999).

PAPYRUS was probably the most common writing medium for official documents, record-keeping, and legal contracts, necessitating the use of a scribal knife (Jer. 36.23) as part of the scribal tool kit (Ezek. 9.2, 3, 11). Nevertheless, the climate of the Levant is not conducive for the survival of papyri; therefore, the Murabba'at Papyrus is a very rare example of a papyrus from the First Temple period (Milik 1961). The ELEPHANTINE PAPYRI and the Samaria Papyri hail from the fifth and fourth centuries BCE and constitute fine exemplars of papyri during the early Second Temple period. Not surprisingly, these are written in Aramaic. Bullae are small pieces of clay that were used as part of the process of sealing a papyrus (or leather) document. A few hundred bullae have been found in Israel and Judah and date to the First Temple period, demonstrative evidence of inscriptions on papyri (Avigad and Sass 1997).

There is no direct evidence regarding the main writing material for long texts used in ancient Israel before the period attested by the Judean Desert documents. Both leather and papyrus were in use in Egypt at a very early period, but it is not impossible that leather was preferred in ancient Israel because it was more readily available than papyrus, which had to be imported from faraway Egypt. It has therefore been suggested that leather was used for the writing of the oldest biblical SCROLLS, a conclusion consistent with Jeremiah's reference to Jehoiakim cutting the columns of Baruch's scroll exactly at the sutures (Jer. 36.23). At the same time, a few allusions in Scripture suggest that papyrus served as the main writing material during the First Temple period, even though no biblical papyrus texts have been preserved from that era and the Qumran corpus contains very few biblical papyrus copies (see Haran 1982).

Stone inscriptions are also attested, including one that seems to have been used for scribal training (Rollston 2012). Inscriptions on plaster are also attested in the First Temple period, with some of the inscriptions from Kuntillet Ajrud demonstrative of this practice (Ahituv, Eshel, Meshel 2012). Inscriptions on metal are also attested, with those from Jerusalem's Ketef Hinnom being among the most important (Barkay, Vaughn, Lundberg, Zuckerman 2004).

The quality of the majority of the Old Hebrew inscriptions from Israel and Judah during the First Temple period is very high, reflecting the fact that SCRIBES, scribal stone-masons, and seal makers had substantial training in scripts, orthographic conventions, the use of hieratic numerals (attested in both Israel and Judah on various inscriptions), and letter formulary (Rollston 2006). The inscriptions produced by those not formally trained in the scribal craft are readily notable for their poorer quality.

Writing and the Documents from the Judean Desert

The writing materials used in the production of the Judean Desert documents (including the DEAD SEA SCROLLS) are very similar to the materials used in the earlier period. The great majority of the texts from the Judean Desert were written on leather and papyrus (the latter comprise some 14 per cent or 131 texts of the 930 Qumran texts). In addition, a large number of ostraca were found, especially at Masada, but also at Murabba'at (Mur 72–87, 165–168), NAHAL HEVER (8Hev 5–6), Nahal Mishmar (1Mish 4–8), as well as at Khirbet Qumran (KhQ Ostraca 1–3) and Qumran cave 10 (10QOstracon). Other materials are used more sparingly.

The use of different writing materials at the various sites in the Judean Desert corresponds to differences in GENRE among the documents found at these locations. The great majority of the literary texts included in the corpora found at Qumran and Masada were written on leather, while papyrus was used for most of the documentary texts, such as LETTERS and various administrative texts, found at Nahal Hever, Nahal Se'elim, Wadi Murabba'at, and the other sites. At the same time, in ancient Egypt and the Greco-Roman world, papyrus was the preferred material for texts of any kind, and writing on various forms of leather was far less frequent.

Although literary works from the Judean Desert were mainly written on leather, many papyrus copies of these compositions are also known, albeit probably without any distinctive features at the content level. The papyri found at Qumran were written during the period of settlement of the Qumran community as well as by several generations prior to that time. At the same time, one of the texts from Wadi Murabba'at, namely the two layers of the palimpsest papyrus Mur 17 (A: papLetter; B: papList of Personal Names), is much earlier, as its two scripts have been dated to the eighth or seventh century BCE. Papyri from Wadi ed-Daliyeh contain fourth-century BCE contracts in Aramaic. Papyrus probably was considered less durable than leather, and the papyri from the Judean Desert appear to be less professional (lines are less straight and no neat column structure can be observed). On the other hand, it was easier for scribes to remove letters from an inscribed papyrus than from leather. Papyrus may therefore have been preferred by some scribes, but it was probably the availability of the writing material that determined the choice of either papyrus or leather, although in the case of the biblical texts, additional factors must have played a role (see below). It is not impossible that papyrus was the preferred medium for private copies of literary compositions, including the many non-biblical compositions discovered at Qumran, especially sectarian texts. It has also been suggested that, during the early stages of their residence at Qumran, the members of the Qumran community may have found it easier to obtain papyrus scrolls from external sources than to produce leather scrolls themselves.

The writing of Scripture on papyrus is forbidden in the rabbinic literature, as indicated, for example, by *m. Meg.* 2.2: 'If it was written with caustic, red dye, gum, or *copperas*, or on paper (i.e. papyrus), or *diftera*, he [the scribe] has not fulfilled his obligation; but only if it was written in Assyrian writing, in a (leather) scroll and with ink' (cf. *y. Meg.* 1.71d). The rabbis viewed that Moses received oral instructions from God on Mt. Sinai that one could write on skins. Additional research is needed to determine from which animal skins the various texts from the Judean Desert were prepared. Partial evidence is available regarding calves, fine-wooled sheep, medium-wooled sheep, wild and domestic goats, gazelles, and ibexes (see PARCHMENT). The sole detail mentioned in rabbinic sources is '… that one should write on the skins of pure domestic and wild animals' (*Sof.* 1.1 = *Massekhet Sefer Torah* 1.1). These considerations suggest that the few Qumran biblical texts written on papyrus did not derive from a milieu that was influenced by the later rabbinic understanding. These instructions were formulated at a later period than the writing of the Qumran papyrus scrolls, but it may be assumed that the Talmudic traditions reflected earlier customs that would have been already followed during the time of Qumran occupancy.

When referring to leather writing materials among the Judean Desert documents, scholars use different terms for the animal skins prepared for writing: skin, hide, PARCHMENT, and leather. There is no firm knowledge regarding the preparation stages, locally and elsewhere, of the leather and papyrus fragments found in the Judean Desert (see Bar-Ilan 2000: 2.996). It is not impossible that the skins from which some Qumran leather documents were prepared were immersed in basins at Ein Fashkha. Other scholars suggest that the process of refining these skins took place at Qumran, but there is no solid evidence in support of this assumption. There is also some evidence for the existence of a tannery at Masada. The tanning techniques applied to the manuscripts found at Qumran were discussed by Haran (1985), who considered the Qumran scrolls to be 'basically parchments, but with moderately tanned surfaces to facilitate writing'.

Rabbinic descriptions distinguish between three types of leather: *gevil* (the thick leather inscribed on the hairy side), *kelaph*, and *dukhsustos* (see Glatzer 2002: 63–4). The latter two are different layers of the same leather that are split apart and prepared differently: *kelaph* is inscribed on the flesh side and *dukhsustos* on the hairy side. Glatzer believes that most of the Qumran scrolls are relatively thick, of the *gevil* type, inscribed on the hairy side. Such is also the instruction in rabbinic literature for Torah scrolls: 'One writes on the hairy side of the skin' (*Sof.* 1.8 and *y. Meg.* 1.71d; cf. *Massekhet Sefer Torah* 1.4). On the other hand, the very thin scroll 11QT[a] (11Q19), of the *kelaph* type, was inscribed on the inside of the skin (the flesh side).

Regardless of the medium (papyrus or skin), it stands to reason that the approximate length of the composition was calculated before writing commenced; with this information, the required number of sheets could be ordered from a manufacturer or prepared to fit the size of the composition. Subsequently, the individual sheets were ruled and inscribed and only afterwards stitched together. The calculation of the number of sheets needed for copying a composition could never be precise, as evidenced by several instances of ruled columns left uninscribed following the final inscribed column of a sheet. The fact that some ruled sheets were used as uninscribed handle sheets (e.g. the final sheets of 11QT[a] and 11QShirShabb) and that some uninscribed top margins were ruled (the second sheet of 1QpHab) shows that the ruling was executed in a process separate from the writing. The numbering of a few sheets probably indicates that they were inscribed individually, to be joined subsequently based on the numerical sequence. On the other hand, some sheets must have been joined before being inscribed.

A further indication of the separate preparation of individual sheets is the different nature of the two surviving sheets of 1QpHab. The first sheet (cols. I–VII) contained regular size top margins of 2.0–3.0 centimetres, while the top margins of the second sheet (VIII–XIII), measuring 1.6–2.0 centimetres, contain one, two, or three uninscribed ruled lines. Since ruled lines are visible in the top margin of the second sheet, while all other sheets from Qumran compositions have unruled top margins, it is evident that the manufacturer of this scroll used an existing ruled sheet of larger specifications than needed for the second sheet of this scroll. When preparing this scroll, he cut the sheet to the size required, in the process removing the unruled top margin of that sheet, and using the ruled area as a top margin.

As noted earlier, in Palestine as well as in the broader ancient Near East stones were used as writing material, inscribed with a chisel or a sharp engraving tool. Less frequent was the writing on stone with ink, sometimes after the surface was first prepared for writing. A well-known specimen of the latter is the so-called Gabriel (or Jeselson) stone that contains a series of prophecies written on a stone probably in the first century BCE. Inscribed weights and seals were also made from stone, often a precious stone. Ostraca, or potsherds, were often used as a medium for writing brief messages, lists, or names. Several ostraca from the Late Second Temple period have been preserved in Qumran and many in Masada (see Lemaire 2003). Most of the inscriptions on clay were written on vessels, indicating the identity of the owners or the contents (see Lemaire 2003 on items from Qumran). Two extant texts were inscribed on wooden tablets: 5/6Hev 54 (P. Yadin 54) and Mas 743 from 73 or 74 CE (Masada II, 90).

Only the two Copper Scrolls from Qumran cave 3 are known to have been inscribed on that material, which is much more durable than papyrus or leather. Holes in the scroll were either meant to tie the scroll with a string to a certain fixed place or to keep it firmly closed.

Although there is variation in the media used for writing and also in the quality of the writing and the orthography, it can be said that the production quality of the documents from the Judean Desert is generally high. The quality of these texts is highlighted by comparison to Second Temple inscriptions on ossuaries. While some ossuaries are inscribed in a beautiful, high quality formal script, many are poorly inscribed, with a fairly high percentage of orthographic problems, inconsistent spacing, and idiosyncratic script morphology. It is reasonable to suggest, therefore, that most of the documents from the Judean Desert were produced by individuals who were trained in the scribal arts, while a fair number of the ossuaries were produced by those without such formal training.

Writing in Early Christianity

Turning to early Christian writing practices, one observes obvious shifts in the choice of writing materials. One example is the complete abandonment of leather: unlike their Jewish predecessors and rabbinic counterparts, the early Christians had an apparent preference for papyrus, which was already the predominant writing material in the Greco-Roman world. The earliest Christian manuscripts, containing both Scripture and non-Scripture, are written on papyrus. Even the finest extant specimens, such as the famous Chester Beatty and Bodmer Papyri, are written on papyrus, which demonstrates a contrast with the Judean practice of using papyrus predominantly for documentary texts. Unlike the leather scrolls of the Judean Desert, papyrus manuscripts were not ruled, and so margins tend to be less defined.

By the fourth century CE, and certainly thereafter, parchment became the standard writing material, even though papyrus continued to be manufactured and used. Made from animal skins through a long process of scraping, stretching, and drying, parchment was a more durable material than papyrus, which had the potential of tearing more easily with time and extended use. The famous Christian Greek manuscripts of the fourth and fifth centuries, such as Codex Sinaiticus, Codex Vaticanus, and Codex Alexandrinus, were all written on finely manufactured parchment.

Another marked difference from Jewish scribal practices was the Christian abandonment of the scroll format. Instead, the early Christians preferred the CODEX, which involved writing on both sides of a page that could be 'flipped', similar to the form of modern books. Despite some images of SCROLLS in Christian ICONOGRAPHY, the codex became a permanent feature of Christian book production. It appears that the earliest example was the so-called *single-quire* codex, which involved folding a single stack of multiple sheets of papyrus. The *multi-quire* codex, which was more complicated to produce, eventually became the standard. This type of codex was produced by folding individual gatherings of sheets (usually four sheets at a time), stacking the folded sheets on top of one another, and then stitching them together.

In the late antique period, Christian scribes made use of many different kinds of writing materials and for various purposes. Christian amulets, ritual artefacts that were considered by their owners to be imbued with divine power, were frequently made from individual pieces of papyrus or parchment (often inscribed with Scripture) that were worn for protection. Liturgical texts, prayers, and doxologies are attested on papyrus, parchment, and ostraca in great numbers. In some cases, mere scraps of material containing brief textual excerpts are preserved, making it difficult to determine their function. In the early twentieth century, a linen shroud containing a single logion from the Gospel of Thomas was discovered near the city of Oxyrhynchus in Egypt.

Scriptures intended for liturgical use continued to be copied by professional scribes, but there is an enormous amount of evidence demonstrating that Christian literature was copied by semi-illiterate scribes and even students. In addition to the various Greek and Latin inscriptions one finds in places such as the catacombs of Rome, Greek and Coptic textual GRAFFITI are attested in Christian monasteries in Egypt. These examples demonstrate the wide range of written media utilized in early Christianity.

Emanuel Tov (Hebrew University of Jerusalem, Israel), Christopher Rollston (George Washington University, USA), and Brice C. Jones (University of Louisiana at Monroe, USA)

Further Reading

Aharoni, Y. 1981. *Arad Inscriptions*. Jerusalem: Israel Exploration Society.

Ahituv, S.; ane Mazar, A. 2014. 'The Inscriptions from Tell Rehov and their Contribution to the Study of Script and Writing during Iron Age IIA'. In *Epigraphy and Daily Life from the Bible to the Talmud: Dedicated to the Memory of Professor Hanan Eshel*. Edited by Esther Eshel and Yigal Levin. Journal of Ancient Judaism Supplements 1. Göttingen: Vandenhoeck and Ruprecht, pp. 39–68.

Ahituv, S., Eshel, E. and Meshel, Z. 2012. 'The Inscriptions'. In *Kuntillet 'Ajrud (Horvat Teman): An Iron Age II Religious Site on the Judah-Sinai Border*. Edited by Zeev Meshel. Jerusalem: Israel Exploration Society, pp. 72–142.

Avigad, N. and B. Sass. 1997. *Corpus of West Semitic Stamp Seals*. Jerusalem: Israel Exploration Society.

Bar-Ilan, Meir. 2000. 'Writing Materials'. *EDSS* 2: 996–7.

Barkay, G., A. G. Vaughn, M. J. Lundberg, and B. Zuckerman. 2004. 'The Amulets from Ketef Hinnom: A New Edition and Evaluation'. *BASOR* 334: 41–71.

Beit-Arieh, I. 1999. *Tel Ira: A Stronghold in the Biblical Negev*. Nadler Institute of Archaeology Monograph Series 15. Tel Aviv: Yass Publications in Archaeology.

Glatzer, Mordechai. 2002. 'The Book of Books: From Scroll to Codex and into Print'. In *Jerusalem Crown, The Bible of the Hebrew University of Jerusalem*. Edited by M. Glatzer. Jerusalem: N. Ben-Zvi Printing Enterprises, pp. 61–101.

Gropp, D. 2001. *Wadi Daliyeh II: The Samaria Papyri from Wadi Daliyeh. DJD* 28. Oxford: Oxford University Press.

Haran, Menahem. 1982. 'Book-Scrolls in Israel in Pre-Exilic Times'. *Journal of Jewish Studies* 33: 161–73.

Haran, Menahem. 1985. 'Bible Scrolls in Eastern and Western Jewish Communities from Qumran to the High Middle Ages'. *HUCA* 56: 21–62.

Lemaire, André. 1992. 'Writing and Writing Materials'. In *Anchor Bible Dictionary* vol. 6. Edited by David Noel Freedman. New York: Doubleday, pp. 999–1008.

Lemaire, André. 2003. 'Inscriptions de Qumrân et Aïn Feshkha'. In *Khirbet Qumrân et Aïn Feshkha II: Études d'anthropologie, de physique et de chimie*. Edited by Jean-Baptiste Humbert, Jan Gunneweg. Novum Testamentum et Orbis Antiquus 3. Göttingen: Vandenhoeck& Ruprecht, pp. 259–306.

Milik, J. T. 1961. *Les grottes de Murabba'at. DJD* 2. Oxford: Oxford University Press.

Reisner, G. A, C. S. Fisher and D. G. Lyon. 1924. *Harvard Excavations at Samaria: 1908-1910, Vol. 1: Text*. Cambridge, MA: Harvard University Press.

Rollston, Christopher A. 2006. 'Scribal Education in Ancient Israel: The Old Hebrew Epigraphic Evidence'. *BASOR* 344: 47–74.

Rollston, Christopher A. 2012. 'An Old Hebrew Stone Inscription from the City of David: A Trained Hand and a Remedial Hand on the Same Inscription'. In *Puzzling Out the Past: Studies in Northwest Semitic Languages and Literatures in Honor of Bruce Zuckerman*. Edited by M. J. Lundberg, S. Fine, and W. T. Pitard. Cultural History of the Ancient Near East 55. Leiden: Brill, pp. 189–96.

Tov, Emanuel. 2004. *Scribal Practices and Approaches Reflected in the Texts Found in the Judean Desert*. STDJ 54. Leiden: Brill.

Tur-Sinai (Torczyner), H., L. Harding, A. Lewis, and J. L. Starkey. 1938. *Lachish I (Tell ed-Duweir): The Lachish Letters*. London: Oxford University Press.

Y

Yavneh/Jamnia Yavneh (Greek name: Jamnia) is a small city (pop. <40,000) in Israel near the coast, 25 kilometres (about 15.5 miles) south of Tel Aviv. According to rabbinic sources, during the first several decades after the TEMPLE's destruction in 70 CE, Yavneh served as the meeting place for a group of Jewish sages (see RABBINIC LITERATURE). Since the late nineteenth century, scholars have often attributed to these Yavnean sages the final closing of the Jewish biblical CANON, and less frequently also the standardization of the Hebrew text of Scripture and certain measures designed to effect a separation between Jews and Christians, though the ancient sources do not explicitly connect Yavneh with such acts. At one time scholars commonly characterized this meeting of sages as a Council or Synod of Yavneh.

Yavneh appears in several pre-rabbinic sources (e.g. Josh. 15.11, 'Jabneel' [cf. 19.33, a different Jabneel]; 2 Chron. 26.6; 1 Macc. 5.58; 2 Macc. 12.8–9, 40; Philo, *Embassy to Gaius* 200). According to legend, at the time of Jerusalem's destruction, Vespasian granted Yavneh 'and its sages' to the early rabbi Yoḥanan ben Zakkai (*b. Giṭ.* 56b; Lapin 2012: 43–4, 49–51). The sages discussed various halakhic issues (cf., e.g. *m. Sanh.* 11.4; *Šeqal.* 1.4; *Kelim* 7.6; *'Ed* 2.4; *Roš Haš.* 2.1–7) in the 'vineyard' of Yavneh (e.g. *m. Ketub.* 4.6), sometimes called the *bet ha-midrash* (e.g. *m. Yad.* 4.4) or *yeshiva* (e.g. *m. Yad.* 3.5). They first collected their traditions there (*t. 'Ed.* 1.1), before the centre of rabbinic authority transferred to Usha in the mid-second century. Cohen (1984) has argued influentially that Yavneh represented the moment when diverse Jewish groups united despite disagreements, thus ending sectarianism.

The MISHNAH attributes to Rabbi Akiva and other Yavnean sages a dispute as to whether Song of Songs and Qoheleth 'defile the hands' (*m. Yad.* 3.5). Later sources mention rabbinic disputes about a few other biblical books (Leiman 1976). In 1871, Heinrich Graetz developed from these hints the theory that a Synod of Yavneh closed the Jewish biblical canon. This idea enjoyed widespread popularity throughout the twentieth century, particularly as a result of its promotion in Herbert E. Ryle's 1892 monograph. A 1964 paper by Jack P. Lewis especially led to the downfall of the theory as unsubstantiated by ancient evidence (see Lewis 2002). However, some scholars continue to see at Yavneh a decisive moment for the Jewish canon, without invoking the idea of a council (Lim 2013).

Edmon L. Gallagher (Heritage Christian University, USA)

Further Reading

Cohen, Shaye J. D. 1984. 'The Significance of Yavneh'. *HUCA* 55: 27–53.

Lapin, Hayim. 2012. *Rabbis as Romans: The Rabbinic Movement in Palestine, 100–400 CE.* Oxford: Oxford University Press.

Leiman, Sid Z. 1976. *The Canonization of Hebrew Scripture: The Talmudic and Midrashic Evidence*. Hamden, CT: Transactions of the Connecticut Academy of Arts and Sciences.

Lewis, Jack P. 'Jamnia Revisited'. In *The Canon Debate*. Edited by Lee Martin McDonald and James A. Sanders. Peabody, MA: Hendrickson, pp. 146–62.

Lim, Timothy H. 2013. *The Formation of the Jewish Canon*. AYBRL. New Haven, CT: Yale University Press.

Y